Lecture Notes in Computer S[...]

Commenced Publication in 1973
Founding and Former Series Editors:
Gerhard Goos, Juris Hartmanis, and Jan van Leeuwen

David [...]
Lancaster University, UK

Takeo Kanade
Carnegie Mellon University, Pittsburgh, PA, USA

Josef Kittler
University of Surrey, Guildford, UK

Jon M. Kleinberg
Cornell University, Ithaca, NY, USA

Friedemann Mattern
ETH Zurich, Switzerland

John C. Mitchell
Stanford University, CA, USA

Moni Naor
Weizmann Institute of Science, Rehovot, Israel

Oscar Nierstrasz
University of Bern, Switzerland

C. Pandu Rangan
Indian Institute of Technology, Madras, India

Bernhard Steffen
University of Dortmund, Germany

Madhu Sudan
Massachusetts Institute of Technology, MA, USA

Demetri Terzopoulos
New York University, NY, USA

Doug Tygar
University of California, Berkeley, CA, USA

Moshe Y. Vardi
Rice University, Houston, TX, USA

Gerhard Weikum
Max-Planck Institute of Computer Science, Saarbruecken, Germany

Maria Francesca Costabile   Fabio Paternò (Eds.)

Human-Computer Interaction – INTERACT 2005

IFIP TC13 International Conference
Rome, Italy, September 12-16, 2005
Proceedings

 Springer

Volume Editors

Maria Francesca Costabile
University of Bari, Department of Computer Science
Via Orabona, 4, 70125 Bari, Italy
E-mail: costabile@di.uniba.it

Fabio Paternò
ISTI-CNR, Pisa
Via G. Moruzzi, 1, 56124 Pisa, Italy
E-mail: fabio.paterno@isti.cnr.it

Library of Congress Control Number: 2005932209

CR Subject Classification (1998): H.5.2, H.5.3, H.5, H.4, I.2.10, K.3, K.4, K.8

ISSN   0302-9743
ISBN-10   3-540-28943-7 Springer Berlin Heidelberg New York
ISBN-13   978-3-540-28943-2 Springer Berlin Heidelberg New York

Springer is a part of Springer Science+Business Media

springeronline.com

© 2005 IFIP International Federation for Information Processing, Hofstrasse 3, 2361 Laxenburg, Austria
Printed in Germany

Typesetting: Camera-ready by author, data conversion by Scientific Publishing Services, Chennai, India
Printed on acid-free paper   SPIN: 11555261   06/3142   5 4 3 2 1 0

General Chair's Welcome

It is my privilege to welcome you to Rome, to our INTERACT 2005 conference where, I hope, you will find interesting and stimulating presentations, tutorials, workshops and demos but, above all, we hope you will meet and interact with researchers to share ideas and projects within our field: human-computer interaction.

As a matter of fact, **interaction** is defined as a "mutual or reciprocal action or influence", and observing the two partners (user and computer) while they interact, we would like our future programs to provide creative (unpredictable) responses, after partial execution of the applications, in order to reach the wanted goal.

We live in a world where our lives are dramatically pre-organized, where we can only choose amongst a pre-emptied set of alternatives, mostly repeating all our actions on a day-by-day basis as if we were…machines.

The purpose of scientific research, in our case Computer Science, is to try to better understand the physical – in this case computational – aspects of true life and, if possible, improve the quality of life itself. Within the six different areas where Computer Science must still move forward [1] (Computation, Communication, Interaction, Recollection, Automation and Design), our field of Human-Computer Interaction may well profit from results obtained in all of them, since the tasks we would like to perform require a blended combination of knowledge from such areas.

Sometimes this research area is within the Departments of Computer Science but in some cases it is within Computer Engineering, Communication Sciences or even Psychology in academic institutions and operates within the research and development divisions of some of the most advanced high-tech software companies.

Many authors have underlined the relevance of a number of natural sciences, in cooperation with computer technology, required to improve the quality of interaction, the understanding of commands for given applications, the state of a multimedia computing system, the focus of attention on the screen during program execution. Cognitive science, learning theory, the roles of short term and long term memory together with perception and attention, constitute the necessary ingredients for a soundly based approach to the design of humane interfaces and interactive systems.

We would like to have programs that help us run our lives, but certainly not to be totally run by them! Programs that help us to choose a doctor, rent a house, book a flight, drive us to the correct location, suggest a book to read, translate a full sentence: all trying to satisfy our personal tastes and needs, yet be constrained by our economical resources.

It is a well-known fact that the number of people that will use computers in the future increases but also that different kinds of persons will depend on such machines. Children, adolescents, adults, senior citizens and handicapped persons, may be helped in their jobs/tasks but need tailored applications and an adequate recognition of their skills. As technology becomes more cost-effective, computers are less used for computing but more as communication devices that help humans to elaborate on facts and processes, to enable distant synchronous and asynchronous cooperation (including e-learning), to display information in a meaningful way (as in maps, graphs, diagrams, etc.) and provide answers to a wide variety of problems encountered in jobs, personal tasks and even entertainment.

We will be, sooner or later, not only handling personal computers but also multi-purpose cellular phones, complex personal digital assistants, devices that will be context-aware, and even wearable computers stitched to our clothes...we would like these personal systems to become transparent to the tasks they will be performing. In fact the best interface is an invisible one, one giving the user natural and fast access to the application he (or she) intends to be executed.

The working group that organized this conference (the last of a long row!) tried to combine a powerful scientific program (with drastic refereeing) with an entertaining cultural program, so as to make your stay in Rome the most pleasant one all round: I do hope that this expectation becomes true.

July 2005   Stefano Levialdi, IEEE Life Fellow
                                             INTERACT 2005
                                             General Chairman

[1] Peter J. Denning, ACM Communications, April 2005, vol. 48, N° 4, pp. 27-31.

Editors' Preface

INTERACT is one of the most important conferences in the area of Human-Computer Interaction at the world-wide level. We believe that this edition, which for the first time takes place in a Southern European country, will strengthen this role, and that Rome, with its history and beautiful setting provides a very congenial atmosphere for this conference.

The theme of INTERACT 2005 is *Communicating Naturally with Computers*. There has been an increasing awareness among interactive systems designers of the importance of designing for usability. However, we are still far from having products that are really usable, considering that usability may have many different meanings depending on the application domain. We are all aware that too often many users of current technology feel frustrated because computer systems are not compatible with their abilities and needs and with existing work practices. As designers of tomorrow's technology, we are responsible for creating computer artefacts that would permit natural communication with the various computing devices, so that communicating with computers would be more like communicating with people, and users might enjoy more satisfying experiences with information and communication technologies. This need has given rise to new research areas, such as ambient intelligence, natural interaction, end-user development, and social interaction.

The response to the conference has been positive in terms of submissions and participation. The contributions, especially the long papers, of which only 70 submissions were accepted out of 264, were carefully selected by the International Programme Committee. The result is a set of interesting and stimulating papers that address such important issues as haptic and tangible interfaces, model-based design, novel user interfaces, search techniques, social interaction, accessibility, usability evaluation, location-awareness, context of use, interaction with mobile devices, intelligent interfaces, multimodal interfaces, visualization techniques, video browsing, interfaces for children, and eye-tracking. The interest shown in the conference has truly been world-wide: if we consider both full and short papers we have authors from 24 countries in 5 continents.

There is a good balance of contributions from academia and industry. The final programme of the symposium includes three technical invited speakers: Bill Buxton on Sketching and Experience Design; Flavia Sparacino on Intelligent Architecture: Embedding Spaces with a Mind for Augmented Interaction; and Steven Pemberton on the Future of Web Interfaces. In addition to the 70 full papers, the programme includes 53 short papers, as well as interactive demos that will allow participants to have direct experience of innovative results, tutorials, workshops, SIGs, panels, and a doctoral consortium.

Particularly noteworthy in the programme are some topics that have been stimulating increasing interest. By way of example, those related to interaction with mobile devices, given that recent years have seen the introduction of many types of computers and devices (e.g., cellphones, PDAs, etc.) and the availability of such a wide range of devices has become a fundamental challenge for designers of interactive software systems. Users need to be able to seamlessly access information and services, regardless of the device they are using. Even when the system or the environment changes dynamically, they would like to see their interfaces migrate dynamically from one device to another, allowing them to continue their tasks from where they left off. In general, the continuous development of new research topics shows how the field is able to dynamically evolve and face both new and longstanding challenges. The results obtained are never an arrival point, but they form the basis for new research and results, and INTERACT is one of the best forums in which to present and discuss them.

We are also happy to announce that for the first time the INTERACT proceedings will be made available in a digital library. This is an important and useful innovation for both authors and the HCI community, as the entire contents will remain accessible and searchable over the years even for all those who have not attended the conference.

Last, but not least, let us thank all those who contributed to the success of the conference, including the authors, the International Programme Committee and the organizers. We are also grateful for the financial support of the sponsoring organizations. A special thanks goes to our collaborators Carmelo Ardito, Silvia Berti, Paolo Buono, Antonio Piccinno and Carmen Santoro for their invaluable support in editing these proceedings and organizing the conference.

July 2005   Maria Francesca Costabile and Fabio Paternò
                                                          INTERACT 2005
                                                      Conference Co-chairs

IFIP TC13

Established in 1989, the International Federation for Information Processing Technical Committee on Human-Computer Interaction (IFIP TC13) is an international committee of 29 member national societies and 5 Working Groups, representing specialists in human factors, ergonomics, cognitive science, computer science, design and related disciplines. INTERACT is its flagship conference, staged biennially in different countries in the world. The next INTERACT conference, INTERACT 2007, will be held in Brazil.

IFIP TC13 aims to develop a science and technology of human-computer interaction by encouraging empirical research, promoting the use of knowledge and methods from the human sciences in design and evaluation of computer systems; promoting better understanding of the relation between formal design methods and system usability and acceptability; developing guidelines, models and methods by which designers may provide better human-oriented computer systems; and, co-operating with other groups, inside and outside IFIP, to promote user-orientation and "humanisation" in system design. Thus, TC13 seeks to improve interactions between people and computers, encourage the growth of HCI research and disseminate these benefits world-wide.

The main orientation is towards users, especially the non-computer professional users, and how to improve human-computer relations. Areas of study include: the problems people have with computers; the impact on people in individual and organisational contexts; the determinants of utility, usability and acceptability; the appropriate allocation of tasks between computers and users; modelling the user to aid better system design; and harmonising the computer to user characteristics and needs.

While the scope is thus set wide, with a tendency towards general principles rather than particular systems, it is recognized that progress will only be achieved through both general studies to advance theoretical understanding and specific studies on practical issues (e.g., interface design standards, software system consistency, documentation, appropriateness of alternative communication media, human factors guidelines for dialogue design, the problems of integrating multi-media systems to match system needs and organizational practices, etc.).

IFIP TC13 stimulates working events and activities through its Working Groups. WGs consist of HCI experts from many countries, who seek to expand knowledge and find solutions to HCI issues and concerns within their domains, as outlined below.

In 1999, TC13 initiated a special IFIP Award, the Brian Shackel Award, for the most outstanding contribution in the form of a refereed paper submitted to and delivered at each INTERACT. The award draws attention to the need for a comprehensive human-centred approach in the design and use of information technology in which the human and social implications have been taken into account. Since the process to decide the award takes place after papers are submitted for publication, the award is not identified in the Proceedings.

WG13.1 (Education in HCI and HCI Curricula) aims to improve HCI education at all levels of higher education, coordinate and unite efforts to develop HCI curricula and promote HCI teaching;

WG13.2 (Methodology for User-Centred System Design) aims to foster research, dissemination of information and good practice in the methodical application of HCI to software engineering;

WG13.3 (HCI and Disability) aims to make HCI designers aware of the needs of people with disabilities and encourage development of information systems and tools permitting adaptation of interfaces to specific users;

WG13.4 (also WG2.7) (User Interface Engineering) investigates the nature, concepts and construction of user interfaces for software systems, using a framework for reasoning about interactive systems and an engineering model for developing user interfaces;

WG13.5 (Human Error, Safety and System Development) seeks a framework for studying human factors relating to systems failure, develops leading edge techniques in hazard analysis and safety engineering of computer-based systems, and guides international accreditation activities for safety-critical systems;

WG13.6 (Human-Work Interaction Design) aims at establishing relationships between extensive empirical work-domain studies and HCI design. It will promote the use of knowledge, concepts, methods and techniques that enables user studies to procure a better apprehension of the complex interplay between individual, social and organisational contexts and thereby a better understanding of how and why people work in the ways that they do.

New Working Groups are formed as areas of significance to HCI arise.
Further information is available at the IFIP TC13 website: http://www.ifip-hci.org/

IFIP TC13 Members

Australia
Judy Hammond
Australian Computer Society

Austria
Tom Gross
Austrian Computer Society

Belgium
Monique Noirhomme-Fraiture
*Federation des Associations
Informatiques de Belgique*

Brazil
Cecilia Baranauskas
Brazilian Computer Society

Canada
Gitte Lindgaard
*Canadian Information Processing
Society*

China
Zhengjie Liu
Chinese Institute of Electronics

Czech Republic
Vaclav Matousek
*Czech Society for Cybernetics and
Informatics*

Denmark
Annelise Mark Pejtersen
 (TC13 Chair)
*Danish Federation for Information
Processing*

Finland
Kari-Jouko Räihä
*Finnish Information Processing
Association*

France
Philippe Palanque
*Société des électriciens et des
électroniciens*

Germany
Horst Oberquelle
Gesellschaft für Informatik

Greece
John Darzentas
Greek Computer Society

India
Mathura P. Thapliyal
Computer Society of India

Italy
Fabio Paternò
Italian Computer Society

Japan
Masaaki Kurosu
*Information Processing Society of
Japan*

The Netherlands
Gerrit van der Veer
*Nederlands Genootschap voor
Informatica*

New Zealand
Mark Apperley
New Zealand Computer Society

Norway
Svein A. Arnesen
Norwegian Computer Society

Poland
Julius L. Kulikowski
Polish Academy of Sciences

Portugal
Joaquim Jorge
Associacão Portuguesa de Informática

Singapore
Kee Yong Lim
*School of MAE, Nanyang Technological
University*

Slovenia
Mirko Vintar
Slovenian Society Informatika

South Africa
Janet L. Wesson
The Computer Society of South Africa

Spain
Julio Abascal
Asociación de Técnicos de Informática (ATI)

Sweden
Lars Oestreicher
Swedish Interdisciplinary Society for Human-Computer Interaction

Switzerland
Markus Stolze
Swiss Federation of Information Processing Societies

UK
Gilbert Cockton
The British Computer Society

USA-based
John Karat
Association for Computing Machinery

USA-based
Nahum Gershon
IEEE Computer Society

Working Group Chairpersons

WG13.1 (Education in HCI and HCI Curricula)
Paula Kotze, *South Africa*
WG13.2 (Methodology for User-Centred System Design)
Jan Gulliksen, *Sweden*
WG13.3 (HCI and Disability)
Monique Noirhomme, *Belgium*
WG13.4 (also WG2.7) (User Interface Engineering)
Morten Borup Harning, *Denmark*
WG13.5 (Human Error, Safety and System Development)
Phillipe Palanque, *France*
WG13.6 (Human-Work Interaction Design)
Annelise Mark Pejtersen, *Denmark*

International Programme Committee

Chairs: Maria Francesca Costabile, *University of Bari, Italy*
Fabio Paternò, *ISTI-CNR, Italy*

Members

Abascal, Julio - *Spain*
Apperley, Mark – *New Zealand*
Ardissono, Liliana - *Italy*
Arrue, Myriam - *Spain*
Avouris, Nikolaos - *Greece*
Balbo, Sandrine - *Australia*
Barbosa, Simone - *Brazil*
Bass, Len - *USA*
Bastide, Rémi - *France*
Baudisch, Patrick - *USA*
Beaudouin-Lafon, Michel - *France*
Bernsen, Ole - *Denmark*
Bevan, Nigel - *United Kingdom*
Blackwell, Alan - *United Kingdom*
Blandford, Ann - *United Kingdom*
Blignaut, Pieter - *South Africa*
Bottoni, Paolo - *Italy*
Bouwhuis, Don - *The Netherlands*
Braendle, Alexander -
    United Kingdom
Brajnik, Giorgio - *Italy*
Brewster, Stephen - *United Kingdom*
Campos, José - *Portugal*
Castells, Pablo - *Spain*
Catarci, Tiziana - *Italy*
Celentano, Augusto - *Italy*
Chittaro, Luca - *Italy*
Cockburn, Andy - *New Zealand*
Cockton, Gilbert - *United Kingdom*
Coninx, Karin - *Belgium*
Correia, Nuno - *Portugal*
Costabile, Maria Francesca - *Italy*
Coutaz, Joelle - *France*
Crowley, James - *France*
Cunha, João - *Portugal*
Czerwinski, Mary - *USA*
Darzentas, John - *Greece*

Davies, Nigel - *United Kingdom*
De Angeli, Antonella -
    United Kingdom
De Carolis, Berardina - *Italy*
De Marsico, Maria - *Italy*
de Ruyter, Boris - *The Netherlands*
de Souza, Clarisse - *Brazil*
Del Bimbo, Alberto - *Italy*
Dewan, Prasun - *USA*
Di Nocera, Francesco - *Italy*
Dix, Alan - *United Kingdom*
Faconti, Giorgio - *Italy*
Felix, Daniel - *Switzerland*
Fogli, Daniela - *Italy*
Forbrig, Peter - *Germany*
Garzotto, Franca - *Italy*
Gea, Miguel - *Spain*
Gershon, Nahum - *USA*
Glavinic, Vlado - *Croatia*
Graham, Nicholas - *Canada*
Gray, Phil - *United Kingdom*
Gross, Tom - *Germany*
Grundy, John - *New Zealand*
Guimaraes, Nuno - *Portugal*
Gulliksen, Jan - *Sweden*
Hammond, Judy - *Australia*
Harning, Morten Borup - *Denmark*
Harper, Richard - *United Kingdom*
Harrison, Michael - *United Kingdom*
Hemmje, Matthias L. - *Germany*
Herczeg, Michael - *Germany*
Hosking, John - *New Zealand*
Hvannberg, Ebba - *Iceland*
Jacko, Julie - *USA*
Jacob, Robert - *USA*
Johnson, Chris - *United Kingdom*
Jones, Matt - *New Zealand*

Jorge, Joaquim - *Portugal*
Kaikkonen, Anne - *Finland*
Karat, John - *USA*
Kazman, Rick - *USA*
Kimani, Stephen - *Italy*
Koch, Michael - *Germany*
Kotze, Paula - *South Africa*
Krishnamurthy, Subramanian - *India*
Leclercq, Pierre - *Belgium*
Lecolinet, Eric - *France*
Leporini, Barbara - *Italy*
Levialdi, Stefano - *Italy*
Lieberman, Henry - *USA*
Lindgaard, Gitte - *Canada*
Liu, Zhengjie - *China*
Lorés, Jesus - *Spain*
Mäntyjärvi, Jani - *Finland*
Mark Pejtersen, Annelise - *Denmark*
Markopoulos, Panos -
    The Netherlands
Marsden, Gary - *South Africa*
Martens, Jean-Bernard -
    The Netherlands
Matousek, Vaclav - *Czech Republic*
Mayora, Oscar - *Mexico*
McCrickard, Scott - *USA*
Moriyon, Roberto - *Spain*
Mussio, Piero - *Italy*
Natale, Domenico - *Italy*
Nicolle, Colette - *United Kingdom*
Nigay, Laurence - *France*
Noirhomme, Monique - *Belgium*
Noldus, Lucas - *The Netherlands*
Nunes, Nuno - *Portugal*
Oberquelle, Horst - *Germany*
Oestreicher, Lars - *Sweden*
Oppermann, Reinhard - *Germany*
Palanque, Philippe - *France*
Panizzi, Emanuele - *Italy*
Paris, Cecile - *Australia*
Paternò, Fabio - *Italy*
Perez, Manuel - *USA*
Pino, Jose A. - *Chile*
Pittarello, Fabio - *Italy*
Plaisant, Catherine - *USA*

Polillo, Roberto - *Italy*
Pribeanu, Costin - *Romania*
Pu, Pearl - *Switzerland*
Puerta, Angel - *USA*
Qvarfordt, Pernilla - *Sweden*
Ranon, Roberto - *Italy*
Rauterberg, Matthias -
    The Netherlands
Rist, Thomas - *Germany*
Roselli, Teresa - *Italy*
Santoro, Carmelina - *Italy*
Santucci, Giuseppe - *Italy*
Savidis, Anthony - *Greece*
Scapin, Dominique - *France*
Schmandt, Chris - *USA*
Schmidt, Albrecht - *Germany*
Schwabe, Gerhard - *Switzerland*
Simone, Carla - *Italy*
Stary, Christian - *Austria*
Stolze, Markus - *Switzerland*
Stuerzlinger, Wolfgang - *Canada*
Sukaviriya, Noi - *USA*
Sutcliffe, Alistair - *United Kingdom*
Thalmann, Nadia - *Switzerland*
Thiran, Jean-Philippe - *Switzerland*
Toffetti, Antonella - *Italy*
Tortora, Genny - *Italy*
Tscheligi, Manfred - *Austria*
Tucci, Maurizio - *Italy*
Tzovaras, Dimitrios - *Greece*
Väänänen-Vainio-Mattila, Kaisa -
    Finland
Van der Veer, Gerrit -
    The Netherlands
Vanderdonckt, Jean - *Belgium*
Vertegaal, Roel - *Canada*
Vetere, Frank - *Australia*
Vitiello, Giuliana - *Italy*
Wesson, Janet - *South Africa*
Winckler, Marco Antonio - *France*
Wittenburg, Kent - *USA*
Wright, Peter - *United Kingdom*
Wulf, Volker - *Germany*
Zancanaro, Massimo - *Italy*
Ziegler, Jürgen – *Germany*

INTERACT 2005 Technical Committee

General Chair
Stefano Levialdi
University of Rome, Italy

Conference Co-chairs
Maria Francesca Costabile
University of Bari, Italy
Fabio Paternò
ISTI-CNR, Pisa, Italy

Tutorials Co-chairs
Mary Czerwinski
Microsoft Research, Seattle, USA
Philippe Palanque
*LIIHS-IRIT, University of
Toulouse 3, France*

Workshops Co-chairs
Tiziana Catarci
University of Rome, Italy
Markus Stolze
*IBM Research, Zurich,
Switzerland*

Short Papers & Demos Co-chairs
Luca Chittaro
University of Udine, Italy
Tom Gross
*Bauhaus-University Weimar,
Germany*

Panels Co-chairs
Julio Abascal
*University of the Basque Country,
Spain*
Piero Mussio
University of Milan, Italy

Special Interest Groups Co-chairs
Joaquim A. Jorge
INESC, Portugal
Monique Noirhomme
University of Namur, Belgium

Doctoral Consortium Co-chairs
John Karat
IBM TJ Watson Research Center, USA
Matthias Rautherberg
*Technical University of
Eindhoven, The Netherlands*

**Organizational Overviews
 Co-chairs**
Paolo Buono
University of Bari, Italy
Carmen Santoro
ISTI-CNR, Pisa, Italy

Technology Co-chairs
Giulio Mori
ISTI-CNR, Pisa, Italy
Emanuele Panizzi
University of Rome, Italy

Sponsors

Organizing Institutions

Table of Contents

Part One: Keynote Speakers

Sketching and Experience Design
William Buxton 1

Intelligent Architecture: Embedding Spaces with a Mind for Augmented Interaction
Flavia Sparacino 2

The Future of Web Interfaces
Steven Pemberton 4

Part Two: Long Papers

Haptic and Tangible Interfaces

An Investigation into the Use of Tactons to Present Progress Information
Stephen Brewster, Alison King 6

Haptizing Wind on a Weather Map with Reactive Force and Vibration
Masaki Omata, Masami Ishihara, Misa Grace Kwok,
Atsumi Imamiya 18

Using ARToolKit Markers to Build Tangible Prototypes and Simulate Other Technologies
Eva Hornecker, Thomas Psik 30

Augmented Reality Painting and Collage: Evaluating Tangible Interaction in a Field Study
Giulio Jacucci, Antti Oulasvirta, Antti Salovaara, Thomas Psik,
Ina Wagner 43

Novel User Interfaces

Hotaru: Intuitive Manipulation Techniques for Projected Displays of Mobile Devices
Masanori Sugimoto, Kosuke Miyahara, Hiroshi Inoue,
Yuji Tsunesada 57

DIZI: A Digital Ink Zooming Interface for Document Annotation
Maneesh Agrawala, Michael Shilman 69

TractorBeam Selection Aids: Improving Target Acquisition for Pointing
Input on Tabletop Displays
*J. Karen Parker, Regan L. Mandryk, Michael N. Nunes,
Kori M. Inkpen* 80

Responsive Interaction Based on Sketch in Concept Styling
Li Han, Giuseppe Conti, Raffaele De Amicis 94

Improving Search Techniques

Natural Language Query vs. Keyword Search: Effects of Task
Complexity on Search Performance, Participant Perceptions, and
Preferences
QianYing Wang, Clifford Nass, Jiang Hu 106

"THAT's What I Was Looking for": Comparing User-Rated Relevance
with Search Engine Rankings
Sameer Patil, Sherman R. Alpert, John Karat, Catherine Wolf 117

Effects of Display Configurations on Document Triage
*Soonil Bae, Rajiv Badi, Konstantinos Meintanis, J. Michael Moore,
Anna Zacchi, Haowei Hsieh, Catherine C. Marshall,
Frank M. Shipman* 130

Searching for Music: How Feedback and Input-Control Change the Way
We Search
Tue Haste Andersen 144

Model-Based Design

Galactic Dimensions: A Unifying Workstyle Model for User-Centered
Design
Pedro Campos, Nuno J. Nunes 158

A Formal Description of Multimodal Interaction Techniques for
Immersive Virtual Reality Applications
*David Navarre, Philippe Palanque, Rémi Bastide, Amélie Schyn,
Marco Winckler, Luciana P. Nedel, Carla M.D.S. Freitas* 170

Analysing User Confusion in Context Aware Mobile Applications
Karsten Loer, Michael D. Harrison 184

Attach Me, Detach Me, Assemble Me Like You Work
Donatien Grolaux, Jean Vanderdonckt, Peter Van Roy 198

Interacting with Mobile Devices

Bringing Dynamic Queries to Mobile Devices: A Visual
Preference-Based Search Tool for Tourist Decision Support
Stefano Burigat, Luca Chittaro, Luca De Marco   213

Mobile Photo Browsing with Pipelines and Spatial Cues
Tero Hakala, Juha Lehikoinen, Hannu Korhonen,
Aino Ahtinen   227

Visual Interface and Control Modality: An Experiment About Fast
Photo Browsing on Mobile Devices
QianYing Wang, Susumu Harada, Tony Hsieh,
Andreas Paepcke   240

Accessibility

The Effect of Age and Font Size on Reading Text on Handheld
Computers
Iain Darroch, Joy Goodman, Stephen Brewster, Phil Gray   253

Fat Finger Worries: How Older and Younger Users Physically Interact
with PDAs
Katie A. Siek, Yvonne Rogers, Kay H. Connelly   267

Flexible Reporting for Automated Usability and Accessibility
Evaluation of Web Sites
Abdo Beirekdar, Marc Keita, Monique Noirhomme,
Frédéric Randolet, Jean Vanderdonckt, Céline Mariage   281

Intelligent Interfaces

The Focus-Metaphor Approach: A Novel Concept for the Design of
Adaptive and User-Centric Interfaces
Sven Laqua, Paul Brna   295

Working Out a Common Task: Design and Evaluation of User-Intelligent
System Collaboration
Daniela Petrelli, Vitaveska Lanfranchi, Fabio Ciravegna   309

Interactivity and Expectation: Eliciting Learning Oriented Behavior
with Tutorial Dialogue Systems
Carolyn Penstein Rosé, Cristen Torrey   323

Large Displays

Put Them Where? Towards Guidelines for Positioning Large Displays
in Interactive Workspaces
  Ramona E. Su, Brian P. Bailey   337

Analysis of User Behavior on High-Resolution Tiled Displays
  Robert Ball, Chris North.....................................   350

Collaboration

Interaction and Co-located Collaboration in Large Projection-Based
Virtual Environments
  *Andreas Simon, Armin Dressler, Hans-Peter Krüger, Sascha Scholz,
  Jürgen Wind*   364

Using Real-Life Troubleshooting Interactions to Inform Self-assistance
Design
  *Jacki O'Neill, Antonietta Grasso, Stefania Castellani,
  Peter Tolmie*   377

Usability Evaluation

Feedback from Usability Evaluation to User Interface Design: Are
Usability Reports Any Good? ✗
  *Christian M. Nielsen, Michael Overgaard, Michael B. Pedersen,
  Jan Stage*   391

Assessing Interaction Styles in Web User Interfaces ✗
  Alistair Sutcliffe, Antonella De Angeli   405

Usability Specialists - 'A Mommy Mob', 'Realistic Humanists' or 'Staid
Researchers'? An Analysis of Usability Work in the Software Product
Development ✗
  Netta Iivari   418

Children's Interfaces and Their Evaluation

Exposing Middle School Girls to Programming via Creative Tools
  Gahgene Gweon, Jane Ngai, Jenica Rangos   431

Exploring Verbalization and Collaboration of Constructive Interaction
with Children
  Benedikte S. Als, Janne J. Jensen, Mikael B. Skov   443

A Structured Expert Evaluation Method for the Evaluation of
Children's Computer Games
  Ester Baauw, Mathilde M. Bekker, Wolmet Barendregt   457

Usability of PDA

Usability Testing of Mobile Devices: A Comparison of Three Approaches
  Adriana Holtz Betiol, Walter de Abreu Cybis   470

Evaluating the Effectiveness of "Effective View Navigation" for Very
Long Ordered Lists on Mobile Devices
  Luca Chittaro, Luca De Marco   482

Social Interaction

Understanding Situated Social Interactions in Public Places
  Jeni Paay, Jesper Kjeldskov   496

Benefits of Social Intelligence in Home Dialogue Systems
  Privender Saini, Boris de Ruyter, Panos Markopoulos,
  Albert van Breemen   510

Evolution of Norms in a Newly Forming Group
  Catalina Danis, Alison Lee   522

Multimodal Interfaces

A Comparison Between Spoken Queries and Menu-Based Interfaces for
In-car Digital Music Selection
  Clifton Forlines, Bent Schmidt-Nielsen, Bhiksha Raj,
  Kent Wittenburg, Peter Wolf   536

A Sketching Tool for Designing Anyuser, Anyplatform, Anywhere User
Interfaces
  Adrien Coyette, Jean Vanderdonckt   550

FlowMouse: A Computer Vision-Based Pointing and Gesture Input
Device
  Andrew D. Wilson, Edward Cutrell   565

Context of Use

Context of Use Evaluation of Peripheral Displays (CUEPD)
  N. Sadat Shami, Gilly Leshed, David Klein   579

Improving Cell Phone Awareness by Using Calendar Information
  Ashraf Khalil, Kay H. Connelly 588

3D and Virtual Environments

Evaluation of 12-DOF Input Devices for Navigation and Manipulation
in Virtual Environments
  *Anke Huckauf, Alexander Speed, André Kunert, Jan Hochstrate,
  Bernd Fröhlich* 601

Integration of 3D Data and Text: The Effects of Text Positioning,
Connectivity, and Visual Hints on Comprehension
  Henry Sonnet, Sheelagh Carpendale, Thomas Strothotte 615

Computer Supported Cooperative Work (CSCW)

The Effect of Operational Mechanisms on Creativity in Design
  Andrew Warr, Eamonn O'Neill 629

The Necessity of a Meeting Recording and Playback System, and the
Benefit of Topic–Level Annotations to Meeting Browsing
  Satanjeev Banerjee, Carolyn Rose, Alexander I. Rudnicky 643

Understanding Users

Key Issues in Interactive Problem Solving: An Empirical Investigation
on Users Attitude
  *Gabriella Cortellessa, Vittoria Giuliani, Massimiliano Scopelliti,
  Amedeo Cesta* 657

Designing Natural Language and Structured Entry Methods for Privacy
Policy Authoring
  John Karat, Clare-Marie Karat, Carolyn Brodie, Jinjuan Feng 671

Questionnaire–Based Research on Opinions of Visitors for
Communication Robots at an Exhibition in Japan
  *Tatsuya Nomura, Takugo Tasaki, Takayuki Kanda, Masahiro Shiomi,
  Hiroshi Ishiguro, Norihiro Hagita* 685

Interface Design

A Toolset for Creating Iconic Interfaces for Interactive Workspaces
  Jacob T. Biehl, Brian P. Bailey 699

Designing Usable Interfaces with Cultural Dimensions
Gabrielle Ford, Paula Kotzé 713

Use of Future-Oriented Information in User-Centered Product Concept
Ideation
Antti Salovaara, Petri Mannonen 727

Eye-Tracking

Wide vs. Narrow Paragraphs: An Eye Tracking Analysis
David Beymer, Daniel M. Russell, Peter Z. Orton 741

Combining Eye Tracking and Conventional Techniques for Indications
of User-Adaptability
Ekaterini Tzanidou, Marian Petre, Shailey Minocha,
Andrew Grayson 753

RealTourist – A Study of Augmenting Human-Human and
Human-Computer Dialogue with Eye-Gaze Overlay
Pernilla Qvarfordt, David Beymer, Shumin Zhai 767

Video Browsing

A Synergistic Approach to Efficient Interactive Video Retrieval
Andreas Girgensohn, John Adcock, Matthew Cooper, Lynn Wilcox ... 781

The Landscape of Time-Based Visual Presentation Primitives for
Richer Video Experience
Yasuhiro Yamamoto, Kumiyo Nakakoji, Takashima Akio 795

Temporal Magic Lens: Combined Spatial and Temporal Query and
Presentation
Kathy Ryall, Qing Li, Alan Esenther 809

User Studies

Logging Events Crossing Architectural Boundaries
Gregory S. Hartman, Len Bass 823

Visualization Techniques

Representing Unevenly-Spaced Time Series Data for Visualization and
Interactive Exploration
Aleks Aris, Ben Shneiderman, Catherine Plaisant, Galit Shmueli,
Wolfgang Jank 835

Multilevel Compound Tree - Construction Visualization and Interaction
    François Boutin, Jérôme Thièvre, Mountaz Hascoët 847

Visualizing Missing Data: Graph Interpretation User Study
    Cyntrica Eaton, Catherine Plaisant, Terence Drizd 861

High-Level Visualization of Users' Navigation in Virtual Environments
    Lucio Ieronutti, Roberto Ranon, Luca Chittaro 873

Location and Context Awareness

How Do People's Concepts of Place Relate to Physical Locations?
    Changqing Zhou, Pamela Ludford, Dan Frankowski, Loren Terveen .. 886

The Territory Is the Map: Exploring the Use of Landmarks in Situ to
Inform Mobile Guide Design
    Nicola J. Bidwell, Jeff Axup 899

Technology in Place: Dialogics of Technology, Place and Self
    John McCarthy, Peter Wright 914

Interaction and End-User Programming with a Context-Aware Mobile
Application
    Jonna Häkkilä, Panu Korpipää, Sami Ronkainen, Urpo Tuomela 927

Part Three: Short Papers

Information Visualization and User Studies

Large Visualizations for System Monitoring of Complex, Heterogeneous
Systems
    Daniel M. Russell, Andreas Dieberger, Varun Bhagwan,
    Daniel Gruhl 938

The Challenge of Visualizing Patient Histories on a Mobile Device
    Carmelo Ardito, Paolo Buono, Maria Francesca Costabile 942

Static Visualization of Temporal Eye-Tracking Data
    Kari-Jouko Räihä, Anne Aula, Päivi Majaranta, Harri Rantala,
    Kimmo Koivunen 946

Analytic Worksheets: A Framework to Support Human Analysis of
Large Streaming Data Volumes
    Grace Crowder, Sterling Foster, Daniel M. Russell, Malcolm Slaney,
    Lisa Yanguas 950

Hundreds of Folders or One Ugly Pile – Strategies for Information
Search and Re-access
Anne Aula, Harri Siirtola 954

Exploring Results Organisation for Image Searching
Jana Urban, Joemon M. Jose 958

Computer-Mediated Communication and Mobility

The SenseMS: Enriching the SMS Experience for Teens by Non-verbal
Means
Alia K. Amin, Bram Kersten, Olga A. Kulyk, Elly Pelgrim,
Jimmy Wang, Panos Markopoulos 962

TextTone: Expressing Emotion Through Text
Ankur Kalra, Karrie Karahalios 966

Lock-on-Chat: Boosting Anchored Conversation and Its Operation at a
Technical Conference
Takeshi Nishida, Takeo Igarashi 970

BROAFERENCE - A Next Generation Multimedia Terminal Providing
Direct Feedback on Audience's Satisfaction Level
Uwe Kowalik, Terumasa Aoki, Hiroshi Yasuda 974

ChatAmp: Talking with Music and Text
M. Ian Graham, Karrie Karahalios 978

The Optimal Focus Position When Scrolling Using a Small Display
James Whalley, Andrew Monk 982

Group Work and Tabletop Interaction

Collaboration with DiamondTouch
Stephen G. Kobourov, Kyriacos Pavlou, Justin Cappos,
Michael Stepp, Mark Miles, Amanda Wixted 986

Preference-Based Group Scheduling
Jiang Hu, Mike Brzozowski 990

Under My Finger: Human Factors in Pushing and Rotating Documents
Across the Table
Clifton Forlines, Chia Shen, Frédéric Vernier, Mike Wu 994

DocuBits and Containers: Providing e-Document Micro-mobility in a
Walk-Up Interactive Tabletop Environment
  Katherine Everitt, Chia Shen, Kathy Ryall, Clifton Forlines 998

Transcription Table: Text Support During Meetings
  Joris van Gelder, Irene van Peer, Dzmitry Aliakseyeu 1002

Common Ground to Analyse Privacy Coordination in Awareness
Systems
  Natalia A. Romero, Panos Markopoulos 1006

3D and Virtual Environments

3D Syllabus: Interactive Visualization of Indexes to Multimedia
Training Content
  Kyuman Song, Surapong Lertsithichai, Patrick Chiu 1010

A Navigation and Examination Aid for 3D Virtual Buildings
  Luca Chittaro, Vijay Kumar Gatla, Subramanian Venkataraman 1014

Virtual Reflections and Virtual Shadows in Mixed Reality Environments
  Frank Steinicke, Klaus Hinrichs, Timo Ropinski 1018

Cooking with the Elements: Intuitive Immersive Interfaces for
Augmented Reality Environments
  Leonardo Bonanni, Chia-Hsun Lee, Ted Selker 1022

Adaptive and Adaptable Systems

Learners' Perceived Level of Difficulty of a Computer-Adaptive Test: A
Case Study
  Mariana Lilley, Trevor Barker, Carol Britton 1026

How to Communicate Recommendations? Evaluation of an Adaptive
Annotation Technique
  Federica Cena, Cristina Gena, Sonia Modeo 1030

Adaptive User Interfaces Development Platform
  Jing-Hua Ye, John Herbert 1034

Adapting the ADS for High Volume Manufacturing
  Connor Upton, Gavin Doherty 1038

Grasping, Gazing, Gesturing

Immersive Live Sports Experience with Vibrotactile Sensation
Beom-Chan Lee, Junhun Lee, Jongeun Cha, Changhoon Seo,
Jeha Ryu 1042

Smooth Haptic Interaction in Broadcasted Augmented Reality
Jongeun Cha, Beom-Chan Lee, Jong-phil Kim, Seungjun Kim,
Jeha Ryu 1046

A Laser Pointer/Laser Trails Tracking System for Visual Performance
Kentaro Fukuchi 1050

Effects of Display Layout on Gaze Activity During Visual Search
Jérôme Simonin, Suzanne Kieffer, Noëlle Carbonell 1054

Eye-Tracking Reveals the Personal Styles for Search Result Evaluation
Anne Aula, Päivi Majaranta, Kari-Jouko Räihä 1058

Hotspot Components for Gesture-Based Interaction
Alejandro Jaimes, Jianyi Liu 1062

Design and Models

Development of Multi-modal Interfaces in Multi-device Environments
Silvia Berti, Fabio Paternò 1067

Analysing Trans-Modal Interface Migration
Renata Bandelloni, Silvia Berti, Fabio Paternò 1071

Inferring Relations Between Color and Emotional Dimensions of a Web
Site Using Bayesian Networks
Eleftherios Papachristos, Nikolaos Tselios, Nikolaos Avouris 1075

Abbrevicons: Efficient Feedback for Audio Interfaces
Matthew Hockenberry, Sharon Cohen, Zachary Ozer, Tiffany Chen,
Ted Selker 1079

Icon Use by Different Language Groups: Changes in Icon Perception in
Accordance with Cue Utility
Siné McDougall, Alexandra Forsythe, Lucy Stares 1083

User Aspects of Explanation Aware CBR Systems
Jörg Cassens 1087

Mobile Devices

Mobile Reacher Interface for Intuitive Information Navigation
Yuichi Yoshida, Kento Miyaoku, Takashi Satou, Suguru Higashino .. 1091

Recognition Errors and Recognizing Errors – Children Writing on the
Tablet PC
Janet Read, Emanuela Mazzone, Matthew Horton 1096

Universal Access

The Design of an Authoring Interface to Make eLearning Content
Accessible
Silvia Gabrielli, Valeria Mirabella, Massimiliano Teso,
Tiziana Catarci 1100

Reducing the Risk of Abandonment of Assistive Technologies for People
with Autism
Peter Francis, Lucy Firth, David Mellor 1104

From Extraneous Noise to Categorizable Signatures: Using Multi-scale
Analyses to Assess Implicit Interaction Needs of Older Adults with
Visual Impairments
Kevin P. Moloney, V. Kathlene Leonard, Bin Shi, Julie A. Jacko,
Brani Vidakovic, François Sainfort 1108

Tools

Supporting Efficient and Reliable Content Analysis Using Automatic
Text Processing Technology
Gahgene Gweon, Carolyn Penstein Rosé, Joerg Wittwer,
Matthias Nueckles 1112

Multi-platform Online Game Design and Architecture
JungHyun Han, Ingu Kang, Chungmin Hyun, Jong-Sik Woo,
Young-Ik Eom 1116

Segment and Browse: A Strategy for Supporting Human Monitoring of
Facial Expression Behaviour
Michael J. Lyons, Mathias Funk, Kazuhiro Kuwabara 1120

iDwidgets: Parameterizing Widgets by User Identity
Kathy Ryall, Alan Esenther, Katherine Everitt, Clifton Forlines,
Meredith Ringel Morris, Chia Shen, Sam Shipman,
Frédéric Vernier 1124

Usability Evaluation and User Studies

Rater Bias: The Influence of Hedonic Quality on Usability
Questionnaires
    Stefanie Harbich, Sonja Auer 1129

Towards the Maturation of IT Usability Evaluation (MAUSE)
    Effie L.-C. Law, Ebba T. Hvannberg, Gilbert Cockton,
    Philippe Palanque, Dominque Scapin, Mark Springett,
    Christian Stary, Jean Vanderdonckt 1134

An X-Ray of the Brazilian e-Gov Web Sites
    Cristiano Maciel, José Luiz T. Nogueira,
    Ana Cristina Bicharra Garcia 1138

An Experiment to Measure the Usefulness of Patterns in the Interaction
Design Process
    N.L.O. Cowley, J.L. Wesson 1142

Testing New Alarms for Medical Electrical Equipment
    Alexandra Wee, Penelope Sanderson 1146

Relevance of Prior Experience in MHP Based Interactive TV Services
    Regina Bernhaupt, Bernd Ploderer, Manfred Tscheligi 1150

Author Index 1155

Sketching and Experience Design

William Buxton

Buxton Design, 888 Queen Street East, Toronto, Ontario, Canada M4M 1J3
http://www.billbuxton.com
bill@billbuxton.com

Abstract. Among others, Hummels, Djajadiningrat and Overbeeke (Knowing, Doing and Feeling: Communication with your Digital Products. Interdisziplinäres Kolleg Kognitions und Neurowissenschaften, Günne am Möhnesee, March 2-9 2001, 289-308.), have expressed the notion that the real product of design is the resultant "context for experience" rather than the object or software that provokes that experience. This closely corresponds to what I refer to as a transition in focus from a materialistic to an experiential view of design. Paraphrasing what I have already said, is not the physical entity or what is in the box (the "material" product) that is the true outcome of the design process. Rather, it is the behavioural, experiential and emotional responses that come about as a result of its existence and use in the "wild".

Designing for experience comes with a whole new level of complexity. This is especially true in this emerging world of information appliances, reactive environments and ubiquitous computing, where, along with those of their users, we have to factor in the convoluted behaviours of the products themselves. Doing this effectively requires both a different mind-set, as well as different techniques.

This talk is motivated by a concern that, in general, our current training and work practices are not adequate to meet the demands of this level of design. This is true for those coming from a computer science background, since they do not have sufficient grounding in design, at least in the sense that would be recognized by an architect or industrial designer. Conversely, those from the design arts, while they have the design skills, do not generally have the technical skills to adequately address the design issues relating to the complex embedded behaviours of such devices and systems.

Hence, in this talk, we discuss the design process itself, from the perspective of methods, organization, and composition. Fundamental to our approach is the notion that sketching is a fundamental component of design, and is especially critical at the early ideation phase. Yet, due to the temporal nature of what we are designing, conventional sketching is not – on its own – adequate. Hence, if we are to design experience or interaction, we need to adopt something that is to our process that is analogous to what traditional sketching is to the process of conventional industrial design.

It is the motivation and exploration of such a sketching process that is the foundation of this presentation.

M.F. Costabile and F. Paternò (Eds.): INTERACT 2005, LNCS 3585, p. 1, 2005.
© IFIP International Federation for Information Processing 2005

Intelligent Architecture: Embedding Spaces with a Mind for Augmented Interaction

Flavia Sparacino

Sensing Places and MIT
flavia@sensingplaces.com
flavia@media.mit.edu

Abstract. Our society's modalities of communication are rapidly changing: we divide our activities between real and digital worlds and our daily lives are characterized by our constant access-to and processing-of a vast quantity and variety of information. These transformations of our lifestyle demand both a new architecture and interaction modalities that support the new as well as old ways of communicating and living.

As a consequence of the prevalent role of information in today's society, architecture is presently at a turning point. Screens are everywhere, from the billboards which dot the contemporary urban cityscape, to the video walls which welcome us in the entry-halls of corporate headquarter buildings, to our desktop computer monitor at home, the PDA in our pocket, or the tiny private-eye screens of wearable computers. Wearable computers are starting to transform our technological landscape by reshaping the heavy, bulky desktop computer into a lightweight, portable device that's accessible to people at any time. Computation and sensing are moving from computers and devices into the environment itself. The space around us is instrumented with sensors and displays, and this tends to reflect a widespead need to blend together the information space with our physical space. "Augmented reality" and "mixed reality" are the terms most often used to refer to this type of media-enhanced interactive space. The combination of large public and miniature personal digital displays together with distributed computing and sensing intelligence offers unprecedented opportunities to merge the virtual and the real, the information landscape of the Internet with the urban landscape of the city, to transform digital animated media in public installations, in storytellers, also by means of personal wearable technology.

To meet the challenges of the new information- and technology-inspired architecture we need to think of the architectural space not simply as a container but as a living body endowed with sensors, actuators, and a brain (a mind), a space capable of assisting people in the course of their activities within such spaces.

On the basis of my work and research I will argue that intelligent architecture needs to be supported by three forms of intelligence: perceptual intelligence, which captures people's presence and movement in the space in a natural and non-encumbering way; interpretive intelligence, which "understands" people's actions and is capable of making informed guesses about their behavior; and narrative intelligence, which presents us with information,

M.F. Costabile and F. Paternò (Eds.): INTERACT 2005, LNCS 3585, pp. 2–3, 2005.

articulated stories, images, and animations, in the right place, at the right time, all tailored to our needs and preferences.

This talk will describe and illustrate a series of models, technological platforms and installations the author developed originally at the MIT Media Lab (1994 to 2002) and later commercially for Sensing Places (2003 to 2005). They contribute to defining new trends in architecture that merge virtual and real spaces, and are currently in the process of reshaping the way we live and experience the museum, the home, the theater, and the modern city.

The Future of Web Interfaces

Steven Pemberton

CWI and W3C
steven.pemberton@cwi.nl

Abstract. The Web took the world by storm, and as a result developed rapidly in many directions. However it still exhibits many aspects of its early development, such as its visual and computer-screen orientation. But the Web is still developing rapidly: there are now more browsers on mobile telephones than on desktops, and there is a vast diversity in types of devices, types and orientations of screens, and sizes (in number of pixels), and resolutions (in dpi) of screens.

Dealing with this diversity is impossible to address just by keeping a list of all the possible devices, or even a list of the most-used ones, and producing different sites for them, since the complexity would be unmanageable, and because once sites started turning away browsers and devices they didn't know, the browser makers responded by disguising themselves to such sites as other browsers.

On top of this diversity there is also the diversity required for accessibility. Although providing access for the visually impaired is an important reason for accessibility, we are all more or less visually impaired at one time or another. When displaying an application on a projector screen at a conference or meeting, the whole audience will typically be visually impaired in comparison to someone sitting behind a computer screen. The existence of separate so-called "Ten-foot Interfaces" (for people controlling their computers by remote control from an armchair ten feet away) demonstrates that the original applications are not designed for accessibility. Furthermore, Google (and all other search engines) is blind, and sees only what a blind user sees of a page; as the webmaster of a large bank has remarked, "we have noticed that improving accessibility increases our Google rating".

The success of the Web has turned the browser into a central application area for the user, and you can spend most of your day working with applications in the browser, reading mail, shopping, searching your own diskdrive. The advent of applications such as Google Maps and GMail has focussed minds on delivering applications via the web, not least because it eliminates the problems involved with versioning: everyone always has the most recent version of your application. Since Web-based applications have benefits for both user and provider, we can only expect to see more of them in the future.

But this approach comes at a cost. Google Maps is of the order of 200K of Javascript code. Such applications are only writable by programming experts, and producing an application is not possible by the sort of people who often produce web pages for their own use.

The Web Interfaces landscape is in turmoil at the moment. Microsoft has announced a new markup language and vector graphics language for the next

M.F. Costabile and F. Paternò (Eds.): INTERACT 2005, LNCS 3585, pp. 4–5, 2005.

version of Windows; probably as a response Adobe has acquired Macromedia and therefore Flash; W3C have standards for applications in the form of XForms, XHTML and SVG and are working on 'compound documents'; and other browser manufacturers are calling for their own version of HTML.

What are we to make of these different approaches? Are they conflicting? Have any addressed authorability, device-independence, usability or accessibility? Is it even possible to make accessible applications? HTML made creating hypertext documents just about as easy as it could be; do any of the new approaches address this need for simplicity, or has power been irretrievably returned to the programmers?

This talk discusses the requirements for Web Applications, and the underpinnings necessary to make Web Applications follow in the same spirit that engendered the Web in the first place.

An Investigation into the Use of Tactons to Present Progress Information

Stephen Brewster and Alison King

Glasgow Interactive Systems Group, Department of Computing Science,
University of Glasgow, Glasgow, G12 8QQ, UK
stephen@dcs.gla.ac.uk
www.dcs.gla.ac.uk/~stephen

Abstract. This paper presents an initial investigation into the use of Tactons, or tactile icons, to present progress information in desktop human-computer interfaces. Progress bars are very common in a wide range of interfaces but have problems. For example, they must compete for screen space and visual attention with other visual tasks such as document editing or web browsing. To address these problems we created a tactile progress indicator, encoding progress information into a series of vibrotactile cues. An experiment comparing the tactile progress indicator to a standard visual one showed a significant improvement in performance and an overall preference for the tactile display. These results suggest that a tactile display is a good way to present such information and this has many potential applications from computer desktops to mobile telephones.

1 Introduction

Progress bars are a common feature of most graphical human-computer interfaces. They are used to indicate the current state of a task which does not complete instantaneously, such as downloading documents from the web or copying files. Myers [14] showed that people prefer systems with progress indicators, as they give novices confidence that a task is progressing successfully, whilst experts can get sufficient information to predict the approximate completion time of the task.

The problem with visual progress bars is that they can become hidden behind other windows on the desktop and often have to compete for visual attention with other tasks the user is trying to perform. Tactile presentation has the potential to solve these problems: progress indicators are temporal and temporal patterns are well perceived through the skin. This paper presents an initial experimental investigation into a vibrotactile progress indicator that does not require visual attention, communicating the progress of a task via a series of tactile pulses.

2 Previous Work

For a progress bar to be effective at keeping the user informed about the state of the task, Conn [6] says that it should have good time affordance, i.e. the user must be able

M.F. Costabile and F. Paternò (Eds.): INTERACT 2005, LNCS 3585, pp. 6–17, 2005.

to tell "when things are okay and when there are problems, and can generally predict when a task will be completed". To do this, Conn suggests a progress bar should give an indication of eight task properties:

1. *Acceptance:* What the task is and whether it has been accepted.
2. *Scope:* The overall size of the task and the corresponding time it is expected to take;
3. *Initiation:* Clear indication that the task has successfully started;
4. *Progress:* Clear indication of the task being carried out, and the rate at which the overall task is approaching completion;
5. *Heartbeat:* Indication that the task is still "alive";
6. *Exception:* Indication that a task has errors;
7. *Remainder:* Indication of how much of the task remains and/or how much time is left before completion;
8. *Completion:* Clear indication of termination of the task and the status at termination.

Several types of progress indicators are commonly used, from 'egg-timer' or 'clock hands' cursors to progress bars (see Figure 1). This paper will consider the latter as they provide more information to the user about the task in progress. They are used when files are copied, transferred or downloaded, etc., and are very common in desktop computer interfaces. They also occur on devices such as mobile telephones or MP3 players, where progress bars are used to indicate the download of web pages or the transfer of photographs or sound files.

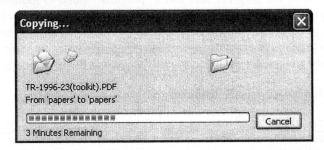

Fig. 1. The progress bar used by Microsoft Windows XP (www.microsoft.com/windowsxp)

Figure 1 shows a progress bar from the Windows XP operating system. In terms of Conn's properties the progress window itself and the type of task indicated in its title bar show *Acceptance*. *Scope* is given by the time remaining indicator under the progress bar. *Initiation* is indicated by the paper icon above the progress bar beginning to fly from the folder on the left to the one on the right. The progress bar itself gives and indication of the *Progress* of the task. The flying paper icon gives *Heartbeat* information. *Exceptions* will be indicated by an error window popping up over the progress bar. *Remainder* is indicated by the amount left on the progress bar and the time indicator. *Completion* is indicated by the disappearance of the progress window.

The indicator presents information about progress very successfully, but there is one problem: users often move progress indicators to the edge of their displays, or cover them up with other windows so that they can get on with other tasks whilst, for example, files copy. This means that the display of information is lost. Users may occasionally bring the progress window to the front to see how things are going, but for much of the time it will be hidden. The problem is that the screen is a limited resource (even with large displays) and users want to maximize the amount they devote to their main tasks. A visual progress indicator must compete for visual attention with a primary task (e.g. typing a report) so the user ends up trying to concentrate on two visual tasks at once. In this paper we suggest that sharing the tasks between two different senses may be a better way to present this information; the user can look at the main task and feel the progress indicator.

2.1 Audio Progress Indicators

There has been some work into the design of sonic progress indicators that give information about progress using non-speech sounds, avoiding problems of screen space. Gaver [10] used the sound of liquid pouring from one container to another to indicate copying in his SonicFinder. The change in pitch of the sound gave the listener information about the how the copy was progressing and how close it was to the end. Crease and Brewster [7, 8] looked at using structured non-speech sounds called Earcons to indicate progress. They designed a system that presented *Initiation*, *Progress, Heartbeat, Remainder* and *Completion*. They used a low-pitched sound to represent the end of the progress task and a 'progress' sound to indicate the current amount of the task completed. This started at a high pitch and gradually lowered until it reached the pitch of the end sound. The listener knew when a task had completed because the two played at the same pitch. The design of our tactile progress indicator was partly based on this, but mapped into the time, rather than frequency, domain.

2.2 Tactile Human-Computer Interaction

There have been some good examples of the use of tactile displays to improve human-computer interfaces. Mackenzie and others have successfully shown that basic tactile feedback can improve pointing and steering type interactions [1, 5]. Tactile cues can aid users in hitting targets such as buttons faster and more accurately. Lee *et al.* [13] and have recently developed a tactile stylus to use on touch screens and PDA's. Poupyrev *et al.* and Fukumoto *et al.* [9, 15, 16] have looked at the use of a tactile displays on handheld computers. Much of the focus of work in this area is on device and hardware development; until recently there were few tactile transducers routinely available and they were often designed for use in different domains (for example, sensory substitution systems [12]). Now many mobile telephones and PDAs have vibrotactile actuators included for alerting. These can be used for other purposes. Poupyrev *et al.* [16] have begun to look at interactions using the devices they have created. They describe a tactile progress bar where progress is mapped to the time between two clicks. They say it "... was easy to relate the tactile feedback to the current status of the process", but very little information is given on the design and no evaluation of its effectiveness is reported.

Techniques for encoding information in tactile cues have been investigated in the area of speech presentation to people with hearing impairments. Summers [17] used temporal patterns along with frequency and amplitude to encode speech information in vibrations, and found that participants mainly used information obtained from the temporal patterns, rather than from frequency/amplitude modulations. This suggests that rhythmic patterns would be a good place to start when designing cues for tactile displays.

Brewster and Brown have proposed *Tactons*, or tactile icons. These are structured, abstract messages that can be used to communicate tactually [2-4]. Information is encoded into Tactons using the basic parameters of cutaneous perception, such as waveform, rhythmic patterns and spatial location on the body. Their early results have shown that information can be encoded effectively in this way. Simple Tactons will be used in our system to indicate the state of progress.

2.3 Audio Versus Tactile Presentation

One disadvantage with the auditory display of progress is that either the user must wear headphones or use loudspeakers. Headphones tie the user to the desk and are not always appropriate, and loudspeaker presentation can be annoying to others nearby if the volume is up too high. The advantage of audio is that output devices are common and cheap and users can hear the display from anywhere around them.

Tactile displays do not have the issue with being public as they make no sound, so information can be delivered discretely. The disadvantage is that they must be in good contact with the skin for information to be perceived. Vibrotactile transducers are also not yet common on most desktop computers. If body location is to be used as a design parameter then transducers need to be mounted on different parts of the body and this can be intrusive. Mice such as the Logitech iFeel mouse (www.logitech.com) or most mobile phones and PDA's have a simple vibrotactile transducer built in. The problem is that if the user's hand is not on the mouse or phone then feedback will be missed.

One other issue is distraction. Carefully designed sounds can be habituated and fade into the background of consciousness, only coming to your attention when something changes (just as the sound of an air conditioner only gets your attention when it switches on or off, the rest of the time it fades into the background). It is not clear how we can design tactile displays to facilitate habituation. We easily habituate tactile stimuli (think of clothes for example) but it is not yet clear how we might design dynamic cues that do not annoy the user. We also, of course, need to avoid numbness by too much stimulation.

The choice of vibrotactile, auditory or visual display of information depends on how and when it will be used. At different times one or the other (or a combination of all three) might be most effective. Detailed study of interactions using tactile is needed to understand how to design them and when they should best be used.

3 Experiment

An experiment was conducted to investigate if progress information could be presented using simple Tactons, and if presenting it this way would be more effective than its standard visual form.

3.1 Design of a Tactile Progress Indicator

The basic design of our progress indicator mapped the amount remaining of a download to the time between two pulses; the closer together the pulses the closer to the end of the download. The download is complete when the cues overlap. The time gap between the pulses is scaled to the amount being downloaded (up to a maximum of a 10 second gap in this case).

An Oboe timbre was used as the waveform for all of the cues. This gave a strong signal when presented through the transducer used. The Tactons were all played at a frequency of 250Hz; this is the resonant frequency of the transducer and also the optimum frequency of perception on the skin. The design of the progress indicator used three simple Tactons (the structure of the Tactons used is shown in Figure 2):

- *Start:* this indicated the start of a new download. A tone that increased in amplitude from 0 to maximum over a period of 1.5 seconds followed by 0.5 seconds at maximum amplitude was used.
- *Current:* this marked the current position of the progress indicator and was a single pulse lasting 0.5 seconds. For a new download this was played directly after the Start cue finished. Figure 3 shows the waveform of this stimulus.
- *Target:* this represented the end of the task. As the download progressed the Current stimuli got closer in time to the Target. When they overlapped the download was finished. The Target cue was a series of 4 short pulses, each lasting 0.6 seconds with a total length of 2.5 seconds. This made the two stimuli feel very different to avoid confusion.

According to Conn's properties this progress indicator gives information on *Initiation* (Start cue), *Progress* (movement of Current cue towards Target), *Heartbeat* (the pulsing of the Current cue), *Remainder* (the difference in time between the Current and Target cues), *Completion* (the combined Current and Target cue). Information was not given on *Acceptance*, in this case the task was always the same: file downloading. No *Exceptions* occurred in this experimental study so no feedback was needed.

A single VBW32 transducer was used (see Figure 4). This transducer was designed for use in tactile hearing aids, and is relatively low cost at US$80. It was mounted on the top of the wrist of the non-dominant hand, under a sweat band to keep it tight against the skin. This kept it out of the way so that it did not interfere with typing. Headphones were worn (but not connected) to stop any sounds from the transducer being heard by the participant. The transducer is simple to use as it plugs into the headphone socket of a PC and is controlled by playing sound files. The use of a single transducer meant that this simple design could be used in a range of different devices, for example on a mobile telephone held in a user's hand.

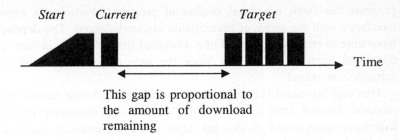

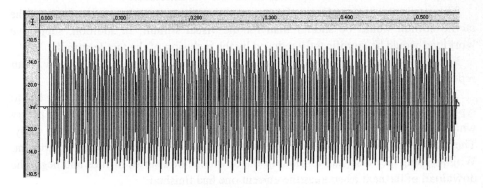

Fig. 2. A schematic layout of the feedback used in the progress indicator for a new download. This would repeat (without the *Start* Tacton) until the download had completed

Fig. 3. Waveform of the *Current* Tacton

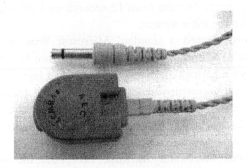

Fig. 4. The Tactaid VBW32 tactile transducer from Audiological Engineering Corporation (www.tactaid.com)

3.2 Experimental Design and Procedure

The experiment was a two-condition within subjects design. The independent variable was interface type with two levels: the standard visual progress bar and the tactile progress bar (with no visual display of progress). Participants experienced both interfaces with the order of presentation counterbalanced. The dependent variables were time to respond to the end of a download (the difference in time from when the download actually finished to when the user clicked the Finished button) and subjective workload.

Hart and Staveland [11] break workload into six different factors: mental demand, physical demand, time pressure, effort expended, performance level achieved and frustration experienced. NASA has developed a measurement tool, the NASA-Task Load Index (TLX) for estimating these subjective factors. We used this but added a seventh factor: Annoyance. In the experiment described here annoyance due to the tactile feedback was measured directly to find out if it was an issue. We also asked participants to indicate overall preference for the two interfaces.

The main experimental hypotheses were that the time taken to respond to the tactile stimuli would be shorter than for the visual stimuli. In addition, subjective workload would be significantly reduced by the inclusion of the tactile stimuli.

Fourteen subjects were used, all students from the University of Glasgow. Four reported themselves as touch-typists; the remainder as 'hunt-and-peck' typists.

The experimental task simulated a typical desktop interaction where the user had to type text and monitor file downloads at the same time. Participants typed in poetry which was given to them on sheets by the side of the computer used in the study. Their task was to type as much poetry as possible in the time of the experiment. Whilst typing they also had to monitor the download of a series of files and begin the download of the next as soon as the current one had finished.

The experimental software was run on a Windows XP machine with a 21 inch monitor set to a resolution of 1600 x 1200 pixels and the application maximized to full screen. Five downloads took place in each condition. These were the same for both conditions and ranged in time from 12 seconds to 1 minute. Two sets of poems were used, taken from the same source.

The Visual condition used a standard Microsoft Windows style progress bar, presented in the right hand corner of the screen (see Figure 5). On the left hand side of the screen was a large area for typing text. The Finished button was pressed when the participant noticed that a download had completed; when pressed it started the next download and recorded time to respond. (The Start button was used to start a condition and the Close button was used to close the application after the last download had been completed.)

The Tactile condition was exactly the same, except that the visual progress bar was not presented. The tactile cues described above were used to present the progress information in this condition.

Subjects were given a brief (approximately 5 minutes) training period before each condition. This gave them some training in the task they were about to perform and the cues they would receive. They received three practice downloads. After each condition they filled in NASA TLX workload charts.

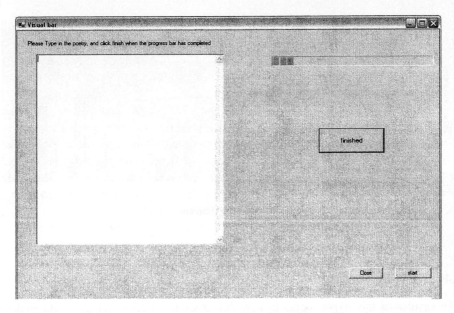

Fig. 5. The experimental interface for the Visual condition of the experiment

3.3 Results

The response times to the downloads are shown in Figure 5. The results show that the participants performed slower in the Visual condition with a mean time to respond of 13.54 seconds (SD 5.2) versus 8.7 seconds (SD 5.6) in the Tactile condition. A T-test showed a significant effect for interface type (T_{13}=3.23, p=0.007), showing that participants noticed the end of a download significantly more quickly in the Tactile condition, confirming the first hypothesis.

In addition, the number of times the participants pressed the Finished button before the current download had finished was counted (this gives some idea of how well users understood the progress cues given). Participants clicked too early 4 out of 70 times in the Visual condition and 8 times in the Tactile. This suggests that users were monitoring well in both conditions, further confirmation that participants could use the tactile progress bar.

The results for subjective workload are presented in Figure 6. Overall workload (computed from the standard six workload factors) showed no significant difference between the two conditions with a mean of 8.5 (SD 2.4) for the Visual condition and 7.5 (SD 2.4) for the Tactile (T_{13}=0.88, p=0.39). The second hypothesis was therefore not confirmed.

Annoyance showed no significant difference between conditions (T_{13}=1.38, p=0.19). Overall preference did show an effect with the Tactile condition significantly preferred over the Visual (T_{13}=4.00, p=0.001).

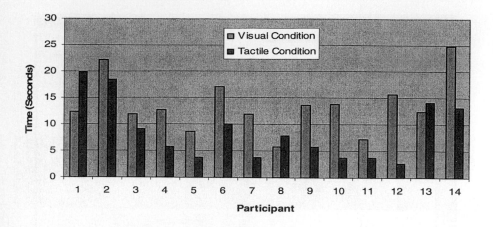

Fig. 6. Mean times to respond to the end of downloads

3.4   Discussion and Future Work

The results of this experiment showed that a simple tactile display could make a successful progress indicator. Participants responded more quickly to the tactile progress indicator than to the visual one. We suggest that this is because the use of the tactile display allowed participants to concentrate visual attention on their primary typing task whilst monitoring the background task of downloading files with their sense of touch, facilitating a sharing of the tasks between senses.

Workload was not significantly reduced by the tactile progress indicator, as predicted. Workload was improved in all categories apart from the mental demand of using the tactile progress indicator. This result may have been due to the unusual task; it is not common to monitor information presented in this way. The effect may be reduced with further exposure to such progress presentation. Participants did prefer the tactile display, which is positive, but this result should be taken with care as there could be some novelty effect. A longer term study would be needed to measure preference over time, but initial results are encouraging. In addition, a further study could look at performance in the typing task to see if users slowed down more or made more typing errors with one type of presentation or another.

Participants took a long time to respond to the end of downloads in both conditions. In Crease's experiment [8] participants responded in 5.3 seconds on average in the visual progress bar condition and 2.8 seconds in the audio. Part of the reason for the difference between this experiment and ours may have been the experimental instructions; in our experiment we told participants that the typing task was their main focus and that they should monitor downloads in the background. Another issue could have been the poetry used. This generally had short lines and it may have been that participants wanted to finish a line before responding to the progress bar (this appeared to happen in informal observations of some users). Therefore the absolute values of response times are less useful than the fact that there was a significant reduction in the Tactile condition. Crease's auditory progress indicator caused a 47% reduction in time to respond. Our tactile progress indicator caused a 36% reduction in time to respond. An interesting study would be to examine all three types of progress displays in one experiment to compare their performance.

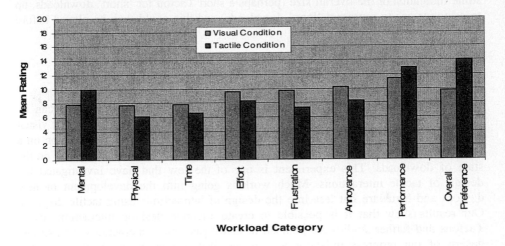

Fig. 7. Mean subjective workload results. Lower scores mean lower workload, except for Performance and Overall Preference where higher scores indicate better performance.

The design we created was simple, using just one transducer. This is beneficial as the cost of adding our tactile display is low so that such a progress indicator could be used in many different situations. Many mobile phones and handheld computers already have a basic tactile transducer in them for alerting purposes. We could use this to present progress information non-visually. This is particularly important as these devices have very limited screen space.

Further work should investigate other designs for the Tactons to see if we can get a faster response from users, for example. These were a first attempt and there is little useful guidance in the literature to facilitate good design. Since this experiment was performed Brown *et al.* [4] have begun to develop some design guidelines for Tactons and these could be incorporated into a future version. We could also make more sophisticated displays of progress information using multiple transducers. For example, a belt of transducers around the waist could be used. In this case a download might start at the front and then move around the body clockwise. When vibration is at the right hip 25% of a download is completed, when at the left hip 75%, and 100% when the vibration reaches the front again. We will need to investigate if this gives a better perception of progress than the simple design presented here.

We have only looked at five of Conn's properties of progress indicators. A further step would be to design cues to represent the others. *Acceptance* might be difficult to present as some form of text is really needed to indicate what type of task has started, unless the possible set of different tasks is small. If that is the case then a Tacton could be included before the progress indicator starts to show its type. *Exception* would be easier as an error Tacton could be created that felt very different to the others to indicate problems and attract the user's attention. *Scope* might also be challenging, especially if the download is very large, as just leaving very long gaps between the tactile cues to show size is likely to confuse users because they will not know if the download has stopped or not. A *Scope* Tacton could be created that gave some indication of the overall size (perhaps a short Tacton for 'short' downloads, up to a longer one to represent 'long' downloads) and this could then be played before the main download started.

4   Conclusions

The experiment reported in this paper has shown that progress indicators can be presented in a tactile form, and that they can be more effective than standard visual progress bars. This is important as it allows users to keep their visual attention on a main task, such as typing, and use their sense of touch to receive information on the state of downloads. This experiment is one of the few that have investigated the design of tactile interactions. Much work is going into the development of new devices and hardware but less into the design of interactions using tactile displays. Our results show that it is possible to create effective desktop interactions using Tactons and further studies are planned to investigate other interactions. The simple design of our progress indicator also means that it may be applicable in other situations, for example handheld computers and mobile telephones could use such an indicator without sacrificing any valuable screen space.

Acknowledgements

This work was funded by EPSRC Advanced Research Fellowship GR/S53244.

References

1. Akamatsu, M., MacKenzie, I.S. and Hasbrouq, T. A comparison of tactile, auditory, and visual feedback in a pointing task using a mouse-type device. *Ergonomics, 38.* 816-827.
2. Brewster, S.A. and Brown, L.M., Non-Visual Information Display Using Tactons. In *Extended Abstracts of ACM CHI 2004*, (Vienna, Austria, 2004), ACM Press, 787-788.
3. Brewster, S.A. and Brown, L.M., Tactons: Structured Tactile Messages for Non-Visual Information Display. In *Proceedings of Australasian User Interface Conference 2004*, (Dunedin, New Zealand, 2004), Austalian Computer Society, 15-23.
4. Brown, L., Brewster, S.A. and Purchase, H., A First Investigation into the Effectiveness of Tactons. In *Proceedings of World Haptics 2005*, (Pisa, Italy, 2005), IEEE Press.
5. Campbell, C., Zhai, S., May, K. and Maglio, P., What You Feel Must Be What You See: Adding Tactile Feedback to the Trackpoint. In *Proceedings of IFIP INTERACT'99*, (Edinburgh, UK, 1999), IOS Press, 383-390.
6. Conn, A.P., Time Affordances: The Time Factor in Diagnostic Usability Heuristics. In *Proceedings of ACM CHI'95*, (Denver, Colorado, USA, 1995), ACM Press Addison-Wesley, 186-193.
7. Crease, M. and Brewster, S.A., Scope for Progress - Monitoring Background Tasks with Sound. In *Volume II of the Proceedings of INTERACT '99*, (Edinburgh, UK, 1999), British Computer Society, 19-20.

8. Crease, M.C. and Brewster, S.A., Making progress with sounds - The design and evaluation of an audio progress bar. In *Proceedings of ICAD'98*, (Glasgow, UK, 1998), British Computer Society.
9. Fukumoto, M. and Toshaki, S., ActiveClick: Tacile Feedback for Touch Panels. in *Extended Abstracts of CHI 2001*, (Seattle, WA, USA, 2001), ACM Press, 121-122.
10. Gaver, W. The SonicFinder: An interface that uses auditory icons. *Human Computer Interaction, 4* (1). 67-94.
11. Hart, S. and Staveland, L. Development of NASA-TLX (Task Load Index): Results of empirical and theoretical research. in Hancock, P. and Meshkati, N. eds. *Human mental workload*, North Holland B.V., Amsterdam, 1988, 139-183.
12. Kaczmarek, K., Webster, J., Bach-y-Rita, P. and Tompkins, W. Electrotacile and vibrotactile displays for sensory substitution systems. *IEEE Transaction on Biomedical Engineering, 38* (1). 1-16.
13. Lee, J.C., Dietz, P., Leigh, D., Yerazunis, W. and Hudson, S.E., Haptic Pen: A Tactile Feedback Stylus for Touch Screens. In *Proceedings of UIST 2004*, (Santa Fe, NM, USA, 2004), ACM Press Addison-Wesley, 291-294.
14. Myers, B.A., The Importance Of Percent-Done Progress Indicators for Computer-Human Interfaces. In *Proceedings of ACM CHI'85*, (San Fransisco, CA, USA, 1985), ACM Press Addison-Wesley, 11-17.
15. Poupyrev, I. and Maruyama, S., Tactile Interfaces for Small Touch Screens. in *Proceedings of UIST 2003*, (Vancouver, Canada, 2003), ACM Press, 217-220.
16. Poupyrev, I., Maruyama, S. and Rekimoto, J., Ambient Touch: Designing tactile interfaces for handheld devices. In *Proceedings of ACM UIST 2002*, (Paris, France, 2002), ACM Press, 51-60.
17. Summers, I.R., Single Channel Information Transfer Through The Skin: Limitations and Possibilities. In *Proceedings of ISAC 00*, (2000).

Haptizing Wind on a Weather Map with Reactive Force and Vibration

Masaki Omata[1], Masami Ishihara[2], Misa Grace Kwok[1], and Atsumi Imamiya[1]

[1] Interdisciplinary Graduate School of Medicine and Engineering,
University of Yamanashi, 400-8510 Kofu, Japan
{omata, grace, imamiya}@hci.media.yamanashi.ac.jp
[2] Graduate School of Engineering, University of Yamanashi,
400-8510 Kofu, Japan
masami@hci.media.yamanashi.ac.jp

Abstract. This paper describes a model for haptizing wind on a weather map. To design the model, we examined the human sensory scale to represent wind speed and direction with appropriate haptic stimuli, and examined parameters of the stimulus that allow a user to easily recognize changes in wind speed and direction. The results of these experiments show that vibration frequency can represent wind speed while a constant reactive force represents direction. The model solves a problem users of reactive force-only systems have difficulty identifying direction when the force is small due to light wind. Based on the model, we have developed a prototype weather information system with visual and haptic information.

1 Introduction

Haptic stimuli are used to present complex scientific information, such as hydrodynamic and weather data, in a readily understandable format. Techniques for haptizing generally provide the fingertips or palms of the user with tactile stimuli by using a kinesthetic feedback device [1].

One application of this technique is haptizing wind. This allows the user to feel wind speed and direction by assigning a reactive force or vibration to these properties [2, 3]. However, in previous systems, which convey direction and speed using the same reactive force, users have had difficulty perceiving direction when wind speed is low, just as with real wind.

To address this problem, we investigate using separate tactile stimuli to represent wind speed and direction. This requires identifying two stimuli that users can perceive changes in simultaneously and without confusion.

In this study, we examined variations in several tactile stimuli and concluded that vibration frequency can effectively represent wind speed while a constant reactive force represents direction. We then apply this combination to a model of haptization.

2 Related Works

Kashiwabara et al. suggested a technique for visualization and haptization of swirling flow in a pipe, implementing contact sensation of virtual particles [2]. The technique

M.F. Costabile and F. Paternò (Eds.): INTERACT 2005, LNCS 3585, pp. 18–29, 2005.

converts velocity and pressure vectors into reactive forces in order to produce haptic data from particle distribution data.

Reimersdahl et al. developed ViSTA FlowLib, which provides haptic information about fluid motion for cases where it is difficult to represent the motion visually, such as local fluid changes [3]. This system provides a scalar field and a vector field of tactile sensation.

A problem with these approaches is that, in faithfully reproducing the relative magnitudes of the variables, they do not consider limitations in the users' sensitivity to tactile stimuli. However, some studies have adapted human sensory scales into haptization. Noma et al. studied a method of representation of volume data using a force-feedback display with haptic sensation [4]. This system uses a reactive force and twisting torque with six degrees of freedom and provides visual information through a head-mounted display. They adjusted the intensity of tactile stimuli to human perception using a difference threshold. However, their system has not been experimentally validated.

Yano et al. developed the VibroGlove and proposed using it to haptize through vibration the direction and speed of a fluid stream [5]. The VibroGlove is a CyberGlove (Virtual Technologies Inc.) mounted with seventeen vibrators. They designed a haptic system based on human perception by correcting the intensity of tactile stimuli using magnitude estimation, sensory accuracy perception, and a difference threshold of vector directions. The VibroGlove has been used to represent the overall flow field of large spaces, such as CAVE [6]. However, it is not clear if it can be used for small spaces, such as PHANToM (SensAble Technologies Inc.). It is still necessary to determine the optimal tactile stimulus type and parameters for haptizing flow at a single point, such as a stylus or fingertip.

3   Perception Experiments with Haptized Wind

This section describes perception experiments to address the problem of haptizing wind. We examined various tactile stimuli to represent wind speed and direction, with consideration of human sensory characteristics and sensitivities. We empirically investigated combined tactile stimuli to simultaneously convey wind speed and direction. We used a two-dimensional vector field on a weather map, employing the Beaufort wind scale for representing speed with sixteen possible directions.

3.1   Experimental Environment

We used PHANToM and a Reachin Display (Reachin Technologies AB) for haptizing wind (Fig. 1). PHANToM provides a stylus with force feedback, allowing a user to feel reactive force, vibration, hardness, roughness, slope and salience. The Reachin system reflects three-dimensional graphics off a semitransparent mirror, so that they appear below the plane of the mirror. The user can see his hands underneath the mirror and "touch" the virtual objects. We presented overall information visually, and local detailed information haptically. The devices were connected to a Windows PC (Intel Pentium III 700 MHz dual CPU, 512 MB RAM, INTERGRAPH Intense3D 4105 graphics card, Microsoft Windows 2000 Professional OS). We used Reachin

API 3.0 to create a three-dimensional space and to develop tactile stimuli for representing wind.

In a subject's differentiation between tactile stimuli is confounded by PHANToM's motor, which produces distinguishable noises. Therefore, subjects wore sound-masking headphones (Fig. 1.).

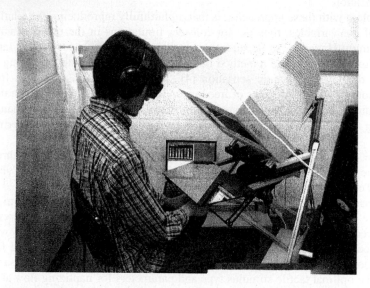

Fig. 1. Experimental environment with PHANToM and Reachin Display

3.2 Appropriateness of Stimuli

We asked subjects to compare the appropriateness of four stimuli for wind flow field, using Scheffé's paired-comparison method. The stimuli tested were those which PHANToM could generate and users could feel changes in without moving the stylus or having to repeatedly "touch" a surface.

Experimental Task. A Subject put the top of stylus on a plate (the size is 5cm x 6cm) and answered appropriateness of a tactile stimulation to wind. Fig. 2 shows six plates assigned two tactile stimulations on the half mirror of Reachin Display. Three of the six plates were placed on upper side, and other three of them were placed lower side. The three plates on upper side were assigned one tactile stimulation of four stimulations, and the three plates on lower side were assigned another tactile stimulation. Moreover, each plate was assigned the different intensity of stimulus.

A subject answered appropriateness between two stimulations on each side separately after he/she touched the six plates about five seconds of each other. While touching the plates, the subject pointed at the same position on the plate without tracing the plate.

We used a 7 point Likert scale as an answer of a trial. A subject, therefore, needed to select one of the 7 points between two tactile stimulations. We also used Scheffé's paired comparison method to analyze subjects' answers between two stimulations.

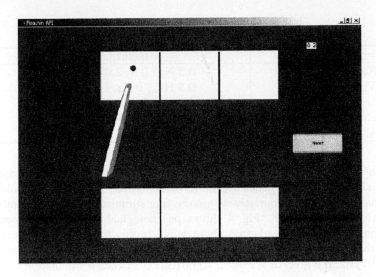

Fig. 2. Display for evaluation for appropriateness

Experimental Stimuli. Fig. 3 and Table 1 show four tactile stimulations of our experiment, which are reactive force, vibration, hardness and slope. Reactive force (0.5, 1.0, 2.0 [N]) is unidirectional force to push the stylus form right to left on a parallel with a plate. Vibration (frequencies: 0.5, 1.0, 1.5 [Hz], amplitude: 1.0 [N]) is simple harmonic oscillation to move the stylus longitudinally on a parallel with a plate. Hardness (50, 100, 200 [N/m]) is normal force on a plate when a subject vertically pushes the stylus on a plate. Slope (0.5 [rad]) is slope of a plate that rotates on its center axis, which divide the plate in half longitudinally. As regarding the slope stimulation, we set the just one condition because we thought that to change an angle of the slope had no effect on subjects when the subjects pointed at the same position on a plate.

The color and the size of all plates are the same each other as visual information, and the differences among the plates are just tactile stimulation as haptic information.

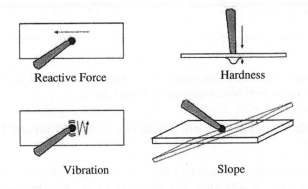

Fig. 3. Four tactile stimuli for evaluation for appropriateness

Table 1. Intensities of four tactile stimuli

Stimulus	Intensities
Reactive force	0.5 N, 1.0 N, 2.0 N
Vibration	0.5 Hz, 1.0 Hz, 1.5 Hz
	Amplitude: 1.0 N
Hardness	50 N/m, 100 N/m, 200 N/m
Slope	0.5 rad

Results and Analysis. Twenty right-handed subjects participated in this experiment. They consisted of fourteen males and six females between 26 and 30 years old.

The main effect of appropriateness among four stimulations is significantly different by ANOVA ($p < 0.01$). Fig. 4 shows psychological scaling of appropriateness among the four tactile stimulations about wind. In this figure, a higher level of the value of the scaling means a higher level of appropriateness about wind, and $Y(0.05)$ and $Y(0.01)$ mean a level of statistical significance between a stimulation and another one.

The analysis shows that reactive force and vibration are equivalent appropriateness about wind. In other words, we can use not only reactive force, which are used in conventional haptization, but also vibration to represent wind with haptic information. Namely, the result and analysis indicate possibility of a new haptization design that allows us to use reactive force to express wind power and to use vibration to express wind direction. Moreover, the design solves the problem that makes it hard to recognize a wind direction when the wind power is low.

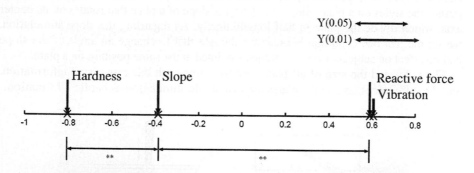

Fig. 4. Psychological scaling of appropriateness for representing wind. A higher level of the scaling means a higher level of appropriateness about wind.

3.3 A Correspondence Examination Between Scale of Wind and Frequency of Vibration

As discussed previously, we revealed that we can represent scale of wind by using change of frequency of vibration. For the next phase, we, therefore, established a model of sensory scales of correspondence between the scale of wind and magnitude of the frequency change. For this purpose, we conducted an experiment to determine the magnitude corresponding to scale of wind represented by numeric value and text as weather information. In this experiment, we used magnitude of the frequency change of wind in formula 1 (contribution ratio: 0.88) that was examined in a prior experiment. The reason why we used this formula is that the rule is Stevens' power law between physical quantity (I) and haptic sensation (S) [7]. In formula 1, I means physical value, and k and α mean constant numbers, which were examined in the prior experiment.

$$I = \left(\frac{S}{k} \right)^{\frac{1}{\alpha}} \qquad \text{[Hz]} \qquad (1)$$

(coefficient: $k = 5.20$, $\alpha = 1.26$, contribution ratio: 0.88)

Experimental Task. A square plate (20 cm on a side) was represented on a half mirror of the Reachin Display (Fig. 5). Numeric value of force of wind and text that explains a situation of wind was displayed on the square (in Japanese). Subjects read the value and text with touching the plate, which was assigned vibration, and adjusted magnitude of the frequency change to his/her sense of the wind by using "Up" button to increase the frequency and "Dn" button to decrease the frequency. Before a subject started performing a task, he/she identified the upper frequency limit and the lower frequency limit, which were adjustable range of a frequency. In addition, we set a frequency randomly in the range when a subject started performing a task.

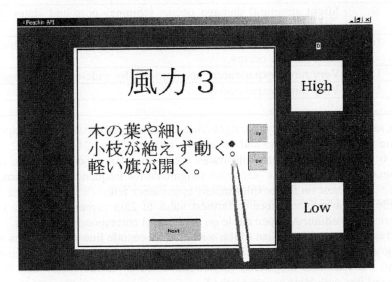

Fig. 5. Display for adjusting vibration frequency to wind speed

Experimental Stimuli. We used the Beaufort wind scale of The Japan Meteorological Agency as value of force of wind and text that represent a state of wind power. The wind scale consists of thirteen degrees of value from 0 to 12 and specification about human activities about wind on land (Table 2) [8] [9]. Amplitude of vibration was 0.83 [N] established in a prior experiment. The 0.83 [N] is the lower limit to recognize a vibration with PHANToM. Direction of a vibration was lengthwise direction of the square, as in the previous experiment (section 3.2).

Table 2. Beaufort wind scale [8]

Force	Description
0	Calm; smoke rises vertically.
1	Direction of wind shown by smoke drift, but not by wind vanes.
2	Wind felt on face; leaves rustle; ordinary vanes moved by wind.
3	Leaves and small twigs in constant motion; wind extends light flag.
4	Raises dust and loose paper; small branches are moved.
5	Small trees in leaf begin to sway; crested wavelets form on inland waters.
6	Large branches in motion; whistling heard in telegraph wires; umbrellas used with difficulty.
7	Whole trees in motion; inconvenience felt when walking against the wind.
8	Breaks twigs off trees; generally impedes progress.
9	Slight structural damage occurs (chimney-pots and slates removed).
10	Seldom experienced inland; trees uprooted; considerable structural damage occurs.
11	Very rarely experienced; accompanied by wide-spread damage.
12	Very rarely experienced

Results and Analysis. Twenty-two right-handed subjects participated in this experiment. They consisted of sixteen males and six females between 20 and 24 years old.

Fig. 6 shows a boxplot that illustrates a correspondence between force of wind (horizontal axis) and subjects' sensation magnitude for frequency of vibration (vertical axis). A whisker on the boxplot means upper inner fence (a farthest value of 75th percentile) or lower inner fence (a farthest value of 25th percentile), and a halfway line represents median. An open circle on the boxplot corresponds to outliers.

The result shows that median of the sensation magnitude linearly increases with increasing value of force of wind. Therefore, the correspondence between force of wind (W) and the sensation magnitude (S) is illustrated by formula 2, which is an approximated line with least-square method.

$$S = aW + b \qquad (2)$$

(coefficient: $a = 10.25$, $b = -2.25$, contribution ratio: 0.97)

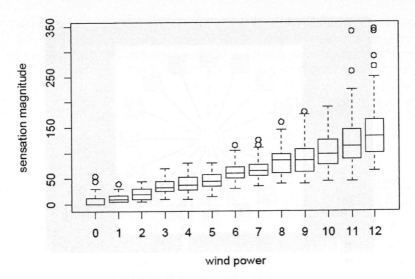

Fig. 6. Vibration frequencies corresponding to wind speeds

3.4 Discrimination of Wind Direction with Reactive Force and Vibration

In section 3.2 we established that it was possible to represent a wind flow field by either reactive force or vibration, and in section 3.2 we established a model of the vibration frequency used to represent wind speed. In this experiment, we investigated subjects' discrimination of wind direction on a wind flow field by representing wind speed by vibration frequency and wind direction by the direction of a constant reactive force. We then compared this system to one using a reactive force to represent both wind properties.

Experimental Task. Subjects were shown a 16-point compass rose on the Reachin Display (Fig. 7). Touching a direction with the stylus produced a randomly directed reactive force. Subjects were asked to push the button corresponding to the direction of the force.

Experimental Stimuli. There were two experimental conditions: one combining a reactive force with vibration, and the other just a reactive force. The vibration amplitude was 0.80 [N] as described in the section 3.3, and the vibration frequency was 10 [Hz], which was the mean value selected by subjects in the experiment of section 3.3. The reactive force was a constant 2.26 [N], which was established in a prior experiment as the minimum constant force detectable using PHANToM. Directions for reactive forces corresponded to the 16 cardinal wind directions (e.g., north-northwest, south-southeast, etc.).

Results and Analysis. Nine right-handed subjects participated in this experiment. They consisted of six males and three females between 21 and 24 years old.

There was no significant difference between the two conditions in either average time to select a direction (5.20 [s] with vibration vs. 5.95 [s] without vibration) or the percentage of correctly identified directions (53.56% with vibration vs. 51.85% without vibration).

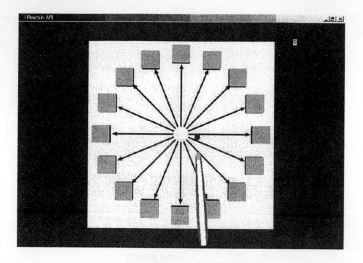

Fig. 7. Display for direction discrimination

The results show that it is difficult for subjects to discriminate among 16 directions for a reactive force. However, when subjects' responses were recalculated using only eight directions, the percentage of directions correctly identified in both conditions was over 90%. Therefore, to allow users a high level of discrimination, our model must be limited to eight wind directions.

4   A Model for Haptizing Wind Using Reactive Force and Vibration

In this section, we propose a model for haptizing wind and a weather information system based on the model.

4.1   A Model for Haptizing Wind with Consideration of Human Sensory Characteristics

Our model for haptizing wind considers human sensory characteristics and sensory scales based on the results of the experiments described above. We limited the wind field to two dimensions, both to simplify evaluation of the model and to simplify integration of visual information for a weather information system.

Formula 3 represents each vector of wind on a grid flow field. In this formula, v_x is vector quantity from east to west and v_y is vector quantity from north to south.

$$v = (v_x, v_y) \tag{3}$$

In our model, wind speed is represented by vibration frequency and wind direction is represented by a constant reactive force. These are established in section 3.2.2.

Changes in vibration frequency are calculated from Formula 2. In addition, we define amplitude of vibration as a simple harmonic motion in order to avoid this force affecting the constant reactive force for wind direction. We use Formulas 4, 5 and 6 to generate simple harmonic motion. In Formulas 5 and 6, t is the time change and f is the frequency of a simple circular harmonic motion.

$$P = (Px, Py) \tag{4}$$

$$P_x = 0.80 \sin(2\pi f t) \tag{5}$$

$$P_y = 0.80 \cos(2\pi f t) \tag{6}$$

Formula 7 is the constant reactive force that represents just a wind direction; it is composed of a unit vector and lower limit of detectable force. $u = (\sin\theta, \cos\theta)$ is a unit vector that is digitized from a wind vector $v = (v_x, v_y)$ to one direction of eight compass directions.

$$D = 2.26u \tag{7}$$

Force F is resultant force transmitted through the stylus to represent wind:

$$F = P + D \tag{8}$$

4.2 A Prototype Weather Information System with Visual and Haptic Information

Using this model, we have developed a weather information system with visual and haptic information. The system allows a user to simultaneously recognize speed and direction of wind by vibration and reactive force, and the system combines the advantages visualization and haptic information. For example, the system allows a user to obtain global information, such as clouds and isobaric lines, as visual information, and local information, such as wind speed and direction at a point, as haptic information. Fig. 8 shows a prototype of the system. When a user indicates a point on the weather map, he or she can feel the speed and direction of the wind at the point with reactive force and vibration, and can see clouds around the point.

We embedded a quantizer and a renderer in this system. The quantizer obtains quantified wind data from WMO DDB (World Meteorology Organization Distributed Data Base) via FTP [10]. The renderer creates a virtual scene with visual and haptic information by using our proposal model with the data from the quantizer. The renderer updates wind data and a virtual scene in response to user's request. The quantizer downloads the latest weather data from the internet in response to update request from the renderer. Fig. 9 shows the data flow from the WMO DDB to PHANToM and Reachin Display.

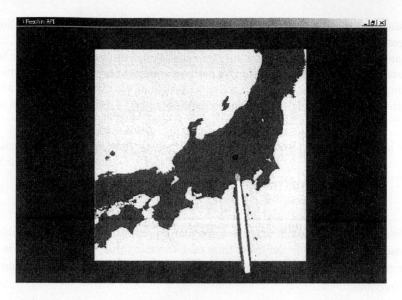

Fig. 8. Prototype weather information system with visual and haptic information

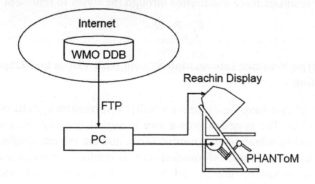

Fig. 9. Data flow diagram of a prototype weather information system

5 Conclusions

In this paper, we have examined a model for haptizing wind on a weather map that
represents wind speed and direction simultaneously using different tactile stimuli,
with a focus on selecting stimuli that are easy for the user to understand. To design
the model, first we conducted experiments to determine appropriate tactile stimuli and
intensities for representing wind. The results showed that vibration frequency can
represent wind speed while constant reactive force represents wind direction. Our
experiments also showed that users can reliably discriminate eight directions of a two-
dimensional wind flow field, even when reactive force and vibration are assigned to
wind simultaneously. The model therefore solves the problem that users of reactive

force-only systems have difficulty identifying direction when the force is small due to light wind.

Using this model we developed a prototype weather information system. The system provides a user with general weather conditions as visual information and wind speed and direction as haptic information. Therefore, this system incorporates a good part of features of both visual perception and tactile perception because users can put the weather in perspective through sight and can perceive a wind at a local point by the sense of touch without the distraction of visual information.

We hope to complete this system soon and then evaluate user interface about tactile stimulations based on our model. After that, we are planning to propose a new haptization model and a new haptic interaction based on human perception.

References

1. Massie, T.H., Salisbury, J.K.: The PHANToM Haptic Interface: A Device for Probing Virtual Objects. Proceedings of the ASME Winter Annual Meeting, Symposium on Haptic Interfaces for Virtual Environment and Teleoperator Systems, Chicago, 55-1 (1994) 295-300
2. Kashiwabara, S., Tanaka, Y., Suzuki, R.: Visualization and Haptization for Swirling Flow in a Pipe. Bulletin of Computational Science Research Center, Hosei University, Vol. 15, (in Japanese) (2002)
3. Reimersdahl, T., Bley, F., Kuhlen, T., Bischof, C.H.: Haptic Rendering Techniques for the Interactive Exploration of CFD Database in Virtual Environments, Proceedings of the Workshop on Virtual Environments (2003) 241-246
4. Noma, H., Iwata, H.: Presentation of Multiple-Dimensional Volume Data by 6 DOF Force Display, Progress in Human Interface, Vol. 3 (1994) 111-120
5. Yano, H.□ Hirose, M.□Ogi, T., Tamura, Y.: Haptization of Flow Field Using Vibroglove. Transaction of Information Processing Society of Japan□ 40 (2), Special Issue on Human Interface and Interaction (in Japanese) (1999) 414-421
6. Cruz-Neira, C., Sandin, D. J., DeFanti, T. A.: Surround-Screen Projection-Based Virtual Reality: The Design and Implementation of the CAVE. Proceedings of SIGGRAPH (1993) 135-142
7. Lindsay, P. H., Norman, D.A.: Human information processing: An introduction to psychology (2nd Ed.). Academic Press (1977)
8. Asano, Y.: Juten Master Kisho-Yohoshi Shiken. Kobunsha (in Japanese) (2000)
9. National Weather Service. http://www.crh.noaa.gov/lot/webpage/beaufort
10. Japan Meteorological Agency, WMO Distributed Data Base /JMA2. http://ddb.kishou. go.jp/

Using ARToolKit Markers to Build Tangible Prototypes and Simulate Other Technologies

Eva Hornecker[1,2] and Thomas Psik[1]

[1] Institute of Design & Assessment of Technology, Technical University Vienna,
Argentinierstr. 8, A-1040 Vienna
[2] Interact Lab, University of Sussex, Falmer, Brighton BN1 9QH, UK
eva@ehornecker.de
tomp@ims.tuwien.ac.at

Abstract. Quick prototyping of tangible user interfaces is currently hampered by availability of toolkits and the double challenge of tinkering with software and hardware. While software may be downloaded, hardware cannot. As a work-around for a class on experimental prototyping of tangible appliances we utilized the ARToolKit that tracks optical markers. By creatively adapting it, our students quickly developed working prototypes, simulating a range of devices and tracking technologies. Our approach enabled a focus on quick prototyping, idea testing and simulation of the interaction process. We explain our reasons for using the ARToolKit, summarize its advantages and disadvantages, present four students projects, and discuss our experiences and conclusions. In particular we found that visual tracking has the advantage not to limit or determine possible interaction styles and thus fosters designing richer interaction. We discuss this as a requirement for future tangible prototyping toolkits.

1 Introduction and Motivation

Quick prototyping of tangible user interfaces is currently hampered by the limited availability of toolkits and the double challenge of bricolaging with software and hardware. Sensing technologies are far from "plug and play" and require time to be mastered while each providing different constraints on what can be tracked [19, 23] and what style of interaction can be designed for. Wiring and soldering electronics requires a lot of time and competencies, which neither computer scientists nor designers usually possess [12]. Existing toolkits often consist of a combination of hardware and software [11,12, 10], only the software being available for free download. With limited budgets one is constrained in selection and often forced to decide on a specific technology too early. For teaching, these problems are even more salient. Such issues turned out as thresholds restricting proliferation of toolkits and accumulation of experience with TUI prototyping (especially for non-computer science communities) during a 2004 workshop about "Toolkit support for interaction in the physical world" [2].

For a class on experimental prototyping of tangible interfaces and appliances we used an existing toolkit widely used for Augmented Reality (short: AR), which relies on visual detection of optical markers ("glyphs"). By creatively adapting this toolkit – the ARToolkit [1], our students managed to quickly develop working prototypes of tangible interfaces, building a range of devices, despite of no budget and almost no

M.F. Costabile and F. Paternò (Eds.): INTERACT 2005, LNCS 3585, pp. 30–42, 2005.

hardware. Using optical markers and vision software, they simulated other kinds of sensing technology, which were not available. As this toolkit is easy to learn, stable and easy to integrate with other software, we avoided many technical problems.

Adapting this existing (and well working) toolkit from another domain and using it for tangible interaction prototypes provides an innovative work-around. Although the ARToolKit has previously been used to develop tangible interaction [8, 20, 21], it has to our knowledge up to now been rarely used *systematically* for "optical simulation" of tangible interaction technologies - in particular not in this variety - and has not been reflected as a teaching tool as well as in its virtues for quick prototyping and focusing on interaction design.

In this article we

- Describe the constraints we had to live with in doing this class
- Present the ARToolKit and the supplementary Open Tracker toolkit used
- Explain the advantages and disadvantages of using this vision technology
- Describe four student group projects, explain the simulated sensing technologies, compare which aspects of the product idea could be prototyped and experienced
- Describe experiences and lessons learned from this class.

1.1 The Class Held and the Constraints Motivating Our Choices

We gave a 3 hour class on "Experimental Design" (6 ECTS) in summer 2004 within the master program media informatics at the Vienna University of Technology. As teacher and practical support person were further involved Prof. Ina Wagner and Kresimir Matkovic. The bachelor program preceding this is technically oriented, providing students with little experience in iterative, user-centered, and creative design approaches. Other students may enter the master degree with other degrees, having less programming experience and different backgrounds.

Our aim was to introduce the students to experimental and creative prototyping methods (mock-ups, theatre and video prototypes) and have them iterate in idea generation and assessment. But we wanted to go beyond a design sketch, students should implement a working (rough) prototype as a proof of concept. With only 3 hours of lecture or presence time, this is – given the high load of classes required and the diversity of students – a wide scope. We needed time for introducing methods, idea generation and design reviews, leaving about a month for implementation. (usual for a technically oriented degree program like ours would be the opposite distribution). In addition we had no budget, could not buy hardware for students, and did not own much to lend away. Given our staff resources we needed to restrict students to a small range of technologies that we could give assistance for.

Having experience with barcode readers and the ARToolKit, we decided to restrict support to these technologies. Nevertheless we wanted the student groups to develop product ideas without feeling constrained by technology. They should focus on the product idea first, iterate and redesign it with consideration of the intended use context instead of being driven by technology. Therefore we introduced the available sensing technology only after the product ideas had been developed.

2 Using ARToolKit and Open Tracker

The main principle of the ARToolkit [1, 5, 15] is as follows. Visual markers (printable with a standard printer) are detected in a live video stream, extracting the 3D position of the marker (relative to camera position) and its rotation (relative to default orientation of the marker). We used the ARToolKit framework as basis, as the hardware needed as tracking device consists only of a web-cam. The markers have to have a certain look and the size of the markers depends highly on the camera resolution being used. It is a well known and often used framework in the AR-community, this ensures that the framework is thoroughly tested and stable. Furthermore we used the Open Tracker library (developed at Vienna University of Technology, IMS Institute [13, 17]) that delivers an abstracted data stream from the tracking device. For our students we provided a compiled version of the software, which reduces the installation process to copying the files. We also included a ready-to-use configuration file for the server, thus reducing the setup procedure to a minimum.

Open Tracker [13, 17] provides an abstraction layer for tracking devices. Support for a number of tracking devices and also other tracking frameworks are included in the library. The library is well documented and is being used as a basis for the AR system Studierstube [13, 14,17]. The library includes a network sink that sends tracking data to the network. The tracking server is configurable through a XML-file, where the tracking devices and the sinks can be defined. The framework also allows transforming the data, before it is sent to the network. This however requires advanced understanding of 3D coordinate system manipulation and calculation. The output is a stream of tracking data including, besides position and orientation, a quality measure of the data. It does not provide support for interpretation of the data or event handling, like "marker appeared" or "marker removed". The detection of these events has to be implemented in the application layer. In order to ease this generic task we provided the students with a small Java class as a template for their own implementation. This already performed some basic functions like reading data from the Open Tracker network stream and producing events.

In [15, 5] the usage of the ARToolKit markers and their restrictions as well as details on the toolkit itself are described in detail, focusing on the application area of augmented reality. Other contexts of usage of the same library are presented in [14]. The ARToolKit has been used to develop several tangible interfaces [8, 20, 21]. One TUI toolkit resembling the ARToolKits capabilities in many respects is Papier-Mâché [16], which integrates different tracking technologies besides vision and provides higher support for programming and debugging.

The tracking technology chosen influences what can be tracked and therefore interpreted (cp. [23, 4]): (a) presence of (unidentified) objects, (b) identity of objects, (c) position, (d) orientation, (e) movement (discrete or continuous) (f) relations of objects to each other (g) activation and other events (besides of movement). „Real" image recognition being slow and difficult, image recognition is usually restricted to attached barcodes or optical markers. Problems result from occlusion through hands, body or other objects, delaying the system reaction until markers are visible again. Further problems are: stability, robustness, and especially changes in light [19, 4, 24], requiring close control of lighting conditions. Clever choice of markers like in the ARToolKit and size of markers improve reliability and speed of recognition. Unfortunately barcodes and markers from a users viewpoint are distracting, not task-related and not aesthetic (see [24]). Besides of barcodes [16] some systems rely on markers reflecting ultra-violet light [6]. We will now reflect on advantages and disadvantages of these ARToolKit markers in the context of prototyping tangible interfaces and appliances.

2.1 Advantages and Disadvantages of the ARToolKit in the Tangibles Context

We were not aware of advantages beyond easy learnability, fast tracking, and price when we decided to use the ARToolKit. We became aware of some of the advantages reported below only in reflecting upon the class and the different student projects. The same holds for disadvantages.

Advantages
When comparing the ARToolKit markers with other kinds of sensing technology, we find several advantages. Unlike most RFID systems, detection is not restricted to adjacent surfaces and very precise. We can detect absence, presence, position and orientation of tags (the last is (almost) impossible with only one RFID). In principle, one can track markers in 3D space, only limited by visibility of the marker within line of sight. Detection is fast, allowing for tracking movement and for simultaneous presence of several markers. In addition there are no cables necessary, which do restrict interaction with some 3D tracking devices. Markers can be attached anywhere and need not be built into objects.

For these reasons prototyping with optical markers allows for a wide range of movements and styles of interaction. The toolkit itself does not restrict interpretation of events to simple event-effect mappings, thus allowing for more sophisticated interaction patterns. This allows pushing tangible interaction design beyond imitating GUI interaction styles (the ubiquitous button pushing and slider shoving) and inventing more varied interaction styles which take account of human bodily skills, are expressive in movement and make interaction enjoyable [7, 9]. Tracking in free space furthermore allows to go beyond shoving objects around on flat surfaces (the dominant interaction style of most existing TUIs). Some larger toolkits like Phidgets [11, 12] which integrate several types of sensors, that allow similar freedom use accelerometers, which can be deployed in three axis which give continuous outputs ss do the force and light sensors

With optical markers we have almost no hardware costs. The software includes a module for printing out new markers and mapping them to an ID. As a video camera most web-cams suffice. The software is highly reliable, being in wide use within the AR community and developed in cooperative effort by several research groups worldwide. By providing a compiled version of the software and a ready-to-use configuration file, we could reduce the installation and setup procedure to a minimum. Unlike many other hardware tracking toolkits, where calibration often takes hours and is vulnerable to many factors (electro fields, metal, water, other materials....) calibration is easy and quickly done, supported by specific software.

In effect our students got going with the ARToolKit in a day or two, being able to concentrate on implementing their idea concept, instead of indulging in the idiosyncratic problems of sensing hardware. Using the optical markers and vision technology, the groups were able to test the core functionality of and the interaction with their product. As will become salient in the presentation and discussion of students' working prototypes, testing the feel of interaction did work for many areas.

2.2 Disadvantages of Using Optical Markers and Vision Tracking

A well known problem of vision tracking is the control of lighting [19]. Changing levels of light and limited contrasts disable correct registration, similar to the problem of the angle between light and camera. The ARToolKit requires relatively large black surfaces, which printed out with some laser printers tend to reflect the light, giving highlights in the video image. A better solution is to use ink-jet printer, or to adjust the angle between light, markers and camera. Related is the problem of tag occlusion. Tags need to be fully within camera view to be detected. Thus occlusion by the inter-actors' bodies or by stacking objects makes tagged objects virtually absent. If one marker overlaps with another marker, the overlapped one will not be detected. Furthermore the camera field determines the interaction space and limits it. Additionally markers in 3D are only registered as long as they are visible within a certain angle of orientation (one cannot turn them around 180°).

Marker tags need to be visible and thus may interfere with aesthetics and intuitive legibility of objects. The looks of a tangible interface, "simulated" with tags, often differ from the intended product and may distract users and evaluators from the general idea. The required tag size (for detection) also limits the smallness of registered objects. And over time tags will deter, fade or get dirty, thus endangering long-term usage of tags (this is less of a problem when prototyping) [24, 19].

For some goal technologies one may need to invent a clever set-up – an example of how this can be done is presented later-on. Nevertheless there are limits to what kind of sensing technology and product idea is simple to prototype and simulate. While for large devices optical markers and the camera may be hidden inside the device, this is not possible for small devices (e.g. a handheld with many buttons). For these a proto-typing toolkit such as CALDER [18] will be more appropriate. As another example, a device that controls lighting would disable its own tracking conditions.

A disadvantage of using the ARToolKit is that it only eases the registration process and the creation of events. Different from tangible prototyping toolkits there is no easy mechanism for connecting events with resulting actions. Interpretation of events and output of interaction (system response) must be implemented in standard pro-gramming languages, requiring some programming experience. Necessary is also programming of basic position calculations. As it is used mostly for Augmented Real-ity, the toolkits eases detection of markers and overlaying an image at the appropriate point in an AR display. When designing tangible interfaces and appliances, there may be different requirements on programming support, better served by toolkits designed specifically for TUI prototyping, as [16, 3, 11, 12].

3   Student Projects

We present four out of six student projects here. These were the best (either in origi-nal idea or in iterating and implementing it) and do suffice for showing the diversity of sensing technology simulated. Two of these are very innovative in simulating mechanical or electrical sensing respectively GPS, the others are variants of common ARToolKit uses. As common theme the class was given "home and household". Some students had attended a previous class on investigation methods, these were allowed to stay with this topic (tourists in Vienna). In total 28 students took part in the course. We describe the basic product idea and the working prototype, focusing on which aspects of the final product (look, handling, interaction process) the prototype helped to experience and assess.

The Mimic Music Maker
This group focused on the selection of music titles from a database. The title selection should be based on the users mood and personal preferences. The user should also be able to enlarge and refine the database on the fly. To enforce the emotional character of the device, the group decided to use a mask as interface, what also gave it a playful aspect. The final device would have the form of a full head instead of only a mask. For identifying oneself (choosing settings) one would put a hat or something else on top (with tracked RFIDs) to identify oneself. The mask should have a well visible switch (with legible state) for selecting the "set track mood" mode. Manipulating its facial expression defines the mood (happy, sad, angry …) the currently playing track is connected with in the database. The group implemented the main functionality of choosing a music style by manipulating the masks facial expression.

This device would be implemented using potentiometers or other kinds of electrical sensing for registering manipulations. Students resorted to mechanical engineering, making use of the fact that a mask has a big backside to hide the mechanics and put up a camera behind. One could move the eyebrows and the mouth to form a smile, a neutral look, or a frown. Levers and sliders manipulated on the face are connected with mechanics behind it and move optical markers. The camera tracks this movement. The group was able to prototype the look of the device and to test a good amount of its interaction feel (restricted by some problems in building the mechanics).

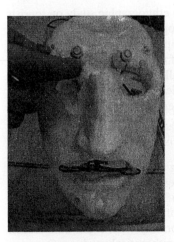
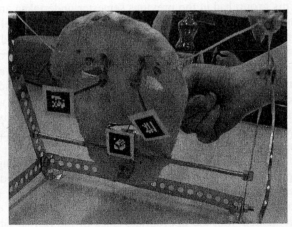

Fig. 1. Mimic Music Maker: Manipulating the mask and optical markers moving at the backside, visible for the web cam positioned behind the mask

Fig. 2. Tourist Navigation Device: Mock-Up with display and vibrating (red) parts on the sides. Demo of working prototype - the system detects a visual marker (camera worn on hat) of a site and spoken text output is triggered.

With some bricolaging many other mechanically manipulated devices could be emulated in a similar way, using levers, strings etc. that move optical markers somewhere on the backside of the device or in a distance. Not for all kinds of devices this will be as easy. Levers and strings must be attached somewhere and optical tags put so they do not interfere with interaction. This limits the smallness of devices that can be designed. A negative effect of using vision detection is that the position of the camera must be fixed relative to markers. The mechanical construction of this combination – movable markers and fixed camera position – is one of the major problems for students not educated in mechanical construction.

Tourist Navigation Device
This group had in the previous semester undertaken an ethnographic study on tourists in Vienna. Building upon this experience, they developed the idea of a device that enables finding interesting sites while walking serendipitously through the city. The device would tell the tourist strolling through the city if (s)he comes close to anything previously marked as interesting so (s)he does not walk past. The device could also enable following a given path, if switching into guided mode. This group initially developed a video prototype showing the use of two versions for their product in the inner district of Vienna (performed and role-played by group members). This in-situ experience helped them in deciding upon form factors (see mock-up in figure 2 left) and interaction style for the device.

The product idea consists of selling the device along with city guides marked with optical codes. City visitors use the device to scan codes for those sites they want to see. If walking through the city, the device vibrates if coming close to a site. The small display would show where to go and the name of the site. This could be complemented with the appropriate sides of the device vibrating (left, right, both sides). Information boards at attractions could be augmented with optical markers. On scanning these, the tourist would hear explanations via earphones.

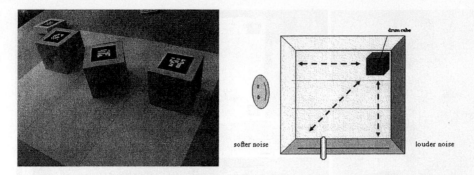

Fig. 3. Composing Cubes: Blocks and playing board. Principle of working.

The goal technology for realizing this device would be GPS (or cell phone cells for identifying location) plus orientation sensors and a bar code reader. The group employed optical simulation of location detection by wearing a camera on the head and strategically placing optical markers in the room. This way they could simulate the interaction process that a tourist would experience and explore potential interaction patterns and problems. This supports iterative software-development. A positive side effect is that testing the software and simulating interaction can occur anywhere, independent of "real" locations by just hanging up markers. For the working prototype, the computer had to be carried around by the test person, as the camera needs to be tethered to it. Therefore the looks of the device did not resemble the design idea at all and the concrete feel of interaction, especially of manual handling, could not be simulated. But the student group had spent a lot of time on deciding on form factors, tinkering a non-functional mock-up well in advance.

Composing Cubes
This group iterated their idea several times, starting from the (too complicated) idea of a puzzle for blind and sighted people with musical feedback which also allows composing music. They eventually decided to focus on a music composing device (c.p. [8, 20]. The system consists of a playing board with different areas. Different cubes represent different musical instruments. The playing board is divided into three visible columns from left to right of the player. These columns represent three different effects (echo, reverb...). Moving cubes on a column controls volume. On the right-hand side a slide-sensor can be moved up and down. This regulates the tempo. For a more advanced version it was envisioned to use three cameras set up at 45° angles from the board, recognizing e.g. stacking of cubes. Turning the cubes over and setting it back on the board activates a different melody.

For such a system one can imagine using either vision or field sensing as implementation technology. E.g. AudioPad (building up on SensePad) uses RFID tracking [19]. Most prototypical systems use optical markers [8]. As students demonstrated, response times are good enough and the system works well under stable lighting conditions. With vision tracking, further forms of manipulation are possible, such as occluding a cube to stop a track from playing. Vision tracking suffers mostly from the big markers on top of elements, making it difficult to place intuitive icons on them

Fig. 4. Interactive TV: The TV magazine has a reservoir of adhesive optical markers. Demo of attaching markers to shows (VCR programming) and selecting a show (starts the TV and selects channel (demoed on computer).

and to make them aesthetically pleasing. Due to stable and quick registration, the prototype system provided a close experience of the interaction feel that a system with field sensing would have.

Interactive TV

The product idea of this group was a TV magazine that enables controlling the TV set and programming the VCR from the magazine. Neither would one need to search the remote control nor remember which channel is placed on what number or how to program the VCR. This group started out in developing this product idea by role-playing situations in a theatre-like way.

The magazine must be placed on a location where it is visible for the camera. Pointing with the finger (or a pointing tool) to any TV show starts the TV and selects the channel, if the show/movie is currently running. Attaching post-its with optical markers to a TV show programs the VCR to record it. Attaching another kind of marker switches the TV and the channel on as soon as the selected show starts. The magazine has a supply of markers on its last page. An advantage of these markers is their persistence, giving an overview of what a family wants to record or see in a week. Browsing through the TV magazine would remain as usual. Deciding upon what to record could take place anywhere, as the magazine is moveable. Zapping would still be easy to do by pointing. Here the goal technology would be vision, albeit probably using infra-red markers, so that visual icons can be legible for laypersons.

The prototype enabled simulating potential looks of such a system, the feel of using it and experiencing the interaction process (albeit without a real TV, using a computer to simulate responses). The prototype served well as a proof of concept. An advantage of using the ARToolKit that here got salient was the possibility of 3D interaction, when selecting shows by pointing.

4   Our Experience with This Class and Lessons Learned

Our students highly enjoyed this class and its experimental character. Although the time given for implementation was considered by most as too short, they would not have missed the time for idea generation and iteration and the exposure to creative prototyping methods. They were proud of their ability to bricolage and to invent work-arounds or tricks in simulating non-available sensing technologies. Getting the tracking working and implementing the product idea in the last month of the semester, which is crowded with hand-ins and exams, challenged students a lot. Student feedback taught us, that despite of the early focus on methods we should give out the ARToolKit framework earlier (done in the new run of the class). This would allow time to experiment with set-up of the system, registration, and calibration. Unfortunately it may also interfere with having groups develop ideas freely (without having in mind technical constraints).

All groups had chosen to focus on home entertainment from the common theme of „home and housekeeping". As we could see from the tourist project group, detailed (ethnographic) investigation of a theme has high impact on the product idea, improving contextual knowledge and awareness of factors affecting use of the device. Most groups were not as aware of factors on usability, desirability or practicability of devices. Yet considering the limited time available, we are happy with the results.

Students programmed in Java, Perl and C^{++}, sometimes using several computers for different aspects of the functionality. Some of the groups needed little support for programming, others needed support in design principles and methods. With basic programming experience the functionality itself was usually easy to implement, as there were no complicated algorithms included in the project ideas. Therefore team building should ensure a sufficient range of competencies within groups. We observed that most groups developed a division of labor with some members responsible for design and physical tinkering and others concentrating on programming. For our class with its focus on process this is fine. If everybody should acquire experience in programming or in visual design, additional exercises and lectures would be necessary and there might be less focus on inspiring and creative design methods. In the new run of the class more emphasis was put on students declaring their competencies and assignment of responsibilities for e.g. documentation, interaction design (responsible for facilitation, approaches of prototyping), programming, project coordination and media design (documents, visuals, sound, video....).

For students with a basic computer science education and some proficiency in programming it was easy to get the ARToolKit working and to develop simple applications using its data input. For students with different backgrounds the challenge is much higher, especially as for some applications geometric calculations for position and orientation are necessary. In standard AR applications the marker is simply visually overlaid in the display with an image. For our purposes, tracking events must go through further processing, extracting appearance, disappearance or movement of markers. As second step these events are mapped with resulting actions. Here a toolkit such as Papier-Mâché [16], or a graphical mapping of events and actions such as in iStuff [3] might be beneficial in lowering thresholds for non-programmers.

The simple technology used for implementation enabled an (uncommon) focus on the design process and idea or scenario generation. Except for one group all were able to present a working prototype showing core functionality. Most groups had started out generating ideas with no particular tracking technology in mind and did manage to implement these. The examples given demonstrate that it was possible to simulate a wide range of tracking technologies and to prototype various kinds of devices.

On reflecting the resulting prototypes another advantage of using optical markers became obvious. The technology does not limit or determine possible interaction styles. One can move markers around freely – or alternatively the camera – resulting in a continuous flow of events. Interaction thus is not restricted to pushing buttons or touching specific sensorized points. Movement can be in 3D and simultaneous. The type of events interpreted thus can differ widely. Effort is moved towards the algorithms making sense of detection events. Such an algorithm may e.g. create meta-events depending on previous events. As indicated earlier, creating such kind of software requires more programming experience.

5 Conclusions and Summary

A major problem of tangible toolkits is that only the software can be downloaded via internet – hardware parts with sensors and actuators must be bought, configured or self-soldered. Tinkering with electronics requires a lot of time (even for people who do this more often) and competence in fields, that computer science and design students and practitioners are not well trained in. The specific quality of Tangibles – to be tangible and physically embodied– renders sharing (of tools, results, systems) more difficult in these respects. Our approach provides a work-around for teachers and researchers, which do not have the resources to buy or develop their own technologies, but want to focus on quick prototyping and idea testing.

Using optical markers and the AR toolkit enabled our students to quickly prototype tangible interfaces while not prematurely closing down the idea space. Student groups invented optical simulations for different tracking technologies and device types. Our choice was originally mostly due to our constraints concerning funding, available hardware and the kind of support we could give to students. Observing the results of student project work revealed additional advantages. Interaction styles are not limited to button pushing and sliders or to shoving objects around on a table. The toolkit allows for interpretation of a continuous flow of events, which can also be simultaneous. Interpretation is not restricted to simple mappings of discrete events with one-click-effects. On the other hand, effort is shifted towards the algorithms interpreting the dataflow, raising demands on programming experience.

Our assumption that the toolkit would be easy to set-up, use and to integrate with other software proved correct – at least for the kind of students we had in this class. We assume that student groups without members having programming experience will experience more problems. A remedy might consist of additional toolkit modules, which enable easy mapping of events with actions, e.g. by graphically connecting event types with actions and devices, as in iStuff [3]. The Phidget toolkit [11, 12] enables mapping incoming physical events with button clicks of standard GUI applications. One such system the Equip Component Toolkit (ECT) [25] allows designers to engage with constructed system components through a GUI that displays the flow of information instigated by a particular action, as it occurs. Nevertheless such mechanisms often tend to predefine what constitutes an event, doing some filtering of events and defining possible kinds of mapping.

Djajadiningrat et al [9] recommend emphasizing the expressiveness of interaction, especially in bodily interaction – that is the how of acting affects the effect. But most toolkits do not support value ranges, combining several inputs, continuous action-event couplings (besides of discrete, button-pushing like events). Hardware toolkits also can limit expressiveness, if they restrict interaction to pushing and sliding – one could also rub, move, hit or stroke a button. Ingenious designers will be able to nevertheless design innovative and expressive forms of interaction. But what is easy to do will be used by those who are less inventive, have less patience or do not know better. Toolkits may, by making it easy to develop an exact, event-based language of interaction, discourage exploring the richness of interaction meaning and style.

We do not consider development of tangible prototyping toolkits to be unnecessary, on the contrary. Yet there is currently only a handful of such toolkits and few research teams developing them. Given that there is only a limited number of people investing time in developing this software, progress is still slow. The AR toolkit on the other hand is being developed as an open source project with lots of people from the Augmented Reality community contributing to it.

We do not claim to be the first using the ARToolKit for developing tangible interfaces/systems. But we (respectively our students) seem to be among the first to use it explicitly for quick prototyping of tangibles and to emulate/simulate such a wide range of different tracking technologies. Most publications focus on one system designed or on the toolkit itself. This paper laid focus on interaction design when analyzing our students' prototypes and discussed toolkits in terms of what style of interaction they lend themselves to design for. Growing experience in using tangible prototyping toolkits and comparing experiences with different toolkits will advance the community in understanding strengths and weaknesses of toolkits and in setting up requirements for future toolkits.

Acknowledgements

Thanks to all participants of the Pervasive 2004 Workshop on Toolkit Support for Interaction in the Physical World, the students participating in our class, Prof. Ina Wagner for teaching the class with us and Krejomir Matcovic for helping us in supporting the students in working with the ARToolKit. Eric Harris from Interact Lab provided comments on technical issues of toolkits and sensor.

References

1. ARToolKit Download Page http://www.hitl.washington.edu/research/shared_space/download/
2. Ballagas, R., Klemmer, S., Sheridan, J.: Toolkit Support for Interaction in the Physical World. Workshop at Pervasive'04. 20.4.2004, Vienna. (2004) http://media.informatik. rwth-aachen.de/tuit/

3. Ballagas, R., Ringel, M., Stone, M., Borchers, J.: iStuff: A Physical User Interface Toolkit for Ubiquitous Computing Environments. Proc. of CHI'03. ACM (2003). pp.537-544

4. Benford, S. et al: Sensible, sensable and desirable: a framework for designing physical interfaces. Tech Report Equator-03-003 (2003)

5. Billinghurst, M., Kato, H., Poupyrev, I.:The MagicBook: A Transitional AR Interface. In: Computers and Graphics, November (2001). pp. 745-753.

6. Brown, L.D., Gao, C., Hua, H.: Toward a Tangible Interface for Multi-Modal Interior Design using SCAPE. Proc. of IEEE VR'04 Workshop Beyond Wand and Glove Based Interaction. (2004). 79-83

7. Buur, J., Jensen, M.V., Djajadiningrat, T.: Hands-only scenarios and video action walls: novel methods for tangible user interaction design. Proc. of DIS'04. ACM (2004) pp. 185-192

8. Constanza. E., Shelley, S.B., Robinson, J.A.: D-TOUCH: A Consumer-Grade Tangible Interface Module and Musical Applications. Proc. of HCI 2003. Bath, UK (2003)

9. Djajadiningrat, T., Overbeeke, K., Wensveen, S.: But how, Donald, tell us how? On the creation of meaning in interaction design through feedforward and inherent feedback. Proc. of DIS'02. ACM (2002). 285-291

10. Gellersen, H., Kortuem, G., Schmidt, A., Beigl, M.: Physical Prototyping with Smart-Its. In IEEE Pervasive Computing 3(3) (2004). pp. 10-18

11. Greenberg, S., Boyle, M.: Interaction in the real world: Customizable Physical Interfaces for Interacting with Conventional Applications. Proc. of UIST'02. ACM (2002). 31-40

12. Greenberg, S., Fitchett, C.: Phidgets: Easy Development of Physical Interfaces through Physical Widgets. Proc. of UIST'01. ACM (2001). 209-218

13. IMS ARToolKit Page http://www.ims.tuwien.ac.at/~thomas/artoolkit.php

14. Kalkusch, et al: Structured visual markers for indoor pathfinding. Proc. of IEEE 1st Int. Workshop on Augmented Reality ToolKit, (2002). technical report TR-188-2-2002-13, Vienna University of Technology.

15. Kato, H., Billinghurst, M., et al.:Virtual Object Manipulation on a Table-Top AR Environment. In: Proceedings of International Symposium on Augmented Reality ISAR 2000, (2000). 111-119

16. Klemmer, S.R., Li, J., Lin, J., Landay, J.A.: Papier-Mâché: Toolkit Support for Tangible Input. Proc. of CHI'04. ACM (2004). pp. 399–406.

17. Lee, J.L, et al: The Calder Toolkit: Wired and Wireless Components for Rapidly Prototyping Interactive Devices. Proc. of DIS'04. ACM (2004). 167-175

18. OpenTracker Download Page http://www.studierstube.org/opentracker/index.html

19. Patten, J., H. Ishii, J. Hines & G. Pangaro (2001). Sensetable: A Wireless Object Tracking Platform for Tangible User Interfaces. Proc. of CHI'01. ACM (2001) 253-260.

20. Poupyrev, I.: Augmented Grooove: Collaborative Jamming in Augmented Reality. Proc. of SIGGraph'00 Conference Abstracts. ACM (2000). 77

21. Sinclair, P., et al.: Links in the palm of your hand: tangible hypermedia using augmented reality. Proc. of Hypertext and Hypermedia. ACM (2002) 127-113

22. 22.Ullmer, B., Ishii, H.: Emerging Frameworks for Tangible User Interfaces. IBM Systems Journal 39(3 & 4) (2000). pp 915-931.

23. Ullmer, B.: Tangible Interfaces for Manipulating Aggregates of Digital Information. Dissertation, Massachusetts Institute of Technology (2002)

24. Want, R., Fishkin, K.P., Gujar, A., Harrison, B.L.: Bridging Physical and Virtual Worlds with Electronic Tags. Proc. of CHI'99. ACM (1999). 370-377

25. ECT http://ubisys.cs.uiuc.edu/proceedings_04/toolkit_rapid_construction.pdf

Augmented Reality Painting and Collage: Evaluating Tangible Interaction in a Field Study

Giulio Jacucci[1], Antti Oulasvirta[1], Antti Salovaara[1], Thomas Psik [2], and Ina Wagner[2]

[1] Helsinki Institute for Information Technology,
P.O. Box 9800, FIN-02015 TKK, Finland
{firstname.surname}@hiit.fi
[2] Vienna University of Technology,
Argentinierstrasse 8, A-1040 Vienna, Austria
iwagner@pop.tuwien.at, thomas.psik@media.tuwien.at

Abstract. Tangible computing applications are rarely evaluated with field studies in real settings, which can contribute as formative studies to understand the challenges and benefits of tangible interfaces in real world practices. We present an AR environment for painting, with a physical brush, digital textures on physical models and creating dynamic stages for the model with spatial collages providing different backgrounds. We report on an evaluation of this AR environment in an architecture school, where 8 groups of students used it as a practical assignment. The evaluation demonstrated the benefits of specific features of the environment and of its tangible interfaces: immersiveness, public availability, supporting collaboration, flexibility, dynamicism and resulting rapidity in creating mixed media representations. Several challenges surfaced from the evaluation especially in connection to the distribution of the interface. The physical, spatial, and computational separation of interface components raised issues on accountability and ergonomics. We link our observations to design guidelines.

1 Introduction

Research on developing augmented environments has been rarely based on naturalistic field trials. Various reasons have been indicated, for example, the difficulty of producing prototypes reliable enough to be introduced in real settings, as they often include the widest range of technology that has to work together: software, middleware, hardware, and physical interface (cf. [1]).

This is also part of a general trend, as Abowd and co-authors indicate that little research is "published from an evaluation or end-user perspective in the ubicomp community" [2, p. 56]. Naturalistic studies in real settings are important not only as summative empirical studies, but also as *formative studies* that can inform the development of applications and interfaces, especially in "pervasive computing in which technologies' potential purposes are not clear". Moreover, even if the purpose is clear, the fits or benefits of a specific application or interface can be only validated through a naturalistic study and specific challenges might only emerge in real use. Following this direction, we report here on a naturalistic evaluation of and environment for AR painting and collage. We use the concepts of "naturalistic or situated evaluation" and

M.F. Costabile and F. Paternò (Eds.): INTERACT 2005, LNCS 3585, pp. 43–56, 2005.
© IFIP International Federation for Information Processing 2005

"real setting" to mean that the technology was used by participants in their own physical environment, to carry out their own projects and goals.

In this AR environment, users can position a physical model on a table, for example on top of a projected plan, and use an application, the Texture Brush, for 'painting' the model using various digital textures. The Texture Brush uses a real brush equipped with a button, which is tracked by an infrared camera. The system projects the virtual 'paint' only where the brush passes by and the button is pressed. In addition, the user can configure an immersive and dynamic stage for the model with three large projections in the background. A simple barcode scanner interface makes it possible to load digital media as texture to be painted or as background. Moreover, painted textures and the background stage can be saved as configurations on a simple barcode, making it possible to load and save sessions with a simple scan of a barcode. After the related work, we present in Section 2 the environment and its components. In Section 3, we report the main findings from the field study, which included 8 groups of architecture students alternatively working in the environment over a period of two weeks. In Section 4, we summarise the lessons learned from the evaluation in terms of the benefits of this tangible interface and of the challenges and problems that emerged during the study.

1.1 Related Work

The related work can be described as being part of these different categories: application demonstrations, comparisons of 2D versus tangible, observational studies, heuristic evaluation and system guidelines.

Application Demonstrations. Physical models have been used as canvases for digital images previously, for example in [3]. Their system, designed with architects and designers in mind, projects imagery onto scale models and contains a real-time location tracking. This allows users to move objects around the table, while the projection is adjusted to follow the movements. Users manipulate the projected images by using a graphics program on an adjacent computer [3]. Another system has a stylus that enables the user to work with the model directly [4]. This model also lets the user move the objects around and hold them in their hands. There is a palette projected onto a table where the user may choose the way he/she manipulates the projection with the stylus. Limitations of the approach, according to the authors, include occlusion and shadows in the model, and the question of catering for objects whose shape may change. Another work reports on a system for learning the principles of pneumatics [5]. In this case, two cameras are positioned over a table, and barcode image recognition is applied to identify the objects on the table, thus enabling the showing of simulations of flow in pneumatic networks as an image overlay. Another similar system visualizes how a laser travels through prisms positioned on the table [6]. The I/O Brush [7] takes an alternative approach. The brush includes a video camera that lets users scan patterns from their environment and paint them onto a digital canvas. The system was developed for children to explore drawing and their surrounding environment.

Comparisons of 2D vs TUIs. The intuitiveness of basic user interface manipulation actions [9] and cognitive support for spatial layout tasks [10]. In relation to interaction and manipulation, the results from controlled experiments suggest the benefits of 3D over 2D interaction in spatial reasoning, [10] and physical interfaces over virtual models [10, 9]. An early study on graspable user interfaces in a multi-target tracking task also suggested specialization of each interface tool so as to serve only one function in a system, as opposed to being a general-purpose controlling tool [11].

Heuristic Evaluations. User requirement and evaluation oriented studies in the field of ambient media have covered the usability and effectiveness of ambient displays [8].

Observational Studies. Open-ended observation studies include an experiment on problem solving in instructed engineering tasks [12], where it was found that physical objects provide situational support for thinking. Naturalistic studies on the use of tangible user interfaces remain very rare and are increasingly needed in order to move interface research beyond what is merely possible to implement towards tangible interfaces for real world use.

These works move from different research approaches and do not provide grounding or investigations into the concept or requirements behind the application from a user point of view, nor do they advance our knowledge in terms of what the challenges and agendas for tangible interfaces are (an exception is [20], which will be examined in the discussion). In addition to addressing these issues our work contributes, to the discussion on how previous system guidelines on table-top displays [20] can be relevant in TUI environments and how they need to be extended and modified.

2   An Environment for AR Painting and Collage

2.1   Components of the Environment

The environment for AR painting that we have developed, supports users in mixing digital media and physical models in an immersive, multi projection set-up.
The main components of the environment are:

- The *hypermedia database*. Users can upload to the database, pictures and videos, which are used to work with their models. When the media files are stored in the database, print-outs are created with thumbnails and barcodes to retrieve the pictures and videos during use (Figure 1a).
- The *Texture Brush*. This is the application that enables the user to paint digital texture on models using a physical brush (Figure 1b). The hardware includes a data projector, an infrared tracking system, and a physical brush augmented with a wireless button and a retro-reflecting surface.
- *Large projection screens*. Three projectors are used to play media on large projector screens behind the models (Figure 1b).
- The *barcode configuration poster*. A barcode Reader is used to perform basic configuration commands in the environment.

Fig. 1. From left: a) A print out with thumbnails of media files and barcodes. b) an example of a painted model with a large projection creating a background

2.2 The Texture Brush

With the *Texture Brush* design, users are able to 'paint' various computer generated visual overlays as textures onto physical 3D models in real time. Different textures are associated with different texture-samples and the actual painting is done by moving the physical "paint-brush" and tracking its position on the physical model. One of the first prototypes of the Texture Brush used a video camera for tracking the physical brush. The lightning conditions were often critical and interfered with the architectural model, so we had to use a white spot, generated by software, to light the retro-reflecting surface of the brush. This spot interfered with the reception of the model. The system was also too slow with this kind of tracking technique. We decided to switch to a professional solution based on infrared technology. With this tracking device, we get faster tracking (60Hz), the tracking module needs much less CPU power, it is easier to install for the user and we get tracking results with higher precision. Users can configure the Texture Brush in many ways. They can manipulate the brush size and shape by selecting these attributes from a menu bar, located at the bottom of the projection area, which is constantly displayed. Working tools like "polygon fill" that are familiar from applications like Adobe Photoshop©, have been integrated into the Texture Brush application. This allows the students to work with the Texture Brush in much the same way they are used to working with applications they know.

They can choose from a number of textures to use, including animated textures (videos), and the projection of the textures can be moved, scaled and rotated. The whole interaction is done using the brush as the only input device. Barcodes can be used to load the textures into the system at run-time. Any image or video that is stored in the Hypermedia database, can be used as a texture to paint the objects with.

A menu bar displays the textures along with four main menu elements. These elements are displayed as a status bar, located at the bottom of the projection area (it is displayed on the vertical border of the table). The menu elements are palette, brush-type/size, and transform (Figure 2):

- From the palette, the user is able to select from ten different layers of textures.
- From brush-type/size, the user is able to specify brush type, brush size and shape of the brush. Flat brushes, round brushes or square brushes will be available. There is a function to create a polygon and fill it with a particular texture. Once an area/polygon is specified it will be filled at once. This helps to paint large areas in one step.
- From the "transform" menu, the user finds functions for transforming the displayed textures. The menu element "scale" allows the user to enlarge or downsize the texture by moving the physical brush at various distances from the model. "Rotate" can turn the texture clockwise or counter clockwise by rotating the physical brush.

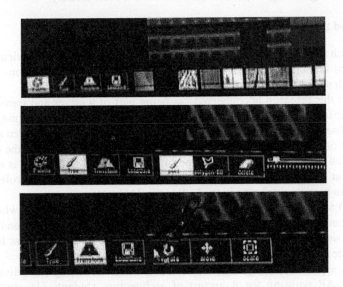

Fig. 2. From above: a) the menu item palette displays all the textures to choose from. b) the menu item "type" with brush, polygon fill, delete, and a bar to adjust the size. C) "transform" with the possibility to rotate, move, and scale.

2.3 The 'Configuration Poster'

Configuration of the space with such a variety of projection possibilities is not trivial. Students have to configure the system so that specific images are projected onto a specific projection screen, or used as a texture in the texture brush. We have designed a simple physical handle to configure the space a configuration poster with a variety of barcodes corresponding to basic configuration and commands:

- Specify an output (texture brush or one of the back projections)
- Saving and loading sessions

Users can specify the receiver of a texture (a picture or video) or any other input. A poster displaying the possible connections between inputs and outputs using barcodes can be used to configure the system. There is a barcode for each command, the barcode reader input can be used to load the media file associated with a specific barcode as a texture with the Texture Brush display.

Additional barcodes have been added to specify printers and background projections on the cave corner as other output components. Other barcodes on the poster serve to save configurations of painted textures on empty barcodes. These connections between input and output persist as long as they are not reconfigured by the students. Configuration and re-configuration can be performed at any time, dynamically changing the set-up of the workspace, using only the configuration poster, barcode reader, and barcodes that correspond to the images stored in the database.

3 Evaluating Tangible Interaction in a Field Study

3.1 Method and Analysis

The approach that guided this field study and its analysis was work-oriented design, this includes combining: "in situ interviewing, workplace observations and video analysis with design interventions" ([13], p. 332).

Design in this research is conceived "as being part of a larger and inevitable cycle of observing use, developing requirements (formal or informal), designing, building and again observing" [14]. In this framework, evaluation and use are seen as being an integral part of the design process and not terminal stages. In particular the evaluation, was organised by introducing a prototype in an on ongoing activity. It is not a set of metrics about the system that have been evaluated but the possible roles of novel technology in participants' activities. As Bannon [14] notes:

"a careful systematic account of what happens in particular settings when a prototype or system is installed, and how the system is viewed by the people on the ground, can provide useful information for 'evaluating' the system and its fitness for the purpose it was designed."

With this approach we organized a field trial in a real setting providing the environment for AR painting for 8 groups of architecture students (16 students). The teams of students used the environment to carry out one of their course assignments. While the course included creating models and collecting material over a whole semester the trail was organized over a period of two weeks. Over this period the teams of students took turns to use of the environment to produce a final presentation. Each team carried out three or four sessions of several hours in the environment and presented their work in a final plenary session at the end of the trial.

Each of the 8 student groups (2 students each) was asked to carry out an analysis of one of the 'icons' of modernist architecture from a selection of "Villas" in the city. They were required to read texts reflecting original and contemporary views on these buildings. They had to build two models 1:50 and 1:20 in scale (of an interesting spatial detail) and use our AR environment for analyzing scale and materiality. They worked with textures expressing the original ideas of the architects as well as with material of their own choice, exploring how materiality and context change the meaning of the building. Each student group was given a brief training of 4 minutes to learn how to operate the environment. Besides this brief training, the groups very rarely required support during their work sessions. A researcher observed the sessions making video recordings, which were used as material for interaction analysis. In addition, each group participated in semi-structured interviews where both members were interviewed simultaneously to collect the participants' views on the benefits and challenges of the environment.

3.2 Working with Immersive and Mixed Media

Each group worked with different physical models and different digital material. The use of the environment also varied significantly. While generally all the groups worked to produce different configurations of textures and background for a model, the following emerging and unanticipated uses were observed:

- installing a second Texture Brush to project textures from two directions, e.g. from the top and change the appearance of the floors or the roof while at the same time 'painting' the façade,
- using a "portable mouse"– a wireless mouse mounted on top of a cardboard box –as there was only one brush this was used especially for operating a second Texture Brush.
- taking pictures with a high resolution digital camera all around the model and also capturing the background,
- making and recording walkthroughs in the model using a web camera,
- using pictures or videos of the models on a large screen, playing with dimensions of small details of the models.

The students rarely used simple colors for painting, but applied colored textures, snapshots or even videos to their models. This notion goes beyond simply enriching a physical artifact by linking it with content in different media. In the case of the Texture Brush the link is such, that the properties of the object itself can be changed, by applying color, inserting movement, varying its dimension in relation to other objects in the physical space, varying context using multiple projections in the background. The participants were generally positive about the environment, expressing interest in working with it more in their studies. They also appreciated the immersiveness of the representations given by the possibility of using multiple large screens in the background. Another benefit was the possibility to rapidly create collages of textures and backgrounds for a model and the possibility to flexibly change it by loading and saving configurations.

3.3 Spatial Distribution of Interface Components

One of the distinctive properties of tangible interfaces is the importance of the spatial organization of users and computer equipment [15]. Through our system, users become immersed in the user interface and the architectural model, but limitations were imposed by our design solutions and the enabling technologies. In our system, the spatial configuration of the scanner, the brush, the model, the projectors, the mouse, and the poster can be re-organized by users so that they too, in a sense become part of the spatial organization. As foreseen in the TUI literature, the spatial distribution of a tangible interface carries many benefits arising from the exploitation of human visio-spatial and motor capabilities. However, e observed many problems and corresponding workaround practices due to difficulties in spatial distribution. We here report and elaborate on four design challenges for others to learn.

First, the *visibility* of interface components is crucial to afford capabilities in different situations. A special challenge arises from the fact that the model, users, and tools can occlude each other in the tangible computing environment. We observed many times an interruption in work caused by searching for the correct tool. The visibility of tools can be accounted for by thinking about dedicated places in the environment for tools and preventing suboptimal places. If there are dedicated areas, such as the desktop in our example, and they can be left in no other place, then users will have a good idea on their probable locations all the time. However, this solution must be pitted against the goal of being able to tailor and configure tangible interface components according to the task at hand.

Second, *referring to* the objects of work is crucial in collaboration. We observed our users having difficulties in knowing to which part of the model some textures in a poster referred to, leading to problems in establishing a shared context or common ground regarding those objects (see [21]). In addition to difficulties in knowing the reference between the physical and the digital, users had difficulties in referring to tangible objects in talk—for example, referring to a particular projector, as they had no known or legible name. Therefore, we suggest considering giving legible names to tangible interface components—"Projector 1", "Scanner" etc. Moreover, we recommend explicating the reference from the physical to the digital where possible (e.g., stating with a picture to what part of the model a texture on the poster refers to), and being consistent in naming conventions across the physical and digital.

Third, *multitasking* in a tangible computing environment such as our system differs significantly from desktop interaction. We observed a user using the barcode scanner, the barcode leaflet, and the brush at the same time–which is obviously quite difficult with only two hands. To support multitasking, rapid switches between tools and tasks must be enabled, by aiming for all necessary tools to be within arms reach and readily usable without more interaction steps than picking up the tool. Our system, for example, had only very limited space for the mouse, which forced some users to pickup a piece of cardboard to extend the pad; likewise dedicated areas could be provided for different tools to be left close to the model. Therefore, to support fluent division of cognitive and motor capabilities, we suggest reflecting the possibility of designing for easily movable objects that can be held in different hands and nearby physical locations. For example, instead of having the palette projected on the desk, which forces the user to constantly shift attention and move between the model and the palette, it could be either integrated into the physical brush or into a separate tool similar to real painting palettes. When projecting the Texture Brush from above, for example, the palette would be projected onto the table or even onto the ground, requiring at times difficult postures from the participant in order to interact with the menu (Figure 3 right). Multimodality and rapid access solutions would also support ergonomic working postures and prevent injuries from long-term use.

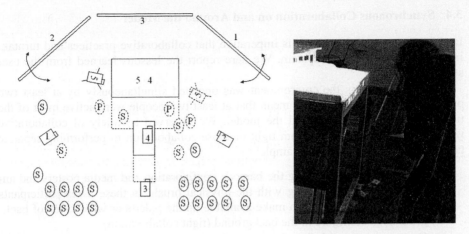

Fig. 3. Left: The physical arrangement of participants and components of the environment in a mixed media presentation. The letter "P" indicates participants operating the environment, the letter "S" indicates spectators. Numbers indicate 5 different projectors used for different purposes. Projectors 1,2,3 are used to provide a stage for the model. Right: a participant bending to operate the palette which is projected on the floor.

Finally, the *spatial configuration of projectors* is a challenge unique to tangible AR environments (Figure 3 left). They are essential for enabling the intermeshing of the digital and the physical, but they differ from other components in the fact that they are merely passive enablers, once set up and running, their initial configuration will most probably not be changed during one project session. Another bottleneck hindering initiation is how to *restore* the physical configuration. We made several observations that may inspire new ideas on how to improve the configurability and restoration of configurations. First, the placement of the projectors must enable convenient group work around the model, with minimum projected shadows due to a user standing in front of the beam. We observed some cases where one user had to command another to move away from the beam. Moreover, it is important that the projectors can reach parts of the model important for the work, different floors or balconies for example, and therefore their placement is significant. Second, the initial set up of the projector is mostly trial and error, and takes considerable time to learn. Our users used adhesive tape to mark the x-y position of their projectors in the room and even to mark the height of the projector. Here, in addition to providing support for marking projector setups in the environment by using group-specific stickers etc, we suggest considering preparing ready-to-hand templates, maybe printed on paper or manuals, for well-known projector configurations to help reduced the initial overload of projector configuration with common types of architectural models. Third, we noted some occasions where users wanted to turn the table, to work on the model from a different perspective, but this was not supported. Our projectors could not automatically adjust the beam to tilted or twisted surfaces, but such projectors now exist.

3.4 Synchronous Collaboration on and Around the Model

In the architectural domain, it is imperative that collaborative practices and turntaking are supported by the system. We here report the lessons learned from the user study.

In all the sessions the environment was operated simultaneously by at least two participants. By "operated" we mean that at least two people were active most of the time carrying out tasks around the model. We observed a variety of collaborative work arrangements ranging from tight or loose collaboration to performing separate tasks on the same model, for example:

- One participant operating the barcode configuration and media posters and another participant painting with the physical brush. In these cases participants discuss which textures to make available on the palette or what kinds of backgrounds to configure in the background (tight collaboration).
- One participant painting the model from one direction (front) another participant painting the model from another direction (above). In these cases, participants engage in brief and sporadic discussions on parts of the models where their work meets up or on the general concept of the model.
- While the one participant changes painted textures and backgrounds the other documents the changes, creating different pictures from the same view.

Fig. 4. Different types of collaborative arrangements

First, in our system, the texture that is worked on is shown as a *cursor* projected on the model. The cursor expresses the current target of operations. This pointer metaphor is adopted from desktop-based paint applications. In order to make it possible to perform operations with the scanner without holding the brush, the cursor is persistent, always there where it was last left. On one hand, this solution promotes shared understanding among group members on the current focus and status of the collaboration, as only one user can operate the system and others know what is happening. On the other hand, one-cursor solutions effectively prevent simultaneous work on the model. We observed that due to this shortcoming, others were rendered non-users of the system, although they were actively commenting on, instructing, or documenting the work. Currently, separate installations of the software have to be set up for separate projectors to enable working on different parts of the model. Here, in addition to the double set up of software being tedious, the system still did not enable simultaneous work on the same projection, which is what some groups wanted to have. Our suggestion is to consider *multi-pointer solutions*. These pointers should be distinctive and could incorporate indications of the brush size and shape and selected texture into the cursor icon. This could help in following what others are doing without extensive questioning and verbalizing. Moreover, *authorship* could be represented in the icon to communicate to others, who is responsible for that particular cursor.

3.5 The Brush, Its Metaphor, and the Portable Mouse

The brush as an interface tool in the setup was used for many purposes: painting, selecting options from the palette, drawing polygons by selecting, erasing paint, zooming and rotating a texture, and issuing commands with a press of a button. This interaction was based on hand movements and button presses, and extended the traditional uses of a brush and a palette remarkably (those of picking paint from a palette and then placing it onto a canvas). It is therefore worthwhile considering how well the brush and palette metaphors align with these uses and what are the implications of bending the concept of a traditional brush.

Two different types of questions emerge from this consideration. The first one is about how intuitive is the concept of a brush providing also non-obvious features. Some of these functions are natural, such as painting with the brush, but zooming is a feature that has to be taught since it is not a part of the brush metaphor. Our data indicates, however, that users are able to be quite adaptive in extending the metaphor. For instance, the technical limitation of not being able to touch surfaces with the brush was exploited opportunistically by painting from a distance of one meter. Another user visualized a Las Vegas like hotel with neon signs, by using textures as separate images. He placed scanned logos onto a surface and erased the paint around the logos, creating a sticker-like visual effect. The use of the palette in carrying out all the menu-related tasks was also natural to the users, although traditional palettes do not contain menus. Therefore, it seems that strict accordance with metaphors is not always required to produce intuitively usable interaction tools. The brush and palette metaphors allowed and constrained the modes of interaction into which all the necessary functionalities could be embedded. For instance, the thinness of a brush did not allow for including a menu into it, but enabled the users to paint areas that would have been unreachable with other tools. The palette metaphor, as a container of textures can be naturally extended to provide other types of selectable functionalities as well.

A portable wireless mouse on a cardboard box was used in some cases (two participants) as a substitute for the physical brush. It was used mainly to manipulate the second Texture Brush from above. Therefore, the palette for the mouse was projected onto the floor or onto the table. The primary difference in using the mouse instead of the brush was that paint was applied to the model from a distance and based on where the user saw the cursor, not by reaching towards it to position where the paint was to be applied. However, positioning the mouse very close to the model is important in order to support visibility and hand-eye co-ordination. Probably, the most important phenomenon was that mouse movements on the box were not easily mapped to cursor movements on the model. While when we operate the mouse on a desktop computer our orientation to the screen does not change, the participants in our case moved around the model, adopting different positions and orientations frequently resulting in a "misalignment" of the mouse with the cursor.

4 Discussion and Conclusions

The main motivation of tangible user interfaces (TUIs) is to move meaningful interaction from digital to physical. Physicality can characterise human-computer interaction in many different and unprecedented ways, including spatiality, artefacts, and various other manifestations of computational resources [16]. While a variety of tangible interfaces and applications are merely presented as demos at conferences and only operated by researchers, there is a growing need for field evaluation in realistic settings. In this paper, we presented an environment for augmented reality painting of physical models and reported on its evaluation in a field trial in a setting with several architecture students working on course projects.

We observed several positive properties of TUIs in the field study. However, our work also revealed many challenges, which remain for future work on making TUIs more usable and attractive. The most vital is the challenge of the *distributed interface*—the physical, spatial, and computational separation of interface components. This distribution cannot be arbitrary but must possess the capability to act meaningfully through the combination of individual multiple input/output devices so that the outcome also makes sense at the level of the system [18]. In a TUI environment like ours, this implies cognitive and creative processes being distributed and coordinated across the members of the group, these processes also being distributed over time and space and at least partly mediated by computer and physical artefacts [17]. A central corollary challenge is to turn the public availability of embodiment (cf. [19]) into real collaborative features of the interface. In our system, collaboration around the model was limited by the single-cursor, single-tool nature of the system. In addition to considering multi-cursor multi-tool designs, we saw that the visibility, labeling, affordance, and accountability of interface components is necessary. At the individual level, multimodality and efficient use of cognitive resources is necessary, also for ergonomical reasons. Finally, intertwining the digital and physical in a bi-directional manner poses a problem for future research. In our field study interfacing the two worked mostly mono-directionally. For example, if the user changed the position of the model, the projection did not adjust accordingly, as the projectors were not sensitive to changes in the real world. Bi-directionality would promise easier set-ups and in-session configurability of the system, but would require rather complex on-line video signal processing to work.

Similar systems have been developed that concentrate on one aspect of the interaction, offering more sophisticated features, such as the possibility of moving, real time, the physical objects and the projected textures using tracking technology [3, 4]. Other studies that compare in detail 2D and tangible interfaces [9, 10] merely state which one performs better using some general criteria (e.g., memory in spatial layout tasks [9] or trial time and user operations [10]). Other work that reports on observational studies of current practices to inform the development of tangible interfaces, provides the motivations but only vague indications of the features to be implemented [12]. Finally heuristic evaluations have been proposed for ambient displays which are weakly applicable in the case of tangible interfaces.

Most relevant to our research are the system guidelines for co-located collaborative work on a table-top display [20]. Our study contributes specific knowledge on how to extend the guidelines for tangible interfaces. In particular, our study contributes to the guideline *support fluid transition between activities*, for tangible interfaces, proving the trade-off between the advantages of specializing tangible interaction (the barcode scanner for "phycons", the physical brush for painting, etc.) and the disadvantages, for fluid transitions, of distributing interfaces across different platforms and tools. For the guidelines *support interpersonal interaction*, *transitions between personal and group work* and *simultaneous user actions* our study highlighted another trade-off between supporting clear divisions of labor and supporting synchronous collaboration while accessing simultaneously shared resources. For example TUIs in our case supported a clear division of labor (one participants selecting textures and backgrounds and the other one applying and modifying textures with the brush, or two participants painting simultaneously), however, with limitations due to missing groupware features and single-tool approaches (a single barcode scanner and a single brush were available). For other guidelines such as *support the use of physical objects, shared access to physical and digital objects* the study demonstrates not only the need to integrate physical objects and affordances (physical models, sheets of papers with icons and visual codes) but the opportunity of mixing digital and physical objects (the model painted with digital textures). Finally, our study provides additional candidate guidelines (requirements) for tangible computing environments. It was possible through a field study to show evidence of the need to support, not only a single interaction scenario, but a whole activity cycle of which painting digital textures might be just a phase. The field study helped us to gain a more "ecological or systemic" perspective, showing the need to support the upload, retrieval and saving of mixed media configurations and also the opportunity to create immersive environments that extended out of a "table-top" with multiple and large scale projections.

References

1. Abowd, G. D., Mynatt, E. D., Charting Past, Present, and Future Research in Ubiquitous Computing, ACM TOCHI, Vol. 7, No. 1, March (2000) 29–58
2. Abowd G D., Mynatt E D., Rodden, T., The Human Experience. In: IEEE Pervasive Computing archive Volume 1, Issue 1 (January 2002) 48 - 57 .
3. Raskar, R., Welch, G., Chen, W.-C.: Table-Top Spatially-Augmented Reality: Bringing Physical Models to Life with Projected Imagery. Proc. IWAR'99. IEEE (1999) 64-73
4. Bandyopadhyay, D., Raskar, R., Fuchs, H.: Dynamic Shader Lamps: Painting on Movable Objects. Proc. ISAR'01. IEEE Computer Society, New York (2001) 207-216
5. Schmudlach, K., Hornecker, E., Ernst, H., Bruns, F.W.: Bridging Reality and Virtuality in Vocational Training. CHI'00 Interactive Posters. ACM Press, New York (2000) 137-138
6. Underkoffler, J., Ishii, H.: Illuminating Light: An Optical Design Tool with a Luminous-Tangible Interface. Proc. CHI'98. ACM Press, New York (1998) 542-549

7. Ryokai, K., Marti, S., Ishii, H.: I/O Brush: Drawing with Everyday Objects as Ink. Proc. CHI'04. ACM Press, New York (2004) 303-310 Mankoff, J., Dey, A.K., Hsieh, G., Kientz, J., Lederer, S., Ames, M.: Heuristic Evaluation of Ambient Displays. Proc. CHI'03, ACM Press, New York (2003) 169-176

8. Mankoff, J., Dey, A.K., Hsieh, G., Kientz, J., Ames, M., Lederer, S.: Heuristic evaluation of ambient displays. CHI 2003, ACM Press, CHI Letters 5(1): 169-176

9. Huang, C.-J.: Not Just Intuitive: Examining the Basic Manipulation of Tangible User Interfaces. CHI'04 Late Breaking Results. ACM Press, New York (2004) 1387-1390

10. Fjeld, M., Guttormsen Schär, S., Signorello, D., Krueger, H.: Alternative Tools for Tangible Interaction: A Usability Evaluation. Proc. ISMAR'02. IEEE (2002) 157-166

11. Fitzmaurice, G.W., Buxton, W.: An Empirical Evaluation of Graspable User Inter-faces: Towards Specialized, Space-Multiplexed Input. Proc. CHI'97. ACM Press, 1997, 43-50.

12. Brereton, M., McGarry, B.: An Observational Study of How Objects Support Engineering Design Thinking and Communication: Implications for the Design of Tangible Media. Proc. CHI'00. ACM Press, New York (2000) 217-224

13. Trigg RH, Blomberg J & Suchman L (1999). Moving document collections online: The evolution of a shared repository. Proceedings of the Sixth European Conference on Computer Supported Cooperative Work (ECSCW'99). S. Bødker, M. Kyng, K. Schmidt (eds.). Dordrecht, The Net-herlands: Kluwer, 331-350.

14. Bannon, L. J.: Use, Design and Evaluation - Steps towards an Integration. In: Shapiro, D., Tauber, M., Traunmueller, R. (eds): The Design of Computer-Supported Cooperative Work and Group-ware Systems. Amsterdam: North – Holland, (1996) 423-442.

15. Dourish, P.: Where the action is: the foundations of embodied interaction. MIT Press 2001

16. Jacucci, G.: Interaction as Performance. Cases of Physical Interfaces and mixed media design. Doctoral Thesis, University of Oulu, Acta Universitatis Ouluensis. (2004)

17. Hollan, J., Hutchins, E., and Kirsh, D.: Distributed cognition: toward a new foundation for human-computer interaction research ACM (TOCHI), (2000) pp.174-196.

18. Binder, T., De Michelis, G., Gervautz, M., Jacucci, G., Matkovic, K., Psik, T., Wagner, I.: Supporting Configurability in a Mixed Media Environment for Design Students. In: Special Issue on Tangible Interfaces in Perspective, Pers and Ubiq Comp, Journal, Volume 8 , Issue 5, Springer Verlag (September 2004) 310 – 325.

19. Robertson, T.,: The Public Availability of Actions and Artefacts', Computer-Supported Cooperative Work, vol. 11, (2002)

20. Scott, S., Grant, K., Mandryk, R.,: System Guidelines for Co-Located, Collaborative Work on a Tabletop Display. In: Proceedings of ECSCW'03, European Conference of Computer Supported Cooperative Work 2003, Helsinki Finalnd, September 14-18, Kluwer, 2003.

21. Kraut, R. E., Fussell, S. R., Siegel, J.: Visual information as a conversational resource in collaborative physical tasks. Human-Computer Interaction, 18, 13-49, (2003)

Hotaru: Intuitive Manipulation Techniques for Projected Displays of Mobile Devices

Masanori Sugimoto, Kosuke Miyahara, Hiroshi Inoue, and Yuji Tsunesada

University of Tokyo, Graduate School of Frontier Informatics,
5-1-5 Kashiwanoha, Kashiwa, Chiba, 277-8561, Japan
{sugi, miyahara, inoue, tsunesada}@itl.t.u-tokyo.ac.jp
http://www.itl.t.u-tokyo.ac.jp/

Abstract. Mobile devices (cellular phone, PDA, etc.) have so far been personal tools. Due to their evolution to multi-functionality, however, the devices have begun to be used by multiple people in co-located situations. This paper discusses near future technologies: a mobile device with a projector and intuitive manipulation techniques by using a video camera mounted on the device. In today's technologies, it is difficult to realize a mobile device with a small and lightweight projector that still retains the feature of mobility. Therefore, we have developed a system to project displays of mobile devices on a table, a floor, or a wall, by tracking their three-dimensional positions and orientations and using an existing LCD projector. The proposed system called *Hotaru* (a firefly, in English) allows users to annotate/rotate a picture or a document in a mobile device by touching its projected display with their fingers. Users can intuitively transfer a file between multiple devices by making their projected displays overlapped. Informal evaluations of *Hotaru* indicated that the proposed manipulation techniques could effectively support multiple people in co-located situations in conducting their tasks.

1 Introduction

Mobile devices (PDA, cellular phone etc.) have rapidly penetrated into our society and many people use them in their daily lives. For example, in Japan in 2003, the number of subscribers of cellular phones has amounted to 86 million, which is about three fourths of Japanese total population[4]. One of the recent trends of cellular phones is multi-functional: not only a phone to communicate with a person in a remote location but also a web browser, a digital video camera, a game machine, a music player, a television, a GPS, and so on. Although the growing trend toward more functions has been remarkably observed in cellular phones, the other types of mobile devices also exhibit the similar tendencies. For instance, various commercial accessories attachable to PDAs for extending their functions are available. This trend makes the differences between a mobile device and a personal computer smaller: a cellular phone or a PDA is becoming a computer that has almost the same functionality of desktop/laptop computers retaining the feature of mobility. Actually, mobile devices have been used as a

M.F. Costabile and F. Patern (Eds.): INTERACT 2005, LNCS 3585, pp. 57–68, 2005.

personal tool such as a personal scheduling assistant, and recently have begun to be used by multiple people in face-to-face or co-located situations.

Let us show you some examples. When you take a photo by using a digital camera mounted on your cellular phone, you may want to show the photo to (more than two) people around you. However, due to a problem of screen real estate of a cellular phone, it is not easy for multiple people to simultaneously look at the photo on your cellular phone. Moreover, when you send the photo to a person who has requested it, you need to conduct unintuitive and bothersome operations on your phone (e.g. search his mail address, attach the photo to a mail, and send it through the user interface of the phone).

Suppose that the display of your cellular phone can be projected on a wall in front of you. If your phone that mounts a projector is as lightweight and small as the recent models of cellular phones, thanks to its mobility, you can make the projected display appear anywhere on a wall, a ceiling, a floor, or a table. Therefore, you can easily look at a photo taken through your cellular phone with people around you. As your cellular phone is equipped with a digital video camera, it may also be possible to capture an image of its projected display. If the cellular phone can recognize manipulations conducted with fingers on its projected display, for example, selecting a file or starting an application program, it will be able to effectively support conversations or collaborative tasks of multiple people in co-located situations. As users can freely change the projected locations of the displays by moving their own cellular phones, the users can conduct data transfer between their phones by overlapping their projected displays.

We believe that a mobile device that mounts a video camera and a projector has the possibility to provide us with a new technique for supporting co-located collaboration in a ubiquitous computing environment. Canesta Keyboard [9] is an one-color projection system designed to be attached to a PDA and used as a personal virtual keyboard (therefore, inappropriate as a shared display for multiple people). Unfortunately, a full-color projector mountable on a mobile device is currently not available due to its weight and power consumption. However, according to the recent news, several researches on portable projectors are in progress and those mountable on mobile devices will become available in near future [5]. In this paper, therefore, we propose a system called *Hotaru* (a firefly in English) that allows users to conduct intuitive manipulations on projected displays of mobile devices by utilizing currently available technologies.

The paper is organized as follows: Section 2 shows the related work to *Hotaru*. In Section 3, the system configuration of *Hotaru* is described. Section 4 shows several manipulation techniques by using *Hotaru*. Section 5 discusses the user studies of *Hotaru*. Finally, Section 6 concludes the paper.

2 Related Work

Hotaru is related to several research topics such as mobile and ubiquitous computing, finger recognition, manipulation techniques for projected displays, and so on. There are too many predecessors related to *Hotaru*. Therefore, some of them which seem similar to and should be differentiated from *Hotaru* are discussed in this section.

iLamps [7] provides users with adaptive projection techniques with a cluster of handheld projectors. iLamps identifies locations and orientations of multiple projectors and creates a seamless and consistent image over a projected surface (e.g. planar, spherical etc.) by correcting an overlapping image given by the projectors. The main purpose of iLamps is different from that of *Hotaru* in that it proposes manipulation techniques for overlapping projected displays of mobile devices.

In [6], the concept of "steerable interface" and its implementation are described. The proposed system (ED: Everywhere Display) uses an LCD projector fixed to a ceiling and can project a display on any surface (e.g. a wall or a floor in a room) by tracking a user's head position and controlling an angle of a mirror attached to the projector. Therefore, ED does not allow multiple users to freely change the locations, shapes, and sizes of their projected displays as the users like, which is possible for users of *Hotaru*.

HyperPalette [1] allows a user to conduct intuitive operations with his PDA. A user can bring a photo projected on a table into his PDA (scoop), or drop a photo in the PDA onto the table (spread) by tilting and moving the PDA. The difference between HyperPalette and *Hotaru* is that *Hotaru* allows a person without a PDA to join collaborative tasks by annotating on a projected display with his/her finger. Moreover, *Hotaru* provides users a more intuitive and direct method by utilizing overlapping projected displays of multiple mobile devices, although HyperPalette proposes a data transfer method between multiple PDAs via a table on which the data to be transferred is projected.

Augmented Surfaces [8] allows users to drag files, such as documents or images, to be shown on a computer desktop, a table or a wall, by using a laser pointer. Users can easily share these files with other users and bring them into their own personal computers. The difference between Augmented Surfaces and *Hotaru* is that *Hotaru* provides users with intuitive methods for supporting their collaborative tasks such as annotating by the users' fingers.

In [2], a system that visualizes a personal and a public spaces on a screen of each user's PDA is described. A user can place a file in the public space to make it visible and accessible to all users, or bring a file from the public space to his personal space. This system does not allow users to specify who can access to which files in an intuitive manner. On the other hand, a user of *Hotaru* can select a person (or PDA) and a file by overlapping their projected displays in an intuitive manner.

3 System Configuration of *Hotaru*

3.1 Design and Implementation Overview

In order to realize projected displays of mobile devices by using existing LCD projectors (most of them weigh more than 1 kg), the following requirements must be satisfied:

1. Three-dimensional (3D) positions and orientations of mobile devices are automatically identified.
2. Based on their 3D positions and orientations, the locations, sizes, and shapes of their projected displays are automatically determined.

In order to fully satisfy the requirement 2, a special apparatus to control the positions and orientations of LCD projectors will be necessary. However, it is almost impossible to implement such an apparatus that can instantaneously change their positions and orientations by following 3D moves of multiple mobile devices. On the other hand, it is possible to investigate the proposed idea by partially (not completely) realizing the feature of projected displays of mobile devices. Therefore, we decided to develop a prototype version of *Hotaru* as shown in Fig. 1. In this figure, a stereo camera is installed above users in order to identify 3D positions and locations of their mobile devices. Based on their 3D positions and locations, the sizes and shapes of the screen images of the devices are calculated and projected onto a table or a wall through an LCD projector.

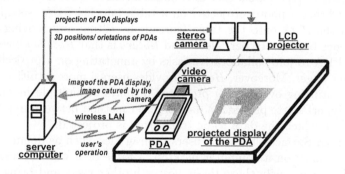

Fig. 1. System configuration of *Hotaru*

In order to capture images of projected displays where users' manipulations are conducted, a video camera attached to a mobile device is used. In the prototype version of *Hotaru*, we use a PDA as a mobile device, because cellular phone vendors do not fully release the technical specification of their devices. Due to the limited computational capability of current models of PDAs, an image processing module for recognizing users' manipulations on projected displays is executed on the server computer.

The current version of *Hotaru* imposes one restriction on its users: displays of users' PDAs are projected only within a specified area (e.g. on a table or a wall) determined by the installation positions and angles of the stereo camera and LCD projector. However, the other functions, such as recognizing a user's manipulation on a projected display through a camera mounted on his PDA, are fully realized. Therefore, when a projector mountable on a mobile device has become available, the techniques described in this paper will also be available without any modification.

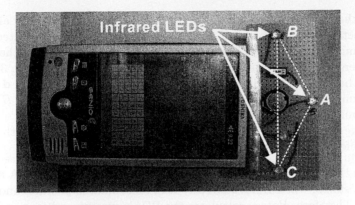

Fig. 2. Infrared LEDs for position and orientation identification

3.2   Location and Orientation Identification

A marker with infrared (IR) LEDs and a stereo camera are used for recognizing the 3D position and orientation of a user's PDA. The IR LEDs on a circuit board are arranged to form an isosceles triangle (A, B, and C in Fig. 2). The position of the PDA is represented as $P = (x_p, y_p, z_p)$ which is the coordinates of the centroid of the triangle. The orientation of the PDA is calculated by the sum of the vector $\overrightarrow{BA}$ and $\overrightarrow{CA}$, and represented as $\mathbf{d} = (x_o, y_o, z_o)$. Different blinking patterns are assigned to LEDs at the vertex A for identifying individual PDAs.

Experimental results to evaluate this method have proved that the position and orientation recognition errors are less than six centimeters and ten degrees, respectively[1]. In the current implementation, it takes less than one second to correctly recognize individual blinking patterns of LEDs. This means that a user is required to hold his PDA steadily for one second so that *Hotaru* can identify the PDA successfully.

3.3   Projection of Displays

In order to emulate a PDA that mounts a projector, the location, size, and shape of its projected display must be determined based on the position and orientation of the PDA. Let the projecting plane (the surface where a display of a PDA at the point P is projected) be Π and its normal vector be $\mathbf{n} = (x_n, y_n, z_n)$, as shown in Fig. 3. From this figure, it is evident that the rotation vector between the planes Π and Π' is the outer product of $\mathbf{n}$ and $\mathbf{d}$ which is the normal vector of Π', and that the shape of the projected display is that of the cutting plane (Π, in this case) of the quadrangular pyramid $\mathbf{Q}$. The algorithm for determining the location, size, and shape of the projected display is summarized as follows:

---

[1] The errors were evaluated by the distance between the estimated and real positions, and by the angle formed by the estimated and real orientation vectors, respectively.

1. Find the crossing point C of the extended line from the point P along with the vector $\mathbf{d}$ and the plane Π. C is the center point of the projected display.
2. Determine the scale k for the projected display on Π', based on the distance between the point P and the plane Π' (the length of $\overline{PC}$ in Fig. 3).
3. Find the rotation vector between the planes Π and Π' by using $\mathbf{d}$ and $\mathbf{n}$.
4. Determine the shape S of the projected display by the plane Π and the quadrangular pyramid $\mathbf{Q}$.
5. Enlarge/reduce the original screen image of the PDA based on the scale k, and deform the image to S.

Due to the errors as described in 3.2, a projected display of a PDA fluctuates and is not stable, when *Hotaru* directly uses its estimated position and orientation data. Therefore, *Hotaru* calculates the PDA's current positions and orientations by averaging over the recent ten consecutive location and orientation data.

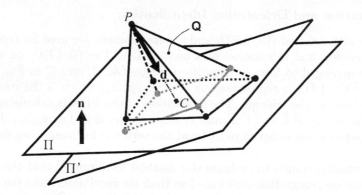

Fig. 3. How *Hotaru* calculates a projected display of a PDA

3.4   Detection of Projected Displays

A video camera attached to a PDA is used for detecting and identifying each of the projected displays and recognizing users' manipulations on them. In order to detect multiple projected displays, a wide-angle lens is mounted on the camera. We first tried to recognize the manipulations by bare fingers as described in [12]. However, the recognition ratio of bare fingers was extremely low without using a special camera such as a thermo-infrared camera [3]. Therefore, in this version of *Hotaru*, we decided to use fingers augmented with an LED light to increase the recognition ratio (as shown in Fig. 5). The recognition process is summarized as follows:

(1) Extract contours and vertices of projected displays from a captured image through a camera mounted on a user's PDA.
(2) Identify projected displays of individual PDAs (discussed in Section 3.5)
(3) Recognize users' manipulations by fingers (discussed in Section 3.6)

Fig. 4 shows a process of extracting contours and vertices of a projected display. The system first performs the distortion correction of an image caused due to the wide-angle lens, and applies the Canny edge detector [10] for detecting contours and vertices in the image When *Hotaru* detects four vertices of individual projected displays, it can successfully recognize the displays. If *Hotaru* cannot find all the vertices due to occlusion by human hands or an overlap of other projected displays (Fig. 4(a)), it applies the Hough transform (Fig. 4(b)) and estimates the unrecognized vertices in order to determine the regions of projected displays (Fig. 4(c)). Finally, by using the four vertices of the projected display in the camera coordinate and those of the PDA screen in the world coordinate, a transformation matrix between the two coordinates is calculated [10].

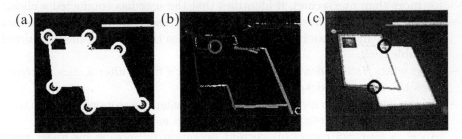

Fig. 4. Extracting a projected display. (a) Three vertices of individual projected displays are determined. (b) The fourth vertex of each projected display is estimated. (c) The region of each projected display is recognized.

3.5 Identification of Individual Projected Displays

Although projected displays are detected from an image captured by a camera of PDA, it is not sufficient because which projected displays correspond to individual PDAs has not been determined. By estimating the locations of the projected displays based on the 3D locations and orientations of individual PDAs, it may be possible to find their correspondence. However, if a portable projector mountable on a mobile device has become available, such location and orientation information will be unnecessary. Therefore, the identification of projected displays is conducted by using an image of multiple projected displays captured by a camera mounted on a PDA.

We first tried similarity matching between an elicited projected display and a screen image of each PDA. However, the success ratio of the matching was not stable. It is suggested that screen images of different PDAs were often similar (in some cases, only folder or file icons appeared on their screens). In the current implementation of *Hotaru*, individual PDAs are given different color markers for their identification. In order to use a screen of a PDA as large as possible, the marker is projected outside of the projected display in Fig. 5 or Fig. 6.

A serious problem of this method is that the number of PDAs to be identified is small (less than ten). To solve the problem, we are now investigating to use a watermark-based method for identifying individual PDAs.

3.6   Recognition of Operations by Fingers

Hotaru allows users to manipulate pictures or file icons on a projected display by using their fingers augmented with an LED light. It elicits a finger-pointing area with a pixel value larger than a specified threshold of brightness. The position of the pointing area on a PDA screen is calculated by using the transformation matrix described in Section 3.4. *Hotaru* uses the Kalman filter [11] to estimate the next pointing area by using the current and previous pointing areas, when users conduct translation or drag operations explained below. The following is a list of the operations:

- click: when *Hotaru* recognizes that a user's pointing area has not changed for more than one second, it identifies that the user has conducted a click.
- double click: when *Hotaru* recognizes that a user's pointing area has not changed for more than two seconds, it identifies that the user has conducted a double click.
- drag: when *Hotaru* identifies a move of a user's finger after a click, it recognizes the move as a drag.
- release: when *Hotaru* identifies that a user's finger has stopped for more than one second after a drag, it recognizes the stop as a release.
- cancel: a user can cancel his current operation by moving his finger away from the projected display.

To identify whether a user has really touched a projected display and conducted a click operation with his finger is difficult. Therefore, two-dimensional moves of a user's finger and its non-moving time are used for recognizing his/her operations as described above. The time required for recognizing the operations has been decided through informal user studies during the development of *Hotaru*. In order to let a user know clearly their current operations, *Hotaru* provides him/her with different auditory feedback corresponding to each operation.

4   Intuitive Manipulations on Projected Displays

Projected displays of mobile devices provide users with new manipulation techniques. Several example techniques are described in the following:

4.1   Annotation

When multiple users share a document or a picture on a projected display, they can directly write comments or draw figures on it with their fingers. In Fig. 5, a group of people shares a map on a projected display, and one of them draws lines or marks on it with his finger. Such an annotation is useful in a co-located situation: when one person accesses a web page to show a map by using his mobile device, the other people can easily suggest, recognize or confirm the direction to their destination.

Fig. 5. Annotation to a projected map

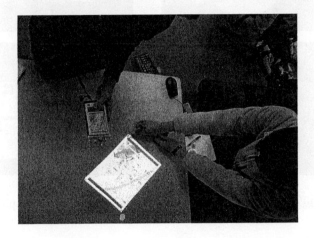

Fig. 6. Rotation of a projected display

4.2   Rotation

When an image file in a PDA is projected on a table which multiple people sit around, it is desirable to allow them to rotate the file so that each of them can easily view and understand the content of the image. As shown in Fig. 6, a user can rotate an image about its center point through any angle, by clicking and dragging at the lower right corner of the image.

4.3   File Transfer by Overlapping Projected Displays

Fig. 7 shows how users can transfer a file between multiple PDAs. In Fig. 7(a), Displays of two users' PDAs are projected on a table. UserA moves his PDA so that its projected display overlaps with that of userB's PDA (Fig. 7(b)), and then drags a image file to be trasferred to the overlapping region of their projected diplays (Fig. 7(c)). The overlapping region is also visualized on the screens of their PDAs. When userA releases the file, a popup window appears on the screen of userB's PDA to confirm if the file transfer is permitted. If userB presses an "ok" button on the popup window, the file is transferred to his PDA as shown in Fig. 7(d). It is also possible for users to write/draw comments on the overlapping region for "carbon-copying" as shown in Fig. 7(c).

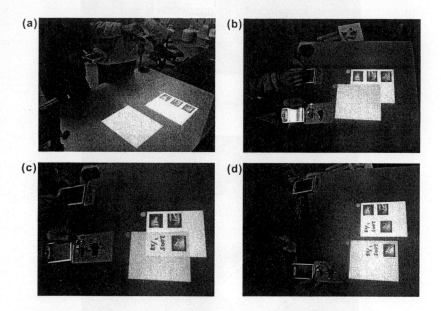

Fig. 7. File transfer between multiple devices by overlapping

5   User Studies

Hotaru were evaluated in informal user studies. Twelve subjects formed three pairs and two groups of three, and were asked to conduct the following tasks: annotation and rotation of an image file, and file transfer between multiple PDAs. The tasks lasted about 30 minutes for each pair and group.

During the tasks, users frequently moved their PDAs, and the locations of their projected displays changed accordingly. When the moves of their PDAs were small (such as a slight tilting), *Hotaru* could almost always recognize their own projected displays correctly. It is suggested that users of *Hotaru* hold their PDAs steadily rather than move them rapidly, when they want to watch their projected displays or conduct collaborative tasks on them. Therefore, we think that a failure of the recognition due to the move of a PDA is not a serious problem practically.

Positive (1-4) and negative (5-7) comments received from the subjects are summarized as follows:

1. Projected displays of PDAs were favored users. The users could easily change the positions, shapes, and sizes of the displays as they like, by moving their own PDAs.
2. *Hotaru* could effectively support multiple people in viewing pictures or documents, because it did not force them to peek at a screen of a PDA over their shoulders.
3. Annotating and rotating a file by fingers were intuitive and useful.
4. Conducting file transfer tasks by overlapping projected displays of PDAs is much more intuitive and easier than other file transfer methods for mobile devices.
5. Slow responses to manipulations by fingers were often irritating.
6. Recognizing users' manipulations failed when a PDA was not held steadily enough (although *Hotaru* succeeded in recognizing the projected displays).
7. It was desirable to identify who conducted which manipulations, in order for *Hotaru* to fully support collaborative tasks.

Comments 1-4 indicated that the idea of *Hotaru* was accepted by the subjects.

The cause of Comment 5 was that the subjects had to stop the moves of their fingers and wait, in order to make click, release, and double click operations recognized by *Hotaru*. The similar reports are found in [13]. As for Comment 6, when a subject holding his PDA by one hand tried to touch its projected display with his finger of another hand, the recognition often failed because he unintentionally moved his PDA. Using inertial sensors (e.g. an accelerometer or a gyroscope) or optical flow analyses may be effective to reduce the influence of user's unintentional small moves of his PDA and fix its projected display at a specified location. As for comment 7, several approaches will be possible, for example, using visual or optical tags attached to fingers, in order for *Hotaru* to identify who has conducted which manipulations.

In the current implementation, *Hotaru* allows only a sender to conduct file tranfer tasks, that is, a sender first selects a file to be transferred, and then releases it in an overlapping region with a projected display of another PDA. All the subjects requested that *Hotaru* should also allows a receiver to conduct file transfer tasks by selecting other users' file that appear on the receiver's PDA screen. We will plan to improve and extend functions of *Hotaru* by examining the issues raised through the user studies.

6   Conclusions

This paper described a system called *Hotaru* and possible intuitive manipulation techniques. The design and implementation of *Hotaru* by using currently available technologies were discussed. Informal user studies for evaluating *Hotaru* proved that it would effectively support collaborative tasks in co-located situations. The studies also clarified several problems to be solved and investigated. In our future work, we will conduct more intensive user studies, improve the performance of *Hotaru*, and explore its possibilities of new applications.

References

1. Ayatsuka, Y., et al: HyperPalette: a Hybrid Computing Environment for Small Computing Device, *Proceedings of ACM CHI2000*, pp.133–134 (2000).
2. Greenberg, S., et al: PDAs and Shared Public Displays: Making Personal Information Public and Public Information Personal. *Personal Technologies*, Vol.3, No.1, pp.54-64 (1999).
3. Koike, H., et al.: Integrating Paper and Digital Information on EnhancedDesk: A Method for Real-Time Finger Tracking on Augmented Desk System, *ACM Transactions on Computer Human Interaction*, Vol.8, No.4, pp.307–322 (2001).
4. Japanese Ministry of Internal Affairs and Communications : *Information and Communication in Japan 2004* (available at http://www.johotsushintokei.soumu.go.jp/whitepaper/eng/WP2004/2004-index.html (2004).
5. New York Times:*For Your Viewing Pleasure, a Projector in Your Pocket* (2004) (available at http://www.nytimes.com/2004/11/04/technology/circuits/04next.html).
6. Pingali, G., et al. (2003): Steerable Computing Interfaces for Pervasive Spaces, in *Proccedings of IEEE PerCom2003*, pp.315-322 (2003).
7. Raskar, R., et al. (2003): iLamps: Geometrically Aware and Self-Configurating, *ACM Transactions on Graphics*, Vol.22, No.3, pp.809–818 (2003).
8. Rekimoto, J., Saito, M.:Augmented Surfaces: A spatially Continuous Work Space for Hybrid Computing Environments, *Proceedings of ACM CHI99*, pp.378-385 (1999).
9. Roeber, H., et al.: Typing in Thin Air: the Canesta Projection Keyboard - A New Method of Interaction with Electronic Devices, *Proceedings of ACM CHI2003*, pp.712-713 (2003).
10. Trucco, E., Verri, A.: *Introductory Techniques for 3-D Computer Vision*, Prentice Hall (1998).
11. Welch, G., Bishop, G.: An Introduction to the Kalman Filter, *SIGGRAPH 2001 Tutorial* (2001) (available at http://www.cs.unc.edu/~ tracker/media/pdf/SIGGRAPH2001_CoursePack_08.pdf).
12. Wellner, P.: Interacting with Paper on the DigitalDesk, *Communications of the ACM*, Vol.36, No.7, pp.87–96 (1993).
13. Zhang, Z., et al.: Visual Panel: Virtual Mouse, Keyboard and 3D Controller with an Ordinary Piece of Paper, *Proceedings of Perceptual User Interface*, pp.1–8 (2001).

DIZI: A Digital Ink Zooming Interface for Document Annotation

Maneesh Agrawala and Michael Shilman

Microsoft Research, One Microsoft Way,
Redmond, WA 98052
{maneesh, shilman}@microsoft.com
http://research.microsoft.com

Abstract. Pen computing devices provide a natural interface for annotating documents with freeform digital ink. However, digital ink annotations are usually larger and sloppier than real ink annotations on paper. We present DIZI, a focus+context interface that zooms up a region of the underlying document for inking. Users write in the zoomed region at a comfortable size for the device. When the zoom region is shrunk back to normal page size, the digital ink shrinks to an appropriate size for the underlying document. The zoom region covers only a small portion of the screen so that users can always see the overall context of the underlying document. We describe several techniques for fluidly moving the zoom region to navigate the document. We show that DIZI allows users to create digital ink annotations that more closely mimic the look of real ink annotations on physical paper.

1   Introduction

One of the goals of pen computing devices, such as Tablet PCs and PDAs, is to provide an inking surface that emulates physical paper. Ideally, using such devices should feel just like writing on paper and the resulting digital ink should look just like real ink. However, a variety of ergonomic factors make it difficult to fully achieve either of these goals. These factors include:

Slip. Digital screens are smoother and slipperier than paper.

Resolution. Digital screens have less visual resolution than paper. In addition, digitizers usually track digital pens at lower resolution than the finest human hand movements.

Screen Size. Digital screens are often smaller than standard letter size paper.

Parallax. Digital screens often contain a protective layer of plastic that creates parallax between the tip of the digital pen and the screen.

Size and Weight. The physical size and weight of pen computing devices makes it hard to position and interact with them like paper.

While hardware designers continue to improve the feel of pen-based devices and make them more like paper, a substantial gap remains.

M.F. Costabile and F. Paternò (Eds.): INTERACT 2005, LNCS 3585, pp. 69 – 79, 2005.

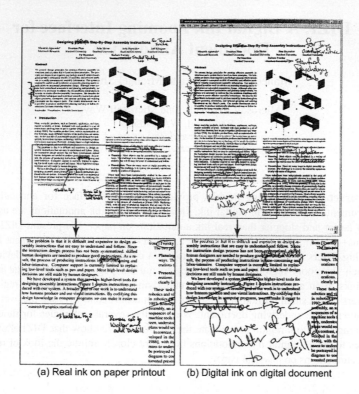

(a) Real ink on paper printout   (b) Digital ink on digital document

Fig. 1. Digital ink annotations are usually much larger and sloppier than real ink annotations on paper. As a result digital annotations may be difficult to read, especially if the reader did not originally write the annotation.

The ergonomic limitations of pen computing devices force users to change the way they write when using such devices. As shown in Fig. 1, digital ink is usually much larger and often sloppier than real ink annotations on paper. Creating legible digital ink is especially difficult when white space is limited, as it usually is when writing between lines, marking up individual characters or words, making comments in margins, or writing long comments. The resulting, larger-sized digital annotations often overlap the underlying text of the document and waste screen space because they are much less dense than real ink annotations.

To maintain context users typically need to see an entire page at a time. Yet, today's pen computing devices have screens that are smaller than a standard sheet of paper, and so pages must be shrunk to fit on the digital screen. The shrinkage only exacerbates the legibility problems due to larger-sized digital ink.

We present DIZI, a focus + context interface that allows users to create digital ink annotations that mimic the look of real ink on paper. DIZI does this by magnifying a region of the underlying document for inking so that users can write at a size that is comfortable for the device. As we will show, we have experimentally found that a scaling factor of 2.0 for the zoomed region allows users to write comfortably and still produces legible natural looking ink when the region is shrunk back to the normal page size. In addition, the zoom region is designed to cover only a small portion of the screen so that users can always see the overall context of the underlying document.

DIZI supports two primary forms of navigation, or moving the zoom region with respect to the underlying document; the user may move the zoom window explicitly to focus on a different part of the document, or the system may move the zoom window implicitly as the user is writing to ensure that the zoom region is always under the user's pen. We consider two strategies for explicit navigation, and we show that there is only one useful strategy for implicit navigation. We describe a simple but effective approach for combining implicit and explicit navigation to give the user full navigational control. Finally we show that the DIZI interface facilitates the creation of natural looking digital ink annotations.

2 Related Work

DIZI builds on two areas of previous work; zoomable user interfaces and free-form digital ink interfaces. We consider each of these in turn.

2.1 Zoomable User Interfaces

Zooming is a standard operation in many applications including document editing (Microsoft Word), photo manipulation (Adobe Photoshop) and vector-based design (Adobe Illustrator). However, these applications usually magnify the entire document and the surrounding context is not visible after the zoom. Thus, navigating in the zoomed view requires tediously scrolling through the document.

A better approach is to allow users to directly navigate a multi-scale focus + context view of the document, in which a magnified focus region show details while the surrounding context also remains visible. Researchers have developed a vast number of focus + context systems. for visualizing different kinds of documents including Fisheye Views[6], Perspective Wall[11] Document Lens[15], and Table Lens[14].

Researchers have also considered navigation in multi-scale space. Magic lenses[4] allow users to directly position a focus region (or lens) over the underlying document. Similarly, zoomable user interfaces such as Pad[12], Pad++[2] and Jazz[3], have applied panning and zooming navigation to a variety of tasks, ranging from viewing web pages, timelines, disk usage and maps, editing text and spreadsheets and presenting slideshows[8]. Users can pan and zoom to quickly reach any point in the multi-scale document space. Furnas and Bederson[7] use space-scale diagrams as a framework for describing this type of multi-scale navigation. Igarashi and Hinckley[9] also use space-scale diagrams to develop an automated zooming algorithm for browsing large documents. However, none of these systems consider the constraints on multi-scale navigation required to support digital inking.

2.2 Digital Ink Interfaces

One common use of freeform digital ink is to annotate digital documents. Schilit et al.[16] have developed xLibris, the first complete paper-like "active reading" system, in which ink annotations are used for collaboration and information retrieval. Follow-on systems include Adobe Acrobat Reader, Microsoft Windows Journal, Multivalent

Documents[13] and Callisto[1]. While some of these systems provide zoomable views and others support digital ink annotations, none of these systems provide both focus+context zooming and digital inking.

Another use of digital ink is note-taking. In work that is most closely related to ours, Davis et al.'s NotePals[5] addresses the problem of writing scale versus display scale. Users specify a focus cursor in the overview area at the top of the screen. As they write in a focus area at the bottom of the screen, the ink is shrunk to 40% of its original size and placed at the focus cursor. Users must explicitly create new writing space when they fill the focus area, which can break the flow of writing. Seni's Treadmill Ink [1] similarly uses a focus area for ink input. In this system the focus area is constantly scrolling from right to left thereby continuously clearing space for new ink. But, users must modify their writing style to accommodate the scroll. Both NotePals and Treadmill Ink are targeted at inking on small-screen devices like PDAs and cell phones. In other work, Lank[10] describes a fisheye lens-based inking system for Personal Digital Assistants. None of these systems is designed for annotating documents.

In this paper we apply the zoomable interface approach to annotate documents with free-form digital ink. We adopt the scale-space framework to explore several strategies for navigating the multi-scale space and we show when each of these strategies may be useful while annotating documents.

3 User Interface

As shown in Figure 2(a), DIZI allows users to interactively magnify a portion of the underlying document for inking. Annotating the document with DIZI in this manner involves a sequence of three interactions.

Initiating the Annotation. To indicate the zoom region users perform an initiation gesture. While holding the pen button users touch a point on the screen, which we call the zoom origin. DIZI generates a rectangular zoom window around this origin and the transition from the unzoomed state to the zoomed state is animated so that the zoom window appears to grow out of the zoom origin. As described in Figure 2(b,c) we have developed a flicking gesture as well as a rectangle gesture to allow the user to specify the orientation and size of the zoom window.

Writing the Annotation. Users then annotate the document by writing within the zoom window. We set a magnification scale factor of 2.0 within the zoom window. As we will describe in the section on implementation design details, we empirically chose this scale factor so that users can write at a size that is comfortable for the device and so that the digital ink appears at a natural size when the zoom window is shrunk back down into the underlying document.

Completing the Annotation. To finish the annotation, users tap the document while holding the pen button. An animated transition shrinks the zoom window along with the fresh ink back into the underlying document.

(a) DIZI interface   (b) Flicking gesture to initiate zoom   (c) Rectangle gesture to initiate zoom

Fig. 2. DIZI interface (a) The user writes at a comfortable size within a magnified region of the document. When zoomed back down the writing appears at a natural size. Zoom initiation gestures (b,c) The user presses the pen button and places it at the zoom origin (red X). The path of the initiation gesture (solid red line from X to pen tip) denotes a region of the document to be magnified (dotted red box) (top). An animated transition shows the zoom window growing out of the zoom origin to produce the focus + context zoom window (bottom). Flicking gesture (b) The user quickly flicks the pen to create the zoom window. The direction of the flick sets the orientation (horizontal or vertical) of the zoom window. Because English is written left-to-right we offset the center of zoom windows so that 70% of the window is lying to the right of the zoom origin. Flicking upwards will generate a vertically oriented window which can be useful for writing in the side margins. Rectangle gesture (c) The user holds the pen button and directly specifies the rectangular region of the document to zoom. This approach allows the user to specify both the size and orientation of the zoom window.

3.1 Navigation

After users have initiated a zoom, they can choose from several strategies for navigating the document (i.e. changing the region that is zoomed). When the user actively chooses the navigation strategy we call this explicit navigation. Two such explicit strategies include:

Move Zoom Origin. One way to move the zoom region is to unzoom and zoom again at another location. However, this approach forces unnecessary switches between zoom mode and unzoom mode. Alternatively, we provide a control that allows users to remain in zoom mode and directly drag the zoom origin to a new location.

Move Document. Instead of moving the zoom origin users may want to leave the zoom window fixed, and simply change the portion of the document that is visible in the zoom window. The move document control allows users to drag the portion of the source document that is visible in the zoom window.

A key design goal for both of these explicit navigation strategies is that users should be able to reach any point in the underlying document. We will show how we achieve this goal in the implementation section of the paper.

In addition to these explicit navigation strategies there is also an implicit strategy that occurs without the user invoking a command:

Create Space. When the user's writing approaches the edge of the zoom window, DIZI automatically repositions the window to create more writing space, as shown in

Figure 3. It is essential that this navigation strategy provide a smooth transition that doesn't disrupt the user's inking experience. As we will show in the implementation section, the only way to achieve this is to keep the zoom origin fixed as the zoom window is moved. Any other transformation will cause the surrounding ink and document to shift in the zoom window and break the user's writing flow.

While other navigation strategies are possible, we have found that these three suffice to accomplish common annotation tasks.

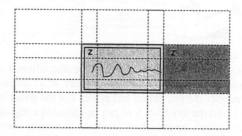

Fig. 3. If the user nears the edge of the zoom window while writing, DIZI automatically repositions the zoom window to create more writing space. We reposition the zoom window Z to one of the eight possible neighboring positions, based on the direction of the stroke. Here, as soon as the stroke exits the slightly smaller internal box (shown in dark blue) on the right side we reposition Z to Z'.

4   Implementation

Aside from inking, the primary form of interaction with DIZI is navigation, or moving the zoom region. In this section we first present a geometric framework for zooming interfaces. We then develop three navigation techniques based on this framework and show how two of them are combined in the default DIZI interface. Finally we describe several implementation design decisions we made in the process of taking DIZI from concept to usable prototype.

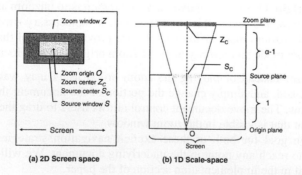

Fig. 4. A 2D screen-space diagram of our zooming interface (a), and a corresponding 1D space-scale diagram for the x-axis (b). The space-scale diagram shows that the mapping between the zoom origin O, the source window S, and the zoom window Z is a projection. The planes are spaced such that the projection scales any region on the source plane by scaling factor α.

4.1 Geometric Framework

Figure 4 shows a diagrammatic representation of our zooming interface. We adopt the space-scale diagrams of Furnas and Bederson[7] to depict the geometric relationship between the zoom region and the source document. In the space-scale diagrams zooming is treated as a projection from the zoom origin O, through the source window S, and into the zoom window Z. The planes are spaced such that the scaling factor α is given by:

$$\alpha = |Z| / |S| \tag{1}$$

where $|Z|$ and $|S|$ denote the width of the zoom window and source window respectively. By similar triangles, the center of the zoom window Z_C, the center of the source window SC, and the zoom origin O are related by the following expression:

$$Z_C = O(1 - \alpha) + S_C \alpha \tag{2}$$

In fact this expression holds for any set of points Z_P and S_P lying on a projector line emanating from origin O. The space of geometric interactions with the system can be expressed in terms of these parameters. Assuming a given scale factor α, we can vary any two of the remaining parameters and the third is fully constrained.

4.2 Navigation

All three of DIZI's navigational strategies are achieved by setting the parameters of this geometric framework in different ways, as shown in Figure 5.

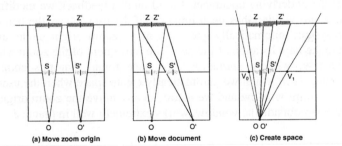

Fig. 5. Navigation strategies described using scale-space diagrams. (a) To move the zoom origin, the zoom window center O is locked to the zoom window center Z_C (b) To move the document, Z_C is fixed while S_C is dragged to S_C'.(c) To create space, the zoom center Z_C is moved to Z_C' while the zoom origin O remains fixed thereby preserving the mapping between the source and zoom planes. Note that since the zoom and source windows partially overlap we have slightly offset them vertically in the diagram. Both the move document and create space strategies shear the projection frustum to generate off-axis projections.

Move Zoom Origin. Our approach to moving the zoom origin is to lock the origin O to the zoom window center ZC. As shown in Figure 5(a), when the user clicks at Z_C' we set $O' = Z_C'$. Using Equation 2 to solve for the new source center S_C' we see that $S_C' = O'$. As the user drags the zoom window, we translate all three parameters equally. This approach ensures that users can zoom up any point in the underlying document as they drag the zoom window.

Move Document. To move the document, the user drags SC to a new position SC', as shown in Figure 5(b). In this case we keep the zoom window fixed by setting ZC' = ZC, and then solve for O' using Equation 2. This approach also ensures that users can zoom up any point in the underlying document but here they are dragging the source window instead of the zoom window.

Create Space. When the user's writing approaches the edge of the zoom window we move ZC to ZC' such that the zoom window remains under the pen and provides more space to continue writing. In order for users to continue writing in a natural way, it is critical that the mapping between the source plane and zoom plane remains fixed. Otherwise the document would shift under the pen and disrupt the user. In the space-scale framework the only way to maintain this mapping is to keep the zoom origin O fixed. Therefore we set O' = O and given the new ZC' we can compute SC using Equation 2. This approach allows the user to continuously draw strokes off the edge of the zoom window. However, because the mapping is fixed, in this case users can only reach a subset of the document as delimited by V0 and V1 in Figure 5(c). To reach other parts of the document users must unzoom and re-initiate the zoom in a new location.

Combining Navigation Strategies. To perform explicit navigation users must enter the appropriate navigation mode (either move zoom origin or move document) by tapping the corresponding button in a button bar. Initially this was the only way to perform explicit navigation. However, our early users pointed out that they sometimes wanted faster access to the move the zoom window mode in order to quickly magnify a new part of the underlying document. Based on this feedback we modified DIZI so that after the zoom window has been initiated, if the user places the pen outside the window, the system automatically goes into move zoom origin mode, and sets the zoom origin to the new location of the pen. The movement of the zoom window takes place immediately, without animation. We have found that this combination of navigation strategies in which we automatically create space when the user writes off the edge of the zoom window and we automatically move the zoom origin when the user places the pen outside the window, works extremely well in practice.

5   Design Details

In building a usable prototype of out zoomable annotation interface we made a number of low-level design decisions. We consider how these decisions affect the DIZI interface.

Initially Positioning Zoom Window. When the initial zoom origin is close to the edge of the document (as it typically is when making margin comments) the zoom window may extend off-screen. Our solution is to translate the zoom window and its center Z_C back on screen while leaving the source window and its center S_C fixed. Then we can again solve for O' using Equation 2. The inset figure shows how the projection geometry changes. If the zoom window is larger than the screen in either dimension, we translate the window so that

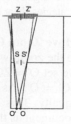

maximum portion of the zoom window is visible, under the constraint that zoom window center Z_C must always be in view.

Default Zoom Initiation Gesture. The default initiation gesture is flicking. In practice we have found that flicking is much faster and easier than the rectangle gesture. The rectangle gesture requires more effort and precision than the flicking gesture because the user has to actively think about the size of the window. With flicking the size of the zoom window is fixed and therefore the user only needs to consider where to place the zoom origin. However, in circumstances where it is important to control the size of the zoom window the rectangle gesture is more appropriate. We provide a checkbutton to allow users to switch to rectangle gesture mode

Setting the Scaling Factor. To determine the appropriate scaling factor α, we conducted an informal study (3 participants) comparing the size of real ink annotations on paper to the same annotations written digitally on a TabletPC without the aid of our zooming interface. We scanned the paper documents and manually drew bounding boxes around each word of the both the real and digital annotations. We found that the digital annotations were between 1.4 and 2.7 times larger than the corresponding ink annotations. We then tried using several different scale factors within this range in DIZI and eventually settled on a scale factor of 2.0. We found that doubling the size of the document allows most users to write comfortably in the zoom window. Larger scale factors force users to deal with a lot more navigation to create long annotations.

The accompanying video shows how our implementation performs in practice. The video is in DivX 5.1.1 format and contains some visual artifacts due to compression.

6   Usage Experience and Discussion

We conducted informal trials in which 6 members of our lab first completed a short training task to learn the DIZI interface and then used DIZI to annotate a set of conference papers. The papers were edited a priori to include spelling and grammatical errors. Participants were instructed to both correct the errors and insert specific alternate sentences and comments.

Our goal was to determine the effect a zooming interface would have on the annotation process: how often users would use the zooming capability versus writing in the standard unzoomed, manner, where would zooming be most useful, how would the zooming interface affect the look of the digital annotations and would users link the interface. These trials confirmed some of the intuitions about the interface, but also included surprises.

While zooming is a primary feature of DIZI, the system also allows users to annotate documents without zooming. Figure 6 shows a typical page with zoomed and unzoomed ink rendered in red and green respectively. Users found zooming most useful when writing text or edit marks in areas of limited white space. Several users commented that their text annotations looked more like their written text on real paper. Users found it less useful to zoom when drawing long, figural annotations such as margin bars, underlines and circles. Such figural annotations usually require less precision than text annotations and can therefore be drawn without zooming.

We were surprised to learn that some users initially preferred the rectangle zoom initiation gesture to the flicking gesture. The rectangle initiation gesture provides full control over the area to be zoomed and is easy to learn because it is similar to selection gestures in many graphical interfaces. Talking with these users afterwards we found that their main complaint with the flicking gesture was that they found it difficult to guess the size of the zoom window. These users also found the gesture a little harder to learn, claiming that it was "unintuitive".

Two of our users were given a longer training task that involved using both the flicking and rectangle gestures to initiate the zoom many times. These users preferred the flicking gesture to the rectangle gesture for its speed. While we believe flicking is a better choice as the default initiation gesture because it requires less effort and precision, these preliminary studies show that users must spend time learning how flicking works before they are comfortable with it. We plan to conduct more in-depth studies to evaluate the effectiveness of these initiation gestures.

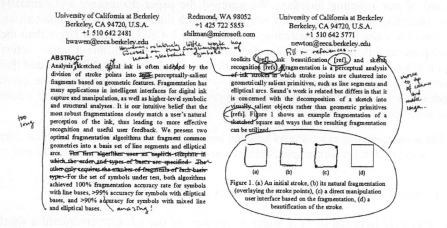

Fig. 6. Visualization of annotations created with DIZI. Text annotations (red) were created using the zooming interface. Figural circles, arrows, and strikethrough annotations (green) were created without zooming. In general we found that zooming was most commonly used in when writing text or edit marks in tightly constrained areas with limited white space. Most of the text in this example, including the long sentence starting, "However,…" would be impossible to fit in the limited white space without the zooming interface. These text annotations remain readable even after they are shrunk back down to page size. Long structural and figural annotations such as margin bars, underlines, arrows and circles are typically created without zooming because they require less precision than text annotations.

7 Conclusions

We have presented DIZI, a digital ink zooming interface that facilitates the creation of digital ink annotations with the same size and look as real ink annotations on paper. DIZI magnifies only a portion of the underlying document for inking so that user can write at a comfortable size of the device but still see the overall context of the page. We experimentally found that a scaling factor of 2.0 allows users to write comfortably and produces legible ink even when into the original document. We have explored several different navigation strategies for moving the zoom region. Based on user feedback we combine an implicit strategy that automatically moves the zoom region so that it stays under the pen while the user is writing, with an explicit strategy that allows the user to directly move the zoom region to any part of the document. We believe that by allowing users to create digital ink that looks more like real ink our interface helps to bridge the gap between pen computing devices and physical paper.

Acknowledgments

We would like to thank Mary Czerwinski for her insightful comments and advice throughout the course of this work

References

1. Bargeron, D. and Moscovich, T. Reflowing digital ink annotations. *Proc. CHI 03*, (2003), 385-393.
2. Bederson B.B. and Hollan J. Pad++: A zooming graphical interface for exploring alternate interface physics. *Proc. of UIST 94*. (1994), 17-26.
3. Bederson, B.B., Meyer, J., and Good, L. Jazz: An extensible zoomable user interface graphics toolkit in Java. *Proc of UIST 00*. (2000), 171-180.
4. Bier, E.A., Stone, M.C., Pierce, K., Buxton, W. and DeRose, T.D. Toolglass and magic lenses: The see-through interface. *SIGGRAPH 93*, (1993), 73-80.
5. Davis, R.C., Landay, J.A., Chen, V., Huang, J., Lee, R.B., Li, F., Lin, J., Morrey, C.B., Schleimer, B., Price, M.N. and Schilit, B.N. NotePals: Lightweight note sharing by the group, for the group. *Proc. CHI 99*, (1999), 338-345.
6. Furnas, G. W. Generalized fisheye views. *Proc. CHI 86*, (1986), 16-23.
7. Furnas, G.W. and Bederson, B.B. Space-scale diagrams: Understanding multiscale interfaces. *Proc. CHI 95*, (1995), 234-241.
8. Good, L. and Bederson, B.B. Zoomable user interfaces as a medium for slide show presentations. *Proc of Information Visualization*. (2002), 35-49.
9. Igarashi, T. and Hinckley, K. Speed-dependent automatic zooming for browsing large documents. *Proc of UIST 00*, (2000), 139-148
10. Lank, E. and Phan, S., Focus+Context sketching on a pocket PC, Extended abstracts of *CHI 2004*, April 24-29, 2004, Vienna, Austria
11. Mackinlay, J.D., Robertson, G. and Card, S.K. The perspective wall: Detail and context smoothly integrated. *Proc. CHI 91*, (1991), 173-179.
12. Perlin, K. and Fox, D. Pad: An alternative approach to the computer interface. *SIGGRAPH 93*, (1993), 57-72.
13. Phelps, T.A., Wilensky, R. Multivalent documents. *Communications of the ACM, 43*, 6(2000), 82-90.
14. Rao, R. and Card, S.K. The table lens: Merging graphical and symbolic representations in an interactive focus + context visualization for tabular information. *Proc, CHI 94*, (1994), 318-322.
15. Robertson G. and Mackinlay, J.D. The document lens. *Proc. of UIST 93*, (1993), 101-108.
16. Schilit, B.N., Golovchinsky, G. and Price, M.N. Beyond paper: Supporting active reading with free form digital ink annotations. *Proc. CHI 98*, (1998), 249-256..
17. Seni, G. Treadmill ink - Enabling continuous pen input on small devices. *Proc. 8th International Workshop on Frontiers in Handwriting Recognition*, (2002), 215 -220.

TractorBeam Selection Aids: Improving Target Acquisition for Pointing Input on Tabletop Displays

J. Karen Parker[1,3], Regan L. Mandryk[2], Michael N. Nunes[1], and Kori M. Inkpen[1]

[1] Faculty of Comp. Sci., Dalhousie University, Halifax, NS, Canada
[2] School of Comp. Sci., Simon Fraser University, Burnaby, BC, Canada
[3] Dept. of Comp. Sci., University of British Columbia, Vancouver, BC, Canada
parker@cs.ubc.ca, rlmandry@cs.sfu.ca
{nunes, inkpen}@cs.dal.ca

Abstract. This paper presents a comparison of several selection aids to improve pointing input on tabletop displays. Our previous research explored the TractorBeam–a hybrid point-touch interaction technique for tabletop displays. We found that while pointing input was preferred (over touch) by users of tabletop displays, it was slower for small distant targets. Drawing from previous work on improving target acquisition for desktop displays, we developed and tested three selection aids to improve pointing selection of small distant targets on *tabletop* displays: expanding the cursor, expanding the target, and snapping to the target. Our experiments revealed that all three aids resulted in faster selection times than no selection aid at all, with snapping to the target being the fastest. Additionally, participants liked snapping to the target better than the other selection aids and found it to be the most effective for selecting targets.

1 Introduction

Tabletop displays have emerged in the past 10 years as an area of interest in HCI research. As this research continues, it is important to develop effective interaction techniques for these types of displays. Although some researchers have developed specialized input devices and techniques for tabletop displays [9, 2, 11, 14], very few have conducted systematic evaluations on the effectiveness of these techniques. Determining appropriate input devices and interaction techniques is critical if tabletop displays are to become mainstream.

In our previous work, we developed the TractorBeam, an innovative technique which seamlessly combines remote pointing and touch – using a stylus – on tabletop displays [9]. Results from this work demonstrated that remote pointing was faster than touch input for large targets, was preferred over touch, and was also employed more often when users were given a choice. However, for small distant targets pointing was slower than touch. In remote pointing, small movements made with the hand are amplified on the screen. This amplification increases as distance to the target increases, so even though users must reach further to touch small distant targets than point to them, it is easier to make an accurate selection using touch.

Due to the amplification of small movements for distant targets, we felt that augmenting the technique with a selection aid might improve acquisition of small, distant targets. Past research into improving target acquisition has focused on desktop

M.F. Costabile and F. Paternò (Eds.): INTERACT 2005, LNCS 3585, pp. 80–93, 2005.
© IFIP International Federation for Information Processing 2005

displays. Researchers have explored methods such as expanding targets [7], area cursors [6], bubble cursors [4], object pointing [5], and semantic pointing [1]. Since the TractorBeam interaction technique for tabletop displays is significantly different than standard mouse-based interaction for desktop environments, we felt it was important to conduct a preliminary investigation of these previously proposed alternatives.

Drawing from this previous research, we developed and tested three selection aids to augment our TractorBeam technique, in order to improve acquisition of small distant targets on tabletop displays:

1. expanding the cursor (expand-cursor)
2. expanding the target (expand-target)
3. snapping to the target (snap-to-target)

All three selection aids, along with a fourth control condition, were evaluated for speed and accuracy, with snap-to-target emerging as the best option; it was fastest, and preferred by participants. The snap-augmented TractorBeam is a very good solution to the problems of reaching small distant targets encountered in our previous work.

2   Related Work

2.1   TractorBeam Technique

The TractorBeam interaction technique is a novel stylus-based input technique that combines close touch and distant pointing, allowing users to interact with nearby parts of the display more naturally with a stylus, and use the pointing functionality when they need to select an item that is beyond their reach. The technique works as follows: Using a stylus, the user points at the tabletop display. A cursor appears on the display to show the current trajectory of the stylus (Figure 1). The user moves the stylus around until the cursor is on the desired item. To select the item, the user clicks the button located on the top of the stylus.

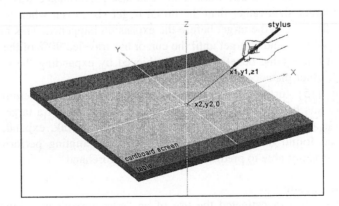

Fig. 1. TractorBeam interaction technique

This allows for seamless interaction with all parts of the display. To interact with a close object, the user touches the stylus to the table, as one would normally use a stylus. To interact with a distant object, the user points the stylus towards their desired target, casting a virtual beam which positions the cursor where the user is pointing.

2.2   Other Tabletop Interaction Techniques

While previous tabletop research has used a wide variety of inputs, few researchers have specifically investigated interaction techniques for tabletop displays. Exceptions to this include Wu and Balakrishnan [14] who developed a suite of hand and finger gestures for multi-touch tabletop displays. Also, tangential to tabletop research, Rekimoto and Saitoh's hyperdragging (dragging an item off one display and onto another with a mouse) and pick-and-drop (picking an item up from one display and dropping it on another with a stylus) techniques allow users to move files between a tabletop and other devices, including distant displays such as large wall screens [10].

2.3   Improving Target Acquisition

Several researchers have proposed solutions to improve target acquisition time on traditional desktop computer monitors with mouse input. In attempting to improve target acquisition on tabletop displays, knowledge of these existing desktop techniques provides insight into possible solutions.

Expanding the Target

Dynamically sized widgets which change size as a cursor approaches them (expanding targets), such as those used in the OS X operating system [8], are becoming more common in current user interfaces. McGuffin and Balakrishnan [7] investigated the effectiveness of expanding targets by comparing them to statically sized targets in a Fitts' task. The results from this work found that task performance was governed by the expanded target size, rather than the initial target size, even when they were already 90% of the way to the target before the expansion happened. This means that it is not necessary to expand a target until the cursor has traveled 90% of the distance to that target, since the same benefits will be achieved by expanding the target at that distance as at further distances.

Zhai et al. [15] further investigated expanding targets to determine whether McGuffin's results held when users did not know whether or not a target would expand. They ran trials in which targets would randomly shrink, expand, or remain unchanged, and found that target expansion improved pointing performance even when the user was not able to predict the expansion beforehand.

Enlarging the Cursor

Kabbash and Buxton investigated the use of an "area cursor" in a Fitts' task and showed that, when using an area cursor to select a point, the action could be modeled with Fitts' law by making W (width of the target in Fitts' equation) the width of the cursor, rather than the target [6]. The authors tested both a single point cursor moving between two large target areas, and a single large area cursor moving between two small target points. They found that the area cursor performed better than a single-point cursor in the task [6]. Worden et al. augmented area cursors with sticky icons in a study of basic selection tasks with older adult users [13] and found significant improvements in target selection times for small targets.

Although an area cursor could provide faster selection, it might be difficult for users to complete finer-grain actions. Grossman and Balakrishnan's bubble cursor solves this problem with its dynamic activation area, which only becomes large when it is close to a viable target [4]. Movement times for the bubble cursor were faster than both a standard point cursor and the object pointing technique [4].

Object and Semantic Pointing
Guiard et al. introduced the idea of object pointing, where the cursor moves between valid targets and never travels in empty space between targets, as a means for improving target acquisition [5]. While object pointing outperforms regular pointing in Fitts' tasks, it may not be appropriate for interactions that require manipulations other than simple selection. For object pointing to work effectively, users would be required to enable it whenever they wanted to make selections, and disable it when they did not.

In semantic pointing, a related technique, targets "expand" in motor space (but not in visual space) according to their importance [1]. For example, as a user moves across a button they will move more slowly than when they move across a blank space because the button is expanded in motor space. Although this technique may be effective with a mouse or another relative input device, is not appropriate for direct input because direct input requires constant mapping of the cursor with the input device.

3 TractorBeam Selection Aids

Our previous work revealed that acquisition of small, distant targets was difficult with the TractorBeam, our hybrid point-touch technique. Thus, we explored three possible selection aids to solve this problem: expanding the cursor (expand-cursor), expanding the target (expand-target), and snapping to the target (snap-to-target).

3.1 Expanding the Cursor

With this selection aid, users make selections using a "selection halo" area which surrounds the cursor, rather than having to use a single cursor point for selection. This is similar to the bubble cursor used by Grossman and Balakrishnan [4], which was shown to improve acquisition of targets. Whenever the cursor travels at least 90% of the distance to a target, a 30mm halo appears under the cursor and immediately expands to 60mm (Figure 2). The halo shrinks and disappears whenever the cursor moves outside of the 90% range. In order to make these changes appear more seamless, both the expansion and shrink are animated. In order to select a target, the selection halo must only overlap the target, not encompass it.

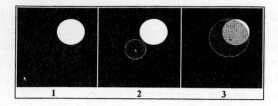

Fig. 2. Expand-cursor: (1) Cursor begins to approach target; (2) Cursor reaches 90% threshold and halo appears and begins expansion; (3) Halo continues expansion until it is full size

3.2 Expanding the Target

Similar to the expanding targets studied by McGuffin and Balakrishan [7], our expanding-target selection aid expands targets from their original size whenever the cursor is within 90% of the total distance traveled to the target (Figure 3). Targets shrink whenever the cursor moves outside of the 90% range. In order to make these changes appear seamless, both the expansion and shrink are animated. In our study, targets started at 30mm, 40mm, or 50mm, and expanded to a final size of 60mm.

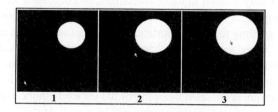

Fig. 3. Expand-target (1) Cursor begins to approach target; (2) Cursor reaches 90% threshold and target begins expansion; (3) Target continues expansion until it has reached full size

3.3 Snapping to the Target

With this selection aid, the cursor "snaps" to the center of the target whenever it comes within 90% of the total distance to the target (Figure 4). It remains in this snapped position unless the "real" cursor position moves outside of this 90% range.

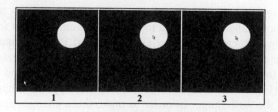

Fig. 4. Snap-to-target: (1) Cursor begins to approach target; (2) Cursor reaches 90% threshold and immediately snaps to centre of target; (3) Cursor remains snapped to target centre until pointer moves outside of 90% range

4 Experimental Design

4.1 Participants

Twenty-four participants, 18 male and 6 female, took part in our study. All participants were university students, staff, or faculty, and were right handed. None had participated in our previous TractorBeam user studies.

4.2 Hardware Setup

The hardware setup included a top-projected tabletop display consisting of a ceiling-mounted projector, mirror, desktop PC, wooden table, and white cardboard "screen" (Figure 5).

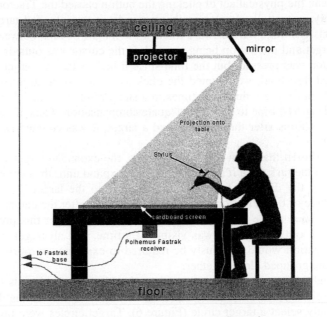

Fig. 5. TractorBeam hardware configuration

The PC was connected to the projector and its output was projected onto the mirror, which reflected the image onto the table. The cardboard screen was used to provide a clearer projection surface than the table alone.

Input for the tabletop display was received via a corded stylus and receiver attached to a Polhemus Fastrak® (a "six degrees of freedom" 3D tracking system). The Fastrak® receiver was secured to the centre of the underside of the table. Using information from the stylus and receiver, the Fastrak® base provided continuous information about the position of the stylus in 3D space to our software through a serial port connection on the PC. Our software then used this information to calculate the spot on the table to which the pen was pointing, and drew the cursor at that location. During our experiments, we experienced no noticeable lag or accuracy issues with the Pohemus.

4.3   Task

A multi-directional task (2D Fitts discrete task) was used to evaluate selection tasks in four conditions: control, expand-cursor, expand-target, and snap-to-target. A Java application was developed to implement the selection aids required for each of the four conditions on our tabletop display.

Participants used the TractorBeam interaction technique throughout the experiment, but used each of the four types of selection aids in four separate conditions. In all conditions, participants selected targets on the table by pointing to them or touching them with the stylus to position the cursor on the target, and clicking the stylus button to indicate the selection.

We had previously used dwell times to indicate target selection with the Tractor-Beam [9]. The stylus button click technique used in the present experiment introduces a small problem: the physical act of clicking the button caused the TractorBeam stylus to shift slightly, potentially displacing the cursor from the intended target. To compensate for this problem, our software tracked the length of time between the cursor exiting the target and the button being pressed. If the cursor was outside of the target when the button was pressed, but the time since it had exited the target was under a pre-determined threshold, we counted the click as a successful target selection. We tested several button-press threshold times in a small pilot study and found 100ms to be a suitable length of time to provide adequate compensation. Thus, if the button was pressed within 100ms after the cursor exited a target, it was counted as a successful target acquisition.

It has been shown that, with expanding targets, the expanded target width dictates the difficulty of the task even if the target does not expand until the cursor has already traveled 90% of the distance from the start position to the target [7]. As such, we designed all three of our selection aids to only take effect after the cursor had traveled 90% of the distance to the target. This design was sufficient for this preliminary investigation since only one target was visible at a time, and all targets were distant. Further investigation would obviously be required to examine appropriate thresholds when targets are grouped close together.

In each condition, participants were presented with a series of trials that required them to first select a home square (located in the bottom centre of the display area) and subsequently select a target circle (Figure 6). Target circles were presented with one of three widths (30mm, 40mm, 50mm), at one of three angles (40 degrees left, midline, 40 degrees right), and at one of three amplitudes (520mm, 650mm, 780mm).

Participants in our previous research were slower with pointing than touching for small, distant targets. Therefore, for this study we chose widths which ranged from slightly smaller than the "medium" sizes in our first study to exactly the "small" sizes used in our first study and amplitudes which ranged from just above the "medium" amplitude in our first study to exactly the "far" amplitude in our first study.

Each individual trial began when a user selected the home square, and ended when they selected the target circle. Selection was defined by a stylus button click in the target circle. Between the users' selection of the home square and the appearance of the target circle, there was a random-length pause of between 500 and 1500 ms.

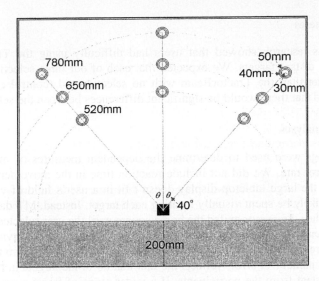

Fig. 6. 2D task setup. The black square is the starting point and the circles represent the targets.

Participants were asked to keep the cursor on the home square until the target appeared. Software logged when a target appeared, when a user moved off the home square, and when a user selected the target circle. As in our earlier studies, movement time was calculated as the difference between the time a user moved off the home square and the time they selected the target.

4.4 Procedure

A within subjects design was utilized with each participant using all three selection aids and a control. To minimize order effects, condition order was counterbalanced.

After a background questionnaire, participants were asked to perform a series of trials using the experimental task software in each of the four conditions. Participants sat at the tabletop display and were asked to remain seated for the duration of the session. For every condition, each participant first completed a warm-up session which required them to select 10 random targets. They then completed exactly five trials of each unique combination of amplitude, width, and angle, for a total of 135 trials. The ordering of the trials was randomized for each participant. On average, participants took 12 minutes to complete each interaction technique (including answering the questionnaire), for a combined session total of approximately 48 minutes for all three interaction techniques.

Following each condition, users completed a post-task questionnaire to gather data on their comfort and perceived performance with the selection aid used. This questionnaire was based on the device assessment questionnaire from the ISO 9241, Part 9 standard [3], which outlines requirements for non-keyboard computer input devices. Once all four conditions were finished, users were given a final questionnaire asking them to rate the selection aids in terms of satisfaction and perceived effectiveness.

4.5 Hypotheses

Our previous research showed that users had difficulty using the TractorBeam to select small, distant targets. We expected that each of our three selection aids would perform better than the TractorBeam with no selection aid (control condition). We also expected that there would be significant differences between the selection aids.

4.6 Data Analyses

Computer logs were used to determine the dependent measures of movement time (MT) and error rate. We did not include reaction time in the movement time, due to the fact that the large tabletop display doesn't fit in a user's field of view and some time would likely be spent visually locating each target. Instead, MT data were calculated from when the cursor exited the home square until the user selected the target.

Errors occurred if the cursor was not on the target when the stylus button was clicked. We removed 1960 (14.7% of total trials) selection errors from the MT analysis. The high number of errors reflects the fact that all of the targets in our study were small and distant from the participants. If a wider range of target sizes and distances had been used, we would have expected a lower error rate.

Movement time data for the five repeated trials at each unique combination of target variables were averaged. Repeated Measures Analysis of Variance (ANOVAs) were performed on the mean MT and entry rate data. All main effects and interactions were tested at $\alpha=.05$. Questionnaires were analyzed using non-parametric statistical tests.

5 Results

Movement time and error data for all conditions are presented in Table 1. For the error rates, totals for each condition are given along with the percentage of total trials constituted by those errors.

Table 1. Mean MT in ms and error rate for each condition

Condition	Movement Time Mean ms (SE)	Error Rate Total (%)
Control	1544 (19.5)	586 (18.1%)
Expand-cursor	1326 (20.5)	313 (9.7%)
Expand-target	1370 (16.3)	429 (13.2%)
Snap-to-target	1060 (15.6)	582 (17.9%)

5.1 Hypothesis 1: Control Condition Would Be Slower Than the Other Conditions

ANOVAs were performed on the movement time data for the 4-condition design. As expected, there was a main effect for condition ($F_{3,69}=14.7$, p=.000, $\eta^2=.39$). Pairwise comparisons revealed our hypothesis was validated, with the control being significantly slower than expand-cursor ($F_{1,23}$=8.6, p=.008, η^2=.27), expand-target ($F_{1,23}$=5.7, p=.026, η^2=.20), and snap-to-target ($F_{1,23}$=51.5, p=.000, η^2=.69).

5.2 Hypothesis 2: There Would Be a Difference Between the Three Selection Aids

ANOVAs were performed on the movement time data for the 3-(selection aid) condition design. There was a main effect for condition ($F_{2,46}$=9.7, p=.000, η^2=.30), which validated our hypothesis. Pairwise comparisons revealed that snap-to-target was significantly faster than both expand-cursor ($F_{1,23}$=9.4, p=.006, η^2=.29) and expand-target ($F_{1,23}$=20.9, p=.000, η^2=.48). However, there was no significant difference between expand-cursor and expand-target ($F_{1,21}$=0.4, p=.556, η^2=.02).

5.3 Error Rates

In order to investigate the number of errors in the various conditions, ANOVAs were performed on the error rate data for the 4-condition design. There was a main effect for condition ($F_{3,69}$=7.2, p=.000, η^2=.24). Pairwise comparisons revealed that the control condition had significantly more errors than both expand-cursor ($F_{1,23}$=34.5, p=.000, η^2=.60) and expand-target ($F_{1,23}$=6.2, p=.021, η^2=.21, but that there was no significant difference with snap-to-target ($F_{1,23}$=.003, p=.956, η^2=.000).

Mean error rates for each condition, separate by amplitude and width, are displayed in Figure 7. A value of zero would indicate no errors occurred for that target. The snap-to-target condition had significantly more errors than the expand-cursor ($F_{1,23}$=20.0, p=.000, η^2=.47) condition, but not the expand-target condition ($F_{1,23}$=3.2, p=.088, η^2=.12). There was no significant difference in errors between the expand-cursor and expand-target conditions ($F_{1,23}$=2.0, p=.170, η^2=.08).

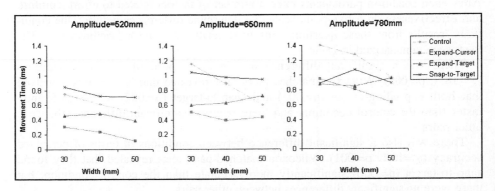

Fig. 7. Mean error rates for each condition, separated by amplitude and width

5.4 Inverse Efficiency

Although snap-to-target was found to be the fastest selection aid in our study, it also had significantly more errors than the slower expand-cursor aid. Thus, we wanted to investigate the speed/accuracy tradeoffs of the various conditions. Townsend and Ashby [12] suggest combining movement time and error measures with the following equation for inverse efficiency (IE): $IE = MT/(Proportion\ of\ trials\ correct)$. For example, a mean movement time of 2000 ms with 4 out of 5 trials successful would result in an inverse efficiency of 2500 (IE = 2000/0.8). A lower IE score corresponds to a more efficient technique.

Inverse efficiencies were calculated using the collected MT and error data. Mean inverse efficiency for each of the conditions is displayed in Table 2.

Table 2. Mean inverse efficiency for each condition

Condition	Inverse Efficiency (IE)
Control	2411
Expand-cursor	1606
Expand-target	2003
Snap-to-target	1446

ANOVAs were performed on the IE data for the 4 condition design. There was a main effect for condition ($F_{3,69}=5.1$, p=.003, $\eta^2=.18$). Pairwise comparisons revealed that snap-to-target had significantly lower inverse efficiency than the control condition ($F_{1,23}=18.2$, p=.000, $\eta^2=.44$). However, while the mean IE for snap-to-target was also lower than that of the other selection aid conditions, it was not significantly different ($F_{1,23}=4.0$, p=.055 $\eta^2=.15$ when compared to expand-target, $F_{1,23}=.95$, p=.341, $\eta^2=.04$ compared to expand-cursor).

5.5 Questionnaire Responses

After each condition participants rated a number of factors related to effort, comfort, and effectiveness on a five-point scale. To determine differences between the conditions, results from these questionnaires were analyzed using a Friedman test. The means are summarized in Table 3.

There was a significant difference in perceived speed of the four conditions ($\chi^2=18.7$, p=.000). Wilcoxon matched-pairs tests revealed that participants perceived that both expanding-cursor (p=.003) and snap-to-target (p=.002) were significantly faster than the control condition, and there were no significant differences between other pairs.

There was also a significant difference between conditions in terms of perceived accuracy ($\chi^2=16.1$, p=.001). Wilcoxon matched-pairs tests revealed that they found snap-to-target (p=.006) significantly more accurate than the control condition, but there were no significant differences between other pairs.

In terms of comfort, there was again a significant difference between conditions ($\chi^2=10.2$, p=.017), with matched-pairs tests showing snap-to-target as significantly more comfortable than the control (p=.008) but no other significant differences between pairs. For ease of use, there was also a significant difference between conditions ($\chi^2=14.5$, p=.002), with matched-pairs tests revealing both snap-to-target (p=.003) and expanding-cursor (p=.004) significantly easier to use than the control, and no other significant differences between pairs.

At the end of the experiment we asked the participants to rate the four conditions according to how effective they were and how much they liked each technique. To determine differences between the interaction techniques, results from these question-naires were also analyzed using a Friedman test. The means are summarized in Table 4. There was a significant difference between the conditions in terms of both effec-tiveness (χ^2=22.96, p=.000) and enjoyability (χ^2=22.94, p=.000).

Matched-pairs tests revealed that snap-to-target (p=.001), expand-cursor (p=.000), and expand-target (p=.001) were all perceived by users to be significantly more effec-tive than the control condition, but there were no significant differences between other pairings. Additionally, users enjoyed using snap-to-target (p=.001), expand-cursor (p=.000), and expand-target (p=.001) significantly more than the control condition, with no significant differences between other pairings.

Participant feedback supported our quantitative finding that snap-to-target was as an effective and enjoyable selection aid:

"The snap helps a lot especially for small targets."
"I liked the fact that the snap-to-target stopped the cursor, as objects far away were harder to select because the cursor became more sensitive."

Table 3. Mean responses from condition questionnaires on a five-point scale where 1 is low and 5 is high. (* denotes p<.05)

	Control Mean (SD)	Expand-Cursor Mean (SD)	Expand-Target Mean (SD)	Snap-to-Target Mean (SD)
Mental Effort	3.21 (.93)	2.96 (.81)	3.08 (.78)	2.58 (.97)
Physical Effort	3.92 (.65)	3.58 (.72)	3.71 (.69)	3.46 (.83)
Perceived Speed*	3.21 (.93)	3.96 (.81)	3.71 (.91)	4.25 (.90)
Perceived Accuracy*	2.96 (1.16)	3.58 (1.11)	3.79 (.88)	4.04 (1.12)
Wrist Fatigue	3.50 (.98)	3.17 (.92)	3.46 (.72)	3.25 (1.03)
Arm Fatigue	2.96 (1.09)	2.75 (.90)	3.13 (1.19)	2.75 (1.03)
Shoulder Fatigue	2.71 (1.09)	2.67 (.96)	2.50 (1.02)	2.37 (.82)
Neck Fatigue	2.33 (.96)	2.54 (.98)	2.21 (.88)	2.29 (.96)
Comfort*	2.96 (.81)	3.50 (.83)	3.42 (.88)	3.67 (.82)
Ease of Use*	3.04 (.96)	3.88 (1.04)	3.46 (1.02)	3.96 (.81)

Table 4. Mean responses from post-session questionnaires on a five-point scale where 1 is low and 5 is high. (* denotes p<.05)

	Control Mean (SD)	Expand-Cursor Mean (SD)	Expand-Target Mean (SD)	Snap-to-Target Mean (SD)
Effective*	2.33 (1.01)	3.71 (.859)	3.63 (.875)	4.04 (1.122)
Enjoy*	2.33 (1.129)	3.75 (.847)	3.62 (1.09)	4.00 (1.103)

6 Discussion

We hypothesized that all three of our selection aids would improve upon the original TractorBeam interaction technique used in the control condition. This hypothesis was validated, as movement times for the control condition were significantly slower than all three selection aids. Additionally, we were able to confirm our hypothesis that there would be a difference between the three selection aids, with snap-to-target being significantly faster than the other two conditions.

There were also differences in the number of errors made by participants in the different conditions. There was no significant difference between the number of errors in the control and snap-to-target conditions. So, although the snap-to-target selection aid improved on movement times it had a higher error rate than the other selection aids. In particular, despite its slower movement time, the expand-cursor selection aid had significantly fewer errors than snap-to-target.

Combining the errors and movement times with an inverse efficiency calculation provided some insight into the speed/accuracy tradeoffs for our four conditions. While our fastest condition, snap-to-target, did have a significantly lower inverse efficiency than the control condition, there was no significant difference between it and the other two selection aids. This suggests that the number of errors that happen with snap-to-target may limit its efficiency to the point of it being on par with our other techniques.

Through our questionnaires, we found that users perceived snap-to-target to be significantly faster, more accurate, more comfortable, and easier to use than the control condition. They also perceived expanding-cursor as significantly faster and easier to use than the control. Additionally, all three selection aids were perceived to be more enjoyable and effective than the control condition.

Overall, snap-to-target was the only selection aid to be perceived as significantly more comfortable and accurate than the control condition. It also had significantly lower movement times than all other conditions, and was as good as the other two selection aids in terms of inverse efficiency. While there were more errors with snap-to-target than some of the other selection aids, future work on the TractorBeam could explore optimal snap thresholds for minimizing error while maximizing movement time, eventually improving on the condition's error rate.

7 Conclusions and Future Work

We explored several methods for improving selection of small, distant targets with the TractorBeam. Augmenting the TractorBeam with each of these selection aids increased our technique's effectiveness for selection of distant items. Additionally, despite no significant difference in inverse efficiency scores between the three selection aids, the positive user feedback from our third study gives snap-to-target an edge over the other solutions. Snap-to-target solves the main problem encountered with the TractorBeam technique in our first study, and further increases its viability as an interaction technique for large tabletop displays.

Although the snap-to-target selection aid had very positive results in our user study, this finding is only the first step. This study explored the effectiveness of many possible selection aids for isolated, distant targets. Having now identified snap-to-target as a very effective technique, we plan to further examine this selection aid for less controlled, more ecologically valid tasks. In particular, we would like to test its effectiveness with groups of targets which are close together, as well as the general usability of the technique for close targets.

Acknowledgements

Thanks to NSERC, Dalhousie University, and Mitsubishi Electric Research Labs for providing funding for this work. Thanks also to members of Dalhousie's EDGE Lab.

References

1. Blanch, R., Guiard, Y., and Beaudouin-Lafon, M. (2004). Semantic Pointing: Improving target acquisition with control-display ratio adaptation. In *Proceedings of CHI 2004*. p. 519-526.
2. Deitz, P. and Leigh, D. (2000). DiamondTouch: A multi-user touch technology. In *Proceedings of UIST 2000*. p. 219-226.
3. Douglas, S.A., Kirkpatrick, A.E., and MacKenzie, I.S. (1999). Testing pointing device performance and user assessment with the ISO 9241, Part 9 standard. In *Proceedings of CHI '99*. p. 215-222.
4. Grossman, T. and Balakrishnan, R. (2005) The Bubble Cursor: Enhancing target acquisition by dynamic resizing of the cursor's activation area. In *Proceedings of CHI 2005*. p. 281-290.
5. Guiard, Y., Blanch, R., and Beaudouin-Lafon, M. (2004). Object pointing: a complement to bitmap pointing in GUIs. In *Proceedings of GI 2004*. p. 9-16.
6. Kabbash, P. and Buxton, W. (1995). The "Prince" Technique: Fitts' Law and selection using area cursors. In *Proceedings of CHI 1995*. p. 273-279.
7. McGuffin, M. and Balakrishnan, R. (2002). Acquisition of expanding targets. In *Proceedings of CHI 2002*. p. 57-64.
8. OS X, Apple Computer.
9. Parker, J.K., Mandryk, R., Inkpen, K.. (2005) TractorBeam: Seamless integration of local and remote pointing for tabletop displays. In *Proceedings of Graphics Interface 2005*. p. 33-40.
10. Rekimoto, J. and Saitoh, M. (1999). Augmented Surfaces: A spatially continuous work space for hybrid computing environments. In *Proceedings of CHI '99*. p. 378-385.
11. Shen, C., Lesh, N.B., Vernier, F., Forlines, C., and Frost, J. (2002). Sharing and building digital group histories. In *Proceedings of CSCW 2002*. p. 3.
12. Townsend, J.T. and Ashby, F.G., (1983). Stochastic modelling of elementary psychological processes. London: Cambridge University Press.
13. Worden, A., Walker, N., Bharat, K., Hudson, S. (1997). Making Computers Easier for Older Adults to Use: Area Cursors and Sticky Icons. In *Proceedings o CHI '97*. p. 266-271.
14. Wu, M. and Balakrishnan, R. (2003). Multi-finger and whole hand gestural interaction techniques for multi-user tabletop displays. In *Proceedings of UIST 2003*. p. 193-202.
15. Zhai, S., Conversy, S., Beaudouin-Lafon, M., and Guiard, Y. (2003). Human on-line response to target expansion. In *Proceedings of CHI 2003*. p. 177-184.

Responsive Interaction Based on Sketch in Concept Styling

Li Han[1], Giuseppe Conti[2], and Raffaele De Amicis[3]

[1,2,3] Graphitech, Via Dei Molini, 2, 38000, Trento (TN), Italy
{li.han, giuseppe.conti, raffaele.de.amicis}@graphitech.it

Abstract. In the CAS/CAD field, the increasing adoption of Spline-based free-form methods to generate surfaces, has introduced a higher degree of freedom into the design process. However, on the other hand, this evolution has made the process of creating and manipulating surfaces more complex. For this reason a much more intuitive and intelligent task-centered and user-centered interaction paradigm is required. This paper presents a responsive interaction technique which adopts a sketch-based interface capable of exploiting the stepwise refinement process typical of conceptual designing. Further it makes use of adaptive user modeling techniques by introducing an innovative adaptive decision-tree structure for top-down designing. We illustrate the implementation of the algorithm and we highlight its efficiency and feasibility for its adoption within Sketch-Based Modeling Systems (SBMS).

1 Introduction

The capability to design innovative products is a key factor to foster the competitiveness of industrial products. In particular, the conceptual design phase plays a strategic role since the creativity and synthesis, which characterize it, are of great importance for the design of an industrial product. Furthermore it has been estimated that up to three quarters of the designing costs are generated during the initial phases. Therefore, it appears clear that, in order to boost efficiency and enhance creativity innovative and adequate tools have to be developed.

In the CAS/CAD field the adoption of Spline-based free-form surfaces has provided designers with greater freedom. However on the other hand, this has introduced a higher complexity in the process of creation and manipulation of shapes since the full exploitation of Splines' advantages it requires knowledge of their mathematical representation.

Recent years' experience suggests that a great improvement to design such tools can be introduced by improving their level of "intelligence", i.e. the capability to discern the commands expressed by the user. This new tendency will yield a new generation of systems capable to dynamically adapt to designers' needs, in opposition to current systems that requires designers to adjust to the technology adopted. The new generation of design system in fact should be able to understand the designer's behavior. That is, they should be able to comprehend the users' actions, the way they identify a shape, the way they interact with the drawing tools during the design process. Finally such a system should present the information consequently provided to the user in a flexible, efficient and supportive manner.

M.F. Costabile and F. Paternò (Eds.): INTERACT 2005, LNCS 3585, pp. 94–105, 2005.

The aforementioned requirements have fuelled recent years' research on sketch-based modeling systems. These allow the user to quickly create 3D models by simple freehand strokes rather than by typing in parameters. The systems developed range from those pursuing a constraint-based or feature-based approach [1-3, 12, 13], to those providing different forms of suggestive feedback and VR rendering [4-5, 14-15]. However, the majority of these systems have been designed as further extension of classical CAD tools. Therefore these cannot be used when information at a higher, semantic level is to be decoded and manipulated. Furthermore these systems propose interaction metaphors far from the designer's traditional approach, typically featuring a top down and stepwise refinement process.

This paper tries to bridge this gap by proposing a formal theory which models the process of comprehension of the user's sketches. Such methodology, applied to conceptual designing, is able to support the stepwise process of sketching by continuously interpreting the flow of data and constraints generated by the designer's actions. Further the approach developed is capable to dynamically adapt to the different users' styles by constantly modeling their personal behaviors. The resulting methodology has being implemented in an architecture described throughout the paper.

The paper is organized as follows: in section 2 we present the related works whilst section 3 introduces a general architecture for sketch-based modeling systems (SMBS) that integrates the *interface module*, the *user adaptation module* and the *rendering module*. In section 4 we will detail the developed interaction algorithm. This is based on sketching and features stroke recognition, dynamic shape modeling and to multi-user adaptation. Finally in section 5 we conclude with the summary and we describe the directions of future work.

2 Related Work

In the last two decades, computer-aided design/styling (CAD/CAS) systems have developed powerful 2D and 3D modeling functionalities. However conventional interfaces based upon the WIMP (Windows Icon Menus Pointer) paradigm have proved to be inadequate being cumbersome, tedious and time-consuming. Sketch-based free-drawing interfaces, combining the ease of freehand drawing with the advantages of computer processing, are becoming prevailing. In particular these allow designers to freely sketch shapes as they would on ordinary paper. This allows designers to fully concentrate on the design process.

Earlier sketch-based systems allowed sketching of geometric models by using a set of pre-defined gestures. Gesture recognition algorithms converted sketches into a series of specific commands to create and manipulate geometric primitives.

The system described in [5] defines geometric features of objects through the drawing of a set of auxiliary lines. It supports over-sketching of lines and both snapping and adjustment are preformed in real time. However the system is not capable to process sophisticated input techniques necessary to generate curve and surface. The work in [4] introduces a new type of so-called "suggestive" interface for 3D drawings: it extends the gesture interface by offering multiple candidates. The system is easy to use although inefficient to understand the user's intentions.

Recently, research has adopted constraint-based methods to resolve unclear sketching input. The work in [3] presents a simple touch-and-replace technique to edit 2D and 3D curves. The authors introduce auxiliary surfaces that allow a reliable interpretation of the users' pen strokes in 3D. The main limitation of this approach is the lack of degrees of freedom, which are restricted by the auxiliary surfaces.

In the literature [6] Teddy proposes an easy way to allow the users to draw 2D silhouettes and the system automatically proposes a 3D surface using polygonal mesh whose projection matches the object contour. However it cannot create multiple objects and it is the impossible to some editing operations.

In [7-8] the authors suggest a Variational Implicit Surfaces (VIS) representation. Here surfaces are defined by a set of constraints that specify the points on the surface boundary. The modeling and editing operations are easily controlled further the method is fast when designing 3D approximate models. However this method is not sufficient for full-featured free-form shape modeling. Furthermore, as the number of constraints increases, the time the algorithm takes to compute the coefficients for the variational implicit surfaces grows considerably.

The main limit of existing modeling tools lies in their lack of the interaction between refinement cycles which take place during the process of designing. Further they show limited intelligence during the decision-making process which takes place during the free-form drawing.

Recently another approach, the so-called declarative designing method, has received increasing interest across the CAD research community [9-10]. As illustrated in Fig. 1, the method provides designers with a more progressive and dynamic model specification based on declarative (rather than imperative) methods. This permits to describe models by means of rules, properties or constraints that are computed by successive refinements, to adopt the logical rules to be dealt with, and finally to provide a solution among the potential ones. To a certain extent this method provides a formalism, which integrates architectural rules and attributes to provide the designer with an interactive graphic language. However, these methods are incomplete, i.e. they do not present specific knowledge representation and, in particular, they do not provide details of the interaction mechanism and of the way the system deals with complex objects.

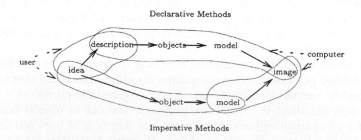

Fig. 1. The comparison between declarative and imperative model [10]

A distinctive feature of current sketch-based interfaces is their continuous visual feedback. This usually involves successive transformations of graphic objects and some form of suggestive rendering between the user and the tools.

3   A General Architecture for Sketch-Based Modeling Systems (SBMS)

We consider the process of sketching as the information flow from/to the designer's brain. For this reason the sketch-based system developed had to be able to show the evolution of the corresponding designing behavior by providing intelligent reasoning of the user's input. As illustrated in Fig. 2, the proposed architecture for such sketch-based modeling system consists of an *interface module*, a *user adaptation module* and *rendering module*.

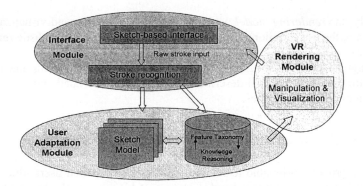

Fig. 2. The proposed architecture for a sketch-based modeling system

The *interface module* provides the interactive behavior and it supports stroke recognition. Since usually the raw stroke input information is unclear, the module plays a key role for the effective extraction of geometric features and constraints. At this stage we analyze the input and we obtain the speed, length, vertex sets, other object attributes so on. Then, based on the evaluation of these features and corresponding fuzzy sets, we assess the shape and save it within a *shapeList*. As illustrated in the class diagram of Figure 3, which shows the main components' features, as a result the system is capable to generate a number of geometric primitives, which are sent, together with other data such as topological constraints, time sequences etc., to the *user adaptation module* for further processing.

The *user adaptation module* accepts such basic information (e.g. geometric and topological constraints, basic geometric entities and time sequences) and it processes it through a stepwise refinement process. To do so the module constantly extracts attributes from the latest sketches arriving from *interface module* through a series of real-time operations. This data is then transformed according to the constraint solving model adopted. This is based on the characteristic features and behaviors typical of the conceptual stage. The *user adaptation module*, which represents the center of the whole system, combines adaptive reasoning with dynamic user modeling in order to deal with the uncertainty typical of hand drawn sketches. As a result, the module, which takes into account the differences between users' drawing styles, decodes the corresponding design behavior and it inserts its different possible interpretations into a ranked probability list. The user then can decide, among those suggested by the system, the most appropriate action to be taken.

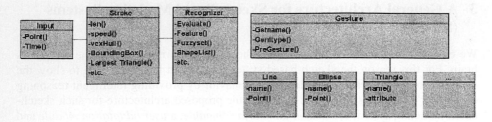

Fig. 3. Class Diagram for the Stroke Recognition

Finally, the *rendering model* performs the post-processing and visualization process allowing the use of tailored representation such as non-photorealistic rendering or alike.

Throughout the following sections we will illustrate the details the interaction mechanism proposed, we will describe the algorithms developed and we will discuss their strengths and weaknesses.

4 Responsive Interaction Based on Sketching

In order to provide to be able to retain the difference between users' drawing styles and to enable user to generate graphic objects of higher complexity, we have introduced a "responsive" interaction mechanism which can dynamically adapt to the constraints defined by the user's input. As described in the following pages, its implementation is based on an innovative decision-tree structure.

4.1 Responsive Interaction Based on Automatic Sketches Identification

In order to deal with the unclarity typical of the sketched input in the initial stages of the designing, we have modeled the data flow which characterizes the early design process according to a mechanism where on-line recognition, user adaptation and decision making are performed at the key stages as illustrated in Fig. 4.

The process of recognition, which is performed at the *interface module* level, is made of a stroke and shape recognition sub-processes. When each stroke is processed by this first stage, the system automatically activates the *user adaptation module* which performs the constraint reasoning and matching process according to the different characteristics typical of each user's drawing style. Finally the system, after suggesting a list of possible solutions, asks the user for feedback to confirm the command.

The adaptive constraint reasoning process takes places at two levels: either by the *stoke recognition process* (for single-stroke identification) or by the combination of *stoke recognition process* and *user adaptation module* (for more complex shape understanding). The latter is responsible to compare the information contained in the relevant model of the user with the information contained in a database of geometric templates organized by parameters and constraints. During this process the stroke represents the base unit of the response mechanism. When the pen is lifted the system automatically reacts by extracting the relevant features and, if required, by performing the adaptive reasoning. As a result of this first process a graphic object is produced. Then the interaction module asks the designer for feedback, i.e. the user has to confirm whether he/she wants to continue renewing the previous stroke or he/she wishes to begin a new object.

The details of this process are illustrated in Table 1 where each raw stroke input information is represented by a 4-tuple G $(L_i,\ S_i,\ P_i,\ V_i)$ where L is the length of the stroke, S is the speed, P is the point set extracted, V is the vertex set extracted. We also assume that T_i represents a graphic object while C_i is a constraint. From Table 1 it is possible to see how, during STEP 2, the basic geometric object T_i which satisfies a series of specific constraints is retrieved through the stroke recognition process. If the user's sketch is not a single stroke (see STEP 4), the constraint solving module is called to analyze the history of the previous strokes and to perform the constraint matching. As a result the T_m, which represents the most suitable graphic object, is selected and used for higher level analysis.

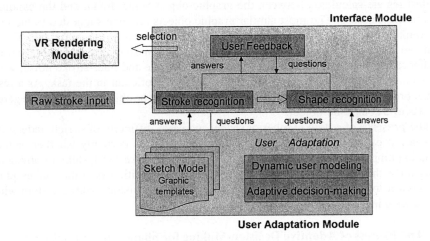

Fig. 4. The framework for the responsive interaction mechanism

Table 1. The responsive interaction algorithm based on adaptive reasoning

STEP1: Raw stroke information $G\ (L_i,\ S_i,\ P_i,\ V_i)$,
STEP2: Stroke recognition: $G\ (L_i,\ S_i,\ P_i,\ V_i) \rightarrow T_i\ (C_j)$
STEP3: If (Single-stroke) then GOTO END.
Else GOTO STEP4
STEP4: Composite constraint reasoning: $C_m\ (T_i\ \wedge \varLambda T_{i-1}\ \wedge\ ...\ T_1) \rightarrow T_m\ (T_j\ (C_k),\ ...T_n(\ C_l)$, $C_m)$
STEP5: Check T_m whether it exists in the pre-defined model database:
If (!existed) then INSERT (T_m)
Else if (Continue) then GOTO STEP1
Else GOTO END.
END: Results confirmation by user's feedback and visualization.

4.2 Intelligent Stroke Interpretation System

It is known that designers tend to draw shapes through several primitive sub-shapes. Likewise they tend define a primitive shape either by a single stroke or by several consecutive strokes. In our recognition algorithm, we first discover latent primitive shapes among user strokes. Then we recognize and regularize them and, finally, we show the regularized drawing on the screen. After being recognized and regularized, the primitive shapes which belong to the same graphic object are grouped together. Eventually they are segmented and combined to form an object skeleton.

In our system the geometric entities are positioned using parameters and constraints rather than using a specific coordinates and spatial orientation. Each time we extract the features' parameters from the free-form drawing and then we match them on the basis of a probability rank.

Specifically, in order to recognize the users' stokes, we employ an SVM-based (Support Vector Machine) incremental active learning method [16]. Partial structural similarities are calculated between the graphic object being drawn and the candidate ones in the database. The most similar graphic objects are then suggested to the users in a ranked list in order for them to choose from and confirm the command. The responsive feedback strategy makes the user interaction smoother and more natural. Further it has the extra advantage to reduce inner-stroke and inter-stroke noise, which are generated when the user is not a professional or proficient in the task. As a result of this process we then get regularized stroke segments or objects, which are regarded as parts of a composite object.

The presence of a high number of shapes increases difficulty of sketch understanding since it can be difficult for the system even to assess correctly whether or not a shape is completely drawn. Likewise it is essential to make the system automatically re-organize the relevant features when a synchronous editing operation takes place. The answer to these issues is provided by the adaptive decision-making system which is described in the following section.

4.3 The Process of Adaptive Decision-Making for Shape Understanding

The process of shape understanding is grounded upon an "ad hoc" internal model which adopts a decision tree to arrange and organize parameters and constraints. As illustrated in Fig. 5 the tree contains basic constraints (geometry primitives, geometric relationships, algebraic relationships) as well as high-level features which are composed of basic constraints used for describing the operation behavior. All the features and parameters are arranged starting from the low-level constraint layer to a high-level feature layer. Sandwiched between these two levels, the constraints are cross-checked and shared, until eventually the semantic descriptions are attached.

This is a reversed tree structure where the top level contains the leaf nodes whilst the bottom level holds the root. Leaf nodes represent a series of basic geometric primitives and constraints. Furthermore, in order to better capture the user's sketching commands, we have adopted an adaptive method which adapts the decision tree according to dynamically upgraded user models. Specifically, we set the attribute of being a "possible shape" to each branch node whilst the root represents the final geometric object which is reached only when the constraint branches are satisfied. The user tree is created to match with the pre-defined decision tree of database. As a result if we find that the model is not present in the pre-defined decision tree within the database, we place the object into the relevant tree as a new node. Then the decision tree within the database is synchronously updated.

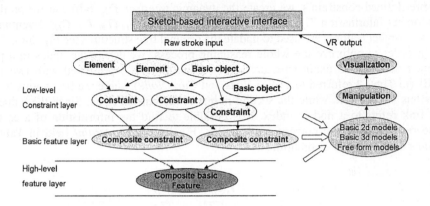

Fig. 5. The structure of the user adaptation module

An example of this process, illustrated in Fig. 6, will help better illustrate the process. In the illustration the indexes from 1 to 11 refer to different constraints. Specifically we suppose that constrains C_7, C_8, C_9, C_{10} are used to obtain general geometrical relationships between graphical objects, whilst C_1, C_2, C_3, C_4, C_5, C_6 are used to recognize the geometric primitives. Let T be a geometric object set, which includes all the nodes in the graph. The raw stroke input information is represented as a 4-tuple G (L_i, S_i, P_i, V_i), where L is the length, S is the speed, P the point set and V the vertex set. As defined in [16], for each single stroke a number of specific features are extracted and the relevant constraints are analyzed. As a result of this process a number of regularized geometric primitives are produced whose relative logic representations are listed below:

- $C_1 (L_1, S_1, P_1, V_1) \rightarrow circle;$ $C_2 (L_2, S_2, P_2, V_2) \rightarrow triangle;$
- $C_3 (L_3, S_3, P_3, V_3) \rightarrow line;$ $C_4 (L_4, S_4, P_4, V_4) \rightarrow square;$
- $C_5 (L_5, S_5, P_5, V_5) \rightarrow rectangle;$ $C_6 (L_6, S_6, P_6, V_6) \rightarrow diamond;$
- $C_7 (X, Y) =(X\ is\ overlap\ to\ Y) \wedge (X\ is\ precede\ Y) \wedge (X \in T; Y \in T);$
- $C_8 (X, Y) =(X\ is\ parallel\ to\ Y) \wedge (X\ is\ precede\ Y) \wedge (X \in T; Y \in T);$
- $C_9 (X, Y) =(X\ is\ Vertical\ to\ Y) \wedge (X\ is\ precede\ Y) \wedge (X \in T; Y \in T);$
- $C_{10}(X, Y) =(X\ is\ touched\ to\ Y) \wedge (X\ is\ precede\ Y) \wedge (X \in T; Y \in T);$
- $C_{11} (C_8, C_9) =(C_8 \rightarrow T_m) \wedge (C_9 \rightarrow T_n) \wedge (T_m\ is\ inside\ T_n);$

We now assume that a decision tree (see Fig. 6-a) is already defined in the database. Each node represents an object and in particular each leaf node (top-level) is a geometric primitive, whilst each branch node is a possible shape (where the index refers to the relevant constraint). For instance in the scene T_9 (Fig. 6-a, second level on the left), where a triangle is adjacent to a circle, the constraints such as C_1, C_2, C_{10}

must be satisfied. This condition is represented with the notation T_9 $(T_2(C_2)$, $T_1(C_1)$, $C_{10})$. This way each node can be represented as a multi-tuple T_i $(T_p(C_j)$, $T_q(C_k)$, C_n, and i, p, q, j k, n, $\in integer$).

When the new object T_{13} is added, a dynamic user model is created. First, based on sketching input, we extract a series of features in time sequence and then, according to the pre-defined constraints, we create the dynamic tree (see Fig. 6-b) and we produce new object information T_{13}, which can be represented as T_{13} (T_9, T_{11}, C_{11}). Eventually, the new object features are used to update the original tree structure (see Fig. 6-c).

In order to optimize the whole reasoning process, we define the nodes in a pre-defined database as chain structures (see). Each node is represented with two link fields (in **Table 2** referred to as *Pre-Node* and *Curr-Node*) where the first points to the previous stroke node while the second points to the current node. Since the value of any link refers to a node's index, it is possible to find the information of a certain node by following the corresponding index. Finally the *Constraint* field in **Table 2** defines the new node's condition.

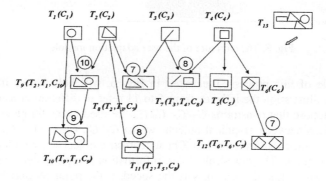

(a)   Before the new object is inserted (pre-defined decision-tree structure)

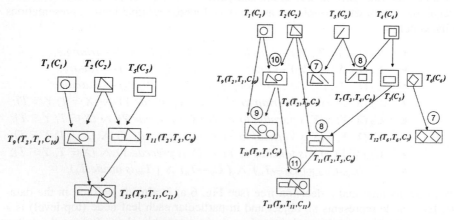

(b) Dynamic user tree for new object T_{13} (c) the new object T_{13} is inserted in database

Fig. 6. The process of adaptive reasoning

Table 2. The structure of the predefined decision-tree storage structure

Index	Name	Pre-Node	Curr- Node	Constraint
1	T_1	NULL	NULL	C_1
2	T_2	NULL	NULL	C_2
3	T_3	NULL	NULL	C_3
4	T_4	NULL	NULL	C_4
5	T_5	NULL	NULL	C_5
6	T_6	NULL	NULL	C_6
7	T_7	3	4	C_8
8	T_8	2	3	C_7
9	T_9	2	1	C_{10}
10	T_{10}	9	1	C_9
11	T_{11}	2	5	C_8
12	T_{12}	6	6	C_7

The specific user modeling and updating process can be described according to the following pseudo-code excerpt:

```
PROCEDURE: USER MODELING
   Begin
      P=NULL,  /*Initialize a node pointer*/
      Stop=0, FindFlag=0
      While (! Stop)
            Q= head    /* head of pre-defined link table*/
            Accept (T)   /* T: the current node pointer*/
            Constraint (P, T) • C_n
            If (P•Pre-Node == NULL) then P• Pre-Node = T,
            P• Constraint= C_n
            Else If (P• Curr-Node == NULL) then P• Curr-
            Node = T
            While (Q! =NULL)
              If (Q= = P) then
                 P• Pre-Node = Q /*set node to prev node*/
                 P• Curr-Node = NULL
                 FindFlag=1
            End while
      If (!FindFlag) then GOTO INSERT(P)/*update table*/
      If (Stop) then END
      End while
END PROCEDURE

PROCEDURE: INSERT (P)
   Begin
      Q=End /* the end of the pre-defined link table*/
      Q=ALLOC (new node);
      Q=P
   End
END PROCEDURE
```

If we assume that the number of nodes in pre-defined database is equal to n, then the modeling algorithm and insert procedure are bound by a complexity of $O\ (n)$. From **Table 2** it is also possible to easily assess the partial structural similarities between users' drawing. This is done by tracking all the pre-node links. If two nodes have the same value then the corresponding nodes will be candidates. For instance, assuming that T_2 is the first stroke, if the system can not extract from the second stroke the exact features then, by tracing the Table 2, it is possible to find that T_8, T_9, T_{11} have the same pre-node link value '2'. As a result of this, T_8, T_9, T_{11} would be offered to the user for selection. The whole process would be still bound to $O\ (n)$.

In general, this adaptive reasoning method effectively solves the stepwise refinement designing process. In fact the approach proposed is truly incremental since each stroke links to the information about the previous and it depends to the constraints defined up to that point. Furthermore the database can be extended through the insertion of new constraints and new nodes.

The dynamic user tree model, which tracks the information on the strokes, focuses on the extraction of features and matching of constraints, and then it efficiently hides the diversity between different users' input style. When an object is finished the tree model is dynamically stored and the tree is replaced by the one corresponding to next free-form drawing.

5 Summary and Future Work

In this paper, we introduce a sketch-based conceptual design system, which aims at achieving the stepwise refinement process which is typical of the early stages of the design process. The system presented features an adaptive decision-making mechanism which is capable of understanding complex objects thanks to an efficient reasoning method. This approach naturally fits within the normal workflow since it seamlessly integrates within the natural process of sketching. The user in fact is not asked to interact with menus or button. Instead the method, based on the analysis of partial structure similarity, is at the same time efficient and user friendly since it provides designer with a series of possible alternatives to choose from while he/she is sketching. Moreover by improving the representation of the graphical object and the logic behind the reasoning technique, the method presented can easily adapt to the designers' graphical styles making it very robust and reliable to use.

However, although the user modeling and the decision making techniques proposed can support stroke recognition through a progressively evolving process they have, in the need for post-processing, their greatest limit. As a result when an object is changed a great computational effort must be spent to update the constraints.

Future developments will try to solve these issues and will try to further improve the constraint reasoning technique. In particular we will look for a better representation of high-level features through semantic description and we will try to provide the required advanced reasoning technique.

References

1. Zeleznik, R. C., Herndon, K. P. and Hughes, J. F: SKETCH: An Interface for Sketching 3D Scenes. In Computer Graphics (Proc. SIGGRAPH 1996) 163-170.
2. Bloomenthal, K., Zeleznik, R. C.: SKETCH-N-MAKE: Automated machining of CAD sketches. In Proceedings of ASME DETC' (1998) 1-11.

3. Michalik, P., Kim, D., Bruderlin, B.: Sketch-and Constraint-based Design of B-spline Surfaces. In Proceedings of the seventh ACM symposium on Solid modeling and applications. (2002) 297-304.
4. Igarashi, T., Hughes, J. F.: A Suggestive Interface for 3D drawing. In Proceedings of the 14th annual ACM symposium on User interface software and technology (2001) 173 - 181.
5. Contero, M.: Smart Sketch System for 3D Reconstruction-Based Modeling. In Smart Graph-ics Proceedings, Springer Lecture Notes in Computer Science (LNCS) vol. 2733 (2003) 58-68.
6. Igarashi, T., Matsuoka, S., Tanaka, H.: Teddy: A Sketching Interface for 3D Freeform Design. In Computer Graphics (Proc. SIGGRAPH 1999) 409-416.
7. Karpenko, O., Hughes, J. F., Raskar, R.: Free-Form Sketching with Variational implicit Sur-faces. In Computer Graphics Forum Volume 21, Issue 3 (2002).
8. Rodrigues de Araújo B., Pires Jorge, J. A.: BlobMaker: Free form modeling with Variational Implicit Surfaces. In Proceedings of 12° Encontro Português de Computação Gráfica, Porto, (2003), 17-26.
9. Hagen, P. J. W. and Tomiyama, T. (Eds.): Intelligent CAD Systems. In Theoretical and methodological aspects. Springer-Verlag, (1987).
10. Flemming, U., Coyne, R. F., Glavin, T., Hsi, H., and Rychener, M.: A Generative Expert System for the Design of Building Layouts. In Technical Report EDRC 48-15-89, Carnegie Mellon University (1989).
11. Lucas, M.: Equivalence classes in object shape modeling. In Proceedings of working conference on Modeling in Computer Graphics (1991), 17-34.
12. Catalano, C. E.: Feature-Based Methods for Free-Form Surface Manipulation in Aesthetic Engineering. Ph.D. thesis - Genoa University (2004).
13. Cheutet, V., Catalano, C. E., Pernot, J. P.: 3D Sketching with Fully Free Form Deformation Features (δ-F4) for Aesthetic Design. In EUROGRAPHICS Workshop on Sketch-Based Inter-faces and Modeling (2004), 9-18.
14. Fiorentino M., Monno G., Renzulli, P. A., Uva, A. E.: 3D Sketch Stroke Segmentation and Fitting in Virtual Reality. In International conference on the Computer Graphics and Vi-sion, GRAPHICON, Moscow, Russia (2003).
15. Wesche, G., Droske, M.: Conceptual Free-Form Styling on the Responsive Work-bench. In ERCIM News No.44 (2001).
16. Peng B. B., Sun, Z. X. and Xu, X. G.: SVM-based Incremental Active Learning for User Ad-aptation For Online Graphics Recognition. In The First International Conference on Machine Learning and Cybernetics, Beijing , Nov. (2002) 73-84.
17. Donikian, S. and Hegron, G.: The kernel of a declarative method for 3D scene sketch mod-eling. In Graphicon '92, Programming and Computer Science, Moscow, Russia, September (1992).

Natural Language Query vs. Keyword Search: Effects of Task Complexity on Search Performance, Participant Perceptions, and Preferences

QianYing Wang, Clifford Nass, and Jiang Hu

Department of Communication, Stanford University,
Stanford, California, USA
{wangqy, nass, huj}@stanford.edu

Abstract. A 2x2 mixed design experiment (*N*=52) was conducted to examine the effects of search interface and task complexity on participants' information-seeking performance and affective experience. Keyword vs. natural language search was the within-participants factor; simple vs. complex tasks was the between-participants factor. There were cross-over interactions such that complex-task participants were more successful and thought the tasks were less difficult and reported more enjoyment and confidence when they used keyword search vs. natural language queries, while the opposite was found for simple-task participants. The findings suggest that natural language search is not the panacea for all information retrieval tasks: task complexity is a critical mediator. Implications for interface design and directions for future research are discussed.

1 Introduction

From punch cards to keyboards to graphical participant interfaces (GUIs) to voice participant interfaces (VUIs), interfaces have evolved to allow increasingly intuitive and natural interactions between participants and computers. Among all the breakthroughs and improvements, the use of natural language (NL) as a means of input and output during human-computer interaction (HCI) is one of the most-researched areas.

One of the potential participant benefits afforded by NL technologies is the reduction in the need for learning and training. The promising future of NL-based conversational interfaces (especially with the presence of computer agents) has been widely lauded by visionaries such as Brenda Laurel [1]. Although no one has yet to be able to claim complete success in natural language generation and processing, progress is continually being made. From text-based software agent (e.g., Microsoft™ Clippy) to speech-recognition customer services automation (e.g., United Airlines' flight information hotline), NL-based technologies have advanced into many areas of daily life.

With the explosion of information brought by the Internet and computers in different forms and sizes, information retrieval has become an integral part of modern life in the information age, demanding participant-friendly and efficient interfaces. In order to provide better search experience for average participants, researchers have applied natural langauge processing (NLP) technology to building information retrieval systems [2-6]. However, usability studies concerning seeking and interacting with information have focused on keyword search (KW) rather than natural language [7-16].

M.F. Costabile and F. Paternò (Eds.): INTERACT 2005, LNCS 3585 , pp. 106–116, 2005.

In this paper, we present a laboratory experiment to examine and compare the usability of two kinds of search interfaces: natural language and keyword search. The study explores how performance limitations of NLP affect participants' perceptions of and preferences for search interfaces. We are especially interested in how *task complexity* affects participants' interaction with information retrieval interfaces.

In the following sections we lay out our experimental design, describe our measured results, offer a discussion of findings, and conclude with design implications.

2   Method

2.1   The Two Interfaces

To ensure that participants would be performing a well-established and typical information acquisition activity, we decided to study interfaces used to obtain frequently-asked information on buying and selling from eBay, which is one of the most successful commercial websites on the Web. Although help with eBay is provided from a single database (enabling us to control content), there are two interfaces for searching the database: My eBay Buddy and eBay Help website. Thus, similar queries will obtain the same answer from both interfaces. Figure 1 shows these two interfaces side by side.

Fig. 1. Screenshots of AIM chat window with My eBay Buddy, and the eBay Help website

My eBay Buddy [17] is a natural language agent provided to AOL Instant Messenger (AIM) participants who can add My eBay Buddy to their buddy lists and chat with it to acquire information. Participants can ask open-ended questions; answers are provided by My eBay Buddy in a conversational manner. Similar agents include AgentBaseball, EllegirlBuddy, and SmarterChild.

The eBay Help website involves a classical keyword-based search paradigm, and returns results in a typical list of ranked links.

2.2 Search Tasks

Participants were given either complex or simple search tasks to find information about buying or selling items on eBay. We pre-tested the complex and simple tasks to ensure that the difficulty of each task was appropriate. The complex tasks were designed to be difficult to accomplish after a single query. In most cases participants had to search for and integrate information about two or more aspects of the eBay services. For example, one complex task was to find out how much one had to pay eBay if s/he were selling a $35 item. To come up with the right answer, participants had to learn about listing fee, final value fee, and the eBay picture service fee.

The following are four examples of the eight complex tasks:

- *Please find out if it is legal to place a bid right before the auction closes.*
- *Please find out what you should do if you don't want a certain person to bid on your item.*
- *Please find out how one can tell if a seller is reliable.*
- *Please find out what happens if the buyer doesn't pay you.*

On the other hand, the simple tasks could normally be accomplished after a single query. To ensure that the net time on task was the same for all complex and all simple tasks, there were 20 simple tasks. Pretests indicated that people completed simple tasks 2.5 times faster than complex tasks.

The following are example simple tasks:

- *Please find out what the gift icon means.*
- *Please find out what the most popular categories of eBay items are.*
- *Please find out what the PIC icon means.*
- *Please find out what the different colored stars mean.*
- *Please find out if it is possible to take back a bid.*
- *Please find out what the difference is between "proxy" and "maximum" bids.*

2.3 Participants

College students (N=52) from an introductory communication class participated in the experiment for course credit. All participants were native speakers of English. Participants were randomly assigned to task complexity, with gender balanced. None of the participants had ever sold anything or bought more than three items on eBay.com. Experiences with AIM were balanced across conditions. All participants signed informed consent forms upon arrival at the lab and were debriefed upon the completion of the experiment.

2.4 Procedure

The experiment was a 2x2 mixed design, with task complexity (simple vs. complex) as the between-participants factor and search interface (keyword vs. natural language search) as the within-participants factor. Participants performed all tasks in a research laboratory equipped with personal computers. Upon arrival to the laboratory, each participant was seated and assigned to a computer with both Internet Explorer and AIM.

Participants read instructions on screen. Half of them were given a list of 20 simple tasks; the other half received a list of 8 complex tasks. Half of the participants with each type of task performed the first half (10 or 4) of their tasks using My eBay Buddy (i.e., NL) and the second half (10 or 4) of tasks using eBay Help website (i.e., KW); other participants with each type of task used the two types of interfaces in reversed order.

Participants typed in an answer when they thought they had successfully accomplished a task. Upon finishing all tasks, participants responded to several questions about their search experiences. Finally, participants were asked to imagine finishing six search tasks. There were two tasks for each of three levels of complexity: high, medium and low. They were all common tasks, such as booking flight tickets, finding out the movie listing in a nearby cinema, and getting a stock quote.

2.5 Measures

Actual performance was the percentage of tasks participants successfully finished. *Perceived performance* was the percentage of tasks participants *believed* that they had successfully accomplished. *Time on task* was the average amount of time spent on each task.

Questions concerning perceived task difficulty, enjoyment of task, and confidence with search interface were asked for each task. Participants used radio buttons to indicate their responses for these questions. Each question had an independent, 10-point Likert scale. *Perceived task difficulty* was an average across task of responses to the questionnaire item, "How difficult did you feel the search was?" *Enjoyment* was an average across tasks to the questionnaire item, "How enjoyable did you find the search?" *Confidence* was an average across tasks of responses to the questionnaire item, "How confident were you with your answer?"

For each search task participants imagined to perform, participants indicated how difficult it would be when using NL and using KW. The questions were answered on 10-point Likert scales anchored by "Very Difficult" (=1) and "Very Easy" (=10).

3 Results

3.1 Manipulation Check

Time to finish the complex tasks and the simple tasks were recorded during the study. Consistent with the pre-test, each complex task took approximately three times longer to finish than did each simple task for both KW [$F(1, 24)=107.6$, $p<.001$] and NL searches [$F(1,24)=55.6$, $p<.001$; see Table 1]. There was no statistical difference for time on task between the two search interfaces ($p>.05$).

Table 1. Time on task

(minutes)	NL Mean (SD)	KW Mean (SD)
Simple	1.21(0.23)	1.33 (0.41)
Complex	3.8 (0.94)	4.17 (0.84)

3.2   Actual vs. Perceived Search Performance

Figure 2 and 3 show results for actual and perceived performance. There was a significant interaction between task complexity and search interface for both actual $[F(1,50)=26.5, p<.001]$ and perceived $[F(1,50)=31.4, p<.001]$ performance. Complex task participants were more successful and perceived themselves to be more successful with KW rather than NL interface. Conversely, simple task participants were more successful and also perceived themselves to be more successful with NL rather than KW interface.

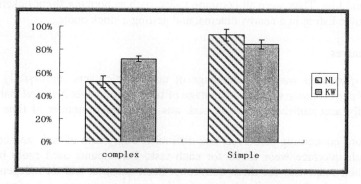

Fig. 2. Actual performance

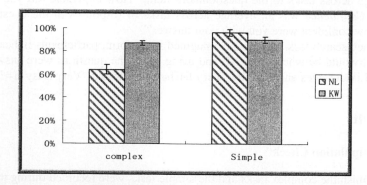

Fig. 3. Perceived performance

There was also a main effect for task complexity on performance: simple task participants had better performance than complex task participants $[M_{simple}=89\%$ vs. $M_{complex}=62\%, F(1,50)=50.1, p<.01]$. Compared with complex task participants, simple task participants also believed that they had more successes $[M_{simple}=93\%$ vs. $M_{complex}=76\%, F(1,50)=41.6, p<.01]$.

3.3 Perceived Task Difficulty, Enjoyment of Search Experience, and Confidence with Answers

Perceived Task Difficulty. Participants' perception of task difficulty was first assessed without including performance as a covariate. There was a significant interaction effect between task complexity and search interface [F(1,50)=105.0, p<.001]. Complex task participants thought that KW made the tasks easier to perform than did NL; conversely, simple task participants thought NL was easier to work with than was KW (see Figure 4). High complexity tasks were perceived to be more difficult than were low complexity tasks (Msimple=3.20 vs. Mcomplex=4.95, F(1,50)=36.4, p<.001), but this was expected. No main effect of perceived difficulty was found for search interface [F(1,50)=.917, p>.34].

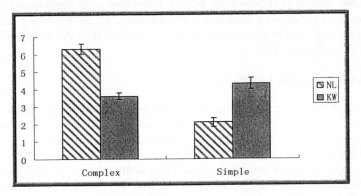

Fig. 4. Perception of difficulty

We re-examined the *perceived difficulty* data with *actual performance* as a covariate. The analysis reaffirmed our finding of an interaction effect between task complexity and search interface on perceived difficulty [$F(1,50)=28.95$, $p<.001$]. That is, even after adjusting for actual performance score, keyword search was perceived as more effective for complex tasks and less effective for simple tasks.

Enjoyment of Search Experience and Confidence with Answers. Participants' enjoyment of search experience and confidence with answers were analyzed. Table 2 presents the means and standard deviations.

There was a cross-over interaction between interface and task complexity with respect to enjoyment of search experience [$F(1,50)=47.6$, $p<.001$]. Complex task participants found using KW to be more enjoyable than using NL, while simple task participants reported the opposite. The effect remained after controlling for actual performance [$F(1,50)=19.9$, $p<.001$]. No main effect was found for search interface on participants' enjoyment of search experience [$F(1,50)=2.01$, $p>.05$]. Overall, complex task participants found the tasks to be less pleasant than simple task participants [$M_{simple}=5.87$ vs. $M_{complex}=4.75$, $F(1,50)=5.61$, $p<0.05$], and this was expected.

There was also an interaction with respect to the participants' confidence with their answers (even after controlling for actual performance). Complex task participants were more confident using KW, while simple task participants were more confident with NL interface [$F(1,50)=70.9$, $p<.001$; control: $F(1,50)=13.1$, $p<.001$].

Table 2. Perceived enjoyment and confidence

	Complex Tasks		Simple Tasks	
	NL Mean (SD)	KW Mean (SD)	NL Mean (SD)	KW Mean (SD)
Enjoyment	4.07 (1.36)	5.43 (1.59)	6.9 (1.71)	4.84 (1.83)
Confidence	5.84 (1.72)	8.03 (1.42)	8.71 (0.81)	7.65 (1.24)

Participant were more confident with their answers while working with KW search than with NL queries [$F(1,50)=8.56$, $p<.01$]. Interviews with participants during debriefing sessions concerning confidence are discussed in the following section. Not surprisingly, complex task participants felt less confident than did simple task participants [$F(1,50)=15.4$, $p<.001$].

3.4 Anticipated Search Interfaces

When participants were instructed to imagine finding answers to six search tasks with either the NL or KW interface, their indications of task difficulty confirmed our categorization of complexity, $F(2,102)=4.34$, $p<.05$. As shown in figure 5, high complexity tasks were viewed as more difficult than medium and low complexity tasks, and medium complexity tasks were viewed as more difficult than low complexity tasks [high vs. medium: $t(51)=4.06$, $p<.001$; high vs. low: $t(51)=5.17$, $p<.001$; medium vs. low: $t(51)=2.50$, $p<.05$].

There was an interaction between task complexity and choice of search interface [$F(1,50)=8.20$, $p<.01$] (Figure 5). Post-hoc tests indicated that for medium and high complexity tasks, participants preferred KW over NL, $t(51)=2.31$, $p<.05$, and $t(51)=2.62$, $p<.05$, respectively; such preference was not reported for low complexity tasks.

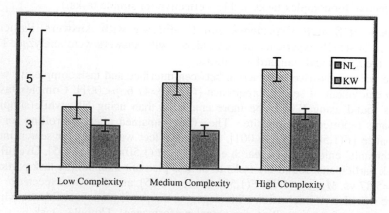

Fig. 5. Perceived difficulty for anticipated search questions

4 Discussion

The present study suggests that the selection of search interface has important and systematic effects on participant performance and perceptions. However, these effects are conditioned by the complexity of search task and the nature of queries. The general pattern we found was that NL interface was better (in both reality and perception) than KW interface for simple search tasks, while KW was better (in both reality and perception) than NL for complex search tasks. The type of search interface had no direct effect on either perceived task difficulty or enjoyment, although participants were in general more confident with KW than with NL search interface. During debriefing, several participants said that they felt more confident with KW because they had browsed pages or links that gave them peripheral affirmation. It is important to note that although there was no difference in terms of actual search performance, participants believed that they obtained more correct answers by using the KW interface than the NL interface.

4.1 Task Complexity Effect and Implications

One clear problem with NL search interfaces is that even high-quality NL systems often fail to understand what users are trying to ask. In the present study, this was true for almost all NL dialogs (i.e., with My eBay Buddy) that involved complex tasks. When My eBay Buddy could not understand the participant, it would generally ask clarifying questions. Unfortunately, the clarifying questions tend to reveal even deeper misunderstandings. Following is a sample dialogue between a participant and My eBay Buddy:

Participant: ok, tell me about your links
My eBay Buddy: What is About Me? A page that tells other eBay participants about yourself.
Participant: I'm asking for links for help
My eBay Buddy: You are asking for links for help, huh?
Participant: ahhhhhhh!
My eBay Buddy: You typed a very weird thing. What's "ahhhhhhh" supposed to mean?
Participant: I'm frustrated at you!
My eBay Buddy: For real?
Participant: for real!!!!!
My eBay Buddy: That right?
Participant: ok... where can I get more help, apart from you?

In human-human conversations, people adjust their communication strategies by asking and responding to questions in order to establish shared understandings, a process known as "grounding." [18]. When a computer agent tries to use language as a real person would, participants likely raise their expectations of the agent's ability to understand. Some previous research [19, 20] has suggested that participants may say things more freely when they have high expectations of the agent as compared to lower expectations. The freer utterances from the participant consequently impose extra burden on natural language processing system. The gap between unconstrained participant utterances and the limited understanding capability of NL agent can lead to a spiral of failure which frustrates the participant and reduces user satisfaction.

When using the Buddy in the present study, participants with complex tasks in general found it difficult to form concise questions. As a result, they had to ask more questions than did simple task participants. Given the limited natural language processing capability of the Buddy, the more questions participants asked, the more likely the Buddy would fail to understand. Also, the more unconstrained the questions were, the more likely the Buddy would appear ignorant. It would be very useful if the agent were able to constrain user utterances by leveraging the "alignment" phenomenon observed in human-human dialogs [21].

On the other hand, simple tasks allowed the NL agent to understand and to offer relevant responses; this led to high levels of participant satisfaction in the present study. The following is a sample dialogue:

Participant: what if no confirmation email?
My eBay Buddy: Do you mean what if I submitted the registration form but didn't get a confirmation email? ......

In fact, during debriefing sessions, several simple-task participants mentioned that they thought the Buddy was smart when it asked questions back to confirm its understanding of participants' queries. Under such circumstances, it seemed to be acceptable for the agent to behave like a human being.

The above findings suggest that a natural language agent should adapt its response style to its confidence level in understanding users' input. A lower confidence level should decrease sentential responses from the system, particularly when there is no conversational history maintained by the system. Large numbers of sentential responses may mislead the participant to expect the same capability and flexibility as they would from a human interlocutor. This raised level of expectation will lead to a decreased level of satisfaction with the system when the system continues with more sentential responses even after serious misunderstandings occur.

4.2 Future Research Directions

In the present study, participants were not given the freedom to choose between the two search interfaces. One potential direction for future research is to investigate how the choice of search interface, and even the switch between search interfaces in the attempts to perform a particular task, influences user performance and perceptions. Task performance and perceptions are likely to be different when participants are able to switch from one interface to the other if they think that their initial approach is ineffective. On the other hand, this might involve duplication of effort. The research question here is whether or not combining two search interfaces/methods could provide a better user experience for information retrieval systems.

As noted earlier, it is important to understand how the response style of an NL agent influences user behaviors and attitudes. Some earlier studies have demonstrated that linguistic variations (e.g., sentence length) generated by NL agents may affect user input by soliciting alignment (i.e., mirroring) behaviors from users [19, 22].

However, linguistic alignment in human-human conversation is a bi-directional process in which two interlocutors converge. How participants would evaluate an aligning agent versus a non-aligning agent is still to be explored. On top of that, researchers must further determine when and in what ways a computer agent should align with the user to achieve or improve user satisfaction.

4.3 Final Words

The design of search methodology requires an understanding of the complex interaction between technology, psychology, and context. The present study demonstrates that any debate concerning keyword versus natural language for search must be contectualized by the complexity of search task.

References

1. Laurel, B.: Interface Agents: Metaphors with Character. In Laurel, B. (ed.), The Art of Human-Computer Interface Design. Addison-Wesley, Reading, MA (1990)
2. Doszkocs T.: Natural Language Processing in Intelligent Information Retrieval. Proceedings of the 1985 ACM Annual Conference on The Range of Computing: Mid-80's Perspective. ACM Press, 356–359
3. Guglielmo E.J., Rowe N.C.: Natural-Language Retrieval of Images Based on Descriptive Captions. ACM Transactions on Information Systems (TOIS), July 1996, Vol. 14, Issue 3, 237–267
4. Jacob, P. S., Rau, L.F.: Natural Language Techniques for Intelligent Information Retrieval. Proceedings of the Eleventh International Conference on Research & development in Information Retrieval (1988), 85–99
5. Meng, F.: A Natural Language Interface for Information Retrieval from Forms on the World Wide Web. Proceeding of the 20th International Conference on Information Systems (1999), 540–545
6. Turtle H.: Natural Language vs. Boolean Query Evaluation: A Comparison of Retrieval Performance. Proceedings of the Seventeenth Annual International ACM-SIGIR Conference on Research and Development in Information Retrieval (1994), 212–220
7. Chen, H., and Dumais, S.: Optimizing Search by Showing Results in Context. Proceedings of CHI 2001. ACM Press, 145 – 152
8. Dumais, S. T., Furnas, G. W., Landauer, T. K., Deerwester, S., & Harshman, R.: Using Latent Semantic Analysis to Improve Access to Textual Information. Proceedings of CHI '88. ACM Press, 281 – 285
9. Woodruff, A., Faulring, A., Rosenholtz, R., Morrison, J., & Pirolli, P.: Using Thumbnails to Search the Web. Proceedings of CHI 2001. ACM Press, 198 – 205
10. Borgman, C. L.: The Participant's Mental Model of an Information Retrieval System: An Experiment on a Prototype Online Catalog. International Journal of Man-Machine Studies, 24(1) (1986), 47-64
11. Borgman, C. L.: Psychological Research in Human-Computer Interaction. In M. Williams (Ed.), Annual Review of Information Science and Technology, Vol. 19. White Plains, NY: Knowledge Industry Publications (1984), 33-64
12. Greene, S.L., Devlin, S.J., Cannata, P.E. and Gomez, L.M.: No IFs, ANDs or ORs: a Study of Database Querying. International Journal of Man-Machine Studies, 32, 3 (1990), 303-326

13. Cleverdon, C.W.: The Significance of the Cranfield Tests on Index Languages. In A. Bookstein, Y. Chiaramella, G. Salton, and V.V. Raghavan (Eds). Proceedings of the 14th Annual International ACM SIGIR Conference on Research and Development in Information Retrieval. ACM Press, (1991), 3 – 12

14. Cooper, W. S.: Getting Beyond Boole. Information Processing & Management 24(3) (1988), 243-248

15. Muramatsu, J., Pratt, W.: Transparent Queries: Investigating Participants' Mental Models of Search Engines. SIGIR: Proceedings of the 24th International Conference on Research & Development in Information Retrieval (2001)

16. Navarro-Prieto, R, Scaife, M, and Rogers, Y.: Cognitive Strategies in Web Searching. Proceedings of the 5th Conference on Human Factors & the Web (1999)

17. Conversagent, Inc. http://www.conversagent.com

18. Clark, H.H.: Using Language. Cambridge University Press, New York (1996)

19. Brennan, S.: Conversation with and through Computers. Participant Modeling and Participant-Adapted Interaction, 1 (1991), 67–86

20. Pearson, J., Pickering, M.J. Branigan, H.P., McLean, J.F., Nass, C.I., Hu, J.: The Influence of Beliefs about an Interlocutor on Lexical and Syntactic Alignment: Evidence from Human-Computer Dialogues. Proceeding of the 10th Annual Architectures and Mechanisms of Language Processing Conference (2004)

21. Nass, C.I., Hu, J., Pearson, J., Pickering, M.J., Branigan, H.P.: Linguistic Alignment in HCI vs. CMC: Do Participants Mimic Conversation Partners' Grammar and Word Choices? Unpublished manuscript (2004).

22. Zoltan-Ford, E.: How to Get People to Say and Type What Computers Can Understand. International Journal of Man-Machine Studies, 34(4) (1991), 527-547

"THAT's What I Was Looking For": Comparing User-Rated Relevance with Search Engine Rankings

Sameer Patil[1], Sherman R. Alpert[2], John Karat[2], and Catherine Wolf[2]

[1] Department of Informatics, Donald Bren School of Information and Computer Sciences,
University of California, Irvine CA 92697 USA
patil@uci.edu
[2] I.B.M. T. J. Watson Research Center, Hawthorne, NY 10532
{salpert, jkarat, cwolf}@us.ibm.com

Abstract. We present a lightweight tool to compare the relevance ranking provided by a search engine to the relevance as actually judged by the user performing the query. Using the tool, we conducted a user study with two different versions of the search engine for a large corporate web site with more than 1.8 million pages, and with the popular search engine Google™. Our tool provides an inexpensive and efficient way to do this comparison, and can be easily extended to any search engine that provides an API. Relevance feedback from actual users can be used to assess precision and recall of a search engine's retrieval algorithms and, perhaps more importantly, to tune its relevance ranking algorithms to better match user needs. We found the tool to be quite effective at comparing different versions of the same search engine, and for benchmarking by comparing against a standard.

1 Introduction

Finding information is a basic task on the Internet. Looking for information on the Internet or on any particular site generally involves a mixture of navigation and search. In order to find information, users typically start at a search engine [13]. Making search better can significantly improve the user experience.

Search engines have typically been assessed in terms of precision and recall. Recall refers to the ratio of relevant records retrieved to the total number of relevant records in the entire database. Precision measures the ratio of relevant records retrieved to the total number of retrieved records. However, as many search developers and researchers now understand:

> "While precision and recall are very helpful in talking about how good search systems are, they are nightmarishly difficult to actually use, quantitatively. First of all, the notion of 'relevance' is definitely in the eye of the beholder, and not, in the real world, a mechanical yes/no decision. Secondly, any information base big enough to make search engines interesting is going to be too big to actually compute recall numbers (to compute recall, you have to know how many matches there are, and if you did, you wouldn't need a search engine)" [2].

M.F. Costabile and F. Paternò (Eds.): INTERACT 2005, LNCS 3585 , pp. 117 – 129, 2005.

Internet users are impatient, and rarely look beyond the first page of search results. In fact, many may scan only those results "above the fold" (visible without scrolling) [10]. Continued improvements in search engine technology have led to a steady rise in user expectations, further decreasing user willingness to look beyond the first few results [10]. Thus, the overall precision and recall of a search engine may be rather meaningless in the face of the user's judgment regarding "Does this result seem to provide the information I am looking for?" In other words, the effectiveness of the search engine is determined by whether the topmost results that are shown on the first page of search results are relevant to the user's goal(s) behind performing the query.

As a result, it is critical that the search engine's determination of which pages are the most relevant to the user's query coincide to the maximum extent with what the user himself or herself judges to be relevant to the task. We believe that the best judge of relevance is the user himself or herself. Given the limitations of keywords in completely and accurately capturing intention [11], the user has a clear advantage of knowing the goal behind the query. Therefore, we argue that asking the user is the most effective way of determining the extent of match between search-engine-rated relevance with actual user-perceived relevance. The tool we describe in this paper provides a lightweight mechanism to capture user-perceived relevance.

2 Related Work

"Search" has always been an important topic in Information Retrieval (IR) research. Initial research focused on algorithmic improvements for better precision and recall in order to retrieve relevant results

Various measures and techniques have been proposed and utilized for evaluating the performance of a search engine, and for comparing different search engines. A typical approach is to use a sample of queries and/or a sample of tasks to compare the relevance of search engine results with the ratings of "expert judges" [20]. As noted before, this approach suffers from the inherent limitation of lacking knowledge regarding user intent and context. Even though independent judges become more proficient with training, as Janes [6] found, "Clearly, there are differences between ratings of users and others, and from this we may infer that there are different processes at work in their judging." Further, the wide range of user queries – a large percentage of which are unique [18] – makes it difficult to select an appropriate sample of queries for evaluation. Indeed, it has been found that such measures may not reflect real world performance [7].

However, relatively little research exists comparing real-life user judgments with search engine relevance rankings [15, 16, 17]. Most notably, Spink [15] conducted a study in which users used a search engine for their own information topics, and rated the relevance of the results. However, the study focused on precision of the first 20 results and ignored how the results were ranked by the engine. Moreover, the study used only a 4-point relevance classification.

The tool we present provides an improvement with a low-burden, cost-effective, and automatic mechanism to capture and compare user relevance ratings with the rankings provided by a search engine. It has been shown that a simple binary classification of "relevant/not relevant" is not adequate to judge the relevance of a document to the user need [1, 5]. Our tool allows the user to make a relevance judgment at a finer grain with a 10-point scale. Also, the user can provide additional input regarding duplicate or non-existing pages as well as include brief comments. While Spink's [15] study involved a single search engine, the user study we conducted with the tool encompassed 2 search engines.

3 SQUARE: Search QUality Analysis by Relevance Evaluation

SQUARE is a tool we have developed to gather user-perceived relevance information. SQUARE wraps itself "around" a normal user search query. It can thus be used to obtain user assessments of relevance for the results of any Web-based search engine. SQUARE executes the user's query using the underlying search engine, presents the results returned by the search engine to the user along with small questionnaire forms, and gathers feedback from the user regarding the perceived relevance ratings of each result entry and the corresponding target document.

SQUARE runs in a standard Web browser, so it can be invoked simply by navigating to its URL. It starts by asking the user to enter a free-form description of his or her information-seeking task, and a search query to find information related to the task. No additional constraints are imposed on user queries, i.e., the form of the query is identical to that the user would enter when using the underlying search engine directly. SQUARE then programmatically queries the underlying search engine using the keywords entered by the user. The results are identical to those obtained if the query is performed directly via the search engine. The top 10 results (or fewer if the query results in fewer than 10 hits) returned by the search engine are collected.

However, instead of presenting the user with the results in the order in which they were ranked by the search engine – as is the case in an actual search – SQUARE presents the results to the user one at a time in random order. First result entries are presented, individually, in random order. By *result entries*, we mean the entries that would normally be displayed by a search engine in the search result hitlist. These entries typically include a title, search-engine-generated snippet of the document, URL, metadata, and classification. The elements that comprise the entry (and the order in which they occur) may vary between search engines, and is also dependent on the target page in question. SQUARE presents all information provided by the search engine.

As shown in Figure 1, each result entry is presented on a page that asks the user to rate its relevance to his or her task on a 10 point scale. Optionally, users can provide an open-ended reason for their evaluation. Users are also asked to indicate whether the entry appears to be a duplicate of one previously presented.

After all result entries have been presented, SQUARE presents the actual target documents associated with the result entries (see Figure 2). As with the result entries, the target documents are shown one after another in random order[1]. The documents are rated in a manner similar to the result entries. Additionally, users can specify whether the document did not display (i.e., an HTTP 404 error).

SQUARE offers several advantages that make it attractive for evaluation of an individual search engine, and comparison of effectiveness of across search engines.

---

[1] The randomization of target documents is independent of the randomization of the result entries.

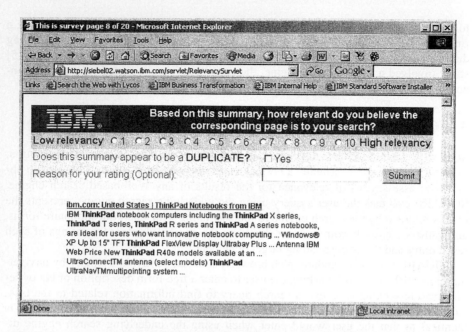

Fig. 1. Sample screen for rating the relevance of a result entry returned by the search engine

Lightweight and Simple. As is evident from the preceding discussion, SQUARE operates in a rather straightforward manner, and fits within the same framework that is used for "normal" searches – using the same Web browser, and the same keywords. Moreover, its simple design allows the user to indicate the rating quickly with minimal effort.

Easily Extensible. To perform searches, SQUARE programmatically forwards queries to the underlying search engine. Thus, it can be extended to any search engine of interest merely by modifying the API (Application Programming Interface) it uses to submit a query, and collect the returned results.

As currently implemented, the search results are formatted in a generic (neutral) fashion, such that any search-engine-specific interface aspects (e.g. text colors, indentation etc.) are ignored, while the search terms that occur within the result entry are bolded. We decided to adopt a neutral approach to eliminate potential bias regarding user ratings of relevance, since a user's relevance perceptions are influenced by form and style as well as the textual content [19]. However, it is relatively straightforward to present a search result "as-is", or to even embed the interface of SQUARE within the results list.

Low-cost, Low-effort. Because SQUARE is deployed via the Web, it eliminates the efforts and costs of arranging for a usability laboratory setting. Users are simply directed to a URL to start the search with SQUARE. SQUARE captures all relevant data to a file for later analysis.

Fig. 2. Sample screen for rating the relevance of the target document of a result entry

Automatic. As SQUARE uses the same framework that is used to conduct actual searches, it is able to simultaneously and automatically capture all relevant metadata along with user input. This results in considerable reduction of effort that would be required for manual capture of this information.

Fast. Finally, SQUARE is able to gather feedback from the user relatively quickly, i.e., in a mere 10-15 minutes per query. As a result, it is easier to attract larger numbers of subjects for a nominal incentive. We were able to gather data from hundreds of users in a very short time frame.

4 Description of Study

We tested SQUARE by conducting a user study that involved two different search engines – the search engine used for intra-site search on the Web-site of a large multinational corporation, and the widely popular Internet search engine Google. In case of the corporate search engine, SQUARE was used to compare two different versions (referred to as Version 1.0 and Version 1.1 in the paper). The two versions of the corporate search engine varied in minor algorithmic details, and in the indexes that they searched. Version 1.1 was, among other things, intended to reduce the number of duplicate pages returned in the result list. Google was chosen because it is widely perceived as the standard in Internet search, and also because it provides a public API making it easy to incorporate it within SQUARE.

4.1 Participants

The study was conducted in three parts – part 1 with Corporate Search 1.0 (CS 1.0), part 2 with Corporate Search 1.1 (CS 1.1), and part 3 with Google. For each of the three parts, an email message was sent to various email lists comprised of employees within the research division of a large technology company. The participants were offered a nominal incentive (a $5 Gift Certificate for the cafeteria) for participation. For the first two parts of the study (i.e. CS 1.0, and CS 1.1), the same email was sent to a different set of employee mailing lists without offering the incentive. Participation rate was about 15% for the employees offered the incentive, and about 2% when no incentive was offered. We received 67 responses for the first part of the study (CS 1.0), 64 for the second part (CS 1.1), and 53 for the third part (Google). As employees of a cutting-edge technology company, all participants are reasonably expected to be highly experienced computer users (and online searchers).

4.2 Methodology

At the beginning, participants were presented with an instruction screen that described the purpose of the study. Participants then proceeded to describe an actual task they might do and to enter keywords to be used for a search engine query. The keywords were then used by SQUARE to gather relevance feedback regarding the search results as described in the previous section. After all result entries and target documents were individually displayed to, and evaluated by a participant, a final screen was shown on which the participants could enter optional overall comments.

Thus, for each participant SQUARE collected participant-specified task description, participant's keywords, evaluations for the result entries (up to 10), and evaluations for target documents of the result entries. Result entry evaluations were comprised of the user's numeric relevance rating (on a 1-10 scale), an optional reason for the rating, and the participant's determination of whether the entry appeared to be a duplicate. Document evaluations were comprised of the same information regarding the target documents with the addition of an indication regarding whether the document did not display.

Along with user evaluations, SQUARE recorded pertinent information such as contents of the result entry, its position in the results list, the URL and the classification of the target document, "keyword" metadata associated with the document, the total number of results returned for the query, and any overall comments from each participant.

4.3 Analysis

After analyzing the queries and tasks that participants had entered for CS 1.0, we found that some were not appropriate for the public (external) corporate Web site, but rather were intended for either the intranet (internal) site (e.g., searches for internal company project names), or for general search engines (e.g. searches for cartoon websites). Such queries were flagged via independent review by three judges, and excluded from analysis. As a result, in CS 1.1, we slightly modified the wording on the instruction screen to ask specifically for tasks relevant to the external corporate Web site. As before, all queries were reviewed for appropriateness independently by three judges. A few non-relevant queries were still encountered. However, possibly due to the modification in instructions, the percentage of inappropriate queries was much lower compared those for CS 1.0

In case of Google, we excluded six queries. Three queries had returned less than 10 results (2, 5 and 6 respectively), and were eliminated for the sake of consistency with the other two parts in which no queries had fewer than 10 results. Of the remaining three, one had a spelling error due to which all results ended up being marked as highly irrelevant. In an actual search using Google, the alternate spelling suggestion feature would have helped to prevent situation. In the second case, the participant had violated the protocol of the study by simultaneously conducting the same search in a separate browser window. This was indicated in the comments: *"I was first presented with 10 URLS one at a time each of which I followed in another browser window so that I could rate them. I was then presented with the actual pages for each of the previously presented URLs. This second set of pages duplicated the URLs."* In the third case, the participant had performed a search on the names of one of the authors. Based on the participant's unfamiliarity with the author in question, we judged that it is unlikely this task is representative of an actual task that the user might perform via Google, as was asked in the study. (This is also evident in some of the comments the participant included with their evaluations for result entries and documents).

Finally, we ended up with 48 queries (72% of total queries performed) for CS 1.0, 54 queries (86% of total performed) for CS 1.1, and 47 queries (89% of total performed) for Google. The findings reported in the next section are based on analysis of these queries.

5   Findings

Using the data gathered by SQUARE, we compared each part of the study. Table 1 summarizes the findings from the numeric portions of the data (Note that the scale presented by SQUARE interface is reversed when the data is recorded so in the data 1 represents "Highly relevant" and 10 represents "Not relevant"). Result entries and target documents that were marked as duplicates by the participants have been excluded from the numeric analyses. The numeric ratings coupled with user justifications and comments lead to a number of interesting insights as discussed below:

5.1   Correlation Between Rated Relevance of Result Entry and Target Document

As Table 1 shows, there was a very high level of agreement between ratings for result entries and corresponding target documents ($r = 0.78$ for CS 1.0 and 1.1, and $r = 0.76$ for Google, all $p \sim 0$). This suggests that the mechanisms being used for generating document snippets for result entries worked adequately in all three cases. Because the correlations were very high, we have restricted the analyses to document ratings only. In general, the two separate ratings are mostly useful in identifying places where there is a discrepancy between the summary and document rating. Such cases could be utilized to help identify where improvements might be made in the generation of result entries.

Table 1. Summary of findings showing comparison of user ratings for CS 1, CS 1.1 and Google (1 = Highly relevant, 10 = Not relevant)

Factor	CS 1.0	CS 1.1	Google
Mean entry relevance	6.14	6.61	5.85
Median entry relevance	7.00	8.00	6.00
Mode entry relevance	10.00	10.00	10.00
Mean document relevance	6.24	6.91	6.18
Median document relevance	7.00	8.00	6.00
Mode document relevance	10.00	10.00	10.00
Duplicates	26.30%	18.30%	13.80%
Correlation between entry & document rating	0.78 $(p \sim 0.0)$	0.78 $(p \sim 0.0)$	0.76 $(p \sim 0.0)$
Correlation between document relevance & ranking	Not. Sig.	0.15 $(p \sim 0.002)$	0.18 $(p \sim 0.0)$
Correlation between document relevance & number of keywords	0.22 $(p \sim 0.0)$	0.17 $(p \sim 0.0)$	0.15 $(p \sim 0.003)$
Average words/Query	2.69	2.98	3.53
Median words/Query	3.00	2.00	3.00

5.2 Correlation Between Search-Engine Ranking and Rated Relevance

Given that the result list is ranked by relevance, a good search engine will place the documents with the highest relevance at the top. As one moves down the list, relevance can be expected to decrease. Thus, for a well-performing search engine, one would expect a correlation between ranking and relevance. As seen in Table 1, relevance was essentially uncorrelated with ranking in CS 1.0, but was positively correlated in CS 1.1. This suggests that although average result quality did not improve in CS 1.1, higher quality results were placed higher in the list. Since most users rarely examine more than a screen (i.e., above the fold), or page of results, this indicates an improvement. The average relevance of the results may not be as important a measure to consider if a highly relevant result appears high in the list. Google results also show a positive correlation of the rankings with relevance. More over, Google performed better than CS 1.1 ($p < 0.01$), although the magnitude of improvement is marginal.

5.3 Average Relevance

Obviously, the better the search engine, the higher the average relevance of all results in the list taken together. However, average relevance may be of limited use when taken by itself. It is more valuable in comparing across different versions of a search engine or between two different search engines, or with a benchmark. We can note from Table 1, that the average relevance in all three parts of the study was below neutral. Although Google performed better than both CS 1.0 and 1.1 (p < 0.01), once again the magnitude of difference seems to be marginal. Similar patterns are observed even if we consider only the top 5 search results returned by the search engines.

A factor that affects the average relevance is the presence of large number of documents marked as not relevant. In fact, the mode of rating in all three cases is 10. It appears that users had little hesitancy in using the lowest rating for documents that seemed irrelevant (CS 1.0: 34.2%, CS 1.1, 31.3%, and Google: 27.4%). This is also reflected in user comments such as: *"Most of the documents found were irrelevant to my specific subject. However, one or two were very helpful."*, *"Most search results are irrelevant, but I did get one result that is exactly what I was looking for"*, *"Search engines continue to optimistically supply huge amounts of irrelevant garbage in their answers."*

The indication of high relevance, on the other hand, was less clear. As a result, we decided to delve a bit deeper into the higher ranked results. Table 2 shows statistics for all documents that were rated within the top 3 (i.e., given a relevance rating of 1, 2, or 3), as well as those that were rated the topmost (i.e., rated 1). We can observe that the percentage of highly relevant documents is much higher in case of Google. In addition, Google seems to do a much better overall job of putting the most relevant results at the very top of the results list, or at least amongst the top 5 results. (Although it may appear as if CS 1.0 is better than Google at listing the highest rated result at the top position, the much lower percentage of such results in CS 1.0 must be taken into account when making an overall comparison.)

Table 2. Comparing highly relevant results

	Top three relevant (Relevance = 1, 2, 3)			Highest relevant (Relevance = 1)		
	CS 1.0	CS 1.1	Google	CS 1.0	CS 1.1	Google
N	100	108	109	34	38	58
%N	20.83	20.00	23.19	7.08	7.03	12.34
Mean rank	5.30	4.77	4.77	4.56	4.68	4.48
Median rank	5	5	4	4	5	4
Mode rank	1	1	1	1	2	1
Range	9	9	9	9	8	9
% at #1	14.00	14.80	16.50	23.50	13.20	17.20
% in top 5	53.00	58.30	58.70	64.70	57.90	65.50

5.4 Duplicates

One frequent user complaint regarding CS 1.0 had been a large amount of "duplicates" in the list, i.e., the same resource being presented as two or more separate results. This was indeed reflected in SQUARE data. More than a fourth of the results were flagged as duplicates by the participants. User comments such as, *"Lots of duplicates. Everything came up at least twice."*, were quite typical. It should be noted that the reported number is actually *lower* than the actual number of perceived duplicates. A duplicate was flagged by the user if he or she believed that it had already been seen before. However, because the user could not specify which already-seen result the current result was a duplicate of, the very first instance seen remained unflagged as a duplicate.

One of the improvements in CS 1.1 was advertised to be duplicate elimination. Again, SQUARE data shows that CS 1.1 resulted in a reduction in the number of duplicates by about a third – an improvement compared with CS 1.0 but significantly worse compared with Google.

Interestingly, reduction of duplicates in CS 1.1 did not improve the average relevance of results in the list. This could be explained by taking into account that duplicate elimination just results in results further down the list being pushed upwards. Given the positive correlation between ranking and relevance, the results being pushed upwards are likely to be of lower relevance.

5.5 Effect of Number of Keywords

Over the past few years, the average query length logged by the corporate search engine has been steadily increasing. We were interested in examining the potential impact of query length on relevance of retrieved results. We found statistically significant positive correlation between rated relevance and the number of keywords in the query. Thus, longer queries result in documents with lower average rated relevance.

6 Discussion

In the previous section, we illustrated how SQUARE can be used to compare search engine performance across versions, and with a benchmark such as Google. We were able to discover that CS 1.1 lived up to its promise of reducing duplicates and pushing highly relevant results up the ranking. Yet, it failed to improve the average relevance of the top 10 results, and fell short of the benchmark that most users are likely to apply to its performance.

Multiple factors may be at play in determining the overall effectiveness of a search engine. For example, merely improving the correlation of the rankings with user ratings may not be sufficient if the overall percentage of highly relevant documents is low. Given that Google is highly reputed for the quality of its search results, it may be surprising that the magnitude of difference (e.g., average relevance, relevance/ranking correlation) for each factor between Google and CS 1.1 was not very large. This suggests that the cumulative effect of all factors taken together could result in substantial differences. In addition, the average query length was longer in case of Google. As discussed in the previous section, longer query lengths are more challenging for a search engine. (There was also some evidence that users deliberately tried to use harder queries to "challenge" Google. For example, one user commented, *"I may be searching for something that doesn't exist we are evaluating whether to patent the idea..."*). Finally, it also begs the question of what part Google's interface plays in user perceptions regarding its effectiveness. It was discussed earlier how one participant failed to notice his spelling error when the spelling-suggestion functionality was stripped off.

Data captured by SQUARE allows us to explore relevance from such multiple angles by allowing us to frame a variety of questions regarding the distribution of relevance judgments in relation to search engine rankings. For instance, one could easily compare the percentage of participants who rated at least one result as relevant. As the above discussion implies, such a multi-dimension perspective is necessary when evaluating overall effectiveness of the search engine. At the same time, each isolated factor represents an area that may be appropriately fine-tuned for better performance.

6.1 Limitations

Although the results presented are quite interesting, we must acknowledge the limitations of the study. For starters, the sample population of technology professionals is not representative of the average user. As a result, we must caution against treating the numeric data in each part of the study in isolation. However, the fact that the samples were drawn from the same population in all three cases allows us to effectively compare the results from the three parts.

Secondly, SQUARE needs to be extended to support query refinement. As several users commented, iterative query refinement is a typical approach used in real-life search behavior:

"I would have probably realized after glancing the top 5 results that I needed to refine the search."

"When I search Google I am able to refine my search by learning better search terms as I read relevant hits. Your test allowed just one iteration."

"I guess I should have added the terms "sale" or "buy"."

7   Implications for Design

We have already highlighted how statistics based on the data captured by SQUARE can be utilized by developers of search algorithms to discover avenues for fine tuning. The findings coupled with user comments provide several additional implications for designers of search engine algorithms and interfaces.

7.1 Algorithmic Implications

Snippet Generation. The high correlations between relevance judgments of result entry and the corresponding target document underscore the importance of generating good document snippets to support effective relevance judgments.

Duplicate Elimination. Frustration expressed by users regarding duplicates coupled with the observed improvement in ranking with reduced duplicate count indicates that eliminating duplicates needs to be paid more attention. In particular, "mirrors" may need to be handled specially.

Personalize by Using Context. A search engine can provide better results if it has some knowledge regarding the user and his or her current context. Such functionality could help avoid frustrating user experiences such as: *"This is in Finland and I am searching from the US. Not useful for me."*, or *"Got lots of warranty stuff when I asked for upgrades. I wanted hardware."*

7.2 Interface Implications

Iterative Query Refinement. As discussed in the previous section, users typically engage in query refinement. Interface improvements that can facilitate this process could make the process more effective and efficient.

Result List Scanning. Presenting the list of result entries in a manner that facilitates quick scanning ensures that users will be able to quickly recognize the most pertinent results. Quick scanning also aids iterative query refinement.

Incorporate User Feedback. Designers may even wish to incorporate parts of the SQUARE interface within the search result list to support gathering impromptu user feedback.

Indeed, approaches to deal with some of the above factors are already being explored [8, 9, 12, 14]. We believe that significant improvements in user experiences could be achieved if designers of search systems treat search as an activity situated in the larger context, rather than an isolated query or session.

8 Conclusion

We have presented SQUARE, a lightweight tool that provides an inexpensive and efficient mechanism for capturing user perceptions regarding how relevant a search result is to the task. SQUARE is interoperable with any search engine that offers access through APIs, provides a standardized presentation of search results across different search engines, and elicits user input regarding perceived relevance of search results. We have described the utility of SQUARE to compare the effectiveness of different versions of the same search engine, and also for benchmarking by comparing against a known standard. We found that relevance needs to be examined from multiple angles in order to gain a thorough understanding of the various factors that affect search engine effectiveness. Based on our findings, we have suggested that search algorithms should provide effective snippet generation, and duplicate elimination, while search interfaces should support quick scanning and iterative query refinement. We urge designers of search systems to treat search as an activity situated in the larger context, rather than an isolated query or session.

Acknowledgements

We would like to thank Pat Velderman, Alfred Kobsa, and all the users who participated in the study.

References

1. Borlund, P. (2003) The Concept of Relevance in IR, Journal of The American Society for Information Science and Technology, 54 (10), pp. 913-925.
2. Bray, T. (2003) On Search: Precision and Recall, http://www.tbray.org/ongoing/When/200x/2003/06/22/PandR

3. Della Mea, V. and Mizzaro, S. (2004) Measuring Retrieval Effectiveness: A New Proposal and a First Experiemental Validation, Journal of the American Society for Information Science and Technology, 55(6), pp. 530-543.

4. Dziadosz, S. and Chandrasekar, R. (2002) Do Thumbnails Previews Help Users Make Better Relevance Decisions about Web Search Results?, In Proc. SIGIR 2002.

5. Eisenberg, E. (1988) Measuring Relevance Judgments, Information Processing and Management, 24(4), pp. 373-389

6. Janes, J. W. (1994) Other People's Judgments: A Comparison of Users' and Others' Judgments of Document Relevance, Topicality, and Utility, Journal of the American Society for Information Science, 45 (3), pp.160-171.

7. Hersh, W. Turpin, A., Price, S. , Chan, B., Kramer, D., Sacherek, L., and, Olson, D. (2000) Do Batch and User Evaluations Give the Same Results?, In Proc. SIGIR 2000.

8. Leroy, G., Lally, A., and Chen, H. (2003) The Use of Dynamic Contexts to Improve Casual Internet Searching, ACM Transactions on Information Systems, 21 (3), pp. 229-253.

9. Liu, F., Yu, C., and Meng, W. (2002) Personalized Web Search by Mapping User Queries to Categories, In Proc. IKM 2002, pp. 558-565.

10. Karat, J. Wolf, C., Alpert, S. R., Velderman, P., and Patil, S. (2003) "Improving Search on IBM.com", IBM Research Technical Report.

11. Kyung-Sun, K. and Allen, B. (2002) Cognitive and Task Influence on Web Searching Behavior, Journal of the American Society for Information Science and Technology, 53(2), pp. 109-119.

12. Muramatsu, J. and Pratt, W. (2001) Transparent Queries: Investigating Users' Mental Models of Search Engines, In Proc. SIGIR 2001.

13. Nielsen, J. (2004) When Search Engines Become Answer Engines, Alertbox, August, 24, 2004, http://www.useit.com/alertbox/20040816.html

14. Paek, T., Dumais, S., and Logan, R. (2004) Wavelens: A New View onto Internet Search Results, In Proc. CHI 2004.

15. Spink, A. (2002) A User-Centered Approach to Evaluating Human Interaction with Web Search Engines: An Exploratory Study, Information Processing and Management: An International Journal, 38(3), pp.401-426.

16. Spink, A. and Greisdorf, H. (2001) Regions and Levels: Measuring and Mapping Users' Relevance Judgments, Journal of the American Society for Information Science and Technology, 52(2), pp. 161-173.

17. Spink, A., and Saracevic, T. (1997) Interaction in Information Retrieval: Selection and Effectiveness of Search Terms, Journal of the American Society for Information Science, 48(8), pp.741-761.

18. Spink, A., Wolfram, D., Jansen, M. B. J., and Saracevic, T. (2001) Searching the Web: The Public and Their Queries, Journal of the American Society for Information Science and Technology, 52(3), pp.226-234.

19. Wolf, C. G., Alpert, S. R., Vergo, J. G., Kozakov, L., and Doganata, Y (2004) Summarizing Technical Support Documents for Search: Expert and User Studies, IBM Systems Journal, 43(3), http://www.research.ibm.com/journal/sj/433/wolf.pdf.

20. Yaltaghian, B., and Chignell, M. (2002) Re-ranking Search using Network Analysis: A Case Study with Google, In Proc. IBM Centre for Advanced Studies Conference.

Effects of Display Configurations on Document Triage

Soonil Bae, Rajiv Badi, Konstantinos Meintanis, J. Michael Moore, Anna Zacchi,
Haowei Hsieh, Catherine C. Marshall[*], and Frank M. Shipman

Center for the Study of Digital Libraries & Department of Computer Science,
Texas A&M University
shipman@cs.tamu.edu

Abstract. Document triage is the practice of quickly determining the merit and disposition of relevant documents. This practice involves selection of documents from a document overview and quick forms of reading: skimming, reading short portions of a longer document, and navigating through headings, indices, and tables of contents. Earlier studies of document triage practice showed considerable overhead related to window management during transitions between the document overview and reading interfaces. This study examines the impact of multiple display configurations on document triage practice. In particular, it compares (1) configurations with same and different size displays, and (2) configurations with and without user control over which activity is performed on which display. Results show a significant increase in the number of transitions between activities when a multi-display configuration is introduced although there is no significant difference between the different multiple display configurations. Additionally, user activity with a document was positively correlated with an overall assessment of document value.

1 Introduction

With the ubiquity of digital documents, users deal with multiple documents when they are looking up information on a particular topic. A student doing a literature survey typically uses a search engine to locate potentially relevant papers for the area of interest. She then skims, scans and evaluates the different documents, making comparisons and/or saving the references. She relies on what Joyce refers to as "successive attendings" to the same materials [5], rather than on scholarly reading and notetaking. Prior research on this triage activity suggests that during information triage, attentional resources are devoted to evaluating materials and organizing them, so they can be read and reread as they return to mind [7].

Document triage is the practice of quickly determining the merit and disposition of relevant documents – including web pages, periodical articles, and other published materials – that one may locate using a search engine, receive from an automated delivery mechanism, or obtain from a human intermediary. This practice necessarily involves quick forms of reading: skimming, reading short portions of a longer document, and navigating through structural elements such as headings, indices, or tables of contents. It also involves comparing documents, integrating results across

---

[*] Microsoft Corporation, Redmond, Washington.

M.F. Costabile and F. Paternò (Eds.): INTERACT 2005, LNCS 3585 , pp. 130–143, 2005.
© IFIP International Federation for Information Processing 2005

documents, noticing missing information, and reconciling conflicting information. Although this kind of triage is related to activities such as managing email, or getting a quick answer to a question by finding the "right" document, there is an important distinction: document triage usually involves a current focal document (or documents) and a periphery or background of other documents relevant to the task at hand.

Document triage gives us a way to investigate tasks in which reading and attention shift from document to document to contextual overview. In other words, we are looking beyond intensive reading (engagement with a single document) to extensive reading (engagement with multiple documents at once) and to hyper-extensive reading (engagement with subdocument components and fragmentary information).

The central issues being investigated in this study are:

- How can display real-estate and multiple displays and devices best be used to facilitate this kind of reading and gathering task?
- How can productivity be defined and promoted in multiple document tasks in which readers must manage their attentional resources?

2 Approach

Our main motivation for this research stems from the results from the study detailed in [12]. This study characterized the shifting attention problem by using a standard document triage task – going through search results and selecting and organizing the items considered valuable. A notable aspect of the data is how many *transitions*, i.e. shifting attention between the overview (in this case the Visual Knowledge Builder [11]) and the full reading window (in this case, Internet Explorer), this task requires.

Table 1. Transitions between document overview and reading application in prior study

Subject ID	1	2	3	4	5	6	7	8
Minutes spent on triage activity	64.1	54.2	22.0	22.8	93.5	80.2	63.8	61.7
Transitions between overview & reading	134	28	78	81	98	106	87	90
Transitions/minute	2.1	0.5	3.5	3.6	1.0	1.3	1.4	1.5

The data suggests that the number of transitions between the overview and reading applications is a profound source of interruption, especially since users had to rearrange or reorder windows at almost every transition. There is an average of more than one transition per minute for most users and this table does not include within-application navigation and reading-related navigation and manipulation that may be disruptive. It is instructive to examine several of the sessions individually to get a sense for this disruption. Subject 2 shows relatively few transitions in a 54 minute session; he or she sacrificed reading in favor of working on the triage task directly from the metadata provided in the overview. By contrast, Subject 4 shows the most transitions of any of the participants in the study. Subject 4 shifted between creating structure in the overview and reading Web pages to see what they were about.

Several questions thus arise from looking at this data:

- Do people try to minimize the number of transitions from overviews to more intensive reading?
- If no transition were necessary (i.e. if there were a stable reading surface like a Tablet PC), would people behave in the same way?
- When do people prefer to work from metadata to perform this kind of task?

To answer these questions and to delve deeper into understanding the approach followed by users during triage activity, we envisioned a scenario with users reading on a tetherless pen-based tablet computer and consulting a secondary peripheral display (possibly a projected image) to see a metadata-based document overview. Figure 1 shows the envisioned configuration with a person reading on a tablet computer with a peripheral display for organizing documents.

Fig. 1. Envisioned setting includes a reading interface on tetherless tablet computer and an organizing interface on a peripheral display

To investigate this document triage configuration, tablet users need to interact with materials on the projected display, since triage ultimately demands that some judgment be made about the documents' relative merit. Current tablet operating systems are limited in that the pen cannot provide direct input to a second display connected to the same computer. Techniques such as Pick-and-Drop [9] and hyperdragging [10] have been proposed to overcome this limitation, but they require considerable additions/modifications in both hardware and software. We decided to focus on hardware configurations that are common in labs or offices. Two factors that are likely to alter the triage task are the number of displays and the assignment of specific user activity to displays.

2.1 Multiple Displays

Research indicates that multiple monitor systems can help users be more productive [2]. Hutchings and colleagues found users with multi-monitors switch windows less frequently than users with single displays [4]. Grudin looks into dual-monitor situations [3] and observes that users do not use the additional monitor as "additional space", i.e. they rarely straddle a window across two monitors. Another observation in Grudin's work is that users distribute tasks among monitors; typically using one monitor for the "main" or "primary" task and using the other monitor for "secondary" or "other" tasks. All this suggests that having multiple displays should be effective for triage activity, wherein the user can use one of the displays for reading and the other display to see the document overview. Even though much work has gone into evaluating the efficacy of multiple displays for primary and peripheral tasks, few evaluations directly compare different display configurations for multi-application tasks requiring frequent shifts between applications.

User practice is likely to be impacted by the size of displays used, the distance between the primary and the secondary displays, and the resolution of the displays. The most common configuration is having two displays placed side by side, as occurs with most dual display desktop computers or when an external desktop monitor is attached to a notebook computer. A less common configuration is to have one display near the user and another larger display a few feet away. This occurs when a laptop computer is brought into a meeting room with a plasma or projected display. The first scenario means that the user will not have to readjust her focus when shifting from one display to another. In the second scenario, the user has to constantly refocus (because of the differing distance from the user to the two displays).

2.2 System/User -Assigned Roles

Subjects in the study referred to earlier [12] used a single monitor, requiring them to use the same display for both reading and document overview. Given the limited screen real estate of a desktop display, users most often used the entire screen for either reading or document overview. In other words, window overlapping was preferred over tiling of windows. With the introduction of dual/multiple displays for the task, there is the question of how the two displays should be controlled and how tasks should be allocated to the different displays. Should the user be able to move across the two screens seamlessly, i.e. is the "extended desktop" metaphor the most effective? For the second "multiple display" scenario mentioned above, would users prefer to read on the primary display and use the farther (bigger) display for document overview? Should fixed roles be assigned to the two displays, i.e. should there be a mechanism whereby the user is restricted to read on a particular display and manipulate the document overview on the other?

The following study includes three configurations with different combinations of positioning dual displays and user choice of activities on them.

3 Study Design

This study investigates the impact of display configuration on document triage practice. The study took place in the Center for the Study of Digital Libraries at Texas A&M University. Twenty four subjects were recruited via flyers and mass email. 96% of subjects were from the Computer Science Department and 87% were graduate students. From discussions with study participants it was determined that some of them had previous experience in working with multiple displays. Additionally, 96% were regular computer users for five or more years. Pre-task interviews indicated that while 80% of the subjects use computers to read informational web pages (i.e. short newspaper articles, reviews, magazines etc.), only 38% read long documents (i.e. a 20 page paper) on the screen.

The subjects were placed in the role of a research librarian that had to select and organize documents for a high school teacher preparing a class on ethnomathematics (the study of a group's culturally-specific mathematical practices as they go about their everyday activities). Subjects started with twenty documents returned from the National Science Digital Library (NSDL) and twenty documents returned from Google placed in lists in the Visual Knowledge Builder (VKB), a spatial hypertext system [11]. VKB allows users to organize information objects (links to websites in this study) in a hierarchy of two-dimensional workspaces. None of the subjects had prior experience with VKB and all were given a brief training session to explain the features considered relevant for this task. The forty links to the NSDL and Google documents as well as their arrangement on the VKB space as objects were the same for all subjects. The documents varied in their level of difficulty, relatedness to the topic and volume of information. Subjects were told to take as much time as necessary to complete the task.

This is the same task, setting, and topic as the study reported in [12]. Some of the documents changed between the two studies as the documents on the Web changed and our caches of these documents did not include all the document subcomponents (e.g. inline images, etc.) These changes were in the content of individual documents and unlikely to influence overall triage practice.

Fig. 2. Group 1 used laptop and tabletop LCD display

Fig. 3. Group 2 used laptop and projected display

Fig. 4. Group 3 used tablet and projected display

Subjects were randomly divided among three display configurations (table 2). In two of the configurations, subjects had a laptop as a focal display with an extra screen forming an extended desktop. The extra screen was a 17" LCD tabletop monitor placed next to the main display (figure 2) for the first group while the extra screen was a large projected display behind the laptop (figure 3) for group 2. In the third configuration, the focal display was a tablet PC while the large projected display was used as the extra screen (figure 4). The subjects of the first two configurations were able to control both screens via keyboard and mouse. They were also free to choose which displays would be for reading and which would be for the document overview. In the third configuration, each display had its own input and control devices (a pen for the tablet PC, and keyboard and mouse for the extra screen). Additionally, the role of each display was predetermined in the third configuration. Hence, subjects had to use the tablet PC for reading documents while the large projected display acted as a working space for organizing the links.

Table 2. Characteristics of three multiple display configurations in the study

Display Configuration	Input Devices	Assignment of Activity
Configuration 1: Laptop and tabletop LCD display.	Extended desktop controlled via keyboard and mouse.	User controls which windows are on which display.
Configuration 2: Laptop and projected display.	Extended desktop controlled via keyboard and mouse.	User controls which windows are on which display.
Configuration 3: Tablet computer and projected display.	Projected display controlled via keyboard and mouse, tablet controlled via pen.	Software assigns document overview to projected display and IE to tablet.

Only basic functionality from IE and VKB was necessary to examine and organize the forty documents. The subjects had to double-click on the VKB objects in order to open the related links and then, based on the content of the documents, organize the links into visual structures for the high school teacher. Participants had to determine their own criteria for including and excluding links and for creating the structures provided to the teacher. They were also free to add text or annotation to their structures in order to make them more understandable and complete.

A variety of data was collected during the study. Screen capture software was used to record on-screen activity on both displays. Video recordings from behind the subjects were recorded to determine the subjects' focus of attention. Additionally, user actions in VKB and IE were logged and provide event times, URLs and Internet Explorer window identifiers. After the task, subjects responded to questionnaires concerning their experience, asked to identify five high-value and five low-value documents from the task, and then took part in an interview based on their activity and answers to the questionnaire.

4   Results

The data below includes the three settings from this study as well as the single-display setting from our prior study when it is directly comparable to the current results. The next section includes results concerning the number of transitions between and time spent in the two applications based on log files and video analysis. After this are results examining the relationship between subjects' assessment of document value and their time and activity spent on documents. Finally, results related to subjects' overall perception of the task, the context, and their performance are presented.

4.1 Time Spent on Task and Number of Transitions

Determining the impact of display configuration on the number of transitions and time spent in VKB and IE required combining the results from the log files and videos. Log files provided data on the user interactions such as opening documents for reading, scrolling and mouse clicks in IE, and changes to the organization of links in VKB. To determine changes in subjects' focus of attention, it was also necessary to analyze the videotapes to identify when subjects switched attention between VKB and IE without causing events logged by either IE or VKB. This was primarily determined by changes in head and body position. One limitation is that it was sometimes difficult to recognize the head movement of subjects according to their individual styles in reading and organizing. This was particularly true in the laptop and LCD screen case because head movement was relatively subtle compared to the projected display configurations. We expect this increases the margin of error about the number of transitions in the laptop and LCD screen configuration.

Table 3. Time spent and number of transitions in four different configurations

	Prior Study	Current Study		
Configuration	Desktop PC	Laptop & LCD screen	Laptop & projected display	Tablet PC & projected display
# of displays	1	2	2	2
Avg. total time (sec)	3,309	3,554	3,642	4,234
Avg. time in VKB (sec)	2,359	2,453	2,627	3,005
Avg. time in IE (sec)	950	1,102	1,015	1,229
Avg. # of transitions	97	193	168	205
Avg. # of documents visited	Data not available	34.38	30.88	31.88

Time on Task. Average total time in the dual display configurations is 3,810 seconds, which is 15% higher than that in the single display configuration of 3,723 seconds. Normality tests indicated that the distribution of total time spent on task was normal but the time spent in IE was not. Thus, different statistical tests were necessary to assess significance. The difference in total time is not significant by t-test (p=0.365). Average total time of Tablet PC and projected display is the highest among the four configurations, but the difference is not significant by ANOVA test (p=0.575). Average time in IE in the dual display configurations is 1,115 seconds, which is 17% higher than that in the single display configuration of 950 seconds. However, this difference is not significant by Mann-Whitney test at significance level 0.05. Average time in IE of Tablet PC and projected display is the highest one among four configurations, but the difference is not significant by Kruskal-Wallis test at significance level 0.05.

In addition, we have examined the percentage of time in IE over total time: the percentage is consistent over the four configurations, around 30%.

Number of Transitions. On average, there were 189 transitions in the dual display configurations, compared to 97 on average in the single display configuration (Figure 5a). The difference is significant by t-test (p=0.002).

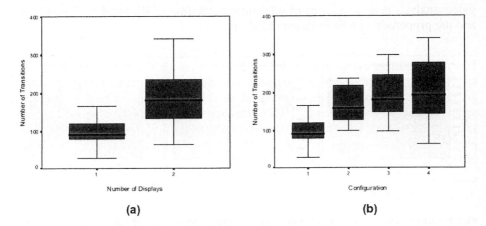

(a)   (b)

Fig. 5. Number of transitions for (a) different numbers of displays and (b) four different display configurations. The configurations in (b) are 1: Single Display (prior study), 2: Laptop and extra screen, 3: Laptop and projected display, 4: Tablet PC and projected display.

ANOVA test shows that average number of transitions among four configurations is not all equal (p=0.013). Post hoc tests (Turkey and LSD) show the single display configuration is significantly different from Laptop and Extra screen and Tablet PC and projected display, but not significantly different from Laptop and projected display at significance level 0.05. The average number of transitions for the Tablet PC and projected display is the highest among the three dual display configurations, but the post hoc tests show that the difference is not significant at significance level 0.05.

4.2   User Behavior in Reading and Evaluation of Documents

Each subject was given 20 documents from NSDL and 20 documents from Google, but did not read all the documents: they did not open 19% of the documents in IE.

Document Value and User Behavior. After subjects finished their tasks, they were asked to select the five least useful documents and the five most useful documents. To estimate overall document value, these results were aggregated. Each time a document was listed among the most useful documents, it was received 2 points. When it was listed among the least useful documents, it received 0 points. If not contained on either list, it received 1 point. We summed up document scores of each document and sorted documents by the document score.

Determining the time spent interacting with a particular document was complicated by the fact that the log files did not recognize transitions from reading in IE to looking at the document organization in VKB when subjects did not generate any events. This resulted in a significant overestimation of the time spent in IE and on reading documents. Video analysis indicated that this problem was primarily at the beginning and end of time spent in IE. Therefore, we built an algorithm to estimate the time spent in IE and the time spent in VKB in between logged events indicating a transition based on the results of the prior study. This estimation better matched the video analysis results in terms of total time, total time in IE, number of transitions, and the proportion of time in IE over total time.

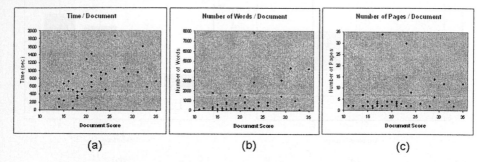

(a)   (b)   (c)

Fig. 6. Graphs showing document score and (a) time on documents, (b) the number of words in a document, and (c) the number of pages in a document

Figure 6a graphs the sum of time spent on each document across the 24 subjects and its accumulated document score. Correlation analysis shows that time spent is positively correlated to document score (Pearson coefficient=0.532 and p=0.001). As for document style, we examined the number of HTML links in a document, the number of images in a document, file size, the number of words in a document and the number of pages of a document, where the number of pages is the number of 1024x768 screens needed to display the document. Correlation analysis shows that the number of words and number of pages are both positively correlated to document score (Pearson coefficient=0.397 and 0.351, p=0.015 and 0.033). These graphs are shown in Figure 6b and 6c. Two subjects mentioned the length of documents as a characteristic when choosing the five most useful documents. We have not found any significant correlation between document score and other document style attributes.

We examined the correlation between document score and five user events: scrolls, mouse clicks, text selections, the number of times subjects followed embedded links on a document, and the number of visits on a document. Correlation analysis suggests that scroll event is highly correlated to document score as shown in Figure 7a (Pearson coefficient=0.632, p<0.0001). The number of visits on a document, mouse clicks, and text selections are positively correlated to document score (Pearson coefficient=0.480, 0.354, and 0.331, p=0.003, 0.034, and 0.049). However, the number of times subjects followed embedded links on a document is negatively correlated to its document score (Pearson coefficient=-0.334, p=0.040).

A variety of user behavior (time spent on documents, scrolls, mouse clicks, text selections, the number of times subjects followed embedded links on a document, and the number of visits on a document) and document attributes (the number of words and the number of pages) are correlated to the perceived value of documents.

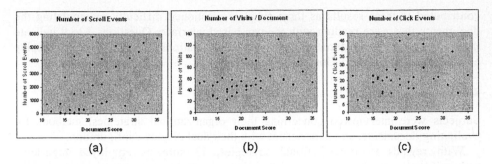

Fig. 7. Correlation between document score and (a) the number of scroll events, (b) the number of visits on a document, and (c) the number of click events

4.3 Questionnaire Results

Table 4 presents the results from five-point Likert scale questions regarding subjects' experience with the hardware and software where 1 was strongly disagree and 5 was strongly agree.

Table 4. User assessment of the display configurations: 1: Single Display (prior study), 2: Laptop and extra screen, 3: Laptop and projected display, 4: Tablet PC and projected display

	1	2	3	4
Q1: I feel comfortable reading documents on a computer.	N/A	4.1	3.3	3.3
Q2: It will be easy for someone else to understand the way I organized the documents.	4.1	3.9	3.5	3.9
Q3: It will be easy to go back later and understand the rationale behind my organization.	4.3	4.4	3.9	4.0
Q4: I enjoyed doing this task.	3.8	3.9	4.1	3.5
Q5: A tablet PC/laptop is effective in reading documents.	N/A	3.0	3.0	3.1
Q6: I was able to operate the tablet PC/laptop as I wanted.	N/A	3.4	4.3	3.3
Q7: It was easy doing the task with two displays.	N/A	4.1	4.4	4.0
Q8: Simultaneously viewing VKB and IE windows on different displays was helpful in reading documents.	N/A	4.1	4.4	4.4
Q9: Simultaneously viewing VKB and IE windows on different displays was helpful in organizing links.	N/A	4.1	4.1	4.1

Question 1 indicates that among the three dual display configurations, the subjects in Laptop and Extra Screen felt more comfortable over the subjects in other two configurations. This could be the result of the display characteristics of projected displays (e.g. decreased contrast and image quality) and the different focal distance for the user. The Tablet PC and projected display users had relatively low assessment of their task enjoyment (Question 4) and ability to operate the computers as they wanted (Question 6). We suspect that the pen-based interface in this configuration contributed to these results as three subjects mentioned difficulty manipulating the documents they were reading with the pen-based interface. Questions 7 to 9 indicate that subjects in all the three dual display configurations felt that the dual display environments were helpful for their given tasks.

4.4 Interview Results

Subjects were interviewed concerning their organizational strategies, methods for evaluating documents, and experiences with their dual display configuration.

With regards to organizational strategies, 13 subjects employed high-level categorization strategies such as dividing resources into books, papers, link collections, and by source of information. These high-level strategies limited the amount of reading required. 17 subjects employed categorization schemes based on an assessment of the content of documents such as their relevance, and whether they were introductory or professional. Notice that six subjects combined both high-level categorizations of documents and an assessment of their contents.

When asked about the evaluation of document value, 16 subjects mentioned characteristics of the content of documents: document providing a good introduction (7), documents giving information directly (7), and the amount of information (2). In contrast, only 3 subjects mentioned document structure or format (hierarchy, embedded links and document file format).

When asked about the role of document metadata provided in VKB, such as page title, page URL and summary, 14 subjects reported that they read the page title before reading documents. Among those 14 subjects, 4 paid attentions page URL as well, and 3 paid attentions to page URL and summary as well. 13 subjects examined the metadata after reading documents, while 4 subjects did not. However, the primary object of revisiting the metadata was to identify documents that they previously read. When we asked subjects what extra information would be useful in the document overview for a better understanding of the web site content, 9 subjects said keywords for the Web pages, while 7 subjects requested thumbnail images of the documents.

When asked about display configurations, 8 subjects preferred the two displays next to each another, while 7 subjects preferred a screen able to display more content. In addition, 5 subjects answered that they preferred one display in front and another display in the background.

5 Discussion

The data gathered from the study lends itself to observations concerning the impact of display configuration on document triage practice and the relationship between user activity and perceived document value.

Our central question on the impact of multiple displays on transitions between applications is partially answered by the data in Table 3. The number of transitions in the single display case is almost half the number of transitions in the dual display case (averaging over the three dual display cases). This would seem surprising at first, given that transitions were sources of interruption as the users had to deal with window management for every transition in the single display case; but the data indicates that users do not see transitioning between the two displays as bothersome, as the effort required in shifting attention between the two displays is negligible. With two displays, users chose to switch between the document overview and the document more often, perhaps working less from metadata. This and the positive responses received about the dual display configurations for questions Q7, Q8 and Q9 in the questionnaire suggest that having two displays is a more "natural" setting for document triage.

Comparing the average number of transitions between the three dual display configurations, it is seen that the number of transitions in the Laptop and Projected Display configuration (LPD) is the least, the number of transitions in the Tablet PC and Projected Display configuration (TPD) is the highest, and the number in Laptop and Extra Screen configuration (LES) was nearly as high as the TPD configuration. Even though the differences are not statistically significant, it is worthwhile to look at the factors influencing them. One difference between configurations LES and LPD is the focal distance between the primary and secondary displays. Since in LES both screens are at the same focal distance, being side by side, the effort required in shifting focus between the screens is lower compared to the LPD case. The qualitative data from the post-task interviews supports this hypothesis. When asked which display configuration they would prefer, many people (9 of the 17 asked, including 6 from the two subjects who had used the projected display configurations) answered "two screens, one next to the other". Some subjects also complained about the size of the projected display saying that it was annoying to look back and forth.

The difference in the number of transitions between configurations LPD and TPD may have been influenced by two characteristics of the configurations. The first difference is that there are two separate input devices in the TPD case (keyboard and mouse controlling the projected display, and the pen controlling the Tablet PC), whereas in the LPD case, the same keyboard and mouse act upon both displays. We expected that the need to switch between the different input devices might reduce the number of transitions in the TPD case. Clearly, this did not deter the subject's from transitioning between the two displays. The second difference between the LPD and TPD configurations is whether users could choose which display to use each activity. In the TPD configuration, the roles of the two displays are fixed, so when the user "opens" a document in the document overview on the projected display it is automatically presented on the tablet computer. This reduced the user's task of window management. Further study is necessary to determine the relative influence of the reduced overhead of window management and the increased effort of switching input devices in the TPD configuration.

The number of documents visited by the subjects in the LES configuration is slightly more than it is for the other two configurations. While not statistically significant, this may further indicate that having two displays at the same focal distance is better suited for a thorough and efficient triage activity.

One unexpected finding was that subjects with a single display took less time to finish the task, although not significantly, than subjects with multiple displays (see table 3). The fastest and the slowest group from those who used multiple screen settings (LES and TPD respectively) performed 7.4% and 28% slower than the group with the single display. A possible explanation is that subjects took advantage of the multiple screen environment and spent more time skimming and reading documents before organizing links. Without the window management disruption, subjects were more willing to switch views and make an effort at evaluating actual document content before judging the document's value.

But willingness to read document content was probably not the only determining factor in the added time for the TPD configuration. Many subjects had complaints and difficulties using the pen as a control device of the tablet PC (scrolling was reported as one of the most painful and time consuming tasks). Comments during post-task interviews as well as the responses to the question about ease of operating the hardware (Q6, table 4), and the question about enjoyment of task (Q4, table 4), indicate subjects preferred the mouse and keyboard while reading documents in IE.

Subjects spent a widely variable amount of time reading/scanning/skimming the content of individual documents. While this was expected, we were unclear how the extra attention a document receives is related to perceived document value. Would subjects quickly assess the best and worst documents and spend more time on those in the "middle of the pack", or would they become more critical of documents as they looked at them longer? The data analysis shows that the time spent in a document is positively related to the user's interest in the document. It is already known that reading time for in-depth reading is an indicator of user interest in a document ([1], [8]). Our data strengthens this previous finding; i.e. time spent in a document is an indicator of interest even when the user is skimming/scanning for the purpose of document triage.

There were also relations between perceived document value and certain user events, as was previously seen by Kelly and Belkin [6]. The number of scroll events to a particular document indicated a higher perceived document value. Also, we find the number of pages in a document and the number of words in a document to be related to user interest, as well. Document length seems to have strongly influenced these findings. In addition to these two objective measurements, document length likely impacted the number of scroll events of subjects.

In the interviews that followed the task, subjects were asked as to how they evaluated the usefulness/scope of documents they skimmed over. From the user feedback, page layout and content of the page play a vital role. Most users considered documents with a lot of text as authoritative. But opinion was divided on the usefulness of such documents based on subjects' interpretation of their task. Some users felt that as they were looking for introductory information on ethnomathematics for the high school teacher and determined that documents with a lot of detail were unnecessary. Others felt that the long and detailed documents provided the most information and thus were useful. Many of the users looked at the metadata information provided in VKB (document title and URL) before and after visiting Web pages. This suggests that they had expectations of what they would find at websites such as ethnomath.org, pages in the .edu domain, amazon.com links, and wordspy.com pages.

Pages of pointers to other documents were not perceived as valuable by subjects, as indicated by the number of followed links being negatively correlated to perceived document value. This was confirmed by subjects' comments indicating websites which simply referred to other sites, or which contained a lot of links without actually containing much information, were not useful.

6 Conclusions

Document triage is the practice of rapidly locating, skimming, selecting, and organizing documents for later use. The combination of the rapid nature of document assessment and the use of separate document overview and reading applications creates a large number of window transitions. By comparing document triage practice under multiple display configurations, it was determined that subjects transitioned between applications more often when using multiple displays than they did when using a single display. Additionally, users evaluated documents more by reading their contents and less often relied solely on metadata. Users spent more time reading and interacting with documents that they valued. This confirms prior research showing such correlations between time spent reading and assessed document value during in-depth reading carry over into the triage activity. [1]

References

1. Chan, P.: A Non-Invasive Learning Approach to Building Web User Profiles. In Workshop on Web Usage Analysis and User Profiling (1999) 7-12.
2. Czerwinski, M., Smith, G., Regan, T., Meyers, B., Robertson, G., Starkweather, G.: Toward characterizing the productivity benefits of very large displays. IOS Press, Proceedings of INTERACT (2003) 9-16.
3. Grudin, J.: Partitioning Digital Worlds: Focal and Peripheral Awareness in Multiple Monitor Use. Proceedings of CHI (2001) 458-465.
4. Hutchings, D.R., Smith, G., Meyers, B., Czerwinski, M., Robertson, G.: Display space usage and window management operation comparisons between single monitor and multiple monitor users. ACM Press, Proceedings of AVI (2004).
5. Joyce, M.: The lingering errantness of place. A talk given at the ACRL/LITA Joint Presidents Program, American Library Association, 114th Annual Conference, (1995).
6. Kelly, D., Belkin, N.J. Display time as implicit feedback: Understanding task effects. In Proceedings of SIGIR '04, Sheffield, UK, (2004) 377-384.
7. Marshall, C.C., Shipman, F.: Spatial Hypertext and the Practice of Information Triage. In Proceedings of ACM Hypertext (1997) 124-133.
8. Morita, M., Shinoda, Y.: Information filtering based on user behavior analysis and best match text retrieval. Proceedings of ACM SIGIR Conference. (1994) 272-281.
9. Rekimoto, J.: Pick-and-Drop: A Direct Manipulation Interface for Multiple Computer Environments. Proceedings of UIST (1997) 31-39.
10. Rekimoto, J., Saitoh, M.: Augmented Surfaces: A Spatially Continuous Workspace for Hybrid Computing Environments. Proceedings of CHI (1999).
11. Shipman, F., Hsieh, H., Airhart, R., Maloor, P., Moore, J.M.: The Visual Knowledge Builder: A Second Generation Spatial Hypertext. Proc. of Hypertext (2001) 113-122.
12. Shipman, F., Hsieh, H., Moore, J.M., Zacchi, A.: Supporting Personal Collections across Digital Libraries in Spatial Hypertext. Proceedings of JCDL (2004) 358-367.

---

[1] This work was supported in part by National Science Foundation grant DUE 02-26321.

Searching for Music: How Feedback and Input-Control Change the Way We Search

Tue Haste Andersen

Department of Computer Science, University of Copenhagen,
Universitetsparken 1, DK-2100 Copenhagen Ø, Denmark
haste@diku.dk

Abstract. The growing amount of digital music available at desktop computers and portable media players increases the need for interfaces that facilitate efficient music navigation. Search patterns are quantified and evaluated across types of feedback and input controllers in an experiment with 12 participants. The way music is searched and the subjective factors varied significantly across input device and type of audio feedback. However, no difference in task completion time was found for the evaluated interfaces. Based on the experiments, we propose several ways in which future designs may improve searching and browsing in recorded music.

1 Introduction

Today it is not uncommon to have a large collection of digital music available, some of which has never been heard by the user before. CD players and PC or mobile based media players offer only limited control of playback for browsing and searching in music. A way to quickly browse a large number of songs to find one that was heard on the radio or one that fits the user's musical preference and mood is needed. Content based retrieval [6] is often identified as the solution to this type of problem. However, content based retrieval requires an extensive amount of computing power and infrastructure, something that is not yet available as services to customers of consumer audio equipment. With better interfaces for browsing and listening to the music at the same time could help improve this situation.

As opposed to the somewhat primitive interface for music navigation offered by CD players and common computer based media players, several interfaces previously presented used information extracted from the audio signal to aid in navigating the music [9,2]. Goto proposed an interface to improve trial listening of music in record stores [7] where visualization and structure information was used. The interface was evaluated in an informal study where it was found that both the visual display and the structure jump functions were more convenient than the traditional CD player interface. However, we do not know if the increase in convenience was due to the use of segmentation information (meta-data), or because the visual display and better means of input control were provided.

M.F. Costabile and F. Paternò (Eds.): INTERACT 2005, LNCS 3585, pp. 144–157, 2005.
© IFIP International Federation for Information Processing 2005

This paper presents a baseline study that investigates the role of different types of aural feedback, along with different types of input control. The evaluation was done on both qualitative measures and observations, and on quantitative measures such as task completion time. The results can serve as guideline for future designs and research in music browsing interfaces.

In section 2 we review current interfaces and research in music browsing. Section 3 presents the experiment. In section 4 we discuss the results and its implications on future designs.

2 Interfaces for Browsing Audio and Music

In this section interfaces for browsing music is briefly reviewed, along with interfaces used in research of this area. A major difference between these interfaces is how the browsing interface is controlled. Different controller types are used, but little is known about how the controller influences the searching of music. Another area where these interfaces differ is in how audio feedback is presented during the search. Different audio synthesis methods for search feedback are described.

2.1 Today's Interfaces

In the following we classify today's interfaces for music browsing and searching based on their input device.

Buttons are probably the most common type of input controller used in interfaces for music browsing and searching. Standard CD players provide a set of buttons to control playback. Audio feedback is provided as the music is being played. In addition, a visual indication of the position in the current playing track is given together with the number of the current playing track. Buttons for play, pause, fast forward, fast backward, and previous and next track are provided. These functions are often combined into fewer buttons which activate different functions based on how long a button is pressed. CD players can play back audio in two modes: Normal playback mode, where the audio is played back at the speed at which it was recorded, and fast forward/backward mode where the audio is played at a faster speed than what is was recorded. Common scale factors are in between 4 and 5 times normal playback speed, although some players allow for even faster playback.

Sliders are most often used to control playback position in digital media players on PCs and portable devices. On PCs sliders are implemented as graphical widgets controlled with a mouse, but on media players the control is often done through a touchpad directly mapped to the graphical representation of the slider. Sliders provide random access to the play position within a track, as opposed to the buttons where the playback position can only be changed relative to the current position. The slider functions both as an input device and as visual and/or haptic display, giving feedback about the current play position relative to the length of the track. Media players also facilitate ways to browse music by title, album, or other meta-data if available.

Rotary controllers are used in DJ CD players, where they are referred to as jog wheels. Here the playback position can be changed relative to the current playback position. The rotary as implemented on DJ CD players allow for fine-grained control of the playback position, while at the same time the inertia of the rotary helps to move the play position to fast forward with little physical effort. The change from playback mode to fast forward or backward mode is not explicit as with the buttons, but continuous. The feedback is also changed continuously by linear interpolation or other interpolation methods that preserve pitch [11,10].

Sliders and buttons or other hybrid controllers are used for example in sound editors. Sound editors are application tools used by musicians and audio engineers that provide several ways to navigate within a music track. The mouse can be used to randomly change play position by clicking on a slider or waveform display, similar to the way play position is changed in a media player. Playback rate can often be adjusted, and finally sound editors provide better means of visual feedback in form of waveform displays supplemented by color codes [12] and spectrograms.

Because audio is tightly related to the time dimension, input controllers or widgets used in controlling audio playback are most often one dimensional. However, the controllers differ on how the absolute position can be changed. Sliders allow for fast random seek while buttons used on CD players do not. Active haptic feedback in input controllers for audio navigation has been used [13]. However it is not entirely obvious if this type of feedback can improve aspects of audio navigation [3].

2.2   Audio Feedback at Different Levels

Little research addresses the searching and browsing of music. For speech, Arons [2] presented an extensive study on the interface design in speech skimming. The design of Arons' SpeechSkimmer interface was based on the notion of a *time scale continuum*, where speech could be auralized using different time compression ratios, based on what type of skimming the user wanted. On the lowest level of the time-scale continuum was uncompressed speech, continuing to pause removal where the same signal was compressed by removing pauses. The highest level was pitch-based skimming where the individual words were no longer audible, but the pitch of the speaker's voice could still be perceived.

Interfaces for music browsing may benefit from a similar time scale continuum, because most music is characterized by repetitions at many different levels. First, most popular music has a beat, where percussive sounds often are repeated with an interval between 0.25 to 2 seconds. Second, music has a rhythm, a certain structure that the beat follows. Third, popular music is divided into sections so that verses are separated by a repeating chorus and other structures such as breaks.

When doing fast forward playback using CD players and sound editors, the sound is transformed in some way to allow for faster playback. In CD players, feedback serves mainly to inform the user that the fast forward mode is activated.

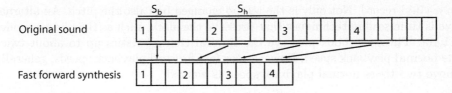

Fig. 1. Figure showing sound synthesis for fast forward as implemented in standard CD players. Blocks of samples (S_b) are copied from the original sound to the fast forward synthesis sound. The hop size (S_h) determines the scale factor.

The average volume level can still be perceived while playing in fast mode, but features such as rhythm, instrumentation and timbre are hard or impossible to perceive. In sound editors time scaling techniques [11,10] are used that preserve timbre and other features, but the interval between consecutive beats is changed. This can be a problem when the listener is searching for a song with a particular style or mood. Using a time scale continuum for music where local features such as rhythm and timbre are still perceivable while searching at high speed could therefore be a way to improve browsing interfaces.

2.3   Synthesizing Audio for Fast Forward Playback

The most widespread method to synthesize audio in fast forward mode from recorded audio is that of playing small chunks of audio with a block size, S_b between 5 and 20 msec, see Figure 1. The method is essentially an isochronous sampling of the audio. Blocks of audio are sampled from the original recording to form a new signal that is used for playback in fast forward mode [14]. Window functions can be used to smooth the transition from one frame to the next [5]. In backward searching, the individual frames are usually played in a forward direction. The method is used in most CD players today as it is suitable for implementing in a CD player with very limited further processing or buffering. The method is most often implemented with a fixed speed of four to five times the normal playback speed, but in principle it can be used at an arbitrary speed factor, by changing the hop size, S_h, shown on Figure 1. The fast forward audio synthesis as implemented on CD players serves at least two purposes: It allows for perception of some acoustic features while scanning, and it gives the user feedback about which mode is activated. When listening to fast forward synthesis on a CD player, the user is not in doubt that the CD is in fast forward mode. On CD players the block size S_b is very short, but it could be increased to allow for better perception of beat, rhythm and instrumentation at the expense of having a strong feedback about which mode the CD player is in. When increasing S_b to be in the range of seconds rather than milliseconds and increasing the speed by increasing S_h, the effect becomes close to a high level skimming of the music, similar to the high level skimming in the time scale continuum used in SpeechSkimmer.

Other alternatives to compressing music exist. Linear interpolation of the sample values effectively scales the audio in a similar way to changing the tempo on a vinyl record. Not only is the tempo changed but also the pitch. An alternative is time scaling techniques that preserve the pitch, such as the phase vocoder [11,10]. These methods preserve the timbral characteristics up to about twice the normal playback speed. However, for fast forward playback speeds, generally above two times normal playback speed is wanted.

3   Experiment: Comparing Interfaces for Mobile and Consumer Devices

In the experiment, participants had to search for a song containing an audio segment heard in advance. The task is similar to searching for a track heard on the radio. The interfaces used in this comparison are all applicable to audio consumer devices and a mobile usage situation. Two independent variables were used in a fully crossed experiment: Input controller and audio feedback. As reference, the CD player interface was compared with three other interfaces. We wanted to test if an input controller such as the rotary controller, which allowed for fast change of playback position when compared to the buttons on a CD player, resulted in fast task completion time and improved satisfaction. Second, we wanted to examine how much time was spent in fast forward mode when searching for a particular song, and how the audio feedback given during fast forward influenced the search performance and satisfaction.

3.1   Interface Design

We used two independent variables: Type of audio feedback (skip, play), and type of input controller (button, rotary). Each variable had two levels as described below.

Audio Feedback. The audio feedback during normal playback was the same in both levels of the feedback variable. When in fast forward or backward mode the audio feedback was synthesized using isochronous sampling as describe above. In the first condition, block size was the same as used on a CD player, $S_b = 10$ msec. The condition is referred to as "skip" because it sounds like the CD read head is skipping. The other level of the feedback variable we choose to refer to as "play" where the block size is one second. In both cases, the step size between each block played is adjusted according to the movement speed. The two types of feedback are fundamentally different, in that "skip" results in a strong sensation of moving forward, but makes it impossible to perceive most features of the music. Play feedback on the other hand does not give a strong sensation of the movement speed, but local features such as rhythm and instrumentation can still be perceived.

Input Control. One level was a set of five buttons, referred to as "buttons," identical to the input method found on most CD players. There was a pair of buttons for switching to previous and next track, a pair of buttons for moving at fast backward or forward, and finally a button controlling playback/pause mode. The fast backward and forward buttons moved at four times normal playback speed. The second condition was the use of a PowerMate[1] rotary controller ("rotary"); moving the rotary knob to either left or right initiated a fast forward or backward operation. The speed at which the rotary was moved determined the movement speed (rate). Playback/pause was controlled by pressing the non-latching button built into the knob. There are two fundamental differences between these two interfaces: The input controller and the mapping. The mapping used with the rotary controller allows for a continuous change of the fast forward playback speed, while the mapping used with the buttons provide one fixed fast forward speed and the ability to do a non-linear jump to the next track. We chose to use different transfer functions for the two input controllers to achieve natural mappings. However, this could have been avoided by mapping the rotary controller to a constant fast forward speed regardless of the speed at which the rotary was operated, and to jump to the next track when above a certain threshold.

Before the experiment, we hypothesized that the play feedback would be superior to skip feedback. The time spent in fast forward mode could be used to listen to local features of the music and could potentially provide more useful information than the skip feedback. Also, we expected the rotary controller to be superior in terms of performance compared to the buttons, primarily because the buttons only allowed a constant, and relatively slow, fast forward speed. With the rotary it would be possible to quickly move to a different part of the track, but on the other hand would require slightly more effort to move to the next track. We decided to do a fully crossed experiment because we did not know if the audio feedback would influence the task performance in any way, depending on the type of controller.

The interfaces were developed using the software Mixxx [1], but with a modified user interface. In the experiment we sought to minimize the influence of visual feedback, and provide a usage situation similar to mobile music devices. Thus we only provided visual information about which track was currently loaded, the absolute position inside the track, and the length of the current loaded track.

3.2   Tasks

We used 20 tasks; each participant completed five tasks in each condition. Each task consisted of a list of nine tracks selected from the Popular, Jazz and Music genre collection of the RWC Music Database [8]. The database was used to ensure that the participants had not heard the music before, and to get a representative selection of popular music. For the 20 tasks, a total of 180 unique music tracks were used. For each task, the list of tracks was constructed in such a way that the tracks were reasonably similar in style, but there was no logical order to the tracks in each list. The music varied in style between tasks, some were instrumental, and some was sung in English and others in Japanese. The 20 tasks were divided into four groups so that each group contained five tasks. In

---

[1] See http://www.griffintechnology.com/products/powermate/

the experiment each group was used in one condition. The four groups were always presented in the same order, but the order of the four conditions was balanced using a Latin square pattern.

The target track of each task was selected randomly, but ensuring that the average target in each group was at position 5 in the track list. This was done to ensure that the groups were close to each other in terms of task complexity.

For each task, the participant was presented with a 10 second long audio excerpt of the target track. The excerpt was chosen to contain the refrain or other catchy part of the song and could be heard as many times as the participant wanted. The participants were required to hear it three times in succession before starting to search for the corresponding song. They were also allowed to hear the except during the search if they had forgot how it sounded. They could navigate the songs using the interface provided, and pressed a button when they had found the song from which the audio excerpt was taken.

3.3   Design and Setup

A fully-crossed within-subjects factorial design with repeated measures was used. Twelve people participated in the experiment. Their musical skills ranged from being a professional musician to having no particular interest in music, with most participants having no musical skill. Independent variables were feedback and input control type. We used two types of dependent variables:

Task Performance. Completion time, error in identification, and time spent in fast forward/backward mode.

Subjective Satisfaction. Rating on five scales based on Questionnaire for User Interface Satisfaction [4] related to ease of use, learning and aesthetics. The scales are shown in table 1.

The experiment was conducted in a closed office, using a computer with CRT screen and attached studio monitors. Studio monitors were chosen over headphones to allow for easy observation of the participants during the experiment. The participants completed one training task followed by five tasks in each condition. After each condition, they rated the interface on the five subjective satisfaction scales before proceeding to the next condition. At the end of the experiment, they could adjust the ratings of all interfaces. The experiment was concluded with an open ended interview. During the experiment, an observer was present and the interaction was logged.

3.4   Results: Task Performance

The data was analyzed using analysis of variance with feedback and input control as independent variables, and task completion time, number of errors and time spent in fast forward mode as dependent variables. To examine how the individual tasks influenced the experiment, and to look for learning effects, an analysis was also performed with task as an independent variable.

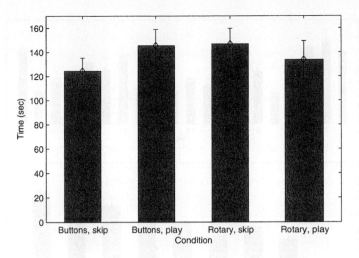

Fig. 2. Mean time used in each condition

Figure 2 shows the mean and standard deviation of the completion time in seconds for each condition. No significant difference was found for feedback, $F(1, 11) = 0.000, p = .998$ or input control, $F(1, 11) = 0.022, p = .885$. However, when looking at the completion time as a function of task there was a significant difference, $F(19, 209) = 4.493, p \leq .001$. This is also shown in Figure 3 (top). A post-hoc comparison using a Bonferroni test at a 0.05 significance level revealed that task 2 and 7 differed significantly at $p = .037$, task 2 and 17 at $p = .039$ and finally task 3 and 19 at $p = .046$. During the experiment, it was observed that for some participants there was a large learning effect in the first few tasks, whereas others did not seem to improve during the course of the experiment. The significant difference between some of the tasks is likely caused by a combination of long completion time (learning) for the first three tasks, as seen on Figure 3 (top), and from the difference in target track position. The target track in task 17 and 19 is track 2 and 3, respectively, which means that the completion time on average is relatively short, since only one or two tracks has to be searched before the target is reached. In comparison, the target track of task 2 and 3 is track number 9 and 6, respectively, where a long completion time is observed.

On figure 3, (bottom) completion time is plotted as a function of target track rather than task. There indeed seems to be a correlation between completion time and distance to target.

Number of errors did not change significantly across feedback, $F(1, 11) = 0.316, p = .585$, and input control, $F(1, 11) = 0.536, p = .496$. Error across task was significant at $F(19, 209) = 2.257, p = .003$, however, no learning effect or other systematic effect was observed.

Figure 4 shows time spent in search mode (fast forward or backward) for the four conditions. The time spent in search mode varied significantly depending on feedback, $F(1, 11) = 9.377, p = .011$, and input control, $F(1, 11) = 7.352, p = .020$. This reveals that even though task completion time did not vary with

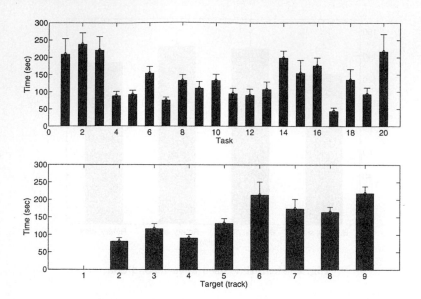

Fig. 3. Completion time as a function of task (top) and as function of target track (bottom)

interface and feedback, the participants' search patterns did. Figure 4 shows that the search time spent in the Buttons, Play condition was almost double that of the other conditions.

Figure 5 shows four examples of the search patterns in task 16, one for each condition. Position is shown as a function of time, and red circles mark where the user is engaged in a search action. Comparing the two button conditions, it is evident that in the examples shown, more time is spent in search mode in the play condition. Comparing the button conditions (top) to the rotary conditions, (bottom) a clear difference in search strategy is visible. In the rotary conditions, more parts of each track are heard by jumping forward in the track. In the button condition this is not possible without spending a lot of time, because the fast forward speed is only four times normal playback speed compared to the adjustable search speed with the rotary controller. In the rotary conditions, no immediate difference that can be explained by other observations is visible. The feedback does not seem to influence the search behavior here.

3.5   Results: Subjective Satisfaction

The ratings on the subjective satisfaction scales were analyzed using analysis of variance on each scale. The scales used in the subjective evaluation are shown in Table 1, along with F and p values for the independent variables interface and feedback. The mean ratings for each condition is shown in Figure 6. The input method influenced most of the scales. Buttons were more frustrating and more terrible than was the rotary. Both input method and feedback type were

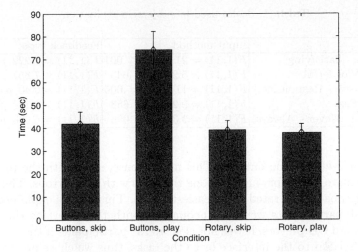

Fig. 4. Mean time used in search mode in each condition

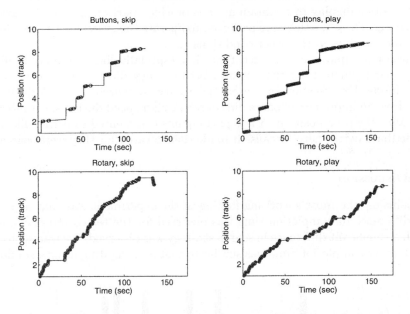

Fig. 5. Example. Position as a function of time plotted for one trial of each condition of task 16.

significantly different on the scale of Terrible-Wonderful, and buttons with play feedback were more wonderful than buttons with skip feedback. The case was the same for the rotary controller, and the rotary controller was overall more wonderful than the buttons. Many participants commented that they did not know how to interpret the responsiveness scale, but there is a significant difference across input type. On average, the participant perceived the rotary to be

Table 1. Scales used in subjective evaluation

Scale	Input method	Feedback type
Frustrating - Satisfying	$F(1,11) = 21.154, p \leq .001$	$F(1,11) = 1.222, p = .293$
Terrible - Wonderful	$F(1,11) = 5.260, p = .043$	$F(1,11) = 7.857, p = .017$
Not responsive - Responsive	$F(1,11) = 11.875, p = .005$	$F(1,11) = 0.40, p = .845$
Difficult - Easy	$F(1,11) = 0.208, p = .658$	$F(1,11) = 0.268, p = .615$
Straightfwd. (Never - Always)	$F(1,11) = 3.313, p = .096$	$F(1,11) = 6.600, p = .026$

more responsive than the buttons. This makes sense, since with the rotary it is possible to move faster forward in a song than it is with the buttons. The buttons with skip feedback was rated to be easiest to use. This can be explained by the fact that all participants were well acquainted with this interface through the use of standard CD players. It was not clear to the participants if the straightforward scale related to the interface or to the tasks; thus we chose not to analyze it further. Finally two participants commented that it was difficult to use the play feedback with the rotary controller because they were forced to look at the visual position display to maintain an idea of which part of the song the system was playing. These participants preferred to operate the system with eyes closed, which was possible in the other conditions.

Three participants commented that they especially liked the play feedback during search when using the buttons, because they did not have to leave the search mode. Few participants used the rotary to search at a relatively low speed. Instead many participants did search at high speed during short intervals to advance the play position. A few participants commented that they liked the skip feedback better here, because it made them aware that they were searching.

3.6   Discussion

In conclusion, the most surprising finding of the experiment was that no significant difference in completion time was observed for the tested interfaces, even though a significant difference in search strategy was observed. We wanted to test if the average completion time was similar to that of navigating using a sound ed-

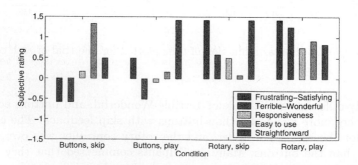

Fig. 6. Subjective ratings of the 4 interfaces on scales ranging between -2 and 2

itor with a waveform display and play position control through a graphical slider widget operated with a mouse. Therefore, we conducted a new experiment with six participants from the previous experiment. An informal comparison showed that no significant difference was observed. This indicated that the task completion times reported in this experiment is not likely to be affected by further improvement of visual feedback or controller input type.

We found that on average participants spent 35% of their time in search mode. There was a significant difference in how people used the interfaces, with participants spending significantly more time in search mode for the condition with button interface and play feedback. In the two conditions with skip feedback, it was hard to perceive features of the music. This explains why less time was used in search mode for these conditions, compared to the Play, Button condition. However, it is somewhat surprising that with play feedback, only the buttons resulted in more time spent in search mode. With the buttons it was only possible to move fast forward in a track by four times the normal playback speed, compared to an almost arbitrary fast forward speed using the rotary. Using the rotary, most users would move forward in a short time interval at fast speed, then stop the rotary motion to hear part of the song. Only a few participants moved slowly forward using the rotary to take advantage of the play feedback. Two problems were evident from the way the participants used the rotary with play feedback: first, no immediate feedback was given that a search was initiated or in progress. Only after one second of spinning the rotary was feedback audible. Second, to keep a constant fast forward speed, the participant would have to spin the rotary at a constant speed, and thus keep the hand in motion, as opposed to using the buttons, where constantly holding down a button would result in a constant fast forward speed. This suggests that a rate based mapping rather than a position based mapping might be a better alternative when using the play feedback scheme.

A large significant difference was found in how participants perceived the interfaces. In general, the play feedback was liked over skip feedback, and the rotary was preferred over the buttons. It is interesting that the responsiveness scale was not influenced significantly by feedback type, but a significant difference was observed for input control. Some participants commented that the perceived responsiveness was influenced by the type of feedback. In particular, one participant commented that he could not use the rotary with play feedback with eyes closed, because he lacked feedback about the playback position in the song. Overall, it seemed that the type of input control was more important than the type of feedback given to how participants liked the interface. The rotary was rated more satisfying and wonderful than the buttons. This may be due to aesthetic factors of the input controller, where the buttons was implemented using a standard keyboard, and the rotary was utilizing the PowerMate controller in aesthetically pleasing brushed metal. Another explanation could be that the mapping used with the rotary allowed for rapidly seeking to an arbitrary position in the track.

4   Conclusions

This study focused on feedback and input when searching in recorded music. We presented a novel feedback method, the "play" feedback, where segments of one second were played during fast forward or backward mode. The "play" feedback allowed for aural scanning of local features of music such as rhythm and timbre, while searching at fast speed. The method allows for perception of local features and seamlessly integration of structural information when available. The feedback method was compared to the "skip" feedback, identical to the feedback given by ordinary CD players. The two types of feedback were compared with two input controllers, one based on buttons and other based on a rotary controller, in a fully crossed experiment.

The most surprising finding of the experiment was that we did not observe a significant difference in task completion time or number of errors between any of the tested conditions. To get an indication of the performance of the tested interfaces we compared them to the performance of a state of the art interface, similar to interfaces implemented in sound editors. In the informal experiment, no significant difference was found in task completion time and number of errors. This indicates that no immediate gain in search performance can be expected by providing better means of input control or visual feedback.

However, we did find a significant difference between feedback type and input control for the time spent in search mode. The interfaces using buttons as input control and the "play" feedback did result in a significantly higher portion of the time spent in fast forward mode compared to the other interfaces. Thus, in this condition, the participants had more time where it was possible to perceive features such as timbre, instrumentation and rhythm. A similar increase in time spent in search mode was not observed for the rotary controller with "play" feedback. This can be explained by the fact that the rotary controller allowed for faster change of playback position. Thus ordinary play feedback was needed earlier than one second after a search action was initiated.

We observed large significant differences in how the interface was perceived by the participants. On average participants found the rotary controller more satisfying, wonderful and responsive than the buttons. The "play" feedback was also significantly more wonderful than the "skip" feedback. During the open ended interviews, several participants commented that the play feedback was better than skip feedback, but did not result in a feeling of moving forward. Future interfaces may thus improve on both satisfaction and responsiveness by mixing the "play" and "skip" audio signal into one. Other ways to further improve the feedback could be to use segmentation information to jump only to places where the music changes, and to use beat information to perform the isochronous sampling relative to the beat phase, to ensure a smooth transition from one block to the next.

We know from research in speech navigation that meta data can improve search performance [2] and that meta data in musical interfaces influences subjective evaluation of the interface in a positive way [7]. However, we do not have any evidence that it will actually improve performance in music navigation in search tasks, even though it intuitively seems likely.

Acknowledgments

I would like to thank members of the HCI group at DIKU, in particular Kasper Hornbæk for his insight during the planning of the experiment and for feedback on the manuscript, as well as Georg Strøm who provided valuable feedback during the writing of the paper.

References

1. T. H. Andersen. In the Mixxx: Novel digital DJ interfaces. In *Proceedings of CHI 2005*, pages 1136–1137. ACM Press, April 2005. Demonstration and extended abstract.
2. B. Arons. SpeechSkimmer: A system for interactively skimming recorded speech. *ACM Transactions on Computer-Human Interaction*, 4(1):3–38, March 1997.
3. T. Beamish, K. Maclean, and S. Fels. Manipulating music: multimodal interaction for DJs. In *Proceedings of CHI*, pages 327 – 334, 2004.
4. J. Chin, V. Diehl, and K. Norman. Development of an instrument measuring user satisfaction of the human-computer interface. In *Proceedings of CHI*, pages 213–218, 1997.
5. G. Fairbanks, W. Everitt, and R. Jaeger. Method for time or frequency compression-expansion of speech. *Trans. Inst. Radio Eng. Prof. Group Audio AU-2*, pages 7–12, 1954. Reprinted in G. Fairbanks, Experimental Phonetics: Selected Articles. University of Illinois Press, 1966.
6. J. Foote. An overview of audio information retrieval. *Multimedia Systems*, 7(1):2–10, 1999.
7. M. Goto. SmartMusicKIOSK: Music listening station with chorus-search function. In *Proceedings of UIST*, pages 31–40, 2003.
8. M. Goto, H. Hashiguchi, T. Nishimura, and R. Oka. RWC music database: Popular, classical, and jazz music databases. In *Proceedings of ISMIR*, pages 287–288, 2002.
9. D. Kimber and L. Wilcox. Acoustic segmentation for audio browsers. In *Proceedings of Interface Conference*, 1996.
10. J. Laroche and M. Dolson. New phase-vocoder techniques for real-time pitch shifting, chorusing, harmonizing, and other exotic audio modifications. *J. Audio Eng. Soc.*, 47(11):928–936, 1999.
11. M. Portnoff. Time-scale modifications of speech based on short-time fourier analysis. *IEEE Transactions on ASSP*, 29(3):374–390, 1981.
12. S. Rice and M. Patten. Waveform display utilizing frequency-based coloring and navigation. U.S. patent 6,184,898, 2001.
13. S. Snibbe, K. MacLean, R. Shaw, J. Roderick, W. Verplank, and M. Scheeff. Haptic techniques for media control. In *Proceedings of UIST*, pages 199–208, 2001.
14. T. Yokota, N. Kihara, and J. Aramaki. Disc playback method. US patent 5,553,055, September 1996. Sony Corporation.

Galactic Dimensions: A Unifying Workstyle Model for User-Centered Design

Pedro Campos and Nuno J. Nunes

University of Madeira,
Campus da Penteada, 9000-390 Funchal, Portugal
{pcampos,njn}@uma.pt

Abstract. This paper describes a new unifying workstyle model for the user-centered design process, comprised of eight dimensions that we claim as fundamental to supporting the UCD process. Our proposal is new because it is the first workstyle model tailored to UCD. We also show the usefulness of workstyle modeling when evaluating the stage/effort of a project at a given time. Our workstyle model was based on the identification of the main obstacles to UCD and SE integration, current research results and extensive observation of HCI students involved in UCD projects. Though simple, it models the designer's behavior and can be effectively and easily used to (a) choose adequate tool support for a given phase of a project and (b) drive the development of new UCD tools.

1 Introduction

User-Centered Design (UCD) is a process that fosters the participation of users in designing and evaluating a system, in order to obtain products that are better suited to users' expectations. However, after almost two decades of UCD tools and techniques research, its adoption remains limited to large organizations and practitioners who recognize its value [6].

Despite all the research efforts dedicated to bringing better tools to the industry, designers still consider tools don't meet their needs [8]. After more than a decade, CASE tools have not been widely used [7], although the market is rapidly growing [6]. Despite of limited CASE tool adoption, there is evidence that the technology improves, to a reasonable degree, the quality of documentation, the consistency of developed products, standardization, adaptability, and overall system quality [4]. It has been argued that future tools should be based on sound models of a software process and user behavior, and should support both creative aspects as well as rigorous modeling [6].

Workstyle modeling [14] has been proposed as a technique to record the interaction style of a group of collaborators during any software development activity. UCD is an iterative, evolutionary process. This means designers often engage in different workstyles as they iterate towards the final design. This is why we claim that modeling the styles of work can be particularly useful in UCD. It has been widely recognized that current User Interface (UI) tools don't support the designers' activities, in particular it has been argued that UI tools suffer from limited combinations of

M.F. Costabile and F. Paternò (Eds.): INTERACT 2005, LNCS 3585 , pp. 158 – 169, 2005.

threshold ("how hard is it to learn?") and ceiling ("how much can be done?") [10]. There is clearly room for benefits here, since it has been shown that a UI development tool has the potential to influence between 50% and 70% of the application code [10].

Constantine and Lockwood [2] described their ideas of "galactic dimensions" as a metaphor change towards fully interconnected and synchronized visual development tools. Traditional CASE tools were based on a metaphor referred to as the "glass drawing board", since they merely represented two-dimensional paper models on the glass surface of a monitor. The "glass galaxy" was then proposed as a multidimensional problem-solving space in which developers could drill down into objects in one dimension, and be taken via software "worm holes" to another. Clicking on a use case could take the developer to its definition in a glossary. Selecting that use case could also show the abstract components that support it, or the concrete widgets for a given realization of that model. Even entries in help files could be linked to the user roles they support, or to the actual code and visual UI controls.

We take this idea further and argue for CASE tools supporting "galactic" dimensions: tools that not only support fast accelerated development through traceability and integration, but also are able to rapidly adjust to any given workstyle in a transparent way. We propose a new workstyle model comprised of eight "galactic" dimensions that we consider as fundamental to supporting the UCD process. Our proposal is new because it is the first time workstyle modeling is applied to UCD and our model can be used to estimate the stage/effort of development in a graphically intuitive way. Another contribution of our paper is that we also show how effective workstyle modeling can be to drive the development of new UCD tools or to choose tool support for a given project phase.

Our workstyle model was based on the identification of the main obstacles to UCD and SE integration [12], current research results and extensive observation of Human-Computer Interaction (HCI) students involved in a UCD project. It incorporates two renamed dimensions from [14], (Asynchrony and Distribution), and two of the modeling-style dimensions from [13] (Perspective and Formality). We introduced three more dimensions (Detail, Functionality and Traceability) and unified these dimensions into a common, coherent model, where the axes fall into one of these categories: collaboration style, notation style or tool-usage style.

This paper is organized as follows: in the next section, we describe related work on models and taxonomies for software design and UI design. Section 3 describes our new workstyle model for UCD and Section 4 illustrates how it graphically conveys information regarding the stage of development of the UCD process. In Section 5, we apply our model to several representative tools and claim that current successful tools are those that can better adjust and support any region of our model. Finally, in Section 6, we draw some conclusions and outline work that might bring benefits to both SE and UCD.

2   Related Work

Software design (which includes interaction design) is often a team activity and most projects involve stakeholders with different backgrounds that must cooperate in many different and interrelated activities.

Wu and Graham [14] describe a novel model for recording the working style of people using an interactive system. Workstyle modeling complements task modeling by providing information on how people communicate and coordinate their activities, and by showing what style of artifact is produced.

The workstyle model was developed in the context of the Software Design Board project, a project aiming to provide better tools for software design. The model was validated through evaluation of existing design tools, and motivated the design of a new software design tool. It is comprised of eight axes: four of them describe collaboration style (Location, Synchronicity, Group Size and Coordination); the remaining four describe the nature of the artifact being produced (Syntactic Correctness, Semantic Correctness, Archivability and Modifiability).

The workstyle model for software design has the advantage of being simple to apply and clearly showing where a tool can fail to match the intended work context. However, it is not sufficient for capturing UI specific activities. Transitions (or shifts) in the workstyles of interaction designers are more frequent and more intense than in any other software design activity.

Traeetteberg [13] claims that current UCD tools should be able to cover a three-dimensional cube of Perspective (moving from problem/requirements space to the solution/design), Granularity (from high level to low level) and Formality (formal, i.e. machine-understandable versus informal i.e. context-dependent). It is suggested that in the course of designing an interface, several languages have to be used to cover all the needed perspectives (see Figure 1).

As an example, Traeetteberg [13] suggests one interpretation of the granularity level across different perspectives, as can be seen on the left side of Figure 1. A task is performed to achieve a goal, and is often supported by a specific component composed of dialogue elements, which is placed in a pane containing widgets.

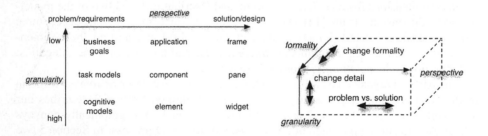

Fig. 1. Left: an interpretation of the granularity versus perspective. Right: movements in the representation framework of Traeetteberg [13].

Cognitive Dimensions [5] have been proposed both as an evaluation technique for visual programming environments and as a discussion tool for designers. This technique concentrates on the activities rather than the finished product. However, it is limited to the information artifacts of visual programming languages.

Prototyping techniques still leave a considerable gap between the inception level models of user intentions (task cases, use cases, scenarios and other requirements level models) and the concrete user interface. The center ellipse in Figure 2 illustrates this gap. A growing awareness of this conceptual gap lead Constantine and colleagues to develop a new language for visual and interaction design, called Canonical Abstract Prototypes [2]. This language fills the gap between existing inception level techniques, such as the illustrated UML-based interaction spaces or visual content inventories, and construction level techniques such as concrete prototypes.

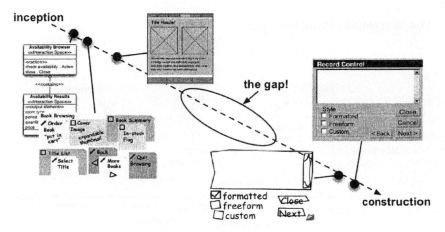

Fig. 2. Prototyping techniques from inception to construction (adapted from [2])

All of these models support the need for a unifying reference framework under the context of UCD processes. They also reflect the importance of considering these several dimensions into the design process of UCD tools. However, these models are too specific and are not expressive enough to be applied more generally to UCD. This is why we expand them and combine the most significant dimensions of some of them: to obtain a more useful and usable model that has more meaning by conveying more information in a better way. In the next section, we will describe our new workstyle model and illustrate its applications.

3   A Workstyle Model for User-Centered Design

There are eight continuous axes in our "galactic" workstyle model for UCD. These axes are grouped under three main categories:

- **Notation** style-related dimensions (Perspective, Formality and Detail),
- **Tool usage** style-related dimensions (Traceability, Functionality and Stability) and
- **Collaboration** style-related dimensions (Asynchrony and Distribution), as shown in Figure 3.

In this section, we briefly describe each of these dimensions and provide a set of questions that can act as guidelines to apply the model to tools, notations or, in general, styles of work adopted by interaction designers.

Perspective. This axis plots the perspective, or view, of the artifact being developed. **Questions:** is the notation capable of expressing business goals? Or non-functional requirements such as customer experience requirements? Does it help define the purpose of the system? Does it describe interaction aspects of the system? How close is it to the final product?

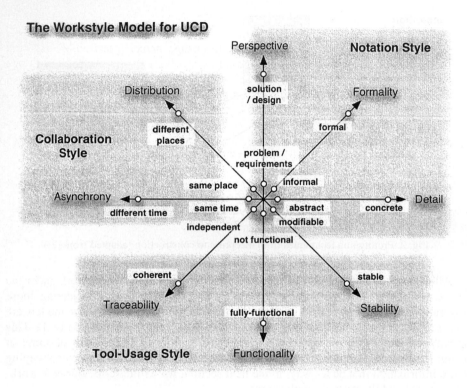

Fig. 3. A unifying workstyle model for user-centered design

Formality. This axis classifies the workstyle of a designer creating artifacts in a formal vs. informal way. In the early stage of the process, designers use rough, ambiguous sketches to freely express ideas quickly [8]. This workstyle also fosters comparison of design alternatives and creativity, since the uncertainty of sketches encourages the exploration of design ideas. As design progresses, a more formal style of work is incrementally adopted, as designers need to focus on the precise meaning of their models. An example of this shift is moving from a whiteboard to a CASE tool. **Questions:** how easy is it to define rough ideas? Does the meaning matter? Does the notation force you to use a rigid syntax/semantics?

Detail. We added this axis to plot the level of detail (or abstraction) the designer is working at. High-level, abstract models facilitate problem solving in organization, navigation and overall structure of the UI, leaving aside the details. On the other hand, realistic (or figurative) prototypes address high-detail design issues [3]. Disciplined designers tend to assume a workstyle that goes from higher-level abstract representations towards more realistic and detailed representations as the process evolves [3].

Questions: can you abstract irrelevant details using the notation? Can you think about navigation and structure of the overall interaction using the notation? Can you incrementally add enough detail?

Stability. This dimension describes how difficult/frequent it is to modify any aspect of the artifact(s) being developed. A content inventory of the UI modeled in a UML tool is highly modifiable because it is easy to change names, positioning, size and other aspects of the elements. This is opposed to drawing a model of the UI with pen and paper, since changes are harder to accomplish. Brainstorming, for instance, is a very unstable workstyle because changes are very frequent. High values in this axis indicate less frequent or less significant changes.

Questions: How easy is it to modify previously created artifacts using the tool? How frequently do you make those changes? Are there particular changes difficult to accomplish with the tool?

Traceability. This is a new dimension we introduce. It describes if the elements of the artifact being developed are consistent and interconnected (thus being highly traceable) or if they are completely unrelated and independent. As an example, developers might adopt a workstyle in which they choose to keep links from task cases steps and the concrete UI widgets that implement those task steps. In this case, it is possible to trace a task step to the concrete widget and to trace a widget to the task step it implements. This dimension is closely related to stability and the number of artifacts produced during a project. As they increase, traceability becomes more important.

Questions: Are you using the tool to maintain interconnections between model elements? How important is it to navigate through your model? Does the tool maintain several different views in a synchronized way (e.g. design view and code view)?

Functionality. This is also a new dimension we introduced. It represents how much functionality is being addressed (by using the tool to build a prototype). There is a barrier between software engineers and usability professionals regarding this matter: software engineers are engaged into building reliable, functional systems, leaving user-friendliness to the usability specialists. Usability and interaction designers, on the other hand, first design and test the interface with end-users, leaving implementation to software engineers, regarded as functionality builders. Those two processes should not be separated [12] and considering this dimension will help overcome that barrier. This dimension is also important because designers combine visual design (presentation issues) with interaction design (behavior issues).

Questions: How much functionality, behavior and dynamics can you add to your prototypes using the tool? How easy is it to test the interaction by using the tool?

Asynchrony. This axis refers to the collaboration style that designers assume: they can make changes to the work being developed at the same time (a *synchronous* workstyle) or they can work at different times (engaging in an *asynchronous* workstyle) [14]. The higher the value in this axis, the more asynchronous is the workstyle.

Questions: do the team members change artifacts at the same time? Or do they make changes at different times? How frequently?

Distribution. This dimension describes whether work is being conducted at the same physical location or at geographically distant locations.

Questions: how far are the team members collaborating? Are they in the same building? Or are they in a different continent, or scattered through a country?

These dimensions can be effectively used to assess a given workstyle adopted by an interaction designer or a team. A single workstyle is plotted as a line (a point in the eight-dimensional space) whereas regions (or planes) represent sets of workstyles.

4   Using the Model to Assess a UCD Project Effort

In general terms, it seems reasonable to say that as the process evolves, designers tend to assume a workstyle that spreads them away from the center of our model.

Under the *perspective* axis, for example, it is clear that as time goes by, developers move from the domain/problem level towards the solution/design space. In terms of *formality*, they start out with informal, ambiguous sketches and move to formal languages later on, when coding increases and functionality becomes more important. Under the *detail* dimension, as we have already seen, skilled designers tend to go from higher-level abstract representations towards more realistic and detailed representations as the process evolves.

Also, as the deadline approaches, prototype *functionality* is added (and is needed for user testing and customer delivery). In an initial phase, designers don't spend much effort on functionality: it is more important to rapidly compare design alternatives. In addition, as time goes by, ideas start to solidify and changes become more incremental, rather than dramatic (thus increasing *stability*). Under the *traceability* axis, the number of artifacts increases, and so does the number of inter-connections between them, which motivates the need for increased traceability. This also happens because developers are not interested in throwing away the models (as in brainstorming) but rather in keeping all models created so far in a coherent state.

Under a collaboration style perspective, the transition may not be so straightforward. Nevertheless, as development tasks get larger and work allocation is made, there is a tendency to work asynchronously and at different places (thus increasing the workstyle value on the Asynchrony and Distribution dimensions), because developers feel the need to focus and split work.

As we will see in Figure 4, one of the advantages of our model is the fact that it graphically conveys implicit information regarding the temporal stage of development (again, in general terms). Figure 4 shows the workstyle model plotted for several phases of a UCD process (in this case the Wisdom process [11]). This is a rough modeling of the styles of work and how they vary according to the activity being performed. In the inception phase, all workstyle dimension values are low: developers think informally in terms of requirements, at the same time and place, without functionality issues in mind, doing many changes to compare alternatives. As they move to elaboration and construction, they start to adopt a workstyle with higher values in all dimensions (although some more than other).

The grey area shows the effort along the time for each activity. The circles show the workstyle adopted by developers along the time as well. When the effort is higher, workstyle transitions become more frequent (the circles thickness plot the frequency of transitions).

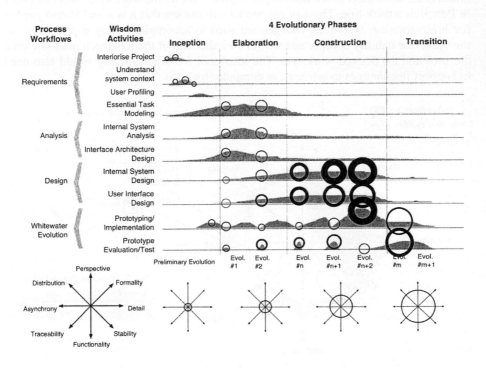

Fig. 4. The workstyle model plotted along the different phases of a UCD process

In practice, this evolution is never translated into a perfect circle, as different projects have different goals and needs. For instance, the larger the organization, the greater the formality and location dispersion. However, if we think in terms of workstyle iterations, as design evolves, there is a general tendency to move away from the center of our model. Also, if regions (instead of lines) become plotted in our model, we have an indication that iterations and workstyle transitions become more frequent, which accounts for higher project effort. Consequently, by checking the plotted regions' size, one can estimate how much effort is being put by a team of UCD developers. The power of our model (over other models such as [5, 13, 14]) is the fact that it can be used to assess the level of development in a graphically intuitive way. An image can convey more information than words or numbers and models should make use of them.

5   Using the Model to Evaluate and Build Better Tools

Our "galactic" model can also be used to identify adequate UCD tools for a given project phase. Let us consider, for instance, brainstorming. In this workstyle all values of our model are very low: problem perspective, informal, low detail, unstable (many ideas and many frequent changes), no functionality at all, no need for traceability and people collaborating at same place and at the same time. Paper & Pencil (or Whiteboards) are often used to brainstorm [2]. Figure 5 shows the workstyle model of Paper & Pencil as a thick line. Through our model, we can see that it is a tool almost perfect for brainstorming. However, changes are hard to accomplish using paper/pencil, so the value for stability is high, and we get an indication of the mismatch point between the tool and the desired workstyle. The ideal tool for brainstorming would also need to support fast changes to artifacts, as computer tools do.

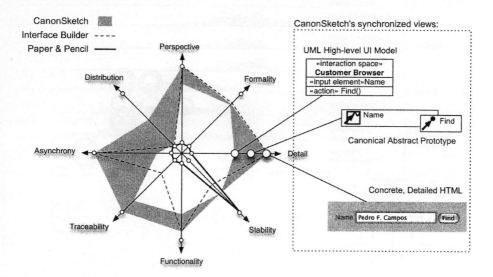

Fig. 5. CanonSketch, Interface Builder and Paper&Pencil under the galactic model

Figure 5 also shows how our model was used to drive the development of a new user-centered tool for designing UI's. CanonSketch [1] is a tool that supports multiple levels of detail by providing the designer three views: UML model of the UI and domain, Canonical Abstract Prototype [3] and HTML concrete prototype (as the right side of Figure 5 exemplifies). The first two views are synchronized and the UML semantic model is used to support traceability. There is also a collaborative version of this tool in which designers can work at the same time on the model and at different places. However, support for distribution is still limited (for instance, there are no awareness mechanisms). Therefore, CanonSketch supports a region in our model, as illustrated in Figure 5. In this way, the tool seamlessly supports designers while switching from high-level abstract views of the UI and low-level concrete realizations [1]. CanonSketch has been tested under a laboratorial setting and has lead to promising results. By contrast, a visual Interface Builder only supports a line in the workstyle model (the dashed line in Figure 5).

Figure 6 illustrates the application of the model to two software modeling tools: ArgoUML and IdeogramicUML. The former is a well-known open-source UML tool and the latter is a commercial tool based on a research project about collaborative software design. ArgoUML has a full-semantic model that allows, for instance, reverse engineering and code generation. IdeogramicUML only supports the syntax of the UML. Thus, ArgoUML is more formal than IdeogramicUML. They both cover part of the perspective, abstraction and modifiability axis; and can even generate some partially functional code. Traceability exists to some extent, since some views are interconnected automatically and there is something like a model navigator in both tools. More differences come in the collaboration-style dimensions. IdeogramicUML uses a sketch recognition language and can be effectively used in electronic whiteboards. There is also a distributed version with awareness mechanisms built in. This way this tool covers a larger region of the model (see Figure 6) than ArgoUML.

Figure 6 also compares the galactic workstyle values for a visual interface builder (VisualBasic) against the popular diagramming tool MS Visio. Visual interface builders became very popular because they support a workstyle in which a functional, concrete prototype can be easily created, thus reducing iteration times. Like ArgoUML, there is no support for collaboration. These tools are limited to a single workstyle (plotted as a single line), so there is no support for abstraction or requirements definition, which is the reason why so many interfaces become rapidly, but poorly designed. On the other hand, Visio supports a wide range of detail, perspective and formality levels and even though it doesn't create functional prototypes, its flexibility in terms of notation quickly became key to its success in rapid prototyping.

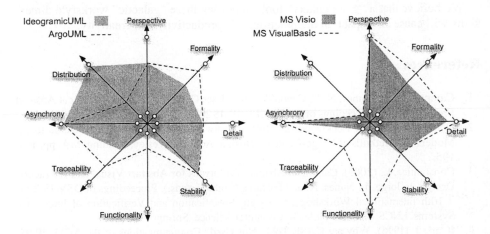

Fig. 6. ArgoUML, IdeogramicUML, VisualBasic and Visio, under the galactic model

These examples show how it is possible to find adequate UCD tool support by applying our model in an easy and intuitive way. It also shows how we can compare and analyze the trade-offs between the dimensions.

More importantly, our model can be used to drive the design of UCD tools, as we have already done with the CanonSketch project [1]. The ideal UCD tool should support the whole space of our "galactic" model as well as shifts between any given workstyle. This could leverage the iterative nature of the UCD process.

6 Conclusions

There is ample room for innovation regarding tool support for UCD processes. Current tools don't fulfill (at least totally) the UI activities of their users: the developers and interaction designers. Support for collaboration and informal communication is even more critical in processes such as UCD. More importantly, supporting transitions in workstyle dimensions can lead to better user-centered tools for user-centered design, given the iterative, evolutionary nature of the process.

Our framework is the first workstyle model tailored to UCD. Current models are too specific and are not expressive enough to be applied more generally to UCD. We expanded them and unified their most significant dimensions in order to achieve a more useful and usable model that could convey more information in a better way. We provided a set of guideline questions that can be used to plot values in the model space. However, our model should be regarded more as an informal discussion tool, rather than a formal method for analyzing workstyles. Contrary to other models, it allows estimating the effort and stage of development of a UCD process by checking the size of the region or line. Its dimensions were specifically designed to allow an easy and intuitive plotting of styles of work. Our model can also be effectively used to (a) choose adequate tool support for a given phase of a project and (b) drive the development of new UCD tools.

We believe that a "glass galaxy" tool supporting these "galactic" workstyle dimensions will cause an impact on the practitioner's productivity and creativity.

References

1. Campos, P. and Nunes, N. J., CanonSketch: a User-Centered Tool for Canonical Abstract Prototyping. In Proceedings of the EHCI/DSV-IS'2004, Hamburg, Germany, 2004.
2. Constantine, L. and Lockwood, L. (1999). Software for Use. A Practical Guide to the Models and Methods of Usage-Centered Design. Addison-Wesley, Reading, MA, pp. 194-195.
3. Constantine, L. (2003). Canonical Abstract Prototypes for Abstract Visual and Interaction Design. In Jorge, J., Nunes, N. and Falcão e Cunha, J. (eds.), Proceedings of DSV-IS'2003 – 10th International Workshop on Design, Specification and Verification of Interactive Systems, LNCS - Lecture Notes in Computer Science. Springer-Verlag.
4. Ilvari, J. (1996). Why are CASE Tools Not Used? Communications of the ACM, 39:94-103.
5. Green, T. R. G. & Petre, M. (1996). Usability analysis of visual programming environments: a 'cognitive dimensions' framework. J. Visual Languages and Computing, 7, 131-174.
6. Jarzabek, S. and Huang, R. (2004). The Case for User-Centered CASE Tools. Communications of the ACM, 41(8):93-99.

7. Kemerer, C. F. (1992). How the Learning Curve Affects CASE Tool Adoption. IEEE Software, 9, 23-28.
8. Landay, J. and Myers, B. (2001). Sketching Interfaces: Toward More Human Interface Design. IEEE Computer, pages 56-64.
9. Lumsden, J. (2001). SUIT - A Methodology and Framework for Selection of User Interface Development Tools, Ph.D. Thesis, Department of Computing Science, University of Glasgow, Glasgow.
10. Myers, B., Hudson, S. and Pausch, R. (2000). Past, Present and Future of User Interface Software Tools. ACM Transactions on Computer Human Interaction, 7(1): 3-28.
11. Nunes, N. J., Cunha, J. F. (2001). WISDOM Whitewater Interactive System Development with Object Models, in Mark van Harmelen (Editor), Object-oriented User Interface Design, Addison-Wesley, Object Technology Series.
12. Seffah, A. and Metzker, E. (2004). The Obstacles and Myths of Usability and Software Engineering. Communications of the ACM, 47(12): 71-76.
13. Traeetteberg, H. (2003). Dialog Modeling with Interactors and UML Statecharts - A Hybrid Approach. In Proceedings of DSV-IS 2003, pages 346-361.
14. Wu, J. and Graham, T. C. N. (2004). The Software Design Board: a Tool supporting Workstyle Transitions in Collaborative Software Design. In Proceedings of the EHCI / DSV-IS'2004, Hamburg, Germany.

A Formal Description of Multimodal Interaction Techniques for Immersive Virtual Reality Applications

David Navarre[1], Philippe Palanque[1], Rémi Bastide[1], Amélie Schyn[1],
Marco Winckler[1], Luciana P. Nedel[2], and Carla M.D.S. Freitas[2]

[1] LIIHS-IRIT (Université Paul Sabatier),
118 route de Narbonne, 31062, Toulouse, France
{navarre, palanque, schyn, winckler}@irit.fr
[2] Informatics Institute, Federal University of Rio Grande do Sul,
Caixa Postal 15.064, CEP 91501-970, Porto Alegre, Brazil
{nedel, carla}@inf.ufrgs.br

Abstract. Nowadays, designers of Virtual Reality (VR) applications are faced with the choice of a large number of different input and output devices leading to a growing number of interaction techniques. Usually VR interaction techniques are described informally, based on the actions users can perform within the VR environment. At implementation time, such informal descriptions (made at design time) yield to ambiguous interpretations by the developers. In addition, informal descriptions make it difficult to foresee the impact throughout the application of a modification of the interaction techniques. This paper discusses the advantages of using a formal description technique (called ICO) to model interaction techniques and dialogues for VR applications. This notation is presented via a case study featuring an immersive VR application. The case study is then used to show, through analysis of models, how the formal notation can help to ensure the usability, reliability and efficiency of virtual reality systems.

1 Introduction

Virtual reality (VR) applications feature specificities compared to classical WIMP (Window, Icon, Menu and Pointers) interactive systems. WIMP interfaces may be considered as *static* (as the number of interactive widgets is usually known beforehand). Besides, they provide users with simple interaction techniques based on the use of the keyboard and/or the mouse, and the events produced (click, double click, etc.) are easy to manage. On the contrary, VR systems are based on 3D representations with complex interaction techniques (usually multimodal) where inputs and outputs can be very complex to manage due to the number of potential devices (data gloves, eye trackers, 3D mouse or trackball, force-feedback devices, stereovision, etc.). Designing or implementing VR applications require to address several issues like immersion, 3D visualisation, handling of multiple input and output devices, complex dialogue design, etc.

As for multimodal applications, when implementing VR applications, developers usually have to address hard to tackle issues such as parallelism of actions, actions sequencing or synchronization, fusion of information gathered from different input devices, combination or separation of information (fission mechanism) to be directed

M.F. Costabile and F. Paternò (Eds.): INTERACT 2005, LNCS 3585 , pp. 170–183, 2005.
© IFIP International Federation for Information Processing 2005

to different devices. These issues make modelling and implementation of VR systems very complex mainly because it is difficult to describe and model how such different input events are connect to the application [21].

Many reports in the literature are devoted to invent new interaction techniques or describe software and hardware settings used in specific applications, most of them presenting also user studies for experimental evaluation. Empirical evaluation of interaction techniques for VR and 3D applications has been addressed recently [6, 7] as well as more general approaches addressing the usability of VR and multimodal interfaces [16, 18, 23]. Usually, interaction techniques for VR applications are described informally sequentially presenting the actions the users can perform within the VR environment and their results in terms of triggered events and modifications of objects appearance and/or location. Such informal descriptions make it difficult finding similarities between different techniques and often result in some basic techniques being "re-invented" [21]. Moreover, informal descriptions (due to their incomplete and ambiguous aspect) leave design choices to the developers resulting in undesired behaviour of the application or even unusable and inconsistent interaction techniques.

The growing number of devices available makes the design space of interaction techniques very large. The use of models has been proved to be an effective support for the development of interactive systems helping designers to decompose complex applications in smaller manageable parts. Formalisms have been used for the modelling of conventional interaction techniques [3, 8, 10, 15], and the benefits of using them for simulation and prototyping are well known [9].

Following the ARCH terminology, this paper presents the modelling of the dialogue part of VR applications and its relationship with the multimodal interaction of the presentation part. The modelling and implementation of the rendering techniques themselves are beyond the scope of this paper.

This paper aims at showing the benefits from using the ICO formalism to model interaction in virtual environments. It presents with details the impact of changing input devices and/or interaction techniques, detecting similarities and dissimilarities in the behaviours, and to allow measurements of the effects of these dissimilarities in the prediction of user performance. Both the interaction techniques and the dialogue part of the application are modelled using the ICO formalism [3], a formalism which was recently extended to support the modelling of multimodal and virtual reality applications. The case study shows the use of this formal notation for modelling a manipulation technique in an immersive virtual environment based on a chess game to allow a deeper discussion of formal notation advantages in the light of quantitative results obtained from experimental evaluation [16]. Such kind of application has also been used for customizing heuristic evaluation techniques for VR environments [1].

The paper is structured as follows. Section 2 informally presents the ICO formalism. The aim of that section is to present the basics of the formalism in order to allow the reader to understand the models presented in Section 4. We also emphasize the extension made on the ICO formalism in order to make it suitable for modelling interaction techniques of VR applications. Section 3 briefly describes the Virtual Chess case study while Section 4 presents its formal modelling using extended ICO. Section 5 is dedicated to related work.

2 Informal Description of ICO

The Interactive Cooperative Objects (ICO) formalism is a formal description technique designed to the specification, modelling and implementation of interactive systems [5]. It uses concepts borrowed from the object-oriented approach (i.e. dynamic instantiation, classification, encapsulation, inheritance, and client/server relationships) to describe the structural or static aspects of systems, and uses high-level Petri nets [12] to describe their dynamics or behavioural aspects.

In the ICO formalism, an object is an entity featuring five components: a cooperative object (CO), an available function, a presentation part and two functions (the activation function and the rendering function) that correspond to the link between the cooperative object and the presentation part.

The **Cooperative Object** (CO) models the behaviour of an ICO. It states (by means of a high-level Petri net) how the object reacts to external stimuli according to its inner state. As the tokens can hold values (such as references to other objects in the system), the Petri model used in the ICO formalism is called a high-level Petri Net. A Cooperative Object offers two kinds of services. The first one is called system devices and concerns to services offered to other objects of the system, while the second, event services, is related to services offered to a user (producing events) or to other component in the system but only through event-based communication. The availability of all the services in a CO (which depends on the internal state of the objects) is fully stated by the high-level Petri net.

The **presentation part** describes the external appearance of the ICOs. It is a set of widgets embedded into a set of windows. Each widget can be used for interacting with the interactive system (user interaction -> system) and/or as a way to display information about the internal state of the object (system -> user interaction).

The **activation function** (user inputs: user interaction -> system) links users' actions on the presentation part (for instance, a click using a mouse on a button) to event services.

The **rendering function** (system outputs: system -> user interaction) maintains the consistency between the internal state of the system and its external appearance by reflecting system states changes through functions calls.

Additionally, an **availability function** is provided to link a service to its corresponding transitions in the ICO, i.e., a service offered by an object will only be available if one of its related transitions in the Petri net is available.

An ICO model is fully executable, which gives the possibility to prototype and test an application before it is fully implemented [4]. The models can also be validated using analysis and proof tools developed within the Petri nets community and extended in order to take into account the specifications of the Petri net dialect used in the ICO formal description technique.

3 Informal Description of the Virtual Chess

The Virtual Chess application is inspired on the traditional chess game. It was originally developed as a testing ground application to support user testing of the selection of 3D objects in VR environments using two interaction techniques (*virtual hand* and *ray casting*) [16]. The Virtual Chess is composed by a chessboard with 64 squares (cells) and contains 32 chess pieces. The interaction includes the manipulation (selecting, moving, releasing) of chess pieces and the selection of the view mode (plan view or perspective view).

The manipulation of pieces can be done either by using a classic mouse or a combination of data glove and motion capture device. When using a mouse the selection is done by first clicking on the piece and then clicking on the target position (x, y). We can replace the mouse by the data glove $5DT^1$ and a motion captor[2] as the ones presented in Fig. 1.a. This data glove has a rotation and orientation sensor and five flexion sensors for the fingers. In this case, the motion captor is used to give the pointer position (x, y, z) while the fingers flexion is used to recognize the user gesture (closing the hand is recognized as a selection, opening the hand after a successful selection is recognized as a release). The selection of the view mode is done by pressing the key 0 (for the top view) or key 1 (for the perspective view) on a classic keyboard. In addition to these input devices, a user can wear stereoscopic glasses (see Fig. 1.b) in order to have a stereo experience. Fig. 1.c provides the general scenario for the user physical interaction with devices.

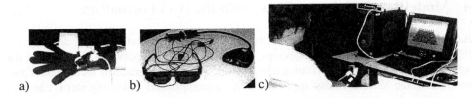

Fig. 1. Some of the devices employed: motion captor attached to a 5DT data glove (a); 3D stereoscopic glasses (b); scenario of user testing (c)

The users can move one piece at a time (horizontally, vertically and/or in diagonal). The Virtual Chess application does not take into account the game rules. All that the users can do are to **pick** a piece, **move** it to a new position and **drop** it. If a piece is dropped in the middle of two squares it is automatically moved to the closest square. Users cannot move pieces outside the chessboard but they can move pieces to a square occupied by another chessman.

In a real chess game, the movement of the pieces over the game board is performed with the hand. This has leaded to the implementation of the *virtual hand* interaction technique which represents the pointer position by a virtual 3D hand as shown in Fig. 2. Visual feedback is given by automatically suspending the selected piece over the chessboard and changing its colour (from grey or white to red).

Fig. 2 and Fig. 3.a show the chessboard in the perspective view mode while Fig. 3.b shows it in the top view mode (2D view).

---

[1] 5DT from Fifth Dimension Technologies (http://www.5dt.com/)
[2] Flocks of Birds from Ascension Technology (http://www.ascension-tech.com/)

Fig. 2. User interaction using direct manipulation (virtual hand technique) with visual feedback. From left to right: *picking*, *moving* and *dropping* a chessman.

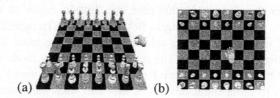

(a)   (b)

Fig. 3. View modes: (a) perspective view; (b) top view

4   Modelling the Virtual Chess with the ICO Formalism

As for other interactive systems, the modelling of VR applications must describe the behaviour of input and output devices, the general dialogue between the user and the application and the logical interaction provided by the interaction technique. Thus, modelling the Virtual Chess application was accomplished following steps 1 to 5 of the modified architecture Arch (the original architecture may be found in [2]) presented in Fig. 4. This model is useful for representing the various architectural components of an interactive application and the relationships between them. However, as the considered application is mainly interactive the left hand side of the Arch is not relevant. Section 4.1 discusses the modelling of steps 1 and 2, covering the treatment of low-level events and logical events from input devices. Section 4.2 describes the dialogue modelling of the Virtual Chess while Section 4.3 discusses the modelling of logical and concrete rendering.

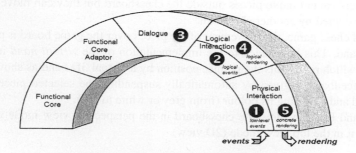

Fig. 4. The modified Arch architecture

4.1 Input Devices Modelling

The behaviour of our application is based on three main logical events: *pick(p)*, *move(p)* and *drop(p)*, where *p* represents the piece being manipulated. In this section we present the different models which describe the way of physical inputs (actions performed by users on input devices) are treated in order to be used as logical events by the dialogue controller. At this point, we need one ICO model for each input device. Fig. 5, Fig. 6, and Fig. 7 present the ICO models describing the behaviour of the mouse, the coupling of motion captor and data glove and the keyboard, respectively.

When using a mouse, these so-called logical events are represented as a composition of the low-level events *move(x,y)* and *click(x,y)*, which are triggered by the physical mouse. Each time the user moves the mouse, a *move(x,y)* event is triggered and captured in the ICO by means of the *Move* service. A service is associated to one or more transitions having similar names in the ICO model; for example, in Fig. 5 the service *Move* is associated to the transitions *Move_1* and *Move_2*. Whatever the actual system state, a mouse's move action triggers a *move(x,y)* event causing a transition in the model.

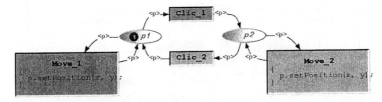

Fig. 5. Logical level behaviour for the Mouse

The logical events *pick(p)* and *drop(p)* are associated to the low-level event *click(x,y)* that is triggered by the physical mouse. The events *pick(p)* and *drop(p)* are determined by the sequence of low-level events (the first *click(x,y)* implies a *pick(p)*, the second *click(x,y)* implies a *drop(p)*, the third implies a *pick(x,y)*, and so on). The incoming events the such as low events *click(x,y)* and *move(x,y)* are described by the Activation Function presented in Table 1.a while the triggered events are described by the Event Production Function presented in Table 1.b. Table 1.a and Table 1.b complete the model by showing the events activating the Petri Net presented in Fig. 5 and the events triggered to other models and/or devices.

Table 1. Event producer-consumer functions as described in Fig. 5.

a) Activation Function

Event Emitter	Interaction object	Event	Service
Mouse	None	*move(x,y)*	Move
Mouse	None	*click(x,y)*	Click

b) Event Production Function

Transition	Event produced
Move_1	*move(p)*
Move_2	*move(p)*
Clic_1	*pick(p)*
Clic_2	*drop(p)*

Figure 6 presents how the events *pick(p), move(p)* and *drop(p)* are produced when using the pair data glove and motion captor. Every time an event *idle( )* is triggered, it enables the transition *init* to capture the current fingers' flexion from the data glove and the spatial hand's position from the motion captor. The information concerning to the flexion of the fingers and the position of the hand are stored on variables *g* and *p*, respectively. The event *idle* is produced in the internal loop implemented by graphic libraries, such as OpenGL, which was used to implement the Virtual Chess. The transitions *pick, notPick, drop* and *notDrop* compare the current and previous positions (which is given by the token from the place *last*). If the current position is different from the previous one, and the hand is opened, the system triggers an event *drop(p)* in the current hand position. If the hand is closed and its position is different from the previous one, then the system triggers an event *move(p)*.

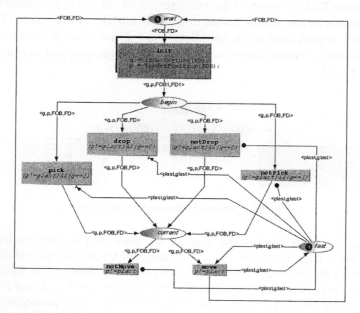

Fig. 6. Low-level behaviour (pick, move and drop) when using a data glove combined with a motion captor

Table 2 presents the list of incoming and triggered events in the model described in Fig. 6. In this model, the data sent back by the data glove and the motion captor can only be individually identified when comparing the current and the previous position.

Table 2. Event production-consumption functions as described in Fig. 6

a) Activation Function

Event Emitter	Interaction object	Event	Service
OpenGL loop	None	*idle*	init

b) Event Production Function

Transition	Event produced
drop	*drop(p)*
pick	*pick(p)*
move	*move(p)*

The role of the keyboard is to allow the users to choose the visualization mode (perspective or top view). The model that describes the keyboard behaviour is presented in Fig. 7. There are only two states available, each one corresponding to one of the pre-defined view modes (perspective or up). The incoming events in ICO for the keyboard are presented in Table 3; this modelling does not trigger any event.

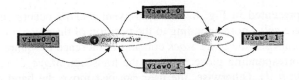

Fig. 7. Logical level modelling of the keyboard

Table 3. Activation Function as described in Fig. 7

Event Emitter	Interaction object	Event	Service
Keyboard	None	*keyPressed(0)*	View0
Keyboard	None	*keyPressed(1)*	View1

4.2 Dialogue Modelling

Independent from the input device employed (mouse or data glove and motion captor), the dialogue controller will receive the same events *pick(p)*, *drop(p)* and

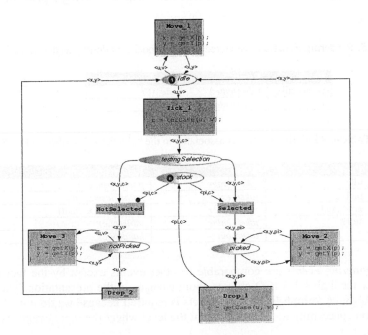

Fig. 8. Dialogue controller modelling

Table 4. Activation Function as described in Fig. 8

Event Emitter	Interaction object	Event	Service
Low-level events from	Chess piece *p*	*move(p)*	Move
mouse or the pair data	Chess piece *p*	*pick(p)*	Pick
glove plus motion captor	Chess piece *p*	*drop(p)*	Drop

move(p). As represented in Fig. 8, when an event *pick(p)* occurs (in the transition *Pick_1*) the square cell *c* corresponding to the position of the piece *p* is captured. If an event *pick(p)* occurs and the place *stock* contains a reference to square *c*, then the user can move the corresponding piece *p* (using the transition *Move_2*) or drop it (using the transition *Drop_1*). Otherwise, the user can just move the hand over the chessboard for a while and then the system return to the initial state. This behaviour is also presented in Table 4.

4.3   Rendering and Interaction Technique Modelling

In this section we introduce the extensions to ICO formalism related to the *rendering events*. We include rendering events in the modelling whenever a change in the state of the system modifies something in the graphical display. We represent this by means of the *Rendering Function*. Table 5 describes the *Rendering Function* associated to the behaviour of the keyboard when selecting the visualization mode (see Fig. 7) and Table 6 presents the *Rendering Function* associated to the behaviour described in Fig. 8 for the dialogue controller. In these examples, the *rendering events* are triggered when entering into a place (a *token-enter* event) or leaving a place (a *token-out* event).

Table 5. Rendering Function associated to the keyboard modelling as described in Fig. 7

Place	Event	Rendering event
perspective	*token-enter*	*view(0)*
up	*token-enter*	*view(1)*

Table 6. Rendering functions associated to the behaviour described in Fig. 8.

Place	Event	Rendering event
idle	*token-enter*	*paintOpen(x,y)*
picked	*token-enter*	*paintClose(x,y,pi)*
notPicked	*token-enter*	*paintClose(x,y,null)*
stock	*token-enter*	*table(pi,c)*
	token-out	*hand(pi,c)*

The *rendering events* are comparable to other events except by the fact that they also notify the high-level ICO objects about changes in the presentation. This kind of events delegation to high-level ICO objects is required because we do not have all the information concerning to the rendering at the level where the input events were originally triggered.

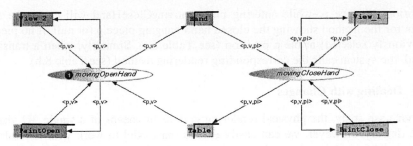

Fig. 9. General behaviour for the rendering

In order to provide a general understanding of how rendering events affect the graphical presentation, Fig. 9 presents another ICO model which describes how the Virtual Chess makes the fusion of events coming from other lower-level ICO models (describing the keyboard's behaviour as well as the mouse and/or the data glove and motion captor's behaviour).

Table 7 presents the activation function for the ICO model presented in Fig. 9. We can notice that the incoming events for that model correspond to rendering events triggered in lower level ICO models (i.e. keyboard and dialogue controller).

Table 7. Activation Function as described in Fig. 9

Event Emitter	Interaction objects	Events	Services
Low-level events from Fig. 7 (keyboard)	None	*view(0)*	View
	None	*view(1)*	View
Low-level events from Fig. 8 (dialogue controller)	None	*paintOpen(x,y)*	PaintOpen
	None	*paintClose(x,y,pi)*	PaintClose
	None	*paintClose(x,y,null)*	PaintClose
	None	*table(pi,c)*	Table
	None	*hand(pi,c)*	Hand

In Fig. 9, the incoming events are fused and translated into classical methods calls to the Virtual Chess application. In this example, each place and each transition is associated to a particular rendering (see Table 8 For example, when entering the place movingOpenHand the system calls the method for showing the open hand at the

Table 8. Rendering functions associated to the model presented in Fig. 9

a) Rendering triggered over places

Place	Event	Rendering
movingOpenHand	Token-enter	*paintOpenHand(v,p)*
movingCloseHand	Token-enter	*paintCloseHand(v,p,pi)*

b) Rendering triggered over transitions

Transition	Rendering
View_1	*changeView(v)*
View_2	*changeView(v)*
PaintOpen	*paintOpenHand(v,p)*
PaintClose	*paintCloseHand(v,p,pi)*
Table	*paintPiece(pi,c)*
Hand	*deletePiece(pi)*

position of piece p, while entering place movingCloseHand will cause the system calls for the method showing the closed hand hanging piece p (or null, if no piece was previously selected) at the p position (see Table 8.a). Similarly, when a transition is fired, the system calls the corresponding rendering method (see Table 8.b).

4.4 Dealing with Changes

In our case study, the physical rendering is done by means of a single 3D visualization display. However, we can easily extend our model to work with several output devices at a time just by replacing the method calls presented in Table 8 by other rendering methods (causing the fission of events) or other events captured by another ICO model describing output devices (in this case, one ICO model is required for each device). More information about the modelling of multimodal application using ICO formalism and how models can be interactively modified is available in the following papers [17, 3].

5 Discussion and Related Work

There are two main issues concerning the modelling of the VR applications: the use of a notation able to represent VR issues and the use of different devices. On one hand, we have extended the ICO notation in order to support the modelling of multimodal aspects such as fusion of several inputs, complex rendering outputs and 3D scenes. On the other hand, we have evaluated how changing input devices might require changes in the modelling and that ICO formalism makes these changes local to the concerned model thus lighten the burden of the designers.

Interaction in virtual environment or, more generally, 3D interaction can not be described using 'conventional' notations for interactive systems due to the inherent continuous aspect of information and devices manipulated in virtual reality applications. Actually, virtual environments are hybrid systems, and researchers in this field tried to extend their formalism to cope with a combination of discrete and continuous components [21]. Flownet [20, 21] is a notation to specify virtual environments interaction techniques using Petri Nets as the basis for modelling the discrete behaviour and elements from a notation for dynamics systems to model the continuous data flow in 3D interaction [25]. The same authors also proposed another formalism [21] so called HyNet (Hybrid High-level Petri Nets), that allows the description of hybrid interfaces by means of a graphical notation to define discrete and continuous concurrent behaviours, the availability of object oriented concepts and the high-level hierarchical description to specify complex systems. Jacob et al. [19] developed another visual hybrid formalism to describe interaction on VE. This formalism results in more compact specifications than HyNet, but the use of separate notations for the discrete and continuous parts makes the comprehension more difficult. More recently, Latoschik [14] introduced tATN (temporal Augmented Transition Network) as a mean to integrate and evaluate information in multimodal virtual reality interaction considering the use of speech and gesture in a VR application, and Dubois et al. [11] have proposed the ASUR notation to describe augmented reality systems in high-level.

The current paper does not address the issue of continuity because, even though the interaction and visualisation can be seen, at a higher level of abstraction, as continuous, when it comes to low level modelling the events produced and processed are always dealt with in a discrete manner. Indeed, both in the modelling and execution phases the explicit representation of continuous aspects was not needed.

VR applications and Multimodal systems have many aspects in common, such as parallelism of actions, actions sequencing or synchronization, fusion of information gathered through different devices to the combination or separation of information to be directed to different devices. In fact, description techniques devoted to the modelling of VR applications are similar to those employed to model multimodal applications.

As far as multimodal interaction is concerned, several proposals have been made in order to address the specific issue of formally describing various elements such as fusion and fission engines. For instance work from Hinckley [13] proposes the use of colored Petri nets for modelling two handed interaction by extending Buxton's work on Augmented Transition Networks [8]. Other work, based on process algebra such as CSP [22], Van Schooten [24] or LOTOS [10] have addressed (but only at a high level of abstraction) multimodal interactive systems modelling.

However, none of the approaches mentioned above are able to define a clear link between application and interaction. Besides, most of them do not have a precise semantics of the extensions proposed while the ICO formalism provides both a formal definition and a denotational semantics for each new construct (see the web site http://liihs.irit.fr/palanque/ICOs.htm). Last but not least, none of the approaches above are executable, i.e. provide a precise enough modelling power to allow for execution. This may not be a problem, as modelling can also be used for reasoning about the models, for instance in order to check whether or not some properties are valid on the models.

6   Conclusion and Future Work

In this paper, we have presented new extensions for the ICO in order to deal with complex rendering output as requested in VR applications. The ICO formalism has been previously extended and presented in [3, 17] to deal with the modelling of multimodal issues in interactive-system (e.g. event-based communication, temporal modelling and structuring mechanism based on transducers in order to deal with low level and higher lever events).

This paper has proposed a multi-level modelling approach for dealing with all the behavioural aspects of multimodal immersive interactive applications. We have shown how to deal with these issues from the very low level of input devices modelling, to the higher level of dialogue model for a 3D application. We presented how models can be gracefully modified in order to accommodate changes in the input devices and also in the interaction technique for such applications. Though relatively simple, the case study presented in the paper is complex enough to present in details all the aspects raised by the modelling of VR immersive applications and how the ICO formalism has been extended to tackle them.

This paper belongs to a long more ambitious research project dealing with the modelling of interactive applications in the field of safety critical application domains such as satellite control operation rooms and cockpits of military aircrafts. For these reasons the ICO formalism has been extended several times in order to address the specificities of such real time interactive applications.

Acknowledgements

The work presented in the paper is partly funded by French DGA under contract #00.70.624.00.470.75.96 and the R&T action IMAGES from CNES (National Centre on Space Studies in France) and CS Software Company.

References

1. Bach, C., Scapin, D. Adaptation of Ergonomic Criteria to Human-Virtual Environments Interactions. In: INTERACT 2003, Zurich. Amsterdam: IOS Press, (2003) 880-883
2. Bass, L., Pellegrino, R., Reed, S., Seacord, R., Sheppard, R., Szezur, M. R. The Arch model: Seeheim revisited. In: User Interface Developer's workshop version 1.0, (1991)
3. Bastide, R., Navarre, D., Palanque, P., Schyn, A., Dragicevic, P. A Model-Based Approach for Real-Time Embedded Multimodal Systems in Military Aircrafts. Sixth International Conference on Multimodal Interfaces (ICMI'04), Pennsylvania State University, USA. October 14-15, (2004)
4. Bastide, R., Navarre, D., Palanque, P. A Model-Based Tool for Interactive Prototyping of Highly Interactive Applications. In: ACM SIGCHI'2002 (Extended Abstracts) (2002) 516-517
5. Bastide, R., Palanque, P., Le Duc, H.; Muñoz, J. Integrating Rendering Specification into a Formalism for the Design of Interactive Systems. In: 5th Eurographics Workshop on Design, Specification and Verification of Interactive Systems (DSV-IS'98), Springer Verlag (1998)
6. Bowman, D., Johnson, D. B., Hodges, L. F. Testbed evaluation of virtual environments interaction techniques. In: ACM Symposium on Virtual Reality Software and Technology (1999) 26-33
7. Bowman, D., Kruijff, E., Laviola Jr., J. J., Poupyrev, I. An introduction to 3-D User Interface Design. Presence: Teleoperators and Virtual Environments, vol. 10, no. 1, (2001) 96-108
8. Buxton, W. A three-state model of graphical input. In: 3rd IFIP International Conference on Human-Computer Interaction, INTERACT'90, Cambridge, UK, 27-31 August (1990) 449-456
9. Campos, J. C., Harrison, M. D. Formally verifying interactive systems: A review. In Design, Specification and Verification of Interactive Systems '97, Springer Computer Science, (1997), 109-124
10. Coutaz, J., Paterno, P., Faconti, G., Nigay L., A comparison of Approaches for Specifying Multimodal Interactive Systems, In Proceedings of ERCIM, Nancy, France, (1993)
11. Dubois, E., Gray, P.D., Nigay, L., ASUR++: a Design Notation for Mobile Mixed Systems, IWC Journal, Special Issue on Mobile HCI, vol. 15, n. 4, (2003) 497-520,
12. Genrich, H. J. (1991) Predicte/Transiion Nets, in K. Jensen & G. Rozenberg (eds.), High-Level Petri: Theory and Applications, Springer Verlag, pp. 3-43.

13. Hinckley, K., Czerwinski, M. and Sinclair, M., Interaction and Modeling Techniques for Desktop Two-Handed Input. http://research.microsoft.com/users/kenh/papers/two-hand.pdf (1998)
14. Latoschik, M. E. Designing Transition Networks for Multimodal VR-Interactions Using a Markup Language. In: IEEE International Conference on Multimodal Interfaces (ICMI'02) Proceedings (2002)
15. Märtin, C. A method engineering framework for modeling and generating interactive applications. In: 3rd International Conference on Computer-Aided Design of User Interfaces, Belgium, (1999)
16. Nedel, L. P., Freitas, C. M. D. S., Jacob, L. J., Pimenta, M. S. Testing the Use of Egocentric Interactive Techniques in Immersive Virtual Environments. In IFIP TC 13 Conference INTERACT 2003, on Human Computer Interaction, Zurich. Amsterdam: IOS Press, (2003) 471-478
17. Palanque, P., Schyn, A. A Model-Based Approach for Engineering Multimodal Interactive Systems. In: IFIP TC 13 INTERACT 2003 conference, Zurich. Amsterdam: IOS Press (2003)
18. Poupyrev, I., Weghorst, S., Billinghurst, M., Ichikawa, T. Egocentric Object Manipulation in Virtual Environments: Empirical Evaluation of Interaction Techniques. Computer Graphics Forum, Eurographics'98 issue, Vol. 17, n. 3, (1998) 41-52
19. Jacob, R., Deligiannidis, L., Morrison, S. A software model and specification language for non-WIMP user interfaces, ACM ToCHI, v.6 n.1, p.1-46, March 1999.
20. Smith, S., Duke, D. Virtual environments as hybrid systems. In Eurographics UK 17th Annual Conference Proceedings, (1999) 113-128
21. Smith, S., Duke, D. The Hybrid World of Virtual Environments. In: Computer Graphics Forum, v. 18, n. 3, The Eurographics Association and Blackwell Publishers. (1999)
22. Smith, S. and Duke, D., Using CSP to specify interaction in virtual environment. In *Technical report YCS 321*, University ok York – Department of Computer Science (1999)
23. Sutcliffe, A., Gault, B., de Bruijn, O. Comparing Interaction in the Real World and CAVE virtual environments. In.: 18th HCI'2004. Leeds Metropolitan University, UK 6-10 September (2004)
24. Van Schooten, B. W., Donk, O. A., Zwiers, J. Modelling Interaction in Virtual Environments using Process Algebra In Proceedings TWLT 15: Interactions in Virtual Worlds, May 19-21, (1999).
25. Willans, J. Harrison, M. A toolset supported approach for designing and testing virtual environment interaction techniques. International Journal of Human-Computer Studies, Vol. 55, n.2, (2001) 145-165

Analysing User Confusion in Context Aware Mobile Applications

K. Loer[1] and M.D. Harrison[2]

[1] Department Strategic Development, Germanischer Lloyd AG - Head Office,
Vosetzen 35, 20459 Hamburg, Germany
loe@gl-group.com

[2] Correspondence address: Informatics Research Institute,
University of Newcastle upon Tyne, NE1 7RU, UK
Michael.Harrison@ncl.ac.uk

Abstract. Mobility of ubiquitous systems offers the possibility of using the current context to infer information that might otherwise require user input. This can either make user interfaces more intuitive or cause subtle and confusing mode changes. We discuss the analysis of such systems that will allow the designer to predict potential pitfalls before the design is fielded. Whereas the current predominant approach to understanding mobile systems is to build and explore experimental prototypes, our exploration highlights the possibility that early models of an interactive system might be used to predict problems with embedding in context *before* costly mistakes have been made. Analysis based on model checking is used to contrast configuration and context issues in two interfaces to a process control system.

1 Background

Mobile interactive technologies bring new opportunities for flexible work and leisure. The fact that the mobile device is context aware means that user interaction can be more natural. The system (that is the whole software, human and hardware infrastructure) can detect where the device and its user are, infer information about what the user is doing, recognise urgency, even be aware of the user's emotional state. As a result user actions may be interpreted appropriately. The benefits that context awareness brings can be obscured by difficulties. Interaction may be confusing, surprising the user, and causing failure to occur.

Context aware systems are still mainly at an experimental stage of development and there is considerable interest in how these systems are used. The cost of user confusion about how action is interpreted may be expensive in terms of poor take up and potential error in safety critical situations. Techniques are required that can help predict these difficulties at design time. An important question therefore is what these techniques should be and whether the cost of using them is justified by the early understanding of design. The work underlying this paper uses formal modelling techniques and model checking. The point of using these techniques is not to suggest necessarily that an industrially scaleable

M.F. Costabile and F. Paternò (Eds.): INTERACT 2005, LNCS 3585, pp. 184–197, 2005.

technique should use them precisely as given in the paper nor that these techniques be used alone. It is instead the purpose to illustrate the type of issues that approaches such as these can help understand. An important question to be asked of any technique is whether early analysis requires a level of effort that can be justified in terms of potential costs of user confusions in business and safety critical systems.

The purpose here is to explore how analytic techniques might be used to:

- analyse differences between different interface configurations, in this case the difference between a central control room and a mobile hand-held PDA.
- analyse contextual effects. A simple model of context based on location is developed to analyse user action and user process.

The structure of the paper is as follows. The next section gives a scenario to illustrate the kind of system that is being considered here. Section 3 discusses the analysis to be performed. Section 4 presents briefly the model of the two user interfaces to the system. Section 5 explores the analysis of the system based on the models. The paper concludes by discussing the relevance of this approach and how future techniques might emerge.

2   A Scenario

A control room contains full wall displays on three sides. Plant schematics are displayed to represent the plant's state and can be manipulated through the control room interface using physical devices (e.g., switches), command line or direct manipulation interaction techniques, through the PDA interface, or through the physical components of the plant itself (e.g., closing a valve). Trend data about the plant is also displayed and helps operators anticipate emerging situations. Workflow information indicating today's schedule for an individual operator is contained in the operator's window also displayed on part of the wall.

A problem occurs in the plant requiring "hands-on" inspection and possible action from one or several operators. Operators (perhaps working as a team) take PDAs as they go to find out what has happened. General situation information and prompts about what to do next can be accessed from the PDA. The PDA can also be used to monitor and control a valve, pump or heater in situ (some of the monitoring characteristics of this device are similar to those described in [16]). A limited subset of information and controls for these components will be "stored" in the PDA to ease access to them in the future – analogous to putting them on the desktop. These desktop spaces are called *buckets* in [16]. The operator can view and control the current state of the components when in their immediate vicinity. Context is used in identifying position of an operator, checking validity of a given action, inferring an operator's intention, checking action against an operator's schedule assessing and indicating urgency.

For example, a leak in a pipe is indicated in the control room by a red flashing symbol over the relevant part of the schematic. Two operators walk out of the control room leaving it empty, one walks to the location of a heater downstream of the leak, the other walks to the valve upstream of the leak. The operator upstream attempts to close off the valve using the PDA but is warned not to, while the other operator is told by the PDA that the heater should be turned off quickly because the first operator is waiting. Both operators, after having carried out their actions, put heater and pump status and controls (respectively) in buckets in their PDAs and move to the location of the leak to deal with it. When they have fixed the leak together they each check and restore the controls that they had previously put in buckets to the state before the leak was identified and walk back to the control room.

This scenario indicates the variety of modes and contexts that can occur. Confusions can arise if there is more than one plant component in close proximity, if the operator forgets which component they have saved, if one operator forgets that another operator is nearby. These problems can be exaggerated by poor design.

3   Analysing the Interface

Given a design such as the one above, it is clear that configuration and context are important to the success of the system. What happens to the interface when the operator moves from the control room to the handheld device and begins to move around the plant? What changes occur between the control room and the hand held device? How is the hand held device affected by the context? An operator will have a number of goals to achieve using these interfaces and the actions that are involved to do this will be different in the two interfaces, and in the mobile case dependent on context.

A typical approach to analysing these differences might be to perform a task analysis in different situations and produce task descriptions that can be used to explore the two interfaces and how the interfaces support the interactions. This might involve considering the information resources that would be required in the two cases [19]. Such an approach would have much in common with [17,7]. Indeed this analysis is performed in Loer's thesis [13]. However there are difficulties with such an approach. Task descriptions assume that the means by which an operator will achieve a goal can be anticipated with reasonable accuracy. In practice a result is that strategies or activities that the operator actually engages in may be overlooked.

A different approach is to take the models and check whether a goal can be reached *at all*. The role of a model checker is to find *any* path that can achieve a user goal. This new approach also has difficulties because the sequence of actions may not make any sense in terms of the likely actions of an operator. In order to alleviate this the analyst's role is to inspect possible traces and decide whether assumptions should be included about use that would enable sequences to be generated that are more realistic. The advantage of this approach is that it means that analysis is not restricted to sequences that are imposed – the presumed tasks. The disadvantage is that in some circumstances there may be many paths that might require such exploration.

A model of context is required, as well as of the devices, that will enable an analysis of the effects of the user interface of the mobile device in this way. Since the problem here is that action or sequences of actions (process) may have different meanings depending on context a clear definition of context is required. Persistently forgetting to restore information when the context has changed could be one effect of context, and can be considered as part of the analysis. In the case study the environment is described simply in terms of physical positions in the environment and transitions between these positions. As the hand-held device makes transitions it is capable of interacting with or saving different plant components onto the device. A model of the plant is included in order to comprehend how the interfaces are used to monitor and control.

Context confusions can be avoided through design by changing the action structure (for example, using interlocks) so that these ambiguities are avoided or by clearly marking the differences to users. Techniques are required that will enable the designer to recognise and consider situations where there are likely to be problems. The process is exploratory, different properties are attempted and modified as different traces are encountered as counter-examples or instances. Traces that are "interesting" are scrutinised in more detail to investigate the effectiveness of the design and the possibility of confusion – discovering an interesting trace does not of itself mean that the design is flawed or is prone to human error. Implications of different configurations are explored by considering simple assumptions about the user. In what follows we describe an experiment in which questions are articulated in LTL (Linear Temporal Logic) and recognised by the SMV model checker [15].

4   Modelling the User Interface

The characterisation of the device and of the control room are both much simplified for the purposes of exposition. The icons on the hand-held device are the only means available to the user to infer the current system state and the available operations. Since the visibility of icons is important to the operation of the plant and the usability of the hand-held device, the basis for the analysis is (i) that all available operations are visible, and (ii) that all visible operations are executable. The analysis uses Statecharts [9]: an example of how an interface can be developed using Statecharts is given in [11]. The Statecharts in the current scenario are structured into different components as suggested by [4] to make interaction with the device and the effect of the environment clearer and is based on a more detailed analysis described in [13].

The interactive system that controls the process is designed: (1) to inform the operator about progress; (2) to allow the operator to intervene appropriately to control the process; (3) to alert the operator to alarming conditions in the plant and (4) to enable recovery from these conditions. A model is required to explore usability issues and design alternatives in the light of these goals of the underlying process. The central control mechanism provides all information in one display (Section 4.1), while the personal appliance displays partial information (Section 4.2).

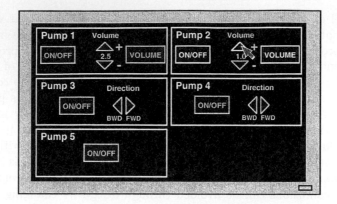

Fig. 1. Control Screen layout

4.1   Representing and Modelling the Central Panel

This paper deliberately glosses over the model of the process. The process involves tanks and pumps that feed material between tanks. The tanks can be used for more than one process and, in order to change processes, a tank must be evacuated before material can be pumped into it. In order to achieve this some of the pumps are bi-directional. In fact the process is expressed as a simple discrete model in which the significant features of the environment can be explored, for more details, see [14] or [2]. Hence the state of the tank is simply described as one element of the set $\{full, empty, holding\}$ — there is no notion of quantity or volume in the model. This is adequate to capture the key features of the process from the point of view of interaction with the system.

The control panel contained in the control room can be seen in Figure 1. All the pumps in the plant are visible and can be adjusted directly using a mouse. As can be seen from the display all the pumps can be switched on and off, some pumps (3 and 4) can be reversed and the volume of flow can also be modified in the case of pumps 1 and 2.

The control room, with its central panel, aims to provide the plant operator with a comprehensive overview of the status of all devices in the plant. Availability and visibility of action will be the primary concern here. Other aspects of the problem can be dealt with by using complementary models of the interface, for example alarms structure and presentation, but analysis is restricted for present purposes. The specification describes the behaviour of the displays and the associated buttons for pump 1 (and equivalently pump 2). The effects of actions are described in terms of the signals that are used to synchronise with the pump description and the states in which the buttons are illuminated.

The control panel is implemented by a mouse-controlled screen (see Figure 1). Screen icons act as both displays and controls at the same time. Hence from Figure 2 we can see that PUMP1USERINTERFACE supports four simple on-off state transitions defining the effect of pressing the relevant parts of the display. The state indicates when icons are illuminated but also shows that the actions trigger

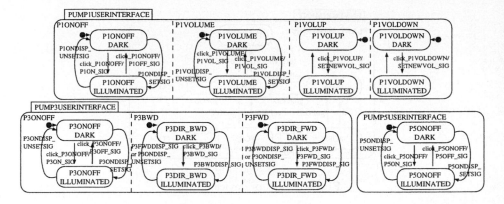

Fig. 2. Initial specification of control screen behaviour

corresponding actions in the underlying process. The Statechart here builds a bridge between actions that relate to the behaviour of the process underneath and actions that correspond to using the mouse to point and click at the relevant icons. A detailed account of what the specification means is not presented here. An indication of what it would look like is all that is intended at this stage – an indication of the scale of the modelling problem using this style of specification. Many other approaches could have been used: Paternò used LOTOS [17], Campos and Harrison used MAL [2]. Notations such as Promela that are supported directly by model checkers are also relatively straightforward to use [10].

4.2 Representing Context and the Hand-Held Control Device

The hand-held device uses individual controls that are identical to those of the central control panel but only a limited amount of space is available for them. As a controller walks past a pump it is possible to "save" the controls onto the display. Thereafter, while the controls continue to be visible on the display, it is possible to control the pumps from anywhere in the system.

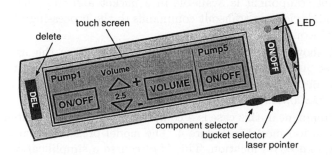

Fig. 3. A hand-held control device (modified version of the "Pucketizer" device in [16])

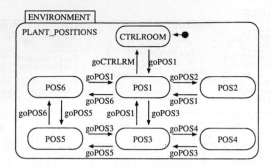

Fig. 4. Model of device positions

The hand-held control device (Figure 3) knows its position within the spatial organisation of the plant. Hence the ENVIRONMENT model to describe the system involving this device is extended to take account of context. A simple discrete model describes how an operator can move between device positions in the plant modelled as transitions between position states, as shown in Figure 4.

By pointing the laser pointer at a plant component and pressing the component selector button, the status information for that component and soft controls are transferred into the currently selected bucket. Components can be removed from a bucket by pressing the delete button. With the bucket selector button the user can cycle through buckets. The intended use of the device has been altered from the description contained in [16] from monitoring and annotating to monitoring and manipulation.

The specification of the hand-held device describes both the physical buttons that are accessible continuously and other control elements, like pump control icons, that are available temporarily and depend on the position of the device. When the operator approaches a pump, its controls are automatically displayed on the screen (it does not require the laser pointer). The component may be "transferred" into a bucket for future remote access by using the component selector button. Controls for plant devices in locations other than the current one can be accessed remotely if they have been previously stored in a bucket. When a plant component is available in a bucket and the bucket is selected, the hand-held device can transmit commands to the processing plant, using the pump control icons.

Figure 5 shows an extract of the specification. Here the user can choose between three buckets and each bucket can store controls for up to two components. In the BUCKETS state the current contents of each bucket x are encoded by variables "BxCONTENT".

The environment in this case is a composition of the tank content model and the device position model in Figure 4. The model presumes that the appliance should always know its location. This is of course a simplification. Alternative models would allow the designer to explore interaction issues when there is a dissonance between the states of the device and its location. A richer model in

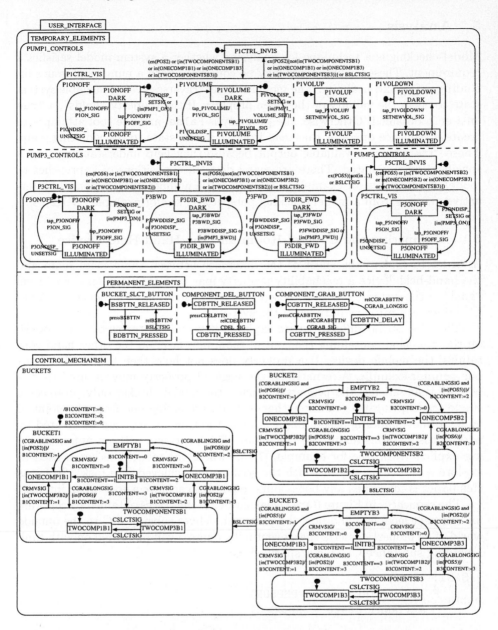

Fig. 5. OFAN model for the hand-held device: The USER INTERFACE and CONTROL MECHANISM modules

which variables are associated with states, and actions may depend on values of the state that have actually been updated, may lead to asking questions of the models as whether "the action has a false belief about the state". These issues are important but are not considered in this paper.

5   Analysis

Model-checking is a technique for analysing whether a system model satisfies a requirement. These requirements may be concerned with a number of issues including safety and usability. The model checker traverses every reachable system state to check the validity of the given property. If the property "holds", a `True` answer is obtained. Otherwise, the property is `False`, and the tool attempts to create a sequence of states that lead from an initial state to the violating state. These "traces" are a valuable output because they help understanding *why* a specification is violated. There are many detailed expositions of approaches to model checking, see for example [3,12,1,10] and a number of treatments of interactive systems from a model checking perspective, see for example [17,7,2,18].

5.1   Comparing the Control Room and the Hand Held Device

In order to explore the effect of the difference between the control room and the hand-held device a reachability property may be formulated for a user level "goal" of the system. The goal chosen here for illustration is "*Produce substance C*" which is a primary purpose of the system.

The idea is that differences are explored between the traces by two models: on the one hand containing the control room interface; on the other hand containing the mobile device. If a property does not hold then the checker finds one counter-example. Alternatively, the negated property may be used to find a trace that satisfies the property. Usually the model checker only produces a single trace giving no guarantee that it is an interesting one from the point of view of understanding design implications. Additional traces can be created by adding assumptions about the behaviour. This contrasts with an approach using explicit tasks (see for example, [7,13]) where the model checker is used to explore a particular way in which the goal can be achieved (the task). So far as this paper is concerned any behaviours required to achieve a goal are of interest.

The sequences in Figure 6 are visualisations of the traces obtained by checking for different models if and how the plant can deliver substance C to the outside world. The property asserts that, eventually, pump 5 will be turned on with tank 1 holding substance C. This is specified as:

```
SAN1:
    F (PUMP5CTRLM.state=PMP5ON)
      & (TANK1.state = HOLDS_C)
```

In this case the negated property "`not SAN1`" is used because instances that satisfy the property are required. The two models involving the different interfaces are checked with the same property. The first sequence in Figure 6 satisfies the control room interface. The second sequence was generated by checking the property against the hand-held device model. While the first two traces assume a serial use of pumps, the third and fourth sequences show the same task for a concurrent use of pumps. Comparison of these sequences yields information about the additional steps that have to be performed to achieve the same goal.

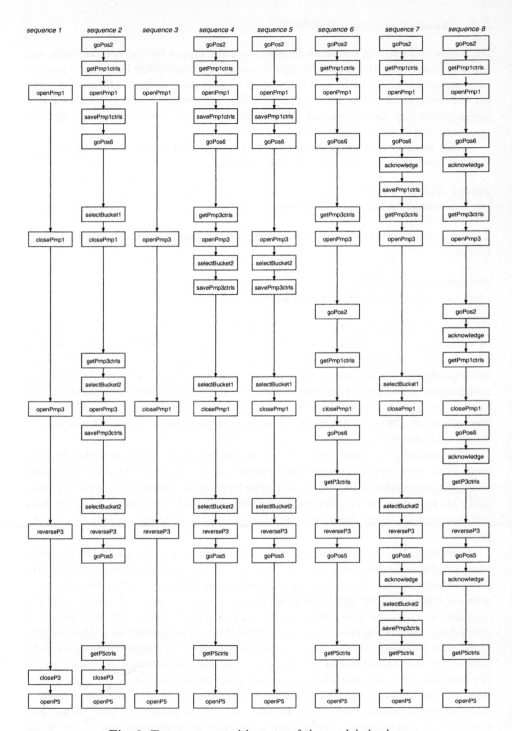

Fig. 6. Traces generated by runs of the model checker

5.2   Analysing Context Effects

As a result of making a comparison between the traces for the control room and
for the hand held, the analyst might come to the conclusion that the repetitive
process of saving controls may cause slips or mistakes, a direct effect of location
on the actions of the hand-held device. To explore the effect of this a further
assumption may be introduced to the property to be analysed, namely that an
operator might forget certain steps.

This assertion "alwaysForget" which states that controls for any of the
pumps are never saved is described as follows:

```
assert alwaysForget:
 G !(savePmp1ctrls| [...] |savePmp5ctrls);
```

The original property SAN1 is checked under the assumption that this assertion
holds:

```
assume alwaysForget;
 using  alwaysForget prove SAN1;
```

Checking this property leads to the sixth sequence in Figure 6. A consequence
of exploring this sequence highlights the likelihood of context confusions and
therefore the need for the redesign of the device. As can be seen, an identical
subsequence of actions at positions 2 and 6 have different effects. An interlock
mechanism is therefore introduced with the aim of reducing the likelihood that
human error arising from forgetfulness might arise. The proposed redesign warns
the user and asks for acknowledgement that the currently displayed control elements are about to disappear.

The warning is issued whenever a device position is left and the device's
control elements are neither on screen nor stored in a bucket. It is straightforward
to adjust the model of the interface to the hand-held device to capture this idea,
and this specification is given in the fuller paper [14]. The design however does
not prevent the user from acknowledging and then doing nothing about the
problem.

Checking the same properties, including the assumptions about the forgetful
user, produces Sequences 7 and 8 in Figure 6. In this example the central control
panel characterises the key actions to achieving the goal since the additional
actions introduced by the hand held device are concerned exclusively with the
limitations that the new platform introduces, dealing with physical location,
uploading and storing controls of the visited devices as appropriate. The analysis
highlights these additional steps to allow the analyst to subject the sequence to
human factors analysis and to judge if such additional steps are likely to be
problematic. The reasons why a given sequence of actions might be problematic
may not be evident from the trace but it provides an important representation
that allows a human factors or domain analyst to consider these issues. For
example, action goPOS6 may involve a lengthy walk through the plant, while
action savePmp4ctrls may be performed instantaneously and the performance

of action `getPmp3ctrls` might depend on additional contextual factors like the network quality. The current approach leaves the judgement of the severity of such differences to the designer, the human factors expert or the domain expert. It makes it possible for these experts to draw important considerations to the designer's attention.

6   Conclusions

The paper illustrates how configuration and context confusions might be analysed in the early stages of design before a system is fielded. We emphasise again that the exploration of these techniques makes no presumption that these would be the only techniques used to explore potential user confusions. The particular method described involves comparing and inspecting sets of sequences of actions that reach a specified goal state. No assumptions are made about user behaviour initially, constraints based on domain and user concerns are used to explore subsets of the traces that can achieve the goals. Experts assist the process of adding the appropriate constraints to the properties to be checked. In order to do this a human factors expert or a domain expert may be provided with sufficiently rich information that it is possible to explore narratives surrounding the traces generated.

Hence traces can form the basis for scenarios that aid exploration of potential problems in the design of mobile devices, e.g. the additional work that would be involved for the system operator if subtasks are inadvertently omitted in achieving the goal. The tool can also be used to find recovery strategies if an operator forgets to store control elements.

Further work is of course needed to devise strategies for appropriate guidance with respect to (i) finding an efficient sequence of analysis steps and (ii) devising a strategy for the introduction of appropriate assumptions. Guidance is also required to help limit the size of the models to be analysed. Suitable techniques and heuristics for semantic abstraction of system models need to be devised to avoid the state explosion problem. However, the size of models that can be dealt with is encouraging and this situation can be improved through appropriate abstraction and consistency checking.

As has been said the case described in the paper involves an oversimplistic model of context for the purpose of presentation. The following questions require exploration:

– What are the key features of the design that are relevant to these context confusions? In the work described here the further step of evaluating whether the properties that are analysed actually cause user confusion is assumed to be carried out by a human factors expert who would assess the traces generated by the technique.
– What are appropriate models of context — what about the information that might be inferred at these different positions? What about knowledge about history or urgency? What about the proximity, knowledge and behaviour of other mobile agents in the environment? What about issues such as the

staleness of data? A number of papers [5,8] classify and critique notions of context.

− If more than one model is appropriate, at different stages of the design or at the same time, how are these different stages and complementary models used together?

More elaborate analysis would involve models of context in which other users and configurations (for example PDAs) may enter or leave dynamically. In order to reason about context such as these, knowledge logics using operators such as the K operator could be used to express what an agent knows in a given context [6]. Since K-logic is described in terms of a Kripke model it is relatively straightforward to perform model checking using it. Hence given the scenario example, a question may be asked such as whether it is common knowledge that the repair has been completed in order that all agents can restore the state of the components they were dealing with to their original states. The model and logic may also be used to ask whether it is possible that an agent can think that the state of their component can be restored before it is time to do it. Hence the logic will be used to express properties that capture potential user confusions in this richer notion of context.

With appropriate models and notions of user context confusion, it becomes possible to consider the pragmatics of modelling and analysis using these techniques. Similar strategies may also be adopted for exploring other aspects of context confusion, for example exploring the significance of the temporal validity of the state of a *bucket* on the user's ability to achieve goals within different timescales.

Acknowledgements

This work was supported by BAE Systems, the EPSRC DIRC project GR/ N13999 and dstl.

References

1. M. Bérard, M. Bidoit, A. Finkel, F. Laroussinie, A. Petit, L. Petrucci, and Ph. Schnoebelen. *Systems and Software Verification. Model-Checking Techniques and Tools.* Springer, 2001.
2. J.C. Campos and M.D. Harrison. Model checking interactor specifications. *Automated Software Engineering*, 8:275–310, 2001.
3. E.M. Clarke, O. Grumberg, and D.A. Peled. *Model Checking.* MIT Press, 1999.
4. A. Degani. *Modeling Human-Machine Systems: On Modes, Error, and Patterns of Interaction.* PhD thesis, Georgia Institute of Technology, December 1996.
5. A.K. Dey, G.D. Abowd, and D. Salber. A conceptual framework and a toolkit for supporting the rapid prototyping of context-aware applications. *Human-Computer Interaction*, 16:97–166, 2001.
6. R. Fagin, J.Y. Halpern, Y. Moses, and M.Y. Vardi. *Reasoning about Knowledge.* MIT Press, 2004.

7. R.E. Fields. *Analysis of erroneous actions in the design of critical systems.* PhD thesis, Department of Computer Science, University of York, Heslington, York, YO10 5DD, 2001.

8. J. Grudin. Desituating action: digital representation of context. *Human-Computer Interaction*, 16:257–268, 2001.

9. D. Harel. Statecharts: A visual formalism for complex systems. *Science of Computer Programming*, 8:231–274, 1987.

10. G.J. Holzmann. *The SPIN Model Checker, Primer and Reference Manual.* Addison Wesley, 2003.

11. Ian Horrocks. *Constructing the User Interfaces with StateCharts.* Addison Wesley, 1999.

12. M. R. A. Huth and M. D. Ryan. *Modelling and reasoning about systems.* Cambridge University Press, 2000.

13. K. Loer. *Model-based Automated Analysis for Dependable Interactive Systems.* PhD thesis, Department of Computer Science, University of York, UK, 2003.

14. K. Loer and M.D. Harrison. Analysing and modelling context in mobile systems to support design. http://homepages.cs.ncl.ac.uk/michael.harrison/publications.htm, 2004.

15. K.L. McMillan. *Symbolic model checking.* Kluwer, 1993.

16. J. Nilsson, T. Sokoler, T. Binder, and N. Wetcke. Beyond the control room: mobile devices for spatially distributed interaction on industrial process plants. In P. Thomas and H.-W. Gellersen, editors, *Handheld and Ubiquitous Computing, HUC'2000*, number 1927 in Lecture Notes in Computer Science, pages 30–45. Springer, 2000.

17. F. Paternò and C. Santoro. Support for reasoning about interactive systems through human-computer interaction designers' representations. *The Computer Journal*, 6(4):340–357, 2003.

18. John Rushby. Using model checking to help discover mode confusions and other automation surprises. *Reliability Engineering and System Safety*, 75(2):167–177, February 2002.

19. P.C. Wright, R.E. Fields, and M.D. Harrison. Analyzing human-computer interaction as distributed cognition: the resources model. *Human-Computer Interaction*, 15(1):1–42, 2000.

Attach Me, Detach Me, Assemble Me Like You Work

Donatien Grolaux[1,2], Jean Vanderdonckt[1], and Peter Van Roy[2]

[1] School of Management, Information Systems Unit, Place des Doyens,
[2] Dept. of Computing Science and Engineering, Place Sainte Barbe,
Université catholique de Louvain, B-1348 Louvain-la-Neuve, Belgium
ned@info.ucl.ac.be, vanderdonckt@isys.ucl.ac.be,
pvr@info.ucl.ac.be

Abstract. Detachable user interfaces consist of graphical user interfaces whose parts or whole can be detached at run-time from their host, migrated onto another computing platform while carrying out the task, possibly adapted to the new platform and attached to the target platform in a peer-to-peer fashion. Detaching is the property of splitting a part of a UI for transferring it onto another platform. AttAaching is the reciprocal property: a part of an existing interface can be attached to the currently being used interface so as to recompose another one on-demand, according to user's needs, task requirements. Assembling interface parts by detaching and attaching allows dynamically composing, decomposing and re-composing new interfaces on demand. To support this interaction paradigm, a development infrastructure has been developed based on a series of primitives such as display, undisplay, copy, expose, return, transfer, delegate, and switch. We exemplify it with QTkDraw, a painting application with attaching and detaching based on the development infrastructure.

1 Introduction

With the advent of ubiquitous computing and the ever increasing amount of computing platforms, the user is encouraged to work in more varying conditions that were not expected before. From a user's perspective, various scenarios may occur:

1. *Users may move between different computing platforms whilst involved in a task*: when buying a movie on DVD a user might initially search for it from her desktop computer, read the reviews of the DVD on a PDA on the train on the way home from work, and then order it using a WAP-enabled mobile phone.
2. *The context of use may change whilst the user is interacting*: the train may go into a dark tunnel so the screen of the PDA dims, the noise level will rise so the volume of audio feedback increases so it can still be heard.
3. *Users may want to collaborate on a task using heterogeneous computing platforms*: the user decides to phone up a friend who has seen the movie and look at the reviews with her, one person using WebTV and the other using a laptop, so the same information is presented radically differently.

There are many other similar situations where these types of interactions may occur, for example, graphic expert teams doing collaborative drawing tasks using

M.F. Costabile and F. Paternò (Eds.): INTERACT 2005, LNCS 3585, pp. 198–212, 2005.

information shared across multiple computing platforms, or a stock market trader who wants to access the same market data on his desktop computer and his mobile phone when she is away from her desk. We can easily extend these scenarios for multi-user communication where users interact from different contexts of use and even the type of coordination and communication that can occur among them depends on a number of aspects related to the context of use. Although more mobile computing platforms exist, they are not always compatible (they do not share the same operating system), communicant (the communication protocols are different), and composable (once together, computing platforms cannot take advantage of the newly available resources to return to another situation when some platform is leaving). Since the User Interfaces (UIs) that are running on these heterogeneous platforms cannot be composed, they are rather inflexible for reconfiguring at run-time and they may impose configurations that are not natural to the user.

For example, when a painter is painting a scene, the painting *is* the main focus of attention, while all tools (e.g., the color palette, the pencil, and the painting tools) remain secondary, available at hand when needed. Unfortunately, this is not the case with most painting/drawing software where the real world is reproduced by a working area representing the painting and a series of menu bars and tool bars containing families of related tools. When many of these bars are displayed, the UI rapidly becomes cluttered so as to reduce the working area to its minimum (Fig. 1). This UI is not considered natural [9] in the sense that tools contained in such bars are not required all the time during interaction, but solely at certain specific moments (e.g., changing the color, increasing the size of the pencil, choosing a painting effect). Of course, the end user can customize the display of tool bars, but this operation remains manual, tedious, repetitive and not related to the main task. Some UIs tend to improve this by displaying toolbars only when they are related to any object manipulated (e.g., an image, a rectangle) and undisplaying them afterwards. For example, PaintShopPro™ includes a 'Tool Options' dialog box that is displayed according the tool currently being selected. Although this partially reduces the screen density, it provokes fast visual change of the UI that may confuse the user [9].

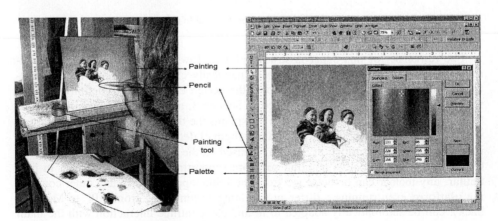

Fig. 1. Natural world vs. user interface world

The availability of today's computing platforms ranging from the traditional PC and the laptop to handheld PC and pocket PC invites us to address this problem by exploiting interaction between multiple surfaces of interaction [5] at the same time. In the painter example, a more natural UI, i.e. a UI that would mimic more the real world depending on availability of platforms, would be the largest screen used as the main painting area and a Pocket PC used only for displaying tool bars and picking there the right tools on demand.

To support this scenario and any similar situation where the user may want to compose, decompose and re-compose the components of a UI on-demand, depending on users' needs, task requirements and platforms availability, we introduce a new interaction paradigm, called *Detachable User Interfaces* that are characterized by the 'Demi-Plat' set of properties (Fig. 2):

- *Detachability*: any UI component of the interactive application of interest can be detached from its host UI, provided it is authorized to do so, while continuing to carrying out the corresponding interactive task.
- *Migratability*: the detached UI component is migrated from the source computing platform running the interactive application to another target platform, possible equipped with totally different operating systems, protocols, screen resolution.
- *Plastifiability*: the migrated UI component is adapted according to the new constraints posed by the new target computing platform, if needed [3].
- *Attachability*: the plastified UI component is attached to any UI running on the target computing platform, if needed.

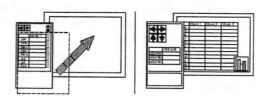

Fig. 2. The basic principle of detachable user interface

The remainder of this paper is structured as follows. The next section 2 summarizes the related work in the domain of dynamically changing UIs on different platforms. Then, the definitions, motivations, the design choices and a definition of the four 'Demi-Plat' properties are provided in Section 3, along with the primitive operations required to support them. Section 4 explains the development infrastructure that we developed to support the interaction paradigm of detachable UIs. Then, a complete implementation is described in Section 5, based on the above scenario of the painter: QTkDraw is an interactive painting software supporting the four properties. In particular, any toolbar can be detached from the initial application to any other computing platform, even running a different operating system (e.g., from a PC to Mac and back), can be automatically adapted to it, and can continue interaction with the main screen. Finally, a conclusion reports on the original points of detachable UIs, some open questions and future work in Section 6.

2 Related Work

In order to uniformly compare existing work we will take the common scenario of the Painter's palette as represented in Fig. 1 and as described in the introduction.

The first steps that have been made towards moving UIs between screens were achieved by virtual window managers capable of remotely accessing an application over the network, such as X-Windows X11 remote displays (http://www.x.org/), Virtual Network Computing (http://www.uk.research.att.com/vnc/), and Windows Terminal Server (http://www.microsoft.com/windows2000/technologies/terminal/default.asp). It is possible to launch an interactive application locally, but to transfer the UI input/output to another workstation. These solutions are controlled by the underlying operating system with a service that is independent of the interactive application. These solutions suffer from the following drawbacks: the UI cannot control its own transfer since it is independent from the service, the UI can only be moved among workstations of the same operating system (e.g., Unix or Windows), there is no adaptation to the target platform, it cannot be dissociated, and it is a client/server solution (a server that has nothing to do with the interactive application is required to run the solution ; if the server disappears, the interactive application also disappears).

Pioneering work in migration has been done by Bharat & Cardelli [2]: their migratory applications are able to move from one platform to another one at run-time, provided that the operating system remains the same. While this is probably the first truly migrating application, the main restriction is that the whole application is migrated. The situation is similar for multi-user applications when an application should be transferred to another user as in [7]. In *The Migration Project* [1], only the UI is migrated, in part or in whole, from one computing platform to another. At run-time, the user can choose the platform where to migrate. But only web pages are migrated between platforms (thus the example toolbar can be run), a migration server is required and all the various UIs for the different platforms are pre-computed.

Remote Commander [11] is an application that supports all keyboard and mouse functions and displays screen images on the handheld PC, so it can serve as a host for our example's toolbars, but the handheld PC is the only platform capable of welcoming the controls. It is not possible to decompose or recompose UI parts, the portion that is migrated needs to be predefined.

The *Pick & Drop* interaction paradigm [12] supports migration of information between platforms, like other interaction techniques and migration environments such as *i-Land* [15], *Stanford Interactive Mural* [8], *Aura* [14], *ConnecTables* [16]. But these solutions do not support the properties of detachability, attachability and plasticity when migrating a UI across platforms. In addition, all the platforms should belong to the same family, which is rarely the case when people meet or for a single person. For instance, the Stanford Interactive Mural enables user to freely move windows from one screen to another, the screens being displayed on walls, side by side or not, but the whole configuration is predefined and described in a topology model that does not accommodate entries and leavings of different platforms. Only I-AM [4,5] today exhibits the capabilities of platform discovery and UI plasticity at the same time. A meta-UI [4] is defined to control the migration process [10] across various platforms and in varying circumstances, thus releasing the user from having a predefined configuration. In contrast, detachable UIs allow people to migrate parts or whole of the UI by direct manipulation of the parts that can be effectively migrated.

3   Definitions, Motivations, and Design Choices

A UI *migration* is hereby defined as the action of transferring a UI from one source computing platform to a target one, such as from a desktop computer to a handheld device. A UI is said to be *migratable* if it holds the migration ability. A migration is said to be *total*, respectively *partial*, when the whole interactive application, respectively the UI, are migrated [1,4]. If we decompose a UI into the control which is responsible for the UI behavior and the presentation which is responsible for presenting information to the user, *control migration* [1] migrates only the control component while the presentation remains. In *presentation migration* [1], the situation is the inverse: the presentation component is migrated while the control remains on the source platform. When the migration is *mixed* [1], different parts of both the control and the presentation are migrated. To support all these different cases of migration, a special UI is required that will perform the required steps to conduct the migration, such as identification of migration possibility, proposal for migration, selection of migration alternative, and execution of the migration itself. Since these types of migrations and underlying steps require complex handling of UI events and procedures, the UI responsible for migration is even more complex and not always visible to the eyes of the end user. This UI is referred to as the *meta-user interface* in [4], i.e. the UI for controlling the run-time migration of the UI of the interactive systems. A meta-UI could be *system initiated* (the system initiates the migration), *user-initiated* (the user initiates the migration), or *mixed-initiated* (the user and the system collaborate to perform the migration).

A UI *component* is hereby defined as any part or whole of a UI of interest. It can be an individual widget (e.g., a control), a composed widget (e.g., a tool bar or a group box with contained widgets), a container (e.g., an area displaying an activity chart), a child or an application window, or any combination of these. The computing platform is referred to as the complete hardware/software environment that is considered as a whole, including the operating system and the input/output capabilities.

A *detachable UI* is a UI from which any allowed portion can be detached at run-time from one platform, migrated and adapted to another one. We now detail the four main properties of detachable UIs, as referred to the 'Demi-Plat' properties:

3.1   Detachability

Any UI component with its current status of interaction can be detached at any time. Detaching a UI is achieved by dragging a portion of the UI and dropping it outside the UI: the migration could be partial or total, presentation-, control-oriented or mixed, and user-initiated. Different types of detachability exist:

1. *Full screen* when the entire UIs of all applications running on the current platform are detached.

2. *Window* when an entire user/system-selected window or any portion of it is detached. For instance, a whole window within the border, along with its title bar, its menu bar, the scroll bar or captions lines.
3. *Active window* when the windows that has the focus of interaction on the desktop is detached when the detach operation is invoked.
4. *Region* when any user-defined rectangular region of the UI is detached. For instance, a user may select by direct manipulation a rectangle surrounding components subject to detachment.
5. *Fixed region* when a user-defined rectangular fixed region of the platform desktop defined by absolute pixel coordinates.
6. *Widget* when any individual widget is detached.

For example, to detach a palette from a drawing application, a region will be selected. When only a particular tool is required to detach, the widget part will be used instead. The fixed region can be used for instance for the menu bar of an application provided that it has been maximized full screen. In addition to the detachability property, any UI component can be declared detachable or not, splittable or not. *Detachability* decides whether a UI component can be detached to another platform or should remain fixed with the main UI. *Splittability* specifies whenever a composed UI component can be detached in itself, but that none of its sub-components can be detached individually. For example, a color palette can be declared *unsplittable* to avoid widespreading of color schemes on different surfaces. Any component that is contained in an upper-level component that is unsplitttable cannot be detached. The detach mode is invoked by triggering a special function which can be tailored on any supported platform, e.g. a function key (F12) on PC and workstation, a menu item on handheld and pocket PCs. Then, by direct manipulation, the user can visually determine the UI component subject to detachment depending on the cursor position: the component subject to detachment is highlighted. When the cursor is inside an undetachable area, respectively a detachable area, it is transformed into a forbidden sign (⃗Ⓗ) (Fig. 3a), respectively a hand (Fig. 3b) before migration.

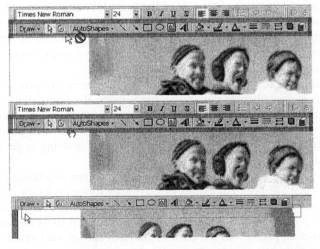

Fig. 3. Detaching a UI component before migration (forbidden area, allowed area, migration)

3.2 Migration

Migration consists of transferring any UI component (presentation and dialogue states) from one platform to another, which can be characterized along four axes:

- Amount of platforms: the migration can be *one-to-one* (from one platform to another one) or *one-to-many* (from one platform to many platforms).
- Amount of users: the migration is said to be *single-user*, respectively *multi-user*, when it occurs across platforms owned by one user, respectively by many users.
- Amount of platform types: the migration is said to be *one-threaded*, respectively *multi-threaded*, when it occurs between platforms of the same type (e.g. between two PCs), respectively of different types (e.g., from a PC to a PDA that does not necessarily run the same operating system).
- Amount of interaction surfaces: the migration can be *mono-surface*, respectively *multi-surface*, when it occurs from one interaction surface to another (e.g., from screen to screen), respectively from one surface to multiple surfaces [5,6] at the same time (e.g., from one screen to several different screens of various sizes).

For example, the QTkDraw is one-to-one (e.g., the tool bars are transferred from the PC to the Pocket PC), single-user (it is expected to be for the usability of the same user), *multi-threaded* (because of different platforms involved), and *mono-surface* (only the tool bars are migrated to a Pocket PC, although separate tool bars can migrate to different Pocket PCs). To support these configurations, a set of primitives is now defined that will be further supported in the implementation.

Display (UI, platform). Any component of the currently being used UI is displayed on a given platform. In the multi-user case, the display is remote on the other one.

Undisplay (UI, platform). Any component of the currently being used UI being on display on a given platform is erased.

Copy (UI, source, target). Any component of the currently being used UI with its current status of presentation (e.g., activated and deactivated parts) and dialogue (e.g., values already entered) is copied from the source platform to a target platform. This primitive results in having two copies of the same UI component with the status preserved, but which can now work independently of each other. The source and target UIs live their life independently. For example, a first drawing is realized and at a certain timestamp, there is a need to continue with two separate versions of the drawing to expand it with different alternatives.

Expose (UI, source, target). Any component of the currently being used UI with its current status is copied from the source platform to the target platform and frozen. Only the source UI can continue to live, the other being merely exposed to the target platform for viewing purpose and being closed afterwards. For example, one user wants to a show to a colleague the current version of a drawing to get her advice, but does not want to allow her to apply any modification.

Return (UI, target, source). Any component of the currently being used UI with its current status that has been copied previously, after living on its own, can be returned to the platform which initiated it. For example, a drawing that has been separately modified at a certain stage by a colleague can be returned to its originator. Then, the UI of concern disappears from the current platform and appears again in its new state of the platform from where it has been copied.

Transfer (UI, source, target). Any UI component with its status is copied from the source to the target and deleted from the source platform to live its life on the target.

Delegate (UI, source, target). A delegation is defined by a sequence of transfer and return. For example, a user wants to completely delegate the realization of a drawing and recuperate the results when done.

Switch (Source UI, source, Target UI, target). Two UI components of two different UIs with their status are exchanged between a source and a target. The source UI is transferred to the target and the target UI is transferred to the source. For example, when two persons working in a collaborative environment need to swap their work and to continue on each others' work.

The Copy, Expose, and Transfer primitives can be made multi-user, multi-platform by repeating the same process for multiple platforms at the same time.

3.3 Plasticity

The property of plasticity [3] is defined as the property of adapting a user interface depending on the change of the context of use, while preserving predefined usability conditions. In our case, the UI that is immigrated in the new target computing platform can be submitted to the process of plastification, if it holds the plastifiability. For instance, if a toolbar is moved from a desktop PC to a handheld PC, and only this component, then the toolbar can be magnified by increasing the size of each button belonging to the toolbar. Or the initial size of the toolbar can be preserved. If the size of the UI element that emigrated from the source platform is larger that the screen resolution of the target platform where it should immigrate, then it can be submitted to a series of plasticity rules, such as widget replacement, size reduction, text summarization techniques, repositioning of widgets, and reshuffling of components. For this purpose, we used the PlaceHolder technique (http://www.mozart-oz.org) to contain any part of the UI that can be submitted to plasticity. Thanks to this system, a container is generated at run-time that only knows its components after firing the appropriate plasticity rules. Once these subcomponents are known, their size and locations can be computed so as to determine the final size of the PlaceHolder.

3.4 Attachability

The *attachability* is defined by analogy with detachability since it is the inverse of detachability. Any UI component of interest can be attached back to its previously detached UI or to any other UI. Thanks to the attachability property, it is possible to support a UI development process by copy/paste. In traditional visual programming, any UI is drawn by composition of widgets dragged from a tool palette onto a working area. This process does not support per se composition of new UI from previously defined UIs. Of course, it is possible to copy/paste parts of the widgets, but there is a need to redraw everything. In Programming by demonstration, a UI that will be implemented is demonstrated and then derived. Here, when a UI component is attached to another UI component, they are automatically merged so as to create an entirely new UI. There is no need to redraw the UI and this operation can be done at run-time rather than at design-time. Or any selected component from one UI can be copied, dragged and dropped into another UI to compose a new UI merging functions which are the sum of functions provided by the individual components.

4 Development Infrastructure for Detachable User Interfaces

To support the above properties, we have developed techniques for making UI detachable by relying on the Mozart-Oz environment (www.mozart-oz.org) that intrinsically supports distributed computing. This environment is multi-platform: a freely downloadable version exists for Linux, Windows, and Macintosh operating systems, thus providing us the advantage that any UI that will be made detachable thanks to this infrastructure will be able to migrate between *any* operating system in a *peer-to-peer* fashion as there is no need to run a server. Each interactive application can manage its own detachability and attachability. We now describe the indirection mechanism that supports at the application level the properties of detachability, attachability, and migration. The toolkit creates a window out of a declarative data structure, called an Oz record, similar in expressiveness to XML. This data structure describes many (if not all) aspects of the window that are specifiable declaratively: the widgets that compose the window, their initial states, their geometry inside the window, their behavior upon window resizing, etcetera. Also, using the handle parameter of the widgets in the description record, controller objects are created that allows a dynamic interaction between the UI and the application once the window has been created. In summary, this toolkit uses first a record DR to create the window in its initial state; during the creation of the window, Oi objects are created to further control individual widgets in an object-oriented imperative way.

Let us build a migratable window from a description record DR (Fig. 4). The handle parameters of DR are bound to P$_i$ proxy objects instead of the usual Oi objects, and a CM communication manager object is created. The original DR record is also stored by CM. At this stage, there is no display D site yet.

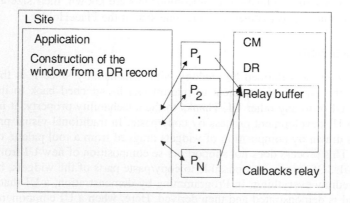

Fig. 4. Definition of a migratable window

The proxy objects will act as the local representatives of the actual `Oi` widget objects. There are at least two ways to implement Pi objects:

1. `Pi` objects reflect the whole semantics of their corresponding `Oi` objects. They don't rely on any `Oi` object to serve their purpose. This requires a huge amount of development and maintenance work: each widget must exist in an actual and proxy flavor.

2. `Pi` objects are generic objects that relay application messages to their currently connected `Oi`. This is the solution used by our toolkit. As a side effect, a `Pi` object cannot work correctly unless it is connected to an actual `Oi` object. When not connected, method invocation messages are buffered; only when connected these messages are processed by the display site.

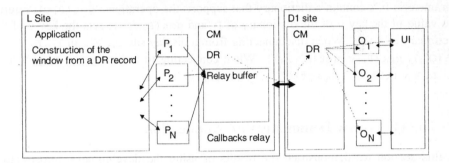

Fig. 5. Configuration of a migrated window

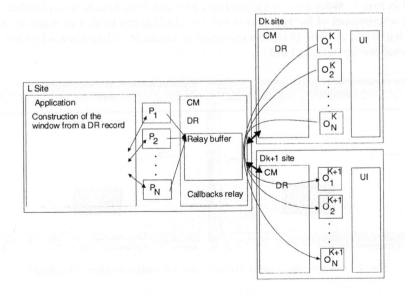

Fig. 6. Migration to another site

When the first remote display site D_1 connects to the CM of L (Fig. 5), the DR record is sent. D_1 creates the effective UI and the O_i's from this DR. At this moment, the application can start working with the migrated UI; the buffered messages are sent first. When migrating to a D_{k+1} site (Fig. 6), the actual user interface and $O^{k+1}{}_i$'s are still created from the DR record. However the visual aspects of the widgets might have changed since their creation time, and the D_{k+1} site should reflect that. Let's define:

- VA(O) = {v | v is a visually observable aspect of the widget controlled by O}
- get(O, v): returns the current value of the visual aspect v of O.
- set(O, v, s): sets the visual aspect v of O to s.

After the user interface and $O^{(k+1)}{}_i$'s are created at D_{k+1}, $\forall$ i in 1..N, $\forall$ v in VA($O^k{}_i$): set($O^{k+1}{}_i$, v, get($O^k{}_i$, v)). In practice, P_i's are used to store the visual parameters: P_i's contain a dictionary that supports the operations: get(P, v): returns the value of the key v of the dictionary of P and set(P, v, s): sets the key v of the dictionary of P to s. When disconnecting from a display site D_k, $\forall$ i in 1..N, $\forall$ v in VA($O^k{}_i$), set(P_i, v, get($O^k{}_i$, v)). When connecting to a display site D_{k+1}, $\forall$ i in 1..N, $\forall$ v in VA($O^{k+1}{}_i$), set($O^{k+1}{}_i$, v, get(P_i, v)).

5   The QTkDraw Demonstration Application

In this section we demonstrate the results of using the development infrastructure explained in Section 4 for the QTkDraw application that serves as a demonstration. We then applied the development infrastructure to obtain the detachable UI reproduced in Fig. 7, where two UI components were declared detachable, splittable. Fig. 7 shows a screenshot of the application before detaching the toolbar (left arrow) and the color bar (right arrow). This demonstration is available at http://www.isys.ucl.ac.be/bchi/members/dgr/palette.html.

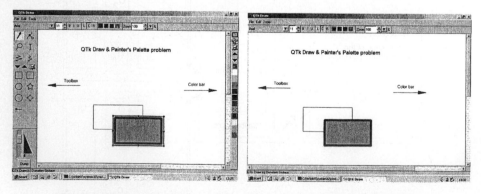

Fig. 7. Detaching the toolbar and the color bar from a desktop to PocketPCs

Since the application is developed on top of Tcl/Tk which is itself running on several computing platforms (i.e., Linux, Windows, and Macintosh) the native Look &

Feel of the platform is preserved. Therefore, the same application can run on all these platforms without changing one line of code: they are simply re-interpreted on top of the development infrastructure.

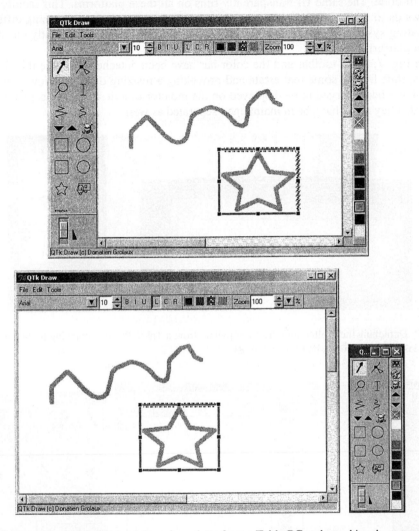

Fig. 8. Detaching the toolbar and the color palette from a TabletPC and attaching them together on a desktop

In Fig. 7 and Fig. 8, the screenshots have been taken in the Windows environment, but they could have been taken in any other environment equally. Even among different platforms running the same operating system and window manager (here, Windows), the application can be run on different devices such as desktop (Fig. 7), TabletPC (Fig. 8), and PocketPC (Fig. 9) by accommodating the different resolutions, with or without plasticity depending on underlying plasticity rules embedded and called. Thanks to the availability of the Mozart software platform for different operating systems (e.g., Microsoft Windows, Apple OS X, and Linux), it is possible to run the same UIs with the same support for Demi-plat properties without changing any line of code. The same UI transparently runs on all these platforms. This facility also allows us to think about migrating a UI across computing platforms running different operating systems since the code of the application can be run indifferently on any of these platforms.

In Fig. 7, 8, the toolbar and the color bar have been detached from the initial windows, thus freeing some real estate and provoking a resizing of the window. The two bars have been merged to be displayed on the monitor of a desktop PC, as pictured in Fig. 9. They could have been maintained separated as well.

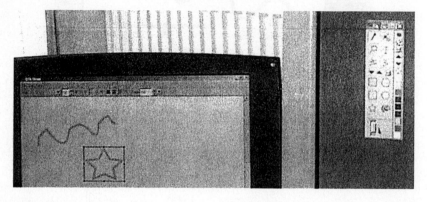

Fig. 9. Detaching the toolbar and the color palette from a TabletPC and attaching them together on a desktop (picture of situation in Fig. 8)

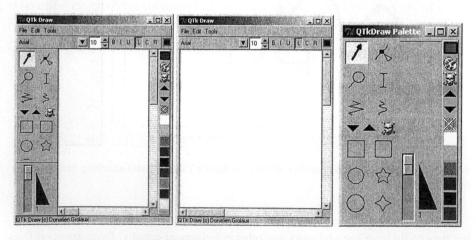

Fig. 10. Detaching the toolbar and the color palette from a PC and attaching them together on another PocketPC

Fig. 10 depicts another configuration in which QTkDraw is executed: first, the complete application is running on a PC, then the toolbar and the color bar are in turn detached from the initial PC and migrated onto a PocketPC. The migration of the second color bar onto the same target PocketPC provokes an attaching of the second bar to the first one, thus leading to repositioning and resizing the bars to fit in a general PlaceHolder. Note that in this case the rule is not detachable, therefore it cannot be migrated onto any other platform. From Fig. 7 to Fig. 10, there is no problem of detaching, attaching the two bars at any time from one platform to another. There is no need of migration server since the application satisfies the 'Demi-Plat' properties itself. The user does not loose the control after detaching and attaching: the UI state is preserved. Actually, there is even no true need to save and restore the UI state since it is simply redirected to another platform wirelessly.

6   Conclusion

This paper presented a development infrastructure supporting detachable UIs. From the application point of view, this is a transparent process: there is no difference between using a stationary UI and a migratable one. A painting application has been changed to behave like the painter's palette (Fig. 2): the tool bar and the color bar can be taken away from the main window, and migrated to any other computer. The difference between the stationary version of the application and the migratable one is around 30 lines of code out of more than 8000. The application that receives the migrated UI is also around 30 lines of code. Note that the core of the application can be extended as if the whole application was purely stationary. As a window can contain an arbitrary amount of migrated UIs at the same time, it is also possible to dynamically compose a UI from different migrated UI components. One could imagine several different applications managing different aspects of a unique problem: their UIs are conveniently migrated to a single place. The system administrator migrates the UIs from all these applications into a single window. This window is migrated between his desktop when he is in front of his desk, and his laptop computer when he is away. Also the development cost of this application is almost the same as the development cost of a stationary version, very little change is required to make the information migrating. This toolkit provides low cost migration mechanism that enables us to have more freedom with multi-platform ubiquitous UIs.

Acknowledgements

We acknowledge the support of the Pirates and Salamandre research projects and the SIMILAR network of excellence, the European research task force creating human-machine interfaces similar to human-human communication (http://www.similar.cc).

References

1. Bandelloni, R., Paternò, F.: Flexible Interface Migration. In: Proceedings of ACM Con. on Intelligent User Interfaces IUI'04 (Funchal). ACM Press, New York (2004) 148–155
2. Bharat, K.A., Cardelli, L.: Migratory Applications Distributed User Interfaces. In: Proc. of ACM Conf. on User Interface Software Technology UIST'95. ACM Press (1995) 133–142

3. Calvary, G., Coutaz, J., Thevenin, D., Limbourg, Q., Bouillon, L., Vanderdonckt, J.: A Unifying Reference Framework for Multi-Target UI. Interacting with Computers 15,3

4. Coutaz, J., Balme, L., Lachenal, Ch., Barralon, N.: Software Infrastructure for Distributed Migratable User Interfaces. In: Proc. of UbiHCISys Workshop on UbiComp 2003 (2003).

5. Coutaz, J., Lachenal, C., Calvary, G., Thevenin, D.: Software Architecture Adaptivity for Multisurface Interaction and Plasticity. In: Proc. of IFIP Workshop on Software Architecture Requirements for CSCW–CSCW'2000 Workshop.

6. Coutaz, J., Lachenal, Ch., Dupuy-Chessa, S., Ontology for Multi-Surface Interaction. In: Proc. of IFIP Conf. on Human-Computer Interaction Interact'2003. IOS Press (2003).

7. Dewan, P., Choudhary, R.: Coupling the User Interfaces of a Multiuser Program. ACM Transactions on Computer-Human Interaction 2,1 (2000) 1–39

8. Guimbretière, F., Stone, M., Winograd, T.: Fluid Interaction with High-resolution Wall-size Displays. In: Proc. of ACM Conf. on User Interface Software Technology UIST'2001

9. Jacobson, J.: Configuring Multiscreen Displays with Existing Computer Equipment. In: Proc. of Conf. on Human Factors HFES'2002.

10. Milojicic, D.S., Douglis, F., Paindaveine, Y., Wheeler, R., Zhou, S.: Process Migration. ACM Computing Surveys 32, 3 (September 2000) 241–299

11. Myers, B.A., Nichols, J., Wobbrock, J.O., Miller, R.C.: Taking Handheld Devices to the Next Level. IEEE Computer 37, 12 (December 2004) 36–43

12. Rekimoto, J.: Pick-and-Drop: A Direct Manipulation Technique for Multiple Computer Environments. In: Proc. of UIST'97. ACM Press, New York (1997) 31–39

13. Rekimoto, J., Masanori, S.: Augmented Surfaces: A Spatially Continuous Work Space for Hybrid Computing Environments. In: Proc. of CHI'99. ACM Press, NY (1999) 378–385

14. Sousa, J., Garlan, D.: Aura: an Architectural Framework for User Mobility in Ubiquitous Computing Environments. In: Proc. of IEEE-IFIP Conf. on Software Architecture (2002)

15. Streitz, N., et al.: i-LAND: An interactive Landscape for Creativity and Innovation. In: Proc. of ACM Conf. on Human Factors in Computing Systems CHI'99. 120–127

16. Tandler, P., et al.: ConnecTables: Dynamic coupling of displays for the flexible creation of shared workspaces. In: Proc. of UIST'01. ACM Press, New York (2001) 11–20

Bringing Dynamic Queries to Mobile Devices: A Visual Preference-Based Search Tool for Tourist Decision Support

Stefano Burigat, Luca Chittaro, and Luca De Marco

HCI Lab, Dept. of Math and Computer Science, University of Udine
Via delle Scienze 206, 33100, Udine, Italy
{burigat, chittaro, demarco}@dimi.uniud.it

Abstract. This paper discusses the design and development of a preference-based search tool (PBST) for tourists, operating on PDA devices. PBSTs are decision support systems that help users in finding the outcomes (e.g., multi-attribute products or services) that best satisfy their needs and preferences. Our tool is specifically aimed at filtering the amount of information about points of interest (POIs) in a geographic area, thus supporting users in the search of the most suitable solution to their needs (e.g., a hotel, a restaurant, a combination of POIs satisfying a set of constraints specified by the user). We focus on the design of an effective interface for the tool, by exploring the combination of dynamic queries to filter POIs on a map with a visualization of the degree of satisfaction of constraints set by the user. We also report the results of a usability test we carried out on the first prototype of the system.

1 Introduction

Mobile computing devices such as PDAs or high-end mobile phones are becoming more and more widespread and powerful. Due to their intrinsic portability, these devices are ideal for traveling users such as tourists or businessmen, who can benefit from a growing number of specific applications. In recent years, for example, there has been a growing interest towards the development of *mobile tourist guides* [1]. These guides provide users with easy access to various classes of information about places (e.g., history, entertainment, dining, transportation, ...), support users during navigation in an area and can allow one to take advantage of the most useful services for a given location (e.g., tour planning, online bookings, weather forecasts and so on). However, current mobile guides provide only limited help as *preference-based search tools* (PBSTs), i.e. applications that assist users in finding multi-attribute products or services that best satisfy their needs, preferences and constraints (e.g., the best hotel for staying overnight, the best place for dining, ...).

Existing PBSTs for tourist decision support on PDAs (e.g., [2]) are still limited in their flexibility and capabilities when compared to similar applications for desktop computers. In this paper, we present our work on the design and

M.F. Costabile and F. Paternò (Eds.): INTERACT 2005, LNCS 3585, pp. 213–226, 2005.

development of a PBST for tourists, operating on PDA devices. Our tool is specifically aimed at filtering the amount of information about points of interest (POIs) in a geographic area, thus supporting users in the search of the most suitable solution to their needs (e.g., a hotel, a restaurant, a combination of POIs satisfying a set of constraints specified by the user). Since device limitations pose constraints on what (and how) information can be visualized, the design of an effective interface for the tool is challenging. Our project focuses on combining dynamic queries to filter POIs on a map with a visualization of the degree of satisfaction of constraints set by the user.

The paper is organized as follows. Section 2 surveys related work on PBSTs. Section 3 presents our approach to the design of a PBST for PDAs, describing requirements and challenges and how we dealt with them. In Section 4, we report the results of a usability test we carried out on the first prototype of the system. Section 5 presents conclusions and future work.

2   Related Work

Searching for a product matching a set of requirements (user's preferences or constraints) is today a frequent task for users, e.g. in e-commerce sites. However, most search tools impose a fixed decision-making sequence on the user and typically visualize the results as ranked lists: products matching the user's request are ordered with respect to some attribute (e.g., alphabetically, by price, etc.). This approach becomes less and less usable as the number of product features and the complexity of user's criteria increase. Thus, researchers are studying how to improve the level of user support. Some of them have focused on modeling user's preferences, studying decision making processes and extending traditional decision theories (see [3] for a survey). Others have studied methods to incrementally elicit user's preferences [4]. Several advanced decision support systems for the search of multi-attribute products have been proposed in different domains (e.g., FindMe [5], ATA [6], Apt Decision [7], SmartClient [8][9]). Most of these systems are based on the *example critiquing* model of interactive problem solving: the system presents candidate solutions to the user based on an initial preference specification and the user either accepts a result or takes a near solution and critiques it by revising the current preference values. For example, using the SmartClient system for finding apartments, users can compose a critique to find a less expensive apartment than those proposed, by clicking on a pulldown menu next to the price attribute and selecting the "less expensive" option. Users can also set the weight of a preference, thus considering tradeoffs while searching for products. While in the real estate domain SmartClient offers only a textual list to visualize the results of a search, in the travel planning domain [8] it employs different visualization techniques such as maps, parallel coordinate plots and starfield displays. ScoreCat [10] does not only rank products as SmartClient, but also displays how each attribute scores in relation to user's preferences. These visualization techniques allow the user to better analyse solutions and augment her confidence level in the choices made.

A different approach to preference-based search is represented by *dynamic queries* [11][12]. Dynamic queries are typically used to explore large datasets, providing users with a fast and easy-to-use method to specify queries and visually present their results. The basic idea of dynamic queries is to combine input widgets (called "query devices" [13]), such as rangesliders, alphasliders [14], check buttons and radio buttons, with graphical representations of the results, such as maps, scatterplots [15] or other visual displays. By directly manipulating query devices, users can specify the desired values for the attributes of elements in the dataset and can thus easily explore different subsets of the data. Results are usually rapidly updated, enabling users to quickly learn interesting properties of the dataset. As shown with user studies [11][16], dynamic queries are more usable and powerful than lists, form filling, or natural language systems, to perform queries. They have been successfully employed in application domains such as real estate [16] and tourism [17].

The previously cited approaches have been developed for desktop systems, and PBSTs are still rare in the mobile computing domain area. The Michelin Guide for PDAs [2] is a commercial application allowing users to search for hotels or restaurants in a specific city by entering their preferences through drop-down lists and checkboxes. Results are then visualized as a ranked list ordered by quality and further information on an element can be retrieved by selecting it in the list. Some steps towards a more complex decision support tool for mobile devices have been recently proposed by Dunlop et al. [18][17]. In [17], they describe CityGuide, an application based on a geographic map that highlights tourist attractions in the city of Glasgow. The aim of the system is to support tourists' unstructured search. The current implementation contains an extensive restaurant guide that can be browsed through a set of dynamic filters. The implemented filters (restaurant type and price) can be activated by selecting them in the application toolbar: the first is controlled through a pop-up menu that provides a list of possible price ranges to choose from; the second through a pop-up window containing a set of check-boxes. The result of a query is immediately displayed on the map as a set of icons displaying the position of restaurants that pass through the filters. Users can then click on icons to obtain further details.

3   The Proposed Solution

The design of our PBST for searching POIs in a geographic area has been guided by different needs. On one side, behavior decision theories and user studies provide requirements that decision search tools and their interfaces should satisfy; in particular, as reported by [9], it should be possible for users to construct their preferences incrementally (that is, without being forced to specify all preferences initially and then examining the results), users should be able to specify their preferences in any order, the decision tool should display partially satisfied results and help users in decision tradeoff analysis, domain knowledge should be revealed whenever possible. Moreover, the development of PDA applications must face both technical and usability challenges with respect to desktop PC applications since mobile devices are characterized by scarce screen size (and resolution), limited computing performance and memory storage, and different input peripherals.

To satisfy all these requirements, we took an approach based on dynamic queries rather than employing the example critiquing model. Instead of letting the application compute the best solutions and propose them to the user (who can then refine her preferences by defining critiques to obtain better solutions), we designed an interface that allows users to specify their preferences incrementally by interactively imposing constraints on POIs attributes (through query devices) and immediately see the effects of their actions. By using this approach, users are in full control of the system, gain flexibility in exploring and analysing the solution space and possibly feel a greater confidence on the obtained results. However, implementing a PBST based on dynamic queries on a PDA is challenging because:

1. The standard behavior for dynamic query systems is to filter out those solutions that do not satisfy all specified preferences. A specific visualization technique must be instead employed to properly display partially satisfied results.
2. Both results and query devices (enabling users to perform searches) must be visualized at the same time. Since screen size is limited and users must be able to easily set various preferences on different attributes, a specific solution is needed.
3. Users must be able to quickly detect relevant attribute values associated with the elements under examination while performing queries. Again, the limited screen size forces to come up with proper solutions.

The following sections discuss how we dealt with these challenges. Section 3.1 will deal with the first issue, presenting our solution for the visualization of partially satisfied results, while section 3.2 will deal with the second and third issues by describing in detail the interface of our system. Finally, section 3.3 presents a typical example of system use.

3.1   Visualizing Partially Satisfied Results

The most common approach in visualizing the results of dynamic queries is to display all and only the elements that satisfy the query. However, as pointed out by Spence [19], this has a major drawback: only those objects whose attribute values satisfy all users' constraints are displayed. It is thus impossible for users to have a global view that shows also partially satisfied results, and to see how changing a query affects the hidden elements. In particular, elements whose attribute values fail to satisfy only a few constraints (e.g., only one) would be especially worthy of more detailed consideration. Moreover, when an empty result is obtained, the user has to backtrack without seeing how to find elements which are closest to the originally derived ones.

We propose a simple visualization technique to help users maintain contextual information on the whole dataset they are exploring. In our system, elements in the dataset (i.e., POIs) are represented by icons superimposed on a map of the geographic area, augmented by a vertical bar representing how much they satisfy users' queries (see Fig. 1).

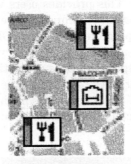

Fig. 1. Each element in the dataset is displayed as an icon representing its category, augmented by a vertical bar showing how much it satisfies users' queries

This technique is an evolution of an idea presented by Fishkin and Stone [20] who introduced the concept of "real-valued queries" by assigning a real-valued score in the [0-1] range to each element in the dataset, based on the value of a specific attribute and on the particular scoring function that is being used. The score is visually presented by showing each element as a partially filled-in bar: the higher the score, the more the bar is filled. Instead of visually displaying a score dependent on the value of an attribute, we display a score dependent on the number of constraints satisfied by an element. We then fill the bar associated with each element with a green[1] area whose size is proportional to the number of satisfied constraints while the remaining area gets filled in red. This way, users can visually compare how much different elements satisfy the specified set of constraints obtaining a deeper understanding of the visualized dataset. Combining this visualization technique with dynamic queries, users can visually perceive the result of their queries by observing changes in the color-filled areas of the bars.

3.2   Interacting with the System

As reported in the previous section, we chose to display POIs as icons superimposed on a map of the considered area (see Fig. 2). This solution is much more natural and powerful than providing a simple ranked list of the results, which is the usual approach in PBSTs, because it provides spatial information by highlighting POIs positions.

---

[1] In the greyscale printed version of this paper, wherever colours are mentioned light grey in the figures corresponds to green, dark grey to red, black to blue.

We devote most of the screen to show the map. The bottom of the screen contains the menu bar and a toolbar which is initially empty except for the zoom icon. The map can be easily panned by dragging the pen on the screen in the desired direction.

Unlike current systems that usually support only one category of POIs at a time (usually hotels or restaurants), our tool allows users to deal with multiple categories at the same time. This provides users with much more information about the domain and is useful to compose more complex queries. Users can choose the categories by tapping on the item "POI" in the menu bar and then checking the proper boxes in a form. Each category is identified by an icon that will be used in the map to display elements. Once the form is closed, the icons of the selected categories appear in the toolbar in the lower part of the screen and the map gets populated with all the elements in those categories. Each element bar is initially fully green because there are no constraints specified.

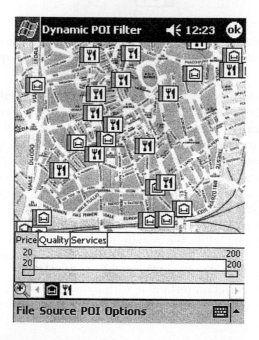

Fig. 2. The map displays all elements of the categories whose icons are shown by the toolbar in the lower part of the screen. A tabbed panel contains the query devices related to the currently selected category in the toolbar.

By tapping on a category icon in the toolbar, the user can specify preferences using the set of query devices associated to that category. These query devices, which are automatically generated by the system according to the type and the range of values of attributes, are organized in a tabbed interface placed above the toolbar, where each tab allows users to specify values for a single attribute of the considered elements. Figure 2 shows an example where the user has selected the "Hotel" category (see the highlighted icon in the toolbar) and can specify preferences for the "Price", "Quality" and "Services" attributes by accessing the corresponding tabs. This layout allows users to specify their preferences in any order while visualizing results at the same time.

We implemented three types of query devices. The first is the classic rangeslider, usually associated with continuous attributes (e.g., price): the user acts on two independent handles to change the range of values of the related attribute. Figure 3 shows an example of this query device where the user has specified a price range between 40 and 80 Euro. The selected range is highlighted by using color and by showing the numeric value of the bounds. The design of the slider is slightly different from what can be usually seen on desktop interfaces. In particular, the handles have been placed under the body of the slider and they are aligned with the borders of the specified range area so as not to overlap when a small range is specified.

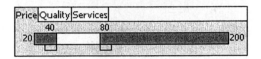

Fig. 3. The rangeslider

The second query device (Fig. 4) is a modification of the rangeslider that can be used to deal with ordinal values (e.g., the number of stars of a hotel). Users operate this device as the classic rangeslider but its behavior is slightly different: when the user stops dragging on one of the two handles, the handle is automatically positioned at the nearest lower limit for the lower handle and at the nearest upper limit for the upper handle.

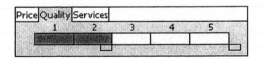

Fig. 4. The "discrete" rangeslider

The third query device is based on the classic checkbox widget and can be used for multiple-choice attributes (e.g., types of services offered by a hotel). An example can be seen in Fig. 5: a POI satisfies the "Services" constraint if it has all the services specified through the checkboxes.

The system provides also a details-on-demand functionality: at any time, the user can tap on any POI on the map to obtain further information about it. As shown in Fig. 6, the tapped icon on the map becomes highlighted and details

Price	Quality	Services	
☐ Air Cond.		☐ Garden	
☐ Credit Card		☐ Internet	
☐ Garage		☐ TV Sat.	

Fig. 5. A group of checkbox widgets

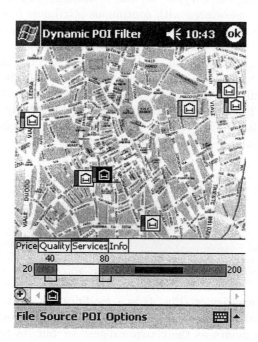

Fig. 6. The interface after the selection of a POI on the map. As shown by the color coded lines on each tab, the "Price" and "Services" constraints are not satisfied. A blue horizontal bar inside the "Price" query device shows the range of prices for the selected POI.

are shown in the tabbed interface. In particular, a color coded line in the upper area of each tab tells if the POI satisfies (green line) or not (red line) the related constraint. In this way, a user can learn at-a-glance which constraints are satisfied (and which ones are not) by the POI, without having to examine the details. Moreover, attribute values for the selected POI are visualized in the query devices by using a blue horizontal bar (the same color as the highlighted POI) inside sliders and marking checkboxes with blue boxes. For example, in Fig. 6, the horizontal bar inside the "Price" query device shows the range of prices for the selected hotel, while, in Fig. 7, blue boxes highlight available services (i.e., "Air Conditioning", "Credit Card", "Garage" and "Garden") for the selected POI. The details-on-demand functionality aims at making the system easier to use by providing rapid access to information which is usually more difficult to obtain in traditional systems and that can be used as a guide for modifying a query. The

Fig. 7. Blue boxes highlight available services for the selected POI in the map

additional tab named "Info" contains contact information on the selected POI such as name, address, phone number, etc.

Our query devices are not tight coupled [15]. In a dynamic query system using tight coupling, results of users' operations on a query device automatically trigger modifications to all other query devices so that only values associated with current solutions can be specified. Since in these systems only fully satisfied solutions are displayed, this behavior does not change the solution set and prevents users from specifying empty queries. On the other hand, tight coupling might influence the percentage of satisfied constraints for partially satisfied solutions, thus it cannot be used in our system. If it were applied, users might not be able to understand why some changes are taking place or they might think that a change is a consequence of their direct manipulation of a query device, while it is a consequence of query devices interrelations.

3.3   Using the System: A Real Scenario

In this section we will describe a typical session with the system, describing the steps needed to obtain the result and pointing out some features that help the user. We will refer to Fig. 8 for illustrative purposes.

The user of the system is a professor visiting a city for a two-day conference. She needs to find a hotel to stay overnight. After selecting hotels as the category of POIs to be displayed, she sets the price range she prefers (40-80 Euro) using the continuous range slider (Fig. 8a). She then sets the Quality constraint (asking for at least a three star hotel) using a discrete range slider (Fig. 8b) and the Services constraint (she wants air conditioning and prefers to pay with her credit card) using checkboxes (Fig. 8c). Then, she looks at the visualization, singles out a hotel satisfying all the specified constraints and taps it on the map to check its attributes (see Fig. 8d) and obtain contact information through the Info tab. She also checks the hotel that is nearest to the conference venue to know why it does not satisfy all her constraints and she immediately notices (by looking at the colored lines on the tabs) that it does not satisfy the Price and the Services constraints (Fig. 8e). In particular, the price range is too high for her. Then she wants to look for a restaurant near the chosen hotel. She thus selects the restaurant category and defines the constraints (she wants a restaurant that is open on Tuesday and does not cost too much, see Fig. 8f - 8h). Looking at the only two restaurants satisfying all the constraints she sees that they are far from her hotel (Fig. 8i). She then examines partially satisfied elements near her hotel and finds one that satisfies all constraints but "Type" (Fig. 8j). Anyway, this seems a good tradeoff for her needs and she proceeds getting contact information through the "Info" tab.

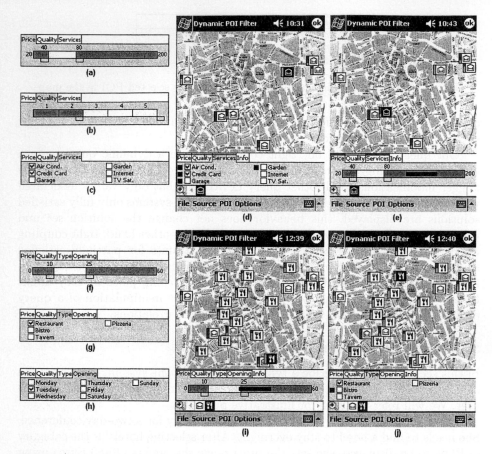

Fig. 8. Example: (a-b-c-d-e) finding a hotel, (f-g-h-i-j) finding the most suitable restaurant near the chosen hotel

4   Usability Evaluation

We carried out a usability evaluation of the system to point out problems with the interface and obtain information to plan possible improvements.

Eight users, six male and two female, were recruited among the staff of our department to participate in the evaluation. The age of subjects ranged from 24 to 30, averaging at 26. All subjects were regular computer users but only two of them had previously used PDAs.

The evaluation procedure was organized in four phases and lasted a total of 30 to 40 minutes for each user. An iPAQ h3970, featuring an Intel XScale 400MHz processor and a 320x240 screen resolution, was used as testing device. During the evaluation, the experimenter observed users' interaction with the system and took notes about their behavior. In the first phase, the experimenter showed to the participant how to use the system, explaining all its features. In the second phase, the user was asked to try the system for a limited period of time (5 minutes) to become familiar with the available functions. In the third phase, users were asked to carry out a series of predefined tasks which took into consideration all system features. In particular, they had to specify some queries, ranging from simple (requiring to specify a single constraint) to complex ones (requiring to specify multiple constraints on different categories), and then point out in the map the elements satisfying all the constraints or, in the case of an empty result (that is, no fully green bar for any POI), those elements which best satisfied the constraints. The fourth phase of the experiment was based on a questionnaire consisting of 28 questions (inspired by user interaction satisfaction questionnaires such as QUIS [21]). Users were asked to rate system features on a 7-value Likert scale, where higher values corresponded to better ratings. More specifically, questions concerned widgets (ease of use, expected behavior, affordance), tabbed interface (ease of use, usefulness of colored tabs), visualization of results (usefulness, understandability), graphical interface (colors, aesthetics, organization), overall system usefulness and ease of use. Users could also add free comments about the system and its features.

4.1 Results

Most of the features received high ratings in the adopted Likert scale and positive comments. The mean value for the 28 questions was 5.6, with mean values for single questions ranging from a minimum of 4.0 to a maximum of 6.9. The worst results concerned the interaction with the rangeslider and discrete rangeslider query devices. In particular, users had difficulties in specifying the range of values in the rangeslider since they were asked to set values precisely and no fine tuning mechanism was available. In the case of the discrete range slider, users considered it too complex and too time-consuming. A more simple implementation based on checkboxes would have been preferred. Users expressed an high degree of satisfaction for the possibility to maintain a global view on all POIs, for the availability of the colored lines on the tabs that informed about the satisfaction of a constraint, for the graphical interface (colors, aesthetics, organization). Globally, the system was judged useful (6.8) and its features were considered easy to use (6.3) and easy to understand (6.3).

From the observation of user interaction with the system and from users' written comments we derived the following major considerations:

1. Users should be able to hide those POIs that do not satisfy constraints they consider to be most relevant (i.e., high-priority constraints).
2. If POIs fall outside the currently displayed part of the map there should be an indication of how many of them satisfy all the specified constraints and where to find them.
3. POIs satisfying all constraints should be made visually more evident.
4. POIs belonging to the currently explored category should be highlighted.
5. The discrete rangeslider would be better replaced by checkboxes.
6. The handles of the rangesliders should have better affordance.
7. Fine tuning of the rangesliders should be available.

All but the first two items require only minor changes to the current implementation and will not change system's behavior. Introducing priorities will allow users to filter out those POIs that do not satisfy constraints that cannot be relaxed. The behavior with high-priority constraints is similar to traditional dynamic query systems but allows the user to control when and on what attributes to apply the filtering. Note that this is different from using soft constraints, that is expressing users' criteria as a scale of preferences using weights [22]. Providing information on out-of-view POIs is a more difficult issue. A possible solution to this problem could be to adapt a technique such as Halo [23], which helps in visualizing off-screen locations on small-screen devices.

5 Conclusions and Future Work

Powerful and flexible PBSTs for PDAs, supporting users while traveling (and complementing existing applications such as mobile tourist guides), are still lacking. The work described in this paper is a first investigation to build such systems, and has been specifically aimed at allowing users to explore and filter data about POIs. We have proposed an approach based on dynamic queries and a constraints visualization technique that allows to better support users in making decisions. PDA limitations, in particular the reduced display area, have been faced in our system by adopting solutions such as tabbed organization, tailored versions of standard query devices, details-on-demand.

We are currently planning an experimental evaluation that will compare our system with a traditional PBST based on the use of form filling to specify preferences and the use of ranked lists to display the results. We will also compare our visualization technique with a slightly modified version of it based on the standard dynamic query paradigm (that is, partially satisfied solutions are not visualized). We will also improve the system by adding other features such as the capability to automatically set preferences based on past user's behavior.

Besides the current application to tourism, we will investigate if the approach we proposed (in particular, the constraint visualization technique) can be applied to other application areas as well in the mobile context.

Acknowledgments

Our research has been partially supported by the Italian Ministry of Education, University and Research (MIUR) under the project "Web-based management and representation of spatial and geographical data", subproject "User Interfaces for the Visualization of Geographical Data on Mobile Devices".

References

1. Baus, J., Cheverst, K., Kray, C.: A Survey of Map-based Mobile Guides. In: Map-based mobile services - Theories, Methods, and Implementations, Springer-Verlag (2005) 197–216

2. Michelin Guide for PDAs, http://www.viamichelin.com/viamichelin/gbr/tpl/psg /produits/htm/pda_guide_michelin.htm
3. Doyle, J., Thomason, R.: Background to Qualitative Decision Theory. AI Magazine **20** (1999) 55–68
4. Pu, P., Faltings, B., Torrens, M.:   User-Involved Preference Elicitation.   In: International Joint Conference on Artificial Intelligence (IJCAI 03) Workshop on Configuration. (2003)
5. Burke, K., Hammond, K., Young, B.: The FindMe Approach to Assistive Browsing. IEEE Expert **12** (1997) 32–40
6. Linden, G., Hanks, S., Lesh, N.: Interactive Assessment of User Preference Models: the Automated Travel Assistant. In: Proc. Conference on User Modeling (UM 97), Springer-Verlag (1997) 67–78
7. Shearin, S., Lieberman, H.: Intelligent Profiling by Example. In: Proc. Conference on Intelligent User Interfaces (IUI 2001), ACM Press (2001) 145–151
8. Pu, P., Faltings, B.: Enriching Buyers' Experiences: the SmartClient Approach. In: Proc. Conference on Human Factors in Computing Systems (CHI 2000), ACM Press (2000) 289–296
9. Pu, P., Kumar, P.: Evaluating Example-based Search Tools. In: Proc. Conference on Electronic Commerce (EC 04), ACM Press (2004) 208–217
10. Stolze, M.:   Comparative Study of Analytical Product Selection Support Mechanisms. In: Proc. INTERACT 99, IFIP/IOS Press (1999) 45–53
11. Ahlberg, C., Williamson, C., Shneiderman, B.: Dynamic Queries for Information Exploration: an Implementation and Evaluation. In: Proc. Conference on Human Factors in Computing Systems (CHI 92), ACM Press (1992) 619–626
12. Shneiderman, B.: Dynamic Queries for Visual Information Seeking. IEEE Software **11** (1994) 70–77
13. Ahlberg, C., Truvé, S.: Exploring Terra Incognita in the Design Space of Query Devices. In: Proc. Working Conference on Engineering for Human Computer Interaction (EHCI 95), Chapman & Hall (1995) 305–321
14. Ahlberg, C., Shneiderman, B.: The Alphaslider: a Compact and Rapid Selector. In: Proc. Conference on Human Factors in Computing Systems (CHI 94), ACM Press (1994) 365–371
15. Ahlberg, C., Shneiderman, B.: Visual Information Seeking: Tight Coupling of Dynamic Query Filters with Starfield Displays. In: Proc. Conference on Human Factors in Computing Systems (CHI 94), ACM Press (1994) 313–317
16. Williamson, C., Shneiderman, B.: The Dynamic HomeFinder: Evaluating Dynamic Queries in a Real-Estate Information Exploration System. In: Proc. Conference on Research and Development in Information Retrieval (SIGIR 92), ACM Press (1992) 338–346
17. Dunlop, M., Morrison, A., McCallum, S., Ptaskinski, P., Risbey, C., Stewart, F.:   Focussed Palmtop Information Access Combining Starfield Displays and Profile-based Recommendations. In: Proc. Mobile HCI 2003 Workshop on Mobile and Ubiquitous Information Access, Springer-Verlag (2004) 79–89
18. Dunlop, M., Davidson, N.: Visual Information Seeking on Palmtop Devices. In: Proc. Conference of the British HCI Group (HCI 2000), Springer-Verlag (2000) 19–20
19. Spence, R.: Information Visualization. Addison-Wesley & ACM Press (2001)
20. Fishkin, K., Stone, M.: Enhanced Dynamic Queries via Movable Filters. In: Proc. Conference on Human Factors in Computing Systems (CHI 95), ACM Press (1995) 415–420

21. Chin, J.P., Diehl, V.A., Norman, K.: Development of an Instrument Measuring User Satisfaction of the Human-Computer Interface. In: Proc. Conference on Human Factors in Computing Systems (CHI 88), ACM Press (1988) 213–218
22. Keeney, R., Raiffa, H.: Decisions with Multiple Objectives: Preferences and Value Tradeoffs. John Wiley & Sons (1976)
23. Baudisch, P., Rosenholtz, R.: Halo: a Technique for Visualizing Off-Screen Locations. In: Proc. Conference on Human Factors in Computing Systems (CHI 2003), ACM Press (2003) 481–488

Mobile Photo Browsing with Pipelines and Spatial Cues

Tero Hakala, Juha Lehikoinen, Hannu Korhonen, and Aino Ahtinen

Nokia Research Center,
P.O. Box 100,
33721 Tampere, Finland
{tero.hakala, juha.lehikoinen, hannu.j.korhonen,
aino.ahtinen}@nokia.com

Abstract. Local memory in mobile devices increases rapidly. Simultaneously, new content creation devices, such as digital cameras, are embedded. As a consequence, the amount of locally stored content is bound to increase in huge numbers. In order to provide support for end-users in managing this ever-growing pile of content, new means of accessing, organizing, and enjoying the content are needed. We investigate techniques that may be used to display more information, especially visual content, on the mobile device screen at once, as well as accessing the content with ease. We focus on visual interaction, with a media manager as a target application. We present the design factors and a prototype application running on a mobile phone. We show that it is feasible to include spatial cues in the design of mobile user interfaces, and report an initial usability study with very encouraging results.

1 Introduction

Currently, one of the most common content types in mobile devices is user-created personal content, such as photos, video clips, contacts, and messages. Personal content has some distinctive features: it is often considered important, it is invaluable (in many cases it cannot be replaced), it has emotions attached to it, and it may be very familiar to the user. These characteristics may imply new challenges and possibilities in managing such content.

Content management is a vast research area, including topics such as content transcoding and transfer, data storage technology, searching, security, archiving, and so forth. In this paper, we focus on yet another aspect of content management – the user interface. We concentrate especially on presentation of and interaction with personal content in mobile domain. Our goals are to provide the user with a broad view over the content stored on his/her mobile terminal, and to allow rapid access to any content object.

Displaying arbitrary graphical images on a mobile terminal screen requires addressing several issues. One of these is providing the user with a proper browsing method. The most straightforward method is to display several thumbnail images (heavily diminished versions of the actual images) on the screen at once. The user can then locate the desired image by identifying the contents of the thumbnail.

The restrictions caused by the small screen are evident especially in the browsing task. On a small screen, only a few thumbnail images may be displayed at once. This

M.F. Costabile and F. Paternò (Eds.): INTERACT 2005, LNCS 3585, pp. 227–239, 2005.
© IFIP International Federation for Information Processing 2005

makes browsing a large set of images a tedious task with a lot of scrolling involved. For a presentation point of view, there are two obvious options to address this issue. Either the image thumbnails are made even smaller, so that more of them can be displayed at once, or screen real estate is conserved by the means of distortion. We set out to study yet another approach: carefully applying spatial cues that would allow more efficient usage of screen space, combined with a new interaction technique.

The paper is organized as follows. First, we review the relevant related work, followed by a presentation of our approach and design. We consider the possibilities and limitations of small screen graphics and mobile interaction, and present the design decisions in detail. We then describe the results of a usability study, followed by discussion and conclusions.

2   Related Research

2.1   Photo Browsing

Several user interface solutions for browsing photos on a large screen have been developed. The most common is inevitably a grid-based layout with thumbnail images, available in Windows XP and virtually every photo application, such as ACDSee [1] and Picasa [12] to name but two. The same approach has been adopted to small screen user interfaces as well, the grid being replaced with a one-dimensional list showing a few thumbnails at a time (Figure 1).

Fig. 1. The Gallery application in current Nokia mobile phones

In addition to thumbnail grids, there are also more advanced browsing user interfaces available. Most photo browsing applications allow the creation of collections. The creation may take place manually, based on, e.g., user-created albums, or automatically, based on, e.g., different categorization techniques. Even though the creation of collections is beyond the scope of this paper, there is one related concept worth noticing: the inclusion of hierarchy, either explicit (e.g., an album) or implicit (e.g., time). What is common to many of these hierarchy-based approaches is dividing the browsing task into two phases:

- the filtering phase and
- the browsing phase.

This means that in order to have a reasonable amount of objects to browse, the user is first expected to filter the undesired content out of view (to zoom in into the hierarchy), and only then start browsing.

A common approach is to replace the traditional folder-based approach with a temporal view, e.g. [4,5]. As an example, Graham et al. [5] present Calendar Browser, which allows viewing images on a single temporal granularity level at a time, such as a year or a month. A maximum of 25 images are displayed at once; therefore, some summarization algorithms are needed to find representative images when more than 25 are available for a chosen timeframe. On a year level, for example, the images are labeled according to months; when a user clicks on a photo, the browser zooms in into the month the photo was taken. Again, 25 photos from that month are displayed. Selecting a photo on this level further zooms in into the day level. On this level, no summarization is applied, but all photos are browsable with a traditional grid view and Next/Previous buttons.

In addition to time, location is also a natural criterion for organization. One photo browser that takes location into consideration is Nokia Album [2]. It allows clustering the images by both time and location. The location information is retrieved automatically from the GSM network and attached to photos as they are taken.

Beyond Nokia Album, we are not aware of any published research addressing image viewers for mobile phones as such. However, photo browsers for PDAs have been studied earlier. For instance, Pocket PhotoMesa [8] uses treemaps for image layout and zooming for navigation. Image browsing on small screen devices have also been studied by Harada et al. [6]. They compared a folder-based traditional layout with a vertical timeline. Among other things they discovered that the zoomable timeline with system-generated time-based hierarchies was at least as effective for browsing as was the traditional layout.

Lifeblog [10] is another example of a timeline-based content browser and organizer. It runs on both select mobile phones and Windows PCs. In addition to browsing photos, Lifeblog can be used to synchronize personal content between the phone and a PC, including photos, messages and videos. In Lifeblog, the timeline is not hierarchical, but linear.

Lehikoinen and Aaltonen [9] present a distortion-based method for displaying more images on a small screen. A perspective distortion is applied to photos, resulting in more screen space available for additional information, such as a menu (Figure 2). The authors found out that a small amount of distortion did not decrease the time it took to recognize an image.

Fig. 2. Perspective distortion frees some screen space [9]

2.2   Information Visualization

Basically there are several techniques for presenting large information spaces in a compressed form. Noik [11] has classified these as follows: implicit (use of perspective), filtered (removal of objects with low degree of interest), distorted (size, shape and position), and adorned (changing attributes such as color).

Many of the current visualization methods suitable for small screens rely on distorting the view; i.e. the viewpoint information is manipulated in a way that enables seeing important objects in detail, while preserving the broader context to which the object belongs. For example, the rubber sheet [13] is a view distortion technique that allows the user to choose areas on the screen to be enlarged. Therefore, the whole information space can be displayed at once with very low amount of detail. Should the user want to see some areas in more detail, he or she stretches the rubber sheet on the particular screen location, effectively zooming into the information on that area.

Zooming and zoomable user interfaces (ZUI), such as PAD++ [3], are another way of presenting large information spaces even on a small screen. The information is presented on a 2D space, and the user can pan the view as well as zoom in and out of any part of that space. The view transition is animated to maintain the broader context of the local detailed information.

Kamba et al. [7] present a way of saving screen space by using pop-up type interface components (the controls are hidden until needed), and movable interaction elements (the elements can be arranged on the screen so that maximum working area is retained).

3   Our Approach

There is an inherent paradox in combining visual interaction and limited screen space. Visual interaction necessarily takes up some screen real estate for the controls, leaving less space for the content itself. There are two basic approaches to maximizing the amount of the content displayed on the screen:

- minimizing the interaction widgets (or hiding, making transparent etc. when not needed), or
- compressing the content into a more compact form.

We combined these two approaches by keeping the interaction elements visible but minimizing their visual appearance, and by applying slight spatial cues in order to make more content fit on the screen. As a result, a photo browsing application named MediaTray was developed.

Visualizing any information on a small screen requires very careful crafting. In order to find the optimum techniques and enhancements, one has to create both conceptual still images and animated sequences. Our study makes no exception: we created dozens of still images and a number of different animated versions of the concept until we were satisfied with the result and were able to proceed.

We aimed at developing a content browsing application that would offer a quick and easy way to browse media objects. The application should be able to show more images on the screen than what is currently possible. Further, we aimed at finding out whether it is feasible to incorporate any spatial cues into a small screen user interface design.

The application should be usable with the current imaging phones equipped with four arrow keys, a selection key, two software keys for application dependent functionality, and a color screen of 176x208 pixels.

3.1 The MediaTray Concept

An early version of the concept was based on folders. However, with initial heuristic evaluations it became quickly apparent that working with folders is not natural in the mobile domain: people are not familiar with using folders in their mobile terminals, not to mention creating them. On the contrary, it appeared that time is one of the most important aspects for classifying digital photos. This is also reported in e.g. [2]. As a consequence, a temporal organizational approach was adopted.

On a concept level, MediaTray consists of two primary screen components: the time bar and the content area (the tray). The time bar is used to filter and control the time span that is displayed on the tray at a time. In addition to these components, some controls for navigation are needed; they are primarily located at the tray frames in order to save screen space. The final version of the application prototype, running on a mobile phone, is shown in Figure 3.

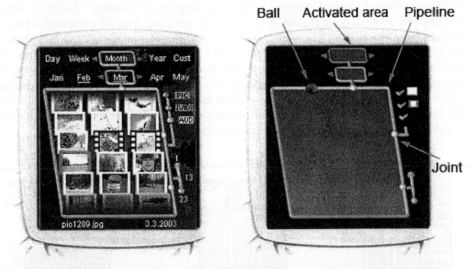

Fig. 3. The MediaTray (on the left) and the user interface components (on the right). The time bar consists of two rows at the top, whereas the tray area fills most of the remaining screen space. The ball is a cursor that is moved along the pipeline.

3.2 Screen Components Explained

The time bar consists of two rows of text on the screen (Figure 3). The first row is used for selecting the temporal granularity level: it determines the time span length within which images on the tray area are displayed. The selection may be based on a day, week, month, or year level. Further, the Cust setting allows creating personalized collections that are not necessarily time-based. It may contain, e.g., pictures of animals only. Rows are horizontally scrollable.

The contents of the second row will change according to the selection made on the first row. For example, if "Month" is selected, the second row shows the names of months (the year will be the one chosen earlier, or this year if no selection has been made). The first and second row selections always remain in the same horizontal position on the screen and are marked with a red frame when focused. The frame will change to blue when the input focus is lost. Underlining is used to indicate that some content exists. For example, in Figure 3 there are some photos taken in February and March, but none in January.

The tray contains the images, filtered according to the time bar settings. The tray is framed; the frame serves also as an input indicator (see the section "Interaction and navigation" below). In addition to the tray area, also the objects are framed. An object's frame indicates its media type. For example, a video clip has a filmstrip-like frame. In this paper, however, only images are considered.

The tray is slightly slanted. This visual design decision serves two purposes: first, it gives a cue of perspective (even though the photos themselves are not distorted), and thus allows the user to organize the thumbnails as if they were very slightly behind each other. Second, the images are easier to differentiate from each other when their borders are not aligned to grid.

We considered several options prior to ending up to slanting. Some of these options are presented in Figure 4 (it is worth noticing that all presented options contain the same amount of images). The leftmost image is the most obvious solution – a grid without any distortion. This takes up a considerable amount of screen space, however. The next option is to decrease the thumbnail spacing (the middle image in Figure 4). This resulted in a crowded-looking, visually unpleasant design where photos seemed to occlude each other without any obvious reason. Finally, we slanted the tray in order to provide a hint of perspective, arranged the images based on a slanted grid, and made them appear very slightly on top of each other.

Fig. 4. A comparison of thumbnail presentation options

It is worth noticing that the first folder-based version had a larger preview of the currently selected image. It was left out from the timeline version, since in heuristic and walkthrough evaluations during the concept creation, we found out that the images were recognized also without the preview, and that when a user wanted to view the whole image, they wished to see it on full screen regardless of the preview.

3.3 Interaction and Navigation

The fundamental design decision concerning interaction and navigation was preventing the user from getting lost. As a consequence, we designed an interaction model where the input focus is always visible, and always presented in a consistent fashion. This is especially crucial in systems based on discrete input with no cursors or pointers. In our prototype the user uses 5-way navigation key for navigating inside the application. Viewing a picture in full screen mode is done by pressing the navigation key.

In order to emphasize the importance of lostness-free navigation even further, we designed visible navigation paths. MediaTray consists of **pipes** and **joints** that indicate the possible navigation paths (pipes) and interactive components (joints).

The navigation is based on a "move the ball in the pipes" metaphor. Any interactive component is connected to others via the pipes. This way, the user not only always knows where the focus is, but immediately recognizes the possible directions for navigating further. The ball is animated and moves fast along the pipe system. This helps the user to follow where the selection is going to or coming from.

When wishing to browse photos, the user simply "jumps" from the pipe to the tray area. The tray area is accessible from any direction and the user presses the navigation key to direction where the tray area is located. When doing this, the target picture (the one closest to the joint from which the jump was made) is framed with red. There are three pictures in a row and an infinite number of rows, depending on how many pictures there are in the selection. Six rows are visible at a time. If the selection is larger than six rows, the first and/or last visible rows are dimmed a little. This gives the user a signal that there are more pictures but they are not visible.

When the user wishes to exit the tray area, they simply move left from the leftmost image, or right from the rightmost image. There are no visible joints for doing this, but what we call **virtual joints** are used. Virtual joints are operative only when moving from tray area back to the pipe. The reason for including virtual joints is that they provide an easy access back to the tray area if the user has accedently exited from there. Otherwise the ball would have moved automatically to the closest joint. This would have been confusing. Furthermore, we did not want to add too many joints along the routes, but to maintain efficiency of movement in the application.

When a picture is selected in the last visible row and the user wants to move further downwards, all visible pictures are scrolled upwards and a new row appears at the bottom of the tray area as the first row disappears. If the amount of browsable images is very high, the user may choose which part of the collection is shown by moving the focus to the scroll lever (on the lower right corner) and adjusting the lever to the desired position. This enables the user to go to the beginning or the end of a large selection very fast. The current position is displayed next to the lever, and the size of the collection below it.

On the upper right corner of the tray area there is a bar for selecting which media types are shown. In the current version there are three possible choices available: picture, video, and audio. This is a multi-select control with at least one selection on all the time. A selected item is marked with green.

3.4 On the Graphical Model

The MediaTray application is based on a pure 3D model (Figure 5). Even though the model is pure 3D, we do not allow free camera nor object manipulation. This is due to practical reasons: the current input capabilities would pose rather huge challenges for easy interaction with a six degrees of freedom manipulation. Therefore, the object manipulation always takes place in two dimensions. The third dimension, in this case depth, is present but is used as a visual cue and aid for cognitively determining an object's location related to others.

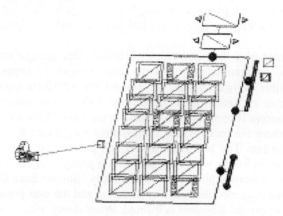

Fig. 5. The graphical model

The object constructions are made by special 3D modeling and rendering software (3DSMax). Only by using this kind of method it is possible to find the best views and appearances of the object; the object orientation is carefully taken into account.

There is a slight shadow effect behind each media object, which gives a feeling of more depth. Also, a blue gradient slide in the first and last row gives a feeling of continuation of the objects; when the gradient is not visible there are no more objects behind.

Using a camera inside the 3D rendering software gives a lot of possibilities to see the objects in a different way. We tried distorted, more slanted, wide-angle views and many other ways to find the best model construction. The conclusion was simple: no distortion in the structure, all media objects of the same size, pipeline always visible (not covered by any objects) and one red spot or frame indicating the selection.

The background of the application turned out to be important. We tried different configurations in early stages and come up with conclusion that it is dark enough to give more contrast, it is fuzzy to give a feeling of floating objects and it can also be slightly animated to give a feeling of non-static environment.

4 Evaluation

In order to assess the usability of the concept, we arranged a qualitative evaluation. The purpose of the evaluation was to find out how easily users could find, browse and view images with the application, and what they subjectively thought about the design.

4.1 Participants

Nine persons, including one pilot user, participated in the evaluation. Their median age was 33 years. Out of the nine participants two were female. All participants had technical background and a university degree. None of the participants has any prior experience with MediaTray and they all volunteered in the evaluation. Each was rewarded with a small gift.

The criterion for the participants was that they should have taken photos with a camera phone. The activity level in taking photos varied between the participants. They had also different ways to store the images. Some participants stored them in the mobile phone, while some transferred them to the computer every now and then. At the time of the usability test, the number of images stored in a mobile phone varied from 0-5 to 20-30. Three participants had created folders for the photos, such as "Work", "Holiday trip" or "Old pictures". Others had left them as a single list.

4.2 Apparatus

The tests were carried out with a prototype application installed in a Nokia 3650 mobile phone (Figure 6). A fixed set of images was used.

Fig. 6. MediaTray application running on a Nokia 3650

4.3 Procedure

There were nine basic tasks in the test. The tasks dealt with browsing and viewing photos, selecting a correct date in the time bar and defining visible file types.

The tests were arranged in a laboratory environment. There were one participant and the moderator present at a time. In the beginning, the test participant was familiarized with the test equipment and procedure. They were also interviewed about their demographics. The participant tried independently navigation and picture selection prior to actual tasks. After the warm-up, the participants were asked to conduct test tasks one by one, and think aloud while proceeding. Finally, there was a discussion about the design.

5 Results

5.1 Tray Area

Our first goal was to display more images on the screen. There was a maximum of 18 thumbnails visible on the tray area, which is remarkably more than normally. Participants were satisfied with that, considering the screen size. None of them commented that slanting the tray would have had any effect on thumbnails. However, shrinking the size of thumbnails had some drawbacks in recognizing them, but that was foreseeable. In some cases thumbnails were considered to be blurry and a little too small, but participants said recognizing images would be easier if they would have taken these photos by themselves. It should be noted that this is only a user comment, not a verified result.

Selecting an image was done mainly based on a small thumbnail. Date taken and the image name were visible at the bottom of the screen, but participants did not use them very often or at least they did not mention that they would have looked at them.

In our design, first and last rows were dimmed in order to indicate that there were more images available either above or below visible images. Participants thought that this was quite an evident method and none of them had any problems in checking all images from the selection.

5.2 The Time Bar

The Time bar is a very crucial part of our user interface since users usually need to filter images to find the ones they are looking for. Participants learned very quickly how to use this control and they found the correct view almost instantly. However, the time bar was not utilized to its full extent: participants accomplished tasks mostly in a month view. Other views were used only if absolutely necessary or specified explicitly in the task description. Participants said that the weekly view is not very important because it is quite a short period, and events usually start during weekend and continue the following week whereas in calendar view the week normally starts on Monday. The day view was used only if the participant needed to check a certain date and look for an image from that day. Year was considered to be too long a period: the large amount of images would make browsing time-consuming.

Dividing the time bar into two halves had both advantages and disadvantages. Participants could easily browse e.g. days or months on the second row once they had selected a view from the first row. Furthermore, the time bar also indicated if there were no images a specific day or month and thus allowed bypassing empty slots quickly. This feature proved to be useful.

Problems were related to selecting the right view; sometimes participants had difficulties in doing that. All broader scale selections in the time bar affected the detailed views and adjusted values on the second row accordingly. For example, the selected month defines available dates in the day view. The current year was indicated at the bottom of the screen, but apparently participants did not notice that until they had tried to look for images taken on a wrong year.

5.3 Navigation

Our second goal was to offer a good and error-free navigation in browsing media objects. The pipeline structure and a red ball as a cursor seemed to work well for this purpose. Participants were quite enthusiastic about the idea of the pipeline structure used for directing cursor movements and some of them found navigation in the application also entertaining and fun. They said that the cursor movements on the pipeline reminded them from some video games from the 80's and some tasks almost turned into a gaming session as participants "drove" around the pipeline.

In addition to visible joints, there were also some virtual joints for specific purposes. In order to provide a smooth exit from the tray back to the pipeline, the participants could just move the cursor from the outermost image to the direction of the pipeline; the cursor jumped on the pipe and stayed alongside the image. From that point it was possible to move to another part of the application, time bar, or return back to the tray area. During the test some participants exited unintentionally from the tray area because they thought that the focus would move automatically to the next row if they press the joystick right on the rightmost image as it would happen in the terminal's menu structure. However, as the cursor just moved to the pipeline but did not move anywhere from there, they could easily return and continue browsing images. Participants noted this behavior very quickly and they did not make this error anymore once they had noticed it.

Transition between the tray area and the pipeline was not completely seamless. Even though it was possible to exit from any outermost media object back to the pipeline, it did not always work the other way around, especially with a small number of images on the tray. For example, from the scroll bar joint it was not possible to move into the tray if there were so few images that the row aligned with the scrollbar joint was empty.

Another problem was related to navigation at the top of the tray area. It was not possible to move directly to the time bar from virtual junctions, but the user had to move first to the right. Some participants tried upward navigation because they thought it would automatically take them to the time bar.

In overall participants learned very quickly how to navigate in the application even if some directions were not so obvious. For instance, navigating down at the scrollbar joint will "drive" the cursor to the time bar joint at the top of the screen because there are no fixed joints at the bottom of the screen or on the left side of the tray area. On the other hand this worked as a shortcut to the time bar almost everywhere from the tray area and hence, it was adopted.

6 Discussion and Future Work

The results from the test were very encouraging. The design goals that we set at the beginning were well met and the participants were satisfied with how the application worked. However, there are some things that could be improved in subsequent versions.

Increasing the number of images on the tray area will evidently have an affect on the size of the thumbnails and thus make recognizing them more difficult.

Furthermore, we did not show image names at all since they are often arbitrary. The creation date was visible, though. It remains to be seen how much familiarity with the photos helps in recognizing small thumbnails and finding the right image. In the post-test interview participants were confident that they could recognize images more accurately if they would have taken them themselves.

Another thing is recognizing different media types on the tray area. In our design we sketched that other media types, like video and audio, could also be browsed in this application. Especially presenting audio files on the tray area is a challenging task because we did not show file names or other textual information, which is traditionally used for identifying audio clips. Videos could be presented in a similar way as images, but the border around a thumbnail (a frame from the video) could be a filmstrip to indicate the media type. For audio files a thumbnail could be some graphical metadata information, an album cover or a picture of an artist. However, such as audio files should have their own border style as well in order to distinguish them from other media types. One possibility is to extend the preview capability of the application required by different media types. The application could play a short video clip or audio sample when a user browses the objects and pauses on one.

The time bar worked well and participants were able to select the correct view smoothly. The visibility of selected views should be improved because some participants had problems, if only minor ones, in selecting a correct view. Most importantly, all selected values should be clearly visible near time bar. This would improve awareness of selections. Also the order of views could be rethought. Currently the time bar has been organized from the most detailed view (day) to the broadest view (year). However, the selection of images on the tray area is first defined by the year and the user can narrow the selection into a more detailed view if necessary.

Based on the results from the usability test, basic navigation in the pipeline structure was very intuitive and easy even though it was new to participants. All problems in navigation were related to virtual joints. Participants did not know for sure how they worked and what were the available navigation directions. Therefore, virtual joints require some more detailed interaction design on how they should work in each case and whether there are any new locations that would require a virtual joint.

One of the key findings was that we are actually able to decrease the icon spacing without losing attractiveness, when some slight spatial cues are applied. The slanted tray enabled more images to be placed on the screen, which is exactly what participants wanted to have. The appearance of the application was also appreciated. It looked different compared to normal applications in the phone, but in a positive way.

7 Conclusions

We have developed a mobile application prototype for photo browsing on a small screen. Our design goal was to provide an application that allows a quick and easy access to all media content on a terminal. Our approach is based on visual interaction; we developed user interface widgets that we call pipes and joints. The design allows the user to move the selection tool, a ball, rapidly through the pipe system. The ball stops whenever there is a joint in the pipe. A joint is an active component where some interaction may take place. The benefits of the piping system are visible navigation paths and the fact that the user never loses sight of the currently focused object.

Another aspect of the UI design is applying slight spatial cues. In this case, we tilted the object plane and arranged objects so that they seemed to appear in three-dimensional space. As a consequence, we were able to arrange the icons representing the objects more efficiently than would have otherwise been possible.

In order to assess usability of the concept, we arranged an evaluation. The results showed that our concept is very easy and even fun to use. One of the key findings was that we are actually able to decrease the icon spacing without losing attractiveness, when some slight spatial cues are applied.

References

1. ACDSee. Online document, availabe at http://www.acdsystems.com/English/index.htm. Last checked Apr 25, 2005.
2. Ahtinen A., Andersson M. Learnability and Automatic Clustering of Images in Mobile Devices. In Proceedings of MobileHCI 2004, pp. 404-408.
3. Bederson B.B, Hollan J.D. Pad++: A Zooming Graphical Interface for Exploring Alternate Interface Physics. In Proceedings of the ACM UIST'94 Symposium on User Interface Software and Technology. 1994. pp. 17-26.
4. Cooper M., Foote J., Girgensohn A., Wilcox L. Temporal event clustering for digital photo collections. In Proceedings of the eleventh ACM International Conference on Multimedia, 2003, pp. 364-373.
5. Graham A., Garcia-Molina H., Paepcke A., Winograd T. Time as essence for photo browsing through personal digital libraries. In Proceedings of the second ACM/IEEE-CS joint conference on Digital Libraries, pp. 326-335.
6. Harada S., Naaman M., Song Y.J., Wang Q.Y., Paepcke A. Lost in memories: interacting with photo collections on PDAs. Proceedings of the 4th ACM/IEEE-CS joint conference on Digital libraries, 2004, pp. 325-333.
7. Kamba T., Elson S.A., Harpold T., Stamper T., Sukaviriya P. Using Small Screen Space More Efficiently. In Proceedings of CHI 1996, ACM, pp. 383-390.
8. Khella A., Bederson B.B. Pocket PhotoMesa: A Zoomable Image Browser for PDAs. Proceedings of the 3rd international conference on Mobile and ubiquitous multimedia, 2004, ACM, pp. 19-24.
9. Lehikoinen J., Aaltonen A. Saving Space by Perspective Distortion When Browsing Images on a Small Screen. In Proceedings of Australasian Computer Human Interaction Conference (OZCHI) 2003, pp. 216-219.
10. Lifeblog. Online document, available at http://www.nokia.com/nokia/0,1522,,00.html? orig=/ lifeblog Last checked Apr 25, 2005.
11. Noik, E. A Space of Presentation Emphasis Techniques for Visualizing Graphs. In Proceedings of Graphics Interface 1994, pp. 225-233.
12. Picasa Photo Organizer. Online document, available at http://www.picasa.com/picasa/. Last checked Apr 25, 2005.
13. Sarkar M., Snibbe S.S., Tversky O.J., Reiss S.P. Stretching the Rubber Sheet: A Metaphor for Viewing Large Layouts on Small Screens. In Proceedings of UIST 1993, ACM, pp. 81-91.

Visual Interface and Control Modality: An Experiment About Fast Photo Browsing on Mobile Devices

QianYing Wang, Susumu Harada, Tony Hsieh, and Andreas Paepcke

Stanford University,
Stanford, CA 94305,
United States of America
wangqy@stanford.edu, {harada, thsieh, paepcke}@cs.stanford.edu

Abstract. We examined the strengths and weaknesses of three diverse scroll control modalities for photo browsing on personal digital assistants (PDAs). This exploration covered nine alternatives in a design space that consisted of three visual interfaces and three control modalities. The three interfaces were a traditional thumbnail layout, a layout that placed a single picture on the screen at a time, and a hybrid that placed one large photo in the center of the display, while also displaying a row of neighboring thumbnails at the top and bottom of the screen. In a user experiment we paired each of these interfaces with each of the following three scroll control modalities: a jog dial, a squeeze sensor, and an on-screen control that was activated by tapping with a stylus. We offer a simple model that classifies our experiment's interfaces by how much they provide visual context within the photo collection. The model also classifies the scroll modalities by how tightly they correlate scroll input actions to effects on the screen. Performance and attitudinal results from the user experiment are presented and discussed.

1 Introduction

As digital cameras become increasingly prevalent, large personal libraries of digital photographs are becoming more and more common. The low incremental cost of digital photography tempts photographers into accumulating photographs faster than they ever did before. This growth in digital photograph libraries has pushed interested parties to seek new ways to store, show, and retrieve digital images. As personal digital assistants (PDAs) with credible processing, storage, connectivity and display capabilities emerge,
these devices are becoming potential platforms that enable users to have their entire digital photo collection available to them at all times.

There are, however, still a number of questions whose answers will lead to improved designs of small-display photo browsers. An appropriate approach needs to take into account two very different, but interacting aspects: the *visual interface* and *physical control modality*. The visual interface refers to the presentation of photos to the human viewer with the goal of facilitating browsing, conducting a focused search, or studying a picture in detail. Control modality refers to the physical mechanism that

M.F. Costabile and F. Paternò (Eds.): INTERACT 2005, LNCS 3585, pp. 240–252, 2005.
© IFIP International Federation for Information Processing 2005

allows viewers to communicate their intentions to the device. Examples of such intentions are "scroll through this deck of photos, or "make this photo bigger."

The most widely used photo interface on PDAs and desktops is a grid of thumbnails that is displayed on the screen. A number of alternative interfaces have been developed for browsing photos on desktops, such as an approach that lets viewers zoom in and out of images [1]. Most desktop interfaces, however, do not perform well when simply replicated on a PDA without modification.

Two of the common control modalities for PDAs are the stylus, which is used to tap or drag items on the screen, and the jog dial. The latter is a small wheel that protrudes from the PDA housing in a position where the user's thumb can reach (see Figure 1-A). The thumb rolls the dial up or down. Some wheels can be rolled indefinitely; others are spring-loaded and have three operating positions: up, down, and neutral. They are sometimes also referred to as *jog wheels* and *scroll dials*, or *scroll wheels*.

 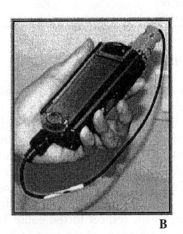

| A | B |

Fig. 1-A. Jog Dial Input Device,   **1-B.** PDA with squeezable input device (circular sensor)

We constructed a different control modality that allows its operator to squeeze the PDA with (usually) the index or middle finger while the device rests in the palm of the hand (Figure 1-B) [2]. The exerted pressure is recorded and transmitted to the PDA software. Applications can use this continuous pressure data to control, for example, the scrolling speed, the frame rate of animations, or the zoom factor of a graphical user interface window. Please see Related Work Section for more references to control modalities.

In an effort to understand the strengths of several diverse interfaces and control modalities, as well as the interactions among them, we implemented three PDA photo browser interfaces and constructed or acquired PDAs with three different control modalities. We then conducted an experiment in which participants were asked to find photos using each combination of interface and control modality.

2 Interfaces and Modalities

We finalized on three modality types, to be compared within the context of three interface types. This arrangement resulted in nine applications, each a unique combination of a particular modality and a particular interface, represented as two-letter abbreviations in Table 1. Table 1 lists the three modality types along the top-most row, and the three interface types along the left-most column.

Table 1. Three modality types and three interface types, and the resulting nine applications (experimental conditions)

Modality Interface	Squeeze (S)	Jog (J)	Click (C)
Thumbnail (T)	TS	TJ	TC
Parade (P)	PS	PJ	PC
Fullscreen (F)	FS	FJ	FC

2.1 Interfaces

The first interface is called the **Thumbnail** interface, in which the thumbnails of the photos are arranged in a grid with a fixed number of rows and columns (Figure 2-A). This interface is, on most existing photo browser applications, the primary presentation style. One difference here is that we replaced the typical scroll bar, which normally allows the user to scroll up and down a multi-page collection, with what we call a context bar. A context bar is a user interface component that is similar to the scroll bar, except for the fact that it does not accept any user input and only serves to provide contextual information about the current position of the corresponding viewing area with respect to the entire length of the content area. We made this change not in advocacy of the context bar as a user interface facility, but to allow proper control over the independent variables of our experiment. The photos are ordered left to right, top to bottom.

The second interface is called the **Parade** interface (Figure 2-B). In this interface there is one photo at the center of the screen that is larger than the rest of the thumbnails. Above and below this central photo, we place one row of smaller thumbnails. The photos in this interface are also arranged left to right and top to bottom. As the user navigates through the photo collection, the photos "parade" along in either direction, following a trajectory of the letter "Z" with the top and bottom horizontal part of the letter corresponding to the top and bottom rows of thumbnails (Figure 2-C). During the diagonal part of the trajectory, the photo enlarges or shrinks, depending on whether it is approaching or moving away from the center of the screen.

The third interface is the **Fullscreen** interface (Figure 2-D), which simply displays each photo at the maximum size that fits within the PDA screen. As the user navigates through the photo collection, the filmstrip scrolls towards the left or right.

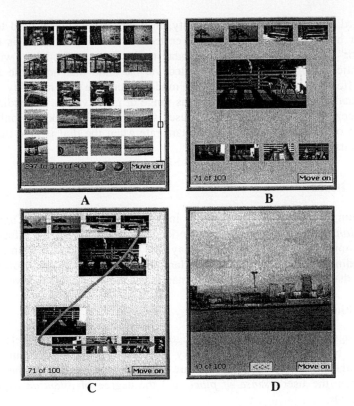

Fig. 2-A. Thumbnail interface. **2-B.** Parade interface. **2-C.** Scolling animation of Parade interface. **2-D.** Fullscreen interface.

2.2 Modalities

The first modality is the **Click** modality, which represents the prevalent modality for flipping through photographs on existing PDA photo browsing applications. The key aspect of this modality is that the user has to explicitly click a "next" or "previous" button repeatedly in order to scroll through the photo collection. Under this modality, the screen shows a pair of left/right arrows (up/down arrows in the case of the Thumbnail interface), which the user can click, using the stylus. One click on either one of the arrows results in the photo collection being shifted by one "increment" in the corresponding direction. One increment corresponds to one photo, except in the case of the Thumbnail interface where it corresponds to one row of photos.

The second modality is the **Squeeze** modality, using the squeeze input device we developed [2]. In this modality, although the manipulation occurs through the external squeezable input device, the mapping between the user's squeeze pressure and the effect on the photos on the screen is unidirectional. That is, as the user squeezes harder, the photos scroll by faster, and if the user releases the squeeze, the photos stop scrolling, but will not change the direction of the scroll. We placed a direction indicator button at the bottom of the screen, which the user can tap with the stylus to toggle the direction of the scroll.

The third modality is the **Jog** modality, in which a jog dial is used to navigate forward or backward through the photo collection. The Jog modality is the closest "competitor" that exists in the market today to the Squeeze modality, with the key characteristic of being able to be operated via the hand that holds the PDA. One marked difference between the Squeeze modality and the Jog modality is that the Squeeze modality allows for a continuous range of input values, depending directly on the squeezing pressure applied by the user, whereas the Jog modality only provides a sequence of up/down events at a constant rate when the dial is held up or down, away from its resting position.

3   Hypotheses

We partition the areas of our concern into two main categories: *Cognition* and *Manipulation*. Cognition refers to characteristics of the *interfaces* that affect the user's ability to comprehend what is on the display, and to apply the information towards the goal of finding a given photograph. By Manipulation we mean aspects of the *control modalities* that affect the user's ability to manipulate the interface effectively.

3.1   Cognition

Both the Cognition and Manipulation categories comprise numerous facets, which are under study by other disciplines of inquiry. For our purposes we concentrate on two aspects of the Cognition category that are particularly important in the context of image search: the user's *sense of place* and the degree of *attention focus* that an interface elicits.

Sense of place refers to the ability of a user to know which portion of the overall collection is being displayed on the screen at any given time. This might be the understanding that the visible images are part of a particular birthday party, or cover some particular time frame. One common method for increasing sense of place is to provide context. For example, fish-eye techniques [3] provide the user with visual clues for what is near a displayed information item of interest.

The degree of **attention focus** is the amount of attentional resource a viewer can allocate to each information unit to absorb in more detail. For example, the thumbnail view requires a broad sweep before the onlooker can pick a photo to examine more closely (low attention focus). In contrast, a single photo on the screen allows for high (sharp) focus. Figure 3-A places the three interfaces of the previous section into this Cognition space. The ordinate tracks sense of place, the abscissa marks attention focus. The values of the two variables are discrete; they can be thought of simply as 'low,' 'medium,' and 'high.'

The figure shows why we chose the three interfaces we introduced earlier. They represent two extremes and one 'compromise' solution in the Cognition space. The thumbnail interface, as pointed out earlier, provides significant sense of place, but requires the viewer to split his attention across the entire display. Fullscreen allows the viewer to examine the (only visible) photo almost immediately, allowing high attention focus at the expense of sense of place. Parade, with its large photo in the center and smaller thumbnails above and below attempts a middle ground for both quantities.

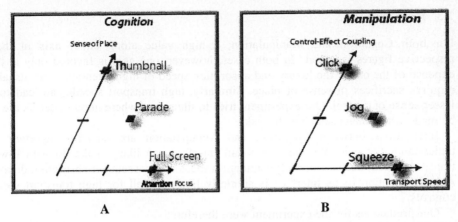

Fig. 3-A. Cognition: Sense of Place vs. Attention Focus. **3-B.** Manipulation: Control-Effect Coupling vs. Transport Speed.

3.2 Manipulation

The quantities we highlight for the control manipulation category are *transport speed* and *control-effect coupling*. **Transport speed** is the speed with which a given control modality allows the user to move between photos. Figure 3-B, analogous to Figure 3-A, places the three control modalities we chose into the Manipulation space. Squeeze enables the viewer to advance a sequence of images at various desired speeds. Pressure controls transport speed on a continuous scale. Transport speed with Click, in contrast, is limited by the operator's rapid tapping ability. While considerable, this speed is no match for the transport blur that a computer can generate. Our compromise between these extremes is the Jog control manipulation. Its on/off nature requires the computer to limit the transport speed such that the 'average' user can follow. Users are therefore not able to accelerate to blurring speed when they know that they are far from the target photo, and to slow down when they reach the image's neighborhood.

Control-effect coupling indicates how closely a discrete manipulative action matches a consequent identifiable event on the display. Click, for example, has high control-effect coupling: one tap with the stylus advances photos by one unit, for instance a single photo in Fullscreen, or one row of thumbnails in the Thumbnail interface. The Squeeze modality has the loosest coupling of the three modalities. Pressure on the sensor controls transport speed, which is a more indirect control than the photo position controlled with Click[1]. We place Jog midway between the extremes because the jog dial's two off-center positions produce a predictable, single-speed transport. It is less coupled than Click because when you hold the jog dial in the up or down position, the transport continues without any further action on the user's part. Jog is more coupled than Squeeze because of its on/off nature.

---

[1] One can think of this relationship as Squeeze impacting the first derivative of the first-order effect, which is what Click controls directly.

3.3 Predictions

For both Cognition and Manipulation, a high value along either axis in their respective figures is `good.' In both cases, however, one goal is favored only at the expense of the other: the luxury and absorption speed of high attention focus usually requires sacrifices in sense of place. Similarly, high transport speeds can lead to a lesser sense of control. Our experiment tries to illuminate where good tradeoffs are to be made when image search is the task.

Interactions between Cognition and Manipulation are equally important to understand. For example, the Thumbnail interface can likely make do with lower transport speed, because of its low attention focus and consequent absorption delays. A high attention focus interface is similarly likely to call for high transport speed controls.

Our predictions for the experiment were therefore:

1. The high sense of place Thumbnail interface will thrive with the low speed Click modality.
2. Squeeze will do well with any interface, because it allows users to control speed continuously.
3. Squeeze will work best with the Fullscreen interface because with a high transport speed the user will need to get a quick understanding of what he is seeing. The only way this can happen is with a high attention focus.

4 Experiment

Photo browsers need to support a number of user activities, ranging from idle browsing, to searching for a particular photograph. We chose search as the task for our experiment, because it demands from the user a large number of interactions with the device. In the interest of avoiding confounding factors, we decided to enable in our experiment only facilities for linear visual search, rather than the kind of sophisticated support that we provided in [4].

We recruited 23 participants for our experiment, ranging from ages 17 to 38, with no special criteria for selection. Of the 23 participants, 17 were male and six were female, with two participants being left handed and 11 without any prior experience with PDAs.

Two PDAs are used for our experiment: a Hewlett-Packard iPaq H5500 and a Dell Axim X3. Both PDAs housed a 400MHz Intel XScale processor running the Microsoft Windows Mobile 2003 operating system, with a 240x320 16 bit color display. The Axim came equipped with the jog dial (Figure 1-A), and the iPaq was adorned with our custom-built squeeze input device (Figure 1-B).

Our experiment followed a within-participant design. We exposed each participant to nine experimental conditions, resulting from the two factors (interface and modality) with three levels each, as shown in the matrix in Table 1. For each condition, the participant performed four search task trials, for a total of 36 trials. At the beginning of each search task trial, the participant was shown a target photo displayed full-screen on a separate PDA. We consistently used the same 1,800 image collection throughout the experiment. The photos were unknown to all participants and were divided among conditions. While using each participant's own collection would have approximated real-life situations better, this collection uniformity was necessary to control for differing familiarity of participants with their own collection. We provided the participants with a sample trial at the introduction of each new condition, where they were given the opportunity to experiment with the particular combination of interface and modality (using separate images from that of the 1,800 images in the collection). Within each interface, we rotated the sequence in which we exposed participants to the three modalities.

We explored two categories of experimental measures: performance and attitudinal. There were two performance measures. The first measure was the average time that participants used to find a target photo under each experimental condition (modality/interface). We did not place any constraints on the amount of time the participants could spend on searching for a photo. The second measure is the success rate. Participants might have difficulty to locate a specific target photo. They could skip any trial by tapping a button labelled "move on".

Participants filled out a questionnaire after the trials of each condition to indicate their subjective evaluations of the nine modality/interface combinations. The rankings for these attitudinal aspects included perceived efficiency, reliability, enjoyment, physical strain, photo size, and screen layout aesthetics.

5 Results

5.1 Performance

The average time to use the Squeeze modality to find a photo was 56.68 seconds. For Jog, the average search time was 52.16 seconds, for Click it was 58.92 seconds. Participants spent significantly less time searching for a photo with the Jog modality than with the Click modality ($t(22)=2.34$, $p<.05$). There was no statistically significant difference between the search time of Jog and Squeeze ($t(22)=1.76$, $p>.01$), and between Squeeze and Click ($t(22)=0.67$, $p>.01$). The success rates for the three modalities were all above 98%. No statistical differences were found among the success rates across modalities ($F(2,44)=0.87$, $p>.1$).

For the Parade interface, the Squeeze and Jog modalities yielded no statistically significant differences; both consumed an average of 48 seconds. Click, on the other hand, at 62 seconds, was slower than Squeeze and Jog by about 23%. Repeated measure ANOVA showed that the difference was highly significant ($F(2,44)=9.14$, $p<.01$). The success rates for Parade were at a very high 98% for all modalities. That is, modality had no significant impact on how many participants were able to find the target photos across trials ($F(2,44)=0.324$, $p>.1$).

The Thumbnail interface was unaffected by modality for both time and success rate. Search time differences were not statistically different ($F(2,44)=0.621$, $p>.1$) and emerged at an average of 75 seconds, no matter whether the participants used Squeeze, Jog, or Click to interact with the photos. The same observation is true for the success rate $F(2,44)=1.0$, $p>.1$). As under the Parade conditions, the rate held steady at 98%.

For the Fullscreen interface, modality did have an impact. This impact differed, however, from the Parade case. When interacting with photos under the Fullscreen condition, there was no significant difference between the Squeeze and Click modalities ($t(22)=0.83$, $p>.01$). Their search times were both at 46 seconds. Jog, in contrast, had participants finding their photos in about 38 seconds. This search speed difference across modalities was highly significant ($F(2,44)=5.82$, $p<.01$). Success rates, again, were not influenced by which input modality the participants worked with ($F(2,44)=1.0$, $p>.1$).

5.2 Attitudinal

Our questionnaire contained a number of questions that we later collapsed into six core indices by means of a factor analysis. Four of the six indices pertained to modality type. They were Perceived Efficiency, Reliability, Enjoyment, and Physical Strain. Photo Size and Screen Layout Aesthetics were the two other indices pertaining to interfaces. All results that are reported as significant are at $p < 0.05$.

Perceived efficiency and enjoyment had similar results across all three modalities. There was no significant difference between Jog and Squeeze for perceived efficiency and enjoyment. Both modalities were rated significantly more efficient and enjoyable to use than the Click modality. Both reliability and strain are inextricably related to modality manipulation. We would expect, for example that strain would likely be caused by the pushing of the squeeze sensor. We therefore examined participants' impressions of reliability and strain separately for each modality. Click was rated as the most strenuous modality to use, followed by Squeeze and Jog. Squeeze was rated as the least reliable modality, followed by Click and Jog. The strain and reliability differences between any two modalities were statistically significant.

Results for interfaces were in agreement with the patterns for individual modalities for both efficiency and enjoyment. That is, for all three interfaces, there was no significant difference between Jog and Squeeze for perceived efficiency and enjoyment. They both were rated significantly more efficient and enjoyable than Click. For Parade and Thumbnail, the perceived efficiency ranking was consistent with the search time performance for the three modalities. A discrepancy between perceived efficiency and search time was found for the Fullscreen interface where participants rated Squeeze more efficient to use than Click, while no search time performance difference was found between these two modalities.

Reliability and strain results for the three interfaces are illustrated by Figure 4-A and Figure 4-B. In these two figures, if two bars are at the same height, there is no significant difference between the two corresponding modalities. In other words, any height difference represents a statistically significant difference for that measure.

The two cross-interface measures we compared were screen layout aesthetics and photo size, (see Figure 5). The Fullscreen interface was rated the best for layout aesthetics, followed by Parade and then Thumbnail. The difference between any two interfaces was significant. Fullscreen and Parade were rated as having a more appropriate photo size than the Thumbnail interface. We measured no significant difference between the Fullscreen and Parade interfaces for photo size.

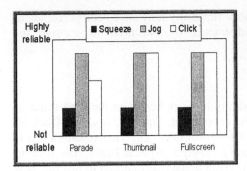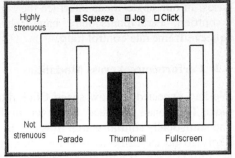

Fig. 4-A. Relative Ranking of Perceived Reliability; **4-B:** Strain Rankings

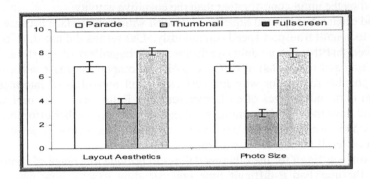

Fig. 5. Subjective measures: (a)layout aesthetics and (b)appropriateness of photo size

6   Discussion

6.1   Search Time and Efficiency Perception

Recall that the participants' perceived efficiency for experimental conditions matched their actual speed performance in all but one case: for the Fullscreen interface, participants in fact performed best on Jog. Squeeze and Click both induced inferior performance.

The participants' perception, however, was that they were less efficient with the Click modality than with Squeeze or Jog. According to our manipulation theory, one explanation is as follows: Jog provides the user with a steady stream of photos, because the jog dial is either in its resting position (no photo movement), or is pushed all the way up or down (single speed photo movement). In the Jog modality, photos thus either move or they don't. This pairing of simplicity with the convenience of single-handed operation may have led to the perception of high efficiency.

In contrast, Squeeze and Click each had one disadvantage on the participants' perception of efficiency. Squeeze requires the operator to consciously control the frame rate. While this flexibility in speed control is presumably welcome in other cases, in our single-focus interface the control flexibility may have been perceived as a burden. Participants may have felt distracted by the need to manage the squeeze/frame rate control loop.

6.2 Performance Across Modalities

We had expected the low speed Click modality to work best with the high sense of place Thumbnail interface. However, in this experiment, Squeeze, Jog, and Click all had statistically similar search times in the Thumbnail interface. The reason for this is likely to be the same as that for Thumbnail's lowered physical strain. The time to assimilate a row of new photos during each screen update, as opposed to just one new addition, may have caused a leveling of the interaction speed across the modalities. Conversely, when only one new image is exposed at a time, the progress speed is dominated by the input control rather than the cognitive activity.

We had originally expected Squeeze to do well with any interface because it allows the users to control transport speed continuously. Our results did not show this and in fact showed that the Jog modality performed well regardless of interface. Utilizing our cognition and manipulation theories to elaborate upon the Jog results, we found that one possible reason for why Jog performed well regardless of interface was its adaptation to the advantages of each interface. For Fullscreen, if the user wanted to go fast and have the photos continue scrolling without any further effort on his part, Jog allowed the user to do this. For Thumbnail, if the user wanted to go slow and be sure that one scroll moved one row of photos, Jog allowed this.

It was more difficult for the other modalities to provide this range of control. With Squeeze, the user had a difficult time understanding exactly how much pressure moved how many photos. With Click, the user could only proceed as fast as he clicked, which required effort and was tedious. These modalities had a difficult time adapting to interfaces that they were not well suited to run with.

To conclude, we learned that Jog's compromise degree of control-effect coupling worked well. Its on/off clarity, combined with the advantage of continuous transport, helped search speed and reduced stress (over Click). Squeeze offered a broader range of control speeds, but its effect-control coupling seems to be too loose. It is always difficult to choose the value for an operating parameter to suit multiple users simultaneously. Jog's single transport speed is such a one-must-fit-all parameter. We had therefore expected the Squeeze modality to offer a clear advantage by allowing each person to control speed continuously. It seems, however, that the price we paid by loosening the control-effect coupling was too high.

We will examine in our follow-on work whether we can modify Squeeze to retain the necessary level of control-effect coupling and still provide high transport speed flexibility. One possibility will be to personalize the slope of the pressure/speed function automatically or by means of a short training run.

6.3 Perceived Lack of Reliability for Squeeze

The results show that most participants perceived Squeeze as the least `reliable' of the three modalities. The squeeze sensor did not break down during the experiments, so the participants' understanding of `reliability' was not technical in nature. Our theory is that the pressure sensor was overly sensitive. This sensitivity, while making the interface feel responsive, also led to frequent 'overshooting' past the target photo.

7 Related Work

There are a number of commercial photo browser applications available for various handheld device platforms. We examined six of the most popular commercial photo browsers on a popular handheld software Website (www.handango.com). The browsers mainly use thumbnail views and Windows-Explorer-style folder views to browse through photos. Clicking or a jog dial can be used to control scroll bars. Several projects have also studied different layouts for browsing photos on the desktop [1, 5, 6, 7].

Various modalities other than Click and Jog have been investigated to provide additional input and control to handheld devices, pressure sensor being one of them. Harrison et al. [8] detect contact with handheld devices using pressure sensors and demonstrate interaction techniques for scrolling, and for automatically detecting the user's handedness. Hinckely and colleagues [9] introduce and integrate a set of sensors, including a pressure sensor, into a handheld device. In the ComTouch project, Chang et al. [10] use a pressure sensor to translate hand pressure into vibration intensity between users in real-time. Tilt sensors have been explored for handheld devices as well. Rekimoto [11] uses tilting for menu selection and map browsing. Harrison et al. [8], Small & Ishii [12], and Bartlett [13] use tilt sensors to scroll through and select information on a handheld device.

Rapid Serial Visual Presentation (RSVP), electronically similar to the activity of riffling through the pages of a book to get a rough idea of the content, is based on the research result that humans have the ability to recognize the presence of a target image in as little as 100 milliseconds or less [14]. Typical RSVP design modes include collage-mode, carousel-mode, floating mode, shelf-mode, and slide show (keyhole) mode.

8 Conclusion

We explored how three alternative interfaces interact with three different control modalities with respect to photo browsing on PDAs. We found that overall, the tri-state Jog modality, with its single speed, off/forward/reverse switch did very well. We had expected that the more flexible Squeeze modality, which allows users to control photo transport speed through finger pressure, would outperform the fixed-speed Jog. Our data indicates that this is not the case with the current implementation of the Squeeze modality. In terms of our design tradeoff model we suspect that the control-effect coupling for Squeeze is currently not tight enough, even when a high sense of place user interface provides context within the collection. Our plan is to explore methods for retaining more control-effect coupling, while still providing good control flexibility.

Photo browsing on small devices poses many user interface design challenges. As the use of digital photography increases, the payoffs for addressing those challenges rise. Mobile photo management should be able to improve on traditional wallet pictures, for example by allowing more images to be portable. This portability is important not just for casual consumers, but also for a number of professionals who rely on image access in the field.

The potential for efficient and satisfying photo management on small devices is there, but additional science is needed to address open issues. These issues include not just linear scanning, but summarization, automatic labeling, effective search over photo collections, and controlled photo sharing. Augmenting these features with intuitive, highly efficient user interface design will empower users with increased portability and accessibility for their digital media collections. All of these are exciting areas to work in.

References

1. Bederson, B.: Photomesa: A Zoomable Image Browser Using Quantum Treemaps and Bubblemaps. Proceedings of the 14th Annual ACM Symposium on User Interface Software and Technology, ACM Press (2001), 71-80
2. Paepcke, A., Wang, Q., Patel, S., Wang, M., Harada, S.: A Cost-Effective Three-in-One PDA Input Control. International Journal of Human-Computer Studies, Volume 60, Issues 5-6, (2004) 717-736
3. Furnas, G. W.: Generalized Fisheye Views. Human Factors in Computing Systems CHI '86 Conference Proceedings (1986), 16-23
4. Harada, S., Naaman, M., Song, Y., Wang, Q., Paepcke, A.: Lost in Memories: Interacting With Large Photo Collections on PDAs, Proceedings of the Fourth ACM/IEEE-CS Joint Conference on Digital Libraries (2004)
5. Kang, H., and Shneiderman, B.: Visualization Methods for Personal Photo Collections: Browsing and Searching in the PhotoFinder. Proc. IEEE International Conference on Multimedia and Expo (2000)
6. Kuchinsky, A., Pering, C., Creech, M.L., Freeze, D., Serra, B., and Gwizdka, J.: otoFile: a Consumer Multimedia Organization and Retrieval System. FProc. CHI (1999), 496-503
7. Platt, J.C., Czerwinski, M., and Field, B.A.: PhotoTOC: Automatic Clustering for Browsing Personal Photographs. Microsoft Research Tech Report Number MSR-TR-2002-17 (2002)
8. Harrison, B., Fishkin, K., Gujar, A., Mochon, C., and Want, R.: Squeeze Me, Hold Me, Tilt Me! An Exploration of Manipulative User Interfaces. CHI (1998), 17-24
9. Hinckley, K., Pierce, J., Sinclair, M., and Horvitz, E.: Sensing Techniques for Mobile Interaction. Proceeding of UIST 2000 (2000), 91-100
10. Chang, A., OModhrain, S., Jacob, R., and Ishii, H.: ComTouch: Design of a Vibrotactile Communication Device. DIS2002 (2002), 312-320
11. Rekimoto, J.: Tilting Operations for Small Screen Interfaces UIST96 (1996), 167-168
12. Small, D., and Ishii, H.: Design of Spatially Aware Graspable Displays CHI97 Companion (1997), 367-368.
13. Bartlett, J.F.: Rock n' Scroll is Here to Stay. IEEE Computer Graphics and Applications, 20(3), (2000), 40-50
14. Healey, C., Booth, K., and Enns, J.: High-Speed Visual Estimation Using Preattentive Processing, ACM Transactions on Computer-Human Interaction, June (1996)

The Effect of Age and Font Size on Reading Text on Handheld Computers

Iain Darroch, Joy Goodman, Stephen Brewster, and Phil Gray

Glasgow Interactive Systems Group, Department of Computing Science,
University of Glasgow, Glasgow, G12 8QQ, UK
{darrochi, joy, stephen, pdg}@dcs.gla.ac.uk
www.dcs.gla.ac.uk/utopia

Abstract. Though there have been many studies of computer based text reading, only a few have considered the small screens of handheld computers. This paper presents an investigation into the effect of varying font size between 2 and 16 point on reading text on a handheld computer. By using both older and younger participants the possible effects of age were examined. Reading speed and accuracy were measured and subjective views of participants recorded. Objective results showed that there was little difference in reading performance above 6 point, but subjective comments from participants showed a preference for sizes in the middle range. We therefore suggest, for reading tasks, that designers of interfaces for mobile computers provide fonts in the range of 8-12 point to maximize readability for the widest range of users.

1 Introduction

Small screen user interfaces, exemplified by personal digital assistants (PDAs), are becoming more popular and more affordable. Uses include web surfing, reading e-books, reading email and listening to music.

The small screen provides challenges for interface designers but we are lacking design guidelines for creating such interfaces [14]. Some information on interface design for handhelds is given by Weiss [22] but few data are available on how this varies with age. According to estimates from the US Census Bureau's International Database (2004), the proportion of those in the UK who are over 60 is expected to increase from 20% in the year 2000 to 27% by 2025. Increasing age leads to declines in various abilities such as losses in visual contrast sensitivity [1]. In a prior study [11] on designing navigation aids for older people, no information on a suitable font size for handhelds for older people could be found. Desktop guidelines were used but were not entirely satisfactory because there was some indication that older people might be able to read smaller text sizes on handheld computers than recommended by the guidelines. Therefore, we felt it was important to investigate this further and clarify whether there are different requirements for handheld computers.

The problem of how best to display textual information on small screens has been studied. For example, presenting text dynamically (e.g. vertical scrolling) [15] and analyzing web design guidelines for applicability to small screen interfaces [14]. In

M.F. Costabile and F. Paternò (Eds.): INTERACT 2005, LNCS 3585, pp. 253–266, 2005.
© IFIP International Federation for Information Processing 2005

this paper we study the effect of the size of the text on readability on small screens, specifically a PDA.

Although few studies exist of text display on small screens there have been a number of studies examining reading text on large screens, such as CRT monitors, (e.g. [2],[19]) and on-line (e.g. [4]). These studies were based on prior reading studies of text presentation on paper (e.g. [20]). Therefore, it is a logical next step to carry out similar text presentation tests on small screen computers. Comparative studies between paper and on-line reading performance have found no significant performance differences [12], but have found differences in users' subjective preferences. Image quality is an important factor in this. It has been found that an increase in image quality results in an increase in subjective performance rating for both paper and on-line reading [13]. Features of CRT monitors, such as screen flicker and luminance, can affect reading performance [10]. Therefore, it may be expected that there will be differences between reading performance on a small screen display compared to a CRT monitor. Recommendations for text sizes from previous studies have indicated font size 14 for children [3], font size 14 for older adults [4], and font size 12 for young to middle-aged adults [2]. This indicates an age-related change in font size on desktop computers but there are no corresponding findings for handheld computers.

In this paper we aim to elicit an indication of a suitable font size to use with text presentation on handheld computers and determine whether different font sizes are required when designing for older people. We also investigate whether the need to scroll when reading text has an effect on which font size should be chosen. We do not consider changing font type in this case to simplify the experiment; it will be investigated in a future study. The next section outlines the experiment used in this study. The results from the experiment are then presented and discussed. Some areas for further investigation are suggested. Finally the conclusions drawn from our experiences are given.

2   The Experiment

The experiment was a 2 x 8 factor within-subjects repeated-measures design. The first factor was age (two levels: younger adults and older adults) the second factor was font size (8 levels: 2,4,6,8,10,12,14 and16 point).

2.1 Participants

Twenty-four participants took part in the experiment and were divided into two groups of 12 with 6 males and 6 females per group. The Younger Adults group was aged 18-29 and the Older Adults group was aged 61-78. All participants were fluent in English as their first language and educated to at least secondary/high school level. A Snellen near visual acuity test for average reading vision at a distance of 40.6cm was used to test participant's near vision before the experiment. All participants had 20/40 vision or better. Participants had no or very minimal experience of handheld computers before the experiment. A £5 book token was given to participants as payment for taking part.

2.2 Equipment

An HP iPAQ hx4700 (www.hp.com) which has a 65,000 colour TFT screen with a resolution of 640x480 pixels was used to present the text (see Figure 1). This has the best quality screen available at the time of writing (January 2005). The screen was backlit and participants sat in a usability lab which was illuminated by overhead fluorescent lights. The iPAQ used the Microsoft Wiindows Mobile™ 2003 Second Edition operating system and had ClearType enabled to anti-alias the edges of fonts to improve quality. Custom software was used to present the experimental texts. An example of the software running on the iPAQ is shown in Figure 2.

Fig. 1. An HP iPAQ hx4700 as used in the experiment

Fig. 2. A screenshot of the application used in the experiment

2.3 Task

Many possible measures could be used to determine the effect of font on reading performance. Setting a task in which participants identify spelling or typographical errors is difficult due to inconsistency in the misspellings used and difficulty in measuring the degree of change in word shape. These types of test also promote skimming behaviour [7]. It has also been found that readers can differ in their ability to detect typographical errors [13]. Post-reading comprehension tests are another option but it is likely that participants will scan passages looking for the main points rather than reading the text. Asking participants to proof read a passage and read the words out loud would ensure that the passage was read but would not be very realistic since the flow of reading would be broken by having to speak continuously. Dillon [8] points out that many studies into reading performance bear little resemblance to normal reading and argues that tasks should be more realistic.

Jorna and Snyder [13] suggest the introduction of word substitution errors in proof reading tasks, making sentences incomprehensible and which force the subject to read and comprehend the sentence. For example, the word "toe" could be substituted for the word "cake" in the sentence "I baked a cake", thus making the sentence incomprehensible to someone reading it. However, Gunjar *et al.* [12] found that subjects sometimes re-read sentences to make sense of them and so constrained the words used for substitution in two ways: the substituted word rhymed with the original word; and the substituted word varied grammatically from the original word. For example, the word "fake" could replace "cake" in the sentence "I baked a cake". This modified proof reading task was successfully used by [2, 3] and was thus chosen for our study (see examples below).

The task ensures a realistic approach because subjects must read the entire passage in order to recognize substituted words. The words chosen for substitution were common English words that were clearly out of context to ensure that fluent English readers would have no trouble in identifying the errors.

2.4 Fonts and Passages

The standard Microsoft Sans Serif font was chosen for displaying text since it has been found that Sans Serif fonts are preferred by subjects in reading computer displayed text [2]. Text was presented to participants at font sizes 2, 4, 6, 8, 10, 12, 14, and 16. Examples of each size are shown in Figure 3. On screen the fonts ranged in size from less than 1mm high for size 2, to 5mm high for size 16.

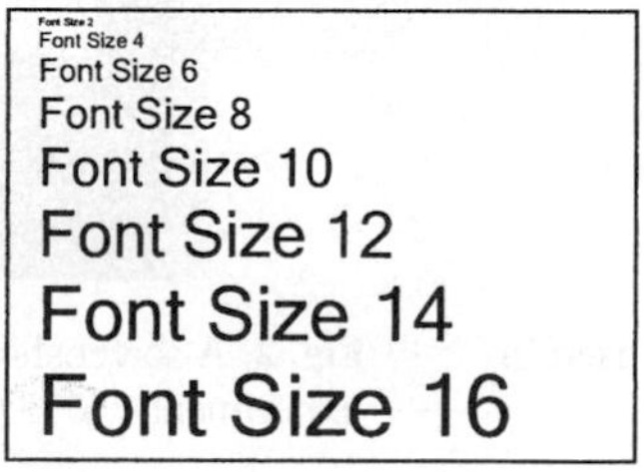

Fig. 3. Examples of the font sizes used in the experiment

Two different lengths of passages were used. The 'short' passages were of a length that fitted on a single screen up to font size 12 but required scrolling at font size 14 and 16. The 'long' passages fitted on a single screen up to font size 8 and required scrolling at font size 10 and above (see Figure 4). The different lengths and sizes required for scrolling meant that we could investigate the effects of scrolling on reading performance. Within the two groups of passages, the length of passages was adjusted to have approximately the same number of characters (Short: M = 230.7 chars per passage, S.D. = 2.9 chars; Long: M = 460.7 chars per passage, S.D. = 4.1 chars).

There was one substituted word in the short passages, and two in the long passages. Text for the passages was taken from Microsoft's Encarta encyclopaedia [16]; specifically from Life Science > Mammals, Birds, Reptiles & Amphibians, Invertebrate Animals. This ensured consistency between passages since all were written at approximately the same level of difficulty and discussed similar topics. Thirty-two passages were created, 16 for each passage length. The order in which the 16 passages were presented was the same for all participants. There was always two of each font size in the sixteen passages with a different font size ordering for long and short passages. No two participants were given the same font size order. Figure 4 shows an example of each passage length. The substitutions are: the word *shore* at the end of the first passage; *plains*, the fifth word on the second line of the second passage; *sneeze*, the eleventh word on the fourth line of the second passage.

Elephant, huge mammal characterized by a long muscular snout and two long, curved tusks. Highly intelligent and strong, elephants are among the longest-lived, with life spans of 60 years or shore.

Monkey, any of about 160 species of primates that have grasping hands, forward-facing eyes and highly developed plains. Most monkeys also have tails, a characteristic that distinguishes them from their larger primate cousins, the apes. Monkeys are highly skilled climbers, and most spend much of their lives in sneeze. Some have prehensile tails - that is, tails capable of grasping - that they can use as a fifth limb whilst foraging for food or climbing.

Fig. 4. One short and one long example passage from the experiment

2.5 Measurements

Both reading speed and reading accuracy were recorded. A timer within the software recorded the time taken to read a passage. Accuracy was measured by the experimenter noting down the words identified as contextual errors by the participant.

It is important, as Dillon [8] argues, that analysis of readability should consider more than reading performance. The use of subjective measures in addition to visual performance should be included in legibility testing [18]. In other reading preference studies it has been found that no difference exists in reading performance, but the subjective view of reading performance did differ between texts [2]. Therefore, participants were asked what they thought of each font size used, and to pick a preferred font size.

2.6 Procedure

After a briefing on the experiment and some background information questions, participants did a number (minimum 6) of training passages to familiarize themselves with the iPAQ and what was required in the task. Participants were asked hold the iPAQ and to read the passages from a comfortable position and were told that they could bring the iPAQ closer to the face if necessary.

The software used to present passages to participants had a "Start" button that was pressed to begin reading the passage and a "Done" button, pressed upon completing the passage (see Figure 2). Users were presented with a series of passages and for each pressed the start button, read the passage (saying out loud any word substitutions), then pressing done. Instructions were given to only say the erroneous word(s) and nothing else while reading a passage and keep questions/comments for the breaks between passages. To avoid effects of eye-strain or fatigue participants were told to rest for as long as they wanted between passages. Furthermore, if a font was unreadable or would cause too much discomfort to read, participants were instructed to tell the experimenter and skip the passage. Participants were asked to read passages once through only and identify any errors. The number of substituted words in passages was not told to the participants.

After being presented with an initial set of 16 passages to read users answered questions on what they thought of the different text sizes and were asked to pick a preferred text size by browsing through the passages. This questioning served a secondary purpose in giving users a rest between sets of passages. Having answered the questions, participants were then given a further 16 passages to read after which they were asked about their views on the text sizes used and to choose a preferred size. The first set of passages was of one length ('short' or 'long') and the second of the other length. The order of presentation of the two lengths was counterbalanced.

3 Results

This section presents the results of the study. Initially the results of the objective measures of reading performance are given before the participants preferred text size and views on the font sizes are presented.

3.1 Reading Performance

Twelve participants from each group read two passages at a given text size for each text length. This gave 24 records of reading time and accuracy per group for the short and long text passages. At the smallest font sizes (sizes 2 & 4) some participants, particularly in the older group, found the text uncomfortable or just impossible to read, so chose not to read it. Font size 2 in particular caused older participants problems, yielding only 2 results for short passages and 3 results for long passages. However, from font size 6 upwards no problems were had with text legibility. Font size 4 posed no problem for younger participants, yielding 24 results while for older participants 19 results were obtained for short passages and 16 for long passages.

Reading Time. Times for completion of reading a passage were recorded to a tenth of a second and then normalized on the fastest completion time. Normalisation was used to remove any effects of base reading speed and reading abilities among participants. For example, those who read regularly would be expected to read faster than those reading infrequently. The graph in Figure 5 illustrates the normalized reading time for both groups for both sets of passages.

The average reading time for older people at font size 2 has not been plotted since there were an insufficient number of data values to get a reasonable representation of the average reading time. The graph shows that there was little difference in reading time between groups for sizes 6-16. However, each group had a lower bound at which reading becomes difficult and times slow, for the younger group this is at size 2 while the older group it is at size 4. An analysis of variance between different passage lengths and age groups found that there was no significant difference in reading times

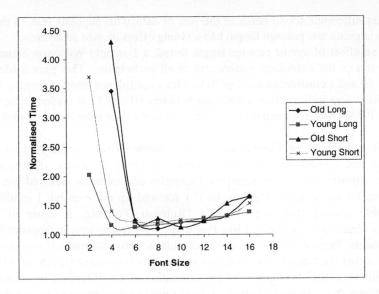

Fig. 5. Time taken to read each passage at each font size by our two user groups

(p > 0.05 in all cases). Though there was a slight increase in reading time at font size 16 it was not statistically significant.

Accuracy. In the tasks there was 1 error per short passage and two errors per long passage. The percentage of correctly identified errors was over 85% in all but 2 cases. It did drop to 66.67% for young people and short passages at font size 2 and 78.13% for older people and long passages at font size 4.

Overall accuracy is very high, over 90% in many cases. There is a small degradation in accuracy for both the older and younger group at the font size where reading speed slowed. This indicates that those sizes are the lower bounds of readability.

Originally it had been planned to follow Bernard's [2] example and calculate an adjusted accuracy measure. That is the ratio of time take to read the passage to the percentage of errors found. However, the ceiling effect seen by the accuracy measure meant that nothing meaningful could be drawn from such results.

3.2 Subjective Results

Font Size Preference. Using a Wilcoxon Signed Rank test the preferences for each age group and passage length was examined. A confidence interval of font sizes from 9-11 (12 for older people) are preferred for reading text on the PDA screen. The younger group has a slightly smaller median (10) to the older group (11). These results are the same for both long and short passages.

It is important to consider whether there are any significant differences between young and old participant's preferences or whether preferences change between long and short passages. A Mann-Whitney test was used to analyse whether there was a difference between the groups. The p-values were all greater than 0.05, with no significant difference found between the sets of data. This suggests that, in this case, neither age group nor passage length had a strong effect on size preference.

With no effect of age or passage length found, a 1-sample Wilcoxon Signed Rank test was run on the combined preferences of all participants. This gave a Median of font size 10 and a confidence level of 95% with a confidence interval ranging from 10 to 11. These data indicate that a font size between 10 and 11 is preferred for reading text on a PDA. (Non-parametric tests were used as the data were based on rankings).

Qualitative Analysis of Comments. Users' comments on specific font sizes were examined and ranked on a five point scale: -2 (very negative), -1 (negative), 0 (neutral), 1 (positive), 2 (very positive). Examples of comments received were: "Just impossible for me to read. Well maybe if I screwed up my eyes but I would not be comfortable reading that size of text", "Rubbish. Too big. A waste of space", "perfectly clear. Nice and bold. I like that one". Two researchers independently rated the comments. Pearson product moment correlation statistical analysis was used and it was found that the ratings from the two researchers correlated ($r > 0.5$; $df = 10$ in all cases). However, this does not show any indication of the difference in magnitude of the two researchers' ratings. Further analysis revealed disagreement in less than 22% of cases and disagreement was never greater than one point on the rating scale. Therefore, there was close agreement between researchers' ratings. The ratings were combined by averaging them. The graph in Figure 6 illustrates the average comment ratings about each font size from the old and young group with respect to the long and short passages.

All groups of participants agreed that sizes 2 and 4 were undesirable. Size 6 had a slight positive comment from all users while size 8 was considered positive. The younger group rated size 10 as positively as size 8 for both long and short passages but were more negative toward size 12 and were negative about sizes 14 and 16. The older group commented most favourably on size 12 for short passages but this was only 0.04 more positive than size 10 (0.08 more than size 8). Sizes 14 and 16, received positive comments but distinctly less positive than sizes 8-12. The comments about the long passages from the older group gave size 10 as the font size most positively commented upon. Sizes 8 and 12 were also given positive comments. Once again sizes 14 and 16 received less favourable comments, both fairly neutral.

A Mann-Whitney test was used to analyse whether there was a difference between the groups. The p-values were all greater than 0.05, with no significant difference found between the sets of data. This suggests that, in this case, neither age group nor passage length has a strong effect on subjective views of font size.

Summary. There was no difference in preference identified due to passage length or between age group preferences. Overall a font range of 10-11 was preferred. This was reflected by users' comments about font sizes where size 10 received high positive comments, as did size 8. In addition, older people also commented positively about size 12. The smaller font sizes (2, 4) were disliked as were the larger font sizes (14, 16) by younger group.

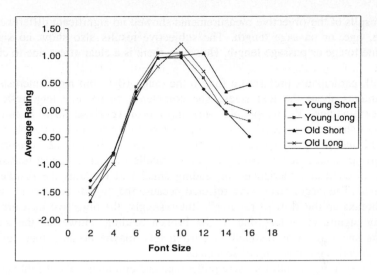

Fig. 6. Average ratings of the comments received about each font size

4 Discussion

The results show that objective measures (time and accuracy) of reading performance are not affected significantly by changes in font size (within limits) or passage length for both the old and young group. This corresponds to the findings of Tinker [21] that varying the typeface and size of text within common parameters only has limited impact on readability. This owes much to the adaptability of the human visual system to be able to process diverse presentation of data. The lower bound for text size appears to be size 4 for the younger group and size 6 for the older group since below that size reading time degrades. However, no upper bound was apparent from the results. However, subjective comments show a negative feeling toward the largest font sizes indicating that there is may be an upper bound, but perhaps we did not go high enough in our font sizes to find the upper bound. Mills & Weldon [17] found that 80 characters per line were easier to read that 40 characters per line. As font size increases the number of characters per line decreases. Therefore, it would be expected that there will be an upper bound to maintain reading performance as the font size increased. At font size 4 we see a large disparity between young and old participants' times for reading passages. These deficits are potentially due to age-related losses in visual contrast sensitivity [1]. This is backed up by some comments from older participants stating that they preferred higher contrast text (e.g. "a decided black is better than grey for text colour the smaller text sizes were lighter").

The ceiling effect seen in the accuracy results was unfortunate since it did not allow analysis of reading time versus accuracy. The effect could be addressed in future experiments by increasing the number of contextual errors per passage. However, too many errors would make the task unrealistic compared to normal reading. Further research is needed to determine an optimum number of errors.

The results of the objective measurements showed no significant difference due to font size, age, or passage length. The subjective results also show no significant effects due to age or passage length. However, there is a clear effect due to change in font size.

Overall, participants preferred a font in the range 10-11 but more interesting were the comments about the text sizes. The comments, to some extent, reflected the preference findings. Young people were most positive about sizes 8 and 10 and preferences showed a range of 9-11. The preferred font size of older people fell in the range 9-12 and they commented positively about sizes 8, 10, and 12. Unsurprisingly neither group commented positively about the smallest (2, 4) or largest font sizes (14, 16). The discomfort experienced in reading small text explains the dislike for the small sizes. The larger sizes were rejected because the "words are spread out more" which "breaks up the flow of reading". Interestingly, the objective measures do not show any significant effect due to the broken reading. However, the subjective comments show this was disliked by participants, maybe because more effort was required to derive the meaning of sentences.

It can be seen from both font size preference and comments about font sizes that a slightly larger range is associated with the older group than with the younger group. This indicates that older users vary more widely in their subjective preferences. Therefore, when considering older users in design, a slightly wider range of fonts should be allowed, including larger ones. This applies particularly to the shorter passages. A possible explanation is that size 12 is the largest font that requires no scrolling with the short passages. However, from the objective measures it was seen that passage length had no significant effect on performance. Therefore, it may be the case that users would prefer not to have to scroll even though it has little effect on their reading performance. Comments from some users reflected this with a preference for "seeing text on one page". Allowing font sizes in the range 8-12 would provide reasonable user satisfaction and ensure good reading performance

The sizes in this range may seem smaller that one would expect based on previous desktop computer based text reading studies. For example, Bernard *et. al.* [2] found size 12 produced greater subjective readability and lower levels of perceived difficulty, therefore, one would expect size 12 to be in the middle of the range. However, font size 10 at a resolution of 640x480 is approximately the same height as font size 12 at a resolution of 1024x768 [2] for the same screen. Therefore, the lower resolution of our screen compared to that of previous desktop computer reading studies could account for the smaller font sizes we found.

4.1 Comparing Our Results to Previous Research

It may have been expected that one font size would come out as the "best" or most favourably commented upon for reading text on handheld computers. Instead, we ended up with a range of sizes. This can be explained by the fact that the reading distance during the experiment was not fixed. Subjects could move the iPAQ closer or further from their eyes as necessary; experimental observation confirms participants varying the distance of the iPAQ from their face. This allowed the angular character size to be changed. Akutsu *et. al.* [1] found that reading speed was maximal for both young and old people within a given angular character size range (0.3° to 1.0°). This would explain the similar performance of all groups from font size 6-16 and possibly the range rather than a specific preference. An analogy to consider is that of reading a book. Publishers use different font sizes (and book sizes), each requiring the book to be held a different distance from the eyes for the most comfortable reading.

The handheld computer used in this study had a screen resolution of 640x480 pixels (currently the best available, and a significant improvement over the previous generation of the iPAQ device where characters below 6 point were not rendered clearly) which is becoming the common screen resolution on handheld computers. Therefore, our findings will continue to apply to handheld technology for the near future. In 2002, Karkkainnen suggested 14 point font for reading text on handheld computers. The resolution of the device he used was 320x240. This is lower than that used in our experiment and is the likely explanation for the different findings. The LCD screen technology for handheld devices is changing rapidly for the better. The anti-aliasing used in the current version of the Windows Mobile operating system makes the characters much easier to see at small sizes. This indicates that our findings may not be applicable to future displays with improved resolutions. However, our findings that a range of sizes is preferred are likely to be the same for future screens, with the bounds of the range changing with resolution changes.

The results in this paper should be taken with the caveat that they only apply to the particular device and screen used in this study, although are likely to apply to other small screen devices with similar displays. The quality of presentational format can have a major influence on both reading speed for learning and comprehension [10]. As the quality of the screens on handheld computers improve, better performance could be expected just as improvements in computer monitors lead to improvements in screen reading such that they are now comparable to print reading speeds.

4.2 Other Observations

At the smallest text size (2), few participants from the older group attempted to read the text. This was because they had been given the option to pass on a passage if it was going to be too much of a strain. However, they may have been able to read it if they had tried. In such a situation the experimenter is faced with a dilemma. There are ethical issues involved in forcing a participant to perform a task that may cause discomfort. However, as in this case, there can be a fine line between extracting useful research results and the comfort of the participant. This adds difficulty in designing tasks and procedure for an experiment, especially involving older people. An alternate view is that gaining a measurement for reading a passage that would never be read in practice is not a useful result. What is useful, however, is finding the limits of what would be read in practice.

A point of interest to those considering doing similar research to this study is to choose words for rhyming carefully. For example, one replacement used in this study was the word "clear" for the word "deer". This meets the requirements of rhyming and sufficiently out of context as to not require rereading of sentences. However, at smaller fonts the letters 'c' and 'l' become less distinguishable and look very much like the letter 'd' (e.g. d). This makes the substituted word very like the original word and means it can easily be missed. The unfortunate choice of word was pointed out by one of the last participants, but it only affected the passage at font size 2. Furthermore, the overall performance of accuracy was such that this did not have a serious impact on the results.

One other import factor is mobility. The research presented in this paper was all done with the participants seated in a quiet usability laboratory. The iPAQ is a handheld computer designed to be used in mobile situations. If the user is mobile then that is likely to have a large impact on the size of font required. As the user moves the device moves, making the screen harder to see. A mobile environment can also have changing lighting conditions which can make the screen hard to see and so change font size requirements. Brewster [6] found a very significant effect on performance when users used a stylus/touch screen interface when on the move. A 32% reduction in tapping performance and a 17% increase in subjective workload were found when users were walking outside as compared to sitting in a usability lab. Therefore the experiments described in this paper should be replicated in a mobile situation to gain more knowledge of appropriate font sizes (something we are planning to do in the near future). However, there are very many cases where users of handheld computers use them when sat down or stood still, so the results described here are significant.

5 Future Work

Our study has given some indications of the text size that should be used and paved the way for further research into suitable text formats to be used for reading on handheld computers. This study used only one font type but previous studies have compared different font types, particularly serif and sans-serif fonts. However, Boyarski *et al.* [5] found that 10 point Georgia (serif) and Verdana (sans-serif) were equally readable. Since these two font types were specifically designed for screen use it is quite possible the same findings would occur if they were used on handheld computers. It was also found that fonts designed for screen that had relatively large x-heights performed well in on-line reading performance [5]. Future studies should investigate reading performance by varying font type (both serif and sans-serif), x-height, and font size. This study has provided bounds within which font size should be varied.

It has been found that line length is a more important factor in reading than line height [9]. Therefore, a future investigation could examine the differences in reading when text is displayed in portrait or landscape format.

As was discussed previously, text reading performance experiments are not always realistic to actual reading. Handheld computers bring another factor to the realism, that of environment. The portability of small screen devices means they can be used in many locations each varying in the distracters it contains. For example, a commuter could read the latest news or novel on a PDA on the train to work. However, the stop-start nature of travel, background noise and vibrations could all have an effect on reading. A planned future experiment is to repeat the study in this paper in a 'real' mobile environment. The difficulty is being able to ensure a consistent environment for comparable results with so many potential variables to account for.

6 Conclusions

The purpose of this study was to examine the effect of different font sizes on reading text on handheld computers and to consider the differences between young and old people. Although there were no significant differences (for sizes 6-16) in reading performance or accuracy due to either passage length or age, there was variation in subjects' preferences on the text sizes used. The range of preferred or positively commented upon sizes was slightly greater (at the large side) for older participants than for younger participants. The amount of text presented and so the amount of scrolling required does not have an effect on reading performance.

We recommend that designers creating applications for reading text on a small screen with resolution of 640x480 should offer the choice of small (font size 8), medium (font size 10), or large (font size 12) sizes to cater for the needs of most users. The choice should consider the amount of text that will be presented at once. Ideally, designers will allow for a range of text sizes to accommodate most users.

Acknowledgements

This work was funded by SHEFC through the UTOPIA project (HR01002).

References

1. Akutsu, H., Legge, G.E., Ross, J.A., Schuebel, K.: Psychophysics of Reading: X. Effects of Age Related Changes in Vision. Journal of Gerontology: Psychological Sciences, 46, 1991, 325-331.
2. Bernard, M.L., Chaparro, B.S., Mills, M.M., Halcomb, C.G.: Comparing the Effects of Text Size and Format on the Readability of Computer-Displayed Times New Roman and Arial Text. International Journal of Human-Computer Studies, 59 (2003) 823-835.
3. Bernard, M.L., Chaparro, B.S., Mills, M.M., Halcomb, C.G.: Examining Children's Reading Performance and Preference for Different Computer-Displayed Text. Journal of Behaviour and Information Technology, 21(2), 2002, 87-96.
4. Bernard, M.L., Liao, C.H., Mills, M.M.: The Effects of Font Type and Size on the Legibility and Reading Time of Online Text by Older Adults. In Vol. II Proceedings of ACM CHI 2001, ACM Press, 2001, 175-176.
5. Boyarski, D., Neuwirth, C., Forlizzi, J., Regli, S.H.: A Study of Fonts Designed for Screen Display. In Proceedings of ACM CHI 98, ACM Press, 1998, 87-94.
6. Brewster, S.A.: Overcoming the Lack of Screen Space on Mobile Computers. Personal and Ubiquitous Computing, 6(3), 2002, 188-205.
7. Creed, A., Dennis, I., Newstead, S.: Proof-Reading on VDUs. Journal of Behaviour and Information Technology, 6, 1987, 3-13.
8. Dillon, A.: Reading from Paper versus Screens: A Critical Review of the Empirical Literature. Ergonomics, 35(10), 1992, 1297-1326.
9. Duchnicky, R.L., Kolers, P.A.: Readability of Text Scrolled on Visual Display Terminals as a Function of Window Size. Human Factors, 25(6), 1983, 683-692.
10. Garland, K.J., Noyes, J.M.: CRT Monitors: Do They Interfere with Learning?. Journal of Behaviour and Information Technology, 23(1), 2004, 43-52.

11. Goodman, J., Gray, P.D., Brewster S.: How Can We Best Use Landmarks to Support Older People in Navigation? Journal of Behaviour and Information Technology, 24(1), 2005, 3-20.
12. Gujar, A.U., Harrison, B.L., Fishkin, K.P.: A Comparative Evaluation of Display Technologies for Reading. In Proceedings of the Human Factors and Ergonomics Society 42nd Annual Meeting, Chicago IL, 1998, 527-531.
13. Jorna, G.C., Snyder, H.L.: Image Quality Determines Differences in Reading Performance and Perceived Image Quality with CRT and Hard-Copy Displays. Human Factors, 33(4), 1991, 459-469.
14. Karkkainen, L., Laarni, J.: Designing for Small Display Screens. In Proceedings of the Second Nordic Conference on Human-Computer Interaction (Aarhus, Denmark, October, 2002), ACM Press, 227-230.
15. Laarni, K.: Searching for Optimal Methods of Presenting Dynamic Text on Different Types of Screens. In Proceedings of the Second Nordic Conference on Human-Computer Interaction (Aarhus, Denmark, October, 2002), ACM Press, 219-222.
16. Microsoft Corporation: Encarta Online Encyclopedia. http://encarta.msn.com, 2004.
17. Mills, C.B., Weldon, L.J.: Reading Text from Computer Screens. ACM Computing Surveys, 19 (4), 1987, 329-358.
18. Mustonen, T., Olkkonen, M., Hakkinen, J.: Examining Mobile Phone Text Legibility while Walking. In Vol. II Proceedings of ACM CHI 2004, ACM Press, 2004, 1243-1246.
19. O'Hara, K., Sellen, A.: A Comparison of Reading Papers and On-Line Documents. In Proceedings of ACM CHI 97, ACM Press, 1997, 335-342.
20. Poulton, E.C.: Letter Differentiation and Rate of Comprehension of Reading. Journal of Applied Psychology, 49, 1955, 358-362.
21. Tinker, M.A.: Legibility of Print. Iowa State University Press, Ames, Indiana (1963).
22. Weiss, S.: Handheld Usability. John Wiley & Sons (2002).

Fat Finger Worries:
How Older and Younger Users
Physically Interact with PDAs

Katie A. Siek, Yvonne Rogers, and Kay H. Connelly

Indiana University, Bloomington, IN 47405, USA
{ksiek, yrogers, connelly}@indiana.edu

Abstract. There has been a steady growth in the global population of elderly people, challenging researchers in the HCI community to design technologies to help them remain independent and preserve their quality of life. One approach has been to create assistive technology solutions using Personal Digital Assistants (PDAs). However, some have questioned whether older people can use PDAs because of age related problems with dexterity, coordination, and vision. This paper presents an initial usability study that shows there are no major differences in performance between older and younger users when physically interacting with PDAs and completing conventional (e.g. pressing buttons, viewing icons, recording messages) and non-conventional tasks (e.g. scanning bar codes).

1 Introduction

Each month, the world's elderly population grows by 795,000. By the year 2030, the world's older population will grow by 847,000 per month [1]. Researchers in the HCI community have taken notice of this trend and are working on applications to help older people live independent and productive lives. Personal Digital Assistants (PDAs) [2, 3] and smart phones [4] are some of the devices researchers use to create *assistive technologies* for older people. Our research is concerned with how PDAs can be used as personal aids for health informatics, in particular, for helping older people who have end-stage renal disease (ESRD) monitor their nutrition more effectively.

When we started our nutrition monitoring project, we were cautioned that older people may not be able to use PDAs given the adverse effects age can have on vision, dexterity, and coordination [5, 6]. If elderly populations have difficulties using traditional personal computers (PCs), as has been found in some studies, how will they fare when interacting with the smaller screen and buttons of a PDA? The lack of literature available on how elderly physically interact with PDAs led us to conduct an initial study to see if there were any differences between older and younger people when physically interacting with PDAs.

In this paper, we present the findings from our study investigating whether elderly people (75-85 years old) have problems using PDAs. As a control to compare older people with, a group of younger people (aged 25-30 years old) participated in the study. Participants were asked to complete three conventional PDA tasks (e.g. pushing buttons, viewing icons, and recording voice messages) and two additional tasks (e.g. scanning bar codes with two kinds of scanners). The scanning tasks were included in the study to

M.F. Costabile and F. Paternò (Eds.): INTERACT 2005, LNCS 3585, pp. 267–280, 2005.
© IFIP International Federation for Information Processing 2005

(1) determine how easy it is to input nutrition information that is found on food items and (2) give insight into how older people would perform on other less familiar PDA tasks, such as taking digital pictures with the device.

The findings from our initial study suggest that older people completed the tasks nearly as well as younger participants. While older people needed more practice before completing each task, their performance was similar to the younger participants.

We begin with a review of related work. The technology, applications, and evaluation techniques we used in the study are discussed in Section 3. In Section 4, we discuss the user study and evaluate the results. We conclude with a discussion of the results and ideas for future work.

2   Related Work

There has been a proliferation of handheld devices designed for the general public, including PDAs, cell phones, remote controls, digital cameras, digital music players, and game playing devices. The interfaces to these vary considerably, suggesting there may be variable age-related performance effects. Hence, when creating applications for older populations that run on these devices, there is a need to consider age-related abilities such as vision, dexterity, coordination, and cognition. HCI researchers have acknowledged that within older populations, there are noticeable differences in abilities and that different design methodologies such as Universal Design [7] and User Sensitive Inclusive Design [8] should be used. Here we discuss some of the research that has been done to better understand older populations interaction with technology.

Bernard et al. found that older people could read faster with a larger, more legible 14-point san serif font on web sites [9]. Researchers at Georgia Tech studied how multimodal feedback (sound, touch, visual effect) could assist participants with varying vision problems perform basic mouse tasks (drag and drop). They found that all groups performed better when sound was added, however groups performed the best when all three modal feedbacks were implemented [10].

A number of recent studies [11, 12, 13, 14] focused on the ability of older populations to use PC input devices. The studies showed that older people completed tasks more slowly when compared to younger groups. Charness et al. evaluated control key, mouse, and light pen input devices and found older people preferred the light pen followed by the mouse and control keys [13].

Smith et al. and Laursen et al. found older people made more mistakes than younger people and had the most difficulty with fine motor control tasks such as double clicking. However, Chaparro et al. found older people performed "point and click" and "click and drag" tasks slower than younger people, but with the same amount of accuracy. The researchers deduced that older people were slower because of the reduced fine motor control, muscle strength, and pincher strength associated with older age.

Most of the human computer interaction studies on elderly and technology have focused on the usability of PCs. As pervasive computing technology applications become more widespread, the usability of handheld devices will be scrutinized more carefully. Researchers are already assessing the needs of older people with respect to mobile phones. Maguire and Osman found that older people primarily considered mobile phones as a way to assist in emergencies, whereas younger people saw mobile phones as a way to interact socially. Older people were interested in small phones with large buttons and location aware systems [15].

Abascal and Civit looked at the pros (safety, increased autonomy, etc.) and cons (social isolation, loss of privacy, etc.) of older people using mobile phone technologies and gave a needs assessment [7]. The pros and cons apply to assistive PDA solutions as well, however the needs assessments differ because PDAs have larger physical interfaces and different input mechanisms.

Smith et al. and Maguire and Osman suggested voice input could assist with difficulties older users have with mouse and mobile phone input. Using PDAs for voice recordings is becoming a popular way to get user feedback in situ. For example, Intille et al. integrated voice recordings into their context-aware experience sampling tool for PDAs to obtain feedback from participants [16]. The natural decrease in pincher strength [17] and difficulty maintaining constant force [18] that accompanies old age may hinder older populations from using voice input technologies.

The findings from these studies suggest that there may be performance differences for older people when using small handheld devices. They may find it hard to manipulate small buttons that are close to one another and read small icons on a screen. PDAs have been designed to allow users to select from two size icons and input information using other kinds of devices besides keypads, keyboards, and mice (e.g. bar code scanners, touch screen). The aim of our study was to assess PDA input mechanisms that do not involved mouse movement or the cognitive mapping between mouse pad coordinates and screen position. PDAs also have the advantage of being all-in-one devices - users can input commands and view output on the same devices. We also wanted to see if older people could successfully record voice messages using a PDA.

In particular, the goal of our usability study was to see whether vision, dexterity, and coordination effects transfer to PDAs or whether the ergonomic design of PDAs is adequately "large" enough to enable older populations who may have more dexterity, coordination, and vision problems. The specific aims were to:

- Compare performance between older and younger participants performing conventional (pushing buttons, viewing icons, and recording voice messages) and nonconventional (scanning bar codes with two different types of scanners) tasks
- Study how older and younger participants physically interact with PDAs (e.g. how they hold the device, how far away they hold the device, etc.) to understand any difficulties participants may have completing PDA tasks

3 Experiment Design

In this section, we discuss why we selected the Tungsten T3 PDA, Socket SDIO scanner and Baracoda pencil as our scanners, and how we developed the usability tasks. Detailed information about the experimental design can be found in our full report [19].

3.1 Hardware

PDA Selection PDAs are the center of our study and the building block of many pervasive computing applications. Most HCI PDA applications use off-the-shelf PDAs to make their application more widely accessible and less expensive. The physical design of PDAs are similar because they have small screens with five buttons. The middle button is usually larger than the other four and (in newer models) is a 5-way navigator buttons. The 5-way navigator buttons allow users to scroll through applications and documents with one hand. We conducted the study with an off-the-shelf PDA so the results would be useful to the HCI community. We chose the Tungsten T3 because it has a 5-way navigator button, four large application buttons, Bluetooth, an SDIO slot, and a voice recorder.

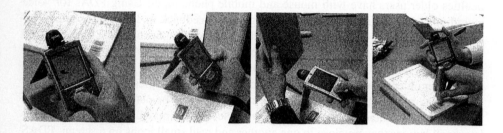

Fig. 1. Usability test tasks: (L-R) button press, icon size, Socket scanning, and Baracoda scanning

Scanner Selection A scanner needs to be small, easy to use, and robust for integration into HCI applications. We found two scanners that met our criteria - Socket SDIO card scanner and the Baracoda pencil. To operate the Socket scanner, users press the predefined PDA scanning button and line up the scanning light with the bar code as shown in Figure 1. The PDA beeps and shows the bar code number on the screen when users have successfully scanned the bar code. To operate the Baracoda pencil scanner, users press a button on the side of the Baracoda pencil and run the pencil tip over the bar code as shown in Figure 1. The users must look at the PDA screen to see if they have successfully scanned the bar code.

3.2   Designing the Applications

People must have a basic level of dexterity, coordination, and vision to use a PDA. We tested these three aspects by asking people to complete a set of tasks summarized in Table 1. The tasks were designed to measure primarily motor control, rather than

Table 1. Types of tasks and the characteristics needed to successfully complete the task

Type of Task	Ability Needed To Complete Task
Push PDA buttons	Dexterity
Selecting an icon	Vision
Recording a voice diary entry	Dexterity & Coordination
Socket Scanning bar code	Dexterity & Coordination
Pencil Scanning bar code	Dexterity & Coordination

mental effort. We chose not to investigate stylus input because we considered it might be too intimidating for first-time users (e.g. learning graffiti). In this section, we discuss how we designed and evaluated the five different input tasks.

PDA Button Press Task. We tested whether participants could press buttons on the PDA because buttons are the primary input method for accessing applications and scrolling through data. We developed an event-driven test modeled after the 1980's Simon Says game, shown in Figure 2, to test the ability to press buttons. The picture on the PDA screen showed the same configuration of buttons as the buttons on the Tungsten T3. The buttons take turns "lighting up" by turning red until the participant selects the corresponding button on the PDA. The task tests if the participant can press each of the nine Tungsten T3 buttons once (four buttons and each of the 5-way navigator buttons). Errors (e.g. if a participant pushes the incorrect button) were recorded as shown on the last screen image in Figure 2. We also recorded how far away the participant held the PDA and what hands and or fingers the participant used to complete the task. We examined how participants held the PDA to see how comfortable the participants were interacting with the device.

Icon Size Task. Icons are used to select PDA applications from the main menu and navigate within applications. Moreover, icons can convey information to users independent of literacy skills. We created a task similar to an eye exam chart, shown in Figure 3, to test what size icons participants prefer to use (vision). Icon sizes ranged from 5mm to 25mm. Current PDA icons are 7.76mm or 5.29mm square depending on the layout

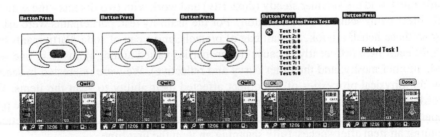

Fig. 2. Button Press Task. The last screen indicates the errors that were made.

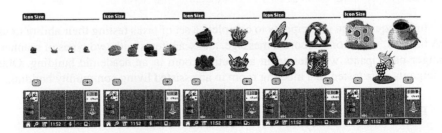

Fig. 3. Icon Size Task. From left to right: 5mm, 10mm, 15mm, 20mm, and 25mm screens.

chosen [20]. When the task was started, a screen with four 15mm icons was displayed. The participant was asked to read the pictures on the screen. We increased or decreased the size of the icons based on the participants answers. The task concluded by recording what size icons the participants preferred, the smallest icon size the participants could read, how far the participants held the PDA from them, and if they had a preference between the realistic pictures or the illustrated drawing icons. We noted preferred icon size and what sizes the participants could read to see if there were any noticeable differences between their preference and vision.

Recording a Voice Diary. For this task, we asked participants to record comments and questions to see how the participants created voice diaries. To do this requires pressing the record button on the side of the PDA, waiting for a beep, and then continuing to hold the button down while recording a voice diary. We asked participants to record three phrases - a short phrase (approximately 1 second), a medium length phrase (approximately 5 seconds), and a longer phrase (approximately 15-20 seconds). After recording each phrase, the participants were asked to play it back. If the participants did not record the message properly, they could try recording the phrase again. We recorded how many times participants successfully recorded each phrase, if the participants waited for the beep before saying each phrase (learning), how far the participants held the PDA away from them, and any difficulties the participants had finding the recording button.

Scanning Items. Scanning bar codes is an easy input mode that does not require intensive cognitive effort to choose items from a menu. However, participants must have a reasonable level of manual dexterity and coordination to scan an object because participants must hold the scanner steady (dexterity) and work with two objects - the scanner and object being scanned (coordination). For the usability test, participants were asked to scan three items: a book, a small bag of pretzels, and a can of soda. Participants had to hold each item differently because the properties varied among items (e.g. one was hard, another mushy, and the other curvy and reflective). We were interested in seeing how the physical properties of the object affected their ability to scan the items. We recorded how many times it took participants to successfully scan each item, if the participants moved the PDA or object being scanned, and how many times they practiced scanning an item after successfully scanning an item the first time.

4   PDA Usability Study

The study required the participants to complete a set of tasks testing their ability to use PDA buttons, view icons, record a message, and scan items with two types of scanners. Younger participants were tested in a meeting room in an academic building. Older participants were tested in a meeting room in an assisted living community building.

4.1   Hypotheses

Based on the literature that showed elderly people can use PCs equally, we hypothesized that there would be no difference between the two age groups. We predicted that:

- Participants of all ages can press buttons on the PDA.
- Participants of all ages prefer medium size (10mm or 15mm) icons.
- Participants can record voice messages of various lengths.
- Participants can scan bar codes with some practice.

4.2 Participants

Twenty participants volunteered for the study. The control group consisted of ten participants 25-30 years old (two female, eight male). The older group had ten participants 75-85 years old (five female, five male). We chose a younger group to compare them with as they have normal dexterity, vision and coordination and therefore, would be able to use PDAs with ease.

Sixteen participants reported using computers a lot. Younger participants used computers primarily for word processing, emailing, and Internet searches. Older participants used computers primarily for emailing and viewing images. We asked how often and what kind of applications participants used to get a more accurate measure on computer experience (scaled 0-3: 0 - not at all; 1- not often with 1 application; 2 - sometimes with 1-2 applications; and 3 - often with various applications). We found participants had similar computer experience ($T_{18} = 1.24$, p = 0.232).

None of the participants in the two groups owned a PDA. However, three younger participants reported they had some experience with PDAs (e.g. occasionally played with a friend's PDA by playing a game or drawing a picture).

All of the older participants and over half of the younger participants wore glasses when using a computer, but did not report any problems reading computer screens. None of the participants had problems using television remote controls. Over three quarters of the younger participants and three of the older participants used cell phones without any difficulty.

4.3 Design and Procedure

Participants completed the five tasks without any time constraints. We did not enforce any maximum amount of viewing time because we wanted the participants to feel comfortable reading the icons and avoid the stress associated with timed events. Laursen et al. found placing time constraints on older people increase the number of errors [14]. Each participant was given a task sheet describing what to do for each task. We let participants hold the PDA for each task as shown in Figure 1.

Since both groups had experience pushing small buttons on cell phones and remote controls, we allowed participants only one chance to complete the button press task. In addition, the button press task gave us insight into how intuitive it was for participants to hold the PDA.

For the icon size task, participants held the PDA and moved the PDA to see the icons clearly. The task administrator or participant changed the size of the icons by pressing PDA buttons.

During the voice diary task, participants read aloud three phrases printed on the task sheet. Participants played back their recording to ensure they successfully recorded the messages. Participants recorded each phrase as many times as they wanted.

During the scanning tasks, participants scanned the bar codes on three items: a book, a small bag of pretzels, and a can of soda. Participants scanned each object as many times as they wanted so they could practice and become familiar with the scanning device. They were encouraged to start the task by scanning the book, then the bag of pretzels, and finally the soda can because each item was increasingly difficult to scan based on bar code material and object size.

At the end of the tasks, we discussed the comments the participants made during the study.

4.4   Findings

As predicted, the key findings from our study were that:

- There were no differences in performance between the older and younger groups for the button press and voice recording task.
- We also found some small differences between the two groups: The younger participants preferred smaller icons (5mm or 10mm), whereas the older participants preferred larger icons (20mm).
- The older participants scanned items more with both scanners, but had the same success rate as younger participants.

In this section, we look in more detail at the results for each task. The results are presented in the order the tasks were completed - button press, icon size, voice recording, Socket SDIO scanning, and Baracoda pencil scanning.

Button Press Task. The button press results supported our hypothesis by showing no significant performance differences between older and younger participants - 8 participants from each group did not make any mistakes during the task. All participants voiced some confusion over the 5-way navigator button. The button press task started by making participants press the middle of the 5-way navigator button, thus participants knew the 5-way navigator button was different than the other buttons. When participants saw the up or down part of the 5-way navigator light up they made comments about how the navigator is an "up and down" button. However, when the left and right part of the 5-way navigator lit up, participants voiced some concerns. Most participants followed their instincts and pressed the left or right part of the large navigation button, but three participants pressed the incorrect button. The participants who pressed the incorrect button learned quickly from their mistakes.

The older male participants voiced concerns about how their "fat fingers" may cause problems when completing the task. They worried that the size of their fingers would cause them to push multiple buttons at the same time. However, the "fat finger" problem was not supported since not many errors were recorded during the task. As previously stated, the only errors were caused by the 5-way navigator button.

Most of the participants held the PDA in their non-dominant hand and selected buttons with their dominant hand. Only three younger participants completed the task by using one hand to hold the PDA and select buttons. This was the first task participants completed with the PDA, thus they were not as comfortable with holding the PDA.

A t-test indicated that there were no significant performance differences in terms of incorrect button presses due to age ($T_{18} = 0.787$, p = 0.442). Participants commented that the task was "easy to follow" - the PDA told them exactly what to press and 9 of the older participants said the button press task was the easiest task they completed during the study.

Icon Size Task. Results from the icon size task were a little surprising. Our hypothesis was confirmed by younger participants who preferred icons 10mm (mean = 10mm, standard deviation = 3.33mm). However, older participants preferred icons 25mm (mean = 18.5mm, standard deviation = 6.687mm). Despite the older participants preferring larger icons, they were all able to read icons ≤ 15mm (younger: mean = 5.5mm, standard deviation = 1.581mm; older: mean = 10mm, standard deviation = 4.082mm). A t-test indicated that there were significant differences in icon size preference ($T_{18} = 3.73$, p = 0.002) and the size icon they could actually see ($T_{18} = 3.25$, p = 0.004).

When we asked participants why they chose a specific size icon, the younger participants were interested in how many icons could fit on the screen. Older participants were primarily interested in larger icons so they could "clearly see details." This accounts for the preferences of size.

The icon size application used scaled photographs and illustrations of food items as shown in Figure 3 to see if participants had a preference. A majority of the younger group did not have a preference, but the older group preferred the photographs because they were "clearer" and "more realistic."

During the icon size task participants were allowed to hold the PDA to view the icons. Both groups of participants held the PDA at about the same distance on average (younger: mean = 14.8", standard deviation = 6.339"; older: mean = 12.5", standard deviation = 4.249"). The only noticeable difference in how the participants held the PDA was the older group tilted the PDA in their hand trying to view the icons with less glare. The younger group did not have a problem with glare.

Recording a Voice Diary Entry Task. Participants were asked to record three phrases during the recording voice diary entry task - a short phrase, a medium length phrase, and a longer length phrase. The voice diary recording task was an easy task for most of the participants - 7 participants from each group were able to record the short message correctly the first time. Participants who could not successfully record the short message during their first try, succeeded on their second try. All of the younger participants and all but one of the older participants successfully recorded the long messages on their first try. Overall, we found no significant performance differences in successfully recording all three messages ($T_{18} \leq 0.5$, p > 0.3 for all three recordings).

Most of the younger participants held the PDA in their left hand and used their thumb to press the button when recording the messages. A majority of the older participants used two hands when recording - the right hand stabilized the PDA while the left hand pressed the recording button. Some older participants expressed a fear of breaking the PDA and held it with two hands to make sure they had a good grip on the device. The fear of breaking the PDA could attribute to why most people in the older group used two hands for some of the tasks. Both groups held the PDA about nine inches away on average from themselves when recording their messages.

Socket SDIO Scanning Task. The older group was more successful in scanning the book on the first try than the younger group (50% versus 40% success rate). Nine younger and 10 older participants were able to scan the book in less than four attempts. Younger participants were able to scan the bag of pretzels on the first try better than older participants (60% versus 50% success rate). All of the participants were able to scan the the bag of pretzels eventually. The can of soda was the most difficult item to scan - only 4 of the younger participants and 2 of the older participants were able to scan the can within three tries. Overall, we found no significant performance differences in all three scannings (book: $T_{18} = 0.958$, p = 0.351; bag: $T_{18} = 0.247$, p = 0.808; can: $T_{11} = 1.30$, p = 0.221).

We observed how practice affects scanning success when we compared the number of successful book scans participants completed before trying to scan the bag of pretzels. Younger participants who practiced successfully scanning the book 3-8 times were able to scan the bag of pretzels more quickly (successfully scanned bag after 1.6 attempts) than those who only practiced successfully scanning the book 1-2 times (successfully scanned bag after 2.6 attempts). Half the younger and older participants practiced scanning the book three or more times before trying to scan the bag. We did not find any relation between overall scanning practice and the ability to successfully scan the soda can. The soda can was an especially challenging item to scan because of its curved edges and reflective material.

Most participants operated the scanner with one hand, using their thumb to press the scanning button on the PDA. The older participants liked the multimodal feedback the scanner provided. They used the scanner light to indicate the distance needed for a successful scan and the beep as a way of ensuring they were successful scanning the bar code. All of the participants exhibited some confusion on what part of the bar code to scan (numbers or lines) and what direction to scan the bar code (sweeping vertically or shine the scanner light across the bar code). When scanning items, older people kept the scanner still and moved the item being scanned, whereas the younger people moved scanner and kept the item stationary. Even though the older participants completed 66% more scans (successful and unsuccessful) than the younger group, they were not frustrated by the activity and felt they did the best they could.

Baracoda Pencil Scanning Task. The Baracoda pencil scanner task was the most difficult task. Only two younger participants and one older participant successfully scanned the book on the first attempt. On average, younger participants attempted to scan the book more than older participants (4.2 times versus 3.3 times) before successfully scanning the bar code on the book. A t-test indicated that there were no significant performance differences due to age when scanning the book ($T_{17} = 0.430$, p = 0.672).

Additionally, older participants attempted to scan the bag of pretzels more than the younger participants before giving up (15.4 times versus 8.8 times). Only three participants were able to successfully scan the bag of pretzels. Participants inability to scan the bag of pretzels and soda can simply shows the limitations of the device.

Two female participants had difficulty scanning with the Baracoda pencil because the length of their nails (the length of nails ranged from an $\frac{1}{8}$" to $\frac{1}{4}$") inhibited them from depressing the narrow button fully. Female participants held the pencil precariously and used the tip of their nail to press the button. Older participants usually pressed the scanner button, reflected the scanner light on their hand, and then scanned the item. They commented that they wish they could see the scanner light while scanning.

Scanning with the Baracoda pencil scanner required the use of a pencil scanner and the PDA. The PDA did not give any audible feedback on successful scans, thus participants had to check the PDA screen to see if they had successfully scanned the object. Participants rested the PDA and item on the table when scanning. From our observations, it appears that the Baracoda pencil scanner would be difficult to use while standing or moving.

5 Discussion

The results of our preliminary study supported our null hypotheses. Concerns that older participants would have difficulty pressing the PDA buttons because of decreases in dexterity with age or the similarity of the layout between PDA buttons and PC control keys [13] were unfounded. Similar to the study by Chaparro et al., we found that older participants were able to select the correct button (fine motor control) and push the button while holding the PDA (pincher strength) with the same accuracy as younger participants [12]. We also found no difference between age groups: both older and younger participants performed at the same level in the button press task.

Participants preference for icon size was the only hypothesis that was rejected - younger participants preferred smaller icons (5mm or 10mm) and older participants preferred larger icons (20mm). The older participants preferred larger icons in comparison with the younger participants because it was easier to see the details. Younger people are also more familiar with distinguishing small graphical images from various applications they use. Our findings are similar to those reported by Czaja and Lee who looked at numerous PC studies on vision and the elderly [21]. During the icon size task, we noted that older people tilted the PDA to view the icons with less glare. Older people's sensitivity to glare was also recorded in a study by Kosnik et al. [5]. The icon size task showed us a one-size-fits all approach to developing PDA applications does not work. Current PDA applications offer two different size icons, but both of these sizes are smaller than the preferences of our two groups.

Similar to the button press results, assumptions that older participants may not do as well recording a message because of age related difficulty maintaining a constant pincher force [18] were not evident in our study. Older and younger participants were able to record voice messages with similar performance rates. The difference in how the two groups held the PDA (two hands for older participants and one hand for younger participants) could be attributed to grip strength. Mathiowetz et al. found high correlations between grip strength in age and observed that younger people had over 50% more grip strength than older people in our age groups [17]. Our participants showed that they could hold down the recording button (dexterity) while interacting with the PDA (coordination).

All of the participants were capable of scanning bar codes with some practice using the Socket SDIO scanner with no major differences in performance. Participants showed that they could hold the PDA steady (dexterity) while interacting with the PDA and object being scanned (coordination). Older participants liked the multimodal feedback (sound, visual effect) the PDA made when participants successfully scanned a bar code. Jacko et al. found that people in various age groups performed PC input tasks better with multimodal feedback (sound, touch, visual effect) [10]. Similar to PCs, PDAs have the ability to emit sound, vibrations, and visual feedback to assist participants perform better.

When we selected scanners for the study, we based our selection on product documentation and reviews. Our study showed the Baracoda pencil's scanning (inability to scan a bag of pretzels and can of soda efficiently) and usability (small button made it difficult to scan with longer nails) limitations. The Baracoda pencil scanner was equally hard for both participants. In future studies we will discontinue the use of the Baracoda pencil and add other tasks such as standing or walking when completing tasks.

This was the first time the participants had used a PDA for an extended period of time. We surmise with more practice, the participants would be able to easily scan all three items. Application developers can learn from our study: (1) older people can complete conventional and non-conventional PDA tasks and (2) applications for a wide range of participants need more icon sizes to select from to ensure universal usability.

The study investigated whether elderly people can physically interact with PDAs as well as younger people. Gick et al. found that the performance of younger and older people are similar when cognitive tasks are not complex [22]. We designed the tasks to emphasize motor control, not mental effort. Thus, we conclude that the participants are performing at similar levels because older participants can physically interact with PDAs at the same level as young novice PDA participants.

6 Future Work

In the future we would like to test more participants and investigate cognitive oriented tasks. We would also like to recruit 25-30 year old people from outside of the university and 75-85 year old people who live on their own or live in a public assisted living facilities instead of private assisted living facilities to diversify the participant pool.

Other avenues of research could include having participants stand and walk during tasks. Testing participants while standing and walking may affect icon size preference [23] and the ability to find and push correct buttons for the button press and voice recording applications. Scanning bar codes may also become more difficult when standing because participants will not have anything to balance their arm or the item on when scanning the bar code. Scanning bar codes while standing is important for us to evaluate because participants using our nutritional monitoring application must be able to input data anywhere - standing while preparing food, buying a can of soda from a machine, etc.

7 Conclusion

Researchers in the HCI community question whether older people can use PDAs given that they can have reduced vision, dexterity, and coordination. Our findings showed this not to be true: older participants can physically interact with PDAs the same as younger participants, with no major impediments. Our results can be used as a guidelines for creating applications for diverse age groups.

Acknowledgments

We would like to thank the participants from Bell Trace Senior Living Community, Meadowood Retirement Community, and Indiana University. Katie Siek is supported in part by a NPSC fellowship and Sandia National Laboratories/CA. This work was supported by NSF grant EIA-0202048 and by a grant from the Lilly Endowment. We would like to thank Dorrie Hutchinson, Yu-Hsiu Li, and Kelli Gehlhausen for their help during usability testing. The authors would like to thank Jeremy Siek and the referees for their careful reading of this paper and for their well-considered comments.

References

1. Kinsella, K., Velkoff, V.A.: An aging world: 2001. Technical report, U.S. Dept. of Health and Human Services, National Institutes of Health, National Institute on Aging, U.S. Dept. of Commerce, Economics and Statistics Administration, and U.S. Census Bureau (2001)
2. Carmien, S., Gorman, A.: Creating distributed support systems to enhance the quality of life for people with cognitive disabilities. In: UbiHealth 2003. (2003)
3. Coroama, V., Rothenbacher, F.: The chatty environment - providing everyday independence to the visually impaired. In: UbiHealth 2003. (2003)
4. Helal, S., Giraldo, C., Kaddoura, Y., Lee, C.: Smart phone based cognitive assistant. In: UbiHealth 2003. (2003)
5. Czaja, S.J.: Computer technology and the older adult. In Helander, M., Landauer, T., Prabhu, P., eds.: Handbook of Human-Computer Interaction. 2nd edn. Elsevier Science, B.V. (1997) 797–812
6. Faye, E.E., Stappenbeck, W.: Normal changes in the aging eye. http://www.lighthouse.org/aging_eye_normal.htm (2000)
7. Abascal, J., Civit, A.: Universal access to mobile telephony as a way to enhance the autonomy of elderly people. In: Proceedings of the 2001 EC/NSF Workshop on Universal Accessibility of Ubiquitous Computing: Providing for the Elderly. (2001)
8. Newell, A., Gregor, P.: Accessibility and interfaces for older people - a unique, but many faceted problem. In: EC/NSF Workshop on Universal Accessibility of Ubiquitous Computing: Providing for the Elderly. (2001)
9. Bernard, M., Liao, C., Mills, M.: The effects of font type and size on the legibility and reading time of online text by older adults. In: CHI 2001. (2001)
10. Jacko, J., Scott, I., Sainfort, F., Barnard, L., Edwards, P., Emery, V., Kongnakorn, T., Moloney, K., Zorich, B.: Older adults and visual impairment: What do exposure times and accuracy tell us about performance gains associated with multimodal feedback? In: CHI 2003. (2003)
11. Smith, M., Sharit, J., Czaja, S.: Age, motor control, and the performance of computer mouse tasks. Human Factors 41 (1999) 389–396
12. Chaparro, A., Bohan, M., Fernandez, J., Choi, S.: The impact of age on computer input device - psychophysical and psychological measures. International Journal of Industrial Ergonomics 24 (1999) 503–513
13. Charness, N., Bosman, E., Elliott, R.: Senior-friendly input devices: Is the pen mightier than the mouse? In: 103rd Annual Convention of the American Psychological Association Meeting, New York (1995)
14. Laursen, B., Jensen, B., Ratkevicius, A.: Performance and muscle activity during computer mouse tasks in young and elderly adults. European Journal of Applied Physiology 25 (2001) 167–183

15. Maguire, M., Osman, Z.: Designing for older inexperienced mobile phone users. In Stephanidis, C., ed.: Proceedings of HCI International 2003, Mahwah, New Jersey, Lawrence Erlbaum Associates (2003) 22–27
16. Intille, S.S., Tapia, E.M., Rondoni, J., Beaudin, J., Kukla, C., Agarwal, S., Bao, L., Larson, K.: Tools for studying behavior and technology in natural settings. In Dey, A.K., Schmidt, A., McCarthy, J.F., eds.: UbiComp 2003: Ubiquitous Computing, Springer (2003) 157–174
17. Mathiowetz, V., Kashman, N., Volland, G., Weber, K., Dowe, M., Rogers, S.: Grip and pinch strength: Normative data for adults. Arch Phys med Rehabil **66** (1985) 69–72
18. Galganski, M., Fuglevand, A., Enoka, R.: Reduced control of motor output in a human hand muscle of elderly subjects during submaximal contractions. Journal of Neurophysicology **69** (1993) 2108–2115
19. Moor, K.A., Connelly, K.H., Rogers, Y.: A comparative study of elderly, younger, and chronically ill novice pda users. Technical Report TR 595, Indiana University (2004)
20. Rhodes, N., McKeehan, J.: Palm OS Programming. 2nd edn. O'Reilly (2002)
21. Czaja, S.J., Lee, C.C.: 21: Designing Computer Systems for Older Adults. In: The Human Computer Interaction Handbook: Fundamentals, Evolving Technologies, and Emerging Applications. Lawrence Erlbaum Associates, Mahwah, NJ (2003) 413–425
22. Gick, M., F.I.M. Craik, R.M.: Task complexity and age differences in working memory. Memory and Cognition **16** (1988) 353–361
23. Hall, A., Cunningham, J., Roache, R., Cox, J.: Factors affecting performance using touch-entry systems: tactual recognition fields and systems accuracy. Journal of Applied Psychology **73** (1988) 711–720

Flexible Reporting for Automated Usability and Accessibility Evaluation of Web Sites

Abdo Beirekdar[1], Marc Keita[1], Monique Noirhomme[1], Frédéric Randolet[1],
Jean Vanderdonckt[2], and Céline Mariage[2]

[1] Fac. Univ. Notre-Dame de la Paix, Institut d'Informatique, Rue Grandgagnage, 21
B-5000 Namur (Belgium)
{abe, mno, mke, fra}@info.fundp.ac.be
http://www.info.fundp.ac.be
[2] Université catholique de Louvain, Information Systems Unit, Place des Doyens, 1
B-1348 Louvain-la-Neuve (Belgium)
{vanderdonckt, mariage}@isys.ucl.ac.be
http://www.isys.ucl.ac.be/bchi

Abstract. A system for automatically evaluating the usability and accessibility of web sites by checking their HTML code against guidelines has been developed. All usability and accessibility guidelines are formally expressed in a XML-compliant specification language called Guideline Definition Language (GDL) so as to separate the evaluation engine from the evaluation logics (the guidelines). This separation enables managing guidelines (i.e., create, retrieve, update, and delete) without affecting the code of the evaluation engine. The evaluation engine is coupled to a reporting system that automatically generates one or many evaluation reports in a flexible way: adaptation for screen reading or for a printed report, sorting by page, by object, by guideline, by priority, or by severity of the detected problems. This paper focuses on the reporting system.

1 Introduction

Since the communication and the information transfer are nowadays predominantly achieved through the World Wide Web, the Web probably represents one of the most largely used channels for information exchange [8]. This observation does not necessarily lead to the conclusion that this channel is appropriately tailored for the wide diversity of users, computing platforms, and environments in which users are working, thus provoking a digital divide [13]. In order to reduce this digital divide, the e-Europe action plan (http://europa.eu.int/information_society/eeurope/action_ plan/ eaccess/index_en.htm), accepted by European Countries in June 2000, foresees that any public site should be made compatible with Web Accessibility Initiative (WAI) recommendations recommended by the W3C. The resolution e-Europe 2002-Public Web Site accessibility and their contents (P5-TAPROV-2002-0325) are very precise on this subject: companies in charge of developing web sites for any public administration will be forced to develop sites adhering to these recommendations.

Among others, Usability and Accessibility (U&A) guidelines have been set up to help designers in the process of creating usable and accessible sites. For instance,

M.F. Costabile and F. Paternò (Eds.): INTERACT 2005, LNCS 3585, pp. 281–294, 2005.

some organizations like W3C consortium promote recommendations for accessible Web Sites: the Web Accessibility Initiative (WAI) recommendations and the Web Content Accessibility Guidelines [21]. But few designers know the existence of these guidelines. When they are aware of their existence, they are confronted with several problems [20]: too many guidelines, conflicting guidelines, various interpretations of these guidelines. When designers and developers are still decided to apply and check such guidelines despite their shortcomings, they do not always have the resources required to conduct this process thoroughly and successfully. To address these needs, several tools have been developed with the hope that by using the tool, the resources required for applying and checking guidelines will be decreased, especially the time will be reduced, while still reaching the target of U&A assessment [20].

Automated evaluation of web sites [12] not only represents a tentative to address both the needs of U&A and the requirements of designers and developers, but also a largely underexplored area [10] that could demonstrate promising results [11], but also reveal several shortcomings [3,5,13]. One of these shortcomings, but not the only one, is the capability of the tool to deliver relevant information after U&A evaluation so that the designers and developers could effectively and efficiently improve the existing version of the web site. Without such formative evaluation, it is likely that the results of the evaluation process will remain without the desired impact [11].

In the context of the DESTINE project (Design & Evaluation STudio for INtent-based Ergonomic web sites – www.info.fundp.ac.be/DESTINE), we have developed a system for automating U&A evaluation of web sites. The system implements a novel approach that we developed for automating the evaluation of a web site against U&A guidelines by checking a formal representation of these guidelines on the web pages of interest [4]. The aim of the approach is to overcome the major shortcomings of existing tools [5], mainly the fact that the evaluation logic (the guidelines to be evaluated) are completely embedded and hard coded in the software [4]. The main characteristic of our approach is the separation between the evaluation logic (i.e. the guidelines to be evaluated) and the evaluation engine (i.e. the engine that performs the evaluation of the guidelines). In this way, the U&A guidelines can be expressed in terms of conditions to be satisfied on HTML elements (i.e., tags, attributes). A formal specification language supporting this approach implements a framework [2] that enables the transformation of such U&A guidelines from their initial expression in natural language into testable conditions on the HTML code. Once expressed, the guidelines can be evaluated at evaluation-time by configuring their formal expression in an improved way depending on the guidelines to be evaluated and the HTML elements contained in the page. This process consequently involves the guidelines that are considered relevant to the targeted evaluation context, and factors out substructures that are common across these guidelines, even if they come from different sets of guidelines. The results of automatic evaluation are presented in a report. A detailed description of the evaluation process and its fundamental concepts are described in [4,20]. Therefore, this paper will focus on the flexible reporting system that is coupled to the engine.

This paper is structured as follows: Section 2 briefly describes some automatic U&A evaluation tools and some examples of generated evaluation reports. Section 3 presents a brief description of the environment. Section 4 explains how different evaluation reports can be generated with different goals in mind. Section 5 concludes the paper by stressing major advantages and the remaining work to be done.

2   Related Work

The general process of performing an automated evaluation of a web site could be decomposed into a sequence of four main steps, that are partially, totally or not at all supported in existing tools for automated evaluation [12]:

1. **Step 1:** Collecting U&A data with their corresponding metrics, such as task completion time, errors, guideline violations, and subjective ratings. A typical manifestation of this step in existing tools consists of conducting a static analysis of the HTML code to ensure that it conforms to U&A guidelines, such as the Section 508 guidelines (US Federal standard) [18], the W3C Content Accessibility guidelines [21], or both. There is a lot of similarity between these two sets of guidelines, because the Section 508 guidelines are based on the W3C guidelines. For this purpose, existing tools collect usage data such as in RemUsine [11], manipulate a task model [11], identify instances of web page components (e.g., widgets, text, graphics, images, fonts) such as in WebTango [12], Kwaresmi [4], A-Prompt [2] so as to perform the U&A analysis. One major shortcoming of this step is that most objects to be evaluated are predetermined according to the evaluation method. It is rarely possible to expand the scope of the existing collecting step.
2. **Step 2:** Analyzing collected U&A data to detect U&A problems in the web site. Existing tools typically attempt to detect deviations between reference values (e.g., a value considered as linked to U&A) and collected values (e.g., the values of the metrics computed in the previous step). Similarly to the previous step, a common shortcoming is that the checkpoints to be evaluated are opportunistically programmed in the software, with little or no possibility to adapt these contents. Bobby (http://watchire.bobby .com), A-Prompt [2], AccessEnable [6], Listener [7], Section 508 verifier [18] cannot handle U&A guidelines other than the one initially implemented (WAI and Section 508). For this reason, a new generation of tools clearly separates the evaluation logic (e.g., the guidelines) from the evaluation engine. These tools typically express guidelines in a structured way, according to a XML-compliant format, that are further parsed and processed on the web pages.
3. **Step 3:** Reporting analysis results to the end user (e.g., web site designer, owner, and visitor). Most tools for automated evaluation, such as Web Static Analyzer Tool (WebSAT) [6], and WebTango [7], report guideline violations in various ways: textually, graphically, numerically, or in some combination. For instance, WAVE [17] produces as output a new web page containing icons added closely to every deviation detected (Fig. 1). Ocawa (http://www.ocawa.com/) displays an accessibility audit report consisting of a series of links leading to individual problems or multiple instances of the same problem type. Ivory [12] observes that the report produced by such tools still demands considerable efforts to interpret the results. For example, WAVE icons are numerous and unintuitive, making their use and interpretation very difficult. Another important observation is that the report format does not vary according to the target user: an evaluator is not the same as a user.
4. **Step 4:** Suggesting solutions or improvements to repair the previously detected problems. The critique tools, such as 508 Accessibility Suite [18], A-Prompt [17], Bobby (http://watchfire.bobby.com), LIFT-NNG, and WAVE [16], also provide recommendations or assistance in repairing violations ([12] provides a detailed dis-

cussion of most of these tools). It is also difficult to explore results or to male repairs with A-Prompt, and LIFT-NNG because each tool presents a list of terse violations within a small window (Fig. 2). The main problems come from the number of structure of a report's page (too many panel in one page increase confusion), its length (difficulty to search information in that kind of page) and the way the errors are identified (many icons are not intuitive to understand).

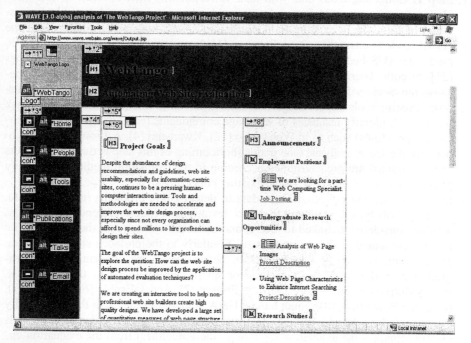

Fig. 1. Evaluation report produced by WAVE, where guideline violations are overlaid on the actual web page by using icons to flag potential issues and also depicts the page reading order (arrows with numbers)

As much effort has already been devoted to covering the scope of steps 1 and 2 (e.g., [4,19]), the remaining of this paper will focus on step 3. For this purpose, we will present a new way of reporting evaluation results generated by our automated evaluation tool by showing that a benefit of the evaluation engine is that not only the evaluation could be automated to some extent, but also that the results issued by this engine could be parameterized so as to produce an evaluation report targeted at different types of users. First, the next section will start by providing a brief description of the DESTINE environment itself. Then, in the forthcoming section, the step of producing flexible reports from the evaluation process will be examined in details.

3   DESTINE Evaluation Tool

The goal of DESTINE [13] is to assist any party interested in evaluating the ergonomic quality (mainly, U&A) of web sites based on existing guidelines gathered in guideline bases (e.g., W3C, Section508, custom guidelines). Interested parties include the end user (i.e., the visitor of the web site to know whether the site could be accessed), the designers and the developers (e.g., to know what they can improve in the web site design), or evaluators (i.e., persons who are in charge of assessing the U&A quality of an existing web site, for information purposes or in order to receive official accreditation or certification). It is based on a formal Guideline Definition Language (GDL) to express and structure formally ergonomic recommendations to guarantee the interoperability of the tool (and is a response to the first problem presented in the beginning of this paper). GDL is also compatible with XML, so the user can use different recommendations base in the same tool. DESTINE is open and does not require any existing development environment. Fig. 2 graphically depicts the global architecture of the system. It will be integrated into a Web design environment (e.g., Macromind DreamWeaver) to maximize its access by a web designer or a web developer. The modules of this software architecture are further detailed in the next subsections.

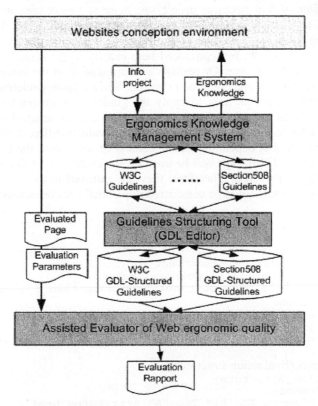

Fig. 2. Global architecture of the DESTINE system

3.1   The Ergonomic Knowledge Management System

This module manages the ergonomic knowledge contained in guidelines bases during the various steps of the life cycle: creating a new base of guidelines (e.g., WCAG, Section508, etc.), inserting new guidelines in this base, distributed and collaborative editing of the existing guidelines (e.g., it is possible to enrich the base by anyone via a Web browser), selecting the guidelines corresponding to a given context (e.g., targeted user stereotypes, type of site, types of tasks, etc.). In addition to managing the information related to U&A guidelines (e.g., the source, the indexing keys, the comments), one particular field contains the guideline specification in a GDL-compliant form that will be parsed afterwards at evaluation-time.

3.2   GDL Editor

This module is used to formally specify a guideline in a GDL-compliant form and to store it in the guidelines base or in a XML file to be exploited later on by the evaluation engine. To exemplify how a guideline initially expressed in natural language is progressively transformed into a formal interpretation, a simple example of a usability guideline "A page must not have more than 8 links" (fictive usability guideline). As the specification of this guideline progresses, more and more tags are added to provide various levels of description of the intended guideline. First, the guideline is assigned to an ID (here, "Test_G1") and its statement in natural language is provided. Perhaps the guideline can be reproduced here exactly in the same way as it is provided by the usability source. Or perhaps a reformulation of the initial guideline according to a special scheme could be preferred. Since a same guideline could lead to different interpretations on how to apply the guideline at design-time and how to assess it at evaluation-time, each original guideline can be attached to one or many interpreted guidelines. In this way, it is possible to evaluate different interpretations of the same guideline, but depending on the context of use. Then, the evaluation structure specify which HTML tags will be used for the evaluation of this guideline. Several tags could be involved. Therefore, they are gathered in evaluation sets so that different evaluation sets could be considered sequentially or concurrently.

Original Guideline

```
<GDL_Specification>
   <Original_Guideline Name="Test_G1"
      EAspect="Usability" Source="Custom"
      Statement="a page must not have more than 8 links"/>
```
Interpreted Guideline
```
   <Interpretation Context="Test">
      <Interpreted_Guideline Name="Max 8 links"
      Statement="Verify that number of text links is less that
      9"/>
```
HTML Elements (Evaluation structure)
```
   <Evaluation_Structure>
   <HTML_Elements>
      <HTML_Element ID="E1" Tag="A" Attribute="href"/>
   </HTML_Elements>
   <Evaluation_Sets>
      <Evaluation_Set S_ID="S1" Name="Links"
         Description="Check all text links"
         Priority="A">
         <Set_Element Id="E1" Mandatory="true">
            <Scope type="Page"/>
         </Set_Element>
```

```
        </Evaluation_Set>
      </Evaluation_Sets>
    </Evaluation_Structure>
Evaluation logic
    <Evaluation_Logic>
        <Basic_Values>
            <Basic_Value V_ID="MaxLinkNumber"
                  Value="8" Type="Integer"/>
        </Basic_Values>
        <Evaluation Set_ID="S1">
        <Vars>
          <Var Name="set" Type="Set"/>
        </Vars>
        <Operation Op_ID="Op1" Symbol="NumberOfInstances"
                Return_Type="Integer">
          <Argument Type="Var" Value="set"/>
          <Action Result="ANY" What="Jump" Where="Op2"/>
        </Operation>
        <Operation Op_ID="Op2" Symbol="less"
                    Return_Type-"java.lang.Boolean">
          <Argument Type="Op" Value="Op1"/>
          <Argument Type="Val" Value="MaxLinkNumber"/>
          <Action Result="True" What="Stop"/>
          <Action Result="False" What="Error"
              Why="This page contains more than 8 links."/>
        </Operation>
      </Evaluation>
    </Evaluation_Logic>
</GDL_Specification>
```

Then comes the most important section of a GDL-expressed guideline: the evaluation logic consists of the full declarative definition of the checkpoints to be processed and the actions that need to be taken when deviation with respect to any checkpoint is detected. Briefly said, the above specification provides the following information:

- Guideline statement, related ergonomic aspect, source, etc.
- Interpretation of the original guideline: context, re-expression of the guideline.
- What HTML elements we must examine in the web page to review the guideline, and where to search them (scope of a set element).
- What logic to apply on captured data in order to verify the respect or violation of any guideline.
- What message to send to the users in case of error.

3.3   The GDL Evaluator

On the basis of some evaluation parameters, this module evaluates the ergonomic quality of a page, a series of pages or a whole site by subjecting it to a set of ergonomic guidelines taken from the databases or XML files. It produces a customizable evaluation report. The pages having ergonomic problems are isolated to be treated by the ergonomic reparation tool. We cannot obviously automate the evaluation of all the guidelines in a complete way (the formal GDL specification provides necessary information indicating their level of automation: partial, total, with a percentage).

4   Reporting of Evaluation Results

After specifying the formal guideline, the evaluation module (Fig. 3) can evaluate any web page against it by parsing the conditions that are involved in each checkpoint, interpreting each condition on each instance of objects contained in a web page. All what is needed is to load the formal representation of the guideline (its GD specification) and to provide the URL of the page to be evaluated. This last step could be performed locally (by evaluating a web page or a series of web pages that have been saved from their original web site – *off-line evaluation* – or by evaluating dynamically a web page or a series of web page whose starting URL is provided along with a depth level – *on-line evaluation*).

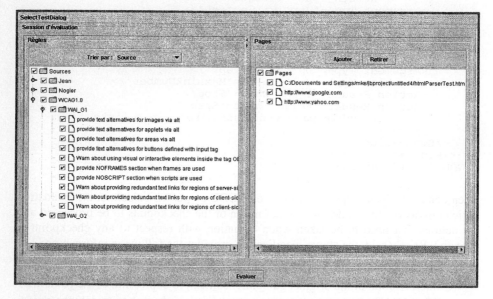

Fig. 3. DESTINE evaluation module

In Fig. 3, the left panel shows a hierarchy of all potential sources of U&A knowledge (e.g., usability guides, style guides, and standards). Each source can be opened to reveal its own table of contents with link to their guidelines. Each section in the table of contents can be selected individually and recursively: any selected entry in the global hierarchy automatically selects all its children (source, section, subsection, guidelines) and vice versa. The design can then select or unselect the evaluation of any guideline depending on the requirements imposed by the evaluation procedure. In this way, the evaluation can be made *on-demand* and can only focus on those guidelines which are considered relevant for this web page. As opposed to a "all or nothing" rule where all guidelines are involved or none. Although a first selection can already be made at this stage, the evaluation engine can also detect guidelines that do not need to be processed depending on the contents of a web page. For instance, if a guideline is assumed to check some properties of a push button, but that the web page of concern does not contain any such push button, the guideline, even if selected, will be left out. The right panel of Fig. 3 gathers in a list all the web pages to be evaluated simultaneously: on-line and/or off-line. As a result of the evaluation, the tool generates a "*dynamic mini-site*" (Fig. 4). The term "mini-site" comes from the composition in a set of HTML pages and the term "dynamic" from the ability of the user in modifying the navigation and the content of the site after the generation of the document (by using "JavaScript" for example). In this way, it is expected that the format of the resulting report could be made adapted to the user profile.

4.1 User Profile

Even if the report has a set of options to modify the presentation of its content, some parameters like the user profile could be specified prior to the report generation. Two different types of user profiles are supported: *expert profile* and *designer profile*. The expert profile is aimed at a human factors expert who does not want to be bothered by the HTML code and who only wants to know information like which guidelines where violated, the seriousness of the errors or their proportions. The *designer profile* will be chosen by a user like a web site designer who needs to know where the errors are located in the HTML code and how to correct them.

4.2 Generated Report

The report, generated for these two profiles, is relatively different to satisfy the needs of the two kinds of user, even if some information will be the same in both versions. The difference between the formats is mainly motivated by to the designer's desire to fix the code depending on the evaluation results, as provided in the report that is automatically generated based on the parameters. For instance, the report presentation may try to optimize its format for printing or for visualization/navigation purposes. In general, evaluation reports produced by other tools are composed by only one block of results, displaying a lot of elements in only one page making it very long to browse. This may prevent the users from viewing the results in an effective way because extracting a clear structure from those heaps of information is not easy.

To obtain a usable navigation, several small and structured HTML pages are produced. The report consists of three main parts: the *menu* (left pane in Fig. 4), the *main frame* (top right pane in Fig. 4), and the page viewer (bottom right pane in Fig. 4) which simply views the evaluated page. The page viewer helps the user to keep an eye on which part of an evaluated page she is working and see what is wrong.

The menu. It is dynamic and can be modified according to the preferences of the user. For example, the guidelines can be sorted by "Source" (as W3C, Section 508), by "Ergonomic Aspect" (as Usability, Accessibility), by "HTML Object" (as tables, images) just by choosing an item in a combination box. In this way, the generated report can accommodate the many variations that may exist between the different potential users of DESTINE. The menu is displayed with the assistance of JavaScript to make it more usable. Even if the browser does not support JavaScript, the menu can still be used without loosing information: all of the menu elements are then shown like a list.

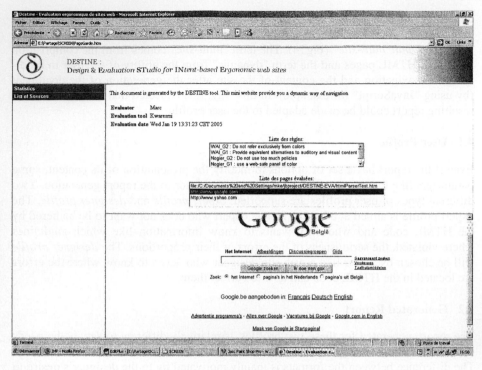

Fig. 4. Generated evaluation report

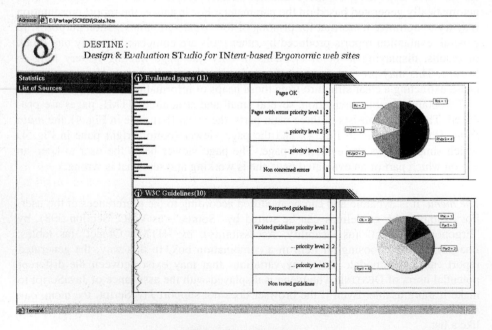

Fig. 5. Page of statistics

The main frame. It contains three different page types. The first page type is linked to the global statistics of the evaluation, the second page type is attached to the selected sorting criteria and the last one, to the evaluated page itself. The first page type contains statistical information like the proportion of pages that have passed successfully all checkpoints of priority 1. Another example of statistical information can be the number of pages that have passed through the entire test successfully for a single guideline source. This page also contains graphics providing a global view of the evaluation helping user seeing which criteria is the most/less respected (Fig. 5). The second type of page contains information about the results corresponding to the criteria for all evaluated pages. E.g., those pages can show for each evaluated page some local statistical graphics and theory about the selected criteria, like shown in Fig. 6. If the user selects the first guideline of the W3C level, the page will show information about the theory, graphics of each page compared to the checkpoints of that guideline.

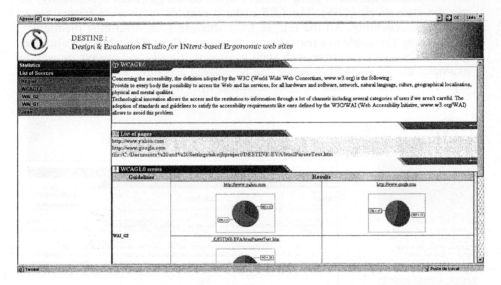

Fig. 6. Statistics by source of guidelines

The last page owns the same type of content as the ones previously found but is focused on one evaluated page at a time. This is the place where the users would retrieve such information as the list of wrong instances and its location in the HTML code, as shown in Fig. 7.

The report as generated by DESTINE therefore presents the following advantages:

1. The navigation within the evaluation results is much more flexible than in existing tools since many navigations correspond to various evaluation intellectual paths, an essential aspect for that kind of document. Information can be found easily (the document is very structured) and in an intuitive way (most of people knows how to navigate through a website) just by clicking on a link and not by scanning a long document. A 'focus+details' navigation scheme can be adopted.

2. The document is structured in several levels of details such as a guideline, a check-point, a U&A criteria, a page widget,…. Each level has its own set of data like statistics, theory and comments directly related with it.
3. The visual aspect of the report can be customized by the user, making it more user-friendly. Parameters like the colors, the type of the graphics and the font could be chosen by the user, thus enabling a personalization of the contents.
4. The type of the document (HTML) can be easily read on all platforms without specific software, just by using a browser which is usually included in most of operating systems. In addition, the internal representation of the evaluation report is made partially compatible with EARL V1.0, a W3C recommendation to uniformly present the results of evaluation across tools. In addition, the HTML code generated for the mini-site is itself made compliant with U&A guidelines as this report in itself consists of a web site.
5. The presentation is compliant with accessibility guidelines. We give hereafter some examples. Instead of using frames , which do not guarantee accessibility, we use the style sheets (CSS). The CSS make it possible to simulate frames but to preserve accessibility. All the images have alternate texts describing themselves, thus making it possible to a textual navigator to read them. The tables are also integrated to be comprehensible with such navigators. Finally and always by way of example, the colors and the police can be adapted according to user's needs. The report was tested on textual navigators such as Lynx (http://lynx.browser.org/).

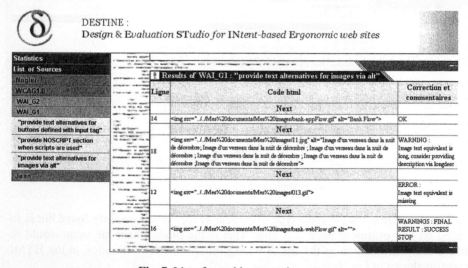

Fig. 7. List of tested instances in a page

It is possible for the user to choose the format of the report as HTML is not imposed. For example, the evaluation report could also be formatted towards printing, such as in plain vanilla text format, in rich text format, and in PDF by automated translation into these formats. In this case, the user reduces the benefits of the navigation on the mini-site, but it is no longer intended to be used with the same level of flexibility as found in the mini-site. Other parameters can be selected such as the corresponding theory, whether to see the lines with the errors identified, etc.

5   Conclusion

In this paper we have presented an environment that supports both designers and evaluators in evaluating any set of quality properties of a web site (in particular, usability and accessibility, but not limited to). In addition, this environment enables the users to parameterize the usability report in such a way that is on-demand, dynamic, and flexible. A user survey has been conducted to determine the most frequently used format of such usability reports in usability organisations. The environment also introduces report navigation, compatibility with W3C standard EARL at level 1, and flexible visual presentation of the report. The profile of the user determines default values of the parameters used to write the usability report, but can be overwritten by custom values stored in a configuration file that can be saved for future usage. In addition, we are now testing the report usability with end users. We will analyse the results and take advantage of these to improve it. For the first time, it is possible to generate usability reports with an unprecedented level of flexibility such as: usability errors sorted by level of importance, of frequency, by page, by origin (e.g. accessibility vs. usability), attached to a web site, a series of web pages, a single page, a section of a page or even a page element. The level of details with which the usability error is reported is also flexible by incorporating more or less information coming from the guideline description, expressed in a XML-compliant language that serves for the computer-aided evaluation. Finally, any generated usability report can be sent through e-mail, viewed and navigated on-line.

Acknowledgement

We gratefully acknowledge the support of the DESTINE research/development project by the Walloon Region, under the WIST (Wallonie Information Société Technologies) convention n°315577.

References

1. Abascal, J., Arrue, M., Fajardo I., Garay, N., Tomas, J.: Use of Guidelines to Automatically Verify Web Accessibility. Universal Access in the Information Society 3,1 (2004) 71–79
2. ATRC: A-Prompt: Web Accessibility Verifier. Adaptive Technology Resource Center (University of Toronto) and Trace Center (University of Wisconsin), Canada & USA
3. Atterer, R.: Where Web Engineering Tool Support Ends: Building Usable Websites. In: Proc. of the 20th Annual ACM Symposium on Applied Computing SAC'2005 (Santa Fe, 13-17 March 2005). ACM Press, New York (2005)
4. Beirekdar, A., Vanderdonckt, J., Noirhomme-Fraiture, M.: A Framework and a Language for Usability Automatic Evaluation of Web Sites by Static Analysis of HTML Source Code. In: Proc. of 4th Int. Conf. on Computer-Aided Design of User Interfaces CA-DUI'2002 (Valenciennes, May 2002). Kluwer Academics Pub., Dordrecht (2002) 337–348
5. Brajnik, G.: Automatic Web Usability Evaluation: Where is the Limit? In: Proc. of the 6th Conf. on Human Factors & the Web (Austin, June 2000). Univ. of Texas, Austin (2000)

294   A. Beirekdar et al.

6. Brinck, T., Hermann, D., Minnebo, B., Hakim, A.: AccessEnable: A Tool for Evaluating Compliance with Accessibility Standards. In: CHI'2002 Workshop on Automatically Evaluating the Usability of Web Sites.
7. Ellis, R.D., Jankowski, T.B., Jasper, J.E., Tharuvai, B.S.: Listener: a Tool for Client-Side Investigation of Hypermedia Navigation Behavior. Behavior Research Methods, Instruments & Computers 30, 6 (1998) 573–582
8. Forrester Research: Why most web sites fail. 1999. Available at http://www.forrester.com/Research/ReportExcerpt/0,1082,1285,00.html
9. Macromedia. Macromedia Exchange - 508 Accessibility suite extension detail page (2001) ACM International Conference Proceedings Series, New York (2004) 117–124
10. Ivory, M.Y., Hearst, M.A.: State of the Art in Automating Usability Evaluation of User Interfaces. ACM Computing Surveys 33, 4 (2001) 470–516
11. Ivory, M.Y., Mankoff, J., Le, A.: Using Automated Tools to Improve Web Site Usage by Users with Diverse Abilities. IT&Society 1,3 (2003) 195–236
12. Ivory, M.Y. Automated Web Site Evaluation: Researcher's and Practitioner's Perspectives. Kluwer Academic Publishers, Dordrecht (2003).
13. Jackson-Sanborn, E., Odess-Harnish, K., Warren, N.: Website Accessibility: A Study of ADA Compliance. Technical Report TR-2001-05. School of Information and Library Science, University of North Carolina at Chapel Hill (2001)
14. Okada, H., Asahi, T.: An Automatic GUI Design Checking Tool from the Viewpoint of Design Standards. In: Proc. of 8th IFIP Conf. on Human-Computer Interaction Interact'2001. IOS Press (2001) 504–511
15. Paternò, F, Ballardin, G.: RemUSINE: a Bridge between Empirical and Model-based Evaluation when Evaluators and Users are Distant. Interacting with computers 13,2 (2000) 151–167
16. Pennsylvania's Initiative on Assistive Technology. Wave V 3.0. Available at http://www.wave.webaim.org/wave/index.jsp
17. Ridpath, C., Treviranus, J.: Integrated Accessibility Evaluation and Repair (The Development of A-Prompt). In: Proc. of CHI'2002 Workshop on Automatically Evaluating the Usability of Web Sites, CHI'2002, Minneapolis (2002)
18. Thatcher, J.: Section 508 Web Standards & WCAG Priority 1 Checkpoints: A side-by-side Comparison. Available at http://jimthatcher.com/sidebyside.htm (2002)
19. Vanderdonckt, J., Beirekdar, A., Noirhomme-Fraiture, M.: Automated Evaluation of Web Usability and Accessibility by Guideline Review. In: Proc. of 4th Int. Conf. on Web Engineering ICWE'04 (Munich, 28-30 July 2004), Springer-Verlag, Berlin (2004) 17–30
20. Vanderdonckt, J.: Development Milestones towards a Tool for Working with Guidelines. Interacting with Computers 12, 2 (December 1999) 81–118
21. W3C Web Content Accessibility Guidelines. Available at http://www.w3.org/

The Focus-Metaphor Approach: A Novel Concept for the Design of Adaptive and User-Centric Interfaces

Sven Laqua[1] and Paul Brna[2]

[1] Northumbria University, Newcastle upon Tyne
slaqua@sl-works.de
[2] University of Glasgow
paul.brna@scre.ac.uk

Abstract. The Focus-Metaphor Approach is a novel concept for the design of adaptive and user-centric virtual environments which seeks to use a form of associativity to adapt the interface to the user whilst keeping one primary focus element and secondary and peripheral focus elements. In this paper, the underlying theory is presented and differentiated from related research. The proposed solution has been implemented as a prototype and tested for usability issues using an online evaluation and in-laboratory eye-tracking to find some evidence that time spent off-communication is reduced. The results are reported briefly, implications considered and the areas for further work are pointed out.

1 Introduction

Collaborative systems require the integration of facilities for a wide range of activities including chatting, exchanging emails, working with a shared application and finding resources for both personal and shared use.

The use of many of these tools involves significant time away from what is often the central focus - communicating effortlessly with others. For example, sending an email address to someone through a chat interface might require firing up an email program and searching through a set of email addresses, then copying and pasting this into a chat box. Even where applications are smarter, many times there is much "off communication" activity.

This raises the issue of whether GUI interfaces could be "smarter", responding to contextual clues without any specific direction from the learner. Can the time spent in navigating the interface be usefully reduced? One possible solution is presented here - the "Focus-Metaphor approach", which seeks to use a form of associativity to adapt the interface to the user whilst keeping one primary focus clement, and many secondary and peripheral focus elements. The proposed solution has been implemented and tested for usability issues and to find some evidence that time spent off-communication is reduced. The results are reported briefly and implications considered.

1.1 Related Work

Interfaces that are more usable, learnable and satisfying may allow people to concentrate on establishing good relationships with each other across the net, freeing them up from some of the tedious navigation tasks to concentrate, for example, on establishing a trusting relationship with other learners or teachers.

Various other researchers have proposed aids to assist navigating through a large information space. In several articles, Card et al. [1+2] describe their research on Degree of Interest (DOI) Trees, aimed to browse through large hierarchies of information. Using a similar approach, TheBrain [3] has developed solutions called PersonalBrain, Web-Brain and BrainEKP (Enterprise Knowledge Platform).

But as these solutions only focus on the visualization of navigation structures the problem which still remains in their approaches is the separation of navigation and information representation. This separation causes abrupt switches between navigation and information, which especially disrupts cognitive processes. The Focus-Metaphor approach aims to overcome this issue to support user orientation and facilitate learning processes.

Moreover, there are examples which make use of the so called fish-eye view technique, like described in work by Gutwin [4] or Thomas [5], the fishnet browser [6] or in a modified form to be seen in the ICQ universe [7]. These fish-eye view implementations allow preserving "the contextual relationship between a large number of objects" [8]. But although the fish-eye view technique shows visual similarities to the Focus-Metaphor approach, there is still a wide difference in the underlying concept. Whereas the fish-eye view tries to provide a visually appealing solution for navigating large amounts of static information, the approach taken here is different - i.e. to reorganise the information space into a focus, secondary foci and peripheral foci, hiding the rest of the space. Doing this in a contextually sensitive manner may well do the majority of the work for the learner so that they can concentrate on their communication with others. Using "cognitive modelling" [9] to organise the information space and using the spreading activation approach to assign information to according foci would be one solution to achieve this goal of an intelligent interface using the Focus-Metaphor approach.

2   The Theory

The Focus-Metaphor approach combines aspects of design theory, cognition psychology and educational theory to create a more natural way of interaction. With the design of the Focus-Metaphor it was intended to achieve advancements over commonly used metaphors (e.g. desktop metaphor, portal metaphor) and counteract effects like "second visit blindness on websites" [10]. This approach uses the principle of cortical connectivity and its importance for cognitive functions [11] to apply them to the design of dynamic and adaptable user interfaces.

2.1   The Connection Between Navigation and Learning Processes

Using hypertext environments like the Internet for the development of learning applications requires an understanding of the importance of navigation, which is more than just the way of orientation and interaction [12]. It is especially an active form of learning, where the way people navigate from one information entity to the next directly influences the way they process this information and possibly acquire new knowledge. Along with Fuster [11], "learning and the acquisition of memory are based on the synaptic linkage of elementary cortical representations".

Everyone has an individual network of personal knowledge which he or she tries to expand through interaction with new information. This individual mental network consists of countless nodes of information entities, organized in topological, non-linear structures [13]. When interacting with virtual spaces like hypertext environments, the mental network of knowledge of an individual is confronted with the virtual network of information of the according environment.

Whereas novel educational research focuses on constructivism [14] and related methods like "experimental learning" [15] or "discovery learning" [14], under the assumption that every individual has a different way to acquire knowledge, information in virtual spaces is mainly static. Of course hyperlinks can provide some amount of flexibility if used in a sensible way, but their advantages are increasingly undermined by overloaded or badly structured screens. This leads to a virtual network of information which forces people to adapt their way of thinking to these static structures. Actual research on semantic web technologies underlines the existence and importance of this problem and tries to give more meaning to information.

The concept of the Focus-Metaphor suggests the design of a dynamic and highly adaptable interface to reduce the gap between people's individual network of knowledge and the presentation of information on the screen. A Focus-Metaphor interface (FMI) bases its visual representation on cognition psychological principles and aims to support learning processes.

2.2   The Hierarchical Structure of a Focus-Metaphor Interface (FMI)

A hierarchical structure is used to manage the visualized elements. The number of these elements should be around five to seven, according to the capacity of short-term memory [16]. "...instructional design for the learning purpose should keep the limits of short-term memory in mind" [17].

In a Focus-Metaphor interface, the element of most interest for the user - the "primary focus element" [18] - is presented in the middle of the screen having the largest dimensions (see fig. 1). Other relevant elements, which are also of interest for the user and which are in context to the 'focused' element, are dynamically grouped and arranged around the primary focus element. These elements represent the "secondary focus". The third hierarchy is called the "peripheral focus" and shows elements which may not be in context of the primary focus element, but still are essential for a fluent and effective interaction of the user with the system (e.g. functions like search, news, contact).

2.3   The Level of Detail of Information

A comparison of the Focus-Metaphor approach to existing but novel user interfaces like the grid- or table-layout approach which are used by myNetscape [19], myMSN [20] and others, reveals a core difference: These approaches allow the user to customize the presented information by arranging and showing or hiding information 'modules', but they are still static and plain two-dimensional, without contextual intelligence.

The wide difference of the Focus-Metaphor approach is the usage of hierarchical information and its hierarchical representation, which should be managed through "information importance level" [18] and the allocation to the according presentation level. Depending on the level of presentation, the amount of presented information in each element is varying.

Only this combination of hierarchical organization of information, dynamically allocated and animated in real-time, as basis for a visual hierarchy, can reasonably enable the Focus-Metaphor approach. This hierarchical order shall help learners to concentrate on one specific and important context and thereby support learning processes. In addition, to limit the amount of information presented to the user through the visual elements in the different importance level, information which is not necessary disappears.

2.4   How the Focus-Metaphor Works

If the user switches his or her focus from the element of primary focus onto an element of secondary or peripheral focus, the interface reacts in an appropriate manner. In the prototype of this project, the described interaction has been realized through mouse-over events, but in future developments an interface implementation might also use eye-tracking data and fixation measurements for the navigation.

Independent of which form of interaction is used, the user needs to 'focus' on an element, which then comes to the front (technically: switches to the top layer) and provides its information completely. This is necessary, as through the possible and likely overlapping of elements of the different foci, the view onto some elements might be restricted. If the user decides to stay with his focus on the new element, he or she 'selects' this element. This has been realized in the prototype via mouse-click, but alternatively an eye-tracking interface could use longer fixations or eye-blink for this interaction. Then, the chosen element takes over the primary focus, presenting its complete information. This forces the other elements to rearrange according to their relation with the new primary focus element. Some presented elements might therefore disappear and others show up. As a result, the user can experience a feeling of involvement and of active interaction where he seems to be a navigator in a networked world of knowledge nodes. As the screenshot of the interface prototype in fig. 1 on the next page shows, the presented elements are specific modules of information, which together build the learning environment. Smooth and continuous motions shall be used to switch focus and rearrange elements.

3   Prototype

In order to evaluate the usability of the Focus-Metaphor Approach, a narrow but high-level prototype, which uses a collaborative story-writing context, has been implemented, tested and evaluated. This prototype has been designed as a virtual, web-based and therefore distributed environment which consists of a back-end using Java and MySQL and a front-end using Macromedia Flash. Within the scope of this project, attention focused on the testing of fundamental usability issues and the general user acceptance in a realistic scenario using a formative online evaluation, experts and as core element an in-laboratory testing with an SMI iViewX eye-tracking system. For the evaluation, test users were instructed to write personal stories. These have been used to find similarities among the contributors communicate these similarities and facilitate interaction within the hopefully emerging community. Fig.1 below shows a screenshot of the prototype, which models the elements of primary and secondary focus. (Also see: http://www.fmi.laqua-consulting.de/Test-Area.html)

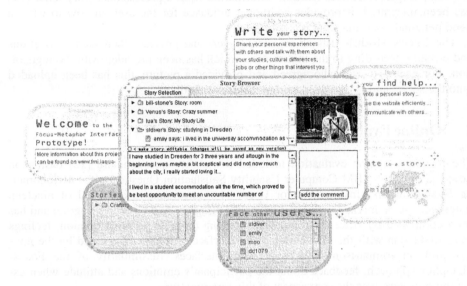

Fig. 1. Screenshot of the Focus-Metaphor Interface prototype

3.1 Modules

For the Focus-Metaphor Interface prototype, nine different modules (also referred to as elements in a specific focus mode) have been developed altogether in order to enable realistic testing scenarios.

The **Welcome Module** provides some general information about the project. It contains a link to the main project website and furthermore gives a brief description of how the online testing works and what the aims are for the user.

In the **Registration Module**, every user who wants to test the FMI prototype needs to fill in the registration form. A nickname and a password are required in order to login. All other entries can be filled in on a voluntary basis.

After a successful registration, the test user can log into the website using the **Login Module**. Nickname and password are required to gain access and thereafter, the user is automatically directed to the FMI testing environment.

With the **Help Module**, the test user can access some guidance on how to work with the FMI prototype. This information is stored in a separate XML file on the webserver, which makes it easy to administrate changes or extensions.

The **MyStories Module** allows the test user to write a personal story about him- or herself including a title and a location in plain text style.

The **StoryBrowser Module** is used to provide an overview on all written stories on which test users can write comments on. A picture of every story- or comment-author is displayed and the test user can optionally choose to display just the five newest stories or his or her stories only.

The **Map Module** visualizes the locations of written stories to provide test users a better feeling for the community.

In the **Expert's Stories Module** information from a professional story-teller [21] has been integrated. It provides additional guidance for the user on how to write a good personal story and what it is useful for.

The **User's Module** lists all registered users and provides their names, locations and e-mails, according to the information which has been provided with the registration. For each test user who agreed and provided a picture, this has been uploaded onto the server and is also displayed in the user's module.

4   Online Evaluation

The formative online evaluation included a usability questionnaire [22] basing on Lewis [23] work: "IBM Computer Usability Satisfaction Questionnaires: Psychometric Evaluation and Instructions for Use." The questionnaire consisted of nineteen statements, to be marked between 1 (strongly disagree) and 6 (strongly agree) and has been completed by fifteen participants, focusing on their personal opinion, feelings and satisfaction with the Focus-Metaphor interface prototype. Reasoned by the novelty and, in comparison with usual web interfaces, dissimilarity of the Focus-Metaphor approach, feedback about the participant's emotions and attitude when using the prototype was the core aspect of this investigation.

The results of this first usability evaluation of a Focus-Metaphor realization showed that the overall feedback on the prototype has been very satisfying. All statements were marked positive (above 3.5), with an overall geometric mean of 4.63 (arithmetic mean = 4.64; harmonic mean = 4.62 and median = 4.68).

Nevertheless, it might be argued that the setting of the evaluation environment caused a shift towards more positive answers due to the fact that the formative part of the evaluation also involved quite some communication flow between participants and investigator. To cope with this, the analysis focused on the high and low peaks of the feedback, which are clearly above or below any of the various means or the median, and therefore ensure reliability of the results.

Table 1. Ranking of the online evaluation feedback

Highest	5.05	The information provided for the system is easy to understand
	4.87	I can effectively complete my work using this system
	4.87	It was simple to use this system
	4.86	The organization of information on the system screens is clear
		...
	4.31	Whenever I make a mistake using the system, I recover easily and quickly
	3.97	This system has all the functions and capabilities I expect it to have
Lowest	3.94	The system gives error messages that clearly tell me how to fix problems

The ranking of feedback given on the statements (see table 1 above) shows the highest and lowest means according to a specific statement. The positive results show that the novelty of the interface has not been an issue for the participants. But the negative results also show that there are still serious issues which can be explained by the very narrow prototype which does not raise any claim to be a finished product. The mentioned problems are important, but obviously would be removed when developing a complete environment using the Focus-Metaphor approach.

Moreover, the online prototype has been developed with two interface options, an 'automated animation' version and a manual version. Whereas the first version provided fixed locations for the modules in primary and secondary focus mode and continuous animation, the second version allowed participants to arrange the modules freely on the browser screen. By voting on these two versions, the participants expressed their preference for the animated version, which as a result has been chosen as the central representation mode for the Focus-Metaphor interface prototype.

In addition, this mode has been chosen to be the fundament for the eye-tracking experiment.

5   Eye-Tracking Experiment

The overall aim of the eye-tracking experiment was to compare an interface using the Focus-Metaphor approach with a common interface which has a static layout like most websites. To have comparable results, the same visual information (factor X) needed to be presented to the participants during the experiment. Accordingly, three different derivatives have been created from the original prototype version of the Focus-Metaphor interface:

X[1] :   The original online version (Focus-Metaphor): animated with secondary focus modules centered around the primary focus module

X[2] :   The adapted static version (grid layout): based on common website structures, using a grid layout and the same information as X[1],

X[3] :   The adapted original version (Focus-Metaphor): similar to X[1] but without animation.

The researched context within the eye-tracking experiment for the versions X[1], X[2] and X[3] was to measure the participants' visual attention (behaviour Y) onto the primary focus module in the middle of the screen, which always provides the 'actual' content.

With the investigation of how X[1], X[2] and X[3] affect Y, the hypothesis "the focus-metaphor improves learning processes in the researched context" has been tested indirectly through the two assumptions: (1) A better (visual) focus on the learning context and (2) an optimized orientation.

For the conduction of the eye-tracking experiment, a population sample of fifteen participants has been used. All participants worked with the real prototypes (X[1], X[2] and X[3]) rather than in predefined paths to allow higher realism of the experiment.

Before the experiment started, participants had been given a scenario form which briefly described the interactions they should undertake whilst conducting the experiment. Along with the three different versions of the prototype (X[1], X[2] and X[3]) the experiment was separated into three sessions. In each session, the participant dealt with one of the prototype versions for five to seven minutes, depending on how quick the participant progressed within the given scenario. The setting of the experiment aimed to allow the participants to explore and work with the prototype in a natural way. The only interfering element has been a chin-rest to improve the quality of the gathered data. The IView X System by SMI, which has been used for the conduction of this experiment, did not require any further disturbing parts like head-mounted elements.

In addition to the recording of the eye-tracking data (gaze path, pupil diameter and fixations), the participant's screen was video-captured in every session and overlaid with the participant's gaze. This method led to 3.5 hours of video data, which was analyzed to define typical interaction sequences like working with the story-browser module, the user's module, the help module, the expert's stories module or the welcome module. These sequences have then been used for the further analysis with the IView X Analysis software.

5.1   Overall Attention Analysis

The overall attention analysis compared the eye-tracking data of the different versions X[1], X[2] and X[3] for the length of a complete session (without the login phase) in order to measure the overall visual attention of participants (Y_all) on the primary focus module. Therefore Y1_all, Y2_all and Y3_all represent the time, which test users in average spend on the primary focus module in each version of the prototype from a successful login until the end of the testing session in percent of the length of the whole session (minus login time). The higher this percentage, the longer test users have dealt with the main content, which they did choose on their own during the session. This measure can provide clues about the effectiveness of the interface versions. The values of Y1_all, Y2_all and Y3_all allow conclusions about how long users needed for navigation tasks. The more time a user spent on the actual content, the less time he required for navigating through the prototype environment. In reverse, less time spent on the content indicates more time consuming navigation, which therefore disturbs the user from studying the desired content.

As expected, the individual results of the participants showed strong variations, but of course the investigation focused on the quantified means of each version. Here, the comparison of X[1] and X[3] (both are Focus-Metaphor Interfaces) shows with the geometric means **Y1_all = 75.9 %** & **Y3_all = 75.7 %** basically identical values. The standard error σ_M for both means, Y1_all and Y3_all, is $\sigma_{Y1\_all} = \sigma_{Y3\_all} = 1.8$. This led to the conclusion that the omission of the animation did not affect the visual attention. Moreover, the result underlines the reliability of the conducted experiment, as the very similar versions deliver nearly the same values. In contrast, the analysis of X[2] delivered with a geometric mean of **Y2_all = 64.1 %** a clearly lower value. The standard error shows a similar result with $\sigma_{Y2\_all} = 3.7$. The relatively high increase of overall visual attention when using the Focus-Metaphor Interface (11.6 % for Y3_all and 11.8 % for Y1_all) instead of the standard grid layout interface is a first indication for an increased attention on the 'learning context' due to less time spent on navigation tasks.

Therefore, the overall attention analysis supports the first assumption of the hypothesis of providing a better focus onto the learning context. Moreover, with the correlation of Y1 and Y3 and time constraints within the project, this led to the decision to investigate only X[1] and X[2] for the further analyses (see fig. 2).

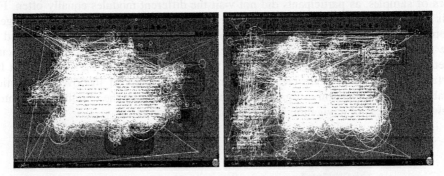

Fig. 2. Visualization of Gaze Paths of all Eye-Tracking Participants for Focus-Metaphor Interface X[1] (left) and Grid-Layout Interface X[2] (right) for the overall session

5.2 Study Phase Analysis

The study phase analysis aimed to find differences in the participants' visual focus on the learning context while working with the versions X[1] and X[2]. In contrast to the prior overall attention analysis, the study phase analysis refers only to the time, in which the participants worked with a specific module. This means, that the small periods of "loading" new content have been neglected. Only the time, which a user spent on the modules in primary focus mode to read stories or comments, study information in general or watch pictures, has been considered. As some modules did not provide enough information to study them for a longer period, only relevant modules had been included in the investigation. These modules were the welcome module, the help module, the story browser module, the user browser module and the expert's stories module, which contained most of the content and also showed average the longest study times. The results of the study phase analysis show that the visual attention in X[1] is noticeably higher than in X[2] (see geometric means for the different modules, according standard errors and confidence intervals in table 2).

Table 2. Comparison of attention on the according moduls during study phases

modules	Focus-Metaphor			Grid Layout		
	in %	σ_{Y1}	Conf. Interval	in %	σ_{Y2}	Conf. Interval
Welcome	79.3	1.9	$71,3 \leq \mu \leq 87,3$	49.4	4.5	$35,6 \leq \mu \leq 64,3$
Help	80.6	2.4	$75,1 \leq \mu \leq 86,0$	73.4	3.0	$66,6 \leq \mu \leq 80,2$
Story browser	84.9	1.1	$82,7 \leq \mu \leq 87,2$	73.8	2.4	$68,8 \leq \mu \leq 78,7$
User browser	79.0	3.2	$70,6 \leq \mu \leq 87,3$	63.1	7.5	$46,2 \leq \mu \leq 80,1$
Expert stories	79.4	2.5	$73,5 \leq \mu \leq 85,2$	74.3	3.2	$66,4 \leq \mu \leq 82,2$

These means, for the modules which have been studied by the participants, show that the Focus-Metaphor Interface delivered higher results in every module. But as the results for the separate modules show relatively high variations (see the confidence intervals in table 2), they have to be regarded as less valid, due to partly small numbers of samples, as participants did not visit the different modules equally often. For this reason, the study phase analysis concentrates on the quantification over the geometric means of each participant's attention during his or her study phase and led to the general geometric means of $Y1\_study = 82.5$ % ($\sigma_{Y1\_study} = 1.4$) for the Focus-Metaphor Interface and $Y2\_study = 70.0$ % ($\sigma_{Y2\_study} = 3.2$) for the Grid Layout Interface. These findings are clearly higher than the results of the overall attention analysis (see comparison in fig. 3) which can be deduced by the elimination of interfering sequences of navigation from one module to another.

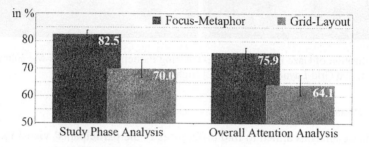

Fig. 3. Comparison of User attention

Nonetheless, the findings of the study phase analysis correspond to the ones of the overall attention analysis and therefore corroborate the first assumption of providing a better focus onto the learning context. In addition, this analysis points out the decreased disruption by navigational elements when using the Focus-Metaphor Interface to study information.

Table 3. Comparison of user attention

	Focus-Metaphor			**Grid Layout**		
	in %	σ_{Y1}	Conf. Interval	in %	σ_{Y2}	Conf. Interval
Study Phase Analysis	82,5	1,4	$79{,}3 \le \mu \le 85{,}6$	70,0	3,2	$63{,}1 \le \mu \le 76{,}9$
Overall Attention Analysis	75,9	1.8	$72{,}0 \le \mu \le 79{,}7$	64,1	3,7	$56{,}0 \le \mu \le 72{,}2$

5.3 Pre-switch Analysis

The second assumption of the hypothesis, "an increased orientation", has been investigated mainly through the pre-switch analysis. This analysis compared the participants' attention onto the primary focus module (again in X[1] and X[2]) in short time frames before the participant switches from one module to another. This switch is defined through initialization of a change for the primary focus module by clicking a module which at this point of time is in secondary focus. The pre-switch analysis uses the time frames: eight seconds, four seconds and two seconds before a switch to analyze the participants' decreasing attention on the primary focus module while looking for "new" information with an accuracy of at least 0.1 seconds.

As expected, both versions, X[1] and X[2], show a decrease of visual attention, the shorter the time frame gets. This reflects the efforts of the participants to 'scan' other modules for potentially interesting information, which logically increases, when the participants approach the moment where they finally switch the focus.

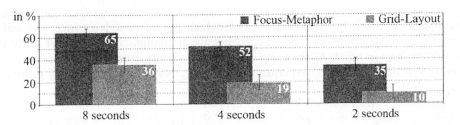

Fig. 4. User Attention before a switch of the primary focus

The comparison between X[1] and X[2] reveals, that the Focus-Metaphor Interface showed conspicuously higher values than the grid layout interface. Table 4 on the next page shows the geometric means of user attention for the specific time frames together with the according standard errors and confidence intervals. The results point out that participants needed clearly less time with the Focus-Metaphor Interface to decide on where they want to switch their focus to. As a result, they can spend more time onto the content they want to study. Moreover, it can be concluded that navigation decisions have been easier for participants with the Focus-Metaphor Interface. These aspects lead to an optimized orientation, as claimed in assumption two. Nevertheless it should be mentioned that participants switched content in the Focus-Metaphor scenario 7.1 times in average, and therefore slightly more often than in the grid layout scenario with 6 times over the length of the session.

Table 4. User attention before a focus switch

Time before a focus switch	Focus-Metaphor			Grid Layout		
	in %	σ_{Y1}	Conf. Interval	in %	σ_{Y2}	Conf. Interval
8 seconds	65	3.5	$57,0 \leq \mu \leq 72,1$	36	6.4	$22,1 \leq \mu \leq 49,5$
4 seconds	52	3.8	$43,8 \leq \mu \leq 60,3$	19	6.6	$5,0 \leq \mu \leq 33,6$
2 seconds	35	6	$22,1 \leq \mu \leq 47,8$	10	6.4	$-3,6 \leq \mu \leq 24,1$

6   Discussion

The Focus-Metaphor Approach gives users an interface with clearly defined elements of information, which aims to match their cognitive capacity. Arranging these elements in a circular way around users' visual center and hosting the information they 'asked for' in this center, reflects their natural perception.

The conducted testing and evaluation of the Focus-Metaphor interface prototype tried to prove its usability through comparison with a standard design approach and assess general acceptance by the test participants. Both aspects are regarded as generally essential for the success of a novel approach towards user interface design. In the concrete case of the Focus-Metaphor approach, they have been investigated through an objective experiment and a subjective evaluation by potential users to decide on the worthiness of further work. The results of the online evaluation reveal the affection of participants towards the interface prototype. Moreover, the results of the eye-tracking experiment are promising in that they show advantages for the Focus-Metaphor approach in all measures. The calculation of confidence intervals adds some further significance to the results, but the limitations of the overall analysis should be kept in mind. As the sample sizes allowed only estimated measures, a second run of the eye-tracking experiment could add great value to the already gathered data.

In addition, it is the novelty of this approach, which needs careful consideration when evaluating the results. As Baudisch et al. [6] pointed out for their project: "A long term study is required to investigate whether users' subjective preference may reverse itself as users gain more experience with this still fairly uncommon visualization style."

Nevertheless the described work provides a detailed picture of the significance of the Focus-Metaphor approach, including the first usable implementation of a Focus-Metaphor interface and testing results.

With regard to further work, the Focus-Metaphor interface prototype can be regarded as a very early stage of a framework which will allow the development of online environments, which are user-centric, adapted to cognitive processes and fully dynamic. Adding, removing or changing information or functionality will be easily possible through integration of new modules.

Moreover, a Focus-Metaphor framework could offer different visualisation modes according to users' preferences or device-side boundaries. Besides the centred animated one, used for this prototype, a further development of a manual mode, which has briefly been mentioned, seems to be of high potential and is definitely worth ongoing efforts.

The emerging research on mobile learning could likely profit from interface solutions which are applicable across platforms. Here, a framework solution of an adaptable and flexible user interface, which the Focus-Metaphor Approach is able to offer, could deliver additional value.

Within online environments, communities become increasingly important in form of communities of interest or communities of practice. As the core of a community is always to exchange information, collaborative information environments [24] for the Internet are actually of great interest. One big issue in the design of respective environments is the visualisation of collaboration, also referred to as community memories [24].

It has already been pointed out how the Focus-Metaphor Approach aims to model individual memories through flexible organisation of information, adaptive navigation and a visualisation which reflects the actual short-term memory. Under the assumption that this will work after spending a considerably large amount of effort on the further development of this approach, in a next step, which might be considerably small, visualizations of individual networks of knowledge could be incorporated into the visualization of a network of group knowledge.

Acknowledgements

This work was conducted by the first author as part of an MSc [25] with the second author as supervisor.

Further work on the Focus-Metaphor approach is planned and will most likely be conducted by the first author as part of a PhD at University College London.

References

1. Card, S. K. et al. (2000). Browse Hierarchical Data with the Degree of Interest Tree. Palo Alto Research Centre & National Security Agency.
2. Card, S. K. & Nation, D. (2002). Degree-of-Interest Trees: A Component of an Attention-Reactive User Interface. Palo Alto Research Centre.
3. TheBrain Technologies Corporation, http://www.thebrain.com/
4. Gutwin, C. (2002). Improving Focus Targeting in Interactive Fisheye Views. Proceedings of the ACM Conference on Human Factors in Computing Systems (CHI'02), Minneapolis, pp. 267-274.
5. Thomas, C. (2002). Fisheye Strategy. Theories in Computer human interaction, University of Maryland, USA. http://www.cs.umd.edu/class/fall2002/cmsc838s/tichi/fisheye.html
6. Baudisch, P. et al. (2004). Fishnet, a fisheye web browser with search term popouts: a comparative evaluation with overview and linear view. Microsoft Research, USA.
7. ICQ Universe, http://www.icq.com
8. Demaine, J. (1996). Library and Archives Canada - Information Visualization http://www.collectionscanada.ca/
9. Hornof, A. J. (2002). Cognitive modelling, visual search, and eye tracking. ONR Attention, Perception and Data Visualization Workshop, George Mason University.
10. Wirth, T. (2002). Missing Links. Hanser publishing, Germany.
11. Fuster, J. M. (1998). Linkage at the Top. In: Neuron, Vol. 21, pp. 1223-1229.
12. Schulmeister, R. (2002). Grundlagen Hypermedialer Lernsysteme. Oldenbourg Verlag, Germany.
13. Kuhlen, R (1991). Hypertext, ein nicht-lineares Medium zwischen Buch und Wissensbank. Springer: Berlin.
14. Bruner, J. S. (1966) Toward a Theory of Instruction. Harvard University Press: Cambridge, Mass., USA.
15. Kolb, D. A. (1984). Experiential Learning: Experience as the source of learning and development. New Jersey: Prentice Hall.
16. Miller, G. A. (1956). The Magical Number Seven, Plus or Minus Two: Some Limits on our Capacity for Processing Information. In: Psychological Review, Vol. 63, pp. 81-97.
17. Pastor, M. - Short-Term Memory. San Diego State University http://coe.sdsu.edu/eet/Articles/stmemory/start.htm
18. Laqua, S. (2003). Concept and user interface design for a cscl-environment for intercultural communication. Bachelor Dissertation at University of Technology, Dresden.

19. MyNetscape, http://my.netscape.com/
20. MyMSN, http://my.msn.com/
21. O'Callahan, J. (2004). Crafting Personal Stories. Reprinted from Storytelling Magazine, May/June 2004. On: www.ocallahan.com
22. Perlman, G. (1998). Web-Based User Interface Evaluation with Questionnaires. http://www.acm.org/~perlman/question.html
23. Lewis, J. R. (1995). IBM Computer Usability Satisfaction Questionnaires: Psychometric Evaluation and Instructions for Use. In: International Journal of Human-Computer Interaction, Vol. 7, pp. 57-78.
24. Stahl, G. (2004) "Collaborating with Technology: Studies in Design & Theory of Online Collaboration". Book preprint from MIT Press.
25. Laqua, S. (2004). "Creation of Virtual Social Networks in Distanced, Informal Learning Settings through collaborative Story Writing - Implementation and Testing of a New Metaphor Prototype". Master Dissertation at Northumbria University in Newcastle.

Working Out a Common Task: Design and Evaluation of User-Intelligent System Collaboration

Daniela Petrelli[1], Vitaveska Lanfranchi[2], and Fabio Ciravegna[2]

[1] Information Studies, Sheffield University, Regent Court, 211 Portobello St,
Sheffield S1 4DP, UK
d.petrelli@shef.ac.uk
[2] Computer Science, Sheffield University, Regent Court, 211 Portobello St,
Sheffield S1 4DP, UK
{v.lanfranchi, f.ciravegna}@dcs.shef.ac.uk

Abstract. This paper describes the design and user evaluation of an intelligent user interface intended to mediate between users and an Adaptive Information Extraction (AIE) system. The design goal was to support a synergistic and cooperative work. Laboratory tests showed the approach was efficient and effective; focus groups were run to assess its ease of use. Logs, user satisfaction questionnaires, and interviews were exploited to investigate the interaction experience. We found that user' attitude is mainly hierarchical with the user wishing to control and check the system's initiatives. However when confidence in the system capabilities rises, a more cooperative interaction is adopted.

1 Introduction

Intelligent interfaces have been proposed as a way to help users dealing with information overload, complex decision making, and topic learning. However there are other areas of human interaction with computers that can be lightened by means of artificial intelligence. Repetitive tasks, like text annotation or classification [7, 12], can be carried out by computers under human supervision. An analogy is the role robots have taken in assembly-belt activities: humans are no longer required to execute the same action hour after hour but only to monitor that the machine is working properly.

Machine Learning (ML) has been demonstrated to be a successful technique to enable computers to become skilled at simple human tasks. In the context of assisted text annotation, ML systems have demonstrated to be efficient (annotation time: -80%), and effective (interannotator agreement: +100%) [3]. However, good algorithms are not enough for setting up a synergistic collaboration. The user interface has to intelligently split the work between the two agents and has to orchestrate their activities by properly deciding when computer intervention is appropriate. The interaction must be designed in such a way that users perceive the benefit of a proactive system that progressively takes over a tedious task but at the same time they do not feel ousted.

This paper describes our experience in designing and evaluating such an intelligent interface. The next section (2) introduces text annotation and discusses the proposed approach. Some considerations on collaboration are presented in section 3. Interface layout and interaction are discussed in section 4, the user evaluation in 5. Section 6

M.F. Costabile and F. Paternò (Eds.): INTERACT 2005, LNCS 3585, pp. 309–322, 2005.
© IFIP International Federation for Information Processing 2005

discusses data analysis and observations. Reflections on cooperative user-intelligent system interaction conclude the paper (section 7).

2 Computer-Assisted Text Annotation

Semantic annotation is used to structure information in a document in order to support information access by content rather than via keywords. For example, "20 Jan 1998", "20th January 1998", and "20-1-1998" all represent instances of the same concept, a date. Annotating the three snippets as *date* makes such a correlation explicit. Adding semantic transforms sequence of words into knowledge ready to be reused. Areas such as Semantic Web and Knowledge Management need text annotation, e.g. for document indexing, for populating ontologies with instances extracted from text [1, 2].

Text annotation is performed by trained users who work on restricted domains, e.g. annotators at intelligence agencies look for details of crimes in hundreds of documents a day. Manual annotation is critical and knowledge intensive: the text must be read in full, relevant snippets must be identified and the appropriate concept assigned. The process is slow and time-consuming; it rapidly becomes tedious, tiring and thus potentially error prone. Adaptive Information Extraction (AIE) can help automating the annotation task, either in an unsupervised (e.g. automatic annotation of documents [5]) or semi-automatic way (e.g. as support to human annotators [3, 8, 13]).

Computer-assisted (or semi-automatic) text annotation is a two-phases process that requires both users and AIE to accomplish tasks:

1) **Training**: the AIE observes the annotations made by a user and the context they occur in; it infers rules and generalizes them (i.e. learning by examples).
2) **Active annotation**: using the rules learnt, the AIE system identifies potential annotations (i.e. similar cases were seen in training) and marks them. This is when the advantage of a computer-assisted annotation becomes apparent as the amount of manually inserted annotations decreases. Correcting annotations is simpler than annotating raw texts and is less time consuming.

How and when user and AEI system are involved in a semi-automatic process vary greatly. Sequential and collaborative models are discussed below.

2.1 The Sequential Model

In the sequential mode documents are managed in batches and user and system work in a rigid sequence [8][1][13]: the user annotates a batch of texts; then the AIE is trained on the whole batch. When the user annotates another batch of texts the system proposes annotations. Additional learning can occur if the second batch of annotated text is re-entered in learning mode. The role of the user interface is solely to pass the output of an agent as input to the other (Fig. 1).

---

[1] S-CREAM uses the same AIE algorithm but has a different interface and interaction mode.

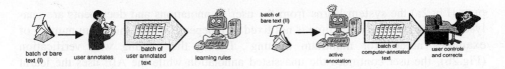

batch of bare text (I) — user annotates — batch of user annotated text — learning rules — batch of bare text (II) — active annotation — batch of computer-annotated text — user controls and corrects

Fig. 1. The simplistic turn-taking interaction (training left, active annotation right). The grey arrows represent the user interface that mediates between user and AIE.

This sequential, turn-taking organization is not the most efficient and effective. Training on blocks of texts implies a time gap between when the user inserts annotations and when the system learns from them, with drawbacks for both. If the batch contains similar documents, users spend time annotating without any help from the system, as no learning session has been scheduled. The AIE system does not benefit from the user effort either: very similar cases do not offer the variety of phenomena that empower learning. The bigger the size of the batch the worse become the problem.

How timely the system learns from the user's actions is an essential user-centred measure of interaction efficacy: ideally the system should use each example provided by the user for learning or checking purposes. Moreover the more dissimilar the examples the better the learning: ideally the user should annotate first those texts that are more problematic for the system thus supporting a faster learning. We call this feature *timeliness*. It is the responsibility of the intelligent user interface to organize user and AIE system work and to properly and promptly react to the user's annotations, i.e. to increase timeliness.

In a sequential model (Fig.1) it is difficult to avoid annoying users with wrong annotations generated by unreliable rules (e.g. induced using an insufficient number of cases). A way of letting the user controlling this behaviour is by setting a confidence threshold: suggestions are provided only when those are good enough. Designers have to mediate between the numerical value needed by the system and a qualitative definition that can be easily grasped by the user.

Another source of annoyance for the user is the rigid sequencing itself as it hampers user annotation activity while the AIE system is learning as the CPU is allocated to it. Scheduling the learning as a background activity is a better design choice. This level of disturbance of the AIE system in the user's natural flow of activity is called *intrusiveness* and represents the second user-centred principle we considered when designing the interaction.

More integrated work between user and AIE system can lead to the better accomplishment of the common goal, i.e. the efficient and effective annotation of documents. Fails and Olsen [7] expressed similar criticisms and found a definite improvement in image classification.

2.2 The Collaborative Model

Conversely from the sequential model, the collaborative model does not force explicit turn-taking. Rather the two agents work simultaneously. Collaboration imposes a new organization of the work, with finer grained activities and parallel execution. The training is split into (a) *bootstrapping* and (b) *training with verification*. In bootstrap-

ping (Fig.2a) the system learns from the user's annotations and documents are analysed one by one. Learning time is not fixed as it depends on the minimum number of
examples needed for minimum training[2]. During the training with verification
(Fig.2b), the user continues the unassisted annotation while the AIE uses the learnt
rules to compete with the user in annotating. The two annotations are compared by the
interface, which calculates accuracy. Missing annotations or mistakes are used to
retrain the learner. The training phase ends when the accuracy reaches the user's preferred level of pro-activity leading to the active annotation phase.

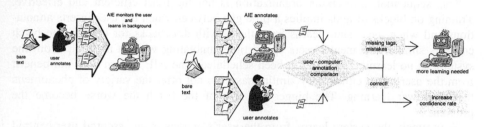

Fig. 2. Training is split into bootstrapping (left) and training with verification (right)

As for the training, the active annotation phase is enriched. The intelligent user
interface monitors the quality of the annotations proposed by the AIE system (Fig. 3)
and decides if these are good enough to be displayed to the user. The user becomes
the supervisor and their task is to correct and integrate the suggested annotations.
Human actions are returned to the AIE system for retraining. This is when the real
user-system cooperation takes place: the system helps the user in annotating; the user
feeds back mistakes and confirmations to help the system perform better.

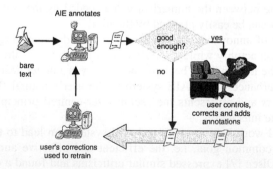

Fig. 3. Active annotation with revision

To summarise, an intelligent user interface that supports collaboration between the
user and the AIE system must act at different points:

---

[2] Features like text variety and complexity impact on the time needed to learn.

- During the bootstrapping it collects all the annotations made by the user and passes them to the learning agent;
- In the training with verification it compares the texts annotated by the learning agent against the same ones annotated by the user; it provides feedback to the learner on how good its performance was and requires retraining if needed;
- During active annotation with revision it filters the annotations proposed by the AIE system and displays the good ones; collects the user's amendments and feeds them back to the learner.

It is therefore the responsibility of the interface to decide if the general quality of suggestions is good enough (intrusiveness) and to manage the timing of the display of these suggestions (timeliness). We consider these user-centred criteria to be the base for effective user intelligent-interface collaboration[3].

3   Key Points in Interactive Collaboration

The intelligent user interface is in charge of synchronising activities into a synergistic effort. To improve the timeliness in the collaboration model we propose that learning is a continuous activity that goes on in the background. This way the system can start proposing annotations as soon as the level of accuracy is reached. It is a case of simple concepts with few variations, e.g. the location where an event takes place. The accuracy increases as the training progresses and more cases and corrections are seen by the learner. Conversely in the sequential mode, the quality of suggestions improves during the active annotation phase. The positive effect is that the more accurate the suggestions are, the less intrusive is the system.

As stated before, timeliness represents how timely the system learns from the user's actions. The best learning occurs when completely new examples are shown. Thus the best collaboration between annotator and learner occurs when the user annotates documents that are problematic for the system. Given a corpus, the interface can rank the texts with respect to the global annotation confidence: texts can then be listed starting from the most promising in terms of knowledge acquisition (i.e. those for which the number of suggestions is low). This scheduling is recalculated when a new annotated text is saved and a new learning step has occurred. How this principle has been included in the interaction is presented in section 4. Laboratory experiments [3, 4] showed that when ranked documents are chosen, annotating 30 documents gives the same performance as annotating 50 random ones. However this policy might affect the user's judgement of system usefulness, since when annotating the most problematic texts the number of suggestions is fewer. This was taken into account when the data of the user evaluation were analysed.

A key factor in the failure of user-intelligent system interaction is the quality of suggestions; whereas giving users control of their own system is a success factor [9]. To

---

[3] Eric Horvitz [9] discusses many more factors besides these two; however many of those are not relevant here, for example, the user's goal or attention are fixed and defined by the nature of the annotation activity.

let the user decide on the quality of displayed suggestions and thus to control system intrusiveness, a qualitative slidebar has been designed (see section 4).

4   Interface Layout and Interaction

How the principles of timeliness and intrusiveness have been captured inside the design has been discussed in sections 2 and 3. This section presents the interface layout and discusses the interaction. The design rational follows Horvitz's principles of "minimizing the cost of poor guess" while "providing genuine value over [...] direct manipulation [i.e. manual annotation]" [9]. The interface in displayed in Fig.5:

1. **The ontology**, on the left, contains the description of the domain. Each item in the hierarchy is a concept in the ontology and is colour coded (e.g. visitor is green, date is pink)[4]. To insert an annotation the user selects a concept by clicking on it and highlights the text in the right hand side. Colour crowding is controlled by the user by ticking off concepts thus preventing the display of those annotations.
2. **The document under annotation**, on the right, shows user inserted annotations as well as system suggestions. Users' annotations are shown by changing the background of the annotated text portion into the colour of the ontology concept (e.g. the background for a date becomes pink). The same colour coding is used to show system suggestions; but the layout depends on the current certainty matched with the acceptance levels set by the user in the slidebar (Fig. 4):

   - *High confidence*: if the blue line is over the 'reliable suggestions' threshold then the suggestion is assumed correct and is displayed by colouring the background; a black border distinguishes it from the user's annotations. No confirmation is needed to have this suggestion recorded when the file is saved.

   - *Lower confidence*: if the blue line is in between the two thresholds (over the 'tentative suggestions' but below the 'reliable suggestions') the suggestion is displayed by colouring just the border around the text; the user is required to explicitly accept it by clicking inside the border (a double click will instead remove it). No action by the user is interpreted as a reject of the suggestion which will not be recorded at saving time.

3. **The command bar** displays some useful commands: 'accept all' and 'reject all' (paper-and-pen icons) accept/reject all suggestions with a single click; the two arrows allow moving between documents. Those buttons implement the policy (discussed in section 3) of ranking the remaining texts respect to how difficult they are for the system to annotate. The most problematic document is displayed when clicking the 'next document' button (a right-pointing arrow). The list of documents with their confidence values can also be displayed.

---

[4] Colours are set by the system as each must uniquely represent a concept; allowing users to choose colours would require a separate negotiation as the system must insure consistency.

4. **The Setting Slidebar:** a qualitative slidebar has been designed (Fig. 4) to allow users controlling the quality of suggestions. It shows the current level of confidence on a % scale, i.e. a blue bar overlaps the scale as in a thermometer metaphor. Two markers set the preferred level of proactivity. The lower sets the minimum level for 'tentative suggestions', the higher sets the level of 'reliable suggestions'. Users can tune the system accuracy to their preference by moving the markers: those who find it annoying to receive wrong suggestions will set both markers very high, others may accept a big gap between the levels if they want to receive more suggestions sooner. The system displays a suggestion when the blue

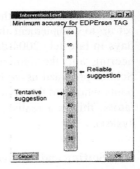

Fig. 4. Accuracy setting affects intrusiveness

line is over the low confidence level, but the layout and the interaction differ when the line is over the high certainty level. A bar is available for each concept in the ontology; a global one to tune the whole system at once is also provided.

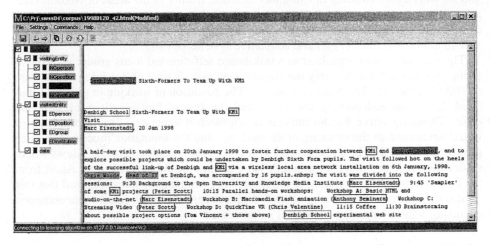

Fig. 5. The interface: concepts listed in the ontology (left) are annotated in the text (right)

5   The User Evaluation

The whole interaction was designed to support a real collaboration between the user and the AIE system. Two extensive quantitative evaluations of the performance had already been done at the time of this study (on corpora of 250 job announcements [4] and 483 seminar announcements [3]). Those assessed efficiency and effectiveness (measured by Precision, Recall and f-measure). Results showed that the cooperative model considerably reduces the number of annotations needed for triggering reliable suggestions (a minimum of 75% correct was set). However it was discovered that the minimum of documents needed widely varied from concept to concept, from a low 5 documents needed to detect 'salary' or 10 for 'city' and 'country', to a top 75 documents needed to identify 'speaker' or 100 for the 'employer'.

Those tests proved the system to be efficient and effective. A user evaluation was set up to complement those results with user satisfaction. It was conducted over two days in late July 2004 during the 2nd European Summer School on Ontological Engineering and the Semantic Web held in Cercedilla (Spain). Being at the Summer School provided us with a good sample of sufficiently knowledgeable naïve participants who used the system in an explorative way. As potential users are trained annotators, this is a realistic setting that resembles the initial approach of users to the system.

5.1 Setting and Participants

The annotation interface (the client) was installed on six computers used by students during the practical session. The AIE and the coordination core, on the other hand, were installed on two servers, each serving three clients[5].

Thirty-one students participated in the study as part of a practical tutorial on the use of annotation tools for the Semantic Web. They came from different Universities and all were Ph.D. students in Computer Science, mainly in the areas of Natural Language Processing, Knowledge Representation, Information Retrieval, Web Services, or the Semantic Web. 68% of them knew about Semantic Web annotation, but were new to annotation tools (77%) and adaptative systems (88%).

The evaluation was organized as a task-based self-directed focus group: working in groups participants had to carry out the assigned task. A total of 7 valid sessions were recorded: 2 the first day, 5 the second day. The condition of working in groups stimulated discussion and participants discovered the system functionalities by trial and error. Though positive for the inquisitive approach it generates, groupwork requires initial agreement on the meaning of the ontology and the annotation process. For three groups this proved to be a problem as recorded in two questionnaire-interviews where students complained that they couldn't work as they would have liked to. Apart from the first disappointment relating to the limited log availability, we recognized that this represents the natural "inter-annotator disagreement", a well known phenomenon occurring when comparing individual judgements.

5.2 Procedure, Tasks, and Data Recording

Initially a 20 minutes introductory lecture on the tool interface and functionalities was given and a printed manual distributed. Participants filled in a brief personal profile questionnaire and received written instruction on the task. Working in groups they had to annotate 10 documents using a provided ontology. The corpus consisted of 42 news reports on visits in a research centre; concepts to annotate where (among others) date of visit, name of visitors and visited persons, visiting and visited institutions.

The evaluation task was articulated in two parts corresponding roughly to the training and the active annotation discussed above:

---

[5] This configuration is not the best one for the highly demanding computation; problems of instability raised the fist day and affected the results of the user satisfaction questionnaire. We kept this in mind when analysing the data and, if needed, we distinguish the data collected the first day from that of the second.

1. to annotate (at least) 5 documents without any AIE help[6]. Suggestion display was inhibited to let students better familiarise with the interface without the further hurdle of understanding adaptivity;
2. to annotate further 5 documents with the help of the AIE. Suggestions from the system were displayed and the group had to decide which action to take, i.e. accept or reject the suggestions, add new ones.

The groups were requested to start with the same specified document, they had 90 minutes to complete the task.

It must be noted that 5 documents provide a very limited amount of learning material for the AIE system. Compared to the recommended 30 documents [3, 4], this number was largely insufficient to produce robust and correct suggestions. However marking 30 documents with an average of 5 minutes each would require at least 2 and a half hours, an excessively high time for any user evaluation. As efficiency and effectiveness had already been addressed [3, 4] we focused on users' first impression and satisfaction, aspects of user-intelligent system interaction never analysed in detail.

Groups' activity was logged and time stamped. Data included: user's annotations, system suggestions, annotations accepted ("accept all" included); annotations rejected ("reject all" included); file opened and saved. After the exercise participants were asked to fill in a user satisfaction questionnaire (derived from QUIS [11]) and, if willing, to participate in an individual interview.

During the evaluation an experimenter was unobtrusively walking around the room observing groups' behaviour. Different strategies were recorded and were later compared against the log files.

6 Data Analysis and Results

This study focuses on first time users, on their behaviour and perception. Therefore the analysis is qualitative and inductive.

6.1 Annotation Strategies

Log analysis was used to extract patterns of behaviours and to infer annotation strategies. This data was compared with the observations noted by the experimenter. We expected a decrease in the annotation time as the interaction progresses and more suggestions were given by the system. The first 4 documents[7] were annotated in an average time of 12 minutes each (min 2.15, max 17), while the remaining ones were done far more quickly, around 3 minutes per document (min 50 sec., max 8.17). This is a combination of having learnt how to use the system plus the suggestions being displayed.

When suggestions started, Group 1, 5, and 6 carefully considered each suggestion for the rest of the evaluation, rarely using the 'accept all' button. Group 2, 3, and 4 started by carefully considering each suggestion in the first few documents, then ac-

---

[6] This condition was relaxed when group discussion dragged over 45 minutes.
[7] As 2 groups did not annotate the 5 assigned documents in 45 minutes, the number of documents included as training was reduced from 5 to 4.

cepting all the suggestions. Group 7 sometime accepted all system suggestions, sometime considered every single suggestion before accepting it. It appears that all groups were monitoring the system behaviour at first and then started accepting suggestions when they trusted the system; when this shifting occurred depended on the group.

A few behaviours are worth a deeper discussion:

- Group 3 and 5 seem to follow in their annotation process a precise, and different, mental model. Group 3 annotated following the order of concepts as listed in the ontology (concept-driven annotation); whereas Group 5 followed the textual structure and selected the concepts in the ontology accordingly (text-driven annotation).

- When the learning algorithm was enabled and the suggestions started to appear, Group 4 always used 'accept all' but then deleted the disliked ones. They also browsed through all the files just watching the suggestions made and then started a new annotation on the one that (apparently) had the most done, thus ignoring the ranking. Then they stopped to actively annotate and simply accepted all system suggestions. This may show an excessive confidence in system's capabilities but may also indicate boredom or carelessness. Indeed a check of their tagged documents revealed that the system suggestions were correct but further annotations were possible.

- Group 2 and Group 3 used the 'reject all' button as a way to clear the document. Their use was not the intended of rejecting wrong suggestions but of restarting the process, of clearing the document, as confirmed in interviews. As the system would actually re-display the suggestions, clicking the 'reject all' would only remove user's annotations.

6.2 User Satisfaction

The questionnaire had 5 main sections discussed below. Questions to address the distinctiveness of interacting with an intelligent system were included.

All questions asked the user to judge a specific statement on a 5 point scale. Ad-hoc opposites were used for each question, e.g. "system speed" ranged from "too slow" to "fast enough"; "quality of the suggestions provided" had "extremely poor" and "excellent". At the end of the questionnaire users were invited to state their opinion on the most positive and most negative aspects of the system. A total of 31 questionnaires were used in the analysis.

Overall Judgement: The overall reaction to the system was positive, though the result of the first day was more critical. The system was judged easy to use by the majority of participants, with more satisfaction among the second day users (40% found it easy, 13% very easy). Only 10% gave a negative opinion, while 37% were neutral.

The questions "frustrating-satisfying" collected a total of 29% satisfied participants, 49% were neutral and 21% felt frustrated.

The "dull-stimulating" question was less critical: 38% considered the system stimulating, while 49% were neutral and 13% thought it was dull.

The opinions on the cooperativeness of the system were again positive: 42% were satisfied, and 13% very satisfied, and 45% were neutral (no negative opinion recorded). This result is consistent with the questions on timeliness, and quality of suggestions discussed below in System Capabilities and Performance.

Layout: Users were satisfied with the layout (16% positive, 45% neutral), organization (55% satisfied, 35% neutral), and position of information (61% satisfied, 25% neutral). Difference opinion on menu vs. the toolbar was recorded: the majority preferred using the toolbar (75%) as opposed to the menu (50%). This result challenges designers of intelligent user interfaces as commands for controlling or setting system features should be represented with a single, small icon. While we were helped in this task by the known icons Word uses for accepting/rejecting changes, this design phase may not be as easy when complex behaviours have to be controlled.

Terminology and System Information: In average the user considered the terminology used to be consistent and related to the task in hand. Participants thought the system status was not made clear enough: almost 40% of participants reported that the system was not keeping them updated on what was going on, and only 3% of the users were satisfied by the error messages (though 39% did not experience any error condition). As the installation configuration made the system reactions very slow, this point needs a reassessment in a more appropriate setting. However this may also be an indication of the violation of the principle of transparency: let the user (partially) see/understand what the adaptive system is doing [10].

Getting Acquainted: Learning to use the system was easy for the majority (62%), 29% were neutral and 5% had difficulties. Performing tasks was considered straightforward by 51%, while 26% were neutral. Opinions on the easiness of correcting mistakes were less positive: 39% were not satisfied, 32% were neutral and only 19% were positive (10% did not answer). Similar numbers for the questions on the usefulness of help messages: 36% not satisfied, 26% neutral (38% no answer).

System Capabilities and Performance: Questions on system speed and reliability showed the lowest satisfaction, particularly among users of the first day when slowness and system instability occurred most. The system speed was largely criticized with only 12% moderately satisfied users (21% were neutral and 67% were not satisfied). The opinions from the first day were more negative, with 90% of not satisfied users and 10% of neutral users. Reliability was also a weak point: 29% users were satisfied, 26% were neutral, 29% were not satisfied. Worst judgement the first day: 10% satisfied, 60% not satisfied (30% no answer).

Answers to questions specifically related to the system intelligence were instead encouraging even though not always positive. Notably numbers are consistent in the two days showing that participants were able to distinguish and prize the innovativeness of the tool despite the technical problems. Users had a good opinion of the quality of the suggestions, with 46% of satisfied/very satisfied users (40% and 6% respectively), 26% of neutral, and only a 25% of not satisfied. The timing in providing suggestions was satisfying for 24%, while half were neutral (49%) and the remaining

27% was not satisfied. System intrusiveness was unobtrusive for 16% and neutral for 49%, while 32% considered the system too intrusive.

As each group annotated a different number of documents in the assigned time (4 min, 10 max, 6.7 average) a Sperman's Rho test was applied to statistically address a possible correlation between the number of documents annotated and the satisfaction. The assumption was that, as the quality of suggestions increases with the number of documents used for learning, the more documents a user has annotated the more positive the judgement would be. Questions were tested separately. The quality of suggestions positively correlates with the number of document seen (r=.414, n=24, p<.04); timeliness positively correlates as well but there is no statistical significance (r=.381, n=25, p<.06); instead intrusiveness correlates just weakly (r=.176, n=24, p<.411). As the number and accuracy of suggestions increases proportionally with the number of example seen (i.e. documents annotated), these numbers show how the user satisfaction increases with the interaction (i.e. better system performance); we expect these values to be much higher under correct conditions. Indeed the minimum threshold was set to 5% against a suggested minimum of 60%, possibly 75%, while the number of documents used in the training was 5 against a suggested minimum of 20, possibly 30 [3].

6.3 Interviews

Six users volunteered for the interview and, quite obviously, were positive about their experience. Features appreciated were the easiness of selecting and highlighting concepts, the possibility of accepting all the suggestion and the opposite of removing them all.

The different layout used to display which agent inserted the annotation was also pointed out as a useful feature, however it was suggested to distinguish user's from system's annotations in the long term, e.g. when re-opening an annotated file. Currently when the user accepts a suggestion the layout is turned into the user one under the assumption that after acceptance the two would be equally true. Keeping a different layout indefinitely would help in assessing the content of an annotated file. A similar idea of keeping and showing who-marked-what comes from another interviewee who did not agree with the group choices, showing once more the effect of the "inter-annotator disagreement". Interestingly both comments required more transparency not at interaction time, but at a more generic and wide level of task.

A user commented on the ontology (Fig. 5): all the levels are displayed equal but only some can be meaningfully used. The proposal was to "grey-out" the abstract levels while keeping visible the relations with the concrete ones. Indeed the ontology is actually a separated entity developed outside the annotation tool though this comment clearly shows how it is perceived as part of it. Ontology creation and use should then be coordinated to create a more consistent context of use.

7   Conclusions

Designing collaboration was our goal, but other forms of interaction could emerge depending on the degree of inter-relationships the user would establish with the intelligent system. Options include: *Collaboration* a relation between peers working together towards the same goal; *Coordination* a hierarchical relation where actors (or actions) are in a specific position respect to each other; *Conflict*: clashing of opposed principles, statements, or goals.

Coordination was prevalent at the beginning. The many checking behaviours displayed during the evaluation indicate the need of building trust before a partnership, therefore a true collaboration, can be set up. How long this would take seems to be very subjective and may also never materialise in full, as for the student who wanted to keep distinguished computer suggestions from human annotations. Factors like transparency, predictability, and trust deeply affect the interaction with intelligent user interfaces (as discussed by Höök [10] and confirmed by Cortellessa et al [6]) even in the simple and narrow context of shared annotation of text.

A second point is that commands can be interpreted and used in an unpredicted way. Indeed both 'accept all' and 'reject all' were used differently from what intended. This has an effect on the granularity of the adaptation strategy: to prevent misinterpretation of user's acts a fixed chunk of actions (as for coordination) should be preferred to a single one (as for collaboration). Only in this way the strategy adopted by Group 4 (accepting all and then correcting the wrong ones) or Group 2 and 3 (rejecting all was a way of clearing their own annotations) can be properly interpreted.

'Accept all' showed to be a very useful command, but also a risky one as accepted and closed files did not contained only correct annotations. Although fully trusting the system might appear as a good cooperation, the negative side effect is that the system will stop learning and the quality of suggestions might decrees. This phenomenon is expected to mitigate with professional users as neglecting behaviors should be rare, however strategies to rise user's attention (e.g. explicitly ask the user to check tricky phrases) should be considered.

Definitely encouraging for us and intelligent interface designers is the fact that conflicts occurred only when problems in the system usability were faced (e.g. frustrating system speed) while the acceptance of and satisfaction with the system intelligence was good. This reinforces the opinion that intelligent features should gracefully integrate into a well designed direct manipulation interface. An effective intelligent interface design should then consider both levels of *tasks scheduling* and *user interaction*. When organising the tasks scheduling, designers should try to exploit system capabilities (e.g. timeliness and intrusiveness) whereas when planning the interaction user needs and preferences should be the leading criteria (e.g. guidelines in [9]). However our work shows that applying generic guidelines is not enough as the use of commands can be different from the intended. As user actions are interpreted by the intelligent interface in a certain way the correspondence must be correct to avoid misinterpretations that could mine the collaboration.

Acknowledgements

EPSRC AKT partially supported this research. We thank the organizers of SSSW-2004 and all the students who participated in the study. Our gratitude to Dr. Alexiei Dingli who developed the intelligence core used in the experiment.

References

1. Alani, H., Kim, S., Millard, D. E., Weal, M. J., Hall, W., Lewis, P. H. Shadbolt, N. R. Automatic Ontology-Based Knowledge Extraction from Web Documents. *IEEE Intelligent Systems* 18(1) 14-21. 2003
2. Celjuska, D. Vargas-Vera, M. Semi-Automatic Population of Ontologies from Text. In Paralic J., Rauber A. (eds.) *Workshop on Data Analysis WDA-2004*, Slovakia, 2004.
3. Ciravegna, F., Dingli, A., Wilks, Y., Petrelli, D. Using Adaptive IE for Effective Human-Centred Document Annotation. Franke J, Nakhaeizadeh, Renz I. (eds.) Text Mining, Theoretical Aspects and Applications. Physica-Verlag, 153-164. 2003.
4. Ciravegna F., Dingli A., Petrelli D. Wilks Y. User-System Cooperation in Document Anntation based on Information Extraction. *Proc. EKAW02*, 2002.
5. Ciravegna F., Chapman S., Dingli A., Wilks Y. Learning to Harvest Information for the Semantic Web. *Proc 1st European Semantic Web Symposium*, Heraklion, Greece, May 10-12, 2004
6. Cortellessa, G., Cesta, A., Oddi, A., Policella N. User Interaction with an Automated Solver: The Case of a Mission Planner. PsychNology Journal (2004) 2 (1) 140-162.
7. Fails, J. Olsen, D. Interactive Machine Learning. *Proc. IUI'03*, ACM Press, 39-45, 2003.
8. Handschuh S., Staab S. Ciravegna F. S-CREAM - Semi-automatic CREAtion of Metadata, *Proc. 13th EKAW02*, Sigüenza, Spain, 2002.
9. Horvitz., E. Principles of Mixed-Initiative User Interfaces. *Proc. CHI99*. 159-166, 1999.
10. Höök, K.: Steps to Take before Intelligent User Interfaces Become Real. Interacting with Computers (2000) 12 (4) 409-426
11. Chin J., Diehl V., Norman K. Development of an instrument measuring user satisfaction of the human-computer interface. Proc. CHI '88 (1988) 213-218
12. Segal R., Kephart J. Swiftfile: An intelligent assistant for organizing e-mail. *AAAI 2000 Spring Symposium on Adaptive User Interfaces*. Stanford CA.
13. Vargas-Vera M., Motta E., Domingue J., Lanzoni M., Stutt A. Ciravegna F. MnM: Ontology driven semi-automatic or automatic support for semantic markup, *Proc. 13th EKAW02*, Sigüenza, Spain (2000)

Interactivity and Expectation: Eliciting Learning Oriented Behavior with Tutorial Dialogue Systems

Carolyn Penstein Rosé and Cristen Torrey

Human-Computer Interaction Institute, Carnegie Mellon University,
5000 Forbes Avenue, Pittsburgh PA, 15260
{cprose, ctorrey}@cs.cmu.edu

Abstract. We investigate the reasons behind students' different responses to human versus machine tutors and explore possible solutions that will motivate students to offer more elaborated responses to computerized tutoring systems, and ultimately behave in a more "learning oriented" manner. We focus upon two sets of variables, one surrounding the students' perceptions of tutor qualities and the other surrounding the conversational dynamics of the dialogues themselves. We offer recommendations based on our empirical investigations.

1 Introduction

Recent classroom and laboratory evaluations of a wide range of learning technologies have revealed a disturbing phenomenon of unproductive student behavior [4,11,17,15] where students approach their interactions with them in a "performance oriented" manner, i.e., resorting to shallow strategies for getting through material as quickly as possible, rather than a "learning oriented" manner, i.e., trying to learn as much as possible. In this paper we explore the extent to which these patterns may be the result of a combination of a priori expectations and attitudes about the technology and features of the technology that enable students to engage in performance oriented behavior. We focus our investigations on tutorial dialogue systems [2,22,14,3,13,12]. A tutorial dialogue system is a type of state-of-the-art learning technology modeled after one-on-one human tutoring that engages students in natural language dialogues.

In tutorial dialogue interactions, the distinction between learning oriented and performance oriented behavior can be characterized in terms of patterns of student verbal behavior. For example, it may be manifest in terms of extremely terse, and sometimes non-existent, student responses to tutor questions, and an almost total lack of elaboration. Comparing student verbal behavior in response to humans and to tutorial dialogue systems both employing an equivalent typed chat interface, it was observed that students do not spontaneously offer the kinds of self-explanations they freely offer to human tutors when responding to equivalent questions from a computer tutor [21,22]. This poverty of self-explanation has a detrimental effect both on the tutoring system's ability to create an accurate model of student understanding and on the student's ability to master the material.

In this paper, we investigate the reasons behind students' different responses to human versus machine tutors and explore possible solutions that will motivate

M.F. Costabile and F. Paternò (Eds.): INTERACT 2005, LNCS 3585, pp. 323–336, 2005.
© IFIP International Federation for Information Processing 2005

students to offer more elaborated responses to tutoring systems, and ultimately behave in a more "learning oriented" manner. Effecting a change in student behavior is one important step along the path towards increasing the effectiveness of tutorial dialogue technology. We focus upon two sets of variables, one surrounding the students' perceptions of tutor qualities and the other surrounding the conversational dynamics of the dialogues themselves. Our hypothesis is that the elaborations students freely offer to human tutors are motivated by interpersonal factors and by the interactive nature of dialogue with the tutor. Neither is commonly part of one's experience with computers. Thus, we hypothesize that we can induce students to generate more elaborated verbal responses generally, and self-explanations in particular, by elevating their a priori perceptions of the computer-based tutoring systems, by making the tutors more responsive and interactive, and especially by a combination of these two strategies.

2 Tutorial Dialogue Technology

We conduct our investigations of tutorial dialogue systems using a popular framework originally developed at the University of Pittsburgh, called Knowledge Construction Dialogues (KCDs) [22]. KCDs were motivated by the idea of Socratic tutoring, a highly interactive tutoring style evaluated favorably in comparison to a less interactive didactic tutoring style in [23]. KCDs are interactive directed lines of reasoning that are each designed to lead students to learn as independently as possible one or a small number of concepts, thus implementing a preference for an "Ask, don't tell" strategy. When a question is presented to a student, the student types a response in a text box in natural language. If the student enters a wrong or empty response, the system will engage the student in a remediation subdialogue designed to lead the student to the right answer to the corresponding question. Once the remediation is complete, the KCD returns to the next question in the directed line of reasoning.

3 Learning Oriented Versus Performance Oriented Behavior in Tutorial Dialogue Systems

Explanation is one of the key learning oriented behaviors students may engage in in a tutorial dialogue context. From a scientific viewpoint, one of the best substantiated educational findings in cognitive science research is the educational benefit of explanation, and in particular, the self-explanation effect [8,19]. Self-explanation benefits learners by revealing knowledge gaps, abstracting problem specific knowledge into schemas that can be applied to other relevant cases, and elaborating the representation of knowledge in the learners mind so that it can be more easily retrieved [26]. The self-explanation effect appears to be related to the process of constructing an explanation. Previous studies of human tutoring have revealed a significant correlation between amount of student explanation and learning [21,10].

Self-explanation has been frequently studied in connection with studies of the educational benefit of studying worked out example problems for mathematics and other problem solving domains. When students possess sufficient background knowledge and are sufficiently engaged, presenting them with correctly worked example problems in math and science and directing them to "self-explain" has been proven highly effective, even more effective than problem solving at early stages of skill acquisition in the context of laboratory studies [19,16]. Nevertheless, in classroom settings neither the appropriate level of background knowledge nor the ideal level of engagement with the material can be assumed. Thus, an important question for improving the state of education is how to design interactions with instructional technology that are effective for keeping students engaged and for supporting productive explanation activities in a way that would be practical to place in a classroom setting.

Explanation in a tutorial dialogue context is also important from an assessment standpoint. Previous studies of student-tutor interactions in a human tutoring setting have demonstrated a strong correlation between length of student response and likelihood for negative feedback offered from the tutor [21]. Thus, elaborate student explanations create more opportunities for valuable instruction by revealing knowledge gaps that might not otherwise come up. Increased awareness of student knowledge gaps facilitates the tutor's process of effectively adapting instruction to the individual needs of students. It also increases the likelihood that students notice their knowledge gaps and strive for deeper understanding [26].

Human tutors are highly successful at eliciting elaborated explanations from students [21,10] and highly successful at educating students [7,9]. In response to equivalent questions from a tutor, we have observed human tutors typically eliciting an order of magnitude more talk in a typed chat environment, including verbal self-explanation, from learners than a tutorial dialogue system in the same domain using similar prompts with an identical text-based chat interface. See Figure 1 for a typical interaction from the WHY-Atlas physics explanation tutor [25]. Notice the student offering a typical, one-word reply. Figure 2 presents an analogous interaction in a human tutoring scenario in the same domain using an equivalent typed chat interface. Not only does the student answer in a complete sentence, but, more importantly, the student also offers a justification for the answer. Since both of these interactions are typed, rather than in speech, the difference between student behavior with a human tutor and with a tutorial dialogue system cannot be explained as a modality difference.

Tutor: In order for your hand to feel pain from the impact, there must be a force acting on it. What force is acting on your hand?
Student: wall

Fig. 1. This example illustrates a typical typed KCD interaction

---

Tutor: There is need for some clarification. A body's motion is determined by the forces acting on it. So, what are the forces acting on earth?
Student: Since space has no gravity, then the only force acting on the earth is the pull of the sun.

Fig. 2. This example illustrates a typical human tutoring interaction

In this paper we describe two studies, each of which explores an alternative explanation for this phenomenon in an attempt to understand better the reasons for unproductive student behavior with tutorial dialogue systems and to formulate a recommendation for a solution. First we explore the issue of the differences in student expectations of human tutors and of instructional technology. As a starting place, one potential explanation for the difference in behavior in response to human tutors and to tutorial dialogue systems is that the same norms of cooperativeness and politeness that strongly influence dialogue behavior in human-human discourse do not routinely apply in human-machine discourse. In addition to frequent one or two word answers in response to tutor questions in a tutorial dialogue system context, we have also observed students offering sarcastic comments about the system rather than answers or sometimes entirely neglecting to answer tutor questions when they figure out that the system will continue to offer instruction even in the total absence of student effort to offer an answer. In rare cases, students proceed in this fashion for an entire dialogue.

Thinking about the issue of a priori expectations more broadly, some previously published evidence already supports the position that the perception of computers as different from humans is a key factor leading to lack of explanation with tutorial dialogue systems specifically, and perhaps "performance oriented" behavior with computer tutors in general. Whereas a series of human-computer interaction studies by Reeves and Nass (2002) suggests that on some level people subconsciously treat computers like people, others have found that humans speak differently when they believe they are speaking to a computer rather than to a human, even when their partner uses identical language with them [24]. Schechtman and Horowitz (2003) focused on social issues such as politeness rituals, and not learning oriented behavior such as explanation. A similar recently published comparison between student verbal behavior with human tutors and with computer tutors shows that students not only display more politeness indicators in their natural language contributions to human tutors, but more "hedges" as well, perhaps as a face saving device [6]. Nevertheless, none of these previous studies focus on the specific issue of student explanations, although the specific issue of eliciting deep explanation behavior from students is particularly important for designing effective tutorial dialogue environments. We hypothesize that students will offer more explanation to an agent they believe is a human because of differences in expectations students bring with them about how they typically interact with humans versus how they typically interact with computers. Note that we are not attempting to overturn "The Media Equation" [18]. We are addressing HCI issues that affect the extent to which students engage in productive behavior for learning with instructional technology. Here we are simply arguing that while previous studies touch on similar issues, they do not specifically address this question, which is an important initial step for improving the effectiveness of instructional technology, particularly tutorial dialogue technology. Thus, our first study explores the impact of student expectations on explanation behavior.

From a different angle, we explore the contribution of limitations in the capabilities of the technology as a contributing factor to the problem. An alternative hypothesis along these lines is that students will offer more explanation to a tutor agent that is more interactive because it will be perceived as more interested in their thoughts. One can easily hypothesize, for example, that the reason why students behave differently with tutorial dialogue agents than with human tutors is simply because the technology is still too rigid to engage in realistically natural dialogue interactions. Focused feedback is one important aspect of human tutorial discourse that sets it apart from tutorial dialogue agents. Human tutors exhibit a high degree of responsiveness to students. In contrast to human tutoring dialogues, no current tutorial dialogue systems are capable of acknowledging and offering tailored feedback for extended explanations that do more than answer a direct question asked by the tutor [2,22,12]. Focused feedback is one way that human tutors demonstrate to students that they are listening and understanding what the student is saying. Previous studies have substantiated the benefits of tutor feedback in assisting students in problem-solving tasks [5]. For this reason, our second study explores the impact of focused feedback on student explanation behavior.

4 Experimental Setup

The two studies reported in this paper shared many common experimental setup features, which we will describe in this section. Features that are specific to a single study will be described in the section below related to the specific study.

In both studies, students interacted independently with a tutor agent through a text-based chat interface at a computer terminal in a small student lab space. The chat setup can be configured in three different ways. In one mode, the student receives only automatically generated messages, produced by the KCD engine. In another, a human can edit each automatically generated message before sending it to the student. In a third mode, a human can compose the entire message. All three modes appeared identical to the student. Both the student and the tutor were able to view the history of the conversation in a scrolling dialogue history window at the top of the chat interface. A separate text input window was used for entering a text, and in the case of the tutor, entering and/or modifying an automatically generated text, before it was submitted.

The tutoring domain was basic college-level Newtonian physics, a domain in which the first author has researched the relative effectiveness of alternative instructional technologies for the past five years [20,21,22]. In both studies, the instructional manipulation was short, consisting of exactly one KCD dialogue designed to teach the concept of normal force, which is the force that every hard surface exerts on any object resting on its surface. As is common practice for tutoring studies, learning was assessed using a pre and post test. We used the same test for pre and post-test, which consisted of 5 multiple choice conceptual physics questions related to the concept of normal force covering all major points raised in the dialogue on normal force that is part of the experimental manipulation.

5 The Impact of Expectations Related to Humanness

In the first study we measured the impact of student expectations on student explanation behavior by comparing students interacting with a computer agent in two conditions. 40 university students participated in the experiment, one at a time, randomly assigned to each of the two conditions. In the experimental condition, students were told that they would be chatting with a human tutor. For the initial segment of their interaction through the chat interface, they conversed freely with a human about their extra-curricular interests. The purpose of this social interaction was to reinforce the idea that they were talking to a human. After several turns, the human shifted the chat mode to automatic tutoring using the KCD engine so that the topic shifted to the dialogue about normal force, and the tutor turns were generated completely automatically. The human remained in the loop just to introduce a delay in order to maintain the illusion that the student was still interacting with a human. In the control condition, the students were told that they would be chatting with a computer agent. There was no initial conversation about extra-curricular interests. And there was no delay introduced between when the student entered a conversational contribution and the tutor's automatically generated response was delivered. Note that there were two differences between the experimental and control conditions in this study. For our purposes it is not important to disentangle the source of elevated student expectation. The important point was to measure the impact that expectations about a tutor agent formed before a tutoring interaction affect student's behavior within that interaction.

After signing a consent form, each student took the pretest. The students then read a set of instructions that explained that they would be engaged in a dialogue about physics with a tutor agent. The only difference in the instructions between the two conditions was that in the experimental condition the students were told they would be interacting with a human tutor and in the control condition the students were told they would be interacting with a computer tutor. After the dialogue, the students took the post-test. After the post-test, the students filled out a questionnaire assessing the students' perceptions of the tutor agent as a manipulation check. One-on-one interviews with students after filling out the questionnaire served as an additional manipulation check. 90% of the students participating in the study believed what they were told about the tutor agent being either computer or machine. During this time the deception was also explained to the students, and they had the opportunity to make comments or ask any desired questions.

5.1 Contrasting Dialogue Behavior in Experimental and Control Conditions

While student verbal behavior in the control condition (see Figure 3) was similar to that observed in previous evaluations of KCDs [20], behavior in the experimental condition (see Figure 4) was strikingly different and much more like what had been observed in human tutoring corpora.

Notice in Figure 3, the control condition student answers two of the tutor's questions with one word answers. The third question, which is a why question, elicits a longer response as expected. Nevertheless, even the longer student response does not offer much discussion. In contrast, in Figure 4, we see a student in the experimental condition answering the same three questions. Notice how much additional discussion the student offers in response to the second tutor question.

Two separate factors distinguished the control condition from the experimental condition and may have separately or jointly contributed to elevated student expectation in the experimental condition. First, the instructions explained that students would be talking to a human. Secondly, the initial portion of the chat discussion that was about their extra-curricular interests was highly interactive, showing great interest in the details of student interests. As mentioned above, for our purposes it is not important to disentangle the source of elevated student expectation. See Figure 5 for an example of one of these social interactions. Note that this initial conversation was completely devoid of physics content and could not contribute to the students' learning nor demonstrate any specific knowledge of physics on the part of the tutor.

Tutor: Ok, ...So think about this: when a rock is falling, what force is acting upon the rock to make it fall?
Student: gravity
Tutor: Good. If a rock is resting on a table, is there still a gravitational force acting on the rock?
Student: Yes
Tutor: Correct. If gravity is pulling the rock down, why does the rock not fall through the table?
Student: Because the table is exerting a force as well
Tutor: Hard surfaces can support objects because they exert a normal force on the objects. That normal force opposes the gravitational force ...

Fig. 3. This example illustrates a typical interaction from Control Condition

---

Tutor: Ok,...So think about this: when a rock is falling, what force is acting upon the rock to make it fall?
Student: Gravity.
Tutor: Good. If a rock is resting on a table, is there still a gravitational force acting on the rock?
Student: Well, the force is present but the rock is not moving. I used to think of acting as requiring movement, so I am confused about this. I would think in this case the answer is supposed to be yes.
Tutor: Gravitational force exists everywhere on earth. If gravity is pulling the rock down, why does the rock not fall through the table?
Student: An equal and opposite force is acting on the rock.
Tutor: Hard surfaces can support objects because they exert a normal force on the objects. That normal force opposes the gravitational force...

Fig. 4. This example illustrates a typical interaction from then Experimental Condition

We compared average student turn length between conditions focusing only on the portion of the dialogue interactions that were managed by the tutorial dialogue system so that the stimulus was the same between conditions and only the expectation set up prior to the physics interaction influenced the difference in students' verbal behavior.

As mentioned, average student turn length in the control condition was consistent with that in previous evaluations of KCDs (mean = 3.6, standard deviation = 2.3). In the experimental condition, average turn length was much larger. Although it was not as large as previously reported average turn lengths of between 10 and 15 with human tutors in the same domain [20], it was significantly longer than in the control condition (mean = 8.6, standard deviation = 4.2, $t(38) = 4.78$, $p = 0.000$, effect size computed with Cohen's $d=1.49$). Thus, we observed a strong main effect of condition on raw amount of student talk per turn. Note that all t-test presented in this paper are unmatched 2-tailed t-tests except where otherwise noted.

Tutor: So before we get started with the physics part of the experiment, I would like to find out more about you. What do you like to do on the weekends?

Student: I only like to work on Artificial Intelligence. I am rather unusual in this regard. I spend all my time working on software.

Tutor: What kind of software are you working on right now?

Student: Well, I have written software that makes Debian packages semi-automatically out of large quantities of online software which is locates mainly using spidering and information extraction.

Tutor: Do you have a dream job? If so, what would it be?

Student: I would enjoy working at the higher end of military AI systems where I have access to all the tools and resources and can be isolated and develop so-called autistic states of consciousness.

Tutor: Sounds interesting! Ok, let's talk some physics now…

Fig. 5. This example illustrates a typical social interaction

We decomposed student turns into idea units at clause boundaries in order to take inventory of how much additional information was communicated in the experimental condition. In the experimental condition, students uttered on average 1.86 idea units of elaboration per turn beyond the direct answer to the tutor's question (standard deviation = 1.93). In the control condition, students uttered only .5 idea units of elaboration per turn (standard deviation = .89). The difference was statistically significant ($t(38) = 2.87$, $p < .05$, effect size = .9 standard deviations).

5.2 Learning Gains Analysis

Our learning gains analysis provides some limited evidence that simply eliciting more explanation without any change in the actual interaction with students in the experimental condition yielded an increase in instructional effectiveness of the KCD technology. On average, students in both conditions knew about the same amount about the concept of normal force prior to their interaction with the instructional manipulation. Out of 11 possible points, students in the control condition earned a mean score of 7.8 on the pre-test, with a standard deviation of 2.44. Mean pre-test score in the experimental condition was lower, although it did not differ significantly from this (mean = 6.9, standard deviation = 1.51). There was a significant main effect of test phase on learning over the whole population. Mean pre-test score was 7.34 with standard deviation 2.04. Mean post-test score was 9.73 with standard deviation 1.48. $t(38) = 6.06$, $p < .05$. So although the instructional manipulation as well as the pre/post test was short, students learned a measurable amount of physics knowledge from their interaction with the system. Based on previous results demonstrating a significant correlation between average student turn length and learning gains, and based on the large effect of condition on average student turn length, we expected to see a significant improvement in instructional effectiveness between the experimental condition and the control condition. What we found was less conclusive. There was a marginal effect approaching significance in favor of the experimental condition on learning gains in terms of adjusted post-test score using a 1-tailed t-test (Mean(experimental) = .66, standard deviation = .33, Mean(control) = .47, standard deviation = .44, t(39) = 1.55, p = .06).

Because KCDs use very simple language understanding technology to process student input, automatically generated tutor responses were not always appropriate to the student's answers. However, we verified that occasional inappropriate KCD feedback did not lead to a significant detrimental effect on student learning. For each student we computed eight separate tallies indicating number of correct answers treated as correct, correct answers treated as incorrect, incorrect answers treated as correct, incorrect answers treated as incorrect, correct elaborations treated as correct, correct elaborations treated as incorrect, incorrect elaborations treated as correct, and incorrect elaborations treated as incorrect. Since the KCD treated every answer as completely correct or completely incorrect, we treated each idea unit that was part of an answer as having been treated as correct or incorrect depending upon whether the answer to the question was classified as correct or incorrect by the KCD. The reliability of the human judgment for correctness versus incorrectness of idea units computed using Cohen's Kappa was computed at .78, so these tallies can be treated as reliable. We did not find any significant correlation between percentage of idea units treated correctly and adjusted post-test score or raw post-test score with or without effect of pre-test score factored out, either within or across conditions. Thus, we did not find any evidence that inappropriate feedback negatively impacted learning.

As in the KCDs used in [22], the KCD used in this study stepped students through a line of reasoning where students were lead through a series of applications of rules of physics in order to provide a foundation for an understanding of an individual conceptual rule of physics. Students answered questions about things they experienced in their every day lives to help them understand. For example, "If you hold a book in your hand, which way do you feel the book pushing?" Students can answer these questions even if they don't know any physics. They simply require students to think about their experiences. And yet, these questions help them to see laws of physics at work. The ultimate goal of a KCD is to bring students to a place where they can remember and articulate a single rule of physics. As part of that line of reasoning, students are eventually asked to go one step further and apply that rule. For example, after discussing the concept of normal force applied by a horizontally oriented object, students were asked to predict what would happen if the object was now tilted. If students were not able to make the conceptual leap, their understanding was scaffolded using a subdialogue, which is an embedded line of reasoning. Eventually, if the students were not able to apply the rule with help, the rule was applied for them. The focus of this work was to provide conceptual help when students displayed a gap in their understanding with faulty problem solving actions. In the study reported in this paper, students were able to answer the KCD question most of the time. In fact, overall, only 10% of direct answers to KCD questions were incorrect, with equal numbers in both conditions. Thus, based on answers to questions in the main line of reasoning of the KCD, little need of remedial instruction was indicated. This is an indication that students were able to follow the KCD's line of reasoning effectively. However, it might also be an indication that the material was too simple to observe a difference in instructional effectiveness due to our experimental manipulations.

6   Study 2: Raising Expectations Through Feedback

The results of Study 1 confirmed our hypothesis that student expectation was a major factor leading to a lack of explanation behavior in previous tutorial dialogue research. Simply elevating expectations without any change in the technology significantly impacted the amount of learning oriented student behavior. However, while the experimental manipulation was effective for testing our hypothesis, using deception to raise student expectations is not a viable solution in practice, and thus is not sufficient by itself to provide the HCI community with specific interface design recommendations. Furthermore, while the increase in student explanation in the first study yielded a marginal increase in learning, an ideal solution would produce a statistically reliable effect on learning.

We hypothesized that offering additional feedback to students in response to their explanation behavior would yield a larger impact on learning. Thus, in a follow-up study we directly tested a second hypotheses, namely that increased interactivity in the form of focused feedback would yield an increase in student explanation behavior. We predicted that the enhanced interactivity and closer coordination would raise student expectations about the technology and communicate to the student more interest in their thoughts. We predicted this would lead to a similar increase in learning oriented behavior to what we observed in the previous study.

6.1   Experimental Design of Study 2

In the experimental condition, students received targeted feedback in addition to typical KCD responses, whereas in the control condition students received only typical KCD responses. Using the same chat setup but in a mode that allowed a human in the loop to edit tutor turns before they were presented to students, a human inserted focused feedback at the beginning of each tutor turn in the experimental condition, wherever possible. Thus, only in the experimental condition the tutor turns would contain more explicit connections with the particulars of what students said.

During a pilot testing phase, we noticed that increased interactivity by itself was not effective, in large part because the students' default taciturn behavior did not offer the tutor many opportunities to offer feedback. Thus, we introduced a modeling phase in both the experimental and control conditions in which students spent 5 minutes prior to their interaction with the tutor agent viewing a screen capture video of a student interacting with the tutor agent on an unrelated physics topic (i.e., the concept of displacement) and offering productive, learning oriented behavior.

In order to rule out the possibility that a difference in learning gains we observe between conditions is the result of additional instruction offered in the experimental condition, we assigned students to matched pairs when we randomly assigned them to conditions. We tallied the list of idea units offered to each student in the experimental condition and offered the same instructional content to the student's matched pair student in the control condition formulated as a reminder at the end of the KCD. Thus, we controlled for information presentation between conditions. Note that students were randomly matched. Thus, paired students did not necessarily have the same instructional needs. This is an important point since one key distinction between feedback per se and additional instruction more generally is whether it is tailored to the specific needs of the student. 20 local university students and staff participated in the study, 10 in each condition. Thus, there were 10 matched pairs of students.

Table 1. Types of Focused Feedback Used in Study 2

Category	Tag Line
Missing Answer	"You have not answered the question about___"
CloseAnswer	"___ is close. I would say ___."
CorrectAnswer/No Elaboration	"You're right, but let's think about why that is correct." "You're right, but let's think about the implications."
CorrectElaboration	"That's a good point about ___."
CorrectAnswer/ Incorrect Elaboration	"You're answer is correct, but your reasoning is not correct. It's not true that ___."
Wrong Answer	"That's not correct. It's not true that ___."

In order to ensure that students in the experimental condition were treated equally, we developed a set of tag lines to use with different categories of feedback (See Table 1). This allowed us to control for tone so that the tutor's feedback would have a consistent feel with the automatically generated KCD responses. Correct Answer and Correct Elaboration feedback was meant to affirm students for positive behavior and encourage them to elaborate. These two types of feedback did not contain any instruction since they were not directed at any specific deficiency in the student's contribution by definition. The other classes of feedback were all forms of negative feedback, thus each referring specifically to at least one specific piece of content.

6.2 Impact on Student Explanation Behavior

As in the previous study, we found an effect of condition on student explanation behavior. In particular, there was a reliable difference in terms of number of idea units per turn included in elaborations according to a 1-tailed t-test (mean(experimental) = 3.5, standard deviation = 3.5, mean(control) = 1, standard deviation = 1.6, t(19) = 2.3, p < .05, effect size = 1.0). Thus, there is evidence that focused feedback has an impact on how much students say. As a rough, informal comparison, the effect size for difference in number of idea units was consistent across studies. However, in terms of raw average student turn length, the difference was only a statistical trend according to a 1-tailed t-test (Mean(experimental) = 5.83, standard deviation = 3.8, Mean(control) = 4.45, standard deviation = 2.3, t(19) = 1.4, p=.17). Note that raw average student turn lengths in both conditions were in between the two extremes observed in the previous study.

Another unexpected result was that a linear regression analysis demonstrated a stronger connection between positive feedback and average turn length and that between negative feedback and turn length. There was no significant correlation between amount of negative feedback and average student turn length (N=10, R-squared=.04, t=.53, p=.55). However, there was a reliable correlation between amount of positive feedback and student turn length (N=10, R-squared=.54, t=3.07, p < .05). It could be hypothesized that students who were correct more often became more confident because of their success at answering the tutor's questions, and their success was more of a factor leading to their increased levels of explanation rather than the feedback itself. Thus we examined explanation behavior in the control condition to assess whether there was a correlation between number of correct student answers and average student turn length, but there was no significant correlation. This supports the interpretation that it was the feedback and not the number of correct responses that influenced how much students explained in the experimental condition.

6.3 Learning Gains Analysis

There was no difference in learning between conditions. Difference in adjusted post test scores was not significantly different even with a 1-tailed t-test (Mean(experimental) = .64, standard deviation = .38, Mean(control) = .75, standard deviation = .33, t(19) = 1.2, p = .24). There was, however, a significant correlation between amount of explanation and learning within the control condition, even with effect of pretest score factored out (N=10, R2=.45, t=2.6, p < .05).

We then examined more closely the substantive feedback offered to students in connection with deficiencies on their pre-tests and corresponding performance on their post-tests. Only 3 students in the experimental condition received any substantive negative feedback. For two of those students the substantive feedback was directed at topics that were not tested on the post-test. The other student showed a knowledge gain between pre-test and post-test on the relevant concept addressed by the tutor's feedback. Thus, further exploration on the topic of feedback is required.

7 Recommendations and Future Work

While the results in this paper do not offer the final solution for overcoming the problem of unproductive student behavior and dramatically improving the instructional effectiveness of the technology, these studies yield some new insights and promising directions for continued investigation. We have presented two studies that demonstrate that both expectation and interactivity have a measurable impact on the extent to which students engage in productive behavior with instructional technology. The strong impact of artificially elevated expectations on explanation behavior and weak impact on learning observed in the first study offers confirmation that exploring ways of elevating student expectation is promising for improving student behavior and potentially contributes to enhancing the effectiveness of instructional technology, although it is not sufficient in itself for yielding a significant impact on learning gains. While increasing the amount of targeted feedback offered to students is a more viable option in practice than artificially elevating expectations through deception, the impact on student behavior based on that manipulation was not quite as pronounced and yielded no effect on learning. However, since our analysis from the second study demonstrated that only the types of feedback offered in response to correct answers in this study correlated with average student turn length, we plan to continue to investigate the potential use of this form of feedback in connection with other types of answers in order to yield a stronger impact on behavior overall. Here we only explored the use of positive feedback in connection with correct answers, but it is possible that similar forms of feedback in connection with incorrect responses would encourage students to elaborate more when they were less certain.

Acknowledgements

This work was funded by NSF SGER REC-0411483 and ONR Cognitive and Neural Sciences Division, Grant number N000140410107.

References

1. Aleven, V., Ogan, A., Popescu, O., Torrey, C., & Koedinger, K. Evaluating the Effectiveness of a Tutorial Dialogue System for Self-Explanation. *Proc. ITS 2004,* Springer Verlag (2004), 443-454.
2. Aleven V., Koedinger, K. R., & Popescu, O. A Tutorial Dialogue System to Support Self-Explanation: Evaluation and Open Questions. *Proc. AI-ED 2003*, IOS Press (2003).
3. Ashley, K. D., Desai, R., & Levine, J. M. Teaching Case-Based Argumentation Concepts Using Dialectic Arguments vs. Didactic Explanations. *Proc. ITS 2002*, Springer Verlag (2002), 585-595.
4. Baker, R.S., Corbett, A.T., Koedinger, K.R., Wagner, A.Z. Off-Task Behavior in the Cognitive Tutor Classroom: When Students "Game The System". *Proc. CHI 2004*, ACM Press (2004), 383-390.
5. Bangert-Drowns, R., Kulik, C., Kulik, J., & Morgan, M. The Instructional Effect of Feedback in Test-Like Events. *Review of Educational Research 61*, 2(1991), 213-238.
6. Bhatt, K., Evens, M. & Argamon, S. Hedged Responses and Expressions of Affect in Human/Human and Human/Computer Tutorial Interactions. *Proc. Cog. Sci. Soc. 2004,* Erlbaum (2004).
7. Bloom, B. S. The 2 Sigma Problem: The search for methods of group instruction as effective as one-to-one tutoring. *Educational Researcher 13*, 1984, 4-16.
8. Chi, M. T. H., de Leeuw, N., Chiu, M. H., LaVancher, C. Eliciting self-explanations improves understanding. *Cognitive Science 18*, 3(1984), 439-477.

9. Cohen, P. A., Kulik, J. A., & Kulik, C. C. Educational Outcomes of Tutoring: A Meta-analysis of Findings. *American Educational Research Journal 19*, (1982), 237-248.
10. Core, M. G., Moore, J. D., Zinn, C. The Role of Initiative in Tutorial Dialogue. *Proc. European ACL 2003*.
11. Davis, J. M., Leelawong, K., Belynne, K., Bodenheimer, R., Biswas, G., Vye, N., & Bransford, J. Intelligent User Interface Design for Teachable Agent Systems. *Proc. IUI 2003*, ACM Press (2003), 26-33.
12. Evens, M. and Michael, J., (in press). *One-on-One Tutoring by Humans and Machines*, Lawrence Erlbaum and Associates, Mahwah, NJ.
13. Graesser, A., VanLehn, K., the TRG, & the NLT. Why2 Report: Evaluation of Why/Atlas, Why/AutoTutor, and Accomplished Human Tutors on Learning Gains for Qualitative Physics Problems and Explanations, LRDC Tech Report, University of Pittsburgh, 2002.
14. Graesser, A. C., Bowers, C. A., Hacker, D.J., & Person, N. K. An anatomy of naturalistic tutoring. In K. Hogan & M. Pressley (Eds.), *Scaffolding of instruction*. Brookline Books, 1998.
15. Hietala, P. & Niemirepo, T. The Competence of Learning Companion Agents. *International Journal of Artificial Intelligence in Education 9*, (1998), 178-192.
16. Hummel, H., and Nadolski, R. (2002). Cueing for schema construction: Designing problem-solving multimedia practicals. *Contemporary Educational Psychology 27*, 2(2002), 229-249.
17. Leelawong, K., Davis, J., Vye, N., Biswas, G. The Effects of Feedback in Supporting Learning by Teaching in a Teachable Agent Environment. *Proc.ICLS 2002*.
18. Reeves, B., & Nass, C. *The Media Equation: How People Treat Computers, Television, and New Media like Real People and Place*, Cambridge University Press, 1996.
19. Renkl, A. Learning from worked-out examples: Instructional explanations supplement self-explanations. *Learning & Instruction 12*, (2002), 529-556.
20. Rosé, C. P., Bhembe, D., Siler, S., Srivastava, R., & VanLehn, K. Exploring the Effectiveness of Knowledge Construction Dialogues. *Proc. AI-ED 2003*, IOS Press (2003).
21. Rosé, C. P., Bhembe, D., Siler, S., Srivastava, R., VanLehn, K. The Role of Why Questions in Effective Human Tutoring. *Proc. AI-ED 2003*, IOS Press (2003).
22. Rosé, C. P., Jordan, P., Ringenberg, M., Siler, S., VanLehn, K., & Weinstein, A. Interactive Conceptual Tutoring in Atlas-Andes. *Proc. AI-ED 2001*, IOS Press (2001), 256-266.
23. Rosé, C. P., Moore, J. D., VanLehn, K., Allbritton, D., A Comparative Evaluation of Socratic versus Didactic Tutoring. *Proc. Cog. Sci. Soc. 2001*, Erlbaum (2001).
24. Shechtman, N., & Horowitz, L. Media Inequality in Conversation: How People Behave Differently When Interacting with Computers and People. *Proc. CHI 2003*, ACM Press (2003).
25. VanLehn, K., Jordan, P., Rosé, C. P., and The Natural Language Tutoring Group. The Architecture of Why2-Atlas: a coach for qualitative physics essay writing. *Proc. ITS 2002*, Springer Verlag (2002).
26. VanLehn, K., & Jones, R. M. What mediates the self-explanation effect? Knowledge gaps, schemas or analogies? *Proc. Cog. Sci. Soc. 1993*, Erlbaum (1993), 1034-1039.

Put Them Where? Towards Guidelines for Positioning Large Displays in Interactive Workspaces

Ramona E. Su and Brian P. Bailey

Department of Computer Science,
University of Illinois,
Urbana, IL 61801 U.S.A.
{ramonasu, bpbailey}@uiuc.edu

Abstract. Multiple large displays are being increasingly used in interactive workspaces to enhance individual and group work. However, little research has been conducted to determine whether various configurations of large displays impact users or their tasks differently. We show that such an impact exists, and take steps towards developing guidelines for how to effectively arrange large displays in interactive workspaces. For two large displays, we manipulated their physical separation, angle between them, and symmetry when facing each other and measured time on task, subjective workload, and satisfaction for application relocation tasks. From the results, we produced three useful guidelines: (i) displays can be separated on a horizontal plane up to a subtended visual angle of 45°, (ii) a display should not be placed behind a user, but if necessary, it should be offset relative to the user, and (iii) displays should be positioned at a 45° angle relative to each other rather than being orthogonal. As the use of large displays is increasing, these guidelines should have a broad, practical impact.

1 Introduction

Multiple large displays are being increasingly used in workspaces such as meeting rooms, design studios, and research labs to improve individual and group work. For example, large displays enable juxtaposition of alternative ideas [3], support awareness of peripheral information [27], and enable more effective discussion of digital information [25]. Workspaces that are equipped with multiple large displays and other, interconnected computing devices are known as *interactive workspaces* [15].

Upon acquiring large displays, however, one faces the practical and significant question of whether or not their position in the workspace has an impact on their use. For example, does a gap between displays adversely affect users? If so, how much of a gap is allowable? If the physical limits of a room do not allow displays to be placed adjacent to each other, does changing the angle or symmetry between the displays affect their use? If so, how much of an angle is appropriate or how much would placing displays behind users affect them? In addition, as large displays are often affixed to a wall, the impacts associated with display placement can be permanent.

While researchers have investigated how people use multiple desktop monitors in work practice [8] and have developed guidelines on how to configure multiple small

M.F. Costabile and F. Paternò (Eds.): INTERACT 2005, LNCS 3585, pp. 337–349, 2005.

displays [2, 12, 13], our research seeks to provide guidelines – supported by empirical evidence – for how to effectively configure large displays in interactive workspaces.

In our experiment, we empirically compared several configurations of large displays; we varied the distance between displays along a horizontal plane, oriented displays at different angles, and positioned displays with varying amounts of symmetry. To test these configurations, we selected the task of moving an application window between displays – a common and frequent task when arranging information or managing applications among multiple displays in interactive workspaces [3, 20].

We compared the configurations based on task performance, subjective workload, and user satisfaction for performing application relocation tasks. For these tasks, our results produced three practical guidelines for configuring large displays: (i) displays can be separated on a horizontal plane up to a maximum visual angle of 45° (Figure 1a-b), (ii) a display should not be placed behind a user, but if necessary, it should be offset relative to the user (Figure 1h-i), (iii) displays should be positioned at a 45° or possibly lower angle relative to one another (Figure 1d). These guidelines are important because they show that following common practices such as positioning displays symmetrical or orthogonal to each other may result in less effective configurations.

2 Related Work

In this section, we describe how our work fits with interactive workspaces, the use of multiple small and large displays, and the ergonomics of computer monitors.

2.1 Interactive Workspaces

An interactive workspace is a physical space where users interact with small/private and large/shared displays to perform individual or group work. Several distributed infrastructures have been developed that enable multiple, heterogeneous devices to function as a single, connected workspace – these include Gaia [21], iRos [14], and Aura [24]. On top of these infrastructures, many interfaces have been developed to enable seamless redirection of input and relocation of applications [3, 4, 7, 16, 17, 19, 20]. However, our work is the first to investigate how different configurations of large displays affect performance, workload, and satisfaction on relocation tasks.

While the design space encompasses many different types of tasks, interfaces, and movements between displays, we focused on a realistic but specific scenario. This allowed for a large and necessary degree of experimental control. Our scenario is the intersection of the three activities commonly performed in interactive spaces: relocating an application [3, 17], using a virtual paths interface [4, 16], and interacting between large displays [5, 22, 26].

2.2 Use of Multiple Small and Large Displays

In a study of multiple monitor usage in the workplace [8], Grudin found that most users divide information between the monitors – the focal monitor is used for main tasks while the peripheral monitor is used for secondary tasks. Because information is now divided between multiple monitors, users employ different window management techniques as seen in Hutchings et al [10, 11]. In these configurations, a common and frequent task is the moving of applications between the displays. Our choice of the experimental task was selected to reflect this scenario of use and show how performing this task may be affected by different configurations of large displays.

In [27], a user study was performed to test how separating information by various visual angles and monitor bezels affects performance for comparing text and detecting changes to information. In contrast, our study measures the impacts of wider visual angles and other configurations of large displays, and uses a task that requires actively moving an application across displays rather than passive monitoring.

Research has shown that using large displays can improve task performance due to more available screen space [5, 22, 26]. By comparing different configurations of large displays for application relocation performance, our study seeks to recommend how to configure large displays such that these performance gains are maximized.

2.3 Ergonomics of Desktop Monitors

Ergonomics research has developed guidelines for positioning desktop monitors in the workplace [2, 12, 13]. Sommerich found that the viewing angle of a monitor affects posture, performance, and preference [23]. Ankrum investigated the optimal range of viewing distance of desktop monitors and recommends a minimum distance of 25" [1]. This area of work supports our hypothesis that the manipulation of angle and distance of large displays will have an impact on users and also demonstrates how the application of a few specific guidelines could have a large practical impact. Our research focuses on developing guidelines for positioning multiple large displays in an interactive workspace to improve performance and satisfaction on a common task.

3   User study

The purpose of our user study was to evaluate how different configurations of large displays affect users when moving applications among them. Specifically, the study was designed to answer the following questions:

- How does the physical separation between large displays affect performance, subjective workload, and satisfaction when moving applications?
- How does the angle between large displays affect performance, subjective workload, and satisfaction when moving applications?
- How does the symmetry between a large display in front of a user and another behind the user affect these same measures when moving applications?

From the results, we want to begin developing guidelines on how to configure large displays for effective use in interactive workspaces.

3.1 Experimental Design

The study used a partial-factorial, within-subjects design. There were four factors– Distance (63", 109", 300"), Angle (45°, 60°, 90°), Symmetry (no-offset, half-offset, one-offset), and Trial (each of the sixteen application movements). The Distance,

Angle, and Symmetry factors were tested as three separate experiments in which three physical configurations of the displays were compared. The ordering of the factors and the configurations within each factor followed a Latin Square design. Because configurations were a function of the factor, they were not crossed in the design.

Twenty users (10 female) participated in the study. Users consisted of undergraduate and graduate students from various non-engineering departments at our institution, and members of the surrounding community. Ages ranged from 18 to over 40.

3.2 Interactive Workspace

The interactive workspace used in this study was comprised of a meeting table and two 61" plasma displays with resolution 1360×768. A workstation running Windows XP equipped with a multi-head graphics card was used to drive the displays. Camtasia was used to record a user's screen interaction on both displays.

To achieve the necessary level of experimental control, we limited the number of large displays used in the experiment to two. The displays were mounted on moveable stands to enable them to be quickly re-positioned in the workspace. A key property of our experimental design is that while the *physical* position of the displays was changed, the *virtual* distance between the displays always remained the same.

3.3 Geometric Properties and Configurations of the Large Displays

We varied the physical configurations of two large displays by varying the distance between the displays along the same horizontal plane (Distance), the amount of angle between the displays (Angle), and the amount of overlap between the displays (Symmetry). The configurations are shown in Figure 1. We selected these geometric properties because they represent how large displays are often configured in practice - displays positioned along a horizontal plane, displays positioned orthogonal to each other, and displays positioned so that they are aligned when facing each other. While these configurations are often selected based on aesthetics or physical dimensions of a workspace, our goal is to provide guidelines backed by empirical evidence that can be used to help determine how to arrange large displays for effective use.

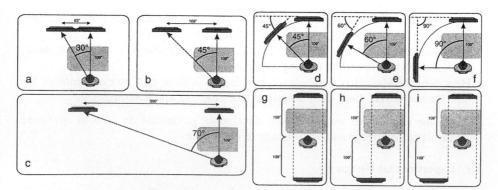

Fig. 1. The physical configurations of Distance (a-c), Angle (d-f), and Symmetry (g-i). One display always remained directly in a user's field of view at a distance of 109", while the location of the other display was manipulated.

In the study, one display always remained directly in front of a user seated at the table, as users would ostensibly want at least one display to be directly in their field of view. The distance to the fixed display was 109", which allowed content on the display to be easily viewed when seated at the table. The position of the other display was manipulated according to the configurations discussed next. Positions of the second display were marked on the floor to ensure consistency across users.

Distance. We compared distances of 63" (Fig. 1a), 109" (Fig. 1b), and 300" (Fig. 1c) between the centers of the displays. Distances were calculated based on two parts of a user's visual field [6, 18]—the useful field of view (extends to 30°) and peripheral field of view (extends to 100°). We positioned the second display so that it would be within the useful visual field (30°), slightly outside the useful visual field (45°), and close to the periphery (70°). We could not place the display at the edge of a user's periphery (100°) due to the physical limitations of our workspace. The display was positioned such that lines drawn from the user to the centers of the displays subtended the desired visual angle. We then measured the distance between the centers of the displays: 30° mapped to 63", 45° mapped to 109", and 70° mapped to 300".

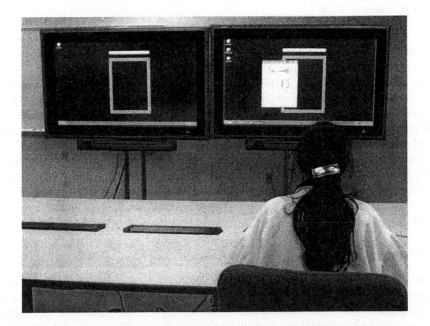

Fig. 2. A user is performing the experimental task for the 63" distance configuration. The user is moving an Internet Explorer application from the display on the right to the display on the left. After moving the application into the target box on the left, the user selects the rectangular bar above it. Each movement was a single trial and sixteen trials (resulting in a back and forth movement of the application) were performed in each configuration. The target boxes were used to ensure that the application was moved the same virtual distance.

Angle. We compared angles of 45° (Fig. 1d), 60° (Fig. 1e), and 90° (Fig. 1f). Because large displays are often wall-mounted, they are typically constrained to be on the same (0°, or orthogonal planes (90°). We wanted to investigate how other angles would affect a user within this range. Since a 0° configuration was similar to Distance, we started with the minimum angle that our pilot users felt was noticeably different from 0°, which occurred at 45°. The maximum angle selected was 90°, as this represents many existing configurations, and 60° was used as a median case. To create the angles, we moved the second display along a circular path from the fixed display until it reached the desired angle.

Symmetry. We compared three configurations of symmetry—the two displays aligned (no-offset, Fig. 1g), one display half overlapping the other (half-offset, Fig. 1h), and one display fully offset from the other (one-offset, Fig. 1i). The second display was positioned and moved along a horizontal plane behind the user. While these configurations may not be ideal, they are *realistic* since the physical limits of a workspace may cause one or more displays to be placed behind a user. We have informally observed displays configured this way in many research labs.

3.4 Experimental Task

The experimental task was to move an Internet Explorer application, with the resize and maximize buttons disabled, from the target box of one display to the target box of the other display. Figure 2 shows a user performing the task. This task was selected because relocating applications to spread information or to manage screen space across displays is a common and frequent task in an interactive workspace [3]. To ensure that a user performed a focused movement as opposed to a ballistic movement, which is a rapid, involuntary movement (e.g. a quick flick of the wrist) [28], a user selected a rectangular bar just above the target box after moving the application.

A target box was 20% larger than the application window and was located in the center of a screen. The target boxes provided a consistent starting and stopping point for each movement of the application and ensured that the application was always moved about the same virtual distance. A user performed this task sixteen times in each configuration to compensate for learning effects on the early trials.

3.5 Procedure

Upon arriving at the lab, we went through an informed consent process with the user. The user filled out a demographic questionnaire, was given a demonstration of the task, and practiced the task. Then, the user was instructed to perform the experimental task as quickly and accurately as possible for a specific configuration of the displays. A user performed the task sixteen times in each configuration. Once complete, the user filled out a NASA-TLX and satisfaction questionnaire. This process was repeated two more times for the other two configurations of the geometric property (e.g. Distance). A user then ranked the difficulty of performing the task in the three configurations. This entire process was then repeated two more times for the remaining geometries. The orders of the geometries and the configurations within each geometry followed a Latin Square design. The study lasted no more than an hour for a user.

3.6 Measurements

In this study, we measured:

- *Time on task (TOT)*. The time on task was measured from when the title bar of the application was selected to when the application was located in the target box and the mouse started moving towards the horizontal bar. Measurements were made from analysis of the timestamps in the screen interaction videos.
- *Subjective workload*. The NASA-TLX was used to measure subjective workload along the standard dimensions of *mental demand, physical demand, own perform-ance, effort*, and *frustration* [9]. While the user was asked to complete the task as quickly and as accurately as possible, no external time limit was imposed, thus we did not include *temporal demand* on the TLX. A continuous scale from Low to High was used for each dimension to allow fine-grained responses from the user.
- *User satisfaction*. A user rated their annoyance, confusion, and overall satisfaction for performing the tasks in each configuration. A user also rated how natural the connection was between the displays. Ratings were made using the same response structure as the TLX. Also, a user ranked the difficulty of performing the tasks in each configuration (e.g., Distance) and explained why they gave the rankings.

4 Results

In this section we discuss how the configurations of Distance, Symmetry, and Angle affected time on task, subjective workload, and user satisfaction. Trial did not affect any of the measures, so it will not be discussed further. To account for any learning effects, the first six trials of a user's performance data in each configuration were removed, leaving ten experimental trials in each configuration for the analysis.

The results for time on task, subjective workload, and user satisfaction for Distance and Symmetry are shown in Figures 3 and 4, respectively.

4.1 Distance

Time on Task. An ANOVA showed that Distance had a main effect on TOT ($F(2,36)=43.63$, $p<0.001$). Post-hoc analysis showed that users moved the application faster at distance 63" ($\mu=1.17s$) and distance 109" ($\mu=1.26s$) than at distance 300" ($\mu=1.84s$, $p<0.001$, $p<0.041$, respectively). There was no significant difference between 63" and 109".

Although the virtual distance between the target boxes was held constant, users performed the task about 57% slower when the displays were furthest apart than when they were closest together. The decrease may be attributed to users perceiving having to move the application across the gap between the displays or to increased difficulty positioning the application within the target box when the display was further away.

For distance 109", however, users completed the task as quickly as for distance 63" despite the physical separation. This shows that separation of displays does not affect relocation performance as long as the visual angle formed for a user is less than 45°.

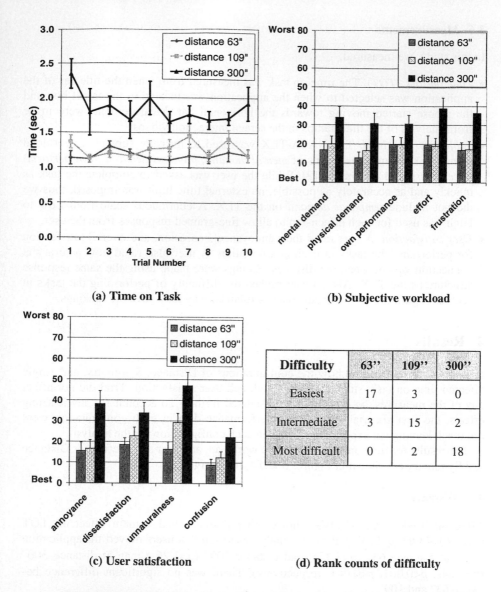

(a) Time on Task

(b) Subjective workload

(c) User satisfaction

(d) Rank counts of difficulty

Fig. 3. Time on task, subjective workload, and user satisfaction results for Distance

Subjective Workload. A MANOVA showed that Distance had a main effect on subjective workload (Wilks' $\Lambda=0.44$, $\underline{F}=(10,68)=3.43$, $\underline{p}<0.001$). Univariate analysis showed that there was a main effect on mental demand ($\underline{F}(1.33, 25.26)=15.61$, $\underline{p}<0.001$), physical demand ($\underline{F}(1.28, 24.22)=12.24$, $\underline{p}<0.001$), own performance ($\underline{F}(2,38)=4.59$, $\underline{p}<0.016$), effort ($\underline{F}(2,38)=11.57$, $\underline{p}<0.001$), and frustration

($\underline{F}$(2,38)=12.54, $\underline{p}$<0.001). Post-hoc analysis showed that for distance 300", users reported more mental demand (μ=34.0), physical demand (μ=30.9), performance demand (μ=30.7), effort (μ=39.0), frustration (μ=36.5) than both distance 63" (μ=16.95, μ=12.75, μ=19.9, μ=19.4, μ=17.0, respectively, with $\underline{p}$<0.014 in each case) and distance 109" (μ=20.05, μ=16.6, μ=19.7, μ=19.0, μ=17.25, respectively, with $\underline{p}$≤0.020 in each case). There was no difference between distances 63" and 109".

Results show that physical separation of displays does not cause an increase in subjective workload as long as the user's visual angle of the displays was less than 45°.

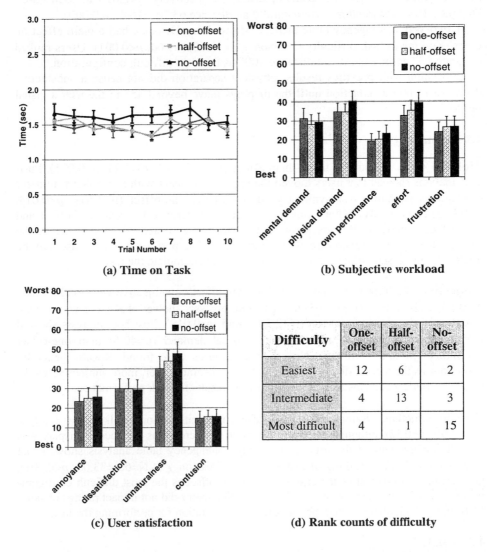

(a) Time on Task   (b) Subjective workload

(c) User satisfaction   (d) Rank counts of difficulty

Fig. 4. Time on task, subjective workload, and user satisfaction results for Symmetry

User Satisfaction. A MANOVA showed that Distance had a main effect on user satisfaction (Wilks' $\Lambda=0.38$, $\underline{F}(8,70)=5.52$, $p<0.001$). Univariate analysis showed that Distance had a main effect on annoyance ($\underline{F}(1.54, 29.17)=15.10$, $p<0.001$), satisfaction ($\underline{F}(2,38)=10.80$, $p<0.001$), naturalness ($\underline{F}(2,38)=23.71$, $p<0.001$), and confusion ($\underline{F}(2,38)=7.23$, $p<0.002$). Post-hoc analysis showed that distance 300" caused more annoyance ($\mu=38.3$), dissatisfaction ($\mu=33.9$), unnaturalness ($\mu=47.0$), and confusion ($\mu=22.3$) than distance 63" ($\mu=15.5$, $\mu=18.5$, $\mu=16.4$, $\mu=8.9$, respectively, $p<0.002$ in each case). Distance 300" caused more annoyance, dissatisfaction, and unnaturalness than distance 109" ($\mu=16.6$, $\mu=22.8$, $\mu=29.3$, respectively, $p<0.016$ in each case). Distance 109" was rated more unnatural than distance 63" ($\mu=16.4$, $p<0.009$).

A two-way contingency table analysis showed that Distance had a main effect on users' ranking of task difficulty (Pearson $\chi^2(4,N=60)=69.60$, $p<0.001$). Users ranked distance 63" as the easiest and distance 300" as the most difficult configuration.

Consistent with previous results, physical separation did not cause a substantive decrease in user satisfaction until the displays move beyond 45° in the user's visual field.

4.2 Symmetry

Time on Task. Symmetry had a main effect on TOT ($\underline{F}(2,38)=6.21$, $p<0.005$). Post-hoc analysis showed that users moved the application faster with one-offset symmetry ($\mu=1.45s$) and half-offset symmetry ($\mu=1.47s$) than no-offset ($\mu=1.61s$, $p<0.014$, $p<0.022$, respectively). There was no significant difference between half-offset and one-offset symmetry. Results show that performance decreased about 11% as the second display was moved directly behind a user. The performance decrease may be due to the increased amount of head turn required to complete the task.

Subjective Workload. Symmetry had a main effect on subjective workload (Wilks' $\Lambda=0.59$, $\underline{F}(10,68)=2.09$, $p<0.037$). Univariate analysis showed that there was a main effect only for physical demand ($\underline{F}(2,38)=4.45$, $p<0.018$). Post-hoc analysis showed that no-offset symmetry caused more physical demand ($\mu=40.6$) than one-offset symmetry ($\mu=34.8$, $p<0.059$). No other differences were found. Results generally show that as the second display is moved further behind a user, more subjective workload is experienced. This is consistent with the results for task performance.

User Satisfaction. Symmetry did not affect user satisfaction (Wilks' $\Lambda=0.82$, $\underline{F}(8, 70)=0.90$, $p<0.52$), although satisfaction tended to decrease as the second display was moved further behind the user. A two-way contingency table analysis showed that Symmetry did affect ranking of task difficulty (Pearson $\chi^2(4,N=60)=33.00$, $p<0.001$). Users ranked one-offset as the easiest and the no-offset as the most difficult configuration for performing the task. While changes in Symmetry did not impact ratings of satisfaction, users highly preferred the one-offset configuration for performing the task.

4.3 Angle

Angle had no main effect on TOT ($\underline{F}(2,9)=0.80$, $p<0.46$). Users required about the same time to perform the task across configurations. Angle did not affect subjective workload (Wilks' $\Lambda=0.79$, $F(10,68)=0.84$, $p<0.59$), though ratings of workload tended to increase as the angle between the displays increased.

While satisfaction tended to decrease as the angle between the displays increased, Angle did not affect user satisfaction (Wilks' $\Lambda=0.73$, $F(8,66)=1.39$, $p<0.22$). However, a two-way contingency table analysis showed that Angle did affect ranking of task difficulty (Pearson $\chi^2(4,N=60)=32.10$, $p<0.001$). Users ranked 45° (count=13) as the easiest configuration and 90° (count=14) as the most difficult configuration for performing the task.

While changes in Angle did not impact ratings of satisfaction, users highly preferred the smallest angle between the displays for performing the task.

5 Lessons Learned

From the results of our study, we learned that:

- *Different configurations of large displays have different impacts on users and their tasks.* Results show that various configurations of large displays affect time on task, subjective workload, and user satisfaction differently when performing application relocations tasks. This validates a need for guidelines for how to physically arrange large displays for effective use in interactive workspaces.
- *Displays can be physically separated on a horizontal plane as long as the visual angle subtended is less than 45°.* Results show that increasing the physical separation between the displays from the edges touching (a user's visual angle of 30°) to a small gap (45°) did not cause a negative change in performance, subjective workload, or satisfaction. Beyond a user's visual angle of 45°, however, each of these measures meaningfully changed in the negative direction. This suggests the allowable distance between the outermost displays should subtend a visual angle of no more than 45° for a user. Our results contradict the accepted intuition that displays must be positioned with their edges adjoined in order to be used effectively.
- *A display should not be placed behind a user, but if necessary, it should be offset relative to the user.* In the one-offset configuration (Figure 1i), users performed tasks faster, experienced less workload, and gave higher rankings than in the other configurations. Despite this preference, users overall disliked having a display positioned behind them (Figure 1g-i). Several users commented that they did not like having to turn their head or rotate their body to perform the task—"Why would you want to do this [placing display behind the user]?", "This is terrible". These comments are consistent with other research [3], which indicates that head turns and body movement can provide additional metrics by which to evaluate user interfaces in interactive workspaces.
- *Displays should be positioned at a 45° or possibly lower angle relative to each other.* The orthogonal (Figure 1f) configuration tended to be worse on all measures and was overwhelmingly ranked as the worst configuration. One user commented, "the relationship between the two displays [at 90°] was awkward; I had to turn my head more." However, the 45° configuration was ranked the best because users felt they could view the displays more easily. One user stated "the 45 angle didn't involve much turning, it was easy to glance from one to the other". Thus, if displays

cannot be positioned along the same horizontal plane, they should be placed with the smallest angle between them rather than orthogonal to each other, which may require the use of moveable stands.

These guidelines are most applicable when users want to rapidly spread information among displays in an interactive workspace, and may not be applicable when users want to visualize large, contiguous data sets such as an architectural design across multiple displays. However, because the former is a common use of interactive workspaces, our guidelines will have a broad and practical impact.

6 Conclusion and Future Work

Large displays are being increasingly used in interactive workspaces to enhance individual and group work. However, there are few, if any guidelines to draw upon when considering how to physically arrange large displays. Through an experiment comparing different configurations of large displays, our work has made two significant contributions. First, our results show that different configurations of large displays have meaningfully different impacts on users and their tasks, validating the need for guidelines about effective arrangement. Second, our results have produced an initial set of practical guidelines on how to arrange large displays for effective use in interactive workspaces. These guidelines are important because they show that following some common practices such as positioning displays symmetrical or orthogonal to each other may result in less effective configurations.

In the future, we want to compare configurations of large displays for additional tasks such as redirecting input, juxtaposing ideas, and monitoring information. Also, we want to evaluate how various configurations of the displays impact interaction techniques for performing those tasks. Results from future work will continue to provide guidelines that will facilitate more productive use of interactive workspaces.

References

1. Ankrum, D. Viewing Distance at Computer Workstations. *Workplace Ergonomics*, 10-12, 1996.
2. Ankrum, D.R. Visual Ergonomics in the Office: Guidelines. *Occupational Health and Safety*, 68 (7), 64-74, 1999.
3. Biehl, J. and B. Bailey. Aris: An Interface for Application Relocation in an Interactive Space. *Conference on Graphics Interface*, 2004, pp. 107-116.
4. Booth, K., B. Fisher, C. Lin and R. Argue. The "Mighty Mouse" Multi-Screen Collaboration Tool. *UIST*, 2002, pp. 209-212.
5. Czerwinski, M., G. Smith, T. Regan, B. Meyers, G. Robertson and G. Starkweather. Toward Characterizing the Productivity Benefits of Very Large Displays. *Interact*, 2003, pp. 9-16.
6. Duchowski, A. *Eye Tracking Methodology Theory and Practice*. Springer, London, 2003.
7. Greenberg, S., M. Boyle and J. Laberg. Pdas and Shared Public Displays: Making Personal Information Public, and Public Information Personal. *Personal Technologies*, 1999, pp. 54-64.

8. Grudin, J. Partitioning Digital Worlds: Focal and Peripheral Awareness in Multiple Monitor Use. *CHI*, 2001, pp. 458-465.
9. Hart, S.G. and L.E. Staveland. Development of a Nasa-Tlx (Task Load Index): Results of Empirical and Theoretical Research. In Hancock, P.A. and Meshkati, N. (eds.) *Human Mental Workload*, North-Holland, Amsterdam, 1988.
10. Hutchings, D., G. Smith, B. Meyers, M. Czerwinski and G. Robertson. Display Space Usage and Window Management Operation Comparisons between Single Monitor and Multiple Monitor Users. *AVI*, 2004, pp. 32-39.
11. Hutchings, D. and J. Stasko. Revisiting Display Space Management: Understanding Current Practice to Inform Next-Generation Design. *Conference on Graphics Interface*, 2004, pp. 127-134.
12. ISO. International Organization for Standardization, 1998.
13. ISO. International Organization for Standardization, 2004.
14. Johanson, B. and A. Fox. The Event Heap: A Coordination Infrastructure for Interactive Workspaces. *IEEE Workshop on Mobile Computing Systems and Applications*, 2002, pp. 83.
15. Johanson, B., A. Fox and T. Winograd. Experience with Ubiquitous Computing Rooms *IEEE Pervasive Computing*, 2002, 67-74.
16. Johanson, B., G. Hutchins, T. Winograd and M. Stone. Pointright: Experience with Flexible Input Redirection in Interactive Workspaces. *User Interface Software Technology*, 2002, pp. 227-234.
17. Johanson, B., S. Ponnekanti, C. Sengupta and A. Fox. Multibrowsing: Moving Web Content across Multiple Displays. *CHI*, 2001, pp. 346-353.
18. Monty, R. and J. Senders. *Eye Movements and Psychological Processes*. Lawrence Erlbaum Associates, Hillsdale, New Jersey, 1976.
19. Rekimoto, J. Pick-and-Drop: A Direct Manipulation Interface for Multiple Computer Environments. *UIST*, 1997, pp. 31-39.
20. Rekimoto, J. and M. Saitoh. Augmented Surfaces: A Spatially Continuous Work Space for Hybrid Computing Environments. *Proceedings of the ACM Conference on Human Factors in Computing Systems*, 1999, pp. 378-385.
21. Román, M., C. Hess, R. Cerqueira, A. Ranganat, R. Campbell and K. Nahrstedt. Gaia: A Middleware Infrastructure to Enable Active Spaces. *IEEE Pervasive Computing*, 2002, 74-83.
22. Simmons, T. What's the Optimum Computer Display Size? *Ergonomics in Design*, 2001, pp. 19-24.
23. Sommerich, C., S. Joines and J. Psihogios. Effects of Computer Monitor Viewing Angle and Related Factors on Strain, Performance, and Preference Outcomes. *Human Factors*, 43 (1), 39-55, 2001.
24. Sousa, J.P. and D. Garlan. Aura: An Architectural Framework for User Mobility in Ubiquitous Computing Environments. *IEEE Conference on Software Architecture*, 2002, pp.
25. Streitz, N.A. and e. al. I-Land: An Interactive Landscape for Creativity and Innovation. *CHI*, 1999, pp. 120-127.
26. Swaminathan, K. and S. Sato. Interaction Design for Large Displays. *Interactions*, 1997, pp. 15-24.
27. Tan, D. and M. Czerwinski. Effects of Visual Separation and Physical Discontinuities When Distributing Information across Multiple Displays. *Interact*, 2003, pp. 252-255.
28. Woodworth, R.S. The Accuracy of Voluntary Movements. *The Psychological Review, Monograph Supplements*, 13, 1-114, 1899.

Analysis of User Behavior on High-Resolution Tiled Displays

Robert Ball and Chris North

Center for Human-Computer Interaction,
Department of Computer Science,
Virginia Polytechnic Institute and State University,
Blacksburg, VA 24061
{rgb6, north}@vt.edu
http://infovis.cs.vt.edu

Abstract. The use of multiple monitors for personal desktop computing is becoming more prevalent as the price of display technology decreases. The use of two monitors for a single desktop has been shown to have performance improvement in several studies. However, few studies have been performed with more than three monitors. As a result, we report an observational analysis of the use of a large tiled display containing nine monitors (in a 3x3 matrix). The total resolution of the large display is 3840x3072, for a total of 11,796,480 pixels. Over the course of six months we observed the behavior and actions of five users who used the display extensively as a desktop. We relate our observations, provide feedback concerning common usage of how people do and do not use the display, provide common scenarios and results of interviews, and give a series of design recommendations and guidelines for future designers of applications for high-resolution, tiled displays.

1 Introduction

Historically, large high-resolution tiled displays have been reserved for control rooms and large government facilities. However, using multiple monitors for one computer is becoming more common in both business and home life as monitors become less expensive and more research is done on productivity gains. With a small amount of extra effort and cost, a single computer can operate several monitors. For example, Microsoft Windows easily supports up to 10 monitors on a single machine.

Tiled displays, with greater numbers of pixels, have the potential to increase the quantity and granularity of displayed information. They allow more information, more applications, and high-resolution images and visualizations to be viewed. Along with additional screen space, they pose problems of being physically larger, more difficult to navigate, and often have bezels between tiled monitors that distort the image (see figure 1). A bezel is the plastic covering around the edges of the monitors.

Our motivation for this paper is to assess how large, high-resolution, tiled displays help individuals or small groups of users with everyday tasks, such as word processing, programming, and viewing images. Our goal is to gather initial basic evidence about how users adapt to the increased screen space and larger physical size of the displays, how they utilize the space and strategically organize their work, how they deal with the bezels between tiles, and the benefits and difficulties they have.

M.F. Costabile and F. Paternò (Eds.): INTERACT 2005, LNCS 3585, pp. 350–363, 2005.
© IFIP International Federation for Information Processing 2005

Fig. 1. Picture of the tiled display used in this analysis

In our analysis, a number of people extensively used a tiled display to view high-resolution images, GIS data, and perform rudimentary tasks such as using word processors, email clients, and spreadsheets over the course of six months.

This paper differs from other studies on large displays in two ways. First, this paper looks at the use of large, high-resolution displays, not just physically larger displays such as projectors. Second, this paper evaluates the use of such a display for a long period of time, not just for 30 minute to 1 hour segments. In this paper we explain previous work, our analysis method, key observations, and a list of suggestions for user interface designers.

2   Previous Work

A variety of studies have been performed on large screens and multiple screens to compare their effectiveness to that of small or single screens. Figure 2 visually shows the different categories of research on different types of displays. In general, there are two independent variables that researchers look at: physical size of the display, and resolution (total number of pixels, not pixel density) of the display.

2.1   Standard Projectors and Monitors

Several studies have suggested that the increase of the physical size of a screen helps with memory. Lin, et al. [11] suggests that an increase of one's field of view increases one's sense of presence and memory. Raja, et al. [12] suggests benefits of being surrounded by large low-resolution screens (CAVE) when dealing with data visualization (information visualization).

Tan et al. show how performance on a large low-resolution screen can be better than a conventional small screen even at the same resolution. They show that with the same visual angle participants in a study were able to perform better on a large screen compared to a single monitor for both spatial performance [17] and 3D virtual navigation [16]. However, large, low-resolution screens have the problem that they can only show the same amount of data as small screens because they have similar resolutions. As a result, the data on the screen is simply enlarged.

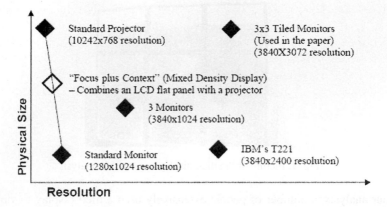

Fig. 2. The configuration space of displays, showing how several instances relate to each other with respect to physical size and total resolution (number of pixels)

Terri Simmons [14] conducted a study comparing performance on different-sized monitors (17 inch to 21 inch), with slightly differing resolutions. His results were unsurprising in that they suggest that people perform faster with the largest monitor, and slightly higher resolution, as opposed to the smaller monitors.

2.2 Two to Three Monitors

Czerwinski et al. [4] explain the current state of performance measurements and explain that their own study showed conclusively that participants using a multi-monitor configuration affording increased resolution (3 monitors wide) performed better than on a single monitor. Tan, et al. [18] also show how retention can be increased by using extra screen space to display different images in the user's periphery to help recall more from a particular task session.

Some studies have also shown that gender can have an effect with spatial performance. Some studies by Czerwinksi, Tan, and Robertson show that the effects of an increase of field of view can offset gender bias [5]. Their findings indicate that women need a wider field of view than men to achieve the same performance.

2.3 Mixed Density Displays

In a unique study, Baudisch et al. [3] performed an experiment using their "Focus plus Context" screen to study the effects of having a small LCD screen embedded within a large projection screen (both standard low-resolution). In effect, they created a focus+context visualization using pixel density distortion instead of spatial distortion.

2.4 Large Tiled Displays

Few studies have reported findings on large tiled displays. Guimbretière, et al. [8] describe new interactive techniques for direct pen-based interaction on high-resolution displays, and reviews several other interaction techniques. A preliminary study on basic perceptual and navigational techniques shows that for fine-detailed information it is faster to find and compare information on high-resolution displays than low-resolution displays [1]. Our behavioral analysis falls into this category. Since little is known about how people use large high-resolution tiled displays, we chose to observe a variety of people using it for common tasks in a longitudinal study.

3 Analysis Method

In order to analyze everyday use of physically larger, high-resolution displays, we first constructed a 3x3 tiled display of LCD flat panels approximately 37 inches (94 cm) tall and 44.4 inches (113 cm) wide. We put the display on a standard desktop table approximately 30 inches (76 cm) off the ground. We then allowed a variety of people to use it, and observed its use over a six month period.

With modern plug and play technology, creating a large high-resolution tiled display takes relatively little expertise and is fairly low cost. Modern operating systems such as Windows and Linux have built-in support for multiple monitors.

Our tiled display was constructed from nine 17" Dell monitors affixed to a wooden frame (see figure 3). We used one computer, a Dell Optiplex GX270, to support all nine monitors. In addition to the dual head AGP video card that came with the computer we installed four additional PCI video cards. All video cards were NVidia GeForce FX 5200.

Figure 3 show various aspects of the tiled display. The picture on the left shows a side angle of the monitors as mounted on a wood frame. The same display could also be mounted on a supported wall or other more permanent place. However, we desired to have a display that could be easily relocated or adjusted. The picture on the right shows a front view of the tiled display with one of the monitors removed to show the underlying frame.

Five participants used the nine-monitor tiled display for at least three months in a form of time sharing. These users will be referred to hereafter as power users. One power user was designated time to use the tiled display during morning and early afternoon and used it as his primary workspace while the other four participants routinely reserved time during all other hours of the day and night on a first come, first serve basis as a secondary workspace. Each of these participants were researchers that used the tiled display for a variety of reasons from normal daily activities such as reading/writing email, browsing the Internet, writing papers, programming, viewing images, and running experiments. Each of these participants was a graduate student conducting research in computer science. In addition, there were four undergraduate users that used it for collaboration work in setting up experiments that also used the display on a first come first serve basis after the first three months of the analysis.

Fig. 3. The left figure shows the side view of the tiled display, showing how the monitors connect to the frame. The right figure shows the front view of the tiled display, with one monitor disconnected to show the underlying wooden frame. The sole computer powering the display is shown to the right.

During the six month period we performed three experiments on how well individuals performed and interacted on the tiled display at different configurations – using one, four, and nine monitors. Although these experiments were not done for the purpose of this paper, we were able to take our observations from the different experiments and apply them here. There were approximately 65 individuals that participated in the three experiments. Each of these individuals spent between 30 minutes to an hour interacting with the tiled display. Our analysis also draws from our experiences with dozens of other people that were given demonstrations. Such people included high school students, people from the community, government officials, business professionals, and university students, faculty and staff.

Our observations in this paper are a result of a broad range of observations with the above mentioned people, ranging in form from the following methods:

- Direct observations as individuals interact with the tiled display.
- Formal interviews involving question and answer.
- Informal interviews to let the user talk about their experience without asking leading questions.

4   Observations

This section enumerates key observations during the course of our analysis. In this section we only highlight common benefits and disadvantages.

4.1   Performance

From the previous work section, many researchers have shown the advantages of having larger displays. Several researchers have shown that larger displays improve performance with different tasks including multi-tasking [4], spatial orientation [17], and general usability [14][7] to name a few.

Our observations show that users clearly referenced back and forth between primary tasks and secondary tasks on a regular basis. Also, interviews show that people reported having to do less window management and were more satisfied with the display as a result.

Our experience concurs with [7], showing that having a larger high-resolution desktop decreases the time switching between applications, allowing for a decrease in cognitive load. When a user is performing a specific task they often have the need for supporting tasks. For example, when writing a document, support information (e.g. references) is often needed. By having extra screen space, a user is capable of simply glancing at the supporting information instead of the need of switching between applications. By not performing extra virtual navigation, less concentration is lost.

Another example of decreased cognitive load is viewing large images and visualizations. Many large images are too large for the entire image to be shown at once on one or two monitors, requiring additional navigation to see the entire image. With a large display there often is no need to navigate the image as the entire image can be seen all at once.

4.2 More Viewable Information at Once

With an increase in screen space comes many different opportunities for increased spatial positioning. With one monitor, users can only have a few applications viewable at a time. In contrast, with multiple monitors there arises an opportunity to not only have more applications viewable, but have each of those applications taking up more screen space than is available to one monitor.

Our actual observations show that users often take advantage of the increased screen space. An observed scenario that represents common usage among most users follows: A user logs into the machine running the large display. He then opens up his remote desktop (for the purpose of using his own email client) and positions it in the lower-right monitor as he always does. He then opens a word processor to continue writing a report. Over the course of writing his report he also opens three Internet browsers, and a spread sheet. All the different opened applications, including the remote desktop, support his main task of writing the report. The different applications each occupy a monitor with the remote desktop always remaining in the lower-right monitor and his word processor always being in the middle monitor.

This actual scenario taken from a session of a user that uses the display as a secondary workplace accurately represents most users. Key results from observations and interviews show that users prefer to use the middle monitor for their main application, surround the main application with support applications, and maintain constant positioning for certain applications (e.g. email, instant messengers, etc.).

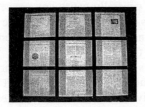 

Fig. 4. The picture on the left shows three documents being displayed at once for easy comparison. The picture on the right shows a user's programming environment.

Two examples of using the increased screen space can be seen in figure 4. The picture on the left shows three PDF applications open side by side. Three different conference papers are viewed simultaneously allowing for easy comparisons of the documents. The picture on the right is a picture of actual usage while programming. Several applications can be seen including a command prompt for compiling purposes in the center, several programming editors, and one file explorer.

4.3 Categorization of Regions

After time, users tend to dedicate certain regions of the screen for certain applications. For example, one power user always positioned his email client application on the middle-right monitor while another power user always positioned his remote desktop (to get to his email client) on the lower-right monitor. After a period of time, users tend to develop preferences of where certain applications should be located. This preference of positioning applications in the same place relies on people's spatial memory abilities. This use of spatial memory is similar to the concept explored in Robertson's Data Mountain [13].

This use of positioning of applications was also observed to follow categories. In other words, power users tended to keep many personal or nonessential tasks in the same regions of the screen. Email, calendars, and instant messengers tended to have positions that were further away from the center of the screen and more toward the periphery.

4.4 Focus on Center

The primary task at any given time with the tiled display tended to be in the center column of the tiled display. It was observed that if a secondary application that was initially further away from the center column became more important and commanded more attention then it tended to be moved closer to the center column.

4.5 Bezel Adaptations

Bezels, the plastic border separating monitors, are often considered a distraction to users. Current LCD technology makes it very difficult to construct a large tiled display without bezels (figure 5). However, interviews from users and observations appear to differ as to how much a distraction they are. Key results from observations and interviews show that users do not generally like bezels, but that they use them very efficiently to their advantage to align, segregate, and differentiate applications.

With a single monitor the bezel does not generally cause any concern and usually goes unnoticed. On the other hand, the bezels around tiled monitors are usually one of the first things that people notice. The thickness of the bezels between monitors is a limiting factor on how close monitors can be tiled.

Interviews from users indicate that bezels are an inconvenience, irritation, and a point of frustration. Users have pointed out that bezels can distort the size of a document or an image. This distortion gives documents or images an artificial lengthening and can be confusing. As one user explained, "It can be really tough to mentally block the bezels out of your mind."

However, our observations show that bezels tend to help users quickly segregate applications between monitors. A common scenario for all users, whether first time users or power users of the display follows: Users first open the primary application in the center monitor. Users then either maximize the application to fill the center monitor with the maximize button or drag the application by hand to approximately fill the center monitor. All subsequent applications that are opened are usually maximized in a monitor that is not in use.

Fig. 5. Comparison of an image with and without bezels splitting up the image

Only the most experienced user, the power user who used the display as a primary workspace, consistently used applications across bezel boundaries. The primary power user gradually became more comfortable crossing bezel boundaries and was able to grow accustomed to text and images being separated by bezels over a course of months. In contrast, our observations and interviews show that most users were able to use bezels to separate applications from the first time they used the display.

4.6 Adjustment Period - From Small to Large

Key difficulties that new users struggle with are moving beyond the paradigm of one monitor, finding the cursor, using space efficiently, and other unpredicted behavior from diverse applications.

One example scenario that took place is when a student showing a demo on the tiled display had two applications open. One application was a control panel driving the other application, which showed a visualization of data. The student had nine monitors of screen space, but only utilized one of them. The student had the two applications maximized to fit on the center monitor. He constantly brought the control panel to the front (over the visualization application), modified one or two parameters and then brought the visualization back to the front. As the student had eight other monitors to use, he could have easily used another monitor to show and interact with the control panel without the need to block the visualization window. When asked about it, the student responded with surprise and simply had not considered the possibility of spreading out the application over multiple tiles.

Adjusting to the larger display takes a variable amount of time. For example, moving beyond the paradigm of using only one monitor usually took less than an hour while finding the best strategies to finding the cursor usually took weeks to learn.

As learning how to use the display takes time and is not instantaneous, a new user may get discouraged by actual loss of productivity at first. As a few applications no longer appear to act as they did, or do not act as the new user would think, the experience can be frustrating. Unlike the noted publications that claim performance boosts with larger displays, new users are not necessarily given a lengthy tutorial at the onset for each application they might use, as was the case in the publications.

4.7 Adjustment Period - From Large to Small

Although not intuitive, we have also noted a definite frustration when using smaller-sized displays after using the larger display for an extended period of time. One scenario from the primary workspace follows: After approximately four months of using only the tiled display as his desktop he encountered a time when he had to prepare for a presentation on a laptop. When trying to change a small program and write notes about the changes, he encountered a great deal of frustration when not being able to see both the program he was editing and the word processor he was using for taking notes at the same time. It was also necessary at the time to have several more applications open at the same time on the laptop and he found himself frustrated and confused as to how to best manage the different applications.

When using only one monitor one power user reported "feeling cramped." Another power user said, "[I would] get really close to the laptop to make it bigger." Users had unlearned their previous organization strategies and had difficulty relearning them.

4.8 Collaboration Usage

Through the increase in actual screen size, more people can gather around the display at once. However, although the display affords many uses for collaboration, we observed only the following collaborations in the order of most often to least often: image viewing, visualization viewing, Internet browsing, and document writing.

A normal scenario of collaboration usage is two people working on a document. One person drives the display while the other person is on the right of the first person. Most of the applications are found in four monitors to the bottom and right as any applications found on the left of the person driving the display are hard to see for the person on the right. These users found it helpful to be able to review long documents together by stretching the windows vertically across multiple monitors and pointing with their hands to portions of the text.

4.9 Maximizing an Application

There are several assumptions that operating system and application writers have made that do not hold true for displays of more than one monitor. Many different assumptions about having only one monitor have been made that appear anti-intuitive with several monitors.

For example, a scenario that occurred with almost every user follows: When a user tries to maximize an application across all nine monitors, they usually click on the "maximize" button in the top right-hand corner of the application. Most users expect to have the application maximize to the full screen size. However, what occurs is that the application maximizes to fill up a single monitor.

4.10 Dialogue Boxes

A problem with applications is their dialogue boxes. Dialogue, or pop-up boxes, may appear any where on the screen space and may be difficult to find. Using only one monitor it is often trivial to find a dialogue box as there is very little area for it to appear. However, with multiple monitors, such as the tiled nine that we used, it can be difficult to find or even notice that a dialogue box was opened if not expecting it. It has been the experience of some users to feel frustrated when suddenly it appears that their application is no longer responsive, when in fact there exists a modal dialogue box some where in the screen space that requires attention.

4.11 Navigational Issues

Interviews with users, including power users and new users, indicate that losing one's mouse cursor on the screen is common and frustrating. To find the mouse cursor on the screen, users would perform one of the following common strategies, listed from most often used to least often used: Quickly moving the mouse back and forth in a small area to use human visual motion detection, simply scanning the entire display until finding it, and moving the mouse to an extreme edge (e.g. moving the mouse down and right until finding it in the bottom right corner of the screen).

Using even two monitors at a time can lead to confusion when using a mouse. Simply put, users can easily lose track of where the cursor is on the screen. For nine monitors the problem is further exacerbated. Several ideas have risen to solve this problem, such as increasing the visibility of the mouse cursor at all times [3].

Windows XP has a feature that helps the user to detect the mouse when it is lost. By pressing and releasing the "CTRL" key without any other key combination, an animated circle grows and shrinks around the cursor. However, our experience shows that such a feature is practically useless on a large tiled screen because the user has to be looking at the correct display tile to detect the animation. For example, if a user is looking for the cursor at the top right of the display and the cursor is in the bottom right then the animated circle cannot be seen by peripheral vision.

However, in general, less navigation is required in large high-resolution displays. By having a larger display, the needs to navigate at all are decreased. For example, as mentioned before, looking at a large high-resolution image, the entire image, or a greater percent of the image can be shown at once, decreasing the need to navigate as much as on a smaller display. The same is also true for documents, web browsing, etc.

4.12 Physical Size and Layout

A disadvantage of the high-resolution tiled display is its cumbersome physical size. Common questions such as where one should put the display are nontrivial. Often office space is considered sacred and not easily granted at many businesses and universities. Although most tiled displays are tiled LCD's (liquid crystal displays), and thus take up less room than CRT's (cathode ray tubes), most tiled displays would not fit in office cubicles.

Also, there is a potential for additional physical stress and pain. If using a keyboard or a mouse for extended periods of time cause problems, then it is also logical that extended use with a large display may cause physical injury or discomfort to the neck or back although we have not observed any problems yet. More research is needed in this area before concluding anything about physical stress caused by large displays.

5   Suggestions and Recommendations

Through the course of our analysis we have learned many things about the use of large high-resolution displays. In this section we discuss several suggestions and recommendations as guidance to future designers.

5.1   Number of Monitors and Physical Layout

Although biased, we concur with [7 that people should use two monitors as a minimum for each desktop. As a maximum, the layout and size of the monitors come into play. For example, experimenting with different layouts we found that six monitors side by side, is very difficult to use. However, the same 6 monitors can be used very efficiently when stacked on top of each other in a 2x3 array.

Several papers including [7] show performance increases with as few as two or three monitors. Also, Simmons [14] shows that just modestly increasing the resolution helps. [17] shows that just increasing the physical size is better for spatial performance. In general, abundant literature exists to show that modern desktop displays are inadequate for maximum performance.

As we have shown previously, we believe that unless a user has needs to view large images on a constant basis, no more than six monitors is recommended. This recommendation is based on physical size of the monitors and not on resolution density. However, with curved displays the number of useful monitors may increase. Our preliminary studies show that having a curved display helps people use more of the outer regions of the display.

5.2   Notification Systems and Controls

Small notifications are not seen on a large, high-resolution display. As a result, we suggest that notifications should be redesigned for large, high-resolution displays. They should be larger, and grouped together in a central area instead of being spread out. For example, an application that has notification systems and controls that are located on the edges of the application might be acceptable for one monitor; however, for large high-resolution displays the controls or notification systems might be several feet from each other. Also, dialog boxes (e.g. popup windows) should be presented in a more uniform manner [10].

5.3   Use of Bezels

Bezels are the plastic surrounding the outside of monitors. Bezels provide natural separations between applications and tasks and can be regarded as helpful. Currently operating systems hide all knowledge of more than one monitor from applications. However, if applications were aware of where the monitor separations are they could take advantage of that information and display things more intelligently.

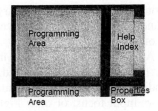

Fig. 6. An example of using bezels to separate work spaces in the Microsoft Visual Studio .NET programming environment

Users can also take advantage of bezels by segregating their work. As explained earlier, users reported using different regions of the screen to separate tasks and ideas. This concept can be taken farther by using bezels to also separate parts of the same application. As briefly mentioned by [7], movable taskbars can increase the amount of available screen space. Also, even with taskbars are not moveable, bezels can be used in such as way to increase work areas as can be seen in figure 6. Internal sub-windows can be maximized to an entire tile, pushing toolbars and supporting frames across the bezel to other tiles.

5.4 Mouse

It is clear that the current state of interaction with computers, with only the mouse as input, is inadequate. Interviewing users of another large tiled display (with 40 tiled displays) from another organization confirms the need. For example, scrolling the mouse across 10 feet of high-resolution screen space is absurd.

Finding the mouse can be problematic. One suggestion is to increase the size of the mouse or the animation finder to be more helpful. In Microsoft Windows' "CTRL" key solution, the animation circle size should be more noticeable and larger as the screen size is larger. It should also be customizable for different sized displays.

For the time being, our recommendation to users for quickly locating one's mouse is to scroll to a corner. For example, if the user chose the bottom right corner of the screen then the user would rapidly scroll down and right. After about two quick scroll movements, the cursor can be found at the desired corner.

Using other interactive techniques, such as laser pointers, pen-based interactions, touch sensitive panels, etc. may be more appropriate than using a mouse for large displays. Unfortunately, these other techniques are either found only in research environments or are prohibitively expensive for common use.

6   Conclusion

Our behavioral analysis shows that a large high-resolution display affords a number of advantages. This section summarizes the broad range of advantages and disadvantages explained in this paper. Advantages include: Improved user performance for task switching or viewing large documents, increased ability to spatially position applications and shortcuts for quick access and recall, bezel adaptations for easy separation of tasks, increased ability to work collaboratively, increased screen space for awareness for secondary tasks (e.g. Email, instant messengers, news, etc.), and enjoyment – interviewed users almost unanimously prefer multiple monitors to one.

Disadvantages include: Adjustment periods (both from one monitor to multiple monitors, and vice versa), more screen space wasted, unpredicted behaviors with software applications including notification systems and dialog boxes, navigational issues with losing the mouse, input focus, or other highlights, and physical size and layout may require more physical strain

Acknowledgements

This research is partially supported by the National Science Foundation grant #CNS-04-23611. This study was also supported and monitored by the Advanced Research and Development Activity (ARDA) and the National Geospatial-Intelligence Agency (NGA) under Contract Number HM1582-05-1-2001. The views, opinions, and findings contained in this report are those of the authors and should not be construed as an official US Department of Defense position, policy, or decision, unless so designated by other official documentation.

References

1. Ball, Robert and North, Chris. "Effects of Tiled High-Resolution Display on Basic Visualization and Navigation Tasks." In *Extended Abstracts CHI'05*, p. 1196-1199.
2. Baudisch, P. Good, N., Bellotti, V., Schraedley, P. "Keeping things in context: a comparative evaluation of focus plus context screens, overviews, and zooming." In *Proc. of CHI '02*. p. 259 – 266.
3. Baudisch, P. Cutrell, E., Robertson, G. "High-Density Cursor: A Visualization Technique That Helps Users Keep Track of Fast-Moving Mouse Cursors." *Proc. of INTERACT '03*. p. 236-243.
4. Czerwinski, M., Smith, G., Regan, T., Meyers, B., Robertson, G., Starkweather, G. "Toward characterizing the productivity benefits of very large displays." In *Proc. of Interact '03*.
5. Czerwinski, M. Tan, D., Robertson, G. "Women take a wider view." In *Proc. of CHI '02*, p. 195 – 201.
6. Furnas, G., Bederson, B. "Space-scale diagrams: Understanding multiscale interfaces." In *Proc. of CHI '95 Human Factors in Computing Systems*, p. 234 – 241.
7. Grudin, J. Partitioning Digital Worlds: Focal and Peripheral Awareness in Multiple Monitor Use. *Proc. CHI 2000*. p. 458-465.
8. Guimbretière, F. Stone, M. and Winograd, T. "Fluid Interaction with High-resolution Wall-size Displays." In *Proceedings of UIST* 2001, 21-30, ACM Press.
9. Healey, C., Booth, K., Enns, J. "High-speed visual estimation using preattentive processing." *ACM TOCHI*, volume 3 (2), June 1996, p. 107 – 135.
10. 10. Hutchings, D., Stasko, J. "mudibo: Multiple Dialog Boxes for Multiple Monitors. " In *Extended Abstracts of CHI '05*. p. 1471-1474.
11. Lin, J., Duh, H., Parker, D., Abi-Rached, H., Furness, T. "Effects of view on presence enjoyment, memory, and simulator sickness in a virtual environment." In *Proc. of IEEE Virtual Reality 2002*.

12. Raja, D., Bowman, D., Lucas, J., North, C. "Exploring the benefits of immersion in abstract information visualization." In *Proc. Of IPT (Immersive Projection Technology)*, 2004.
13. Robertson, G., Czerwinski, M, Larson, K., Robbins, D., Thiel, D., van Dantzich, M. "Data Mountain: Using Spatial Memory for Document Management." *Proc. of UIST '98*. p. 153-162.
14. Simmons, T. "What's the optimum computer display size?" Ergonomics in Design Vol. Fall 2001, p. 19 – 25.
15. Tan, D., Czerwinski, M. Robertson, G. "Women go with the (optical) flow." In *Proc. of CHI '03*, p. 209 – 215.
16. Tan, D., Gergle, D., Scupelli, P., Pausch, R. "Physically large displays improve path integration in 3D virtual navigation tasks." In *Proc. of CHI '04*. p. 439 – 446.
17. Tan, D., Gergle, D., Scupelli, P., Pausch, R. "With similar visual angles, larger display improve spatial performance." In *Proc. of CHI '03*. p. 217 – 224.
18. Tan, D., Stefanucci, J., Proffitt, D., Pausch, R. "The infocockpit: providing location and place to aid human memory." In *Proc. of PUI 2001*. p. 1 – 4.

Interaction and Co-located Collaboration in Large Projection-Based Virtual Environments

Andreas Simon[1], Armin Dressler[1],
Hans-Peter Krüger[1], Sascha Scholz[1], and Jürgen Wind[2]

[1] Fraunhofer IMK Virtual Environments, Sankt Augustin, Germany
ansimon@gmail.com
{armin.dressler, hans-peter.krueger,
sascha.scholz}@imk.fraunhofer.de
[2] Vertigo Systems, Köln, Germany
juergen.wind@vertigo-systems.de

Abstract. Conventional interaction in large screen projection-based display systems only allows a "master user" to have full control over the application. We have developed the VRGEO Demonstrator application based on an interaction paradigm that allows multiple users to share large projection-based environment displays for co-located collaboration. Following SDG systems we introduce a collaborative interface based on tracked PDAs and integrate common device metaphors into the interface to improve user's learning experience of the virtual environment system. The introduction of multiple workspaces in a virtual environment allows users to spread out data for analysis making use of the large screen space more effectively. Two extended informal evaluation sessions with application domain experts and demonstrations of the system show that our collaborative interaction paradigm improves the learning experience and interactivity of the virtual environment.

1 Introduction

Since the introduction of the CAVE [4] over ten years ago, large, projection-based stereoscopic displays have become a commodity item. Wide-screen stereoscopic walls, CAVEs or even bigger theatre-like installations like the i-Cone [18] are an established part of the infrastructure for 3D graphics visualization, not only at research labs and universities, but also in large corporations, in particular in the automotive and in the oil-and-gas industry. Although these systems are large, expensive and difficult to maintain, they have eclipsed the use of small, inexpensive, personal head mounted displays (HMDs) in all but a few application areas. In part this is due to the fact that they are large, single screen displays, allowing multiple users to directly view and share the experience of a virtual environment in a group; all this without the immediate need to make changes to the software or hardware.

The use of head mounted displays for doing real work in a virtual environment certainly is an acquired taste. We would argue that user preference for projection-based displays over HMDs is not just influenced by display quality, but is motivated by collaboration aspects and the learning experience for new or casual users. First-time

M.F. Costabile and F. Paternò (Eds.): INTERACT 2005, LNCS 3585, pp. 364–376, 2005.

users of HMDs get to wear a heavy helmet (smaller, still obtrusive Sony Glasstron-style goggles have a narrow field of view and no stereoscopic viewing), isolating them from their familiar environment and from other people. It is difficult for a demonstrator to teach and guide a new user, since it is hard to know exactly what she really sees and does. For projection-based display systems, instead of experimenting on their own, new users typically join an experienced demonstrator who is guiding them through the environment. At some point the demonstrator may carefully hand over controls, remaining alert to immediately help whenever the learner gets lost. Unfortunately this is where the story typically ends. Although in a projection-based system a group of viewers can share the experience of the virtual environment, in current applications only one user can interact and control the application at a time.

In order to correctly match real and virtual space and to achieve fully correct spatial viewing, the projection of a stereoscopic image must match the exact location of the viewer. This image has to be continuously updated to the viewer's current viewing position and orientation. Since practically all display systems are only capable of projecting a single stereoscopic image, only the one head-tracked user in a display sees a correct spatial image. Other participants in the same display share this view, leading, from the individual user's perspective, to parallax: distortion and a mismatch between the real and the perceived virtual space.

The single head-tracked user in a display is often called the "master user" of the application, and operates specialized interaction devices that are unfamiliar and usually hard to learn. All other participants are practically only looking over the shoulder of the master user, without tools to interact on their own. In typical theatre-like demonstration centers, the master user even sits at a desk outside the display, steering the application from a conventional desktop interface. In this case, the "interface" operates by viewers inside the virtual environment asking the master user at the keyboard to change parameters in the application.

Recently, we have presented two rendering techniques—omnistereo projection [19] and multi-viewpoint images [20]—that allow the projection of different image elements with different perspectives in a single, consistent, stereoscopic image. This allows displaying virtual interaction elements in each user's perspective, correctly aligning real devices and their virtual representations to overcome the parallax problem for multi-user interaction.

Based on the concept of Single Display Groupware (SDG) systems [22][13], we develop a new interaction paradigm for co-located collaboration in large projection-based virtual environments. We apply this concept to the VRGEO Demonstrator, an application for the review of volumetric data sets in the oil-and-gas industry. Following Buxton et. al [3], the overriding issue for the successful use of large displays is ultimately a story about interaction, not displays. For the system to be of value, viewers must be able to create, manipulate, explore, and annotate in the environment. Key goals for the development of our interaction paradigm for projection-based virtual environments are to improve the level of interactivity and the learning experience by introducing a co-located collaborative interface and using common device metaphors in a virtual environment; also we want to exploit the screen space for large virtual environment displays better by introducing multiple workspaces that can be arranged to structure the display volume.

The remainder of this paper is organized as follows: Section 2 introduces techniques to support co-located collaboration in a projection based virtual environment. Sections 3 and 4 present spatial interaction techniques with a 3D tracked PDA and the PDA GUI interface; section 5 discusses related work. In section 6 we present experiences from trials and demonstrations with the VRGEO Demonstrator. Finally, section 7 presents conclusions and discusses opportunities for future work.

2 Co-located Collaboration

We introduce three techniques to support co-located collaboration. Multi-viewpoint images solve the parallax problem for direct interaction with multiple users in a panoramic projection-based display. Multiple workspaces—in the case of the VRGEO Demonstrator boxes containing geoscientific volumetric data sets—allow users to spread out the data over the whole display and make better user of the large display surface. Finally, we introduce PDAs into the interface, to implement a common private interface for each user.

2.1 Multi-viewpoint Images

We use multi-viewpoint images [20], composed out of different image elements projected from multiple viewpoints, to overcome the parallax problem in non-head-tracked applications and to enable multi-user interaction in the i-Cone projection-based display.

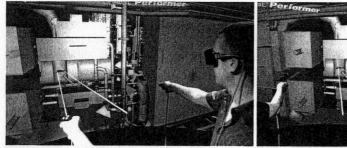

Fig. 1. Left user's vs. right user's view of a multi-viewpoint image: Picking rays align correctly from the respective user's viewpoint

The multi-viewpoint image in Figure 1 is one and the same image. It combines three different viewpoint projections: One for the main scene and one for each of the two users. The main scene, containing engines and pipes, is rendered without head tracking from a static viewpoint centered in the middle of the display. For each of the two users, the user's picking ray is rendered from the respective user's head-tracked viewpoint. This places the picking ray, seen from that user's perspective, in correct alignment with his tracked interaction device.

2.2 Multiple Workspaces

Conventionally, projection-based virtual environments displays like the CAVE are used with a single active scene and a single focus of attention. There are no simultaneous, competing applications, the application complexity is typically quite low, and there is no notion of spatial dividers and of separate workspaces, since there is only one "master user" equipped with interaction devices.

Fig. 2. A group of users working with multiple workspaces in a 240° i-Cone™ display

Large display surfaces are essential for supporting collaborative, or even individual activities [9] because they allow users to simultaneously spread out and arrange several data items. In our multi-user paradigm, we have introduced the concept of multiple work areas in a virtual environment, allowing users to work with multiple 3D data sets side by side, but also allowing them to split into subgroups or work on specific problems independently of each other (Figure 2). In the VRGEO Demonstrator, we use boxes—separate 3D workspaces—each containing one 3D volumetric data set. Inside a box visualization tools like volumetric rendering lenses or texture slices allow to view and analyze different aspects of the data set, set markers and take snapshots. The boxes work as spatial separators and allow users to arrange and partition different visualizations. They are a spatial analogue to windows in a conventional 2D interface and allow users to easily grab a coherent part of the scene and move it next to another for comparison.

By introducing workspace boxes, we establish multiple foci of work in a panoramic environment. Users use this by forming different work areas and alternating between different solutions, using the large screen area for direct comparison and as a visual memory. Alternatively, the large screen and the spatially distinct work areas allow a larger group to split up temporarily to analyze different sub-problems, enabling users to alternate between collaboration and individual work and preparation. The boxes also form a clear visual background and separation for the individual data sets, avoiding confusion, and allow users to easily layout a spatial arrangement of data sets around them.

2.3   Public vs. Private Display

Introducing PDAs into a large immersive projection display as an additional individual and private display for each user, introduces the separation of public and private data into our virtual environment (Figure 3). It also solves the problem of separating the representation of the application state and the individual contexts and modes for each user [13] by allowing us to put all the individual application state information on each user's PDA interface.

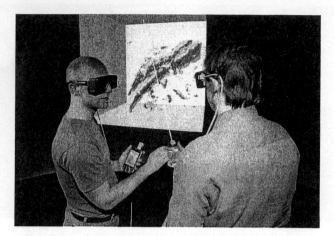

Fig. 3. Teaching the interface in a collaborative environment

In some situations, for example reviewing numerical or textual data on the PDA or to follow the interaction of a user, we would like to share the information on another user's PDA directly. We have implemented a function to explicitly share the state and "jump" to the interface pane of another user's PDA, joining the private interfaces by connecting both PDA interfaces (Figure 4). When a user jumps to the interface of a colleague, he will share the state and display of the other PDA's GUI. In shared mode, both PDAs will behave exactly the same, if one user is changing a value with a slider, the other user's slider will move simultaneously to the same value. Both users stay connected (when one user changes a pane or selects an object, the other PDA follows) until one of them explicitly disconnects.

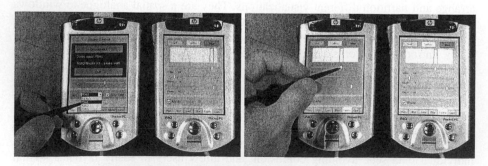

Fig. 4. Connecting (*left*) and sharing (*right*) two PDA interfaces

Joining the PDA GUIs allows transparency for other users for the manipulation of complex interfaces on the PDA (temporarily sharing the private interface) and allows users to very effectively teach each other the application.

3 3D PDA Interface

Tracking of 3D position and orientation of the PDA as part of the spatial interface enables us to integrate the device as a functional prop into the three-dimensional virtual world. This allows us to relate to interface metaphors of common devices in the real world, making the interface accessible to new and infrequent users of virtual environments.

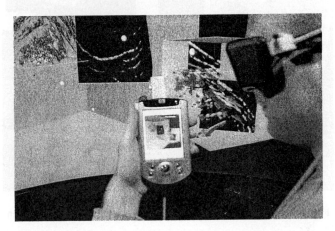

Fig. 5. Taking a snapshot using the PDA like a *real camera* in the virtual environment

3.1 Snapshot Camera

The use of a tracked PDA as a virtual environment display device of its own was proposed by Fitzmaurice [6], who has investigated the use of Chameleons. Chameleons are small-screen devices that provide a small but mobile window to a virtual world behind the screen. The position and orientation of the device is used to determine the view-frustum into the virtual scene. In our application, we use the same technique to render an image to the PDA, using it as a virtual camera to provide a natural and direct interface to take snapshots of the virtual environment. The PDA screen acts as the finder, reacting to the orientation and position of the PDA in the same way as a real camera would (Figure 5). As with a real camera, the user can frame the image, zoom and take a snapshot by pressing a button. The resulting image is transmitted and stored locally on the file system of the PDA, providing the user with a personal copy.

3.2 Virtual Light

In similar fashion to using PDA's display as a camera finder, we use the backlight of the screen to act as an interface to a moving virtual light source. For rendering, a directional light with a 180° light cone is attached to the position and orientation of the tracked PDA, facing the same direction as the light cone of the PDA screen's real backlight. In order to highlight some close-up object, the user turns his PDA around—with the screen facing into the scene—and shines *virtual light* onto the rendered scene. This interaction produces a very strong illusion and suspension of disbelief [5], since the backlight on the PDA acts on real objects (e.g. the users hand) in the same way as the virtual light source acts on virtual objects.

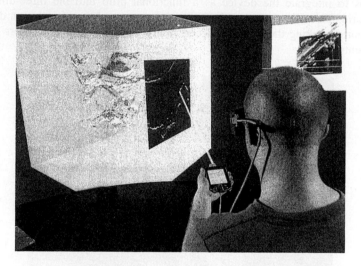

Fig. 6. Using the PDA as a virtual laser pointer for object selection

3.3 Laser Pointer

The tracked PDA is also used as a pointing device for 3D object selection by ray casting [10], extending a virtual lightsaber [11] from the tip of the PDA. For selection, the user points the lightsaber at a virtual object (Figure 6) and clicks the top-left PDA button. This 3D object selection will also set the state of the PDA GUI and places the corresponding 2D interface pane on the PDA on top. Laser pointing is also a common device metaphor from the real world—digital projector remote controls typically incorporate real laser pointers in a similar fashion.

3.4 Scaled Grab Motion

We want to place objects at a comfortable viewing distance and spread them out over a large field of view; therefore, users need to be able to perform interaction and object motion at a distance in an effective way. In a collaborative environment, we cannot use travel to move larger distances inside the virtual environment, since this would disturb other users—similar to collaboratively browsing a rotating postcard stand—instead, we have to be able to select (grab) distant objects and pull them close or push them back with minimum effort.

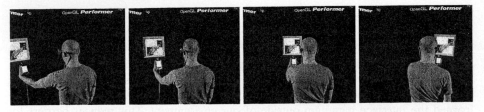

Fig. 7. Large object motion with Scaled Grab: Note alignment between PDA and virtual object

Selecting an object by ray casting with the PDAs Laser Pointer automatically places a pivot point at the intersection of the lightsaber and the object's surface. After selection, a user can drag the selected object, holding the top-left PDA button and moving the PDA.

For effective dragging and moving objects over large distances, we have developed a virtual motion technique we call Scaled Grab. Scaled Grab combines image plane selection and motion techniques and is similar to world-in-miniature (WIM) object manipulation [23]. Unlike Mine's Scaled-world Grab [12], which scales down the world to bring the selected object within reach of the user, Scaled Grab scales up the users range of hand motion, to extend to the selected object (Figure 8). In this respect it behaves like a WIM, but without introducing an explicit miniature representation of the object. Scaled Grab rather uses the PDA as a handle on the selected object instead.

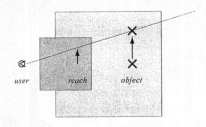

Fig. 8. Scaled Grab to extend the user's reach

The distance of the selected pivot point on the object's surface to the user's eye point determines the scale-ratio for hand to object motion. This ensures constant alignment in the image plane of the virtual object's motion with the tracked point on the PDA. Note that in Figure 7 the tip of the PDA and the workspace box on the screen remain aligned in the image, although the box is about 3m away from the user. Also, using this technique, the ratio between the subtended angle—the relative size in the image plane—of the PDA and the dragged object remains constant. This behavior gives very good and consistent feedback of the synchronized motion between object and handle (PDA) to the user.

Rotation of virtual objects presents a challenge, since rotation with a far away center of rotation can result in large, unwanted motion of the object. This is known to lead to confusion since the object can *rotate* out of the field of view and magically disappear. With Scaled Grab we use the pivot point that the user has placed by selecting the object as center of rotation and rotate the virtual object around a meaningful, user-defined center.

4 PDA GUI Design

The primary motivation for introducing PDAs as an interface into our collaborative virtual environment is the same as for Myers et. al [13] who have introduced PDAs into single display groupware (SDG) systems: The PDA as personal device allows us take advantage of the fact that users are familiar with the device and have already learned the interface paradigm outside of our environment. This reduces barriers for new or infrequent users to join a team.

When using a PDA-based GUI interface in a virtual environment, we have to consider a number of issues that influence the design of the PDA interaction. Major issues concern the viewing of the PDA screen. Shoemaker [17] has noted that using a PDA display forces a rapid change in the focus of attention over different displays and over a wide depth range, when a user is manipulating or reading something on the PDA screen in his hand and has to look back into the environment to see the result. In our case this environment even consists of a stereoscopic virtual image on a screen. Stereo glasses—needed for stereoscopic viewing of the projected images—further reduce the contrast and readability of the PDA's screen.

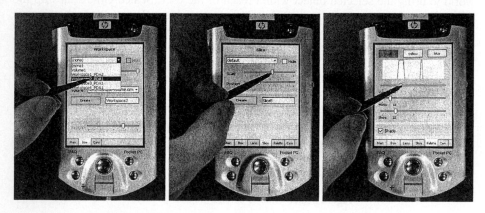

Fig. 9. PDA GUI organized in simple hierarchically ordered panes

Another issue concerning the design of the PDA GUI is the possible disruption of context in the interface. The 3D ray-casting object selection allows the selection of objects by pointing directly at them in the virtual environment. Displaying the corresponding PDA interface for the selected object (just as if the user had selected this object with the GUI on the PDA) produces a jump in context on the PDA that may be unexpected to the user, since she is not looking at the PDA while performing the selection.

With the concerns for readability and the need for a simple, clear design to enable the user to follow external context switches as a result of the 3D selection interface, we have structured the PDA GUI in simple, static panes that are selected through tabs. Only a single tab set, with tabs aligned with the lower edge of the screen, is used (Figure 9). An additional bold headline on top of each pane indicates the name of the currently selected pane and makes external context switches better visible. Tabs order the panes in a sorted, hierarchical fashion that corresponds to the object relationships in the application: After creating a new workspace Box, panes for Lens, Slice and Palette open up and are ordered directly after the Box tab of the workspace pane.

5 Related Work

Stewart et al. [22] have coined the term Single Display Groupware (SDG). Stewart's KidPad [21] is a SDG environment for kids, where multiple mice are connected to a single computer. It uses "local tools" on Pad++, a drawing program, where each tool does exactly one thing. Background studies showed that children often argue and fight when trying to share a single mouse, but when using separate mice, cooperated more effectively. The Pebbles project by [13] connects multiple PDAs to a main computer in a SDG scenario. In the applications, the PDAs are primarily used to control multiple mouse and keyboard input to whiteboard applications. Greenberg has studied the role of public and private information in a SDG application with PDAs [7]. In this system, mobile individuals carry PDAs and can create personal notes at any time. When these individuals gather in a meeting, they can selectively publicize these notes by transferring them to the shared display. Rekimoto has developed a similar system involving a shared display and private mobile devices [18]. Rekimoto introduces mobile computers and PDAs as common, spatially tracked interaction devices into his shared environment. With this system, a PDA is used as a tool palette and as a data entry palette. At any time a user can "pick and drop" private information from the PDA with a special stylus and place it on the shared, public display.

Most of the work on co-located collaboration in virtual environments focuses on head mounted displays (HMDs) since they are inherently suitable for multi-user display. Studierstube [24] was one of the first systems to show the potential of AR for co-located collaboration. [14] describes an HMD based Augmented Reality (AR) system which allows multiple participants to interact with two- and three-dimensional data using tangible user interfaces. The system is based on a tabletop metaphor and uses camera-tracked markers on paper cards or props to provide a tangible interface to virtual objects. As in [15] PDAs are used as a data entry palette, using "pick and drop" to drag virtual objects onto the table.

Only a few multi-view projection-based displays, to allow multiple users to interact and collaborate in a virtual environment sharing a common viewspace, have been developed. These systems allow the display of more than one stereoscopic image, displaying individual perspective views for each user to overcome the parallax problem. The duo-responsive workbench [1] is a multi-view display system that supports two users by sequentially displaying four images on the screen of a responsive workbench. Both users wear tracked data-gloves and use direct manipulation techniques to select, grab and move objects. A static menu, shared by both participants is attached to the edge of the tabletop surface. Other multi-view projection displays use a spatial barrier to achieve multiple views in a shared view-volume, but on different screens. The PIT [2] consists of an L-shaped arrangement of two screens, with each user looking at one of the screens. With the Illusion Hole [8], a view barrier separates the different views of users standing around a small hole over a workbench, each user looking through the hole at a different part of the workbench screen. Both papers concentrate on the technical aspects of the displays and do not discuss interaction or collaboration.

It is interesting to note, that previous virtual environment scenarios deal exclusively with outside-in viewing in round table situations and concentrate on the use of direct manipulation interfaces. We use the PDA GUI interface independently and concurrently to a 3D interface on the shared screen, combining PDA meeting style applications with a multi cursor SDG application. This is a more complex paradigm than PEBBLES [13], similar to the situation of [15] who in turn primarily connects devices through data, and not through their interface. For our application, we combine two very different application and interaction paradigms—3D spatially tracked vs. PDA GUI—in a single environment.

6 Experiences and Observations

We have presented the VRGEO Demonstrator on numerous occasions to groups of three to eight visitors. In two 60 minute evaluation sessions, four members of the VRGEO consortium, representing several mayor oil companies, have used the demonstrator. These evaluations sessions have retuned the most valuable feedback.

In the current set up, because of limitations with the Polhemus Fastrack tracking system, we use two fully tracked PDAs, and one additional non-tracked PDA.

There is practically no need to explain the interface of the application at all. Most visitors would grab the PDA and immediately start exploring the interface on their own. We would only explain the use of the top-left PDA button as the select/execute button and demonstrate the conceptually more complex "joining" of two PDAs.

As expected, learning of a new interface in a co-located environment is much more relaxed than in a single user environment. New users would take their time to look and browse the interface, not feeling rushed even in a demo situation. We would frequently observe users discussing functionality with each other. Sharing of the PDA interface through the "jump" function has been effective for teaching, since it allows two users to closely follow each other's actions. Test users liked this function a lot, but report minor problems: they would assume that they were connected when they were not, completely missing the other user's actions. Connect and disconnect functions, placed on the Main pane, are currently too slow to "jump" to the neighbors PDA GUI just to have a peek.

With the introduction of separate workspaces that can be spread out in the display, we have seen that users make much better use of the large screen space, and tend to spread out various boxes over the whole field of view. The ability for a single user to separate a part of the visualization, adjust the viewing parameters to clearly bring out and mark some detail, and quickly rejoin the discussion, changes the possible work flow in this type of application. Tedious adjustments do not have to be performed while the whole group is watching.

In our evaluation scenarios, it was difficult to actually observe true active collaborative behavior. With the oil-and-gas experts we could see that while one user was moving and turning the data set around, another would adjust the color palette of the same volume to segment out new structures. With non-experts we would observe more individual viewing of the data and exploration of the interface and less interaction. Occasionally users would "steal" workspace boxes from each other.

The Scaled Grab technique has proven to be very effective and completely transparent to the users. We did not receive any negative feedback on this technique; most users were completely unaware that there was something special going on until we switched the scaling off.

Most users would handle the PDA in their non-dominating hand, to be able to use the PDA GUI with the pen in a normal fashion. For some users this would lead to problems with the 3D PDA interface since they had to handle ray-based object selection and Scaled Grab motion with their non-dominating hand. Although we have not seen severe problems with this issue, the interface seems to favor ambidextrous users.

Overall, using the i-Cone in a collaborative fashion delivers a very different experience than the conventional single user paradigm. Feedback about this was enthusiastic. Although the ergonomics are difficult (handedness problems, tethered tracking, problematic button placement on the iPAQs) the overall effect of introducing the PDA interface into the virtual environment has been very positive.

7 Conclusions and Future Work

We have introduced an interaction paradigm for co-located collaboration in large projection-based display systems. Based on the concept of SDG systems, it introduces PDAs as personal interface for users in a virtual environment. Informal observations show that the introduction of co-located collaboration improves the overall user experience and interactivity of the virtual environment. Despite some ergonomic problems with the use of the tracked PDAs, the introduction of common devices and common device metaphors, together with sharing a common interface in a co-located application environment, seems to have a very positive effect on the learning experience of new and casual users.

In the future we will use a wireless optical tracking system, allowing us get rid of all the wires and to support a larger number of active users. With a clip-on mechanism for the optical tracking target, users would be able to bring their own PDAs into a virtual environment session. We would like to develop a more complex application scenario based on our interaction paradigm that encourages more immediate collaboration between users on a demanding collaborative planning and design task.

References

1. Agrawala, M., Beers, A., Fröhlich, B., Hanrahan, P., McDowall, I., and Bolas, M.: The Two-user Responsive Workbench: Support for Collaboration through Individual Views of a Shared Space. Proc SIGGRAPH'97. ACM Press (1997) 327–332
2. Arthur, K., Preston, T., Taylor, R., Brooks, F., Whitton, M., and Wright, W.: Designing and Building the PIT: A Head-Tracked Stereo Workspace for Two Users. Proc. 2nd International Immersive Projection Technology Workshop (1998)
3. Buxton, W., Fitzmaurice, G., Balakrishnan, R., and Kurtenbach, G.: Large Displays in Automotive Design. IEEE Computer Graphics and Applications (2000) 68–75

4. Cruz-Neira, C., Sandin, D., DeFanti, T., Kenyon, R., and Hart, J. The CAVE Audio-Visual Environment. ACM Trans. on Graphics 35,1 (1992) 65-72
5. Coleridge, S. (1817). Willing Suspension of Disbelief. Samuel Taylor Coleridge, ed. Jackson, H. (1985) ch 14, 314
6. Fitzmaurice, G. Situated Information Spaces and Spatially Aware Palmtop Computers. Communications of the ACM 36,7 (1993) 38-49
7. Greenberg, S., Boyle, M. and LaBerge, J.: PDAs and Shared Public Displays: Making Personal Information Public, and Public Information Personal. Personal Technologies, 3, 1 (1999)
8. Kitamura, Y., Konishi, T., Yamamoto, S., and Kishino, F.: Interactive Stereoscopic Display for Three or More Users. Proc SIGGRAPH 2001. ACM Press (2001) 231–240
9. Lange, B., Jones, M., and Meyers, J. Insight Lab: An immersive team environment linking paper, displays, and data. Proc CHI'98 ACM Press (1998) 550-557
10. Liang, J., and Green, M. JDCAD: A highly interactive 3D modeling system. Computers & Graphics, 18,4 (1994) 499-506
11. Lucas, G. Star Wars. Motion Picture (1977)
12. Mine, M., Brooks, F., and Sequin, C. Moving Objects in Space: Exploiting Proprioception in Virtual Environment Interaction. Proc Siggraph'97 (1997)
13. Myers, B., Stiel, H., and Gargiulo, R.: Collaborations using multiple PDAs connected to a PC. Proc ACM CSCW'98. ACM Press (1998) 285–294
14. Regenbrecht, H., and Wagner, M.: Interaction in a collaborative augmented reality environment. Proc CHI 2002. ACM Press (2002) 504–505
15. Rekimoto, J.: Pick-and-Drop: A Direct Manipulation Technique for Multiple Computer Environments. Proc ACM UISF'97. ACM Press (1997) 31–39
16. Rekimoto, J.: A Multiple Device Approach for Supporting Whiteboard-based Interactions. Proc CHI'98. ACM Press (1998) 18–23
17. Shoemaker, G.: Supporting Private Information on Public Displays. Proc CHI 2000. ACM Press (2000) 349–350
18. Simon, A., and Göbel, M. The i-Cone™ – A Panoramic Display System for Virtual Environments. Pacific Graphics '02 (2002) 3-7
19. Simon, A., Smith, R., and Pawlicki, R. OmniStereo for Panoramic Virtual Environment Display Systems. Proc IEEE Virtual Reality'04 (2004) 67–73
20. Simon, A., Scholz, S. Multi-Viewpoint Images for Multi-User Interaction. Proc IEEE Virtual Reality'05 (2005)
21. Stewart, J., et al.: When Two Hands Are Better Than One: Enhancing Collaboration Using Single Display Groupware. Proc SIGCHI'98. ACM Press (1998) 287–288
22. Stewart, J., Bederson, B. and Druin, A.: Single Display Groupware: A Model for Co-present Collaboration. Proc ACM CHI'99. ACM Press (1999) 286–293
23. Stoakley, R., Conway, M., Pausch, R. Virtual Reality on a WIM: Interactive Worlds in Miniature. CHI'95 (1995) 265–272
24. Szalavari, Z., Schmalstieg, D., Fuhrmann, A., and Gervautz, M. Studierstube: An Environment for Collaboration in Augmented Reality. Virtual Reality, 3-1 (1998) pp. 37–48

Using Real-Life Troubleshooting Interactions to Inform Self-assistance Design

Jacki O'Neill, Antonietta Grasso, Stefania Castellani, and Peter Tolmie

XRCE, 6 Che de Maupertuis, 38240 Meylan, Grenoble, France
{name.surname}@xrce.xerox.com

Abstract. Technical troubleshooting is a domain that has changed enormously in recent years. Instead of relying on visits from service personnel end users facing technical problems with machinery, for example computers and printers, can now seek assistance from systems that guide them toward an autonomous solution of the problem. Systems that can be offered to them are wide in their range, but typically fall either in the category of Expert Systems or searchable databases that can be queried with keyword searches. Both approaches present advantages and disadvantages in terms of flexibility to address different levels of user expertise and ease of maintenance. However, few studies explicitly address the issue of how best to design for a balance between guidance and user freedom in such systems. In the work reported here an office equipment manufacturer's call centre was studied in order to understand the mechanisms used when *human* agents guide users toward a resolution. The overall aim here is not to reproduce the agent behaviour in a system, but rather to identify which interactional building blocks such a system should have. These are assessed in relation to the existing online knowledge base resources offered by the same company in order to exemplify the kinds of issues designers need to attend to in this domain.

1 Introduction

In recent years a number of systems which support end-users in self-troubleshooting problems with their machines have become available. This is especially noticeable amongst companies where there is a heavy service commitment and a concomitant desire to minimize the costs associated with that [5] [8] [9]. There is therefore a strong impetus towards providing better tools for users who are willing to try to solve autonomously the problems they face. In large part troubleshooting activities are based on using technical expertise to identify causes and ways to proceed beyond the evident symptoms people might be witnessing. Because of this many of the proposed tools and systems are based on Artificial Intelligence techniques, which allow the machine to embody a model of the domain and let the user navigate within it, even where they lack any deep technical knowledge. Examples of such systems are the SACSO system [6], based on Bayesian networks and the NaCoDAE system [1], based on Conversational Case Based Reasoning. A wide review of Intelligent Help Desk systems is provided in [7].

M.F. Costabile and F. Paternò (Eds.): INTERACT 2005, LNCS 3585, pp. 377–390, 2005.

These systems, while different in the particular models they choose to use, nonetheless all share the assumption that to build a model based upon their explorations of the domain is the correct way to proceed. Thus they all exhibit an engine that embodies a description of how symptoms and faults could be correlated that is directly derived from such a model. This underlying modelling presents several advantages, for example offering the possibility to guide the users toward the solution through a number of fixed steps. However, these AI-based systems often appear too rigid, since the interaction model often forces the user to follow the predefined steps without easy shortcuts. Sometimes motivations such as wanting to make one system fit all and keep down the costs of different implementations results in the same system needing to address a range of expertise from qualified experts to novice users. In such cases the rigidity of an AI-based system can be even more problematic. A useful example of this kind of problem, where a case-based reasoning system proved to be inadequate for the use of call centre troubleshooters is presented in [10]. At the opposite end of the scale, following advances in full-text Web search engines, systems have been proposed that are based on Information Retrieval techniques where the content is structured in terms of cases and solutions. An example of such a category of systems is Eureka [3] where a database of tips for service engineers can be accessed through the entry of a query. Benefits of the latter approach appear to be the possibility for a user to express a query in his or her own words, together with the possibility of freely navigating the content without a rigid structure. An additional benefit of such systems is that they can easily be dynamically modified by field engineers or troubleshooters, in order to insert new content expressed with their own wording and fitting exceptional cases that were not originally taken into account by the knowledge base designers. Aside from a number of drawbacks to such solutions we will be discussing throughout the course of this paper, other possible downsides are a certain redundancy and heterogeneity of style in their contents.

In addition to the above some systems have been proposed that make use of both the AI and the Information Retrieval approaches. This is the case with the MCRDR system discussed in [7], where a case-based reasoning system is complemented with keyword search to provide both quick navigation and guided interaction when the user is unclear about appropriate keywords. This latter approach is certainly promising as it seems to offer the best of the two approaches: guidance and flexibility.

In this paper we aim to contribute to the design of such hybrid systems by drawing upon real-life observations of troubleshooting activities and the insights that have grown out of them. In particular we will be proposing that design in this domain needs to properly attend to the way such interactions currently proceed. This is not to be undertaken simply to replicate every feature of current human-human troubleshooting interactions. Rather, it is that this is the only way to effectively identify the interactional building blocks that a system *will* have to support if it is going to truly meet the requirements of online users.

In order to meet this objective we investigated both the keyword based online Knowledge Base of a leading supplier of office equipment and the telephone interactions between troubleshooters and users at its European support centre. Our initial step here was to gain access to customers' troubleshooting practices and understandings by undertaking an extended ethnographic study of the work of troubleshooters (see [3] and [4] for an a exposition of the rationales for conducting these kinds of studies in a design context). The troubleshooters in question work through problems and the solutions with customers whilst at the same time drawing upon a knowledge base to underpin their expertise. The knowledge base we are referring to here has recently been made available to customers so that they can troubleshoot for themselves without calling technical support or an engineer. It is typical of many databases, consisting of a repository of information which the customer accesses through a word search. Although troubleshooters have access to some additional materials the knowledge base used by both troubleshooters and online users is to all intents and purposes the same and utilises the same search mechanisms. Analysis of the work of the company's troubleshooters therefore offered two important elements. First of all it gave us access to the methods and reasoning customers and troubleshooters engage in together to successfully troubleshoot failed devices. Secondly, it gave us the opportunity to explore the ways in which troubleshooters might be providing a resource for successfully *working the knowledge base* that stands above and beyond the knowledge base itself. Our other activity was to explore how *non-expert* users engage with the company's knowledge base in order to try and fix problems for themselves. This offered us a way to both compare on-the-phone and self-assisted troubleshooting with access to the same online resource, and to assess the ways in which the knowledge base currently provides support in its own right.

In this paper we will be focusing on the ways in which observations derived from these studies have highlighted fundamental interactional features of troubleshooting that have clear implications for how the existing keyword-based system could be enhanced to support its online users. To do this we will begin with a brief outline of the online resource. This will be followed up with a discussion of the various findings from our study, findings that indicate a number of issues to do with the tension between people's practices and the existing organisation of the knowledge base. These will be shown to centre upon the character of problem descriptions, terminology, the ways in which problems and causes get constituted, and how solutions actually get located and implemented. This will be followed by a number of suggestions for how the design of systems might be informed by these insights and might locate ways of supporting both structure and flexibility at the same time.

2   The Knowledge Base

The troubleshooting knowledge base we have been referring to here is an online resource provided to the customers of a major office equipment supplier in order to facilitate the resolution of problems with their machines without recourse to phoning a troubleshooter or calling out a service engineer. It is made accessible from the support pages of the company's website, and both customers and troubleshooters can use it as a resource for finding solutions to their technical problems.

The knowledge base is organized around products, each providing a similar entry page where two main troubleshooting areas are provided: search area and a sidebar with links to related resources (see Figure 1). Using the search area customers can issue searches using multiple keywords. Tips for searching are also provided on the page, giving advice about how best to formulate queries, e.g. 'Install toner cartridge', 'Paper tray not recognized', and 'Read the meter'. In addition to this main interaction area, a sidebar provides links to resources like procedures and manuals, as well as an entry point to the content of the knowledge base for pre-categorized problems.

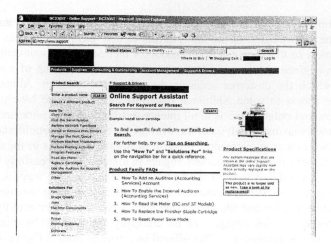

Fig. 1. The Troubleshooting Knowledge Base

3   Users' Practices and the Organization of the Knowledge Base

As we have already outlined, the customers of the office equipment company are provided with both an online knowledge base and access to one of several large support centres which they can telephone in order to request help from troubleshooters. The troubleshooters they are passed on to then seek to establish the nature of the problem and talk the customer through to possible solutions. The cornerstone of our initial investigations into the possible issues in this domain was a three week ethnographic study of troubleshooting work in one of these support centres, responsible in this case for the whole of Europe. Troubleshooters across a range of teams were observed intensively throughout their working day in order to be able to record and acquire a deep understanding of how troubleshooting is accomplished in actual working practice. Data collected included field notes, audio records of the troubleshooters side of the conversation and video of the troubleshooters interaction with the knowledge base and other tools. Multiple interactions with customers, across a range of problems and products, were witnessed from beginning to end, and analysed in order to uncover the way those troubleshooting interactions are organised. Out of this we evolved a clear picture of both how troubleshooting stands as a methodic accomplishment, and the problematics that the actual practice of troubleshooting over the telephone must overcome. One example of such a problematic is that customers are often not by the machine when they call in and in many cases the only solution is to give piecemeal instruction as a customer goes to and fro to their machine. Another problematic of this order is the need for troubleshooters to resolve their own inability to see the troubled device. In this paper, however, we shall be concentrating upon the implications of how troubleshooting is organised as an interactional practice for those situations where people can only interact with *troubleshooting systems* rather than other human beings. In the course of this we shall be directly considering how these might relate to the same company's existing provision of such support, their online knowledge base. These considerations are underpinned by our own observations of the use of that knowledge base by non-expert users and of its use by expert troubleshooters in the support centre.

3.1 Symptoms, Causes, Faults and Solutions

Our first observation here relates to the way in which customers encounter and describe problems with their devices in terms of symptoms. When they make contact with troubleshooters they then work through the problem together making use of symptoms *and* causes. Symptomatic description is a commonsense way of reasoning about a trouble in the absence of the necessary technical knowledge, e.g. 'the copier machine isn't stapling'; 'the machine blocks up with paper'. Symptomatic understanding can be contrasted with the technically oriented 'fault' understanding displayed in the knowledge base. The following is a simple example offered to illustrate the distinction between faults and symptoms. When taking a car to a garage there are some faults an owner can just plainly see and report to the mechanic. For example, it is possible to see that the headlight glass and bulb are smashed. However, owners often also report things like 'it makes a knocking noise when I go round the corner'. The owner may have no idea what fault could cause such a noise so they report the symptom. Not possessing a technical understanding of cars and their faults, the owner resorts to a commonsense symptomatic description of the car's adverse behaviour. With sufficient knowledge they might well describe the fault in the same way as for the smashed headlight. So, the very fact they describe the matter symptomatically displays the absence of such knowledge, making it unlikely they would be able to reason through from the symptom to the cause. The mechanic, of course, when asked by a colleague about the same problem, will not in all likelihood answer 'it makes a knocking noise when it goes round a corner'. Instead he or she might say something like 'the kingpin is worn'. The very act of describing the fault here displays a technical knowledge of cars.

When using the knowledge base customers are being asked to act like the car mechanic and make those orders of interpretations without necessarily possessing the relevant expertise. In one exchange during our observations we witnessed the following description:

> **Customer**: it screws it up ... in the paper tray.

However, when using the same starting point and searching for 'screwed up paper' in the knowledge base, it brings up 42 results, the first seven of which are shown in the screenshot in Figure 2.

None of these obviously describe the problem, but it is possible that 1, 2, 3, or 4 might be the issue. However, from neither the titles nor the solutions beneath them is there any information on what the printer would do when it has that problem. That is, would it screw up the paper? The only way to discover whether one of these is applicable is to try all the suggested steps for each of these to see if they solve the problem.

Troubleshooters work to *mediate* between the symptomatic reasoning deployed by customers and the organisation of the knowledge base. With customers they will happily engage with and use symptomatic accounts themselves, but when it comes to using the knowledge base they use the requisite technical search term that they believe may lead to the fault giving rise to the symptom. For example, when a customer described a squealing noise from her device the troubleshooter was able, through further symptom

g & Outsourcing   Account Management   Support & Drivers

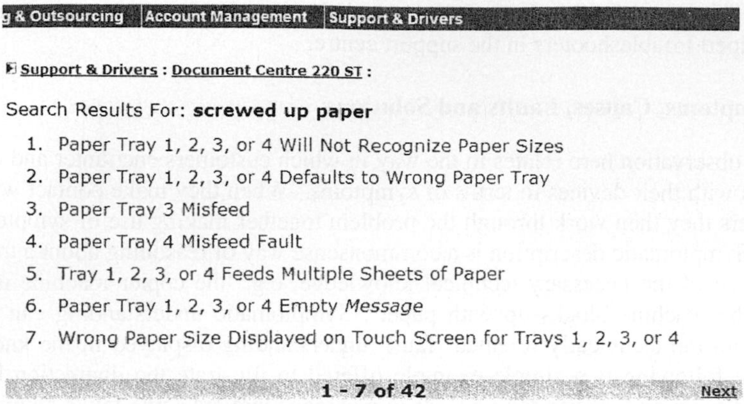

▶ **Support & Drivers** : <u>Document Centre 220 ST</u> :

Search Results For: **screwed up paper**

1. Paper Tray 1, 2, 3, or 4 Will Not Recognize Paper Sizes
2. Paper Tray 1, 2, 3, or 4 Defaults to Wrong Paper Tray
3. Paper Tray 3 Misfeed
4. Paper Tray 4 Misfeed Fault
5. Tray 1, 2, 3, or 4 Feeds Multiple Sheets of Paper
6. Paper Tray 1, 2, 3, or 4 Empty *Message*
7. Wrong Paper Size Displayed on Touch Screen for Trays 1, 2, 3, or 4

1 - 7 of 42   <u>Next</u>

Fig. 2. First seven results for "screwed up paper"

elicitation, to come to the conclusion that the fault resided in the processor. By entering 'processor' into the search field the troubleshooter was able to bring up the requisite solution. Utilising their technical knowledge of devices troubleshooters are able to turn everyday commonsense symptomatic descriptions into the necessary technical vocabulary of the knowledge base. Troubleshooters are then able to select the most appropriate terms to enter into the knowledge base from the multiple symptoms described by customers. At the same time, troubleshooters are able to translate knowledge base instructions into symptoms which the customer can look for. They mediate between the commonsense, symptomatic *and vernacular* understanding of problems displayed by customers and the technical understanding of machine faults displayed by the knowledge base.

3.2 Vernacular and Technical Terminology

As we described above customers use vernacular terminology whereas the terminology of the knowledge base is highly technical. Machine parts are referred to by their technical names, e.g. 'duplex module', 'finisher', 'upper paper path', 'document feeder rollers', and so on. In addition, technical terminology is also used to describe the faults that occur, such as 'spooling', 'postscript errors', or 'guest authentication pass code lockout error'. When customers phone in the troubleshooters can act as translators between them and the knowledge base. However, if customers are using the knowledge base on their own they must already have the right kind of terminology available to them. This applies to both searching the knowledge base and interpreting the results of their searches. The use of a technical vocabulary is not limited to obviously technical language; it is also manifest in the fact that vernacular terms are given a technical meaning in the context of the knowledge base. For example, what is the difference between a black line and a black band? When does a line become a band, and vice versa? The importance of this question can be seen if one uses 'lines' to refine a search within the 'image quality' field offered by the knowledge base. This brings up 45 results, towards the end of which one finds results that include the term 'bands'. However, searching for 'bands' instead brings up five results all of which relate directly to bands. Lines and bands are obviously considered different image quality problems as can be seen when selecting 'Black Lines on Copies From the Glass Only' which produces the following solutions:

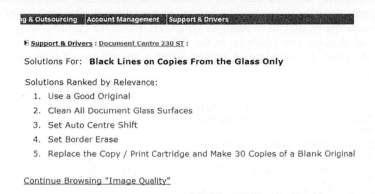

Fig. 3. Results for Black lines

Selecting 'Black Bands on Copies From the Glass Only', however, leads to just these three solutions instead:

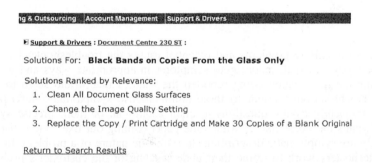

Fig. 4. Results for black bands

Only some of the solutions are the same for both of the options, thus lines and bands have a precise and different meaning in the technical parlance of the knowledge base. Reasoning technically about the matter may enable an engineer to distinguish different faults and the different appropriate actions to be taken depending upon whether the mark is a line or a band, but that distinction is not one that is available to customers in their everyday encounters with technology. Here, what turns on the distinction between a line and a band may not be readily apprehended.

3.3 Constituting Problems and Causes

The customers and the troubleshooters have to build up a description of the problem and its range of causes between them because the problem the customer is encountering is not immediately available to troubleshooters. Instead they have to elicit the character of the problem through their interactions with the customer and the customer's reported interactions with the machine. Customers do not simply describe problems. Instead a customer's telling of problems may have several aspects. They offer up symptoms that need to be resolved with technical descriptions. Wrapped around such symptoms there will be other information that may be redundant from a troubleshooter's point of view. In addition, problems may have multiple symptoms, which the customer may not necessarily tell all at once. For example, in the following extract C describes that there's a jam, that the paper is not going in properly, that it doesn't sound right, and that it is making a noise.

> *Troubleshooter*: Hi Shan how can I help you then
> *Customer*: it's the high capacity feeder
> *TS*: Yeah
> *C*: it says there's jams but there's not
> *TS*: Right
> *C*: When we put the paper in
> *TS*: Um hmm
> *C*: and it's as if it is not going in properly
> *TS*: Yeah
> *TS*: You You're talking about where the tray actually lifts itself up doesn't it?
> *TS*: Um and can you tell me when you look in is the tray still lying flat or is it er a bit off does it look as though it's skewed by any chance?
> *TS*: It does look? Ok I just wonder if we can sort that out now
> C: And it doesn't sound right
> *TS*: Yeah
> *C*: It's making a noise

In order to constitute problems and potential causes the troubleshooter has to work with the customer to both reconfigure symptoms in appropriate ways and to uncover from within the information being reported the features that would seem to be most relevant. Troubleshooters orient to these commonsense symptomatic descriptions of problems frequently asking questions to elicit additional, or more precise symptoms such as "what's the noise like", "what's the paper coming out like", etc. That is, they will readily use symptomatic descriptions to refine the nature of a problem. In addition the troubleshooters work to refine their understanding of the customer's problems by asking 'when' or 'where' questions which may require the customer to carry out tests on the machine. For example, a commonly asked question is one designed to determine when the problem occurs. For example, if a problem occurs when printing from the glass the operator may ask, 'does the problem occur when using the document feeder as well?'. Customers may need to carry out tests on the machine to answer these questions, having reported only their initial impression of the problem (e.g. they were printing from the glass, so they knew this was where the problem occurred). The answers to such questions help troubleshooters to narrow down the problem space.

If one takes in comparison the resources currently offered by the company's knowledge base they are evidently more limited. Rather the customer locates solutions through searching the knowledge base. These searches can be effected through the use of keywords or phrases or via a side bar which specifies pre-categorised problems such as 'image quality'. This side bar can be used for category searches but these tend to have the disadvantage of producing large numbers of results. As an example, for one machine, selecting 'image quality' produces 113 results. When it comes to using keywords or phrases we have already seen how the technical terminology can have an impact. Furthermore, the knowledge base does not allow for a ready concatenation of symptoms. Instead, it searches on each symptom individually. If one is searching in a category such as 'image quality', adding a new symptom from another category (e.g. 'noise') leads to results which are difficult to interpret in the light of the symptoms. Indeed, as we shall see below, the search results often bear little apparent relationship to the search term. Nor does the knowledge base help with the reformulation of problems. It does indicate some questions which could be used to refine the list of causes. However, these are not clearly presented as questions, but rather as options within a mass of other possibilities which may not even all appear on the same page.

3.4 Locating and Implementing a Solution

Customers are not, of course, unthinking automatons blindly following the advice of troubleshooters. Instead they use their own knowledge and understandings of the machine and its troubles to make sense of the troubleshooting procedure. Thus troubleshooters must offer 'visibly' good advice to customers that is relevant to the problem at hand. One way of doing this is by talking about causes. Causes may be brought into troubleshooting sessions for a number of reasons, e.g. educating the customer, but also crucially as a means of demonstrating that the advice they are giving is good advice and relevant to the problem. They can be used as a way of persuading sometimes reluctant customers to troubleshoot. In the observations of troubleshooting work troubleshooters were often explicitly asked to account for their proposals in these terms, e.g.:

> *Customer*: why should that work then? Will it clean it?
> *Troubleshooter*: Exactly yeah yeah could be a build up of dust or something like that you know

In another example we can see how a customer is given pause by advice that at first sight seems to contradict their commonsense expectations about what a reasonable procedure should consist in:

> *Troubleshooter*: 'Ok have you cleaned the pick pad and the pick roller on the machine? ...in the tray there's a pick pad and pick roller that need to be cleaned basically that's what um takes the paper out of the tray and if there's dirt on them then it won't actually pick the paper out of the tray'
> [troubleshooter directs the customer to the location of the pick pad]
> *TS*: Ok? So what we do need to do is urm basically clean this pick pad and there's also a roller then that er kinda comes down on top of it (.) ok?
> [troubleshooter instructs the customer in cleaning the pick pad]
> *TS*: yeah Ok and then once you've got that done we need to do the very same with the actual roller that corresponds to the pad that takes the pa the paper out ok? So
> *Customer*: Ok let me get a bit of tape
> *TS*: Sure
> (pause)
> *C*: OK done that
> *TS*: Ok so what I want you to do now is if you you can put the paper tray back in
> *C*: in?
> *TS*: Yeah you can put the tray back in
> (pause)
> *C*: OK

Here the troubleshooter has told the customer that they need to clean both the pick pad and the pick roller which comes down on top of it. Having completed the cleaning of the pick pad the troubleshooter has instructed the customer to put the tray back in. However, the customer queries this instruction, so the troubleshooter has to confirm it.

After a telling pause the customer acknowledges the instruction and proceeds to carry it out. But why query the instruction and hesitate about it? Here the customer can be seen to be actively reasoning, making sense of the instructions on the basis of his/her commonsense understanding of them. They have cleaned the pick pad and are now about to clean the adjacent roller. This, to them, would appear to be a constituent part of the tray assembly, so putting the tray back does not seem to make sense. However, it does make sense once one is in possession of more technical knowledge for it turns out that the roller is accessed via another area of the machine.

Whilst the solutions offered in the knowledge base might be understood to be premised upon the causes of certain kinds of problems these causes are never made explicit. Thus customers are never able to directly relate the actions proposed to what might be underlying the symptoms they have witnessed and are denied another resource integral to the reasoning about problems they engage in. In addition there is the afore-mentioned and more serious problem of the lack of an apparent relationship between the search query and the presented results. Search results, in this case, frequently do not have the keyword(s) used, or even anything obviously related to the keywords. Indeed they often have no visible relation to the problem to which a solution is being sought. For example, if we look back to Figure 1, which was about a search for "screwed up paper", we can see how it brought up several apparently unrelated results, such as number 6: "Paper Tray 1, 2, 3, or 4 Empty Message".

However, results which are not apparently related, from the customer's point of view, may be related from the technical point of view. In this particular case the proposed solution related to the possibility of a type of jam where some fragments of paper affect the sensor detecting the size of the sheets, resulting in a message for an empty tray. Thus, to understand such relationships between search query and search results the customer must have a considerable technical knowledge. If the customer does not possess such knowledge the results appear nonsensical. Even where results obviously relate to the query, more often than not a search will result in multiple options and it is necessary to choose between them. However, it may be that the differences between the options are not, from a commonsense point of view, readily understandable and again require a technical orientation for someone to understand. To illustrate, in Fig. 5 are the results of a search under 'noise' for one machine:

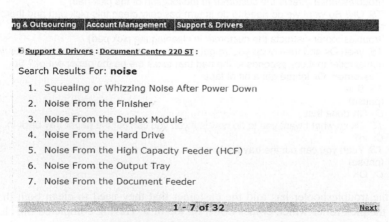

Fig. 5. First seven results for "noise"

The problem with this set of results is that it requires a certain (relatively advanced) knowledge of printers to decide which option to choose. It is necessary to know both what the various parts referred to on the printer are and exactly where the noise is coming from. To address the first issue, the customer could click on the various options in the hope of seeing pictures of them (and thus identifying what, for example, a Duplex Module is). But this is onerous, putting extra work on customers when they could just ring for help. In addition, only one solution here gives any kind of indication of the sort of noise the different problems could make, which could substantially help to narrow down the search for the customer. Indeed in the 'noise from the processor' example above the troubleshooter was swiftly able to identify the location of the noise from the customers' description of its sound. For the customer to select the correct, or even the most likely option from those presented, requires them to be knowledgeable about both the printer and the problem, rather than enabling the customer to explore the problem from the most basic understanding of it. One can see in that case how the organisation of results in this manner does not enable the customers to make use of their common-sense understandings of the problem or even to learn how to couch their problems from a technical viewpoint.

In the above discussion of the work practices of troubleshooters and customers when troubleshooting, and the extent to which these are reflected in the current organisation of this particular company's online support knowledge base, we have indicated a number of potentially significant concerns regarding the design of knowledge bases for customer-only troubleshooting. In the next section we will outline some design recommendations to address these issues. It is important to note that these recommendations could be applied to the *existing* knowledge base through the creation of a new interface, thereby enabling customers to be better supported in customer-only troubleshooting at a relatively low overhead. As is the case here, many such knowledge bases are already up-and-working and available to customers, making the overhead involved in making changes one of the important 'real-world' considerations that must be attended to.

4   Design Recommendations for Knowledge Base Redesign

When we had completed the investigations reported above, we came to the conclusion that the design of keyword based search systems should not simply follow the design of typical Web engines. This is because the vast majority of customers troubleshooting are not able to assess the technical character of their problem or what a solution could look like. They are therefore hugely dependant upon additional guidance and support for the exploration of their problem beyond their constrained understanding of it. We believe that the interaction mechanisms that have been described in this paper can guide the design of such systems by bringing the expertise of the troubleshooters to the user-machine interactions. Using an understanding of these interactions can inform the design of interfaces for knowledge bases, in order to support both guidance and flexibility. This interface would provide mechanisms to better enable the customer to interrogate and interpret the knowledge base and thus solve their problems. This involves taking into account a number of interaction principles:

*   Organisation around a symptomatic taxonomy, where the structure reflects the symptoms and causes of problems, along with their solutions, rather than being

organised on the basis of faults and solutions. Currently troubleshooters translate customers' reported symptoms into search terms appropriate for the knowledge base. As it stands online users have to manage without any such provision. Organising the knowledge base in terms of symptoms and causes would enable a search to be done according to initial symptomatic understandings of the problem.

* Enabling customers to work up an appropriate problem description within the problem space for themselves out of their own understanding of the problem. Nontextual representations of symptoms could be presented where relevant, enabling easier identification of symptoms than through subjective textual descriptors alone. In relation to this it should be possible to add more symptoms and thereby systematically refine their original problem description. In a similar vein, it should be clarified where 'when/where' tests need to be carried out by clearly showing these options to the customer, thus enabling them to narrow down the problem space through testing the device.

* Providing the possibility of searching on either vernacular or technical terms or a mixture of both. This will enable customers to utilise the technical knowledge that they have, but where they do not have such knowledge to be able to describe the problems in the terms they *do* have available to them.

* Providing support for understanding the results of searches, with technical terms being given a lay description or an indication associated symptoms.

* Presenting search results in a way which clearly displays the relationship between them and original search terms that were entered. For instance, if one of the symptoms of a problem is a noise and this underlies why results are displayed, even if the result titles themselves do not appear to be noise-related, then a list of the symptoms you get with that kind of problem could be provided underneath.

* Beyond the search terms themselves, making clear how the results relate to the problem the customer is experiencing. One possibility here is that causal information could be provided that would enable a customer to see just why a set of instructions might apply to their problem. Explanations of what carrying out such instructions does would also help. Symptomatic and causal information could assist in establishing a clear link between symptoms/problems and solutions.

5 Discussion

It is evident that there are a number of usability issues with the kinds of purely keyword based knowledge bases for troubleshooting problems we have been discussing in this paper. It is also evident that on-the-phone troubleshooters do a lot of work to mediate between customer locutions and the content of such resources. This latter observation carries particular force when one considers the fact that customers have to use the knowledge base on their own, deprived of the very resources and competences that provide for the knowledge base being an effective working tool. In that case there is a clear need for self-assisted troubleshooting systems that attend to and articulate around the critical interactional concerns outlined above. To review the issues here: 1) The information in the knowledge base is organised in terms of faults and solutions rather than symptoms. This makes it necessary for customers to have a high level of knowledge about their devices. 2) Troubleshooters currently translate customer symptoms into search terms and, where necessary, enrich this with their own understanding of causes. This is something customers are not necessarily well-equipped to do on their own. 3) On-the-phone customers often report more than one symptom and troubleshooters work to take these into account. However, the knowledge base itself does not provide an intuitive way of collating symptoms or incorporating new symptoms into a search. 4) Troubleshooters work with customers to elaborate and refine problems into something implicative of a solution. In the case of the knowledge base there is little support for this kind of iterative development of the understanding of a problem by lay users. 5) Customers are likely to vary in their technical ability, yet they must all use the same interface. In that case the terminology and information display are likely to prove difficult for novice users and tedious for experts. 6) To use the knowledge base it is necessary both to be able to interrogate it *and* to interpret the results. As it stands results are expressed technically and can require a significant knowledge of devices to interpret them.

All of this underscores the fact that systems using pure keyword-based searches like this one are not truly sufficient to provide the kinds of online support many users will require. However, as we indicated at the outset, heavily structured systems run the risk of proving too rigid, as well as being expensive to construct. In the light of this we have turned our own attention to working on retaining the flexibility of a keyword-based engine, whilst creating a user interface that can properly take into account the interactional components we have discussed. This will be accomplished through means of *in situ* linguistic analysis of user input that is coupled with a linguistic analysis of the contents of the online knowledge base. Amongst other things this provides for things like the reconciliation of symptomatic and technical terminologies, the addition of symptoms, and the iterative refinement of the description of a problem. Thus it can be seen that hybrid systems do not by any means always necessitate going back to the drawing board. Instead there are ways to devise solutions that can stand on top of existing knowledge bases, something that in its own right would seem to merit further research.

Acknowledgements

We thank members of the field work site for their patience, cooperation and help.

References

1. Aha, D., W., Maney, T., and Breslow, L. A. (1998) Supporting Dialogue Inferencing in Conversational Case-Based Reasoning. *Proceedings of EWCBR '98: Proceedings of the 4th European Workshop on Advances in Case-Based Reasoning*, 1998. 262-273.
2. Anderson, R. J., (1994), Representations and Requirements: The Value of Ethnography in System Design. *Human-Computer Interaction*, Vol. 9. 151-182.
3. Bobrow, D. G., and Whalen, J. (2002) Community Knowledge Sharing in Practice: The Eureka Story, Reflections. *Journal of the Society for Organizational Learning*, Vol. 4 Issue 2.
4. Hughes, J, King, V, Rodden, T and Andersen, H, (1994) Moving Out from the Control Room: Ethnography in System Design, in R Furuta and C Neuwirth (eds), *Proceedings of the Conference on Computer Supported Cooperative Work*, October 22-26, 1994. 429-440

5. IDC Report #28967 (2003) *Worldwide and U.S. Software Support Services Forecast and Analysis, 2002-2007*, IDC Publications.
6. Jensen, F. V., Skaanning, C. and Kjærulff, U. (2001) The SACSO System for Troubleshooting of Printing Systems. *Proc. of SCAI 2001*. 67-79.
7. Kang, B. H., Yoshida, K., Motoda H., and Compton, P. (1997) Help Desk System. *Applied Artificial Intelligence*, 1 December 1997, Vol. 11, No. 7, 611-631(21).
8. Kolsky, E, (2004) *MarketScope: E-Service Suites*, 27 February 2004, Gartner Research
9. Ragsdale, J, (2005) Trends 2005: Customer Service And eService. *IT View and Business View Trends*, November 1, 2004, Forrester Research
10. Whalen, J. (1995) Expert systems versus systems for experts: computer-aided dispatch as a support system in real-world environments. *The social and interactional dimensions of human-computer interfaces*. 161--183, 1995.

Feedback from Usability Evaluation to User Interface Design: Are Usability Reports Any Good?

Christian M. Nielsen[1], Michael Overgaard[2], Michael B. Pedersen[2], and Jan Stage[1]

[1] Aalborg University, Department of Computer Science,
Fredrik Bajers Vej 7, DK-9220 Aalborg East, Denmark
{monrad, jans}@cs.aau.dk
[2] ETI A/S,
Bouet Moellevej 3-5, DK-9400 Nr. Sundby, Denmark
michael@netmo.dk, mbp@least.dk

Abstract. This paper reports from an exploratory study of means for providing feedback from a usability evaluation to the user interface designers. In this study, we conducted a usability evaluation of a mobile system that is used by craftsmen to register use of time and materials. The results of this evaluation were presented to the designers in different forms. First, the designers were presented with a traditional usability report. Second, we facilitated a dialogue where the results of the evaluation were discussed. During this process, we collected opinions from the designers on the main strengths and weaknesses of the system. The findings indicate that detailed descriptions of problems and log descriptions of the user's interaction with the system and of system interaction are useful for the designers when trying to understand the usability problems that the users have encountered.

1 Introduction

The purpose of a usability evaluation is to assess the quality of a user interface design and establish a basis for improving it. Usability evaluations and the related activities can help designers make better decisions, and thereby allow them to do their jobs more effectively [25].

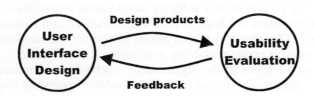

Fig. 1. The interplay between user interface design and usability evaluation.

The interplay between user interface design and usability evaluation activities can in a simplified manner be illustrated as in Fig. 1. The design process produces a vari-

M.F. Costabile and F. Paternò (Eds.): INTERACT 2005, LNCS 3585, pp. 391–404, 2005.
© IFIP International Federation for Information Processing 2005

ety of user interface designs. Usability evaluations are conducted on some of these products, and the results are subsequently fed back into the design process.

There are many different design products that can be examined in a usability evaluation. The most apparent product is the system itself. A usability evaluation based on the final system has been denoted as a validation test [28]. The most typical product that is used for a usability evaluation is a less complete but still operational prototype of the system. This has been denoted as an assessment test [28]. It has also been suggested to use very early design sketches, e.g. paper prototypes. This form of evaluation has been denoted as an exploratory test [28].

The feedback also takes a variety of forms. By far the most typical one is a traditional written report that presents a number of usability problems. Other forms have also been explored, such as meetings with designers, edited videos, re-design proposals, etc.

In this paper we study and discuss different forms of feedback from usability evaluation to user interface design. The main focus is on the qualities of a written report, but we also deal with other means for feedback. In the following section 2, we provide a survey of previous work on the means for providing feedback. In section 3, we describe the experiment that we have conducted in order to examine the relevance of some forms of feedback. Section 4 presents the results of this experiment. In section 5, the results are discussed in a broader context, and section 6 concludes the paper.

2   Related Work

The interplay that is illustrated in Fig. 1 involves two different roles: designer and evaluator. The literature on usability engineering includes a significant body of research that deals with the relation between the designers and the evaluators on an organizational level. We have identified three different ways of structuring the relation between designers and evaluators: (1) the evaluators are integrated in the development teams and conduct evaluations as part of the work in the team, (2) the evaluators form a separate organizational unit within the development organization and they conduct evaluations as a service to development teams, and (3) the evaluators are employed by a different organization and evaluations are outsourced to this organization from the development organization.

The integration approach (1) focuses on the organizational and interpersonal aspects of usability evaluation in a software development organization. Some describe how usability engineers are best adopted and introduced into existing development groups [15, 16]. There have also been efforts to simplify the integration problem by training designers to conduct usability evaluations. Others attend to how organizational focus, on all levels of the organisation, can be directed towards usability [8, 25]. When the organizational setup is based on usability specialists being a part of the development team, there is little need for formalized forms of feedback, because results are taken directly into the development process by the evaluators [2]. The only need for feedback is save the results for later reference.

The separate unit approach (2) has been discussed by many authors. Rohn [27] portrays a usability engineering group inside SunSoft, which provide support and performs usability evaluations *across* the organization. Several authors describe the use of specialized usability groups/departments employing usability professionals [4, 10, 14, 19, 23, 29, 32]. With this organizational form, there is a manifest need for some form of formalized feedback.

The outsourcing approach (3) has had less attention. One of the contributions states that an alternative to being either centralized or distributed is third-party vendors providing services to other companies [6]. There are also documented examples of projects where the evaluation has been outsourced [20]. This approach requires even more formalized feedback compared to the second approach.

For several years, the primary focus has been on the second approach (separate unit). A study of software organizations emphasized a tendency toward separating designers and usability specialists in distinct organizational units. It is also reflected in the amount of literature that deals with this approach. More recently, there has been an increasing interest in the third approach (outsourcing) [6, 20].

The literature on strengths and weaknesses of different forms of feedback is very limited. A reason for this is that most of the research that report on design and evaluation of specific systems employ the first approach (integration). A review of papers that present usability evaluations of mobile systems showed that in all of the 58 papers examined, the designers and the evaluators were the same individuals [21]. Thus in research experiments it is often the designers themselves, who perform the usability evaluation. This approach has both advantages and disadvantages concerning the outcome of a usability evaluation. The advantage is that the evaluators are familiar with the application domain as well as the functionality and design of the system [12]. On the other hand, the lack of independence between the designer and the evaluator might result in a less objective evaluation since the designer is biased towards the system [1].

When the second (separate unit) or third (outsourcing) approach is employed, there is a need for formalized feedback. In that case, most of the literature seems to take for granted that this feedback must be a written report. In Dumas & Redish [7], Rubin [28] and Molich [17] usability reports are suggested as a mean for communicating the results of a usability evaluation. A study has shown that test reports are very common and standardized documents [5]. Muller & Czerwinski [19] also describe the use of reports within Microsoft to share findings and usability engineers' recommendations, by making them available on the company intranet.

When feedback is based on a report, the literature provides some guidance on the structure and contents of that document. A few authors present specific advice on the structure and content of a usability report. The advices presented in Sy [31] are: include the goals of the test, order usability problems according to how critical they are and use bulleted lists, tables, and graphical presentation for quick retrieval of information. Redish et al. [26] and Perfetti [24] mention the following advice: the report should not be too long, present a manageable number of problems, include an executive summary, include severity classifications, include the number of users, who experienced the problem, and include positive findings.

Formalized forms of feedback like the report emphasize the relationship between evaluators and designers. Receiving feedback which describes problems in a system that the designers have personal involvement in, can be a discouraging task. When usability issues in a design are pointed out as being problematic, the designers will sometimes make an effort to defend the design, described as 'design defensiveness' [30]. These problems are often caused by the lack of basic understanding about what usability really is [15:414]. This prompts for the need to investigate the communicative mechanisms at play, when this form of feedback is provided to designers.

3 Experimental Design

In this section we present our experiment. The focus is on the experimental procedure and the structure of the usability reports that were the foundation of the experiment.

3.1 Participants and System

Our experiment involved two groups: designers and evaluators. For the experiment to be as realistic as possible, we collaborated with developers from a software company, who were working on the development of a mobile system. We could involve two developers from the company in the experiment. They were responsible for the design of the user interface of the system we evaluated. They described themselves as experienced interface designers based on their educational background and their work.

The system that was evaluated is a system that is used for registering use of time, materials, mileage, and equipment and for providing online access to the inventory, while working in the field. The system runs on a regular mobile phone with a barcode scanner attached. Most of the registrations and interactions with the system are based on barcodes that are taken from a small book. The target user group is for example servicing engineers, home-helpers, carriers, crafts- and workmen.

Table 1. The structure of the usability reports. Bold numbers denotes chapters and letters sections.

Usability report structure		
1. Summary	**3. Results**	**4. Conclusion**
2. Method	a) Workload (NASA-TLX)	**5. Appendix**
a) Purpose	b) Time used	a) Tasks
b) Procedure	c) Problem overview	b) Interview guide
c) Test participants	d) Detailed description of problems	c) Questionnaires
d) Test procedure		d) Video log-files
e) Location & equipment		e) System log-files
f) Identification & categorization of problems		f) Task solutions

3.2 The User-Based Usability Evaluation

The purpose of the experiment was to examine how usability reports could change the developers' opinions about the major challenges and advantages of the system. The basis was two usability reports that were made as part of a related experiment.

The two usability reports were from two different usability evaluations of the mobile system described above. One of the evaluations was conducted in a state-of-the-art usability laboratory at Aalborg University and the other in a field setting at Vitus Bering CEU (technical high school) in Horsens. Yet the fact that the two reports were from evaluations in different settings is not important for this experiment.

Usability reports are often very extensive, take a long time to produce, and involve a heavy workload for the author [5]. Therefore, it is paramount that the feedback designers receive from such reports are useful. Otherwise, producing the report would be a waste of resources. The structure of our usability reports are illustrated in Table 1. Apart from minor adjustments, this structure is based on Rubin's [28:288-293] description on how to structure a usability report. The enumeration in this structure will be used as a reference later on in this paper, where the developers' opinion on what parts of the report they found the most important is presented.

3.3 Data Analysis and Problem Descriptions

The two usability evaluations were conducted by two different teams of two persons. The entire process of analyzing the data and writing the reports were done by the same persons that conducted the test. The two teams were not allowed to discuss any results or findings before the entire process was complete. In advance, a common severity rating procedure was agreed upon, which was based on three ratings proposed in Molich [17]. Table 2 shows the number of usability problems documented, described and rated according to severity in the reports.

Table 2. Number of usability problems found in both evaluations according to severity

	Field	Laboratory
Critical	15	14
Severe	16	14
Cosmetic	17	6
Total	48	34

As the table illustrates, the number of critical and severe problems found is almost identical in the two evaluations. A more through comparison of the results can be found in [22].

3.4 Developer Opinions

Table 3 shows the 5 steps of the experiment and the involvement of the two developers. In the first step, they were asked to write down their initial understanding of usability and usability evaluation. In addition, their expectations to the usability reports were uncovered. Following this, they were interviewed about their initial opinion on strengths and weaknesses in the system (step 2). Then they were presented with the two usability reports one and a time and in opposite order. The task of describing and explaining strengths and weaknesses in the system was repeated after each of the reports had been read. Each time strengths and weaknesses had been identified, the developer was also asked to rank them relative to each other.

The usability reports from the two evaluations were presented to each developer in opposite order (step 3 + 4) to see if the order in which they were read would influence how the developers perceived them. The developers were kept separate until they made the final common list. This list (step 5) was compiled by the two developers in cooperation. First the final list from each developer was written on a white-board without ratings. Then the developers were asked to discuss and finally agree on a rating for all of the items of the two lists. The rating was important, but it also served the purpose of forcing the developers to discuss and reflect on each item.

Table 3. An overview of the structure of the experiment

Step	Developer A	Developer B
#1	Outline the process for the developers, without revealing details.	
#2	Semi-structured interview on initial opinions on advantages and disadvantages	Semi-structured interview on initial opinions on advantages and disadvantages
#3	Recieve and read the **laboratory** usability report. Semi.structured interview based on step #2. Interview is conducted by one of the writers of the **laboratory** report.	Recieve and read the **field** usability report. Semi.structured interview based on step #2. Interview is conducted by one of the writers of the **field** report.
#4	Recieve and read the **field** report. Semi.structured interview based on step #3. The developer is asked to comment on the usefulness of the reports and the individual parts. Interview is conducted by one of the writers of the **field** report.	Recieve and read the **laboratory** report. Semi.structured interview based on step #3. The developer is asked to comment on the usefulness of the reports and the individual parts. Interview is conducted by one of the writers of the **laboratory** report.
#5	Group discussion where the developers are presented with each others list of advantages and disadvantages. The two developers are asked to agree on a joint list.	

3.5 Conducting and Analysing the Interviews

The developers were interviewed when they made the lists with strengths and weaknesses. Our approach was a semi-structured interview, also known as a qualitative research interview [13]. In this type of interview the interviewer starts out with the most general questions in order to gain some initial knowledge concerning the interviewee. He then moves on to ask follow-up questions, which leads on to specific questions on specific topics. Based on the answers from the interviewee, the interviewer finishes of by asking questions, which indirectly aim at interpreting the statements made.

To analyze the interviews, we used opinion condensation as described by Kvale [13:186-206]. This was done two days after the interviews. Through this kind of transcription, opinions expressed by the interviewees are transformed into shorter and more precise formulations. The intention of the condensation is to be as precise as possible, which means that we maintain the keywords that the interviewee use. Longer pieces of speech are condensed into a single or few sentences. The advantage of opinion condensation is that is can help present a relatively large amount of empirical data in an easy-to-read fashion, while both preserving and clarifying important issues. Opinion condensation can never be considered equal to 'traditional' transcription of the interview, which has significantly higher level of detail and involves less processing of the original text (audio recordings).

4   Results

This section presents the key findings from the experiment. When referring to sections in the usability reports notations like '(3a)' are used, which refers to the section on workload in Table 1. Steps in the experiment are referred to by '(step x)'. Quotes from the interviews are in '*italics*'.

4.1 The Concept of Usability

Before reading the usability reports both developers were asked to express how they understood the term usability. Both of them were able to formulate this in specific terms. Developer A found that 'intuitive' is the word that described it best, but also mentioned 'easy' and 'straightforward' to use, without having to read several manuals. Developer B defined usability as the specific screens in the system, where the design of the screens should target the user and the information presented should be relevant. Additionally, the user interface should be easily understood and nice to look at. The developers stated that usability is and always has been important in their daily work, but that time issues prevent them from analysing and considering different ideas.

Table 4. The problem lists that developer A generated

List	Advantages	Disadvantage
Developer A		
#1 Before Reading Reports	1. Online: The system can provide relevant real time information. 2. Barcode scanners: All interaction begins with the user scanning. 3. No software on the mobile phone.	1. GPRS: Limited coverage. 2. Barcodes are used to interact with the system instead of the mobile phone. 3. Online: problem when no connection is available.
#2 After First Report	1. Online / No software on mobile phone. 2. The use of barcode technology. 3. Customizable.	1. No manual or documentation. 2. Error messages. 3. Handling of logical errors. 4. Input of data through the mobile phone is problematic in relation to target user group. 5. Human resistance towards the system.
#3 After Second Report	1. Online / No software on mobile phone. 2. Customizable. 3. The use of barcode technology. 4. Hardware: mobile phone. Everybody knows it.	1. Human resistance towards the system. Employees feel that they are under surveillance. 2. No manual or documentation. 3. Many barcodes needed to navigate the system. 4. Browser technology/phone restrictions: Input of data through the mobile phone is problematic in relation to target user group. 5. Error messages and handling of logical errors.

4.2 Developers´ View on System Advantages and Disadvantages

Developer A had, especially in the beginning, some difficulties in naming five advantages and disadvantages in the system and actually never succeeded in mentioning five, see Table 4. He was also somewhat reluctant in prioritizing the items in the lists His advantages reflected the arguments that the system was sold upon, whereas the disadvantages reflected the technical issues encountered in the development process.

After reading the first report, developer A did not change his list of advantages noticeable; the points were merely rephrased. On the contrary his list of disadvantages was completely altered as he adapted many of the issues described in the usability report and was able to expand the list to five items and more reflected issues that concerned interaction with the system. Furthermore social implications caused by the usage of the system became evident to the developer.

The second usability report did not have a profound influence on his belief about strength in the system. It made him rearrange two subjects, but also ad the use of daily technology as an advantage. Regarding disadvantages reading the report made him rearrange the rankings in the list and expand and rephrase the descriptions of two subjects.

Table 5. The problem lists generated by developer B

| List | Developer B | |
	Advantages	Disadvantage
#1 Before Reading Reports	1. Hardware: mobile phone. 2. Few scans necessary. 3. Customizable. 4. Online – real time. 5. Simple solution with limited interaction.	1. Screen size 2. Problems with GPRS. Often slow. 3. No manual or documentation. 4. Only works on some types of mobile phones.
#2 After First Report	1. Hardware: mobile phone. Everybody is familiar with the technology. 2. Displays only necessary information. 3. Customizable. 4. Online all the time. 5. The system is simple and uniform.	1. The text describing each of the barcodes. 2. More user education in needed. 3. System reply time. 4. Screen size. Difficult to maintain an overview. 5. System is interpreted differently on different phones.
#3 After Second Report	1. Hardware: mobile phone. Everybody knows it. 2. The system is simple and uniform. 3. Customizable. 4. Displays only necessary information. 5. Online all the time.	1. The text describing each of the barcodes. 2. More user education in needed. 3. System reply time. 4. Screen size. Difficult to maintain an overview. 5. System is interpreted differently on different phones.

Unlike his colleague, developer B was from the beginning able to list five subjects in the list of advantages and four in disadvantages. Most of his initial subjects were kept through the entire process and was only slightly altered and rearranged, as seen in Table 5.

After reading the first report the description of the highest ranking advantage was elaborated and the second highest subject was replaced. His list of disadvantages on the other hand was expanded with a problem of understanding the possibilities of interaction as a new highest ranking problem. The remaining subjects were rephrased and rearranged. Reading the second usability report did not influence developer B enough to make noticeable changes. Only alterations to advantage list the description and ranking of the two last subjects were made.

The elaboration of the joint list, depicted in Table 6, included both developers and gave rise to discussion between the two, where especially the ranking process served as fuel for the fire. The developers discussed each subject on their lists until an agreement was reached. It is noticeable that all the advantages in the final list can be back traced to the developers' initial lists, either in one or both lists. Some subjects have been rephrased but depict in general the same advantage. The story is different when it comes to the disadvantages. Here the two top subject also originates from both developers initial lists, but the third subject is A's final top disadvantage. The two last subjects are derived from developer B's final list and are subjects that were added to list in the experimental process.

Table 6. The joint problem list, which was made in cooperation between both developers

List #4 After Group Interview	Joint List - Developer A & B	
	Advantages	**Disadvantages**
	1. Online – real time.	1. Online: Problems with GPRS.
	2. Customizable.	2. No manual or documentation.
	3. Rely on commonly known technology: mobile phone.	3. Human resistance towards the system. Employees feel that they are under surveillance.
	4. Simple and small barcode-scanner.	4. More user education in needed.
	5. The system is simple and uniform.	5. Error messages and handling of logical errors.

4.3 Usefulness of the Reports

Regarding the reports both developers used the same approach when reading them. Basically the reports were read from the beginning to the end. Occasionally the appendices (5) were used to see the design of the tasks. The log-files (5d + 5e) were not read in their entirety, but were used to examine details concerning a problem, if they were uncertain why a problem had occurred. Developer B stated when asked: '*I used the log-files to gain further insight into what happened*'.

Both developer A and B mentioned that the overview of the usability problems (3c) and the elaborating descriptions (3d) were important in the future work on the system: '*I really like the problem list and it is something I can use concretely in my work*'. The log-files (5d) were good, because '*they describe what they (the test participants) did. It provided a better feel of what they did, why they could not figure it out, and what they did next*'. This shows that log-files are useful, for providing further insight when trying to understand some of the problems in detail.

Log-files can provide almost firsthand insight into what specific actions the user performed. Although they cannot be used directly to resolve the problems, the developers find them important to understand the conditions under which the tests have been conducted (2). This was mentioned by both developers as being very important in respect to how they rate the validity of the evaluation. On the contrary, developer B mentions that: '*The other assessments and similar are quite fun to read, but they are not very useful*', referring to the summary (1) and the conclusion (4). It is important to note that executive summaries may still be important in a more general organizational context.

The developers found the NASA-TLX (3a) method interesting, but they experienced some problems in interpreting tables displaying NASA-TLX results. Developer B found that one of the usability reports, the one based on the field evaluation, lacked a transcription of the debriefing conducted at the end of each test. This was important, since: '*It would provide me with a better insight into the participants' attitude towards the system*'.

During the final interview (step 5), the developers brought up the issue of using video recordings. In relation to some of the problems encountered in: '*the first few minutes, when the user for the first time was presented with the mobile phone*', it would have been beneficial if the video material had been available. This would have given him a chance to see the test participants' first reactions.

When asked, which of the two reports, they found to be the best, they both replied that it was the one they read as the first one. Developer B said that the laboratory-based report was the best because transcriptions of the debriefing following each test were available in the log (5d). He also mentions that: *'it reflects the reality I know best'* and that the field report appears more *'critical'*. Developer A found the field based report to be the best, as he found that it was more detailed in it descriptions of the problems (3d).

4.4 Social and Organizational Aspects

Limited time is an overall issue throughout the interviews and in several occasions the two developers use this as an excuse for some of the existing usability problems. In the beginning, before having seen any of the reports (step 2), developer A said: *'We know that many of the things are there – many things that we would really like to correct if we had the time'*. Numerous times both developers mentioned that designing the user interface is an important and necessary part of their job, but that they cannot spend much time on analyzing and considering different ideas. They are simply too busy and therefore have not got the necessary time. Developer A expressed that this should be taken into account when evaluating the usability of a system.

As developers, they often find themselves thinking in 'states' and 'actions', but according to both developers, the reports can help them to gain further insight into how the users think, when they use the system.

4.5 Evaluation Setup

One of the issues frequently referred to during the interviews was that the users were very inexperienced, and if they were more experienced, the result of the evaluation would have been different. This is probably correct, but it does not imply that usability problems found by relatively inexperienced users do not exist. We see this more as a defensive reaction towards, a perhaps, overwhelming number of usability problems seen from the developers point of view. This is supported by the developers accepting that many of the problems were relevant and should be fixed. When developer A was asked about his general opinion on the evaluations, he replied that: *'Many of the things mentioned have applicability in our further work'* and added that he: *'can relate to the findings and use them positively'*.

Another point of critique presented by the developers was that the tasks were not realistic and that this might have affected the outcome of the tests. According to Molich [18] this is a typical objection raised by developers. Still developer A mentioned: *'I am impressed with how many strange errors the users manage to provoke, which we have never thought of ourselves'*.

5 Discussion

Before reading any of the usability reports developer B expressed that he had great expectations to the usability evaluation. However, he was somewhat worried that we as evaluators might not have had enough experience in using the system, whereas a potential user has a need for doing the things that the system can. He thought the evaluation might have had another outcome, if we had done the evaluation one more time. We find this as an example of the developer being defensive [30].

Developer A expressed that the time pressure, they work with every day, should be taken into account when evaluating the usability of the system. In relation to usability evaluations this makes little sense. Usability problems exist in a system regardless of the time that has been available for development. The issue of designers being reluctant to allocate time in their schedule for HCI activities has been described before, for example by Radle & Young [25] and Spencer [30].

Regarding the structure and content of usability reports, a question about whether to include an edited videotape as part of the feedback for the designers, to allow designers a first hand view of the problem, arose. This has been tried at IBM [9]. Traditional reports are still utilised, but video clips can 'provide compelling evidence to developers who are reluctant to correct usability problems' [9]. A drawback associated with the use of video recordings is that it is very time-consuming task to edit such a tape [5].

Very few positive findings were presented in the two reports. When the developers were asked, whether they would have liked the evaluation to focus more on positive findings, they replied that positive findings are always nice, but they cannot really use them for improving the system. Hence they do not find any reason for spending a lot of time and energy on finding positive aspects. Both Perfetti [24] and Redish et al. [26] support the idea of including positive findings in usability reports. Frøkjær and Hornbæk [11] on the other hand report from a series of interviews where practitioners criticized the form of traditional usability reports, that developers were much more interested in constructive proposals for redesign.

Alternative approaches to usability reports as a mean for providing feedback have been proposed. This experiment has actively included the developers in generating an additional usability problem list, hereby succeeding in forcing the developers to take a stand towards the usability problems presented to them. Redish et al. [26] takes the cooperation with the designers a step further by suggesting that they are brought in and made a part of the planning and conducting of the evaluation, analysis of the data, and the communication of the results.

Moving feedback from the written to spoken language changes the criteria for giving good feedback. Radle & Young [25] recognize the importance of interpersonal skills when addressing usability in relation to development teams. Sy [31] also presents additional advises on how communication of the evaluation results can be improved apart from a usability report. If possible, a meeting should be held to go through the findings with the appropriate people. During this meeting, it is important to refrain from any kind of confrontational attitude, and if possible, the meeting should be ended with a list of actions derived from a co-operative discussion. This is important in order to involve designers more actively in the resolution of usability problems

6 Conclusion

Through the experiment we have learned a number of lessons, which are relevant in providing feedback to designers through usability reports and interviews about usability problems. This leads us to conclude that:

- A problem list providing overview of usability problems combined with detailed descriptions is important in a report and essential for the designers when trying to understand a problem.
- Results of NASA-TLX, which are not explained and put into context, are difficult for the designers to relate to.
- Log-files of user interaction, based on video recordings combined with system-logs, are used and considered important by the developers to understand specific details of the usability problems.
- Information on test setup, users, tasks, and test users' subjective opinions are important to the developers, but these are also the point of critique, when developers explain, why they find problems more or less real.
- General assessments and evaluations in usability reports have limited usefulness for the designers.

The reports were useful for the designers in understanding the usability evaluation and as a mean for references in redesign and further development. They enriched the developers with insight into how users interact with their product and what strengths and weaknesses there were. For the developers the usability reports did not alter their initial belief of the system to a great extent, but it did expand their list and made them consider other topics. The reports had a more substantial effect on the developers' conception of the weaknesses of the system.

In this experiment, we rely heavily on qualitative data collected through interviews with two participants. In addition, the two developers can in no way be representative for all user interface designers.

Based on the results of our experiment, we find that it would be interesting to perform similar feedback experiments with other ways of providing feedback to designers. Inspiration can be found in the area of interpersonal communication. The other important avenue of research is to conduct similar experiments with other designers to broaden the empirical basis for more general conclusions.

References

1. Bachrach, C. & Newcomer, S. F. (2002). *Addressing Bias in Intervention Research*, in Journal of Adolescent Health, Volume 31, Number 4, 2002.
2. Bærentsen, K. B. & Slavensky, H. (1999). *A Contribution to the Design Process*. Communications of the ACM, May 1999, Vol. 42, No. 5.
3. Baillie, L. (2003). Future Telecommunication: Exploring actual use, INTERACT 2003.
4. Blatt, L., Jacobsen, M. & Miller, S. (1994). *Designing and equipping a usability laboratory*, In BIT Volume 13, Numbers 1 & 2, January –April 1994, Special Issue 'Usability Laboratories'
5. Borgholm, T. & Madsen, K. H. (1999). *Cooperative Usability Practices*. Communications of the ACM, May 1999, Vol. 42, No. 5.
6. Dolan, W. R. & Dumas, J. S. (1999). *A Flexible Approach to Third-Party Usability*. Communications of the ACM, May 1999, Vol. 42, No. 5.
7. Dumas, J. S. & Redish, J. C. (1993). *A practical guide to usability testing*, Norwood, NJ: Ablex Publishing.

8. Ehrlich, K., Beth, M. B. & Pernice, K. (1994). *Getting the Whole Team into Usability Testing*, IEEE Interface – January 1994.

9. Fath, J. L., Teresa, L. M. & Holzman, T. G. (1994). *A practical guide to using software usability labs: lessons learned at IBM*, In BIT Volume 13, Numbers 1 & 2, January –April 1994, Special Issue 'Usability Laboratories'

10. Fowler, C., Stuart, J., Lo, T. & Tate, M. (1994). *Using the usability laboratory: BT's experiences*, In BIT Volume 13, Numbers 1 & 2, January –April 1994, Special Issue 'Usability Laboratories'

11. Frøkjær, E. and Hornbæk, K. (2004) Input from usability evaluation in the form of problems and redesigns: results from interviews with developers. In Hornbæk, K. and Stage, J. (Eds.) Proceedings of the Workshop on Improving the Interplay between Usability Evaluation and User Interface Design, NordiCHI 2004, pp. 27-30. Aalborg University, Department of Computer Science, HCI-Lab Report no. 2004/2.

12. Hartson, H. R., Shivakumar, P. & Pérez-Quiñones, M. A. (2004). *Usability Inspection of Digital Libraries: A Case Study*, accepted for publication in the Special Issue of Journal of Digital Libraries on Usability

13. Kvale, S. (1997). Interview – En Introduction til det Kvalitative Forskningsinterview, Hans Reitzels Forlag, 1. udgave, 1997.

14. Lund, A. M. (1994). *Ameritech's usability laboratory: from prototype to final design*, In BIT Volume 13, Numbers 1 & 2, January –April 1994, Special Issue 'Usability Laboratories'

15. Mayhew, D. J. (1999). *The Usability Engineering Lifecycle*, Morgan Kaufmann Publishers Inc. San Francisco, California.

16. Mayhew, D. J. (1999). *Strategic Development of the Usability Engineering Function*, ACM Transactions – September /October 1999.

17. Molich, R. (2000). *Brugervenlige edb-systemer*, Teknisk Forlag.

18. Molich, R. (2004). E-mail correspondence with Rolf Molich 18/05/04.

19. Muller, M. J. & Czerwinski, M. (1999). *Organizing Usability Work To Fit the Full Product Range*. Communications of the ACM, May 1999, Vol. 42, No. 5.

20. Murphy, J., Howard, S., Kjeldskov, J. and Goschnick, S. (2004) Location, Location, Location: Challenges of Outsourced Usability Evaluation. In Hornbæk, K. and Stage, J. (Eds.) Proceedings of the Workshop on Improving the Interplay between Usability Evaluation and User Interface Design, NordiCHI 2004, pp. 12-15. Aalborg University, Department of Computer Science, HCI-Lab Report no. 2004/2.

21. Nielsen, M. C., Overgaard, M., Pedersen, M. B. & Stenild, S. (2004). *A Review of Literature on Usability Evaluation Methods for Mobile Systems*, Department of Computer Science, Aalborg University, 2004.

22. Nielsen, M. C., Overgaard, M., Pedersen, M. B. & Stenild, S. (2004). *Usability Evaluation of a mobile system: Comparison of a Laboratory and Field Evaluation*, Department of Computer Science, Aalborg University, 2004.

23. Palmiter, S., Lynch, G., Lewis, S. & Stempski, M. (1994). *Breaking away from the conventional 'usability lab': the Customer-Centered Design Group at Tektronix, Inc.*, In BIT Volume 13, Numbers 1 & 2, January –April 1994, Special Issue 'Usability Laboratories'

24. Perfetti, C. (2003). *Usability Testing Best Practices: An Interview with Rolf Molich.* Originally published: 07/24/2003, Found 10/05/04: http://www.uie.com/articles/molich_interview.

25. Radle, K. & Young, S. (2001). Partnering Usability with Development: How Three Organizations Succeeded, IEEE Software – January/February 2001.

404   C.M. Nielsen et al.

26. Redish, J., Bias, R. G., Bailey, R., Molich, R., Dumas, J. & Spool, J. M. (2002). *Usability in Practice: Formative Usability Evaluations – Evolution and Revolution*. Usability in Practice Session, CHI 2002.
27. Rohn, A. J. (1994). *The usability engineering laboratories at Sun Microsystems*, In BIT Volume 13, Numbers 1 & 2, January –April 1994, Special Issue 'Usability Laboratories'
28. Rubin, J. (1994). Handbook of usability testing: How to plan, design, and conduct effective tests, New York, NY: John Wiley & Sons.
29. Salzman, M. C. & Rivers, S. D. (1994). *Smoke and mirrors: setting the stage for a successful usability test*, In BIT Volume 13, Numbers 1 & 2, January –April 1994, Special Issue 'Usability Laboratories'
30. Spencer, R. (2000). The Streamlined Cognitive Walkthrough Method, Working Around Social Constraints Encountered in a Software Development Company, CHI Letter 2000 Volume 2 Issue 1.
31. Sy, D. (1994). Bridging the Communication Gap in the Workplace With Usability Engineering, ACM 1994.
32. Zirkler, D. & Ballman, D. R. (1994). *Usability testing in a competitive market: lessons learned*, In BIT Volume 13, Numbers 1 & 2, January –April 1994, Special Issue 'Usability Laboratories'

Assessing Interaction Styles in Web User Interfaces

Alistair Sutcliffe and Antonella De Angeli

Centre for HCI Design, School of Informatics, University of Manchester,
P.O. Box 88, Manchester M60 1QD, UK
a.g.sutcliffe@co.umist.ac.uk

Abstract. An evaluation of two websites with the same content but different interface styles (traditional menu-based and interactive metaphors) is described. A formative usability evaluation was carried out with heuristic assessment of aesthetics followed by post-test memory. The subjects had more problems with the metaphor-based site, but rated it more favourably on the aesthetics heuristics. There was no difference in free memory recall between the sites. The implications for website design and evaluation are discussed.

1 Introduction

Conceptions of "new usability" propose that overall satisfaction with user interfaces involves not only traditional usability but also other factors such as user engagement, experience, and aesthetics [5] Some heuristic evaluation techniques make reference to aesthetics and user engagement [8], [12], [13]. However, few experimental investigations into aesthetic components of usability have been carried out apart from those by Tractinsky [17], who demonstrated that users' perception of aesthetic qualities was an important, and culturally variable, component in the rating of quality in experiments with ATM user interfaces. Further evidence for the importance of aesthetics can be found in the study by Hassenzahl et al. [6], who asked users to compare six different designs of a process control application, with questionnaire inventories for experience, hedonic and appeal qualities. Hassenzahl et al. concluded that both experience and hedonic qualities contributed approximately equally to the overall judgement of appeal. However, these studies either did not specify which design features they varied to test aesthetic quality or varied on simple aspects such as colour and layout consistency as in Tractinsky's studies.

To our knowledge, no comparative studies have been undertaken on how interaction might influence aesthetics or user judgement of their "experience". One design feature which may attract users' attention, animated banner adverts, has been extensively researched. Bayles [1] found that animation in banner adverts was not effective in promoting memorability, while Guan and Zhang [4] and Diaper and Waeland [3] reported that although attention was directed towards animated adverts in terms of eye-tracking fixations, users did not comprehend or remember the information. Hornof and Halverson [7] have demonstrated that even fixations on animated adverts are not reliable indicators of attention, let alone comprehension of content. However, other factors which might contribute to the users' overall satisfaction, such as interaction and aesthetics have received less attention.

M.F. Costabile and F. Paternò (Eds.): INTERACT 2005, LNCS 3585, pp. 405–417, 2005.
© IFIP International Federation for Information Processing 2005

This paper reports an evaluation of two websites with different design styles, one traditional, the other with interactive metaphors and more aesthetic design features. The study also investigates the link between design, usability, user perception and memory. In the following section we describe the experimental methods and materials. Section 3 reports the results of the usability, aesthetics heuristics and memory tests. The discussion then reviews the implications of the results for website evaluation and design.

2 Method

Two live websites were selected from the ThinkQuest Library, a collection of educational sites entered in an international competition sponsored by the Oracle Education Foundation. These websites presented the same content on Astronomy with very different design styles, one exploiting animated metaphors and more aesthetic features (metaphor-based), the other a traditional menu-based style. Example screen-shots are shown in Fig. 1.

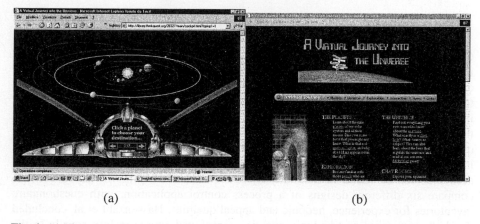

(a)   (b)

Fig. 1. (a) Metaphor-style interface showing the planets and cockpit metaphors, and (b) Menu-based user interface

The sites had 210 content pages organised in four main sections – planets, universe, exploration, news, resources and glossary with further pages linking to mainly disabled interactive features such as chat rooms and feedback forms. From the home page (http://library.thinkquest.org/28327/), the user can select which style she/he prefers. In the interactive metaphor version, an animated representation of the solar system is displayed with a "cockpit" metaphor of controls at the bottom of the screen (see Fig. 1a). Moving the mouse over the planets causes an orbit to highlight, then clicking on the planet or its orbit causes the planet's name to appear in the cockpit display. Information about the planet can then be accessed by "Go" in the cockpit metaphor. Some fast moving planets such as Mercury were difficult to access, while Uranus and Neptune were not easily visible. The side panels in the cockpit contain other navigation links to chat rooms, universe, exploration, etc., although the user has to mouse over the panel to display the option name. The menu interface style, in contrast, (Fig. 1b) has a standard link menu structure to access information without any intervening displays. The top-level menu leads to sub-menus for the planets, and each planet has an introductory text followed by a sub-menu of information relevant to that planet. The key differences between the two interface styles which we hypothesised should influence user perception of engagement and aesthetics are summarised in Table 1.

Table 1. Informal assessment of the aesthetic/user engagement differences between the two interface styles

	Menu-based style	Metaphor-based style
Interaction	Menu and links	Interactive planets and cockpit metaphors
Use of colour	Black background, green and white text	Black background, green and white
Layout & presentation	Conventional block structures layout	Shape and shading emphasised
Use of media	Text plus still image	Animation in several places, interactive captions on images
Background image	Starfield display borders	Starfield display background

Table 2. Instruments and techniques used during the evaluation

Usability	• Self-report and severity rating of usability problems (1 minor problem; 5 major problem) • 5-item usability scale on a 7-point Likert scale [9]
Memorabilty	• Free recall memory test and attitude rating on 5 point scale (5 very negative, 1 very positive)
Aesthetics	• Heuristics for attractiveness [15], [16]) • 10-item perceived website aesthetic scale on a 7-point Likert scale [9]
Service quality	• 3 items measuring service quality on a 7-point scale [9]
Engagement	• 3 items measuring engagement on a 7-point scale
Willingness to use	• Post-test group discussion

To summarise the informal assessment, the two interfaces had minor differences in the layout, presentation, and graphics/font aspects of aesthetics; both used the same fonts and colour scheme, although the metaphor site used more interesting graphical and shading on titles and layout frames for the information. The clear differences lay in the interactivity, such as the solar system metaphor for accessing information, and information presentation with animation and pop-up captions on images. There was a slight difference in the use of background image to frame displays, with the metaphor site using the starfield space image more extensively.

The websites were evaluated for usability, memorability of content and interface features, aesthetics, service quality, entertainment and willingness to use. A list of the techniques and instruments used in the study is reported in Table 2; details of the experimental procedure are reported in the following sections.

2.1 Subjects

Twenty-five undergraduate and postgraduate students (21 male and 4 female) from the School of Informatics, University of Manchester participated in the experiment. They all had basic knowledge of HCI, usability evaluation techniques and the aesthetic heuristics used in the experiment from the Multimedia and Virtual Reality course they had recently attended.

2.2 Procedure

Data were collected in a group setting, with each participant working individually for almost three hours. On arriving for the experimental session, the subjects received verbal and written instructions followed by a brief pre-test questionnaire recording personal data, Internet experience, and level of interest and knowledge of Astronomy. Then each subject was randomly assigned to one of the two websites and had to perform six information-retrieval tasks (e.g. what is the orbital period of Jupiter, what is the percentage of hydrogen in the composition of Jupiter) reporting their answers on a task sheet. Optimal task performance required visiting 17 pages in the menu-based condition and 14 pages in the metaphor condition, the difference being pop up menus in the cockpit metaphor which allowed a shorter path.

While performing the tasks, subjects were invited to describe the usability errors they encountered and rate their severity. Once they had completed the tasks, subjects completed a free recall memory test. This required listing the first ten facts/items/issues they could remember about the website, and rating the quality of these memories on a five point scale as favourable, neutral or adverse. Then, they briefly revisited the site and completed the attractiveness heuristics and a questionnaire combining the remaining measures listed in Table 1. After a short break, the procedure was repeated with the other website and a new set of equivalent tasks which varied the planet chosen as subject (Jupiter, Uranus/Saturn, Neptune). Finally, a group discussion was run to investigate overall preferences and reasons behind them.

Interaction style was manipulated within-subjects, so that each participant evaluated both the menu-based and the metaphor-based interfaces. Evaluation order and tasks were counterbalanced among subjects and conditions.

3 Results

All scales and measures showed high reliability (Cronbach alpha > .78), thus comparative analyses were based on scale averages. Unless otherwise specified, inter-site differences were tested by paired samples t-test.

3.1 Task Performance

None of the subjects had any prior knowledge of the websites, and the overall knowledge and interest in the topic matter was moderately low. Nevertheless, information-retrieval performance was extremely accurate, with only 6% of 300 tasks resulting in inaccurate or wrong information. No difference between experimental conditions emerged.

3.2 Usability

Overall the usability evaluation favoured the menu-based website. On average, subjects reported significantly more problems when evaluating the metaphor-based site (mean/subject = 4.2) than the menu-based design (mean/subject = 2.32) $t_{(24)} = -3.41$, $p < .01$. The problems associated with the metaphor-based style were also judged to be more severe (mean = 3.65) than those associated with the menu-based style (mean = 3.02), $t(160) = 3.10, p < .01$. Usability problems were clustered in five general categories according to their cause, as illustrated in Table 3.

Table 3. Percentage frequencies of usability problems and average severity rating on a 1 to 5 scale (5 worst) classified by cause

	Menu-based			Metaphor-based		
	Freq	%	Severity	Freq	%	Severity
Poor menu/navigation	25	43	2.80	71	68	3.54
Poor graphical design	16	27	2.60	18	17	3.17
Poor information	8	14	3.00	9	8	3.44
Unexpected effect	5	9	4.20	4	4	4.50
Other	4	7	2.50	3	3	3.67
Total	**58**	**100**	**3.02**	**105**	**100**	**3.65**

As can be seen from Table 3, problem frequency is significantly affected by interaction style ($\chi^2_{(2)} = 6.62$, $p < .05$) and the metaphor style encountered twice as many problems. Poor menu/navigation were usability problems which caused operational difficulties, i.e. critical incidents [11], whereas poor graphical design reflected adverse comments on aesthetic aspects and the subjects' design preferences, and poor information covered adverse comments on the clarity and completeness of the information architecture and content. Unexpected effect refers to unpredictable system behaviour that interrupted the user's task flow (e.g. unexpected pop-up window) or functionality failures.

When evaluating the metaphor-based interface, it was found that subjects reported 25% more poor menu/navigation problems than with the menu-based interface. However, with evaluation of the menu-based interface, subjects were 10% more likely to complain about graphical design than with the metaphor-based interface. It is worth noting that this distribution difference is not responsible for the difference in severity rating between the two styles. Indeed, an Anova on individual errors with style (2) and error category (3) as between-subjects factors indicated a significant effect for style, but neither for category nor for the interaction (F < 1). The metaphor-based style was consistently evaluated more seriously in every problem category than the menu-based style; see the average severity scores in Table 3.

In the menu-based style, the most frequent problems in the poor menu/navigation category were the need for scrolling (N = 6 events) and inconsistent use of the back and home button (7). In poor graphical design, the most common complaints were the unpleasant colour combination of green on black (6) and inconsistent use of text fonts (8). In this style most problem reports related to overall dissatisfaction with the design, and less frequently content, rather than problems with particular design features, apart from links (7).

In the metaphor-based style the more common problems were the lack of a caption for the planet name in the solar system metaphor (N = 14); the difficulty of selecting a planet (double click procedure) (10) and the obscure interaction in the cockpit menu (8). The most troublesome design features were the solar system and planets metaphor, which was responsible 22% of the total errors, followed by the cockpit metaphor with 7%. In contrast to the menu style, usability problems were frequently associated with specific design features.

The trend emerging from the objective usability analysis is reflected in the subjective evaluation. As shown in Fig. 2, subjects in the metaphor-based condition evaluated the usability of the site as significantly worse than in the menu-based design, $t(23) = 3.02, p < .01$.

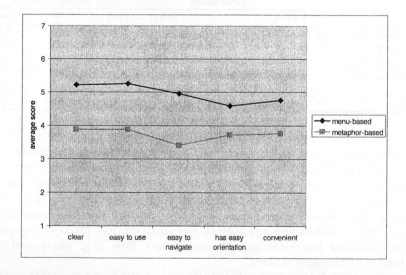

Fig. 2. Ratings in a post-test questionnaire on usability as a function of interaction style

3.3 Aesthetics

Following the factorial configuration proposed and validated by Lavie and Tractinsky [9], two dimensions were used: classical and expressive aesthetic. The classical aesthetics dimension included questions on pleasant, clear, clean, symmetric and aesthetic design; while expressive aesthetic dimension consisted of creative,

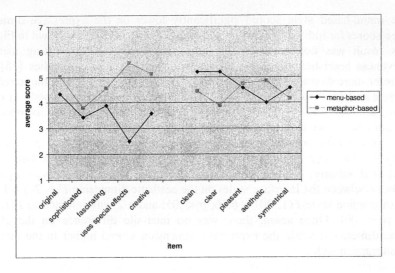

Fig. 3. Average scores on aesthetic evaluation factors as a function of interaction style

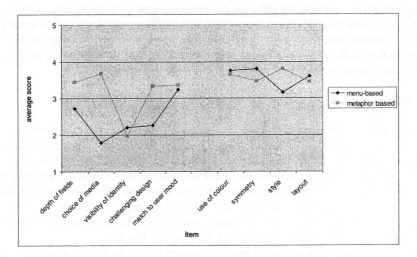

Fig. 4. Average scores on the expressive and classic clusters of the attractiveness heuristics

fascinating, original and sophisticated design with use of special effects. These two factors were then entered as dependent variables in a repeated-measure Anova with aesthetic dimension (2) and interaction style (2) as within-subjects factors. Both the main effects and their interaction were significant, namely aesthetic dimension: $F(1, 22) = 8.06$, $p < .01$; interaction style: $F(1, 22) = 4.75$, $p < .05$; 2-way interaction $F(1, 22) = 30.01$, $p < .001$.

The effect of the interaction style on aesthetics is modulated by the dimension considered. There were no inter-site differences on the classical aesthetic dimension, but the menu-based style scored significantly lower on the expressive dimension. Average scores for individual items of the two aesthetic factors are shown in Fig. 3.

This result was confirmed by the analysis of the subjects' rating using the attractiveness heuristics which have been validated in previous studies [15], [16]. These refer more directly to design features which should promote aesthetic reactions than Lavie and Tractinsky's dimensions. The ten heuristics were grouped in two sets, reflecting classical and expressive dimensions, as illustrated in Fig. 4. Given the small size of our sample, we could not statistically confirm this configuration.

However, satisfactory Cronbach alpha and significant correlations ($p < .01$) with the corresponding factors extracted from the questionnaire appealed to both internal and external validity. Results of the Anova on the heuristics showed significant differences between the interface styles on the aesthetic dimension $F(1, 20) = 16.34$, $p < .01$; interaction style $F(1, 20) = 6.56$, $p < .05$; and a 2-way interaction $F(1, 20) = 20.62$, $p < .001$. Once again, there was no inter-site difference on the classical aesthetic dimension, while the expressive dimension scored higher in the metaphor-based interaction style.

3.4 Service Quality and Engagement

Interaction style significantly affected the perception of website quality, $t(23) = 2.57$, $p < .05$, the menu-based website being perceived as more reliable and less error prone than the metaphor-based site. Conversely, the subjects' assessment of engagement tended to favour the metaphor-based site, $t(23) = -2.7$, $p < .05$, which was perceived as significantly more entertaining, engaging and enjoyable.

3.5 Memory

Overall, subjects reported 289 items in free recall memory of the two websites. No effect of interaction style emerged on the number of memory items retrieved or the memory valency in the different memory categories. However, a content analysis of these memories suggested that interaction style affected the content of retrieved items. Recalled items were categorised into reports relating to the user interface, sub-divided into visual design, use of colour, use of multimedia, comments on links and navigation features, labelling and feedback, and content memory, including reference to the subject matter and information architecture (see Fig. 6).

The menu-based style triggered more memories related to site content (56% versus 44% in the metaphor-based condition). Conversely, the metaphor-based style invoked more memory related to UI elements and features, in particular multimedia elements (24% total items) and feedback mechanism (see Table 4). Memory valency, which we interpret as attitude, towards the more aesthetically related aspects of the design (graphics, use of colour and multimedia) were worse in the menu style, in contrast the metaphor style invoked adverse memory for interactive features such as navigation and feedback. The difference in subject attitude to information content between the two styles is strange since the content was the same; however, its presentation was more adventurous in the metaphor style with interactive titles and captions, so we conjecture this may have had a positive influence on the subjects' attitude. In the metaphor style the most frequently remembered features were the solar system/

planets metaphor (14 reports, average valency 2.71) followed by the cockpit (12 reports, average valency 3.61) so it appears that even though both these features caused high frequencies of usability problems, the solar system metaphor resulted in memory with a slightly negative attitude, whereas the cockpit metaphor provoked a more adverse reaction. No particular design features were remembered noticeably more than others in the menu condition, where memories related more to content.

Table 4. Frequencies and valency of items in free recall memory by category

		Menu-based			Metaphor-based		
		Freq	Valency	Std. error	Freq	Valency	Std. error
Content	Subject-matter	37	2.57	.18	32	2.60	.24
	Info architecture	23	2.23	.25	14	1.93	.29
UI	Graphical design	16	3.13	.35	15	2.33	.40
	Use of colour	18	2.71	.29	6	2.67	.61
	Multimedia	12	2.92	.42	35	2.91	.24
	Link and navigation	29	2.74	.30	34	3.22	.22
	Labelling/feedback	2	2	0	12	3.92	.31
	Other	1	1	0	3	4	.58
	Total	**138**	**2.41**	**0.22**	**151**	**2.95**	*0.36*

A total of 138 memory items were explicitly related to the aesthetic dimensions, namely information quality, usability, expressive aesthetic and classical aesthetic. For the menu-based interface subjects tended to retrieve memory related to information quality (31%), classical aesthetic (30%), usability issues (25%) and finally expressive aesthetic (14%); in contrast, the most common items for the metaphor-based interface related to usability (36%), followed by expressive aesthetic (30%), information quality (21%) and classical aesthetics (13%). The quality of these memories was not significantly different, with the clear exception of usability, which generated more negative memories in the metaphor-based condition than in the menu-based one ($t(61)=-2.66$, $p<.01$).

3.6 Group Discussion

During the group discussion, all subjects agreed that the metaphor-based website was worse for usability and many subjects pointed out problems with using the design. Nevertheless, when asked which of the two sites they personally preferred and might be willing to use again in the future, all but one subject voted for the metaphor-based style. Their preference was explicitly driven by an increase in engagement and pleasure experienced during the interaction, even though this came at the cost of increased initial workload to understand interaction procedures. It is worth noting that subjects were mostly attracted by the planet animation on the front page which strongly appealed to their curiosity even though it was clearly recognised as the worst usability feature of the design. However, when asked to assess which of the two sites was more suitable for teaching secondary school pupils, the subjects were evenly divided between the two interaction styles. The main reasons cited in favour of the menu-based style were simplicity and clarity; while the reasons in favour of the metaphor-based style were engagement by interaction and motivation.

3.7 Summary

The matrix reporting correlations between the main dimensions under investigation is reported in Table 5. Correlation values are reported separately for the two style conditions. Metaphor style values are in the upper part of the table; menu values are in the lower part of the table. Note that as the high correlations between aesthetic dimensions assessed by questionnaires and heuristics have already been discussed in section 3.3, in the table we report only questionnaire values, for consistency with the other measures.

Table 5. Correlation matrix of the study's measures. $* = p < .05$; $** p < .01$; $*** p < .001$

		Metaphor measure combination.					
		1.	2.	3.	4.	5.	6.
Menu measure combin- ation	1. Memory valency		*	**			*
	2. Usability	**		**	*	**	**
	3. Classical_A		**		**	**	**
	4. Expressive_A		**	**		*	*
	5. UI_quality		**	**			*
	6. Engagement		**	**	**	*	

Table 6. Summary of the differences between the two interactive styles, + denotes better style for the dimension, - worse style, = no difference between the styles

Dimensions	Metaphor-based style	Menu-based style
Usability	-	+
Aesthetic classic	=	=
Aesthetic expressive	+	-
Information quality	-	+
Engagement	+	-
Memory	Content-based	Interface-based

The overall correlation trend demonstrates the inter-relationships between the different evaluation dimensions. The most striking difference between the two styles regards memory valency, which in the menu-based condition correlates only with usability; whereas the metaphor-based condition correlates also with classical aesthetic and engagement. A summary of the results of the different evaluation dimensions assessed is given in Table 6.

The menu style was superior for usability and perceived to have better information quality, even though both sites had exactly the same content. Both sites were rated positively for classic aesthetics in both the attractiveness heuristics and Tractinsky's dimension. However, the metaphor style was superior for the expressive aesthetics on both measures and was preferred overall. This preference was partially reflected in the subjects' memory which was slightly more positive for the metaphor site, but it appears that the subjects' judgement of overall quality differed from their attitude to specific design features and recall of separate aspects of each site. In conclusion, aesthetics does appear to have an important effect, since the subjects preferred the site they rated as being better designed aesthetically even though they were aware of its poor usability.

4 Discussion

Advocates of the new usability [5] argue that aesthetics should be an important determinant of users' satisfaction with a design; however, there have been remarkably few experimental studies to determine which design features may aesthetically enhance users' experience. We have demonstrated that interactive metaphors do contribute strongly to users' attitude and rating of website design even though the users' usability experience was worse with the more aesthetic design style. Furthermore animation and interaction may have had a positive effect on user perception of content which is an important finding for education related web sites.

The attractiveness heuristics [15], [16] we proposed assess design features which should contribute towards positive aesthetic expression, unlike previous evaluation instruments which have assessed users' judgement of qualities that can be clustered under the umbrella of aesthetics perception [9]. The aesthetics heuristics we describe correspond most closely to the expressive aesthetics dimension which Lavie and Tractinsky [9] found in a factor analysis of evaluation questions; however, their questions focused on users' perception of user interface qualities, such as "beautiful", "challenging", "fascinating", whereas our questions are judgements on the quality and use of more specific design features and media. The correlation of the aesthetic heuristics and dimensions suggests that the attractiveness heuristics may be reasonable indicators of design qualities for expressive aesthetics, although we can not exclude other factors, such as user reaction to the specific metaphor, which may influence individuals' judgement.

Tractinsky [17] demonstrated that users' perception of aesthetic qualities was an important, and culturally variable, component in the rating of quality and experience in experiments in ATM user interfaces. However, the study varied only low-level graphical design (e.g. colour button format) and visual layout features, whereas we have demonstrated that interaction and metaphors also have a powerful effect not only on user perception of aesthetics but also on their judgement of satisfaction and engagement. The questionnaire assessment study by Hassenzahl et al. [6] does not detail the changes they made to the six design variations used in their study so it is difficult to assess the causal factors influencing user perception.

The strong effect of interaction on aesthetic judgement and satisfaction which we found can be explained by affective interpretations of user judgement [14], in that the metaphors invoke user curiosity and pleasure even if they are clearly more difficult to use. Our study provides some evidence that aesthetic design and interactive metaphors do form an important influence on users' overall judgement of their experience, which overrides a poor usability experience. However, users may not forget such poor experiences since their memory for problematic features was adverse; furthermore, they make different judgements about the interfaces for scenarios of serious educational use. Further investigations need to be carried out to assess the impact of different metaphors and design qualities on user perceptions of engagement, and to assess the relative contributions of "static" aesthetics (e.g. layout, colour, graphics), use of media and interactive effects.

References

1. Bayles, M. Designing online banner advertisements: Should we animate? *CHI Letters*, *4*(1), (2002) 363-366.
2. Beier, B., & Vaughan, M. W. The bull's-eye: A framework for web application user interface design guidelines. In V. Bellotti, T. Erickson, G. Cockton, & P. Korhonen, (Eds). *CHI 2003 Conference Proceedings: Conference on Human Factors in Computing Systems, Fort Lauderdale FL 5-10 April 2003*. New York: ACM Press, (2003), 489-496.
3. Diaper, D., & Waelend, P. World Wide Web working whilst ignoring graphics: Good news for web page designers. *Interacting with Computers*, *13*(2), (2000) 163-181.
4. Guan, S. U., & Zhang, X. The design and implementation of a web-based personal digital library. *Journal of the Institution of Engineers*, *44*(3), (2004) 59-77.
5. Hallnas, L., & Redstrom, J. From use to presence: On the expression of aesthetics of everyday computational things. *ACM Transactions on Computer-Human Interaction*, *9*(2), (2002) 106-124.
6. Hassenzahl, M., Platz, A., Burmester, M., & Lehner, K. Hedonic and ergonomic quality aspects determine a software's appeal. In T. Turner, G. Szwillus, M. Czerwinski, & F. Paterno, (Eds). *CHI 2000 Conference Proceedings: Conference on Human Factors in Computing Systems, The Hague 1-6 April 2000*. New York: ACM Press, (2000), 201-208.
7. Hornof, A., & Halverson, T. Cognitive strategies and eye movements for searching hierarchical computer displays. In V. Bellotti, T. Erickson, G. Cockton, & P. Korhonen, (Eds). *CHI 2003 Conference Proceedings: Conference on Human Factors in Computing Systems, Fort Lauderdale FL 5-10 April 2003*. New York: ACM Press, (2003). 249-256.
8. IBM. *Ease of use: Design principles.* http://www.ibm.com/ibm/easy/ eou_ext.nsf/Publish/6. (20 November 2000).
9. Lavie, T., & Tractinsky, N. Assessing dimensions of perceived visual aesthetics of websites. *International Journal of Human-Computer Studies*, *60*(3), (2004) 269-298.
10. Lynch, P. J., & Horton, S. *Web style guidelines* (2nd ed.). New Haven CT: Yale University Press, (2001).
11. Monk, A., Wright, P., Haber, J., & Davenport, L. *Improving your human-computer interface: A practical technique.* London: Prentice Hall, (1993).
12. Nielsen, J. *Designing web usability: The practice of simplicity.* New Riders, (2000).
13. Nielsen, J. *Usability engineering.* New York: Academic Press, (1993).
14. Norman, D. A. *Emotional design: Why we love (or hate) everyday things.* New York: Basic Books, (2004).

15. Sutcliffe, A. G. Assessing the reliability of heuristic evaluation for website attractiveness and usability. In *Proceedings HICSS-35: Hawaii International Conference on System Science*. Honolulu: University of Hawaii, (2002). 1838-1847.
16. Sutcliffe, A. G. Heuristic evaluation of website attractiveness and usability. In C. W. Johnson (Ed.), *Proceedings: 8th Workshop on Design, Specification and Verification of Interactive Systems, Glasgow 13-15 June 2001*. Berlin: Springer-Verlag, (2002). 188-199.
17. Tractinsky, N. Aesthetics and apparent usability: Empirically assessing cultural and methodological issues. In Pemberton S. (Ed.), *Human Factors in Computing Systems: CHI 97 Conference Proceedings, Atlanta GA 22-27 May 1997*. New York: ACM Press, (1997), 115-122.

Usability Specialists - 'A Mommy Mob', 'Realistic Humanists' or 'Staid Researchers'? An Analysis of Usability Work in the Software Product Development

Netta Iivari

Department of Information Processing Science, University of Oulu,
PO BOX 3000, 90014 Oulu, Finland
netta.iivari@oulu.fi

Abstract. Users should be involved in the interactive systems development. However, involving users is difficult and rare, especially in the product development context. Guidelines for the facilitation of user involvement have been produced. However, a critical review shows that the guidelines rely on naïve notions of people and change in organizations. In this paper an interpretive research approach is utilized in the analysis user involvement in software development organizations operating in the product development context. User involvement is indirect in the organizations, and labelled as usability work. Usability specialists are conceptualized as a specific community of practice, usability work being their practice. Analysis reveals divergent ways usability work has been organized in the organizations, and divergent meanings attached to usability work. Both practical and theoretical implications are discussed.

1 Introduction

This paper analyzes strategies for organizing usability work in the organizational context of software (SW) development. Therefore, the interactive systems development context is under examination. This context is one of the main research areas in the field of Human Computer Interaction (HCI) [17]. Usability work refers to the work of usability specialists, who 'represent the users' [8] in the development. This task of 'representing the users' has been crucial for the whole legitimacy and identity of the field of HCI [8]. Usability work advocates user involvement of indirect type. Users are assigned a consultative or informative role [10]: users comment on predefined design solutions or act as providers of information and objects of observation. They do not actively participate, but are represented in the design process. In this paper the focus is limited to usability work in the development of interactive systems in the product development context (as contrasted with the in-house development context). In-house development has been the traditional context for user involvement. Product development, on the other hand, is the context the HCI community has worked with. [15], [25].

It has been reported that usability work is quite challenging and rare in the product development context, not even to mention more participative user involvement [4], [15], [25]. This is because in this context even identifying and making contact with the prospective users is difficult. The development is also often totally organization-

M.F. Costabile and F. Paternò (Eds.): INTERACT 2005, LNCS 3585, pp. 418–430, 2005.

ally isolated from users and the requirements are transmitted to the development via marketing. The development cycle is also typically very short and therefore there is no time for usability work or for iteration [15], [16]. The literature also highlights the difficulty of having usability work accepted in organizations. The position of usability specialists is often weak, their credibility questioned and their work undervalued [2], [3], [13], [25], [27], [32]. The development organizations lack knowledge about users and about appropriate ways to involve them [13], [14], [25], [32] and often the development proceeds without any user feedback [14], [16], [30]. If users are involved, it often takes place too late with no effects on design [2], [4], [14], [16], [25], [30].

This indicates that usability work has proven to be difficult, especially in the product development context. Regarding user involvement in organizations, empirical studies have been carried out mainly in the context of in-house development. This paper analyzes usability work in SW product development context. Usability specialists are conceptualized as a specific community of practice in the SW development organizations. The concept of community of practice has gained increasing attention in HCI literature and designers have been analyzed as a specific community of practice [19], [28]. This paper continues this work by analyzing the work of professionals who have labeled themselves 'usability specialists'. Focus is specifically on their work, which is related to the 'representing the users' in the interactive systems development. This community, their practice, and their interaction with other communities in the SW development organizations will be illuminated in the empirical part of the paper.

The paper is organized as follows. The next section presents literature on the facilitation of usability work. Afterwards, the literature is critically reviewed. It is shown that the literature relies on naïve notions of organizations and facilitation of usability work. In section three the concept of community of practice is introduced. In the fourth section the interpretive research approach utilized in this study is presented. In the fifth section empirical results are presented. Last section discusses the findings, outlines the limitations of the study and suggests paths for future work.

2 Literature on the Facilitation of Usability Work

Related to the challenge of facilitating usability work in organizations, HCI community has already produced literature addressing specifically this problem. Part of the literature implies that there is a 'one best way' to successfully introduce usability work into organizations. These studies outline a set of activities and principles that should and could be applied in any organization. Generally this literature suggests the following aspects as critical. Developers are seen as the most important target group [2], [3], [12], [27]. The development team should perceive usability specialists as allies [12], [27], [32]. Developers' involvement in the usability work is seen as a very important factor [2], [3], [12]. However, also the management commitment and support is seen as an important criterion for success [12]. Furthermore, a strong, centralized group of usability specialists is recommended [12], [27], [38] and the importance of experienced, professional usability specialists highlighted [2], [12].

The literature also identifies as important the creation of documentation on best practices [2], printed materials describing the methods and techniques for usability work [12] and a formal development process with usability work included [12], [27], [38]. Moreover, the results of usability work should be documented and made available [2]. As an addition to the facilitation of usability work, there usually are other change and improvement initiatives in organizations. Usability specialists should be perceived as allies to these initiatives [3], [27]. In addition, marketing, training and documentation should be addressed and cooperation initiated. Usability specialists should act as change agents addressing many different target groups in their organizations. [3], [21], [27], [32]. Altogether, it is argued that usability work should be 'sold' into organizations [27]. Presentation of the things you do and especially of the results achieved is recommended [3], [32]. Quick results are important [3]. One should also be able to show the benefits achieved [27], [32]. The business perspective is highlighted [3], [12], [27], [32] - usability work should make sense from the business perspective and be related to achieving key business goals [3], [12]. Also cost-benefit tradeoffs may play a major role in the adoption of usability work - low cost methods are preferred [38]. Finally, the resources for usability work should be planned and budgeted [2] - usability work should not increase development costs and time [3].

On the other had, other studies argue that one should understand the context in which usability work is to be facilitated more thoroughly in order to select the most suitable strategy. Processes should not be followed religiously. [1], [33], [35] Processes should be used as guides not to be executed mechanistically. Instead, a highly adaptive approach is recommended. [21] Generalizable guidelines for the facilitation of usability work are not good, and instead the emphasis should be on supporting developers' ingenuity, reflection and improvisation. [4], [29], [35] Furthermore, it is also highlighted that the social and organizational context should not be neglected [6], [16], [18], [33], [34], [35]. In addition, organizational politics and conflicts should be acknowledged [1], [6], [18], [21], [23], [33], [34]. Also the role of organizational culture should be understood and addressed [3], [6], [7], [21], [27], [29], [32], [34]. Finally, some studies warn that very different meanings have been attached to user involvement – it has been used only as a buzzword [7], [23], [33].

2.1 Critical Review of the Guidelines

The advice can be categorized by utilizing the distinctions between realism vs. nominalism and determinism vs. voluntarism [5], [22]. Realist, deterministic position 'implies that reality is predictable and at least in principle manipulable, prescribable and designable' [22]; human beings are postulated as responding to the external events in a mechanistic or even deterministic way [5]. Nominalist, voluntarist position, on the other hand, views 'social phenomena largely as emergent and not directly designable' [22]; human agent is viewed as a creator of the environment and as a controller rather than as controlled [5]. The studies outlining mechanistic, universally valid activities and principles for usability work that should and could be applied in any organization can be labeled as relying on a realist, deterministic orientation. The only problem is to figure out how to exploit usability work the most efficient way (cf. [20]). This position can be criticized of relying on very mechanistic assumptions about organizations and people. On a more practical level there is a risk that facilitation strategies and models relying on this type of assumptions cannot take into account the complexity involved in the facilitation of usability work in any organizational context. There is a risk in their application in real life environments, in which one cannot escape the complexity.

On the other hand, other studies highlight that processes should not be followed religiously and improvisation, reflection and ingenuity are always needed. The one facilitating usability work should always be aware of the multitude of factors (cultural, organizational, social, political) that affect usability work in organizations. Furthermore, it is highlighted that very divergent interpretations can be attached to usability work in practice. Therefore, within this position usability work is seen as raw material that can be tailored and modified by human actors (cf. [20]). It is argued that management can never directly control this process, but instead a multiplicity of meanings will be attached to it in practice. Furthermore, also paradoxical, ironic and unexpected reactions and consequences are possible, since interpretations cannot be controlled or directed. (cf. [31]) This advice relies on more nominalist, voluntarist orientation. The emergent, context-specific nature of the facilitation of usability work is highlighted. One could argue that adopting this position might provide more realistic basis for the facilitation of usability work, since the complexity is at least acknowledged, even though the process might never be controllable or directly manipulable.

3 Communities of Practice

As mentioned, the organizational context of the facilitation of usability work needs to be acknowledged. Recent literature in organizational studies highlights that organizations should be characterized by differentiation and diversity. A view of organization as a harmonious, unified phenomenon is criticized of being too simplistic and static. Instead, organizational reality needs to be seen as contested, changing and emergent. Researchers should examine how meanings are created, recreated and negotiated in organizations. [9], [31]. Altogether, organizations should be seen as multicultural, and clashes and conflicts as distinctive features. Researchers should pay attention to the inconsistencies and lack of consensus in any organizational context [9]. Also the inevitable multitude of subcultures and occupational communities should be acknowledged [9], [36]. Especially occupational communities and divergent communities of practice are influential within organizations [9], [36], [37].

A community consists of individuals who interact with each other and consider themselves as a group - a collective identity has evolved [26], [36], [37]. A community of practice necessitates a community to have a joint enterprise, and a practice supporting the enterprise. [26], [37] A community of practice is also characterized by mutual engagement of the members and by shared repertoires of resources (tools, techniques, language etc.). Membership necessitates interaction between the members and existence of mutual relationships. Characteristic are feelings of solidarity and construction of boundaries against outsiders. Members also have a mutually defining identity and common styles or ways of displaying it. Use of specific language expresses membership and status, and thus provides a basis for identification. [26], [36], [37]

In this paper usability specialists are conceptualized as a specific community of practice within the context of SW development organizations. This community of practice, their practice, and their interaction with other communities within the larger organizational context will be illuminated in the empirical part of the paper.

4 Research Design

In this research effort we have gathered empirical research material related to the process of usability work and to the context of usability work from three product development units (case units A-C) from three SW development companies during three years time. Units A and C are organizational units of large global corporations. Unit B is an organizational unit of a Small to Medium Sized Enterprise. The units have from 16 to 30 employees. In the research effort we utilized an interpretive case study method, in which researchers attempt to make sense of the world, not to explain in the sense of predicting. In the focus are the meanings attached to the phenomenon studied. Aim is to capture the native's point of view, to produce 'thick descriptions', and to gain thorough understandings of particular cases. Theories are used only as sensitizing devices; they are not to be falsified, as is the case in the positivist case studies. [11], [24].

The research material was gathered while conducting process assessments in the units, and while supporting the units in the facilitation of usability work by offering workshops and training. In the process assessments we interviewed the personnel of the units related to their ways of working in a selected project, and evaluated whether usability work was carried out in the projects. The research team has also regularly had meetings with the personnel of the units. Memos from the meetings, the assessment reports, and all e-mail correspondence with the personnel of the units have been saved for the purposes of the research. Research team has also written down field notes after all joint events. Furthermore, we have gathered specifically contextual data from the units. We have experimented with different techniques for data gathering - organizational culture surveys, themes interviews and workshop sessions. In the interviews we gathered feedback from the survey results, and discussed the context and process of usability work in the units. In the workshops we discussed and evaluated the interview results. Therefore, the technique of member checking was utilized extensively.

The data analysis proceeded in different phases. Case study write-ups were produced related to each unit, and commented by the interviewees and by the workshop participants. In the analysis of usability work in the units we went through all the empirical material gathered during 3 years time, and listed the usability activities carried out in the units and the preferences for the future the units had expressed during the years. The workshop participants commented also on this material in the workshop sessions. Afterwards, we used the concept of community of practice as a sensitizing device. We analyzed usability specialists as a specific community of practice, and usability work as their practice. This community of practice, their practice, and their interaction with other communities in their organizations were under examination.

5   Empirical Examinations

In all case units there were one or more usability specialists hired. However, they had divergent educational backgrounds (e.g. in information systems, engineering, psychology, design science) and amounts of work experience (from a couple of years to over ten years). All had some familiarity with the field of HCI, but not necessarily through education. The practical ways of involving the users resembled that of the consultative type [10] in all the case units. The usability specialists 'represented the users in the development'. They had carried out customer visits (interviewed and observed the users) and evaluated design solutions by using methods such as laboratory usability testing, paper prototyping and different kinds of usability inspection methods. Next the specific features of each unit are reviewed.

In unit A the first usability specialist was hired six years ago. Now there is a team of four usability specialists in the unit. In addition to the usability specialists, the manager of the unit has emphasized the importance of usability work a lot: "the path has been smoothened a lot probably because management has had such a positive attitude and has marketed this thing (usability work). Due to this also workers have at least at some level quite a positive perception of this" (Usability specialist A). The rest of the personnel are SW developers whose responsibilities include designing, coding and testing the SW – including the user interface (UI) SW.

In this unit the usability specialists label themselves as a *'mommy mob'* (Usability specialist A). They view their role to be a 'controlling mommy mob' in their unit:

> "When you bring usability orientation into an organization you have to be a police in the beginning. The developers don't have the knowledge needed in their head, and you have to act as a police." (Usability specialist A)

> "Here we have a quality organization who perceives quality within a rules oriented approach. Numerical things are highlighted; bugs and stuff like that. We have quality plans and report the bugs and follow the projects. (...) We have these control mechanisms, and they're very powerful. If you try to compete with them, and you aren't in the control mechanisms, then you are left out. Because these control mechanisms set the pressures." (Usability specialist, A)

In unit A 'what is measured, that is done'. Usability work has to be measured and included in the control mechanisms, otherwise 'it is left out'; "in the same way as SW metrics are gathered, they should be gathered for usability" (Developer A). Also the developers have quite a positive perception of this controlling effort:

> "If things can be measured one can show how well one has succeeded and where one can improve and what went wrong. All measured things are concrete. It can be bugs in the SW or usability. (...) Things are prioritised and those that are measured and controlled, those can't be left out. (...) Controlling, constant controlling and monitoring, its part of normal project work. (...) If usability work can be measured and controlled, then it's more natural, then its just part of your job." (Team leader A)

However, usability and UI design will not be the main concern of the developers: "our work involves a lot of investigation of new things. Most of our time is spent on investigating things when we are designing new things and new interfaces. And when someone has thought of a new part for the system, then we have to investigate how it affects our part of the system. Most of our time is spent on investigating things. Quite little time is spent on coding or on designing the UI." (Developer A)

Related to the facilitation of usability work, the 'grand mission' in this unit is to "solve how usability can be very effectively integrated with other processes" (Project documentation). Another challenge is the development, evaluation and documentation of methods, tools and techniques for usability work (Project documentation). Altogether, "we have put a lot of effort on the improvement efforts and meta-level work related to context of use knowledge. We have spent a lot of time on that. And less time on concrete work with products and projects" (Usability specialist A). This is because: "we are used to having these tools before we start our work. We miss them and want to have them also here (in usability work)" (Manager A).

However, problematic is that the developers do not appreciate usability work; they perceive usability work as pedantic decoration in the last phase of the project:

"A coder is not excited about things like that. If you have a passion for coding, then you code. And some senior, for example architects, especially here the important things are the functionality of the SW and the interfaces. It is so technical here. You don't then necessarily think that the most important thing of the UI is that it is usable." (Developer A)

"Projects have always limited resources and one must decide whether to invest in the finishing touch (usability) or in bugs and functionality. (Project manager A)

"Yes, sure, sometimes it feels like the usability issues become kind of useless speculation. (...) Sometimes the usability work is over emphasized. If we are in a hurry, it might be that we don't have time for these speculations." (Developer A)

Also the larger organizational context is brought up. Unit A alone can't ensure usability of the system. Cooperation with other units is needed, but the other units don't understand the importance of this nor have the knowledge for doing this:

"If you think of the problem, it is that our unit develops the UIs, and due to this the whole usability is our responsibility. They (other units) don't understand that all stakeholders should put effort into making the product usable. If the other parts of the project do not support usability, we can only decorate in here." (Usability specialist A)

The usability specialists have taken the responsibility to organize cooperation with other units. However, in this case organization facilitating usability work: "is extremely painful and persevering job. You must proceed slowly and take small steps. You can't change the direction of a ship of this size very fast." (Manager A)

Unit B, on the other hand, has very long history in usability work; it started over ten years ago. There has been a team of usability specialists and graphical designers in the unit, but currently there is only one usability specialist and few graphical designers left. However, both a team leader and a manager are former usability specialists. The graphical designers and usability specialists formed a very tight group within this unit: "we had a lot of co-operation, especially when we had more people in our team" (Usability specialist B). However, most of the personnel also in this unit are SW developers. A couple of developers focus specifically on UI development.

In this unit the usability specialists identify themselves as 'humanists working with engineers' (Usability specialist B). Their strategy for usability work can be characterized as 'sneaking in, in secret':

"I think that it is very important from the point of view of user centeredness that our manager is a usability specialist; that there is that kind of competence. We can avoid a lot of unnecessary work, because our manager makes the decisions. We can trust her. (...) This user-centered viewpoint kind of affects other things in secret. (...) I think that it is better that all know little about it than we have a dozen of usability specialists and rest of the personnel know nothing about it. Because this situation it is a battlefield. Or there should be a developer and usability specialist doing things together all the time. But in this situation the developer becomes a usability specialist almost naturally." (Team leader B)

The 'sneaking in, in secret' is perceived as the most efficient way in this unit, since: "we do what we want. We have this traditional culture. X (a product) wouldn't have been invented if we had obeyed the managers. But people did it in the lab" (Team leader B). "Doing things together, it is the most effective way to teach. It is much more efficient that to produce fancy guidelines for how things ought to be done. At least for part of our personnel. Some people might be good in following written work descriptions, but those are quite rare here." (Manager B) One of the former usability specialists further argues: "I have been doing this job so long that the utopia has disappeared. You understand the realities. I have spent here ten years with the engineers and worked with them. You learn to take new perspectives and don't fancy vain things. You learn to live with it and adjust your own ways of working." (Manager B)

Also in this context it is the developers who have problematic perceptions of usability work. Technological development 'wins' and usability is seen as decoration:

"Truly, we have a feeling that the development service people (including usability specialists and graphical designers) are the 'second rate' people. We are, our history is technocratic, and technology is appreciated here. (...) I understand that the technology is important; it has to be there. But when we compete of the resources, it is always the technology that wins." (Team leader B)

"Our team got into a rut because usability specialists and graphical designers cannot alone affect anything. People thought that our team could do everything. But we ran out of steam, because it is the developer who actually implements everything. (...) People thought that UI developers are not needed and technical skills are not needed. Like our team could do it, like it could just make a decoration over the top of the technology." (Team leader B)

This is one of the reasons the team of usability specialists and graphical designers does not exist anymore: "the fact that the team existed created an illusion that usability issues are taken care of. There were people who took care of these issues and had knowledge of these issues, but the knowledge didn't necessarily have any contact with the end product or how it was developed" (Graphical designer B). Furthermore, some of the developers strongly maintain that it is not their job to think about the user:

"These java coders, quite many of them have a strong opinion that they don't touch the UIs. Someone else has to do that. They won't do it. And this reflects their professionalism. They have different type of design problems. (Manager B)

There are a couple of UI developers in the unit. One of them cooperates considerably with the usability specialist; she has participated in the customer visits and paper prototyping sessions, and writes a style guide together with the usability specialist. However, 'not all developers participate like her' (Usability specialist B). Furthermore: "here has not been much UI development. We don't have that tradition in here. We haven't even had a strong team here who would have developed them. We have only had few individuals and they have been quite alone in here." (Team leader B)

Related to the larger organizational context, unit B functions very independently. However, the usability specialists have adopted a responsibility to educate also other units, i.e. sales and marketing: "it spreads through my and Ellen's (both former usability specialists) personalities, what we are able to tell about it. We forcefully talk about user centeredness, when they (sales and marketing) want to hear what we do" (Team leader B). Finally, in this unit the usability specialists highlight that usability work should especially contribute to the strategic level planning and decision-making. The business strategy and vision should be influenced by user orientation: "here the most important targets for improvement are not related to making the position of the usability specialists better or their work easier, but they are related to the strategic level (...) Related to the decision making, for example when you are defining what to include in the next release" (Manager B).

Finally, in unit C usability work has been part of the development from the establishment of the unit. Actually, usability work has been defined as one of the main competences the unit excels in (Project documentation). The personnel of this unit are all labeled as specialists focusing either on usability, or interaction, graphical or SW design. The usability specialists are labelled *'staid researchers'*, who are supposed to carry out the 'burdensome and dull' usability work in the unit:

"There are 'staid researchers', research oriented people, and in some other projects there are these 'careless designers'. (…) This 'research gang' questions existing things and wants to examine things. On the other hand, these designers like to do things that are fun. They don't have, like arguments, behind their decisions. Designers produce designs from a very creative point of view, not from the point of view of the user." (Usability specialist C)

"There exists some unwillingness to carry out usability tests, because usability activities are perceived to be burdensome and dull. (…) Brainstorming sessions are their (designers) favorite sessions, those sessions in which relatively lightweight methods are used. (…) Ideating is fun, but systematically using certain methods seems to be unappealing to some of these 'ideators' (designers)" (Usability specialist C)

The 'careless designers' have condemned usability work as burdensome and dull. Furthermore, there are problems with management commitment to usability work – the personnel complain that the management doesn't demand usability work: "management has not understood to demand for quality, which, together with the lowering of the competence level has resulted in degradation of usability" (Usability specialist C).

In this context there is not much control of work and the project work is chaotic: "we have a lot of freedom to do things in new ways. (...) Processes, we don't have anything agreed on, like officially. Everything is informal. (…) I have to say out loud that project work is chaotic. (…) I think that the motive behind this is that we do creative work. And creative work necessitates freedom" (Usability specialist C). However, the usability specialists wish for more control. Their preference for future action is related to: "how to evaluate the product as an addition to the process? It is easy to evaluate a process, but how about its effectiveness?" (Project documentation) The problem is that in this unit "qualitative criteria (easy to use) are readily proposed, but they can not be verified" (Project documentation). Furthermore:

"We have bad quality measures. And when targets for individuals are defined and afterwards evaluated whether they are met, they are always quantitative. It is always certain document: whether it is produced. But the question should be: how has the content been produced, what methods have been used, and are they rational and generally acknowledged methods? We don't have measures for this type of things." (Usability specialist C)

"The (usability) specialists have done these things, for example things to do with strategic planning. And they have initiated these process improvement efforts. Those have come from bottom up rather than top down. Probably too much. And the specialists shout that there should be more quality and improvement." (Usability specialist C)

Furthermore, more cost-effective methods are called for, since the methods currently used have proven out to be very resource demanding:

"It (a method) is so resource-costly. From the viewpoint of the project it is a risky method. It is a big risk to choose. As a method it is fine and fun and includes everything. But when you are planning the project, you are taking a big risk from the viewpoint of the schedules (…) Things are prolonged, prolonged, prolonged" (Project manager C)

"It (usability testing) is also a risk. It takes time to prepare, it takes time to carry out, and its analysis takes time. This time is taken away from other issues." (Usability specialist C)

6 Discussion

The paper conceptualized usability specialists forming a specific community of practice within the context of SW development organizations. In the analysis of this community of practice the focus was on the joint practice of this community (usability work). Table 1 summarizes the findings that are related to the collective identity (who are we?); to the joint practice (what do we do?); and to the helping and hindering 'outsider' groups (who do we work with?) in the case organizations.

Table 1. Usability Specialists as a Community of Practice

Unit	Unit A	Unit B	Unit C
Identity (who are we?)	'A controlling mommy mob'	'Realistic humanists working with engineers'	'Staid researchers'
Joint Practice (what do we do?)	- Meta-level work - Control people	- 'Sneak in, in secret', cooperate with designers and developers - Participate in strategic decision making	- Carry out usability work alone in projects - Participate in the strategic level planning and quality improvement
Helping outsider groups	- Management: strong management support	- Graphical designers: team mates - UI developers: cooperate in usability work	-
Hindering outsider groups	- SW developers: usability work pedantic decoration - Other units: don't support usability	- SW developers: usability work decoration - Management: usability as a buzzword	- Designers: usability work pedantic, dull and burdensome - Management: usability as a buzzword

Regarding the facilitation of usability work, the existing HCI literature suggests that one should especially involve and educate the developers, have a strong group of usability specialists, document the methods and tools for usability work, incorporate them into the development process, involve other organizational units and change efforts, carry out cost-benefit analyses and show the business benefits of usability work. However, in the case organizations there clearly are divergent strategies for usability work. The formal development process with usability work integrated and the documentation of methods and tools can be associated with unit A, the importance of cooperation with the developers with unit B, the interest in strategic level decision-making with B and C, the importance of low cost methods with unit C and the cooperation with other organizational units with A and B. Therefore, the empirical results seem to suggest that in different contexts different strategies to usability work are adopted.

Related to the difference between the realist, deterministic and the nominalist, voluntarist position to the facilitation of usability work, the results seem to provide support for the latter. The results show that divergent interpretations have been attached to usability work in divergent settings: usability work has been perceived only as a buzz-word (B and C), as decoration in the last phase of the project (A and B), as pedantic, delaying factor (A and C) and as a strategic level factor contributing to the business success (B and C). Furthermore, also the attributes attached to usability specialists show that usability work can be perceived in clearly divergent ways in organizations; 'a mommy mob', 'realist humanists' and 'staid researchers' clearly advocate different interpretations of usability work. Furthermore, these divergent interpretations emerged in divergent contexts: the mommy mob operates in a context is which 'constant con-trolling is normal project work', the realist humanists try to 'sneak in, in secret' in a context in which 'technology always wins' and people 'do what they want' and the 'staid researchers' work in a context in which 'everything is informal' and 'project work I chaotic', but in which they try to demand for more quality and control.

Finally, divergent 'outsider groups' seem to provide helping and hindering factors to the usability work in different contexts. Designers might be either teammates or the worst criticizers of usability work. Developers altogether seem to have rather prob-lematic perceptions of usability work, but if the responsibility of the UI development is assigned to specific UI developers, they might also show clear interest in the usabil-ity work. Therefore, the facilitation of usability work might be conceptualized as a dynamic, volitional, context-dependent process in which mechanistic, universal, con-text-free strategies will not work, at least as they are expected to work. Based on this study and the existing literature one could also suggest that it should be acknowledged that usability work, while introduced into organizations, will be interpreted and rein-terpreted in these contexts in an emergent process of sense making that is not manipu-lable or directly controllable. Furthermore, the results also suggest that paradoxical and unexpected consequences are possible, since interpretations cannot be controlled. In the case organizations several 'outsider groups' were identified, and they had also surprising and conflicting interpretations of usability work.

As an implication for practice, we argue that sensitivity to the contextual issues in the facilitation of usability work is important. The problem of selecting a fitting strat-egy for the facilitation is brought up. Especially practitioners introducing usability work into their organization could benefit from the insights presented in this paper. Furthermore, the paper advocates the nominalist, voluntarist position related to the fa-cilitation of usability work. Mechanistic, universal, context-free strategies for the fa-cilitation of usability work seem to rely on naïve notions of people and change in or-ganizations. Acknowledging this can provide a more realistic basis for the facilitation of usability work, since the complexity related to this phenomenon is at least ac-knowledged, even though one might never be able to control or directly manipulate the process. Regarding the limitations of this study, the paper is based on the analysis of only three cases. In the future this type of analyses should be carried out in more varying contexts employing a larger amount of cases. The results of this paper are to be utilized in a NOMADIC MEDIA project in which multiple European partners par-ticipate in the development of new technologies and services for nomadic users. Paths for further work include also a further analysis of usability work in the case organiza-tions. Follow up data related to the facilitation of usability work is to be gathered – this paper provides only one snapshot of dynamic, continuous process of the facilita-tion of usability work in the SW development organizations.

References

1. Allen, C. D. (1995): Succeeding as a Clandestine Change Agent. Communications of the ACM 38(5). Pp. 81-86
2. Aucella. A. (1997): Ensuring Success with Usability Engineering. Interactions May + June. Pp. 19-22
3. Bloomer, S. – Croft, R. (1997): Pitching Usability to Your Organization. Interactions November + December. Pp. 18-26
4. Bodker, S. – Buur, J. (2002): The Design Collaboratorium – a Place for Usability Design. ACM Transactions on Computer-Human Interaction 9(2). Pp. 152-169
5. Burrell, G. – Morgan, G. (1979): Sociological Paradigms and Organizational Analysis. Elements of the Sociology of Corporate Life. London: Heinemann Educational Books Ltd.
6. Butler, T. – Fitzgerald, B. (1997): A Case Study of User Participation in the Information Systems Development Process. In Kumar, K., DeGross, J. (Eds.): Proc. ICIS 1997, Atlanta, USA. Pp. 411-426
7. Catarci, T. – Matarazzo, G. – Raiss, G. (2002): Driving usability into the public administration: the Italian experience. International Journal of Human-Computer Studies 57. Pp. 121-138
8. Cooper, C. – Bowers, J. (1995): Representing the users: Notes on the disciplinary rhetoric of human-computer interaction. In Thomas, P. (Eds.): The Social and Interactional Dimensions of Human-Computer Interfaces. Cambridge: Cambridge University Press.
9. Czarniawska-Joerges, B. (1992): Exploring Complex Organizations. A Cultural Perspective. Newbury Park: Sage Publications.
10. Damodaran, L. (1996): User involvement in the systems designs process - a practical guide for users. Behaviour & Information Technology 15(16). Pp. 363-377
11. Denzin, N. K. – Lincoln, Y. S. (2000): Introduction: The Discipline and Practice of Qualitative Research. In Denzin, N, Lincoln, Y. (Eds.): Handbook of Qualitative Research. 2nd edition. Thousand Oaks: Sage Publications Inc.
12. Fellenz, C. B. (1997): Introducing Usability into Smaller Organizations. Interactions September/October. Pp. 29-33
13. Gould, J. D. – Lewis, C. (1985): Designing for Usability: Key Principles and What Designers Think. Communications of the ACM. Vol. 28(3). Pp. 300-311
14. Gronbak, K. – Grudin, J. – Bodker, S. – Bannon, L. (1993): Achieving Cooperative System Design: Shifting From a Product to a Process Focus. In Schuler, D., Namioka, A. (Eds.): Participatory Design: Principles and Practices. New Jersey: Lawrence Erlbaum Associates.
15. Grudin, J. (1991): Interactive Systems: Bridging the Gaps Between Developers and Users. IEEE Computer 24(4). Pp. 59-69
16. Grudin, J. (1993): Obstacles to Participatory Design in Large Product Development Organizations. In Douglas Schuler – Aki Namioka (Eds.): Participatory Design: Principles and Practices. New Jersey: Lawrence Erlbaum Associates. Pp. 99-122
17. Grudin, J. (1996): The organizational contexts of development and use. ACM Computing Surveys 28(1). 169-171
18. Gärtner, J. – Wagner, I. (1996): Mapping Actors and Agendas: Political Frameworks of Systems Design and Participation. Human-Computer Interaction 11(3). Pp. 187-214
19. Halstead-Nussloch, R. – Konneh, D. – Woodruff, R. (2003): Communities of Design Practice in Electronic Government. In Cockton, C., Korhonen, P. (Eds.): Proc. CHI 2003. ACM Press. Pp. 744-745

20. Hirschheim, R. (1986): The Effect of A Priori Views on the Social Implications of Computing: The Case of Office Automation. ACM Computing Surveys 18(2). Pp. 165-195

21. Hutchings, A. F. – Knox, S. T. (1995): Creating Products - Customer Demand. Communications of the ACM 38(5). Pp. 72-80

22. Iivari, J. – Hirschheim, R. (1996): Analyzing information systems development: a comparison and analysis of eight IS development approaches. Information Systems 21(7). Pp. 551-575

23. Kirsch, L. J. – Beath, C. M. (1996): The enactments and consequences of token, shared, and compliant participation in information systems development. Accounting, Management, & Information Technologies 6(4). Pp. 221-254

24. Klein, H. K. – Myers, M. D. (1999): A Set of Principles for Conducting and Evaluating Interpretive Field Studies in Information Systems. MIS Quarterly 23(1). Pp. 67-94

25. Kyng, M. (1994): Scandinavian Design: Users in Product Development. In Adelson, B., Dumais, S., Olson, J. (Eds.): Proc. CHI 1994. ACM Press. Pp. 3-9

26. Lave, J. - Wenger, J. (1991): Situated learning: Legitimate peripheral participation. Cambridge: Cambridge University Press

27. Mayhew, D. J. (1999): Business: Strategic Development of Usability Engineering Function. Interactions 6(5). Pp. 27-34

28. Muller, M. J. - Carey, K. (2002): Design as a Minority Discipline in a Software Company: Toward Requirements for a Community of Practice. In L. Terveen (Eds.) Proc. CHI'02. ACM Press. Pp. 383-390

29. Nandhakumar, J. – Jones, M. (1997): Designing in the Dark: the Changing User-Developer Relationship in Information Systems Development. In Kumar, K., DeGross, J. (Eds.): Proc. ICIS 1997, Atlanta, USA. Pp. 75-86

30. Poltrock, S. – Grudin, J. (1994): Organizational Obstacles to Interface Design and Development: Two Participant – Observer Studies. ACM Transactions on Computer-Human Interaction 1(1). Pp. 52-80.

31. Robey, D. – Azevedo, A. (1994): Cultural Analysis of the Organizational Consequences of Information Technology. Accounting, Management & Information Technology 4(1). Pp. 23-37

32. Rosenbaum, S. – Rohn, J. A. – Humburg, J. (2000): A Toolkit for Strategic Usability: Results from Workshops, Panels, and Surveys. In Turner, T., Szwillus, G., Czerwinski, M., Paterno, F., Pemberton, S. (Eds.): Proc. CHI 2000. ACM Press. Pp. 337-344

33. Symon, G. (1998): The Work of IT System Developers in Context: An Organizational Case Study. Human-Computer Interaction 13. Pp. 37-71.

34. Taylor-Cummings, A. (1998): Bridging the user-IS gap: a study of major information systems projects. Journal of Information Technology 13. Pp. 29-54.

35. Thoresen, K. (1993): Principles in Practice: Two Cases of Situated Participatory Design. In Douglas Schuler – Aki Namioka (Eds.): Participatory Design: Principles and Practices. New Jersey: Lawrence Erlbaum Associates.

36. van Maanen, J. – Barley, S. R. (1984): Occupational communities: Culture and control in Organizations. In Staw, B., Cummings, L. (Eds.). Research in Organizational Behavior 6. Greenwich: JAI Press.

37. Wenger, E. (1998): Communities of Practice: Learning, Meaning and Identity. New York: Cambridge University Press.

38. Vredenburg, K. – Mao, J - Smith, P. W. – Casey, T. (2002): A survey of user-centered design practice. In D. Wixon (ed.) Proceedings of CHI'02. ACM Press. Pp. 471-478.

Exposing Middle School Girls to Programming via Creative Tools

Gahgene Gweon, Jane Ngai, and Jenica Rangos

Carnegie Mellon University, Pittsburgh, PA USA
{gkg, jngai, jrangos}@cmu.edu

Abstract. This paper explores design concepts and principles to engage middle school girls in learning preliminary programming concepts through different media and interaction techniques. Creating a greeting card and creating a personal avatar for an Instant Messenger (IM) were two approaches that were examined. Findings suggest that an IM avatar creation tool, with guiding principles including partial manipulation of code, immediate feedback, engaging content, reinforcement exercises, and transition from concrete to abstract examples, may interest girls to start learning programming concepts.

1 Introduction

Gender imbalance with male domination in the professional IT workforce has long been observed, as the number of female graduates in Computer Science majors or similar disciplines remains low. Efforts have been made to promote Computer Science in high schools. Yet, statistics reveal that the number of female computer science graduates has been declining each year from 32.5% in 1980[15] to 27.6% in 2002 [8]. The root of this phenomenon traces back to a low enrollment rate in High School, where programming classes have been traditionally dominated by boys [15].

There has been a lot of research towards investigating reasons for a lack of female interest in Computer Science. Currently, promotions and educational campaigns are trying to correct girls' perception of Computer Science as a "male" domain, and the stereotype that programming is a "nerdy" activity. Prior research indicates that girls prefer collaboration more than competition. Furthermore, girls view the computer as a tool used to achieve an end result, while boys see the computer as a toy for enjoyment [4, 15]. As of 2000, girls seem to be more familiar with technology. They are more "computer literate"; many understand common widgets in software applications. They use computers frequently as a social tool, as they use email and instant messengers. They also use computers to perform tasks such as doing research, writing papers, handling graphics, and drawing with visual tools [5].

So, what distinguishes girls from boys? Programming is difficult for all beginners and although girls are computer literate, they still don't go into computer professions as much as boys. Since girls envision the computer as a tool, the materials covered in traditional introductory programming classes become mundane and impractical [6]. For example, typical assignments in beginner programming classes may include an exercise to calculate the sum of numbers using loops and conditions. Summing up

M.F. Costabile and F. Paternò (Eds.): INTERACT 2005, LNCS 3585, pp. 431–442, 2005.

numbers may seem irrelevant to an interesting end result. Even if gender differences are disregarded, programming is difficult for all novice users. This is shown by a study done at the University of Michigan that estimates the percentage of novices that will continue to program after taking a programming class is less than 1 percent [11] One reason could be that the distance between the programming world and the problem world is too large [10]. Programming languages are not presented in a way that matches the users' mental model. Creating an interesting end result requires more advanced programming skills, and girls may decide that programming is not interesting before they can learn sufficient programming skills to apply to a problem with a practical and "interesting end-goal".

The purpose of this study is to expose middle school girls to some preliminary programming concepts through some attractive means. Although many studies have been done in exploring reasons for the low female involvement rates in technology, work in exploring ways to motivate young girls to programming is still at a relatively pioneer stage. Middle school girls from 5th to 8th grade were chosen to be the target audience for this study. At this point of their education, they are not settled on the path they will pursue in High School and later in college. These years are the critical stage when girls are introduced a variety of subject areas, and likely the period when many girls decide not to pursue computer science [6].

A tool to entice girls to learn programming concepts would require compelling, engaging content that would produce a concrete end result. Over the course of this study, two approaches were considered and carried out in this study to address the needs of teenage group – a Greeting Card tool and an avatar for Instant Messaging.

2   Phase I – Greeting Card Tool

The greeting card tool would provide means of creating a greeting card with simple animations and text while exposing girls to introductory programming concepts. Greeting cards have a large capacity in fulfilling girls' desire to construct an interesting product.

2.1   Our Hypothesis and Design Realization

In order to meet the main goal of introducing girls to programming and sparking their interest in computer science, a greeting card application seemed to hold potential as an excellent introduction. We hypothesized that greeting cards would provide social connection between people and a motivating factor in making something for specific recipient(s). Our tool consists of 3 sections: step-by-step wizard, code, greeting card stage.

Four guiding principles were used to aid in achieving the main objective. The first principle is to enable learning by direct manipulation of graphical user interface (GUI). Generating code is a difficult activity, especially for beginners who are first introduced to the subject of programming [9]. Generating code that produces an entertaining or engaging product proves more difficult. To enhance the girls' ability to learn programming, a GUI might serve as a mediating tool between the girl and the code. Participants do not need to write the code directly, but can manipulate the GUI

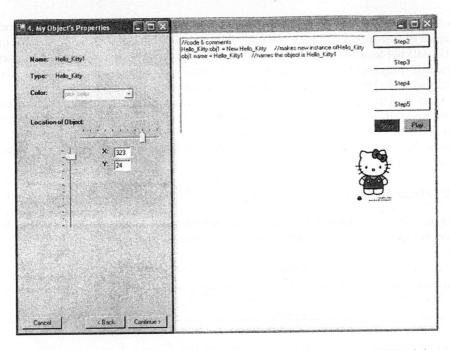

Fig. 1. Greeting Card Tool interface. The left pane is the step-by-step wizard. The right pane consists of code section on top and greeting card stage on the bottom.

in order to change the code. The aim is for users to see code, understand that it can change and produce an action. This is achieved with a step-by-step wizard in the interface. Users can select an object from a cupboard filled with popular characters, change the object's various properties, animate the object by manipulating its x and y coordinated in addition to changing the background color and type text.

The second principle is to produce practical and concrete results. Tangible results are important to girls as seen in literature [4, 5, 15]. Unlike their male counterparts, girls do not view programming or using the computer as a game; instead, they view the computer and programming as a tool used as a means to an end. Greeting cards are useful and fun end products, since girls enjoy making greeting cards for special occasions for friends and family as evidenced in our surveys.

The third principle is to provide visual feedback. Feedback provided during programming is often neither visual nor immediate. Users must first program and then compile to see the results. In most programming environments, abstract text errors provide the only source of feedback. It is difficult to understand what is going on just with the textual feedback, especially for novices. In this interface, visual feedback is provided in two ways in this interface: in both the code and greeting card stage sections when the user makes a change via the wizard section. For example, manipulating the x and y coordinates to change the character position or the background color of the card from the wizard section updates both the code and the greeting card sections instantly. Users can immediately see changes on the screen as a result of their manipulation. Traditional feedback, analogous to that of compiling is also provided. In the final wizard step, the user should press a "Play" button, placed in the code section, to see the final animation of the card. This is an attempt to convey the correct mental model of programming - to compile programs before they are run - so that the girls will not have to unlearn concepts when they program without the aid of our tool. Moreover, comments are shown in the code section as an additional source of feedback, with the intention of encouraging good programming practice.

Our final principle is to have engaging and entertaining content. Programming greeting cards appears to be inherently more entertaining than many other first activities introduced in beginner level programming courses. Popular characters such as "Hello Kitty" and "Baby Cheese" were used in the tool. The user may choose a character of his/her choice from the repository.

2.2 Methods

Research began with a structured field interviewing method based on understanding the context in which a product is used, known as Contextual Inquiries (CI) [1].

Table 1. Methods used in Phase I

Method	Number of Users	Age	Location
Contextual Inquiry 1	12 girls	11-12	Fox Chapel Middle School
Contextual Inquiry 2	20 boys & girls	6-13	Carnegie Science Center
User Test	6 girls	6-13	Carnegie Science Center
Survey	14 boys & girls	11-12	Fox Chapel Middle School

There were 12 girls interviewed in the first CI and 20 boys and girls in second CI. During both CIs, children made greeting cards with materials such as pencil, construction paper, glitter glue, and other paper products. The goal was to observe the students' creative process, the components children believed were essential to their greeting card, the characters they chose, the quantity of text used, and the occasion for which they made the card. Subsequently, we conducted think-aloud usability testing with 6 girls. A survey with 14 boys and girls was also conducted to understand teenagers' card making habits, their favorite holidays, and their exposure to computers and the Internet. Participants were asked to create a greeting card using the greeting card tool. During the think aloud usability testing, participants were encouraged to think aloud while creating a greeting card by animating the character object chosen, changing the properties of their choice, and adding text to the card. Due to time constraints and the process required to recruit students to participate in user testing, we performed pilot testing with fellow master students before testing it with the target population to catch main usability problems.

2.3 Findings and Lessons Learned

Direct manipulation of GUI helped the girls engage in programming activity more easily. Yet, it had an unexpected side effect. It did not help girls understand the relationship between the manipulated objects and the code. To complete the task, participants relied on direct manipulation provided by the wizard. No participants manipulated the code, asked what the code section of the screen did, or why it changed. However, 5 of 6 girls tried to manipulate objects on the greeting card stage in relation to the change in the wizard. Of the three main portions of the interface, the code portion was the only part that the participants did not touch, aside from when they pushed the play button to animate the card. During the debriefing section, one participant said, "I don't care about that [the code], I want to just play with this [wizard]". It was also unclear if they even noticed the code change as they manipulated the object. Placing the "play" button in the code portion of the scene did not encourage the users to look at the code. None of the users remarked on any of the dynamic changes in the code during the task. Our attempt to encourage the girls to the code by placing the "play" button in the code section failed. In sum, participants did not appear to learn any programming concepts from interaction with the interface.

Regarding the second principle of producing practical and concrete results, we observed from both contextual inquiries that greeting cards are something that users would make normally. A greeting card tool was shown to be a practical and concrete medium to use. During our first CI, all of the girls spent time before starting their card thinking of an occasion for which they could make their greeting card. Most girls made greeting cards for upcoming holidays, such as Mother's day, Father's day or St. Patrick's Day. None of the girls made cards for distant holidays such as Christmas, despite the fact that it was a popular favorite holiday among the participants according to the survey. Most girls made cards for their family members, while none of the girls made cards for their peer friends. 10 out of 12 girls took the cards with them. These observations seem to support that girls preferred to create something useful, if not immediately useful. However, in our subsequent contextual inquiries, greeting cards seemed to be not compelling enough for our target audience. The second CI that took place at the Science Center is a very different environment compared to a school environment where the first CI took place. The participants of the second CI were self-selected and the greeting card project had to compete with many other entertaining activities. Surprisingly, our greeting card table attracted both boys and girls who were approximately 6 years old who were much younger than our target audience. It was possible that the materials used afforded the interest of younger children. Nevertheless, overall evidence from our user testing also supports that the audience attracted to this activity were younger than intended. Not one middle school girl chose to make a greeting card unless solicited. The two middle school girls that participated in the user test indicated that they do not create greeting cards on a regular basis. It seemed that they were not interested in making greeting cards with the provided material, and even when asked to use the prototype, the majority preferred to engage in other activities at the science center such as viewing the exhibits or going to the Omnimax theatre.

The third principle of providing visual feedback worked well. Users were amused when they saw an object appearing or moving when they clicked the "Next" button in the wizard. Providing visual feedback at each step gave the users a sense of progress and kept them in context.

For the fourth principle to provide entertaining content, the use of characters such as "Hello Kitty" was successful. All girls chose well-known characters over alternative pictures. The younger users enjoyed the experience. From the girls' smiles, it seemed that they were reasonably impressed with the application's functionality, and were excited. Younger girls in particular had all expressed content and excitement. Some of them mentioned that the animation is "cool", "nice", or "fun". A noteworthy observation was that younger girls (age 9 or under) enjoyed the experience more. The middle school girls that participated in the study appeared to be less amused.

The greeting card interface had 2 general usability problems. First, none of the participants could add text to the card easily. In order to add text, the participant had to select the text object from the cupboard (the repository with character and text objects). The text object was not easily identified or distinguished from the other objects, because none of the participants saw this object immediately. Second, some of the objects in the cupboard seemed to afford dragging and dropping onto the stage; however, this functionality was not available. The participant could only manipulate the object by using the cupboard. Younger children accepted this functionality, but older girls who had more experience using the computer, had difficulty not trying to directly manipulate the object of the stage. These problems were previously revealed in the pilot test. The nature of these problems was thought to be mainly limitations of the prototype and did not affect the presentation of the main ideas of the interface. When participants reached the glitches and clearly demonstrated that they experienced the difficulties, the facilitators guided them through this step. These problems did not yield an unusable application; the interface also had some aspects that worked well. For example, the x and y axis scroll bars used to select the beginning and of an objects path, used in animation, seemed to be easy to use. Due to the visual feedback, most girls understood that manipulating the x or y scroll bar would move the object. Also, none of the girls had difficultly selecting a color for their card.

3 Phase II – Avatar for Instant Messaging

To address the concerns of motivating girls to programming through greeting cards, another medium was introduced in the second phase – a tool to create an avatar for Instant Messaging.

A study on what appeals to teenagers revealed that girls often identify themselves with characters; they like to be represented by characters, as if they were in a hypothetical story [4]. In addition, girls enjoy social interaction. 43% of surveyed 7th graders reported that they use instant messenger (IM) "all the time". This medium allows girls to socialize in cyberspace, while helping girls overcome shyness in talking with boys or about difficult topics [12]. Teenage girls often search for characteristics that identify themselves as a unique person, while conforming to trends and group standards [13].

An avatar for IM tool allows girls to design and customize a picture displayed on a chat window. This tool, when fully developed, could be used for various tasks in the context of an IM. Programming concepts are introduced through simple statements in changing properties and conditions. For example, using this tool, girls can create and customize a character that would represent themselves. They can use this tool to customize messages and pictures according to self-defined conditions by executing programming statements. This tool is predicted to satisfy girls' desire to identify themselves with characters, to see visual representations of themselves, while fitting into their social lives.

3.1 Our Hypothesis and Design Realization

For phase II, six principles are selected in total. Most of the hypotheses from phase I persist with slight modifications.

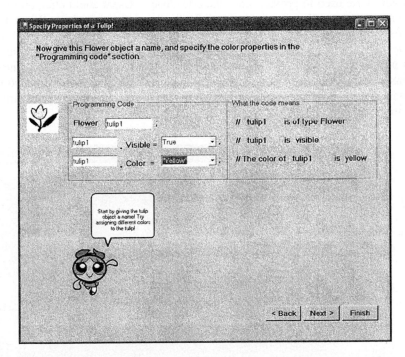

Fig. 2. IM avatar Tool Interface. The color and visibility of the tulip change as the user manipulates the dropdown menus. The line-by-line comments are changed to reflect the partial code.

The fist principle is to use manipulation of partial code. As discussed in phase I, direct manipulation did not encourage girls to look at actual code with programming syntax, for it allowed girls to complete the activity without looking at the code. Therefore, in phase II, the girls must complete code that is partially filled out. Manipulation directs girls' attention to code-like syntax, and also conveys the message that they are not using a tool with a GUI, but dealing with programming. Furthermore, "Partial" manipulation provides guidelines for beginners, so they only work within a valid set of possibilities. This introduces simple syntax and semantics, and prevents errors that discourage them.

The second principle is to produce practical and concrete results, which persists from the first phase. An IM avatar tool may be more practical to girls than a greeting card tool. The survey indicates that many girls use IM frequently, whereas they would only make greeting cards on special occasions. According to the survey, most girls make a greeting card approximately once a month and use IM daily or at least weekly.

Furthermore, the avatar for IM is predicted to be more socially compelling as it supports a two-way communication, while greeting cards only support one-way interactions.

The third principle is visual feedback. As mentioned in Phase I, visual feedback is necessary for better understanding of materials [3, 14]. In the previous interface, the code was placed above the result, which could not be seen until the last wizard step. In phase II, the code and its results are placed adjacently to establish the connection. Rollovers were used to provide immediate feedback. Users could click on the button "Check my answers" to receive visual feedback on the exercises. When the user presses a button "Refresh", the altered code will update, showing visual feedback.

The fourth principle of having engaging and entertaining content is also carried from phase I. The team tried to keep the project less like a dry textbook. Interactive lessons were used to keep girls engaged. Cute and funny graphics were also used to entertain the girls. For example, popular characters such as "power puff girls" were used in the lessons.

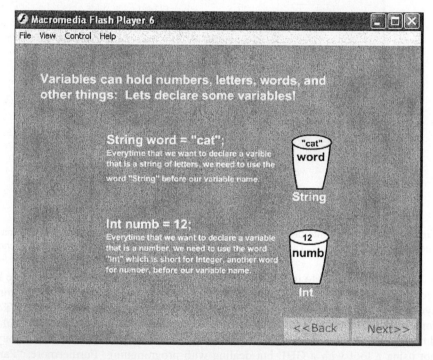

Fig. 3. Programming Concepts Lesson. In an introductory lesson, concrete examples in everyday language are used to enhance understanding of abstract concepts.

The next principle is to reinforce concepts through examples and applications. Students learn better by working through examples rather than strictly reading text [2]. The interface consisted of lessons that teach concepts in programming, and "projects" with exercises to reinforce concepts previously taught. The IM tool consists of 4 lessons and 3 projects. Lessons are used to teach the concepts in programming. Projects that follow contain exercises that help the user to try out the lesson just learned. Since alternating lessons and projects are more efficient than having lessons and examples grouped together [3], we placed each project immediately after each lesson.

The final principle is the transition from concrete to abstract. To lessen the intimidation to learn programming, efforts have been made "to close the gap" between programming languages and natural languages for beginners [7]. Most lessons have concrete examples, often making analogies between code and everyday items. For example, when introducing the concept of a variable, metaphors of cups holding different items were used. To introduce the concept of objects and property, an example of a girl and her dress color was used. Eventually, the tool advanced into the concepts that are more abstract and mathematical in nature, such as "for" loops are taught with Java-like syntax.

3.2 Methods

Questions about Instant Messenger were added to the survey. Phase II included two iterations with 3 sets of user tests using the most recent version of interface incorporating the concept of IM system. The number of students in each user testing was 3, 2, and 3 respectively. After hands-on experience using the prototype, the girls were also asked 4 questions to test their understanding of the concepts learned.

Table 2. Methods used in Phase II

Method	Number of Users	Age	Location
User Test	3girls	11-12	Fox Chapel Middle School
User Test	2 girls	11, 14	Fox Chapel Middle School
User Test	3 girls	11-12	Fox Chapel Middle School

3.3 Results and Discussions

Testing with the updated prototype that used manipulation of partial code proved to be more successful than the version made in phase I in introducing programming concepts. Users had to look at the code with the IM tool in order to complete the task. In the quiz that followed the user test, most questions testing the programming concept were answered correctly. In addition, 75% (6/8) of phase II users completed the tasks while only 50% (3/6) of the Phase I users were successful. Some users commented "This is easier than I thought", indicating that we were approaching a better way to communicate the programming concepts.

The second principle of producing practical and concrete results worked better as well. Girls were positive about the concept of making an avatar for IM. In the post interview, three girls commented that "the idea is cool" and they would use it if such a tool was implemented. Based on such observations and the survey revealing the girls' frequent use of IM, it seems that the tool used in phase II is more practical than the greeting card tool used in phase I.

Better visual feedback also improved the prototype. The wizard metaphor provided a stronger path cue that helped the participants stay on the correct path to complete the task in phase II. Additionally, various forms of visual feedback informed participants when they had completed the task. For example, the participants were given the task of changing the type and property of a flower. Real-time feedback showing the effects of their code manipulations help the participants determine when they had selected the proper type of flower and its color.

Users were also engaged when they saw the results changing when they changed colors and properties of an object. 6/8 participants said "this is neat", when they saw the color of the tulip or the look of the Power Puff Girl changing. The if/else lesson seemed particularly interesting, 3/8 girls went back to try different mood combinations, to see how the power puff girl would dress depending on her mood.

The principle of reinforcing concepts with examples and applications seemed to improve understanding. Users indicated they understood concepts better. In the quiz, 71% (5/7) of users could verbally explain what the code means, and how they would change a "For" loop. In addition, 2 girls wrote down "comments" with "//" on the quiz. This showed attempts to apply knowledge out of initiative. However, it appeared that some girls understood what simple code would do and how to do tasks according to examples, yet they did not understand the concept of objects clearly. Furthermore, it seemed that some girls could still finish lessons without learning the concepts completely. This is a design flaw. When creating a GUI, participants should not be able to easily bypass the lesson without understanding the concepts. "Step-by-step" error messages can be used when participants do not complete a field, to help them make better decisions.

Table 3. To assess how much concepts were retained by the end of all lessons, a post user test quiz was given to the girls during the debriefing session. 7 of 8 participants performed the quiz, while one participant did not have time to do it.

Question Description	# Correct Responses	% Correct
1a. Explain verbally what a small section of code means. (Naming an object and assigning a property)	5/7	71%
1b. A small section of code was given, and the girl is asked to modify a For loop to change the number of executions.	5/7	71%
2. The girl is asked to distinguish statement(s) that are not "If" Statements.	6/7	86%
3. True or False question about whether an object has to have a name.	2/7	29%
4. True or False question about identifying different kinds of loops.	5/7	71%

Lastly, in applying the principle of transition from concrete to abstract, some of the ideas worked well, such as introducing familiar objects before mathematical concepts. Only 1/8 girls were hesitant about starting the activity. They might be less intimidated by the code, for they were first introduced with familiar and concrete concepts. Girls were quicker in reading the beginning lessons compared to the later, more abstract lessons. The learning curve from the everyday pseudo-code to "Java-like" code was steeper than expected, as reflected in the quiz results. Three girls expressed that the curly brackets were "confusing" during debriefing. They said that they had to think twice to understand when a curly bracket appeared. Some girls did not want to read the screen, which contained such programming symbols.

Some user interface problems were revealed in the user testing, such as placement and color of buttons that were not prominent enough. Some other UI issues were cluttered screen in which the user could not find an obvious place to start. Another problem was use of difficult vocabulary. Use of words such as "initiate" and "emotion" confused the users. These words changed to "set" and "feelings" respectively. After this initial phase of testing, easier ways were discovered to explain some concepts. For example, our last project has 2 types of loops combined into one exercise. This turned out to be too much information. Therefore, users suggested separating them. Visual cue of where the users can start reading was also provided to help user parse the complex text after first iteration.

4 Conclusions and Future Work

The goal of this study is to kindle girls' interest in programming via lessons and projects that appeal to both girls' entertainment and social needs. Overall, we have achieved the goals as seen in the girls' expression of interest and comprehension of the concepts introduced in the lessons. Yet some girls still seemed slightly intimidated in touching the projects. They asked the experimenters questions to confirm their answers before completing a blank field although they were correct. They were reluctant in exploring different types of combinations beyond instructions. A friendlier interface, a more robust set of lessons, and a more comfortable environment may reduce this sensitivity.

One way to bring this concept of enticing girls to program into realization of concrete application is to introduce a finished product into a classroom setting, where the users would learn introductory programming skills and interaction methods. After acquiring some level of proficiency acquired in classrooms, users might be motivated to make characters in their own time outside the required school work.

Additionally, there is a great potential of this project on a broader scale. Currently, some online communities allow each member to create and personalize a character that represents them (avatar). An existing example is cyworld, which is a very popular online community in Korea. Future work can be done to develop similar communities in which the user can program to change their avatars.

Acknowledgement

We thank Ken Koedinger for his support and guidance.

References

1. Beyer H., & Holtzblatt K. *Contextual Design*. San Francisco: Morgan Kaufmann, 1998.
2. Chi, Michelene T. H., Bassok, Miriam. Knowing, Learning & Institution; Essays in Honor of Robert Glaser. Ch.8. Lawrence Erlbaum Assoc, 1989.
3. Clark, R. C, Mayer, R. E. E-Learning and the Science of Institution. Pfeiffer. San Francisco, CA, 2003.
4. Gorriz, C., Medina, C. Engaging Girls with Computers Through Software Games. Communication of the ACM (Jan 2000), 43, 1 42-49.
5. Kelleher, C., Pausch, R. Lowering the Barriers to Programming: a survey of programming environments and languages for novice programmers. ACM surveys (Oct 2004).
6. Kelleher, C. Motivating Programming: using storytelling to make computer programming attractive to more middle school girls. PhD Thesis, Carnegie Mellon University, Pittsburgh, PA 2004
7. Lane, H.C, VanLehn, K. Coached Program Planning: Dialogue-Based Support for Novice Program Design. SIGCSE '03.
8. 8.National Center for Education Statistics. Digest of Education Statistics. U.S. Department of Education, Washington, D.C.,(2003) Available at http://nces.ed.gov//programs/digest/d03/tables/dt255.asp
9. Norman, D, Draper, E. Cognitive Engineering. User Centered System Design, Mew Perspectives on Human-Computer Interaction. Lawrence Erlbaum Associates Publishers, 1986. P.31-61
10. Pane, J. F., Ratanamahatana, C. A., and Myers, B. A. Studying the Language and Structure in Non-Programmer's Solutions to Programming Problems. Human-Computer Studies, 2001, 54, 237-264.
11. Smith, D., Cypher, A., Tesler, L. Novice Programming Comes of Age. Communications of the ACM, (March 200), 43, 3, p.75-81.
12. Schiano, D., Chen, C., Ginsbery, J., Gretarsdottir, U., Huddleston, M., and Isaacs, E. Teen use of messaging media. In Proc. CHI 2002, ACM Press (2002), 594-595.
13. Talbot, M. Girls just want to be mean. New York Times Magazine, 2002, 27, 24-65.
14. Taylor, R. Cunniff, N. Uchiyama, M.Learning, research, and the graphical representation of programming. IEEE 86'.
15. Verbick, T. Women, Technology, and Gender Bias. Journal of Computer Sciences in Colleges, (Feb 2000), 17, 3, 240-250

Exploring Verbalization and Collaboration of Constructive Interaction with Children

Benedikte S. Als, Janne J. Jensen, and Mikael B. Skov

Department of Computer Science, Aalborg University,
Fredrik Bajers Vej 7, DK-9220 Aalborg East, Denmark
{als, missj, dubois}@cs.aau.dk

Abstract. Constructive interaction provides natural thinking-aloud as test subjects collaborate in pairs to solve tasks. Since children may face difficulties in following instructions for a standard think-aloud test, constructive interaction has been suggested as evaluation method when usability testing with children. However, the relationship between think-aloud and constructive interaction is still poorly understood. We present an experiment that compares think-aloud and constructive interaction. The experiment involves 60 children with three setups where children apply think-aloud or constructive interaction in acquainted and non-acquainted pairs. Our results show that the pairing of children had impact on how the children collaborated in pairs and how they would afterward assess the testing sessions. In some cases, we found that acquainted dyads would perform well as they would more naturally interact and collaborate while in other cases they would have problems in controlling the evaluations.

1 Introduction

Children have been characterized as not just short adults, but as independent individuals with their own strong opinions, needs, likes, and dislikes, and they should be treated as such. The design and evaluation of children's technologies have received increased attention during the last several years [7, 8]. Druin [9] provides a classification of involvement where children play the roles of users, testers, informants, or design partners. The four roles encompass different levels of engagement and impose different opportunities and limitations. All roles involve different kinds of usability tests where children participate as subjects, for example user [29], tester [19], informant [10], and design partner [6].

Some research studies have started to investigate the roles of children in usability tests, cf. [18, 21]. Nielsen [26] suggests that evaluators should use a variation of think-aloud called constructive interaction [16, 23] (also known as co-discovery learning), since it may be difficult to get children to follow the instructions for a standard thinking-aloud test. Constructive interaction involves two test subjects collaborating in trying to solve tasks while using a computer system [27]. Even though constructive interaction with children seems appropriate, the relationship between think-aloud and constructive interaction in usability testing with children is poorly understood. A number of questions still need to be addressed and answered: 1) How do children think-aloud and collaborate in constructive interaction 2) How should pairs of chil-

M.F. Costabile and F. Paternò (Eds.): INTERACT 2005, LNCS 3585, pp. 443–456, 2005.
© IFIP International Federation for Information Processing 2005

dren be configured in constructive interaction? 3) How do children perceive the testing situation during constructive interaction?

In this paper, we investigate and address the above stated questions by looking at how children perform and behave in constructive interaction during usability testing. Our particular focus is on how the children behave and perceive a testing situation when involved a traditional think-aloud test compared to constructive interaction tests. First, we present an experimental design involving 60 children participating in two different configurations of constructive interaction and a traditional think-aloud. Secondly, we present results from the evaluations by illustrating how the children applied the think-aloud protocol and collaborated and further how they perceived the situation. Finally, we outline three lessons on involving children in usability testing.

2   Constructive Interaction in Usability Testing with Children

Nielsen [26] claims that constructive interaction is preferable over think-aloud when conducting usability evaluations with children. Where children face difficulties in following the instructions for a think-aloud test, constructive interaction comes closer to their natural behaviour, since the children work in pairs and collaborate in solving the tasks. Due to the fact that different the children's ability to verbalize their thoughts and feelings during a test, Hanna et al. [13] propose some adjusted guidelines where they reflect upon common target age ranges. Jensen and Skov [15] found that 67% of the research on interaction design and children applied some sort of systematic field or laboratory evaluations. Furthermore, some studies have explored different methods for conducting usability evaluations with children; one studied the effectiveness of co-operative evaluations (think-aloud) and co-discovery evaluations (constructive interaction) [1, 21], where another studied different method's effectiveness to elicit verbal comments from children [18]. The first compared the difference in total number of identifies usability problems identified by four subjects or four pairs, and found only negligible differences between the two methods.

Miyake [23] states that constructive interaction inherently integrates a number of opportunities and limitations. An advantage is that the test subjects naturally use think-aloud in their collaboration, one of the disadvantages is that the might aim for different strategies for learning and using computers. Furthermore, since constructive interaction requires twice as many test subjects as think-aloud, in order to conduct the same number of usability sessions, it is typically more expensive [26]. Configuring pairs for construction interaction includes two important steps [16]. First, test subjects must be selected and acquired for the usability test [27]. Secondly, usability evaluators are further faced with challenges of pairing subjects when adapting constructive interaction as evaluation technique. A number of challenges seem to influence the configuration of subjects in constructive interaction.

First, one challenge concerns the level of expertise. The level of expertise is important, as argued by O'Malley et al. [27], since the test subjects' knowledge of specific work tasks is quite often corresponding to their level of expertise. Nielsen [26] recommends that the test subjects have the same level of experience, whereas having one of the test subjects enabled to guide the interaction, is an argument used by Kahler [16] when stating advantages by pairing test subjects with different levels of experience. Usually children do not posses expertise of work that might influence the outcome of the usability test, which makes the issue of expertise subtler when working with children. Most studies involving children do not explicitly consider the level of expertise [19, 25], one of the exceptions is a study where the participating children are profiled according to their scripting level [28]. Where age does not seem to matter when testing with adults, it has a more eloquent impact when conducting tests with children, since the children's level of maturity changes more quickly than adults. Most studies equalize the children's age, with their level of expertise. It is not obvious how children's ages influence results of a usability test.

Secondly, level of acquaintance is another important aspect in constructive interaction. Previous studies have indicated that children behave quite differently according to how well they know each other. In a study where adult test subjects were asked to bring a friend, co-worker, or family member to the usability test provided a positive experience [16] while other studies stress the importance of using non-acquainted test subjects [17]. Most studies involving children seems to prefer acquainted pairs of children; this is often achieved through involvement of children attending same school classes or kindergartens [10, 25, 28]. In the Eco-I project [30], the pairing goes beyond acquaintance, since a participating teacher had configured the pairs of children according to how well they worked together. Few studies indicate that the pairs of children were unacquainted, but this might have been the case in the StoryMat project [5] since the children attended different schools.

Thirdly, gender is potentially important when working with children; for example illustrated by girls and boys preferring different types of computer games [12]. Gender can also play a subjective role with children's preferences and attitudes towards technologies [4, 14]. But it is not apparent if and how gender influences other other issues of usability testing, such as effectiveness, efficiency, or number of identified usability problems. Several studies involve both genders in the design processes [3, 6, 19, 20, 30, 32, 33]. Some studies adapted imbalanced numbers of girls and boys [2, 25], while others deliberately chose an equal number of boys and girls [19]. Furthermore, some studies intentionally use same-sex pairs [10, 24].

Analyzing previous research on interaction design and children, we found several studies in which children participated as test subjects applying think-aloud [7, 8, 9, 28, 33], constructive interaction [24, 25, 30, 31], or both approaches [2, 6]. However, none of these studies present results related to how well the children adapted to think-aloud or constructive interaction. Summarized, we need a deeper understanding of involving children in the evaluation of software products to assess some of the opportunities and limitations related the different evaluation methods.

3 Experimental Method

The purpose of our experiment was to explore the impact of involving children in the evaluation of a software product. The idea was to place children in different settings or conditions to see how this affects their performance. Thus, in this paper we do not measure the performance of the different setups in terms of usability problem identification (please refer to [1] for this aspect of our study).

Table 1. 60 children participated in our experiment in three different setups: constructive interaction as acquainted dyads or non-acquainted dyads and think-aloud as individual testers

	Constructive Interaction		Think-Aloud
	Acquainted Dyads (N=24)	Non-Acquainted Dyads (N=24)	Individual Testers (N=12)
Girls	6x2	6x2	6
Boys	6x2	6x2	6
Total	12x2	12x2	12

We designed the experiment as a 3x2 matrix consisting of three types of sessions: individual testers using think-aloud, acquainted dyads (pairs) using constructive interaction, and non-acquainted dyads using constructive interaction. Furthermore, we configured the usability test sessions with same-sex dyads having sessions with girls and boys for each of the three setups. This is illustrated in table 1.

3.1 Participants

60 children (30 girls and 30 boys) at the age of 13 and 14 years old (M=13.35, SD=0.48) participated as test subjects in the experiment. The children were all 7th grade pupils from five different elementary schools in the greater Aalborg area. The children did not receive compensation for their involvement in the experiment.

The children were assigned as test subjects to one of the three test setups e.g. individual testers, acquainted dyads, or non-acquainted dyads. Each setup had twelve individual testers (six girls and six boys), twelve acquainted dyads (six pairs of girls and six pairs of boys), and twelve non-acquainted dyads (six pairs of girls and six pairs of boys). Assignment of the children to the three test setups was done randomly under two conditions 1) all acquainted dyads attended the same school class and 2) all non-acquainted dyads attended different schools. The acquainted pairs had known each other for at least five years except for one pair of girls and one pair of boys who had been acquainted for one year (M=6.25, SD=2.5). None of the non-acquainted dyads knew each other in advance.

3.2 System

The selected system for our experiment was an inno-100 mobile phone by innostream. This particular mobile phone was selected since it had not been released on the European market at the time of our experiment. Thus, all children would have to learn to use the mobile phone.

The inno-100 integrates a range of standard mobile phone features, such as making and receiving phone calls and short text messages, and more advanced features, including speed dial functions and options for creating personalized ring tones. The inno-100 has two separate screens with a main 128x144 pixel 16 bit colour screen and 64x80 pixel sub screen on the cover. The navigation is primarily based on icons in the two upper menu levels. The lower levels are textual based including choice menus for setting values. Furthermore, the inno-100 integrates a number of games.

3.3 Procedure

Children from five schools in Aalborg, Denmark were introduced to the experiment by two of the participating researchers. The researchers explained the children's roles in the experiment and how their participation would contribute to our research. Participation in the experiment was voluntarily and interested children got an information sheet describing the experiment in detail and a consent form that had to be signed by a parent or a guardian. After receiving signed consent forms from a total of 60 children, we scheduled the usability evaluation sessions.

The sessions were held at the usability laboratory at Aalborg University. We adapted the guidelines for usability testing with children proposed by Hanna et al. [13]. Particularly, we focused on greeting the children, stressing the importance of the participation, and stressing that they were not the object of the test. The purpose of the evaluation was explained in detail to the children and they were shown the facilities of the usability lab. Test subjects intended for roles as non-acquainted dyads were kept separate before the test sessions. The children received questionnaires on which they had to provide answers to such as age, name, school, and mobile phone experience. The usability test sessions were conducted in a specialized usability laboratory. The laboratory integrated two rooms; an observation room in which the evaluations took place and a control room where one of the researchers would handle electronic equipment for recording the sessions. The two rooms were separated with a one-way mirror allowing people in the control room to see what was going on in the observation room. All sessions were recorded on video tapes for later analyses including perspectives of the children and of their interactions with the mobile phone.

The children were asked to solve twelve tasks one at a time addressing standard and advanced functionalities in the inno-100 mobile phone. This included making a phone call, sending a short text message, adjusting the volume of ring tones, and editing entries in the address book. We did not specify any time limits for the tasks, but required the participants to try to solve all tasks. All children were able to solve all specified tasks. On average, the children spent 26:45 minutes (SD=06:39) on the twelve tasks. The individual testers were asked to think-aloud while solving the tasks. We explained think-aloud to the individual testers in terms of the descriptions in [26, p. 195-198]. The acquainted and non-acquainted dyads were asked to solve the tasks by constructive interaction where they should collaborate with each other in order to solve the tasks. We explained constructive interaction to the dyads in terms of the descriptions in [26, p. 198].

After the usability sessions, the children completed a subjective workload test (NASA-TLX) [22]. The children filled in the test individually even though the participated in pairs. This was done to evaluate the workload as experienced by the children in order to compare the different setups. We translated the test into the children's native language, Danish.

3.4 Data Analysis

After conducting all 36 sessions, the sessions were analyzed in a collaborative effort between two of the authors of this paper. The sessions were picked randomly for the analysis to avoid bias in the analysis. We analyzed the sessions according to how well the children collaborated (in constructive interaction sessions) and recorded their verbal interaction and comments. The six different aspects of our analysis were: 1) Level of verbalization, 2) quality of verbalization, 3) interaction between test subject(s) and test monitor, and 4) influence of test monitor on the solving of tasks. The two setups of constructive interaction were additionally analyzed according to: 5) Level of collaboration between the dyads and 6) quality of the collaboration between the dyads. We analyzed and marked each of the six aspects on a scale from 1 to 5 where 1 being the lowest score and 5 being the highest score. For example, for the level of verbalization, a session was marked 1 if the children made none or very few verbalizations during their interaction with the system, and a sessions was marked 5 if the children constantly or almost all time made verbalization during interaction.

The NASA-TLX tests were further analyzed. 55 tests were answered correctly by the children while 5 were incomplete answered. Data from our assessment of think-aloud and collaboration and the NASA-TLX tests were analyzed with one-way ANOVAs, followed by post hoc comparisons using Tukey tests.

4   Results

The 60 children in the 36 usability test sessions solved all 12 assigned tasks. Even though the constructive interaction sessions with acquainted dyads (M=29:54, SD=06:57) spent most time on the assignments in our experiment; the individual testers (M=25:34, SD=03:44), and the non-acquainted dyads (M=24:48, SD=07:53), we found no significant differences for the task completion times. The children performed and behaved differently in the three setups and the following sections present our assessment of their interaction and collaboration and the NASA-TLX test.

4.1   Assessment of Think-Aloud and Collaboration

As a part of our assessment of the three setups, we applied six different aspects of the verbalization and collaboration in usability tests. These six aspects are illustrated in table 2. Not surprisingly, we found that the level of verbalization was considerably higher for the constructive interaction sessions compared to the think-aloud sessions. The acquainted dyads scored rather high (M=4.58, SD=0.90) especially compared the individual testers who scored rather low (M=2.17, SD=1.19). An analysis of variance shows significant differences between the three setups on level of verbalization $F_{(2,33)}$=13.421, p=0.001. A post-hoc test showed significant difference at the 0.1% level between the acquainted dyads and the individual testers and at the 5% level between the non-acquainted dyads and the individual testers. Furthermore, we found a tendency towards a higher level of verbalization for the acquainted dyads compared the non-acquainted dyads, but this difference is not significant (p=0.090).

Looking further at verbalization in the test sessions, we analyzed the quality of the verbalization primarily defined as the ability of the verbal comments to facilitate the identification and classification of usability problems. Considering the quality of the verbalization the differences between the setups are less apparent than for the level of verbalization. For the acquainted dyads (but also for some non-acquainted dyads), several verbal comments did not concern the actual test; a lot of the verbal comments did not facilitate the identification of usability problems. Summarized, the differences between the setups on quality of verbalization were not significant $F_{(2,33)}$=2.171, p=0.130.

Table 2. Assessment of verbalization and collaboration in the three setups. A plus indicates a significant difference to the setup marked with a minus according to an ANOVA test.

	Constructive Interaction		Think-Aloud
	Acquainted Dyads (N=12)	Non-Acquainted Dyads (N=12)	Individual Testers (N=12)
Level of verbalization	4.58 (0.90) +	3.58 (1.31) +	2.17 (1.19) -
Quality of verbalization	3.58 (1.00)	3.25 (1.48)	2.50 (1.38)
Interaction between test subject(s) and monitor	2.75 (0.87)	3.08 (0.79)	3.25 (0.87)
Influence of test monitor on the solving of tasks	2.17 (0.39)	1.67 (0.65)	1.83 (0.58)
Level of the collaboration between the dyads	4.75 (0.62)	3.83 (1.47)	N/A
Quality of the collaboration between the dyads	3.67 (1.56)	3.58 (1.56)	N/A

We further analyzed the influenced of and interaction with the test monitor. Constructive interaction provides potentially natural thinking-aloud as test subjects collaborate in pairs to solve tasks and therefore, one could expect less influence and interaction with a test monitor. We found that the test monitor has slightly more interaction with the think-aloud subjects compared the constructive interaction subjects, but the difference is not significant $F_{(2,33)}=0.134$, $p=0.875$. On the other hand, we identified a higher influence form the test monitor on the solving of tasks for the acquainted dyads compared both non-acquainted dyads and individual testers, but again this difference is not significant $F_{(2,33)}=0.282$, $p=0.756$.

As constructive interaction have test subjects collaborate in pairs to solve tasks, we finally assessed the level and quality of collaboration. Most of the acquainted dyads collaborated during the entire sessions ($M=4.75$, $SD=0.62$) and we identified a tendency towards a higher collaboration between them than the non-acquainted dyads ($M=3.83$, $SD=1.47$), but this difference is not significant according to a Student's t-test $t_{(22)}=1.993$, $p=0.059$. Considering the quality of the collaboration, we found no difference between the two setups $t_{(22)}=0.131$, $p=0.897$.

4.2 Assessment of Subjective Workload

Table 3 summarizes mean values for the six factors of the NASA-TLX test as assessed by the 60 children in the three setups. As the table illustrates, minor differences could be observed between the different setups, however we found no significant differences between them. Even though not significant, we can however see that the individual testers found the effort factor more important than the dyads, but large variances were identified for the individual testers on this factor.

On the other hand, more factors were assessed to almost the same mean values for the three setups e.g. frustration and mental demand. While the absolute values of the

Table 3. Subjective workload (NASA-TLX test) for think-aloud and constructive interaction illustrating the mean values for the six factors as assessed by children

| | Constructive Interaction | | Think-Aloud |
	Acquainted Dyads (N=20)	Non-Acquainted Dyads (N=24)	Individual Testers (N=11)
Effort	38.5 (19.7)	41.9 (20.3)	52.7 (23.8)
Frustration	34.3 (25.4)	35.8 (22.4)	39.5 (23.4)
Mental	43.5 (16.2)	42.1 (19.3)	50.0 (12.2)
Performance	27.0 (21.7)	25.8 (17.7)	35.0 (24.5)
Physical	41.0 (25.8)	39.4 (25.9)	27.3 (13.8)
Temporal	38.5 (20.1)	27.5 (18.9)	37.7 (25.7)

factors provided no significant differences between the three setups, we analyzed the inter-relative importance of the factors.

The assessment of the relative importance of the factors (table 4) showed significant difference between the three setups on the effort factor $F_{(2,52)}=5.693$, p=0.006. A post-hoc comparison showed significant difference at the 1% level between the acquainted dyads and non-acquainted dyads and at the 5% level between the acquainted dyads and the individual testers. Additionally, sitting with an acquainted influenced the importance of performance as acquainted dyads found this significantly more important than the individual testers and the non-acquainted dyads $F_{(2,52)}=3.775$, p=0.029. A post-hoc test showed significant difference at the 5% level between the acquainted and non-acquainted dyads.

Table 4. Inter-relative assessment of workload factors for the three setups. A plus indicates a significant difference to the setup marked with a minus according to an ANOVA test.

| | Constructive Interaction | | Think-Aloud |
	Acquainted Dyads (N=20)	Non-Acquainted Dyads (N=24)	Individual Testers (N=11)
Effort	2.30 (1.17) -	3.38 (1.10) +	3.45 (1.29) +
Frustration	1.75 (1.25)	2.54 (1.59)	2.64 (0.92)
Mental	2.90 (1.48)	3.38 (1.28)	3.73 (1.49)
Performance	3.15 (1.60) +	2.08 (1.18) -	2.09 (1.38)
Physical	2.35 (1.66)	2.08 (1.79)	1.36 (1.75)
Temporal	2.55 (1.50)	1.54 (1.47)	1.73 (1.27)

We found that the acquainted dyads assessed frustration as the least important factor while both individual testers and non-acquainted dyads rated it as the third most important factor, but this difference was not significant $F_{(2,52)}=2.337$, p=0.107. For the remaining three factors, we found only minor differences between the three setups and no significant differences, mental demand $F_{(2,52)}$=1.357, p=0.266, physical demand $F_{(2,52)}$=1.160, p=0.322, while we identified a tendency for temporal issues $F_{(2,52)}$=2.800, p=0.070.

Table 5. Calculated workload for the three setups. A plus indicates a significant difference to the setup marked with a minus according to an ANOVA test.

	Constructive Interaction		Think-Aloud
	Acquainted Dyads (N=20)	Non-Acquainted Dyads (N=24)	Individual Testers (N=11)
Effort	99.8 (80.0) -	148.7 (90.7)	190.9 (126.3) +
Frustration	61.0 (63.1)	108.8 (97.5)	116.8 (91.5)
Mental	120.8 (65.1)	132.5 (69.5)	186.8 (90.7)
Performance	83.8 (88.4)	51.7 (56.0)	65.0 (50.0)
Physical	118.8 (113.8)	80.0 (104.4)	40.5 (61. 6)
Temporal	90.0 (60.7) +	42.1 (55.6) -	58.2 (59.3)

Combining the two measures, we calculated the overall score for the workload for the participating children. As discovered above, we found that the individual testers had to put much more effort into the testing situation and an ANOVA test showed a significant difference between the three setups $F_{(2,52)}$=3.464, p=0.039. A post-hoc comparison showed significant difference at the 5% level between the individual testers and the acquainted dyads. On the other hand, the acquainted dyads in total assessed temporal demand rather high compared to the two other setups and we found a significant difference between the three setups $F_{(2,52)}$=3.737, p=0.030. A post-hoc test showed significant difference at the 5% level between the acquainted dyads and the non-acquainted dyads.

We identified a tendency for mental demand as the individual testers in general assessed this factor higher than both constructive interaction setups, however the difference was not significant for our test $F_{(2,52)}$=3.114, p=0.057. Again and as above, we found that the level of frustration is much lower for the acquainted dyads compared the two other setups, however the difference is not significant $F_{(2,52)}$=2.247, p=0.116. Furthermore, we found no significant differences for the other calculated values; physical demand $F_{(2,52)}$=2.198, p=0.121 and performance $F_{(2,52)}$=1.190, p=0.312.

5 Discussion

This section provides qualitative results from the study. We have identified a number interesting lessons related usability testing with children.

Lesson 1: *Constructive interaction did not necessarily facilitate natural think-aloud as the dyads tended to talk-aloud and not think-aloud.* Constructive interaction in usability testing with children potentially provides natural thinking-aloud as the children collaborate in pairs to solve tasks. Our study illustrated that children in pairs using constructive interaction had a much higher level of verbalization, but often they were more talking-aloud than actually thinking-aloud. We further experienced that the individual testers applying think-aloud tended to be quieter during the sessions compared to the dyads; they expressed themselves noticeably fewer times than the dyads. When asked about their choices, more of them would mostly answer our questions in very few words without giving further insight into their behaviour and choices. On the other hand, the non-acquainted dyads had less interaction with each other compared to the acquainted dyads; they mainly kept focus on the task they were solving. The interaction of the acquainted dyads was partially related to the task, but we identified some interaction as noise as this was irrelevant to the solving of the task, for example some would have long discussions on what to name the melody they had just composed. These observations resemble the discussion by Ericsson and Simon of think-aloud and talk-aloud [11]. It was very difficult to get the children to explain their interaction and motivation even though they had been carefully instructed before the session. Thus, this can be seen as a contradiction to benefits of constructive interaction as stated by Nielsen [26] as we found only minor differences between the think-aloud sessions and constructive interaction sessions.

Lesson 2: *Dyad configuration in constructive interaction influenced the children's behaviour and assessment of the testing situation according to their acquaintance.* Our study indicated that there were a significant difference between how the acquainted and the non-acquainted dyads experienced the assessment of effort and performance. Our results showed that the acquainted dyads were significantly more satisfied with their own performance and they did not feel it demanded a lot of effort from them. It was just the opposite for the non-acquainted dyads. Even though the acquainted dyads sometimes would try to pull the phone out of the hands of their co-solver, they rated performance of minor importance compared to the non-acquainted dyads. From our study, we also found that the non-acquainted dyads acted rather polite against each other and in general they were more polite to each other than the acquainted dyads. Consequently, they collaborated quite differently compared to the acquainted dyads and they did not argue explicitly for the control of the tested phone. This is also indicated in our results as we found a tendency, however not significant, towards better collaboration between the non-acquainted dyads. Further, the non-acquainted dyads separated the roles between them during the test. Even in the cases were they did not collaborate very well, they would some times read the task aloud, or they would take turns by shifting in between tasks. The acquainted dyads' interaction were influenced by the fact that the children knew each other in advance, they referred to each others by nick-names, remarked their co-solvers intelligence etc. They would also physically try to grab the phone and thereby preventing their co-solver from helping to solve the task. The acquainted dyads would easily get distracted from the task they were solving, they would discover something interesting in the menu, and would spend time discovering such aspects. Some of the non-acquainted dyads did not collaborate very well while solving the task; we found no significant differences between the girls and the boys in this issue. The children took turns in operating the system and the child who was not in control of the interaction had sometimes difficulties in seeing what was going on the screen of the phone.

Lesson 3: *Gender issues might play important roles in the configuration of dyads in constructive interaction.* Our study utilized pairs of same sex dyads as adapted in several studies with children [10, 24]. Even though we haven't summarized the results gender wise, our study showed a tendency towards that the boys collaborated better than the girls. Especially the acquainted dyads of boys collaborated rather well and had a fruitful and successful collaboration whereas the acquainted dyads of girls experienced several situations where their collaboration was rather poor. Thus, while it seems to be of less importance if the boys tested in acquainted or non-acquainted dyads, the girls should test in non-acquainted dyads. For some of the specified tasks, we observed that the acquainted dyads of girls would more easily get distracted from the task they were solving, they would discover something interesting in the menu, and would spend time discovering what it was, for example acquainted dyads quite often used several minutes to compose a melody, for example "Itsy Bitsy Spider".

6 Conclusion

In this paper, we investigate and address the above stated questions by looking at how children perform and behave in constructive interaction during usability testing. Our particular focus is on how the children behave and perceive a testing situation when involved a traditional think-aloud test compared to constructive interaction tests. Thus, we did not treat the performance of the different setups in terms of usability problem identification (please refer to [1] for this aspect of our study).

Our results show that the pairing of children had impact on how the children verbalized and collaborated in pairs during the testing sessions. First, we found that constructive interaction did not necessarily facilitate natural think-aloud as the dyads tended to talk-aloud and not think-aloud. Our children in pairs had a high level of verbalization, but often they were more talking-aloud than actually thinking-aloud. This issue resembles some of the discussions by Ericsson and Simon of think-aloud and talk-aloud [11]. Secondly, dyad configuration in constructive interaction influenced the children's behaviour and assessment of the testing situation according to their acquaintance. The acquainted dyads were significantly more satisfied with their own performance and they did not feel it demanded a lot of effort from them. It was just the opposite for the non-acquainted dyads. Thirdly, gender issues might play important roles in the configuration of dyads in constructive interaction. Our study showed a tendency towards that the boys collaborated better than the girls. Especially the acquainted dyads of boys collaborated rather well and had a fruitful and successful collaboration whereas the acquainted dyads of girls experienced several situations where their collaboration was rather poor. Thus, while it seems to be of less importance if the boys tested in acquainted or non-acquainted dyads, the girls should test in non-acquainted dyads.

Our study suffers from a number of limitations which could form further research with children. First, our results of our experiment cannot simply be generalized for all ages of children. Thus, replicating the experiment with younger children may show a different kind of relationship between think-aloud and constructive interaction. Secondly, we recorded that the non-acquainted dyads continuously took turns with the mobile phone making it difficult for the other child to see what was going on at the interface. This could probably be different for desktop-based applications.

Acknowledgements

The work behind this paper received financial support from the Danish Research Agency (grant no. 2106-04-0022). We would especially like to thank all the participating children and their parents. Furthermore, we want to thank several anonymous reviewers for comments on drafts of this paper.

References

1. Als, B. S., Jensen, J. J., and Skov, M. B. (2005) Comparison of Think-Aloud and Constructive Interaction in Usability Testing with Children. In *Proceedings of the 4th International Conference on Interaction Design and Children (IDC'05)*, ACM Press
2. Benford, S., Bederson, B. B., Åkesson, K-P, Bayon, V., Druin, A., Hansson, P., Hourcade, J. P., Ingram, R., Neale, H., O'Malley, C., Simsarian, K. T., Stanton, D., Sundblad, Y., and Taxén, G. (2000) Designing storytelling technologies to encouraging collaboration between young children. In *Proceedings of the Human Factors and Computing Systems CHI'00*, ACM Press, pp. 556 - 563
3. Bers, M. U., Gonzalez-Heydrich, J., and DeMaso, D. R. (2001) Identity Construction Environments: Supporting a Virtual Therapeutic Community of Pediatric Patients Undergoing Dialysis. In *Proceedings of the Human Factors and Computing Systems CHI'01*, ACM Press, pp. 380 - 387
4. Cassell, J. (2002) *Genderizing*. The Handbook of Human-Computer Interaction
5. Cassell, J. and Ryokai, K. (2001) Making Space for Voice: Technologies for Supporting Children's Fantasy and Storytelling. *Personal and Ubiquitous Computing*, Springer-Verlag, vol. 5(3), pp. 169 - 190
6. Danesh, A., Inkpen, K. M., Lau, F., Shu, K., Booth, K. S. (2001) Geney: Designing a collaborative activity for the Palm handheld computer. In Proceedings of the Human Factors and Computing Systems CHI'01, ACM Press, pp. 388 - 395
7. Druin, A. and Solomon, C. (1996) Designing Multimedia Environments for Children. Wiley & Sons, New York
8. Druin, A. (1999) The Role of Children in the Design of New Technology. HCIL Technical Report No. 99-23, University of Maryland, USA
9. Druin, A. (1999) The Design of Children's Technology. Morgan Kaufmann Publishers, Inc., San Francisco, CA
10. Ellis, J. B. and Bruckman, A. S. (2001) Designing Palaver Tree Online: Supporting Social Roles in a Community of Oral History. In Proceedings of the Human Factors and Computing Systems CHI'01, ACM Press, pp. 474 - 481
11. Ericsson, K.A. and Simon, H.A. (1990) *Protocol Analysis. Verbal reports as data*, Cambridge Massachusetts
12. Gorriz, C. M. and Medina, C. (2000) Engaging Girls with Computers through Software Games. Communications of the ACM, vol. 43, No. 1, pp. 42 – 49
13. Hanna, L., Risden, K., and Alexander, K. J. (1997) Guidelines for Usability Testing with Children. In interactions, September + October, pp. 9 – 14

14. Inkpen, K. (1997) Three Important Research Agendas for Educational Multimedia: Learning, Children, and Gender. In Proceedings of Educational MultiMedia '97
15. Jensen, J. J. and Skov, M. B. (2005) A Review of Research Methods in Children's Technology Design. In Proceedings of the 4th International Conference on Interaction Design and Children (IDC'05), ACM Press
16. Kahler, H. (2000) Constructive Interaction and Collaborative Work. interactions, May + June, pp. 27 - 34
17. Karat, C.-M., Campbell, R., and Fiegel, T. (1992) Comparison of Empirical Testing and Walkthrough Methods in User Interface Evaluation. In Proceedings of the Human Factors and Computing Systems CHI'92, ACM Press, pp. 397-404
18. van Kesteren, I. E. H., Bekker, M. M., Vermeeren, A. P. O. S., and Lloyd, P. A. (2003) Assessing usability evaluation methods on their effectiveness to elicit verbal comments from children subjects. In Proceeding of the 2003 conference on Interaction design and children (IDC'03), ACM Press, pp. 41 - 49
19. Lester, J. C., Converse, S. A., Kahler, S. E., Barlow, S. T., Stone, B. A., and Bhogal, R. S. (1997) The Persona Effect: Affective Impact of Animated Pedagogical Agents. In Proceedings of the Human Factors and Computing Systems CHI'97, ACM Press, pp. 359 - 366
20. Lumbreras, M. and Sánchez, J. (1999) Interactive 3D Sound Hyperstories for Blind Children. In Proceedings of the Human Factors and Computing Systems CHI'99, ACM Press, pp. 318 - 325
21. Markopoulos, P. and Bekker, M. (2003) On the Assessment pf Usability Testing Methods for Children. Interacting with Computers, Elsevier, Vol. 15, pp. 227 – 243
22. Miller R. C. and Hart, S. G. (1984) Assessing the Subjective Workload of Directional Orientation Tasks. In Proceedings of 20th Annual Conference on Manual Control, NASA Conference Publication, pp. 85 – 95
23. Miyake, N. (1986) Constructive Interaction and the Iterative Process of Understanding. Cognitive Science, vol. 10(2), pp. 151 - 177
24. Moher, T., Johnson, A., Ohlsson, S., and Gillingham, M. (1999) Bridging Strategies for VR-based Learning. In Proceedings of the Human Factors and Computing Systems CHI'99, ACM, pp. 536 - 543
25. Montemayor, J., Druin, A., Farber, A., Simms, S., Churaman, W., and D'Amour, A. (2002) Physical Programming: Designing Tools for Children to Create Physical Interactive Environments. In Proceedings of the Human Factors and Computing Systems CHI'02, ACM Press, pp. 299 - 306
26. Nielsen, J. (1993) Usability Engineering. Academic Press
27. O'Malley, C. E., Draper, S. W., and Riley, M. S. (1984) Constructive Interaction: A Method for Studying Human-Computer-Human Interaction. In Proceedings of IFIP Interact '84, pp. 269 – 274
28. Rader, C., Brand, C., and Lewis, C. (1997) Degrees of Comprehension: Children's Understanding of a Visual Programming Environment. In Proceedings of the Human Factors and Computing Systems CHI'97, ACM Press, pp. 351 - 358
29. Resnick, M., Martin, F., Berg, R., Borovoy, R., Colella, V., Kramer, K., and Silverman, B. (1998) Digital Manipulatives: New Toys to Think With. In Proceedings of the Human Factors and Computing Systems CHI'98, ACM, pp. 281 – 287
30. Scaife, M., Rogers, Y., Aldrich, F., and Davies, M. (1997) Designing for or Designing with? Informant Design for Interactive Learning Environments. In Proceedings of the Human Factors and Computing Systems CHI'97, ACM Press, pp. 343 - 350

31. Skov, M. B., Andersen, B. L., Duhn, K., Garnæs, K. N., Grünberger, O., Kold, U., Mortensen, A. B., and Sørensen, J. A. L. (2004) Designing a Drawing Tool for Children: Supporting Social Interaction and Communication. In Proceedings of the Australian Computer-Human Interaction Conference 2004 (OzCHI'04)
32. Stewart, J., Bederson, B. B., and Druin, A. (1999) Single Display Groupware: A Model for Co-Present Collaboration. In Proceedings of the Human Factors and Computing Systems CHI'99, ACM, pp. 286 - 293
33. Strommen, E. (1998) When the Interface is a Talking Dinosaur: Learning across Media with ActiMates Barney. In Proceedings of the Human Factors and Computing Systems CHI'98, ACM Press, pp. 288 - 295

A Structured Expert Evaluation Method for the Evaluation of Children's Computer Games

Ester Baauw, Mathilde M. Bekker, and Wolmet Barendregt

TU Eindhoven, Department of Industrial Design,
P.O. Box 513, 5600 MB Eindhoven, The Netherlands
{E.Baauw, M.M.Bekker, W.Barendregt}@tue.nl

Abstract. Inspection-based evaluation methods predicting usability problems can be applied for evaluating products without involving users. A new method (named SEEM), inspired by Norman's theory-of-action model [18] and Malone's concepts of fun [15], is described for predicting usability and fun problems in children's computer games. This paper describes a study to assess SEEM's quality. The results show that the experts in the study predicted about 76% of the problems found in a user test. The validity of SEEM is quite promising. Furthermore, the participating experts were able to apply the inspection-questions in an appropriate manner. Based on this first study ideas for improving the method are presented.

1 Introduction

1.1 Evaluation Approaches

Evaluation plays a crucial role in user-centred design in general, and also in the development of computer games for children. Globally two types of evaluation approaches exist for assessing interactive products: empirical evaluation methods and predictive or analytical evaluation methods. The main advantage of applying empirical methods is that real users are likely to find real problems. Overall, the strengths of predictive methods are that they are cheap to apply and they can be applied more easily early in the design process when only prototypes of products exist [17]. We are developing a predictive method for assessing usability and fun of children's computer games. This paper describes a study in which we assess the quality of the proposed method.

1.2 Predicting Problems in Computer Games

When developing games, the most important evaluation criterion is whether the game provides a fun experience. However, as indicated by Pagulayan et al. [19] usability should also be taken into account. They stated: 'The ease of use of a game's controls and interface is closely related to fun ratings for that game. Think of this factor as the gatekeeper on the fun of a game'. Thus, our predictive method should focus both on usability and fun.

Some well-known and frequently used predictive evaluation methods, focusing on usability are the Cognitive Walkthrough, Heuristic Evaluation and Guideline-based

M.F. Costabile and F. Paternò (Eds.): INTERACT 2005, LNCS 3585, pp. 457–469, 2005.

evaluation [6]. While the Cognitive Walkthrough is based on an underlying theory of exploratory learning, Heuristic Evaluation and Guideline-based evaluation are based on exploring an interface for breaches of design guidelines. Globally, these methods can be divided into two types of methods: the first group of types is based on underlying models of human behaviour (like the Cognitive Walkthrough) and the second group is based on collections of separate guidelines.

Not many specific predictive evaluation methods exist for evaluating computer games. Some of the existing methods are heuristic-based and focus on computer games for adults [9]. Other heuristics have been specifically developed for children's computer games, but are intended for design purposes, and not specifically for evaluating games [15]. Federoff [10] organized many of these existing guidelines. This set is quite large which is a disadvantage since the probability of conflicting statements increases with an increasing number of guidelines [16]. Another issue is that most guidelines are at a high level of abstraction, e.g. 'get the player involved quickly and easily', while others cover very specific design issues, e.g. 'minimize control options'. This makes these guidelines hard to use for predicting problems.

As far as we know, there are, to date, no existing predictive evaluation methods based on theory for the evaluation of (children's) computer games. Considering the drawbacks of applying guideline-based methods, we decided to develop a predictive method for identifying problems in children's computer games.

1.3 Predictive Method

First, a pilot study was executed to test the assumption that it is possible at all for adults to predict problems that children will encounter in computer games. Two adults, both with a good understanding of evaluation methods in general, (usability testing with) children and computer games, predicted problems in children's computer games without the use of a standard predictive method. The results of this pilot study will not be discussed in detail in this paper; however they showed that it is indeed possible for adults to predict problems in computer games for children. Even without the use of a standard evaluation technique the evaluators predicted about 40% of the problems that children encountered during user tests of this game.

In search of an appropriate theoretical basis for a predictive method, Norman's theory-of-action [18] was selected. This general model allows a systematic analysis of user product interaction. The model has two main aspects: the first aspect is Execution that covers planning the actions, translating the plans into actions, and executing the actions on the product. The second aspect is Evaluation, which covers both perceiving and interpreting the feedback and evaluating the outcome of the previous actions on the product. The model has the assumption of goal-driven behaviour. Goal-driven behaviour is also applicable for both children and computer games. To play a game successfully children have to reach certain goals (e.g. to collect all the right tools from various parts in the game in order to free the princess).

This model was employed for the construction of our predictive method, called Structured Expert Evaluation Method (SEEM). SEEM's checklist consists of questions based on Norman's stages complemented with questions based on the fun-related concepts from Malone [15], Challenge, Curiosity and Fantasy.[1] The general predictive questions were divided in a) questions for each screen of a computer game and b) more global questions that should be answered after evaluating the game. The following questions have to be checked at all screens:

1. Do children understand the goal?
2. Do children know what to do in order to accomplish the goal?
3. Are children able to perform the physical actions easily?
4. Can children perceive the feedback? This includes feedback (if any) from both correct and wrong actions, and whether children can click to stop the feedback.
5. Do children understand the feedback? This holds for both visual and auditory feedback from correct and wrong actions.
6. Will children keep on going until they reach the goal? This includes whether children will like the sub game and if the level of difficulty is okay for young children.
7. Are the navigation possibilities and the exits from a (sub) game clear?
8. Are there other objects in the Game Interface that will cause problems?

The global questions are:

1 a. Is the challenge right for the target group?
  b. Is the curiosity of children stimulated?
  c. Are the story and the interface tuned to the fantasies of children?
2 a. Is it clear whether a sub game is optional or obligatory?
  b. Does the flow of the game meet the expectations? Is the story line logical?
  c. Is it clear when a child should be either passive or active during the game?

As preparation for applying these questions to predict problems in children's computer games, a tutorial is provided. To get acquainted with the predictive method, the tutorial also provides many examples related to each of the predictive question.

1.4 Assessing the Quality of SEEM

To assess the quality of SEEM, two performance measures were used: thoroughness and validity [12] [7]. These measures were determined by having experts apply SEEM to evaluate two computer games. The resulting lists of problems were compared to the lists of problems obtained from User Tests (UT) of these games. Furthermore, the experts' understanding of SEEM's questions was examined by checking the appropriateness of the questions they used to identify problems. The problem predictions that did not match problems uncovered in UT were analyzed in detail. Based on these analyses suggestions for improvements of SEEM are made.

2 Method

2.1 Procedure

The participants in this study were experienced in at least one of the following areas: children, usability and/or usability testing methods and computer games. Their

---

[1] We have also used the combination of Norman's model and Malone's concepts of fun to structure design guidelines for children's computer games [3].

experience varied from 6 months to 20 years, with a mean of 4.4 years. In sum 10 male and 8 female participants (from now on called experts) from 11 different companies participated in the study. The youngest expert was 25 years old; the oldest was just above 40 (mean age was 30.3 years).

The experts evaluated two different Dutch computer games, 'Milo and the magical stones' [1] (from now on referred to as Milo) and 'Roger Rabbit, Group 3: Fun in the Clouds' [2] (from now on referred to as Roger).

The experts read a written tutorial before the test took place. This tutorial contained SEEM's questions with corresponding examples from other computer games, descriptions of the computer games to be evaluated and the procedure experts had to follow. During the first meetings with experts (in small groups at the same time) they received a short training with another computer game, in which two sub games had to be evaluated in the correct manner. The problems obtained from UT of these sub games were shown and discussed. The aim of the tutorial and training was to increase experts' understanding of SEEM. Understanding of the method is important since analysts who do not understand an inspection method can readily both come up with many false positives and fail to predict problems [8].

After this training, the actual evaluation started. The first game had to be evaluated for one hour. Evaluators were told to go at least once through the questions at each screen. After 55 minutes experts were asked to take a closer look at the global questions. Experts took a short break when they were finished analyzing and reporting problems that related to the two final questions. After the break experts were given the instruction to look specifically at predetermined sub games for a further 45 minutes. These sub games were selected because about 50% or more of the children visited these screens during UT and these screens contained many uncovered problems. After 40 minutes experts once again were requested to focus on the two global questions.

The order of the games was randomly determined. Experts took the second game home and evaluated it there. The instructions for the evaluation did not change.

2.2 Problem Report

For each predicted problem evaluators filled in an Interaction Problem Report (IPR). The format for IPR's is based on Lavery et al. [14]. Experts had to fill in the screen number, the predictive question the problem referred to, a short problem description, expected causes of the problem and expected outcomes of the problem. By constraining experts to use this format, the comparison of their predictions to the problems uncovered by children became easier.

3 Analysis of the Data

3.1 Creating the Actual Problem Sets

To determine the thoroughness and validity of SEEM, standard problem sets were needed for both computer games. UT was used to generate these touchstone sets of usability problems [12]. For both computer games children participants played the game as they liked in sessions that lasted about 30 minutes.

Twenty-six children participated in the UT of Milo, which makes it likely that almost all problems were detected because the total number of usability problems found levels off asymptotically as the number of participants increases [12]. Only seven children participated in the UT of Roger. All children were between 5 and 7 years old. For information of the study set-up and data analysis see Barendregt et al. [4]. The data analysis resulted in a list of 86 actual problems for Milo, and a list of 39 actual problems for Roger.

3.2   Determining the Thoroughness

The thoroughness of SEEM was assessed with the following formula [7]:

$$\text{Thoroughness} = \frac{\text{hits}}{(\text{hits} + \text{misses})} \qquad (1)$$

Hits are predictions matched to problems found in UT, and misses are problems found in UT that are not predicted. Two researchers judged whether a prediction from an expert matched with an actual problem (which made the problem prediction a hit). When they disagreed, they discussed the problem prediction until they both agreed whether it was a hit or not. The thoroughness of SEEM was compared to the thoroughness for another inspection method.

3.3   Determining the Validity

The validity of SEEM was determined with the following formula [7]:

$$\text{Validity} = \frac{\text{hits}}{(\text{hits} + \text{false positives})} \qquad (2)$$

As stated before, hits are predictions from experts that are matched to actual problems from UT. False positives are predicted problems that do not occur in the actual problem set derived from UT. The validity of SEEM was compared to the scores of another existing method.

3.4   Determining the Appropriateness of SEEM's Questions

As Cockton and Woolrych [8] stated: "For heuristics to be shown to have a role in problem discovery or analysis, appropriate heuristics must be associated with problems". The same applies for the questions of SEEM. Therefore two evaluators checked the appropriateness of the questions that the experts had filled in on the IPR. The following categories were used:

1. Correct use: when an expert used a correct question, or when the choice was not optimal, but this question was possible in relation to the problem
2. Incorrect use: when experts did not fill in any question, or when they used a wrong question in relation to the problem.

4   Results

4.1   Thoroughness

Table 1 shows the thoroughness of SEEM. Thoroughness scores have a range from 0 to 1, with an optimal value of 1.

Table 1. Thoroughness of SEEM

	Lowest score	Highest score	Median	Mean	Sum (n=18)
SEEM Milo	0.08	0.29	0.15	0.17	0.77
SEEM Roger	0.05	0.28	0.15	0.18	0.74
SEEM	0.10	0.29	0.16	0.17	0.76

The third row is not simply an average of the two computer games, e.g. the lowest score for SEEM is higher than the average of the two scores above. An explanation is that the expert with the lowest thoroughness at Milo compensated this with a higher thoroughness at Roger. The lowest scores are from different experts. The same goes for the other numbers. The sum shows that for the two computer games together about 76% of the actual problems were predicted by experts while using SEEM. The sum is much higher than the individual scores from experts. Based on a study that compared three predictive evaluation methods, Sears [20] also concluded that the thoroughness increases as more evaluators participate. This is due to the increasing number of hits whereas the number of hits plus misses (the actual problem set) remains unchanged.

These numbers can be compared to values from other studies to give a global impression of their quality. Cockton et al. [7] conducted a Heuristic Evaluation with many participants (31 analysts divided over 10 groups in the latest study compared to 96 analysts divided over 16 groups in an earlier version of the study) to validate the DARe model. They compared the predictions from the Heuristic Evaluation with problems uncovered with UT. In the latest study 5 users were included in UT; in the earlier study 15 users were included. They found a thoroughness of 0.70 in the latest study; in the earlier study they found a thoroughness of 0.63. Compared to these thoroughness scores for a Heuristic Evaluation, the results from SEEM are promising.

Apart from overall thoroughness, we determined separate thoroughness scores per severity category, similar to Hartson's approach [12]. Frequency severity stands for the number of children that experience a problem, impact severity stands for the seriousness of the consequences a problem has for children [4]. Table 2 shows the thoroughness of the different severity categories.

Table 2. Thoroughness of SEEM per severity category

	Frequency severity			Impact severity		
	High	Medium	Low	High	Medium	Low
SEEM Milo	1	0.88	0.70	1	0.94	0.70
SEEM Roger	1	1	0.70	0.80	0.78	0.72
SEEM	1	0.90	0.70	0.91	0.88	0.71

Striking is that for both computer games none of the high frequency severity problems were missed. The two medium frequency severity problems that were not predicted both have a low impact severity.

Experts failed to predict only one high impact severity problem, however only one child found this problem. In Milo one medium impact severity problem was not predicted, however only one child out of 26 found this problem. The two problems with medium impact severity from Roger also have a low frequency severity; only one child found them. Besides this, these problems were very detailed and therefore hard to predict. So by far most misses have a low frequency or impact severity.

Separate thoroughness scores per question were determined to examine SEEM's quality in more detail. All problems uncovered with UT were distributed over the different predictive questions. Table 3 shows the thoroughness scores only for the predictive questions which had related misses.

Table 3. Thoroughness of SEEM per predictive question

	1 Goal	2 Translation	3 Physical actions	5 Understanding feedback	8 Other
SEEM Milo	0.88	0.80	1	0.38	0.78
SEEM Roger	1	0.56	0.80	0.67	- *
SEEM	0.92	0.74	0.83	0.47	0.78

* Because there were no actual problems for this category, no thoroughness score could be determined.

Only a few problems regarding the Goal, Translation, Physical Actions, and Other (they were all technical problems) were not predicted by SEEM. The number of misses regarding Understanding Feedback is relatively high. Zapf et al. [21] investigated the error detection of computer users using word processing. They also found that errors in the feedback phase were particularly hard to detect for users. A possible explanation is that experts experienced a problem but did not realize it. Only when a person really knows a computer game very well, it is possible to predict whether someone else will see and understand the feedback.

4.2 Validity

Table 4 shows the validity of SEEM, the validity scores range from 0 to 1 with 1 being the optimal score.

Table 4. Validity of SEEM

	Lowest score	Highest score	Median	Mean	Sum (n=18)
SEEM Milo	0.54	0.90	0.71	0.69	0.47
SEEM Roger	0.15	0.63	0.39	0.37	0.19
SEEM	0.34	0.66	0.57	0.53	0.33

The validity of SEEM for Roger is much lower than the validity for Milo. This is due to the number of false positives; for Roger this number (124) is much higher than the number for Milo (73). This can be partly explained because it is likely that the problem set of Roger is not complete yet, since only 7 children participated in the UT. Kanis and Arisz [13] show that it is possible to calculate how many participants should be included in a test to be able to detect 80% of all usability problems. It turned out that UT for Roger should have been done with 11 children (instead of 7), and then the number of uncovered problems would have been 61 (instead of 39).

The validity decreases (but not as much as the thoroughness increases) as the number of experts increases. This means that in terms of percentage the number of false positives increases faster than the number of hits. This is in line with Sears' findings [20].

Compared to values from other studies SEEM's scores are still promising. Cockton et al. [7] found a validity of 0.31 for the Heuristic Evaluation, which in a later version increased to 0.50. This means that SEEM scores about equally good as their first version, but improvements are still desirable.

4.3 Appropriateness of SEEM's Questions

Table 5 shows the numbers and percentages of both the correctly and incorrectly applied questions.

Table 5. SEEM's (in-)correctly applied questions by experts

	Correct		Incorrect	
	Number	Percentage	Number	Percentage
SEEM Milo	203	75.2	67	24.8
SEEM Roger	86	70.5	36	29.5
SEEM	289	73.7	103	26.3

The results show that almost 74% of the problems were related to a correct question. Cockton et al. [7] found percentages of 31% and 57% in their experiments with the Heuristic Evaluation, meaning that the appropriate application of SEEM's questions is very good.

5   Improving SEEM

5.1   Increasing the Thoroughness

Although the thoroughness is quite high, there were quite a few misses. A possible explanation for not predicting some of the actual problems is that the experts did encounter some problems but they did not write them down. It is possible that this happened because the experts realized faster than children what went wrong and what they were supposed to do. This hypothesis was confirmed by observing some experts during their evaluations and by statements from experts made after the evaluation. By stressing the importance of immediately writing down the problem predictions and by urging experts to constantly imagine how children would use the game; the number of missed problems due to not writing them down could be decreased.

5.2 Increasing the Validity

The results show that validity is somewhat disappointing. This is due to the many false positives predicted by the experts. This number is relatively high and should decrease. Probable causes for the list of false positives were determined to see how SEEM could be improved. Two possible causes were frequently found:

1. Under- or overestimation of children. Many experts made wrong assumptions about the (cognitive) level of understanding from children.
2. Incorrect assumptions about the game. Most of these predictions occurred because there are multiple solutions to reach a sub goal in the games. For example it is almost never necessary to click at exactly one small hotspot; clicking beside the hotspot will also make the feature work. It is possible that experts did not realize this and therefore still reported this as a problem.

To decrease the number of false positives caused by incorrect assumptions of the game a suggestion is to make sure that experts evaluate sub games more than once. That way it is possible for experts to try more things in the game and get to know the game better. This could also decrease the relatively high number of Understanding Feedback problems. Giving experts more specific information about children and their cognitive level of understanding could decrease the number of false positives caused by over- or underestimating children.

Finally, the questions were analyzed and some of them were changed. Some problem predictions were described at such a high level that it was hard to judge their realness. An example is: 'The flow of the game is not logical' with no further information given. Problem predictions that were too general were mainly due to the format of the global questions. It would be better to let experts have a look at these aspects (if still necessary) at each screen to make it possible to write down detailed and complete problem predictions. Furthermore, questions that were often used in the wrong manner or that generated many false positives had to be changed. Based on these considerations and comments from the experts, the new questions are the following:

1. Goal: Can children perceive the goal? Do children understand the goal? Do children think the goal is fun?
2. Planning and translation into actions: Can children perceive and understand the actions they have to execute in order to reach the goal? Do children think the actions they have to execute in order to reach are fun?
3. Physical actions: Are children able to perform the physical actions easily?
4. Feedback (after correct and wrong actions): Is the feedback (if any) perceivable? Do children understand the feedback? Is the feedback motivating?
5. Continuation: Is the goal getting closer fast enough? Is the reward in line with the effort children have to do in order to reach the goal?
6. Navigation: Are the navigation possibilities and the exits from a (sub) game clear?
7. Are there other (e.g. technical) problems?

These new questions will be tested in a follow-up study.

6 Discussion

6.1 Generalizability

To increase the generalizability of our results experts had to evaluate two computer games. Although both games are adventures, one (Roger) focuses more on education than the other (Milo). Together they cover a wide range of activities that are often presented in adventure games for children, like motor skill games and cognitive challenges. Therefore the combination of these two games is a good representative of the genre. The results on thoroughness, validity and the understanding of SEEM show similar trends for the two games. Thus, SEEM is likely to perform similarly for other computer games as well.

6.2 Comparing Evaluation Methods

There are several issues related to conducting quality assessments of evaluation methods, among other things the number of experts participating in the study and the assumption that UT uncovers all actual problems. The large number of experts may have influenced the validity and thoroughness scores of SEEM. If every subsequent expert finds relatively more false positives than extra hits, then the validity score will decrease with more experts. In contrast, the thoroughness score is likely to increase with more experts, since the number of hits is likely to increase. This is one of the reasons why it is difficult to compare validity and thoroughness scores of different predictive evaluation methods when the studies are conducted with different numbers of experts. Therefore, SEEM's quality scores were compared to those of the Heuristic Evaluation as determined by Cockton et al. [7]. This has been done because our assessment approach is similar to theirs in terms of judging the realness of problems, the definition of the quality criteria and the number of experts (in their study groups).

We applied a similar approach as used by Hartson [12] and Cockton et al. [7] to assess the quality of SEEM. This assessment approach assumes that UT is capable of finding all problems in a game. However, various researchers have argued that predictive methods can predict actual problems not found in UT. As Gray and Salzman [11] already stated: 'It is a sure bet that no usability evaluation method (both empirical and analytical) is perfect; any method will detect some problems while missing others'. Nielsen [17] argues that predictions not found in UT were not false positives for the Heuristic Evaluation but were due to the characteristics of the users who were involved in UT. Finally, Chattratichart and Brody [5] introduce the term *false negatives* to describe the real problems uncovered by a predictive method, which are not uncovered by the UT. Thus, SEEM may have been able to uncover additional real problems that were not uncovered by UT. An example of such a problem is the following: in Milo children have to click at two crabs that make the same sound. However, these crabs walk around and all look alike, so it is impossible to follow any tactic. Children just clicked the crabs randomly until they clicked the right ones. The experts predicted that it would be more fun when children could use a tactic to solve this sub game. However, none of the children explicitly indicated this. Thus, while this problem was not found in UT, it could very well be true.

Because the validity measure is based on all false positives including those that may be real problems, it is a conservative estimate of SEEM's validity. To investigate this effect, we re-analysed the set of false positives. Two researchers independently determined whether a false positive was a true false positive or a false negative. Of the 73 false positives for Milo 45 were judged to be *false negatives*, and 77 of the 124 false positives were judged to be *false negatives* for Roger. As a consequence the validity score of SEEM would increase because the number of false positives would decrease.

6.3 Number of Experts

In this study many more experts were involved than e.g. the 5 that are normally advised for conducting a Heuristic Evaluation [17]. This was done because the aim was to test and further develop SEEM, and not to test the computer games. Another reason for including a large number of experts in this study was to decrease the influence of experts performing either very well or very poorly.

6.4 Type and Amount of Expertise

Nielsen [17] states that usability specialists were better than non-specialists at performing a Heuristic Evaluation. Nielsen distinguishes three levels of expertise; novice, single expert or double expert. In our study none of the participants can be determined as novice. All the 18 experts in this study were experienced in at least one of the following areas: children, usability and/or usability testing methods and computer games. A preliminary analysis of the results in relation to the expertise gives the impression that the scores for thoroughness and validity do not differ much as the expertise increases. A possible explanation could be that the experts do not differ greatly in their level of expertise and therefore there are no clearly marked differences in thoroughness and validity.

However, none of the experts can be categorized as novices. It is possible that the promising results of SEEM are only practicable with experts and not with novices. The differences between experts and novices regarding the thoroughness, validity and appropriateness of SEEM's questions will be investigated further in a follow-up study with novices.

7 Conclusion

The study shows that SEEM predicts actual problems quite well, the thoroughness of SEEM is 0.76. The problems from UT that are not predicted by experts can mainly be assigned to the Understanding Feedback question. Only very few severe problems from UT were not predicted by experts while using SEEM. Unfortunately the number of false positives is also rather high, resulting in a fairly low validity. The results show that experts understood SEEM quite well; almost 74% of the problem predictions were correctly related to a predictive question. Based on the analyses of the missed problems, the appropriateness of the questions, the causes of the false positives, and the useful comments from experts, the method was improved. Because the findings are very promising, we intend to conduct another study to evaluate the quality of the new version of SEEM.

Acknowledgements

First of all we thank all the experts for participating in our study. We also thank Professor Bouwhuis from the TU Eindhoven for his useful comments on an earlier version of this paper. Finally, we thank the Innovation-oriented Research Program Human-Machine Interaction (IOP-MMI) of the Dutch government that provided the grant that has made this research possible.

References

1. Milo and the magical stones (Max en de toverstenen). MediaMix Benelux (2002)
2. Roger Rabbit, Group 3: Fun in the Clouds (Robbie Konijn, Groep 3: Pret in de Wolken). Mindscape (2003)
3. Barendregt, W. and Bekker, M.M.: Towards a Framework for Design Guidelines for Young Children's Computer Games. Proceedings of the 2004 ICEC Conference, September 2004 The Netherlands, Eindhoven, Springer-Verlag (2004) 365-376
4. Barendregt, W., Bekker, M.M., Bouwhuis, D. & Baauw, E.: Predicting effectiveness of children participants in user testing based on personality characteristics. Submitted to Behaviour & Information Technology (Unpublished manuscript)
5. Chattratichart, J. and Brodie, J.: Applying User Testing Data to UEM Performance Metrics. Late Breaking Results Paper, 24 April 2004 Vienna, Austria (2004) 1119-1122
6. Cockton, G., Lavery, D. & Woolrych, A.: Inspection-based evaluations. In: Jacko, J. and Sears, A. (Eds.): The Human-Computer Interaction Handbook: Fundamentals, Evolving Technologies and Emerging Applications. Lawrence Erlbaum Associates (2003) 1118-1138
7. Cockton, G., Woolrych, A., Hall, L. & Hindmarch, M.: Changing Analysts' Tunes: The Surprising Impact of a New Instrument for Usability Inspection Method Assessment. In: Palanque, P., Johnson, P. and O'Neill, E. (Eds.): People and Computers, Designing for Society (Proceedings of HCI 2003). Springer-Verlag (2003) 145-162
8. Cockton, G. and Woolrych, A.: Understanding Inspection Methods: Lessons from an Assessment of Heuristic Evaluation. In: Blandford, A., Vanderdonckt, J. and Gray, P.D. (Eds.): Springer-Verlag (2001) 171-192
9. Desurvire, H., Caplan, M. & Toth, J.A.: Using heuristics to evaluate the playability of games. CHI extended abstracts 2004, Vienna, Austria (2004) 1509-1512
10. Federoff, M.A.: Heuristics and usability guidelines for the creation and evaluation of fun in video games. Msc Department of Telecommunications of Indiana University (2002)
11. Gray, W.D. and Salzman, M.C.: Damaged merchandise? A review of experiments that compare usability evaluation methods. Human-Computer Interaction, 13(3) (1998) 203-261
12. Hartson, H.R., Andre, T.S. & Williges, R.C.: Criteria for evaluating usability evaluation methods. International Journal of Human-Computer Interaction: Special issue on Empirical Evaluation of Information Visualisations, 13(4) (2001) 373-410
13. Kanis, H. and Arisz, H.J.: How many participants: A simple means for concurrent monitoring. Proceedings of the IEA 2000/HFES 2000 Congress, (2000) 637-640

14. Lavery, D., Cockton, G. & Atkinson, M.P.: Comparison of Evaluation Methods Using Structured Usability Problem Reports. Behaviour and Information Technology, 16(4) (1997) 246-266
15. Malone, T.W.: What makes things fun to learn? A study of intrinsically motivating computer games. Technical Report CIS-7, Xerox PARC, Palo Alto (1980)
16. Nes, F. v.: On the validity of design guidelines and the role of standardisation. In: Nicolle, C. and Abascal, J. (Eds.): Inclusive Design Guidelines for HCI. London and New York, Taylor & Francis Group (2001) 61-70
17. Nielsen, J. and Mack, R.L.: Usability Inspection Methods. New York, John Wiley & Sons, Inc. (1994)
18. Norman, D.A.: The design of everyday things. London, MIT Press (1998)
19. Pagulayan, R.J., Keeker, K., Wixon, D., Romero, R. & Fuller, T.: User-centered design in games. In: Jacko, J. and Sears, A. (Eds.): Handbook for Human-Computer Interaction in Interactive Systems. Mahwah, NJ, Lawrence Erlbaum Associates (2003) 883-906
20. Sears, A.: Heuristic Walkthroughs: Finding the problems without the noise. International Journal of Human-Computer Interactions, 9(3) (1997) 213-234
21. Zapf, D., Maier, G.W. & Irmer, C.: Error Detection, Task Characteristics, and Some Consequences for Software Design. Applied Psychology: an international review, 43 (1994) 499-520

Usability Testing of Mobile Devices: A Comparison of Three Approaches

Adriana Holtz Betiol[1] and Walter de Abreu Cybis[2]

[1] Department of Computer Science, Pontifical Catholic University of Paraná, Brazil
abetiol@netpar.com.br
[2] Department of Computer Science, Federal University of Santa Catarina, Brazil
cybis@inf.ufsc.br

Abstract. This paper describes a study that compares the results of usability testing of mobile interfaces based on three different evaluation approaches: (i) using a computer-based mobile phone emulator inside the laboratory (ii) using a mobile phone inside the laboratory (iii) using a mobile phone linked to a wireless camera in the field. The results regarding user performance and usability problem identification showed the existence of more similarities than significant differences between the results of the three evaluation contexts. Moreover, in the simplest evaluation context of the emulator it was possible to identify a large percentage of the overall set of usability problems found.

1 Introduction

The usability of the mobile devices and their applications is a key factor for the success of mobile computing. The needs and characteristics of the mobile user, the usage context of the mobile devices, the characteristics of the applications and the physical limitations of these equipments are factors which can influence the interaction and should be considered in the design of the interfaces, as well as in the usability evaluation.

An important issue currently presented in the area of Human-Computer Interaction addresses the importance of the context of use of mobile devices in their usability evaluation, so that the traditional HCI evaluation criteria and methods should be reconsidered in order to meet the requirements of mobile interaction.

Johnson [1] addresses the difficulties in reproducing inside the lab all the elements which belong to a context so dynamic and diversified as that of the mobile user. Researchers like [2,3,4] highlighted the importance of measuring usability outside the lab, in more realistic situations. As Brewster [4] suggests "it is important that mobile devices are not tested only in the lab as many potential problems may be missed". Some authors [5] also state that the use of mobile device emulators on a desktop computer cannot provide reliable indications for the usability measured. However, we don't have a good understanding about how usability measures done inside the lab differ from similar studies in the field.

From these findings, this research was proposed to compare the results of usability testing of mobile interfaces based on three commonly used setups, inside and outside the lab.

M.F. Costabile and F. Paternò (Eds.): INTERACT 2005, LNCS 3585, pp. 470–481, 2005.

2   Experimental Design

The usability tests were conducted for the purpose of evaluating the overall usability of the user interface of a Wireless Application Protocol (WAP) portal accessed through a mobile phone. This portal offers access to various typical mobile services such as leisure information, news and e-mail. All these services may be consulted anytime, anywhere, provided the user is in the area of coverage of the mobile phone operator. There is no pre-requisite necessary to access this service and any person who owns a mobile phone compatible with the WAP technology can be considered a potential user.

Three distinct approaches were defined to conduct the usability tests based on the evaluation contexts. These contexts differed only in three aspects: the equipment used for navigation on the WAP portal (mobile phone or emulator), the location for conducting the tests (usability lab or field) and the equipment used to register the interaction (computer, document camera or wireless camera). The remaining components of the evaluation contexts such as criteria for choice of participants, tasks, measures and metrics of usability were exactly the same for the three approaches.

A total of 36 participants (18 men, 18 women) between 21 and 40 years, with different educational backgrounds and professions were split into three groups of 12 persons, so each one of the users participated in one only usability test. All participants were mobile phone users with at least one year of computer experience, but none of them had used WAP or the mobile phone model used in this study.

2.1   Context of Evaluation 1: In the Laboratory, Using an Emulator

The first group performed the usability tests inside the lab using a computer-based emulator. Even though the emulator permitted the use of a keyboard, the participant was instructed to use only the mouse. The entry of data was only possible by clicking on the keys of the mobile phone simulation on the computer screen. All the user interactions with the interface and verbal comments were recorded in videotape. There were no cameras filming the participant, the image recorded on tape was only that of the computer screen. The evaluator was in the same room as the participant observing the interaction on the TV screen. From now on this context will be referred as "emulator context".

2.2   Context of Evaluation 2: In the Laboratory, Using a Mobile Phone and a Document Camera

The second group performed the usability tests inside the lab using a mobile phone fixed to a tripod which was positioned under a document camera. The tripod was developed with dimensions that enabled the users to handle the phone in the palm of their hands and touch the keypad with their thumbs (Fig. 1). However, they could not move the tripod from its initial position, so the mobile phone could not leave the visualisation area of the camera. The degrees of freedom of the supporting base were also carefully defined to enable the best angle of view for the user and for recording the phone display and keypad.

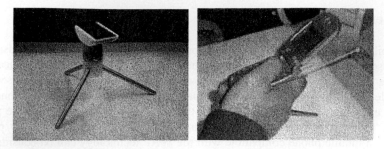

Fig. 1. Tripod for fastening the mobile phone

All the user interactions with the interface and verbal comments were recorded in videotape. There were no cameras filming the participant, the image recorded on the tape was only that of the mobile device. The evaluator was in the same room as the participant observing the interaction on the TV screen. From now on this context will be referred as "document camera context".

2.3 Context of Evaluation 3: Outside the Laboratory, Using a Mobile Phone and a Wireless Camera

The third group performed the interaction tests outside the lab, in a busy and distracting environment that reproduced several possible locations pertaining to the usage context of this type of equipment, such as airports, shops, restaurants, etc.

The system which was designed to record the interaction in an open environment was developed specially for this research inspired by the work from Nyysonen [6]. The system consisted of a wireless mini-camera (Fig.2) with a built-in microphone that communicated with a receiver on a portable digital video camera (Fig.3). The camera was fixed to a support so its movements would accompany the movements of the mobile phone. The support had several degrees of freedom of movement, which enabled the camera several different adjustments to obtain the image of the phone desired without hampering the users view and quality of filming.

Fig. 2. Wireless mini-camera system   **Fig. 3.** Reception and recording system

The participant could operate the mobile device normally. This condition contributed with greater fidelity to the reproduction of the real usage context. The evaluator was seated close to the participant observing the interaction through the video camera screen. There were no cameras filming the participant. The image recorded on tape was only that of the mobile phone. From now on this context will be referred as "wireless camera context".

2.4   The Emulator and the Mobile Phone

Several models of mobile phones and various emulators were studied with the purpose of finding the pair that presented the greatest number of similarities in terms of: disposition and functionalities of the keys and the visualisation of the application. Based on these criteria, an Openwave [7] emulator was selected, with a standard phone mask. The mobile phone model selected was the BD4000 by LG [8] operating in the 2.5G network in the CDMA 1X technology. The disposition and functionalities of the keys for data entry, selection and navigation were rigorously the same in the emulator and the mobile phone. The texts and menus of application were presented on the display following the same disposition. However, there were two main differences in relation to the two displays: the number of lines on the display and the scroll bar. The emulator presented two more lines of text on the display in relation to the mobile phone and the indication of the scroll bar for text that appeared on the right-hand side of the mobile phone did not exist in the emulator.

Table 1. Description of tasks

#	DESCRIPTION
1	You are in a restaurant having dinner with friends and you're talking about soccer. One of your friends cheers for "Internacional" and would very much like to know when his team is next playing in the Brazilian championship. You volunteer to find this information. Your objective: Find the date, time and opponent in the next "Internacional" game in the Brazilian soccer championship.
2	You are seated in the departure lounge of the airport awaiting your flight to Rio de Janeiro. You would like to go to the theatre tonight. Your objective: Find the names of all the plays on show tonight in the theatres of Rio de Janeiro.
3	You are participating in an important business meeting when a colleague asks you for updated information on the dollar rate. Your objective: Find the value of the commercial dollar, the percentage of increase or decrease and the date and time that this information was referred to.
4	You are with a client visiting a firm in the Cabral district. You do not know this district very well and would like to know which are the options of restaurants so that you can have lunch/dinner now. Your objective: Find the name, address and opening hours of a restaurant in the Cabral district.
5	You notice there is a voice message in your mobile phone. It is from a friend of yours living in New York. He asks you to call back at a certain phone number still today at 9:00 pm punctually. You are not very sure of the difference in time between Curitiba and New York, and would like to know at what time you should make this call. Your objective: Find the time in New York now.
6	I called you yesterday and said that I would send you an e-mail with the information on our meeting. You did not have time to read your e-mails in the computer today. Now you're out of the office and remember that you need to read this e-mail because the meeting may have been set for today. Your objective: Find the e-mail that I sent you, read it through, checking what time, date and where our meeting will be held. Your e-mail is: wqoliveira@ig.com.br Your password is: senha
7	You read the e-mail and are in agreement with the date and time appointed. You now need to confirm your presence at the meeting. Your objective: Reply to this e-mail with the text: Ok, confirmed!

2.5 Procedure

The usability tests were rotated among the contexts of evaluation and performed during two weeks. Each usability test took an average of 1 1/2 hour and rigorously followed the same test script.

After being introduced to the test environment the participant was requested to fill out a screening questionnaire. He was instructed on the main functionalities of the mobile phone or emulator and also asked to familiarise himself with the basic commands of WAP navigation. The user was asked to accomplish seven independent tasks concerning information search over the WAP portal (Table 1).

The evaluator did not interfere in the user's performance. He took notes of verbal comments and reactions of the participant. At the end of each task a quick interview was held with the participant to clarify possible doubts with regard to the interaction incidents observed. The participant was also requested to fill out the satisfaction and workload questionnaires. A debriefing was held to obtain general comments on the evaluation and to clarify possible difficulties that the participant may have faced during the test.

The sessions generated a total of 32 hours of videotapes that were analysed with the following purposes: measure the total task time; analyse the task outputs to determine whether the task goals where achieved; identify the interaction problems faced by the user, classifying them by degree of severity.

2.6 Criteria for Comparison

The results were compared according to two criteria: (i) the user performance in each context and (ii) the context performance in identifying usability problems.

The definition of usability for mobile devices adopted in this study was that of ISO 9241-11 [9]: "The extent to which a product can be used by specified users to achieve specified goals with effectiveness, efficiency and satisfaction in a specified context of use". Once the usability components (effectiveness, efficiency and satisfaction) were determined by this definition, the Performance Measurement Method [10], integrating part of the MUSiC project [11], was used to establish the definitions and methods of measurement of these components.

As well as the differences between equipment used to navigation (emulator X mobile phone) and to register the interaction (computer X document camera X wireless camera), the users were exposed to different environments (inside the lab X outside the lab) and situations (quiet location X noisy and busy location). So it was also decided to evaluate the workload perceived by the participants in each of the three evaluation contexts using the NASA Task Load Index [12].

The context performance in identifying usability problems was compared in terms of the number of usability problems identified, the severity of these problems and the number of hours spent in performing the evaluations.

To be able to identify the capacity of the context in identifying more serious problems, to each usability problem identified a degree of severity was attributed. The degree of severity was defined as a function of two factors: the impact that the problem caused on the user and the frequency with which it occurred [13]. The impact was defined as a scale of three points: impact 1: the user becomes a little confused or disappointed and hesitates briefly; impact 2: the user makes an error, which he manages to recover; impact 3: the user makes an error which he does not manage to recover, making it impossible for him to complete the task with success [14]. The frequency was defined as a result of the number of users that faced the same problem during the interaction. As a cost measurement, we considered the hours spent by the evaluator in the performance of usability tests and in the analysis of the videotapes. In this way it was possible to determine a benefit/cost ratio for each context, which would indicate the severity of problems found per hour of evaluation.

3   Results

One-factor ANOVA tests were conducted across the three evaluation contexts results. Table 2 presents a summary of the comparison of usability results measured in the three evaluation contexts, indicating where a statistically significant difference occurred.

Table 2. Summary of statistically differences in usability measured

	Document Camera X Emulator							Document Camera X Wireless Camera							Emulator X Wireless Camera						
	Task							Task							Task						
	1	2	3	4	5	6	7	1	2	3	4	5	6	7	1	2	3	4	5	6	7
Effectiveness	X	=	=	=	=	=	=	=	=	=	=	=	=	=	=	=	=	=	=	=	=
Efficiency	=	X	X	=	X	X	=	=	X	=	=	=	=	=	=	=	=	=	=	=	=
Satisfaction				X							X							=			
Workload				=							=							=			
X = lower results in the document camera context																					

3.1   Task Effectiveness

The statistical analysis revealed there was no difference in effectiveness measured in the three evaluation contexts, with exception of task 1 which presented a smaller effectiveness in the document camera context in comparison with the emulator context (α=5%, F(3,32) = 5.28, p=0.01).

Fig. 4. Task 1 screens on the emulator and mobile phone

To understand better these results it is necessary to analyse task 1 content. This task had as objectives to find the opponent, the date and time of the next soccer game which the "Internacional-RS" team would play in the Brazilian Soccer Championship. All participants managed to find the correct card where this information was found and hence the effectiveness value was determined in view of the quantity of information found. The quantity was calculated as 30% for the correct opponent, 35% for the correct date, and 35% for the correct time. Fig. 4 illustrates two examples of screens for this task in the emulator and the mobile phone.

All participants answered the correct opponent (Guarani-SP) however the majority got confused with the date. On reading the information the participants thought that the date would be 21/09. This is the date which appears close to this game information but it refers to the next games set (no dot line was provided to separate information sets). In fact the correct date was 20/09, which was no longer visible on the screen. The same confusion happened with the time of the game when many people thought it would be at 16.00h, when in reality the correct time was 18.00h.

In the emulator context 50% of the participants found all the correct information whereas the other 50% got the correct opponent and time, but failed on the date. In the document camera context only 8.3% (1 participant) managed to find all the correct information, 33.3% got the correct opponent and time, while 58.3% got only the correct opponent. In the wireless camera context 41.6% found all the correct information, 8.3% got the correct opponent and time, while 50% got only the opponent right. These results could be attributed to the difference that existed between the emulator and mobile phone user interface. On the smaller phone display the participant could have greater difficulty in identifying the correct date and time. However this difference between sizes of screens did not cause a significant difference in averages in the emulator and wireless camera contexts. In the wireless camera and document camera contexts, where the participants visualised the same mobile phone display, there was also no significant difference between the averages.

The results for effectiveness also showed that in the document camera context users gave up completing the tasks with greater frequency in comparison with the other two evaluation contexts.

3.2 User Efficiency

The averages of user efficiency for tasks 1, 4 and 7 presented no statistically difference in the three evaluation contexts ($\alpha=5\%$, $F(3,32)=1.58$, $p=0.22$; $F(3,32)=1.33$, $p=0.27$; $F(3,32)=3.28$, $p=0.046$ respectively). The user efficiency was lower in the document camera context in relation to the emulator context for tasks 2, 3, 5 and 6 ($\alpha=5\%$, $F(3,32)=9.91$, $p=0.0004$; $F(3,32)=9.01$, $p=0.0007$; $F(3,32)=4.27$, $p=0.022$; $F(3,32)=3.62$, $p=0.0378$ respectively).

Efficiency was defined as the ratio effectiveness/task time. Since the effectiveness for tasks 2, 3 and 6 was 100% in the three contexts, we may conclude that the lower efficiency in these tasks was due to the fact that in the document camera context the participants took more time to achieve the task objectives in comparison with the participants that performed the same tasks in the emulator context. This statement was confirmed when we performed the ANOVA for the average times in the three contexts and found that the time in the document camera context was always longer for tasks 2, 3 and 6 ($\alpha=5\%$, $F(3,32)=5.96$, $p=0.0061$; $F(3,32)=3.87$, $p=0.03$; $F(3,32)=5.11$, $p=0.01$). The lowest efficiency for task 5 may be attributed to the fact that three participants gave up completing this task in the document camera context and those who managed to complete the task took more time in this context than in the emulator context.

Between the document camera and the wireless camera contexts there was no significant difference for the task efficiencies except for task 2, where the user efficiency was lower in the document camera context. Since the effectiveness of this task was 100% in the two contexts, this difference in efficiency can be attributed to the longer time that the users took to perform it in the document camera context in comparison with the wireless camera context (α=5%, F(3,32)=5.96, p=0.0061). There was no significant difference between the efficiency measured in the emulator context and the wireless camera context in any of the tasks.

3.3 User Satisfaction

The results of applying the SUS Questionnaire [15] to measure user satisfaction in relation to the interaction with the system was reduced significantly in the document camera context in relation to the other two evaluation contexts (α=5%, F (3,32)=4.60, p=0.01). The SUS values were 72.92 in the emulator context, 58.33 in the document camera context and 71.88 in the wireless camera context.

3.4 Workload

ANOVA tests showed that there were no statistical differences in the results obtained for the NASA TLX general value in the three evaluation contexts (α=5%, (F(3,32)=2.40, p=0.10)). There was also no statistical differences among the factors isolatedly, the Mental Demand (α=5%, F (3,32)=0.82, p=0.44), Physical Demand (α=5%, F (3,32)=1,14, p=0,33), Temporal Demand (α=5%, F (3,32)=0.60, p=0.55), Effort (α=5%, F (3,32)=1.69, p=0.19), Performance (α=5%, F (3,32)=2.31, p=0.12) and Frustration (α=5%, F(3,32)=1.63, p=0.21). These results show that through the participants' perspective, the subjective experience of the workload was the same in the three evaluation contexts.

3.5 Quantity of Usability Problems

Considering the three evaluation contexts, a total of 43 unique usability problems were identified in the interaction with the system. The usability problems were distributed among the different evaluation contexts as showed in Fig. 5.

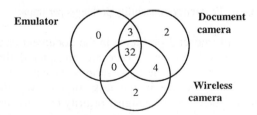

Fig. 5. Usability problems distributed according to evaluation contexts

These results show that the document camera context was the context in which it was possible to identify the greatest number of usability problems, 95.35% of all the problems found. This value corresponds to 8% more usability problems identified in relation to the wireless camera context and 17% more than the emulator context. However in the emulator context it was possible to identify more than 80% of the total problems.

There was no usability problem identified exclusively in the emulator context. However, the contexts of the document camera and the wireless camera detected 2 exclusive problems each. From the total of 8 problems not identified in the emulator context only one was a problem relative to the characteristic of the mobile phone being used and could not have happened in the emulator. This problem refers to prompting a field for text entry. In the emulator this field already appears as prompted, while in the mobile phone it is necessary for the user to press a key before starting to enter text. Since there is no indication that it is necessary to take this one extra step to prompt the field, the participants were very confused. The emulator interface eased the usability in this context since the field already appeared as prompted.

3.6 Severity of Usability Problems

The document camera context was the context that totalled the highest degree of problem severity with a result 23% superior in relation to the wireless camera context and 59% superior in relation to the emulator context. Between the contexts of the wireless camera and the emulator, the context of the wireless camera presented a result 29% superior. The analysis of Fig. 6 shows that the usability problems identified occurred with much greater frequency in the document camera context, for all impact degrees of the problem.

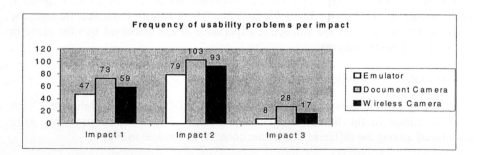

Fig. 6. Frequency of usability problems per impact

The greatest visibility of impact 3 problems in the document camera context is an important aspect to be considered since these are considered the most important problems to be detected for they are the most serious. When they occur, the user is incapable of achieving his objectives in the task. In this way they are related to usability aspects in the interface that have higher priority to be modified.

The difference between the frequency of occurrence of impact 3 problems in the emulator and the wireless camera context was significant, a value of 113%, indicating that the most serious problems appear with greater frequency on the mobile phone. However, we may consider that in spite of appearing with less frequency in the emulator context it was possible to identify 75% of the problems of greater impact (impact 2 and 3) in this context. While in the document camera and in the wireless camera contexts 100% of these problems were identified.

3.7 Benefit/Cost Ratio

Considering the hours spent on evaluation, the document camera was the context which presented the best benefit/cost ratio since it was able to identify the greatest number of usability problems, including the most serious, per hour of evaluation. The benefit/cost ratio greater advantage for the document camera context was 82% greater in relation to the emulator context and 30% more in relation to the wireless camera context. Table 3 presents a summary of the contexts performance in identifying usability problems.

Table 3. Contexts performance in identifying usability problems

	Emulator 3rd	Document Camera 1st	Wireless Camera 2nd
Usability problems	81.4%	95.35%	88.37%
Severity degree	229	363	296
Benefit/cost	7.49	11.38	8.79

4 Discussion

Overall, the results show that user performance rates were lower and that usability problems appeared with a higher frequency in the document camera context. These results can not be attributed only to the fact of using different interfaces such as the emulator vs. the mobile phone, and performing the tests inside the lab vs. in the field. Otherwise comparing the results from the emulator and wireless camera setup could have shown statistically significant differences, which didn't happen. This suggests that the fact of needing to operate the phone that was positioned on the tripod which could not be moved, since it might be out of the visualization area of the document camera, caused an extra concern to the user. This concurrent cognitive task ended up influencing the test results.

The emulator context was the simplest evaluation setup since it did not require special equipment for recording the interaction and there was no need to use the real phone. However, the use of the emulator places a restriction on the choice of participants, since it is necessary for the participant to be a computer user. Otherwise the difficulties with the use of the mouse and other devices for interaction will be the principal ones faced by the user. Generally speaking, the emulator context attained excellent performance rates in identifying usability problems. In the emulator context it was possible to identify more than 80% of the total usability problems and three out of the four most severe problems. This suggests as stated in [16] that many important usability problems can be found in simpler laboratories approaches. However, the validity of the usability problems identified in the emulator setup may depend on the similarity between the emulator and mobile phone interfaces. It was found that a slight change in the emulator interface, such as a greater number of lines, for example, may cause a large effect in the usability measured, for better or worse.

The solution of the wireless camera to record the interaction in the external environment was satisfactory, since it was capable of generating high quality images and did not hamper the participant interaction with the mobile phone. Although the external environment was busy and noisy, in the field the user was not as susceptible to outside interference as expected. The fact that the users knew that they were participating in an evaluation, that the test administrator was nearby, and that they could see the equipment used to record the interaction may have helped to increase their concentration in the tasks at hand. This data suggests the research development of new evaluation techniques which enable the user to handle a mobile device in real situations, in movement, in several different environments, being exposed to concurrent tasks, without the presence of the evaluator, and at the same time enabling to record the interaction.

This experiment was based on three representative evaluation contexts for usability tests of mobile devices. However, its results are limited in a number of ways. First the users were not exposed to explicitly concurrent tasks. The document camera context results showed that the appearance of a concurrent cognitive task, as small as it may be, had a negative impact on the usability measured.

Secondly, although the participants performed the usability tests seated, which also corresponds to a possible real context once "mobile user" doesn't necessarily mean that the user is "in movement", the mobility aspect of the user was not directly evaluated.

Finally, based on its results, this experiment should be repeated using the wireless camera and real phone in the laboratory and in the field, with the user standing or walking, for better test the effects of the mobility aspect and of these two different contexts over usability evaluations.

References

1. Johnson, P. Usability and Mobility: Interactions on the Move. First Workshop on Human Computer Interaction with Mobile Devices. Glasgow, UK (1998)
2. Petrie, H., Furner, S., Strothotte, T. Design Lifecycles and Wearable Computers for Users with Disabilities. First Workshop on Human-Computer Interaction with Mobile Devices. Glasgow, UK (1998)
3. Waterson, S., Landay, J.A., Matthews, T. In the Lab and Out in the Wild: Remote Web Usability Testing for Mobile Devices. Extended Abstracts of ACM CHI 2002 Conference on Human Factors in Computing Systems. Minneapolis, MN (2002)
4. Brewster, S. Overcoming the Lack of Screen Space on Mobile Computers. Personal and Ubiquitous Computing (2002) 6 (3):188-205
5. Chittaro, L., Cin, P. Evaluating Interface Design Choices on WAP Phones: Single-Choice List Selection and Navigation Among Cards. Proceedings IHM-HCI Mobile HCI 2001. Lille, France (2001)
6. Nyyssönen, T., Roto, V. Kaikkonen, A. Mini-camera for Usability Tests and Demonstrations. Demonstrated at Mobile HCI 2002 – Fourth International Symposium on Human-Computer Interaction with Mobile Devices. Pisa, Italy (2002)

7. Openwave Developer Network web site: Tools and SDK. Available at: http://developer. openwave.com/dvl/ (February, 2004)
8. LG Corporate web site: BD4000 Mobile Phone Characteristics. Available at http://www. lge.com.br/produtos/ (February, 2004)
9. ISO 9241-11 – Ergonomic Requirements for Office Work with Visual Display Terminals (VDT)s – Part 11: Guidance on usability (1998)
10. Cooper, D. - Performance Measurement Handbook. National Physical Laboratory, Teddington, Middlesex, UK (1995)
11. Macleod, M., Bowden, R., Bevan, N., Curson, I. The MUSiC Performance Measurement Method. Behaviour & Information Technology (1997) 16 (4/5): 279-293
12. NASA TLX - NASA Task Load Index. Human Performance Research Group, NASA Ames Research Center. Moffett Field, California, USA (1986)
13. Jeffries, R., Miller, J., Wharton, C., Uyeda, K. User Interface Evaluation in the Real World: a Comparison of Four Techniques. Proceedings of CHI'91, New Orleans, USA (1991)
14. Desurvire, H. W. Faster, Cheaper!! Are Usability Inspection Methods as Effective as Empirical Testing? In: Nielsen, J., Mack, R.L. Usability Inspection Methods. John Wiley & Sons, USA (1994) 173-202
15. Brooke, J. SUS – A Quick and Dirty Usability Scale. In: Jordan, P.W. et al., Usability Evaluation in Industry. Taylor & Francis, London, UK (1996) 189-94
16. Kjeldskov, J., Skov, M. Creating Realistic Laboratory Settings: Comparative Studies of Three Think-Aloud Usability Evaluations of a Mobile System. Interact 2003. Zurich, Switzerland (2003)

Evaluating the Effectiveness of
"Effective View Navigation" for
Very Long Ordered Lists on Mobile Devices

Luca Chittaro and Luca De Marco

HCI Lab, Dept. of Math and Computer Science, University of Udine,
via delle Scienze 206, 33100 Udine, Italy
{chittaro, demarco}@dimi.uniud.it

Abstract. Searching for an item in a long ordered list is a frequent task when using any kind of computing device (from desktop PCs to mobile phones). This paper explores three different interfaces to support this task on the limited screen of mobile devices (e.g., PDAs, in-car systems, mobile phones). Two of the considered interfaces are based on the idea of tree-augmentation of a list proposed in Furnas' *Effective View Navigation* theory [6] and differ in their depth versus breadth ratio. The third interface adopts the traditional technique of list scrolling based on keyboard entry. We compare them in terms of search time, number of errors, and user's satisfaction. Results show that list scrolling based on keyboard entry outperforms both tree-augmented lists and that the broader tree-augmented list is better than the deeper one.

1 Introduction

In recent years, mobile devices such as personal digital assistants, smart phones and in-car navigation systems have become more and more widespread among consumers. These devices offer the user the opportunity to access a great deal of information coming from local or remote databases, anytime and anywhere. In this context, the small screen of mobile devices is a serious limitation, because it restricts the user's ability to view and interact with large amounts of information. This information is often organized into long ordered lists, e.g., contact information in address books, alphanumeric index entries in databases or multimedia catalogs, destinations in navigation systems, etc. Various mechanisms have been proposed to facilitate list scrolling, e.g., buttons for moving up and down, thumbwheels on the side of devices, scrollbars on touch-sensitive screens. Besides scrolling mechanisms, many interfaces support list scrolling based on keyboard entry. The idea is to select list items by combining the use of a (virtual or physical) keyboard and a scrolling list: pressing any key will automatically scroll the list up to the first item whose first character matches the pressed key, and any subsequent keypress will further refine the search considering also the second character, then the third and so on. Although this mechanism is an obvious, widely adopted and efficient solution (assuming the user is familiar with the keyboard layout), very few mobile devices offer a complete physical keyboard and many can require multiple keypresses to select a single character (e.g.,

M.F. Costabile and F. Paternò (Eds.): INTERACT 2005, LNCS 3585, pp. 482–495, 2005.
© IFIP International Federation for Information Processing 2005

mobile phones), while adopting a virtual keyboard has the disadvantage of wasting precious screen space.

In general, the literature proposes alternative techniques to search items in long lists that are especially valuable in contexts where screen space is at premium, e.g., Alphaslider [1], Popup vernier [2], Fish-eye views [5] and, in a broader context, Zooming interfaces such as PAD++ [4]. In particular, Furnas [6] discussed how to improve the efficiency of retrieving an item in a long ordered list from a theoretical point of view. Among the alternatives he proposed, fisheye sampling has been recently explored by Bederson [3], while tree-augmentation techniques have been partially explored in previous studies ([7] and [8]) with encouraging results that motivate further investigation.

In our study, we focused on the latter idea and implemented two interfaces for mobile devices, inspired to those proposed in [7] and [8]. We then implemented a more traditional interface employing list scrolling based on keyboard entry. We carried out an experiment to compare the three interfaces, in terms of both users' performance and satisfaction, with a twofold goal. First, we wanted to compare the tree-augmentation technique versus list scrolling based on keyboard entry. Second, we wanted to compare tree-augmented lists that differ in their breadth versus depth ratio (as in [7]) on the limited screen of a mobile device.

The paper is organized as follows. In Section 2, we introduce Furnas' *Effective View Navigation* theory [6]. Section 3 describes the tree-augmentation algorithm we adopted. In Section 4, we summarize related work on evaluating item search interfaces for long lists. Section 5 and 6 respectively present the interfaces we implemented and their evaluation. Experiment results are illustrated in Section 7, while Section 8 presents conclusions and future work.

2 Theoretical Foundations: Effective View Navigation [6]

In this section, we will briefly illustrate the core ideas of Furnas' [6] *Effective View Navigation*.

Effective View Navigation is a theory of navigation in information spaces that explores some basic issues in moving around and finding data in different information structures (e.g., webs, trees, tables, simple lists). The focus is particularly on issues that arise when such structures get very large, and interaction is seriously limited by available space (e.g., screen real estate) and time (e.g., number of actions required to get somewhere).

The theory (for a complete description of it, see [6]) defines the two requirements that an information structure must satisfy to be *Efficiently View Traversable* (EVT); a comparison of several EVT structures is then made by means of a formal worst case characterization and suggestions about how to fix non-EVT structures (in particular, ordered lists) by laying over them an EVT structure are given; finally, the two requirements for *View Navigability* are discussed.

The basic assumption of Effective View Navigation theory is that the user navigates an information structure to find a specific *target*. The information structure can be represented by a *viewing graph*. At any given time, the user is *at* some *node* in the viewing graph. Each node represents a *view* that contains *items* (e.g., a window that shows a subset of items of a list). Users can make *selections* in a view to reach other nodes of the viewing graph (e.g., a click on a displayed item could change the set of displayed items).

A structure is defined to be *Efficiently View Traversable* (EVT) if the following two requirements are met:

- EVT1: the number of available selections at each view is small compared to the size of the structure.
- EVT2: the number of selections needed to travel from one view to any other is small compared to the size of the structure.

Moreover, a structure is defined to be *View Navigable* (VN) if the following two requirements are met:

- VN1: all views must contain enough information to make clear which is the correct selection to find the target.
- VN2: each available selection must make its outcome clear by presenting a small amount of information.

These last two requirements conflict with each other so that a View Navigable structure results only from a proper balance between them.

Finally, a structure is defined to be *Effectively View Navigable* if it is both Efficiently View Traversable and View Navigable.

Among the Efficiently View Traversable structures analyzed in [6] (by means of a worst case characterization), the balanced tree turns out to be one of the best with respect to EVT requirements and, for this reason, Furnas suggests that the efficiency of view-traversal of a long list could be improved by means of tree-augmentation. In the next section, we will see how tree-augmentation works.

3   The Adopted Tree-Augmentation Algorithm

In this section, we present the algorithm for tree-augmentation of ordered lists that we employed in two of the interfaces we studied.

The algorithm considers the n alphabetically ordered items of a list as the leaves of a tree, and generates a number (linear in n) of nodes to build a balanced tree of degree k and depth $d = \lceil log_k n \rceil$. Obviously, if the number of items n in the list is not a power of k, not all the subtrees rooted at the same level of the tree will contain the same number of nodes (and in particular leaves) as we will see in the following.

We call $L(i,j)$ the number of leaves that are descendants of the i-th node at level j. We start by creating the root of the tree at level 0 and all n list items as its descendants (i.e., $L(1,0)=n$). We then repeat the following iterative process until we reach the leaves level. We consider level j (starting from level 0) and for each node i at that level we create k children. Then, for each node i at level j, we organize the $L(i,j)$ leaves that are descendants of that node as follows: each of the first $k-1$ children of node i will have $\lceil L(i,j)/k \rceil$ leaves in its descendants and the remaining leaves (i.e., $L(i,j)-(k-1)\lceil L(i,j)/k \rceil$) will be descendants of its rightmost child. Then we move to the $j+1$ level and repeat the process, unless we have reached the leaves level. In this way, we guarantee that every pair of subtrees rooted at the same level will differ at most by $k-1$ leaves.

Fig. 1 illustrates an example where the list had $n = 594$ items, and we wanted to build a tree of degree $k = 5$ (and thus depth $d = \lceil log_5 594 \rceil = 4$). Each of the first $k - 1$ children of the root has $\lceil L(1,0)/k \rceil = 119$ leaves in its descendants, while the remaining 118 leaves are descendants of the rightmost child. Analogously, each of the first $k - 1$ children of the first node at level 1 has $\lceil L(1,1)/k \rceil = 24$ leaves in its descendants and the remaining 23 leaves are descendants of the rightmost child of that node. The resulting number of nodes in the example is 1 at level 0; 5 at level 1; 25 at level 2; 125 at level 3; 594 at level 4.

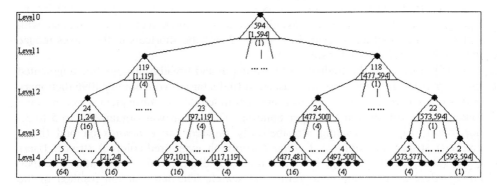

Fig. 1. A tree-augmented structure of degree 5. A triangle at each node provides numerical information about the subtree rooted at the node: (inside the triangle) number of leaves in the subtree and their range; (below the triangle) number of subtrees with the same structure contained in the whole tree.

The tree we produce for a list can be used to navigate the list as follows. Every *internal* node of the tree corresponds to a view where the user is able to select which of the k subtrees to visit by choosing among k ranges of list items. A range is identified by its bounds (i.e., by a pair of list items), and indicates which range of leaves is included in the corresponding subtree. At each node, the user has also the opportunity to go back to the father of the current node.

The obtained tree structure is *Efficiently View Traversable* for $1<k<<n$, because:

- EVT1: the number of selections at each view (being less or equal to $k+1$, i.e., the maximum number of children k, plus the back-link to the father), is small compared to the size of the structure (that is linear in n).
- EVT2: the number of selections needed to travel from one view to any other (being upper-bounded by the distance between two leaves, which is twice the depth of the tree that is logarithmic in n) is small compared to the size of the structure (that is linear in n).

4 Related Work

In this section, we summarize the results of two user studies [7,8] that applied tree-augmentation techniques for item search tasks in long lists and we compare them with the results of another study [1], that used Alphaslider and traditional scrollbars.

In [7] and [8], the employed tree-augmented structures are similar to the one described in Section 3. Besides range selection, selection of a range bound as target was supported (fully by [7] and only for a central item by [8]). Note that adding this possibility corresponds to adding shortcuts in the tree structure that allow one to jump from internal nodes to some descendant leaves. Each range bound (except for the first one and the last one) was used for two adjacent ranges as the upper bound of the lower range and the lower bound of the upper range (see e.g., Fig. 2a). Both EVT requirements are still met. In fact, with respect to EVT1, the number of available selections remains constant (being equal to k ranges plus $k+1$ bounds) and thus small compared to the size of the structure. With respect to EVT2, the upper bound for the number of selections needed to travel from one node to another does not change with respect to the structure described in Section 3, but the shortcuts to the leaves reduce the number of selections for some items.

In [7], a study of the tradeoff between depth and breadth in large tree-augmented lists is presented. Eight users were asked to find a target word among 4096 dictionary words (each one between 4 and 14 characters in length) by subsequent selections on a touch screen, carried out by finger pointing. The screen was organized into 5 to 33 horizontal stripes alternating alphabetically ordered *range bounds* on odd (blue-colored) stripes and unlabeled *range-buttons* on even (red-colored) stripes. Users could select one of the range bounds if it already displayed the target, otherwise they could select a range-button to refine the search. The latter action resulted in the display of a new set of alternating range bounds and range-buttons (or only words, if the leaves level of the tree was reached). The procedure was repeated until the target word was found. To study the depth versus breadth trade-off, the number of ranges in a single screen was varied. There were a total of 4 sessions (consisting of 5, 10, 15, and 20 trials) with 2, 4, 8 and 16 ranges, which required 12, 6, 4 and 3 selections per trial, respectively. The average search time varied from 23.4 down to 12.5 seconds as the number of ranges increased from 2 to 16, thus demonstrating the advantage of using a broad and shallow structure over a narrower and deeper one. Subjects went through a long training time, consisting in 30 trials with 6 ranges at the beginning of the experiment and a supplementary training session before each of the 4 test sessions.

In a more recent study [8], a binary search method (called *BinScroll*) for finding a target item in long ordered lists was tested on 24 users. The method employed a specific instance ($k=2$) of the general tree-augmentation technique we described in Section 3. Consequently, the resulting structure was a binary tree. Participants were asked to find a target movie title among 10000 movie titles in English (with an average length of 17 characters) by subsequent selections carried out with the four arrow buttons of a standard keyboard. A CRT display showed three movie titles in a single column. The top and middle items were, respectively, the lower and upper bound of a range of movie titles. The middle and bottom items were, respectively, the lower and upper bound of another range. The right arrow was used to select the middle item when it was the target; the up and down arrows were used to refine the search, selecting the upper or the lower range, respectively; the left arrow was used to go back to previous screens one by one. The average selection time for a search with the *BinScroll* technique turned out to be 14 seconds, which is close to the best result obtained in [7]. Participants were given a long training time also in this study, consisting of 15 minutes of training before the 25 test search tasks.

In [1], three different versions of the well-known Alphaslider were compared with each other and with a traditional scrollbar on a list item search task. 24 users were asked to find a target movie among 10000 movie titles in English (with an average length of 19 characters) by means of three Alphaslider versions and a traditional scrollbar. A CRT display was employed and selections were carried out by moving the slider-thumb of the Alphaslider or the scrollbar using a mouse. The interfaces' appearance and behavior was very similar to traditional horizontal scrollbars. The slider-thumb of each Alphaslider or scrollbar could be moved by directly dragging it or by clicking in the slide area. Below the slide area, an index provided cues about the alphabetical distribution of the elements, while above the slide area, the currently selected item was displayed. The three Alphasliders differed from the scrollbar because the granularity of mouse movements (and consequently slider speed) could be varied by clicking on different segments (top, center and bottom) of the slider-thumb or by moving the mouse at different speeds. The average selection time with the fastest of the Alphaslider versions was 24 seconds, while the average selection time with the traditional scrollbar was 25 seconds. Unlike the two previous studies, there were only 5 training trials per interface.

Although the results of the three studies cannot be directly compared, because they used very different input techniques (finger pointing, keypresses and mouse point-and-drag, respectively), the following considerations can be made:

- The interfaces described in [7] and [8] were both based on a tree-augmented list, resulting in an *Effectively View Navigable* structure, following the theory formulated by Furnas in [6].
- The *BinScroll* technique [8] seems to be very efficient with respect to the other ones; only the interface showing 16 ranges used in [7] offered a better performance, but the number of items was less than half (4096 vs. 10000 items); however, it must be pointed out that the input technique used in [8] might have improved performance, because users did not need to move their hand on the screen to select the displayed items, but just keep it on the 4 arrow keys.
- The two tree-augmented lists proposed in [7] and [8] seem to offer a notable advantage with respect to Alphasliders and scrollbars employed in [1], although it must be pointed out that in the latter study the training time was much shorter.
- The study by Landauer and Nachbar [7] suggests that increasing the number of ranges can lead to total task time reduction.

5   The Interfaces Considered

5.1   6-Ary Tree-Augmentation of a List ("Six-Tree" Interface)

The first interface ("Six-Tree") exploits the tree-augmented structure obtained by applying the algorithm described in Section 3 and is inspired to the one presented in [7]. The screen is organized into 13 horizontal stripes alternating range bounds on odd stripes and range-buttons on even (dotted) stripes. An example of a starting screen is shown in Fig. 2a.

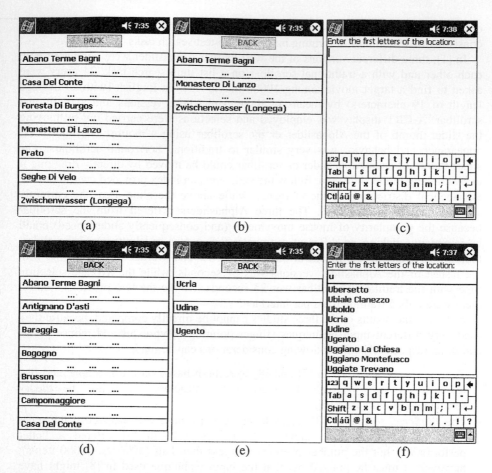

Fig. 2. Starting screens of Six-Tree (a), Bin-Tree (b) and Keyb (c); Six-Tree after the selection of the first range-button (d); example of last selection screen in Six-Tree and Bin-Tree (e); Keyb after entering a first character (f)

Each screen presents up to 6 range-buttons and 7 (directly selectable) range bounds. If the target is not one of the displayed range bounds, the user has to select the proper range-button (e.g., Fig. 2d shows the effect of selecting the first range-button of Fig. 2a). The "BACK" button allows users to recover from possible errors by going back to previous views. Each selection produces a "click" sound, to give the user auditory feedback.

When the last selection screen is reached (which means that the number of possible choices is less or equal to 7) a screen without range-buttons is presented (see e.g., Fig. 2e). This event produces a "ding" sound, to give the user auditory feedback. After selecting a list item, a final confirmation screen is presented to the user. The same screen is presented when a range bound is selected as a shortcut to the last level. This screen (used also in the other interfaces we implemented) allows the user to check that the selected item was really the desired target, pressing an "OK" button to confirm her choice or a "BACK" button to return to the previous screen.

The adopted structure is Effectively View Navigable, because it is both Efficiently View Traversable (as already discussed in Sections 3 and 4) and also View Navigable. The two VN requirements are indeed met:

- VN1: in each screen, the range bounds make it unambiguously clear which selection is needed to reach the desired target.
- VN2: the outcome of each available selection is made clear by presenting only a small amount of information (specified by a single list item or by a pair of range bounds).

"Six-Tree" differs from the interface described in [7] in the following details:

- The range-buttons are distinguishable from the range bounds because they contain dots, instead of using a different color; this avoids undesirable effects due to possible color perception problems of users and takes into account the case of mobile devices with monochrome displays.
- The number of items in a screen has been determined by the available space of a typical PDA screen.
- The selections are carried out on a PDA touch screen by means of a stylus pen, instead of finger pointing on a larger touch screen.

5.2 Binary Tree-Augmentation of a List ("Bin-Tree" Interface)

The second interface ("Bin-Tree"), inspired by the one in [8], is operated exactly as "Six-Tree" and differs from it only in the number of range bounds and range-buttons (Fig. 2b). Each screen presents 3 range bounds on odd stripes and 2 range-buttons on even stripes.

"Bin-Tree" differs from the interface described in [8] in the following details:

- User input is based on stylus pointing instead of arrow-keypresses to become consistent with "Six-Tree" and thus allow a fair comparison between the two tree-augmented structures; stylus pointing is also typical of PDAs and high-end smartphones.
- Due to the change in user input style, range-buttons have been introduced between range bounds; range-buttons were unnecessary in [8], where ranges were selected by pressing the up or down arrow keys.
- While only the central range bound could be selected as the target item in [8], in our design all three range bounds are directly selectable for consistency with "Six-Tree".

5.3 List Scrolling Based on Keyboard Entry ("Keyb" Interface)

The last interface ("Keyb") implements the traditional idea of list scrolling based on keyboard entry described in the introduction of this paper.

This interface (Fig. 2c and 2f) employs the default QWERTY virtual keyboard of Pocket PCs to allow one entering characters of the target item. The text entry field is devoted to display entered characters and it is initially blank (Fig. 2c). A list of 9 items that can be directly selected appears after entering the first character (Fig. 2f) and contains only items starting with that character. The "BACKSPACE" button of the keyboard allows the user to delete the most recently entered characters one by one. At each selection of a character, accompanied by a "click" sound, the list is automatically scrolled down until reaching the first entry whose first characters match those entered by the user. This process continues until the user recognizes the target item in the displayed list and selects it.

6 Experimental Evaluation

6.1 Experimental Design

We recruited 48 subjects, 28 males and 20 females, from diverse backgrounds (e.g., university students, office clerks, engineers). Age ranged from 20 to 59, averaging at 30. Participants had at least a basic computer knowledge: only a few subjects used computers rarely (a few times in a year for 2 subjects and once in a month for 3 subjects), some subjects used computers at least weekly (7 subjects), while most subjects used computers daily (36 subjects). However, only five subjects owned a PDA and used it almost every day, while most of them (30 subjects) had never used a PDA, the remaining ones (13) had the opportunity to try a PDA for a very limited time (e.g., in shops or with a friend that owned one).

For our test we employed a Pocket PC with 320x240 screen resolution. Logging code automatically collected data about the number of selections and task completion times. The interfaces were operated by means of a stylus.

A between-subjects design was adopted, with interface type as the only independent variable (with three levels: "Six-Tree", "Bin-Tree" and "Keyb"). Subjects have been carefully assigned to the three groups to minimize differences in computer experience, age and sex among groups. Two subjects have been excluded from the data analysis due to their behavior during the test: one from the "Bin-Tree" group became confused by the binary search and one from the "Keyb" group stopped and began talking to the experimenter.

The following dependent variables were measured to characterize efficiency and usability:

- *Search time* to find a given target.
- *Number of errors* in terms of wrong range selections (for "Six-Tree" and "Bin-Tree"), wrong characters entered (for "Keyb"), and wrong list item selections (for all three interfaces).
- *Subjective assessment* of the ease of learning and using the interface, the ease of finding the target item (all on a five-point Likert scale, ranging from "Difficult" to "Easy") and the appropriateness of the number of items displayed on the screen (on a three-point scale: "Too few", "Appropriate", "Too many").

The list used for the evaluation contained all the 13926 unique names of Italian locations. This list is employed in real applications such as navigation systems that run on in-car devices and subsets of it are employed in applications such as automatic ticket vending machines in railway stations. A detailed analysis of all list items was carried out to identify a set of locations that were representative of the average complexity of selection. In particular, for each item and for each interface, the following data has been calculated:

- N_TAPS: the number of taps (each corresponding to a selection) needed to have the searched target displayed on the screen; in the interfaces based on tree-augmentation, this corresponded to the number of range selections needed; in "Keyb", this corresponded to the number of characters that needed to be entered.
- N_MOVES: this parameter measured the number of times a user must move the stylus to a different area of the screen to carry out the needed (N_TAPS) selections. It was calculated by subtracting from N_TAPS the number of times that a tap must be made on the same position of the previous tap.

Only locations with N_TAPS and N_MOVES values close to the mean or modal ones (shown in Table 1) were chosen as targets for the test and trial sessions (the "Chosen" rows in Table 1 shows the resulting ranges of values for the chosen target locations).

Table 1. Mean, mode and values for the chosen targets of N_TAPS and N_MOVES in the three different interfaces

Interf.	Stats	N_TAPS	N_MOVES
Six-Tree	Mean	4.35	2.79
	Mode	5.00	3.00
	Chosen	4-5	2-3
Bin-Tree	Mean	11.82	5.47
	Mode	13.00	5.00
	Chosen	12-13	5-6
Keyb	Mean	4.40	3.28
	Mode	3.00	2.00
	Chosen	3-4	2-3

During each test session, subjects completed 20 training trials (to familiarize with the assigned interface) and 10 trials during which dependent variables were measured. This high number of training trials is deliberately consistent with the studies in [7] and [8]. At the end of each test session, the previously described subjective assessment was collected by means of a questionnaire.

Based on the results reported in [7], we expected that users' performance at finding an item in the list by means of a tree-augmented structure would have been better in the broad and shallow "Six-Tree" with respect to the narrow and deep "Bin-Tree". As anticipated in Section 4, we conjectured that the better performances reported in [8] for the binary search interface could be due to the arrow-keypresses input technique. We also hypothesized that users' performance at finding an item in the list and their assessment of the ease of use of the interface would have been better in "Keyb" than in the interfaces based on tree-augmentation, for the following reasons:

- "Keyb" requires a smaller number of selections than the interfaces based on tree-augmentation (especially "Bin-Tree", as it can be seen from Table 1).

- In [8], many users reported difficulties and frustration in dealing with the alphabetical ordering in the interfaces based on tree-augmentation.
- Despite the familiarity with the alphabetical search task (frequently performed by anyone with dictionaries, phone directories, etc.), retrieving an item in a tree-augmented ordered list requires a large number of comparisons between the target and list items and, for this reason, it seems to be more cognitively demanding than the simpler task of (possibly partially) spelling and typing a name, as in list scrolling based on keyboard entry.

7 Results

7.1 Mean Search and Selection Times

For each test subject, the mean search time has been calculated considering all the 10 different test trials (Fig. 3a). A one-way ANOVA pointed out a significant effect of interface type ($F(2,43)=35.09$, $p<0.001$). A Tukey post-hoc test pointed out that the effect was significant for all pair-wise comparisons. In particular, "Keyb" (6.06s) was better than both the interfaces based on tree-augmentation ($p<0.001$) and "Six-Tree" (21.57s) was better than "Bin-Tree" (28.89s) ($p<0.05$). These results are consistent with our hypotheses and with the results of [7].

We also studied the time to make single selections (Fig. 3b) by dividing the search time by the number of selections, taking into consideration only error-free trials (those with no selection errors). It is interesting to note that tree-augmented list structures require more time than list scrolling based on keyboard entry. A one-way ANOVA pointed out that the effect was significant ($F(2,43)=18.48$, $p<0.001$) and the Tukey post-hoc showed that it was significant for all pair-wise comparisons ($p<0.05$). Mean selection times are: 1.78s with "Bin-Tree", 2.96s with "Six-Tree", 0.95s with "Keyb". The longer selection times of the interfaces based on tree-augmentation with respect to "Keyb" can be explained by a higher cognitive load required to perform each selection. The longer selection time of "Six-Tree" with respect to "Bin-Tree" is explained by the need to make a greater number of comparisons per screen. However, mean search time of "Bin-Tree" is anyway larger with respect to "Six-Tree" due to the higher number of selections needed to find the target item.

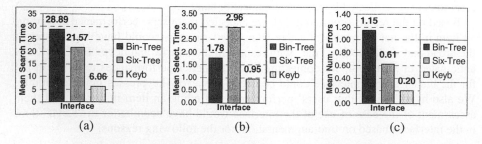

(a)   (b)   (c)

Fig. 3. Means: search time (a), selection time in error-free trials (b), number of errors (c)

7.2 Number of Errors

For each subject, the mean number of errors has been calculated considering all the 10 different test trials (Fig. 3c). A Kruskal-Wallis test, pointed out a significant effect ($p<0.05$). A Dunn post-hoc comparison showed that subjects made less errors with "Keyb" than with the interfaces based on tree-augmentation at a significant level ($p<0.05$), while no significant differences ($p>0.05$) were found between "Six-Tree" and "Bin-Tree".

Moreover, it is interesting to note that more than half of the subjects (9 out of 15) did not make selection errors at all with "Keyb" and the remaining subjects in the "Keyb" condition (6 out of 15) made at most 6 errors (considering all the 10 trials). On the contrary, nearly all subjects made at least one selection error with "Bin-Tree" and "Six-Tree", and the number of errors made was also higher, as shown in Table 2.

Table 2. Number of subjects making errors with the different interfaces

Number of errors	Bin-Tree	Six-Tree	Keyb
No errors	1	0	9
From 1 up to 6 errors	6	11	6
More than 6 errors	8	5	0

7.3 Subjective Assessment

For each question on a 5-point scale, a Kruskal-Wallis test was employed to analyze data (Table 3 reports the means). With respect to ease of learning and ease of use, the different interfaces were all rated positively with no significant differences ($p>0.05$).

With respect to the ease of finding the target item, the Kruskal-Wallis test pointed out a significant effect ($p<0.05$). Dunn post-hoc showed that "Keyb" was better than "Bin-Tree" and "Six-Tree" at a significant level ($p<0.05$), while there were no significant differences between the two interfaces based on tree-augmentation ($p>0.05$).

Table 3. Mean scores of the subjective assessments per interface

Assessment	Bin-Tree	Six-Tree	Keyb
Ease of learning (1-Difficult; 5- Easy)	3.60	3.19	3.87
Ease of use (1-Difficult; 5- Easy)	3.33	3.00	3.80
Ease of finding target item (1-Difficult; 5- Easy)	3.60	3.38	4.53

With respect to the appropriateness of the number of items displayed on the screen (rated on a three-point scale: "Too few", "Appropriate", "Too many"), it is interesting to note that most users of "Bin-Tree" and "Keyb" (respectively 12 and 13 out of 15) thought that the displayed number of items was appropriate, while nearly half of "Six-Tree" users (7 out of 16) thought that the interface displayed too many items.

8 Conclusions and Future Work

The experimental study presented in this paper provides designers with useful information to help them in choosing structures to improve item search tasks in long lists on the small screen of mobile devices. In the following, we outline the most important considerations about the findings of the experiment.

First, the idea of tree-augmentation of lists proposed by Furnas' [6] does not offer - in the context we considered - any benefit to the task of finding a target item in an alphabetically ordered list with respect to the more traditional technique of list scrolling based on keyboard entry. With respect to "Keyb", the two interfaces based on tree-augmentation were found to have a significantly longer task completion time (approximately three and four times greater) and to lead to a significantly greater number of errors. Moreover, they imposed a greater cognitive load on users as highlighted by both the significantly longer selection time and by the difficulties in dealing with the alphabetical ordering, directly observed by the experimenters on many users and explicitly reported by some of them. These results suggest that list scrolling based on keyboard entry should be preferred to tree-augmented lists, when it is possible to have a virtual (or physical) keyboard available. Nevertheless, techniques based on tree-augmentation of a list could still be useful when no full keyboard (either virtual or physical) can be provided (e.g., in some wearable computer scenarios as those envisaged in [8]).

With respect to the breadth versus depth trade-off in tree-augmentation techniques, task completion time was shorter with the broad and shallow tree-augmented list (21.6s with "Six-Tree"), rather than the narrow and deep one (28.9s with "Bin-Tree"). This confirms the results presented in [7], but in the different context of mobile devices. In particular, the advantage of breadth versus depth, shown with finger pointing on a large touchscreen in [7], holds also using stylus pointing on a PDA (the conditions of our study).

We are currently planning to investigate in more detail the following two interesting aspects, highlighted by the obtained results. First, the fact that nearly half of "Six-Tree" users thought that the interface displayed too many items seems to suggest that they perceived it as imposing a greater cognitive demand (at least for a single selection) with respect to the narrower "Bin-Tree". Intermediate breadth levels would thus be worth investigating. Second, the mean single selection time of "Bin-Tree" (1.78s) was found to be much longer than that found in [8] (1s). This fact might be due to the different kind of input techniques used in the two experiments (respectively, stylus pointing versus arrow-keypresses). An experimental study would be necessary to directly compare these two different input techniques.

Finally, we are considering to carry out additional experiments to contrast tree-augmentation techniques with other techniques that are currently employed when no full keyboards (either physical or virtual) are available. For example, some mobile phones implement a sort of list scrolling based on keypad entry where pressing a keypad key corresponds to specifying an "OR" among the letters associated to that key (e.g., pressing the "2" key followed by the "3" key displays only list items whose first letter is "a", "b" or "c" and whose second letter is "d", "e" or "f").

References

1. Ahlberg, C., Shneiderman, B.: The Alphaslider: A Compact and Rapid Selector. Proc. Conf. on Human Factors in Computing Systems (CHI '94), ACM Press (1994) 365-371
2. Ayatsuka, Y., Rekimoto, J., Matsuoka, S.: Popup Vernier: a tool for sub-pixel-pitch dragging with smooth mode transition. Proc. Symp. User Interface Software and Technology (UIST '98), ACM Press (1998) 39-48
3. Bederson, B. B.: Fisheye Menus. Proc. Symp. User Interface Software and Technology (UIST '00), ACM Press (2000) 217-225
4. Bederson, B.B., Hollan, J.D.: Pad++: a zooming graphical interface for exploring alternate interface physics. Proc. Symp. User Interface Software and Technology (UIST '94), ACM Press (1994) 17-26
5. Furnas, G. W.: Generalized Fisheye Views. Proc. Conf. on Human Factors in Computing Systems (CHI '86), ACM Press (1986) 16-23
6. Furnas, G. W.: Effective View Navigation. Proc. Conf. on Human Factors in Computing Systems (CHI '97), ACM Press (1997) 367-374
7. Landauer, T., Nachbar, D.: Selection from alphabetic and numeric menu trees using a touch screen: breadth, depth, and width. Proc. Conf. on Human Factors in Computing Systems (CHI '85), ACM Press 73-78 (1985)
8. Lehikoinen, J., Salminen, I.: An Empirical and Theoretical Evaluation of BinScroll: A Rapid Selection Technique for Alphanumeric Lists. Personal and Ubiquitous Computing Vol.6, Issue 2, Springer-Verlag (2002) 141-150

Understanding Situated Social
Interactions in Public Places

Jeni Paay[1] and Jesper Kjeldskov[2]

[1] Department of Information Systems, The University of Melbourne,
Victoria, 3010, Australia
jpaay@unimelb.edu.au
[2] Department of Computer Science, Aalborg University,
9220 Aalborg, Denmark
jesper@cs.aau.dk

Abstract. Designing context-aware mobile information systems for supporting sociality requires a solid understanding of the users' context, situated interactions, and the interplay between the two. Currently such understanding is lacking in the field of HCI research and is sought after by several authors. Addressing this gap we conducted a field study of small groups socialising in a public place. Based on a grounded analysis of our findings we present a conceptual framework of situated social interactions in public. Finally, we illustrate how this framework informed design of a mobile context-aware prototype.

1   Introduction

Mobile computer technologies are increasingly being appropriated and used to support people's social life outside the work domain. Mobile phones, and especially SMS (Short Messaging Service), have changed the way people communicate with each other, interact in the physical world and coordinate their social activities [10] [18]. Smart Phones and Personal Digital Assistants (PDAs) connected to the Internet bring web services to the mobile user and extend the potentials of SMS through Internet-chat capabilities and facilities for video-based communication. By adding advanced positioning technology and short range network capabilities (such as Bluetooth) mobile services are beginning to appear which adapt their content to the user's physical and social context. SMS messages are being sent to customers in shopping centres and airports on the basis of their position. Mobile dating services exist which alert the user when they are in the proximity of a potential partner who matches their own pattern of attributes [6]. In the more experimental domain mobile guide systems provide information about the location of friends in vicinity [9], take into consideration the user's social context [4] and enable people to attach small messages for each other (virtual graffiti) to physical locations for other people to find when they enter that specific place [16].

When developing such systems designers are faced with a huge challenge. How do we take into consideration the user's physical and social context in our interaction design in a way that makes sense and is useful to the user? In order to answer this question we need to understand better the user's physical and social context, their

M.F. Costabile and F. Paternò (Eds.): INTERACT 2005, LNCS 3585, pp. 496–509, 2005.
© IFIP International Federation for Information Processing 2005

situated social interactions [14], the role of human activity within the built environment [5] and the interplay between context and user actions [8]. We need to study how physical and social affordances of a place influence the situated interactions that occur there and we must understand the relationship between interactions in the built environment and the social roles and rules of the people who inhabit that space [1]. Also, we need to understand the social processes that surround our everyday interactions with others [22].

This paper addresses this challenge by providing an understanding of peoples social interaction in a public place derived through grounded theory from a field study of small groups of people socialising in public. It also illustrates how this understanding informed the interaction design of a prototype system. The paper is structured in the following way. Section 2 briefly introduces the concept of situated interactions and the typology of situated interactions proposed by McCullough [12]. In section 3 we present our field study of socialising in public, describing the details of our empirical method and data analysis. In section 4 we present the findings from our study in the form of a conceptual framework of situated interactions in public places. Illustrating the use of this model for informing interaction design, section 5 describes the basic design ideas of an implemented prototype system for Federation Square which adapts to the user's physical and social context. Section 6 concludes on this study and outlines our current research directions.

2   Situated Interactions

Recent research approaches into context-aware computing have focused on recurrent patterns of everyday life and the relation between interactions of people and technology and the social settings in which these interactions take place [7]. Dourish regards context as a central concept in social analyses of interaction and says that social and cultural factors affect how the user makes decisions about actions and interprets a system. It seems important therefore to understand the social context of use for a mobile system to be able to predict how users will perceive it. This approach to defining context is further explored by Dourish [8] where he regards the operational situation of context-aware technology as "varied" with context being particular to each occasion of activity or action, requiring mobile and ubiquitous systems to be more responsive to the different social settings in which they might be used. Studying people's "everyday action" is one way to be able to provide designers with a sense of the meaning associated with user activities, an understanding of people's experience of place and knowledge about what they actually do in a particular situation.

One of the challenges of modelling social situated interaction is finding a method of representation to capture the situational and social aspects of a space that influence people's ability to achieve their intended activities within that built environment. In response to this McCullough [12] offers the idea of using typology (the study of recurrent forms) as a design philosophy and provides types of everyday situations as a way of abstracting context for context-aware computer applications. In his recent book McCullough [14] elaborates on this set of situational types and talks about computing as consisting of situations, rather than objects, and context as not being just the setting in which computing is embedded, but rather the user's engagement with that setting affecting the interactions that occur there. He characterizes a new era in information technology that focuses on experience and the need to understand how people play out situations. Social situations are seen as providing design precedents and problems from which to build types that can be used in creating a new form of context-centred design. Better modelling of people in contexts is the best way towards more human-centred design of mobile and pervasive computing systems.

In providing a preliminary list of everyday situations that may be transformed by technologies McCullough [12] presents a rudimentary typology of 30 different situations, a typology of "life's habitual places", grouped to reflect the usual categories of place: at work, at home, on the town and on the road. However, the use of this typology for informing interaction design for sociality is yet to be explored. As a starting point, and with the aim of understanding sociality in public places, we have focused on the situated interactions associated with being "on the town". These can be summarised briefly as: 1) eating, drinking, talking (places for socializing); 2) gathering (places to meet); 3) cruising (places for seeing and being seen); 4) belonging (places for insiders); 5) shopping (places for recreational retailing); 6) sporting (places for embodied play); 7) attending (places for cultural productions); and 8) commemorating (places for ritual).

3   Field Study: Socialising at Federation Square

Exploring the categories of McCullough's typology of "on the town" everyday situations listed above, we conducted a field study of social interaction at Federation Square, Melbourne, Australia. Federation Square is a new civic structure covering an entire city block, providing the people of Melbourne with a mixture of digital and architectural elements that provides a variety of activities to visitors including restaurants, cafes, bars, a museum, galleries, cinemas, retail shops and several public forums. The intention for the space was to incorporate digital technologies into the building fabric creating a combination of virtual information space and physical building space for people to experience.

3.1   Participants, Procedure and Data Collection

Our field study consisted of a series of contextual interviews [2] and ethnographic field observations [3] on location at Federation Square. Three different established social groups participated in the study. Each group consisted of three young urban people, mixed gender, between the ages of 20 and 35, who had a shared history of socializing at Federation Square together. Prior to the field visits each group received a 10 minute introduction to the study followed by a 20 minute interview about their socializing experiences and preferences, about places familiar to the group. One of the members of the group was then taken to Federation Square and asked to contact the other members of the group and arrange to meet up with them as they would usually do when out on the town. When the group had met at Federation Square they were not given any further assignments but were asked to simply undertake the same activities that they would usually do as a group when socialising at Federation Square. Furthermore, the participants were asked to "think aloud" as they moved around the space and respond to an interviewer interjecting with questions on points of clarification about things that had been said or decisions and interactions that were not so explicit, as they involved themselves in different interactions and activities (see figure 1). The contextual interviews and observations lasted approximately three hours for each visit.

One researcher managed and conducted the contextual interviews while the other recorded the interaction between the group and the interviewer on digital video and audio. The outcome from the field visits amounted to: 8 hours of digital video documenting all questions, responses, initiation of activities and movement of the group around the square; notes of field observations; and diary reflections about each visit recorded immediately after it.

The first group participated in two visits to Federation Square. However, during the repeat visit their enthusiasm for participation in the study observably waned and the observers learned only very little new about their social interactions relative to the time commitment required from the participants. On the basis of this lesson, the second and third groups were only asked to do a single visit each.

Fig. 1. Contextual Interview   **Fig. 2.** Affinity Diagramming

3.2 Transcriptions and Data Analysis

Shortly after the field visits all video recordings were reviewed, transcribed and analysed. The review and transcription process consisted of three steps. Firstly, each recording was viewed in its entirety during which hand written notes were made noting the place of situated interactions and any interesting events observed. These notes were combined with field notes made during the visit. Secondly, an electronic log-file was created noting the time stamp on the tape where each situated interaction event started. Thirdly, all spoken interactions between interviewer and participants including gestures and actions (such as pointing and the group forming a closed circle) were transcribed. The full transcription only covered conversations related to the participants' situated interactions. The transcription files contained the following columns: 1) time stamp (derived from the video recording); 2) situated interaction (listing situated interaction type); 3) transcript (the spoken words and actions relating to that situated interaction); and 4) margin note (notes made during transcription about initial analytical thoughts or identifying interesting trends in the data). During the later analysis phase the following columns were added: 5) codes (created through open coding); and 6) themes (higher-level categories and themes).

The analysis of the transcript involved open coding adapted from the grounded theory analysis method [15] [21] and affinity diagramming [2] (see figure 2). The open coding of the first field visit began before the field visits with the other two groups were completed. Identifying key words or events in the transcript and analyzing the underlying phenomenon being represented created the codes. To ensure consistent use of codes, each code was supplemented with a brief explanation. By reviewing the codes higher-level categories were drawn out, describing situated interactions and actions, with properties and dimensions of the category carrying the detail of the phenomenon. On the basis of this, high-level themes were then extracted from the data using axial coding and looking at the relationships across the data and between occurrences of composite descriptive categories.

The transcript from the first group produced 73 novel themes. The second group produced 34 novel themes and the third group did not contribute with any significantly new themes. One researcher did the transcription, coding and themeing. Following the coding of the data the themes were transferred to individual pieces of paper for the process of affinity diagramming. Another researcher carried out axial coding and independently analyzed and grouped the themes to produce a set of higher-level concepts. Both authors then worked cooperatively on this grouping, debating and refining each cluster of themes until consensus was reached. Affinity diagramming was used to draw successively higher levels of abstraction from the data by grouping and sorting the themes until a small set of high-level concepts, representing the essence of the data and encompassing all lower level themes, was extracted.

This affinity diagramming process resulted in a conceptual framework containing four levels of grouped themes abstracted above the themes identified in the transcripts. The outcome of the analysis is described in section 4 below.

4   Situated Social Interaction in Public Places

The conceptual framework that emerged from the analysis of situated interactions at Federation Square is called SOPHIA (SOcial PHysical Interaction Analysis). SOPHIA encapsulates a formalized understanding of every day social interaction in the situation of a public place. At the same time SOPHIA also contains a rich understanding of the role of physical and social context in the form of a structured qualitative story about how people experience physical space and how they interact with each other while socializing in these spaces.

SOPHIA consists of seven high level themes grouped into three main aspects of social interaction in the physical setting of a public place: knowledge, context and motivation. The complete SOPHIA framework is presented in Table 1 and explained in detail below.

4.1   SOPHIA: Knowledge

People socially interacting in public places draw on their knowledge using their understanding of the world around them, that is, their knowledge-in-the-world. They use physical affordances to operate in the world recognizing places for entering or places for gathering or they use landmarks as focal points. People also operate in public places using a set of social affordances. They look to what other people are doing to find cues about what to do in a place. Following crowds or people queuing is a way for people to work out where they are supposed to go.

Table 1. SOPHIA conceptual framework

Knowledge	knowledge-in-the-world	physical affordances	places to enter
			places for gathering
			landmarks as focal points
		social affordances	cues for what to do
			cues for where to go
	history	physical familiarity	familiar paths
			familiar places
		social experience	past experience
			shared experience
			recommendations (experience of others)
			preferences
Context	people	us and them (group and others)	interaction by maintaining group
			interaction by proximity
			interaction by watching
			discomfort of waiting (waiting alone)
	situation	setting matters	others (social)
			environment (physical)
			convenience
	surroundings	indexing to surroundings	index to shared knowledge
			index to visible elements
			index to events
			index to physical objects
Motivation	reflection	sizing up the situation	getting an overview
			pausing before committing
			making sense of a place
			making sense of what's happening
		seeking information	different levels of information
			media screens as decoration
			what's new
			uncertainty (lack of information)
	extension	directed movement	transition through spaces
			dynamics of a place
			wayfinding
		exploring	exploration for the sake of it
			wandering and browsing
	negotiation	making decisions	discussing suggestions
			someone takes the lead

People rely on their past history with a place to determine the activities they participate in and the way that they operate in the place. Physical familiarity with a place means that they approach specific places using familiar paths, the way that they "usually come". They also tend to choose places to socialize based on places they are familiar with. They use social experience of places as a basis for selecting places to socialize in with friends using their personal past experience, their shared experience with this group of friends or recommendations from the friends they are with or others. Sometimes they have a preference for something that they know they like. When socializing with a particular group of friends, people often arrange to meet in a place where they "usually meet" together.

4.2 SOPHIA: Context

When socializing the presence of people, including friends and strangers, influence the way that people behave and move through public places. A group of friends maintains their sense of "group" by the way that they physically locate themselves. As they move through a public place they walk abreast and when they stop to negotiate they gather in a circle. People like to be near others but not necessarily interacting directly with them, they prefer "socializing by proximity" to others without feeling the need to speak to them. People watch others, especially if they feel unobserved or they are waiting on their own. Waiting alone is an uncomfortable situation eased by appearing occupied or by being in a busy or familiar place.

Situation is important for socializing. The setting in which a particular activity takes place matters. The presence of others and the types of people influences the acceptability of a place. Physical comfort is also important, whether a place is sunny, sheltered, etc., influences the choice of location to socialize. A place may also be chosen for the convenience of its location to other activities. Personal preferences for types of activity or types of food also guides place selection.

Surrounds are part of people's context. They describe a location of a place unknown to a friend in terms of the places and activities of shared experience that they hold with that person. They also use visible elements and point to them or they might refer to generally known events or physical objects, including landmarks.

4.3 SOPHIA: Motivation

Reflection on current experience is part of socializing in a place. People try to size up the situation. They like to get an overview of what is happening in a place. Before entering a situation, they tend to stand on the outside to understand what is happening. They stand back and familiarize with situations and they pause before entering. People strive to make sense of things and places around them. This includes making sense of what is happening in a place by assessing the activities of others. Different levels of information are often required by different people for different activities. People want to know what is new. Media screens while ostensibly informative are often regarded as decoration. Lack of appropriate information in a place leads to uncertainty in understanding that place.

Extension of knowledge about a place motivates social activity. Movement by transition through spaces involves paths that have people and activities of interest along the way. These places are dynamic and paths can be altered by the presence of crowds and ad-hoc structures. In way finding people navigate by familiar paths and they look ahead for familiar objects or ask others. People spend time exploring, both physical space and shared knowledge. Exploration for the sake of it and wandering and browsing extend their knowledge of the space. Friends spend time negotiating as they move around a space deciding what to do and where to go next sometimes discussing suggestions as a group, other times someone takes the lead and others follow.

5 Implications for Design

Inquiring into the usefulness of the knowledge represented by SOPHIA for informing interaction design we conducted a two-day design workshop with the aim of developing design ideas for a context-aware mobile information system supporting sociality when "out on the town". Following the design workshop several iterations of paper-prototyping [20] turned the most promising design ideas into a high-fidelity paper prototype. Subsequently, the paper prototype was implemented as a functional web application running in Microsoft Pocket Internet Explorer on HP iPAQ h5550 using mySQL, PHP, pushlets and server-side applications for handling context-awareness and dynamic generation of maps and graphics. The system keeps track of the users' location, their current activity and friends within close proximity. It also keeps a history of the users' visits to places around the city. The technical details of the prototype are described in [12].

In the following sub-sections we describe four of the seven design ideas emerging from SOPHIA and illustrate some of the resulting paper prototype design:

- Indexing content to history and context;
- Indexing directions for way finding to familiar places;
- Representing current activities within close proximity;
- Supporting meeting up by communication about places, activities and time.

Each design idea was drawn directly from themes and categories in SOPHIA. These are italicized in the descriptions below.

Indexing Content to History and Context. Evidenced in the data by the way people make decisions about where to go, one of the most interesting findings was the importance of people's past experiences in terms of their existing *knowledge*, *history* of visits and *social experience* with places and their current social group. In the design workshop this finding was explored further using, among others, a Venn diagram to examine the relationship of experience between two people, A and B (see figure 3). Looking at the diagram from A's point of view, A has a past history which includes a number of *familiar places*. These places play an important role in A's mind, in comparison to non-familiar places, as places A knows very well, likes to go to, might recommend to others and knows the location of. A subset of A's history may be shared with B and represents *shared experience* which can be referred to through indexical relational descriptions such as "where we met last time". Finally, B may have a past history of familiar places that A has not been to. When A and B are socialising these places may be brought up by B as *recommendations* for new places for A to go (and visa versa).

On the basis of the overall design idea of indexing [11] content to the users' individual and shared histories, the paper prototype was designed to rank recommendations about places to go the basis of the user's *knowledge* and current *context*.

When a member of a social group (the user) selects a specific activity on the device (such as e.g. "having coffee", "having a drink", "eating" or "attending a cultural event") it presents a list of recommendations of places to go (see figure 4). Rather than sorting the list of places alphabetically, for example, it is sorted on the basis of the systems knowledge about user's *familiar places* (history), current *physical and social setting* (where the user is and who he is with) and the current *environmental setting* (e.g. weather conditions). Firstly, the list contains places where the user has been to before together with the people that he is currently socializing with *(shared experiences)*. This is followed by places that all people in the current social group have been to before but have not been to together. Thirdly, the list contains places where the user has been before that none of the other people in the social group have visited *(past experience)*. This is followed by places that the user has not been to but that other members of the current social group have *(recommendations)*. Finally, the remaining places in the vicinity of the social group are displayed.

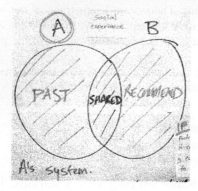

Fig. 3. Design workshop notes informed by SOPHIA: indexing to the users' individual and shared histories

Fig. 4. Paper prototype: ranked list of recommendations

Within these sub-listings, places are ranked in consideration to the frequency of past visits, the proximity of places *(convenience)*, the current activity at places and how well the weather situation of past visits to a place fits the current conditions. The highest scoring places are highlighted with a star next to the name. Furthermore, each place contains an "activity-meter" displaying the current busyness and primary activity. This ranking was informed by the findings that *places and spaces are dynamic* and that *setting matters* specifically in relation to *environment, others* and *convenience*. By providing this information the system supports the *pervasive negotiation* that happens when people are socializing together and *exploring* a space. It *indexes to shared knowledge* and gives the social group a chance to *pause before committing* to an activity or a place.

Indexing Directions for Way Finding to Familiar Places. In a somewhat similar fashion the data also evidences that people use their *history* and especially *physical familiarity* with a space as well as *the knowledge-in-the world* supported by *physical affordances* such as *places to enter* and *landmarks* to find their way around a space. Rather than requiring GPS-like instructions for way finding, people rely on simple indexing to their *familiar places* and prefer to follow their *familiar paths* from A to B even if this may not be the most time-efficient route. Furthermore, people often make use of their *surrounds* and *index to visible elements and objects* in their physical context. In the design workshop this finding was used to develop the idea of basing way finding on simple, indexical references to *landmarks* and *familiar places* with consideration to the user's history of *familiar paths* rather than efficiency (figure 5). This extends the mobile guide design presented in [16].

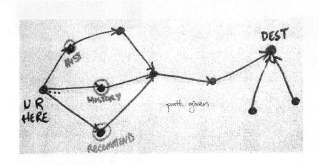

Fig. 5. Notes from design workshop informed by SOPHIA: indexing directions for way finding to familiar places and paths

Fig. 6. Paper prototype: Indexical directions for way finding

Whenever the user accesses information about a place a "Getting There" pane becomes available. Clicking on this tab displays information about how to get to that place from the user's current location based on references to places where the user has been to before such as "Chocolate Buddha is located next to ACMI Cinemas opposite Arintji". If the place is not in the vicinity of anything known by the user the wayfinding descriptions indexes to places visible from both the destination and a familiar place or visible landmarks. If the place is not within close proximity to the user directions are divided into a series of sub pages guiding the user to the nearest familiar place or landmark. The way finding directions are combined with photographs of places, landmarks and transition points referred to in the text.

In this way, the system provides information that takes into consideration what people already know about the environment they are situated in and acknowledges their ability to make sense of an unfamiliar place on the basis of a few simple cues.

Representing Current Activities within Close Proximity. Another important observation made from our field study was the importance of knowing about the existence of other people in a space and what they are doing. Other people cohabiting a space play an important role in defining the social context by constituting an external frame of reference for the social group. The interaction between a social group and the other co-inhabitants of a space is complex. It involves maintaining a boundary between *us and them* while also allowing for a certain level of *interaction between the group and others,* either *by proximity* or *by watching.* Observing where other people are gathering and what they are doing there helps in *getting an overview* of a place, *making sense of what is happening* and *sizing up the situation,* which are a very important part of *pausing before committing* to enter a place. Observing, for example, other people gathering in an unfamiliar place may invoke *exploration* that in turn may result in an *extension* of a person's knowledge of that place. In the design workshop this finding was used to discuss and develop the idea of represent current activities of others within close proximity (figure 7).

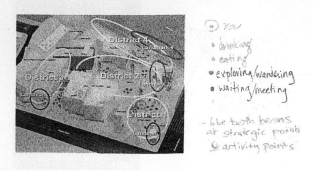

Fig. 7. Notes from design workshop informed by SOPHIA: representing current activities of others within close proximity

Fig. 8. Paper prototype: Dynamic activity map of places in vicinity

When the user clicks on the "NOW" icon on the main menu bar it displays a minimalistic map of the user's immediate surroundings. On this map superimposed, dynamically updated, circular coloured circles indicate the approximate location, current busyness and activities of places within proximity to the user. The radius of the circles represents the number of people at a place while the colour represents their primary current activity (e.g. "having coffee", "having a drink", "eating" or "attending a cultural event"). The colours of the circles match the system's general colour coding of activities and are explained through the legends at the bottom of the screen. The map also shows the location of the user. By clicking on the coloured circles the user can access more information about a place: detailed descriptions, photos, menus, programs, directions for way finding, etc.

In this way, the system supports *making sense of a place* through the *social affordances* provided by what others are doing and through access to *different levels of information* about places. It also accommodates people's desire for *interaction between the group and others by proximity*.

Supporting Meeting Up by Communication about Places, Activities and Time. A fourth finding from the data that had a major influence on the paper prototype is related to the activity of coordinating a rendezvous with your friends prior to socialising out on the town and the *discomfort of waiting* for the others to arrive at the agreed meeting point. When coordinating a rendezvous we found that people spend considerable effort on negotiating where to meet based on sometimes very complex and interrelated considerations about who they are meeting up with *(people)*, what they want to do, where the others are coming from and how long they will be *(convenience)*, where they have been together before *(history)*, the weather conditions and what other people are doing around the considered meeting place *(environmental and social setting)*. In extension of this, *the discomfort of waiting* recognizes peoples' need to look occupied and have something to do while waiting for their friends. When waiting alone people like to read newspapers, text their friends, talk on their mobile phones or watch the activities of others in order to look occupied.

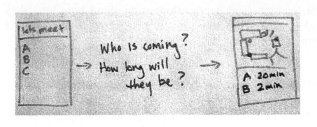

Fig. 9. Notes from design workshop informed by SOPHIA: supporting communication about people, places, activities and time

Fig. 10. Paper prototype: Context-aware chat w auto-text functions

When the user selects the "Contact" option on the top menu bar of the screen it displays a list of friends similar to the contacts list in e.g. MSN Messenger. The list is divided into three main parts: 1) friends who arc online and within proximity of the user; 2) friends who are online but further away; and 3) friends who are offline. If two or more friends are currently together (within very close proximity of each other) they are displayed as a group. When the user selects a friend or group of friends the "Meet up" pane is activated and an Internet chat session is established (figure 10). At the receiving end this causes a brief ringing tone and a flashing telephone icon on the top of the screen. Apart from supporting free text input, the chat screen more importantly also supports automatic generation of small pieces of text with the purpose of supporting communication about people, places, activities and time. At the top of the screen a minimalistic map represents the user's immediate surroundings and the location of the participants in the chat (absolute if within the map area and relative if not). Next to this the user can choose between the activities supported by the places on the map. After selecting an activity, recommended places (generated on the basis of the user's history and context using the same algorithm for recommendations described earlier) are shown on the map by means of different sized coloured stars.

Having initiated a chat from John to Frank selecting, for example, the "coffee" checkbox, clicking on the star on the map representing "The Wine Bar" and choosing "10 min" from the time drop down menu will cause the following text "Hey Frank, do you want to meet at Federation Square for coffee at the wine bar in 10 minutes?" to be generated in the outgoing message window. Here the user can subsequently edit it. When an automatically generated text message is sent it causes the selected place, activity and time to be synchronized among the participants in the chat. The other participants in the chat can then modify the original suggestion by selecting another place, activity and time, causing a counter suggestion to be generated in the outgoing message window such as "No, but what about a drink at Transport Hotel in 25 minutes?". As in a traditional Internet chat people can leave the conversation and new people can be invited to participate along the way. The conversation continues indefinitely until everyone leaves.

This design supports interaction *maintaining the group* and limits *the discomfort of waiting* by providing an open communication channel to one's friends as well as information about their present location (and hence information about how long they will be). Furthermore, it makes use of the user's *history, physical familiarity* and *social experiences* in supporting coordination of where to meet.

6 Conclusions and Further Work

In this paper we have presented a field study of small groups socialising in a public place aimed at providing a better understanding of the users' context, situated interactions and the interplay between the two. Based on a grounded analysis of our findings we have presented a conceptual framework of situated social interactions in public. Finally, we have illustrated how this conceptual framework informed the design of a mobile context-aware prototype for supporting sociality by providing a grounded understanding of people's situated social interactions in public places in an abstract form that inspires broad design solutions rather than specifying narrow system requirements.

The research presented in this paper is ongoing. The described paper prototype has been implemented in a functional prototype, which is scheduled for a large-scale field evaluation at Federation Square throughout February 2005. The focus of the evaluation is not as much on the usability of the design but rather on the usefulness of the underlying design ideas discussed above. On the basis of the findings from the evaluation the prototype will be refined and subjected to further evaluations.

Acknowledgements

This research is supported by the Danish Technical Research Council's talent project "Indexical Interaction Design for Context-aware Mobile Computer Systems" (project reference 26-04-0026). The authors thank Steve Howard and Bharat Dave for input into the design of the field study.

References

1. Agre, P.: Changing Places - Contexts of Awareness in Computing. Human-Computer Interaction. 16 (2001) 177-192
2. Beyer, H., Holtzblatt, K.: Contextual Design - Defining Customer Centred Systems. Morgan Kaufmann, San Francisco (1998)
3. Blomberg, J., Burrell, M.: An Ethnographic Approach to Design. In: Jacko, J., Sears, A. (eds.): Handbook of Human-Computer Interaction. Lawrence Erlbaum Associates Inc., Mahwah New Jersey (2003) 964-986
4. Bornträger, C., Cheverst, K.: Social and Technical Pitfalls Designing a Tourist Guide System. Proceedings of HCI in Mobile Guides, Udine, Italy (2003)
5. Ciolfi, L.: Understanding Spaces as Places: Extending Interaction Design Paradigms. Cognition Technology and Work 6. 1 (2004) 37-40

6. CNN.com: Japan's Lonely Hearts Find Each Other with "lovegety". CNN.com, 7 June 1998, http://www.cnn.com/WORLD/asiapcf/9806/07/fringe/japan.lovegety/ (1998) (accessed 16 January 2005)
7. Dourish, P.: Seeking a Foundation for Context-Aware Computing. Human-Computer Interaction. 16 (2001) 229-241
8. Dourish, P.: What We Talk About When We Talk About Context. Personal and Ubiquitous Computing. 8(1) (2004) 19-30
9. Fithian, R., Iachello, G., Moghazy, J., Pousman, Z., Stasko, J.: The Design and Evaluation of a Mobile Location-Aware Handheld Event Planner. Proceedings of Mobile HCI 2003, Udine, Italy, LNCS. Springer-Verlag, Berlin (2003) 145-160
10. Grinter, R. E., Eldridge, M.: y do tngrs luv 2 txt msg? Proceedings of the Seventh European Conference on Computer-Supported Cooperative Work ECSCW'01, Bonn, Germany. Kluwer Academic Publishers, Dordrecht Netherlands (2001) 219-238
11. Kjeldskov, J.: Just-In-Place Information for Mobile Device Interfaces. Proceedings of Mobile HCI 2002, Pisa, Italy, LNCS. Springer-Verlag, Berlin (2002) 271-275
12. Kjeldskov, J., Paay, J.: Just-for-Us: A Context-Aware Information System Facilitating Sociality. (2005) forthcoming
13. McCullough, M.: On Typologies of Situated Interactions. Human-Computer Interaction. 16 (2001) 337-347
14. McCullough, M.: Digital Ground - Architecture, Pervasive Computing, and Environmental Knowing. The MIT Press Cambridge, Massachusetts London (2004)
15. Neuman, W.: Social Research Methods: Qualitative and Quantitative Approaches. Allyn and Bacon, Boston (1994)
16. Paay, J., Kjeldskov. J.: Understanding and Modelling the Built Environment for Mobile Guide Interface Design. Behaviour and Information Technology. 24 (2005) 21-35
17. Persson, P., Espinoza, F., Sandin, A., Coster, R.: GeoNotes: A Location-based Information System for Public Spaces. Proceedings of Mobile HCI 2002, Pisa, Italy, LNCS. Springer-Verlag, Berlin (2002) 151-173
18. Rheingold H.: Smart Mobs. The Next Social Revolution. Perseus Publishing, Cambridge (2003)
19. Schmidt, A.: Implicit Human Computer Interaction Through Context. Personal Technologies. 4(2) (2000) 191-199
20. Snyder C.: Paper Prototyping. The Fast and Easy Way to Design and Refine User Interfaces. Morgan Kaufmann, Amsterdam (2003)
21. Strauss, A., Corbin, J.: Basics of Qualitative Research. Sage Publications, Newbury Park, California (1990)
22. Tamminen, S., Oulasvirta, A., Toiskallio, K., Kankainen, A.: Understanding mobile contexts. Proceedings of Mobile HCI 2003, Udine, Italy, LNCS. Springer-Verlag, Berlin (2003) 17-31

Benefits of Social Intelligence in Home Dialogue Systems

Privender Saini[1], Boris de Ruyter[2], Panos Markopoulos[3], and Albert van Breemen[2]

[1,3] User System Interaction Programme/ Industrial Design, Eindhoven University of
Technology, Den Dolech 2, 5600 MB Eindhoven, The Netherlands
{p.k.saini, p.markopoulos}@tue.nl
[2] Philips Research, Media Interaction, Prof.Holstlaan 4 (WY 2.01),
5656 AA Eindhoven, Netherlands
{boris.de.ruyter, albert.van.breemen}@philips.com

Abstract. This paper reports an exploration of the concept of social intelligence in the context of home dialogue systems for an Ambient Intelligence home. It reports a Wizard of Oz experiment involving a robotic interface capable of displaying several human social behaviors. Our results show that endowing a home dialogue system with some social intelligence can (a) create a positive bias in user's perception of technology in the environment, (b) increase user acceptance for the home dialogue system, and (c) trigger social behaviors of the user towards the home dialogue system.

1 Introduction

A defining characteristic of the vision of Ambient Intelligence is that humans will be confronted with an ever-increasing population of devices and applications embedded in our environments and in our everyday activities. There appear to be two prevalent and probably complementary views upon how humans will interact with such environments [14]: one is that interaction will be through a multitude of task specific information appliances [16]; the other is through a centralized user interface anticipating user needs through adaptivity and intelligence [17]. In the home domain, *home dialogue systems* are expected to fulfill this latter role by acting as intermediaries between systems embedded in the home and the people within them.

This research examines the effect of endowing *social intelligence* to a home dialogue system; it sets out to verify whether designing such a system so that it is perceived as socially intelligent will lead to a more positive experience for the users. In particular we expect that users will not only have higher acceptance of the home dialogue system, but also of the technology embedded within the home environment.

2 Social Intelligence and User Experience

In its widest definition social intelligence is a person's ability to "...get along with people in general, social technique or ease in society, knowledge of social matters, susceptibility to stimuli from other members of a group as well as insight into the temporary moods and underlying personality traits of strangers." [25].

M.F. Costabile and F. Paternò (Eds.): INTERACT 2005, LNCS 3585, pp. 510–521, 2005.
© IFIP International Federation for Information Processing 2005

There is a large body of psychological literature on Social Intelligence. However, there does not seem to be a single list of characteristics or behaviors that constitute Social Intelligence. An important reason for this is that Social Intelligence is manifested in many different ways according to the context at hand. Socially intelligent behaviors may range from being nice and pleasant to interact with, admitting mistakes, displaying curiosity, to being able to read non-verbal cues of interlocutors, etc. This complex nature of social intelligence has two consequences. First, it means that there are multiple ways in which we can try to make a system exhibit social intelligence. Second, that it is not straightforward to assess whether a particular system or behavior is indeed socially intelligent.

In recent years, research into computational and robotic characters has demonstrated an increasing interest into the topic of social intelligence. Nevertheless, the benefits that social intelligence might offer to users are to this point only hypothesized. It is well known that people have a tendency to attribute human like properties to interactive systems [18]. Various works have shown that endowing on-screen computational characters with human-like behaviors, e.g., from eye-gaze to emotional facial expressions and from hand gestures to full body posture adjustments, may lead to enhancing the likeability of the character, trust in the character, satisfaction with interaction, naturalness of interaction, ease of use, efficiency of task completion, and closeness to human characteristics [4, 11, 22]. Similar effects have been found in research on social robots. Effects like the appropriateness of movements [19], joint attention [12], attention getting and cooperation elicitation from strangers [5], and invested effort in interaction task [3] have been measured, with the results in favor of the socially expressive robot. Such piecemeal results show a constant pattern in favor of the more 'colorful' and 'human-like' behaviors of the computational character.

Recent research has focused on examining the effect of singular factors conducive to social intelligence. This study examines what broader benefits could be brought upon the interaction experience by a more socially rich and coherent home dialogue system that is perceived to be socially intelligent. Such a holistic examination that would show the relevance and importance of social intelligence in the domain of human computer interaction has not been attempted before.

In this paper we report a controlled study into the effects of perceived social intelligence in a home dialogue system addressing the following questions:

- Will test participants be able to perceive the level of social intelligence implemented in the home dialogue system?
- What is the effect of bringing the concept of social intelligence into a home dialogue system on the perception of quality of the interactive systems (other than the home dialogue system) in the environment?
- Will the participant's acceptance for home dialogue systems increase if the concept of social intelligence is implemented into these systems?

In the following sections we present, a home dialogue system using a robotic interface, the iCat. We describe an experiment addressing the research questions raised above. The results of this experiment are discussed leading to conclusions in the final section.

3 The iCat as an Embodied Home Dialogue System

The home dialogue system used in our study takes the form of an "interactive Cat", or just iCat. The iCat is a research platform for studying social robotic user-interfaces. It is a 38 cm tall user-interface robot that is stationary, i.e. it has no mobility facilities (see figure 1). The robot's head is equipped with 13 standard R/C servos that control different parts of its face, such as the eyebrows, eyes, eyelids, mouth and head position. With this setup we are able to generate many different facial expressions that are needed to create an emotionally expressive character.

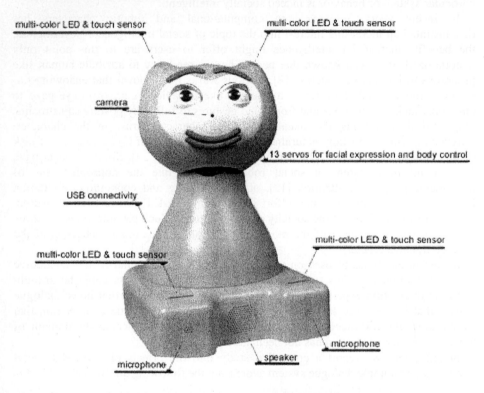

Fig. 1. Hardware setup of the home dialogue system "iCat"

A camera installed in the head of the iCat supports a range of computer vision capabilities, such as recognizing objects and faces. The iCat's foot contains two microphones to record the sounds it hears, perform speech recognition, and determine the direction of the sound source. By determining the direction of a sound source, the iCat can exhibit 'turn-to-speaker' behavior. Also, a loudspeaker is installed to play sounds and generated speech. Furthermore, the iCat is connected to an in-home network to control devices, e.g., light, VCR, TV, radio, and to access the Internet. Finally, touch sensors and multi-color LEDs are installed in the feet and ears to sense whether the user touches the robot and to communicate further information encoded by colored light. For instance, the operation mode of the iCat (e.g. sleeping, awake, busy, listening, etc.) is encoded by the color of the LEDs in the ears.

4 Experiment

4.1 Participants

The experiment involved 36 paid participants, 14 women and 22 men, $\underline{M}$ = 28.7. 80 % of the people were either attending or had graduated from university. The rest had at least attended high school. Of these 20% all had office jobs. All participants were selected to have at least some basic experience with E-mail and Internet. Participants were recruited through an external agency.

4.2 Setting

The experiment took place at HomeLab, a dedicated laboratory that simulates a home, but which is equipped with an extensive observational infrastructure that allows testing of innovative technologies at home at a naturalistic setting [9].

Participants would be left with the iCat in the living room of HomeLab, while the experimenter would observe and control the experiment from the observation station of the HomeLab.

4.3 Design

We adopted a one-factor between-subjects design in which social intelligence was manipulated. There were two conditions. Participants were randomly assigned to one of the conditions. There were 18 participants in each condition.

Condition 1 can be called the 'social intelligence' condition. During this condition the robot talked (using synthesized speech) with lip synchronization. It blinked its eyes throughout the session and displayed facial expressions while exhibiting the following selected social intelligence aspects:

- *Listening attentively*: by looking at the participant when s/he is talking and occasional nodding of the head.
- *Being able to use non-verbal cues the participant displays*: responding verbally to repeated wrong actions of the participant by offering help.
- *Assessing well the relevance of information to a problem at hand*: by stating what went wrong, before offering the correct procedure to the user
- *Being nice and pleasant to interact with*: by staying polite, mimicking facial expressions (smile when participant smiles for example), being helpful.
- *Not ignoring affective signals from the user*: by responding verbally or by displaying appropriate facial expressions to obvious frustration, confusion, or contentment.
- *Displaying interest in the immediate environment*: the immediate environment being the participant and the equipment used in tasks, by carefully monitoring the person and the progress of the tasks.

- *Knowing the rules of etiquette*: by not interrupting the participant when s/he is talking.
- *Remembering little personal details about people*: addressing the participant by name, remembering login information, and passwords if asked.
- *Admitting mistakes*: by apologizing when something has gone wrong, but also when no help can be provided upon participant's request.
- *Being expressive*: by showing facial expressions while talking, if appropriate.
- *Thinking before speaking and doing*: by showing signs of thinking (with facial expression) before answering questions or fulfilling the participant's request.

Fig. 2. Snapshot from the test sessions showing respectively: the participant (LIV1), an overview of the living room (LIV2 and LIV3) and a close up of the iCat

The behaviors for the social intelligence condition were available as pre-programmed blocks. In the socially intelligent condition the experimenter would observe and listen to the participant and would type in responses for the iCat to utter. Further, the experimenter would initiate (press of a button) these pre-programmed social behaviors at appropriate moments in a Wizard of Oz fashion.

Condition 2 was the 'socially neutral' condition. The iCat did not display any facial expressions and did not blink its eyes. It talked and used lip-synchronization, but the talking did not support the above listed aspects of social intelligence. It responded verbally only to explicit questions from the participant. The only self-initiated help was when the participants really got stuck (when after 12 minutes no progress was made) and could not continue without help.

We underline that contrary to studies listed in the previous section, we did not seek to assess the impact of each of the low level behaviors listed here. Rather, we hoped that their combination would lead the iCat to be perceived as socially intelligent and it is the impact of this perception that we aimed to assess.

4.4 Tasks

Participants were asked to perform 2 tasks. The first task was to program a DVD recorder to record 3 broadcast shows for the upcoming week. The iCat would sit on the table while participants performed the task. Participants could elicit help from the iCat by talking to it. The time allotted for this task was 10 minutes.

The second task was an online auction. An auction website was built for this purpose. The task was to register with the auction site and buy several items on a list. Participants could bid on the items, but that did not mean that they had bought them. Other people (in reality the experimenters) could out-bid them. For registration as a new user, the site required the participants' E-mail address (should be web-accessible). The E-mail was used in the experiment to notify participants when other people in the auction (in reality the experimenters) had outbid them on the listed items. In order to avoid having to check their E-mail for these outbid messages, participants could give iCat their E-mail details (login and password) if they wanted iCat to monitor their bid-on items. In other words: in asking iCat's help, participants would also need to entrust it with their E-mail password. The participants were allowed 20 minutes for this task.

4.5 Measures

A set of multiple measures was designed to test both the direct effects of the iCat's behaviors and the potential implicit "spillover" effects like satisfaction with the DVD recorder.

Social Behaviors Questionnaire (SBQ). In the absence of existing validated instruments to assess social intelligence in interactive systems a questionnaire was developed for the purpose of this study. Its purpose was to verify whether we succeeded in creating two separate conditions that the participants would rate differently in terms of social intelligence. The questionnaire (described in a separate publication) was built up of 5-point scales rating the degree of agreement (agree, somewhat agree, not agree or disagree, somewhat disagree, disagree) of participants to statements like:

- The robotic cat takes others' interests into account.
- The robotic cat does not see the consequences of things.
- The robotic cat says inappropriate things.
- The robotic cat is not interested in others' problems.
- The robotic cat tells the truth.

User Satisfaction Questionnaire (USQ). The USQ is an instrument developed previously in-house for assessing user satisfaction with consumer products [8]. It is a 54-item questionnaire that requires answers on a 5-point rating scale (agree to disagree). The USQ was used to assess the satisfaction with a DVD recorder that participants had to operate during the experiment.

The Unified Theory of Acceptance and the Use of Technology (UTAUT). [24] The UTAUT is a measure of technology acceptance. It was used with some adaptations for the home domain, to measure the extent to which participants expected to use iCat at home, if that were a possibility. It also requires participants to rate each item on a 5-point rating scale (agree to disagree).

In a post-experimental interview participants were asked some questions about what they thought abut their own performance on the auction task. The answers were scored by the experimenter on 5-point scale ranging from not happy to happy about performance.

Finally we recorded the number of times participants asked the robot general questions and the number of times they asked task-related questions. We also recorded the number of times that participants looked at the robot during the entire session.

4.6 Procedure

Participants were welcomed and it was explained that they were going to do two tasks. They were also told that while they did those tasks there would be a robot cat on the table that could be addressed if they needed or wanted its help. There would be times that the robot would initiate conversation when it thought it might be able to help. The instruction was such that emphasis was placed on completing the tasks, whereas interaction with iCat was secondary.

While participants did the tasks iCat was always sitting on the table facing them, available for input. When the opportunity arose iCat offered to monitor their E-mail account for outbids if the participants authorized it by giving it their password. The iCat was there to help in many other ways as well. If, for example, participants could not manage to register as a new user, the iCat could register on their behalf. This was done in both conditions when participants would not succeed in registering within 12 minutes. The iCat could also give information on the items that were offered in the auction. If authorized it could place bids for the participants.

After the experimental session the participants were taken to a separate room. They gave their first impressions of the experiment in an interview and filled in the questionnaires.

5 Results

Questionnaires. In light of the number of participants and the questionnaires having ordinal rating scales, Kruskal-Wallis one-way analyses of variance were performed to see whether responses on the three questionnaires differed from each other in the two conditions. An $\alpha = 0.05$ was set for all analyses.

SBQ. The difference between conditions for the SBQ was significant ($\chi^2 = 5.938$, df = 1, p < 0.05). Inspecting the means (see table 1) indicated that our hypothesis was confirmed. Participants thought the socially intelligent iCat was indeed socially more intelligent than the neutral iCat.

USQ. The difference in user satisfaction with the DVD recorder was also significant ($\chi^2 = 4.294$, df = 1, p < 0.05). Participants, who interacted with the socially intelligent iCat, were more satisfied with the DVD recorder.

UTAUT. The responses on the UTAUT also resulted in a significant difference ($\chi^2 = 9.633$, df = 1, p < 0.05). Participants who worked with the neutral iCat were less inclined to want to continue working with iCat at home.

Table 1. Questionnaire results

Questionnaire	Socially intelligent	Neutral
SBQ	1.98	2.34
USQ	1.92	2.49
UTAUT	1.71	2.33

* Lower ratings mean socially more intelligent, more satisfied, and more likely to use technology.

Interviews. From the semi-structured interview it became clear that there is no difference between the two conditions on how participants evaluated the way they performed on the auction. On a scale from 1 (not happy about performance) to 5 (very happy about performance), the average for both conditions was 3.8 ($\chi^2 = 0.170$, df = 1, p > 0.05). In response to the question: *"If you had iCat at home, what would you like it to do for you?"* many participants mentioned things like operating all their electronics and electrical appliances (such as lights, home heating system, household appliances, and home entertainment equipment). Many mentioned more privacy-sensitive tasks like having their E-mail checked for them, screening telephone calls, and Internet banking. The number of people that mentioned this was equal for both conditions.

However, when probed deeper there was a difference in the constraints posed before authorizing iCat to access personal information. Out of the 11 participants in the socially intelligent condition that would like iCat to handle their private tasks, six would like some user research data that tells them that it is safe and secure to use iCat for such tasks. The other five would use iCat without further evidence.

Participants in the neutral condition felt differently. There were 12 participants that would authorize iCat for personal tasks. 4 of them would like research evidence before using iCat. Only one participant would use iCat as is. But 7 participants were not sure if research was enough: they wanted to have further experience with iCat before allowing it more extensive access to their data. They stated that they would first give it small tasks. They would grant it full authorization only over the longer term and after proven success.

From the 36 participants, only 2 suspected the experiment was a Wizard-of-Oz.

Observations. Contrary to our expectations, there were no significant differences in the query behavior of subjects in the two conditions. The Wilcoxon-Mann-Whitney test was used to analyze the data. Participants asked questions to the iCat 13.6 times in the socially intelligent versus 11.1 in the neutral condition ($Z = -0.954$, $p > 0.05$). On average 4.9 questions were posed about items in the auction in the socially intelligent condition versus 3.2 in the neutral condition ($Z = -0.486$, $p > 0.05$). Participants looked at the iCat 11.6 times (average) in the social intelligence condition and 6.0 in the neutral condition ($Z = -1.134$, $p > 0.05$). In many cases participants looked at the robot in anticipation of an answer.

6 Discussion

The results from the SBQ confirm the distinctness of the experimental conditions that we wanted to create: Participants rated the socially intelligent iCat as more social than the neutral one. This corroborates the selection and the design of behaviors of the iCat to exhibit social intelligence.

The USQ also had a differential effect between the two conditions. Since the USQ was developed to test satisfaction with a consumer product after thorough interaction with that product and the DVD recorder task only consisted of exploring one function in a time frame of 10 minutes, the significant difference found between the two experimental conditions is remarkable.

The UTAUT was applied to the iCat and shows an explicit positive effect of the social intelligence manipulation.

There was no significant effect regarding the perceived auction performance; most participants in both conditions thought they did pretty well. The task of buying items was for most of them not a hard one. As such, many of them felt they did very well. Participants would have liked to delegate more chores to iCat and to ask it more questions. Most participants asked the iCat to monitor their items for bids from others (83% of participants). The only participants who were not very satisfied with how they had performed were those who in their daily lives do not spend much time on the web or on the computer.

Overall our impressions were that participants were more 'social' with the socially intelligent iCat. They were much more inclined to laugh, and (make small) talk, than with the neutral iCat. People generally talked more and more elaborately in the social intelligence condition. They were also more curious about the reasons the social robot said the things it said. For example, when asked which LCD monitor was a good one (to buy in the auction task) they were content with an answer. But in the socially intelligent condition they were also curious about how it knew this and why it was the best. They were also more inclined to ask about the iCat's opinion regarding other LCD monitors. They asked these questions politely and using full sentences. In the case of the neutral iCat, they were more inclined to take the suggestion of the best LCD monitor for what it was and not continue asking further. In cases that they did ask more, it was usually in shorter and more to-the-point command-like sentences than it was in the social condition.

Participants in the socially intelligent condition liked the fact that the robot was expressive in terms of facial expressions, that it nodded and shook its head in response to their talking. Overall they agreed that it was only natural for the iCat to use its potential this way. However, participants in the neutral condition also liked iCat with its more neutral behavior. After all, they argued, it is a robot and it should not try or pretend to be anything other than that. Moving and facial expressions would only look like a poor attempt to seem alive and it would likely annoy and distract from whatever you are doing. This finding shows how hard it can be to imagine something you have not experienced. Neither group of participants could imagine the iCat being different than the way they had experienced it. This has important implications for future user-system interaction research. It is simply not helpful to just ask people what they like.

7 Conclusion

Participants in this study had the experience of a robot that could 'see' what the participant was doing, whether this was a task on the TV and DVD recorder or on the Internet. Although the participants were well aware of the level of invasion technology like this would have on their lives – should it be allowed into their homes – many of them welcomed this fact. Our study has shown that a few social behaviors in a robot may be sufficient to remove some discomfort that is brought about as domestic environments become richer in technology. One plausible explanation is that participants are more inclined to accept a single centralized interface for an Ambient Intelligence environment rather than a distributed set of separate products. Adding some thoughtful implementations of social intelligence to a perceptive robot that takes this role can make the robot easier to communicate with and more trusted by users.

Whereas most research on social robotic characters concerns the interaction with the robot as the focus of attention, this study has concentrated on the role of a robot as an intermediary, a home dialogue system. The interaction with the iCat was not the participants' priority. Despite its background function, the iCat and the behaviors it displayed had significant effects on satisfaction with the systems embedded in the home environment, their acceptance by users, and the sociability users exhibit towards the system. It was shown that social intelligence is not just important in the context of direct interaction with robotic or even screen characters, but it has relevance in systems that do not necessarily have a social function.

Concerning research in social intelligence of on-screen and robotic characters, this study has made a three-fold contribution. First we have shown how a collection of human-like behaviors can lead the character to be perceived as socially intelligent. Second, by means of the social behaviors questionnaire we developed, we have provided the means with which this perception can be evaluated. Third we have demonstrated the relevance of social intelligence as a concept for studying interaction between humans and computational characters. Researchers often assume this relevance implicitly; by showing how an increase in perceived social intelligence impacts people's perception positively of a system we can substantiate this assumption. On the basis of our results, it is possible for future research to explore the most effective ways to achieve social intelligence and to forge the links between lower level behaviors of robots or on-screen characters and the resulting experience of social intelligence.

References

1. Aarts, E, and Marzano, S (Editors) (2003), *The New Everyday: Vision on Ambient Intelligence*, 010 Publishers, Rotterdam, The Netherlands.
2. Banham, K. M. (1968). *Social competence inventory for adults : a social competence inventory for older persons*. Durham : Family Life Publications.
3. Bartneck, C. (2003). Interacting with an embodied emotional Character, *Proceedings of the DPPI2003 Conference*, Pittsburgh.
4. Bickmore, T., & Cassell, J. (2001). Relational agents: A model and implementation of building user trust. Proceedings. ACM CHI 2001, Seattle, Washington, 396-403.
5. Bruce, A., Nourbakhsh, I. R., &. Simmons, R. G. (2002) The Role of Expressiveness and Attention in Human-Robot Interaction. *ICRA 2002*, 4138-4142.
6. Cañamero, L., & Fredslund, J. (2001). I Show You How I Like You – Can You Read it in My Face? IEEE Transactions on Systems, *Man and Cybernetics – Part A: Systems and Humans, 31(5),* 454-459.
7. De Ruyter, B. & Aarts, E. (2004). Ambient Intelligence: visualising the future, *AVI 2004 - Advanced Visual Interfaces*, May 25-28, Gallipoli, Italy.
8. De Ruyter, B. & Hollemans, G. (1997). *Towards a User Satisfaction Questionnaire for Consumer Electronics: Theoretical Basis.* Eindhoven: Natuurkundig Laboratorium Philips Electronics N. V., NL – TN, 406/97.
9. De Ruyter, B., Markopoulos, P., Aarts, E., IJsselsteijn, W. (2004). Engineering the user experience, In: W. Weber, J. Rabaey, and E. Aarts (Eds): *Ambient Intelligence.* Springer-Verlag.
10. Fong, T., Nourbakhsh, I., & Dautenhahn, K. (2003). A survey of socially interactive robots. *Robotics and Autonomous Systems,* 42, 143-166.
11. Heylen, D., Van Es, I., Van Dijk, E. M. A. G. & Nijholt, A. (2004). Experimenting with the Gaze of a Conversational Agent. In J. van Kuppevelt, L. Dybkjaer and N.O. Bernsen (Eds.) *Natural, Intelligent and Effective Interaction in Multimodal Dialogue Systems.* Dordrecht: Kluwer Academic Publishers.
12. Imai, M., Ono, T., & Ishiguro, H. (2001) Physical relation and expression: joint attention for human-robot interaction. *Robot and Human Interactive Communication, 2001.* Proceedings. 512-517.
13. Keating, D.K. (1978). A search for social intelligence. *Journal of Educational Psychology,* 70, 218-233.
14. Markopoulos, P., (2004). Designing ubiquitous computer human interaction: the case of the connected family. In Isomaki, H., Pirhonen, A., Roast, C., Saariluoma, P., (Eds.) *Future Interaction Design*, Springer.
15. Moos, F. A., Hunt, K. T., Omwake, K. T. & Ronning, M. M. (1927). *Social Intelligence Test.* Washington, D.C.: The Center for Psychological Service.
16. Norman, D. A. (1998). The Invisible Computer. Cambridge,MA: MIT Press.
17. Pentland, A. (2000). Perceptual Intelligence. *Communications of the ACM*, 43(3), 35-44.
18. Reeves, B., and Nass, C. (1996). *The Media Equation: How People Treat Computers, Television, and New Media Like Real People and Places*, Cambridge: Cambridge University Press.
19. Sidner, C. L., Kidd, C. D., Lee, C. H., & Lesh, N. B. (2004). Where to Look: A Study of Human-Robot Engagement, *ACM International Conference on Intelligent User Interfaces (IUI),* pp. 78-84, January 2004.
20. Strang, R., Brown, M. A., & Stratton, D. C. (1942). *Test of knowledge of social usage,* New York: Columbia University.

21. Sternberg, R.J., & Smith, C. (1985). Social intelligence and decoding skills in nonverbal communication, *Social Cognition*, 3, 168-192.
22. Thórisson, K. R. (1997). Gandalf: An Embodied Humanoid Capable of Real-Time Multimodal Dialogue with People. First ACM International Conference on Autonomous Agents, Marina del Rey, California, February 5-8, 536-7.
23. Van Breemen, A.J.N. (2004a). Bringing Robots to Life: Applying principles of animation to robots, *CHI2004 workshop Shaping Human-Robot Interaction*, Vienna.
24. Venkatesh, V,. Morris, M. G., Davis, G. B., & Davis, F. D. (2003). User Acceptance of Information Technology: Towards a Unified View. *MIS Quaterly, 27(3)*, 425-478.
25. Vernon, P.E. (1933). Some characteristics of the good judge of personality. *Journal of Social Psychology*, 4, 42-57.

Evolution of Norms in a Newly Forming Group

Catalina Danis and Alison Lee

IBM TJ Watson Research Center 19 Skyline Drive Hawthorne, NY 10532 USA
{danis, alisonl}@us.ibm.com

Abstract. Norms are expected to make significant contributions towards enabling discourse in cyberspace among people of different backgrounds, just as they do in the physical world. Yet many distributed, electronically mediated groups fail to form norms successfully. Causes range from open discord to the more insidious lack of comfort people experience in groups that fail to openly address disagreements about what constitutes appropriate behavior in the online environment. We present a case study of the evolution of norms about what constitutes appropriate posts to an online discussion forum for a newly forming group. We trace the discussion sparked by a critical incident and show how a design of an online environment that promotes visibility of participants contributed towards overcoming the forces for dissolution and promoted progress towards coalescing as a group with a shared identity.

1 Introduction

Behavioral norms are viewed as a way to bring governance to online environments [7]. They tell group members what they can and cannot do [10]. Being associated with possible sanctions against violators, they contribute to the regulation of behavior in a social or work setting [5, 7, 10]. While often discussed as a way of decreasing the incidence of intentionally disruptive behaviors, ambiguity about what constitutes appropriate behavior and the consequent unintended violation of norms can also result in much harm to productivity and sociality [4, 15]. Thus, norms are fundamentally important to the formation of agreements that underlie the smooth operation of distributed cooperative work [9, 12].

In face-to-face interaction, norms are developed implicitly over time, through observation [1, 13]. The lack of awareness and presence cues in many Computer-Mediated Communication (CMC) systems precludes observation of other people's behaviors and hinders the process of norm formation [9, 12, 13]. One response to this has been for owners of online sites to post and enforce standards for Internet behavior and provide sanctions for undesirable behavior [5, 7, 8, 12]. However, netiquette is only a starting point. There also needs to be a means for group members to evolve norms in response to new environmental conditions that require adaptations [7, 13].

This paper examines the norms development process of an emerging online group, where the need for norms definition and evolution is particularly acute [9]. Social psychological theories hold that new groups inevitably pass through a stage where disagreement about matters critical to the group are surfaced and must be resolved before they can become a coherent, productive force [17].

M.F. Costabile and F. Paternò (Eds.): INTERACT 2005, LNCS 3585, pp. 522–535, 2005.

Our case study makes two important contributions. First, it documents the negotiation that takes place as a group grapples with the process of evolving a set of norms that the participants will be willing to adhere to. Prior naturalistic studies have generally shown the end results [3, 13] but rarely examine the norms evolution process. Second, our case study demonstrates how common, easily deployable technologies that make the actions of online participants "visible" to others can create an online environment in which people become aware of the actions of others. As we will show, this visibility makes people become accountable and plays a principal role in the negotiation of governance of our online group. Consequently, this case study is a successful example of the conditions that other researchers have argued is critical for norm development to occur [9, 12]. We show how the combination of awareness of behavior and a "remedial episode" – a construct used to analyze behavior correcting episodes in online discussions [15] – can serve as the mechanism for the negotiation of norms.

2 Related Work

Groups commonly develop norms about matters that have significance to them [5]. Thus, the introduction of new technology often creates circumstances under which groups need to build new norms or elaborate existing ones. Ackerman et al. [1] studied an established group's response to the introduction of an audio-only media space for interaction. The process of norm development was largely conflict-free in the group described as being "largely cohesive" at the time the technology was introduced. This may have been further aided by the immediate adoption of the technology by the "socially central" members of the group. However, there were some occasions where sanctions had to be applied and even the loss of some users when the group failed to reach consensus on one issue on one issue [1]. Participants successfully created norms to communicate signing on, signing off and inattention.

Others have reported cases of open disagreement about norms. Cherny [3] reports on a MUD environment where an established power elite reacted against external participants and on the unsatisfactory experiences of the non-elite with attempting to modify norms. MUD environments have been criticized for providing tools to participants that address the misbehavior of others (e.g., 'gag' and 'refuse' commands) which circumvent group processes. Sproull and Faraj [16] note that by failing to deal with participants as members of a social entity, these types of individual measures reinforce the view of such spaces as "informational" spaces rather than "social" spaces. Furthermore, such tools "... benefit the individual who may use it, but it may be socially dys-functional for the group" because they preclude the education of the group and allow individuals to shirk social responsibility [16].

Of particular relevance to our discussion are case studies of norm development among newly forming electronic groups [9, 13]. Postmes et al. [13] identify groups on the basis of linguistic usage in emails written to instructors and other students in an online, self-paced course. In this case, the form of the communication, but not the content served to differentiate groups. This demonstrates Feldman's point [5] that norms can serve an expressive function which clarifies what is distinctive about the group. Differences among groups observed by Postmes et. al. [13] became more pronounced over time, although the authors do not provide insights as to how this happened and what role technology support might have played in it.

Mark [9] presents an analysis of the long-term adoption of a complex electronic technology by a distributed group and documents the failure of the development of norms. This group was effectively constituted through the introduction of a new group-ware system. She observes that it took members of the group more than two years to realize that they had dependencies on each other and needed to develop norms to govern interaction. She attributes the failure to develop norms to several factors, including the inability of members to observe each others' behavior, the lack of mechanisms to monitor adherence to norms, and the inability to apply peer pressure to sustain commitments to the norms that have been agreed to. All of these, she argues, depend on awareness mechanisms. We show in our case study that surfacing disagreements about appropriate conduct occurs in a site which makes awareness mechanisms available. Further, the case study illustrates how participants were able to explore different norm perspectives and then begin to formulate a set of norms agreeable to the group.

3 The Case Study

This case study examines an online environment developed to support summer interns at a large industrial laboratory with 1500 people located in two buildings that are 10 miles apart. Interns were typically assigned to 5 to 7 person project teams comprised of permanent researchers. They had contact with other interns through a few company-planned social gatherings and through smaller intern-organized outings. The corporation's Human Relations (HR) department wanted to create a Web site to supplement the face-to-face contact with electronic opportunities for interns to meet.

The Web site deployed in prior years had been unsuccessful in holding the interns' interest beyond the first few weeks. They looked to us as researchers with expertise in supporting collaboration among distributed team members to create a more compelling online environment. We ascertained from a dozen pre-design interviews with former and returning interns that they were interested in a discussion space where they could learn from each other. They wanted to be able to supplement the official, management version of the information with their peers' experiences. Previous research has discussed this requirement (e.g., empathic online communities [14]).

Our interest in creating the Web site was the opportunity to study the course of interaction among members of a "concocted" [2] group (put together by external agents) as they begin to develop ties. The Web site, called Portkey, was created to address both the service and the research goals. This dual focus was discussed in HR's email introduction of the site to interns and was advertised on the site as well. Interns who were not comfortable with participating under these terms were able to extract the value created by other interns by reading, but not contributing to, the discussion. We, as the researchers behind the Web site's creation, were visible and accessible both through the Web site and at the interns' social gatherings.

3.1 Portkey's Design

Portkey consisted of a discussion space, called Peertalk, profile pages, called People Pages and official information about the laboratory and living in the surrounding area. The Web site was open to all summer 2001 interns, their mentors, and managers.

A main design goal was to support accountability by providing visibility of participants and their behavior [4]. We therefore provided a discussion venue and integrated it with participant profile information. A participant's demographic information (e.g., name, school, research interests, project), their manager, their photograph, and their personal and professional interests appeared in a profile page. Entries beyond name, school, and manager were optional. Accountability was promoted by linking discussion contributions to the author's profile page. A running count of each contributor's posts appeared next to their name and, in response to requests by interns later in the summer, we made it possible to list the content of all posts made by an individual.

A second main design feature was a monthly contest used to encourage participation. Interns who volunteered the optional profile information and made at least three posts in a month were eligible for a monthly drawing of $1000 in the corporate sponsor's products. Each subsequent post resulted in an additional contest entry. Figure 1 shows that between 23 and 49 (of the 284 active) interns were eligible for the four monthly drawings. Interns earned an average of 6.5, 8.3, 13.7, 5.6 ballots per month from May through August. The spike in July's ballot number reflects the controversy which provided the occasion for the norms discussion we report on in this case study.

3.2 Methods and Data

We collected three types of data. The first type is the content of posts made by the interns over the 15-week period from May 14 - Aug 19 (calendar weeks 20 to 34). While the site operated from May 4 until October 31, our data analysis is focussed on the 15-week period when 96% of the interns were around. The second type is log records of Web site page requests. The data was used to find patterns of usage that answer questions such as "do interns tend to look at people profiles after they read the posts?" The third type is from three group interviews with interns (8 each). The groups consisted of a) a randomly selected set of Portkey users, b) interns who had only read but not posted to Peertalk, and c) high frequency posters. The interviews were loosely structured around a series of questions aimed at uncovering how well the site met their needs and how they felt about its social features. Only information gleaned from the third interview, on August 15th, is used in this report.

Usage of the Portkey site was widespread among the interns during the 15 week case study period. 284 interns out of the 340 Summer 2001 interns logged onto the Web site. Of the 284 interns, 124 posted to and read from Peertalk, 132 only read Peer-talk, while 28 others only examined areas other than Peertalk. The 124 interns (44% of total) made 1473 posts. The remaining 25, or 2% of the total 1498 posts were made by 14 permanent researchers. Other participation by the eligible permanent researchers was also low. The 398 permanent researchers accounted for only 4% of the Web-page requests and less than 40% (155) of them logged on to the Web site.

Our analyses make use of two sets of analytic methods. The first is the construct of *remedial episodes* which is used to analyze conduct around disagreements – *conduct-correcting episodes* – in Usenet newsgroups [15]. We use it to analyze the disagreements surrounding the appropriateness of content of Peertalk posts. The first component of the four-part remedial episode is the *failure event,* which is the remark

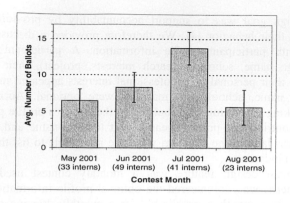

Fig. 1. Average number of contest ballots per intern along with standard error bars for each of the four months of the contest. A total of 78 interns qualified for the contest in the 4 months.

around which a disagreement coalesces. A *reproach* from one or more individuals follows. This may be explicit or implicit depending on the individual and the group dynamics. A *response* from the "offender" may or may not occur. The final component is an *evaluation of the account* by the reproacher, which either accepts or rejects it.

The second method is Holeton's message categorization scheme for classifying email distribution list messages according to one of three larger social purposes: *housekeeping dialogue, social dialogue, critical dialogue* [6]. *Housekeeping dialogue* is for minimal, social purpose discussions such as work-related activities and informational requests. *Social dialogue* is lightweight social purpose discussions related to social activities, to people's outside interests, and to relieving stress. *Critical dialogue* is higher-order social purpose discussions of a substantive, reasoned, constructive nature such as norms discussion in Portkey. We analyzed 1022 messages from the 1473 intern posts created in 9 of the 21 Peertalk fora during the study period. The messages were divided in half and each half was assigned to two raters for categorization.

4   A Conduct Correcting Episode Begins the Norms Discussion

The opportunity to examine a norm evolution discussion surfaced as a result of disagreements with what constituted an appropriate post to Peertalk and was, in part, motivated by the contest. As Feldman notes [5], groups will only bother to develop norms about behaviors that are important to them. While the monthly prize was substantial, it is interesting to note that in any given month no more than 40% of the posting interns became eligible for the contest. The norms discussion we present will show that the contest was a strong motivator for some, but not most, of the interns.

The trigger for the discussion occurred ten weeks into the study period. It was an indexical remark, a short comment that acknowledges a previous remark but does not advance the conversation, made by a recently-arrived intern. The intern, P1, became the object of a *reproach* by two other interns but did not respond for two weeks. We learned during the third of the group interviews, four weeks later, that several seemingly unrelated threads that were started after the *reproach* were in fact part of a growing effort to elicit a *response* from P1. The reason for this collective effort to *reproach* P1 was because he quickly surpassed all others on the total number of posts in spite of having arrived more than a month later than most other interns. An intern's productivity was visible to others as the number of posts made by each intern was displayed by their name. A less direct measure could be obtained from the frequency with which a person's name was encountered while reading the posts. We learned in the August 15th interview that the general feeling among the interns was that P1's postings were largely motivated by a desire to win the July drawing. Figure 2 confirms what the interns concluded about P1's extreme posting behavior. It shows the number of posts per week P1 made since his arrival in week number 27 relative to the next highest Port-key poster. The average poster made 2.9 posts per week. Clearly, P1 is an outlier.

4.1 Start of the First Remedial Episode

The context for the first reproach against P1 was a post alerting interns of a possible confusion about the location where some experiments were being held. Interns are often solicited to participate as paid subjects in experiments being run at the laboratory so the alert would have been generally informative. P3 posts the alert and is thanked by P4. P1's reiteration of the indexical remark made by P4 is viewed as the *failure event* that started the remedial episode and is followed by two *reproaches* by P4 and P5.

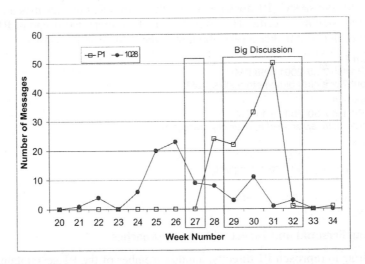

Fig. 2. Number of posts per week for top posters from May 14 to Aug 19 (weeks 20 to 34)

>> **Person P3**
>> Date Posted 7-01-2001 8:52 PM
There are about 3 different people at *<Building 2)>* and a few at *<Building 1>* conducting experiments. If you sign up to participate make sure you know what location it is at. People have signed up for the wrong location and missed appointments.

>> **Person P4**
>> Date Posted 7-11-2001 3:06 PM
Thanks for the heads up.

>> **Person P1**
>> Date Posted 7-18-2001 9:47 AM
yeah, thanks

>> **Person P4**
>> Date Posted 7-18-2001 2:52 PM
Will you all be doing that again?

>> **Person P5**
>> Date Posted 7-18-2001 4:48 PM
yeah...
will u be doing it again,
when its nice, do it twice!!!

Initial *reproaches* are followed by others that may either scold or, as in this case, reinforce the reproacher [15]. P1 does not offer a *response* to the *reproach* until two weeks later. In the meantime, a sub-group (P1-accountability group) formed with the goal of eliciting a response from P1. He was the target of a subsequent *reproach* which was expressed very opaquely and he again failed to acknowledge it. Smith et. al. [15] found that only 25% of their remedial episodes included a *response* to the *reproach*.

4.2   The Second Remedial Episode with the Same Protagonist

The second remedial episode began when another intern wrote what he called an ode to a local bar called the Thirsty Turtle. P1 responded with a binary question about the nature of the Thirsty Turtle establishment, to which a third intern, an established critic of P1's behavior, spelled out "BOTH" in four separate posts (reproduced below as a single post to save space). P1 does not accept the *reproach,* but uses it as an occasion to level a *reproach* at his critic. However, P2, an office mate and friend of P1 realizes what is happening and makes a joke alluding to the volume of P1's posts.

>> **Person P1**
>> Date Posted 7-30-2001 3:58 PM
is this a pub? or a club or something like that?

>> **Person P10**
>> Date Posted 7-30-2001 5;11 PM
B-O-T-H *(actually appeared in four separate posts)*

>> **Person P1**
>> Date Posted 7-30-2001 6:07 PM
Are you desperately trying to put in posts?

>> **Person P2**
>> Date Posted 7-31-2001 3:06 PM>
you will not catch <P1>

4.3   Getting Personal and Direct with the Reproaches

Still unwilling to reproach P1 directly, another member of the P1-accountability sub-group of interns, took the next step in this extended remedial episode by starting a new thread to ostensibly recognize interns who make high quality posts. The thread was entitled *Vote for your favorite Portkey poster/discussion* to focus attention on what the sub-group considered to be valuable posts rather than the noise that began to dominate Portkey. This thread generated only 2 responses including one by P1.

>> **Person P7**
>> Date Posted 7-30-2001 5:43 PM

Forget the *<Name>* contest - finally, here is a forum to recognize those people who provide posts of quality to Portkey (not necessarily quantity). If you've found someone's posts to be helpful and of relevant substance ... then let everyone know!

In another response, P1's office mate (P2) started a thread entitled *Vote for your favorite Portkey useless poster/discussion*. When this thread degenerated into name calling and jeering, the originator of the "favorite Portkey poster/discussion" thread tried to get the participants to focus on the real issue: a *reproach* against P1 for his undisguised chase of the contest prize.

>> **Person P7**
>> Date Posted 8-01-2001 11:35 AM Come on guys, this was the underlying intent of my original thread. This and *<the thread>* posting ethics. I was really hoping that a certain someone who has endeared himself to the Portkey community would be the first to be nominated. But kudos to those who stated outright what i could only hint to :-).

With his comment, P7 articulates the difficulty the group of disgruntled interns had in confronting P1 directly about his behavior. The restraint these interns showed for two weeks after the original critical incident occurred is remarkable in comparison to the swift *reproaches* reported in Usenet settings [8, 15]. One likely source of this restraint is that Portkey was a work-based site that was open to the interns' management. Secondly, unlike on the open Internet where an individual can usually find alternatives, Portkey was the only site available that addressed the interns' concerns. A third reason may have been that since P1 arrived after the group had established implicit norms as indicated by stable posting during the first two contests, they could, as Feldman [5] notes, be "charitable or tolerant towards deviant behavior." After two weeks, one of the interns finally made a direct reproach that, however, included a hedge to soften the accusation. It came in the form of a new thread entitled *Congratulations, <P1>!*

>> **Person P8**
>> Date Posted 7-31-2001 10:13 AM
You've made it to a whopping **100 posts**[1]. You are now eligible to start working! ;-) Wow, this forum is getting out of hand...

Eventually P1 responds to the mounting *reproaches* that have been aimed at him for over two weeks by offering an excuse. His *response* is mediated by his office mate, P2, who had earlier encouraged P1's behavior.

>> **Person P2**
>> Date Posted 7-31-2001 10:50 AM
Hey *<P1>* you need a project ASAP!! :-)

>> **Person P1**
>> Date Posted 7-31-2001 11:40 AM
Yeah! Thanx. I have had some problems lately with my supervisor being sick, and work has been a bit slow in arriving, so I just spend my days in portkey...I am the ever present poster.

In a subsequent post, P1 offers a more direct *response* to the *reproach*. He acknowledges his pursuit of the contest prize, but also surfaces the posting norm that governs his behavior on Portkey. An *evaluation* of his response by P11 articulates the different norm he, and others in the P1-accountability sub-group, hold.

---

[1] P1's 100th post represents 7.1% of the total posts to-date (1415 posts) achieved in just 3 weeks.

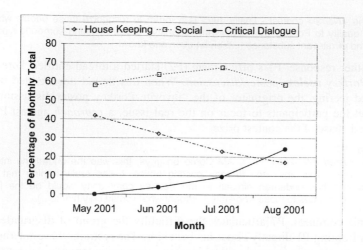

Fig. 3. Percentages of the three categories (i.e., housekeeping, social, and critical dialogue) in each of the four months. 751 of the 1022 messages with same ratings were considered. The 1022 messages were selected from 9 discussion fora during the period of May 14 to Aug 19.

>> **Person P1**
>> Date Posted 7-31-2001 1:42 PM
I think that this site was a place to socialize, and many of us are starting to know each other by names, encouraging us to meet personally. Isn't this the aim? ... We are about 200 interns, and many of us like internet chatting, as well as communicating through forums. Portkey is a fun place. Even if there were no prize, trust me that there would be the usual 5 or 6 people spending a lot of time posting, meeting other people and having fun.

>> **Person P11**
>> Date Posted 7-31-2001 4:09 PM
If I wanted free-form back-and-forth conversation, I would follow <P9>'s suggestion and go find a chat room somewhere [set one up here, maybe?] Discussion lists are for constructed thought, funny, un-funny, reverent, irreverent whatever. Otherwise the system becomes no better than the unsolicited deluge of e-mail we had to cope with last summer.

This interchange surfaced the divergent norms held by the two groups and marks the transition from a personal, behavior-correcting episode [15] to a broader discussion about the norms that should govern the group's posting behavior on Portkey.

5   Developing Ties on Portkey

Before we document the group norms discussion in the next section, we next examine more closely the interns' use of the technology and the accompanying evolution of social ties among members of this concocted group. Discussion fora are a simple but powerful tool to give expression to people's beliefs. In this context, Postmes et. al. [13] note, people's words have two functions, "... simultaneously defining and reflecting group norms." The use of signed posts and the ease with which interns could monitor an individual's output created the opportunity for accountability to emerge [4]. We should note that we had not expected that the running count of posts would figure so prominently in the social interaction that unfolded. It appears to have functioned as a socially translucent [4] piece of data that was appropriated [13] by the interns to fit the needs that emerged from their particular use of the technology.

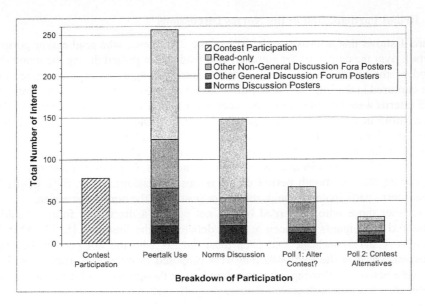

Fig. 4. Breakdown of forms of participation. Number of interns a) eligible for contest in the four months (column 1), b) posting and/or reading on the site (column 2), c) posting and/or reading the norms discussion (column 3), d) voting to alter the contest (column 4), and e) voting among contest alternatives (column 5).

5.1 Growing Intimacy Reflected in Poster Content

The behavior-correcting episode occurred against a backdrop of developing intimacy through online and face-to-face interactions. To measure how this might be reflected in changes in the nature of the posts, we had a sample of 1022 messages categorized into Holeton's [6] three social-purpose categories. These are intended to capture a progression of intimacy in the discussions. The initial results produced an agreement level of 73% (Cohen's Kappa = .511). Rather than try to resolve the disagreements, we present the data for observations where agreement was observed.

Figure 3 shows the percentage of messages assigned each month to each of the three categories. It shows that *social dialogue* messages were the most frequent, accounting for approximately 60% of the monthly posts throughout the life of the site. *Housekeeping dialogue* messages were common at the start of the summer but their frequency decreased as the summer progressed. The opposite pattern occurred for the *critical dialogue* messages, which did not exist at the start, but equaled the number of *housekeeping* messages at the end of the summer. The growth in *critical dialogue* posts came at the expense of both *housekeeping* and *social* posts. We believe that the *critical dialogue* category was underestimated because many of the posts generated to get P1 to respond to the reproaches leveled against him were indirect. Given that the raters were unfamiliar with the study, they were not privy to the communicative purpose of a thread that discussed, for example, "your favorite Portkey poster/discussion." The data nevertheless indicates that the interns were developing a degree of intimacy among themselves as the summer progressed.

5.2 Broad Participation in the Norms Discussions

Figure 4 shows that approximately 60% of the 256 interns who read and/or posted in Peertalk over the course of the summer, also read and/or posted during the month-long period of the norms discussion. The data is based on analyses of page requests that were captured in the logs. Column 1 provides a baseline measure and shows that a total of 78 interns were eligible in the four contests. Column 2 shows the number of interns participating in various ways in Peertalk. The bottom-most section corresponds to 21 interns involved in the norms discussions while the middle-two sections represent the number of interns involved in postings in other fora. The top section of column 2 shows that 132 of the 256 interns read but did not post. Column 3 shows comparable data during the one-month period of the norms discussions. Fully, 58% of the 256 active interns participated through reading or posting in the norms discussion.

Whether those who only read but do not post in a discussion forum should be considered participants has been actively debated in the literature [8, 11]. Our data (columns 4 and 5) indicate that even those interns who did not post in the norms discussion voted in the two polls that were proposed in the norms discussion. Thus, they were actively following what transpired, even though they did it in a less visible manner than through posting. We discuss the polls further in the next section.

6   Towards Establishing Group Identity

Several themes emerged in Peertalk in the three remaining weeks that followed P1's response to his reproachers. These ranged from the concrete question of which of the two norms – chat room or discussion forum behavior – is desirable, to criticisms of the contest and discussions of alternative prizes, to discussions of their status as a group. Thus, the remedial episode rather than simply correcting the offender's behavior functioned to focus the group's attention on the more fundamental issue of themselves as a group with shared issues to address. Feldman [5] notes that groups often attempt to enforce norms to "...express the central values of the group and clarify what is distinctive about the group's identity."

6.1 Group Discussion of Competition Norms

After a few more interns added *reproaches* about P1's large number of posts, the attention of the interns turned to a discussion of the effect of the contest on the group and the need for the participants to evolve a norm that all would abide by. One of the original complainants began a discussion thread entitled *ethics for posting?!* with a post that addressed norms, the effect of the contest and his anger at what he called the *"end-of-the-month get-your-post-in-for-the-draw phenomenon"*. The thread generated 50 responses from 13 interns over the next four days. The lead post was:

>> **Person P9**
>> Date Posted 7-31-2001 11:13 AM
I think the Portkey forum has grown large enough for people to start self-imposing some sort of restraint on their postings. Alternatively, maybe the forum should itself come up with a code that every poster would be urged to stick to.

Another poster succinctly summarized the change taking place in recent weeks.

>> **Person P10**
>> Date Posted 7-31-2001 11:54 AM

The majority of posters have abided by the silent social contract that you are supposed to post signal instead of noise, but it only takes one selfish individual to break the contract and all hell breaks loose. Even social pressures such as satire (which I have tried to direct at certain posters, whom I need not name) and outright jeering will not discourage someone who has his/her eye on the prize.

A number of other posters openly confronted P1 for his posting behavior, accusing him of selfishness and challenging him to give up his chance for the prize. He, in turn, did not deny his intentions to win the prize, but joined others in arguing that the contest was the root of the difficulty.

6.2 Towards Resolving the Conflict

The discussion that ensued was varied in tone, at times logical and well-argued, often impassioned and full of frustration. Eventually the discussion turned away from a focus on P1 and generalized to what standards the entire user population should adopt.

At first, the interns wanted the resolution to be imposed from outside. As the disagreement was beginning to surface in early August, some of the interns passed a message to us through two interns who worked on the project with us that we *"have to do something"* as administrators of the site. Our decision to maintain our role as "sentinels" rather than moderators was debated in a number of the posts, with the interns being divided on which role they wanted us to play. When we did not step in, various interns adopted a different strategy and began to work with their peers on the site. After much debate and anger in the thread name *ethics for posting?!*, an intern made a suggestion for a different algorithm for contest eligibility.

>> **Person P12**
>> Date Posted 7-31-2001 7:43 PM
Lets borrow some tricks from game theory. Make the top 10 (in the number of posts) people not available for the prize, and the others still randomly choose based on their ballots.

This led to a lot of debate about the rules for contest eligibility and even for the contest prize. After a week of such debate, we violated our decision to not get involved and offered them a voting mechanism which they could use to make some changes. In the first vote (column 4 in Figure 4), 49 out of 69 people voted to change the contest. In the second vote, interns voted on three contest change options.

Our decision was not taken lightly. We realized that our intervention would put an end to our ability to collect unbiased data from the site. However, most interns were nearing the ends of their internships and we wanted to give them some closure on the controversies they had been embroiled in for the previous month.

6.3 Reflection on What Transpired

As the storm engendered by the contest began to die down, some interns began to reflect more broadly on what had happened on the site over the course of the summer. While some interns criticized the occurrence of the playful threads that were meant to model P1's behavior, more interns defended them. Overall, there seemed to be a recognition that there had been some change that took place and this was positive.

>> **Person P14**
>> Date Posted 8-01-2001 4:09 PM
< *P6's*> post was I think the first true nonsensical one. It as revolutionary and, dare I say, brilliant. Without posts like these can change ever occur? I don't think portkey will ever be the same, and for that I am grateful.

>> **Person P15**
>> Date Posted 8-03-2001 12:08 AM
every post you make is also a reflection on yourself and also on the portkey community in general. And this certainly has a pronounced effect. Many of my fellow interns have been put off from portkey because of this rising trend of nonsensical posts.

Further discussion of governance and of group issues was unfortunately cut off by the ending of the summer internship period. But while the interns did not reach a complete resolution to their norms discussion, they did make substantial progress.

7 Discussion

This case study documents what many observers of CMC suspect: developing norms is difficult work that needs to be supported by technology [1, 9, 12]. In the Portkey environment, broaching the topic openly required the concerted effort of more than twenty interns. The discussion fora provided the mechanism that enabled interns to observe the behavior that they disagreed with, to surface the disagreement through dialogue, and finally to work towards resolving it. This study supports Mark's hypothesis [9] that awareness is important for mediating the opportunity to negotiate norms. Of course, the nature of case study data is correlational, not predictive.

We also demonstrate that the diagnosis of a conflict is difficult. Even though we had been monitoring the site for almost three months, we did not recognize the significance that certain threads played in surfacing the norms discussion until we happened to include some of the members of the disaffected group of interns in one of the group interviews. We believe that this caused our colleagues who rated the content of the posts to incorrectly categorize some of the posts as social rather than critical dialogue.

This raises the question of how to surface conflict and disagreement among members of an online group and how to support their resolution. Particularly, if the social psychologists' contention is correct that groups must pass through a period of "storming" before "norming"[17], conflicts among members of online environments need a way to surface. Certainly tools such as those available in MUDs and MOOs [3, 16] for individually rather than socially handling conflict could shortchange the process of norms development. Without addressing the difficult issues that matter to the group, the group does not progress through to a level where they can form a productive force.

Clearly, not all groups need to progress to becoming a productive force. Participants in Portkey were a loosely coupled, concocted group [2] whose joint work was optional. Without the motivation of the structure of the contest, this group may never have found reason to engage in "storming." And consequently might have missed out on moving beyond being a concocted group, functioning as individuals [17].

Our case study revealed that visibility made it possible for the group to be made aware of issues and problems. As a result, a small group of people took the lead to raise the issue that led to vibrant discussion. Would this happen in other groups? We surmise that there are at least two important factors in our case study. First, we had group of moderate where people could notice what was happening. In a larger group, it may be necessary to develop surfacing mechanisms across all activities. Second, there were individuals who stepped forward to raise and to resolve the issues. Without these two factors, visibility would be a benign mechanism. In larger online environments, reputation systems have the potential to fill both of these needs: a) to surface diverging behaviors and b) to enable social governance through collective actions of people.

The remedial episode construct studied by Smith et al. [15] was a useful analytic tool for analyzing and surfacing the conflict. Our case study and the instrumental application of the analytic method supports their hypothesis that studying incidents of breakdowns can provide a means to study emergent standards of behavior.

Acknowledgments. We owe a great debt of gratitude to all the interns who participated so fully in the Port-key site. Special thanks also go to Unmil Karadkar and Jun Zhang for their work as summer interns on the Portkey project. Many thanks to Tom Erickson for his insightful comments on a previous draft of this paper.

References

1. Ackerman, M.S., Hindus, D., Mainwaring, S.D., and Starr, B. Hanging on the 'Wire: A Field Study of an Audio-Only Media Space. In ACM Transactions on Human-Computer Interaction, 4, 1, 1997, 39-66.
2. Arrow, H., McGrath, J.E., and Berdahl, J.L. Small Groups as Complex Systems. Sage Publications, Inc.: Thousand Oaks, 2000.
3. Cherny, L. Conversation and Community: Chat in a Virtual World. CSLI Publications: Stanford, 1999, chapter 6.
4. Erickson, T. & Kellogg, W. Social Translucence: An Approach to Designing Systems that Support Social Processes. *ACM Transactions on Computer Human Interaction 7*, 1, ACM: New York, 2000, 59-83.
5. Feldman, D.C. The Development and Enforcement of Group Norms. In Academy of Management Review, 9, 1, 1984, 47-53.
6. Holeton, R. Constructive 'Noise in the Channel": Effects of Controversial Forwarded E-mail in a College Residential and Virtual Community. Presented at ED-MEDIA 1999 (http://www.stanford.edu~holeton/edmedia/noise.html).
7. Kim, A. J. *Community Building on the Web*. Peachpit Press: Berkeley, CA. 2000. '
8. Kollock, P. and Smith, M. Managing the Virtual Commons: Cooperation and Conflict in Computer Communities. In S. W. Herring (ed.), *Computer-Mediated Communication: Linguistic, Social, and Cross-Cultural Perspectives*. J. Benjamins: Amsterdam, 1996, 109-128.
9. Mark, G. Conventions and Commitments in Distributed CSCW Groups. Forthcoming inCSCW: The Journal of Collaborative Computing, Special Issue on Awareness.
10. McGrath, J. E. *Groups: Interaction and Performance*. Prentice-Hall College Division, 1984.
11. Noonecke, B. and Preece, J. Lurker Demographics: Counting the Silent. In *Human Factors in Computing Systems, CHI'00 Conference Proceedings*. ACM: New York, 2000, 73-80.
12. Pankoke-Babatz, U. and Jeffrey, P. Documented Norms ans Conventions on the Internet. In International Journal of Human-Computer Interaction, 14 (2), 2002, 219-235.
13. Postmes, T., Spears, R. and Lea, M. The Formation of Group Norms in Computer-MediatedCommunication. In Human Communications Research, 26, 3, 2000, 341-371.
14. Preece, J. Empathic Communities: Balancing Emotional and Factual Communication. *Inter-acting with Computers, 12*, 1999, 63-77.
15. Smith, C. B., McLaughlin, M. L., and Osborne, K. K. Conduct Control on Usenet. *Journal of Computer-Mediated Communication 2*, 4. 1997, 90-111.
16. Sproull, L. and S. Faraj. Atheism, Sex and Databases: The Net as a Social Technology. In S.Kiesler (Ed.), *Culture of the Internet*. LEA: NJ, 1997, 35-51.
17. Tuckman, B. W. Developmental Sequence in Small Groups. In Psychological Bulletin, 63, 1965, 384-399.

A Comparison Between Spoken Queries and Menu-Based Interfaces for In-car Digital Music Selection

Clifton Forlines, Bent Schmidt-Nielsen, Bhiksha Raj,
Kent Wittenburg, and Peter Wolf

Mitsubishi Electric Research Laboratories,
201 Broadway, Cambridge, MA 02139 USA
{forlines, bent, bhiksha, wittenburg, wolf}@merl.com

Abstract. Distracted driving is a significant issue for our society today, and yet information technologies, including growing digital music collections, continue to be introduced into the automobile. This paper describes work concerning methods designed to lessen cognitive load and distracting visual demands on drivers as they go about the task of searching for and listening to digital music. The existing commercial paradigms for retrieval—graphical or spoken menu traversal, and text-based search—are unsatisfactory when cognitive resources are limited and keyboards are unavailable. We have previously proposed to use error-tolerant spoken queries [26] combined with direct modalities such as buttons mounted on the steering wheel [7]. In this paper, we present in detail the results of an experiment designed to compare the industry standard approach of hierarchical graphical menus to our approach. We found our proposed interface to be more efficient and less distracting in a simulated driving task.

1 Introduction

It was estimated in 2001 by the U.S. National Highway Traffic Safety Administration that at least 25% of police reported accidents involve some form of driver inattention. A study by Stutts et al. [24] estimated that at least 13% of the drivers whose state was known at the time of the crash were distracted. Adjusting the audio system of the car accounted for 11% of these distractions. Since these studies, a number of electronics manufacturers have introduced products that incorporate personal digital music collections into automobile audio systems. Some automobile manufacturers have gone as far as bundling a personal digital music player with the purchase of a new car. The additional complexity of navigating and selecting music from large music collections while driving is thus a cause of concern.

In general, there are two basic paradigms for retrieving an item from some large set: (1) menu-based traversal and (2) search. For drivers whose hands and eyes are mostly occupied, each of these paradigms has its challenges. Menu-based traversal can be maintained using buttons or touch screens; however, the growing size of the selection set (tens of thousands of songs already) requires hierarchical menus of increasing breadth and/or depth. The need to navigate ever-larger sets of menus may require too much time and visual attention to allow for safe driving.

M.F. Costabile and F. Paternò (Eds.): INTERACT 2005, LNCS 3585, pp. 536–549, 2005.
© IFIP International Federation for Information Processing 2005

The combination of speech input with menus might seem promising, and it has been shown to be effective compared to mouse-based menu selections in earlier studies [6][15]. However, speech interfaces need to address not only the issue of misrecognition errors in noisy environments, but also the issue of habitability, i.e., the ease with which a user can stay within the sublanguage understandable by the system. Users need to learn what to say to a speech interface since no speech recognition system can deal with unrestricted language. VoiceXML [25] has been proposed as a rather direct translation of menu selection to the speech domain and addresses the issue of habitability through prompting. However, the enumeration of all menu choices with speech would be time-consuming and frustrating for drivers, and, again, as the size of the set increases, its efficacy diminishes.

More advanced speech interfaces aim to create flexible dialogs in order to avoid the tedium of mechanistic menu traversal and the need for a rigid command syntax. A good example is the automotive interface introduced in [20]. The approach incorporates sophisticated prompting while also allowing for shortcuts once the user has learned the sublanguage of the system. Dialogs are carefully crafted in order to minimize errors and misunderstandings. While promising, a drawback for such approaches is the cost and complexity of development. Each deployment requires extensive language-specific efforts to collect speech natural to the application in question and also requires much iteration to refine the dialogs. Some researchers have suggested that the adoption of universal conventions by speech interfaces could eventually help reduce application and language- specific dialog development [21], but in the meantime, other alternatives should be considered.

What about search UIs? Search interfaces require the entry of a query term and manipulation of a result list. The entry of a query term is the primary challenge in the automobile. For text-based queries, a keyboard is inappropriate for an in-car device, and the entry of text without use of a keyboard is notoriously difficult. Character entry by menu is, again, time-consuming and visually demanding.

A promising approach lies in the utilization of speech in search UIs. Examples proposed previously include Cohen et al.'s system ShopTalk [5]. The historical approach is to prompt the user with a query box, apply speech understanding, and then input the disambiguated result to the query system. The habitability problem is still in evidence here — users need to know the sublanguage of query terms in order for the speech recognizer to achieve successful recognition rates. As the domain becomes less restricted and more "Google like," the challenge of disambiguating the speech becomes more severe since there are few language constraints that can be imposed on queries.

In previous work, we have proposed using speech input for search UIs without direct conversion to disambiguated text [7][26]. In this approach, the spoken query is converted to a probabilistic query vector that is input directly into the search process. Instead of requiring the spoken input to be converted to an unambiguous form, the spoken input is converted to a probabilistically scored "bag of words" that serves the purpose of defining the query. The user never sees the query specification, but only the list of query results. We call this approach "Speech In, List Out" or SILO.

Our proposal for an automotive UI for digital music selection utilizes the SILO approach in combination with a set of simple buttons for manipulating query results [7].

The buttons can be mounted directly on the steering wheel. The simplicity of the resulting interactions between the user and the system is expected to result in a lower cognitive load on the user, an important consideration when the user is simultaneously involved in other attention-critical tasks. In the remainder of this paper we review the basic elements of the proposed SILO-based interface for an automotive digital music player. We then relate the full details of an experiment in which we compare our interface to a graphical menu-based interface that is today's industry norm. Our preliminary findings support the claims that a SILO-based interface can be more efficient and impose less cognitive overhead than a menu-based graphical one. We finish by discussing the ramifications of this work on future study.

2 SpokenQuery

The enabling technology for our experiments is the SpokenQuery speech-based search engine [26]. While a detailed description of SpokenQuery is outside of the scope of this paper, we present a summary here for the convenience of the reader. SpokenQuery is similar to familiar web-based information retrieval engines such as Google, AltaVista, etc., except that the user speaks his or her query instead of typing it. The user may speak whatever words he/she thinks best describe the desired items and there is no rigid grammar or vocabulary. The output of SpokenQuery is an ordered list of items that are judged to be pertinent to the query. As with other IR techniques, there is no guarantee that the desired item(s) will be the top choice(s) in the output list.

Contrary to the conventional approach of using speech recognition to convert the spoken input to disambiguated form, SpokenQuery uses the probabilities in a word lattice returned by a speech engine as input to a probabilistic document index. SpokenQuery uses speech to input a set of words with associated probabilities, which can in turn be used to return a list of best matches.

SpokenQuery stands in contrast to conventional recognition techniques that convert the spoken input into a single disambiguated phrase, or as is often the case, a list of the N-best phrases for the speaker to choose among. Instead, the speech recognizer converts the spoken query into a graph of words, called a lattice, where the nodes correspond to possible words and the edges correspond to the probability of transition between the words. All the words in this lattice are weighted by their probability and used in the search. The output of the system is a list of the N-best documents found by this search. Unambiguous identification of the query words is never required.

A noteworthy feature of recognizers is that the actual words uttered by a user are usually included in the recognition lattice and have high expected counts, even when they are not included in the final word sequence output by the recognizer. As a result, SpokenQuery is able to perform remarkably well in highly noisy conditions (such as automobiles) under which conventional speech UIs that depend on the recognizer's text output break down [7]. Table 1 lists some example phrases and their (often poor) interpretation by the speech recognizer along with the performance of the Spoken-Query search.

2.1 A SILO Interface Model

Here we consider a SILO-based UI for an application we refer to internally as Me-diaFinder. It is intended for retrieving music from large collections using multimodal input. Digital music players designed for automobiles currently allow for 10s of thousands of songs (and growing). The UIs provided on these devices today provide a display of up to about 10 lines of text and a few buttons or touch surfaces to navigate a tree of choices in order to play a desired piece of music. The collection may be navigated by artist/album/song as well as by genre and other organizations. In contrast, MediaFinder is not menu-driven. Instead, it recasts the music retrieval problem as information retrieval: the system responds to spoken requests with a list of songs that are deemed pertinent to that request. Here are four design principles we followed:

1. Appropriate use of speech. Speech input is used only for choosing from a very large set when the use of buttons (for scrolling and selection) is inefficient or impossible. All choices from a small set are performed with direct manipulation [13].

2. Speech in, graphics out. While speech input is used by the user to describe the desired item(s), the result of the query is rendered as graphics or text. Speech output is not the most efficient way to communicate a list of results to the user—text or graphics is quick to display and convenient to browse.

3. Pure pull model. The user interface never prompts the user. It always waits for the user to initiate the next interaction. The pace of the interaction is entirely set by the operator, which is an important feature of an automotive system.

4. A recognition of the limitations of speech recognition. In a command and control system, poor speech recognition often results in the system responding with "I did not understand that" or, worse still, with the system issuing an incorrect command. With MediaFinder, the result of poor speech recognition is the same as that of a poor query — a degraded result list (i.e., the desired item(s) may be further from the top or missing all together). As with IR (e.g., Google), it is the responsibility of the user to speak a query that distinguishes the desired item.

3 Experiment

While driving, perception and attentional resources are highly constrained. Recent studies have shown significant driving impairment by cell phone use and navigational aids [8]. Any search mechanism that interferes with driving's complex balance of motor, cognitive, and perceptual skills may result in unacceptable performance penalties, leading to unsafe conditions. A successful search in this environment not only means finding the desired information quickly, but also means generating less interference while doing so.

Our initial plan was to compare the SILO speech interface to a command and control speech interface for in-car music selection. At the time of this experiment, we surveyed available in-car and handheld voice activated music players and found no systems that we felt could be used in a meaningful comparison. High error rates and limited storage capacity eliminated all contenders. We considered developing our own using an off-the-shelf speech recognition system, but this proved to be problematic, as shown in Table 1. The lack of a successful commercial product became in our minds comparison enough.

Table 1. While the disambiguated phrase output by the speech recognition system is often wildly inaccurate, SILO manages to return the desired song near or at the top of the list

Driver says...	System hears...	SILO search result
"Play Walking in my shoes by Depesh Mode"	layla [NOISE] issues [NOISE] [NOISE] load	1
"Depesh Mode, Walking in my shoes"	e [NOISE] looking [NOISE] night shoes	1
"Walking in my shoes"	law(2) pinion mae issues	1
"Walking in my shoes by Billy Joel" (partially incorrect information)	walking inn might shoes night billie joel	1
"um, uh, get me Credence Clearwater Revival... um... Who'll stop the Rain" (extra words)	fall(2) [UH] dead beat creedence clearwater revival [UM] long will stop it rains	1
"Credence Clearwater Revival, Who'll stop the Rain" (very noisy environment)	[NOISE] [COUGH] clearwater revival [COUGH] down [COUGH] [BREATH]	6

One might pose the question, *"Why compare a speech-based system to a menu-driven system? Clearly, any speech-based system that allows drivers to keep their eyes on the road should "beat" any menu-driven system that demands lots of visual attention, right?"* The answer to this question is unclear in our minds. Cell phone use while driving is now a well known cause of distraction, and even hands-free, eyes-on-the-road dialing does not eliminate the cause for concern. A purely voice-based music-retrieval system with no visual display or manual input might seems like a good idea at first glance, but such a system requires that the operator keep track of the state of the system in their working memory. A deeply nested menu-tree, presented aurally, is very demanding in terms of cognitive load. Knowing that a quick glance at a screen can recover forgotten information relieves the user from having to keep close track of the system's state in their mind. In-car systems must strive to not only keep their user's eyes on the road, but also keep their minds on the driving task.

With this in mind, we designed an experiment to test the multimodal SILO interface against what is widely available today, an interface based on hierarchical menus. We compared quantitative measurements of simulated steering and braking while searching for music with the two different interfaces. Our hypotheses were:

H1: Subjects will more accurately track a moving target with a steering wheel while searching for songs using the SILO interface than while searching for songs using the menu-driven interface.

H2: Subjects will react faster to a braking signal while searching for songs using the SILO interface than while searching for songs using the menu-driven interface.

H3: Subjects will be able to find songs faster while using the multimodal interface than while using the menu-driven interface while driving.

3.1   A "Driving-Like" Task

Although testing subjects in a real automobile while they engage in highway driving would lead to a more accurate study, ethical considerations prevented us from exposing subjects to a potentially lethal combination of activities. We relied on a simple driving simulator, such as those in [4][9], that mimicked two important facets of driving — steering and braking. An experiment using a high-fidelity simulator or real automobile is left for future work. Eyes-off-the-road gaze time is difficult and expensive to measure; however, steering and braking measurements are good proxies for gaze since both require visual attention, and may well be a better proxy for driving performance.

The simulator (Figure 1) had both a "windshield" and "in-dash" display. Subjects steered, braked, and controlled the searching interfaces with a Microsoft Sidewinder [16] steering wheel and its gas and brake pedals. A microphone (not shown) was placed on top of the main monitor. Steering was measured with a pursuit tracking task in which the subject used the wheel to closely frame a moving target [23]. The simulator recorded the distance in pixels between the moving target and the user controlled frame 30 times a second. Braking was measured by recording subjects' reaction time to circles that appeared on screen at random intervals. Subjects were asked to only react to moving circles and to ignore stationary ones. Moving and stationary circles were equally probable.

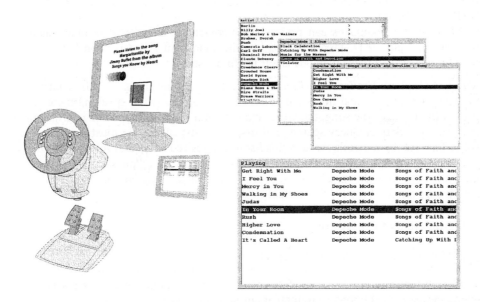

Fig. 1. The hardware setup (*left*). Subjects controlled the interfaces using the buttons on the steering wheel. The three levels of the menu-driven interface (*top right*). The SILO interface (*bottom right*). Three columns display song name, artist, and album for the search results.

3.2 Two Music Searching Interfaces

We built two interfaces for this study. The first interface was based on a sampling of currently available MP3 jukeboxes and used a traversable menu organized by artist, album, and song; the second was a SILO multimodal interface. Both interfaces ran on the same "in-dash" display and were controlled using buttons on the steering wheel.

Both interfaces searched the same music database of 2124 songs by 118 artists, and both were displayed at the same resolution in the same position relative to the subject. Additionally, both interfaces displayed the same number of lines of text in identical fonts. Neither interface dealt with many of the controls needed for a fully functional in-car audio system, such as volume, power, and radio controls.

The Menu-driven Interface. The menu-driven interface was designed to be familiar to anyone who has used an MP3 jukebox (such as the Apple iPod [1]) that uses an artist/ album/song hierarchical structure. When searching for a song, the user first scrolls through a list of the artists with music on the device. The user then selects an artist from this list, and the device displays a list of albums by that artist. After traversing and selecting an album, the user is presented with a list of the songs on that album. Finally, the user selects and plays a specific song from that list. By moving in and out within this three-level tree, the user is able to traverse to any song stored on the device. This interface was controlled with four buttons — one for scrolling up in a list, one for scrolling down in a list, one for moving "up" a level (such as moving from a list of an artist's albums to the list of all artists), and one for selecting the currently highlighted artist or album. To simplify the interface, the selection button doubled as a play button when in the song listing. A picture of the menu-driven interface is shown in Figure 1.

Many music jukeboxes can present their content in alternative fashions such as user defined play lists, favorites, anti-favorites, etc., but a comparison between the SILO interface and these methods is left for future study.

The SILO MediaFinder Interface. To search for a song using the SILO interface, the user first presses and holds the "push-to-talk" button while speaking a combination of the name of the song, the artist, and the album in any order. The interface then performs the SpokenQuery search, and displays a list of the ten most promising results. The user then scrolls through this list to the desired song, and selects the song to play it. This interface was controlled with four buttons - the "push-to-talk" button, a button for scrolling down, a button for scrolling up, and a play button. A screenshot of the visual portion of the SILO interface is shown in Figure 1.

3.3   Method and Procedure

Fourteen subjects participated in this experiment and were paid $20 for about 45 minutes of their time. Of the fourteen subjects, eight were male and six were female, and their ages ranged from 18 to 37. Four of our subjects spoke English as a second or third language. All but one were regular automobile drivers.

Subjects were first given instructions on how to correctly perform the steering and braking tasks and were given as much time as they wanted to practice "driving". They were then asked to perform a four-minute driving-only trial during which they performed no music searches.

Next, subjects were instructed to search for and playback specific songs while performing the driving task. Subjects used both the SILO and menu-driven interface, and completed 8 search trials with each condition. Before each block of 8 trials, subjects were given instructions on how to use the current interface and allowed to practice searches while not driving. The order that the interfaces were used, and the order of the songs that were searched for were randomized. During each trial, the testing application displayed the steering and braking signals along with instructions that the user would read asking them to search for a specific song (*e.g.* "Please listen to the song Only the Good Die Young by Billy Joel from the album The Stranger"). Subjects were allowed to take a break between trials for as long as they wished.

The application logged the distance between the moving target and the subject-controlled black box, as well as the reaction time to any brake stimulus presented during each trial. The task time was also logged, measured from the moment that the instructions appeared on the screen to the moment that the correct song started playing. To reduce learning effects, only the last 4 of each set of 8 trials contributed to the results. At the end of the session, subjects were asked to fill out a questionnaire designed to measure subjective preference between the two interfaces. Subjects rated their agreement with a collection of statements on a 7- point Likert scale, and listed the "best three things" and "worst three things" about the SILO interface.

3.4 Results

Our data supports hypotheses H1 and H3 and rejects H2.

H1: Subjects were significantly better at the steering task while using the SILO interface than while using the menu-driven interface. During each trial, the testing application recorded the average distance between the moving target and the subject-controlled frame. Subjects were able to steer more accurately while searching for music using the SILO interface than while searching with the menu-driven interface (on average, 9.2 vs. 11.6 pixels of error respectively, $t(13) = 3.15$, $p=0.003$). Additionally, nine out of our fourteen subjects listed variations of "it was easier to keep your eyes on the screen" as one of the "best three things" about the SILO interface. Searching with the SILO interface was not without its penalties; subjects steered more accurately while driving without searching than while using the SILO interface (on average, 7.4 vs. 9.2 pixels, $t(13)=2.5$, $p=0.013$). The average error for each condition is shown in Figure 2 (*left*).

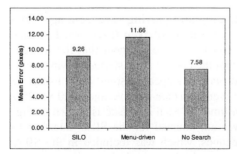 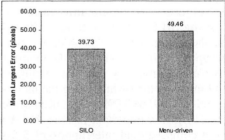

Fig. 2. The SILO interface had both a significantly lower mean steering error (*left*) and a significantly lower mean largest steering error (*right*) than the menu-driven interface

The SILO interface had a significantly lower maximum steering error as well (39.7 pixels vs. 49.4 pixels, $t(13)=2.27$, $p=0.02$). This measurement of error roughly

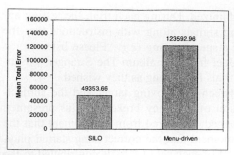 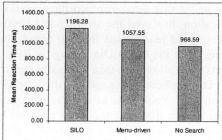

Fig. 3. The SILO interface had a significantly lower mean total steering error (*left*). There was no significant difference in mean break reaction times between the search conditions (*right*).

corresponds to the point when the subject was most distracted from the steering task. If actually driving, this point would be the point of greatest lane exceedence. The average maximum error for the two interfaces is shown in Figure 2 (*right*).

Finally, to measure the total steering error attributable to each search, we first subtracted the average no-search error from each of the average search errors and then multiplied these differences by the respective task times. On average, subjects accumulated 2.5 times the error while using the menu-driven system than while using the SILO interface (49,300 vs. 123,500, t(13)=1.95, p=0.03). The total errors for the two interfaces are show in Figure 3.

H2: There was no difference in subjects' brake reaction times for the SILO and menu-driven interfaces. During each trial, the testing application recorded the reaction time of the subjects to the randomly occurring brake stimulus. The mean reaction times were indistinguishable between the multimodal and menu-driven conditions (on average, 1196 ms vs. 1057 ms, t(13)=1.66, p=0.12); however, subjects were significantly faster at braking while not searching for music than while searching using the SILO (p=0.008) or the menu-driven (p=0.03) interface. The mean reaction time to the brake stimulus for each condition is shown in Figure 3 (*right*).

H3: Subjects were significantly faster at finding and playing specific songs while using the SILO interface than while using the menu-driven interface. For each trial, the test application recorded the time taken from the moment that the instructions appeared on the screen to the moment that the correct song started playing. Subjects were significantly faster at finding and playing a specific song while using the SILO interface than while using the menu-driven interface (on average, 18.0 vs. 25.2 sec., t(13)=2.69, p=0.009). The mean search time for each interface is shown in Figure 4 (*left*). It is important to note that it was not unusual for the SILO interface to have a computational interruption of 3-6 seconds, which was included in the SILO search time. A faster CPU or better microphone could decrease this time.

Six out of our fourteen subjects listed variations of "it often put the song you were looking for at the top of the list" as one of the "best three things" about the interface. 35 out of the 56 SILO trials returned the correct song at the top of the list on the first try. The average position for the correct song for all SILO trials was 5.1.

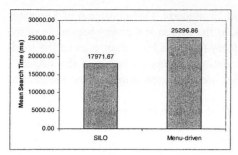 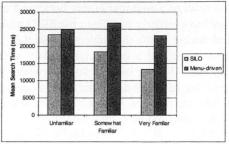

Fig. 4. Subjects were significantly faster at finding songs with the SILO interface (*left*). Familiarity with the music affected the SILO condition, but not the menu-driven condition (*right*).

3.5 Non-hypothesized Findings

Subject's familiarity with the music significantly affected the speed with which they were able to locate a song using the SILO interface, but did not affect the time taken to find a song using the menu-driven interface. At the end of each session, we asked subjects to rate their familiarity with the music that they had been asked to search for. Being familiar with the search content lead to faster searching using the SILO interface ($F(2,53)=8.25$, $p=0.0008$), but not with the menu-driven system ($F(2,53)=1.13$, $p=0.32$). We speculate that this difference is largely due to knowing the correct pronunciation of names in the database, and we would expect that searching through a familiar set would increase the hypothesized performance differences between the two interfaces. The average time for each familiarity group for each interface is shown in Figure 4 (*right*).

3.6 Experimental Discussion

We are pleased to be able to report evidence that our SILO multimodal interface for music finding does have measurable advantages for users operating a simulated automobile over the standard menu-based approach. Although a few other studies have shown advantages in task performance for speech input over mouse and keyboard [15], this is the first as far as we know that has found an advantage for speech input for search tasks. The findings of this preliminary study were encouraging; however, as is often the case, many questions arose.

We were surprised by the lack of any statistical difference between mean break reaction times between the SILO and menu-driven search conditions. A closer inspection of the results shed light on this issue. Because the time between brake stimuli was randomized, many trials were finished without the subject encountering any brake signals. Because SILO trials were faster than menu-driven trials, subjects were 20% more likely to finish a SILO trial without encountering a single brake stimulus than with the menu-driven interface. These cases, in which no brake reaction times were recorded, did not factor into the mean brake reaction times; however, one would think that shorter tasks times would lead to safer driving. Additionally, after each brake signal and at the beginning of each trial, the amount of time between brake signals was reset to a random number between 5 and 15 seconds. This minimum of 5 seconds may have unfairly penalized the SILO trials, as the period at the very beginning of the trial during which the subject speaks their query (and can keep their eyes on the road) never contained a brake signal. Only after the query was spoken, and the subject's eyes turned to the in-dash display (where they were focused from the first moment of menu-based trials) did brake signals occur.

The instructions for each task included all of the available information for a particular song. While a song title is enough to perform a SILO search, it would not have been fair to ask subjects to find the song "Never Die" without telling them it is by the artist "Creed" on the album "Human Clay" while using the menu-based interface. An informal evaluation of the SILO interface found that it performed quite well using incomplete and even partially incorrect information. A future study might incorporate searching with incomplete information.

The song library we used for the study contained only 2124 songs. It is now possible to buy a handheld music player that holds over 10,000 songs, and we can count on this number increasing. As the number of available artists, albums, and songs grows, we would expect the time needed to search through a menu-driven interface to grow as well. Since this experiment was conducted, we have increased the size of the database in our prototype. An informal evaluation of the SILO interface searching a database of 250,000 songs shows no noticeable differences in search time.

Several subjects noted in their questionnaires that they would like to be able to search for and play an entire album rather than an individual song. MediaFinder is easily modifiable to handle this additional task by including a heterogeneous collection of individual songs and playlists in its database. Playlists would be indexed by the artist and album name, as well as keywords like "album" and "record". A driver searching for "Beatles, Yellow Submarine" would receive a listing for both the song and the album.

It is well known that speech recognizers have more trouble with female and heavily accented voices than with male and native English speaker voices. We were surprised that the SILO interface performed just as well for female and non-native speakers as it did for our male and native English speakers. A formal exploration of the differences between these groups is left for future study.

Finally, in preparing the study, we found that the menu-driven interface was more susceptible to inconsistencies in the music files metadata. Because the music files had been generated over a long period of time using several conversion tools, the metadata itself was not uniform. For example, music by the group "The B-52s" was erroneously split into many artists: "The B-52s", "B-52s", "The B52s", etc. While problematic for the menu-driven interface, these types of errors do not affect the performance of the SILO interface. For the purpose of this study, we cleaned up the metadata in the database, but these issues must be taken into consideration for any menu-driven interface.

Limitations of this study include the fact that an actual in car environment that included environmental noise was not used. Other tests have shown that the Spoken-Query information retrieval engine is very robust to high levels of environmental noise [7]. We are therefore optimistic about the performance of the SILO interface in real in-car environments, but will have to confirm this expectation with future experiments. Finally, we look forward to a comparison between SILO and other speech based audio selection systems.

4 Conclusion

In this paper we have advocated for a particular model of using speech in interfaces when text-entry methods are unavailable or inadvisable. The paradigm of including spoken queries in SILO interfaces narrows the role of unstructured speech to a search subtask while employing direct manipulation for other functions in the interface. We believe that such a model can address the problems of misrecognition and habitability that limit the use of speech interfaces today, particularly in stressful or cognitively demanding environments such as driving an automobile. As evidence, we conducted an experiment in which we measured task-related performance on a simulated driving task as well as task completion time while asking users to find songs from a music collection. We compared an interface designed with our SILO paradigm with an industry standard graphical menu-based interface and were able to show statistically significant superiority for the SILO approach in two of the measures.

Future work will include the consideration of more complex user interfaces than the one we presented here. Our model was restricted to the simplest type of query in which the users' input is considered to be a "bag of words". It is an open question as to whether this model of direct-manipulation and speech can be extended to include more complex types of queries, which could include negation and other operators. Also, there are other challenges for interfaces in the automobile when more precision is required than in the examples we discussed here. We would like to consider, for example, whether our model can be extended to encompass destination entry in navigation systems, in which a particular street number, for instance, must be specified.

From our perspective, one may consider both search-based and menu-based systems as generators of lists of plausible responses from which the user must choose. The smaller and more accurate the list (where accuracy may be defined as the probability that the desired response is actually in the list), and the smaller the number of intermediate steps to getting there, the more user-friendly and less taxing the system is likely to be. As the set of choices gets larger, menu based systems often tackle the problem by setting up hierarchies. The user must generally navigate several levels of menus to get to the appropriate item. A search-based interface, on the other hand, returns a dynamically configured list of responses to the user's request. If the desired response is not on the presented list, the next list of possible choices can be immediately presented based on the scores attributed to the various choices by the system. In the worst case, the user must repeat the query in order to generate a fresh list of choices; a single step as opposed to the navigation of menus required by a menu-based system.

Safe interfaces for operation of communications and entertainment systems while driving are of concern as the complexity of such systems grows. The multimodal Speech-in List-out (SILO) paradigm shows promise over conventional GUI-based approaches for accommodating the inevitable introduction of large personal music collections into the automobile. The paradigm itself is applicable for retrieval of digital information other than music — recorded news, weather, and other radio programming, for instance. An intriguing idea is whether the SILO model that we have presented here can be generalized to handle many more of the functions in off-the-desktop interfaces than just the ones that we think of today as search. It will be interesting to see whether our approach provides an alternative to the mixed-initiative dialog approach, which has captured the attention of most of the researchers in our field, or whether some sort of integration of the flexible dialog approach with SILO will prove most effective.

References

1. Apple iPod, http://www.apple.com/ipod/.
2. Baeza-Yates, Ricardo, Ribeiro-Neto, Berthier, (1999) *Modern Information Retrieval.* Addison Wesley, p. 27.
3. Bolt, R.A. (1980) Put-that-there: Voice and Gesture at the Graphics Interface, Computer Graphics 14,3, 262 - 270.
4. Beusmans, J., & Rensink, R. (Eds.) (1995). Cambridge Basic Research 1995 Annual Report (Tech. Rep. No. CBR-TR-95-7). Cambridge, MA: Nissan Cambridge Basic Research.
5. Cohen, P. (1991) Integrated interfaces for decision-support with simulation. In *Proceedings of the 23rd Winter Conference on Simulation*, Phoenix, Arizona, pp. 1066 - 1072.
6. Cohen, P. R., McGee, and D. R., Clow, J. The efficiency of multimodal interaction for a map-based task. *Proc. Applied Natural Language Processing Conference* (ANLP'00), Seattle, WA, April 29-May 4, 2000, Morgan Kaufmann, pp. 331-338.
7. Divi, V., Forlines, C., Van Gemert, J., Raj, B., Schmidt-Nielsen,B., Wittenburg, K., Woelfel, J., Wolf, P., and Zhang, F. (2004) A Speech-In List-Out Approach to Spoken User Interfaces, in Proc. Human Language Technologies 2004, Boston MA.
8. Driver distraction with wireless telecommunications and route guidance systems. [DOT-HS-809-069]. Washington, DC: USDOT, NHTSA.
9. Driving Simulators, http://www.inrets.fr/ur/sara/Pg_simus_e.html
10. Geller, V.J., and Lesk, M.E. (1983) User Interfaces to Information Systems: Choices vs. Commands, in Proc. ACM SIGIR, 130-135.
11. Green, P. (1997). Potential safety impacts of automotive navigation systems, in *Proceedings of the Automotive Land Navigation Conference*, June 18, 1997.
12. Hauptmann, A. G. (1989) Speech and Gestures for Graphic Image Manipulation. In *Proc. CHI '89*, pp. 241-245.
13. Hutchins, E.L, Hollan, J.D., and Norman, D. A. (1986) Direct Manipulation Interfaces, in D. A. Norman and S. W. Draper (eds), *User-Centered System Design*, Lawrence Erlbaum, 87-124.
14. Kaljuvee, O., Buyukkokten, O., Garcia-Molina, H., and Paepcke, A. (2001) Efficient Web form entry on PDAs, *Proc. World Wide Web Conf.*, 663 - 672.
15. Leatherby, J.H., and Pausch, R. (1992) Voice Input as a Replacement for Keyboard Accelerators in a Mousebased Graphical Editor: An Empirical Study, *Journal of the American Voice Input/Output Society*, 11, 2.
16. Microsoft Sidewinder Wheels - Precision Racing Wheel, http:/ /www.microsof t.com/hardware/sidewinder/PrecPro.asp.
17. Oviatt, S.L. (2003) Multimodal Interfaces, in J. Jacko and A. Sears (eds.), *The Human-Computer Interaction Handbook: Fundamentals, Evolving Technologies and Emerging Applications*, Lawrence Erlbaum, 286-304.

18. Oviatt, S.L. (2002) Breaking the Robustness Barrier: Recent Progress on the Design of Robust Multimodal Systems, in M. Zelkowitz (ed.), *Advances in Computers,* 56, 305-325.
19. Oviatt, S.L., Cohen, P., Vergo, J., Duncan,L., Suhn, B., Bers, J., Holzman, T., Winograd, T., Landay, J., Larson, J., and Ferro, D. (2000) Designing the User Interface for Multimodal Speech and Pen-based Gesture Applications: State-of-the-Art Systems and Future Research Directions, Human Computer Interaction 15,4, 263-322.
20. Pieraccini, R., Dayanidhi, K., Bloom, J., Dahan, J-G., Phillips, M., Goodman, and B. R., Prasad, K. V. Multimodal Conversational Interface for a Concept Vehicle. *Proc. Eurospeech 2003,* pp. 2233-2236.
21. Rosenfeld, R., Olsen, D., and Rudnicky, A. (2000) Universal Human-Machine Speech Interface: A White paper. Technical Report CMU-CS-00-114, School of Computer Science, Carnegie Mellon University.
22. Silfverberg, M., MacKenzie, I.S., and Korhonen, P. (2000) Predicting text entry speed on mobile phones, in *Proc. SIGCHI,* 9-16.
23. Strayer, D. L., Drews, F. A., Albert, R. W., & Johnston, W. A. (2001). Cell phone induced perceptual impairments during simulated driving. In D. V. McGehee, J. D. Lee, & M. Rizzo (Eds.) Driving Assessment 2001: International Symposium on Human Factors, in *Driver Assessment, Training, and Vehicle Design.*
24. Stutts, J.C., Reinfurt, D.W., Staplin, L.W., and Rodgman, E.A. (2001) The Role of Driver Distraction in Traffic Crashes. Washington, D.C.: AAA Foundation for Traffic Safety. Full text at: http://www.aaafts.org/pdf/distraction.pdf.
25. VoiceXML Forum, http://www.voicexml.org
26. Wolf, P.P., and Raj, B. (2002) The MERL SpokenQuery Information Retrieval System: A System for Retrieving Pertinent Documents from a Spoken Query, in *Proc. IEEE International Conference on Multimedia and Expo (ICME),* Vol. 2, 317-320.

A Sketching Tool for Designing Anyuser, Anyplatform, Anywhere User Interfaces

Adrien Coyette and Jean Vanderdonckt

Université catholique de Louvain, School of Management (IAG),
Place des Doyens, 1 – B-1348 Louvain-la-Neuve, Belgium
{coyette, vanderdonckt}@isys.ucl.ac.be

Abstract. Sketching activities are widely adopted during early design phases of user interface development to convey informal specifications of the interface presentation and dialog. Designers or even end users can sketch some or all of the future interface they want. With the ever increasing availability of different computing platforms, a need arises to continuously support sketching across these platforms with their various programming languages, interface development environments and operating systems. To address needs along these dimensions, which pose new challenges to user interface sketching tools, SketchiXML is a multi-platform multi-agent interactive application that enable designers and end users to sketch user interfaces with different levels of details and support for different contexts of use. The results of the sketching are then analyzed to produce interface specifications independently of any context, including user and platform. These specifications are exploited to progressively produce one or several interfaces, for one or many users, platforms, and environments.

1 Introduction

Designing the right User Interface (UI) the first time is very unlikely to occur. Instead, UI design is recognized as a process that is [15] intrinsically *open* (new considerations may appear at any time), *iterative* (several cycles are needed to reach an acceptable result), and *incomplete* (not all required considerations are available at design time). Consequently, means to support early UI design has been extensively researched [16] to identify appropriate techniques such as paper sketching, prototypes, mock-ups, diagrams, etc. Most designers consider hand sketches on paper as one of the most effective ways to represent the first drafts of a future UI [1,8,10]. Indeed, this kind of unconstrained approach presents many advantages: sketches can be drawn during any design stage, it is fast to learn and quick to produce, it lets the sketcher focus on basic structural issues instead of unimportant details (e.g., exact alignment, typography, and colors), it is very appropriate to convey ongoing, unfinished designs, and it encourages creativity, sketches can be performed collaboratively between designers and end-users. Furthermore, the end user may herself produce some sketches to initiate the development process and when the sketch is close enough to the expected UI, an agreement can be signed between the designer and the end user, thus facilitating the contract and validation. Van Duyne *et al.* [16] reported that creating a low-fidelity UI prototype (such as UI sketches) is at least 10 to 20

M.F. Costabile and F. Paternò (Eds.): INTERACT 2005, LNCS 3585, pp. 550–564, 2005.
© IFIP International Federation for Information Processing 2005

times easier and faster than its equivalent with a high-fidelity prototype (such as produced in UI builders). The idea of developing a computer-based tool for sketching UIs naturally emerged from these observations [6,12]. Such tools would extend the advantages provided by sketching techniques by: easily creating, deleting, updating or moving UI elements, thus encouraging typical activities in the design process [15] such as checking and revision. Some research was carried out in order to propose a hybrid approach, combining the best of the hand-sketching and computer assisted interface design, but this marriage highlights five shortcomings:

- Some tools only support sketching activities, without producing any output: when the designer and the end user agreed upon a sketch, a contract can be signed between them and the development phase can start from the early design phase, but when the sketch is not transformed, the effort is lost.
- Sketching tools that recognize the drawing do produce some output, but not in a reusable format: the design output is not necessarily in a format that is directly reusable as development input, thus preventing reusability.
- Sketching tools are bound to a particular programming language, a particular UI type, a particular computing platform or operating system: when an output is produced, it is usually bound to one particular environment, therefore preventing developers from re-using sketches in new contexts, such as for various platforms.
- Sketching tools do not take into account the sketcher's preferences: as they impose the same sketching scheme, the same gestures for all types of sketchers, a learning curve may prevent these users from learning the tool and efficiently using it.
- Sketching tools do not allow a lot of flexibility in the sketch recognition: the user cannot choose when recognition will occur, degrading openness [15] and when this occurs, it is difficult to return to a previous state.

To unleash the power of informal UI design based on sketches, we need to address the above shortcomings observed for existing UI sketching tools. The expectation is thus that UI sketching will be lead to its full potential. SketchiXML is a new informal prototyping tool solving *all* these shortcomings, letting designers sketch user interfaces as easily as on paper. In addition, SketchiXML provides the designer with on-demand design critique and assistance during early design. Instead of producing code specific to a particular case or environment, SketchiXML generates UI specifications written in UsiXML (User Interface eXtensible Markup Language – www.usixml.org), a platform-independent User Interface Description Language (UIDL) that will be in turn exploited to produce code for one or several UIs, and for one or many contexts of use simultaneously.

In this paper Section 2 demonstrates that state-of-the-art UI sketching tools all suffer from some of the above shortcomings. Section 3 reports on an experimental study conducted to identify the sketchers' preferences, such as the most preferred and appropriate UI representations. These results underpin the development of SketchiXML in Section 4, where these widgets are recognized on demand. The multi-agent architecture of SketchiXML is outlined to support various scenarios in different contexts of use with examples. Section 5 discusses some future work and Section 6 demonstrates that the seven shortcomings above are effectively solved in SketchiXML.

2 Related Work

UI prototypes usually fall into three categories depending on their degree of fidelity, that is the precision to which they reproduce the reality of the desired UI.

The *high-fidelity* (Hi-Fi) prototyping tools support building a UI that looks complete, and might be usable. Moreover, this kind of software is equipped with a wide range of editing functions for all UI widgets: erase, undo, move, specify physical attributes, etc... This software lets designers build a complete GUI, from which is produced an accurate image (e.g., Adobe Photoshop, PowerPoint) or code in a determined programming language (e.g., Visual Basic, DreamWeaver). Even if the final result is not executable, it can still be considered as a high fidelity tool given that the result provided looks complete.

The *medium-fidelity* (Me-Fi) approach builds UI mock-ups giving importance to content, but keeping secondary all information regarding typography, color scheme or others minor details. A typical example is Microsoft Visio, where only the type, the size and the contents of UI widgets can be specified graphically.

Low-fidelity (Lo-Fi) drafting tools are used to capture the general information needed to obtain a global comprehension of what is desired, keeping all the unnecessary details out of the process. The most standard approaches for Lo-Fi prototyping are the "paper and pencil technique", the "whiteboard/blackboard and post-its approach" [16]. Such approaches provide access to all the components, and prevent the designer from being distracted from the primary task of design. Research shows that designers who work out conceptual ideas on paper tend to iterate more and explore the design space more broadly, whereas designers using computer-based tools tend to take only one idea and work it out in detail [6,12,15]. Many designers have reported that the quality of the discussion when people are presented with a Hi-Fi prototype was different than when they are presented with a Lo-Fi mock up. When using Lo-Fi prototyping, the users tend to focus on the interaction or on the overall site structure rather than on the color scheme or others details irrelevant at this level [16].

Consequently, Lo-Fi prototyping offers a clear set of advantages compared to the Hi-Fi perspective, but at the same time suffers from a lack of assistance. For instance, if several screens have a lot in common, it could be profitable to use copy and paste instead of rewriting the whole screen each time. A combination of these approaches appears to make sense, as long as the Lo-Fi advantages are maintained. This consideration results two families of software tools which support UI sketching and representing the scenarios between them, one with and one without code generation.

DENIM [6,10] helps web site designers during early design by sketching information at different refinement levels, such as site map, story board and individual page, and unifies the levels through zooming views. DEMAIS [1] is similar in principle, but aimed at prototyping interactive multimedia applications. It is made up of an interactive multimedia storyboard tool that uses a designer's ink strokes and textual annotations as an input design vocabulary. Both DENIM and DEMAIS use pen input as a natural way to sketch on screen, but do not produce any final code or other output.

In contrast, SILK [8], JavaSketchIt [2] and Freeform [11,12] are major applications for pen-input based interface design supporting code generation. SILK uses pen input to draw GUIs and produce code for OpenLook operating system. JavaSketchIt proceeds in a slightly different way than Freeform, as it displays the shapes recognized in real time, and generates Java UI code. JavaSketchIt uses the CALI library [6] for the shape recognition, and widgets are formed on basis of a combination of vectorial shapes. The recognition rate of the CALI library is very high and thus makes JavaSketchIt easy to use, even for a novice user. Freeform only displays the shapes recognized once the design of the whole interface is completed, and produces Visual Basic 6 code. The technique used to identify the widgets is the same than JavaSketchIt, but with a slightly lower recognition rate. Freeform also supports scenario management thanks to a basic storyboard view similar to that provided in DENIM.

Table 1. Comparison of software for low-, medium-, and high-fidelity UI prototyping tools

Fidelity	Appearance	Advantages	Shortcomings
Low	- Sketchy - Little visual detail	- Low development cost - Short production time - Easy communication - Basic drawing skills needed	- Is facilitator-driven - Limited for usability tests - Limited support of navigational aspects - Low attractiveness for end users - No code generation
Medium	- Simple - medium level of detail, close to appearance of final UI	- Medium development cost - Average production time - May involve some basic graphical aspects as specified in style guide: labels, icons,... - Limited drawing skills - Understandable for end user	- Is facilitator-driven - Limited for usability tests - Medium support of navigational aspects - No code generation
High	- Definitive, refined - Look and Feel of final UI	- Fully interactive - Serves for usability testing - Supports user-centered design - Serves for prototype validation and contract - Attractive for end users - Code generation	- High development cost - High production time - Advanced drawing and specification skills needed - Very inflexible with respect to changing requirements

Table 1 summarizes major advantages and shortcomings of existing UI prototyping tools depending on their level of fidelity. In addition to the shortcomings in the last column, the shortcomings outlined in the introduction should also be considered to elicit the requirements of SketchiXML. SketchiXML's main goal is to combine in a flexible way the advantages of the tools just presented into a single application, but also to add new features for this kind of application. Thus SketchiXML should avoid the five shortcoming above by: (R1) producing UI specifications and generate from them UI in several programming languages to avoid binding with a particular environment and to foster reusability; (R2) supporting UI sketching with recognition and translation of this sketching into UI specifications in order not to loose the design effort; (R3) supporting sketching for any context of use (e.g., any user, any platform, any environment) instead of only one platform, one context; (R4) being based on UI widget representations that are significant for the designer and/or the end-user; and

(R5) performing sketch recognition at different moments, instead of at an imposed moment. R4 is addressed in Section 3, the others, in Section 4.

Others vital facilities to be provided by SketchiXML are handling input from different sources (R6), such as direct sketching on a tablet or a paper scan, and also receiving real time advice on two types of issues (R7), if desired: the first occurs in a post-sketching phase, and provides a set of usability advice based on the UI drawn. For the second type of advice, the system operates in real time, looking for possible patterns, or similarities with previously drawn UIs. The objective of such an analysis is to supplement the sketching for the designer when a pattern is detected. Since the goal of SketchiXML is to entice designers to be creative and to express evaluative judgments, we infer the rules enunciated in [15] to the global architecture, and let the designer parameterizes the behavior of the whole system through a set of parameters (Section 4).

3   Building the Widgets Catalogue

This section presents the method used to define the widget catalogue. The first subsection introduces the method itself. Subsection 2 provides a short analysis of the results.

3.1   Method

To address requirement R3, SketchiXML recognizes different representations, different sketches for the same UI widget. Indeed, the advantage of such a tool lies in the fact that it imitates the informality of classical low-fidelity tools, and is thus required to be easy and natural to use. For this purpose, we have conducted an experimental study aimed at collecting information on how users intuitively sketch widgets. Two groups of 30 subjects were randomly selected from a list: the first group had relevant experience in the computer science domain and interface design, while the second were end users with no specific knowledge of UI design or computer science. The second group was considered because SketchiXML' goal is to involve the end user as much as possible in the early prototyping process to bridge the gap between what they say and what the designer understands. Thus, the representations may vary between designers and end users. Fig. 1 depicts the various domains of expertise of each group.

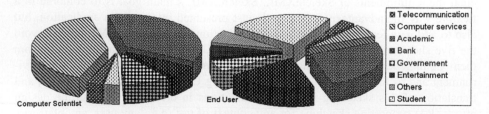

Fig. 1. Distribution of the subjects according to their domain of expertise

A two phase analysis was carried out on both groups. The scope of the first part was to determine how members of each group would intuitively and freely sketch the widgets to be handled by SketchiXML. From a cross-platform comparison of widgets, a catalogue was identified comprising the following 32 widgets: text, text field, text area, push button, search field, login, logout, reset form, validate, radio button, check box, combo box, image, multimedia area, layer, group box, table, separator, frame, hyperlink, anchor, list box, tabbed dialog box, menu, color picker, file picker, date picker, hour picker, toggle button, slider, progress bar, spinner. Each widget was documented with its English and French name, a screen shot and a small textual definition (see first three columns of Table 2). For each widget, subjects were asked if they had ever seen this widget before and to provide a sketching representation. Then, from the widget representations provided during the first phase, we tried in a second phase to extract the most common representations, in order to build a second questionnaire. In this questionnaire, 5 representations were associated with each widget, and participants were asked to rank the different representations (last column of Table 2) according to their representativeness and preference as a five point Likert scale. Fig. 2 depicts the propositions for a list box that will be examined as a representative example in the next subsection.

Table 2. Definition of the widgets catalogue (excerpts)

Widget	Graphical presentation	Textual definition	Potential sketchings
Search Field	submit	This widget is composed of a text field and a button. It allows the users to submit a search.	
Tabbed Dialog Box	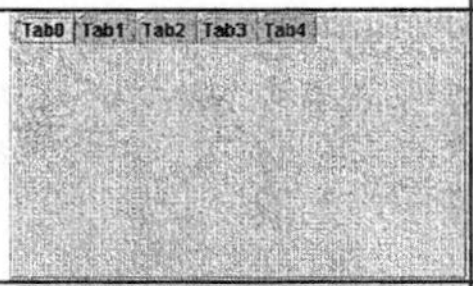 Tab0 Tab1 Tab2 Tab3 Tab4	This widget allows the user to switch from one pane to another thanks to the tab.	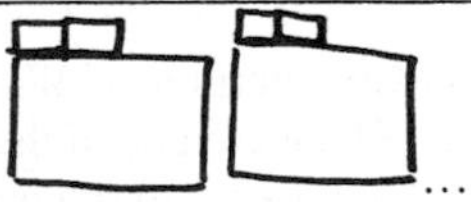
Date Picker	 mars 2004	This widget allows the user to pick a date on an agenda.	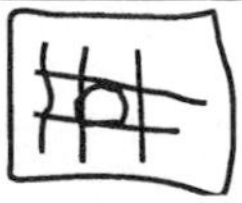

Fig. 2. Sketching propositions for the list box widget

3.2 Results and Discussion

Due to space restriction, we mainly focus on the list box widget. Based on the result distribution showed in Fig 3, we establish the best representation with the following method. Firstly we assess whether any dependence exists between the participants. If this first step's results established a significant dependence, then we proceed to the second phase and we compute the aggregate preference of both groups and the global preference. For each widget, the Kendall coefficient of concordance W test was computed. This coefficient expresses the degree of association among n variables, that is, the association between n sets of rankings. The degree of agreement among the 60 people who evaluated the representations is reflected by the degree of variation among the 6 sums of ranks.

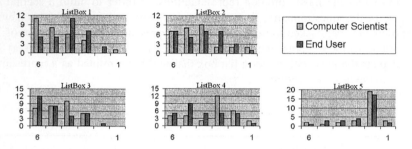

Fig. 3. Result frequency of the survey regarding the list box

$$W = \frac{\sum_{i=1}^{N}(\overline{R}_i - \overline{R})^2}{N(N^2-1)/12} = 0,36238$$

Fig. 4. Computation of W where k is the number of judges, N the number of objects being ranked, RI the average of the ranks assigned to the ith object, R the average of the rank assigned across all objects or subjects and $N(N^2-1)/12$ represents the maximum possible sum of the squared deviations

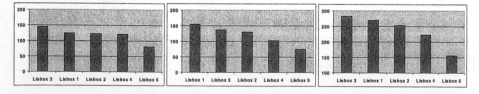

Fig. 5. Borda Count results for end users, computer scientists and both categories aggregated

The comparison of the value obtained from this computation to the critical value shows that the null hypothesis (independence between participants) has to be rejected. We can thus proceed to the second phase of the analysis and establish a ranking among all representations using the Borda Count method [14]. The principle of the Borda Count method is that, each candidate gets 1 point for each last-place vote received, 2 points for every next-to-last-place vote, etc., all the way up to N points for each first-place vote where N is the number of candidates. On basis of this analysis we observed that both groups have almost the same preferences among the representations (Fig. 5). Most of the time, the set of well considered representations is the same, even if small changes in the sequence occur. Out of this set, we chose preferred representations on the basis of intrinsic complexity, which is defined on basis of a set of criteria such as the number of strokes, the need of new vectorial shapes, high probability of confusion with other widget... For instance, list box 4 obtained a good score compared to the other representations, but its intrinsic complexity is very high, since it requires hand writing recognition, that is not supported for the moment. List box 4 and 5 were thus discarded from the final selection. Often, representations selected for the list box are composed from the three first representations in Figure 2.

4 SketchiXML Development

After meeting requirement R3 in the previous section, we have to address the remaining requirements, i.e. the application has to carry out shape recognition (R2), provide spatial shape interpretation (R2), provide usability advice (R7), handle several kinds of input (R6), generate UsiXML specifications (R1), and operate in a flexible way (R5). To address these requirements, a BDI (*Belief-Desire-Intention*) agent-oriented architecture [4] was considered appropriate: such architecture allows building robust and flexible applications by distributing the responsibilities among autonomous and cooperating agents. Each agent is in charge of a specific part of the process, and co-operates with the others in order to provide the service required according to the designer's preferences. This kind of approach has the advantage of being more flexible, modular and robust than traditional architecture including object-oriented ones [4].

4.1 SketchiXML Architecture

The application was built using the SKwyRL-framework [7], a framework aimed at defining, formalizing and applying socially based catalogues of styles and patterns to construct agent and multi-agent architectures. The joint-venture organizational style pattern [7] was applied to design the agent-architecture of SketchiXML [3]. It was chosen on basis of non-functional requirements Ri, as among all organizational styles defined in the SKwyRL framework, the joint venture clearly matches the requirements defined in Section 2 as the most open and distributed organizational style.

The architecture (Fig. 6) is structured using $i*$ [17], a graph where each node represents an *actor* (or system component) and each link between two actors indicates that one actor depends on the other for some goal to be attained. A dependency describes an "agreement" (called *dependum*) between two actors: the *depender* and the *dependee*. The *depender* is the depending actor, and the *dependee,* the actor who is depended upon. The type of the dependency describes the nature of the agreement. *Goal* dependencies represent delegation of responsibility for fulfilling a goal; *softgoal* dependencies are similar to goal dependencies, but their fulfillment cannot be defined precisely; task dependencies are used in situations where the dependee is required.

When a user wishes to create a new SketchiXML project, she contacts the *Broker* agent, which serves as an intermediary between the external actor and the organizational system. The *Broker* queries the user for all the relevant information needed for the process, such as the target platform, the input type, the intervention strategy of the *Adviser* agent,... According to the criteria entered, the coordinator chooses the most suitable handling and coordinates all the agents participating in the process in order to meet the objectives determined by the user. For clearness, the following section only considers a situation where the user has selected real time recognition, and pen-input device as input. So, the *Data Editor* agent then displays a white board allowing the user to draw his hand-sketch interface. All the strokes are collected and then transmitted to the *Shape Recognizer* agent for recognition. The recognition engine of this agent is based on the CALI library [5], a recognition engine able to identify shapes of different sizes, rotated at arbitrary angles, drawn with dashed, continuous strokes or overlapping lines.

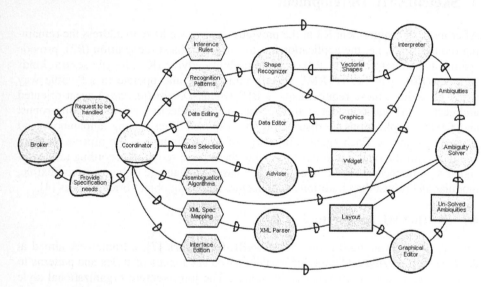

Fig. 6. i* representation of SketchiXML architecture as a Joint-Venture

Subsequently, the *Shape Recognizer* agent provides all the vectorial shapes identified with relevant information such as location, dimension or degree of certainty associated to the *Interpreter* agent. Based on these shape sets, the *Interpreter* agent attempts to create a component layout. The technique used for the creation of this layout takes advantage of the knowledge capacity of agents. The agent stores all the shapes identified as his belief, and each time a new shape is received all the potential candidates for association are extracted. Using its set of patterns the agent then evaluates if shape pairs form a widget or a sub-widget. The conditions to be tested are based on a set of fuzzy spatial relations allowing to deal with imprecise spatial combinations of geometric shapes and to fluctuate with user preferences. Based on the widgets identified by the *Interpreter*, the *Adviser* agent assists the designer with the conception of the UIs in two different ways.

Firstly, by providing real-time assistance to the designer by attempting to detect UI patterns in the current sketch in order to complete the sketch automatically. Secondly in a post operational mode, the usability adviser provides usability advice on the interface sketched. If the *Interpreter* fails to identify all the components or to apply all the usability rules, then the *Ambiguity Solver* agent is invoked. This agent evaluates how to solve the problem according to the initial parameters entered by the user.

The agent can either attempt to solve the ambiguity itself by using its set of disambiguation algorithms, or to delegate it to a third agent, the *Graphical Editor* agent. The *Graphical Editor* displays all the widget recognized at this point, as classical element-based software, and highlights all the components with a low degree of certainty for confirmation. Once one of these last three agents evoked has sufficient certainty about the overall widget layout, the UI is sent to the *XML Parser* agent for UsiXML generation.

4.2 Low-Fidelity Prototyping with SketchiXML

The first step in SketchiXML consists of specifying parameters that will drive the low-fidelity prototyping process (Fig. 7): the project name, the input type (i.e. on-line sketching or off-line drawing that is scanned and processed in one step-Fig. 8), the computing platform for which the UI is prototyped (a predefined platform can be selected such as mobile phone, PDA, TabletPC, kiosk, ScreenPhone, laptop, desktop, wall screen, or a custom one can be defined in terms of platform model [9]), the output folder, the time when the recognition process is initiated (ranging from on-demand manual to fully automatic each time a new widget can be detected- this flexibility is vital according to experiments and [15]), the intervention mode of the usability advisor (manual, mixed-initiative, automatic), and the output quality stating the response time vs. quality of results of the recognition and usability advisor processes. In Fig. 7, the UsiXML parsing is set on fully manual mode, and the output quality is set on medium quality. The quality level affects the way the agents consider a widget

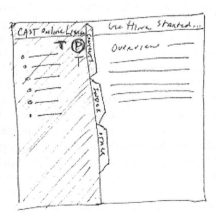

Fig. 7. Creating a new SketchiXML prototype   **Fig. 8.** Scanned UI sketching

layout to be acceptable, or the constraints used for the pattern matching between vectorial shapes. The sketching phase in that situation is thus very similar to the sketching process of an application such as Freeform [11]. Of course, the designer is always free to change these parameters while the process is running.

Fig. 9 illustrates the SketchiXML workspace configured for designing a UI for a standard personal computer. On the left part we can observe that shape recognition is disabled as none of the sketches is interpreted, and the widget layout generated by the *Interpreter* agent remains empty. The right part represents the same UI with shape recognition and interpretation. Fig. 10 depicts SketchiXML parameterized for a PocketPC platform and its results imported in GrafiXML, a UsiXML-compliant graphical UI editor that can generate code for HTML, XHTML, and Java (http://www.usixml. org/index.php?view=page&idpage=10).

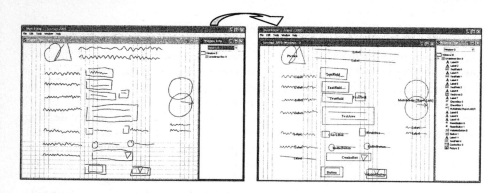

Fig. 9. SketchiXML workspace

When shape recognition is activated, each time a new widget is identified the color of the shapes turns to green, and the widget tree generated by the *Interpreter* is updated. Changing the context has a deep impact on the way the system operates. As an example, when a user builds a user interface for one platform or another, adaptations need to be based on the design knowledge that will be used for evaluation, by selecting and prioritizing rule sets [15], and on the set of available widgets. As the size of the drawing area is changing, the set of constraints used for the interpretation needs to be tailored too, indeed if the average size of the strokes drawn is much smaller than on a standard display, the imprecision associated with each stroke follows the same trend. We can thus strengthen the constraints to avoid any confusion.

Once the design phase is complete, SketchiXML parses the informal design to produce UsiXML specifications. Fig. 11 gives an overview of the UsiXML specifications generated from UI drawn in Fig. 10. Each widget is represented with standard values for each attribute, as SketchiXML is only aimed at capturing the UI core properties. In addition, the UsiXML specifications integrate all the information related to the context of use as specified in the wizard depicted on Fig. 7: information for the user model, the platform model, and the environment model [9]. As UsiXML allows defining a set of transformation rules for switching from one of the UsiXML models to another, or to adapt a model for another context, such information is thus required.

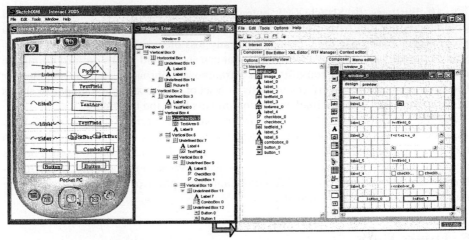

Fig. 10. SketchiXML workspace configured for a PDA and its import in GrafiXML

```
<?xml version="1.0" encoding="UTF-8"?>
<uiModel id="Interact_2005" name="Interact 2005"
    creationDate="2005-01-06T14:51:31.656+01:00" schemaVersion="1.6.1"
    xmlns="http://www.usixml.org">
    <version modifDate="2005-01-06T14:51:31.656+01:00" xmlns="">1</version>
    <authorName xmlns="">SketchiXML</authorName>
    <cuiModel id="Interact_2005_6-cui" name="Interact 2005-cui">
        <window id="window_0" name="window_0" isVisible="true"
            isEnabled="true" fgColor="#000000" bgColor="#ece9d8"  borderWidth="0" width="400"
            height="350"
            isAlwaysOnTop="false" windowLeftMargin="0"  windowTopMargin="0" isResizable="true">
            <box id="box_0" name="box_0" isVisible="false"
                isEnabled="true" width="400" height="350" type="horizontal" isFlow="false"
                isFill="false"
                isScrollable="false" isSplitable="false"  isDetachable="false"
                isResizableVertical="false"
                isResizableHorizontal="false" relativeMinWidth="0" relativeMinHeight="0"
                isBalanced="false"
                relativeWidth="0" relativeHeight="0">...
                <textComponent id="label_0" name="label_0"
                    isVisible="true" isEnabled="true" fgColor="#000000" bgColor="#ece9d8"
                    visitedLinkColor="#000000"
                    activeLinkColor="#000000" isBold="true" isItalic="false" isUnderline="false"
                    isStrikethrough="false" isSubscript="false" isSuperscript="false"
                    isPreformatted="false"
                    textColor="#000000" textSize="12" textFont="Dialog" textMargin="0"
                    textVerticalAlign="middle"
                    textHorizontalAlign="left" scrollStyle="scroll" scrollDirection="left"/>...
                <imageComponent id="image_0" name="image_0" isVisible="true" isEnabled="true"
                defaultHyperLinkTarget=""/>...
                <button id="button_1" name="button_1" isVisible="true" isEnabled="true"
                fgColor="#000000" bgColor="#ece9d8"/>...
            </box> </window>
    </cuiModel>
    <contextModel id="interact_2005-contextModel_0" name="interact_2005-contextModel_pda">
        <context id="interact_2005-context_0" name="interact_2005-context_pda">
            <userStereotype id="interact_2005-user_US_0" language="en_US"
            stereotypeName="interact_2005-user_US"
            taskExperience="1" systemExperience="1" deviceExperience="1" taskMotivation="1"/>
            <platform id="windows_mobile_2003" name="windows_mobile_2003">
                <softwarePlatform OSName="Windows" OSVersion="2003"  OSVendor="Microsoft Corp."/>
                <hardwarePlatform screenSize="240x320" />
            </platform></context></contextModel>
    <resourceModel id="Interact_2005_6" name="Interact 2005"/>
</uiModel>
```

Fig. 11. Excerpt of the UsiXML specifications generated by SketchiXML

Fig. 10 illustrates the SketchiXML output imported in GrafiXML, a high fidelity UI graphical editor. On basis of the informal design provided during the early design, a programmer can re-use the output without any loss of time to provide a revised version of the UI with all the characteristics that can and should not be defined during the early design phase. This contrasts with a traditional approach, where a programmer had to implement user interfaces on basis of a set of blackboard photographs or sheets of paper, and thus start the implementation process from the beginning.

As the Usability Advisor intervention time has been specified as "automatic" (Fig. 7), each time a usability deviation is detected with respect to usability guidelines, a tool tip message is produced in context, attached to the widget on concern. For this purpose, a set of form-based usability guidelines have been encoded in GDL (Guideline Definition Language), a XML-compliant description of guidelines that can be directly related to UsiXML widgets.

5 Future Work

Although SketchiXML already provides a wide set of features, many evolutions could be imagined. Out of many ideas, three major ones retain our attention:

1. One drawback of SketchiXML is the lack of a scenario editor allowing to represent transition between screen. Capturing such information could be very profitable, and is quite natural to represent for a novice designer. Moreover such information can be directly stored in the UsiXML model and be reused just as easily as the code generated for each UI.
2. A second high potential evolution consists in developing an evolutionary recognition engine. SketchiXML uses the CALI library [5] and a set of spatial constraints between the vector shapes recognized to build the widget. Even if the recognition rate is very high, the insertion of new widget representation is restricted to a combination of the set of the vector shapes supported. To this aim, research in a biometric domain such as handwriting recognition [13] could provide valuable answers, taking full advantage of the multi-agent architecture.
3. During the sketching process, the possibility to instantly switch to a runnable version of the current UI is useful. Indeed, all informal design tools providing code generation allow easy switching from design to run mode, while SketchiXML requires to invoke a third application. Right now, SketchiXML only supports import in GrafiXML. So, we would like to support existing external interpreters that produce Flash, Java, XHTML and Tcl-Tk interpretations (see www.usixml.org for a list of such interpreters)

6 Conclusion

With SketchiXML we have introduced a new and innovative tool. Firstly, SketchiXML is the first informal design tool that generates a user, platform, and environment independent output and thus provides a solution to the language neutrality weakness of existing approaches. Secondly, the application is based on a BDI multi-agent architecture where each requirement is assumed by an autonomous and collaborative agent part of an organizational system. Based on the criteria provided by the designer at the beginning of the process, the experts (agents) adapt the way they act and interact with the designer and the other agents in order to meet the global objectives. We have shown that SketchiXML meets requirements R1-R5 that were identified as important shortcomings of existing tools. Through this research, we have also conducted a survey on 60 people from different activity sectors with different backgrounds, in order to identify how these people would intuitively represent the widgets to be handled by SketchiXML. From these results we have associated a set of sketching representations to each widget. Moreover, this set of representation is not hard coded and can be reconfigured by the user through an external configuration file. SketchiXML will extend a set of tools initiating the design process from the early design phase to the final concrete user interface, with tools supporting every stage. The complete widgets catalogue, screen shots, demonstration of SketchiXML and implementation are available at www.usixml.org. SketchiXML is developed in Java, on top SKwyRL-framework [7] and JACK Agent platform, with recognition based on CALI library [5].

Acknowledgements

We gratefully acknowledge the support of the Request research project under the umbrella of the WIST (Wallonie Information Société Technologies) program under convention n°031/5592 RW REQUEST). We warmly thank J.A. Jorge, F.M.G. Pereira and A. Caetano for allowing us to use JavaSketchIt and the CALI library in our research, Mickaël Nicolay for conducting the user survey and providing the results, and Gilbert Cockton for helping us in the preparation of this manuscript.

References

1. Bailey, B.P., Konstan, J.A.: Are Informal Tools Better? Comparing DEMAIS, Pencil and Paper, and Authorware for Early Multimedia Design. In: Proc. of the ACM Conf. on Human Factors in Computing Systems CHI'2003. ACM Press, NY (2003) 313–320
2. Caetano, A., Goulart, N., Fonseca, M., Jorge, J.: JavaSketchIt: Issues in Sketching the Look of User Interfaces. In: Proc. of the 2002 AAAI Spring Symposium - Sketch Understanding (Palo Alto, March 2002). AAAI Press (2002) 9–14
3. Coyette, A., Faulkner S., Kolp, M., Vanderdonckt, J., Limbourg, Q.: SketchiXML: Towards a Multi-Agent Design Tool for Sketching User Interfaces Based on USIXML. In: Proc. of TAMODIA'2004 (Prague, November 2004). ACM Press, New York (2004) 75–82
4. Faulkner, S.: An Architectural Framework for Describing BDI Multi-Agent Information Systems. Ph.D. Thesis, UCL-IAG, Louvain-la-Neuve (May 2004)
5. Fonseca, M.J., Jorge, J.A.: Using Fuzzy Logic to Recognize Geometric Shapes Interactively. In: Proc. of the 9th Int. Conf. on Fuzzy Systems FUZZ-IEEE'00 (San Antonio, 2000). IEEE Computer Society Press, Los Alamitos (2000) 191–196
6. Hong, J.I., Li, F.C., Lin, J., Landay, J.A.: End-User Perceptions of Formal and Informal Representations of Web Sites. In: Extended Abstracts of CHI'2001, 385–386

7. Kolp, M., Giorgini, P., Mylopoulos, J.: An Organizational Perspective on Multi-agent Architectures. In: Proc. of the 8th Int. Workshop on Agent Theories, Architectures, and Languages ATAL'01 (Seattle, 2001).
8. Landay, J., Myers, B.A.: Sketching Interfaces: Toward More Human Interface Design. IEEE Computer 34, 3 (March 2001) 56–64
9. Limbourg, Q., Vanderdonckt, J., Michotte, B., Bouillon, L., and Lopez-Jaquero, V. USIXML: a Language Supporting Multi-Path Development of User Interfaces. In: Proc. of 9th IFIP Working Conf. on Engineering for Human-Computer Interaction EHCI-DSVIS'2004 (Hamburg, July 11-13, 2004). Kluwer Academics, Dordrecht (2004)
10. Newman, M.W., Lin, J., Hong, J.I., Landay, J.A.: DENIM: An Informal Web Site Design Tool Inspired by Observations of Practice. Human-Comp. Interaction 18 (2003) 259–324
11. Plimmer, B.E., Apperley, M. Software for Students to Sketch Interface Designs. In: Proc. of IFIP Conf. on Human-Computer Interaction INTERACT'2003. IOS Press (2003) 73–80
12. Plimmer, B.E., Apperley, M.: Interacting with Sketched Interface Designs: An Evaluation Study. In: Proc. of CHI'04. ACM Press, New York (2004) 1337–1340
13. Schimke S., Vielhauer C., Dittmann J.: Using Adapted Levenshtein Distance for On-Line Signature Authentication. In: Proc. of ICPR'2004. Springer-Verlag (2004) 931–934
14. Sidney Siegel and Jr. N. John Castellan. Nonparametric Statistics for The Behavioral Sciences. McGraw-Hill, Inc., second edition, 1988.
15. Sumner, T., Bonnardel, N., Kallag-Harstad, B., The Cognitive Ergonomics of Knowledge-based Design Support Systems. In: Proc. of CHI'97. ACM Press, New York (1997) 83–90
16. van Duyne, D.K., J.A. Landay, and J.I. Hong, The Design of Sites: Patterns, Principles, and Processes for Crafting a Customer-Centered Web Experience. Addison-Wesley (2002).
17. Yu, E.: Modeling Strategic Relationships for Process Reengineering. Ph.D. thesis. Department of Computer Science, University of Toronto, Toronto (1995).

FlowMouse: A Computer Vision-Based Pointing and Gesture Input Device

Andrew D. Wilson and Edward Cutrell

Microsoft Research,
One Microsoft Way, Redmond, WA
{awilson, cutrell}@microsoft.com

Abstract. We introduce FlowMouse, a computer vision-based pointing device and gesture input system. FlowMouse uses optical flow techniques to model the motion of the hand and a capacitive touch sensor to enable and disable interaction. By using optical flow rather than a more traditional tracking based method, FlowMouse is exceptionally robust, simple in design, and offers opportunities for fluid gesture-based interaction that go well beyond merely emulating pointing devices such as the mouse. We present a Fitts law study examining pointing performance, and discuss applications of the optical flow field for gesture input.

1 Introduction

Today's computing environments are strongly tied to the availability of a high resolution pointing device, and, more fundamentally, to the notion of a single, discrete two-dimensional cursor. Modern GUIs (graphical user interfaces) combined with devices such as mice and track pads are extremely effective at reducing the richness and variety of human communication down to a single point. While the utility of such devices in today's interfaces cannot be denied, there are opportunities to apply other kinds of sensors to enrich the user experience. For example, video cameras and computer vision techniques may be used to capture many details of human shape and movement [24]. The shape of the hand may be analyzed over time to manipulate an onscreen object in a way analogous to the hand's manipulation of paper on a desk. Such an approach may lead to a faster, more natural, and more fluid style of interaction for certain tasks [10], [28].

The application of video cameras and computer vision techniques as an interface component to today's computing architecture raises many questions. Should the new device be designed to replace the mouse? In what ways might such a device complement the mouse? Will the added functionality of the new device be incorporated into today's computing experience [15], [27] or does the entire interface need to be rethought [16], [26]?

Unfortunately, most computer vision-based user interface systems are poorly suited to the task of emulating the mouse. To begin, the resolution of video-based techniques is far less than today's mouse. While it is difficult to directly compare the resolution of an optical mouse to a computer vision-based tracking system, we note

M.F. Costabile and F. Paternò (Eds.): INTERACT 2005, LNCS 3585, pp. 565–578, 2005.
© IFIP International Federation for Information Processing 2005

that a typical optical mouse has a resolution of about 400 dpi and frame rate of 120 Hz. A typical video camera produces 640×480 pixel images at 30 Hz. Assuming a full view of a 9" wide mousing surface, a computer vision tracking algorithm with tracking precision equal to that of the input image yields a resolution of only about 71 dpi.

The lack of spatial and temporal resolution is not the only difficulty. Often with computer vision-based user interfaces, it is difficult to determine the precise relationship between the object being tracked and the resulting output position information. For example, in tracking the hand, which part of the hand should indicate cursor position? If the tip of the finger is chosen, which point is exactly the "tip" of the finger? A lack of agreement between the user and the sensing system on what is being tracked further limits resolution and can be the source of breakdowns in interaction. A number of related works pursue finger tracking approaches to recover absolute finger position [25], [21], [15], [19]. Another approach is to design a handheld prop which is tracked unambiguously [7], [4].

A related issue is that vision-based systems often have difficulty in providing natural ways for the user to enable or disable the device. Mice and trackpads both provide unambiguous and simple mechanisms that require little or no thought on the part of the user. It is important for vision-based systems to adopt mechanisms that are similarly natural and failsafe, or the trouble of unintentional input will outweigh any benefit provided by the interface.

Finally, many vision techniques make strong assumptions about the appearance of the tracked object and the background or are sensitive to lighting conditions. In the case of computer vision systems trained on hands, often much effort is placed on developing models of skin color and hand shape. The *segmentation* problem of separating foreground from background, based on color or otherwise, is very difficult in general. While the field of computer vision has techniques that can address these problems, the resulting systems can be complex and provide no guarantee on robustness.

In this paper we present a pointing device and gesture input system based on computer vision techniques. To capture the motion of the hand, FlowMouse uses optical flow techniques rather than traditional absolute position-based tracking methods, and so avoids many of the difficulties mentioned above. In a laptop configuration, a natural mode switching mechanism is provided by a touch-sensitive strip placed on the mouse button just below the keyboard. The flow computation performed at each point in the input image is roughly analogous to that performed by a typical optical mouse sensor, in which mouse velocity is determined by image correlation between successive captured images. In aggregate these individual motion estimates provide a robust estimate of the relative motion of the hand under the camera. This approach avoids the fragility of absolute tracking techniques as discussed above.

Flow fields are able to express patterns of motion beyond a simple translation of the hand, and in that capability there is opportunity to explore new interaction scenarios while maintaining support for traditional two-dimensional pointing. Our goal is to demonstrate that FlowMouse is a capable pointing device for today's interfaces while outlining its potential to simultaneously support novel interactions that take advantage of the richness and subtlety of human motion.

Fig. 1. Left: FlowMouse prototype with screen-mounted camera facing down on keyboard and user's hands, and touch sensitive strip on left mouse button. Right: Example image capture from camera.

In the following, we outline the configuration of the device, detail the image processing used, present a Fitts law analysis of FlowMouse pointing performance, and discuss how FlowMouse enables interaction scenarios beyond traditional two-dimensional pointing.

2 FlowMouse

Fig. 1 illustrates a FlowMouse prototype installed on a laptop computer. A USB web camera is attached to the top of the display such that the camera image contains a view of the laptop keyboard and the user's hands when they are on the keyboard and mouse buttons. When FlowMouse is enabled, images are acquired from the camera and processed to determine motion information useful for pointing and gesture. In our experiments, we have relied on ambient office lighting for illumination, but we envision that future implementations may include light emitting diodes (LEDs) to be used when ambient light levels are inadequate.

It is important to have a reliable and natural *mode switch* which can be used to enable and disable FlowMouse, such that only intentional gesturing is processed by the system, but also to allow for a "clutching" action that a relative pointing scheme requires [5]. In our prototype, a touch sensor is affixed to the surface of the left mouse button. We chose this placement based on the desire to find a mode switch method that requires very little modification of the user's behavior: we have observed that while moving the cursor using keyboard-integrated devices (e.g., a trackpad or isometric joystick), most users rest their left thumb or left forefinger on the left mouse button so that they are prepared to quickly click the mouse button. We believe that touching the left mouse button is an adequate indicator for using the mouse rather than the keyboard. A similar application of touch sensors is presented in [11] and [22].

The loading of the mode switch on the left mouse button also avoids the problem that many vision-based user interface designs face: if the hand used for positioning is also used to effect a click action, the motion for the click action may be confused with the motion used for positioning. In this case, the clicking action is likely to bump the cursor off the target just as the user has finished positioning the cursor.

In our prototype, a simple capacitance-based touch sensor relies on a copper electrode taped to the mouse button. Such a sensor can also be placed under the plastic shell of the mouse button itself.

3 Image Processing

While the user touches the left mouse button, FlowMouse sensing is enabled. During this time, grayscale images are acquired from the USB camera attached to the top of the display. These images are then processed in real time to determine the optical flow field corresponding to the motion of the hand under the camera. Optical flow is a standard representation used in computer vision which indicates the direction and magnitude of motion at each point on a regular grid defined on the input image [1], [2].

Part of the goal of FlowMouse is to explore the advantages of optical flow over a more traditional approach based on segmentation of hands against the keyboard and subsequent absolute position tracking processes. Optical flow computations make very few assumptions about the nature of the input images and typically only require that there be sufficient local texture on the moving object. We avoid the difficulties of developing a reliable absolute position-based tracker by only computing simple statistics that summarize the flow field and restrict ourselves to computing relative motion information. As with traditional mice and track pads, a key to the success of this approach is the effectiveness of the clutching mechanism.

During the time the user touches the left mouse button, optical flow is computed from the most recently acquired image and the previous image. There are a number of methods to compute optical flow. Our prototype uses a simple block matching technique in which, for each point (x, y) on a regular grid in the image, the integer vector quantity (dx, dy) is determined such that the image patch centered on (x, y) at time $t-1$ most closely matches the image patch centered on $(x + dx, y + dy)$ at time t. In this calculation, image patches are compared by computing the sum of pixelwise absolute differences (low values indicate close match). For a given patch in the image, we select (dx, dy) that minimizes

$$\sum_{x,y \in \text{patch}} |I_{t-1}(x, y) - I_t(x + dx, y + dy)| \tag{1}$$

Our current implementation acquires 640×480 pixel grayscale images at 30Hz. Flow vectors are computed every 32 pixels on a regular grid, yielding a 20×15 flow field. Each of dx and dy are allowed to vary by 6 pixels in either direction on 16×16 pixel patches, and the optimal (dx, dy) for each grid point is found by exhaustive search over this range. The flow field is computed at full frame rate (30Hz) on a 1.1GHz Pentium III Mobile. An example flow field for hand motion is illustrated in Fig. 2.

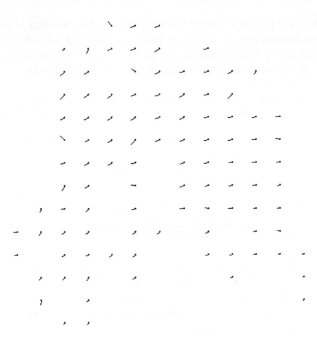

Fig. 2. Example optical flow field, with hand undergoing translation left and down

There are a few details to note about the optical flow computation. First, correct values (dx, dy) are attainable only if there are adequate features such as edges or corners in the image patch under consideration. In practice, it is necessary to determine the merit of the computed (dx, dy) at a patch. We compare the match score corresponding to $(dx, dy) = 0$ against the best score for any (dx, dy) and discard the flow information at this patch if the best score is not significantly better than that corresponding to $(dx, dy) = 0$. This typically avoids the problem of spurious flow vectors computed on regions of the image without adequate texture, such as may be found on the smooth area on the back of the hand.

A second consideration is that this method finds integer values for dx and dy. This would seem to limit the overall precision of motion information derived from the flow, but typically a hand under the camera will generate many valid flow observations. While a single flow observation may be a noisy estimate of motion, when averaged together the collection of flow vectors result in a more stable estimate of motion.

4   FlowMouse as Pointing Device

4.1   Mouse Acceleration Profile

A simple averaging of the nonzero flow field vectors may be used to obtain a grand mean (dx, dy) suitable for cursor movement. In our experience it is necessary to transform this raw velocity to incorporate acceleration such that it is possible to finely position the mouse cursor. Whereas in previous studies such velocity transfer functions are motivated by minimizing the range of motion [14], we adopt an acceleration profile in an attempt to mitigate the lack of resolution of the camera compared to the mouse.

We adopt a sigmoidal (logistic) acceleration profile, where the speed s is computed as the norm of (dx, dy). The acceleration factor scales input (dx, dy) to obtain mouse movement offsets (m_x, m_y) on a display of resolution 1024×768:

$$s = \sqrt{(0.5dx)^2 + (0.7dy)^2} \tag{2}$$

$$(m_x, m_y) = \left(\frac{80}{1 + e^{-(s-4)/0.6}} \right)(dx, dy) \tag{3}$$

where the scaling factors on dx and dy were added to differentially scale movement in the horizontal and vertical directions, respectively, to account for the fact that vertical motion of the hand in the plane of the keyboard appears to be more difficult than horizontal motion. This disparity is probably due to the rotation of the wrist as a component of horizontal movement.

This acceleration profile is more aggressive than the usual profile used in Windows XP [3]. This change reflects the fact that FlowMouse has significantly less sensor resolution than a typical mouse, we require fine positioning of the cursor as well as the ability to move the cursor across the entire screen with little or no clutching.

5   Laboratory User Study

To objectively evaluate the performance of FlowMouse used as a pointing device, we performed a user study using a Fitts Law task. Fitts Law is a standard method for evaluating, optimizing, and studying properties of pointing devices and techniques that is well-accepted by the HCI community [20], [9]. We tested the FlowMouse against the default trackpad included in the laptop the prototype was installed on.

5.1   Hypotheses

Because the FlowMouse technique is quite novel for most users and the prototype is not highly optimized for pointing (as opposed to the trackpad), we expected that the performance of FlowMouse would be significantly worse than the trackpad. Nevertheless, we thought that inexperienced users would be able to complete all trials with little difficulty. In addition, we expected that the performance difference between FlowMouse and the trackpad would be considerably less for users who have a bit more experience. That is, experienced users would show substantially improved performance over novice users.

5.2 Participants

We recruited 6 participants between the ages of 30 and 55 from coworkers. All had extensive experience using trackpads on laptop computers, and none had ever used the FlowMouse. All rated themselves as advanced computer users and had normal or corrected to normal vision with no color blindness. In addition, all were right handed and used the mouse in their right hand. Two other participants who had several hours practice using FlowMouse were recruited to compare the effect of experience on performance.

5.3 Method

The Fitts Law task was administered using a modified version of WinFitts (courtesy of the Dept. of Computer & Information Science, University of Oregon). For each device, participants performed a block of practice trials to familiarize them with the task and device. They then performed a block of trials for that condition. Each block consisted of 2 trials for each of the 12 distance-width combinations at 8 different target angles for a total of 192 trials per block. Error conditions (where a target was missed) were repeated in a random order at the end of the block. The Fitts parameters used in the experiment were: Width: 5, 10, 20 mm; Distance: 20, 40, 80, 160 mm; Angle: 0, 45, 90, 135, 180, 225, 270, 315 degrees from start point. This yielded Fitts index of difficulty measures ranging from 1 to 5.04 bits (according to the formula $ID=log_2(D/W +1)$).

5.4 Results

All data analyses for movement times were performed on the log transformed movement times to normalize the typical skewing associated with response time data. These were converted back to normal time for all figures below to make the results more intelligible. Movement times were first cleaned by removing error trials and outliers (movement times greater than 4 standard deviations larger than the mean for each condition), about 2% of all trials. We collapsed across angle to yield the means of 16 repetitions of each distance-width combination for each participant. The error rate was very low: 1.7% for the trackpad and 2.2% for FlowMouse.

We performed a 2 (Condition) x 4 (Distance) x 3 (Width) Repeated Measures ANOVA on the log-transformed movement data. The typical finding of increased movement time as D increases and W decreases was confirmed (i.e., as the task got more difficult: for D, $F(3, 15) = 709$, $p \ll 0.01$; for W, $F(2, 10) = 275$, $p \ll 0.01$). There was also a small interaction between Distance & Width, $F(6, 30)=8.9$, $p<0.01$—as D decreased, the size of the target, W, had a smaller effect on movement time. As hypothesized, there was large difference between conditions; the trackpad was faster than FlowMouse by 700 ms, $F(1, 5) = 555$, $p \ll 0.01$ (see Table 1).

Because FlowMouse was quite novel for our participants, we were interested in the performance of users with a bit more experience in using the device. Therefore, we looked at two other users who had several hours of practice using FlowMouse. As we hypothesized, a bit of practice resulted in a substantial improvement in performance, reducing the mean difference in conditions almost in half (only 400 ms difference for the experienced users, see Table 1).

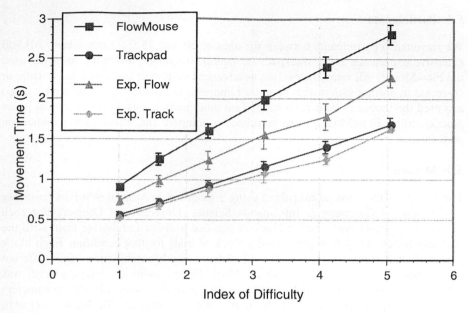

Fig. 3. Mean movement time (±SEM) versus Fitts index of difficulty ($ID=log_2(D/W +1)$)..
Circle & squares represent performance for the 6 novice users of FlowMouse. Triangles &
diamonds represent the performance for the 2 experienced users of FlowMouse.

To better characterize FlowMouse, we calculated the Fitts Index of Performance
(IP) for FlowMouse and the Trackpad. Fitts Law states that movement time is related
to the distance and width of the target being acquired ($MT = a + b \ log_2(D/W +1)$,
where a and b are device-dependent empirically derived constants. The inverse slope,
$1/b$, is referred to as the Index of Performance (IP) for a given device. This is often
used to compare the "bandwidth" of different devices (see [20] and [9] for more details). Fig. 3 plots the mean movement time versus ID for each device and participant
group (the 6 novice and 2 experienced users). IP was calculated from a linear regression on each line (see Table 1).

Note that the performance on the trackpad is very similar for both novice and experienced FlowMouse users. This is not surprising because both groups were very
experienced at using the trackpad. However, a few hours' practice resulted in a substantial improvement for the FlowMouse. This is very encouraging, as it suggests that

Table 1. Fitts index of performance (IP, the inverse slope of each line in) and the mean movement time (±SEM) for each condition. Note the large improvement in IP for the FlowMouse with
a small amount of practice.

	FlowMouse	Trackpad	Exp. Flow	Exp. Track
IP (bits/s)	2.15	3.70	2.76	3.84
Move Time (s)	1.70 (±0.11)	1.00 (±0.07)	1.33 (±0.15)	0.93 (±0.10)

a combination of device optimization and modest practice could result in performance similar to that of the trackpad.

Participants made several interesting subjective observations after using Flow-Mouse. All noted that it took a little while to "get the hang" of using it, but after 5 minutes or so, all of them found it quite intuitive. Surprisingly, the most common complaint was not with the FlowMouse *per se*, but the implementation of the touch sensor used to turn it on and off. The sensor was somewhat noisy and participants often had a hard time maintaining contact when they intended to.

Perhaps related to this issue with the touch sensor, the main difficulty for most users was in clutching. Most initially tried to clutch in the same way they would do so with a mouse or trackpad, but because the system tracked the movement of their hand as they clutched, this technique was generally frustrating. Most used the left hand touch sensor to turn off tracking during the clutch motion, but this coordination was somewhat difficult and unintuitive. One novice and both experienced participants adopted a different behavior for clutching. By exploiting the acceleration profile, it was possible to use differential slow and fast movement of the pointing hand to reset the hand position relative to the cursor. This was more intuitive and seemed to result in a generally better performance.

6 Beyond Pointing

For two-dimensional pointing tasks, it is sufficient to collapse the flow field information to a single direction and magnitude by averaging all nonzero points of the flow field. This average indicates the translation of the hand. But flow fields are able to express patterns of motion beyond translation and have been shown to be useful in gesture recognition tasks [8]. Fig. 4 shows flow field motions other than a simple translation. We consider a variety of interaction scenarios that are enabled by simple calculations on the flow field:

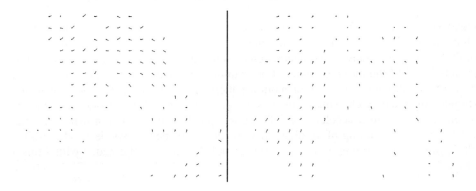

Fig. 4. Flow fields represent more than translation. Left: Flow field generated by clockwise rotation of the hand. Note how the flow field vectors lie along circles about the point of rotation. Right: Flow field generated by hand raising over keyboard. Here the flow vectors indicate an expansion about a point.

Freeform rotation, scaling, translation. An onscreen object may be simultaneously rotated, scaled and translated in 2D by constructing the transform matrix for a graphics object as the composition of rotation, scaling and translation parameters. In the appendix we present a mathematical framework for computing the simultaneous rotation, scaling and translation of the hand by computations on the flow field. If an application requires it, one or more of the three transforms may be ignored. For example, general object manipulation in a CAD program may make use of all transforms simultaneously, while rotating an onscreen knob may require only rotation information.

Change in hand height to zoom. By the same mathematical technique a change in the height of the hand over the keyboard can be detected as a scaling of the flow field. This may be useful for interfaces with zooming functionality, such as mapping programs or other spatial displays.

Tilt. By extension of the mathematical framework presented in the appendix, it may be possible to extract the hand's tilting in and out of the plane of the keyboard. This could be useful for "open" or "reveal" gestures, as well as with CAD object manipulation. Tilt could be used to change the attitude of the user's viewpoint in a virtual environment for navigation, including games in which the player controls a vehicle (e.g., airplane). See [4] for related mathematical techniques for extracting object pose in a controller device setting more generally.

Two-dimensional scrolling or panning. FlowMouse may be used for pointer based interactions that are complementary to cursor control. For example, the average (dx, dy) may be mapped to two-dimensional scrolling. This panning mode may be triggered by detecting that the user has spread the hand fully, to effect a rather direct analogue of the hand icon found in many drawing and mapping applications. Scrolling or panning with FlowMouse with the non-dominant hand may complement simultaneous use of the conventional mouse for precise selection tasks [12].

Gesture modulation based on size or shape. The approximate size of the moving object under the camera may be determined by counting the number of nonzero points in the flow field. Many of the interactions discussed here may be modulated based on detected size of the moving object. For example, the mouse acceleration profile may be related to object size: smaller motion patterns resulting from the movement of a single finger can yield small amounts of acceleration, while whole hand motion results in the greatest acceleration. This corresponds with the notion that in the real world, gross positioning of an object may be accomplished by whole-hand grasping, while precise positioning may be better accomplished by a gentle nudge with a finger or two.

Simple gesture recognition. Strong motion patterns detected over a short duration of time may be set to trigger application commands such as "next", "previous", "up", "down", "delete", "dismiss", "minimize", "reveal", etc. [27]. Simple gestures may have their use in short fleeting interactions that do not warrant the burden of fully acquiring the mouse and keyboard, such as in advancing a slide during a presentation, changing the track or volume on media playback, and in other "casual" computing settings.

Marking menus. Marking menus typically arrange menu options in a circular fashion around a given point on the screen, like slices of a pie, and so do not require precise cursor positioning along the usual menu items [17]. As such, the coarse relative motion provided by FlowMouse may be well suited to marking menus. The application of marking menus to vision-based UIs is discussed in [18].

Two handed interactions. Simple clustering techniques on the position of flow vectors or on their dominant directions of movement (as in [8]) may be used to detect the motion of two hands under the camera. Various two-handed interactions would thus be enabled (see [6] and [12] for examples).

Finally we note that the camera enables a variety of other camera-based interaction scenarios not limited to optical flow. For example, visual tags or barcodes placed on documents on other objects may be recognized [23]. For a fixed camera looking at the keyboard, it would be possible to detect which key the user is about to press and exploit that in some interaction, perhaps in presenting tooltips or status. A camera that can be re-oriented can be used in video conferencing scenarios.

7 Conclusion

FlowMouse is a computer vision-based pointing and gesture input device which relies on optical flow computation where most previous related works uses more fragile object tracking techniques. FlowMouse makes few assumptions regarding the appearance or color of the user's hand, but instead is driven by analysis of the motion patterns indicated in the optical flow field.

The relative motion indicated by the optical flow field may be used for cursor positioning tasks much in the same manner that an optical mouse recovers velocity by image correlation techniques. Our first FlowMouse prototype relies on a touch sensor on the left mouse button for a clutching mechanism. We conducted a Fitts law study which demonstrated that while pointing performance with FlowMouse was significantly worse than with a trackpad, subjects were able to use FlowMouse successfully. Encouragingly, there is some indication that users are able to improve performance dramatically with practice.

The optical flow field derived from hand motion is able to express more than simple translation. We outline a number of interaction scenarios which make use of the rich motion information present in the optical flow field, such as rotation and scaling effects. Furthermore, we note some scenarios where FlowMouse may complement the mouse, such as simultaneously pointing and panning.

In the same way that today's pointing devices are the product of years of engineering refinement, FlowMouse can take advantage of numerous technical improvements to enhance pointing performance. For example, faster cameras are available today, and better optical flow techniques can be used to obtain flow fields of higher quality.

However, we believe that FlowMouse and related devices will ultimately make the most impact in providing a channel of input that is richer and more expressive than that of today's pointing devices. FlowMouse in particular is focused at capturing the richness and subtlety of human motion for novel interactions while offering a kind of "backwards compatibility" with today's point-and-click interfaces. By way of extending today's interfaces, rather than replacing them completely, we hope that novel devices such as FlowMouse will find easier paths to adoption and present opportunities for significant user interface innovation.

References

1. Anandan, P., *A Computational Framework and Algorithm for the Measurement of Visual Motion*. International Journal of Computer Vision, 1989. **2**: p. 283-310.
2. Barron, J., D. Fleet, S. Beauchemin, and T. Burkitt. *Performance of Optical Flow Techniques*. in *Computer Vision and Pattern Recognition*. 1992.
3. Bathiche, S., *Pointer Ballistics for Windows XP*, in *http://www.microsoft.com/whdc/device/input/pointer-bal.mspx*. 2002.
4. Bradski, G., V. Eruhimov, S. Molinov, V. Mosyagin, and V. Pisarevsky. *A Video Joystick from a Toy*. in *Proceedings of the 2001 Workshop on Perceptive User Interfaces*. 2001.
5. Buxton, W. *A Three-State Model of Graphical Input*. in *INTERACT '90*. 1990.
6. Buxton, W., and B. Meyers. *A Study in Two-Handed Input*. in *Proc. of CHI '86: ACM Conference on Human Factors in Computing Systems*. 1986.
7. Cao, X., and R. Balakrishnan. *VisionWand: Interaction Techniques for Large Displays Using a Passive Wand Tracked in 3D*. in *ACM Symposium on User Interface Software and Technology*. 2003.
8. Cutler, R., and M. Turk. *View-based Interpretation of Real-time Optical Flow for Gesture Recognition*. in *IEEE Conference on Automatic Face and Gesture Recognition*. 1998.
9. Douglas, S., A. Kirkpatrick, and I. S. MacKenzie. *Testing Pointing Device Performance and User Assessment with the ISO 9241, Part 9 Standard*. in *Proc. CHI'99*. 1999.
10. Fitzmaurice, G.W., H. Ishii, and W. Buxton. *Bricks: Laying the Foundations for Graspable User Interfaces*. in *Proceedings of CHI 1995*. 1995.
11. Hinckley, K., and M. Sinclair. *Touch-Sensing Input Devices*. in *ACM CHI 1999 Conference on Human Factors in Computing Systems*. 1999.
12. Hinckley, K., R. Pausch, D. Proffitt, and N. Kassell. *Interaction and Modeling Techniques for Desktop Two-Handed Input*. in *ACM UIST 1998 Symposium on User Interface Software & Technology*. 1998.
13. Horn, B.K.P., *Closed Form Solution of Absolute Orientation Using Unit Quaternions*. Journal of the Optical Society, 1987. **4**(4): p. 629-642.
14. Jellinek, H.D., and S. K. Card. *Powermice and User Performance*. in *SIGCHI Conference on Human Factors in Computing Systems*. 1990.
15. Kjeldsen, R., and J. Kender. *Interaction with On-Screen Objects Using Visual Gesture Recogntion*. in *CVPR '97*. 1997.
16. Krueger, M., *Artificial Reality II*. 1991: Addison-Wesley.
17. Kurtenbach, G., and W. Buxton. *The Limits of Expert Performance Using Hierarchic Marking Menus*. in *Proceedings of InterCHI '93*. 1993.
18. Lenman, S., L. Bretzner, and B. Thuresson. *Using Marking Menus to Develop Command Sets for Computer Vision Based Hand Gesture Interfaces*. in *Proceedings of the Second Nordic Conference On Human-Computer Interaction*. 2002.
19. Letessier, J., and F. Berard. *Visual Tracking of Bare Fingers for Interactive Surfaces*. in *ACM Symposium on User Interface Software and Technology*. 2004.

20. MacKenize, I.S., *Fitts' Law as Research and Design Tool in Human-Computer Interaction*, in *Human-Computer Interaction 1992*. 1992. p. 91-139.
21. Quek, F., T. Mysliwiec and M. Zhao. *FingerMouse: A Freehand Computer Pointing Interface*. in *Proc. of Int'l Conf. on Automatic Face and Gesture Recognition*. 1995.
22. Rekimoto, J. *ThumbSense: Automatic Mode Sensing for Touchpad-based Interactions*. in *CHI 2003 Late Breaking Results*. 2003.
23. Rekimoto, J., and Y. Ayatsuka. *CyberCode: Designing Augmented Reality Environments with Visual Tags*. in *Designing Augmented Reality Environments (DARE 2000)*. 2000.
24. Turk, M., and G. Robertson, *Perceptual User Interfaces*. Communications of the ACM, 2000.
25. Wellner, P., *Interacting with Paper on the DigitalDesk*. Communications of the ACM, 1993. **36**(7): p. 86-97.
26. Wilson, A. *TouchLight: An Imaging Touch Screen and Display for Gesture-Based Interaction*. in *International Conference on Multimodal Interfaces*. 2004.
27. Wilson, A., and N. Oliver. *GWindows: Towards Robust Perception-Based UI*. in *First IEEE Workshop on Computer Vision and Pattern Recognition for Human Computer Interaction*. 2003.
28. Wu, M., and R. Balakrishnan. *Multi-finger and Whole Hand Gestural Interaction Techniques for Multi-User Tabletop Displays*. in *ACM Symposium on User Interface Software and Technology*. 2003.

Appendix

We present a technique where a flow field may be characterized as simultaneous rotation in the image plane, uniform scaling, and two-dimensional translation. If the hand is mostly rigid, this technique can be used to determine change in the hand orientation in the image plane, change in height above the keyboard, and so on.

For the flow field described by $\mathbf{x}_i = [x_i \quad y_i]^T$ and $\mathbf{dx}_i = [dx_i \quad dy_i]^T$, each point $\mathbf{x}_i$ moves to $\mathbf{x}_i' = [x_i' \quad y_i']^T = \mathbf{x}_i + \mathbf{dx}_i$ by rotation θ in the image plane, uniform scaling s and translation $\mathbf{t}$:

$$\mathbf{R} = \begin{bmatrix} \cos\theta & -\sin\theta \\ \sin\theta & \cos\theta \end{bmatrix} \tag{4}$$

$$\mathbf{x}_i' = s\mathbf{R}\mathbf{x}_i + \mathbf{t} \tag{5}$$

We first solve for rotation. With means $\bar{\mathbf{x}} = \dfrac{1}{N}\sum_i \mathbf{x}_i$ and $\bar{\mathbf{x}}' = \dfrac{1}{N}\sum_i \mathbf{x}_i'$ we may solve for θ [13]:

$$\tan\theta = \left[\frac{\sum_i (x_i - \bar{x})(y_i' - \bar{y}') - (y_i - \bar{y})(x_i' - \bar{x}')}{\sum_i (x_i - \bar{x})(x_i' - \bar{x}') + (y_i - \bar{y})(y_i' - \bar{y}')} \right] \tag{6}$$

Scaling factor s and translation $\mathbf{t} = \begin{bmatrix} t_x & t_y \end{bmatrix}^T$ may be recovered by least squares:

$$\mathbf{z} = \begin{bmatrix} s & t_x & t_y \end{bmatrix}^T \tag{7}$$

$$\mathbf{M}_i = \begin{bmatrix} \mathbf{Rx}_i & \begin{matrix} 1 & 0 \\ 0 & 1 \end{matrix} \end{bmatrix} \tag{8}$$

$$\mathbf{x}_i' = \mathbf{M}_i \mathbf{z} \tag{9}$$

$$\mathbf{z} = \left(\sum_i \mathbf{x}_i'^T \mathbf{M}_i \right) \left(\sum_i \mathbf{M}_i^T \mathbf{M}_i \right)^{-1} \tag{10}$$

It may not be obvious that this formulation allows for rotation and scaling about any point. For example, consider rotation about a point $\mathbf{t}_R$:

$$
\begin{aligned}
\mathbf{x}_i' &= s(\mathbf{R}(\mathbf{x}_i - \mathbf{t}_R) + \mathbf{t}_R) + \mathbf{t} \\
&= s\mathbf{R}\mathbf{x}_i + \mathbf{t}'
\end{aligned}
\tag{11}
$$

where with $\mathbf{t}' = -s\mathbf{R}\mathbf{t}_R + s\mathbf{t}_R + \mathbf{t}$ we arrive at the original form of equation 5.

Context of Use Evaluation of Peripheral Displays (CUEPD)

N. Sadat Shami, Gilly Leshed, and David Klein

Cornell University Information Science Program,
301 College Ave., Ithaca, NY 14850, USA
{sadat, gilly, dik4}@cornell.edu

Abstract. A gap exists between the growing prevalence of peripheral displays and appropriate methods for their evaluation. Mankoff et al. [11] present one attempt to bridge this gap by adapting Nielsen's Heuristic evaluation to the defining characteristics and goals of peripheral displays. In this paper, we present a complementary approach that depends on active user participation and emphasizes the experience of using peripheral displays. The Context of Use Evaluation of Peripheral Displays (CUEPD) captures context of use through individualized scenario building, enactment and reflection. We illustrate the CUEPD method in a study to evaluate two peripheral displays. The evaluation using CUEPD revealed important design recommendations, suggesting that the method may be an important advance in evaluation methods for peripheral displays.

1 Introduction

Increasingly, information is being displayed in the periphery of our attention. These *peripheral displays* are designed to move back and forth between the center and periphery of a user's attention since they require minimal cognitive processing. As a result, they allow users to focus on a primary task while maintaining opportunistic awareness of a secondary task [15]. McCrickard et al. suggest a classification of these types of displays, according to three critical parameters – interruption, reaction and comprehension (IRC) [13]. Each display receives a rating between 0 and 1 on each of the three IRC parameters. For example, an onboard vehicle navigation system invokes moment to moment reaction by prompting turns along the road without causing interruption or requiring deep comprehension about the route. As such, it will receive an IRC rating of (010). An instant messaging program notifies users of arrival of new email and when a contact logs in. A user can then attend to important emails or communicate with a contact by redirecting activity as necessary. Such an instant messaging program would receive an IRC rating of (110). In this paper, we focus on the set of displays that receive ratings of 0 on interruption and between 0 and 1 on both reaction and comprehension.

The research on peripheral displays has focused primarily on their design rather than on methods of evaluating them [11]. These displays are difficult to evaluate [1,11,13]. Traditional HCI evaluation methods focus on productivity oriented metrics such as successful task completion rates, time taken for completion, error rates etc. It

M.F. Costabile and F. Paternò (Eds.): INTERACT 2005, LNCS 3585, pp. 579–587, 2005.
© IFIP International Federation for Information Processing 2005

is difficult to use these metrics for measuring perception and attention [10,11]. Furthermore, traditional evaluation methods focus on how successfully a system supports a user's primary task. But peripheral displays are about secondary tasks. For example, results obtained from a study that had users simply use a vehicle navigation system as a primary task would not be as meaningful as a study that had users drive while using the navigation system. This difference in the nature of peripheral displays compared to other systems highlights the need for an evaluation method tailored for peripheral displays.

Most of the designs of peripheral displays published in the literature have been evaluated through ethnographic methods [2,8,9], some through controlled experiments [12,18], others by a combination of the above [3], while some have not been evaluated at all [4,5,7,17]. To the best of our knowledge, only one method has been explicitly developed to evaluate peripheral displays. Mankoff et al. extend Nielsen's Heuristic Evaluation by modifying his set of heuristics to fit peripheral displays. Their discount evaluation method provides guidance during the early stages of design by reminding designers about usability principles [11]. Typically, different evaluation methods are used at different stages of the design process [14]. In this paper, we introduce the Context of Use Evaluation of Peripheral Displays (CUEPD – *pronounced cupid*), which can be used when designers have at least a working prototype and are interested in improving its future design. As such, CUEPD is complementary to Mankoff et al.'s method as it is used later on in the design process.

2   Context of Use Evaluation of Peripheral Displays (CUEPD)

As one of two research challenges facing the ubiquitous computing field, Abowd & Mynatt emphasize the importance of developing evaluation methods that capture the context in which a system is used [1]. Context of use refers to the setting in which a display is employed and it is assumed to influence our attention and perception. For example, the human 'spotlight of attention' may or may not focus on the information a display attempts to convey because of its surrounding context. It is noteworthy that moving from a primary to a secondary task and back is not only about switching visual focus, but also about the cognitive processing necessary to perform such action.

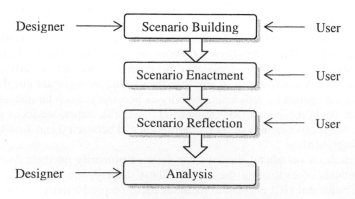

Fig. 1. Conceptual model of CUEPD

We describe the stages of CUEPD below, explaining how context of use is captured at each stage. A conceptual model of CUEPD is displayed in Figure 1. We stress the fact that users need not be familiar with the evaluation method or have evaluation experience to participate. The only requirement is that they be potential users of the display.

2.1 Scenario Building

The first step of CUEPD is a question and answer session between the designer and a user with the purpose of creating a scenario that captures how the information presented in the display is accessed. The designer asks questions on how the user accesses the *information* presented in the display, rather than the display itself. For example, in an evaluation of a peripheral network monitor displayed on a computer desktop, the designer would ask a system administrator about ways she monitors network traffic. Based on the answers that the user provides, the designer creates a scenario of use that the user will act out. Within the scenario, the designer will identify one or more primary tasks for the user to complete while providing the opportunity to access the peripheral display. In the network monitor evaluation example, the designer could create a scenario where installing software patches and creating new accounts on the system are primary tasks, and keeping track of network traffic is the secondary task. This manner of scenario building is a departure from traditional scenario-based design since a designer and user collaboratively construct a scenario, as opposed to designers doing it themselves. Working together with the user to build a scenario allows the peripheral display to be evaluated in the context of how an individual would use it in a real situation.

2.2 Scenario Enactment

Once the scenario has been developed and described to the user, the user performs the primary task while having the opportunity to access the display. Note that accessing the display is never the primary task. In fact, during the primary task, the peripheral display should not be at the center of a user's attention. However, once the peripheral display is noticed and accessed, it then moves from the periphery of a user's attention to the center. Evaluating if and how users use a peripheral display within the context of a primary task allows designers to determine how easily the display moves back and forth between the periphery and center of a user's attention.

2.3 Scenario Reflection

After acting out the scenario, users are given a 10 item questionnaire to fill out. The questionnaire design was informed by our literature review of defining attributes of peripheral displays. We believe the best way to get users to articulate strengths and weaknesses of the design of a peripheral display are to frame questions based on its defining attributes. Mankoff et al. took a similar approach when they focused on definitional attributes of peripheral displays to modify Nielsen's Heuristics [11]. We used an iterative approach to determine the questions on the questionnaire. Certain questions were modified based on initial responses from participants. We identified five categories representing definitional attributes of peripheral displays, and developed questions that address our categories, as listed in Table 1. The categories reflect the trade-offs in designing peripheral displays. For example, a peripheral display should be *noticeable* and allow for *division of attention* at the same time. It should provide *comprehensible* and *relevant* information yet be *engaging*. Rating high on all these categories is a challenge for designers.

Table 1. Questionnaire questions grouped by category

Noticeability
Q 1. Did you notice the display?
Q 7. While performing your primary task were you aware of the opportunity to access the display?
Comprehension
Q 2. Were you able to understand the information in the display?
Q 5. Were you able to understand the information just by glancing at it?
Relevance
Q 3. Did the display provide you the information you needed?
Division of attention
Q 4. Was the display located outside the focus of your attention?
Q 6. Were you able to adequately focus on your primary task?
Q 8. Were you able to shift your attention between your primary task and the display smoothly?
Engagement
Q 9. Did you find the design of the display attractive?
Q 10. Did you enjoy using the display?

Each question in our questionnaire was followed by a 'Yes/No' option and space for an open-ended response. By asking users to choose between 'Yes' and 'No' we attempted to give designers clear feedback regarding aspects of design, while at the same time allowing participants to express themselves in the open-ended portion of the response. In the end, we found that the explanations were the most useful part of the questionnaire because they provided more information about how the display mapped onto the user experience.

2.4 Analysis

The analysis focuses on how well the display addresses the five categories described above. For each question, the designer assigns 1 for a positive and 0 for a negative response, based on the 'Yes/No' answer and explanation provided in the open-ended response. Next the numeric values are averaged in the following way for each category:

$$\frac{\text{positive responses}}{\text{questions in category} \times \text{users}} \tag{1}$$

A high or low rating is an early indicator of which category's open ended responses should be looked at first. Those explanations then allow for in-depth interpretation regarding the user's experience. The numeric values also provide approximations on how well the display performs on the five categories.

3   Testing the CUEPD Method

We subsequently tested CUEPD on real peripheral displays. Gray and Salzman argue that comparative studies of evaluation methods often suffer validity weaknesses, following different settings and metrics measured by each method [6]. As a result, relative effectiveness of one method over the other can hardly be trusted. Therefore, we tested our method independently to see whether it was effective in capturing context of use in peripheral displays.

3.1   Displays Used

We evaluated two displays, which are both relatively common. One was a peripheral display for a computer desktop called 'Weather Watcher' (a free download at http://www.singerscreations.com/), as shown in Figure 2. The other display was a stock ticker located along the entrance corridor of the Business School of a large northeastern university (Figure 3). We chose these two because we wanted to check the validity of CUEPD on both 'virtual' and 'tangible' peripheral displays. Our focus was not to evaluate these displays *per se*, but rather to determine whether CUEPD was effective in evaluating them. The Weather Watcher and stock ticker both act as passive displays providing information that needs to be comprehended without interrupting users and sometimes requiring them to react to the information. Consequently, they would both receive IRC rankings of (0/0.5/1) in the context of our evaluation.

Fig. 2. Weather Watcher display showing 31 degrees

Fig. 3. The stock ticker is above the TV screens

3.2 Participants

The participants we recruited were undergraduate, graduate and MBA students of the same large northeastern university. They received a $10 gift certificate in exchange for their participation. 95% of participants had been using computers and the internet for more than 5 years. In the Weather Watcher evaluation, we had 7 undergraduate and 3 graduate students, with 80% having little or no self reported experience evaluating a system/software, and 20% having between 1 and 3 years of experience. In the stock ticker evaluation, we had 9 MBA students and 1 fourth year undergraduate business student, with 60% having no evaluation experience at all and 40% having between 1 and 3 years of experience. None of the Weather Watcher participants were previously familiar with the software while the business students were acquainted with the stock ticker at the entrance to their building.

3.3 Procedure and Task

The Weather Watcher evaluation was conducted on a laptop computer that had the software installed on it. The stock ticker evaluation took place near the location of the stock ticker at the Business School. After filling out a pre-task questionnaire on demographics and prior evaluation experience, participants were guided through the stages of CUEPD. Typical scenarios for the Weather Watcher included checking email and reading online news as primary tasks. Typical scenarios for the stock ticker included entering the business school to go to class or to the library as primary tasks. Accessing information from the displays was a secondary task in all these scenarios. With permission of participants, the scenario building conversation was recorded. Participants then acted out the scenario and completed our questionnaire.

4 Results

Table 2 presents the category ratings for the Weather Watcher and stock ticker using CUEPD. To verify the reliability of the results, the questionnaire data was coded independently by two coders. Inter-coder reliability using Cohen's Kappa was a satisfactory 0.905 and 0.865 for Weather Watcher and stock ticker evaluations respectively.

Table 2. Weather Watcher and Stock Ticker ratings

Category	Weather Watcher	Stock Ticker
Noticeability	71%	62%
Comprehension	67%	69%
Relevance	56%	13%
Division of attention	80%	63%
Engagement	60%	73%

We report how CUEPD allowed us to arrive at design recommendations. From Table 2, we see Weather Watcher received the highest favorable rating on *division of attention*. That alerted us to look at the open ended responses in that category to determine why. One Weather Watcher participant reported that it was "small enough not to distract a lot but big enough to be readable and noticeable." Since *division of attention* involves a trade-off with *noticeability*, we then read explanations in that category. We found participants reporting that "I forgot it was there" and "it did not 'jump' at me", which might explain why it rated high in *division of attention* but lower in *noticeability*.

For the stock ticker, we see that it received its lowest rating on *relevance*. According to the open ended responses in that category, users reported that "the individual company stickers were pretty random" and lacked "overall levels of indexes". It also ranked relatively low in *noticeability*. Participants reported that it was located "too high." As location is part of context, CUEPD was successful in creating a contextual setting that facilitated such responses.

To improve *noticeability* in the Weather Watcher, we suggest adding a meteorological symbol in the background of the temperature figure, i.e. a cloud or the sun, to emphasize the relation of the number to weather information. The *relevance* of the stock ticker can be improved by presenting both specific stock information in a predetermined order and general trends/indexes of the market. Suggestions for *noticeability* include relocating the display lower and in front of the entrance rather than on the side wall. These suggestions illustrate how CUEPD provides practical design recommendations for peripheral displays.

5 Discussion

Our study suggests that CUEPD is a functional evaluation method for peripheral displays that captures context of real use through scenario building, enactment, and reflection. Rosson & Carroll describe the use of scenarios as a basis for usability evaluation [16]. We take this approach further, allowing for potential individual differences and preferences by customizing the scenarios to each user. This 'participatory' evaluation advances traditional scenario-based methods as the designer and user collaboratively construct the scenario. If recorded, as we did in our study, a repository of scenarios is produced, facilitating the understanding of typical uses, as well as unintended ones. Under CUEPD, there is a possibility that each participant might receive a different scenario, which we believe would produce a set of valuable information for the designer. In particular, the different scenarios would qualify the numeric ratings, and illustrate the importance of the qualitative responses in evaluating a display within its context of use. In that sense, CUEPD is in the direction of evaluation methods that go beyond usability and attempt to measure experience.

The primary vs. secondary task is an important distinction for capturing context of use. For example, Plaue et al. successfully evaluated recall of data presented in peripheral displays in a *primary task* setting [15]. In contrast, CUEPD requires users to focus on a task apart from the display, which enables an evaluation of the ease of switching between primary and secondary tasks, an important characteristic of peripheral displays. Maglio & Campbell evaluated scrolling text displays through a series of experiments using a primary task/secondary task distinction [12]. However, their study was not intended to be a formal evaluation method for peripheral displays.

Since time to market is a critical factor nowadays, CUEPD is useful in eliciting valuable user feedback without requiring a lot of time commitment. It took on average half an hour for us to conduct our study with each participant. Furthermore, CUEPD can be easily applied with average users that have little or no evaluation experience. The majority of participants in our study did not have substantial evaluation experience. With increasing demand for discount evaluation methods, CUEPD is similar to the endeavor of Mankoff et al. to produce such methods [11].

6 Conclusion and Future Work

In this study, we combined an approach of tailoring an existing evaluation method for specific systems, e.g. in [11], with the call to develop evaluation methods that capture context of use [1]. The result, CUEPD, can either be used to evaluate already deployed systems, such as the stock ticker, or working prototypes, as demonstrated by the Weather Watcher. We fully expect that as our method is used and tested, it will evolve, as other evaluation methods have evolved. While we have focused on McCrickard's [13] parameters of reaction and comprehension, future work could extend to displays having high levels of interruption as well.

Designers select methods for evaluating their design from a repository of evaluation methods [14]. Our method serves as a useful addition to the evaluation methods designers of peripheral displays have at their disposal.

Acknowledgements

This research was supported by the funding of Jeff Hancock. We thank Kirsten Boehner, Nathan Bos, Matt Brochstein, Anind Dey, Geri Gay, Jeff Hancock, Elaine Huang, and Joseph Kaye for their valuable comments on previous drafts.

References

1. Abowd, G.D., Mynatt, E.D. Charting past, present, and future research in ubiquitous computing. *ACM Trans. Comp.-Hum Inter. 7, 1,* (2000), 29-58.
2. Cadiz, J. J., Venolia, G., Jancke, G., Gupta, A. Designing and deploying an information awareness interface. In *Proc. CSCW 2002,* ACM Press (2002).
3. Denoue, L., Nelson, L., Churchill, E. AttrActive windows: dynamic windows for digital bulletin boards. *Ext. Abstracts CHI 2003,* ACM Press (2003).
4. Dieberger, A. Supporting collaboration through passing informal notes to peripheral displays. *Ext. Abstracts CHI 2002,* ACM Press (2002).
5. Gaver, B. Provocative Awareness. *Computer Supported Cooperative Work, 11,* (2002), 475-493.
6. Gray, W.D., Salzman, M.C. Damaged Merchandise? A review of experiments that compare usability evaluation methods. *Hum. Comp. Inter. 13,* (1998), 203-261

7. Heiner, J., Hudson, S., and Tanaka, K. The Information Percolator: Ambient Information Display in a Decorative Object. In *Proc. UIST 1999,* ACM Press (1999), 141-148.

8. Huang, E. M., Mynatt, E. D. Semi-public displays for small, co-located groups. In *Proc. CHI 2003,* ACM Press (2003).

9. Huang, E. M., Tullio, J., Costa, T. J., McCarthy, J. F. Promoting awareness of work activities through peripheral displays. *Ext. Abstracts CHI 2002,* ACM Press (2002).

10. Karat, J. Beyond Task Completion: Evaluation of Affective Components of Use. In J. Jacko and A. Sears (Eds.), *The Human Computer Interaction Handbook.* LEA, 2003.

11. Mankoff, J., Dey, A. K., Hsieh, G., Kientz, J., Lederer, S., Ames, M. Heuristic evaluation of ambient displays. In *Proc. CHI 2003,* ACM Press (2003).

12. Maglio, P. P., Campbell, C. S. Tradeoffs in displaying peripheral information. In *Proc. CHI 2000,* ACM Press (2000).

13. McCrickard, D. S., Chewar, C.M., Somervell, J.P., Ndiwalana, A. A model for notification systems evaluation – Assessing user goals for multitasking activity. *ACM Trans. Comp.- Hum. Inter. 10, 4,* (2003).

14. Olson, J. S., Moran, T. P. Mapping the method muddle: Guidance in using methods for user interface design. In M. Rudisill, C. Lewis, P. B., Polson, and T. D. McKay, (Eds.), *Human-Computer Interface Design: Success Stories, Emerging Methods and Real-World Context,* Morgan Kaufmann, San Mateo, Calif, 1996.

15. Plaue, C., Miller, T., Stasko, J. Is a picture worth a thousand words? An evaluation of information awareness displays. In *Proc. Graphics interface* (2004).

16. Rosson, M., and Carroll, J., M. Scenario-based design. In J. Jacko and A. Sears (Eds.), *The Hum. Comp. Inter. Handbook.* LEA, 2003.

17. Skog, T. Activity wallpaper: ambient visualization of activity information. In *Proc. DIS 2004,* ACM Press (2004).

18. Tyman, J., Huang, E. M. Intuitive visualizations for presence and recency information for ambient displays. *Ext. Abstracts CHI 2003,* ACM Press (2003).

Improving Cell Phone Awareness by Using Calendar Information

Ashraf Khalil and Kay Connelly

Department of Computer Science, Indiana University,
Bloomington, IN, 47405
{akhalil, connelly}@cs.indiana.edu

Abstract. The many benefits that cell phones provide are at times overshadowed by the problems they create, as when one person's cell phone disrupts a group activity, such as a class, meeting or movie. Cell phone interruption is only highlighted by the ever increasing number of mobile devices we carry. Many tools and techniques have been proposed in order to minimize interruption caused by mobile devices. In the current study, we use calendar information to infer users' activity and to automatically configure cell phones accordingly. Our in-situ experiment uses PDAs that run a cell phone simulator to examine the feasibility and design factors of such a solution. Our results show that both structured activities and appropriate cell phone configuration can be predicted with high accuracy using the calendar information. The results also show consistent mapping of activities to configuration for each individual. However there was a poor consistency of mapping activity to configuration across different participants. We discuss the results in relation to inaccuracy, spontaneous activities, and user reactions.

1 Introduction

With the increasing number of mobile devices that seek users' attention, it is essential to minimize interruptions and distractions caused to the users and the surrounding environment. Garlan et. al. notes that human attention is becoming the most precious and scarce resource, considerably more so than computational power [1]. Cell phones, with all the services they provide such as phone calls, reminders, text and instant messages, are the prime example of mobile devices that demand constant cognitive attention from the user and also serve as a frequent source of interruption and distraction. Cell phones are currently the most ubiquitous communication device the world over [2]. The tremendous growth of cell phones' usage and their location-free nature have helped to establish a new social order. This social order has been described as a shift from Place-to-Place communication to Person-to-Person communication [3].

The benefits offered by cell phones, such as flexibility and accessibility, seem to inevitably come with the cost of increased interruption and interaction demands. Interruption caused by inappropriate notification such as ringing in a meeting can cause inconvenience, disruption and embarrassment for the owner. The effect of interruptions has been shown to be disruptive to task performance even when the

M.F. Costabile and F. Paternò (Eds.): INTERACT 2005, LNCS 3585, pp. 588–600, 2005.
© IFIP International Federation for Information Processing 2005

interruption is ignored [4]. Even worse, interruption may also lead to an increased level of stress and errors [5, 6]. Interruption is not limited to the owner of the cell phone only but extends to the surrounding environment as well. Kern et al [7] have introduced and validated a model for interruptibility wherein they distinguish between interruption to user's environment "social interruptability" and interruption to the user him or herself "personal interruptability". The cell phone's social interruptibility is further confirmed by studies that show most people consider the use of cell phones in public places to be annoying [8, 9]. Bautsch, et. al [10] found that most people think there should be etiquette guidelines created for public mobile phone use.

All the problems mentioned above are usually caused by the static nature of cell phone configurations and their inability to automatically change their setting according to the context of the surrounding environment. This, in turn, creates a mismatch between a phone's setting and the context of the space it occupies. Many people change their cell phone setting every time they are in a new context. This solution is both inconvenient and inadequate since in many cases the user forgets to change the setting. Other people just keep their cell phone in silent mode, but that results in their missing many important calls.

In this paper, we present an approach that aims to improve the awareness of cell phones by using information from the calendar book, which already exists in most cell phones and all current smart phones. The information in the calendar book is used to determine the most suitable configuration for the cell phone. In order to examine the validity and effectiveness of this solution, many questions need to be explored first. Its real value greatly depends on the accuracy of the predicted context based on the scheduled activities. Given the inevitable fact that people's actions do not always mirror their intentions, scheduling events and activities does not necessarily ensure attendance.

With this in mind, the accuracy of the information provided by the calendar must be carefully considered, along with the tendency of users to carry out their plans as written in the calendar. A related question to be asked concerns the effect of spontaneous and unscheduled activities on the predictability of calendar-based configuration. Further, can users predict the best configuration for specific activities? Is there consistent mapping between context and configuration? Given that people's sense of control decreases as a cell phone's autonomous capabilities increases [11], and given the personal connection people feel toward their cell phones, would people welcome the idea of more aware and autonomous cell phones? How much control are users willing to give up in exchange for the convenience offered by the system? Finally, how can we account for the differences in people's perception of the appropriateness of the same level of interruption?

To answer the above questions, we have conducted an in situ experiment in a dynamic campus setting. During the experiment, participants were asked to fill in their calendar information regularly in the PDA we supplied. Every PDA ran an application designed to simulate a smart cell phone. The application simulated phone calls at random times during the day, prompting participants to evaluate the appropriateness of the configuration and to specify their current activity and location. The application acquired and stored evaluation data from participants during the study. More data was collected through end-of-study interviews to examine the overall evaluation of the calendar-based solution.

Section 2 examines the existing solutions to this problem at hand. We describe the strengths of the calendar book as a solution in Section 3, and give the details of our in-situ user study in Section 4. Section 5 documents our results, including the accuracy of calendar information, the consistency of the mappings between context and configuration in our user population participants', and evaluations of calendar-based configuration. We conclude our findings in Section 6.

2   Calendar as a Context Provider

All current smart phones and most other regular cell phones come equipped with a calendar book. The calendar book usually serves as a personal organizer and is a valuable resource for organizing daily activities and schedules. Naturally, calendar information provides very important and reliable cues about the availability, location, and surrounding environment of the user. For example, if the calendar has a meeting appointment from 1pm to 2 pm we know with a high degree of probability that the user is unavailable and he is in a place with at least one other person. Such information indicates that any incoming interruption should be kept minimal and only the most urgent ones should be allowed to go though with a very discreet notification mechanism. Such cues are available for free and we predict they are usually accurate.

Calendars provide simple and inexpensive contextual information. By inexpensive, we mean that no sensors or computations are needed to infer the contextual information. Furthermore we predict this information to be highly accurate since in most cases the user fills in the entries that are of high importance and that she intends to attend. This information can be used by cell phones in order to dynamically and automatically change their configuration, or settings, in a way that received calls are least disruptive to both the user and the surrounding environment.

It remains unclear, however, to what extent cell phone calendars are actually used. We have not found any studies that examine the usage pattern of a cell phone's calendar, although many studies have been conducted to examine the mobile Personal Information Management's (PIM) usage behavior, task management, and efficiency of information retrieval [12]. PIM is an essential set of tools that exists in almost all personal digital assistants (PDAs) as well as many smart phones and includes a calendar application in addition to task list, contact, and memo applications. In a recent study we conducted involving 20 cell phone users, we found that a cell phone's calendar is rarely used, or when it is used, it serves as a reminder rather than as a scheduler. However, we expect this to change in the near future as regular cell phones converge into smart phones that include many PDA-like capabilities. Smart phones usually offer better user interface and communication capabilities. Enhanced interaction capabilities such as bigger touch-screen displays and a QWERTY keyboard provide for easier user input and enable users to make better use of PIM applications, including the calendar. Moreover, the enhanced communication capabilities such as Bluetooth and infrared enable users to synchronize their calendar information and other data with their PC. Thus, even if users utilize other electronic calendar devices, the information can easily be transferred to and used by their smart phone.

3   Related Work

Calendar information has long been used as a valuable resource for information in several research projects. The Coordinate system, for example, uses the calendar information and previous computer activities to predict the availability of a person on a particular computing device [13]. MyVine system uses calendar information in addition to many other cues, such as a speech detection sensor, to model a person's availability for communication [14]. The Ambush system extends the calendar via a Bayesian approach to predict the likelihood of one's attendance at the event listed in one's calendar [15]. The context-aware Office Assistant uses a person's calendar to inform a personal agent of available meeting times for visitors at the person's office door [16].

Many approaches have been developed aiming to minimize interruptions caused by mobile devices. One approach is to empower the caller to make better decisions about the appropriateness of the call before making it by providing him information about the receiver's context [17-19]. The Calls.calm system uses the web to activate an interaction webpage that provides the caller with a set of available communication channels as well as information about the receiver's current situation and leaves it up to the caller to make an educated choice [17]. Milewski and Smith used the address book to display dynamic information about the recipient's availability and whereabouts [19]. The solution applies the same concepts of "Buddy list", used in instant messengers. This approach, however, raises many privacy concerns that may prevent the receivers from publishing useful information about their context. Also the approach does not address the question of what type of contextual information provides the best cues about the receiver's availability.

Another approach is to empower cell phone owners by improving the capabilities and awareness of cell phones. Quiet Calls is a system that enables users to have a private conversation in a public place by using a quiet mode of communication such as voice mail and prerecorded messages [20]. Such a system decreases social interruption but does not affect personal interruption since the user is still expected to receive the call and act upon it. SenSay is a system that uses input from different sensors such as accelerometers, light detectors, and microphones to capture the context of the user [21]. The context is then used to adjust the modality of cell phone configuration (i.e. vibration, ringer). Schmidt et. al. have introduced an adaptive cell phone that changes its profile automatically based on the recognized context [22]. The phone chooses to ring, vibrate, adjust the ring volume, or keep silent depending on whether the phone is on a table, in a suitcase, outside, or in hand. Solutions which acquire context information through augmented sensors are somewhat expensive in terms of the computational needs of inferring the context information given the scarce resources of cell phones. Moreover, usability studies have yet to be conducted to study the effect of inaccurate context prediction on users, as well as the issue of how much control users are willing to give up in exchange for convenience.

4 Experiment

The main goal of the experiment was to assess the likely value of the calendar-based automatic cell phone configuration approach and the various factors affecting it. We examined the accuracy of calendar information, configuration predictability, and the consistency of mapping activities to configurations for individuals and across different individuals. We examined whether automatic cell phone configuration, based on the user's calendar information, improves the overall user experience. Finally, we investigated the approach to automatic configuration and whether it should be passive, where users are aware of the change and have more control over it, or active, where the change is made without any notification and the user has less control over it.

4.1 Preliminary Survey

The experiment was conducted in two stages. Preliminary data was collected using a survey in the first stage to help us better design the main part of the experiment. The benefit of a two-stage experimental approach in the context of interactive and ubiquitous systems was argued by Antifakos et al. [23]. The goal of the survey is to investigate how people categorize their daily activities as well as the variation of this categorization across different groups. The data was gathered by an online survey. We had a total of 72 participants divided among graduate students, undergraduates, professors and staff. The participants were distributed among 7 different majors or areas of study. The survey results show that the participants tend to do very similar activities irrespective of their major or occupation. However, we found that the frequencies of activities are different among different groups. We used the list of collected activities to categorize them according to the most suitable cell phone configuration corresponding to that activity.

4.2 Method

Design: The study consists of a context-aware cell phone configuration application. The application simulates a cell phone that changes its configuration (loud ring, quiet ring, vibrate, on, off) depending on the context of its owner. The context is derived from the calendar book. During the study, the participant carries a Palm PDA that runs the application, and during the day she receives simulated phone calls at random times (Figure1). According to the context of the participant, the application notifies the user differently about the received call. The cell phone configuration can be in any of four different states: Loud, Quiet, Off, and Normal. In the loud state, the phone rings loudly when a call is received, while it vibrates in the Quiet state. Normal state is the default state that takes whichever configuration has been set up by the owner. In the Off state, the phone is off, and if a call is received then a voice mail message will be generated the next time the phone is in any other state. Moreover, if the participant misses a phone call, he will be notified of that missed call the next time he answers a phone call. The four different states were identified from the online preliminary survey mentioned in the previous section. After receiving the notification of either an incoming call, a missed call or a voice mail message, the participant is asked whether the configuration of the cell phone, reflected by the notification mechanism, is appropriate or not. If the answer was inappropriate, then she is asked to select the most appropriate configuration. After that, the participant is asked to select his location and activity.

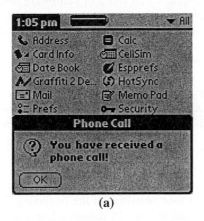
(a)

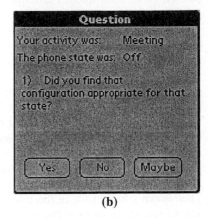
(b)

Fig. 1. Figure (a) shows the notification message that appears once a call is received. Figure (b) shows the question asked once the user presses the "OK" button on figure (a).

We chose to use a cell phone simulator that is running on a Palm PDA instead of using a real cell phone because the PDA provided us with more programming flexibility and with greater means to collect, store and manage in-situ data. At the same time, the selected PDAs had the same notification capabilities as cell phones, such as ringing, vibrating, LED, and volume control. We were only interested in measuring the appropriateness of the configurations in terms of their social ramifications rather than identifying the callers or any other factors. The simulation provided us with more control over the study, which enabled us to examine only the factor of interest while eliminating others such as caller identity. Moreover, it would have been very expensive and inefficient to provide participants with real cell phones with calling plans for the duration of the study.

Conducting the experiment in a natural setting is a crucial part of our study and for Ubicomp systems in general because of their inherent mobile nature and the fact that, in real life, they interact with users in a natural environment. We have chosen to conduct the experiment in a college environment because of its dynamics and the ease of subject recruitment. Moreover, college campuses have always been on the forefront of adopting new technologies. In fact, Weiser [24] predicted that the compact nature of the campus environment will put it at the forefront of ubiquitous computing.

Duration: The experiment duration was chosen to be 5 working days. This period was selected because most activities are repeated in either daily or weekly intervals. In addition, we conducted the experiment only during the week rather than on the weekends because we were mostly interested in the days when the participants are busy and interactive in a campus environment. In this case, the cost of interruption or misconfiguration is rather high for both the user and the surroundings and thus the value of the application is highlighted.

Participants: 11 students both graduate and undergraduate from Indiana University participated in the study. Participants were aged 20-28 and 3 of them were males. All participants reported to have owned cell phones for more than a year and have busy daily schedules with many different activities throughout the day. 10 participants fully completed the study. One participant collected very little data due to a family emergency. This data was not considered in the evaluation process.

Equipments: The study was conducted using Tungsten T3 running Palm OS 5.2 and our cell phone simulator. The devices are equipped with ringing, vibration and volume control capabilities as well as a color display. Each participant was provided with a PDA for the duration of the study.

Procedure: Participants were individually given a brief overview on how to use the PDA, and then they were introduced to the cell phone simulator and how to use it. They were asked to fill in the calendar with their activities at the beginning of every day of the study with all the activities that last at least 15 minutes. Every activity is mapped by the participant to the cell phone state that best fits that activity. The participants were advised to think of the PDA as their own cell phone that is changing its configuration dynamically depending on the context. After finishing with the experimental study, end-of-study interviews were conducted in one-on-one sessions that lasted approximately 40 minutes.

Design Tradeoffs: The fact that participants received simulated phone calls rather than real ones may have introduced some bias in their evaluation of the calls. In order to treat all calls with the same level of importance and factor out personal preferences, we asked participants to think of the calls as received from anonymous callers. With the simulated phone calls, participants still had to deal with the social ramifications of receiving calls in public spaces and with inappropriate alerts that could have been caused by the calls. Also, activity to configuration mapping in most cases should not be affected by the fact that the calls are simulated.

5 Results and Discussion

During the study, a total of 340 calls were made, all generated by the simulator. Participants received an average of 30 calls and 4 voice mails. Even though participants missed 31% of the initial calls, they received reminders about many of the missed calls, and thus they had the chance to evaluate them. Overall participants evaluated 85% of the calls; the rest were not evaluated due to the fact that the application only stored a partial list of missed calls and the participants were reminded only about the last three missed calls. In addition, in some cases, the Palm device had to be reset during the study, and thus a few stored reminders were lost.

5.1 Evaluating Calendar-Based Automatic Cell Phone Configuration

During the end-of-study interview, all participants reported they were willing to use such an application if their cell phones were equipped with it. Participants were also asked to rate the usefulness of the application on a scale of 1 to 6, with 1 being the most useful and 6 being annoying. 40% of the participants rated it 1 (very useful) while the rest rated it 2 (useful). These results are particularly interesting given the fact that 9%-13% of the calls were evaluated as having an inappropriate or inexact configuration. Since these calls were received in a real-life environment, they could have caused frustration or embarrassment for the participants. The fact that evaluation occurs after notification makes the evaluation very accurate and reflects the real feelings of the participants that could not be obtained otherwise. One participant commented that: *"I like how it changes state without you having to tell it to. I always forget to turn my cell [off] in class and turn it on after"*.

Overall, participants rated 87% of the evaluated calls as having the appropriate configuration and 9% as having an inappropriate configuration. The rest were evaluated as having an inexact configuration but not inappropriate which was another option. Out of the missed calls that were later evaluated, 36% were missed unintentionally due to the fact that participants failed to notice the alert, usually due to low volume, and the rest were missed intentionally. We interpreted both intentionally and unintentionally missed calls as having an inappropriate configuration. In most cases participants did not mind missing the calls because they did not want to be interrupted. Only 14% of the missed calls were evaluated as having an inappropriate configuration. One participant commented that the embarrassment of having the phone ring in the middle of a meeting is worse than missing a phone call. Most of the calls with inappropriate configuration were received when the participants were either in transition between activities or dealing with unplanned activities such as 'on the phone', 'taking a break' or 'having a conversation'.

Even though this approach did not produce perfect accuracy, it did not appear to affect the participants' perception about the usefulness of the applications since any inaccuracy is a predictable one and they have total control over it. People's reaction to inaccuracies and uncertainty in context-aware applications varies from one person to another. However, if Bellotti and Edwards' [25] design principles of intelligibility and accountability are followed, which include the user in the decision making process, then we expect people will adopt context-aware applications. In our case, participants were included in the decision making process by having them initially map different states to configuration rather that using different inference techniques to map them automatically.

Our study also examined the preferred level of interactivity between the user and any potential application that could provide context-aware configuration for cell phones. This question must be dealt with for most of the context-aware applications because of the fact that they are dynamic and proactive [26]. When asked about their interaction preferences in the end-of-study interviews, all participants stated that they would like to be involved in deciding on the configuration for a given context. Most participants wanted to be notified whenever certain configuration transitions occur. However, the level of involvement varies from one participant to another. A detailed discussion of this can be found in [27].

5.2 Accuracy of Calendar Information

Participants were asked to fill in a more detailed account of their daily activities than they would usually do in real life. We asked them to schedule in advance all the activities that were expected to last more than 15 minutes. The purpose was to gather as much data as we could about the different activities and the way participants choose to configure these activities. Participants filled in 9 different activities on average. The most common activities were meeting, work, homework, watching TV, class, working out and eating. During the study, participants were asked to specify their current activity. Participants accurately predicted 62% of their activities and inaccurately predicted 29% of activities. 9% of participant activities were spontaneous. The relatively low value for accuracy was not unexpected given the fact that it is very hard to predict a detailed account of our daily activities in advance. The calendar is designed to function as an organizer of important, well-structured events and not activities part of one's daily routine. Not surprisingly, the activities that contributed to most of the inaccuracies in calendar predictability were the loosely structured home activities such as "food", "watching TV", "homework" and "relaxing". When such activities were ignored, a much higher accuracy rate of 93% was obtained. This result highlights the importance of using calendar information as a source of contextual cues with high level of accuracy for structured activities.

5.3 Mapping Activities to Configuration

One main goal of the experiment was to examine how people map their activities to different configurations and to check for consistency in the mappings. In order for the configuration to be determined automatically by the cell phone (i.e. inferring it from the description field in the calendar entry) and not as specifically directed by the owner as in our experiment, there needs to be a predictable pattern of mapping from activities to configuration.

Table 1. Activity to configuration mapping by one participant

Activity	Loud	Normal	Quiet	Off
Meeting	0	2	6	1
Work	0	6	5	1
errands	0	1	0	0
Class	0	0	3	5
Homework	0	10	0	0
Lunch	0	3	0	0
Watching TV	0	1	0	0
Work Out	0	0	1	1
Walking	0	1	0	0
Shopping	2	0	0	0

A typical example of the mapping data that was collected is shown in Table 1. Upon initial observation, it appears that most activities have a dominant desired configuration, but that there exist activities that have 2 or more preferred configurations. Upon closer examination, however, we find that individuals have a predictable desired configuration for 89% of the activities. For example, the "work" activity in Table 1 shows two different dominant configurations. This particular case was due to the fact that the user happened to configure the "Normal" state to the same setting as the "Quiet" configuration. Thus, the "work" activity for this participant is counted as consistent. Further, configurations other than the dominant ones were usually chosen at the beginning of the study when participants were experimenting with the settings and were not yet sure which was the best fit for a particular activity. This behavior tended to diminish toward the end of the study period. This shows that the mapping process can be easily automated after the initial period where the user is more involved and she is part of the decision making.

The mapping was less consistent across different participants than for each individual participant. Table 2 shows the activity to configuration mapping data for the eight most common activities among participants. Even though certain activities such as "Homework" showed consistent mapping, many other activities were not as consistent. For example, many participants chose to have their cell phone "Off" during class, but others chose the "Quiet" configuration. As a result of this and in order for the automatic configuration to be useful, it should be tuned and customized to specific preferences for each user. However, results from this type of study can be used to choose intelligent default settings for different activities. For example, the default setting for "Work" could be "Quiet" because it is the most popular configuration. The users who desire "Normal" can change this default.

Table 2. Activity to configuration mapping across all participants

Activity	Loud	Normal	Quiet	Off
Meeting	2	25	23	6
Homework	8	57	2	0
Class	1	0	18	29
Food	1	21	9	0
Work Out	2	2	2	1
Travel	24	29	2	0
Watching TV	3	9	2	0
Work	0	17	38	4

Kern. et. al obtained very similar results in their study of the differences between personal and social interruptability [7]. Their experiment found that there were differences among people in the way they assess personal and social interruptability and they argue for interruptability estimation systems to better adapt to individual users' preferences. This may well be the case for all other interactive, context-aware applications. Making general conclusions about the desired behavior of context-aware applications within certain contexts is a problematic practice that many researchers have fallen into. In fact this is the same practice that Bellotti and Edwards have warned about, and they have proposed following the guidelines of intelligibility and accountability when designing context-aware systems to avoid such problems [28]. We expect that providing the capability for participants to choose their own mapping from activities to the desired configuration has had a substantial effect on the way participants perceive the application as well as on the very positive evaluation of its usefulness.

6 Conclusion

Our results suggest that automatic configuration based on calendar information provides both an effective and desirable solution to the interruption problem caused by cell phones. The results show that both structured activities and appropriate configuration can be predicted with high accuracy using the calendar information. The results also show consistent mapping of activities to configuration for each individual. However there was a poor consistency pf mapping activity to configuration across different participants. The results show that people are willing to accept a certain level of inaccuracy which comes as a side effect of any context-aware application in exchange for good services and convenience.

Calendar information does not provide accurate context all of the time, and even if the context is predicted accurately, the desired configuration for a certain context is not always the same and there are many factors that might affect it. However, even with an inaccuracy rate of 9-13%, participants still liked this solution and said they are willing to adopt it in real life. We believe this inaccuracy rate can be greatly reduced if reinforcement learning tools were used over a longer period of time. Moreover, the fact that people use the calendar for important activities and appointments and not to record a detailed account of their daily activities as they were asked to do during the study, is expected to increase the accuracy of context predictability and the consistency of activity to configuration mapping.

The fact that mobile phone calendar usage might not be very common due to the very limited inputting capabilities should not undermine the importance of our results. Mobile phones are developing at a very fast pace and smartphones are gaining more and more popularity. Smartphones offer more interaction capabilities, coupling phone capabilities with the functionalities of a PDA, and short-range wireless connectivity such as Bluetooth. The PDA functionalities of the smartphones are expected to drastically increase the use of the mobile calendar application as well as other PIM applications. Moreover, the short-range connectivity is expected to further contribute to the popularity of the mobile calendar due to the fact that people can use their computers to fill in the entries and use the wireless connection to synchronize with their smartphones.

The goal of future work should be to study the relationship between the caller and the receiver and its effect on how people evaluate the appropriateness of different phone configurations given different roles of the caller. In addition, we are planning to do the same experiment with real cell phones in order to validate the results and avoid any biases that could be introduced by the simulation. It is also important to examine the preferred direction of error in a context-aware configuration. The error of such an application can be of two sorts: fewer missed calls but higher probability of inappropriate interruption or fewer inappropriate interruptions but more probability of missed calls. In our experiment, most participants were not annoyed by missing calls since the caller was assumed to be anonymous. That the calls were not real may have contributed to this factor; however, this may not be the case in real life. We would like to investigate whether it is more important for people not to be interrupted inappropriately or not to miss certain calls. It is also important to study the effect of using real mobile calendar information as opposed to using a structured list of activities, as was the case in our study. A real strength of our study, however, is that it provided valuable insight regarding activity-to-configuration mapping and its consistency, as well as validity and usefulness of the calendar-based approach to decrease cell phone interruptions. We thereby hope to influence the design of future applications' aims regarding context-aware configuration.

Acknowledgments

This work was supported in part by NSF (EIA-0202048) and by a grant from the Lilly Endowment. We would also like to thank the subjects who provided us with valuable data and feedback.

References

1. Garlan, D., et al., *Project Aura: Toward Distraction-Free Pervasive Computing.* IEEE Pervasive Computing, 2002(April-June).
2. REUTERS, *Mobile phone users double since 2000.* Dec, 2004.
3. Wellman, B., *Physical Place and Cyber Place: The Rise of Personalized Networking.* International Journal of Urban and Regional Research, 2001. **25**(2): p. 227-52.
4. Cutrell, E., M. Czerwinski, and E. Horvitz. *Notification, Disruption, and Memory: Effects of Messaging Interruptions on Memory and Performance.* In Proceedings of *Interact 2001.* 2001. Tokyo, Japan.
5. Eyrolle, H. and J. Cellier, *The effects of interruptions in work activity: Field and laboratory results.* Applied Ergonomics, 2000. **31**: p. 537-543.
6. *Study: All cell phones distract drivers.* August 16, 2001, CNN.
7. Kern, N., et al. *A model for human interruptability: experimental evaluation and automatic estimation from wearable sensors.* In Proceedings of *IEEE International Symposium on Wearable Computers.* 2004.
8. Monk, A., et al., *Why are Mobile Phones Annoying?* Behaviour and Information Technolog, 2004. **31**(1): p. 33-41.
9. Lasen, A., *A comparative Study of Mobile Phone Use in London, Madrid and Paris.* 2002
10. Bautsch, H., et al., *An investigation of mobile phone use: a socio-technical approach.* 2001
11. Barkhuus, L. and A.K. Dey. *Is context-aware computing taking control away from the user? Three levels of interactivity examined.* In Proceedings of *UBICOMP 2003, 5th International Symposium on Ubiquitous Computing.* 2003.
12. Bellotti, V., et al. *What a to-do: Studies of task management towards the design of a personal task list manager.* In Proceedings of *CHI 2004.* 2004: ACM Press (2004).
13. Horvitz, E., et al. *Coordinate: Probabilistic Forecasting of Presence and Availability.* In Proceedings of *National Conference on Uncertainty and Artificial Intelligence (UAI 2002).* 2002.

14. Fogarty, J., J. Lai, and J. Christensen, *Presence versus Availability: The Design and Evaluation of a Context-Aware Communication Client.* International Journal of Human-Computer Studies (IJHCS), 2004. **61**(3): p. 299-317.

15. Mynatt, E. and J. Tullio. *Inferring Calendar Event Attendance.* In Proceedings of *the International Conference on Intelligent User Interfaces (IUI 2001).* 2001.

16. Yan, H. and T. Selker. *Context-aware office assistant.* In Proceedings of *International Conference on Intelligent User Interfaces.* 2000. New Orleans, LA.

17. Pedersen, E.R. *Calls.calm: Enabling Caller and Callee to Collaborate.* In Proceedings of *CHI 2001.* 2001.

18. TANG, J.C., et al. *ConNexus to awarenex: extending awareness to mobile users.* In Proceedings of *CHI 2001.* 2001.

19. Milewshi, A.E. and T.M. Smith. *Providing Presence Cues to Telephone Users.* In Proceedings of *CSCW 2000.* 2000. Philadelphia, PA.

20. Nelson, L., S. Bly, and T. Sokoler. *Quiet Calls: Talking Silently on Mobile Phones.* In Proceedings of *CHI 2001 Conference on Human Factors in Computing Systems.* 2001.

21. Siewiorek, D., et al. *SenSay: A Context-Aware Mobile Phone.* In Proceedings of *IEEE International Symposium on Wearable Computers (ISWC).* 2003. New York, NY.

22. Schmidt, A., et al. *Advanced interaction in context.* In Proceedings of *First International Symposium on Handheld and Ubiquitous Computing (HUC'99).* 1999. Karlsruhe, Germany.

23. Antifakos, S., A. Schwaninger, and B. Schiele. *Evaluating the Effects of Displaying Uncertainty in Context-Aware Applications.* In Proceedings of *Ubicomp'04. 6th International Conference on Ubiquitous Computing.* 2004. Nottingham, UK.

24. Weiser, M., *The Future of Ubiquitous Computing on Campus.* Communications of ACM, 1996. **41**(1): p. 41-42.

25. Bellotti, V. and K. Edwards, *Intelligibility and accountability: Human considerations in context-aware systems.* Human-Computer Interaction, 2001. **16**: p. 193-212.

26. Chen, G. and D. Kotz, *A survey of context-aware mobile computing research.* 2000, Department of Computer Science, Darthmouth CollegeTR2000-381.

27. Khalil, A. and K. Connelly. *Context-aware Configuration: A study on improving cell phone awareness.* In Proceedings of *Context 05.* July 2005. Paris, France.

28. Bellotti, V. and W.K. Edwards, *Intelligibility and accountability: human considerations in context aware systems.* Human Computer Interaction, 2001. **16**(2-4): p. 193-212.

29. Dourish, P. and V. Bellotti. *Awareness and Coordination in Shared Workspaces.* In Proceedings of *ACM Conference on Computer Supported Cooperative Work (CSCW).* 1992.

Evaluation of 12-DOF Input Devices for Navigation and Manipulation in Virtual Environments

Anke Huckauf, Alexander Speed, André Kunert, Jan Hochstrate, and Bernd Fröhlich

Faculty of Media, Bauhaus-University Weimar, Germany
{anke.huckauf, alexander.speed, andre.kunert, jan.hochstrate,
bernd.froehlich}@medien.uni-weimar.de

Abstract. Navigation and manipulation in virtual environments may require up
to six degrees of freedom each. Input devices with twelve or more degrees of
freedom can avoid explicit changes between navigation and manipulation and
may therefore perform well in certain situations. However, usability of already
existing 12-DOF devices is still unclear. For evaluating such handheld devices,
we developed an extended docking task based on docking tasks designed for
examining the usability of 6-DOF devices. In addition to the usually
investigated object manipulation, the task requires navigation. We compared
docking performances of two 12-DOF devices, the CubicMouse and the YoYo.
Additionally, performance with a newly developed 12-DOF input device, the
SquareBone, was under study. The SquareBone, a variation of the YoYo idea
combined with some potentially beneficial features of the CubicMouse,
provides 2 * 6 elastic DOF which can be controlled simultaneously. The study
revealed that the isotonic CubicMouse, although preferred by novice users, was
outperformed by the elastic SquareBone and the YoYo. The new SquareBone
was shown to bear the potential of becoming superior to the YoYo, possibly
because it enables simultaneous control of the 2*6 DOF.

1 Introduction

Navigation and object manipulation are central interaction tasks for three-dimensional
virtual environments. In most virtual reality (VR) systems these tasks are controlled
through a single 6-degree of freedom (DOF) input device. In this case, switching
between navigation and manipulation requires a mode change through a menu, button
press, or some type of command. This additional operation may not only be time-
consuming, but may also lead to confusion between modes. Input devices with 12 or
more DOF could avoid this explicit mode change and may perform better for tasks
which require frequent changes between navigation and manipulation.

Input devices can be classified according to the range of motion and their
manipulation resistance. Isotonic devices (e.g., the 2-DOF computer mouse) allow
forceless movements while measuring travel. Isometric devices are controlled by
using force and provide infinite movement resistance. Elastic devices allow slight
force-requiring movements. Isometric and elastic devices measure the applied force.
The input is mapped onto the movement of objects via position control (i.e., the
position of the device is used to control the position of the object) or via rate control

M.F. Costabile and F. Paternò (Eds.): INTERACT 2005, LNCS 3585, pp. 601–614, 2005.

(i.e., the force applied to the device is used to control the velocity of the object). Zhai [16] showed that the combinations of isotonic sensors and position control, and of elastic or isometric sensors and rate control produce superior performance when compared to other combinations.

Another important factor is the compatibility of integral attributes of a task with simultaneously available DOF of the input device [9]. If a task requires movement in all three spatial directions, the input device should support these translations in multiple axes. Therefore, to make and understand design decisions, one should also consider typical applications for the evaluation. This is especially the case for the multiple-DOF devices presented here which are controlled by both hands.

Hinckley and co-workers [8] use a head prop for neurosurgical visualization. Users hold a small rubber sphere or a doll's head with an embedded tracker in one hand. This head prop is used to control the orientation of a head model on the screen. The other hand holds a second prop which can be used to position a cutting plane relative to the head prop. Although using two separate input devices is certainly an alternative, we focus on approaches where both hands manipulate a single device. A variety of systems using two-handed interaction techniques is based on handheld widgets. In [13], for example, users hold a virtual widget in one hand and operate it with the other. In [14], users hold a miniature model of the virtual world in one hand and manipulate objects in the miniature with the other. These systems often employ tracked data gloves in combination with direct manipulation techniques which are difficult to use with large projection systems.

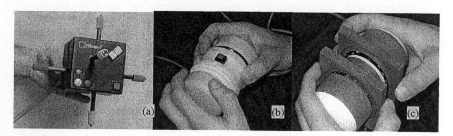

Fig. 1. (a) The CubicMouse is commercially available. The cube-shaped box is held with the non-dominant hand, while the dominant hand manipulates the rods. (b) The YoYo consists of two SpaceMouse sensors attached to a handle in the middle. (c) The SquareBone's handles attached to the contained SpaceMouse sensors can be simultaneously manipulated with the finger tips.

1.1 The CubicMouse

The CubicMouse [4,5] is a handheld interface device consisting of a cube-shaped box with a 6-DOF tracking sensor and three orthogonal rods, each offering 2 DOF (Fig. 1a). It can thus be described as a 6+(3*2) DOF device, basically a handheld 3-D coordinate system, for which the rods represent the X, Y, and Z axis. The rods can be pushed, pulled, and twisted. Pushing or pulling a rod is used for translating an object in the respective direction. Twisting a rod rotates an object around the corresponding axis. The 6-DOF sensor tracks the device movements used for view manipulations. The CubicMouse employs position control for all DOF. It is mostly used for data visualization applications, where the box represents a three-dimensional model, and translations and rotations of the box are directly applied to the model. The rods manipulate data probes such as cutting planes. The device allows simultaneous manipulation of up to eight DOF; six DOF offered by the cube plus operation of one of the rods which adds another two DOF.

1.2 The YoYo

The YoYo [15] consists of two symmetric elastic 6-DOF SpaceMouse sensors attached to a grip in the middle (Fig. 1b). This 2*6 DOF device is used with rate control techniques. The device is operated with the caps of the SpaceMouse sensors. The left SpaceMouse is typically used for navigation, the right SpaceMouse for object manipulation. Switching between navigation and manipulation requires changing the grip on the device. It is common to embed a 6-DOF tracker in the grip to compensate for rotations of the YoYo against the world coordinate system. The tracker may also be used for isotonic input and position controlled rotation or translation. This mode was not enabled in our study.

1.3 The SquareBone

We aimed at examining the usability of the CubicMouse and the YoYo; both, however, differing in various features: Whereas the CubicMouse offers isotonic control, the YoYo provides elastic control for all 12 DOF. Hence, position control is applied for the CubicMouse, and rate control for the YoYo. The CubicMouse is a 6+3*2 DOF device, and the YoYo offers 2*6 DOF. Besides these principal differences, navigation and manipulation can occur simultaneously only with the CubicMouse by moving one rod simultaneously with the cube. The YoYo allows only sequential control due to re-grasping necessary to shift between left and right 6-DOF sensors. Furthermore, due to its cubic shape, the CubicMouse provides a tactile coordinate system which might serve as a reference for navigation, whereas the round YoYo does not provide information about its current orientation.

In order to differentiate between potentially important features for 12-DOF devices, we developed the SquareBone (Fig. 1c). The SquareBone belongs to the YoYo family and consists of 2*6 DOF SpaceMouse sensors as well. The caps of the SpaceMouse sensors are replaced by square handles, providing a distinct tactile coordinate system. As for the YoYo, the handles are manipulated with the fingertips. Contrary to the YoYo, both handles can be operated simultaneously by both hands. The SquareBone has its grip on the outside and rests comfortably in the user's hands.

2 The Extended Docking Task

The manipulation of an object in a virtual world is one necessary and main objective for an evaluation task of 12-DOF devices. Several standard tasks have been developed to study the usability of 6-DOF devices under controlled conditions [e.g., 11, 16]. Typical tasks measure docking performance. Docking requires the manipulation of one object (the cursor) which has to be moved to another position or object (the target). To avoid that objects obscure each other, stimuli are usually presented with transparent surfaces. In real environments, such occlusions are less problematic since one can easily change the point of view. Hence, inducing a feeling of real world presence should be increased via allowing for changes of the view point, that is, via navigation. Navigation is provided by devices allowing for 12-DOF input. A standard task to study performance within 12 DOF should require to change the view in addition to the manipulation of an object. Our suggested solution is the extended docking task (Fig. 2). In this task, participants have to manipulate a part of a cube (the cursor) to dock it onto a larger static counter-part (the target). The target is positioned so that participants are forced to change their view point for fast and precise docking.

One problem with such an extended docking task is its increased complexity compared to a typical 6-DOF docking task [e.g., 16]. As a consequence, task performance is harder to interpret with respect to device features: Since the task is rather difficult and might require a lot of cognitive processing, completion times can be also due to various task difficulties. In addition, task difficulty may produce a large variability so that even in case of existing differences between various devices or device features, their effects may be masked. Various approaches were included for best possible control of such effects. We used a within-design in which participants worked with several devices. Although this requires careful control of transfer effects, equal task difficulties can be supposed when comparing the devices.

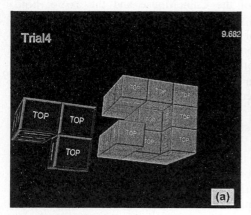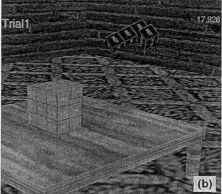

Fig. 2. Stimuli in the extended docking task consist of a larger bright (red) target composed of 3^3 small cubes minus five adjacent small cubes, which represent the dark (blue) cursor. Cursor and target may appear (a) in front of a black background, or (b) inside a virtual room.

In addition, we investigated two possible modes for navigation, an egocentric and an exocentric one. Egocentric mode means that the own point of view is manipulated. That is, pushing the device to the left results in movements of the view to the left. Thus, the world moves to the right (i.e., the device input is interpreted relative to the current view position). In exocentric mode, the world is moved with the device. Hence, moving the device to the left results in a movement of the world to the left (i.e., the device input is interpreted relative to a position of an object in the world). Obviously, the exocentric mode implies that the one point in the world serving as centre of all navigation movements is being interpreted as the centre of attention [1]. In fact, this mode reduces the potential navigation trajectories. However, the CubicMouse has been designed to be used in an exocentric mode, and egocentric navigation turned out to be hard to understand with this device. This can be attributed to the isotonic navigation in that the cube of the CubicMouse serves as a prop for the referenced object.

To gain information of whether there is a similar preference for devices employing elastic navigation, we collected some first preliminary data with the SquareBone. Besides the kinds of navigation control (exocentric, egocentric), we varied the structure of the virtual world. Exocentric navigation (i.e., moving the world) might be supported by displaying a certain isolated object, whereas egocentric navigation (i.e., moving one's own view) might benefit from a virtual world around the target, which may provide a reference frame. Preliminary data of 16 novice users showed that exocentric navigation was about 30% faster when presenting the target in front of a black background compared to being presented inside a virtual room. For egocentric navigation, the opposite effect was observed, although the effect was much smaller (about 2%). In addition in more than 20% of trials, neither the cursor nor the target have been visible on the screen for more than 10 sec suggesting that the user got lost within the virtual world. As already the TCTs, these aberrant movements were systematically affected by the interaction of the navigation mode and the background: About 35% occurred in the egocentric, and 65% in the exocentric mode of navigation. From all aberrations in the egocentric mode, 75% occurred with the black background, whereas from all aberrations in the exocentric mode, more than 90% occurred within the room.

This finding led to two consequences: First, a bounding box around the scene was implemented in order to avoid aberrant movements. Second, exocentric navigation was always presented with a black surround, whereas egocentric navigation was performed within a room. Another important factor is the compatibility between integral and separate parts of task and the simultaneously available DOF of a device [9]. For the task at issue, navigation and object manipulation can be considered to be separate parts which are therefore to be controlled by separate subsets of the totally available DOF. The less frequent navigation was assigned to the subdominant hand known to perform movements of higher amplitude and lower frequency than the dominant one [7].

3   Experiment 1

Experiment 1 aimed at establishing the usability of the isotonic CubicMouse, the elastic YoYo, and the elastic SquareBone with our new task. Training functions were assessed over nine sessions within five weeks. In addition, subjective ratings of various device features were collected. All three devices were tested with the exocentric navigation mode. Since egocentric navigation typically implemented using rate control techniques does not work well with isotonic devices [16], egocentric navigation was studied with the Yoyo and the SquareBone only.

3.1 Methods

The stimuli consisted of a large cube composed of 3^3 small cubes (Fig. 2). Five small cubes were removed from the large cube and formed the cursor. The remaining cubes served as target. The target's cubes were red, whereas the cursor's cubes were blue and changed to red individually once they were positioned within the docking tolerance. The change in color served as feedback for the participants. The target was always placed with its missing part on the back-side so that it was almost impossible to dock the cursor without manipulating the view. There were five different starting positions of the cursor each with a certain orientation of the view of approximately equal difficulty. Translation and rotation values of the device were recorded at 20 Hz.

Eight students already experienced with various input devices for three-dimensional virtual environments volunteered to participate in the experiment. The order of devices was balanced across participants. All three devices were used by half of the participants with the exocentric mode of navigation (10 trials per session), and the other half used the SquareBone and the YoYo with the egocentric mode (15 trials per session). Participants were assigned to each group according to their performance in a mental rotation test [6] to assure for comparable task difficulty in both groups. For the exocentric mode, target and cursor were presented before a black surround. Egocentric navigation was performed within the room environment. Participants performed the task on nine days with a two or three days break in between.

Participants were seated in front of a 22" monitor and performed the task in monoscopic display mode. In the first session, the task and the device were explained by performing two training trials. The participants´ right hand was measured, and preliminary experience with computers and various input devices as well as handcrafting skills were assessed. After the first, the fourth, and the eighth session, the participant filled out written questionnaires about the devices asking about various features, each on a four-point scale. The experiment ended with a last questionnaire consisting of three questions designed to compare the tested devices. One experimental session took about 45 minutes.

3.2 Results and Discussion

Device performance and learning. Data was averaged across sessions and entered into a 9 (session: 1 to 9) * 2 (device: YoYo, SquareBone)-ANOVA with repeated measures and the between factor navigation mode (exocentric, egocentric). Only for the exocentric group, an additional 9 (session) * 3 (device: YoYo, SquareBone, CubicMouse) was performed. Effects not reported failed to reach significance.

Mean TCTs for all participants using the YoYo and the SquareBone decreased from session 1 (27.46 sec, se=3.06) to session 9 (15.09 sec, se=.53; $F_{(8,48)}=18.10$; p<.001, see Fig. 3). The SquareBone tended to produce better performance than the YoYo, but only during some sessions within the exocentric mode of navigation (interaction between session, device, and mode: $F_{(8,48)}=1.90$; p<.10). The analysis only for the group performing the task with all three devices revealed that mean TCTs for the CubicMouse were significantly larger than for the other devices ($F_{(82,6)}=266.44$; p<.001). The interaction between session and device was of significance ($F_{(16,48)}=2.95$; p<.05).

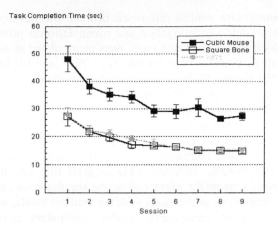

Fig. 3. Mean task completion times and standard errors as a function of session separately for the three devices in Experiment 1

Table 1. Mean estimated intercept and exponent values of the individually fitted power functions as well as the determination coefficient R^2. Standard errors are given in brackets.

Navigation mode	Device	Intercept [sec]	Exponent [sec]	R^2
egocentric	SquareBone	26.98 (5.51)	-.22 (.09)	.81 (.14)
	YoYo	29.11 (4.73)	-.27 (.08)	.88 (.11)
exocentric	SquareBone	25.13 (4.84)	-.27 (.07)	.69 (.12)
	YoYo	26.88 (4.10)	-.26 (.07)	.64 (.09)
	CubicMouse	46.87 (4.06)	-.26 (.02)	.84 (.05)

To further examine the question whether the learning progress differs between devices, power functions were fitted. As the intersection values confirmed (see Tab. 1), the CubicMouse performed worse than the other devices. There was a tendency of the SquareBone to produce better performance than the YoYo. However, exponents did not differ showing that performances declined at about the same rate for all devices.

Learning should not only result in faster docking performance, but also in a reduction of variability. Standard deviations for all participants using the YoYo and the SquareBone were reduced from 9.17 sec in session 1 to 3.37 sec in session 9 ($F_{(8,48)}=10.31$, p<.01, see Fig. 3). The decrease was marginally more pronounced in the egocentric mode than in the exocentric mode ($F_{(8,48)}=1.95$; p<.10) in that it decreased from 9.89 sec to 3.54 sec in the egocentric, and from 8.45 sec to 3.20 sec in the exocentric group. For the exocentric group, variability was shown to depend on sessions ($F_{(8,24)}=5.56$, p<.01), on the device ($F_{(2,6)}=14.25$, p<.01), and on their interaction ($F_{(16,48)}=2.36$; p<.05): Whereas variability for the SquareBone decreased from 8.60 sec to 2.66 sec, for the YoYo the decline was less steep (from 8.30 sec to 3.74 sec). For the CubicMouse, variability decreased steeper on a higher level (from 15.75 sec to 6.62 sec).

Simultaneous control. One central difference between the devices is the degree to which simultaneous control of navigation and manipulation is possible. The portions of time during which both, cursor and view, were manipulated at the same time, were compared. Over all participants, this portion was 1.78% (se=.49) for the SquareBone, and 0.45% (se=.16) for the YoYo – a marginally significant difference ($F_{(1,6)}$=3.97, p<.10). In addition, the exocentric group produced more simultaneous control (6.93%) than the egocentric group (1.05%; $F_{(1,6)}$=5.33; p=.06). Moreover, a significant interaction between session and device ($F_{(16,48)}$=1.90, p<.05) revealed that whereas simultaneous control with the YoYo slightly decreased over sessions (1.52%:1.29% in session 1:9), its portion increased for both other devices (SquareBone: 1.37%, 2.14%, CubicMouse: 9.42%, 16.07%). This suggests that simultaneous control is learned over sessions. One might wonder about the simultaneous control observed for the YoYo: This is due to two participants with the smallest hands, who also stated that the YoYo was too large accidentally causing involuntary movements with the grasping hand.

However, it is still unclear whether simultaneous control is of general advantage. If simultaneous control can produce an advantage, then TCTs should become shorter with increasing simultaneous control; that is, a negative correlation between TCTs and the fraction of simultaneous control is to be expected. For the trials of session 9, TCTs and portion of simultaneous control significantly correlated for the SquareBone with r=-.49 (p<.001), whereas for the YoYo, there was with r=.10 no significant correlation (p=.30). This confirms the interpretation that the amount of simultaneous control with the YoYo was mainly due to involuntary movements. It further supports the assumption that simultaneous control can produce advantages at least for experienced users, and therefore can be assumed to provide one important feature of a 12-DOF input device. But, it should be noted that the correlation for the SquareBone traces back mainly to two participants. For the CubicMouse, however, TCTs and the fraction of simultaneous control of cursor and view did not correlate (r=-.13, p=.42). This can be attributed to the users' reports of problems in stabilizing the view with the CubicMouse: Since changing ones own position leads to changes of the view with the CubicMouse, one has to control not only arms and hands, but also feet and body postures. That is, the way of how simultaneous control is enabled severely affects performance. For precise manipulation of an object with the CubicMouse, it might be effective to temporarily disable navigation by clutching.

Times of inactivity and subjective ratings. For all participants using the YoYo and the SquareBone, the fraction of times in which no movement was visible for any DOF was in mean 13.62% (se=.95) and decreased with increasing training from 16.82% in session 1 to 12.18% in session 9 ($F_{(8,48)}$=4.09; p<.01). Only for the exocentric group, except the effect of session, also an effect of device was obtained ($F_{(2,6)}$=54.15; p<.001) showing that the relative amount of time in which no signal was transferred to any DOF was for the CubicMouse with 30.94% twice as large as for the two other devices. This difference, which is even larger if one takes the absolute (longer) docking times with the CubicMouse into consideration, is very likely to reflect times of re-grasping, which are much longer for the CubicMouse where each rod has to be accessed and moved separately. Correlations between TCTs and the fraction of inactivity did not reach significance for any device (SquareBone: r=-.08. YoYo:

r=-.09, CubicMouse: r=.04). This suggests that times of inactivity seem in part due to cognitive processing. This interpretation is supported by the fact that the fraction of time of inactivity correlated between devices (r=.43; p<.01).

Subjective ratings of usability (on a four-point scale ranging from 1=very poor to 4=very good) showed that ratings increased with increasing training from 2.7 (se=.10) to 3.4 (se=.08) for all participants and the YoYo and the SquareBone. Only for the exocentric group, there was an additional effect of device in that the CubicMouse received worse usability ratings (1.8, se=.09) than the YoYo (3.0, se=.23) and the SquareBone (3.1, se=.21).

Taken together, the results show that docking performance with the SquareBone and the YoYo is better than with the CubicMouse. The data tend to demonstrate small advantages for the SquareBone over the YoYo in mean docking duration, in variability during performing the task, and in adequate size. Nevertheless, reducing the size of the YoYo might be an option to overcome these slight advantages of the SquareBone.

4   Experiment 2

The input devices have been developed for being used with large projections screens and potentially stereoscopic virtual environments. Since the data in Experiment 1 was collected under monoscopic viewing conditions using a monitor, the participants of Experiment 2 performed the task again using a monitor as well as a large projection screen (4*3m²), both under monoscopic as well as stereoscopic viewing conditions. For the monitor, we used active stereo and shutter glasses. For the large screen, we used passive stereo with linear polarization.

4.1   Results and Discussion

As can be seen in Fig. 4, performance did not differ between conditions (all F<1). This indicates that the results of our long term Experiment 1 can be transferred to large screens and stereo conditions. Over all participants using the SquareBone and the YoYo, there was one significant interaction between the device, the mode of view, and the output device ($F_{(1,6)}$=42.36, p<.001). This interaction is due to the relatively large difference between the YoYo and the SquareBone when the task is performed in stereoscopic mode at the projection screen. The group working with the exocentric mode of navigation produced the interaction between device, and the output device ($F_{(2,6)}$=7.28, p<.05) due to the fact that performance with all devices except the SquareBone was worst under stereoscopic viewing conditions at the large projection screen. In addition, a main effect of device ($F_{(2,6)}$=119.64, p<.001) showing that performance with the CubicMouse of 26.60 sec (se=.42) was again worse than with the other devices (SquareBone: 12.75 sec, se=.95; YoYo: 14.18 sec, se=1.13).

In summary, the effects of devices already observed in Experiment 1 were replicated in Experiment 2 in that performance with the CubicMouse was worse than performance for the SquareBone and the YoYo. Again, slight advantages for the SquareBone relative to the YoYo were obvious. Moreover, the data gave rise to the assumption that the SquareBone might produce even more advantages under more typical stereoscopic viewing conditions using a large projection screen. Of course, it cannot be ruled out that participants trained in stereo on the projection screen produce better performance under these conditions. But, we can at least proceed on the assumption that the fundamental differences between performances for the devices under study hold for immersive three-dimensional environments as well.

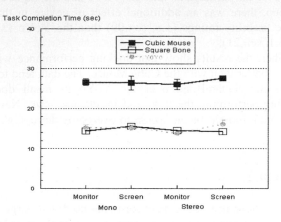

Fig. 4. Mean docking performance for monoscopic and stereoscopic mode of view and monitor and large projection screen for all three devices

5 Experiment 3

Experiments 1 and 2 have shown that the isotonic CubicMouse is clearly outperformed by the elastic devices. However, for 6-DOF devices Zhai [16] reported comparable, for novice users even superior performances for isotonic relative to elastic or isometric control. Therefore, in Experiment 3, novice users performed the extended docking task with the SquareBone and the CubicMouse. Eight users performed ten trials with exocentric navigation; four of them first operated the CubicMouse, four the SquareBone.

5.1 Results and Discussion

Mean TCT with 67.90 sec as well as variability with a standard error of 2.49 sec were quite high over all 10 trials. This can be attributed to the high task difficulty, especially for the completely inexperienced users.

To study short term learning effects, the first and the last (i.e., tenth) trial were statistically compared. Both devices produced comparable performances (CubicMouse: 74.33 sec, se=8.05; SquareBone: 75.92 sec, se=8.44; F<1). Performance in the last trial was better than in the first one ($F_{(1,6)}$=9.82, p<.05, Fig. 5) revealing training effects already within ten trials. However, this was not observed when the CubicMouse is operated as the first device (interaction devices* trial* order of devices: $F_{(1,6)}$=4.59, p=.08). The interaction thus indicates that the ease of usage of the CubicMouse is indeed inherent in the data, but disappears already after ten trials.

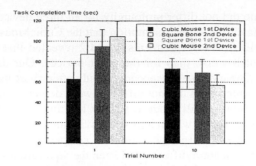

Fig. 5. Mean task completion times (TCTs) and standard errors for the CubicMouse and the SquareBone obtained in trials 1 and 10 separately for the group beginning with the CubicMouse and the one beginning with the SquareBone

Mean usability ratings were with 3.24 (se=.18) for the CubicMouse marginally better than for the SquareBone (2.70; se=.16; $F(1,6)=5.28$; p=.06) confirming the slightly better performances with the CubicMouse. Better evaluations of the CubicMouse were also observed in other ratings of task difficulty, of device features, and especially of the difficulty of navigation. Hence, although the CubicMouse requires rather long times for re-grasping since each rod has to be manipulated separately, it seems to have, at least for novice users, several advantages.

6   General Discussion

The extended docking task, although very difficult for novice users, provides reliable and valid measures of performance for 12-DOF devices. The results of the experienced users clearly revealed several factors as important for the design of 12-DOF devices.

The isotonic CubicMouse was inferior relative to the SquareBone as well as to the YoYo. One important factor for this is certainly the relatively long time it takes to change the grip when manipulating the three separate rods. But, even when subtracting these times, the CubicMouse did not produce docking times as fast as the other two devices. This suggests that some more profound deficit of the CubicMouse leads to its lower performance. One possible factor is that due to the separation of the rods, diagonal movements require so-called "city block" movements which alternate between x, y, and z axis control. This requires not only grip changes, but probably also more complex mental processing.

However, the CubicMouse has been preferred by our novice users. Moreover, navigation with the CubicMouse was also regarded by all experienced users as extremely easy. This suggests that an isotonic position control device can serve as a kind of prop for the manipulated object thus facilitating exocentric navigation. But, it cannot be denied that the very intuitive navigation with the CubicMouse led to several impairments due to the fact that it forces the user to maintain a stable body position. Therefore, clutching to disable navigation for precise manipulation of an object should be allowed with the CubicMouse.

The learning rate did not differ profoundly for all three devices. Although the data of Experiment 3 gave rise to the assumption that the CubicMouse can be more easily controlled by novice users, Experiments 1 and 2 revealed that performance for the CubicMouse is much worse than for the other devices. Our data suggests that the superiority of the CubicMouse disappears already after short usage. In other words, the fact that the learning rates did not differ between devices cannot be interpreted as indication that all devices will produce similar learning rates also for novice users. This has to be studied further within long-term evaluations with novices.

The YoYo and the SquareBone produced comparable performances over five weeks. One important feature differing between the SquareBone and the YoYo is that the former allows for simultaneous control whereas the latter does not. Although simultaneous control might save docking time, different movements with both hands can also lead to interferences. As the data for the SquareBone revealed, lower task completion times go ahead with a higher degree of simultaneous operation. That is, simultaneous control was partly successfully applied by our experienced users arguing for the SquareBone as being principally superior over the YoYo. However, simultaneous navigation and object manipulation occurred only in 2% of the time. Thus, even if this fraction increases with further expertise, we cannot exclude that the potential saving might be of minor practical importance. To get further estimations about the usefulness of simultaneous control, the conditions under which asymmetric bimanual control can lead to advantages must be explored further [2, 10, 12].

The comparable performances of the SquareBone and the YoYo in Experiments 1 and 2 suggest that a tactile coordinate frame does not facilitate performance. Nevertheless, as some users objected, our design of the tactile coordinates in the SquareBone can also produce disadvantages. Since the square handles of the SquareBone require to grasp one of the corners in order to move diagonally, the degree to which diagonal movements are possible is reduced. This uncomfortable position of one of the fingers might have produced trajectories avoiding such movements and thus an increase of docking times. Therefore, long-term performance for experts using a Bone with round handles (Fig. 6) would be desirable to assess.

Fig. 6. A new version of the SquareBone: The manipulated handles are round allowing comfortable manipulation of diagonal movements. The square caps on the left and right side provide a tactile coordinate system.

Another fact might argue in favor of the YoYo. Since controlling the YoYo needs time to switch the grip when switching between navigation and object manipulation, one should expect docking times to be about the switching times longer when using the YoYo relative to the SquareBone. But, these additional costs could not be observed. Instead, even the fraction of time in which no movement was observed did not differ between both devices. This suggests that switching between navigation and object manipulation produces costs, perhaps due to mental processes, which can hardly be avoided even if a device enables simultaneous performance. The subjective ratings argue also slightly in favor of the YoYo. After all sessions, five of eight participants preferred the YoYo, whereas three favored the SquareBone. Even those who claimed the device was too large leading to accidental movements favored the YoYo suggesting a more fundamental advantage for the YoYo.

7 Conclusions and Future Work

This paper presented the results of a first series of user studies for 12-DOF input devices. For the studies, we developed an extended docking task requiring navigation as well as object manipulation. As a main result, we found that for such a complex task, the elastic devices performed significantly better than the isotonic CubicMouse. The newly developed SquareBone is competitive to the YoYo. It allows for simultaneous navigation and manipulation used by very experienced users only. The disadvantage of our current SquareBone lies in prohibiting certain diagonal movements. Nevertheless, with only a few design changes as suggested in Fig 6, the SquareBone holds the potential of becoming an alternative device to the commercially available CubicMouse.

We have investigated the use of these devices for a specific navigation and manipulation task only. Most real world applications additionally require the control of selection and system control tasks besides navigation and manipulation. It is still unclear how well devices can support such interaction modes. There are many more combinations possible to reach 12 or more DOF. The CubicMouse and the Yoyo family are only a starting point for exploring this design space. The combination of isotonic and elastic input bears a lot of potential to support novice and experienced users appropriately, for example by constraining the DOF. This points to reconfigurable smart input devices, which can be adapted or ideally adapt themselves to the task and user.

Acknowledgements

Thanks to Andreas Simon for providing us with a YoYo, Alexander Kulik for building the SquareBone, David Paneque for keeping the devices in shape, Sonja Gutzeit and Timo Göttel for assisting in data collection, Verena Skuk in data analysis. This work was supported by the VRIB project funded by the German government.

References

1. Bowman, D., "Interaction Techniques for Common Tasks in Immersive Virtual Environments, Design, Evaluation and Application", PhD-Thesis, Georgia Institute of Technology (1999).

2. Buxton, W. and Myers, B.A., "A study in two-handed input", Proceedings of CHI 1986 (1986), 321-326.
3. Fitts, P., "The information capacity of the human motor system in controlling the amplitude of movement", Journal of Experimental Psychology, 47 (1954), 381-391.
4. Froehlich, B. and Plate, J., "The CubicMouse: A new device for 3D input", Proceedings ACM CHI 2000 (2000), 526-531.
5. Fröhlich, B., Plate, J., Wind, J., Wesche, G., and Göbel, M.: Cubic-Mouse-Based Interaction in Virtual Environments, IEEE Computer Graphics&Applications (2000)
6. Gittler, G., "Dreidimensionaler Würfeltest [Three-dimensional cube test]" Weinheim, G, Beltz (1990).
7. Guiard, Y., "Asymmetric division of labor in human skilled bimanual action: The kinematic chain as a model", Journal of Motor Behavior, 19 (1987), 486-517.
8. Hinckley, K., Pausch, R., Downs, J.H., Proffitt, D., and Kassell, N.F., "The Props-Based Interface for Neurosurgical Visualization", Medicine Meets Virtual Reality, 5th Global Healthcare Grid, Amsterdam, NL, IOS Press (1995), 552-562.
9. Jacob, R., Sibert, L., McFarlane, D., and Mullen, M. 1994.Integrality and separability of input devices. ACM Transactions on Computer-Human Interaction, 1(1), p. 3-26.
10. Leganchuk, A., Zhai, S. and Buxton, W., "Manual and Cognitive Benefits of Two-Handed Input: An Experimental Study", ACM Transactions on Computer-Human Interaction, 5 (1999), 326-359.
11. Masliah M. and Milgram P. Measuring the allocation of control in a 6 degree-of freedom docking experiment. Proceedings of CHI 2000 (2000), 25-32.
12. Mechsner, F., Kerzel, D., Knoblich, G., and Prinz, W., "Perceptual basis of bimanual coordination", Nature, 414 (2001), 69-73.
13. Mine, M., Brooks, F.P., and Sequin, C., "Moving Objects in Space: Exploiting Proprioception in Virtual-Environment Interaction" Proceedings of ACM SIGGRAPH 1997 (1997), 19-26.
14. Pausch, R., Burnette, T., Brockway, D., and Weiblen, M.E., "Navigation and Locomotion in Virtual Worlds via Flight into Hand-Held Miniatures", ACM SIGGRAPH 1995 (1995), 399-400.
15. Simon, A. and Froehlich, B., "The YoYo: A Handheld Device Combining Elastic and Isotonic Input", Interact 2003 (2003).
16. Zhai, S., "Human Performance in Six Degree of Freedom Input Control", PhD-Thesis, University of Toronto (1995).

Integration of 3D Data and Text: The Effects of Text Positioning, Connectivity, and Visual Hints on Comprehension

Henry Sonnet[1], Sheelagh Carpendale[2], and Thomas Strothotte[1]

[1] University of Magdeburg, Dept. of Simulation and Graphics,
D-39016 Magdeburg, Germany
[2] University of Calgary, Dept. of Computer Science,
Calgary, Alberta, Canada T2N 1N4

Abstract. 3D computer graphic models hold much promise as illustrations that can be interactively explored. These 3D illustrations often need to be linked to labels, annotations and sometimes more lengthy textual explanations. Achieving effective integration of the 3D illustration and its textual information is a difficult task and has resulted in a variety of proposed approaches. However, the comparative effectiveness of these approaches has not been studied. To address this issue, we have conducted a study in which we have compared methods of associating text with its 3D model: attaching the text directly to the object, placing the text in the object's shadow, using symbols to make the correlation between the object and the text, and using a line to make the visual connection from the text to the object with and without additional hints in the shadow. During the first part we were interested in whether a graphical method can clarify the correlation between a part of the 3D model and its associated text. The second part focused on whether the text remains comprehensible during a scene exploration. Based on our results, we suggest design implications for developing interactive 3D illustrations.

1 Introduction

Data for 3D models exists in a large number of domains such as medicine, automotive engineering, and architecture. Often, it is accompanied by textual information that explains the components of the model or provides further information. In this regard, BRINKLEY et al. [1] distinguish between spatial information (e. g., images, 3D models, or animations) and symbolic information (metadata about the images and 3D models). They state that both types of information are of equal importance in understanding the data presented.

In 3D illustrations, the two distinct types of information, 3D data and text, need to be arranged in a single *layout*. According to LOK and FEINER [2], the term *layout* refers to the process of determining each visual object's position and size. FEKETE and PLAISANT [3] have identified a number of basic principles concerning an adequate layout. They state that text should be readable, non-ambiguously related to its graphical object, and not hide any other pertinent information. In order to follow those principles in illustrations that allow for interactive scene exploration (*dynamic layouts*), the textual

M.F. Costabile and F. Paternò (Eds.): INTERACT 2005, LNCS 3585, pp. 615–628, 2005.

information continuously needs to be adapted (e. g., position, size, text layout) according to the current view of the data. Several techniques for an interactive information exploration of 3D models and their textual annotations have been proposed.

In most applications, image or model components and their associated labels are connected with lines (e. g., [4,5]). Additional relational data can be provided in context menus [6]. It can also be accessed in separate areas, for instance, a user can browse through extensive textual description that explains an explorable 3D model, in a separate window [7]. Alternatively, instead of directly integrating the words into a scene, *annotation markers* can serve as a reference to the textual information (e. g., [8,9]). There are also a number of dynamic techniques, in which labels move, appear, or disappear during interaction (e. g., [3,10]). In other approaches, an alternative representation of the original scene is used to provide additional explanation (e. g.,[11,12,13]). Here, scene components are projected onto a plane in order to be highlighted and annotated in the background without disturbing the view of the scene. SONNET et al. [14] have proposed a technique in which annotations are directly connected to their corresponding scene objects.

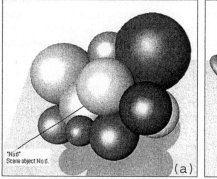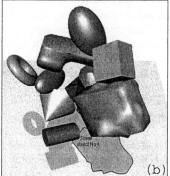

Fig. 1. Two examples of 3D scene and text integration

We were interested in gaining a better understanding of the usability of these types of techniques. In particular we were interested in the clarity of the correlation between the object in the 3D model and its associated text, the effect of including additional visual hints, and whether the text remains readable and comprehensible during scene exploration. Figure 1 shows examples of two different techniques for linking text with objects in a 3D scene. A common method, linking text and its associated object with a line, is shown in Fig. 1(a). Notice how this scene is also an example of an unclear correlation between object and text. Is the green, red, or another sphere referenced? Figure 1(b) shows a method of augmenting shadows to provide information. The effectiveness of these types of techniques has not been studied.

In this paper, we present a user study that has been designed to explore the issues involved when integrating 3D data and textual information. During the study, participants were given tasks that involved the exploration of 3D scenes. These tasks included finding the correct object-text correlations and following 3D scene exploration instructions that where embedded in the 3D scene. All of the 3D models were composed of arbitrary geometric objects. Data was collected through recording participant activities, questionnaires and the participant's comments and opinions.

This paper is organized as follows: In Section 2, we describe the purpose of our study. Basic aspects regarding the study are given in Section 3. Section 4 contains the individual tasks and designs. Results of the study are included in Section 5. In Section 6, these results are discussed before Section 7 summarizes the evaluation.

2   Study Goals

Static layouts can be more easily designed than dynamic layouts. In a static layout, text labels can be positioned carefully so that they do not occlude relevant parts of the image and so that it is clear which image parts are referenced by which labels. But when a static layout is turned into a dynamic layout, the formerly clear layout may become confusing. Image parts may now be located at new positions while associated texts have not been transformed appropriately. As mentioned above, while several techniques have been proposed with the intention of creating adequate dynamic layouts, it is not clear to what extent they achieve these goals. For example, a 3D scene that is supplemented by text may be complex, in that it may have many interleaved components. In a complex scene like this, creating a useful text integration is already complicated in static layouts, let alone dynamic layouts. In particular, we were interested in:

- the effect of text integration techniques and scene complexity on people's ability to correctly correlate a scene object with its associated text,
- the effect of including the additional hint of highlighting an object's shadow on people's ability to correctly correlate a scene object with its associated text, and
- the readability and comprehension of presented text.

3   Study Method

3.1   Participants and Setup

Thirty-six voluntary participants (10 female / 26 male), aged between 16 and 32, were recruited from the local computer science department. All of the participants were familiar with mouse navigation and 11 % of them had no or little experience with 3D interaction, 25 % had some experience navigating 3D scenes, and 64 % had considerable experience in 3D navigation from playing 3D computer games or using 3D modeling software.

All tasks were performed at a *SGI Octane Workstation* with a 21" display. The software used for all tasks differed only in the method used to correlate the textual information with the objects in the 3D scene and in whether or not additional visual hints were included. All the environments allow for interactive exploration of 3D scenes. By exploration we mean the capability to view the scene from arbitrary viewpoints while acquiring information from texts. There were no differences in the techniques that enabled a user to spatially explore the 3D scenes, that is, all other interactions, rotations, etc. were identical. In the software, each 3D scene has a model, which is a 3D arrangement of 3D geometric objects of different colors and a setting, which is the manner by which the textual information is correlated to the objects in the model.

3.2 Description of the Settings and Models

We chose three different types of settings to evaluate. Setting I was chosen because it integrates the text into the 3D scene. It is an example of the commonly used *object-line-label* technique, except that the line is replaced by a translucent polygon. Setting II was chosen because it represents an unusual text integration approach and Setting III was chosen because it represents the common separation between text and 3D model. These three settings were used for Tasks 1 and 3 (see Sect. 4).

- *Setting I—Object-attached labels.* Annotations are directly connected to their respective scene objects in *Setting I*. As can be seen in Fig. 2(a), a translucent polygon, intersecting with the scene object, provides a visual link between annotation and object. During scene exploration, annotations remain attached to their associated scene objects. The annotations' size is adapted to their scene objects' bounding box sizes, which gives additional hints regarding connectivity. A detailed description of this technique can be found in [14].
- *Setting II—Shadow annotations.* In *Setting II*, annotations are located within a shadow plane [13]. The annotations are bordered by the outlines of the respective scene objects after they have been projected onto this plane (see Fig. 2(b)). Since annotations may be occluded by scene objects, they can be temporarily displayed in the foreground on user request. Also, since the available space for text strongly depends on the object projections' shapes, text may not entirely fit into its assigned space. The available space may only be enlarged by zooming into the scene.
- *Setting III—Separated annotations.* In contrast to the previous settings where annotations are integrated within the same window as the 3D scene, in *Setting III* text is located in a separate window. As can be seen in Fig. 2(c), the textual information is shown within the windows on the right hand side. In order to identify individual objects, a clear textual description of all the scene objects is provided.

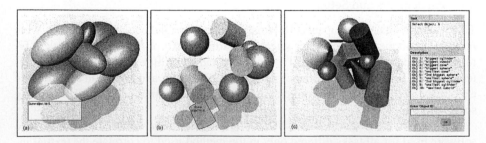

Fig. 2. (a) *Setting I (Model 1)*: annotations are directly attached to scene objects using translucent polygonal shapes. (b) *Setting II (Model 2)*: annotations are located within the objects' shadows in the scene. (c) *Setting III (Model 3)*: area showing the 3D model and text area are separated. Textual information—including scene object descriptions—is displayed in the window on the right hand side.

For Task 2 we explored whether what is perhaps the most common method of labeling—attaching the text to its associated object by means of a simple line—can be improved with the addition of visual hints. From our own experience and from pilot studies we knew that this method could be ambiguous. Therefore for Task 2, the settings, A, B and C, vary in regards to the type of visual hint used.

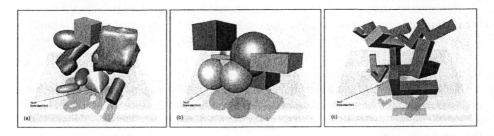

Fig. 3. All these settings use a simple line and text label annotation technique: (a) Setting A, (Model 4) makes use of no additional hints, (b) Setting B, (Model 5) the shadow of the object is highlighted using a gray tone, and (c) Setting C, (Model 6) the highlighting uses the diffuse color of the respective scene object

- *Setting A.* Object and text are only linked with a line. There are no further hints that may help to find a correlation between scene object and annotation (see Fig. 3(a)). The text remains at a static position during scene exploration. Only the line end that is connected to a point inside the corresponding scene object moves with the object.
- *Setting B.* Beside the line that connects scene object and annotation, the respective projection of the annotated scene object (object's shadow) is highlighted using a gray value that differs from the general shadow color (see Fig. 3(b)).
- *Setting C.* The only difference to *Setting B* is that the annotated object's shadow is highlighted using the diffuse color of the corresponding scene object. To this end, the shadow color as well as the position of the shadow relative to the respective scene object can be used to locate the annotated scene object (see Fig. 3(c)).

The models used during the study were composed of arbitrary geometric objects. Basically, there were two reasons for why we decided to use arbitrary models: (1) to prevent previous knowledge from aiding some participants when objects were to be found on the basis of descriptions and (2) each model was constructed to consciously stress specific aspects to be analyzed during the study. For example, we were interested in the different effects of compact models and models whose objects were arranged more apart. Or what would be the difference between models composed of similarly and variously shaped objects?

4   The Tasks

Each participant performed three tasks and each task had three different settings. So that familiarity with the 3D model did not affect the results, for each setting, one of three different models was used. The order in which the participants saw the settings and which model was used with which setting was counterbalanced. Before each task, participants were given a careful explanation of the task and were given practice runs. In addition to these interaction tasks, participants were asked to complete three questionnaires: at the beginning, the end, and after completing Task 1. The participants were also asked if they had any comments they would like to make.

Participants were told that their actions would be recorded. This included the time taken for each task, which objects were selected and text annotations that were preformed. They were also told that it was more important to solve the tasks correctly rather than to be quick. The participants were observed during the tasks and notes were taken about their actions and comments.

Problems that may occur when integrating textual information into a scene include: unclear correlation between scene object and text, scene occlusions, or other interferences during scene exploration. The following three tasks were designed to explore these issues.

4.1   Task 1: Object-Text Correlations

Using Settings I-III and three different 3D models, participants were asked to find the correlations between the scene objects and the annotations. Specifically a participant was asked to identify the scene object that the annotation currently displayed referred to, by selecting that object. For that purpose, eight annotations were shown for each setting (see Fig. 2). A new annotation appeared every time the participant had completed the subtask of selecting a scene object. In Settings I and II, the annotations were displayed together with the rendered model within the same window. Setting III differed from the other settings in that scene object descriptions were shown in a window on the right hand side. Instead of eight annotations integrated into the scene, successively the descriptions of eight objects were shown in the annotation window. The participant found the objects being referred to by their descriptions (see Fig. 2(c)). Prior to each recorded study run a practice run with a test model was performed. The two attributes *Setting* and *3D model* have been varied such that each participant performed the task with Settings I-III and three different models.

4.2   Task 2: Object-Text Correlations with Additional Hints

This task was designed to discover whether there are benefits to be gained when additional hints are included with simple labels attached by straight lines. The task used Settings A-C, see Fig. 3. We expected that the ancillary hints would help a user to find correct object-text correlations.

The basic task was the same as Task 1. Participants were asked to find the correlations between the scene objects and the annotations. Again, successively eight annotations appeared that should be assigned to the scene objects. The 3D models differed from those of Task 1 as can be seen in Fig. 3. The setting-model pairs were varied such that no participant performed the task with the same model twice.

4.3   Task 3: Task-Based Scene Exploration

This task was designed to explore reading and understanding the displayed text information and this was followed by a task-based scene exploration. The task itself was displayed to the participant in the text annotation of the setting that was in use. The participants were asked to read the text and then to follow the instructions it contained. There were two aspects we addressed with this part of the study: Can the participants gather the provided information properly and are there potential interferences between 3D model and text during scene exploration?

Fig. 4. Task 3: Setting I (Model 4). (a) The description of the scene object that is to be found is displayed attached to a different scene object. The participant uses this information to find and select the described scene object; on selection a second annotation that contains the object ID appears (b). Finally, this object ID is then appended to the first annotation (c).

The task had three components:

1. Read the complete information given by a displayed text.
2. Find the scene object according to the information gathered from the displayed text.
3. Append an ID—associated with the found scene object—to the displayed text.

With component (1) we wanted to find out if participants would have problems when reading the complete displayed information. Whether the participants understand the information could be observed by how they carried out the instructions for the second part of the task (2). Carrying out component (3) was included to shed some light on possible interferences between 3D model and text such as model/text occlusions that might occur during the search for the described objects with their IDs and during the annotation of the text information with this ID. Figure 4 illustrates this task.

Task 3 proceeded as follows: After an annotation—attached to an arbitrary scene object—was displayed (see Figs. 4(a) or 5(a)), the participant read the complete text. Note that the textual description referred to a different scene object from the object that the annotation was attached to. When the participant found and selected the described scene object, an annotation with the found object's ID appeared (see Figs. 4(b) or 5(b)). At this point both annotations were integrated into the scene and remained visible during interaction. The last step was to enter the found object's ID into the first annotation. When this annotation had been selected, its new text was "Enter Object ID here:" instead of the task description (see Figs. 4(c) or 5(c)). This procedure was repeated 5 times each for Settings I and II. In Setting III, annotations were not integrated into the render area. Hence, the procedure differed from Settings I and II (see Fig. 6) in that readings were preformed in the side window.

Fig. 5. Task 3: Setting II (Model 5). The same procedure as in Fig. 4 with the difference that all text is displayed within the shadow plane.

Fig. 6. Task 3: Setting III (Model 6). (a) The scene object's description is shown in the top right window. When the described object has been selected, its object ID is temporarily displayed at the mouse cursor (b). In a final step, the object ID needs to be entered in the bottom right text field (c).

As during Tasks 1 and 2, practice runs were performed prior to the recorded runs. The recorded attributes were elapsed times for each task as well as user interactions such as object selections and text inputs. Settings and models were varied such that no participant performed a task under same conditions twice.

5   Study Results

The results for all three tasks including the logged data and the participants' ratings and comments are included in this section.

5.1   Task 1: Object-Text Correlations

The elapsed times for each setting and model are visualized in the diagrams of Fig. 7. Altogether, the participants needed the most time to perform this task with Setting III (Mean: 77.92 sec, SD: 39.98) compared to Setting I (Mean: 39.99 sec, SD: 33.25) and Setting II (Mean: 58.55, SD: 34.61). Model 1 was the most complicated model (Mean: 69.59, SD: 37.48) compared to Model 2 (Mean: 47.68, SD: 24.25) and Model 3 (Mean: 59.20, SD: 49.06). *Two-Way ANOVA* (factors: model and setting) shows that there is a significant interaction between the respective factors ($F_{4,99,\gamma} = 7.39$, $p - Value < 0.01$).

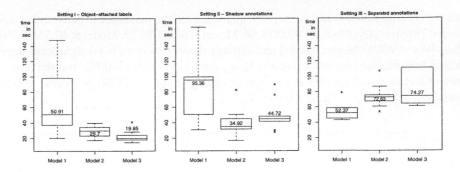

Fig. 7. Task 1: Elapsed times for Settings I-III and Models 1-3. The boxes indicate the lower and upper quartiles of the measured times as well as the Medians. In addition, smallest and largest values are shown together with outliers.

$F_{2,99,\alpha} = 3.47$ (factor: type of model, $p - Value = 0.036$) indicates that the type of model has less effect on the time than the type of setting ($F_{2,99,\beta} = 10.39$, $p - Value < 0.01$).

After this first task had been performed, participants were asked to give a ranking of the individual settings. As can be seen in Table 1 (in Sect. 5.3), 70 % favored Setting I whereas 50 % gave Setting III the worst rating.

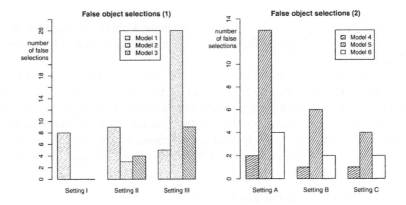

Fig. 8. Incorrectly selected scene objects

Figure 8(left) illustrates the number of incorrectly selected scene objects for each setting and model. The number of wrong selections varies for each setting depending on the model. In Settings I and II, Model 1 caused the most incorrect selections, whereas in Setting III participants had most problems with Model 2.

5.2 Task 2: Object-Text Correlations with Additional Hints

Again, user interactions and elapsed times were recorded. The diagrams in Fig. 9 show that participants performed this task fastest in Setting C for each model (Means/SDs: Setting A: 52.24/24.40, Setting B: 49.34/25.39, Setting C: 41.19/17.59). Model 5 was the most complicated model since participants needed the most time to perform the task with it (Means/SDs: Model 4: 40.0/15.88, Model 5: 62.23/28.28, Model 6: 40.51/15.29). *Two-Way ANOVA* (factors: model and setting) shows that there is no significant interaction between the respective factors ($F_{4,99,\gamma} = 0.43$, $p - Value = 0.79$). But the type of model has more influence than the type of setting ($F_{2,99,\alpha} = 13.67$, $p - Value < 0.01$ and $F_{2,99,\beta} = 2.79$, $p - Value = 0.07$).

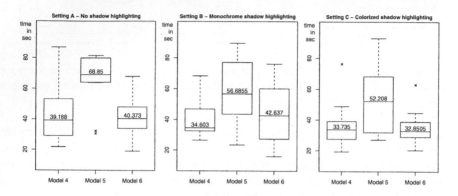

Fig. 9. Task 2: Elapsed times for Settings A-C and Models 4-6

The number of false object selections significantly decreased in Settings B and C, as is illustrated in Fig. 8(right). Model 5 was the model that caused the most incorrect selections in all settings.

Participants used various techniques during this task, in which the search for object-text correlations was supported by highlighted shadows. Some of them were quite fast in Setting C. When an annotation appeared, they compared scene object colors with the highlighted shadow color and quickly made their choice. However, other participants did not adapt their strategy to the type of setting. Some of them (14 %) even did not consider the highlighted shadows or stated that the shadows were not very helpful.

5.3   Task 3: Task-Based Scene Exploration

Task 3 was the most complex and time-consuming task. Since the settings were the same as in Task 1, we were primarily interested in a ranking. As can be seen in Table 1, it significantly differs to the ranking given after Task 1. A clear majority of 97 % rated Setting II to be the worst setting. Also, in contrast to the first rating, a majority of 64 % favored Setting III. Furthermore, when participants were asked if they felt disturbed by annotations during scene exploration, nearly all said no.

The number of false object selections as well as incorrectly entered object IDs was marginal for each setting. But there were considerable elapsed time variations (see Fig. 10). Independently from the type of model, Setting II was the setting for which participants needed most time to perform this task (Means/SDs: Setting I: 98.35/25.06, Setting II: 176.00/43.08, Setting III: 93.89/24.37). *Two-Way ANOVA* yields that there is no significant interaction between the type of setting and the type of model ($F_{4,99,\gamma}$

Table 1. Ratings for Settings I-III: after Task 1 (left) and Task 3 (right)

Setting	1st place	2nd place	3rd place
I	70 %	22 %	8 %
II	11 %	47 %	42 %
III	19 %	31 %	50 %

Setting	1st place	2nd place	3rd place
I	36 %	64 %	0 %
II	0 %	3 %	97 %
III	64 %	33 %	3 %

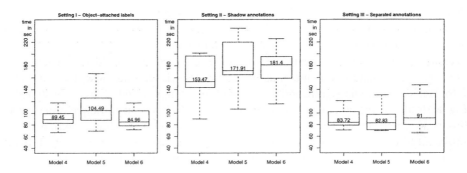

Fig. 10. Task 3: Elapsed times for Settings I-III and Models 4-6

$= 0.78$, $p - Value = 0.54$). But the type of setting had a significant influence on the measured time ($F_{2,99,\beta} = 56.89$, $p - Value < 0.01$) whereas the influence of the model's type was marginal ($F_{2,99,\alpha} = 1.97$, $p - Value = 0.15$).

6   Discussion

The purpose of this study was to increase our understanding about the assets and drawbacks of different techniques that integrate 3D data and text. We found that none of the evaluated techniques was perfect and that several factors had significant impact on how successfully certain tasks were completed. This included as expected the type of setting and it included the type of 3D model and the type of task.

6.1   Task 1: Object-Text Correlations

The diagrams in Fig. 7 show that participants needed most time to perform this first task with the setting-model pairs: Setting I - Model 1, Setting II - Model 1, and Setting III - Model 3. To shed light on these observations, Figure 2, in which the individual models are depicted, can be analyzed. Model 1 is quite compact and the individual model components intersect with each other. Hence, using visual techniques to link between model component and text (as in Settings I and II) may not always be perfectly clear. Often, participants needed to ascertain their choices by time-consuming camera rotations. In contrast, Model 3 is more wide-spaced and composed of similarly shaped components. These visual features may make it more compatible with Settings I and II. However, Model 3 caused longest times in Setting III. This was probably due to descriptions such as "2nd biggest sphere" or "smallest cylinder" with which model components could be found. Even though the descriptions were clear, participants had problems evaluating the differences in size. False object selections (see Fig. 8(left)) correlated with the elapsed times. The more time a participant needed to perform a particular task the higher the rate of false selections.

6.2   Task 2: Object-Text Correlations with Additional Hints

When the search for object-text correlations was combined with hints in the shadow, 75 % of the participants stated explicitly that highlighted shadows facilitated the search. They first tried to find out where the annotation line ended before they ascertained their decision by including the shadow. However, some participants did not benefit from the highlighted shadows as much as we had expected. On one hand, the number of false object selections significantly decreased in Settings B and C, as is illustrated in Fig. 8(right). On the other hand, the diagrams in Fig. 9 show that participants performed this task significantly faster only in Setting C for each model. Since Setting B also provided hints in the shadow, we expected significant faster times here as well. It still has to be studied whether a longer practice period would yield other results.

6.3   Task 3: Task-Based Scene Exploration

This was a quite complex task. Basically, we aimed at provoking interferences between model components and annotations. As the rating in Table 1(right) and the diagrams in Fig. 10 show, Setting II was the worst setting for this task. There were two main reasons for this result: (1) the text did not always fit completely into the annotation shape causing participants to zoom into the scene to enlarge the text area and (2) annotations did often overlap.

Since the model render area and text were separated in Setting III, participants could not be disturbed by annotations during scene exploration. However, the measured times in Setting I and Setting III do not differ that much. This indicates that annotations, integrated into the 3D scene, have not such a high impact on a task-based scene exploration as we had expected. The post-questionnaire, in which participants were asked if they felt disturbed by annotations, confirmed these results. But nevertheless, as an observer, one often had an impression contrary to the participants' self-evaluations, especially in Setting I. One possible explanation might be that participants were so focused on searching for scene objects that they did not notice how much the annotations overlapped with the model. This aspect could be analyzed within another study.

6.4   Design Suggestions

After participants had performed the tasks, they were asked to itemize the features they would include if they were to design an information system. They could choose from a list of the techniques used during the study (multiple selections were possible) and they could make other suggestions. The results are: technique in Setting I: 83 % of the participants would include this technique; technique in Setting II: 11 %; technique in Setting III: 89 %; and technique of highlighting objects in the shadow (Settings B and C): 69 %. In addition to these techniques, some participants suggested techniques such as using context menus (compare [6]) or displaying text only on explicit user request. These would be interesting suggestions to consider in a future study.

Furthermore, here are some comments participants gave for Settings I-III: *Setting I* "uses the most intuitive technique. It was helpful that the annotation size was adapted to the associated scene object's bounding box". The technique used in *Setting II* "was unaccustomed and requires practice. It was not suited for displaying text". In *Setting III*, "reading the scene object descriptions was time-consuming. Also, sometimes it was not clear which scene object was meant. But this setting was the most clearly arranged setting".

Our suggestions for the design of an information system, in which textual information is to be integrated, strongly depend on the application. When both short text labels and extensive texts are to be integrated, we suggest a combination of different techniques. The technique in Setting I seems to be suited for short labels. Using this technique scene objects referred to by annotations can be quite clearly identified. Also, there are no long distances between objects and annotations. However, "only" short labels because the use of this technique with longer texts may cause important parts of the scene to become occluded. An improvement of the *object-line-text* technique in Setting A (e. g., [10]) may be appropriate as well, although it is difficult to maintain an adequate scene layout during the scene exploration. For extensive texts, Setting III seems to be applicable because a user can explore a scene without any occlusions from the text. Furthermore, providing additional hints in the background can be helpful when object-text correlations need to be identified. The technique of highlighting the appropriate shadows (e. g., Settings B and C) could be a useful enrichment in an information system.

7   Summary

We have reported the results of a user study, in which we have examined three different techniques for providing textual information in interactive 3D illustrations. These techniques are: text labels directly attached to scene objects, texts located within a shadow plane, and textual information displayed in a window separated from the area in which the 3D model is rendered. Basically, we were interested in the effects when a 3D model and text are integrated into an appropriate layout and certain tasks are to be performed.

The study—with thirty-six participants—had three tasks. For Task 1, participants were asked to correlate the displayed annotations with the model components to which the annotations referred. For Task 2, we were interested in the accessorial benefits when the additional hints of highlighted shadows are provided in the background. Finally, Task 3 aimed at text readability, text comprehension, and interferences between model components and text such as occlusions. All tasks required the interactive exploration of the 3D scene. As well as recording their actions, the participants were asked to answer questionnaires and to give further comments. As a result we found that none of the evaluated techniques was without drawbacks during all the tasks. But each technique has features that make it particularly applicable in certain situations. Based on our findings, we were able to point out some of those features.

For the future, we plan to investigate other techniques that give a user support during the navigation in interactive 3D illustrations. Unclear object-text correlations and scene occlusions are important issues in this regard. Concerning the design of a second study of that kind, it would be interesting to recruit participants who do not have any experience in the field of 3D computer graphics. Also, even though we had reasons for choosing arbitrary models, using real models may reveal results that can be more directly applied on specific interactive information systems.

References

1. Brinkley, J.F., Wong, B.A., Hinshaw, K.P., Rosse, C.: Design of an Anatomy Information System. IEEE Computer Graphics & Applications **19** (1999) 38–48
2. Lok, S., Feiner, S.: A Survey of Automated Layout Techniques for Information Presentations. In: Proc. of the 1st International Symposium on Smart Graphics. (2001) 61–68
3. Fekete, J.D., Plaisant, C.: Excentric Labeling: Dynamic Neighborhood Labeling for Data Visualization. In: Proc. of the SIGCHI Conference on Human Factors in Computing Systems. (1998) 512–519
4. Golland, P., Kikinis, R., Halle, M., Umans, C., Grimson, W.E.L., Shenton, M.E., Richolt, J.A.: AnatomyBrowser: A Novel Approach to Visualization and Integration of Medical Information. Computer Aided Surgery **4** (1999) 129–143
5. Bell, B., Feiner, S., Höllerer, T.: View Management for Virtual and Augmented Reality. In: Proc. of UIST'01, ACM Symp. on User Interface Software and Technology. (2001) 101–110
6. Pommert, A., Höhne, K.H., Pflesser, B., Richter, E., Riemer, M., Schiemann, T., Schubert, R., Schumacher, U., Tiede, U.: Creating a High-Resolution Spatial/Symbolic Model of the Inner Organs Based on the Visible Human. Medical Image Analysis **5** (2001) 221–228
7. Schlechtweg, S., Strothotte, T.: Generating Scientific Illustrations in Electronic Books. In: Smart Graphics. Papers from the 2000 AAAI Spring Symposium. (2000) 8–15
8. Loughlin, M.M., Hughes, J.F.: An Annotation System for 3D Fluid Flow Visualization. In: Proc. of the Conference on Visualization '94. (1994) 273–279
9. Jung, T., Gross, M.D., Do, E.Y.L.: Annotating and Sketching on 3D Web Models. In: Proc. of the 7th International Conference on Intelligent User Interfaces (IUI 2002). (2002) 95–102
10. Ali, K., Hartmann, K., Strothotte, T.: Label Layout for Interactive 3D Illustrations. Journal of the WSCG (13th Int. Conf. in Central Europe on Computer Graphics, Visualization and Computer Vision) **13** (2005) 1–8
11. Herndon, K.P., Zeleznik, R.C., Robbins, D.C., Conner, D.B., Snibbe, S.S., van Dam, A.: Interactive Shadows. In: Proc. of ACM Symposium on User Interface Software and Technology. (1992) 1–6
12. Ritter, F., Sonnet, H., Hartmann, K., Strothotte, T.: Illustrative Shadows: Integrating 3D and 2D Information Displays. In: Proc. of the 8th International Conference on Intelligent User Interfaces (IUI 2003). (2003) 166–173
13. Chigona, W., Sonnet, H., Ritter, F., Strothotte, T.: Shadows with a Message. In: Proc. of the 3rd International Symposium on Smart Graphics. (2003) 91–101
14. Sonnet, H., Carpendale, M.S.T., Strothotte, T.: Integrating Expanding Annotations with a 3D Explosion Probe. In: Proc. of the Working Conference on Advanced Visual Interfaces (AVI 2004). (2004) 63–70

The Effect of Operational Mechanisms
on Creativity in Design

Andrew Warr and Eamonn O'Neill

Human-Computer Interaction Group, Department of Computer Science,
University of Bath, Bath, UK
+44 (0) 1225 3374/3216
{cspaw, eamonn}@cs.bath.ac.uk

Abstract. Creativity is frequently referred to as an important dynamic of design. However, over 50 years of empirical research has suggested that social influences have a detrimental effect on creativity in collaborating groups. The results of this research indicate that design teams may not be as creative as they could be, resulting in a negative impact on the design process. In this paper we build upon previous research to identify what effect operational mechanisms have on creativity, in order to determine how best to support the creative process in design.

1 Introduction

The Human Computer Interaction (HCI) community has long been concerned with the design of usable software applications and computer systems. Over the years a consensus has developed that involving users directly in the software development process can lead to more useful and usable systems. This has found its clearest expression in the Participatory Design (PD) movement. PD initially grew out of Scandinavian concerns to bring democracy into the work place [1], by involving users in the design stage of the software development process. Since the 1970s, the focus of PD has shifted from introducing democracy into the work place to a belief that 'active user involvement in the software development process leads to more useful and usable software products' [2]. PD epitomizes the collaborative nature of design, bringing together stakeholders from diverse backgrounds to work together in both the analytical and creative practices of systems development. Design in PD is a social rather than an individual activity. However, even in design processes that do not encourage user participation, an individual designer rarely works in isolation.

The collaborative processes of generating design requirements and envisioned system designs remain something of a 'magic art', within both PD and other systems development approaches. In the PD literature, this 'magic art' is frequently referred to using terms such as *creativity* and *innovation* [e.g. 2-8]. However, while participatory design may be viewed as a collaborative or social creative process and PD researchers and practitioners use the term 'creativity' when referring to the design process, they provide little definition of what this term means and what is actually involved in this process of social creativity, although many researchers [e.g. 9, 10] have argued the importance of creativity in design.

M.F. Costabile and F. Paternò (Eds.): INTERACT 2005, LNCS 3585, pp. 629–642, 2005.
© IFIP International Federation for Information Processing 2005

In our research [11, 12] we have built upon previous research in creativity [e.g. 13-15], to develop a unified definition of creativity:

'Creativity is the generation of ideas, which are a combination of two or more matrices of thought, which are considered unusual or new to the mind in which the ideas arose and are appropriate to the characteristics of a desired solution defined during the problem definition and preparation stage of the creative process'.

With respect to design, creativity is the generation of design ideas, to solve a given design problem, which are both: (i) new or unusual to the mind in which they arose (novelty); and (ii) conform to the requirements of the design problem (appropriateness).

In this paper, we report the results of an experiment we conducted to investigate creativity in design; specifically, we investigated the effect of operational mechanisms (i.e. altering the group composition in the design process) on creativity for both individuals and groups. Many researchers [e.g. 16] have studied the effects on creativity due to procedural mechanisms (i.e. production blocking); social psychological mechanisms (i.e. evaluation apprehension); and economic mechanisms (i.e. free-riding). We extend this consideration to include a fourth type: operational mechanisms. We define operational mechanisms to include, for example, group size and group composition. Building upon previous research we discuss the findings of our experiment observing the effect on creativity due to the operational mechanism of group composition, and provide a focus for future research on supporting creativity in design.

2 Experiment Overview

In 1958 Taylor et al [9] conducted a study comparing real groups (i.e. face-to-face interacting groups) with nominal groups (i.e. individuals working on their own and then collating their outputs to form a cumulative output), to test Osborn's claim that 'the average person can think up twice as many ideas when working within a group than when working alone' [17]. Taylor et al found that nominal groups produced nearly twice as many non-replicated ideas as real groups – refuting Osborn's claim. Since the Taylor et al study, over 50 years of empirical studies have shown nominal groups to outperform real groups. Hence, Taylor et al and other researchers have shown that collaborating groups, such as design teams, are not being as creative as they could be.

Since the Taylor et al [9] study, there has been an abundance of research investigating why real groups are not as effective as nominal groups with respect to creativity [e.g. 18]. However, the findings of such research have only increased the effectiveness of creativity in real groups over nominal groups slightly in some conditions, while there are still many cases where nominal groups outperform real groups. Therefore some researchers [e.g. 18, 19] have suggested that the process of idea generation should be performed by nominal groups alone.

Rotter et al [20] conducted a study observing the effects on creativity due to different group compositions in the design process (i.e. operational mechanisms). Rotter et al [20] hypothesized that the number of solutions would be greater when participants worked consecutively in an individual and a group setting (nominal-real or real-nominal conditions) rather than either a group (real condition) or an individual (nominal condition) setting alone. It was also hypothesized that for all conditions the number of ideas generated should be greater when working individually than when working within a group. The first hypothesis was not supported, as there were significantly more ideas produced in the nominal condition than either of the mixed conditions or the real condition. Their second hypothesis was supported, showing nominal groups to be more creative than real groups.

However, the Rotter et al [20] study had a few fundamental flaws. In the individual condition the participants were told to write down their ideas. However, in the other conditions involving a group component the participants were also allowed to communicate verbally. This form of asynchronous interaction adds a variable of production blocking, resulting in a difference between the conditions [12]. Secondly, if group members can verbally express their ideas rather than just writing them down, a variable of evaluation apprehension is also introduced [12]. The resultant effect of these confounding variables between the conditions means that the results cannot be relied upon. In addition to this, in the nominal-real and real-nominal group conditions, the participants were not allowed to bring up ideas they had previously generated in the latter half of the experiment. According to our theory [12], if the externalization of matrices of thought (i.e. ideas) is prohibited, there is a resultant detrimental effect on creativity.

In our study it is hypothesized (H1) that the number of novel and creative ideas generated in response to a given design problem should be greater when participants work in a nominal-real condition rather than in a real, nominal or real-nominal condition. The rationale for this hypothesis is that an individual will initially (in the nominal sub-condition) be able to exploit the matrices of thought in her own domain of knowledge. Upon transferring to the real sub-condition, the participants in the group will be exposed to other matrices of thought allowing them to combine and generate new matrices of thought, or improve upon the ideas of others. Whereas in the real-nominal condition and the real group condition participants may be influenced by group norms [21], and in the nominal condition an individual will exhaust her domain of knowledge compared to those groups who have the ability to interact with each other and externalize their matrices of thought. It is also hypothesized (H2) that the nominal condition will generate more novel and creative replicated ideas compared to the other conditions and the real condition will generate fewer novel and creative replicated ideas compared to other conditions. Rotter et al [20] argued that the expression of an idea in a group causes all the members to think along the same lines, leading to the duplication of ideas. However, we argue that being in a setting which allows other members to see what ideas are being generated will cause less duplication as members are aware of what has already been reported.

3 Method

The experiment had a between participants experimental design. The experiment manipulated one independent variable, the operational mechanism of group composition, which consisted of four levels: 1) Nominal Groups; 2) Nominal-Real Groups; 3) Real-Nominal Groups; and 4) Real Groups. The dependent variable was creativity – the number of novel and appropriate design ideas generated [12]. It was predicted that: the number of novel and creative ideas generated in response to a given design problem would be greater when participants worked in the nominal-real condition rather than in a real, nominal or real-nominal condition (H1); and the nominal condition would generate more novel and creative replicated ideas compared to the other conditions and the real condition would generate fewer novel and creative replicated ideas compared to the other conditions (H2).

3.1 Participants

Forty-eight participants, seven of whom were female, took part in this experiment, twelve per condition. The participants varied in age from 18 – 37, with a mean of 20.65 years. All participants were computer scientists from the University of Bath, with the majority of them being undergraduates. The participants were recruited personally by the experimenter from lecture rooms and mailing lists and were each paid £5 for participating in the experiment.

3.2 Apparatus

The set up of the apparatus can be seen in fig. 1. On each participant's desk was a 12" display IBM x31 ThinkPad and a USB Microsoft IR Mouse. Each of the ThinkPads' had an internal 802.11g wireless connection which allowed it to communicate with a server. An A4 piece of paper was stuck to the desk, giving information relevant to the experiment: Osborn's four brainstorming rules, the rules of the experiment, and the design problem which was covered by an overlay until the experiment started (see Sect. 3.3). Each participant's desk was shielded by tall dividers to prevent communication between participants.

Each ThinkPad was running a custom built stand-alone Windows application – the Idea Generator (see fig. 2). In the top right of the screen is the generated ideas textbox – this is where a participant writes her idea when she thinks of one. To submit an idea, participants could either press the 'submit' button located in the bottom right of the screen, or press the 'enter' key on the keyboard. The generated ideas textbox could be cleared by pressing the 'clear' button in the bottom right of the screen. In the bottom

Fig. 1. Experimental set up on a Participant's Desk

left of the screen is a condition label that indicates to the user which condition they are currently in – individual (i.e. nominal) or group (i.e. real). In the top left of the screen is the pooled ideas textbox. This textbox displayed recorded ideas dependent on the current condition and could not be edited. In the nominal condition, only the participant's own ideas could be viewed. In the real condition, all participants could see the ideas generated by themselves and others. In the nominal-real condition, when the condition changed from the nominal sub-condition to the real sub-condition all ideas generated by each participant during the nominal sub-condition were pooled into the pooled ideas textbox. In the real-nominal condition, when the sub-condition changed from the real sub-condition to the nominal sub-condition, all ideas generated by the group during the real sub-condition remained in the pooled ideas textbox during the nominal sub-condition.

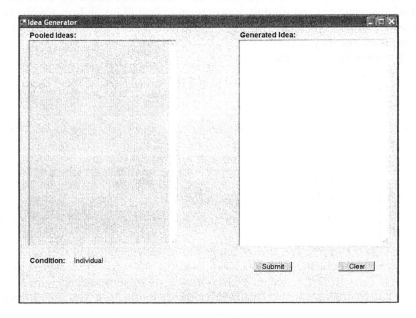

Fig. 2. Idea Generator Software

In a separate room to the experiment was the experimenter's table. The experiment was recorded here. In the participants' room were two cameras which each viewed two participants. The output from these cameras was fed through a monitor displaying a real-time image to the experimenter. The image was also captured via a DVC recorder for future analysis. The experimenter also had access to a HP Tablet PC that ran the Windows Remote Desktop application to access the server remotely. This allowed the experimenter to change the sub-condition during the nominal-real and real-nominal experimental conditions.

The server was a standard desktop PC that ran Microsoft's SQL Enterprise Server version 8.0. An SQL database ran on this server, storing ideas generated by the participants and other information: who generated the idea; the condition in which the idea was generated; and the date and time the idea was recorded. The server was also used to play audio files of instructions to the participants via Windows Media Player.

3.3 Procedure

Participants were run in groups of four in a secure, sound-proof lab. At the outset the participants were taken to the back of the lab where the pre-recorded instructions were played. Pre-recorded instructions were used to minimise the experimenter's contact with the participants. The start of the pre-recordings gave an overview of the experiment: the condition the participants had been assigned to; a description of Osborn's brainstorming rules; some rules to abide by during the experiment; a description of the software; the warm-up exercise; and the design problem for the actual experiment. After each audio file the experimenter asked the participants if they had any questions and tried to answer them to best of his ability. Creativity was never mentioned, as Amabile [14] argues that participants' performance changes if they are aware that they are being assessed on creativity.

The groups were assigned to one of four conditions:

1) *Nominal Condition*: Participants work individually for 16 minutes.
2) *Nominal-Real Condition*: Participants work individually for 8 minutes and then as a group for 8 minutes.
3) *Real-Nominal Condition*: Participants work as a group for 8 minutes and then individually for 8 minutes.
4) *Real Condition*: Participants work as a group for 16 minutes.

Osborn's brainstorming rules were given to the participants to help them with the idea generation process:

1) *Criticism is ruled out*. Adverse judgement of ideas must be withheld. No one shall criticism anyone else's ideas. Say anything you think of.
2) *Freewheeling is welcomed*. The wilder the idea the better. It is easier to tame down than think up. Do not be afraid to say anything that comes to mind. The further out the idea the better, this will stimulate more and better ideas.
3) *Quantity is wanted*. The greater the number of ideas, the greater the likelihood of winners. Come up with as many as you can.
4) *Combination and improvement are sought*. Suggest how the ideas of others can be joined into still better ideas.

In contrast to previous experiments, these brainstorming rules were included on the information sheet attached to each participant's desk. This was done to relieve the cognitive load on each participant, so that they could focus more on the design problem at hand.

Based on previous research [18], participants were told three rules by which to abide in order to control confounding variables:

1) You may not communicate with anyone else once the experiment has started – to control production blocking.
2) All ideas contributed will be anonymous – to control evaluation apprehension.

3)   We are assessing the ideas of individuals, not the group collectively – to control free-riding.

Once again, unlike other experiments, instead of just verbalising this information it was also included on the information sheet attached to the participant's desk so they could reference it when desired.

Once the background information was provided to the participants, they were asked to gather round one of the ThinkPad's which was running the Idea Generator software. While an audio recording played a description of the software (see Sect. 3.2 for software description) the experimenter pointed to the relevant parts of the screen.

The software was designed to externalise ideas in a textual form. While it could be argued that some aspects of design are more oriented towards sketching ideas rather than writing then, van der Lugt [22] argues how sketching and writing ideas are quite different in nature (i.e. brainsketching vs. brainstorming). van der Lugt [23] has shown how sketching causes a breakdown in the process of activities like brainstorming. To make a valid comparison with previous research [20], we controlled this confounding variable of representation by using a textual representation of ideas for all conditions.

The warm-up exercise was utilized to get the participants used to the experiment and the software they would be using. The exercise lasted two minutes and was based on an adaptation of the tourism problem [9] for the European community:

'Each year a great many European tourists go to America to visit. But now suppose that Europe wanted to get many more Americans to come to Europe during their vacations. What steps can you suggest to get many more Americans to come to Europe as tourists?'

The experimenter asked all the participants if they understood the problem and gave an example idea of 'providing cheaper trans-Atlantic flights'. Once all queries had been dealt with, the experimenter asked the participants to take a seat at a desk and open up the Idea Generator software. Once the experimenter was happy, the two minute warm-up exercise began.

After the two minutes all participants were asked to come to the back of the lab. The experimenter checked for erroneous responses, closed the Idea Generator software on each IBM ThinkPad and cleared the SQL Server of all ideas from the warm-up exercise. If the experimenter found erroneous responses, he explained to all the participants why this was so. After dealing with all queries by the participants and upon being satisfied that everyone was happy, the experimenter began the design problem experiment.

Unlike other experiments which gave non-specialist problems such as the tourist problem [9], it was decided to give a design problem within the domain of computer science, in order to relate the findings of the experiment more to design in that domain. The problem was named the Pervasive Computing Scrolling Problem and was like other design problems in that it was open-ended and ill-defined:

'You have been asked to design an interaction technique for scrolling on a pervasive computer system with a 61" plasma screen. The technique should allow the user or users to scroll up, down, left and right.'

The experimenter asked all the participants if they understood the problem and answered any questions without giving information as to possible solutions to the problem. Once all queries had been dealt with, the experimenter asked the participants to take a seat at a desk and open up the Idea Generator software by selecting the appropriate icon on the desktop. Participants were then informed that they could remove a partial overlay on the information sheet that revealed the experimental problem. This allowed the participants to reference the problem as they worked. The experimenter told the participants that the experiment would last sixteen minutes. Before the experiment started the experimenter started recording the participants and then informed them that they could begin.

For those participants who were in the nominal-real or real-nominal condition, the experimenter changed the condition after eight minutes via the experimenter's computer. Upon the change in condition, the label on the participant's computer changed to indicate which condition the participant was in, and the experimenter also verbally communicated this from the experimenter's room to make the participants aware of the change in condition.

After the sixteen minutes were completed, the experimenter asked all participants to stop typing; close down the Idea Generator software; and remain seated. The experimenter then stopped the recording and handed each participant a questionnaire.

While the participants were completing the questionnaire, the experimenter printed off a form for a post-analysis of each participant's ideas. The post-analysis was designed to assess if the ideas generated were novel. Previous research [e.g. 16, 25-31] considers every idea generated to be creative, however in order for an idea to be considered creative it must be both novel and appropriate [12]. The experimenter went round each participant and asked them to say for each of their ideas whether it was: (i) a new idea – a combination of two or more existing ideas; (ii) an old, existing idea applied to a new context; or (iii) other, and if other could they specify. This classification of ideas is similar to that used by Benami and Jin [10].

4   Results

The dependent variable we observed in the experiment was creativity. According to Torrance [24] we can measure creativity in terms of fluency, flexibility and quality. Fluency is the number of creative ideas that were generated. Flexibility is the number of categories of ideas that were generated. Quality is a subjective rating by two or more independent judges who are considered experts in the domain in question [14]. It is beyond the scope of this paper to analyse all these factors of creativity, therefore we are going to consider fluency as a factor of creativity.

We analysed the effect of the operational mechanisms upon creativity in terms of the number of creative ideas generated and the number of replicated ideas. The findings are reported in terms of the effect upon the individual and the group.

Most other studies when considering the number of creative ideas just assume every idea to be creative – taking into account replications. However, in accordance with our definition of creativity [11, 12], in order for an idea to be deemed creative we first assessed all generated ideas for their novelty by using the retrospective protocol administered after the experiment and then assessed all novel ideas to determine if they were appropriate. Appropriateness was determined using a simple checkbox list to make sure each idea conformed to the characteristics defined during the problem statement – the interaction techniques should allow the *user* or *users* to scroll *up*, *down*, *left* and *right*.

4.1 The Effect of Operational Mechanisms on the Creativity of Individuals

The number of novel and creative ideas was assessed for each participant. The mean number of novel and creative ideas, replicated and non-replicated, can be seen in table 1.

Table 1. Mean (and SD) number of novel and creative ideas for all four conditions for individuals

	N	N-R	R-N	R
Novel Ideas (Replicated)	10.08 (3.34)	8.5 (2.24)	12.08 (4.77)	10.25 (4.33)
Novel Ideas (Non-Replicated)	7.08 (4.31)	6.17 (2.79)	9.75 (3.94)	9.25 (3.91)
Creative Ideas (Replicated)	9.75 (3.42)	8.5 (2.24)	11.58 (4.01)	9 (5.34)
Creative Ideas (Non-Replicated)	6.75 (4.30)	6.17 (2.79)	9.33 (3.94)	8 (3.91)

The data were analysed using a one-way unrelated ANOVA. No significant differences were found between the four conditions: novel ideas, including replications ($F_{3,44} = 1.97$, $p = 0.133$); novel ideas, with no replications ($F_{3,44} = 2.63$, $p = 0.062$); creative ideas, including replications ($F_{3,44} = 1.43$, $p = 0.247$); and creative ideas, with no replication ($F_{3,44} = 1.57$, $p = 0.210$). Therefore, with respect to the effect of operational mechanisms on the creativity of individuals, hypothesis H1 was not supported.

Using these data, the number of replications made by individuals was calculated for both novel and creative ideas. The mean number of novel and creative ideas that were replicated can be seen in table 2.

Table 2. Mean (and SD) number of replications for both novel and creative ideas for individuals

	N	N-R	R-N	R
Novel Ideas	3 (1.91)	2.33 (1.07)	2.83 (1.72)	1 (1.21)
Creative Ideas	3 (1.91)	2.33 (1.07)	2.25 (1.66)	1 (1.21)

Using a one-way unrelated ANOVA, significant differences were found between the four conditions for both novel ($F_{3,44} = 3.67$, $p = 0.019$) and creative ($F_{3,44} = 3.72$, $p = 0.018$) ideas. In order to detect where the significance occurred, we performed a Tukey Test. From the data for the number of replicated novel ideas we found that there was a significant difference only between the nominal and real group conditions (mean N – mean R = 2, T = 1.66, 2 >1.66, $p < 0.05$). For the number of replicated creative ideas, we also only found there to be a significant difference between the nominal and real group conditions (mean N – mean R = 2, T = 1.64, 2 > 1.64, $p < 0.05$). Therefore, with respect to the effect of operational mechanisms on the creativity of individuals, hypothesis H2 was partially supported, as a significant effect was found between the nominal and real group conditions, but no significant effect was found between either the nominal or real group conditions and either the nominal-real or real-nominal conditions.

4.2   The Effect of Operational Mechanisms on the Creativity of Groups

The numbers of novel and creative ideas were assessed for each group. The mean number of novel and creativity ideas, replicated and non-replicated, can be seen in table 3.

Table 3. Mean (and SD) number of novel and creative ideas for all four conditions for groups

	N	N-R	R-N	R
Novel Ideas (Replicated)	41 (3)	34.33 (2.31)	49 (13)	40.33 (10.41)
Novel Ideas (Non-Replicated)	26.33 (4.61)	25 (2.31)	38.67 (7.57)	36.33 (8.50)
Creative Ideas (Replicated)	39.67 (4.51)	33.33 (3.51)	47.66 (11.02)	32.33 (13.80)
Creative Ideas (Non-Replicated)	25.22 (4.04)	25 (2.65)	38 (7.21)	32.33 (11.15)

The data were analysed using a one-way unrelated ANOVA. No significant differences were found: novel ideas, including replications ($F_{3,8}$ = 1.49, p = 0.298); novel ideas, with no replications ($F_{3,8}$ = 3.64, p = 0.064); creative ideas, including replications ($F_{3,8}$ = 1.21, p = 0.365); and creative ideas, with no replications ($F_{3,8}$ = 2.33, p = 0.151). Therefore, with respect to the effect of operational mechanisms on the creativity of groups, hypothesis H1 was not supported.

From this data, the number of replications made by the group for both novel and creative ideas was calculated. The mean number of novel and creative ideas that were replicated can be seen in table 4.

Table 4. Mean (and SD) number of replications for both novel and creative ideas for groups

	N	N-R	R-N	R
Novel Ideas	14.66 (5.51)	9.33 (0.58)	10.33 (5.69)	4 (2)
Creative Ideas	14.33 (5.03)	8.33 (1.16)	8.66 (5.03)	3 (2.65)

Using a one-way unrelated ANOVA, no significant differences were found between the four conditions for novel ideas ($F_{3,8}$ = 3.44, p = 0.072), but significant differences were found between the four conditions for creative ideas ($F_{3,8}$ = 4.36, p = 0.043). To detect where the significance occurred between the conditions for the number of replicated creative ideas, we performed a Tukey Test. For the number of replicated creative ideas, we found there to be a significant difference between the nominal and real group conditions (mean N – mean R = 11.33, T = 10.04, 11.33 >

10.04, $p < 0.05$). Therefore, with respect to the effect of operational mechanisms on the creativity of groups, hypothesis H2 was also partially supported, as a significant effect was found between the nominal and real group conditions, but no significant effect was found between either the nominal or real group conditions and either the nominal-real or real-nominal conditions.

5 Discussion

A lot of research [e.g. 16, 25-31] over the years has explored how to reduce the impact of social influences upon creativity in collaborating groups – removing the factors of production blocking, evaluation apprehension and free riding. However, the findings of such research have only increased the effectiveness of real groups over nominal groups slightly in some conditions, while in many cases nominal groups continue to outperform real groups. In this study, we built on previous research to reduce the social influences upon creativity to see what the effect of the various operational mechanisms would be without the social influences acting as confounding variables.

Creativity in terms of fluency – the number of creative ideas generated – was assessed as a result of altering the operational mechanism from the perspective of the individual and the group. In addition to looking at the fluency of creativity, we also analysed the number of replicated ideas for both novel and creative ideas. It was hypothesized that: the number of creative ideas generated in response to a given design problem would be greater when participants worked in the nominal-real condition rather than working in either a real, nominal or real-nominal condition (H1); and that the nominal condition would generate more replicated ideas compared to the other conditions and the real condition would generate fewer replicated ideas compared to other conditions (H2).

We found that there were no statistically significant differences between any of the four conditions in terms of the fluency of creativity for both individuals and groups; therefore H1 was not supported. This is in itself an important finding since, compared to the large body of previous research [e.g. 16, 25-31], we substantially increased the creative performance of real groups. We produced a change from the creativity of real groups being statistically less significant than that of nominal groups, as reported by previous studies, to there being no statistical differences between these conditions.

The experimental hypothesis H1 was based on our theory [12] that real groups should be able to generate more creative ideas due to more effective sharing of domains of knowledge. Despite our increasing the creative performance of real groups, we did not confirm the experimental hypothesis that the nominal-real condition should be most creative. Hence, we must ask why there were no statistically significant differences in creativity due to different operational mechanisms as predicted?

So, why is it the case that real groups still did not reach their theoretical potential when social influences upon creativity were removed in our study? The representation of the externalization of matrices of knowledge (i.e. a list of ideas represented as text) may not have been effective enough. Other possible explanations relate to the time taken by the participants. Perhaps the time allowed was sufficient for the participants in each of the conditions to reach their maximum threshold of productivity, therefore being equally productive across conditions; or it could also have been the case that participants were suffering from fatigue and had lost the motivation to continue [14]. Our experiment followed Rotter's [20] which assumed that a 16-minute session is equivalent to 2 8-minute sessions. That is, the nominal and real conditions each ran for an uninterrupted 16 minutes while the nominal-real and real-nominal conditions each had a change in operational mechanism halfway through the session. The changeover may have had effects on the participants' creativity. While the change itself was minimally disruptive, as described above, each participant in the nominal-real condition was suddenly faced at the beginning of the real sub-condition with the accumulated ideas from the other participants in the nominal sub-condition. The participants may have concentrated on "catching up" on the others' ideas, thus incurring a form of production blocking. To explore these potential explanations for our results, further research is required.

It was also found that there were statistically significant differences between the nominal group condition and the real group condition for the number of replicated ideas, supporting hypothesis H2 for both the effect on the individual and the group. Rotter *et al* [20] argued that the expression of an idea in a group causes all the members to think along the same lines, leading to the duplication of ideas. However, this study has contradicted Rotter *et al* [20], as real groups replicated fewer ideas than nominal groups. It was also no surprise that there were no statistically significant differences between the nominal-real and the real-nominal group conditions, since each condition had an equal amount of time in the nominal condition and the real condition – therefore the effects of replicated ideas for each condition could have cancelled each other out. It is possible that statistically significant differences were found only between the nominal and real group conditions because of the effects of increasing and decreasing duplicated ideas respectively for each condition. Yet when comparing either the nominal or real group conditions with either the nominal-real or real-nominal conditions, there were no significant differences.

Therefore, although we have shown that there is no statistically significant difference between the fluency of creativity when considering the effects of operational mechanisms in terms of individuals and groups, we have shown a significant change in the perform of real groups compared to previous research [e.g. 16, 25-31] and also shown real groups to be more effective during the design process compared to the nominal group compositions, when social influences upon creativity are controlled. Hence, our findings have contradicted an abundance of previous research [e.g. 16, 25-31] showing real groups to be inferior to nominal groups.

6   Conclusions and Future Work

In this paper we report an experiment investigating the effect of operational mechanisms on creativity from the perspective of both the individual and the group in a design scenario. In the experiment we manipulated operational mechanisms that consisted of four levels: nominal; nominal-real; real-nominal; and real group conditions.

The results of the experiment are that there was no significant difference in creativity between any of the conditions although a significant change in performance has been found compared to other research, and significant differences were found when looking at the number of replicated ideas, showing real groups to be more efficient in terms of the number of non-replicated ideas – refuting an abundance of previously reported research [e.g. 16, 25-31].

In our future work we plan to conduct further analyses of the data: assessing creativity between the different conditions in terms of flexibility and quality. In addition to this, we are also going to analyse the performance of the individuals' and groups' creativity.

Further research questions which we have so far identified from the analysis presented in this paper are: why is it the case that real groups are still not reaching their theoretical potential when social impediments to creativity are removed?; does the form of representation of externalized matrices of knowledge affect creativity; and is it the case that there is an upper limit on a person's creative productivity before task motivation falls below some threshold and fatigue sets in?

With answers to such research questions, we can look towards supporting social creativity and improving the practice of design, ultimately leading to more usable and useful software applications and computer systems.

References

1. Floyd, C., Mehl, W., Reisen, F., Schmidt, G. & Wolf, G. Out of Scaninavia: alternative approaches to software design and system development. Human-Computer Interaction 4 (1989) 253-350
2. O'Neill, E. User-developer cooperation in software development: building common ground and usable systems. Springer Verlag, London (2000)
3. Alborzi, H., Druin, A., Montemayor, J., Platner, M., Porteous, J., Sherman, L., Boltman, A., Taxén, G., Best, J., Hammer, J., Kruskal, A., Lal, A., Schwenn, T. P., Sumida, L., Wagner, R., & Hendler, J., Designing StoryRooms: Interactive Storytelling Spaces for Children. in DIS (Brooklyn, New York, 2000) 95-104
4. Buur, J. & Bødker, S., From Usability Lab to "Design Collaboratorium": Reframing Usability Practice. in DIS (Brooklyn, New York, 2000) 297-307
5. Bødker, S. & Iverson, O. S., Staging a Professional Participatory Design Practice - Moving PD beyond the Initial Fascination of User Involvement. in NordiCHI (Arhus, Denmark, 2002) 11-18
6. Kyng, M., Scandinavian Design: Users in Product Development. in CHI (Boston, Massachusetts, 1994) 3-9
7. Shneiderman, B. Creating Creativity: User Interfaces for supporting innovation. ACM Trans. on Computer-Human Interaction, 7, 1 (2000) 114-138
8. Streitz, N., Geißler, J., Holmer, T., Konomi, S., Müller-Tomfolde, C., Reischl, W., Rexroth, P., Seitz, P. & Steinmetz, R., I-LAND: An interactive Landscape for Creativity and Innovation. in CHI (Pittsburgh, PA, 1999) 120-127
9. Taylor, D.W., Berry, P. C. & Block C. H. Does Group Participation When Using Brainstorming Facilitate or Inhibit Creative Thinking? Administrative Science Quarterly, 3, 1 (1958) 23-47

10. Benami, O. & Yan, J., Creative Stimulation in Conceptual Design. in ASME Design Engineering Technical Conferences and Computer and Information in Engineering Conference (Montreal, Canada, 2002) 1-13

11. Warr, A. & O'Neill, E., Getting Creative with Participatory Design. in Participatory Design Conference, 2 (Toronto, Canada, 2004) 57-60

12. Warr, A. & O'Neill, E., Understanding Design as a Social Creative Process. in Creativity and Cognition (London, UK, 2005)

13. Boden, M. The Dimensions of Creativity. MIT Press Cambridge, London (1994)

14. Amabile, T.M. The Social Psychology of Creativity. Springer-Verlag, New York (1983)

15. Guildford, J.P. Creativity. American Psychologist, 5 (1950) 444-454

16. Mullen, B., Johnson, C. & Salas, E. Productivity Loss in Brainstorming Groups: A Meta-Analytic Integration. Basic and Applied Social Psychology, 12, 1 (1991) 3-23

17. Osborn, A.F. Applied Imagination: Principles and procedures of creative thinking. Scribeners and Sons, New York (1957)

18. Diehl, M. & Stroebe, W. Productivity Loss in Brainstorming Groups: Toward the Solution of a Riddle. Journal of Personality and Social Psychology, 53 (1987) 497-509

19. Lamm, H. & Trommsdorff, G. Group versus individual performance on tasks requiring ideational proficiency (brainstorming). European Journal of Social Psychology, 3 (1973) 361-387

20. Rotter, G.S. & Portugal, S. M. Group and Individual Effects in Problem Solving. Journal of Applied Psychology, 53, 4 (1969) 338-341

21. Terry, D.J. & Hoog, M. A. Attributes, behavior and social context the roles of norms and group membership. Lawrence Erlbaum Associates, Mahwah, NJ (2000)

22. van der Lugt, R., Functions of Sketching in Design Idea Generation Meetings. in Creativity and Cognition (Loughborough, UK, 2002) 72-79

23. van der Lugt, R. Developing a graphic tool for creative problem in design groups. Design Studies, 21, 5 (2000) 505-522

24. Torrance, E.P. Influence of Dyadic Interaction on Creative Functioning. Psychology Reports, 26 (1970) 391-394

25. 25. Cohen, D., Whitmyre, J. W. & Funk, W. H. Effect of Group Cohesiveness and Training upon Creative Thinking. Journal of Applied Psychology, 44, 5 (1960) 319-322

26. Demhis, A.R. & Valacich, J. S. Computer Brainstorms: More Heads Are Better Than One. Journal of Applied Psychology, 78, 4 (1993) 531-536

27. Dillon, P.C., Graham, W. K. & Aidells, A. L. Brainstorming on a "Hot" Problem: Effects of Training and Practice on Individual and Group Performance. Journal of Applied Psychology, 56, 6 (1972) 487-490

28. Kraemer, T.J., Fleming, G. P. & Mannis, S. M. Improving Face to Face Brainstorming through Modelling and Facilitation. Journal of Small Group Research, 32, 5 (2001) 533-557

29. McGlynn, R.P., McGurk, D., Effland, V. S., Johll, N. L. & Harding, D. J. Brainstorming and Task Performance in Groups Contained by Evidence. Journal of Organisational Behaviour & Human Decision Processes, 93, 1 (2004) 75-87

30. Paulus, P.B. & Yang, H. Idea Generation in Groups: A Basis for Creativity in Organisations. Journal of Organisational Behaviour & Human Decision Processes, 82, 1 (2000) 76-87

31. Valacich, J.S., Dennis, A. R. & Connolly, T. Idea Generation in Computer-Based Groups: A New Ending to an Old Story. Journal of Organisational Behaviour & Human Decision Processes, 57, 2 (1994) 448-466

The Necessity of a Meeting Recording and Playback System, and the Benefit of Topic–Level Annotations to Meeting Browsing

Satanjeev Banerjee, Carolyn Rose, and Alexander I. Rudnicky

Language Technologies Institute,
Carnegie Mellon University
{banerjee+, cprose, air+}@cs.cmu.edu

Abstract. Much work in the area of Computer Supported Cooperative Work (CSCW) has targeted the problem of supporting meetings between collaborators who are non-collocated, enabling meetings to transcend boundaries of space. In this paper, we explore the beginnings of a proposed solution for allowing meetings to transcend time as well. The need for such a solution is motivated by a user survey in which busy professionals are questioned about meetings they have either missed or forgotten the important details about after the fact. Our proposed solution allows these professionals to transcend time in a sense by revisiting a recorded meeting that has been structured for quick retrieval of sought information. Such a solution supports complete recovery of prior discussions, allowing needed information to be retrieved quickly, and thus potentially facilitating the effective continuation of discussions from the past. We evaluate the proposed solution with a formal user study in which we measure the impact of the proposed structural annotations on retrieval of information. The results of the study show that participants took significantly less time to retrieve the answers when they had access to discourse structure based annotation than in a control condition in which they had access only to unannotated video recordings ($p < 0.01$, effect size 0.94 standard deviations).

1   Introduction

Meetings in modern organizations play a crucial role as the forum where information is shared, alternatives are discussed, and decisions are made. Much research has therefore focused on facilitating the conduct of meetings when all the participants are not collocated (e.g., [10], [11], etc). A secondary role that meetings play is in the bringing together of a large amount of project–relevant information, and also being the source of new kinds of information (such as decisions, action items, etc). Some recent research has focused on capturing this information, both old and new, and making it available for later access by interested parties (e.g.: [1], [4], [7], etc.) Such technology has several potential uses. First it can be of use to parties that were absent during the actual meeting. While such *non–contemporaneous* meeting participants may not be able to contribute

M.F. Costabile and F. Paternò (Eds.): INTERACT 2005, LNCS 3585, pp. 643–656, 2005.

to the meeting itself, they can at least benefit from the information discussed at the meeting using such technology, and then be included as a more informed participant in resulting ongoing discussions. A second use of this technology is as an aid to participants' memories of past meetings. Participants forget details of meetings, or worse, have erroneous recollections of past meetings. Meeting capture and play back technology, if appropriately designed, can be used to efficiently retrieve details of past meetings. Thus, this technology can be viewed as improving Organizational Memory [8], which has been shown to enhance productivity [9]. Note that recording meetings raises several privacy and confidentiality issues. Cutler and colleagues (2002) report finding that participants are "generally comfortable having their meetings recorded", although they caution that this could be the result of participant self selection in their pilot study.

Our first goal in this paper is to explore the problem of reconstructing information discussed at a meeting. How often do busy professionals need to reconstruct details of past meetings? What kinds of documents do they typically have access to? Are those documents sufficient? What kinds of information are they typically seeking from past meetings? How much time does it take to do the reconstruction? To gain an understanding of these issues, we have run an interview–based survey with 12 faculty members at Carnegie Mellon University. We have chosen this user population since university faculty typify professionals whose lives are dominated by meetings. Interviewees were asked to narrate specific instances of situations when they were trying to catch up on a meeting that they had missed, or were trying to reconstruct forgotten details of a meeting they had attended in the past.

Our second aim is to assess through a controlled study how helpful topic–level annotations are to meeting browsing. The Carnegie Mellon Meeting Recorder [1] can be used to create rich multi–modal records of meetings, while the MockBrow can be used to manually annotate a meeting record, and also play back both the meeting record and any associated annotations. Both these tools are being developed as a part of the CALO (Cognitive Agent that Learns and Organizes) project [14]. The ultimate goal is for the discourse structure based annotation that we evaluate the utility of in this paper to be applied to recordings of meetings automatically by making use of easily detectable cues such as shifts in word frequency distributions that are indicative of topic shifts.

2   Related Work

Three previously published lines of research form the foundation for the investigations reported in this paper.

The Distributed Meetings (DM) project [4] involves a system that can be used to broadcast and record meetings, and also view pre–recorded meetings. Unlike our system, the DM does not attempt to automatically identify the structure of the meeting. Cutler and colleagues (2002) evaluated the DM by conducting a user study involving real meetings between real participants at Microsoft Research. At each meeting, a person was asked to remain absent, and to later come in

and view the meeting recording using the DM viewing software, and then fill
out a questionnaire. The questionnaire data did not present a strong case for
the desirability of the solution although it did provide evidence that users were
satisfied with the information they received from it. What the paper lacks that
we attempt to provide is insight into the specific types of information needs
people have regarding missed or forgotten meetings.

Another similar project is the WorkspaceNavigator [5] that attempts to capture many different sources of digital information as a meeting proceeds inside a
"smart room". Recording involves taking regular snapshots of different computer
displays, the meeting room itself, filenames of open files and URLs of visited web
pages from participant laptops, etc. Users are allowed to label the snapshots, or
just mark snapshots as being important as they are being recorded. Two qualitative user studies were conducted to provide a detailed view of patterns of actual
use of the technology. The paper provides convincing evidence that users were
able to index and retrieve portions of meetings when needed. What this previous paper lacks that we offer in this paper is a controlled experiment in which
the magnitude of the impact of a general class of annotations on the speed of
information retrieval from meeting recordings is precisely measured.

Closely related to our project is the survey [6] of potential users of a meeting
browser, conducted as a part of the IM2.MDM (Interactive Multi-modal Information Management, Multi-modal Dialogue Management) project. The goal of
this survey was to elicit a set of questions that users may ask of an intelligent
meeting browser. While this survey provides some broad insights, it differs from
ours in both its goals and its methodologies, especially in that it does not adhere
to strong HCI methodology for survey research. One of the goals of our survey
is to assess how *useful* a meeting browser would be, how urgently its need is
currently felt by busy professionals, and in what range of their actual situations
they could potentially benefit from the use of a meeting browser. In contrast, the
survey reported in [6] makes the implicit assumption that if busy professionals
had access to an intelligent meeting browser, they would indeed use it! In our
survey interviewees were asked to recall recent instances of actual situations.
The resulting analysis of the interviews is therefore grounded in real experiences
as opposed to potentially erroneous generalizations. The survey questionnaire
in [6] asked participants to imagine themselves in a situation they have never
been in before, namely, in possession of a system using which they could "ask
questions about the actual content of the meeting". Thus, it is not clear how
many of the questions collected in that study would indeed be asked by users of
a future meeting browser in actual use.

3   User Survey

3.1   Goals

Efforts towards creating a meeting recording and play–back system can clearly
drive research on a large number of fronts including speech recognition, spoken

language understanding, vision–based gesture recognition, multi–modal information integration, and others. In this paper, however, we are interested in evaluating whether there is a *need* for such a meeting browsing application. Intuitively, such an application would be useful to busy professionals who need to catch up on missed meetings or recall forgotten details of meetings they have attended in the past. To understand how professionals currently perform these tasks we have conducted an interview based survey. Specifically, the survey was conducted to find answers to the following questions:

- How often do busy professionals miss important meetings that they need to catch up on?
- How often do users need to reconstruct forgotten details of meetings they did attend?
- What kind of information/documents do they typically have access to in each of the above two cases?
- What kind of information do they typically seek?
- What processes do users currently employ in obtaining this information and how effective/costly are they?

3.2   Survey Methodology

Our survey was based on face–to–face interviews conducted with 12 faculty members at Carnegie Mellon University. We chose faculty members since they attend many meetings as a part of their daily routine, and would be the likely targets of a meeting recording and playback application. Since not all missed meetings are important enough to bother catching up on, we defined a meeting as *important* if the interviewee indicated that he would indeed make an attempt to find out about it if he missed it. Interviewees were asked to describe instances of two kinds of situations: situations when they had missed important meetings, and those in which they were trying to recollect details of a meeting they had attended in the past. For each instance, interviewees were asked to name and describe the meeting artifacts they had access to, what specific pieces of information they were seeking about the meeting, whether and how they found the information, and whether they were satisfied with the information they did find. To avoid bias, interviewees were not informed about the reasons for this interview until the very end of the interview. To ground the interview in real experiences, interviewees were strongly and repeatedly encouraged to avoid replying in potentially erroneous generalities, and instead were asked to recall specific situations from their experiences in answering questions.

3.3   Analysis of Non-missed Meetings

The 12 interviewees reported a total of 19 instances of situations when they were attempting to recall details of a meeting they had attended in the past (1 interviewee reported no such instances, 3 interviewees reported 1 each, and the rest reported 2 each). Interviewees were asked to report both when they were attempting to recall details of a past meeting, as well as when the meeting took place (which was normally within the past few months).

Information Sought from a Meeting: Interviewees were asked to specify the information they were attempting to reconstruct about the meeting; table 1 lists the frequencies of the various categories of information sought across all the instances of non–missed meetings reported by the interviewees. Note that interviewees were not shown the categories listed in the table, but were simply asked to recall all the pieces of information they were seeking about the meeting. These answers were later manually clustered into the groups in table 1. For example, the category *Specifics of the discussion on a topic* include questions like "What was the name of the algorithm we discussed?". These categories are not directly comparable to the questions generated by the study in [6] which asked respondents to visualize scenarios where they had *missed meetings*.

While interviewees were not specifically asked to explain why they needed the information they were seeking, for several of the 7 instances of the category *What the decision was regarding a particular topic*, interviewees spontaneously mentioned that the reason they were attempting to recall the decision was not because they thought they had forgotten the detail, but because their recollection of the detail differed from that of another co-participant of that meeting. We believe that this phenomenon of needing verification of information is an important motivation for meeting recording and play–back technology.

Table 1. Information Sought from Meeting

Information sought	# meetings
Specifics of the discussion on a topic	11
What the decision was regarding a particular topic	7
What task someone else was assigned	4
Who made a particular decision	2
What the participants' reactions were to a particular topic	1
What the future plan is	1

Reconstructing from Available Documents: The interviewee was asked to list the documents he had access to while he was attempting to make the reconstruction; table 2 lists the documents. In 14 of the 19 meetings, the users had access to notes taken at the meeting, typically the notes they had taken during the meeting. In the remaining instances, interviewees had not taken notes at the meeting, and further did not have access to notes taken by any other meeting participants. Interviewees were also asked to rate on a scale of 0 to 5 whether the piece of information they sought about the meeting was satisfactorily answered by the meeting documents they had at their disposal, where 0 implied their question remained unanswered, and 5 implied they were completely satisfied with the answer they got. The average rating was 3.0 (std. dev.: 1.7).

Additional Steps Taken to Find Information: Interviewees were asked what additional steps (besides perusing the meeting documents) they took to find

Table 2. Documents the Interviewee Had Access To

Documents interview had access to	# meetings
Notes	14
Nothing	2
Minutes	1
PowerPoint Slides	1
Excel Sheet	1
Project proposal document	1
Whiteboard content	1
Email	1

the information they needed from the meetings. In 8 cases the interviewees asked someone in a face–to–face conversation. This was particularly the case when the question was about a specific detail about the meeting. In 5 cases interviewees reported that they reconstructed from memory, in consultation with a meeting co–participant (note that this is not the same as simply *asking* someone else about a detail). Finally interviewees were asked to rate on a scale of 0 to 5 their quality of reconstruction of the information they were seeking, after they took the additional steps, where 0 implied they could not do any reconstruction at all. The average rating was 4.0 (std. dev.: 0.6) – this was significantly higher than the satisfaction before perusing the meeting documents (p $<$ 0.0005). 5 interviewees stated that the additional steps took less than 15 minutes, 7 said between 15 minutes and an hour, while for 2 interviewees, the additional steps took more than an hour.

Summary and Conclusions:

- Interviewees mostly sought very detailed pieces of information from the meetings they had attended in the past.
- Very often the interviewees had access to notes that they could consult.
- Interviewees sometimes felt satisfied with the information they were able to retrieve from available documents.
- When the documents did not suffice, interviewees spoke to co–participants, or took other additional steps, which took up to an hour of time. At the end of these steps, interviewees largely felt that their information needs had been satisfied. Nevertheless, this does not guarantee that the information that they received was accurate since meeting co-participants may have different recollections of what was discussed at a meeting.

3.4   Analysis of Missed Meetings

The 12 interviewees reported a total of 22 instances of meetings they had missed in the past that they needed to catch up on. 9 interviewees reported 2 instances each, while 1 interviewee reported 3, 1 2, and 1 none (that is, one interviewee could not recall any specific instance of an important meeting that he had missed and later attempted to catch up on). 2 of these 22 missed meetings had occurred in the week prior to the interview, while 10 had occurred within the preceding month. Thus, on average interviewees reported missing one important meeting in the month prior to being interviewed. Of the remaining instances, 9 had occurred within six months prior to the interviews, and 1 between six months to a year before the interview. Note that based on the frequency of missed important meetings reported within the month prior to the survey, it would not be unrealistic to estimate that the population used in the survey misses on average about 1 important meeting per month.

Understanding of Expected Meeting Content Prior to Meeting: A person's overall understanding of the information discussed at a meeting is likely to be affected by his prior knowledge and expectations about the meeting before it takes place. Of the 22 reported instances of missed meetings, in 2 cases the interviewee did not receive any notification about the meeting (such as an email announcing the meeting). In one of these cases the meeting had already taken place by the time the interviewee received the notification, while in the other case the meeting was a regularly scheduled one and notifications weren't usually sent out. In 12 of the remaining cases the interviewee received an agenda and/or a description of what would be discussed, while in the remaining cases he received a notification email announcing the meeting. Each interviewee was asked to rate on a scale of 0 to 5 how well he felt he knew the contents of the meeting would be, where 0 implied he had no idea what the contents would be, and 5 meant he knew exactly what would be discussed. The average rating was 3.5 (std. dev.: 1.3).

Information Sought from a Missed Meeting: For each instance of reported missed meetings, interviewees were asked why they wanted to catch up on the meeting. In particular, they were asked to list all the pieces of information they needed from each missed meeting. Table 3 presents the frequency of each category of information sought by the interviewees across all the instances of missed meetings. Thus in 10 of the 22 missed meetings, the interviewee wished to find out what was discussed about a specific topic. As with non–missed meetings, participants were not provided with the categories in table 3; the categories were constructed based on their responses.

Observe that the first 3 categories in table 3 together make up the majority of categories of information sought about missed meetings; note also that these three categories are related in that they are all concerned with seeking information about a particular topic of interest. This suggests that when a person misses a meeting, he is often more interested in catching up on the discussions regarding a specific topic of interest rather than the entire meeting. Thus, perhaps an automated topic detection and segmentation mechanism that lets the viewer of a recorded meeting focus only on the topic he is interested in will be well received.

The most salient difference between the questions asked in "real world" situations by our interviewees and the questions proposed by [6] is that none of

our interviewees reported asking any "hard" questions that require deep understanding of the meeting context, such as "3-Y-7-2 Why X changed his mind on
issue Y in the current meeting?", or "3-N-5-9 Why was topic #5 not resolved?"
([6]). We believe this is the case because when people miss meetings, they are
unlikely to be aware of enough context to ask these questions. That is, the user
will not ask why X changed his mind if he is unaware that X changed his mind.
Also, while it is possible to imagine that each of the large variety of questions
in [6] may be asked under some circumstance, perhaps these conditions are rare
enough that they did not arise in our limited set of interviews.

Table 3. Information Sought from Missed Meetings

Information sought	# meetings
What was discussed about a particular topic	10
What decisions were made about a particular topic	7
Whether a particular topic was discussed	5
Whether I was assigned a new task	4
Whether a particular decision was made	3
What decisions were made	2
If there were any new issues/announcements	2
Reasons for a decision	1
What the participants' reactions were to a particular topic	1
The backgrounds of the other participants	1

Understanding of Meeting Content After the Meeting: To understand
what kind of information about the meeting the interviewees could access without having to make an effort at locating the information, we asked the interviewee
to list the documents he received from the meeting after the meeting took place,
without him prompting for them. Note that by "document" we included *any* piece
of information that the interviewee may have received without prompting, including orally communicated information from other participants of the meeting,
emailed documents, etc. The aim in asking this question was to understand what
kind of documents are routinely sent around – one can presume that (at least
a large subset) of these documents would be available even when participants
have access to a meeting browsing system. Table 4 lists the documents reportedly
received by the interviewees. Observe that in more than half the meetings, no
document was received at all. Since these meetings are important enough to the
interviewee that he wants to catch up on them, not receiving any information
from the meeting implies that the interviewee is forced to either actively search
for information about the meeting, or give up and not learn anything about the
meeting at all.

Interviewees were further asked to rate on a scale of 0 to 5 how well the
documents they received (if any) answered their question(s) about the meeting,
where 0 meant they either did not receive any documents, or that the documents
they received did not answer their questions at all. The average rating was a very

low 1.7 (std. dev.: 1.9). This low number is partly explained by the fact that to a large extent interviewees received nothing from the meetings. In cases where the interviewee did receive notes etc from the meeting, they were often not sufficiently detailed to answer their questions regarding the meeting.

Table 4. Documents Received after the Meeting

Post–meeting document received	# meetings
Nothing	12
Notes	7
Minutes	3
Email from meeting participant (not official notes)	2
Document containing draft of a proposal	1

Additional Steps Taken to Find Information from Missed Meeting
Interviewees were asked what additional steps, if any, they took to find answers to their questions regarding the meetings. Table 5 shows the steps taken. Consistent with our findings about non-missed meetings, in connection with 15 meetings interviewees either asked someone face to face about the meeting, or emailed someone.

Table 5. Additional Steps Taken

Additional step	# meetings
Asked someone face-to-face	9
Emailed someone	6
No additional steps	5
Caught up at next meeting	3
Looked up information on the Internet	1

When asked how long these steps took, in 11 instances the interviewee said it took less then 15 minutes, in 5 cases between 15 minutes and an hour, and in 1 case more than an hour (this information was not collected for 5 instances). These times were self reported by the interviewees and are rough estimates only: the interviewees often reported having discussed other issues with their interlocutors while catching up on the missed meeting.

Finally the interviewees were asked to rate on a scale of 0 to 5 how much they believed their information need was met after taking the additional step, where 0 meant their information need was not met at all. The average rating in this case was 3.4 (std. dev.: 1.3).

Summary and Conclusions:

- Interviewees were more interested in catching up on discussion regarding specific topics rather than the entire meeting.
- Very often no documents were received, even though the meetings were important.
- Typically interviewees had a low level of understanding of the meeting from the documents received.
- Most interviewees attempted to answer their questions regarding the meeting by asking or emailing a co-participant. This extra effort took around 15 minutes.
- Even after taking additional steps to find information about the meeting, the interviewees' levels of understanding about the meeting were felt to be far from perfect.
- Based on the fact that information is often sorely lacking about a missed meeting, we conclude that a meeting recording and playback system would be useful for busy professionals to catch up on missed meetings. Further, if the meeting recording is segmented into discussion topics, users can focus on only their particular topics of interest, thus increasing their efficiency of extracting information from the meeting.

4   Meeting Browsing Using Topic Annotations

In the second part of this paper we report on our investigation into the effect of meeting annotation on the time it takes for a user to retrieve information from a meeting.

4.1   Meeting Annotation

We are interested in automatically detecting the structure of a meeting. For the purposes of this paper, we define meeting structure on two levels: A coarse level consisting of meeting states and participant roles, and a finer level consisting of discussion topics.

We build upon a previously published ontology of meeting states and participant roles [2] based on extended observation of natural meetings between human beings. In this ontology, there are three kinds of meetings states, as follows: (1) Discussion state, which is described as being a state in which a group of two or more meeting participants are involved in quick back and forth of discussion on a topic; (2) Presentation state, which is described as being a state in which one particular meeting participant is presenting information to the others in a formal setting; and (3) Briefing state, which is described as being a state where one participant is giving information to one or more meeting participants, but without involving either the formality of the presentation state, or the quick back and forth of the discussion state. Within each meeting state, the possible roles of the meeting participants are defined as follows: within the discussion state, participants may take the role of discussion participants or of the observer; within the presentation state, presenter or observer are the two possibilities; and within the briefing state, information-provider, information consumer and observer are the possible roles.

Discussion topic regions are defined as all the times of the meeting that are devoted to discussing a certain topic. Although "topic" itself can be defined on various levels of granularity, in general we are interested in broad high level topics such as those that typically form different agenda items. For example "buying a printer" may be considered a topic. Research has been done on automatically finding topics both in written texts [13] and in broadcast news [12]. While we are currently applying the text topic detection techniques described in [13] to media recorded at meetings, in this paper we use only manually annotated meetings to ensure high quality topic boundaries.

4.2   Brief Description of the MockBrow

Meetings can be manually annotated using the meeting annotation and playback tool *MockBrow* implemented at Carnegie Mellon University. This tool allows human annotators to select a time interval within a recorded meeting and associate it with one or more labels. For example, an annotator may mark an interval of the meeting as being a "presentation", or as belonging to the discussion on "buying a printer", etc.

MockBrow is also intended as a platform to play back all the time–stamped media streams recorded at a meeting (such as close–talking microphone audio, video from multiple cameras, captured whiteboard markings, etc), along with all annotations generated either automatically or manually as described above. The interface allows viewers to quickly jump backwards and forwards within the meeting, as well as play only small portions of interest within the meeting. For example, a viewer may choose to only play back the portion of the meeting labeled as "buying a printer". Currently MockBrow does not support any automatic searching mechanism.

4.3   User Study Goals and Methodology

In order to assess the value of developing technology to automatically annotate meeting recordings with discourse structure based annotations in order to facilitate extracting information from recorded meetings, we designed a within subjects user study.

Materials: We created an audio-video record of two ten-minute-long meetings, each involving three participants. Next we manually annotated each meeting with meeting states, participant roles and discussion topics using MockBrow. The same meeting could then be viewed either with the annotations or without. Finally, based on findings from the questionnaire, we prepared for each meeting a set of five factual questions, with answers that are easy to evaluate the answer as correct or not. (To avoid biasing the questions, the annotations were not consulted while constructing the question set).

Participants: 16 Carnegie Mellon graduate students participated in the within subjects experiment. Note that while the survey was conducted on faculty members who would be the most likely target population for a meeting recording and playback application, the career status of the participants is not likely to affect the speed with which they are able to retrieve answers to questions that are provided for them from recorded meetings. Our plan is in the future to invite busy faculty members to participate in a long term longitudinal study of meeting recording and playback.

Experimental Manipulation: Each participant was asked to answer the questions for each of the two meetings by viewing the meeting's video using Mock-Brow while searching for the answers. In order to control for ordering effects, subjects were randomly assigned to 4 configurations in which half of the subjects viewed the first meeting and then the second meeting whereas the other half of the subjects viewed the meetings in the opposite order. Furthermore, half of the subjects viewed the annotated version of meeting one and the unannotated version of meeting two, whereas the other half of the subjects viewed the annotated version of meeting two and the unannotated version of meeting one.

In all cases, participants were encouraged to answer the questions as fast as possible, and their time to completion of each meeting viewing and question answering was recorded.

4.4   User Study Results and Analysis

The timing data collected in the experimental manipulation was sufficient for comparing average speed of answering questions with and without discourse structure based annotations. The control group (the group that did not have access to the annotations) took an average of 10.0 minutes (std. dev. = 2.6) to answer the given questions, while the experimental group took 7.5 minutes (std. dev. = 1.4). A two-tailed Student's T-Test assuming unequal variance shows that this difference in the means is significant with $p < 0.01$. Further the effect size (using the standard deviation of the control group as the denominator) is 0.94. This establishes that the difference in time taken to answer the questions when the participants could view the annotations versus when they could not is a reliable difference. Specifically, the annotations allowed participants to take on average 2.5 minutes less time to retrieve the answers to 5 questions in meetings that were 10 minutes long, when compared to those who had no access to the annotations.

In this experiment we did not record and analyze participants' browsing behavior. However it was clear that different participants used different strategies to retrieve information from the meeting record. When not provided with any annotations, some participants were content to listen to the entire meeting, while some others tried to randomly jump back and forth within the meeting. Several participants who did so complained that they had difficulty keeping track of which parts of the meeting they had already seen and which parts they had not. When provided with annotations, no participant viewed the entire meeting. Instead all participants viewed those annotated portions of the meeting they believed they would find the answer in. In future work we plan to minutely record and observe participants' browsing behavior to find useful patterns.

5   Conclusions and Future Work

In the first part of this paper, we have reported on a user survey aimed at understanding how busy professionals such as faculty members deal with situations when they are attempting to catch up on missed meetings, or attempting to recall details of meetings they have attended in the past. One important finding was that the busy professions participating in our survey research missed on average 1 important meeting per month. Furthermore, they frequently discovered that their recollection of a discussion at a meeting was not consistent with another group member's recollection. The most frequent recourse when faced with a perceived need to recover meeting was to talk to a group member who was at the meeting. However, even in the case where people felt satisfied with the information received from a group member, it is not clear to what extent the information they receive based on another's recollection is accurate. Thus, the survey research provides some support for the usefulness of a meeting browser. It also provides an ontology of question types that represent the types of information typically sought by our target user population.

In the second part of this paper we have reported on a within-subjects user study performed to quantify the impact that discourse structure based annotations have on the time it takes users to retrieve the answers to focused questions from recorded meetings. We have shown that in our experiment, participants on average took 2.5 minutes less to find answers when given the annotations than when not, and that this is a highly significant difference ($p < 0.01$ using Students' two tailed T-Test, assuming unequal variance). This encouraging result is only a first step towards understanding the impact of discourse based annotations on retrieval of information from recorded meetings. We plan to perform a larger study with longer meetings, and with two populations of participants – those who have been in the meeting and need to recall details about the meeting, and those that have missed the meeting and need to find out about the meeting. As a part of this larger "real–world" experiment we will also be able to investigate potential privacy issues with recording meetings, such as answering questions.

References

1. Banerjee, S., Cohen, J., Quisel, T., Chan, A., Patodia, Y., Al-Bawab, Z., Zhang, J., Black, A., Stern, R., Rosenfeld, R., Rudnicky, A.I., Rybski, P., Veloso, M.: Creating Multi-Modal, User-Centric Records of Meetings with the Carnegie Mellon Meeting Recorder Architecture. In: Proceedings of the ICASSP 2004 Meeting Recognition Workshop, May 17, 2004, Montreal, Canada.
2. Banerjee, S., Rudnicky, A.I.: Using Simple Speech-Based Features to Detect the State of a Meeting and the Roles of the Meeting Participants. In: Proceedings of the 8th International Conference on Spoken Language Processing (Interspeech 2004 - ICSLP), October 4-8, 2004, Jeju Island, Korea.

3. Rybski, P., Banerjee, S., Torre, F., Vallespi, C., Rudnicky, A.I., Veloso, M.: Segmentation and Classification of Meetings using Multiple Information Streams. In: Proceedings of the Sixth International Conference on Multimodal Interfaces, October 14th-15th, 2004, State College, Pennsylvania.

4. Cutler, Rui, Gupta, Cadiz, Tashev, He, Colburn, Zhang, Liu, Silverberg: Distributed Meetings: A Meeting Capture and Broadcasting System. In: Proceedings of the ACM Multimedia Conference, 2002.

5. Ionescu, A., Stone, M., Winograd, T.: WorkspaceNavigator: Tools for Capture, Recall and Reuse using Spatial Cues in an Interactive Workspace. In: Stanford Computer Science Technical Report 2002-04 (2002).

6. Lisowska, A.: Multimodal Interface Design for the Multimodal Meeting Domain: Preliminary Indications from a Query Analysis Study. In: Technical Report IM2.MDM-11, November 2003.

7. Chiu, P., Kapuskar, A., Wilcox, L., Reitmeier, S.: Meeting Capture in a Media Enriched Conference Room. In: Proceedings of the Second International Workshop on Cooperative Buildings, Integrating Information, Organization, and Architecture, Pages 79-88, 1999.

8. Stein, E. W., Zwass, V.: Actualizing Organizational Memory with Information Systems. In: Information Systems Research, Volume 6, Number 2, June 1995, pp. 127-137.

9. Jennex, M. E., Olfman, L.: Organizational Memory/Knowledge Effects on Productivity, a Longitudinal Study. In: 35th Annual Hawaii International Conference on System Sciences (HICSS'02) - Volume 4, January 07-10, 2002, Big Island, Hawaii.

10. Ackerman, M. S., Starr, Brian, Hindus, Debby, Mainwaring, Scott: Hanging on the 'wire': a field study of an audio–only media space. In: ACM Transactions on Computer–Human Interaction (TOCHI), 4, 1 (March 1997), 39–66.

11. Ahuja, S. R., J. Ensor, Robert, Horn, David N.: The Rapport multimedia conferencing system. In: ACM SIGOIS and IEEECS TC–OA Conference on Office information systems, ACM SIGOIS Bulletin, 9, 2-3 (April 1988).

12. Allan, J., Carbonell, J., Doddington, G., Yamron, J., Yang, Y.: Topic detection and tracking pilot study: Final report. In: Proceedings of the DARPA Broadcast News Transcription and Understanding Workshop, 1998.

13. Hearst, M.: TextTiling: Segmenting Text into Multi–Paragraph Subtopic Passages. In: Computational Linguistics, 23(1), pp. 33–64, March 1997.

14. http://www.ai.sri.com/project/CALO.

Key Issues in Interactive Problem Solving: An Empirical Investigation on Users Attitude*

Gabriella Cortellessa, Vittoria Giuliani,
Massimiliano Scopelliti, and Amedeo Cesta

ISTC-CNR, Institute for Cognitive Science and Technology,
Italian National Research Council, I-00137 Rome, Italy
{name.surname}@istc.cnr.it

Abstract. This paper explores the interaction between human and artificial problem solvers when interacting with an Intelligent Scheduling System. An experimental study is presented aimed at investigating the users' attitude towards two alternative strategies for solving scheduling problems: automated and interactive. According to an automated strategy the responsibility of solving the problem is delegated to the artificial solver, while according to an interactive strategy human and automated solvers cooperate to achieve a problem solution.

Previous observations of end-users' reactions to problem solving systems have shown that users are often skeptical toward artificial solver performance and prefer to keep the control of the problem solving process. The current study aims at understanding the role played by both the users' expertise and the difficulty of the problem in choosing one of the two strategies. Results show that user expertise and task difficulty interact in influencing this choice.

A second aspect explored in the paper concerns the context in which the end-users rely on explanations to understand the solving process. Explanations are in fact expected to play an important role when artificial systems are used for cooperative and interactive problem solving. Results support the hypothesis that explanation services are more often called into play in case of problem solving failures.

1 Introduction

The introduction of intelligent systems for solving complex problems in real world domain has been characterized by the raising consciousness that in most cases a completely automated approach is neither applicable nor suitable for a successful deployment of solving technologies. Traditionally, the main concern of scholars in the problem solving field has been to develop efficient and powerful algorithms for finding solutions to complex problems. This is true for both Artificial Intelligence and Operations Research approaches. A usually neglected issue has been the lack of effective front end design through which an end user can benefit from the potentialities of the artificial tools, taking, at the same time, an active role in the resolution process. In fact, on the

---

* This research is partially supported by MIUR (Italian Ministry of Education, University and Research) under project ROBOCARE (A Multi-Agent System with Intelligent Fixed and Mobile Robotic Components).

M.F. Costabile and F. Paternò (Eds.): INTERACT 2005, LNCS 3585, pp. 657–670, 2005.
© IFIP International Federation for Information Processing 2005

one hand the development of automated algorithms to solve difficult problems can relieve a user from complex or tedious tasks, on the other it needs to be combined with the design of effective and usable instruments for the users to maintain a level of control over the solving phase.

An integrated system ⟨*human, artificial solver*⟩ would create a powerful and enhanced problem solver applicable to the resolution of difficult real world problems. In this light, a new solving paradigm has been proposed in the literature, which promotes a collaboration between human and artificial solvers during the problem solving process. This emerging paradigm is known as mixed-initiative approach [2,4] and fosters the human-computer cooperation during the resolution of complex problems. The approach is based on the idea that experienced users and automated technologies bring complementary problem-solving strengths to the table, and the goal is to synergistically blend these combined strengths. Hence, successful technology application requires effective integration of decision-making and representation models of the user and the system. However, several problems, stemming from the composite nature of the system user-machine, need to be addressed.

This work investigates the interaction between human beings and computer-based decision support systems for the resolution of difficult problems. In particular we consider the case of an intelligent scheduling system that is endowed with different levels of interactivity with the user.

The design of mixed-initiative planning and scheduling systems has mainly to do with the general problem of interfacing the user with the automated system and placing him/her into the problem-solving loop. One basic task is to show system outcomes in user-comprehensible terms to save users the cognitive burden of understanding the internal representation usually inherent to specialized solving techniques. An additional feature, very relevant for human problem solving, is the ability to provide explanatory support in different problem solving phases . Unfortunately, most current systems provide no guidance in such cases, and force the user to diagnose the problem using the system's internal model. The ability of the system to provide user-level rationalizations of generated solutions may promote user acceptance [21]. Current proposals for mixed-initiative systems (see [2] for example) are very often presented as system description, whereas less work has been devoted to understanding how it is possible to evaluate the utility of the whole approach and the different features. This paper offers a methodological contribution in this direction, applying an experimental approach to the problem of understanding users' attitude toward interactive problem solving features.

Two main issues will be considered, concerning (a) users' preferences in selecting the solving strategy and (b) their willingness to rely on explanation. It is worth emphasizing that while several works on the mixed-initiative paradigm claim that end-users of automated systems prefer to maintain control over the problem solving, thus appreciating mixed-initiative systems, nonetheless, no empirical evidence is given to support this statement.

Plan of the Paper. The paper is organized as follows. The reference problems are introduced and the aims of the study are spelled out in Section 2. Section 3 describes the methodology used in the experiment. The results of the research are illustrated in Section 4. A general discussion and some final conclusions end the paper.

2   Preface to the Study

Before describing the methodology and results of the study we first introduce some definitions and notions that prepare the ground to better understand the context of the work. In particular this section introduces the type of problems we will consider in the study, then briefly describes an Artificial Problem Solver by which this work has been inspired and outline the main aims of the research.

2.1   Planning and Scheduling Problems

For the purpose of this paper we shall first give a definition of the reference problems which will be used in the study. The problems we are referring to, are known in literature as *planning* and *scheduling* problems. Planning and scheduling problems are present in many different applicative contexts, and are the object of many applicative computer-based systems. Considering that in most cases a clear distinction between the two categories is very difficult, definitions aiming at highlighting some crucial differences are given. While *planning* is concerned with the problem of deciding *what* to do – which actions are to be executed– to reach some *goals*, without any particular attention to the resources needed to execute the actions, the main concern of *scheduling* is to determine when to execute the actions and which resources are to be used to complete the whole set of actions. In other words planning consists of synthesizing a sequence of actions that enable us to reach a desired final state of the world, starting form a given initial state. The sequence of actions is called *plan* and it allows to reach a goal. Scheduling specializes the plan adding information about *time* and resources needed to execute the actions. A scheduling problem, see for example [1], consists of a set of activities, a set of resources and a set of temporal and resource constraints the activities should satisfy in order to be correctly executed. A solution of such problem is a *schedule*, that is an assignment to the start time of the activities such that all the specified constraints are satisfied.

2.2   COMIREM: A Reference Planning/Scheduling System

The mixed-initiative system we have used as a reference for our work is COMIREM [19], a web-based mixed-initiative problem solver devoted to the resolution of planning/scheduling problems.

The system is based on a CSP paradigm [20] and promotes a problem solving process that combines the actions of the automated solver and the human planner. COMIREM is composed of two main modules, named respectively *Automated Solver* and *Interaction Module*. The first is devoted to modeling domain entities through a CSP representation and provides the *automated* problem solving strategy. The Interaction Module directly interacts with the user, and allows him/her to take part in the process of finding a solution via advanced interactive facilities. It represents the communication channel between the user and the automated solver and a means to exploit various features of the automated system. Due to its interactive nature, the system can exploit human-planner knowledge and decision making, and in fact promotes a mixed-initiative problem solving process. Through the Interaction Module a user can choose to either generate a solution automatically or iteratively build one through a *step by step* mixed-initiative procedure that interleaves human choices with system calculation of consequences. In the first case a user decides to completely delegate the system, in the second case he/she takes an active role in the problem solving. In accordance with the mixed-initiative theory, the ambitious idea behind COMIREM is to capture the different skills that a user and an automated system can apply to the resolution process, by providing both powerful automatic algorithms to efficiently solve problems and interactive facilities to keep the human solvers in the loop. For the purpose of our study we developed a simplified and simulated version of COMIREM, which is devoted to solve scheduling problem instances in a TV broadcasting station domain.

2.3   Objectives and Hypothesis

The aim of this study is twofold, addressing both user strategy preferences and use of explanations.

Empirical Investigation on Users' Solving Strategy Selection. Previous research on human problem solving procedures has mainly addressed either the influence of the type of problem [14] or the users' assessment of different strategies (e. g., how successful different strategies are or how costly they are to apply), focusing on how success/failure resulting from previous trials influence solving processes [13]. This work aims at investigating the influence of both human solvers' expertise and problem difficulty on the selection of interactive vs automated strategy. In addition, contrary to traditional research in the field of problem solving, where the object of study has usually been mathematical or logic problems, in this case "real world" problems will be considered. In our research, the user is presented an alternative between a completely automated procedure and an interactive approach. By choosing the first alternative, the user will delegate each action to the artificial solver, thus keeping no control over the problem solving process, whereas in the second case the system and the human solver will actively cooperate to produce a solution to the problem.

There is some evidence that humans do not always adopt an optimal strategy in getting help from artificial tools, ignoring advices or solutions proposed by the system [10]. A possible explanation for this behavior is provided by some research in the field of human-computers interaction, reporting that humans tend to attribute a certain degree of anthropomorphism to computers, assigning to them human traits and characteristics. In [12,16] a series of experimental studies are reviewed, showing that individuals mindlessly apply social rules and expectations to computers. It is plausible to hypothesize that human problem solvers show the same tendency toward artificial solvers, and refuse to delegate the solution of the problem, for many reasons. For instance, they could mistrust the automated agent's ability to solve the problem or they could enter in competition with it. However, we have no data on possible differences in the behavior of users with different levels of expertise. Experts are people with some knowledge of the design of artificial solvers and they are aware of the limits and merits of the system. We assume they would adopt a more pragmatic strategy, thus delegating the machine to solve the problem in order not to waste time. On the other hand they may be interested in understanding the procedure applied by the system. Hence, when facing difficult tasks, they might be motivated to test themselves and actively take part in the process. Conversely, non-experts do not know the mechanisms behind the automated algorithms and thus might have a different degree of trust. Nonetheless the greater the difficulty of the problems, the more likely the choice to commit the problem solving to the machine. For these reasons we believe that some differences might exist between experts and non-experts while interacting with an artificial problem solver. In particular we formulate the following hypotheses:

Hypothesis 1. *Solving strategy selection (automated vs interactive) depends upon user expertise. In particular it is expected that scheduling expert users use the automated procedure more than non-experts. Conversely, non-expert users are expected to use the mixed-initiative approach more than experts.*

Hypothesis 1b. *In addition it is expected that when solving easy problems, inexperienced users prefer the mixed-initiative approach, while expert users have a preference for the automated strategy. Conversely, for solving difficult problems inexperienced users may prefer the automated strategy while expert users have a tendency to choose the mixed- initiative approach.*

Explanation Recourse. The term explanation usually means "to make something plain or understandable", to "give the reason for some event, be it expected or not". In AI, explanation has been investigated from a variety of different perspectives.

The traditional notion of explanation in expert systems is based on the early work on the MYCIN system [5] developed at Stanford in the 1970s to diagnose and recommend treatment in the medical field. In that case, explanation was devoted to answering "how" and "why" questions, based on a trace of the system's reasoning. In knowledge-based system explanations facilities have been designed to teach and clarify systems' intentions or to convince the users of the reliability of system results [8].

Explanations, by virtue of making the performance of a system transparent to its users, are influential for user acceptance of intelligent systems and for improving users' trust in the advice provided [9]. In systems where explanation is provided as a part of problem solving, it is important to consider how it relates to the problem solving process. In fact it is possible that explanations can either be based on problem solving, in which case they elucidate reasoning and problem solving methods, or be used as a dialogue with the user to allow him/her to influence the problem solving progress. This second alternative is appropriate in those contexts in which the user and the system are collaborating to solve a problem. In these cases explanations are seen as an effective means to cooperate in the problem solving process [11]. In previous research [3] expectation of failures and perceived anomalies have been identified as an occasion for accessing explanations [6,17]. According to these results we formulate the following hypotheses:

Hypothesis 2. *The access to explanation is more frequent in case of failure than in case of success.*

Hypothesis 2b. *The access to explanation is positively associated with the number of failures and negatively associated with the number of successes.*

In the context of knowledge-based systems, the role of explanations in cooperative problem solving has been investigated [7] and results show that participants in cooperative problem solving conditions, made a greater use of explanations. In accordance with the Mixed-Initiative Theory we hypothesize that the human solver, actively participating in the problem solving, possesses a higher level of control in the problem solving, thus showing a lower need to access the explanation. In particular we formulate the following hypothesis:

Hypothesis 3. *Access to explanation is related to the solving strategy selection. In particular participants who choose the automated solving strategy access more frequently the explanation than subjects who use the mixed-initiative approach.*

In addition to the hypotheses expressed above, we want to investigate the relationships between the user's level of expertise and the use of explanation. Evidence has been provided that experts are more likely to use explanations for resolving perceived anomalies [15] or because they are surprised by conclusions [21]. In accordance with cognitive learning theory, we expect that non experts will use explanation more frequently than experts when solving problems with automated systems. In particular we formulate the following hypothesis.

Hypothesis 4. *During problem solving non experts access explanations more frequently than experts.*

Finally we also expect that the difficulty of problems will affect the recourse to explanation. In particular we hypothesize that:

Hypothesis 5. *Access to explanation is more frequent in case of difficult problems.*

Based on the taxonomy of explanation types provided in [3] the explanation we will use in our experiment will have the following features: it aims at explaining problem solvers' choices, it is expressed in textual form and has a user-invoked provision mechanism.

3   Method

The general experimental design of this research aims at investigating the influence of the variables *expertise* and *problem difficulty* on the solving strategy selection and access to explanation. The variable *expertise* is a *between* factor with two levels, expert or non-expert, while the *problem difficulty* represents a *within* factor with two levels, low and high[1]. A further independent variable is represented by *failure* during the problem

---

[1] The two levels of this variable have been determined considering the problems dimension in terms of number of activities to be scheduled and alternative resources available for each activity.

solving. This last variable has two levels, present or absent. As general measures, the choice of the solving strategy and the frequency of access to explanation have been considered. With respect to the solving strategy, two general scores were computed (*choice_auto* and *choice_mixed*). They measure the overall frequency of choice of each strategy in the experiment.

As regards the access to explanation the following indexes were calculated:

- *access_failure* which represents the frequency of access to explanation in case of failure during problem solving;
- *access_success* which measures the frequency of access to explanation in case of correct decision during problem solving;
- *access_low_difficulty* indicating the frequency of access to explanation in case of problems of low difficulty;
- *access_high_difficulty* indicating the frequency of access to explanation in case of problems of high difficulty.

3.1 Tools

A web-based software has been developed, inspired by the software COMIREM described in 2.2. The simulated system allows users to solve instances of scheduling problems by means of two alternative procedures, automated and mixed-initiative. The system is accessible through a web browser and is organized as follows:

- *Presentation*: A general description of the study and the list of software requirements.
- *User data input form*: Data collected through this input form were registered in a data base implemented in MySQL Language. For each participant the following data were registered: identifier, profession, education, sex, age, language, expertise in planning & scheduling and participant's problem solving pattern.
- *Instructions*: A list of instructions to be followed during the experiment.
- *Training session*: This session was implemented through a sequence of animated web pages showing the actions necessary to use the system. The layout of the screen has been subdivided into two parts. On the left part the list of instructions was presented, which described the interface of the system and called upon the users to actively use the system. The right part of the screen was devoted to presenting the Problem Solver and its behavior consequently to user actions. The training session also allowed users to use and practice the system.
- *Session 1*: It was implemented through a sequence of web pages showing an instance of a scheduling problem to be solved. A textual description of the problem was shown, followed by a graphical presentation. Consequently to the user's actions, the system showed updated results.
- *Questionnaire 1*: an 11-item questionnaire was presented at the end of the first session. The questionnaire was subdivided into three sections:
  1. the first section was devoted to the *manipulation check* of the variable *difficulty*;
  2. the second section was devoted to verifying how clear the two description modalities (textual and graphic) were;

3. the last section aimed at investigating users' strategy selections and the reasons for their choices.

The first two sections included 6 items on a 5-step Likert type response scale (from "not at all" to "very much"). For the remaining items, related to reasons for the strategy selection, participants were asked to choose among different options. Participants were given the possibility to indicate possible suggestions or general comments.

– *Session 2*: It was implemented through a sequence of web pages showing the instance of a scheduling problem to be solved.
– *Questionnaire 2*: The first three sections were the same as for questionnaire 1. In addition a fourth session was added designed for investigating the access to explanations during the experiment and their perceived utilities. Questions related to explanations were evaluated on a 5-step item Likert scale.

3.2 Participants and Procedure

A group of 46 subjects was contacted, aged from 23 to 58 years (Mean 33,3). The sample was balanced with respect to expertise in planning and scheduling (23 experts and 23 non experts) and with respect to gender, education, age and profession.

All subjects participated in the experiment by connecting from their own computer to the experiment web site[2].

At the beginning of the experiment, an animated tutorial provided subjects with instructions on how to use the software, and showed which type of problems were to be solved. Then, it solved an example of scheduling problems by using both the automated and the mixed-initiative procedure. Participants could repeat the tutorial session until they felt confident with the use of the system. Then a problem was presented to the subjects and they were asked to choose between one of the two available solving strategies. During the problem solving, participants could either access explanations through the *explanation* button or go to the next step. User's interactions with the system were registered in the data base. At the end of the first session subjects were asked to fill in Questionnaire 1. The same procedure was followed for session 2. In order to avoid effects due to the order of the presentation, the two sessions (which corresponded to different degrees of difficulty[3]) were randomly presented to the users.

3.3 Stimuli

Four scheduling problems were defined in the field of a broadcast TV station resources management. Two solvable problems (1 low difficulty and 1 high difficulty) were presented during the first and the second session to all subjects, and two unsolvable problems (1 low difficulty and 1 high difficulty) were presented only to subjects who chose the automated procedure. The reason for adding these further problems in case of automated selection is twofold:

---

[2] http://pst2.istc.cnr.it/experiment/
[3] Results of a preliminary analysis showed that our classification of difficult and easy problems coincides with the one perceived by the participants.

- the mixed-initiative selection entailed more time to solve problems. In this way all subjects had a comparable workload in term of time spent in solving problems.
- the mixed-initiative selection entailed that almost all participants encountered some failures during the problem solving, thus introducing unsolvable instances (failure) which were also necessary to the automated procedure.

4   Results

4.1   Solving Strategy Selection

The first analysis investigated the influence of *expertise* on the solving strategy selection. A between subjects ANOVA was performed to test Hypothesis 1, separately for the two different strategies. The dependent variables used in this analysis were the indexes *choice_auto* and *choice_mixed* respectively (see Section 3). With respect to the strategy selection no significant difference was found (F(1,22)=1.94, n. s.).

To test Hypothesis 1b a χ^2 test was performed, separately for low and high level of difficulty. In case of low difficulty problems, a significant effect was found (χ^2=5.58, df=1, $p < .05$) . In particular the analysis of standardized residual shows that when solving easy problems, experts prefer the automated strategy, while non-experts prefer the mixed-initiative approach (see Fig. 1).

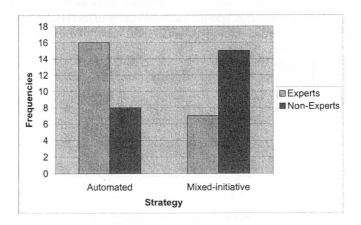

Fig. 1. Strategy selection preferences: easy problems

The analysis shows no significant difference between the two groups in case of difficult problems (χ^2=0.11, df=1, n.s.) (see Fig. 2).

4.2   Access to Explanation

To test Hypothesis 2 which aimed at investigating the relationship between failures and access to explanation, a repeated-measures ANOVA was performed using as dependent

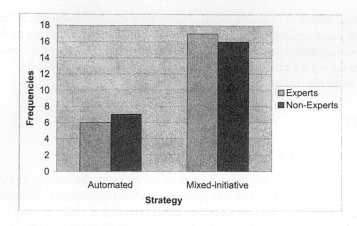

Fig. 2. Strategy selection preferences: difficult problems

variables the indexes *access_failure* and *access_correct*, introduced in Section 3. Results show a significant effect of failure on the access to explanation ($F(1,41)=24.32$, $p <$ .001). In particular users rely on explanation more frequently in case of failure than in case of success (see Table 1).

Moreover, a correlation analysis between number of failures (and successes) and number of accesses to explanation was performed in order to test Hypothesis 2b. Results show a significant correlation between failures and number of accesses to explanation ($r=0.623$, $p <$ .001). Conversely there is no significant correlation between number of correct choices and number of accesses to explanation ($r=.01$, n.s.).

Table 1. Access to explanation: failure and success (statistics)

	N	Mean	Std. Deviation
access_failure	42	.6794	.4352
access_success	42	.3141	.3174

To test the relationship between the selected strategy and the access to explanation (Hypothesis 3), an ANOVA for independent groups was performed separately for the two levels of difficulty. The indexes *access_low_difficulty* and *access_high_difficulty*, defined in Section 3, were used as dependent variables. A significant effect of the strategy selection on the recourse to explanation was found . In particular the access to explanation is higher when the automated strategy is chosen both in case of easy problems ($F(1,43)=67.22$, $p <$ .001), see Table2, and in case of difficult problems ($F(1,44)=10.97$, $p <$ .05), see Table 3.

Finally, to test Hypothesis 4 and 5 a mixed-design ANOVA was performed considering *expertise* as a between-subjects factor and *difficulty* as a within-subjects factor. The indexes *access_low_difficulty*, and *access_high_difficulty* were used as dependent variables. Results show a significant effect of expertise on recourse to explanation

Table 2. Index of access to explanation: easy problems

	N	Mean	Std. Deviation
automated	23	.8043	.2915
mixed-initiative	22	.1667	.2242
totale	45	.4926	.4128

Table 3. Index of access to explanation: difficult problems

	N	Mean	Std. Deviation
automated	13	.5769	.3444
mixed-initiative	33	.2625	.2666
total	45	.3513	.3204

(F(1,43)=4.76, $p < .05$). Experts were found to access explanation significantly more than non-experts. An effect of problem difficulty on the recourse to explanation was also found (F(1,43)=6.48, $p < .05$). Access to explanation was found to be significantly higher when an easy problem is to be solved. No significant interaction effect was found (F(1,43)=0.89, n.s.) (see Table 4).

Table 4. Index of access to explanation: effect of expertise and problem difficulty

	expertise	N	Mean	Std. Deviation
	Non-experts	23	.3696	.3407
access_low_difficulty	Experts	22	.6212	.4489
	Totale	45	.4926	.4128
	Non-experts	23	.2768	.2994
access_high_difficulty	Experts	22	.4193	.3360
	Total	45	.3465	.3223

5   Discussion

The overall results of the present research are consistent with the expectation that non-expert users prefer the mixed-initiative approach rather than the automated strategy, while experts rely more frequently on the automated strategy. Moreover, the explanation is frequently used and the frequency of access is higher in case of failure than in case of success. More specifically, the study showed that non experts prefer the mixed-initiative procedure independently from the problem level of difficulty. Conversely, experts prefer the automated strategy when solving easy problems, while tend to move to the mixed-initiative approach while solving difficult problems.

As expected non-expert users show a tendency to actively solve problems keeping control over the problem solving process. This result can be considered in accordance with the idea that non-experts tend to be skeptical toward the use of an automated system, probably because they do not completely trust the solver capabilities. One possible explanation, consistent with [16], refers to the tendency to anthropomorphise machines and to believe that they can make mistakes just like human beings.

Conversely, expert users show a higher trust toward the automated solver. Nonetheless, they find it stimulating to actively participate in the problem solving process when a difficult task is given. The relevance of the problem difficulty emerged to be a key variable in their choice. Expert users are usually system designers and are used to implementing automatic algorithms, thus knowing how effective machines can be in solving problems. When an easy task is to be solved they are likely to consider the mixed-initiative approach as a time-wasting choice. On the other hand the idea of facing a puzzling problem can drive them to conceive alternative methods to generate solutions.

Results confirmed previous studies [6,17] according to which access to explanation is more frequent in case of failure and the main reason for accessing explanation seems to be the will to understand the artificial solver. Interestingly we found that, as expected, the more the failures the more the accesses to explanation; on the other hand no relationship was found between success and access to explanation. As a consequence it is possible to assert that success is not predictive of any specific behavior with respect to access to explanation.

In contrast with what was found in [7], our Hypothesis 3 asserting a greater use of explanation in case of automated solving strategy selection was confirmed. However a key difference between the two studies needs to be highlighted. In this contribution participants were asked to choose their preferred strategies while in [7] the automated vs. interactive strategy was treated as a between-subjects condition. In both sessions of our experiment it was found that participants who choose the automated strategy access explanation more frequently than subjects who chose the mixed-initiative approach. It is possible to speculate that by selecting the mixed-initiative approach, subjects actively participate in the problem solving and keep a higher control on the solving process. As a consequence the need for explanation might decrease. Conversely, participants who chose the automated strategy delegate the artificial solver but at the same time they need to understand solvers's choices and decisions. A somewhat surprising finding of the study was that experts access explanation more frequently than non experts; in addition the access to explanation is more frequent when facing an easy problem than in case of a difficult problem.

6   Conclusions

This paper introduces an experimental approach to evaluate key features of mixed-initiative systems to problem solving.

In particular we have given attention to basic users attitude concerning the choice of automated rather than interactive strategies and the bias toward the use of explanation. As a result, we have empirically proved that the mixed initiative approach responds to the willingness of end users to keep control over automated systems. Additionally, evidence has been found that non expert users prefer to adopt a mixed-initiative approach rather than delegate the automated system to solve a problem. Conversely, expert users prefer to entrust the system with the task of problem solving. The existing difference between individuals with different levels of expertise highlights the need for different styles of interaction in the development of intelligent problem solving systems.

It was also demonstrated the utility of explanation during problem solving, and the achievement of a *failure* state has been identified as a main prompt to increase the frequency of explanation access.

Several points remain open for future investigation, in particular we would like to use the same experimental apparatus to evaluate different types and depths of explanation. Additionally we are interested in the automated synthesis of explanation from the internal representation of the intelligent scheduling system. (see [18] for some preliminary results).

References

1. P. Baptiste, C. Le Pape, and W. Nuijten. *Constraint-Based Scheduling*, volume 39 of *International Series in Operations Research and Management Science*. Kluwer Academic Publishers, 2001.
2. Mark Burstein and Drew McDermott. Issues in the development of human-computer mixed-initiative planning. In B. Gorayska and J.L. Mey, editors, *Cognitive Technology*, pages 285–303. Elsevier, 1996.
3. B. Chandrasekaran and Sanjay Mittal. Deep versus compiled knowledge approaches to diagnostic problem-solving. *Int. J. Hum.-Comput. Stud.*, 51(2):357–368, 1999.
4. R. Cohen, C. Allaby, C. Cumbaa, M. Fitzgerald, K. Ho, B. Hui, C. Latulipe, F. Lu, N. Moussa, D. Pooley, A. Qian, and S. Siddiqi. What is initiative? In S. Haller, S. McRoy, and A. Kobsa, editors, *Computational Models of Mixed-Initiative Interaction*, pages 171–212. Kluwer Academic Publishers, 1999.
5. R. Davis. Application of Meta-Level Knowledge to the Construction, maintenance and Use of Large Knowledge bases. In R. Davis and D. Lenat, editors, *Knowledge-Based Systems in Artificial Intelligence*. McGraw-Hill, Inc., NY, 1982.
6. N. Gilbert. Explanation and dialogue. *Knowledge Engineering Review*, 4(3):205–231, 1989.
7. S. Gregor. Explanations from knowledge-based systems and cooperative problem solving: an empirical study. *International Journal of Human-Computer Studies*, 54:81–105, 2001.
8. P. Hayes and R. Reddy. Steps toward Graceful Interaction in Spoken and Written Man-Machine Communication. *Internal Journal of Man-Machines Studies* , 19:231–284, 1983.
9. F. Hayes-Roth and N. Jacobstein. The state of knowledge-based systems. *Communications of the ACM*, 37:27–39, 1994.
10. D. R. Jones and D. Brown. The division of labor between human and computer in the presence of decision support system advice. *Decision Support Systems*, 33:375–388, 2002.
11. L. Karsenty and J. Brezillon. Cooperative problem solving and explanation. *Expert Systems with Applications*, 8(4):445–462, 1995.
12. E. J. Langer. Matters of mind: Mindfulness/mindlessness in perspective. *Consciousness and Cognition*, 1:289–305, 1992.
13. M. C. Lovett and J. R. Anderson. Making heads or tails out of selecting problem-solving strategies. In J. D. Moore and J. F. Lehman, editors, *Proceedings of the Seventeenth Annual Conference of the Cognitive Science Society, Hillsdale, NJ*, pages 265–270. Erlbaum, 1995.
14. P. G. Polson. M. E. Atwood, M. E. Masson. Further explorations with a process model for water jug problems. *Memory and Cognition*, 8(2):182–192, 1980.

15. J. Mao and I. Benbasat. Exploring the use of explanations in knowledge-based systems: a process tracing analysis. Working Paper 96-MIS-002. Faculty of Commerce, University of British Columbia, Canada , 1996.
16. Clifford Nass and Youngme Moon. Machines and mindlessness: Social responses to computers. *Journal of Social Issues*, 56:81–103, 2000.
17. R. C. Schank. Explanation: A first pass. In J. L. Kolodner and C. K. Riesbeck, editors, *Experience, Memory and Reasoning*, pages 139–165. Erlbaum Associates, Hillsdale, NJ, 1986.
18. S.F. Smith, G. Cortellessa, D.W. Hildum, and C.M. Ohler. Using a scheduling domain ontology to compute user-oriented explanations. In L. Castillo, D. Borrajo, M.A. Salido, and A. Oddi, editors, *Planning, Scheduling, and Constraint Satisfaction: From Theory to Practice*. IOS Press, 2005.
19. S.F. Smith, D.W. Hildum, and D.A. Crimm. Interactive Resource Management in the Comirem Planner. In *IJCAI-03 Workshop on Mixed-Initiative Intelligent Systems*, Acapulco Mexico, August 2003.
20. E.P.K. Tsang. *Foundation of Constraint Satisfaction*. Academic Press, London and San Diego, CA, 1993.
21. L. R. Ye. The Value of Explanation in Expert Systems for Auditing: An experimental Investigation. *Expert Systems with Applications*, 9(4):543–556, 1995.

Designing Natural Language and Structured Entry Methods for Privacy Policy Authoring

John Karat[1], Clare-Marie Karat[1], Carolyn Brodie[1], and Jinjuan Feng[2]

[1] IBM T.J. Watson Research Center, Hawthorne, NY 10532, USA
{jkarat, ckarat, brodiec}@us.ibm.com
[2] University of Maryland Baltimore County, Baltimore,
MD 21250, USA
jfeng2@umbc.edu

Abstract. As information technology continues to spread, we believe that there will be an increasing awareness of a fundamental need to seriously consider privacy concerns, and that doing so will require an understanding of policies that govern information use accompanied by development of technologies that can implement such policies. The research reported here describes our efforts to design a system which facilitates effective privacy policy authoring, implementation, and compliance monitoring. We employed a variety of user-centered design methods with 109 target users across the four steps of the research reported here. This case study highlights our work to iteratively design and validate a prototype with target users, and presents a laboratory evaluation aimed at providing early support for specific design decisions to meet the needs of providing flexible privacy enabling technologies. This paper highlights our work to include natural language and structured entry methods for policy authoring.

1 Introduction

The rapid advancement of the use of information technology in industry, government, and academia makes it much easier to collect, transfer, and store personal information (PI) around the world. This raises challenging questions and problems regarding the use and protection of PI [13]. Questions of who has what rights to information about us for what purposes become more important as we move toward a world in which it is technically possible to know just about anything about just about anyone. As stated by Adams and Sasse [2]: 'Most invasions of privacy are not intentional but due to designers' inability to anticipate how this data could be used, by whom, and how this might affect users.' Deciding how we are to design privacy considerations in technology for the future includes philosophical, legal, and practical dimensions – any or all of which can be considered as within the domain of the field of human-computer interaction (HCI).

Privacy can and does mean different things to different people. We are primarily focused on a view of privacy as the right of an individual to control personal information use rather than as the right to individual isolation [15, 16, 22]. Organizations commonly provide a description of what kind of information they will

M.F. Costabile and F. Paternò (Eds.): INTERACT 2005, LNCS 3585, pp. 671–684, 2005.
© IFIP International Federation for Information Processing 2005

collect and how they will use it in privacy policies. In some areas (e.g., the collection and use of health care information in the US or movement of personal information across national boundaries in Europe) such policies can be required, though the content of the policy is not generally specified in legislation. While there has been considerable consensus around a set of high level privacy principles for information technology [16], we do not think it is likely that a single privacy policy can be created to address all information privacy needs. For example, there will likely be considerable differences in privacy legislation in different regions of the world [14]. Similarly, organizations in different fields (e.g., healthcare, banking, government) need to tailor policies to their domains and needs [6, 7]. While we will focus on privacy policy, we acknowledge that privacy is not entirely about "setting rules and enforcing them" [18]. To implement privacy within an organization, the coordination of people, business processes, and technology is required. Still we do believe that privacy policies are essential when interacting with technology and/or organizations in that they enable people to better understand just how the boundary between public and private information is impacted by technology [3].

It is interesting to note that while privacy policy is not new to most organizations, very little has been done to implement the policies through technology [21]. Usability has been identified as a major challenge to moving the results of security and privacy research to use in real systems [8]. One reason seems to be that there has been only limited research into how to make complex security and privacy functionality understandable to those who must use it.

Privacy policy enforcement remains largely a human process, and privacy policies which organizations present to customers are generally very vague (e.g., "We will only use your personal information for the efficient conduct of our business"). There are emerging standards for privacy policies on websites [9], but these address machine readable policy content without specifying how the policy might be created or implemented. The reality is that there is very little capability to have technology actually implement access and use limitations we might expect from a policy statement like "We will not share your information with a third party without your consent". Our research focus has been on how organizations could create a wide range of machine readable policies, and how technology might enable the policies to be enforced and audited for compliance. We have elected to focus on technology to enable usable privacy policy authoring and enforcement, rather than trying to directly address what privacy rights people should have [e.g., 23] or how to de-identify information stored in systems [e.g., 20]. This does not mean that we think these aspects of privacy are not important social issues. Rather it points to our belief that technology can enable flexible, reliable and accountable privacy policy (i.e., be privacy enabling) and not just be a force which reduces individual rights. We hope our work contributes positively to this goal.

1.1 Privacy Policy Structure

Research from the International Association of Privacy Professionals (IAPP) reports that 98% of companies have privacy policies. Often organizations have both internal policies, which state rules about information handling within an organization, and external policies which describe the policy in terms intended to inform the data subjects about use of their information. We focus here on internal policies, largely because they describe actual data handling procedures in organizations. These policies have been found to have a fairly specific structure which describes who can use what information for what purposes [19]. First of all organizations generally have a number of internal privacy policies; some to address use of data about internal employees, and others to address use of data about individuals with which the organization interacts (e.g., customers, patients, clients). Any policy includes a number of rules governing the use of data-subject's information. The rules in a privacy policy include data user, data element, purpose, use, condition, and obligations [5]. The first four of these elements can be said to be required of any good policy rule, and the last two are optional. The data user who accesses the data may be acting in a particular role in regard to a purpose. For example, doctors may read protected health information for medical treatment and diagnosis. In many privacy policies and legislation, granting or denying access incurs an obligation on the data user to take additional actions. For example, a medical researcher may read protected health information for medical research if the patient has previously explicitly authorized release (i.e., the condition) and the patient is notified within 90 days of the release of information (i.e., the obligation).

1.2 Motivation for Our Privacy Research

Most organizations store PI in heterogeneous server system environments. Currently they do not have a unified way of defining or implementing privacy policies that encompass data collected and used by both Web and legacy applications across different server platforms [4]. This makes it difficult for the organizations to put in place proper management and control of PI, the data users to access and work with the PI inline with the privacy policies, and the data subjects to understand rights regarding use of their PI.

In this paper we present a case study of a user-centered design research program on organizational privacy capabilities. We employed a variety of usability methods to progress from identifying organizational privacy concerns and needs to designing and evaluating prototypes and design trade-offs. This work included four steps: (1) identifying privacy needs within organizations through email survey questionnaires, (2) refining the needs through in-depth interviews with privacy-responsible individuals in organizations, (3) designing and validating a prototype of a technology approach to meeting organizational privacy needs through onsite scenario-based walkthroughs with target users, and (4) collecting empirical data in a controlled usability laboratory test to understand the usability of privacy policy authoring methods included in our proposed design. These activities were completed between the spring of 2003 and summer of 2004 and involved participation of 109 target users from around the world. From the first two steps we identified organizational needs which guided us in our choice of a focus area for the design of a system to improve privacy management for organizations. We focus our presentation here on our prototype development to meet these needs along with a laboratory study to evaluate the feasibility of our direction.

2 Designing and Evaluating a Privacy Policy Prototype

We designed and developed a prototype of a privacy policy workbench called SPARCLE. The overall goal in designing SPARCLE was to provide organizations with tools to help them create understandable privacy policies, link their written privacy policies with the implementation of the policy across their IT configurations, and then help them to monitor the enforcement of the policy through internal audits. Once we designed a prototype, we conducted a series of walkthrough sessions in which we utilized the prototype to discuss an appropriate scenario with representatives of healthcare, government, and finance organizations. In this paper, we will concentrate on the techniques we designed and developed for authoring privacy policies and assisting organizations in understanding the policies that have been created. While we present work on authoring policies in English, the approach and underlying technology allows the development of similar systems for other languages.

2.1 Designing a Prototype for Authoring Privacy Policies

During the survey and interview research, many of the participants indicated that privacy policies in their organizations were created by committees made up of business process specialists, lawyers and security specialists as well as information technologists. Based on the range of skills generally possessed by people with these varied roles, we hypothesized that different methods of defining privacy policies would be desirable. Our design direction was to support users with a variety of skills by allowing individuals responsible for the creation of privacy policies to define the policies using natural language or to use a structured format to define the elements and rule relationships that will be directly used in the machine-readable policy. SPARCLE keeps the two formats synchronized. For users who prefer authoring with natural language, SPARCLE transforms the policy into a structured form so that the author can review it and then translates it into a machine-readable format such as EPAL [5]. SPARCLE translates the policies of organizational users who prefer to author rules using a structured format into both a natural language format and the machine-readable version. During the entire privacy policy authoring phase, users can switch between the natural language and structured views of the policy for viewing and editing purposes. Once the machine-readable policy is created, it is possible to create enforcement engines to ensure the policy is enforced for data stored in the organization's on-line data stores.

Figure 1 contains a screen capture of SPARCLE's natural language interface for deEfining privacy policies. Throughout SPARCLE, the tool provides a task flow in the form of tabs showing the high level task steps to be accomplished and the status of each. The tasks include: Author Policy (step shown in Figures 1 and 2), Transform Policy (step shown in Figure 3), Map User Categories, Map Data Categories, Map Purposes/Actions, Map Conditions, Map Obligations, and Verify Policy. The mapping steps are used to associate policy elements with system objects, and enable separation of high level and detailed policy specification. The page also contains general information about the policy, (the name, date created, and file source of the policy, and a description of the policy authoring task to be performed) a list of privacy policy templates that could be either provided by the tool for particular domains and geographies based on laws or created by the organization for customization and use by its divisions, and an Example Rule Guide describing the elements that make up a privacy policy rule. The privacy policy rule guide is based on analyses of privacy policy rules specified in [5].

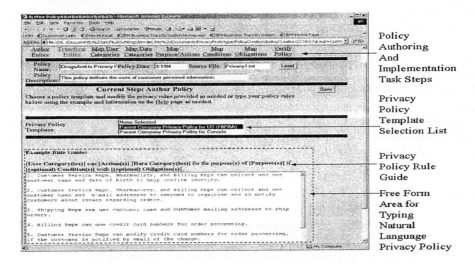

Fig. 1. SPARCLE natural language privacy policy creation screen

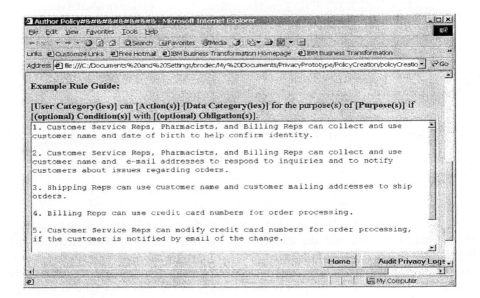

Fig. 2. Expanded view of natural language policy guide and entry field

The guide defines the basic components that are necessary in a privacy policy rule that is enforceable including user categories, allowed actions, data categories, purposes, as well as optional components such as conditions and obligations. Finally, a text entry area is provided for the actual privacy policy. When the user begins the process of creating a new policy, she can create the policy from scratch by typing into the text entry area, copy an existing policy into that area, or select one of the templates provided and modify it. The portion of Figure 1 within the dotted lines is enlarged and shown in Figure 2.

When the author is satisfied with the policy, he clicks on the Transform Policy tab shown in Figure 1. The natural language policy is analyzed and the policy elements (the strings which describe the User Category, Action, Data Category, Purpose, Conditions, and Obligations) in each rule are identified using a natural language parser (a shallow parser with a grammar and a domain dictionary). The natural language entry field area is replaced with a structured privacy policy creation view (shown in Figure 3). On this page, the user is provided with a list containing the parsed rules in the current policy.

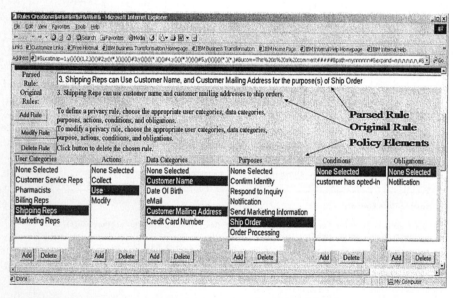

Fig. 3. Expanded view of SPARCLE structured privacy policy rule creation

Whenever a parsed rule is selected in the transformed view, the original unparsed text is also displayed and the elements of the rule that have been identified are highlighted in individual policy element selection lists as shown in Figure 3. There is one policy element selection list for each of the 6 types of rule element. There were two original purposes for this part of the prototype. First, while the natural language parsing technology in a limited domain such as privacy policy creation has promising accuracy, it is not perfect. This page allows users who have created the policy using the natural language technique to confirm that the parsing technology has identified all parts of the rules correctly and to correct anything that is in error. Second, for users who prefer the more structured method for privacy policy creation, this method can be used to create the entire policy. The organization can define policy element lists and then rules can be created by selecting the appropriate elements from each of the policy element selection lists and selecting "Add Rule". Likewise, a rule can be modified or deleted by highlighting the rule in the rule selection list, modifying the selected elements as appropriate and selecting "Modify Rule" or "Delete Rule". Any modification to rules or rule added or deleted using the structured approach is automatically reflected in the natural language version of the rules as well. Therefore, the author is able to go back and forth between the two methods to view the policy either in natural language or the parsed format with the elements identified.

During the course of the scenario-based sessions with target users, they identified an additional use of the combined natural language and structured methods. The users indicated that the natural language parsing and display of parsed policies would be valuable to them for assessing the completeness of their existing privacy policies. Several participants were excited about the possibility of using SPARCLE to analyze their existing natural language privacy policies and then view the elements and rules identified in order to identify gaps and inconsistencies in the policies. For example, if an existing privacy policy rule fails to identify the purpose for which a particular user group is allowed to use a particular piece of data, the parsed rule would contain "none found" where purpose would usually be. The organizational users felt that this would be a valuable tool to ensure the quality of the privacy policies used by the organization and helpful in educating their organizations regarding their privacy policies.

Based on the data collected from interviews with organizational users responsible for the creation of privacy policies, they often find it difficult to understand the policies that they create in order to ensure that policies are complete, able to be implemented, and consistent. Figure 4 shows our design to provide users with easy ways of viewing the privacy policy. The figure contains a table in which two of the policy elements types are used as axes and the other elements that are associated with each row and column are shown in the cells. In the example that is shown, user categories are placed on the horizontal axis and data categories are placed on the vertical access. The cells in the table contain the purposes, conditions, and obligations for rules that apply to that user and data category. Using this table, users can see at a glance what type of users are allowed to access each data element and also see which user groups are never allowed to access particular data items. While the table format was well received by users, we are not yet sure how well a two dimensional table scales up to real organizational policy complexity. Scaling and visualization will be the subject of our future research.

2.2 Validation of Prototype with Target Users

We conducted scenario-based usability walkthrough sessions of two iterations of SPARCLE with people who were responsible for the creation, implementation, and auditing of privacy policies within large organizations in the domains of healthcare, banking, and government. During the course of the 90 minute sessions with 1 to 4 participants, we gathered verbal and written feedback on the usability, design, and value of the privacy tool. For the first iteration of the prototype, walkthrough participants (7 participants in 5 sessions) rated the prototype positively (an average rating of 5.4 on a 7-point scale with 7 indicating "highest value" and 1 indicating "no value"). We present this summary result since it communicates the overall response to the prototype. However, the primary purpose for the sessions was to gather more qualitative responses from the participants about the value of the system to their task of managing privacy (some of which is described below).

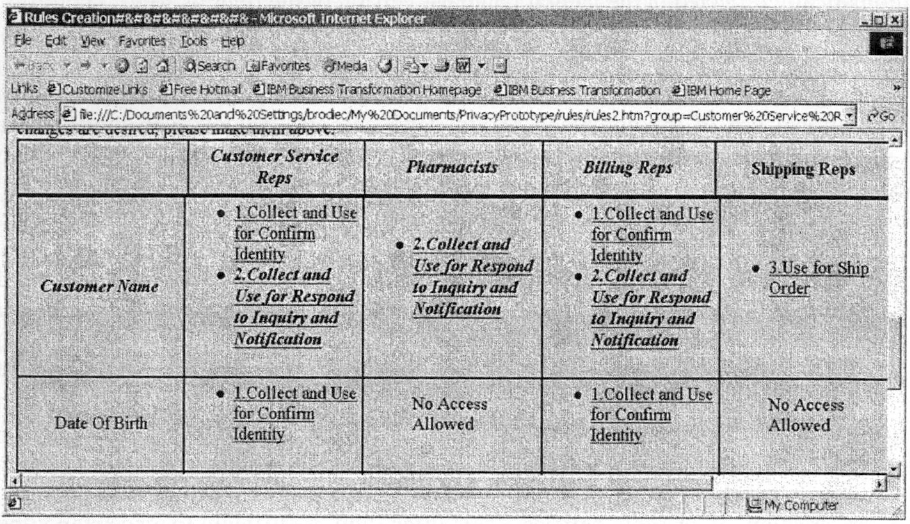

	Customer Service Reps	Pharmacists	Billing Reps	Shipping Reps
Customer Name	• 1.Collect and Use for Confirm Identity • 2.Collect and Use for Respond to Inquiry and Notification	• 2.Collect and Use for Respond to Inquiry and Notification	• 1.Collect and Use for Confirm Identity • 2.Collect and Use for Respond to Inquiry and Notification	• 3.Use for Ship Order
Date Of Birth	• 1.Collect and Use for Confirm Identity	No Access Allowed	• 1.Collect and Use for Confirm Identity	No Access Allowed

Fig. 4. Table showing privacy policy rules that apply to each user and data category

At the conclusion of the first iteration of design and evaluation, we made the following changes: 1) We added the ability to import pre-existing privacy policies into the natural language policy authoring condition to allow SPARCLE to highlight gaps and inconsistencies in the policies, 2) We added the ability to use privacy policy templates as a starting point for authoring privacy policies using either the natural language or structured policy authoring methods, and 3) We improved the readability of the table view of the privacy policy by bulleting entries and making it scrollable (See Figure 4). Additional improvements were made to the mapping and auditing functionality which we will not discuss here. Based on the feedback from our walkthrough sessions, we also decided to conduct an empirical test of the two authoring methods described in Step Four. During the second iteration of walkthrough sessions, the participants (15 participants in 6 sessions) also rated the revised prototype very positively (an average rating of 5.5 on the same scale).

The evaluations included 20 features on which we wanted to obtain feedback from the target users. Figure 5 summarizes the evaluation results over the two iterations of the prototype for 5 of these features which were included in both versions of the prototype and one feature that was added for the second iteration. While the data presented here only represent a small sample, we think that it provided us with a good picture of how the users responded to the prototype. The added feature was the ability to import policy files from other sources and to modify those files. This would enable localization of larger corporate policies or laws. This was seen as a highly valuable feature in itself, and we also believe that it led to a more positive evaluation of the natural language entry in the second iteration of SPARCLE. While structured rule entry seemed to be preferred in the first iteration, Natural Language and Structured Entry had equal ratings in the second iteration (these features were not altered substantially between iterations). It was also important to hear from the target users that they felt there was considerable value in the fairly simply policy table that we included in the prototype. We had viewed this two-dimensional representation as an initial design which we might need to change substantially, but found that users actually found it to be very clear and a powerful tool for understanding policy coverage. Additionally, target users responded very positively to the incremental authoring process which allowed high level specification in natural language followed by detail specification (possibly by a different person at a different time). Finally, the target users provided feedback that the compliance checking capabilities we included in the prototype were in line with what they needed to offer end users details of how PI was being used within their organizations (by enabling records of accesses to specific user's information).

Selected Privacy Feature Value Ratings

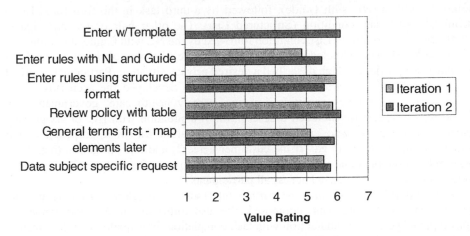

Fig. 5. Summary of Evaluation of Privacy Policy Authoring Features by Target Users

3 Evaluating Natural Language and Structured Policy Authoring

An empirical laboratory study was run to compare the two privacy policy authoring methods illustrated in the prototype. In order to provide a baseline comparison for the two methods (Natural Language with a Guide, and Structured Entry from Element Lists), we added a control condition that allowed users to enter privacy policies in text in any format that they were satisfied with (Unguided NL). The intention of the study was not to strictly resolve which approach was better, but rather to inform the design by asking whether the two methods could easily be used to produce reasonable quality rules. While it is generally important to utilize target users in laboratory studies, we elected to use privacy policy novices in this study for two reasons. First, our earlier work with customers suggested that authoring privacy policies is undertaken by an audience with a variety of backgrounds and with no specific training in privacy policy authoring. We expect this to change over time, and that authors will become skilled as they gain access to the sort of tools we are developing. Second, the population of people skilled at writing policies which can be implemented is small. Thus we felt it practical and appropriate to look at the methods we were designing with a general audience. Our primary goal was to decide whether natural language authoring seemed promising enough to include in future research.

3.1 Experimental Design

Thirty-six employees of a large IT company were recruited through email to participate in the study. The participants had no previous experience in privacy policy authoring or implementation.

A repeated measures design was employed in the study; each participant completed one task in each of the three conditions. All participants started with a privacy rule task in the Unguided NL control condition (Unguided NL). Then, half of the participants completed a similar task in the Natural Language with a Policy Rule Guide condition (NL with Guide), followed by a third task in the Structured Entry from Element Lists condition (Structured List). The other half of the participants completed the Structured List condition followed by the NL with Guide condition.

In each task, we instructed participants to compose a number of privacy rules for a scenario we provided which described a desired privacy situation. Participants worked on three different scenarios in the three tasks. We developed the scenarios in the context of three privacy sensitive domains, namely health care, government, and banking. Each scenario included a description of a situation with five or six privacy rules (statements of who could use what information for what purpose), which included one condition (e.g., "If the customer agrees") and one obligation (e.g., "We will delete your personal information from our databases after one year"). The order of the scenarios was balanced across all participants.

We recorded the time that the participants took to complete each task and the privacy rules that participants composed. We also collected, through questionnaires, participants' perceived satisfaction with task completion time, quality of rules created, and overall experience after participants completed each task.

In order to compare the quality of the rules participants created under different conditions and scenarios, we developed a standard metric for scoring the rules. We counted each element of a rule as one point. Therefore, a basic rule of four compulsory elements had a score of four and a scenario that consisted of five rules, including one condition and one obligation, had a total score of 22. We counted the number of correct elements that participants specified in their rules, and divided that number by the total score of the specific scenario. This provides the percentage of elements correctly identified for comparison across different scenarios and conditions.

3.2 Results and Discussion

There was a significant difference in the task completion time across the three conditions ($F_{(2, 70)}$ = 4.58, p < 0.05). Mean participant time on task was 910 seconds for Unguided NL, 814 secs. for NL with Guide, and 992 secs. for Structured List conditions respectively. Post hoc tests showed that the NL with Guide method took significantly shorter time than the Structured List method. There was no significant difference between the Unguided NL method and the other two methods.

A repeated measures test with post hoc analyses indicated that participants were more satisfied with the quality of the rules created by the NL with Guide method or the Structured List method as compared with the Unguided NL method ($F_{(2, 70)}$ = 6.54, p < 0.005). On a scale of 1 to 7, with 7 indicating highest overall satisfaction, participants mean satisfaction scores were 4.0 for Unguided NL, 4.7 for NL with Guide and 4.6 for Structured List conditions. There was no significant difference between the NL with Guide method and the Structured List method.

A statistical test of the rule quality scores calculated using the standard metric found a significant difference between the three conditions ($F_{(2, 70)}$ = 44.3 p < 0.001) (see Figure 6 below). Post hoc tests showed that the NL with Guide method and the Structured List method helped users create rules with significantly higher quality than the Unguided NL method. There was no significant difference between the NL with Guide method and the Structured List method. Using the Unguided NL method, participants correctly identified about 42% of the elements in the scenarios, while the NL with Guide method and the Structured List method users correctly identified 75% and 80% of the elements, respectively. Since we did not provide feedback on rule quality in any method, we attribute most of the improvement to the authoring methods themselves and not to learning in the first trail.

We examined the readability of the policies created. Jensen and Potts [11] found that privacy policies posted on the Web were generally not easy to read. We adopted the same measurement approach and used the Flesch readability score to evaluate the readability of the rules composed in the study. A repeated measures test suggested that there was a significant difference in the readability of the rules composed in the three conditions (F $_{(2, 70)}$ = 15.89, p <0.001). A post hoc test showed that the rules composed in the NL with Guide condition were significantly more difficult to read than the other two conditions. There was no significant difference between the readability of the rules created under the Unguided NL and Structured List conditions, and they were of similar readability as the majority of the online privacy policies reported by Jensen and Potts [11].

The results of the experiment confirmed for us that both the NL with Guide method and the Structured List method enabled participants to create rules with higher quality than the Unguided NL method. The fact that the percentages of elements identified with these methods almost doubled that of the Unguided NL method suggests that the NL with Guide and the Structured List methods are reasonably easy to learn and use. Our purpose in conducting the study was not simply to select one of the methods as the best method to include in the prototype. Certainly, if one of the methods seemed significantly superior, it would have made us consider going forward with a single method. However, our explorations of the two methods with customers had suggested that going forward with two methods that we complimentary might be a preferred solution. We view the results of this study as giving support to the design direction of including both methods and allowing rule creation in either to accommodate author preferences.

Policy Rule Quality Evaluation

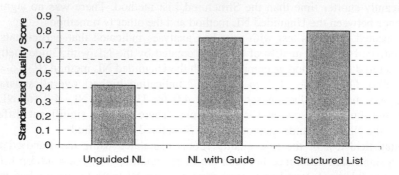

Fig. 6. Average scores of the quality of the rules according to the quality evaluation metric in three conditions

4   Conclusions and Future Research

Privacy is emerging as a powerful issue for people within organizations and individuals who interact with them around the world. In the networked world in which we live today, the topic is of growing concern and importance. Previous research has shown that the general public is concerned about protecting their privacy and often does not understand the implications of the privacy policies published by organizations with which they share their PI [11, 18]. This case study highlights the work of identifying organizational privacy requirements, iteratively designing and validating a prototype with target users in their work settings, and empirical laboratory testing to guide specific design decisions to meet the needs of providing flexible privacy technologies for organizations and their users.

Early work with privacy representatives in this project convinced us to focus on policy authoring, implementation and auditing in our research. We designed and developed a prototype with the overall goal of providing organizations a tool to help them create understandable privacy policies, link their written privacy policies with the implementation of the policy across their IT configurations, and then help them to monitor the enforcement of the policy through internal audits. We explored and iterated on the design with target users and were able to obtain valuable feedback well before we could complete a full implementation of the prototype. While work on the natural language parsing and mapping components of SPARCLE is still underway, we think we have a solid understanding of organizational needs for privacy technology.

We also conducted an empirical usability laboratory test of two methods of authoring policies. Results were promising and showed that in initial use, novice users could use the two methods to identify and cover 75-80% of the policy rule elements.

Coupled with our work with target organizational users, we have concluded that integrating the Structured List and NL with Guide authoring methods along with providing an easy to understand policy coverage view will be important elements of a successful privacy policy tool. We think that the laboratory test was an important component of the overall research in helping to justify the value of including a natural language method and integrating it with a structured authoring approach.

We think that a number of research challenges remain. First, we need to examine how well our authoring environment works for realistically complex organizational privacy policies. Our target users have generally been from large organizations, and they have responded well to the parts of the prototype we present in this paper – authoring and viewing policy coverage. However, working with policies with hundreds of rules might create problems that do not emerge in discussions centered on a single policy involving a few rules. A planned next step and a natural evolution for our work will be to work with several organizations to create complete machine readable policies which reflect their actual internal privacy policies. In doing this we hope to address issues about the use of internal policies in communicating with end users concerning privacy. We suspect that well formed internal policies will also be useful descriptions as external policy documentation. Related to this, is a belief that better tools for policy authoring can enable the creation of clearer privacy related legislation. We are still in a time where there is a considerable gap between what privacy laws say should be done and what technology actually can help make happen.

There are some challenges that future research and professional groups will need to address before our work could contribute to a generally useful privacy technology. First, standards need to advance beyond those currently in place [9] so that it becomes technically feasible for privacy policy information to travel with data within and outside of organizations. Perhaps a focus on the importance of privacy could contribute to changes in system architecture – to enable easier privacy and security. Current world events are providing pressure on the public and private sectors to consolidate data and collect and use more PI for a variety of purposes. At the same time, legislation in countries around the world is providing data users with increased obligations regarding the use of PI and data subjects with rights about the collection and use of their PI by organizations. Technology can help to protect people's privacy in collaboration with social policy. The HCI field can step up to the challenge of creating interfaces and interaction methods that reduce the complexity in defining, implementing, and managing privacy policies for the benefit of all parties.

References

1. Ackerman, M. Darrell, T., and Weitzner, D. (2001) Privacy in context, *Human Computer Interaction*, 16, 2, 167-176.
2. Adams, A. and Sasse, A. (2001) Privacy in Multimedia Communications: Protecting Users, Not Just Data . In A. Blandford, J. Vanderdonkt & P. Gray [Eds.]: People and Computers XV - Interaction without frontiers. *Joint Proceedings of HCI2001 and ICM2001*, Lille, Sept. 2001. pp. 49-64. Springer.
3. Altman, I. (1975). *The Environment and Social Behavior, Privacy, Personal Space, Territory and Crowding*. Monterey, CA: Brooks/Cole Pub. Co., Inc.

4. Anton, A., He, Q., and Baumer, D. (2004) The complexity underlying JetBlue's privacy policy violations. *IEEE Security & Privacy*. August/September, 2004.
5. Ashley, P., Hada, S., Karjoth, G., Powers, C., and Schunter, M. (2003). *Enterprise Privacy Architecture Language (EPAL 1.2)*. W3C Member Submission 10-Nov-2003. http://www.w3.org/Submission/EPAL/
6. Ball, E. (2003). Patient privacy in electronic prescription transfer. *IEEE Security and Privacy*, 1, 2, 77-80.
7. Baumer, D., Earp, J.B., and Payton, F. C. (2000). Privacy in medical records: IT implications of HIPAA. *Computers and Society*, December, 2000, 40-47.
8. CRA Conference on "Grand Research Challenges in Information Security and Assurance". http://www.cra.org/Activities/grand.challenges/security/. November 16-19, 2003.
9. Cranor, L. (2002). *Web Privacy with P3P*. Cambridge: O'Reilly.
10. Hagen, P. (2000). Personalization versus privacy. *The Forrester Report*, Nov., 2000, 1-19.
11. Jensen, C. and Potts, C. (2004). Privacy polices as decision-making tools: An evaluation of online privacy notices. *CHI 2004*, 471-478.
12. Karat, C., Brodie, C., Karat, J., Vergo, J., and Alpert, S. (2003) Personalizing the user experience on ibm.com. *IBM Systems Journal*, 42, 4, 686-701.
13. Kobsa, A. Personalized hypermedia and international privacy. Communications of the ACM, 45, 5, 64-67.
14. Manny, C. H. (2003). European and American privacy: Commerce, rights, and justice. Computer Law and Security Report, 19, 1, 2003, 4-10.
15. National Research Council. (2003). Who goes there? Authentication through the lens of privacy. Washington, D.C: National Academies Press.
16. OECD (1980). OECD guidelines on the protection of privacy and transborder flows of personal data. http://www.oecd.org/home/
17. Office of the Federal Privacy Commissioner of Australia. (2000). *Privacy and Business (2000)*. http://www.privacy.gov.au
18. Palen, L. and Dourish, P. (2002). Unpacking 'privacy' for a networked world, *CHI 2002*. 129-136.
19. Ponemon Institute and IAPP. (2004). 2003 benchmark study of corporate privacy practices.
20. Senior, A., Pankanti, S., Hampapur, A., Brown, L., Tian, Y., and Ekin, A. (2004). Blinkering Surveillance: Enabling Video Privacy through Computer Vision. *IEEE Security and Privacy*, in press.
21. Smith, J. (1993). Privacy policies and practices: Inside the organizational maze. Communications of the ACM, 36, 12, 105-122.
22. U.S. Fair and Accurate Credit Transaction Act. (2003). H.R. 2622, 108th Congress, July 24, 2003.
23. Warren, S.A. and Brandeis, L.D. (1890). The right to privacy. Harvard Business Review, Dec, 4, 195.

Questionnaire–Based Research on Opinions of Visitors for Communication Robots at an Exhibition in Japan

Tatsuya Nomura[1,2], Takugo Tasaki[2,3], Takayuki Kanda[2],
Masahiro Shiomi[2], Hiroshi Ishiguro[2], and Norihiro Hagita[2]

[1] Department of Media Informatics, Ryukoku University,
1–5, Yokotani, Setaohe–cho, Otsu, Shiga 520–2194, Japan
[2] ATR Intelligent Robotics and Communication Laboratories,
2–2, Hikaridai, Seika–cho, Soraku–gun, Kyoto 619–0288, Japan
[3] Graduate School of Corporate Information, Hannan University,
5–4–33, Amamihigashi, Matsubara, Osaka 580–8502, Japan

Abstract. This paper reports the results of questionnaire–based research conducted at an exhibition of interactive humanoid robots that was held at the Osaka Science Museum, Japan. The aim of this exhibition was to investigate the feasibility of communication robots connected to a ubiquitous sensor network, under the assumption that these robots will be practically used in daily life in the not–so–distant future. More than ninety thousand people visited the exhibition. A questionnaire was given to the visitors to explore their opinions of the robots. Statistical analysis was done on the data of 2,301 respondents. It was found that the visitors' opinions varied according to age; younger visitors did not necessarily like the robots more than elderly visitors; positive evaluation of the robots did not necessarily conflict with negative evaluations such as anxiety; there was no gender difference; and there was almost no correlation between opinions and the length of time spent near the robots.

1 Introduction

The aim of communication robots is to act in environments with humans and assist humans through communication with them. Humanoid–type robots are considered to be useful in this communication task by, for example, gesturing with their faces, arms, and eyes in guidance tasks for maps.

One method of implementing communication robots is ubiquitous computing, where robots use information from sensors, not only in the robots themselves but also in the environments in which they exist [1,2,3]. This method assumes that all of the objects in the environments have their own IDs by using wireless tag systems [4,5,6]. The most important characteristic of this method is its reduced computational cost for identification of environments by robots, which is difficult in cases where each robot must act alone.

Guidance in museums is considered an effective application of communication robots using these ubiquitous sensor networks. Although research on this task

M.F. Costabile and F. Paternò (Eds.): INTERACT 2005, LNCS 3585, pp. 685–698, 2005.

has been considered for one robot, it focused on providing information by the robot [7]. From the perspective of communication robots, the interaction between robots and humans via sensor network information is more important.

To investigate the effectiveness of communication robots connected through ubiquitous sensor networks in guidance tasks, an exhibition of humanoid robots, called "Robovie" [8], was held at the Osaka Science Museum [1], Japan, for approximately two months in 2004. At this exhibition, a questionnaire was distributed to visitors to explore their opinions of the robots.

Although there has been some research on psychological evaluations by visitors of robots at science museums [9,10,11], these studies have been limited to individual impressions of specific robots behaving alone. The Osaka Science Museum exhibition focused on interaction between visitors and robots via sensor network information in a guidance task. Thus, the visitors' opinions of the robots are assumed to reflect impressions of this interaction. In particular, the research evaluates not only interest in, friendliness toward, and perceives effectiveness of the robots but also anxiety toward them. In addition, it focuses on relations among these psychological features, concrete behavior such as time spent near the robots, and personal traits such as gender and age. Anxiety toward robots and this feeling's relation to behaviors and personal traits are important factors to investigate when communication robots behave in environments with humans and communicate with them [12].

This paper gives an overview of the communication robot exhibition and then analyzes the results of the questionnaires gathered there.

2   The Communication Robots Exhibition

This section presents an overview of the ubiquitous sensor network, the communication robots, the procedures, and the questionnaire used at the communication robots exhibition.

2.1   Overview of Systems

The ubiquitous sensor network was constructed on the 4th floor of the Osaka Science Museum (see Fig. 1). This sensor network records visitor behaviors, and the information obtained was used by the robots to assist visitors in viewing exhibits at the museum and to encourage their interest in science and technology.

Sensor Systems: In this exhibition, visitors had wireless tags. Signals from these tags were detected by using 20 wireless tag readers. A tag reader can detect signals from tags within a maximum of 10 m. The interpolation of the strengths of signals detected by several tag readers makes it possible to determine the physical positions of tags. Eighteen wireless tag readers were hung on the ceiling near exhibits to detect whether visitors stayed near the exhibits. Two tag readers were installed into the robots.

---

[1] http://www.sci-museum.kita.osaka.jp/

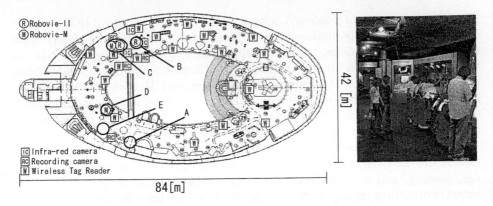

Fig. 1. Overview of the Osaka Science Museum and a Visitor Scene

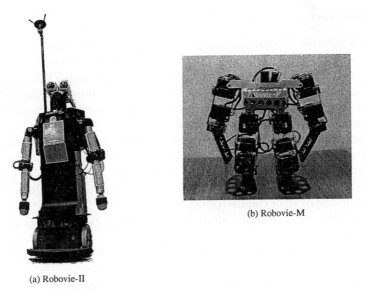

(a) Robovie–II

(b) Robovie-M

Fig. 2. Two Types of Robots Used in the Exhibition: (a) Human–Sized Robot "Robovie–II", (b) Small–Sized Robot "Robovie–M"

In addition, three infrared cameras were assigned to detect positions of the robots and four digital cameras were assigned to record scenes at the exhibition. Each of the cameras and tag readers, except for the ones assigned to the robots, was connected to a PC to control information maintained in a database processed on a central server via ethernet.

Robots: In the exhibition, two types of communication robots were used. Figure 2 shows the humanoid robot "Robovie" [8].

"Robovie–II", shown in Fig. 2(a), is a human–sized robot that stands 120 cm tall. Its diameter is 40 cm, and it weighs about 40 kg. The robot has two arms

(4×2 DOF (degrees of freedom)), a head (3 DOF), two eyes (2×2 DOF for gaze control), and a mobile platform (two driving wheels and one free wheel). This robot has various sensors, including skin sensors covering the entire body, 10 tactile sensors located around the mobile platform, an omni–directional vision sensor, two microphones to listen to human voices, and 24 ultra–sonic sensors for detecting obstacles. It carries a Pentium III PC on board for processing sensory data and generating gestures, including utterances. It is assigned one wireless tag reader.

"Robovie–M", shown in Fig. 2(b), is a small– sized robot that stands 29 cm tall. It has 22 DOF, which allows it to execute various gestures such as walking, bowing, and a handstand (see http://www.vstone.co.jp/top/p_info/robot/robovie-m.html). Since the robot does not have its own function to make utterances, its utterances are performed by the connected PC.

2.2   Procedures

Flow of Visitors: Visitors experienced the exhibition as follows.

First, visitors register for their wireless tags at the reception desk at the entrance to the 4th floor (position A in Fig. 1). At this stage, their names, ages, and birthdates are registered and input to the ID tags provided them. Then, the registered names are automatically transfered into speech information that the robots use in their utterances to visitors.

Visitors are then free to observe exhibits in the museum. All of the wireless tag information is recorded in the database. While viewing the exhibits, visitors interact with robots, each of which has its own role. One provides guidance of the exhibits while moving alone. Two of them communicate with each other to provide guidance of the exhibits (position C in Fig. 1). The other robot executes interaction behaviors, such as calling visitors' names near the exit (position D in Fig. 1).

When visitors finish viewing the exhibits, they are asked to freely respond to a questionnaire on their opinions of the robots and the exhibition at the exit (position E in Fig. 1). The wireless tags are then returned.

Roles of the Robots: At the exhibition, two Robovie–IIs and two Robovie–Ms were used.

One Robovie–II executed exhibit guidance in the museum while moving about (Fig. 3(a)). It explained the contents of exhibits, such as their history.

The other Robovie–II and one Robovie–M executed exhibit guidance while simulating interaction between them by synchronization via the network (Fig. 3(b)). Specifically, the Robovie–M explained an exhibit, the Robovie–II asked questions about it, and finally the Robovie–M responded to the question. Furthermore, these robots interacted with visitors by using information from the ubiquitous sensor network.

The remaining Robovie–M did not provide guidance but instead interacted with visitors by calling their names based on visitor tags and registered information, saying good–bye, asking visitors to return their tags, and so on (Fig. 3(c)).

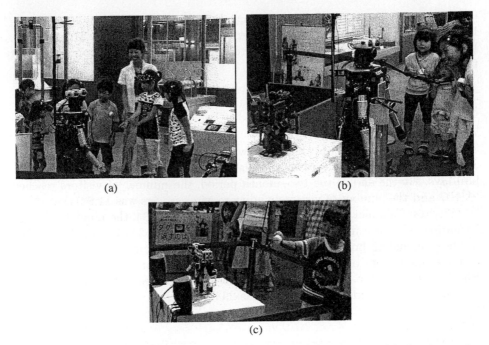

Fig. 3. Scenes of Interaction between the Robots and Visitors: (a) Guidance by Robovie–II, (b) Interaction between Robovie–II and Robovie–M, (c) Interaction with Robovie–M near the Exit

Questionnaire Items: The questionnaire used in the exhibition consisted of the following statements. Respondents indicated the degree to which each statement applies to them by marking whether they (1) "strongly agree", (2) "agree", (3) "are undecided", (4) "disagree", or (5) "strongly disagree".

Item 1 (Interest):
  I am interested in the robots.
Item 2 (Friendliness):
  I felt friendly toward the robots when I faced them.
Item 3 (Effectiveness):
  I find guidance provided by the robots effective.
Item 4 (Anxiety toward Interaction):
  I felt anxiety when the robots talked to me.
Item 5 (Anxiety toward Social Influence):
  I feel anxiety about the possible widespread application of robots to perform tasks such as those shown at the exhibition in the near future.

The 1st, 2nd, and 3rd items measure respondents' interest in the robots, friendliness toward the robots, and evaluation of the robots' effectiveness, respectively. The 4th and 5th items measure the respondents' anxiety toward interaction with the robots and the social influence of the robots, respectively.

The questionnaire also includes items on gender and age. The item on age has seven graded answers (for respondent age categories from the 10's to 70's). In addition, the questionnaire has an item for freely describing opinions about the robots and the exhibition.

3   Analysis of Data

The communication robots exhibition was held at the Osaka Science Museum, Japan, from July to August, 2004. This period included the Japanese summer holidays. By the end of the two–month period, the number of visitors reached 91,107 and the number of visitors who wore wireless tags was 11,927.

The total number of returned questionnaires was 3,034, the number of those including all of the five items shown in section 2.2 was 2,891, and the number of those including both the gender item and the age item was 2,301. Analysis considering factors of age and gender was executed for these 2,301 samples. Finally, the number of questionnaires that included freely described opinions about the robots and the exhibition was 293.

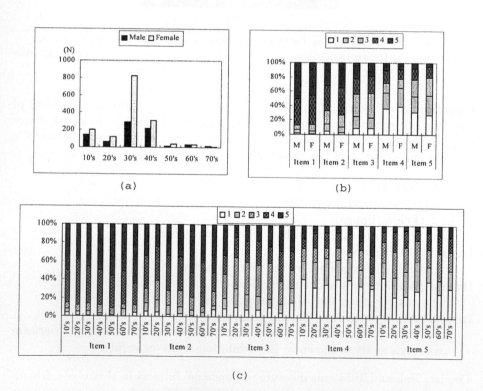

Fig. 4. Distributions of Respondents and Item Scores: (a) Distribution of Respondents based on Gender and Age, (b) Distribution of Item Scores based on Gender, (c) Distribution of Item Scores based on Age

Answers were scored in reverse order of their listing, from 1 ("strongly disagree") to 5 ("strongly agree).

Moreover, the following information was measured as a behavior index, based on tag information from the ubiquitous sensor network:

T3: Time that visitors stayed within 3 m of the point where Robovie–II and Robovie–M simulated their communication.

The relationship between this behavior index and the item scores was also analyzed.

3.1   Item Scores

The number of male respondents was 777 and that of female respondents was 1,524. Moreover, the number of respondents aged in the 10's was 349, that in the 20's was 182, that in the 30's was 1109, that in the 40's was 519, that in the 50's was 56, that in the 60's was 61, and that in the 70's was 25. Figure 4(a) shows the distribution of respondents based on gender and age. This figure

Table 1. Mean Scores and Standard Deviations of Items based on Gender and Age, and Results of Two–Way ANOVA for the Item Scores

			Item 1	Item 2	Item 3	Item 4	Item 5
10's	Male	Mean	4.319	3.882	3.708	2.424	2.243
	(N=144)	SD	0.944	1.087	1.300	1.508	1.360
	Female	Mean	4.171	3.790	3.468	2.307	2.166
	(N=205)	SD	1.064	1.192	1.282	1.434	1.225
20's	Male	Mean	4.203	3.531	3.016	2.313	2.828
	(N=64)	SD	0.858	1.221	1.315	1.296	1.352
	Female	Mean	4.212	3.653	3.093	2.415	2.559
	(N=118)	SD	0.772	1.081	1.094	1.316	1.121
30's	Male	Mean	4.300	3.746	3.174	2.436	2.582
	(N=287)	SD	0.950	1.174	1.182	1.362	1.273
	Female	Mean	4.245	3.960	3.265	2.270	2.519
	(N=822)	SD	0.837	1.002	1.159	1.289	1.150
40's	Male	Mean	4.256	3.786	3.284	2.414	2.335
	(N=215)	SD	0.914	1.077	1.215	1.340	1.152
	Female	Mean	4.372	4.010	3.309	2.141	2.263
	(N=304)	SD	0.729	1.013	1.127	1.334	1.142
50's	Male	Mean	4.368	4.105	3.105	2.316	2.000
	(N=19)	SD	0.684	0.875	1.100	1.416	1.155
	Female	Mean	4.486	4.270	3.459	2.297	2.568
	(N=37)	SD	0.731	1.071	1.304	1.431	1.425
60's	Male	Mean	4.484	4.290	3.710	2.645	2.548
	(N=31)	SD	0.677	0.864	1.131	1.518	1.312
	Female	Mean	4.100	4.200	3.667	2.467	2.900
	(N=30)	SD	1.062	0.714	1.155	1.432	1.322
70's	Male	Mean	4.294	3.941	3.353	3.235	3.000
	(N=17)	SD	1.047	1.345	1.412	1.786	1.458
	Female	Mean	4.750	4.250	3.125	3.000	1.625
	(N=8)	SD	0.707	1.165	1.642	1.604	0.744
F–Values	Gender		0.043	1.689	0.003	1.132	1.609
	Age		0.937	4.186	6.223	1.665	6.514
	Interaction		1.642	1.109	1.027	0.448	2.165
p–Values	Gender		0.836	0.194	0.959	0.287	0.205
	Age		0.467	0.000	0.000	0.126	0.000
	Interaction		0.132	0.355	0.406	0.847	0.044

indicates that there was a bias among respondents aged in their 30's and 40's, in particular, females in their 30's.

Figures 4(b) and (c) show the distributions of the item scores based on gender and age, respectively. These figures show that the rates of respondents scoring more than 4 on items 1 and 2 were more than 80% and about 70%, respectively. Moreover, the rates of the respondents scoring less than 2 on items 4 and 5 were each about 60%. On the other hand, these figures imply that the distributions of the item scores may differ between ages.

Table 1 shows mean scores and standard deviations of the items based on gender and age, and the results of a two–way ANOVA for the item scores with factors of gender and age. There were statistically significant differences for items 2, 3, and 5 between ages. There was no statistically significant difference between genders. A Tukey post–hoc test obtained the following results:

- The scores of item 2 in the 20's group were lower than those in the 30's, 40's, 50's and 60's groups.
- The scores of item 3 in the 20's group were lower than those in the 10's and 60's groups. Moreover, those in the 10's group were higher than those in the 30's and 40's groups.
- The scores of item 5 in the 10's group were lower than those in the 20's, 60's, and 70's groups. Moreover, those in the 40's group were lower than those in the 20's and 30's groups.

3.2   Time That Respondents Stayed Near the Robots

The behavior index T3 may reflect the respondents' interest, friendliness, and anxiety toward the robots to some extent. However, it can also be influenced by external factors, such as congestion on the floor. In fact, the number of visitors per day was widely distributed during the period (maximum: 3,240, minimum: 767, average: 1,898, median: 1,780), due to the fact that this period included the Japanese summer holidays. Thus, the days that more than 2,250 people visited, including summer holidays, were assumed to be congested days and the effect of congestion on the behavior index was analyzed.

First, a two–way ANOVA with factors of the congestion condition and age was executed. Only the congestion condition had an effect (age: $F = 1.186$, $p = 0.083$; congestion: $F = 20.406, p = 0.000$; interaction: $F = 0.885, p = 0.505$).

Next, a two–way ANOVA with factors of congestion and gender was executed. Both congestion and gender had an effect (gender: $F = 8.111, p = 0.004$; congestion: $F = 44.930, p = 0.000$; interaction: $F = 1.171, p = 0.279$). Figure 5(a) shows the mean values and standard deviations of T3 on the gender and congestion conditions. It was found that the T3 values of the visitors on congested days were about 50 sec larger than those on non–congested days, and the T3 values of the female respondents were more than 10 sec larger than those of the male visitors.

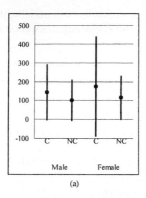
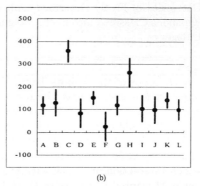

(a)   (b)

Fig. 5. Mean Values and Standard Deviations of T3: (a) on Gender and Congestion Condition (C: Congestion, NC: Non–Congestion, Male–C: $N = 414$, Male–NC: $N = 363$, Female–C: $N = 699$, Female–NC: $N = 825$), (b) on Categories of Freely Described Opinions (A: $N = 14$, B: $N = 6$, C: $N = 9$, D: $N = 5$, E: $N = 26$, F: $N = 5$, G: $N = 12$, H: $N = 5$, I: $N = 6$, J: $N = 6$, K: $N = 18$, L: $N = 10$)

Table 2. Peason's Correlation Coefficient r between the Item Scores and Behavior Index T3

	Item 1	Item 2	Item 3	Item 4	Item 5	T3
Item 1	–	0.521	0.385	-0.095	-0.123	0.077
Item 2	0.521	–	0.459	-0.142	-0.128	0.059
Item 3	0.385	0.459	–	-0.030	-0.100	0.036
Item 4	-0.095	-0.142	-0.030	–	0.372	0.048
Item 5	-0.123	-0.128	-0.100	0.372	–	-0.018

3.3   Correlations Between Item Scores and Behavior Index

Table 2 shows Peason's correlation coefficient r between the item scores and behavior index T3. There were medium–level correlations between items 1–3 and between items 4–5. On the other hand, there were few correlations or low–level correlations between the group of items 1–3 and that of items 4–5. Moreover, there were few correlations between the item scores and behavior index T3.

3.4   Freely Described Opinions

A total of 293 sentences expressing opinions on the robots and exhibition were manually classified into several categories based on the contents of the sentences. This classification was executed by two people who discussed the contents of the sentences and categories until they reached a consensus in their classification results. Finally, 16 categories were established and each sentence was classified into one of them. Table 3 shows these categories, the number of sentences classified into each category, and examples of the sentences classified into each category.

Table 3. Categories of Freely Described Opinions of the Robots and Exhibition, the Number of Opinions Classified into Each Category, and Examples of Opinions Classified into Each Category

Category	N
A. Positive Opinions of the Robots Themselves	23
(Example: "I was glad to have the robots talk me.")	
B. Expectations for Robots and Technology in the Future	16
(Example: "I would enjoy it if there were more kinds of robots."),	
C. Positive Attitudes of Children toward the Robots	17
(Example: "My child seemed to be glad to be called by the robots.")	
D. Desires on Interaction or Touch with the Robots	8
(Example: "I wanted to talk with the robots more.")	
E. Negative Opinions of Communication with the Robots	59
(Example: "The robots' utterances were hard to listen to.")	
F. Negative Emotions toward the Robots	10
(Example: "I felt a little fear toward the robots.")	
G. Fear of Children toward the Robots	20
(Example: "My child seemed to feel fear toward the robots.")	
H. Children's Indifference to or Non–Interest in the Robots	9
(Example: "My child seemed to lose interest in the robots because they did not react to the name tag.")	
I. Other Dissatisfaction with the Robots	12
(Example: "The robots' reactions were slower than what I expected.")	
J. Physical Danger in Interaction with the Robots	7
(Example: "The robot's arm struck my child.")	
K. Positive Evaluation of the Exhibition	27
(Example: "I was happy because I could directly come in contact with the robots.")	
L. Critical Requests for the Contents of the Exhibition	17
(Example: "Please prepare more kinds of robots.")	
O. Other 4 Categories	68

Categories A–D were positive opinions of the robots themselves. A corresponds to sentences expressing positive opinions and emotions toward the robots' appearance, interaction, intelligence, and so on. B corresponds to sentences expressing expectations and desires for robots and technology in the future. C corresponds to sentences expressing positive attitudes held by children toward robots, described by the children themselves or their parents. D corresponds to sentences such as "I wanted to interact with the robots more".

Categories E–J were negative opinions of the robots themselves. E corresponds to sentences expressing dissatisfaction with and negative opinions of the robots' functions of utterance, recognition, communication, and so on. F corresponds to sentences expressing negative emotions toward robots, such as anxiety, fear, and so on. G corresponds to sentences stating that children felt fear or anxiety toward the robots, as written by the children themselves or their parents.

H corresponds to sentences indicating that children were indifferent to or had no interest in the robots, as written by the children themselves or their parents. I corresponds to sentences expressing other dissatisfaction with the robots. J corresponds to sentences about physical danger in interaction with the robots, such as the fact that a robot's arm struck the visitor's body.

Categories K and L were opinions on the exhibition. K corresponds to a positive evaluation, such as "I would like to visit here again". L corresponds to critical requests about the contents of the exhibition, such as types of robots to be exhibited. The other four categories correspond to sentences on dissatisfaction with external factors not related to the robots or content of the exhibition, such as congestion of the floor and waiting time for demonstrations. Thus, these four categories were reduced in analysis.

Respondents of categories A–D and K were grouped as those having positive opinions, and respondents of categories E–J and L as those having negative opinions. The number of positive opinions and that of negative opinions were 91 (31%) and 134 (45.7%), respectively. The opinions classified into A and K dominated more than half of the positive opinions. Moreover, category E had the largest number of opinions among the negative opinions and acounted for 44% of the negative opinions.

In order to investigate the relationship between these opinions and the time that the respondents stayed near the robots, a one–way ANOVA with the opinion categories was executed for the behavior index T3. Since the external factor of congestion may influence the analysis, as mentioned in section 3.2, this ANOVA was limited to the respondents on the non–congested days. Figure 5(b) shows the mean values and standard deviations of T3 on the categories. As a result, there was a statistically significant effect of the categories ($F = 2.930, p = 0.002$). A Tukey post–hoc test found that the T3 values of the respondents classified into C were larger than those in all the other categories except for H.

3.5   Discussion

Influence of Age: The results presented in section 3.1 show that many visitors positively evaluated the robots. More specifically, many visitors had interest in and felt friendliness toward the robots. Moreover, many visitors did not feel anxiety about interaction with the robots and their social influence.

On the other hand, there were differences in these opinions between ages. The results show that people in their 20's feel less friendliness toward robots than those in their 30's – 60's, people in their 20's less positively evaluate guidance by the robots than those in their 10's and 60's, people in their 10's more positively evaluate the guidance than those in their 30's and 40's, people in their 10's feel less anxiety about the social influence of the robots than those in their 20's, 60's, and 70's, and people in their 40's feel less anxiety about the social influence than those in their 20's and 30's. In other words, younger respondents do not necessarily like the robots more than elderly respondents. The above results imply that the design of robots should be changed according to user age.

Relationship to Behaviors: The results presented in section 3.2 show that some external factors influence concrete behaviors in real situations, such as museums. However, the results in section 3.3 show that there is no relationship between opinions of the robots and the concrete behavior of staying near the robots. These results imply that environmental factors may more strongly affect behaviors than psychogical factors in real situations such as museums.

Moreover, the results in section 3.3 also show that interest in, friendliness toward, and evaluation of effectiveness of the robots do not necessarily conflict with anxiety toward them. These results imply that robot designs intended to increase effectiveness and friendliness do not necessarily reduce the anxiety felt toward the robot.

Attitudes of Children Toward Robots: The results given in section 3.4 indicate that there are both positive and negative opinions of the robots and the exhibitions on a concrete level. They also show that there exist several areas of dissatisfaction with the functions of the communication robots, and people, in particular children, may have negative emotions toward the robots at their current level. On the other hand, the results also show that there are children who had interest in and friendliness toward the robots and indicate that these children and their parents stay near the robots longer than others.

The above results can be interpreted as follows. In Japan, there are several types of discourses on robots, and their effect naturally differs between age groups. The results in section 3.1 reflect this. Moreover, many children have never seen actual moving robots, although they are affected by several media. This gap may lead to the fear and anxiety toward the robots shown in section 3.4. If this interpretation is valid, we can conclude that the design of robots for children should be adapted for the image of robots presented in the various media.

Gender Difference: The results in section 3.2 reveal a tendency for females to remain near the robots longer than males. However, there is some doubt as to whether there is a gender difference in behavior toward the robots, as shown in section 3.2, at least in the situation presented in this research. In fact, there was no gender difference in opinions shown for the items, nor any correlation between them and the behavior index.

As a reason, it can be surmised that many of the visitors were females in their 30's and 40's. The period included the summer holidays, and, as a result, many females visited the exhibition with their children. In other words, it can be assumed that their children stayed near the robots longer with them and, as a result, the females appeared to be staying longer. This assumption needs to be investigated through another type of data, such as orbits in which the visitors moved while viewing the exhibits. Such data will be gathered and analyzed in future research.

4   Summary

This paper reported the results of questionnaire–based research conducted at an exhibition of interactive humanoid robots that was held at the Osaka Science

Museum, Japan, with the aim of investigating the use of communication robots connected with a ubiquitous sensor network. More than ninety thousand people visited the exhibition and a questionnaire was given to the visitors to explore their opinions of the robots. Statistical analysis was done for data consisting of 2,301 respondents. It was found that the visitors' opinions of the robots differed according to age, younger people did not necessarily like the robots more than elderly people, positive evaluation of the robots did not necessarily conflict with negative evaluations such as anxiety, there was no gender difference in opinions of the robots, and there was almost no correlation between the opinions and the length of time spent near the robots.

As future research, the relationship between the visitors' opinions of the robots and another behavior index should be explored. Moreover, there was a bias of respondents in assembling samples. Although this bias may be unavoidable in situations such as museums, data from various types of people need to be gathered for analysis.

Acknowledgments

This research was supported by the Ministry of Internal Affairs and Communications. We wish to thank the staff at the Osaka Science Museum for their highly appreciated cooperation and helpful suggestions: Hideaki Terauchi, Toshihiko Shibata, Koutarou Hayashi, Masaaki Kakio, Taichi Tajika, and Fumitaka Yamaoka.

References

1. Ng, K.C., Ishiguro, H., Trivedi, M.M., Sogo, T.: An integrates surveillance system–human tracking and view synthesis using multiple omni–directional vision sensors. Image and Vision Computing Journal **22** (2004) 551–561
2. Ikeda, T., Ishida, T., Ishiguro, H.: Framework of distributed audition. In: Proc. 13th IEEE Int. Workshop on Robot and Human Interactive Communication (RO–MAN). (2004)
3. Murakita, T., Ikeda, T., Ishiguro, H.: Human tracking using floor sensors based on the Markov chain Monte Carlo method. In: Proc. Int. Conf. Pattern Recognition (ICPR). (2004) 917–920
4. Nishimura, T., Itoh, H., Nakamura, Y., Yamamoto, Y., Nakashima, H.: A compact battery–less information terminal for real world interaction. In: PERVASIVE 2004. Number 3001 in LNCS. Springer (2004) 124–139
5. Sumi, Y., Matsuguchi, T., Ito, S., Fels, S., Mase, K.: Collaborative capturing of interactions by multiple sensors. In: Proc. Int. Conf. Ubiquitous Computing (Ubicomp). (2003) 193–194
6. Schulz, D., Fox, D., Hightower, J.: People tracking with anonymous and id-sensors using rao–blackwellised particle filters. In: Proc. Int. Joint Conf. Artificial Intelligence (IJCAI). (2003) 921–926
7. Burgard, W., Cremers, A.B., Fox, D., Hähnel, D., Lakemeyer, G., Schulz, D., Steiner, W., Thrun, S.: The interactive museum tour–guide robot. In: Proc. Nat. Conf. Artificial Intelligence (AAAI). (1998)

8. Ishiguro, H., Ono, T., Imai, M., Maeda, T., Kanda, T., Nakatsu, R.: Robovie: an interactive humanoid robot. Int. J. Industrial Robot **28** (2001) 498–503
9. Shibata, T., Wada, K., Tanie, K.: Tabulation and analysis of questionnaire results of subjective evaluation of seal robot at Science Museum in London. In: Proc. Int. Workshop on Robot and Human Interactive Communication (RO–MAN). (2002) 23–28
10. Shibata, T., Wada, K., Tanie, K.: Subjective evaluation of a seal robot at the national museum of science and technology in Stockholm. In: Proc. Int. Workshop on Robot and Human Interactive Communication (RO–MAN). (2003) 397–407
11. Shibata, T., Wada, K., Tanie, K.: Subjective evaluation of a seal robot in Burunei. In: Proc. Int. Workshop on Robot and Human Interactive Communication (RO–MAN). (2004) 135–140
12. Nomura, T., Kanda, T., Suzuki, T., Kato, K.: Psychology in human–robot communication: An attempt through investigation of negative attitudes and anxiety toward robots. In: Proc. the 13th IEEE International Workshop on Robot and Human Interactive Communication. (2004) 35–40

A Toolset for Creating Iconic Interfaces
for Interactive Workspaces

Jacob T. Biehl and Brian P. Bailey

Department of Computer Science, University of Illinois, Urbana, IL 61801
{jtbiehl, bpbailey}@uiuc.edu

Abstract. To work productively in an interactive workspace, users need effective interfaces for seamlessly sharing, annotating, and juxtaposing digital information across heterogeneous devices. In this paper, we present an interface toolset for constructing and using iconic interfaces for interactive workspaces. Using an iconic representation of the physical workspace, users can quickly and easily relocate applications and redirect input across devices. The toolset provides a graphical tool for rapidly constructing iconic representations for various workspaces, supports an existing interactive workspace infrastructure, and is engineered to be portable to others. A usability evaluation showed that the interaction design of the interfaces created with our toolset is effective for redirection and relocation tasks. Our results provide the first empirical baseline for comparing alternative interfaces for interactive workspaces. The use of our toolset facilitates more productive use of interactive workspaces for both individual and group work and is available for download today.

1 Introduction

An interactive workspace is a physical workspace that connects small and portable devices, and large shared displays through a distributed software infrastructure. Because they enable information to be easily distributed and synchronized across devices, interactive workspaces can dramatically improve how users share, annotate, and juxtapose digital information for individual and group work [7].

Two of the most common and frequent tasks in an interactive workspace are relocating applications and redirecting input across devices. While systems-level services for performing these tasks are fully supported within current distributed infrastructures for interactive workspaces, users need effective interfaces to quickly and easily perform those tasks. To support application relocation and input redirection tasks, several interfaces and supporting toolsets have been developed, e.g., [6, 15, 18]. However, these interfaces are either too heavily tied to a specific infrastructure, making them difficult to port to other infrastructures, or variations of the interfaces are overly difficult to construct for different workspaces. Additionally, for many of these interfaces, the effectiveness of their interaction design has not been evaluated.

In our previous work, we discussed the iterative design of an interface which uses an iconic representation for performing application relocation and input redirection tasks [1]. The iconic representation supports recognition over recall and enables users to utilize their spatial reasoning abilities when performing these tasks. In this work,

M.F. Costabile and F. Paternò (Eds.): INTERACT 2005, LNCS 3585, pp. 699–712, 2005.
© IFIP International Federation for Information Processing 2005

we present a toolset for constructing iconic interfaces for interactive workspaces. We explain how iconic representations are constructed and used, describe the architecture and implementation of the toolset, and discuss results from a usability evaluation.

Our toolset provides a configuration tool that enables users to rapidly construct iconic representations of various physical workspaces. We implemented our toolset to work with an existing infrastructure, Gaia, but engineered it to allow easy integration with other existing infrastructures. The usability evaluation showed that the interaction design of our interface is effective for performing input redirection and application relocation tasks quickly and with minimal error, induces low subjective workload, and supports high satisfaction across users. Moreover, our results provide the first empirical baseline for comparing alternative interfaces for performing these tasks in interactive workspaces. By facilitating the creation of effective interfaces, our toolset enables more productive use of interactive workspaces for both individual and group work and is available for download today.

2 Related Work

In this section, we discuss how our work builds upon distributed infrastructures for interactive workspaces, differs from other interaction designs for performing application relocation and input redirection tasks, and compares to other toolsets for creating and executing user interfaces for interactive workspaces.

2.1 Infrastructures for Interactive Workspaces

Distributed infrastructures such as Gaia [15], iROS [6] and Aura [18] provide systems-level services for application relocation, input redirection, and file sharing in an interactive workspace. Gaia, for example, supports presence detection for users, devices, and services, provides context events and services, and supports an information repository for entities in the workspace [15]. Gaia also provides an application framework to construct or adapt existing applications to execute and be relocated in an interactive workspace [14, 16]. While our toolset was developed for Gaia, it was engineered to be easily portable to other existing infrastructures.

Most modern operating systems enable a single workstation with a multi-head VGA card or multiple VGA cards to provide the ability for a user to seamlessly relocate applications and redirect input among connected screens. By building on top of Gaia, our toolset enables users to redirect input and relocate applications across screens driven by independent, heterogeneous devices that are network connected.

2.2 Interaction Designs for Relocating Applications and Redirecting Input

XWand [20] is a set of wireless sensors packaged in a wand-shaped device that enables a user to control lights, stereos, TVs, and more. VisionWand [4] enables a user to manipulate artifacts on large screens using computer vision to track a passive wand. Although XWand and VisionWand could be extended to relocate applications in an interactive workspace, our interface enables a user to relocate applications not visible to a user, e.g., applications that are on screens turned away from the user, and does not require the user to pick up a separate input device and then switch back.

In [9], researchers extended a browser to enable users to browse web pages across screens driven by independent machines. A user specifies the destination screen from a textual list of available screens. Because our interface provides a visual rather than a textual interface, users can leverage their spatial reasoning abilities to both relocate applications and redirect input.

In I-Land [19] researchers developed several novel interactions to enable a user to relocate applications among screens using gestures. Pick-and-Drop [12] allows users to relocate applications by virtually assigning them to movable physical objects. EasyLiving [3] relocates application windows among screens in a room by passively tracking user movement. Our interface enables a user to relocate an application among screens without being physically close to or physically moving among them.

With UbiTable [17] users can share information on a horizontal work surface using an interface of geometric paths and iconic portals. The shared area of the horizontal surface is used to exchange information among users. In our interface, we enable users to relocate information directly among screens through an iconic, conformal representation of the workspace.

In [13], shared display surfaces are formed by spatially extending a user's local desktop onto the surrounding table surface. To relocate an application, a user hyper drags the application between locations. With our interface, users are able to relocate applications among screens that are not in their field of view. Also, our interface supports both application relocation and input redirection in the same visual interface, allowing users to coalesce these tasks into a single interaction. Finally, our interface is built on top of a toolset that can be ported to other infrastructures, enabling it to be used in a variety of interactive workspaces.

2.3 Toolsets

In Mighty Mouse [2], researchers modified a remote desktop protocol to enable users to redirect input across multiple devices. Users initiate a redirection by selecting a destination screen from a list of identifying icons. To end input redirection, the user performs a special click and key combination. PointRight [8] utilizes the iROS infrastructure to provide configurable geometric paths which enable users to redirect input across devices. In PointRight, users define behaviors to construct the geometric relationship of screens, e.g. moving the cursor off the left side of one screen connects it to the right side of another. In addition to providing support for application relocation, our toolset allows users to visually configure an iconic representation of devices within a physical workspace. This allows users to perform relocation and redirection tasks without having to recall the geometric alignment of screens.

iCrafter [11] automatically generates an interface with a top-down view of the workspace to enable relocation of services. Users access textual lists of services attached to a screen and drag the desired service descriptor to another screen. For example, a user can drag a URL from a laptop to a shared screen to relocate a web browser. In contrast, our work provides effective end user tools that enable iconic representations of various workspaces to be quickly constructed. At runtime, the constructed representation is dynamically updated as events are generated due to changes in the location of applications or devices in the workspace. Additionally, our interface enables a user to visually relocate representations of applications rather than having to mentally map textual identifiers of applications and screens to the corresponding applications and physical screens that they refer to in the workspace.

3   Use and Construction of the Interface

In this section, we describe the iconic representation of our interface, how a user interacts with it to relocate applications and redirect input, and the graphical tool that allows others to rapidly construct iconic representations for their own workspaces.

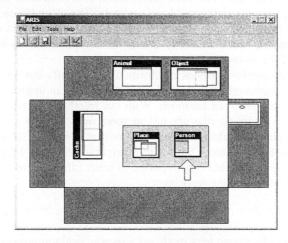

Fig. 1. A screen shot of the iconic representation for our interactive workspace. The representation shows each wall in the workspace pulled down on its back side so that the screens attached to the walls all face upwards. Applications are shown within the screens. The rectangle in the middle of the room represents the table, which has two graphics tablets on it. An arrow shows a user's current location and orientation in the workspace.

3.1   Iconic Representation

As shown in Figure 1, our interface uses an iconic representation of the workspace in a 2-D, foldout view. In a *foldout* view, the walls of the workspace appear pulled down on their back sides so that the screens attached to them all face upwards, providing a complete, distortion-free view of their content. The interface provides representations of all screens connected to the workspace. On each screen, representations of application windows are shown sized and positioned relative to their size and position on the corresponding physical screens. Salient physical objects such as tables, desks and doors are included to enable users to quickly orient the interface's representation to the physical workspace. The representation also contains a yellow arrow indicating a user's current location and orientation in the workspace.

Because the interface provides a spatial representation of the workspace, it supports recognition over recall [10] and enables users to leverage their spatial reasoning abilities to quickly and easily perform relocation and redirection tasks. Our interface is the first to support both of these tasks within a single visual metaphor.

3.2 Relocating Applications and Redirecting Input

A user interacts with the interface's iconic representation to relocate applications and redirect input among screens in the workspace. To relocate an application, a user invokes the interface by selecting a specially added button on the window's title bar, double-clicks its application icon or leaves the interface open indefinitely. The interface receives events from the configuration manager to ensure its representation always reflects the current state of applications, devices, and users in the workspace.

Once invoked, the user selects the representation of the application, drags it to the destination screen in the interface, and drops it. While it is selected, the representation changes color and a rectangular, yellow outline is drawn around the corresponding application in the workspace, which we call a "live outline." As a user is dragging the representation across the screens in the interface, the live outline of the application can be seen moving across the corresponding physical screens in the workspace. If a user looks up from the local screen, the outline provides confirmatory feedback of the ongoing interaction. Once the representation is dropped, the live outline is removed and the interface sends a request to our toolset's Application Manager to relocate and position the application to the destination screen.

Because the iconic representation depicts the *entire* workspace, a user can interact with the interface on a local screen to relocate an application from any screen to any other screen. For example, a user can move an application from one large display to another large display by interacting with the interface executing on their local laptop. Because a relocation task can be completed entirely on a single screen, our interface also supports the use of a stylus input device or touch screen without having to switch it to a relative positioning mode. A relative mode would be required if the cursor had to leave the screen as part of the interaction.

To redirect input using the interface, a user positions the cursor over the destination screen and right-clicks (a stylus and touch panel can also support right-clicks). We chose a right-click interaction for input redirection to disambiguate it from the start of application relocation. The interface sends a request to the runtime engine to redirect mouse and keyboard input to the specified screen. Input can then be redirected back to the local system by performing a similar interaction on the destination screen or by selecting a special key sequence.

3.3 Constructing the Iconic Representation

Since the iconic representation depends on the physical layout of a particular workspace, our toolset offers a graphical tool for rapidly constructing the default representation. In the tool, a user drags representations of walls, displays, doors, and tables from a palette and drops them on the canvas, placing and sizing them as appropriate. To achieve a precise layout, users can enter the exact dimensions of objects in a properties dialog in the construction palette. However, an exact replication is probably not required – the resulting representation just needs to be close enough such that users can quickly associate it with the physical workspace.

Once the default representation is loaded into the runtime system, it can be dynamically updated. For example, when the location or presence of portable devices changes, appropriate events can be sent to the interface to update its representation.

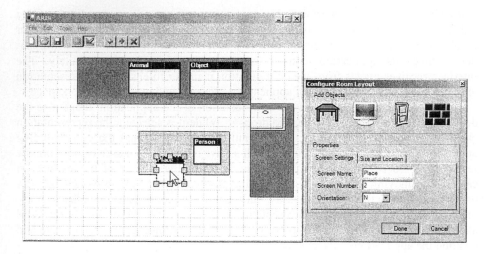

Fig. 2. A screen shot of our graphical construction tool which enables users to quickly construct an initial representation of the workspace. In this screen shot, the user has partially constructed the representation shown in Figure 1.

4   Toolset Architecture and Implementation

In this section we describe the design goals of our toolset, its architecture (shown in Figure 3), and the interface runtime that supports relocation and redirection tasks.

4.1   Design Goals

A design goal of our toolset was to enable it to be used in interactive workspaces driven by different distributed infrastructures. Because there are several such infrastructures for interactive workspaces, e.g. [6, 15, 18], we implemented our toolset for one, Gaia, but engineered the toolset so that it can be easily ported to others. This enables our interface to be used across a variety of existing interactive workspaces.

Another goal was to enable our interface to be used in workspaces with multiple small and large displays driven by a single PC with multi-head graphics cards. While this configuration does not support some of the advanced, real-time features of distributed infrastructures, it does effectively simulate many of the core functions. By supporting this configuration, we offer a low investment mechanism for researchers to use or adapt our interface and compare its use for interactive workspaces. For brevity, the following sections only discuss how our toolset functions with Gaia.

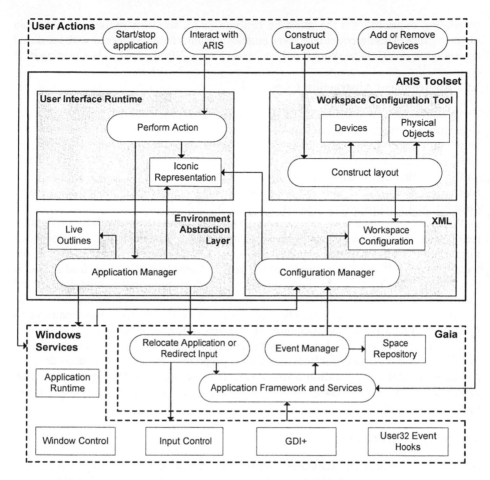

Fig. 3. The architecture of our toolset

4.2 Gaia

Gaia is a distributed infrastructure that manages devices, applications and user state in an interactive workspace. Its application framework [14, 16] provides system support for developing and extending applications which can migrate across heterogeneous devices. Gaia negotiates with the native operating system to acquire application state and coordinate relocation of applications and redirection of input. When users bring devices in or take devices away from the workspace, Gaia's event manager detects the change and notifies our configuration manager (see figure 3). The event manger also notifies the space repository, a service that maintains device, application, and user state for the workspace.

Our toolset extends and abstracts the functionality of Gaia. The toolset's environment abstraction layer (EAL) was created, in part, to provide a simplified relocation and redirection API to the interface runtime. This layer is responsible for translating requests from the interface runtime into a series of requests to the Gaia infrastructure. This intermediate layer enables our interface to execute without direct dependencies on Gaia, making it only necessary to modify the EAL when porting it.

4.3 Environment Abstraction Layer

The Environment Abstraction Layer (EAL) executes on each device in the workspace. In addition to providing a simplified API to the interface runtime, the EAL provides application query services for the interface runtime, coordinates application relocation and input redirection with the underlying infrastructure, and provides support for live outlines. When the interface is invoked, the runtime contacts the EALs executing on each device to acquire information about running applications such as their size, position, and window stacking order.

When the interface runtime sends a request for application relocation or input redirection, the EAL translates the request into the appropriate calls for the underlying infrastructure, which then completes the request. When the EAL executing on the local system receives a completion confirmation from the application framework, it then contacts the EAL on the destination device (which may be the same device) and positions the application window as a function of where it was positioned in the iconic representation. The EAL also coordinates with the configuration manager to update all of the iconic interfaces currently running in the workspace.

To support live outlines for an ongoing relocation task, the EAL is responsible for drawing the rectangular outlines on the appropriate screens. As a user drags a representation of an application across a screen in the interface, the interface runtime contacts the EAL executing on the system driving the corresponding screen to draw or update the outline.

4.4 XML Specification

An XML specification maintains information about the items depicted in the interface's iconic representation. Attributes include object type, location, size, orientation, hostname, screen resolution, etc. The XML specification is created using the graphical tool described in section 3.3.

At runtime, the configuration manager loads the XML specification. When device attributes change, the event manager in Gaia contacts the configuration manger, which updates the specification in memory. The configuration manager notifies the interface runtime, which updates its iconic representation. Through this information loop, the toolset ensures that the iconic representation in each instance of the interface executing in the workspace accurately reflects the current physical state.

4.5 Interface Runtime

The interface runtime draws the iconic representation based on information supplied by the configuration manager. As discussed in section 3.2, a user performs input redirection and application relocation by interacting with the iconic representation. When the user drags an application across screens in the iconic representation, the interface runtime contacts the EAL executing on the system driving the corresponding screen to draw or update the live outline. When a user completes a relocation or redirection interaction, the EAL is contacted to service the request.

5   Usability Evaluation

A user study was conducted to evaluate the effectiveness of the interaction design in our interface and to understand how to improve it. The results also serve another important function – providing an empirical baseline against which the usability of alternative interfaces can be compared. Without the availability of such results, it is difficult to judge the relative quality of alternative interfaces for performing similar tasks. In our study, we used a representative configuration of an interactive workspace and used our graphical tool to construct the corresponding iconic representation.

5.1   Workspace Configuration

Our interactive workspace consisted of three 61" plasma screens and two 20" LCD screens. The LCD screens were positioned 2' apart on a table in the center of the room, faced in the same direction. We positioned two plasma screens in front of the table directly in a user's field of view and physically close together along the same plane. The third plasma screen was positioned just to the left of the table, turned 90 degrees but still within a user's field of view. This configuration is representative of existing interactive workspaces, e.g., [7, 14]. For the study, four of the screens were labeled with a category of image content, Person, Place, Animal, or Object, while the fifth screen (one of the three large displays) was labeled Cache.

A high-end Dell Precision 450n workstation was used to drive the screens. The workstation was equipped with one nVidia Quadro 1000 and two nVidia FX 5200 graphics cards. Camtasia was used to video record a user's screen interaction for later analysis. We chose to use the single PC configuration of our toolset because the Gaia distributed infrastructure is still a research prototype and we did not want slow response times or other errors in the infrastructure to adversely affect the tasks.

5.2   Users and Task Scenario

Sixteen users (7 female) participated in the study. Users consisted of undergraduate and graduate students, and administrative professionals from our institution. The high-level task scenario was to relocate a PowerPoint application among screens in the workspace and to redirect input to perform annotations. The application consisted of four images, one image per slide. A user viewed the image on a slide, relocated the application to the screen labeled with the category that fit that image (e.g., an image with a person in it needed to be relocated to the screen labeled Person), redirected input to the screen closest to them, typed an annotation for the image (e.g., the name of the person in the image), and then redirected input back to the screen with the application. These steps were repeated three more times, as there were four images in the application. The application always started on the screen labeled Cache.

The task scenario is comprised of representative subtasks commonly performed in interactive workspaces, relocating applications based on their content and redirecting input for annotation. Most importantly, these subtasks were sequenced into a meaningful, higher-level task scenario. We had users perform the tasks in rapid succession to stress the use of the interface.

5.3 Procedure and Measurements

Upon arriving at the lab, we went through an informed consent process with the user. The experimenter described the equipment in the room, explained the task and demonstrated the functionality of the interface. The users perform a practice task consisting of six images; and, if requested, a user could perform a second practice to ensure the interface and task was understood. Once questions were answered, the user performed the experimental task and was instructed to perform the task as quickly and accurately as possible. When finished, the user completed a subjective workload and a post-task questionnaire. In our study, we measured:

- *Time to relocate an application from one screen to another.* Computed from the timestamps in the interaction videos, relocation time was measured from when a user first advanced the slide in the application to when the application appeared on the target screen.
- *Time to redirect input from one screen to another.* Computed using the same method, redirection time was the time to redirect the cursor to the local screen to enter the annotation and then to redirect the cursor back to the screen with the application. The time spent performing the annotation was not included.
- *Errors when relocating an application or redirecting input.* An error was any interaction step that did not move a user closer to completing the task. Example errors would be moving the application to the wrong screen or using a left-click rather than a right-click to perform input redirection.
- *Subjective workload.* This was measured using the NASA TLX [5]. The TLX measures workload along continuous scales in six dimensions: *mental demand*, *physical demand*, *temporal demand*, *own performance*, *effort*, and *frustration*. A user responds by marking a vertical line along a continuous scale from Low (0) to High (80) for each dimension, and is measured in 1/16" increments.
- *User satisfaction.* Users rated the interface according to ease of use, appropriateness for the task, and ease of learning. A rating was structured using a 7-point Likert scale where statements were made in neutral form, e.g., the interface was easy to use, and users responded from 1 (Strongly Disagree) to 7 (Strongly Agree). Users were also asked to briefly explain their ratings.

6 Evaluation Results

In this section we present the results from our usability study.

6.1 Task Performance and Error

Users were able to perform the tasks quickly and with minimal error. For application relocation, users completed the task with a mean performance time of 7.99 seconds (SD=6.96 seconds). Users completed input redirection tasks with a mean performance time of 10.56 seconds (SD=5.08 seconds).

When performing the tasks, the number of errors committed was quite low overall. For application relocation, we identified only a single error out of 48 trials. For input redirection, we identified just three errors out of 48 trials. Most importantly, all users were able to successfully complete the tasks after just a few minutes of instruction on how to use the interface.

6.2 Subjective Workload and User Satisfaction

Figure 4 shows the ratings of subjective workload. The average workload was 25.46 (SD=21.88), or 31.8% of the maximum. The average along each workload dimension was well below the midpoint value, with the highest being mental demand with an average of 46.1%. Overall, the interface induced relatively low workload on a user.

Figure 5 shows the ratings of user satisfaction for ease of use, appropriateness, and ease of learning. On each dimension, users rated the interface highly. On a scale of 1 (worst) to 7 (best), users rated ease of use 5.19 (SD=1.47), appropriateness also 5.19 (SD=1.42), and ease of learning 6.50 (SD=0.82). Results show that users experienced reasonably high satisfaction when performing the tasks with the interface.

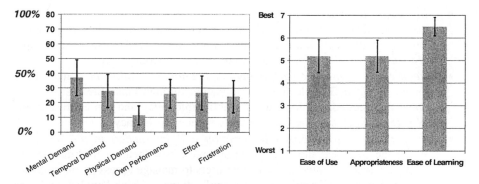

Fig. 4. Subjective workload ratings   **Fig. 5.** User satisfaction ratings

7 Discussion and Future Work

The results of our evaluation show that the interaction design of our interface is effective for performing application relocation and input redirection tasks. After just a few minutes of instruction on how to use the interface, users were able to perform relocation and redirection tasks quickly and with minimal error, reported low subjective workload, and experienced high satisfaction. Also, users found the spatial mapping in the iconic representation useful for performing the tasks:

> "Moving of the application is done very easily, the mapping of the room was very accurate and easy to think about when using."

> "[It's] like the physical environment I am sitting in. So [it's] easier to correlate to the real environment and start where I left off."

"[The interface] clearly depicts the whole space on one screen in a manner that is very accessible"

We attribute the low number of errors to the spatial mapping and direct manipulation interaction, but also to the use of the live outlines. We observed that users often looked up into the workspace to see the effects of the ongoing interaction. Observations also showed that users were able to detect and correct errors while in the midst of performing the task. Of the errors that did occur, they were mostly due to the use of the right-click interaction for redirecting input. Users often left-clicked to redirect input and were confused about why no action was invoked. Several users commented that a different interaction technique would be preferred.

Our toolset supports workspaces driven by an existing distributed infrastructure as well as a single PC equipped with multiple graphics cards, supports both application relocation and input redirection tasks in the same visual metaphor, and provides a graphical tool for rapidly constructing iconic interfaces for various workspaces. Our toolset can be downloaded (http://orchid.cs.uiuc.edu) and used for both research and practice in interactive workspaces. Also, the results from our study provide an initial baseline against which alternative interfaces can be compared.

For future work, we plan to:

- *Investigate alternatives to the use of a right click for redirecting input.* A few users left clicked several times before recalling that a right-click was needed. We are exploring alternative interactions such as the use of an 'input redirection' icon that users can drag to the destination screen.
- *Reduce the latency in performing application relocation in a workspace driven by Gaia.* To relocate an application through Gaia, the system takes about two seconds, which causes a noticeable delay and can confuse users. We are working with the Gaia group to reduce this latency.
- *Support more group-based information and interaction in the interface.* While the interface shows application and cursor location information, we want to extend the interface to enable users to manage access permissions for shared displays, to identify specific applications as being "public" and then only show those applications in the interface, and to view which interactions other users are interacting with to better convey activity awareness.

8   Conclusion

To work productively in an interactive workspace, users need effective interfaces to seamlessly share, annotate, and juxtapose information across independent devices. Our research has made several contributions in this direction. We developed an interface that uses an iconic representation of a workspace for performing relocation and redirection tasks, a graphical tool for rapidly constructing iconic representations for different workspaces, and a toolset that provides runtime support for an existing infrastructure and that can be easily ported to others. A usability evaluation showed that the interaction design of the interface is effective for performing relocation and redirection tasks. The interface enabled users to perform tasks quickly and with minimal error as well as to experience low workload and high satisfaction. Results of the evaluation provide the first empirical baseline against which alternative interfaces can be compared. Our toolset can be downloaded today, enabling others to construct and use iconic interfaces for research or practice in their own interactive workspaces.

Acknowledgements

We thank Steve Saville, Chris Drexelius, Carolyn Van Slyck, and Brian Willard for building the graphical construction tool. We also thank Piotr Adamczyk, Shamsi Iqbal, and Damon Cook for offering insightful comments on early drafts of this paper.

References

1. Biehl, J.T. and Bailey, B.P., ARIS: An Interface for Application Relocation in an Interactive Space. *Graphics Interface*, 2004, 107-116.
2. Booth, K.S., Fisher, B.D., Lin, C.J.R. and Argue, R., The "Mighty Mouse" Multi-Screen Collaboration Tool. *UIST*, 2002, 209-212.
3. Brumitt, B., Meyers, B., Krumm, J., Kern, A. and Shafer, S.A., EasyLiving: Technologies for Intelligent Environments. *Handheld and Ubiquitous Computing*, 2000, 12-29.
4. Cao, X. and Balakrishnan, R., VisionWand: Interaction Techniques for Large Displays Using a Passive Wand Tracked in 3D. *UIST*, 2003, 173 - 182.
5. Hart, S.G. and Stateland, L.E. Development of NASA-TLX (Task Load Index): Results of emperical and theoretical research. in Hancock, P.A. and Meshkati, N. eds. *Human Mental Workload*, North-Holland, Amsterdam, 1988, 139-183.
6. Johanson, B. and Fox, A., The Event Heap: A Coordination Infrastructure for Interactive Workspaces. *4th IEEE Workshop on Mobile Computing Systems and Applications (WMCSA)*, 2002.
7. Johanson, B., Fox, A. and Winograd, T. Experience with Ubiquitous Computing Rooms *IEEE Pervasive Computing Magazine*, 1(4): 67-74, 2002.
8. Johanson, B., Hutchins, G., Winograd, T. and Stone, M., PointRight: Experience with Flexible Input Redirection in Interactive Workspaces. *UIST*, 2002, 227-234.
9. Johanson, B., Ponnekanti, S., Sengupta, C. and Fox, A., Multibrowsing: Moving Web Content Across Multiple Displays. *CHI*, 2001, 346-353.
10. Johnson, J., T. L. Roberts, W. Verplank, D. C. Smith, C. H. Irby, M. Beard, and K. Mackey The Xerox Star: a retrospective. *IEEE Computer*, 22 (9). 11-26.
11. Ponnekanti, S.R., Lee, B., Fox, A., Hanrahan, P. and Winograd, T., iCrafter: A Service Framework for Ubiquitous Computing Environments. *UbiComp*, 2001.
12. Rekimoto, J., Pick-and-Drop: A Direct Manipulation Technique for Multiple Computer Environments. *UIST*, 1997, 31-39.
13. Rekimoto, J. and Saitoh, M., Augmented Surfaces: A Spatially Continuous Work Space for Hybrid Computing Environments. *CHI*, 1999, 378-385.
14. Román, M. and Campbell, R., Providing Middleware Support for Active Space Applications. *ACM/IFIP/USENIX International Middleware Conference 2003*.
15. Román, M., Hess, C., Cerqueira, R., Ranganat, A., Campbell, R. and Nahrstedt, K. Gaia: A Middleware Infrastructure to Enable Active Spaces. *IEEE Pervasive Computing Magazine,* 1(4): 74-83, 2002.
16. Román, M., Ho, H. and Campbell, R., Application Mobility in Active Spaces. *International Conference on Mobile and Ubiquitous Multimedia*, 2002.

17. Shen, C., Everitt, K.M. and Ryall, K., UbiTable: Impromptu Face-to-Face Collaboration on Horizontal Interactive Surfaces. *UbiComp,* 2003.
18. Sousa, J.P. and Garlan, D., Aura: an Architectural Framework for User Mobility in Ubiquitous Computing Environments. *IEEE Conference on Software Architecture,* 2002.
19. Streitz, N.A., et. al., i-LAND: AN Interactive Landscape for Creativity and Innovation. *CHI,* 1999, 120-127.
20. Wilson, A. and Shafer, S.A., XWand: UI for Intelligent Spaces. *CHI,* 2003, 545-552.

Designing Usable Interfaces with Cultural Dimensions

Gabrielle Ford[1] and Paula Kotzé[2]

[1] School of Information Systems and Technology, University of Kwa-Zulu Natal,
King George V Avenue, Durban, South Africa
fordg1@ukzn.ac.za
http://www.ukzn.ac.za
[2] School of Computing, University of South Africa, P O Box 392, Unisa, 0003, South Africa
kotzep@unisa.ac.za
http://www.cs.unisa.ac.za

Abstract. There are as many arguments against as supporting the accommodation of culture into user interface design. One argument suggests that it is necessary to match the subjective cultural profile of the interface to the cultural profile of the users in order to enhance usability and performance. In contrast, we argue that the interface design characteristics required to design interfaces to accommodate one side of four of the five cultural dimensions proposed by Hofstede will result in an increase in usability for all users, irrespective of the users' cultural profile. Secondary data analysis of a prior experiment somewhat supported our argument, but we conclude that further research into the effects of Hofstede's cultural dimensions is required before our hypotheses can be accepted.

1 Introduction

The influence of culture on usability is a controversial issue in the field of human-computer interaction. Those that are in support of accommodating culture into the design of user interfaces do not seem to agree on whether to incorporate objective culture, subjective culture or both into user interface design. Furthermore, the use of cultural dimension models as a way of managing the subjective aspects of user interface design has been severely criticized.

In contrast to the arguments against the use of cultural dimension models, and in particular, Hofstede's [1] model, we argue that the interface design characteristics required to design interfaces to accommodate high power distance, high uncertainty avoidance, masculinity and short-term orientation, would provide a generally more usable interface than one that is designed to accommodate the opposing sides of these dimensions.

This paper presents initial evidence in support of our argument that interfaces that display characteristics relevant to specific sides of four of Hofstede's cultural dimensions increase usability for all users. Section 2 briefly reviews the concept of culture and approaches to culturalisation, while Section 3 focuses on culture in the context of usability and interface design. Section 4 presents details on our research and an experiment conducted. Section 5 concludes and mentions future research.

M.F. Costabile and F. Paternò (Eds.): INTERACT 2005, LNCS 3585, pp. 713–726, 2005.
© IFIP International Federation for Information Processing 2005

2 Culture

To better understand the concept of culture, and how it is related to human-computer interaction, we review below the definitions, metamodels and models that have been proposed in the literature.

2.1 Definitions

There are many definitions of culture in the literature, but there is no agreement on a specific definition of culture [2, 3]. Some examples of such definitions include:

- Culture is conceptualized as a 'system of meaning that underlies routine and behaviour in everyday working life' [4, p 122].
- Culture 'includes race and ethnicity as well as other variables and is manifested in customary behaviours, assumptions and values, patterns of thinking and communication style' [5, p 49].
- 'Culture is communication, and communication is culture' [6, p 186].
- Culture is 'the collective programming of the mind that distinguishes the members of one group or category of people from another, where the mind stands for thinking, feeling and acting, with consequences for beliefs, attitudes and skills' [1, p 5].

Most of the above definitions refer to culture as influencing the way in which communication takes place. Using the computer to perform tasks requires communication between the user and the system, particularly when using an interactive system. Consequently, for the purposes of this paper, we define culture as the patterns of thinking, feeling and acting that influence the way in which people communicate amongst themselves and with computers.

2.2 Metamodels of Culture

Metamodels of culture provide a high-level view of the overriding philosophies surrounding the concept of culture, by defining different layers of culture [2]. Four metamodels have been proposed in the literature, including the Onion Model, the Pyramid Model, the Iceberg Model and the Objective and Subjective Culture Model [2]. For the purposes of this research, we will adopt the latter metamodel.

The Objective Culture and Subjective Culture Model, developed by Stuart and Bennett [2], identifies only two layers of culture, objective culture and subjective culture. Objective culture is the 'institutions and artefacts of a culture, such as its economic system, social customs, political structures and processes, arts, crafts and literature' [2, p 43]. Objective culture is visible, easy to examine and tangible, as it is represented in terms of text orientation, date and number formats, colour and language [7]. In contrast, subjective culture is 'the psychological features of a culture, including assumptions, values, and patterns of thinking' [2, p 43]. Subjective culture is difficult to examine because it operates outside of conscious awareness, for example, in the way in which people accept or reject uncertainty [1], similarities and differences in power and authority [1, 8], and the amount of emotions that people express when dealing with others [9].

Objective culture is abstract, because it is an externalization of subjective culture. Subjective culture is what is real and concrete. However, objective culture tends to be treated as more real and concrete than its source, subjective culture [2].

2.3 Models of Culture

The metamodels of culture form the basis for the development of different models of culture. These models provide a more detailed view of culture, by identifying a number of cultural dimensions that are used to organise cultural data [10]. Hoft [2] describes four models of culture, developed by Victor [8], Hall [6], Trompenaars [9] and Hofstede [1], which are summarised in Table 1.

Table 1. Cultural models and their dimensions

Victor [8]	Hall [6]
• Language	• Speed of Messages
• Environment and Technology	• Context
• Social Organisation	• Space
• Contexting	• Time
• Authority Conception	• Information Flow
• Nonverbal Behaviour	• Action Chains
• Temporal Conception	

Trompenaars [9]	Hofstede [1]
• Universalism vs. Particularism	• Power Distance
• Neutral or emotional	• Masculinity vs. Femininity
• Individualism vs. Collectivism	• Individualism vs. Collectivism
• Specific vs. Diffuse	• Uncertainty Avoidance
• Achievement vs. Ascription	• Time Orientation
• Time	
• Environment	

Hofstede [1] focuses his model on determining the patterns of thinking, feeling and acting that form a culture's mental programming. He conceptualized culture as 'programming of the mind' in the sense that certain reactions were more likely in certain cultures than in others, based on differences between the basic values of the members of different cultures [11].

As reflected in Table 1, Hofstede identified five cultural dimensions that can be used to distinguish among different cultures [12]. All five of Hofstede's dimensions relate to subjective culture, and many of these dimensions also appear in the other three models summarised in Table 1. Each of these dimensions is a dichotomy, in that there are two opposing sides to each dimension. The design characteristics of interfaces that are designed to accommodate each side of these dimensions is presented in Section 3.1.3. The character traits expected of users displaying each side of each dimension is presented below [2, 10, 12, 13]:

- *Power distance* refers to the extent to which less powerful members of a society or group of people expect and accept unequal power distribution within that group. High power distant people are afraid to express disagreement with people in authority such as bosses, parents and teachers. Low power distant people have little difficulty in approaching and contradicting their superiors.
- *Uncertainty avoidance* is the way in which people cope with uncertainty and risk. High uncertainty avoidant users tend to be emotional and aggressive, avoid ambiguous situations, prefer to work in a structured and predictable environment, and consider differences to be threatening and dangerous. It is also believed that high uncertainty avoidant users would prefer to work within a team environment, as this would serve as a support structure in times of uncertainty. In contrast, low uncertainty avoidant users can accept that superiors do not have all the answers, that there may be more than one correct answer, and are curious about differences.
- *Masculinity vs. femininity* refers to gender roles, not physical characteristics, and is primarily characterized by the levels of assertiveness or tenderness in the user. Masculine users tend to be assertive, competitive and tough. Their work goals include high earnings, recognition, advancement and challenge. Feminine users focus on home, children and people. Their work goals include good relations with supervisors, peers and subordinates, good living and working conditions with sense of security.
- *Individualism vs. collectivism* relates to the role of the individual and the group, and is characterized by the level of ties between an individual in a society. Individualist users are expected to look after themselves and their immediate family, but no one else. They value personal time, freedom and challenge, material rewards, honesty and truth, talking things out, maintaining self-respect, and the right to privacy and personal opinion. In contrast, collectivist users are integrated into strong, cohesive groups that protect them in exchange for unquestioning loyalty. Collectivists value training and skills, and group achievement rather than personal recognition. Harmony is valued more than truth and honesty. They are comfortable with an invasion of privacy and restrictions on personal opinions.
- *Time orientation* relates to people's concern with the past, present and future. In essence, short-term oriented people are concerned with the past and the present, while long-term oriented people are concerned more with the future. Long-term oriented users believe that a stable society requires unequal relations, and that older people and men have more authority than younger people and women. They value trying to acquire skills and education, working hard and being frugal. They are prepared to persevere and display a lot of patience in understanding new things. In contrast, short-term oriented users believe in an equality of relationships, and emphasize individualism. They value reciprocity of favours, gifts and greetings, and the ability to achieve quick results.

3   Effects of Cultural Dimensions on Usability and Interface Design

As culture influences the way in which people interact in general, culture will also influence the way in which people will interact with computers. Using interactive systems to perform tasks requires communication between the system and the user. People learn patterns of thinking, acting and communicating from living in a specific social environment, normally typified by national culture [14]. As such, culture partially predetermines a person's communication preferences and behaviours. Communication style, which reflects how a person sends and interprets messages, represents the overall patterns and values of a culture. As the user interface is the means by which the user and the computer interact [15], it stands to reason that the interface should facilitate users to use their particular communication styles [14]. Consequently, global interfaces need to accommodate a diversity of communication styles to provide support for the cultural diversity of the users.

Diversity in culture is particularly relevant where global interfaces take the form of websites [7, 16, 17, 18, 19, 20, 21]. The advent of the World Wide Web (WWW) has resulted in a fundamental technical context of use that now needs to be taken into consideration, namely the difference between traditional software applications and web applications.

From a cross-cultural usability perspective, the primary difference between traditional software and web-based interfaces is that websites are constantly addressing different cultural audiences simultaneously [18]. Within the global information technology environment, cross-cultural usability of websites is about making websites an effective means of communication between a global web site owner and a local user [11]. Because users differ across regional, linguistic and country boundaries, their expectations of websites are driven primarily by their local cultural perspectives. Consequently, user reactions become more predictable and understandable when the user's cultural perspective is taken into account [14, 17]. Websites need to display 'culturability', that is, designing the interface to accommodate the cultural preferences and biases to increase the usability of the interface and the product [17].

3.1 Approaches to Culturalisation

Culturalisation, or preparing a product for use by diverse cultures, requires two steps: internationalization and localization. Internationalisation involves identifying the culturally specific elements of the product, and localization involves substituting those culturally specific elements with a local content [22].

Traditionally, the approaches to culturalisation seemed to focus primarily on objective cultural issues rather than subjective culture.

The Objective Culture Approach. The objective cultural approach concludes that, when dealing with human-computer interaction, meaning is the central issue in culture [23]. Supporters of this approach suggest that designers need only cater for cultural diversity by ensuring that the intended meaning of user interface representations, such as symbols, icons and language, are translated to suit the target cultures, so that they are understood correctly. Thus, this approach is based on the premise that it is the objective, rather than the subjective, cultural aspects that are important. The culturalisation process has concentrated primarily on the translation of the objective cultural aspects [24], such as language and date and time formats [22, 23], to avoid potentially harmful misunderstandings.

The Subjective Culture Approach. It has been argued that whilst objective culture is important, it is also necessary for the interfaces to reflect the values, ethics and morals of the target users [22], in order to make the users more comfortable and accepting of the interfaces [25]. These aspects relate to subjective culture [24], and go beyond the 'surface manifestations of culture that have been widely accepted' [11, p 89]. Del Galdo and Nielsen [7] clearly support this by pointing out that there are three levels of internationalization, namely:

1. Displaying the native language, character set and notations.
2. Translating the user interface and documentation so that it is understandable and usable.
3. Matching the user's cultural characteristics, which goes beyond avoiding offensive icons and must accommodate the way business is conducted and the way people communicate.

Essentially, this approach is based on the premise that culture is about how individuals behave and respond, their beliefs and values, and therefore it is also necessary to reflect subjective culture in the design of interfaces [24]. Consequently, this approach suggests that the interface should be designed to match the users' cultural profile [20].

Accommodating Subjective Culture into the Design of Interfaces. Marcus [26] developed a set of guidelines for accommodating Hofstede's cultural dimensions into the design of user interfaces. These are described below.

- *Power distance*: Interfaces that display high power distance characteristics should provide highly structured access to information, prominence should be given to leaders, security measures should be both explicit and enforced, and there should be a strong focus on authority. The opposite holds true for low power distant sites.
- *Uncertainty avoidance*: Interfaces that display high uncertainty avoidance characteristics should focus on the prevention of user error by providing minimal menu options, simple and descriptive help facilities, and a navigation structure that is focused on preventing users from getting lost. Colours, sounds and images should be used to reinforce the messages. In contrast, low uncertainty avoidant interfaces should encourage user exploration; provide many menu options, and use colours, sounds and images to provide additional information.
- *Masculinity vs. femininity*: Interfaces that are oriented towards the masculine side of this dimension should be focused on allowing for quick results for limited tasks. The navigation structure should support user exploration and control. The content should be suggestive of a challenge for the user to master something, and cater for explicit distinctions between genders and age groups. Graphics and animations should be used for utilitarian purposes. In contrast, feminine oriented interfaces should use aesthetic appeal and poetry as a way of gaining users' attention. There is a blurring of gender roles. In particular, feminine oriented interfaces should support mutual cooperation and the exchange of ideas and support.
- *Individualism vs. collectivism*: Individualist interfaces should use images of materialism and consumerism to denote success, and youth, action and individuals to gain the users' attention. The content should be focused on personal achievement,

new and unique products and concepts, and contain or encourage controversy and personal opinions. Users should not be required to provide personal information. In contrast, collectivist sites should use images of the achievement of socio-political agendas to denote success, and experienced, aged leaders and groups of people to gain the user's attention. The content should be focused on group achievement, history and tradition, and contain official slogans while discouraging personal opinions.

- *Time orientation*: Short-term oriented user interfaces should be structured in a way that allows users to complete tasks quickly. Rules should be used to verify the credibility of information, and information content should be based on truth and certainty of beliefs. In contrast, long-term oriented interface navigation style and content can be more complex, as users will persevere until they gain an understanding. Long-term oriented websites should contain content that is of practical value, and can use relationships to verify the credibility of the information.

However, the use of Hofstede's cultural dimensions model of managing the subjective aspects of cross-cultural interface design has been severely criticized as being too stereotypical [23] or rigid [16]. In addition, previous attempts to apply Hofstede's model to usability has resulted in conflicting and therefore inconclusive findings. For example, Gould et al. [27] found that Malaysian websites contain links on the home page to website administration, which correlates well with the high power distance reported [1] for Malaysia. However, this does not explain why low power distance countries such as the US also contain such links on their websites. In contrast, Forer and Ford [28] reported that accommodating for the user's cultural profile enhanced performance. Consequently, until better proof of their relevance to website design is provided, Fitzgerald [29] suggests that cultural dimension models should be used with care.

4 Research on the Influence of Cultural Dimensions on Usability

In contrast to the arguments put forward against the use of cultural models in general and against the use of Hofstede's cultural model [1] in particular, we believe that the inherent characteristics of a specific side of four of the five cultural dimensions proposed by Hofstede provide a generally more usable interface than the opposing side of the same dimension. For example:

- High uncertainty avoidant sites are designed to reduce uncertainty. According to Marcus [26], the design should provide clear and familiar metaphors, simple, clear articulation and limited menu options, simple and limited navigation controls, precise and detailed feedback of status, simple and clear imagery and highly redundant coding. All these characteristics would naturally cater for more accurate and speedier completion of tasks. This could also increase satisfaction levels as users would feel that the task had been accomplished quickly and correctly.
- Masculine site design incorporates similar characteristics to those of high uncertainty avoidant sites. For example, masculine sites should be designed to provide limited navigation choices, and high-level executive views, and are goal

and work-oriented [26], thus providing for quick results of limited tasks. These characteristics would also naturally increase the speed and accuracy levels obtained, thereby possibly also increasing satisfaction levels.

- High power distant sites should also provide limited navigation choices, and wizards or guides to assist with navigation [26], thereby increasing the speed, accuracy and satisfaction levels obtained.
- Short-term time orientation design incorporates similar characteristics to those of masculine and high uncertainty avoidance site design. For example, short-term sites should be designed to provide bread-crumb trails and quick-results; and focus on the task at hand or the product of interest.

The proposed influence of Hofstede's cultural dimensions on usability has important implications. The subjective cultural approach to culturalisation, as proposed by Smith and Chang [20], and shared by others (for example [21]), is based on the belief that the cultural profile of the interface should be matched to the cultural profile of the users in order to enhance usability and performance. However, if a particular cultural profile is found to increase the usability of interfaces for all users, this would invalidate this belief. Conversely, this would still provide evidence that Hofstede's cultural dimensions are related to usability, just not in the way that was originally hypothesized.

From the above, our research objectives and hypotheses can be drawn and tested.

4.1 Research Objectives and Hypothesis

The aim of this research is to determine whether or not one side of each cultural dimension's dichotomy increases the general usability of user interfaces. In order to achieve this aim, the following hypotheses were tested:

H1   User interfaces designed for high power distance will be more generally usable than interfaces designed for low power distance.

H2   User interfaces designed for high uncertainty avoidance will be more generally usable than interfaces designed for low uncertainty avoidance.

H3   User interfaces designed for masculinity will be more generally usable than interfaces designed for femininity.

H4   User interfaces designed for short-term orientation will be more generally usable than interfaces designed for long-term orientation.

H5   User interfaces designed for collectivism will be as usable as interfaces designed for individualism.

4.2 Research Design and Methodology

Secondary data analysis was used to reanalyse data generated from a previous experiment that we conducted[1]. The aim of the experiment was to establish empirical evidence of a causal relationship between subjective culture and usability. As usability is tested in terms of the resultant performance achieved from using a computer to complete tasks [31], the aim of the experiment was expected to be

---

[1] The experiment is reported on in detail in a separate article [30].

achieved by testing the effects of Hofstede's cultural dimensions on the performance of users using computer-based interfaces.

The experiment was conducted in the form of a formal usability test, supported by the use of questionnaires. Test subjects were sourced from a multi-cultural group of students enrolled for a third-level course in Information Systems and Technology at the University of Kwa-Zulu Natal (South Africa). Using an adapted version of Hofstede's [1] Value Survey Model, the cultural profile of each test subject was assessed. Ten test interfaces were identified using Marcus's [26] design guidelines, one for each side of each cultural dimension. Data on performance measures were collected quantitatively, using a test task instrument that comprised of test tasks and a satisfaction questionnaire. For each test task, the accuracy, speed and satisfaction of users using an interface that corresponded to their side of the cultural dimension were collected and compared to the same performance measures when using an interface with an opposing side of the cultural dimension.

Four statistical tests were used to analyse the data:

1. Related samples t-tests were used to measure whether or not there were significant differences in accuracy, speed and satisfaction levels between users using an interface that displayed design characteristics that corresponded to the subjects' cultural dimension side, compared to the same users using an interface that displayed design characteristics of an opposing cultural dimension side.

2. Independent samples t-tests on the users were used to determine whether one set of users was generally a 'better' set of users than the other. This was done by determining the average score of users of one side of the dimension using both sites, and comparing it to the average score of users of the other side of the dimension. If a significant difference was found, then it was concluded that there were variables in the test subject groups, other than culture, that were causing increased usability.

3. Independent samples t-tests on the interfaces were used to determine whether one of the sites was generally a 'better' site than the other. This was done by determining the average score achieved by all users using the first site and comparing it to the average score achieved by all users on the second site. If a significant difference was found, then it was concluded that one of the sites was better than the other, and therefore the increase in usability could be attributed to variables on the sites other than that cultural dimension.

4. Paired samples t-tests on overall usability were used to confirm the findings of the independent samples t-tests done on the users and the sites, an additional paired samples t-test was performed on the data. The data was arranged to compare the differences in scores between (1) all users using an interface with the same dimension, and (2) all users using an interface with the opposing dimension. Where the sample size of users with one side of the dimension was greater than the sample size of users with the opposing dimension, a random sample of the higher number was taken, equivalent to the smaller number in the opposing side. Because the same number of users was using the potentially superior site and the potentially inferior site, the usability difference between the sites should be nullified. Therefore, if a significant difference was not found, then the test was seen to support the findings of the independent sample t-tests described above.

4.3 Experimental Results

The performance of more than 50 test subjects for four of the five cultural dimensions were measured and compared. Due to the very small sample size of short-term oriented subjects found, it was not possible to analyse the results for the time orientation dimension. The results of the four statistical tests performed on the data obtained on the measures for each cultural dimension are presented next:

1. *Impact of power distance on performance*: The paired samples t-test showed no significant differences in the accuracy or satisfaction levels achieved. Significant differences in speed occurred within the low power distant user group, but not within the high power distant user group. It was noted that the difference within the low power distant user group was positive, indicating that low power distant users using the low power distant site took longer to complete the tasks than when using the high power distant site. The independent samples t-test (site) indicated that irrespective of the user's side of the cultural dimension, it took longer to complete the tasks overall using the low power distant site than when using the high power distant site. This was confirmed by the lack of significant results found in the paired samples t-test used to control for usability. No significant difference was found between the two user groups.

2. *Impact of uncertainty avoidance on performance:* The only insignificant difference found at the 95% level in the paired samples t-test was in the accuracy scores between low uncertainty avoidant users using a low uncertainty avoidant site compared to the same users using a high uncertainty avoidant site. However, this difference fell just short of being significant in terms of the t-crit value, and could be accepted at the 94% level. It was noted that the differences found for the high uncertainty avoidant user group were exactly opposite to the differences found for the low uncertainty avoidant user group. This strongly suggested that the high uncertainty avoidant site was substantially superior to the low uncertainty avoidant site in terms of accuracy, speed and satisfaction levels. The independent samples t-tests (site) confirmed that, irrespective of the user's side of the cultural dimension, that (1) higher levels of accuracy were achieved, (2) less time was taken to complete the tasks, and (3) greater satisfaction levels were reported, when using the high uncertainty avoidant site than when using the low uncertainty avoidant site. This was confirmed by the lack of significant results found in the paired samples t-test used to control for usability. No significant difference was found between the two user groups.

3. *Impact of masculinity vs. femininity on performance:* The only insignificant difference found at the 95% level in the paired samples t-test was in the accuracy scores between masculine users using a masculine site compared to the same users using a feminine site. It was noted that the significant results found for the masculine user group were exactly opposite to the differences found for the feminine user group. This strongly suggested that the masculine site was substantially superior to the feminine site in terms of accuracy, speed and satisfaction levels. The independent samples t-test (site) confirmed that, irrespective of the user's side of the cultural dimension, that (1) higher levels of accuracy were achieved, (2) less time was taken to complete the tasks, and (3) greater satisfaction levels were reported, when using the masculine site than when

using the feminine site. This was confirmed by the lack of significant results found in the paired samples t-test used to control for usability. No significant difference was found between the two user groups.

4. *Impact of individualism vs. collectivism on performance*: The paired samples t-test showed no significant differences in the accuracy or speed levels achieved. Significant differences in user satisfaction occurred within the individualist user group, but not within the collectivist user group. It was noted that the difference within the individualist user group was negative, indicating that individualist users using the collectivist site reported higher satisfaction levels than when using the individualist site. The independent samples t-test (site) indicated that irrespective of the user's side of the cultural dimension, greater satisfaction levels were achieved overall when using the collectivist site than when using the individualist site. This was confirmed by the lack of significant results found in the paired samples t-test used to control for usability. No significant difference was found between the two user groups.

4.4 Analysis and Interpretation

For every significant result obtained from the paired samples t-tests, a significant result was obtained from the independent samples t-tests for site usability differences. This indicates that the increase in performance could be attributable to the cultural dimension of the site, rather than as a result of a user using an interface with a corresponding side of a cultural dimension. In particular, the interfaces that were evaluated to be high power distant, high uncertainty avoidant, masculine or collectivist were found to be the better sites. These results support hypotheses H1, H2 and H3. In contrast to H5 (that neither collectivism nor individualism would increase the usability of the interface), the results show that collectivist sites are more generally usable that individualist sites.

These results are somewhat supported by one other study identified in the literature. Smith and Chang [20] reported that Chinese users preferred interfaces that displayed high power distant, high uncertainty avoidant, masculine and individualist characteristics. Other than the individualism/collectivism dimension, the preferred dimensions correlate to the findings of the experiment. In addition, Smith and Chang expressed surprise at the Chinese users' preference for sites that displayed individualism, in contrast to traditional perceptions of the Chinese as being a collectivist society.

Consequently, at a superficial level, the results of the experiment could allow us to accept hypotheses H1 – H3, and reject hypothesis H5. H4 could not be tested due to the limited number of test subjects that were identified as short-term oriented.

However, it must be noted that the increase in general usability of the masculine, high power distant, collectivist and high uncertainty interfaces could also have been due to variables on the interfaces other than the cultural profile of the interfaces. For example, the user interfaces could have been more generally usable if the design of the interfaces incorporated relevant usability principles, heuristics and guidelines. Furthermore, subjective cultural dimensions other than those tested could have influenced the results of the experiment.

Consequently, to avoid a Type I error, the hypotheses cannot be accepted until further research is conducted.

5 Conclusions and Further Research

Some of the arguments in the literature propose that objective, rather than subjective culture, should be accommodated into the design of user interfaces. Others argue that subjective culture is just as important as objective culture, and that the subjective cultural profile of the interface should match the subjective cultural profile of the intended users. In addition, the use of cultural dimension models as a way of managing the subjective aspects of user interface design, such as the one proposed by Hofstede [1], has been severely criticized as being stereotypical and rigid.

In contrast to the above arguments, we proposed that the interface design characteristics required to design interfaces that accommodate high power distance, high uncertainty avoidance, masculinity and short-term orientation would provide a more usable interface to all users than one that is designed to accommodate the opposing sides of these dimensions. The assumed increase in general usability was translated into the hypotheses on which this research project was based.

Secondary data analysis of an experiment previously conducted to determine the effects of Hofstede's cultural dimensions on usability has indicated that user interfaces designed to accommodate high power distance, masculinity, high uncertainty avoidance and collectivism provide better performance, irrespective of the cultural profile of the users. These results are somewhat supported by one other study [20] identified in the literature.

Although two independent studies have brought to light similar results that support our hypotheses, we noted that the differences in performance measures could have been attributable to variables other than the cultural dimensions tested that were not controlled for. This leads us to conclude that the influence of Hofstede's cultural dimensions on general usability should be considered as a topic for further research. Preliminary work on these issues is reported in [32].

References

1. Hofstede, G.: Culture's consequences (2nd ed.). Sage Publications (2001).
2. Hoft, N.: Developing a Cultural Model. In: Del Galdo, E., Nielson, J. (eds.): International User Interfaces. John Wiley and Sons, New York (1996).
3. Ciborowski, T.J.: Cross-Cultural aspects of Cognitive Functioning: Culture and Knowledge. In: Marsella, A.J., Tharp, R.G., Ciborowski, T.J. (eds): Perspectives on Cross-Cultural Psychology. Academic Press Inc., New York (1979).
4. Bodker, K., Pederson, J.: Workplace cultures: Looking at artifacts, symbols, and practices. In: Greenbaum, J., Kyng. M. (eds): Design at work: Cooperative Design of Computer Systems. Lawrence Erlbaum, Hillsdale, NJ (1991).
5. Borgman, C.L.: The User's Mental Model of an Information Retrieval System: an Experiment on a Prototype Online Catalog. International Journal of Man-Machine Studies, 24 (1986) 47-64.
6. Hall, E.: The Silent Language. Doubleday (1959).
7. Del Galdo, E., Nielson, J.: International User Interfaces. John Wiley and Sons (1996).
8. Victor, D.: International Business Communications. Harper Collins (1992).

9. Trompenaars, F.: Riding the Waves of Culture. Nicholas Brealey Publishing, London (1993).
10. Evers, V.: Cultural Aspects of User Interface Understanding: An Empirical Evaluation of an E-Learning Website by International User Groups. University of Amsterdam (2001).
11. Smith A., Dunckley, L., French, T., Minocha, S., Chang, Y.: A Process Model for Developing Usable Cross-Cultural Websites. Interacting with Computers, 16 (2004) 63–91.
12. ITIM. Geert Hofstede Cultural Dimensions. http://www.geert-hofstede.com/-geert_hofstede_resources.shtml (retrieved January 12, 2005), (2003).
13. Marcus, A., Gould, E.W.: Crosscurrents: cultural dimensions and global web user-interface design. Interactions, 7(4) (2000) 32–46.
14. Massey, A.P., Hung, Y.C., Montoya-Weiss, M., Ramesh, V.: When culture and style aren't about clothes: perceptions of task-technology 'fit' in global virtual teams. In: Proceedings of the 2001 International ACM SIGGROUP Conference on Supporting Group Work. ACM Press, New York (2001) 207 – 213.
15. Dix A., Finlay, J., Abowd, G., Beale, R.: Human-Computer Interaction. Prentice Hall International (UK), Hemel Hampstead (1998).
16. Jagne, J., Smith, S.G., Duncker, E., Curzon, P.: Cross-cultural Interface Design Strategy. Technical Report: IDC-TR-2004-006, Interaction Design Centre, Middlesex University (2004).
17. Barber, W., Badre, A.: Culturability, the merging of culture and usability. In: Proceedings of the 4th conference on Human Factors and the Web. Basking Ridge, NJ, USA (1998).
18. Chau, P.Y.K., Cole, M., Massey, A.P., Montoya-Weiss, M., O'Keefe, R.M.: Cultural differences in the online behavior of consumers. Communications of the ACM, 45(10) (2002) 138–143.
19. Marcus, A.: Cross-cultural user-interface design for work, home, and on the way. Tutorial 5, 10th Annual UPA Conference 25 – 29 June, Lake Las Vegas (2001).
20. Smith, A., Chang, Y.: Quantifying Hofstede and developing cultural fingerprints for website acceptability. In: Evers, V., Röse, K., Honold, P., Coronado, J., Day, D.L. (eds.): Proceedings of the IWIPS 2003 Conference. University of Kaiserslautern, Berlin, Germany (2003).
21. Hall, P., Lawson, C., Minocha, S.: Design patterns as a guide to the cultural localisation of software. In: In: Evers, V., Röse, K., Honold, P., Coronado, J., Day, D.L. (eds.): Proceedings of the IWIPS 2003 Conference. University of Kaiserslautern, Berlin, Germany (2003).
22. Russo, P., Boor, S.: How Fluent is your interface? Designing for international users. In: Proceedings of the INTERCHI '93 Conference on Human Factors in Computing Systems: INTERACT '93 and CHI'93. ACM Press, New York (1993) 342–347.
23. Bourges Waldegg, P., Scrivener, S.A.R.: Meaning, the central issue in cross cultural HCI design. Interacting with Computers, 9(3) (1998) 287–309.
24. Dunckley, L., Smith, A.: Cultural dichotomies in user evaluation of international software. In: Day, D., Del Galdo, E., Prahbu, G. (eds.): Proceedings of IWIPS'00, Designing for Global Markets 2. Backhouse Press Baltimore, MD (2000).
25. Carey, J.M.: Creating global software: A conspectus and review. Interacting with Computers, 9 (1998) 449–465.
26. Marcus, A.: Mapping user-interface design to cultural dimensions. Unpublished paper based on a paper prepared for a CHI 2002 Workshop and a paper prepared for Advanced Visual Interfaces, 2002.

27. Gould, E.W., Zakaria, N., Yusof, S.A.M.: Applying culture to website design: a comparison of Malaysian and US websites. In: Proceedings of the IEEE Professional Communication Society's International Professional Communication Conference and Proceedings of the 18th Annual ACM International Conference on Computer Documentation: Technology and Teamwork. IEEE Educational Activities Department, Piscataway, NJ, USA (2000) 161–171.
28. Forer, D., Ford, G.: User performance and user interface design: Usability heuristics versus cultural dimensions. In: Mende J., Sanders, I. (eds.): Proceedings of the South African Computer Lecturer's Association 2003 Conference. Johannesburg, South Africa (2003).
29. Fitzgerald, W.: Models for Cross-Cultural Communications for Cross-Cultural Website Design. Institute for Information Technology, National Research Council Canada, (2004).
30. Ford, G., Gelderblom, J.H.: The effects of culture on performance achieved through the use of human computer interaction. In: Eloff, J., Kotzé P., Engelbrecht A., Eloff M. (eds): IT Research in Developing Countries - Proceedings of the SAICSIT 2003 Conference ACM International Conference Proceedings Series, SAICSIT, Pretoria (2003) 218–230.
31. Nielsen, J.: Usability Engineering. Academic Press (1993).
32. Ford G.: Researching the Effects of Culture on Usability. MSc Dissertation, University of South Africa (2005).

Use of Future-Oriented Information in User-Centered Product Concept Ideation

Antti Salovaara[1] and Petri Mannonen[2]

[1] Helsinki Institute for Information Technology, P.O.Box 9800, 02015 TKK, Finland
antti.salovaara@hiit.fi
[2] Usability Group, Software Business and Engineering Laboratory,
Helsinki University of Technology, P.O.Box 9210, 02015 TKK, Finland
petri.mannonen@soberit.hut.fi

Abstract. User-centered product concept design aims at creating concepts of new products. Its success is dependent on the design team's ability to use present-day information to come up with concepts concerning future products. This paper takes as its task to investigate and explore what underlies this use of future-oriented information and what challenges it poses at the creative stages of a design process. The proposed solution is based on an analytic division of available information into (1) trends such as company strategies, trends in the society and working life that denote changing conditions, and (2) stable context features that describe issues that are unlikely to change in the timeframe concerned. A small case study is presented that exemplifies how this analytic distinction can be put into use. More broadly, the paper encourages designers to think reflectively about the nature of information on which design decisions are based.

1 Introduction

In an innovation management oriented study measuring the number of raw ideas that are needed to make a new commercially successful product, Stevens and Burley found that as many as 3000 unwritten ideas may be needed to end up with a single successful product [23]. Naturally, in such a process much work effort can be wasted. At present, solutions to the problem are often based on lightweight ideation and screening techniques to create ideas easily, and filter out the probable failures as early as possible during the design process.

From a designer point of view, a better alternative would be to improve the percentage of successful ideas. This calls for techniques to guide ideation in more fruitful directions. To address this issue, this paper investigates how future-oriented information, such as company strategies and trends in users' working life and society can be used more effectively in user-centered product concept design (UCPCD).

This paper first presents an outline of UCPCD and analyzes some of the challenges that lie behind the low hit ratio in the current practice. Based on the analysis, the paper provides suggestions for enhanced deployment of future-oriented information to overcome the problems. A report from a case study follows where the usefulness of the hypotheses was explored in a project that developed product concepts for future

M.F. Costabile and F. Paternò (Eds.): INTERACT 2005, LNCS 3585, pp. 727–740, 2005.
© IFIP International Federation for Information Processing 2005

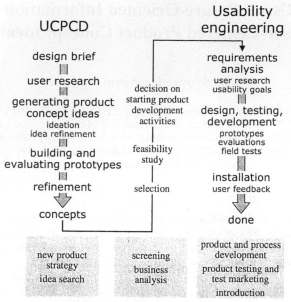

Fig. 1. Relations between user-centered product concept design (UCPCD) and usability engineering, and how they are mapped into a new product development process

maintenance work. This part of the paper is probably most valuable for considerations of contract work, since the focus was on exploratory findings without continuous managerial steering. The paper concludes with evaluation and discussion.

2   User-Centered Product Concept Design

Within the field of user-centered design activities, UCPCD is an early-phase exploratory process that aims at creating ideas concerning future products. It has its origins in empathic design [11] and needfinding [22] , which aim to find product ideas by identifying users' needs that are difficult to articulate directly. It is part of the idea search phase in the new product development process [15], and precedes the decision whether the idea is good enough for the actual product development to commence [10]. If the idea is accepted, usability engineering activities (e.g. [14,17]) are started.

A simplified relation between UCPCD, usability engineering and new product development is shown in Fig. 1. UCPCD has been originally presented as a process with two iteration cycles of prototyping and testing [7]. In the figure, the latter iteration (using high-fidelity prototypes) has been omitted to stress the nature of UCPCD as a lightweight process, and two sub-phases have been added to idea generation, due to the focus of the paper. Idea screening is also moved outside UCPCD and is assigned to managers who "own" the project, as suggested by Khurana and Rosenthal [10]. The usability engineering process is a simplification of Nielsen's [17] and Mayhew's [14] models. The phases of new product development are from Moore and Pessemier [15].

2.1 Design Phases

This section provides a quick overview of the standard phases of the concept design process, described briefly in e.g. [19]. Product concept design starts with drafting a design brief – a short description defining what user group and purpose the product should be designed for, and other company-relevant design issues [7]. The contents of the brief vary depending on whether the team is part of the company, an academic research project, or contract work from a consulting firm. The design brief also defines whether the team should aim at developing a concept of a new discontinuous product, or a new incremental version of an existing product.

The design team conducts a user study, often comprising observations and interviews, supplemented with e.g. role-playing, diaries and cultural probes. Ideally, from the material collected the team can identify contextual phenomena and user needs and is able to generate product concepts that answer these issues. Concepts are concretized as interactive prototypes, storyboards or mockups, and are evaluated with users. The ones considered best are selected for further development in a screening process.

2.2 Challenges in the Process

As a rather new discipline within HCI, UCPCD is still hampered by many factors that are difficult to control. In product concept idea generation, three challenges can be identified, two relating to ideation, and one to idea refinement. Firstly, after having studied users, ideation may be biased with *user data domination*, leading to a partial neglect of company-relevant aspects in the design brief. Secondly, although concepts are developed with the future in mind, what the team observes is present-day activities. This can lead to a *closed-system assumption*: that new forces would not affect user's context in the future, and thus gathered observations would form a reliable basis for design decisions. Studying lead users or other margin segments may alleviate this, but assessing trends in the society and working life should in general play a bigger part in ideation. The problem is addressed in innovation management literature (e.g. [4]) but it is only slowly being distilled into HCI-based concept design.

During idea refinement, *weakly grounded contextualization* may pose the third challenge. Sketchy ideas need more flesh in the form of e.g. use scenarios. If this contextualization has no linkage to the essentials of the present-day activity, the resulting concepts may be disruptive to users. So, contextualization cannot be independent of how tasks are presently accomplished.

Naturally, UCPCD has other challenges in addition to those already listed. In the discussion, two additional challenges relevant to the paper's topic are discussed.

2.3 Addressing Challenges by Reflecting on Future-Oriented Information

The problematization of the standard UCPCD process presented in the previous section is related to how the team reflects upon and uses future-oriented information during the design phases. The connection becomes evident by considering a conceptual division of available information into *stable context features* (meaning issues that are unlikely to change in the timeframe of interest) and *trends* (pointing out the differences between present circumstances and their potential trajectories of change).

The division helps to see which type of information is dominant in the problematic design stages. Stable context features and trends are both future-oriented information, since their division is made based on assumptions about future circumstances.

User data domination during ideation is a result of a narrowly perceived design domain. It could be alleviated by including a wider array of viewpoints to spark creative work. User research observations could be supplemented with company strategies and data on trends in the societal, technological and economic environment. Of the types of future-oriented information, trends seem useful regarding this problem.

Closed-system assumption – another trap during ideation – is also related to the use of trends. Without consideration and explication of what is likely to change in the context, and the team's commitments to such hypotheses, the "creative leap" into the future is not well grounded. Aligning ideas with trends would address the circumstances in the foreseeable future. This can be combined with creative problem-solving methods (such as brainstorming) that are based on an observation that people have difficulties in breaking away from existing solutions and associated restrictions [12]. From the product development point of view, guiding ideation with trends can help focus the innovation towards the foreseeable future without limiting creativity.

The third listed challenge – weakly grounded contextualization – is relevant to the refinement stage where ideas are made more credible and fleshed out. What could be done to avoid disruptive results is to adapt the ideas to present-day features to some necessary extent. The trade-off between the novelty of the concept and conformance to current practice requires balancing. Finding the balance and exploring solutions to other challenges was the target in the case study.

3   Case Study: Making Concepts for Future Maintenance Work

The design team explored how to address the challenges in practice in a project where the task was to ideate proactive computing systems for maintenance work. Proactive computing refers to a vision of technology capable of anticipating users' actions and taking initiative, in this way acting on behalf of the user in a beneficial way. Autonomous cooperation between different computing systems and their close connection to real world phenomena are important parts of the vision [24].

This was an academic concept design project where the participating companies did not intervene in the work during ideation. The design brief was explorative: to "develop a description of future practices in maintenance work based on opportunities in proactive computing. The description should help in foreseeing future challenges and in developing tools and machines to be more easily maintainable by service workers, within a time frame of 5 to 10 years."

The two participating companies provide maintenance on elevators and slot machines. In both cases the company is also the manufacturer of the machines maintained. The promise of proactive computing for maintenance work lies in the ongoing trend of equipping machines with increasing communication capabilities. The goal is to enhance machines' capability of event monitoring, self-diagnosis and malfunction communication to service centres via the Internet, which would reduce downtime and help predict errors. However, the same trend also makes it possible to help service workers by providing context-dependent support in maintenance tasks.

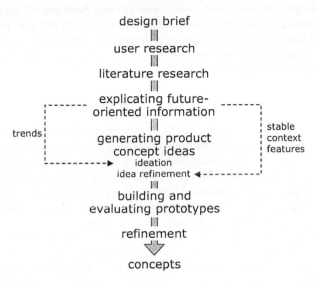

Fig. 2. The user-centered product concept design process, improved with phases for using future-oriented information

3.1 Planning the Study

Recognition of the importance of dividing future-oriented information into trends and stable context features was reflected in the methodology of the process. It was noted that the division of information had to take place before starting ideation. Otherwise, if carried out on an on-demand basis, there would be a risk that the team made biased divisions if they had already identified their favourite product concepts after ideation. With early explication, the temptation to interpret data in a post-hoc manner to support favourable conclusions was decreased.

The consideration in the previous section implies that the use of trends precedes stable context features. This means that the team should probably first aim to make a leap into the future during ideation, and then come somewhat back in the time in refinement phase by using presumably stable features in the context.

The overall concept is visualized in Fig. 2. In this figure a separate stage called "Explicating future-oriented information" has been added immediately before the concept generation tasks. From the explication task, information flows lead to the ideation and refinement subtasks. Except for these modifications, the process is similar to the one presented in Fig. 1.

When planning the study, an exploratory approach to methodology on the use of the future-oriented information was chosen. This also serves the purpose of this paper, because rather than proposing a formal model for a design process, it exemplifies the possible uses of the future-oriented information in a reflective manner throughout the design stages.

However, some decisions were made early on. User research was to be carried out with traditional interviewing and observing methods, to be followed by a literature survey on emerging topics. As the team was familiar with the affinity diagram construction technique, it was chosen as a method in this study and was used during idea refinement. It was known in advance that interactive prototypes would probably be very difficult to build, and therefore the outcome of the project would consist of user-evaluated storyboards or passive mock-ups.

3.2 User Research

Information about service workers and their context was gathered in two ways: studying the users, and based on the findings, deepening the understanding with literature. The project was started with a study of service workers in both companies. The focus was on learning about the use of present tools, describing the main task categories of maintenance activities, and collecting stories. It was assumed that inquiry into these topics would produce understanding both on procedural aspects of work, as well as on social issues in collaboration and attitudes towards work.

The study covered in all 20 persons from the two companies. Daily work was studied with Contextual Inquiry (N=5) [2] and artifact analysis interviews in which workers discussed photographs on their tools (N=11) [13]. In addition, 4 persons from the companies' R&D departments were interviewed to obtain a complementary perspective on service work, and to compare their perceptions of work to those of workers themselves. Information was also gained about companies' future strategies.

Analysis consisted of writing aggregated day-in-the-life scenarios (to gather together different observations from Contextual Inquiry), and listing work tasks, workers' opinions and terminology that were collected with different methods. In total, 145 different work tasks, 81 terms and 63 opinions were listed. At this point the importance of a single site visit as a useful unit of analysis was identified, and task sequence models of such site visits were drawn for both companies.

The rationale for these data gathering and analysis methods was their naturalness from the user point of view: interviewing about tools was a natural discussion topic. It was also both economical in terms of the amount of time invested by the team, and supplementary in a way that it revealed issues that were not encountered in Contextual Inquiry. The list creation was easy after day-in-the-life scenario writing and artifact interviews. What the data helped to see were, for instance:

- The intensely mobile nature of work (frequent driving between installed machines)
- The dualistic nature of site visits (either repair or routine maintenance, both of which contain dirty tasks such as cleaning as well as sophisticated tasks such as parameter tuning with a laptop)
- The dualistic nature of customers (requirements coming from users of the machine vs. people who operate the place where the machine is installed)
- The scarcity of the time available to see colleagues (due to the mobility of work)
- Personal service territories as something to be responsible for and proud of.

Interviews with R&D personnel were helpful in pinpointing topics for literature research, such as questions of changes in expertise requirements of future work, the consequences of rearrangements of service territories, or the possibility of implementing proactive computing systems into the existing environment.

In total, there were 8 task categories and 8 general phenomena of such findings. This served as a sufficient introduction to the nature of present-day work, and provided hints concerning future changes in the work context.

3.3 Literature Research

Researching the literature on maintenance work was important in providing a second opinion on emerging themes from user research, and in learning about service work in similar work domains, such as photocopier repair. Four topics drew special attention:

– *Changing nature of work*. This topic emerged both from comments by workers and remarks on technology trends by R&D. Investigation into the literature on future of work showed an ongoing debate around the question of de-skilling and skill upgrading: is work becoming automated and simpler or more complicated in the future? There appeared to be no consensus on the trend, but with respect to service work, there appeared to be an incentive to increase hardware modularity and improve he diagnostic capabilities of machines, thus increasing automatization but also sophistication of technology. This drew interest to the following two issues.
– *Service work as knowledge work*. Skill upgrading is a phenomenon often combined with discussion on knowledge-intensive work. In the observations it became apparent that especially difficult repair tasks had features that resemble knowledge work: creative problem solving under uncertainties, and using information technology frequently to help in such tasks.
– *The role of a service worker in the work society*. A question was raised also about how workers, customers, and other people in service companies perceive service work. The literature showed workers served two functions: they buffer information between customers and people in the company ("buffers"), and solve maintenance problems for customers ("brokers"). In these roles, technicians are cutpoints in companies' production systems, making companies vulnerable to their loss [1]. As this is not always recognized, tensions tend to form.
– *Information sharing among maintenance workers*. Orr's ethnographic study on service work and work society [20] pointed out the importance of informal coffee table discussions as an important means for learning. This was also observed in both companies in this study. Such occasions led to a search for further information about knowledge management and the question of horizontal information sharing. This was an interesting issue as both companies had organized their information flow channels to support vertical feedback from workers to managers and R&D.

The issues from literature provided a basis for explicating the team's assumptions on future working conditions.

3.4 Explicating Future-Oriented Information

Having gathered a wealth of domain knowledge, commitments on future-oriented information were explicated before proceeding to concept generation. This information consisted of observations on work, workers' opinions, future strategies, information about similar working domains, and discussions found in the literature. Neutrality in moral judgments was found to be important so that trends and features were not selected based on their positive or negative effects on work conditions. Instead, it was within these limits of effects that concepts with positive implications had to be found.

Trends. Section 2.2 suggested trends as a tool to guide ideation into fruitful directions. In the case study, due to the two companies involved, two types of trends were defined. General trends applied to both companies, whereas the rest were company-specific. Although it was not suggested by the literature, a 24/7 society trend was added because of the visions it could open for future work. In total, the general trends were:

– *Increase in surveillance and automatic reporting.* Enhanced telecommunication connections with machines and workers' PDAs to maintenance monitoring systems will provide companies with increased scope to monitor the condition of machine-sas well as workers' actions. This improves information flow and the ability to anticipate faults, but may also result in more stressful work.
– *Increase in evening and night shifts.* The 24/7 society phenomenon has a direct effect on service work, since working is easiest during quiet hours, which become scarce if shop opening hours are being extended.
– *Proactive maintenance.* Technology will support enhanced mechanisms to predict repair needs so that visits are scheduled to take place before faults occur.
– *Information outdating and a need for constant updates.* Proactive maintenance requires each machine to have individual, tailored maintenance. Proliferation of software components increases individualization of installation configurations. This causes a need to update one's knowledge of the machines more frequently.

The five *company-specific trends* were mostly inherited from company strategies, and were more focused on specific work issues. We will skip them for the sake of brevity.

Stable Context Features. In the case of finding stable context features in maintenance work within a 5–10-year time frame, explication was done by simplifying task sequence models about typical maintenance visits. With simplification, the level of abstraction was raised, and the model's commitment to present-day factors was decreased, revealing a task structure that summarizes necessary tasks in maintenance visits also in the future: receiving a call-out message, driving to the site, doing routine maintenance or repair, and completing the visit. This model was also in line with company strategies on future work, and did not conflict with the trends identified. The model is shown in Fig. 3.

Task sequence models were chosen as the basis because of the team's user research focus on task categories and tool use. However, a sociogram-like model was also created, describing broker and buffer positions of a worker in relation to workmates, managers and customers. This model originated from literature research findings.

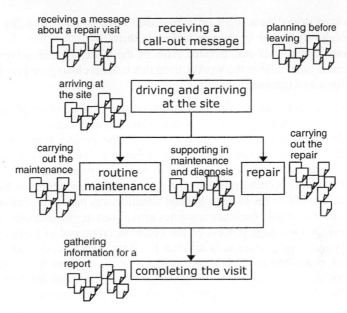

Fig. 3. A schematic visualization a high-level sequence model and its use for providing structure for affinity diagram construction. The clusters of sticker notes denote the main categories of remarks that were identified in the diagram construction process.

3.5 Ideation Based on Trends

For a person familiar with the maintenance domain in question, the trends listed are a quick source of ideas about the implications for activities in future work. This was found to be beneficial during ideation. Therefore, instead of envisioning product concepts directly, activities in future work were brainstormed. In order to create a variety of ideas, each trend was considered separately, without any attempt to form a single unified vision. The session was an intensive half-day two-person session where the focus was on inventing activities with positive implications from trends. The persons participating in the session were already familiar with UCPCD, had done project work together in the past, and had participated in the observations and interviews. The rest of the team members did not have as much experience on creative brainstorming and consequently would have probably found this kind of idea generation difficult. Because successful brainstorming is also dependent on the engagement of the people participating (see e.g. [9]), this selection was considered best by the team members. A bigger might possibly have created more ideas, but that is not guaranteed.

Ideas about activities were formulated in one-sentence long microscenarios. Also ideas with difficult implementation were written down if they came up. This was done in order not to rule out any unexpected opportunities that would require a creative leap into the future 5-10 years ahead. Here are three of the resulting 36 microscenarios (with the originating trends in parentheses):

– Serving companies that are only open at night, not during official working hours ("Increase in evening and night shifts").

- Repairers start doing their work on a freelance basis when it best fits into their daily schedules ("Increase in evening and night shifts").
- Autonomous reporting of maintenance visits by the machines themselves, with the help of sensors, will relieve the worker from this tedious closing-up task ("Increase in surveillance and automatic reporting").

In a subsequent session, microscenarios were reconsidered in a contemplative session where the whole team was present. With this setup, the microscenarios could be enriched with feedback from all the ethnographers in the project (amounting to four persons in total). Microscenarios were presented one at a time, and PostIt notes were written when ideas came up. This resulted in notes on improved product concept ideas, detailed remarks on design issues, and considerations on future working conditions, amounting to 200 notes in total. Special attention was paid to proactive computing opportunities that would facilitate activities envisioned in microscenarios.

The effect of the two-stage process on the outcome, compared to a straightforward single-stage brainstorming session, is difficult to assess. Trends could have also been cross-tabulated, providing possibly more inspiring starting points for scenario creation. The opportunities to use trends in lightweight idea generation are many, and the methods can be adapted to suit each project's individual requirements.

3.6 Idea Refinement Based on Stable Context Features

At this point of the project, a wealth of ideas about proactive computing products had been created in the form of microscenarios and related remarks by team members, but they needed refinement because each idea with its remarks was linked only to the microscenario and the trend from which it had originated. The analysis at the beginning of the paper raised weakly-grounded contextualization as an imminent challenge to idea refinement, and suggested applying stable context features to align ideas with firm contextual data. From previous projects, the team was familiar with affinity diagrams [2,8] as a technique to organize pieces of information into bigger structures. Collecting remarks on PostIt notes in the preceding stage was done with this in mind.

Fig. 3 shows a schematic visualization of the approach taken when refining ideas. A high-level task sequence model of a single site visit was used as a structural backbone to help in organizing the PostIt notes. Each note was placed into its contextually relevant position in the task sequence, and if an idea fitted into multiple positions, the note was duplicated. The organization process resulted in seven note clusters (headings shown in the figure), and gave rise to seven contextualized product concepts. In this stage, care was given to preserve proactive computing opportunities.

3.7 Evaluation with Users and the Companies

The refined concept ideas were concretized in storyboard scenarios, and iterated by discussing them with maintenance workers. As a result, two concepts were merged and minor changes were made to each of the concepts. The underlying trends and stable context features were not disclosed to the workers, because they could have been easily interpreted as providing insider information on company strategies. The team felt that it was crucial to avoid any unnecessary misunderstandings.

To company representatives, full background information was provided. Trends combined with the possibility of proactive computing proved useful in inspiring discussions. As a negative feedback, a bigger emphasis on economic considerations would have been preferred. Although relevant to project success, this feedback does not undermine the validity of this paper's approach, that of the need for explicating trends and stable features. With closer cooperation with companies, such issues could have been included in the future-oriented information and used in idea generation.

4 Discussion

The contribution of this paper can be discussed from various viewpoints: are the identified challenges general, and can more challenges be found based on the analytic distinction of future-oriented information? What are the implications of the paper to design practice? Can alternative approaches be suggested to overcome the same challenges? This section addresses these questions.

4.1 Generalizability of the Identified Challenges

Predicting the future lies at the heart of any design of future products. By making conscious decisions on the use of available information, the probability of developing successful concepts should be increased. The issues raised in this paper attempt to map out the questions on which such decisions could be based. The generalizability of the contribution can then be partly evaluated by considering whether it helps reveal more of the kind of challenges presented at the beginning of the paper. Indeed, during the study, two new challenges were noted where a division of information into trends and stable features might provide a solution. Both are related to idea refinement.

One is about the risk of *inspiration depletion*. Coming up with creative ideas requires effort, and doing it repeatedly is difficult and unmotivating. This is, however, the case with unproductive brainstorming results that do not qualify for further development. Inspiration depletion can be overcome if new task-specific information becomes available, thus providing an escape from a fixation to previous problem-solving strategies [6]. In doing this, stable context features can be helpful. As has been seen, user research and literature data can be used to create multiple models. In the case study, the sociogram-like model of buffer and broker relationships could have been used as such an alternative and new viewpoint.

The other challenge is related to internal concept evaluation. Product concepts need to be validated after their generation. But UCPCD is a lightweight process and therefore trials with interactive prototypes and real users cannot always be carried out. There is a need to be able to assess the validity of concepts by other means. With internal evaluation there is a potential problem of *within-team evaluation bias*, due to the subjective basis of available information. Comparison with identified phenomena and user needs does not qualify, since they have been design drivers for ideation and thus biased for evaluation. Sometimes evaluation is possible by getting feedback from domain experts who are not part of the team, but even before this it would be helpful to be able to do a within-team iteration round. Bias may be decreased with cross-validation using stable context feature models: one can check if concepts refined with one model have conflicts with other models. In the case study, the sociogram would have been such an evaluation basis, since concepts had been refined using the task sequence model. This type of evaluation does not of course replace real evaluations and it requires also that stable models are created before the start of idea generation.

4.2 Evaluation of the Approach

As the focus of the paper is essentially on the use of information during the concept design stages, its implications are mostly independent of selected concept design methods or the results of the case study. The case study has merely served as a medium for reflective analysis of the use of available information at different stages of the process. What then needs to be evaluated is the perspective provided by the paper, and the usefulness of its epistemological implications for UCPCD in general.

The implications are of four types. Firstly and most generally, problematization of the use of information in concept design provides a designer with analytical tools that facilitate reflective thinking during the design process. These are the ideas of trends, stable context features, and the described challenges. With these concepts, a designer can assess if false commitments on available information are being made, or if the information on which to base decisions is biased or incomplete.

Secondly, the paper has presented an analytical division of future-oriented information into trends and stable context features. This conceptualization provides more understanding of the nature of information on which concept creation for future products is always based. This helps to choose methods for user and literature research, and also for analysis, in order to distill the right type of information from the context.

Thirdly, by analyzing at what stages each type of future-oriented information is most valuable, the designer can make informed decisions on the methodology to apply when using the information to produce (e.g., brainstorm) good ideas. The transformation of the information and knowledge from user and literature research to the final refinement and evaluation of the concepts can then be streamlined more easily.

Fourthly, the use of trends in guiding ideation into fruitful directions, and giving stable context features in refinement and contextualization, provides an analytical tool for estimating the degree of open-endedness at the concept generation stage. If the focus is on inventing radically new concepts, then the trends can be broad and they can point far into the future, thus widening the design space. If the focus is on minor improvements, the trends can address issues in a 2–3-year time frame, and the stable context features can also describe rather detailed activities.

4.3 Alternative Approaches to the Challenges

It is worth considering if alternative approaches exist which provide better solutions for overcoming the listed challenges, and does the use of such approaches exclude the use of the approach presented in this paper. However, this can be done only cursorily.

The case study has three characteristics that need consideration. The first, relating to the project's contract work nature where the companies did not intervene in its progress, has already been mentioned. But there is no reason why defining trends and stable context features should not be possible in within-company projects as well. It may, however, be more challenging to avoid trends which conform too closely to company strategies. Involving outside participants in the explication may be useful.

The second characteristic is the low involvement of users in the concept generation stages, contrary to the spirit of Participatory Design. While involving users is certainly possible, neutral assessment of future trends may prove problematic. This may result in risk-averse concept development or worker-manager tensions in the team. Therefore, it may be more useful to involve users in the design process when the more traditional development process has started, as shown on the right side of Fig. 1.

The third characteristic is the small number of people involved in the project. Could a bigger team with a multi-disciplinary line-up ensure that no information is misused or forgotten in the process? The answer is that such manning certainly makes it easier to overcome the challenges, but does not conflict with the approach proposed in the paper. Multi-disciplinarity and the explication of future-oriented information can be seen as complementing each other.

Finally, some brief remarks can be made on the techniques applied to overcome individual challenges presented in the paper. These include using scenario methods of futurology (e.g. [3]) to counter user-data domination, or bodystorming [21] to counter within-team evaluation bias. However, these issues must be left for future research.

5 Conclusions

The general aim of this paper has been to explore new ways for reflective meta-level thinking during the concept design process, and through analysis to show how that can be beneficial in producing informed ideas about future products. The analysis started by problematizing current approaches and continued with a suggestion to overcome the identified challenges. It was shown to be useful to explicate the gathered information about future use situations with respect to the assumptions made on changes and stable features in the future use context. The suggestion also provided an analysis concerning what stages of a project each type of information would be of most value. A small case study was provided to describe in more detail what the suggestion can imply in practice in terms of epistemological commitments at each level of the process and the methods chosen thereby, especially during ideation and the idea refinement stages. With this treatment, it has been shown how important for any design team it is to consider the nature of information on which the concept design is based, and in this way manage the design space in concept generation.

Acknowledgments

The authors would like to thank Sirpa Riihiaho and Hannu Kuoppala for their help, and The Finnish Work Environment Fund for funding the project.

References

1. Barley, S.R.: Technicians in the Workplace: Ethnographic Evidence for Bringing Work into Organization Studies. Administrative Science Quarterly 41(3) (1996) 404-441
2. Beyer, H., Holtzblatt, K.: Contextual Design: Defining Customer-Centered Systems. Morgan Kaufmann, San Francisco (1998)

3. Coates, J.H.: An Overview of Futures Methods. In: The Knowledge Base of Futures Studies 2, DDM Media Group, Hawthorn Australia (1996) 57-75
4. Craig J., Vogel, C.M.: Creating Breakthrough Products: Innovation from Product Planning to Program Approval. Prentice-Hall PTR, Upper Saddle River (2002)
5. Dahlbäck, N., Jönsson, A., Ahrenberg, L.: Wizard-of-Oz Studies – Why and How. Proc. Intelligent User Interfaces (IUI'93). ACM Press, New York (1993) 193-200
6. Duncker, K. On Problem Solving. Psychological Monograms 270(5) (1945) 1-113
7. Kankainen, A.: UCPCD - User-Centered Product Concept Design. Proc. Designing for User Experiences (DUX'03). ACM Press, New York (2003)
8. Kawakita, J.: The Original KJ Method. Kawakita Research Insitute, Tokyo (1982)
9. Kelley, T., Littman, J.: The Art of Innovation. Doubleday, New York (2001)
10. Khurana, A., Rosenthal, S.R.: Towards Holistic "Front Ends" in New Product Development. Journal of Product Innovation Management 15(1) (1998) 57-74
11. Leonard, D., Rayport, J.F.: Spark Innovation through Empathic Design. Harvard Business Review 75(6) (1997) 102-113
12. Lumsdaine, E., Lumsdaine M.: Creative Problem Solving: Thinking Skills for a Changing World. McGraw-Hill, New York (1995)
13. Mannonen, P., Kuoppala, H., Nieminen, M.P.: Photograph-Based Artefact Analysis. Proc. Interact'03. IOS Press, Amsterdam (2003) 833-836
14. Mayhew, D.J.: The Usability Engineering Lifecycle. Morgan Kaufmann, San Francisco (1999)
15. Moore, W.L., Pessemier, E.A.: Product Planning and Management: Designing and Delivering Value. McGraw-Hill, New York (1993)
16. National Research Council: The Changing Nature of Work: Implications for Occupational Analysis. National Academies Press, Washington (1999)
17. Nielsen, J.: Usability Engineering. Academic Press, Boston (1993)
18. Nielsen, J.: Scenarios in Discount Usability Engineering. In Carroll, J.M. (ed.) Scenario-Based Design: Envisioning Work and Technology in System Development. John Wiley & Sons, New York (1995)
19. Nieminen, M., Mannonen, P., Turkki, L.: User-Centered Concept Development Process for Emerging Technologies. Proc. NordiCHI'04. ACM Press, New York (2004) 225-228
20. Orr, J.E.: Talking about Machines: An Ethnography of a Modern Job. ILR Press, Ithaca (1996)
21. Oulasvirta, A., Kurvinen, E., Kankainen, T.: Understanding Contexts by Being There: Case Studies in Bodystorming. Personal and Ubiquitous Computing 7(2) (2003) 125-134
22. Patnaik, D., Becker R.: Needfinding: The Why and How of Uncovering People's Needs. Design Management Journal 10(2) (1999) 37-43
23. Stevens, G.A., Burley, J.: 3,000 raw ideas = 1 commercial success! Research Technology Management 44(3) (1997) 16-27
24. Tennenhouse, D.: Proactive Computing. Communications of the ACM 43(5) (2000) 43-50.

Wide vs. Narrow Paragraphs: An Eye Tracking Analysis

David Beymer[1], Daniel M. Russell[1], and Peter Z. Orton[2]

[1] IBM Almaden Research Center, 650 Harry Road,
San Jose, California 95120 USA
[2] IBM On Demand Learning, 20 Old Post Road,
Armonk, New York 10504 USA
{beymer, daniel2, porton}@us.ibm.com

Abstract. How wide should paragraphs be formatted for optimal reader retention and ease of reading? While everyone is familiar with the narrow, multi-
column formatting in newspapers and magazines, research on the issue is not
consistent. Early work using printed media favored narrow formatting, while
more recent work using computer monitors has favored wider formatting. In
this paper, we approach this issue by using eye tracking analysis of users reading material on instructional web pages. In our experimental system, subjects
read the material using an instrumented browser that records all HTML content
and browser actions, and their eye gaze is recorded using a nonobtrusive, "remote" eye tracker. Comparing the wide and narrow formatting conditions, our
analysis shows that for narrow formatting, subjects (a) read slightly faster, (b)
have fewer regressions, (c) retain more information in a post-test of the material, but (d) tend to abandon the ends of longer paragraphs.

1 Introduction

In this paper, we address the question: how is reading behavior affected by narrow
vs. wide paragraph formatting? Are there observable differences between readers
given the same material, but differing paragraph widths? Early work by typogra-
phers, psychologists, and designers focused on printed material. Using reading speed
as a metric, these experiments favored shorter line length (Tinker [6] favored 80 mm),
which is recognizable today in the narrow columns typically seen in newspapers and
magazines. The intuition is that the "return sweep" from the end of one line to the
beginning of the next is more difficult in wide paragraphs because of the longer eye
movement required by the reader. More recently, however, researchers in ergonomics
and human factors have re-visited the issue with reading from computer screens
[1,3,4,5,14]. In contrast with print studies, reading speed on computer screens favored longer lines (e.g. most of the monitor width) or at least showed no preference
for shorter lines. To help reconcile these differences, it has been noted that monitors
are typically further from the reader than hardcopy pages, so a narrow printed paragraph may subtend a similar visual angle on the eye as a wider paragraph on a
monitor.

M.F. Costabile and F. Paternò (Eds.): INTERACT 2005, LNCS 3585, pp. 741–752, 2005.

Eye gaze tracking provides a valuable tool for objectively measuring reading behavior. In eye gaze tracking systems, a camera records the eye gaze of a user, which in the case of reading is mapped to the words and lines of text being read. Amazingly, eye tracking technology has a history that stretches back 100 years, with early work coupling photographic recording methods with a "corneal reflection" technique that bounced light beams bounced off the subjects' eyes. Indeed, early application of this technology was used to study reading behavior. While readers intuitively may think that their eye gaze follows a continuous left-to-right motion, eye tracking studies showed that eye motion advances in discrete chunks across the page. A reader's eyes will actually stop, or fixate, on a set of characters for about 250 ms. This *fixation* is followed by a *saccade*, an eye movement of about 10 characters to the right, where the eyes will stop at the next fixation. A *regression*, or backwards eye movement in the text, is a sign that the reader is having difficulty understanding the material.

Given the tool of eye gaze tracking, what does it tell us about reading performance? Eye tracking has confirmed the intuitive notion, for instance, that the difficulty of reading material has an effect on reading. For example, material from a physics or mathematics textbook will cause longer fixations and more regressions than material from light fiction or newspapers [7]. Eye gaze tracking has also been used to study the effects of typography on reading [8]. In 1940, Patterson and Tinker [9] studied eye movements when subjects were presented with text formatted with different line lengths. From eye gaze, they measured fixation frequency and perception time (the sum of time spent in fixations), measures that have been found to correlate with reading speed. These measures favored an intermediate line length of just over 3 inches. In a longer line length tested (7 inches), the slowness of subjects was found to be explained by increased regressions and difficulty in return sweeps. These tests were done with printed text, not text presented on computer screens.

Eye tracking systems have evolved greatly since the photographic techniques used by Paterson and Tinker. While the corneal reflection method is still used today, the light beams now use nonobstrusive infrared light and recordings are measured using video techniques. A number of commercial eye gaze trackers exist, with some software systems performing reading analysis on recorded eye gaze.

In this paper, we revisit the question of how typography affects reading, focusing on the issue of line length. Relative to the 1940 study by Tinker and Paterson, we think that (a) the maturation of eye gaze tracking technology makes the recording less obtrusive and the analysis more automatic and less error-prone, and (b) given the earlier disagreement between print-based and computer-based line length studies, a study of online reading from monitors may provide a different result.

We have developed a tool, WebGazeAnalyzer (WGA) [10], for recording and analyzing the eye gaze of a user during a web browsing session. A nonobtrusive camera mounted inside the computer monitor bezel observes the eye gaze of the computer user, estimating where on the screen the user is looking. Reading is detected in the eye gaze by looking for the characteristic horizontal pattern of fixations and saccades. By intersecting the eye gaze location with the location of words on the web pages, we can tell what the user is reading, the reading speed, what they are re-reading, skipping, etc. Our recording tool records multiple data streams using a special instrumented version of Internet Explorer. We record: a movie of the computer screen, all

URLs visited by the user, a parsed version of the HTML content, and all Windows events such as scrolling and mouse clicks. After recording the data, we can browse it as a movie using a playback tool, or we can batch analyze a number of sequences to analyze reading behavior across different experimental conditions. In this paper, we use WebGazeAnalyzer to study reading behavior under wide and narrow formatted paragraphs.

2 Measuring Reading Using Eye Tracking

Given that WGA's recording system has recorded the eye gaze and web content from a particular experiment, how does WGA analyze the eye gaze to report reading statistics? While the mechanics of the recording system and reading analysis were largely reported in [10], we expand upon some of the details of how time, distance, and speed are measured, since those are the important statistics reported in this paper.

2.1 Low-Level Gaze Processing

From the raw eye gaze, our analysis system first detects fixations in the gaze stream using a dispersion-based approach [13]. Because of the 0.5 degree of error in the gaze estimate from our eye tracker, assigning fixations to URL text for reading analysis may be ambiguous – given the uncertainty region around a fixation, the fixation may potentially map to multiple lines of text. As detailed in [10], we address this uncertainty with a robust, line-based matching algorithm that assigns fixations to lines of text from the recorded web page. After this matching process, the system can map each fixation to a single line of text, allowing reading analysis to proceed.

After matching, the analysis system next parses the fixation data into *forward reads*. A forward read is a grouping of consecutive fixations moving forward through the text with typical reading saccades (see Fig. 1). When processing the fixations to form forward reads, a forward read will be stopped when (1) a regression is encountered, (2) a forward saccade is too large and likely a forward skip through the text, or (3) the eye gaze moves to another line of text. Intuitively, forward reads are designed to capture when and where subjects are actively reading the text in detail. As shown in Fig. 1, the ith forward read detected, fr_i, covers a distance d_i that is padded to the left and right by the perceptual span [7]. Furthermore, let time t_i be the time spent in the forward read, defined as the time difference between the beginning of the first fixation and the end of the last fixation.

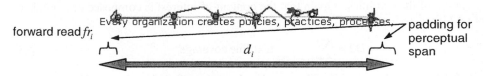

forward read fr_i padding for perceptual span d_i

Fig. 1. For forward reads, the reading distance is padded by the perceptual span. Detected fixations are shown with small circles, interconnected by the raw gaze.

Typically in an experiment, the researcher is only interested in reading behavior for particular content-of-interest, whether it be specific sentences or entire paragraphs from the URL. While WGA offers flexibility in specifying content-of-interest down to the word level, in this paper we will analyze reading statistics over paragraphs. We now explain how forward reads are processed over the specified paragraphs-of-interest.

2.2 Instantaneous Measures

Given the short amount of time covered by forward reads, typically 1 to 2 seconds, measuring reading using forward reads alone gives us a raw, instantaneous measure of reading. Given a line of text from a paragraph-of-interest, the gaze matcher will assign some number of forward reads $fr_0 \dots fr_{n-1}$ to the line. We measure the time

$$T1 = \sum_{i=0}^{n-1} t_i \qquad (1)$$

as the total time the subject's eyes are actively reading forward through the text. Note that $T1$ does not count time spent in regressions, return sweeps, or distractions like scrolling or scanning. The text distance covered by these forward reads

$$D1 = \sum_{i=0}^{n-1} d_i \qquad (2)$$

will include re-reads of the same material.

Our instantaneous speed measure $D1/T1$ is a low-level measure of eye velocity while reading. Given the low-level nature of this speed measure, it may be most useful as an input to some modeling process as opposed to a final reporting statistic.

2.3 Overall Measures

In measuring the overall speed of reading, we want to include the effects of regressions and return sweeps. Also re-reading the same material should count against the reader, as this slows down his or her overall performance. To account for this, we can re-use the forward reads as follows. For time, measure the **elapsed time** between and including the first and last forward reads

$$T2 = (\text{end time of } fr_{n-1}) - (\text{begin time of } fr_0) . \qquad (3)$$

For distance, we only measure the first time material is read by projecting the forward reads onto the text lines and ignoring overlapping segments—we call this the reading coverage of the text lines. Given that the content-of-interest is composed of a number of text lines, we compute

$$D2 = \sum_{\text{all text lines}} \text{text line coverage} \qquad (4)$$

which measures the amount of text read at least once (but does not double count re-reads).

Finally, the overall speed is computed as *D2/T2*. If the subject re-reads the same material in multiple passes separated by non-reading activities, each pass is treated separately with its own *T2* measurements, and speed is measured by $D2 / \Sigma\, T2$.

3 Experiment

Because our experimental system is designed to record and analyze web browsing sessions, we developed web pages with the same text content, but different paragraph widths. The two conditions used in our experiment include:

Cond. A: *Wide paragraphs*. Paragraphs width was 80% of screen width, measuring 9 inches on our monitor.

Cond. B: *Narrow paragraphs.* Paragraph width was 40% of screen width, measuring 4.5 inches.

The font used was Verdana 10 pt, and subjects are positioned approximately 60-70 cm from the monitor. In both conditions, scrolling is required to read the entire page. The experimental web page describes the different stages of "culture shock" of employees on overseas assignments, and it is a real page from IBM training course material. Fig. 2 shows an example of one paragraph in each of the two conditions.

Subjects were volunteers from a group of new managers attending management training school, so the web material was relevant to their background, motivations and interests; each subject had extensive practice (on the order of tens of hours) with these course materials before our test. There were 8 subjects in condition A (6 male, 2 female) and 8 subjects (1 male, 7 female) in condition B.

Before seeing the culture shock page, each subject read through 2 practice pages, and had to answer several basic data collection questions (e.g., native language, handedness, etc.) Subjects were told there would be a post study test of their retention of the content and that they should study the materials in anticipation of the test just as they had during their normal course of instruction.

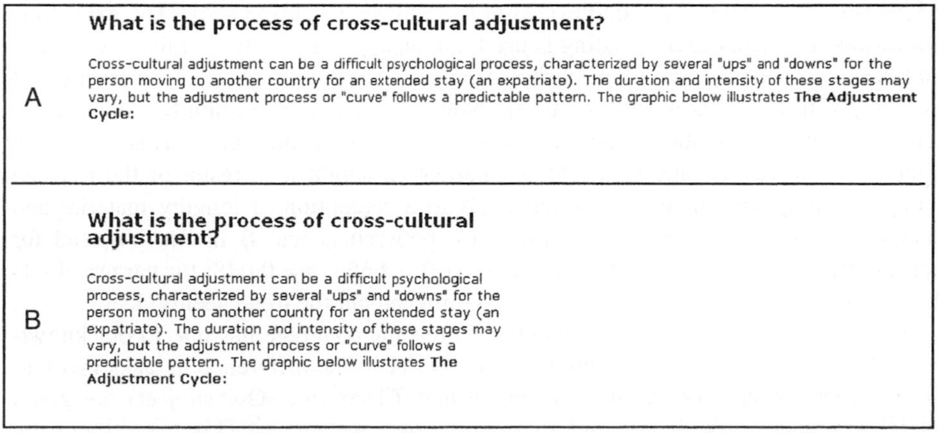
A

What is the process of cross-cultural adjustment?

Cross-cultural adjustment can be a difficult psychological process, characterized by several "ups" and "downs" for the person moving to another country for an extended stay (an expatriate). The duration and intensity of these stages may vary, but the adjustment process or "curve" follows a predictable pattern. The graphic below illustrates **The Adjustment Cycle:**

B

What is the process of cross-cultural adjustment?

Cross-cultural adjustment can be a difficult psychological process, characterized by several "ups" and "downs" for the person moving to another country for an extended stay (an expatriate). The duration and intensity of these stages may vary, but the adjustment process or "curve" follows a predictable pattern. The graphic below illustrates **The Adjustment Cycle:**

Fig. 2. In condition A, paragraph formatting is wide (9 inches on our monitor), while in condition B, paragraphs are narrow (4.5 inches on our monitor)

Eye tracking was done with the Tobii 1750 eye tracker [11] and two IBM T41 laptop computers. One laptop, the "gaze server", was devoted to running the Tobii eye tracking software. The second laptop, the "user machine", was the machine used by our subjects. On it ran our instrumented Internet Explorer browser, which records all URLs visited, HTML content (through the Document Object Model), and dynamic events such as scrolling [10]. We also record an event-driven movie recording of the user's screen through an adapted version of the VNC remote desktop system (see [12] for a related screen capture system).

4   Results

Reading analysis focuses on the first 5 paragraphs of the culture shock URL, looking for reading differences between the wide and narrow conditions. As mentioned in section 2, reading analysis proceeds by detecting fixations, matching them to lines of URL text, and finally grouping them into forward reads, which are the characteristic reading pattern of fixations and saccades in the eye gaze stream. Thus, for each paragraph, we can measure reading speed, regressions, the fraction of material read (vs. skipped), and return sweeps from one line of text to the next.

Comparing conditions A and B (the wide and narrow conditions, respectively), our reading analysis does show a slight speed advantage for B, but this is not caused by A being slowed down by return sweeps. One surprising result is that narrow paragraphs encourage the readers to skip material.

4.1   Reading Time and Coverage

Subjects in condition A (wide) spend more total time reading and read more of the material than B (narrow). For the first five paragraphs in conditions A and B, we measured reading time using the $T1$ and $T2$ metrics measured defined in section 2.

Subjects in condition A spend more time in both measures ($T1$: 13.22 sec, $T2$: 15.80 sec) than subjects in condition B ($T1$: 9.28 sec, $T2$: 11.35 sec). The extra time condition A subjects spend reading is used to read a greater fraction of the material, as compared to condition B. Fig. 3 shows time measure $T1$ (top) and the fraction of paragraph material that is read (bottom). Note that those in condition B progressively read less and less of the paragraphs as they move down the page. This paragraph abandonment may be due to the longer paragraph height as a result of the reduced width. Perhaps this increased height leads to a perception of lengthy material and encourages skipping ahead. The difference between A and B in fraction read for paragraph 5 is statistically significant, $F(1, 14) = 4.655$, $p = 0.048$; for paragraphs 1-4, the differences in fraction read are not significant, but the trend seems clear.

This relationship between line length and reading coverage has not, to our knowledge, been examined before. This is primarily due to the difference in tasks given to our subjects versus, for instance, Paterson and Tinker [9]. Our subjects are given an open reading task, being told to freely read a web page. This gives them the

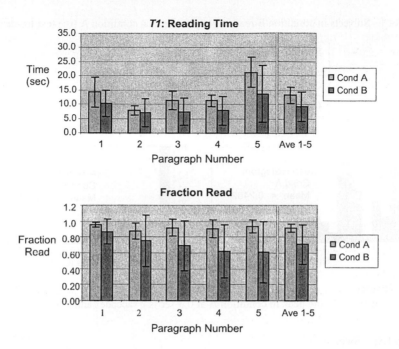

Fig. 3. Subjects spend more time reading the text under condition A (top chart). Thefraction of paragraphs read remains high for condition A, but deteriorates for condition B (bottom). In this bar graph and subsequent ones, the error bars indicate the standarddeviation in the distribution.

opportunity to skip around in the material, perhaps deciding to ignore some material. In [9], subjects are essentially forced to read all the material by the nature of the test used – the "Chapman-Cook Speed of Reading Test". In that test, subjects read a paragraph where a single word "spoils" the meaning, and the subjects are asked to identify the word. Thus, any influences of typography on *whether* to read the text are eliminated from [9].

4.2 Reading Speed

Subjects in condition B are slightly faster than those in condition A. Referring back to section 2, we measure speed in two different ways, an instantaneous measure of eye reading velocity and an overall measure of reading speed.

Subjects in condition B read faster than condition A under both metrics (see Table 1). As the table shows, condition B is faster by about 7% for instantaneous speed and 15% for overall speed, but, unfortunately, even the latter difference is not statistically significant ($F (1, 14) = 1.035$, $p = 0.32$). The instantaneous speed result is in rough agreement with [9], where they saw a 7.8% difference in fixation frequency favoring short line lengths over long (fixation frequency is correlated to speed).

Table 1. Subjects in condition B read slightly faster than condition A (see text for details)

Speed	Instantaneous (pix/sec)	Overall (pix/sec)
Cond. A	275, $\sigma = 37$	161, $\sigma = 35$
Cond. B	295, $\sigma = 68$	185, $\sigma = 52$

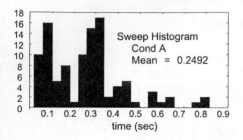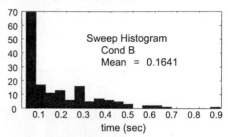

Fig. 4. Histograms of return sweep times for conditions A and B. The peaks near 0.1 sec are single saccades, while the peak in condition A at 0.3 sec is 2 saccades and a fixation.

4.3 Return Sweeps

The long return sweeps in condition A take more time than condition B and often require an additional positioning fixation. As shown in Fig. 4, the histogram on return sweep times is bimodal for condition A and unimodal for condition B. For the short distance covered by return sweeps for condition B, the eye makes a single saccade from the end of the previous line to the beginning of the next line (see Fig. 5). Similarly for condition A, sometimes the eye performs the return sweep in a single saccade, yielding the first histogram peak. But quite often the eye requires an additional fixation and saccade to position the eye for reading the next line (Fig. 5). This additional fixation is always close to the beginning of the next line, and usually undershoots the return. This type of return sweep yields the second histogram peak in

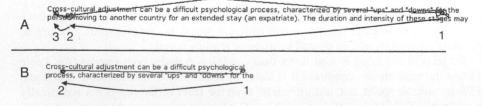

Fig. 5. In condition A, the long return sweep often requires an additional fixation (fixation 2 above) to position the eye for reading the next line. In condition B, the return sweep is most often performed with a single saccade. Detected fixations are shown with small circles, interconnected by the raw gaze.

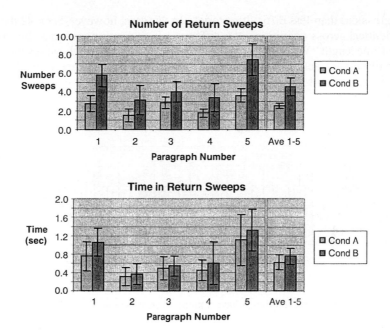

Fig. 6. Condition B has more return sweeps than A (top chart), and requires more total processing time from the subjects (bottom)

Fig. 4 for condition A. (Bouma [2] also noticed "correction saccades" after "line saccades" in his eye tracking studies.) For the first five paragraphs in the test web page, the average sweep times are 0.25 sec for condition A and 0.16 sec for condition B.

4.4 Time in Return Sweeps

For condition B, the advantage of shorter return sweeps is outweighed by their increased number. While return sweeps require less time in condition B, the shorter paragraph formatting creates more of them for the reader to process. In Fig. 6 (top), we show the number of return sweeps detected for the first five paragraphs in the text; the numbers correlate well with the number of lines in each paragraph. Fig. 6 (bottom) shows the average time in return sweeps for conditions A and B, which is basically the product of the number of sweeps with the mean sweep time. Because subjects in condition A spend less time in return sweeps but have a lower speed, they must have some other speed handicap. This turns out to be increased regressions.

4.5 Regressions

As shown in Fig. 7, the subjects in condition A have a higher rate of regressions. Averaged over the first five paragraphs, the regression rate under condition A is 0.54 reg/sec, while it is only 0.39 reg/sec for condition B. The regression rate is computed by dividing the total number of regressions by $T2$, the total elapsed time. Regressions are used as a cue for reading difficulty – more difficult reading material will generate more regressions than less difficult material. In this case, however, because the material is identical across conditions, the difference in regression rate must be from the increased line length. We hypothesize that the increased line length causes the eyes to occasionally make tracking mistakes, which requires backing up and re-reading. The increase in regressions for the longer line length condition is in agreement with Paterson and Tinker [9].

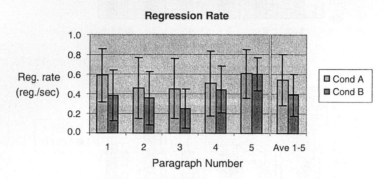

Fig. 7. Subjects in condition A have a higher regression rate than condition B

4.6 Retention

Subjects in condition B have better retention than condition A on a post test of the URL material. After reading the web page on culture shock, the subjects are given a 3-question multiple-choice test on the material. On average, subjects in condition A get 1.25 questions correct, while those in condition B score an average of 1.75 correct. This difference is even more interesting in light of the fact that condition A subjects spend more total time reading the material than condition B. Given this observation, another relevant statistic is the score divided by elapsed time with the material – getting a high score using less time is ideal. After normalizing each subject's score by $T2$, the elapsed time, we get an average normalized score of 0.081 points/sec for condition A and 0.191 points/sec for condition B. Using this time-normalized metric, there is a significant difference between the two conditions, $F(1, 14) = 6.798$, $p = .0207$.

5 Discussion

The experiment described here presents some basic tradeoffs in choosing paragraph width. Making the paragraph width wider reduces the number of return sweeps required for reading, but increases regressions and decreases retention. While the experiment presented here used two specific paragraph widths for testing, paragraph width can be finely tuned. It would be interesting to repeat the histogram analysis of return sweeps for a variety of widths to see when the auxiliary "positioning" fixation begins to appear as a function of width. This would suggest choosing a width just below this threshold.

Relative to the earlier work of Paterson and Tinker [9], our work is in agreement on (a) reading speed favoring shorter lines, and (b) increased regressions being recorded for longer lines. Moving beyond the results in [9], we showed that shorter line length tends to cause paragraph abandonment and hence less reading coverage. Also, a post-test of retention showed that the subjects performed better with shorter line length. Interestingly, with regards to reading speed, our results were more in alignment with the earlier work with print media as opposed to more recent work with online reading from monitors.

An interesting question arises as to why readers of the narrow widths did not continue reading as far to the end of the material as the readers of the longer widths. As noted, one possibility may be perception of a greater amount of material to be read in the tall columns. Another possibility may be that narrow-width text is associated with newspaper columns, which are almost universally written in the "inverted triangle" style. That is, newspaper stories put the most important information at the top of their column inches and become progressively less important as the column grows longer. Perhaps readers familiar with newspaper-style writing associated the narrow column widths to be written the same way, and thus concluded that the material near the end of the column was far less important to read. From a design perspective, important information should not be put in the second half of narrow-width paragraphs.

But perhaps the most important implication for message senders is that the shorter line lengths produced significantly greater retention. Instructional designers ought certainly to know that certain configurations of text provide a greater opportunity for material to be remembered, because learning is directly correlated with retention. The importance of this finding alone warrants further investigation of the implications of wide versus narrow column length web text.

References

1. Bernard, M., Fernandez, M., and Hull, S., The Effects of Line Length on Children and Adults' Online Reading Performance. *Usability News*, 4:2 (2002).
2. Bouma, H. Visual Reading Processes and the Quality of Text Displays. In *Ergonomic Aspects of Visual Display Terminals*, E. Grandjean and E. Vigliani, Eds. (1980), 101-114.
3. Duchnicky, R.L. and Kolers, P.A. Readability of Text Scrolled on Visual Display Terminals as a Function of Window Size. *Human Factors*, 25:6 (1983), 683-692.
4. Dyson, M.C. and Kipping, G.J. The Effects of Line Length and Method of Movement on Patterns of Reading from Screen. *Visible Language*, 32:2 (1998), 150-181.
5. McMullin, J., Varnhagen, C., Heng, P., and Apedoe, X. Effects of Surrounding Information and Line Length on Text Comprehension from the Web. *Canadian Journal of Learning and Technology*, 28:1 (2002).
6. Tinker, M.A. and Patterson, D.G. Studies of Typographical Factors Influencing Speed of Reading: Length of Line. *Journal of Applied Psychology*, 13:3 (1929), 205-219.
7. Rayner, K. and Pollatsek, A. The Psychology of Reading. Lawrence Erlbaum Associates, Hillsdale, NJ (1989)
8. Tinker, M. Legibility of Print. Iowa State University Press, Ames, Iowa (1963)
9. Paterson, D. and Tinker, M. Influence of Line Width on Eye Movements, *Journal of Experimental Psychology*, vol 27, pp. 572-577 (1940)

10. Beymer, D. and Russell, D. WebGazeAnalyzer: A System for Capturing and Analyzing Web Reading Behavior Using Eye Gaze. In *CHI 2005 Extended Abstracts*, ACM Press, pp. 1913-1916 (2005)
11. Tobii 1750 Eye-Tracker, Tobii Technology, http://www.tobii.se, April, 2005.
12. Li, S.F., Spiteri, M.S., Bates, J., and Hopper, A., Capturing and Indexing Computer-based Activities with Virtual Network Computing. ACM Symposium on Applied Computing, 601-603 (2000).
13. Salvucci, D.D. and Goldberg, J.H. Identifying Fixations and Saccades in Eye-Tracking Protocols. *Proc. of the Symposium on Eye Tracking Research & Applications* (ETRA), 2000.
14. Dyson, M. and Haselgrove, M. The Influence of Reading Speed and Line Length on the Effectiveness of Reading from Screen. *Int. J. Human-Computer Studies*, vol 54, pp. 585-612 (2001)

Combining Eye Tracking and Conventional Techniques for Indications of User-Adaptability

Ekaterini Tzanidou[1], Marian Petre[1], Shailey Minocha[1], and Andrew Grayson[2]

[1] Department of Computing, The Open University, Walton Hall,
Milton Keynes MK7 6AA, UK
{e.tzanidou, m.petre, s.minocha}@open.ac.uk
[2] Division of Psychology, Nottingham Trent University, Burton Street,
Nottingham, NG1 4BU, UK
andy.grayson@ntu.ac.uk

Abstract. We have captured and analysed users' eye movements by means of an eye-tracking device to re-visit existing web design guidelines. The study reported here examines how quickly users adapt to an unfamiliar design layout and, in particular, how quickly they adjust their expectations of where to look for a given target link during repeated exposures to a new layout. Eye movement-based metrics such as time to target fixation, location of first fixation and scan path (sequence of fixations) were applied to capture users' eye movements. These metrics were then applied to analyse the effects of repeated exposures and of design layouts of websites. More exposures led to decreased time to target fixation, indicating that *user-adaptation* occurred. The visual characteristics of the target link also influenced visual search behaviour. Qualitative complementary data such as the users' frequency and purpose of internet usage, users' expectations about the target link added value to the eye-movement data.

1 Introduction

As Jones and Dumais [21] stated it *"it is not enough to know what we are looking for, we must also know where to look for it"* (pg.43). This is evident when users encounter web pages where they are often presented with an overwhelming amount of information, with a mix of visual and textual design elements clamouring for attention. Thus, understanding the factors that influence user's visual search behaviour on the user interface is important so as to design usable user interfaces.

Existing design guidelines embody assumptions that visual search behaviour is shaped by expectations, hence they suggest designing user interfaces that conform to conventions. Nielsen et al. [26] underlines the importance of maintaining consistency with other websites and pages. *"All web pages are much the same from the user's perspective, they share interaction techniques, they are downloaded (slowly) from the internet, and they have relatively similar layouts. Those similarities are in fact good because they allow users a measure of transfer of skill from one site to the next. Users complain bitterly when a site doesn't try to use navigation from the majority of other sites"* (pg. 189). But how do users learn conventions and develop expectations? Ehret

M.F. Costabile and F. Paternò (Eds.): INTERACT 2005, LNCS 3585, pp. 753–766, 2005.
© IFIP International Federation for Information Processing 2005

[5] suggests that when locations of design elements remain constant, performance improves over exposures as users learn placements of design elements and focus/limit the scope of their visual search behaviour. The consistent placement of design elements influences visual search.

But a recent eye tracking study by McCarthy et al. [25] investigated the impact of changing the placement of design elements and how users performed when viewing the element in unexpected placements. The authors found that following conventions with other websites did not matter, as users quickly adapted to design layouts with unexpected placement of design elements.

So is it important to follow consistency with other websites or is it acceptable to place design elements in non-consistent locations on the user interface? The study reported in this paper used an eye tracking device to capture users' eye movements and investigated how quickly users adapt to different placements of a design element over repeated exposures. Specifically, the study focused on one design element, the 'About Us' link on a website, and addressed the following questions:

Q1: Do users adapt their expectations of where to look for when presented with repeated exposures of the 'About Us' link in a consistent, but unconventional, position?

Q2: Do users adapt quickly to alternative design layouts such as finding the 'About Us' link in an unconventional position?

Q3: Where do users look first, after the repeated exposures, on pages that do not contain any 'About Us' link?

Previous research as conducted by McCarthy et al. [25] had investigated whether placing design elements, such as menu items, in unexpected positions has an impact on visual search behaviour in terms of search performance. Variations of simple and complex web pages presented menu items in 3 different locations (top, left, right) for 3 different tasks. Each type of web page received three page visits. We have applied a different experiment design: consistent placement of a design element over repeated exposures but placed the design element at an unconventional position (that is, not as per the guidelines) to explore user adaptation. Moreover users were also presented with web pages that didn't contain the 'target' design element (About Us link) in order to explore users' expectations of its location. Complementing eye movement data and conventional techniques, such as self-reports of expectations and preferences as elicited from pre- and post-session questions, has enabled a better understanding and interpretation of the eye-movement data. User-adaptation occurred over repeated exposures of the web pages and a change in user's expectations was detected by where the users looked for the target link on web pages on which the target link was absent.

1.1 Visual Search Behaviour

Theories of visual search, as reported by Horowitz and Wolfe [17], conclude that visual search relies on accumulating information about the identity of design elements over time. This knowledge enables designers to structure the user interface effectively and influence the user's visual search behaviour. Post-cognitive modelling research, as cited in [17], has demonstrated that people use anticipatory location information to guide visual search, and that visual features sometimes guide the visual search (i.e., expectations and salience) [18]. It is through visual search primarily that users locate the content and control for their web-based tasks. Despite extensive research into visual search behaviour in disciplines such as psychology, recent research in HCI [15, 18] has underlined the importance of developing a unified understanding of the visual search in HCI. Visual search behaviour on websites is influenced by expectations about what is being looked for and where it might be located. Pirolli and Card [30] talks about the design layout of the display as a bottom-up influence and expectations as a top-down influence. Bottom–up processing refers to the design elements influencing the visual scene itself, such as presentation format, colour, position, whereas top-down processing refers to the expectations the users develop such as the cognitive processes when viewing a scene. The interactions between top-down and bottom-up influences is identified as *Information Scent* or *Information Foraging* [30]. Unless the design elements such as colour, menu items, graphs (bottom–up) are looked at, there is no 'scent', and therefore there is no basis for selection.

2 Eye Tracking to Assess Usability

Conventional usability evaluation techniques such as user-observations, think-aloud protocols, questionnaires and interviews focus more on the activities of user performance rather than understanding the cognitive processes of the users [12]. Therefore, aspects of task performance such as ease of navigation, efficiency of selecting the 'right' menu item, or time taken to complete a task can be captured but the inferences of cognitive processes are more difficult to explain. Eye tracking studies in cognitive psychology have established that eye movements give an insight into the users' cognitive processes (e.g. [23]). Eye movements in reading and information processing have been studied by Rayner and Pollatsek [31] and they concluded that eye movements indicate how easy or difficult it is to process a display. The use of eye tracking in HCI is not a new concept, as Jacob and Karn [20] have illustrated in their recent review of eye tracking studies. In 1954, Fitts [7] was the first to conduct a systematic eye tracking study of pilots using cockpit controls and instruments. In recent years eye tracking devices have become more affordable, and the technology has improved, enabling an increasing number of HCI researchers to engage in eye tracking studies [4]. In general eye tracking data is used to support recommendations for how a user interface should be designed for usability, rather than provide a broad assessment of the interface's overall usability [12].

Previous research [3, 9, 10, 32] has established that specific design elements influence eye movements in a predictable way, and they demonstrate that eye tracking metrics are sensitive enough to detect them. The authors have compared eye tracking data with performance times, completion rates, and accuracy of task responses. For example, Goldberg and Kotval [10] manipulated items' grouping labelling on the tool bars of several versions of a simulated drawing package which were shown to interface designers for their (subjective) usability ratings. The eye tracking data as captured from real users was then correlated with the designers' subjective ratings. Eye tracking metrics such as duration of fixations, saccadic amplitude and fixation/saccade ratio were not found to be useful in predicting the differences in usability ratings. Metrics such as scan path length, number of fixations, and number of saccades were found to be more sensitive in highlighting the differences in the usability ratings.

The effectiveness of eye movement-based metrics has been explored to suggest ways of applying them in order to answer specific research questions regarding visual search behaviour. For example, Fitts et al. [8] distinguish between frequency and duration of fixations with duration reflecting difficulty of information extraction and frequency reflecting the importance of that area of the interface.

Eye tracking has been applied in HCI in two ways: as a real-time input device and its use as a usability evaluation technique [20]. In the study reported in this paper, eye tracking has been applied for usability evaluation of websites.

2.1 Eye Tracking Studies of Websites

Granka et al. [13] have reported that only a small number of studies have been conducted on eye movement behaviour on web pages. Visual preferences of text and images have been explored by two studies [6, 24]. Ellis et al. [6] demonstrated that users completed tasks more quickly and easily on text-based screens, although they preferred image-based screens. The Stanford Poynter Project study [24] examined how users read on-line and off-line news; they found that text was viewed more than images for readers who read on-line news, whereas the opposite occurred for readers who read off-line news.

Two studies [11, 22] have examined the navigational styles on user interfaces of web pages. Josephson and Holmes [22] examined users' scan paths on different kinds of images widely used on the internet to test Norton and Stark's scan path theory and identified strong similarities among scan paths, suggesting that different users' eye movements may follow a 'habitually preferred path'. Goldberg et al. [11] captured navigational styles of users freely navigating web portal pages. They concluded that headers of links are not always viewed before the main body. This research went on to develop specific design recommendations for portal pages and suggest design changes based on eye movement data.

The studies discussed above explored navigational styles that users apply on both offline and online channels but these studies did not investigate the factors that influence the navigation styles. More recent studies [e.g. 27, 29] have aimed to understand the factors that influence visual search behaviour. Pan et al. [29] investigated some of these factors, such as individual differences, design characteristics of the web pages, the order in which web pages are viewed and different tasks that were given to the users to complete. Gender and viewing order were found to be the key determinants of visual search behaviour. Men applied different scan paths from women and the order in which the stimuli were presented influenced the scan paths as well.

The Stanford Poynter Project [27] extended their previous work [24] on how users read news websites. They applied a more methodological approach in their latter study. Some of the key points of their latest study [27] suggest that users navigate more on the upper part of news websites rather than left or right of the page. The size of text was found to be influential in terms of encouraging focused viewing behaviour; smaller text drew more fixations while larger sizes promoted lighter scanning. The users fixated more on headlines with large text rather than headlines with small text.

2.2 Eye Movement–Based Metrics and Terminology

As there is no standard way of defining a single fixation operationally, and there are different psychological theories about the relationship between eye movements and cognitive processes [16]; there is a need to ensure a common understanding of the use of terms and definitions related to eye-tracking in the context they are used. The following eye movement-based metrics were applied in our study being reported here: i) *Time to target fixation*: the time users need to fixate on the target link gives a basis of performance measurement when a specific search target exists. Since we are interested in investigating how quickly or slowly the target link is fixated, the time to target fixation is an indication of user performance. The target link in our study is the 'About Us' link; ii) *Location of fixation*: the location of fixations is used as an indicator of where users look on a web page to locate the target link; iii) *Initial gaze*: initial gaze measures the user's first gaze during the first 50 milliseconds of the web page appearing on the screen in order to examine where users expect to find the target link; iv) *Entry point*: entry point measures the user's first fixation within the first 250 milliseconds of the web page appearing on the screen in order to examine which design elements first draw user's visual attention; v) *Scan path*: the sequence of fixations indicates the order in which the user looked at areas on the web page.

3 Method

The eye tracking study reported here collected four types of data: i) *A background questionnaire* to elicit the participants' internet experience and typical frequency of usage; ii) *Pre-session questions* to elicit expectations about the target link (About Us link); iii) *Eye tracking data* to measure visual search behaviour; and iv) *Post-session questions* to address perceptions and preferences about the About Us link.

3.1 Experiment Design

A counterbalanced experiment design [2] was applied varying the ten exposures of web pages to eliminate possible order effects. Ten web pages of E-Commerce sites were selected and amended so that they would appear in each of the three different exposure styles. So, for example, each web page was amended in order to have: i) The 'About Us' link at the bottom of the page, ii) The 'About Us' link at the top of the page, and iii) No 'About Us' link. The description of each exposure and purpose is presented in Table 1.

The study had two sets of hypotheses: The *first set* addressed the effect of the consistent placement of the target link (About Us link) for exposures 2 to 7 and predicted that the placement of the target link at the bottom of the page over six repeated exposures would result in the participants' decrease in the time to target fixation and also change in participant's expectations of where to find the target link.

The *second set* examined the effect of the alternative placement of the target link (About Us link) and predicted that the placement of the target link at the top of the page in Exposure 8 would result in quick adaptation to an unexpected design layout. Specifically we anticipated that the two first sets of hypotheses will be evidenced by shorter times to target fixation, modifications of scan patterns, change of location of first fixations and self-report of preferences and expectations.

Table 1. Description and purpose of exposures

Exposures	Description	Purpose
Exposure 1	Did not include the 'About Us' link	To explore users' expectations of where to find the 'About Us' link before the repeated exposure session
Exposure 2-7	Six repeated exposures where the 'About Us' link appeared at the bottom of the page	To examine the effect of consistent design element placement on visual search behaviour.
Exposure 8	The 'About Us' link appeared at the top of the page	To capture the users' visual reactions when introduced to an alternative design layout after being presented with the repeated exposures in which the 'About Us' link appeared at the bottom of the page
Exposure 9	The 'About Us' link appeared at the bottom of the page again	To assess persistence of any affect of repeated exposures on visual search behaviour
Exposure 10	Did not include the 'About Us' link	To explore users' expectations where to find the 'About Us' link after the repeated exposure session

3.2 Participants

Ten volunteers (5 male and 5 female) with age range of 22-56 from the staff and postgraduate student population of the Open University participated in this study. Five participants were regular (using the internet 2-3 times per day) internet users and five participants were frequent (using the internet throughout the day as part of their job) internet users. None of the participants had viewed the homepages used in the study prior to their participation.

3.3 Stimuli and Equipment

Prior to the selection of the stimuli, a survey was conducted to identify the position of the 'About Us' link on homepages. Fifty European and fifty US E-Commerce sites were chosen on the basis of their sales. 80% of the homepages placed the 'About Us' link on the top of the page as a global navigation its position in the navigation bar varied on different websites. On the basis of this survey, we concluded that the convention is to place the 'About Us' link at the top of the page. This led to the assumption that Web users will be used to finding the 'About Us' link on the top of the page or at least expect to find it around that position based on their previous experiences. Therefore, the position of the target link in the repeated exposures session (exposures 2-7) was on the bottom of the page.

Ten UK E-Commerce homepages were selected as stimuli for this study: Cover4students www.cover4students.com (campus insurance), Hatton Garden Online www.hattongardenonline.com (jewellery), Diamond Daisy www.diamonddaisy.com (jewellery), Travelodge www.travelodge.co.uk (accommodation), Travel Bag www.travelbag.co.uk (travel), Train Line www.thetrainline.com (travel), Saga Holidays www.sagaholidays.com (holidays), Hotel net www.hotelnet.co.uk (accommodation), Past Times www.past-times.co.uk (gifts),To Book www.tobook.com (accommodation). The criteria for choosing homepages was that pages should have: i) a design layout that fits within the computer screen (17 inches flat screen with a resolution of 1024 by 768 pixels) without requiring scrolling; and ii) having both a top- and bottom-page navigation bar where the 'About Us' link could appear.

The pixel size of the target design element 'About Us' along with its presentation format (emboldening) and position within navigation bar slightly varied across homepages. For example, the Past Times homepage had the three navigation bars at the bottom of the page and the 'About Us' link appeared in the middle one.

Eye movements were recorded using an ASL (Applied Science Technologies) 504 eye tracking remote pan-tilt camera [1] capturing eye movement data at a sample rate of 60Hz. The presentation of the stimuli was controlled by means of the Gaze Tracker™ software and presented on the screen viewed by participants from a distance of 55 cm from the screen. The Gaze Tracker™ software also records the eye-movements and enables viewing the data and output statistics based on researcher-definable regions of interest on the web page (e.g. A-F in Figure 2).

3.4 Procedure

The duration of a session including the briefing and calibration process was approximately thirty minutes. The session started by the researcher giving an introduction of the eye tracking equipment and the study to the participant. The participant completed a consent form and a background questionnaire. The questionnaire captured age, gender, previous internet experience, and frequency and purpose of internet use. The participant was asked the following questions regarding the 'About Us' link: *Where do you look when you want to find information regarding the company? Where do you prefer to find it?* These questions were aimed to collect information about the user's expectations and preferences regarding the placement of the 'About Us' link before the eye-tracking session.

The researcher then calibrated the eye tracking camera for the participant. The participant was asked to look at each web page and find the 'About Us' link. The participant was asked to say aloud where on the interface they found the 'About Us' link in order to indicate that the task had been completed, so that the researcher could press the 'enter' key on the keyboard for the next page to appear. There was no time limit for the task so as to encourage a natural navigation of the web page. To avoid the researcher's reaction times influencing the data, the eye movement data were used as a measure of the task completion times. After the eye tracking session, the participants were asked: '*Where would you like to find the 'About Us' link? What do you think about the web pages you just saw? Was it easy to find the 'About Us' link'?* These questions aimed to collect information about the user's perceptions and preferences regarding the 'About Us' link after the repeated exposures session.

4 Results

4.1 Repeated Exposures Effect

The study's first question aimed to examine whether users adapt their expectations of where to look when presented with repeated exposures of the 'About Us' link at the bottom of the page (an unconventional position). The qualitative data from the pre- and post-session questions along with eye tracking measures such as time to target fixation were analysed. The descriptive statistics of the scores to target fixation across repeated exposures are shown in Table 2. There is a difference between the sum of time to target fixation for the first of the repeated exposures (exposure 2) *179.10* and the last of the repeated exposures (exposure 7) *38.70*.

Table 2. Descriptive statistics of sums of time to target fixation for repeated exposures in milliseconds

Exposures	N	Minimum	Maximum	Sum	Mean	Std. Deviation
Exposure 2	10	3.52	38.86	*179.10*	*17.90*	11.41
Exposure 3	10	1.44	44.97	120.16	12.01	13.11
Exposure 4	10	0.72	17.98	64.63	6.46	5.65
Exposure 5	10	1.53	31.64	83.26	8.32	9.99
Exposure 6	10	1.20	41.13	122.62	12.26	14.09
Exposure 7	10	0.91	6.80	*38.70*	*3.86*	1.61
Exposure 8	10	2.53	16.16	58.48	5.84	3.99
Exposure 9	10	1.80	22.86	91	9.09	6.79

A non-parametric Trend test [28] was applied to test for a trend of learning where to look when presented with a sequence of six repeated exposures of homepages where the 'About Us' link appears on the bottom of the page.

A Page's L trend test [28] on the ranked scores of time to target fixation for the repeated exposures revealed a significant trend across exposures: L (10, 6) =792, $p<0.05$. A trend of time to target fixation decreases as the number of exposures increases is shown in Figure 1.

The eye tracking measures were complemented by the qualitative data as retrieved from the pre- and post–session questions. When the participants were asked before the eye tracking session where they expected to find the 'About Us' link they answered 'on top of the page' or it doesn't matter as long as they can see it. But, when the participants were asked after the eye tracking session where would they like to find the 'About Us' link they answered 'on the bottom of the page'. In addition to the eye tracking data where a trend of adaptation was found as exposures increased, the modification in answers from the pre- and post-session questions suggests an influence of change in preferences of where the 'About Us' link is expected to appear.

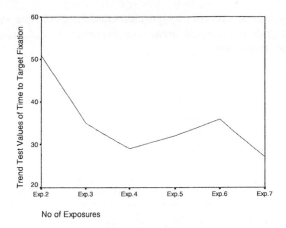

Fig. 1. Trend Test of time to target fixation across exposures

4.1 Alternative Design Layout Effect

The study's second question aimed to examine if users adapt quickly to alternative design layouts such as finding the 'About Us' link in an unconventional position.

A two-tailed paired t-test was used to establish whether there were significant differences between the time to target fixation before the repeated exposures (About Us link at the bottom of the page) and after repeated exposures (About Us link at top of the page) at the 5% alpha level of confidence. There is evidence that the users found the target link quicker when the 'About Us' link was placed at the top of the page even after having seen it on the bottom of the page in the repeated exposures session as t (9) = 3.351, p < .05.

After transforming the raw scores using a two related samples Wilcoxon test, the distributions between the time to target fixation after the repeated exposures (About Us link at top of the page) and after the alternative exposure (About Us link at bottom of the page again) were compared at the 5% alpha level of confidence. Despite the significance difference found when the About Us link is presented on the top of the page, when it is then presented again at the bottom of the page there is a significant difference as t (9) = 1.98, p < .05.

The results indicate that when placing the 'About Us' link on the top of the page, users find it quicker than when placing it at the bottom of the page which might be the effect of their previous experiences as indicated in their self-reports and also as per the normal conventions of the About Us link's placement that we found in our survey of leading E-Commerce sites. But when presented with the 'About Us' link at the bottom of the page again after the repeated exposure a second expectation has been developed possibly caused by the consistent placement of the 'About Us' link on the bottom of the page over the repeated exposures.

4.2 Before and After Repeated Exposures Effect

Granka et al. [14] used a location grid to analyse eye movements in relation to position on the user interface. This enabled the classification of initial expectations and visual attraction to specific design elements. Similarly our study reported here used a location grid of six equal areas (see Figure 2) to determine the locations of 'initial gaze' and 'entry points'.

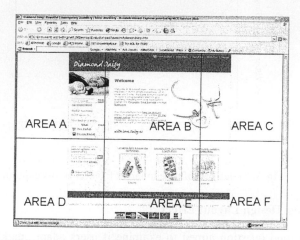

Fig. 2. Sample location grid to assess effect of design element location

The location of 'initial gaze' for each participant was measured during the first 50 milliseconds of the homepage appearing on the screen to determine where the participant expected to find the 'About Us' link. 'Initial gaze' for all participants was always in areas A or B (i.e. the top left or top middle of the screen) for both exposures 1 and 10. None of the 'initial gazes' focused on the right side or bottom of the screen (areas C, D, E, F in Figure 2). This is more of an indication of similar visual search strategies of initial gazes starting from the upper part of the page rather than any indication of user-adaptation across exposures. The very small amount of time (50 milliseconds) during which 'initial gazes' where measured might not have allowed the observation of any possible scan path modification. Therefore, the location of the 'entry point' for each participant was measured during the first 250 milliseconds of the homepage appearing on the screen to indicate where the participant first fixated. The 'entry points' were not consistent across participants and varied from homepage to homepage. Nevertheless none of the 'entry points' were in the right side of the screen (areas C and F in Figure 2). This might be influenced by the visual attraction of specific design elements rather than purely consistent placement of the 'About Us' link.

By comparing the users' scan paths in Exposure 1 and Exposure 10, five users where found to have modified their scan patterns from the first to the last exposure after being presented with the repeated exposures session. They started their scan paths in the upper area of the screen (areas A and B) whereas after the repeated exposures session they started their scan paths in the lower part of the screen (areas D and E) suggesting user-adaptation after finding the 'About Us' link at the bottom of the page. When looking at the profile of these five users we found that they were frequent internet users (regularly throughout the day) and used the internet as part of their everyday work activities suggesting that they were highly skilled internet users which might explain their quick adaptation to consistent placement of specific design elements such as the 'About Us' link. Despite a trend of user-adaptation during the repeated exposures session was found, the variance of scores of time to target fixation lead to the examination of the effect specific design characteristics of the target link.

4.3 Effect of Design Characteristics

Despite a trend of decrease in time to target fixation as exposures increased the variance of scores to target fixation lead to the examination of the effects of particular design characteristics of the target design element.

Table 3. Descriptive statistics of sums of time to target fixation for homepages regardless exposure in milliseconds

Web Pages	N	Minimum	Maximum	Sum	Mean	Std. Deviation
Cover4students	10	1.20	17.78	56.30	7.03	4.94
Hatton	10	1.88	32.80	99.19	12.39	12.00
Past-times	10	2.95	44.97	*190.22*	23.77	17.50
To book	10	2.23	22.86	56.45	7.05	7.25
Travel bag	10	1.53	13.94	46.77	5.84	4.15
Diamond	10	3.49	22.86	84.77	10.59	6.30
Hotel net	10	1.80	17.86	49.80	6.22	5.99
Saga	10	0.91	17.98	54.57	6.82	6.30
Train line	10	1.44	5.21	*27.23*	3.40	1.13
Travelodge	10	0.72	26.38	88.34	11.04	8.88

It is apparent that certain web pages required more time for the 'About Us' link to be identified. This was measured for each homepage, regardless of its place in the exposure order (Table 3). The Past Times homepage had the highest scores for the time to target fixation *190.22*, whereas the Train line homepage *27.23* had the lowest scores for the time to target fixation.

When considering the possible effect of specific visual characteristics design elements, three characteristics were explored: a) pixel size, b) text appearing bold or not, and c) the position of the 'About Us' link within the navigation bar.

The pixel size of the target design element 'About Us' link was measured using JRuler Pro [19]. A relationship between time to target fixation and pixel size was found, but it was not significantly correlated ($r = -.189$, $p > 0.05$). So, small size in pixels did not always lead to increased time to target fixation.

When the 'About Us' link did not appear in bold or distinctive colour (the formatting effects used in the example websites), the time to target fixation increased, implying that without distinctive formatting the target was more difficult to locate. The position of the 'About Us' link within the navigation bar did not appear to influence the time to target fixation. However, when more than one navigation bar appeared on the bottom of the screen, the time to target fixation increased.

5 Conclusions

5.1 User-Adaptation

When placing the target link in a consistent position over a series of exposures, the results show that users adapt to consistent placement of the target link and improve their visual search performance. A trend was found of more exposures leading to decreased time to target fixation. Eye movement data was complemented by self reports of change in expectations and preferences of where the target link was expected to be found. The reported results comply with previous research as conducted by Ehret [5] suggesting that users learn the locations of design elements over series of repeated exposures. On the contrary, McCarthy et al. [25] had found no evidence that performance improves when the target link is placed in expected positions. They found that users adapt quickly to unexpected design layouts.

When placing the About Us link at the top of the page as per the norm on most websites as shown by our survey, the results indicate that users' visual search performance is quicker than when placing the target link at the bottom of the page. It is assumed that primacy effects of the users' exposure to web pages might have influenced their visual search performance whereas influence of the repeated exposures develops as a secondary effect which was found to improve visual performance but does not override the effect from previous experiences.

5.2 Impact of Design Layout Characteristics

Distinctive formatting of design elements (e.g. emboldening and position within navigation bar) also influences users' visual search behaviour and shortens time to target fixation. However, this influence is secondary to the learning effects: the learning effects associated with consistency of placement of the design element over repeated exposures were observed regardless of the complexity and visual characteristics of the design elements.

5.3 Utility of Results for Designers and Researchers

This study should encourage designers to aim for consistency not only *within* a website but also consistency *across* websites. However, just placing design elements in similar positions on the user interface within or across a website does not guarantee efficient visual search. The presentation format of the design element influences user visual search behaviour as well. The results of the reported study indicated that design elements such as the 'About Us' link are not only located more quickly when presented in a consistent position over exposures, but also when they are presented in a distinctive format. For researchers the study demonstrates the usefulness of applying eye tracking as a usability evaluation technique for user interface designs. Although the reported study is limited to visual search of homepages, the methodology can be applied to other web pages and to a wide range of tasks. In addition, it shows how eye movement data can be triangulated with data from other evaluation techniques, including qualitative elicitation, to enrich the study's outcomes. Eye tracking contributes to design knowledge and evaluation by providing detailed capture of user interaction behaviour.

Acknowledgments

The research in this paper is being supported by an EPSRC Research Studentship. Our thanks to Dr. Alvaro Faria (Open University, UK), Professor Robert Jacob (Tufts University, US), Dr. Ewald Kaluscha (University of Klagenfurt, Austria), Dr. James A. Renshaw (Leeds Metropolitan University, UK) and, Mr. Jonathan P. SanDiego (Open University, UK) for their feedback and advice.

References

1. ASL (Applied Science Laboratories) Model 504. http://www.a-s-l.com/model504.htm last visited 29th April, 2005
2. Campbell, D. and Stanley, J. Experimental and Quasi- experimental designs for research on teaching. In Gage, N. (Eds.), Handbook of Research on teaching. Rand McNally Company, Chicago, (1963), 171-216
3. Cowen, L., Ball, L., Delin, J. An eye movement analysis of web page usability. In Proc. of the BCS-HCI, (2002), 317-335
4. Dix, A., Finlay, J., Abowd, G. D., Beale, R. Human –Computer Interaction. Third edition, Prentice Hall, England, (2003)
5. Ehret, B., D. Learning where to look: location learning in graphical user interfaces. In Proc. of CHI (2002), 211-218
6. Ellis, S., et al. Windows to the soul? What eye movements tell us about software usability? In Proc. of the Usability Professionals' Association Conference (1998), 151-178
7. Fitts, P. M. The Information capacity of the human motor system in controlling the amplitude of movement. In Journal of experimental psychology, 47, (1954), 381-391
8. Fitts, P. M., Jones, R. E., and Milton, J. 1. Eye movements of aircraft pilots during instrument landing approaches. Aeronautical Engineering Review (1950), 9 (2), 24-29
9. Goldberg, J. and Kotval, P.X. Computer interface evaluation using eye movements: methods and constructs. International Journal of Industrial Ergonomics 24 (1999), 631-645
10. Goldberg, J. and Kotval, P.X. Eye movements and interface component grouping: an evaluation method. In Proc. of the human and ergonomics society 42nd annual meeting, (1998), 486-490
11. Goldberg, J. H., Stimson, M. J, Lewenstein, M., Scott, N. and Wichansky, A. M. Blink response, visual attention, and the www: Eye tracking in web search tasks: design implications. In Proc. of ETRA (2002), 51-58
12. Goldberg, J. H. and Winchansky, A. M. Eye tracking in usability evaluation. The Mind's Eyes: Cognitive and Applied Aspects of Eye Movements. R. R. J. Hyona, and H. Deubel. Oxford, Elsevier (2003), 493-516
13. Granka, L., Joachims, T., and Gay, G. Eye-Tracking Analysis of User Behaviour in WWW Search. In Proc. SIGIR (2004), 478-479
14. Granka, L., Hembrooke, H. Gay., and Feusner, M. Correlates of Visual Salience and Disconnect. Unpublished research report, Cornell University Human-Computer Interaction Lab (2004) http://www.stanford.edu/~granka/research.html last accessed 29th April, 2005
15. Halverson, T., and Hornof, A. J. Link colours guide a search. In Proc. of CHI, ACM Press, (2004), 1367-1370
16. Hansen, D., W. Committing eye tracking. PhD. Thesis, IT University of Copenhagen (2003)

17. Horowitz, T.S., and Wolfe, J.M. Visual Search Has No Memory. In Nature, 357, (1998) 575-577

18. Hornof, A. J. and Halverson, T. Cognitive strategies and eye movements for searching hierarchical computer displays. In Proc. CHI 2003, ACM Press, (2003), 249-256

19. JRuler Pro. http://www.spadixbd.com/jruler/ last accessed 2nd August, 2004

20. Jacob, R., and Karn, K. S. Eye Tracking in Human-Computer Interaction and Usability Research. The Mind's Eyes: Cognitive and Applied Aspects of Eye Movements. R. R. J. Hyona, and H. Deube (eds.). Oxford, Elsevier (2003), 572-605

21. Jones, W. P. and Dumais, S. T. The spatial metaphor for user interfaces: experimental tests of reference by location versus name. ACM transactions on Office Information systems, 4, 1 (1986), 42-63.

22. Josephson, S. and Holmes, M.E. Visual attention to repeated internet images: testing the scan path theory on the World Wide Web. In Proc. of ETRA., ACM (2002), 43-51.

23. Just, M. A., Carpenter P. A. Eye Fixations and Cognitive Processes. Cognitive Psychology 8, 9 (1976), 441-480

24. Lewenstein, M., Edwards, G., Tatr, D., and De Vigal, A. The Stanford Poynter Project. (2002). Available at http://www.poynter.org/eyetrack2000/ last accessed 29th April, 2005.

25. McCarthy, J. Sasse, M.A. & Riegelsberger, J. Could I have the menu please? An eye tracking study of design conventions. In Proc. of BCS-HCI, (2003), 401- 414

26. Nielsen, J., Molich, R., Snyder, C. and Farrell, S. E-Commerce User Experience. Nielsen Norman Group, Fremont, CA (2001)

27. Outing, S., and Ruel, L. Eye Track III, The Poynter Institute available at http://www.poynterextra.org/eyetrack2004/ (2004), last accessed 29th April, 2005

28. Page, E. B. Ordered hypotheses for multiple treatments: A significance test for linear ranks. Journal of the American Statistical Association, 58 (1963), 216-230

29. Pan, B., Hembrooke, H., Gay, G., Granka, L., Feusner, M., and Newman, J. The determinants of web page viewing behaviour: An eye tracking study. In S.N. Spencer (Ed.), Proc. of ETRA, ACM SIGGRAPH (2004), 147-154

30. Pirolli, P. and Card, S. Information foraging in information access environments. In Proc. of SIGCHI (1995), 51-58

31. Rayner, K. and Pollatsek, A. The Psychology of Reading. Lawrence Erlbaum Associates (1994)

32. Renshaw, J., A., Finlay. J. E., Tyfa D and Ward R D. Designing for visual influence: An eye tracking study of the usability of graphical management information. In Proc. of Interact (2003), 144-151

RealTourist – A Study of Augmenting Human-Human and Human-Computer Dialogue with Eye-Gaze Overlay

Pernilla Qvarfordt[1], David Beymer[2], and Shumin Zhai[2]

[1] Department of Computer and Information Science, Linköping University,
SE-581 83 Linköping, Sweden
perqv@ida.liu.se
[2] IBM Almaden Research Center, 650 Harry Rd, San Jose, CA 95120, USA
{zhai, beymer}@almaden.ibm.com

Abstract. We developed and studied an experimental system, RealTourist, which lets a user to plan a conference trip with the help of a remote tourist consultant who could view the tourist's eye-gaze superimposed onto a shared map. Data collected from the experiment were analyzed in conjunction with literature review on speech and eye-gaze patterns. This inspective, exploratory research identified various functions of gaze-overlay on shared spatial material including: accurate and direct display of partner's eye-gaze, implicit deictic referencing, interest detection, common focus and topic switching, increased redundancy and ambiguity reduction, and an increase of assurance, confidence, and understanding. This study serves two purposes. The first is to identify patterns that can serve as a basis for designing multimodal human-computer dialogue systems with eye-gaze locus as a contributing channel. The second is to investigate how computer-mediated communication can be supported by the display of the partner's eye-gaze.

1 Introduction

In face-to-face conversation, much can be felt from the conversational partners' eye-gaze—whether they are interested or bored, attentive or preoccupied, engaged or unmindful, in doubt or in agreement, wanting to continue or trying to finish the conversation. Indeed, research has confirmed that eye-gaze plays an important role in face-to-face conversation. It enables us to assess a conversational partner's under-standing, what he or she is looking at, and his or her feelings [2].

In this paper we present the design and study of RealTourist, an experimental on-line tourist information service. RealTourist allows a tourist to consult a remote tourist consultant with shared visual information on computer screens. In addition, the system overlays the tourist's gaze locus onto the tourist consultant's view of the shared workspace (see Fig. 1). By superimposing eye-gaze, a direct and accurate indication of the tourist's trajectory of visual attention on the visual spatial stimuli is displayed for the consultant. Potentially, such a paradigm gives rise to opportunities for better awareness of the partner's attention, more assurance that the partner is "on the same page", less communication ambiguity, and another channel for grounding—a fundamental characteristic and need in human conversation [7].

M.F. Costabile and F. Paternò (Eds.): INTERACT 2005, LNCS 3585, pp. 767–780, 2005.
© IFIP International Federation for Information Processing 2005

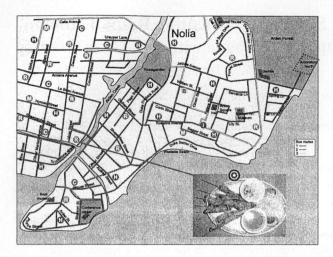

Fig. 1. The tourist consultant's view of the RealTourist system. The red and blue bull's-eye pattern above the photo is the tourist's gaze.

The purpose of this study is two-fold. First, we attempt to contribute to an empirical foundation of future multimodal human-computer interaction systems with eye-gaze as a critical channel of input. RealTourist can be considered a "Wizard of Oz" simulation of an intelligent multimodal system that can see the user's eye-gaze. Second (and compatible with the first purpose), this study contributes to the under - standing of RealTourist as a paradigm of computer mediated human-human communication system augmented with eye-gaze overlay. Given the exploratory nature of this work, our research methodology is a combination of system development, literature analysis and qualitative empirical study.

2   Real Tourist – An Experimental System

RealTourist has two views, one for the tourist and one for the tourist consultant. The tourist could talk to the tourist consultant by voice and see a map of a city on an 18" 1024 x 768 pixel TFT display integrated with a Tobii ET-17 eye-tracker (Fig. 2). The

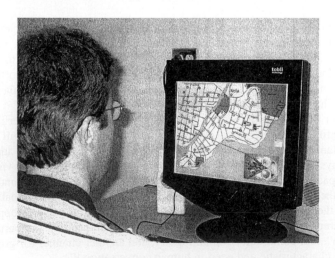

Fig. 2. The "tourist" side of the RealTourist system

eye tracker operated at 30 Hz and its output was sent to the tourist consultant's computer. The tourist consultant's computer ran an application, TGuide, which displayed the interactive map of the city with the tourist's eye-gaze overlaid on the map. The map, driven by the tourist consultant, was shared on the tourist's side. With TGuide the consultant could access tourist information of the city through pull down menus and control a photo display of places such as a restaurant or a museum (Fig. 1). The two computers were connected by local area network (TCP/IP). RealTourist was developed in a combination of Macromedia Director and C++.

The tourist consultant could see the tourist's eye-gaze on the map as a multi-colored dot. We found that superimposing instantaneous eye-gaze was too jittery and hard to follow. A simple recursive filter, which made the eye-gaze location subjectively easier to perceive, was adopted:

$$y(i) = 0.1x(i) + 0.9y(i-1) \; . \tag{1}$$

where $y(i)$ was the current displayed 2D position of the eye-gaze; $x(i)$ was the current measured gaze position, and $y(i-1)$ was the past (last sample) location.

Tourist information and maps of two imaginary cities, Vapour Bay and Nolia, were created. Each city had a number of hotels (13), restaurants (12), attractions (9), nightclubs (5) and movie theaters (3). Each hotel, restaurant, attraction and nightclub had a small body of information text. In addition, general information about transportation and tourism were made available to the tourist consultant via the TGuide pull down menu.

When the tourist consultant and tourists talked about a place, the tourist consultant could show a photo of it on the tourist's map. The photo had a line connecting to the location of the places in the map (Fig. 1).

3 Related Work and Research Implications

There is a rich body of literature that bears relevance to the current work. For the sake of brevity, in this section we only review work in HCI and CSCW that sets the general background of this study. We will review the literature in the broader cognitive sciences later when discussing our empirical findings.

Researchers have long explored using eye-gaze both as alternative computer input methods and for computer mediated communication. Eye-gaze as a modality for human-computer interaction has primarily been explored in the tradition of direct manipulation interfaces in which eye-gaze is used as a pointing device, either explicitly [13, 26] or implicitly [28, 29]. In multimodal interaction, eye-gaze has either been used for the purpose of disambiguation [23, 30], or as a complement to the speech channel [15]. We are interested in eye-gaze as a general channel in multimodal human-machine dialogue system beyond the function of pointing. Given the fundamental ambiguity in natural language [27], developing human-computer dialogue system is very challenging. Of particular difficulty is for computer systems to take initiative relevant to the user's need and interest in conversation. "Knowing" where the user is looking at on its "face" (the interface), a computer system should have more contextual clues on what topics to start and carry a dialogue. In order to develop multimodal dialogue systems with eye-gaze as a contributing channel, we have to understand how eye-gaze patterns are related to discourse in human-human communication.

The benefit of seeing a communication partner's eye-gaze has motivated many well known CSCW design solutions. For example, Buxton & Moran [6] used half-silvered mirror to optically align camera with video screen to enable eye contact ("video tunnelling"). Vertegaal used virtual faces (avatars) that could rotate depending "who is talking to whom" [25]. For tasks that involve visual spatial information, research suggests that a shared view of the workspace is more important than a view of the partner's face /gaze [8, 16]. People tend to look more at the shared workspace than their communication partner [3]. With advances in technology it is possible to bring the view of the partner's face and the view of the shared work pace closer in location. For example by presenting graphical information on a "clear board" which superimposes the partner's image over common work surface in a video tunnel, Ishii and colleagues [12] made both the collaborator and drawings visible in the same visual space. Monk and Gale [18] have shown that the number of turns and numbers of words spoken decreased when the collaborators could see each other's gaze through this type of set-up, although no improvement on task completion time was found.

Instead of displaying partner's whole face, only displaying the eye-gaze is an interesting alternative. While not the focus of their research, Vertegaal [25] displayed all participants' tracked eye-gaze as light spots in a shared document view. As another example, Velichkovsky [24] conducted a pioneering study in which one party's eye-gaze was superimposed onto a computer puzzle game. Velichkovsky was interested in how joint attention may facilitate the performance of a team in which the expert gave suggestions to a novice on how to move the scattered parts around. Since such a puzzle game requires frequent deictic referencing, the improved team performance over voice-only condition is quite plausible.

The literature also indicates that communication (human-human or human-computer) is complex and plastic. In general simple measurements are not sensitive to experimental manipulation and do not give a good sense of what is going on. For example the impact of being able to see a partner's gaze is not easily measurable in task completion time (Ochsman and Chapanis [19]). When the conversational partners could not see each other, they compensated the lack of visual feedback from the partner's face with more verbal feedback [5, 10].

4 An Empirical Study

To observe how user's verbal and gaze behavior were related, we conducted an empirical study in which "tourists" talked with "tourist consultants" using the Real-Tourist system. With the tourist consultant's help and advice, the tourist was asked to plan a conference trip to two cities.

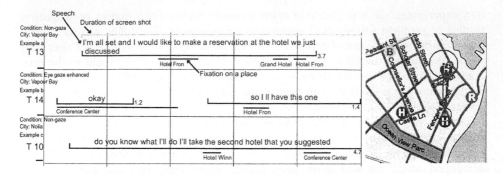

Fig. 3. Examples of the correspondence of eye-gaze and verbal deictic expressions, screen shot for example (a)

4.1 Experimental Design

Seventeen participants volunteered to act as tourists in the study; however, only twelve participants, one woman and eleven men, could be used in the study, since the eye tracker had problem tracking five of the participants. (The most recent model of eye-tracker from the same vendor has improved significantly.) Their ages ranged from 27 to 40, and the median age was 34. Two additional participants, one woman and one man, acted as tourist consultants. The tourist consultants had extensive training on the two imaginary cities used in the tasks and on the TGuide interface.

The specific subtasks for the tourist included finding a suitable hotel that was not too far away from the Conference Centre and within a price limit, a restaurant within a price limit and attractions to visit during the weekend. The tourists were also asked to consider their personal preferences in making his or her plans.

Working with one of the two tourist consultants, each tourist made trip plans for both cities, one with eye-gaze overlaid on the tourist consultant's screen and other without. The tourists did not know whether or how their eye-gaze was displayed before and during the experiment, but were informed after the test. The city and gaze conditions were balanced across participants.

4.2 Set-Up and Procedure

The tourists and the tourist consultant were located in the same room. They were separated by a physical divider so they could hear but not see each other.

The experimental session started with an introduction of the study and eye tracker calibration (Fig. 2). This was followed by the trip planning for the two cities. After completion, the tourist was asked to fill in a questionnaire. The consultant also filled a questionnaire and took notes after each tourist participant completed his or her test.

4.3 Data Collection and Analysis Method

Although the study used a classical experimental set-up, it did not follow the classical quantitative experimental paradigm that compares performance difference between two conditions. The study was inspective in nature, and can be regarded as a "qualitative experiment." It was closer in spirit to ethnographic field studies or inspective studies of problem solving skill analysis in chess playing. The focus was to observe and identify patterns and phenomena rather than performance, which is a necessary phase of scientific inquiry. As Simon argued, "Perhaps we need to add to the textbooks a chapter, or several chapters, describing how to observe the world intently, in the laboratory or outside it, with controls or without them, heavy with hypotheses or innocent of them". [22, p. 394]

During the experiment, the conversation between the tourist and the tourist consultant, the tourist's eye-gaze (in both conditions), and screen events were all recorded. After the experiment, the data were played back in real time by a toolkit we developed which allowed us to play, pause, repeat, transcribe and annotate what happened in the experiment. The main body of the analysis was done on these playbacks. They were inspected, segmented and annotated with regards to different events, such as a change of focus in the conversation. Events or parts of events exemplifying reoccurring patterns found in the inspection were then further segmented, annotated and transcribed. The purpose of the transcriptions was to confirm the findings from the inspections of the playbacks. In the transcribed segments the tourist's fixations were analyzed with a dispersion-based fixation algorithm [21].

For this study we developed a special notation system composed of speech-gaze transcription graphs. In these graphs, verbal dialogue is transcribed and coded on a time line with the tourist's eye-gaze marked (Fig. 3). The dialogues were segmented into 5 second "pages". At occasions, the speech-gaze transcription graphs were supplemented with a still image of the tourist's eye-gaze on the map. The time period shown in the still image is marked with a gray line in the speech-gaze transcription graph (Fig. 3). Due to space constraints, only a few examples of speech-gaze transcription graphs are presented in this paper.

5 Results, Analysis, and Discussion

This section presents findings based on data from our experiment as well as related eye-gaze behavior literature in the cognitive sciences such as psycholinguistics. We organize our findings around a non-exhaustive and often mutually dependent list of plausible impacts of eye-gaze overlay on human-human communication and human-machine conversation.

(1) Eye-gaze carries deictic and spatial reference information; hence, displaying it may reduce effort of frequent referencing.
When communicating about spatial tasks one often needs to make reference to an object, a location or a path. This can be done either by giving complex verbal descriptions, such as "in the north east part of town, close to the Cathedral", or by deictic references in a combination of an utterance and a gesture, such as saying "here" and pointing at a place. Deictic information in fact is also naturally carried in eye-gaze. It is obvious that in explicit deictic pointing, one has to look at an object before gesturing at it. More generally, people look at the object they talk about even when they are not pointing at it [11, 17, 20]. Thus, the eye-gaze locus can serve as an

implicit pointer when a person utters a spatial reference. Velichkovsky's [24] focused on using eye-gaze as an explicit pointer during cooperative problem solving by an expertise-novice team. He showed that when the expert's eye-gaze position was represented by a dot in the puzzle on a computer screen, the number of overall words used decreased.

The fact that eye-gaze could support deictic or referencing functions is also quite evident in our experiment. Fig. 3 shows the speech-gaze transcription graph of three such examples. In example (a) (top row, with screen image on the right), after discussing a number of restaurant choices close to one of the hotels on the map the tourist decided to book "Hotel Fron". During the utterance "I'm all set and I would like to make a reservation at the hotel we just discussed", his eye-gaze fixated on Hotel Fron more frequently (twice) and over longer periods than other objects. Similarly in the next example in the same figure, Tourist 14 also referred to Hotel Fron by an utterance while glancing at it, which again shows that the eye-gaze could have served as implicit deictic reference if the tourist consultant could have seen the eye-gaze locus. These examples show that "pointing with the eye" is a quite natural and subconscious behavior.

The subconscious role eye-gaze plays as a pointer to locations in the map was also demonstrated by the tourist consultants' experiences. They often felt more lost in the non-gaze condition: "I was more lost in the non-gaze condition. The tourist was very inquisitive and asked information about specific places that I did not know their location." (*Tourist consultant B*). In sum, displaying eye-gaze onto the workspace can reduce the need to make explicit and effortful references (either verbal or gesture), since often the partner will know exactly what is being referred to based the eye-gaze.

Beyond supporting deictic and spatial references in human-human conversation, the eye-gaze as a pointer to the current focus of the conversation can also benefit human-computer communication. It can help disambiguating the users' speech both at the speech recognition level and the semantic interpretation level.

(2) Eye-gaze reflects a listener's interest and can be used to judge whether to continue on the current conversation topic.

The partner's eye-gaze can play a role also when the partner is listening. Previous research has shown the eye-gaze tended to correlate with objects related to the verbal message heard. The pioneering research of eye movements during listening was done by Cooper [9]. He found that people look at objects that were relevant to what they listened to. For example, when they heard the word "lion", they looked at the lion in the picture. When they heard the word "Africa", they looked at the lion, the zebra and the snake. Not only the eye-gaze follows the speaker's instruction, it may also anticipate what the speaker is going to talk about next. Altmann and Kamide [1] and Kamide et al [14] showed that when the speaker says "the boy will eat the cake" the listener already looked at the cake when the speaker starts uttering "cake."

In our study, we found that the tourist looked at what the tourist consultants talked about at least for a while. In addition we found a tight coupling between eye-gaze patterns and interest level. How interested the tourist was in a topic (a club, a museum, etc) was reflected by the duration and intensity of the tourist's eye-gaze on a particular place.

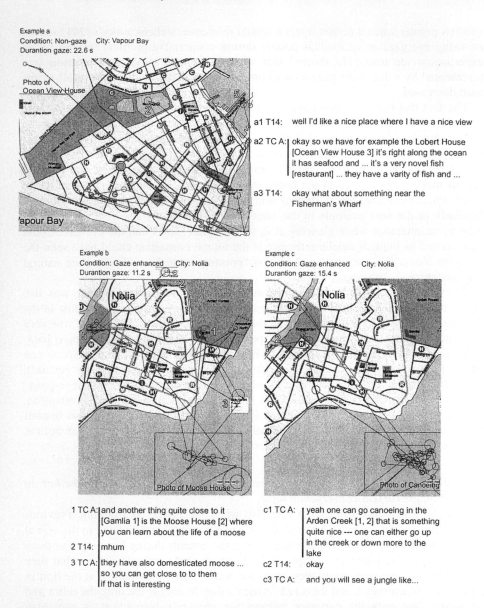

Example a
Condition: Non-gaze   City: Vapour Bay
Durantion gaze: 22.6 s

Photo of Ocean View House

'apour Bay

a1 T14:   well I'd like a nice place where I have a nice view

a2 TC A: okay so we have for example the Lobert House
           [Ocean View House 3] it's right along the ocean
           it has seafood and ... it's a very novel fish
           [restaurant] ... they have a varity of fish and ...

a3 T14:   okay what about something near the
           Fisherman's Wharf

Example b
Condition: Gaze enhanced   City: Nolia
Durantion gaze: 11.2 s

Nolia

Photo of Moose House

Example c
Condition: Gaze enhanced   City: Nolia
Durantion gaze: 15.4 s

Nolia

Photo of Canoeing

1 TC A: and another thing quite close to it
         [Gamlia 1] is the Moose House [2] where
         you can learn about the life of a moose
2 T14:   mhum
3 TC A: they have also domesticated moose ...
         so you can get close to to them
         if that is interesting

c1 TC A: yeah one can go canoeing in the
          Arden Creek [1, 2] that is something
          quite nice --- one can either go up
          in the creek or down more to the
          lake
c2 T14:   okay
c3 TC A: and you will see a jungle like...

Fig. 4. Three examples from Tourist 14's conversation with Tourist Consultant A that indicate changes of focus and different interest levels. The vertical lines in transcription indicate the time periods used for the gaze fixation trace.

The three examples in Fig. 4 illustrate the eye-gaze relation to interest level. As we can see example (c) is very different from the other two examples: Tourist 14 looked more intensely on the photo and location of the attraction in example (c) than in example (b). Notwithstanding the longer duration of the segment in example (c) compared to example (b), Tourist 14 hardly looked at anything else other than the

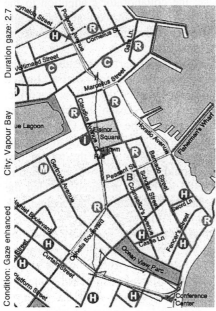

On the left side of the map image, running vertically:

Duration gaze: 2.7

City: Vapour Bay

Condition: Gaze enhanced

TCB: So that is a pretty good choice

[break]

Yeah, you can take the yellow bus line.
It is quite accessible.

Fig. 5. Tourist 3 looked up north and Tourist Consultant B changed the focus accordingly

photo of canoeing or the location of the canoeing. The long time period that Tourist 14 spent looking at the photo of the canoe is best explained by his interest in that activity. Indeed Tourist 14 eventually decided to sign up for a canoe trip.

The tourist consultants also interpreted the tourist's interest as high when they saw a high intensity or long duration of the tourist's eye-gaze on places representing the current conversational focus. For example, when Tourist Consultant A observed that Tourist 14 was no longer looking at the Moose House (example b), she finished off the topic by saying " ...if that is something interesting." In contrast, in example (c) she observed Tourist 14's high gaze intensity and continued to talk about canoeing for another 10.3 seconds after Tourist 14 uttered "okay."

Subjectively, the tourist consultants felt that they often could tell what the tourists were interested in based on the eye-gaze display. Typically the tourist consultants interpreted a long dwell time over an object or an area as interest: "It was easy to see if he was interested. He looked very focused on those things" or "He did look around elsewhere quite a bit when I talked about these attractions...he did not seem to be interested." (*Tourist consultant A*)

The fact that a person's interest in the current topic is reflected in the eye-gaze can be used by multimodal systems to adapt the information given to the user. This issue is further explored in [4].

(3) Common focus coordination and topic switching
Closely related to interest detection is the coordination of the common focus and topic switching. Displaying a partner's eye-gaze may enable mutual awareness of each other's loci of focus, hence fostering a common focus when needed. Velichkovsky [24] has argued that eye-gaze tracked and displayed to the partner could support joint attention because it constantly communicates where the conversational partner's attention is.

Eye-gaze may also help the dialogue partners to switch the topic of conversation. We have not found much in the literature in this regard, but it was evident in our experiment. When the tourist was no longer interested in a particular place the tourist consultant was talking about, the tourist started to look at new places (see e.g. Fig. 4, Example (a)). The drifting eye-gaze may give the consultant a clue on either moving on to other topics, or increasing the effort to get the collaborator's attention to the "right" place. In the gaze enhanced condition of the experiment the consultant could take advantage of the displayed gaze trajectory and predict the change of focus or what the tourist was interested in hearing about next.

Fig. 5 shows an example of this behavior. While the Tourist Consultant talked about a restaurant in the northern part of Vapour Bay, he noticed that Tourist 3 looked at the Conference Center. When Tourist 3 next roughly followed the yellow bus route, Tourist Consultant B told the tourist that it was possible to reach the restaurant by bus. This episode shows that the eye-gaze overlay enabled the Tourist Consultant to adapt the dialogue to the Tourist's changing interest. Subjectively, the tourist consultants noticed that they could use the eye-gaze to infer what the tourist was going to ask or talk about next: "[With eye-gaze] I could see what he was interested in and what he was going to talk about." and "I could be better prepared on what the person was interested in...the communication seems to flow better in the second task [with eye-gaze]" (*Tourist consultant A*).

In contrast, for the non-gaze condition, the tourist consultant was more driven by the tourist information tool and the map: "With the non-gaze condition I was more driven by the menu, going down the list since I do not know where the tourist was looking at." and "In the non-gaze condition I was more driven by what ever happened to pop up to me, e.g. I see Museum of Modern Art and I will talk about it." (*Tourist consultant B*)

The extent to which eye-gaze information could be used to steer the conversation also depended on the tourist's personality and style. Some tourists let the consultant drive the conversation, while others wanted to get very specific information themselves. With both these styles, the eye-gaze helped the tourist consultant but in different ways.

When the tourist consultant drove the conversation, the tourists' eye-gaze was used to determine what the tourist consultant should talk about. "I could see places he was interested in and talk about them. He was not talking a lot so I had to drive the conversation." (*Tourist consultant A*) "I tried to use his eye-gaze more this time to drive our conversation. I could use it sometimes effectively." (*Tourist consultant B*)

When the tourist drove the communication, the tourist consultant did not need to rely on the eye-gaze as much for topic switching, but the eye-gaze still could be used for its deictic and reference function discussed earlier: "I could see which places he was talking about. I lacked that in the second city (without eye-gaze). He switched often between different hotels when making up his mind. The eye-gaze would have been very helpful in the second city." (*Tourist consultant A*)

These findings indicate that an eye-gaze overlay can play an important role in the process of grounding [7] in human-human communication. In addition, these findings show that eye-gaze information can provide additional information in human-computer communication for selecting information to present to the user.

(4) Reduced ambiguity and increased redundancy in communication.
While face-to-face communication in natural language is often ambiguous, tele-communication or human-computer communication can be more so. Since people often look at what they talk about, displaying eye-gaze may increase redundancy and reliability in communication.

In the experiment, the tourist's eye-gaze was tightly connected to what was said about objects on the map. The utterance could be a proper name or a referring expression. At occasions these utterances were ambiguous. Instead of referring a hotel by name, a tourist might say "the hotel we just discussed" or "this one" (Fig. 3), which could be interpreted in more than one way if one attended to these words alone. Sometimes what said verbally was not what the tourist really meant. For example in Fig. 3 example (c), Tourist 10 said "you know what? I'll take the *second* hotel you suggested" while he actually meant the *third* hotel. In all these cases, the tourist's eye-gaze could have provided information to either resolve the ambiguity, or to warn the consultant to disambiguate a disparity between eye-gaze and verbal utterance. In all these cases, additional verbal information was needed to resolve the ambiguities.

(5) Completion time, assurance, engagement, confirmation, understanding and confidence in communication.

Task completion time in the experiment did not differ significantly between the gaze conditions ($F_{1, 10}$ =.001, p=.982). This mirrors other results in communication or collaboration studies between different interfaces, such as the study by Monk and Gale [18]. Individual communication style was a more dominant factor on completion time in our study. The conversations with Tourist Consultant B lasted on average longer than with Tourist Consultant A ($F_{1, 10}$ =21.596, p=.001). Tourist Consultant B spent more time introducing the cities and gave more alternatives, while Tourist Consultant A was more targeted. Tourist Consultant A also knew the cities and the TGuide tool better than Tourist Consultant B.

Rather than task completion time, the major impact of an eye-gaze overlay was on confirmation, assurance, understanding and confidence of the tourist consultants when they saw the eye-gaze overlay. Comparing the two conditions used in the experiment, the tourist consultants felt that their communication with the tourists was qualitatively different. They found the gaze-enhanced condition more engaging: "With eye-gaze I was more engaged with the tourist" (*Tourist consultant B*) "It is easier to feel connected with the person when I see the eye-gaze." (*Tourist consultant A*). On the question of how much the eye-gaze helped the communication, they rated on average across all sessions, 72.7, on a 100-point scale (with 50 being neutral).

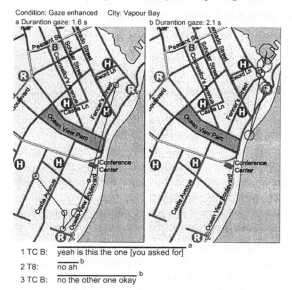

Condition: Gaze enhanced   City: Vapour Bay
a Durantion gaze: 1.6 s   b Durantion gaze: 2.1 s

1 TC B: yeah is this the one [you asked for]
2 T8:   no ah
3 TC B: no the other one okay

Fig. 6. Tourist Consultant B uses the tourist's eye-gaze to confirm his understanding of the tourist's request

One could be more sure if his or her partner really "got

the point" by looking at the partner's eye-gaze response. If the speaker's statement about a particular object was followed by the listener's eye-gaze on or around the same object, the speaker can be more confident that the statement is heard. We found that the tourist consultants repeatedly used the eye-gaze overlay to confirm either their own understanding of what the tourist meant, or to confirm that the tourist was following their instructions. Fig. 6 shows an example of how Tourist consultant B first used Tourist 8's eye-gaze in addition to his spoken response to determine that the alternative (Restaurant 2) he showed to the tourist was wrong; and then he used it to determine which was the right alternative (Restaurant 1).

When commenting on the general effects of eye-gaze overlay, the consultants said: "Mostly ensuring me that we are on the same page" (*Tourist consultant B*) "I could make sure that the person followed and understood what I was talking about" (*Tourist consultant A*) "The eye-gaze gives me confidence that the tourist is with me. I felt more presence of the tourist." (*Tourist consultant B*)

Although eye-gaze overlay was a novel and synthetic phenomenon, the tourist consultants were overall positive towards it and found it helpful. Similar to what was found by Velichkovsky [24], they did not find the overt display of eye-gaze confusing, disturbing, or unnatural. Note we used a processed (filtered) display of the eye-gaze in the study. On the other hand, we have observed in some cases the eye-gaze could attract too much attention. For example, consultant A felt that sometimes she had to focus on finding information needed by the tourist and deliberately ignored the tourist's eye-gaze for a while.

6   General Discussion and Conclusions

Being a "window to the mind", human eye-gaze is tightly coupled with mental processes and plays important roles in face-to-face communication [2]. Focusing on the functions of eye-gaze in dialogue, we investigated RealTourist both as a computer-mediated communication paradigm and as a study (simulation) of intelligent multimodal interaction with the user's eye-gaze as a critical channel of input. Our analysis of data and literature identified various functions that the eye-gaze plays including: (1) The overlaid eye-gaze can serve natural deictic and referencing functions that help one partner to keep track of what the other partner talks about, hence reducing the need and effort of frequent explicit verbal or gesture referencing; (2) The eye-gaze information reveals the partner's interest, which helps one to determine how much to talk about a particular topic; (3) Eye-gaze display can help synchronize the two partners' attention and form a common task focus. One may also use the eye-gaze information to switch topics and steer the conversation to the partner's need; (4) Information carried in eye-gaze can help to increase communication redundancy and resolve some of the ambiguities in verbal expressions; (5) Eye-gaze overlay gives one increased assurance or confidence that his or her conversational partner is engaged and indeed getting the information communicated.

Although using RealTourist is a novel experience, the tourist consultants were able to take advantage of it and reacted positively. They felt that it made a qualitative difference in communicating about spatial tasks. Aiming at an inspective pattern identification of new phenomenon rather than an evaluative performance comparison of well established constructs, the research presented here was not necessarily definitive or complete. As a computer mediated communication paradigm, the eye-gaze augmentation was simplex in the RealTourist system. Although this did not prevent us from observing some of the functions afforded by eye-gaze overlay, a full duplex experiment may reveal more complex and more interesting behavior.

As a Wizard of Oz experiment of multimodal human-computer dialogue system in which the computer may communicate with the user based on speech and eye-gaze information, this study provides a rich source of empirical information on how eye-gaze can be used in the future. In fact, we have taken some of the patterns observed and knowledge gained in this study and embodied them in a prototype system, iTourist, which replaced the human tourist consultant with eye-gaze pattern-based interaction algorithms and databases. We found that iTourist users could successfully accomplish the same trip planning task as in this study [4].

Acknowledgement

Pernilla Qvarfordt was supported by the Stockholm-Linköping Graduate School in Human-Machine Interaction, the Swedish Agency for Innovation Systems (VINNOVA), the Centre for Industrial Information Technology (CENIIT), and the IBM Almaden Research Center. We thank Arne Jönsson and Tue Andersen for their input.

References

1. Altmann, G.T., and Kamide, Y. Incremental interpretation at verbs: Restricting the domain of subsequent references. *Cognition, 73*, (1999). 247-264.
2. Argyle, M. and Cook, M. *Gaze and Mutual Gaze.* Cambridge University Press (1976).
3. Argyle, M. and Graham, J. The central Europe experiment - Looking at persons and looking at things. *Journal of Environmental Psychology and Nonverbal Behaviour, 1*, (1977). 6-16.
4. Blank-for-blind-review. Conversing with the User Based on Eye-Gaze Patterns. *blank for review* (to appear).
5. Boyle, E.A., Anderson, A. H., and Newlans, A. The effect of visibility on dialogue and performance in a cooperative problem solving task. *Language & Speech, 37*, 1 (1994). 1-20.
6. Buxton, W.A.S. and Moran, T.P. EuroPARC's integrated interactive intermedia facility (iiif): Early experience. in Gibbs, S. and Verrijn-Stuart, A.A. (ed). *Multi-User Interfaces and Applications,*, Elsevier, Amsterdam (1990), 11-34.
7. Clark, H.C. and Schaeffer, E.F. Contributing to discourse. *Cognitive Science, 13*, (1989). 259-294.
8. Clark, H.H. and Krych, M.A. Speaking while monitoring addresses for understanding. *Journal of Memory and Language, 50*, (2004). 62-81.
9. Cooper, R.M. The control of eye fixation by the meaning of spoken language - a new methodology for the real-time investigation of speech perception, memory, and language processing. *Cognitive Psychology, 6*, (1974). 84-107.
10. Doherty-Sneddon, G., Anderson, A., O'Malley, C., Langton, S., Garrod, S. and Bruce, V. Face-to-face and video mediated communication: A comparison of dialogue structure and task performance. *Journal of Experimental Psychology: Applied, 3*, (1997). 105-125.

11. Griffin, Z.M. and Bock, K. What the eye says about speaking. *Psychological Science, 11*, 4 (2000). 274-279.
12. Ishii, H. and Kobayashi, M., ClearBoard: A Seamless Media for Shared Drawing and Conversation with Eye-Contact. *Proc. ACM CHI Conference on Human Factors in Computing Systems (1992)*, 525-532.
13. Jacob, R.J.K. The Use of Eye Movements in Human-Computer Interaction Techniques: What You Look At is What You Get. *ACM Transactions on Information Systems,, vol. 9*, no. 3 (1991). 152-169.
14. Kamide, Y., Altman, G. T. M., and Haywood, S. L. The time-course of prediction in incremental sentence processing: Evidence from anticipatory eye movements. *Journal of Memory and Language, 49*, (2003). 133-156.
15. Kaur, M., Tremaine, M., Huang, N., Wilder, J., Gacovski, Z., Flippo, F. and Mantravadi, C.S., Where is "it"? Event synchronization in gaze-speech input systems. *Proc. Fifth International Conference on Multimodal Interfaces (2003)*, 151-157.
16. Kraut, R.E., Gergle, D. and Fussell, S.R., The use of visual information in shared visual spaces: Informing the development of virtual co-presence. *Proc. ACM Conference on Computer Supported Cooperative Work (CSCW) (2002)*, 31-40.
17. Meyer, A.S., Sleiderink, A.M. and Levelt, W.J.M. Viewing and naming objects: Eye movements during noun and phrase production. *Cognition, 66*, (1998). B5-B33.
18. Monk, A. and Gale, C. A look is worth a thousands word: full gaze awareness in video-mediated conversation. *Discourse Processes, 33*, 3 (2002). 257-278.
19. Ochsman, R.B. and Chapanis, A. The effects of 10 communication modes on the behaviour of teams during co-operative problem-solving. *International Journal of Man-Machine Studies, 6*, (1974). 579-619.
20. Richardson, D.C. and Dale, R., Looking to understand: The coupling between speakers' and listneners' eye movement and its relationship to discourse comprehension. *Proc. the 26th Annual Meeting of the Cognitive Science Society (2004)*.
21. Salvucci, D.D. and Goldberg, J.H., Identifying fixations and saccades in eye-tracking protocols. *Proc. ACM Eye Tracking Research & Application Symposium (ETRA) (2000)*, 71-79.
22. Simon, H.A. The scientist as problem solver. in Klahr, D. and Kotovsky, K. (ed). *Complex information processing: The impact of Herbert A. Simon*, Lawrence Erlbaum, Hilsdale, NJ (1989), 376-398.
23. Tanaka, K., A robust selection system using real-time multi-modal user-agent interactions. *Proc. 4th International Conference on Intelligent User Interfaces (1999)*, 105-108.
24. Velichkovsky, B.M. Communicating attention-gaze position transfer in cooperative problem solving. *Pragmatics and Cognition, 3*, 2 (1995). 99-224.
25. Vertegaal, R., The GAZE Groupware System: Mediating Joint Attention in Multiparty Communication and Collaboration. *Proc. CHI'99: ACM Conference on Human Factors in Computing Systems (1999)*, 294-301.
26. Ware, C. and Mikaelian, H.H., An evaluation of an eye tracker as a device for computer input. *Proc. CHI+GI: ACM Conference on Human Factors in Computing Systems and Graphics Interface (1987)*, 183-188.
27. Winograd, T. and Flores, F. *Understanding computers and cognition*. Ablex Publishing Corp, Norwood, NJ, (1986).
28. Zhai, S. What's in the Eyes for Attentive Input *Communications of the ACM* (2003), 34-39.
29. Zhai, S., Morimoto, C. and Ihde, S., Manual and gaze input cascaded (MAGIC) pointing. *Proc. CHI'99: ACM Conference on Human Factors in Computing Systems (1999)*, ACM Press, 246-253.
30. Zhang, Q., Imamiya, A., Go, K. and Gao, X., Overriding errors in speech and gaze multi-modal architecture. *Proc. 9th International Conference on Intelligent User Interfaces (2004)*, 346-348.

A Synergistic Approach to Efficient Interactive Video Retrieval

Andreas Girgensohn, John Adcock, Matthew Cooper, and Lynn Wilcox

FX Palo Alto Laboratory, 3400 Hillview Avenue, Bldg. 4, Palo Alto, CA 94304, USA
{andreasg, adcock, cooper, wilcox}@fxpal.com

Abstract. A video database can contain a large number of videos ranging from several minutes to several hours in length. Typically, it is not sufficient to search just for relevant videos, because the task still remains to find the relevant clip, typically less than one minute of length, within the video. This makes it important to direct the users attention to the most promising material and to indicate what material they already investigated. Based on this premise, we created a video search system with a powerful and flexible user interface that incorporates dynamic visualizations of the underlying multimedia objects. The system employes an automatic story segmentation, combines text and visual search, and displays search results in ranked sets of story keyframe collages. By adapting the keyframe collages based on query relevance and indicating which portions of the video have already been explored, we enable users to quickly find relevant sections. We tested our system as part of the NIST TRECVID interactive search evaluation, and found that our user interface enabled users to find more relevant results within the allotted time than other systems employing more sophisticated analysis techniques but less helpful user interfaces.

1 Introduction

Users such as intelligence analysts often need to find video clips related to a particular topic that is described using both text and images. This type of video search is difficult, because users need visual information such as keyframes or even video playback to judge the relevance of a video clip and text search alone is not sufficient to find the desired clip within a video. While searching text documents is a well-studied process, it is less clear how to best support search in video collections. Typically text documents are treated as units for the purpose of retrieval, so that a search returns a number of relevant documents. The user can then easily skim the documents to find parts of interest. In cases where documents are long, there are techniques to search for just the relevant sections [16].

However, treating entire videos as units of retrieval will often not lead to satisfactory results. After retrieving relevant videos, the task still remains to find the relevant clip, typically less than one minute of length, within the video. Even when such videos are broken into sections, or stories of several minutes in length, it is still time consuming to view all those video sections to find just the relevant clip.

M.F. Costabile and F. Paternò (Eds.): INTERACT 2005, LNCS 3585, pp. 781–794, 2005.
© IFIP International Federation for Information Processing 2005

Our approach to this problem is to support users in rapidly searching through such video collections. Our target users are analysts who need both visual and textual information or video producers who want to locate video segments for reuse. While the latter will frequently use libraries that support retrieval with extensive meta-data describing properties such as location, included actors, time of day, lighting conditions, our goal is to support the search in video collections where such meta-data is not available. In this work, we assume that time-aligned text, such as transcripts, automatically recognized speech, or closed captions, is available.

Our system design uses a synergistic approach that has the system and the user collaborate on improving the search results. We automate certain parts of the system but to let the users directly perform tasks that humans can do better. For example, the system can retrieve all video containing a particular keyword, but the user can more easily look through keyframes representing the video and find just those of interest. Our system makes novel contributions for the user interface design for video search systems. We use several visualization techniques to direct the users' attention to potentially relevant material and to let them judge quickly what is truly relevant. We also make novel contributions to the video search back-end by providing a story segmentation for automatically recognized speech and by determining terms related to the query in latent semantic text search where the retrieved text passage might not share any terms with the query.

In the next section, we discuss related work. We then describe the setup for a retrieval experiment and our search user interface. Next, we present the components of the back-end search system. Finally, we present the results of the TRECVID evaluation and conclude with a discussion of the implications.

2 Related Work

There is currently a great deal of interest in video search, as evidenced by recently unveiled web-based video search portals by Yahoo [20] and Google [9]. 2004 marked the 4th year of the TRECVID [19] evaluations which draws a wide variety of participants from academia and industry. Some of the more successful ongoing efforts in the interactive search task draw upon expertise in video feature identification and content-based retrieval. The Dublin City University effort [6] includes an image-plus-text search facility and a relevance feedback facility for query refinement. The searcher decides which aspects of video or image similarity to incorporate for each query example. The Imperial College interactive search system [11] likewise gives the searcher control over the weighting of various image features for example-based search, a relevance feedback system for query refinement, and notably incorporates the NN^k visualization system for browsing for shots "close" to a selected shot. The MediaMill, University of Amsterdam system [18] is founded on a very powerful semantic concept detection system and searchers can search by concept as well as keyword and example. Likewise the Informedia system from Carnegie Mellon University [5] incorporates their very mature technology for image and video feature detection and puts the searcher in control of the relative weighting of these aspects. We previously reported preliminary results of our approach [8].

Our effort is distinguished from others primarily by the simplicity of our search and relevance feedback controls in favor of an emphasis on rich interfaces and intuitive paths for exploration from search results. Our scenario is not so much one of query followed by refinement as it is query followed by exploration. Whether explicitly stated or not, a goal in all of these systems is a positive user experience. That is, an informative and highly responsive interface cannot be taken for granted when handling thousands of keyframe images and tens of gigabytes of digital video.

3 Retrieval Experiment

To validate our approach, we participated in the interactive search component of a video retrieval evaluation called TRECVID sponsored by the National Institute of Standards and Technology (NIST) [19]. In the interactive search, participants have access to broadcast news video from four months from the U.S. ABC and CNN networks (128 videos; about 60 hours). The TRECVID evaluation consists of 24 topics such as "find shots of Bill Clinton speaking with at least part of a US flag visible behind him." Users are given 15 minutes for each topic, and must find all video passages relevant to the topic. Some of the TRECVID participants use very elaborate video analysis techniques to support the search [10]. For example, one very successful system allows the user to search for visual features such as animals, buildings, or people [4].

For our retrieval experiments, we used automatically recognized speech from the news videos as time-aligned text. A few errors in the recognized speech do not have a major impact on the retrieval results because stories tend to include important terms repeatedly. We provided both literal and latent semantic text search. The former uses the term frequency (tf; the count for a term in a document) and the inverse document frequency (idf; the count of documents containing a term) as measures of relevance [17]. The latter maps all terms into a reduced-dimensional space such that related terms are placed near each other [1]. Literal search is well suited to searching for proper names whereas latent semantic search is more useful when searching for concepts that can be described with different words, and the exact words appearing in the transcript are unknown to the searcher.

The basic retrieval units are video shots that are uninterrupted sequences with strong visual coherence, generally taken by a single camera [2]. In the news video collection, shots have an average length of six seconds. Those shots are of insufficient length for performing text retrieval on the text associated with them. Because each half hour news video deals with a wide variety of topics, using whole videos as text documents for retrieval is not appropriate, either. Instead, our system pre-processes the text transcript to segment each video into smaller semantically-related units (stories) that are of a length better suited for standard text retrieval techniques. Each story has several associated video shots that can be accessed through the story. Videos, stories and shots form a three level hierarchy. Our application can also support hierarchies with more or fewer levels if that is more appropriate for the video material to be searched.

We also provide support for image similarity search to deal with situations where the visual information is more important than the associated text (e.g., to find sunsets). In this case, the user selects an image that represents his visual information need and the system searches through the keyframes representing the individual video shots. The system returns those shots whose keyframes have a strong visual similarity to the image supplied by the user. We use color correlograms [12] for our similarity measure. To support our hierarchy of stories and shots, the visual similarity search results are propagated from shots to the stories containing them.

4   User Interface

A typical search in a moderate to large video collection can return a large number of results. This is the result of returning relatively short segments of video that are visually and/or semantically coherent. Our user interface directs the user's attention to the video segments that are potentially relevant. We present results in a form that enables users to quickly decide which of the results best satisfy the user's original information need. Our system displays search results in a highly visual form that makes it easy for users to determine which results are truly relevant.

The basic retrieval units in our system are video shots. Because the frames in a video shot are visually coherent, each shot can be visualized with a single keyframe. A keyframe is an image that visually represents the shot, typically chosen as a representative from the frames in the shot [2]. Time-aligned automatic speech recognition (ASR) output is used to assess the semantic content of each shot. But because shots are too short to be used as units of meaningful content, we use automatically segmented stories as the main retrieval units. Adjacent shots with relatively high text-based similarity are grouped into stories. These stories form the organizing units upon which video shots are presented in our interface. Because each story consists of several shots, it cannot be well represented by a single keyframe. Instead, we represent stories as collages of shot keyframes.

Figure 1 shows the interface for the interactive search. The user enters a query as keywords and/or images (Figure 1B). Keywords are typed and images are dragged into the query section from other parts of the interface. For the TRECVID task, the topic is displayed in Figure 1C. In this case, the user can select keywords and images from the topic description. Once the user has entered a query and pressed the search button, story results appear in Figure 1A, displayed in relevance order. The size of each story icon is also determined by query relevance. A novel feature of our system is that retrieved stories are represented by keyframe collages where keyframes are selected and sized by their relevance to a query so that the same story may be shown differently for different queries. When the user wants to explore a retrieved story, he clicks on the collage. The parent video is opened and the selected story is highlighted in the video timeline (Figure 1E). Below the timeline the keyframes from all the shots in the selected story are displayed (see Figure 1F). The shot or story under the mouse is magnified in the space in Figure 1D. A tool tip provides additional information for the shot or story under the mouse. When the user finds a shot of interest, he drags it to the area shown in Figure 1G to save relevant results. Another novel aspect of our system is that we mark visited stories so that the user can avoid needless revisiting of stories. We present the three types of UI elements that we developed to surface the novel features:

Fig. 1. The interactive search interface. (A) Story keyframe summaries in the search results (B) Search text and image entry (C) TRECVID topic display (D) Media player and keyframe zoom (E) Story timeline (F) Shot keyframes (G) Relevant shot list.

1. Three visualizations provide different information perspectives about query results.
2. Tooltips and magnified keyframes provide users with document information relevant to the query.
3. Overlays provide cues about previously visited stories, current story and shot in video playback, and the degree of query relevance on story and shot.

4.1   Query Result Visualizations: Story Collage, Shot Keyframe, Video Timeline

Query results are returned as a set of stories, sorted by relevance to the query. Each story is represented by a collage of keyframes from the video shots contained in the story. The size of the collage is determined by the relevance to the query so that one can see at a glance which stories are most relevant. We use a collage of four keyframes to give a flavor of the different shots in a story without making the keyframes too small for recognizing details. We use rectangular areas for the keyframes for the sake of fast computation but we could instead use other collages such as a stained glass window visualization [3].

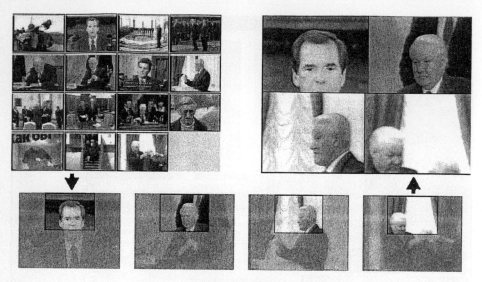

Fig. 2. Story keyframe montage example. The keyframe montage at the right is constructed from the 15 shot keyframes of the story at the left selected and cropped based on their relevance to the query "Boris Yeltsin".

In addition to determining the relevance of stories with respect to the query, we also determine the relevance of each video shot. While the shot relevance does not provide good results on its own, it can be used to determine which shots in a story are the most relevant ones. The most-relevant shots are selected and their keyframes are combined to form a story keyframe-collage. The size allotted to each portion in this 4-image montage is determined by the shot's score relative to the query. Figure 2 shows an example of this where the query was "Boris Yeltsin" and the shots most relevant to the query are allocated more room in the story thumbnail, in this case the 2 shots of the 9 total shots in the story that depict Boris Yeltsin. Rather than scaling down the keyframes, they are cropped to preserve details in reduced-size representations. In the current implementation, the top-center portion of the cropped frame is used but we plan to crop the main region-of-interest with face or motion detection.

Because the automatic story segmentation is not always accurate and related stories frequently are located in the same part of the video, we provide access to the temporal neighborhood of the selected story. First, the timeline of the video containing the story color-codes the relevance of all stories in the video (see Figure 1E and Figure 3). This color-coding provides a very distinct pattern in the case of literal text search because only few stories contain the exact keywords. After a latent semantic text search, all parts of the timeline indicate some relevance because every term has some latent relationship to all other terms. We experimentally determined a nonlinear mapping of the relevance scores from latent semantic text search that highlights the most related stories without completely suppressing other potentially related stories. Immediately below the timeline in Figure 1E collages of neighboring stories around the selected story are displayed. This provides quick

Fig. 3. Timelines for the query "Boris Yeltsin". Brighter colors indicate more relevance. The literal text search timeline above displays two distinct relevant areas whereas the latent-semantic search timeline below indicates some amount of relevance everywhere.

access to keywords in those stories via tool tips. By clicking on the timeline or the neighboring collages, the corresponding story can be selected.

The keyframes for the shots comprising the selected story are shown in a separate pane (see Figure 1F and Figure 4). Double-clicking a keyframe plays the corresponding video shot. The expanded view provides access to the individual shots for play-back, for adding them to the results, and for displaying information about the shots. One or more keyframes of shots can be dragged into or out of the result area to add or remove them from the result list, or into or out of the image search area to add or remove them from the image search. Shots can also be marked explicitly as irrelevant. Such shots are excluded from being automatically added to the results when the user selects the "Add related" button.

4.2 Document Relevance Feedback: Tooltips and Magnified Keyframes

It is useful to provide feedback to the user to indicate why a particular document was deemed relevant to the query and how the document is different from other documents. Tooltips for story collage and video shot keyframes provide that information to the user in the form of keywords that are distinctive for the story and keywords related to the query (see the plain text in Figure 4). Terms that occur frequently in the story or shot and do not appear in many other stories or shots are most distinguishing. While words such as "lately" do not really help in distinguishing the video passage from others, words such as "russia" are helpful. By displaying five keywords, it is likely that at least one or two are truly useful.

The terms in bold are most related to the query and indicate why the document is relevant to the query. We decided against displaying the terms with surrounding text as it is frequently done in Web search engines. The reason is that we do not want the tool-tips to be overly large. Furthermore, the automatic speech recognition makes mistakes that are more noticeable when displaying whole phrases.

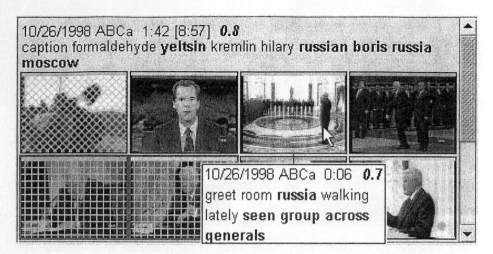

Fig. 4. Tool tip showing distinguishing keywords and bold query keywords

With a literal text search approach, the terms most related to the query are the query terms appearing in the story. When latent semantic text search is used, a relevant document may not contain any of the query terms but terms that are closely related to them. We use the latent semantic space to identify terms in the document that are most similar to the query.

In an earlier version of our application, we displayed keyframes as part of the tool-tips. Users interacting with that version of the application found that the keyframes were either too small to be useful or that the tooltips covered up too much the window. To address this issue, we decided to reuse the video player area as a magnifier for the keyframe under the mouse or the selected keyframe (see Figure 1D). Usually, the video player will be stopped while the user inspects keyframes so that the user can see a magnified version of the keyframe or collage without the need to dedicate some window area for that purpose.

4.3 Overlay Cues: Visited Story, Current Playback Position, Query Relevance

Semi-transparent overlays are used to provide three cues. A gray overlay on a story icon indicates that it has been previously visited (see Figure 1A and E). A translucent red overlay on a shot icon indicates that it has been explicitly excluded by the user from the relevant shot set. A translucent green overlay on a shot icon indicates that it has been included in the results set (see Figure 1F). Figure 4 shows the use of patterns instead of translucent overlays for color-blind users and grayscale reproduction of the image. Red diagonal lines indicate exclusion and green horizontal and vertical lines indicate inclusion.

While video is playing, the shot and the story containing the current playback position are indicated by placing a red dot on top of their keyframes. The playback position is also indicated in the timeline by a vertical red line.

Horizontal colored bars are used along the top of stories and shots to indicate the degree of query-relevance, varying from black to bright green. The same color scheme is used in the timeline depicted in Figure 3.

5   Back-End Search System

We pre-process videos to segment them into stories with a text-based latent semantic analysis (LSA) of the text transcripts [1]. For a topic of interest such as the topics provided by TRECVID, users need to issue several queries to find the relevant video shots. We give users the choice among literal keyword text search, LSA-based text search, visual similarity search, or a combination of text and visual similarity search.

At the completion of a topic, the system uses the query history and list of relevant shots to automatically find additional relevant video shots to add to the results.

5.1   Data Pre-processing

As the lowest-level unit, we use video shots that are provided as a reference by TRECVID [15]. Video frames in a shot have strong visual coherence, i.e., the video only changes because of movement in the scene or pans and zooms. We perform an automatic pre-processing step to identify topic or story units from the automatically recognized speech. We use latent semantic analysis (LSA) [1] to improve the performance of the segmentation. LSA turns a large matrix of term-document association data into a "semantic" space wherein terms and documents that are closely associated are placed near one another. Singular-value decomposition allows the arrangement of the space to reflect the major associative patterns in the data, and ignore the smaller, less important influences. We use a reduced space of with 100 dimensions because that accounts for most of the variance. As a result, terms that did not actually appear in a document may still end up close to the document.

For the story segmentation, we build a latent semantic space (LSS) treating the stopped and stemmed [14] text tokens for each video shot in the testing corpus as a separate document. We then project the text for each shot into this shot-based LSS. This results in a low-dimensional representation for each shot in term of its projection coefficients in the LSS. We then group adjacent video shots into stories following the similarity-based approach of [7]. The similarity between pairs of shots is quantitatively assessed using the cosine similarity between the corresponding vectors of projection coefficients. A similarity matrix is constructed with the (i,j) element equal to the similarity between the ith and j^{th} shots. Areas with high self-similarity appear as dark squares along the diagonal of the matrix. Boundaries between groups of shots with high similarity appear as checkerboards in the similarity matrix (see the left of Figure 5). This is because shots contained in the same story exhibit high (within-story) similarity. Shots from different stories exhibit low (inter-story) similarity. A checkerboard kernel is moved along the main diagonal of the matrix to locate boundaries. Only the part of the matrix that overlaps the moving kernel needs to be computed. The checkerboard kernel acts as a matched filter; the shot-indexed kernel correlation score exhibits local maxima at the boundaries between stories. The points of highest kernel correlation are chosen as story boundaries subject to heuristic constraints on the minimum and maximum length of a story. After determining story boundaries, we create a new LSS treating each story as a document.

5.2 Search Engine

Queries are specified as a combination of text and images. The searcher can opt to perform a text-only or image-only search by leaving the image or text query area empty. For the text portion of the query, the searcher can choose either a literal keyword text search or a LSA-based text search. Literal text search performs better for proper names (e.g., of persons) whereas latent semantic search can find related concepts.

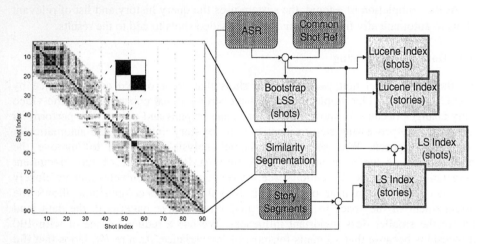

Fig. 5. Data preprocessing flow. A story-level segmentation is derived from the reference shot boundaries and the self-similarity matrix of the text transcripts. Dark areas in the similarity matrix on the left indicate high similarity and a checkerboard kernel finds boundaries between those areas. Both LS and Lucene indices are created at both the shot and story levels.

When determining text-query relevance for shots, the shots inherit part of the retrieval score of their parent stories to properly handle terms that co-occur in the same story but in different shots. We use only automatically recognized speech to provide text for story and shot segments. The literal text search is based on a Lucene [13] back end and ranks each story based on the tf-idf values of the specified keywords [17]. In this mode the story relevance, used for results sorting and thumbnail scaling and color coding as described in Section 4, is determined by the Lucene retrieval score. When the LSA-based search is used [1], the query terms are projected into a latent semantic space (LSS) like the one used in the story segmentation created from the detected stories. The query terms are scored in the reduced dimension space against the text for each story and each shot using a cosine similarity function. In this mode, the cosine similarity value becomes the query relevance score.

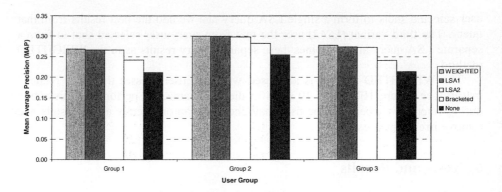

Fig. 6. Overall mean average precision (MAP) performance by user group and post-processing system type employed. The "None" column is the MAP performance of the user selected shots without any automatic augmentation.

For a literal text search, it is common to highlight the matching keywords from the query in the search results to provide an indication of the context in which the document and the query matched. To achieve a similar effect for a latent semantic text search, we project the query term vector (which is likely to have very few entries since most user-entered queries use few terms) into the reduced dimension space and expand it back into the full term-vector space with the inverse of the projection matrix. This produces a dense query vector. Next, to identify keywords, first eliminate terms from the dense query vector that do not occur in the search document, then choose some number of the remaining terms with the highest corresponding values in the dense query vector as query-related "keywords". These terms can now be used to highlight the context of the similarity between the query and the returned document.

An image similarity matching capability is provided using color correlograms [12]. Correlograms provide signatures for color groupings in images and tend to produce better image search results than color histograms or similar measures. During a visual search, the correlograms of the search images are compared to the correlograms of the keyframes of the video shots. To generate an image-similarity relevance score at the story level, the maximum score from the component shots is propagated to the story.

5.3 Post Query Processing

The goal of the TRECVID interactive search evaluation is to find all relevant shots. To aid the user in this, the system attempts to find additional relevant shots after the searcher finishes searching for video shots relevant to a topic. We use two strategies to select additional shots. First, we address the fact that shots are sometimes segmented at the wrong place by adding all shots bracketing the shots selected by the user *(Bracketed)*. Second, we issue additional queries to find shots similar to the ones the user selected. We use three variants for the second strategy. The first variant *(WEIGHTED)* uses the weighted average of the scores of all queries issued by the user to compute a new score for every video shot in the collection. Each individual query's scores are weighted by the recall of that query as judged against the user-identified list of relevant shots. The second variant *(LSA1)* combines the text from all user-selected shots to form a single LSA query and we add the best results from that query. The third variant *(LSA2)* uses the text from every user-selected shot to form a separate LSA query and combines these separate query results as in the WEIGHTED method.

The WEIGHTED method is also used when the user presses the "Add related" button (see Figure 1F) to add 10 shots to the result area. By performing this action during interactive operation the user may check the automatically added results and remove irrelevant ones.

6   Tests and Results

The TRECVID evaluation consists of 24 topics (one of which had no relevant shots in the test set and was discounted). 15 minutes are allowed for answering each topic. Since answering all topics would take 6 hours, we assign subsets of topics to individual searchers. We employed 6 searchers (5 male; 1 female) to each answer 12 topics. All searchers have experience with video processing but most of them had not used the user interface before their 30-minute training session with a different news video collection. None of the searchers had seen the test collection or the topics before the search session. We grouped the topics into quarters and assigned them to the searchers in a standard latin square arrangement such that every searcher had a different combination of quarters. We then grouped searchers who had answered complementary sets of topics to create 3 groups of 2 searchers.

We evaluated search results by computing the average precision for each topic. This is the average of the precision values obtained after each relevant shot is retrieved. Relevant shots that are not retrieved are assumed to have a precision of 0. The mean over all topics (mean average precision; MAP) is used to compare results.

Figure 6 shows the mean average precision results for the three groups of searchers. In addition to the results for the user-selected shots, the figure also shows the results of bracketing shots and the three post-processing strategies described in the previous section. The post-processing strategies have similar performance (*WEIGHTED* is best and *LSA2* worst) and increase the MAP by 0.054 on average. While there are significant differences in performance between the groups of searchers, those differences are fairly small compared to the overall range of submitted results.

Figure 7 shows the MAP performance of our system with different post-processing strategies compared to all TRECVID submissions. Our best submission placed 3rd overall and only 4 submissions from 3 groups performed better than our worst performing submission [19]. Those 3 groups (University of Amsterdam/MediaMill, CMU, and IBM) have very mature image retrieval efforts and employ very sophisticated semantic image processing and feature detection. For example, the top-scoring MediaMill system uses a semantic lexicon with 32 concepts such as aircraft, bicycle, or Bill Clinton. This allows them to do well in TRECVID 2004 topics such as *"find shots of one or more bicycles rolling along."*

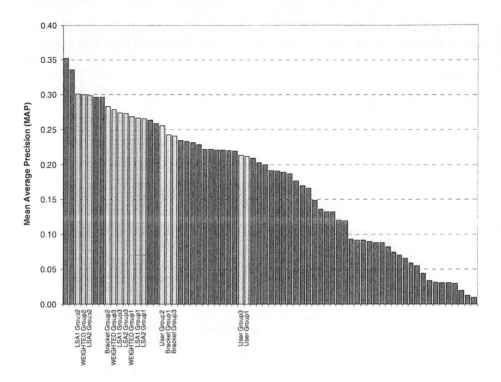

Fig. 7. Interactive search MAP scores for the entire set of TRECVID submissions. Scores or our 3 user groups with and without automatic post-processing are shown as striped bars. Other TRECVID participants' submissions as solid bars.

7 Conclusions

We presented an approach to supporting users in searching video collections. Our novel contributions fall into two areas. First, we use visualization techniques to draw the users' attention to promising results and support them in selecting relevant results. Second, we process the unstructured text associated with the videos and segment it into stories. We also determine keywords to present to the user. This is a difficult problem with latent semantic search.

Rather than using elaborate media analysis techniques, we provided an efficient user interface that enables users to quickly browse retrieved video shots and to decide which of those are truly relevant. Several visualization techniques were used to cue users to likely candidates for relevant video passages. We grouped video shots automatically into stories and represented those stories as keyframe collages where the more relevant keyframes were allotted more space. Redundant coding of size, position, color, and brightness were used to indicate document relevance to the users. We also marked already-visited stories across multiple searches to enable users to determine at a glance which results still had to be explored. This was especially important because the appearance of stories changed for different queries.

These features enabled the TRECVID participants in the interactive search evaluation to find many of the relevant video shots within the allotted time. Our evaluation results were very competitive with systems employing more sophisticated analysis techniques. We are currently looking beyond the TRECVID evaluation to determine how our system can be best adapted to real-world usage scenarios and plan to incorporate our current design into a larger video reuse system.

References

1. M.W. Berry, S.T. Dumais, G.W. O'Brien, Using Linear Algebra for Intelligent Information Retrieval, *SIAM Review*, 37(4), p. 573-595, 1995.
2. J.S. Boreczky and L.A. Rowe. Comparison of video shot boundary detection techniques. *Proc. SPIE Storage and Retrieval for Image and Video Databases*, 1996.
3. P. Chiu, A. Girgensohn, and Q. Liu. Stained-Glass Visualization for Highly Condensed Video Summaries. *Proc. IEEE Intl. Conf. on Multimedia and Expo*, 2004.
4. M. Christel and N. Moraveji. Finding the Right Shots: Assessing Usability and Performance of a Digital Video Library Interface. *Proc. ACM Multimedia*, pp. 732-739, 2004.
5. M. Christel, J. Yang, R. Yan, A. Hauptmann. Carnegie Mellon University Search. TREC Video Retrieval Evaluation Online Proceedings, 2004.
6. E. Cooke, P. Ferguson, G. Gaughan, C. Gurrin, G.J.F. Jones, H. Le Borgue, H. Lee, S. Marlow, K. McDonald, M. McHugh, N. Murphy, N.E. O'Connor, N. O'Hare, S. Rothwell, A.F. Smeaton, P. Wilkins. TRECVID 2004 Experiments in Dublin City University, TREC Video Retrieval Evaluation Online Proceedings, 2004.
7. M. Cooper and J. Foote. Scene Boundary Detection Via Video Self-Similarity Analysis. *Proc. IEEE Intl. Conf. on Image Processing*, pp. 378-381, 2001.
8. A. Girgensohn, J. Adcock, M. Cooper, and L. Wilcox. Interactive Search in Large Video Collections. *CHI 2005 Extended Abstracts,* ACM Press, pp. 1395-1398, 2005.
9. Google Video Search. http://video.google.com
10. A.G. Hauptmann and M.G. Christel. Successful Approaches in the TREC Video Retrieval Evaluations. *Proc. ACM Multimedia*, pp. 668-675, 2004.
11. D. Heesch, P. Howarth, J. Megalhaes, A. May, M. Pickering, A. Yavlinsky, S. Ruger. Video Retrieval Using Search and Browsing. TREC Video Retrieval Evaluation Online Proceedings, 2004.
12. J. Huang, S.R. Kumar, M. Mitra, W.-J. Zhu, and R. Zabih. Image Indexing Using Color Correlograms. *Proc. IEEE Comp. Soc. Conf. Comp. Vis. and Patt. Rec.*, pp. 762-768, 1997.
13. Jakarta Lucene. http://jakarta.apache.org/lucene/
14. M.F. Porter. An Algorithm for Suffix Stripping. *Program*, 14(3), pp. 130-137, 1980.
15. G.M. Quénot, D. Moraru, and L. Besacier. CLIPS at TRECvid: Shot Boundary Detection and Feature Detection. TREC Video Retrieval Evaluation Online Proceedings, 2003.
16. G. Salton, J. Allan, and C. Buckley. Approaches to passage retrieval in full text information systems. *ACM SIGIR conference on R&D in Information Retrieval*, pp. 49-58, 1993.
17. G. Salton and C. Buckley. Term-weighting approaches in automatic text retrieval. *Information Processing and Management*, 24(5), pp. 513-523, 1988.
18. C.G.M. Snoek, M. Worring, J.M. Geusebroek, D.C. Koelma, F.J. Seinstra. The MediaMill TRECVID 2004 Semantic Video Search Engine. TREC Video Retrieval Evaluation Online Proceedings, 2004
19. TRECVID. http://www-nlpir.nist.gov/projects/tvpubs/tv.pubs.org.html
20. Yahoo! Video Search. http://video.search.yahoo.com

The Landscape of Time-Based Visual Presentation Primitives for Richer Video Experience

Yasuhiro Yamamoto[1], Kumiyo Nakakoji[1], and Takashima Akio[2]

[1] KID Laboratory, RCAST, University of Tokyo,
4-6-1 Komaba, Meguro, Tokyo, 153-8904, Japan
{yxy, kumiyo}@kid.rcast.u-tokyo.ac.jp
http://www.kid.rcast.u-tokyo.ac.jp/
[2] Meme Media Laboratory, Hokkaido University,
N-13, W-8, Sapporo, Hokkaido, 060-8628, Japan
akiota@meme.hokudai.ac.jp
http://km.meme.hokudai.ac.jp/akiota/

Abstract. As technology advances, we have increasingly more opportunities to use video for our knowledge work, such as monitoring events, reflecting on physical performances, learning subject matter, or analyzing scientific experimental phenomena. Existing video-related software tools are either for as-is viewing or editing and do not support such knowledge-intensive processes. We argue for a variety of interactive presentation tools for richer video experiences in active watching. Based on the Time-based Visual Presentation (TbVP) framework, which separates presentation from content and views interaction methods as transformations between temporal and visual media data properties and user experience properties, this paper presents twenty-seven TbVP primitives and provides the landscape of rich interaction methods for videos. The primitives are illustrated with five scenarios that use videos for knowledge work.

1 Introduction

As technology advances, we have increasingly more opportunities to use video for our knowledge work, such as monitoring events, reflecting on physical performances, learning subject matter, or analyzing scientific experimental phenomena. The focus on most existing video viewing tools for interacting with video data, such as Quick-Time Player, RealPlayer, or Windows Media Player, has not been on supporting such processes. Such tools presume that viewers passively watch videos from the beginning to the end, appreciating it as a complete work of art or entertainment on an as-is basis. Video editing tools, such as Final Cut Pro or Premier, allow users to produce a variety of ways to interact with video data and to explore the space of visual effects. However, their goal is to save the results of such interactions and produce another set of videos. They do not help users to simply interact with video data without changing the original content.

We argue that we need a variety of interactive presentation tools for richer experiences in using videos for our knowledge work. Our tools are intended to support *active watching* in contrast with *passive watching*. By applying Adler's notion of active

M.F. Costabile and F. Paternò (Eds.): INTERACT 2005, LNCS 3585, pp. 795–808, 2005.
© IFIP International Federation for Information Processing 2005

reading to the video viewing experience [1], we argue that richer interaction schemes are necessary for active watching (Fig. 1).

Viewers need to be able to interact with videos in various presentations depending on the purpose of their tasks: whether they are (1) checking for anomalies in events recorded over a long period of time (e.g., a surveillance video); (2) trying to identify a trend in the entire event recorded on video (e.g., a video record of a soccer game); or (3) learning the process recorded in a video (e.g., a video of a cooking procedure).

In the first case, a user may want to quickly skim the entire movie to look for possible distinctively different frames. The user may then want to focus more on those frames by very slowly looking at them. In the second case, such as a video of a soccer game, the user may want to skim the entire video, develop an overview of how the game went, and then focus on particular frames that show a certain player doing something spectacular. Those focused frames need to be situated within the context of the game as a whole. With the third case, a user may want to repeat a certain part of the video that shows crucial steps in a process. The user may also want to view multiple parts of the frames simultaneously to compare "before" and "after" procedures.

The goal of our research is to enable a user to interact with a video in a variety of ways: by interactively changing temporal and visual properties of a video, to identify trends, to discover unexpected phenomena, or to deeply examine a particular segment of a video. Our approach is to separate the presentation of a video from its content. A video presentation has both temporal and visual properties. Temporal properties include the playing speed and which part of the video to play. Visual properties include the size, opacity, or rotation of a video frame. Interaction methods on how to control speed and the appearance of frames while the video is being played have not been studied much. Combinations of multiple controls over temporal and visual properties would open up a vast space of possible presentation styles.

Our Time-based Visual Presentation (TbVP) model uses the notion of *media data values* and *user experience values*. Interacting with a video and changing its temporal properties can be expressed as a transformation from the video's Media Data Time (MDT) to the User Experience Time (UET). Changing the visual properties is expressed as a transformation from the video's Media Data Visualization (MDV) to the User Experience Visualization (UEV). We have designed interaction methods for various transformations from MDT to UET and from MDV to UEV to develop TbVP primitives. This paper shows how combinations of the TbVP primitives support rich-video viewing experiences.

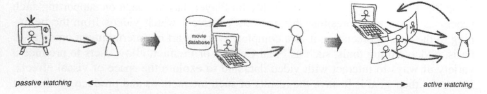

passive watching ⟵————————————————————————————⟶ active watching

Fig. 1. Opportunities have been widened for people to be engaged not only in passively watching videos but also in more actively watching videos

2   Rich Video Experiences for Active Watching

2.1   Tools for Active Watching

Our research has explored how people interact with materials and external representations in creative knowledge work, and we have developed interaction design methods for such processes [14][18][21][22]. Understanding depends not only on the experiences or the knowledge that each viewing person already has, but also on the dynamically emerging relation between the person and the representations. How people interact with text and images in everyday life involves not mere naive information-receiving processes but complex knowledge-construction processes. Videos as knowledge materials are no exception.

Adler and Doren used the phrase *active reading* to refer to reading with critical thinking and learning [1]. Active reading involves not only interactively changing the appearance of the reading material through highlights and annotations, but also changing reading styles, such as riffling through pages to overview its content, layout, and atmosphere; or poring over the specific parts of a book in which the reader has an interest. Schilit et al. developed a touch panel device named XLibris that supports the former process [16]. Speed-dependent Automatic Zooming for a document browser [3][9] has proved to be an effective approach supporting the latter process. The view automatically zooms out when the user scrolls rapidly so that the perceptual scrolling speed in screen space remains constant.

The experience of reading a book differs among readers, depending on the representation or what kind of interaction is possible [8]. We argue that the same holds for watching videos. In the same way as with reading, watching video data, such as a movie or animated visualization [12], can be *active watching* as well as *passive watching*.

Some studies have supported active watching, even though they might not have used this particular phrase. Video summarization and annotation tools, many of which are developed as research tools [4][10][19][22], allow users to bookmark frames in video; to associate text, images, video, URLs or other materials (such as presentation slides) with some frames or parts of videos as annotations, to use 2D-spatial positioning to represent relationships among segmented frames, and to insert XML tags. Those approaches serve for video viewing as knowledge construction by adding more information and context for video data to enrich the video viewing experience.

In contrast, few studies have addressed changing the temporal and visual aspects of video data to help knowledge construction. Visual and temporal aspects are the two fundamental properties of video data. Manipulation of time has had much fewer studies compared to the field of visualization. Our research goal addresses this challenge in designing interaction methods for both temporal and visual properties.

2.2   Separation of Presentation from Content

Presentation and content have been separated in traditional media. By using a document browser, for instance, one can change the appearance of the text by enlarging the font size, increasing the line spacing, highlighting certain phrases, or converting text from a single column into multiple columns, all of which are possible without changing the content of the text. Or, by using an image viewer, one can view images in various sizes, as a thumbnail list, or in a slide show, depending on what kind of experiences the viewer desires through viewing the images.

Viewing thus does not necessarily assume that data are presented in an as-is manner. Compared to these kinds of text and image changes, however, many existing video viewing tools support almost only as-is viewing. The few variations include half-size viewing, full-screen viewing, or repeating a certain part. They do not support viewing in varieties of different presentations.

This paper presents our approach to provide richer video viewing experiences. Although such experiences could be enabled by using high-functionality video editing tools, we argue that when the goal is to view videos and not to produce different video contents, such editors would be too cumbersome in the same way as it is too cumbersome to use Photoshop for viewing a set of images and not for editing. A variety of visual effect systems have been developed [5][6]; however, many of these are for production of new forms of media, and not for understanding the video content.

One example of an approach that shares our goal involves Rapid Serial Visual Presentation (RSVP) techniques [17]. RSVP is a presentation method that serializes a number of images and stacks them into a pile that a user can interactively flip through. Wittenburg et al. applied the method for consumer video devices [20], in which a sequence of image frames are generated from a video into a 3D trail, and as the user plays forward or backward, the trail advances or recedes while the image in the foreground focus position is replaced.

This paper argues for the need for such types of viewing options for users. We do not provide a single viewing mechanism suitable for a specific task. Rather, this paper provides a framework and the landscape of possible interaction methods for richer video experiences.

2.3 TbVP Model

Our approach uses the properties of Media Data (MD) and User Experience (UE) to distinguish between what the data originally have and what a user actually experiences. Interacting with media is viewed as transforming MD values into UE values. For example, zooming into a frame is regarded as changing a given value of a visual property (e.g., size, resolution) into different values of the properties (e.g., larger size, higher resolution). Changing the visual appearances of a representation is explained as a transformation from MDV into UEV. In the same manner, fast-forwarding the video is regarded as changing a given value of a temporal property (e.g., playing speed) into different values of the properties (e.g., faster play), which is explained as a transformation from MDT into UET.

Numerous systems have been developed to summarize and visualize video data by automatically transforming the raw video data into alternative temporal, or visual representations. For example, Video Manga identifies key frames of a video, and then adjusts their sizes to pack them on the page in a style reminiscent of a comic book [19]. Stained-Glass visualizations identify important areas in the key frames and emphasize them in irregular shapes [2]. Nam and Tewfik introduced the Dynamic Video Summarization technique for summarizing video data, a system that modifies the local sampling rate to make it directly proportional to the amount of visual activity in localized sub-shot units of the video [15]. Girgensohn et al. described detail-on-demand hypervideo, which allows users to watch short video segments and to follow ‹ hyperlinks to see additional details [7].

The goal of these approaches, however, is not to enrich video experiences but rather to enable a faster, more effective grasp of the video content than a user can get by watching the original video.

As described in the previous section, we view knowledge construction as a dynamic process by which people interact with external representations. Because no system will be able to generate appropriate visualizations and interaction methods for every conceivable need and situation, our goal is to create a system by which users can actively watch video data.

3   TbVP Landscape and Its Primitives

This paper presents twenty-seven TbVP primitives that we have developed by using Macromedia Director. Each TbVP primitive is a video viewer for a particular type of interactive presentation of a video with a basic set of video manipulations. In the course of the development of the TbVP primitives, we have developed the landscape of TbVPs (Fig. 2), which guides the design and development of further video viewing interaction methods based on the TbVP framework.

The primitives are described under the following six different areas of interaction methods for richer video experience:

(1) direct temporal transformation
(2) direct visual transformation
(3) integrated views
(4) instrumental temporal transformation
(5) instrumental visual transformation
(6) integrated presentations

Note that these primitives presume the video viewer archetype, TbVP000, consisting of (a) the video-file-selection pane; (b) the play, pause, and go-back-to-start buttons; (c) the frame-viewing pane; and (d) the horizontal tracker-bar. The length of the tracker-bar corresponds to the entire video, and the bar has an indicator that allows a user to select a particular frame of the video. All TbVP primitives are based on TbVP000, and have these same four fundamental interface elements. See Fig. 2 for the landscape of all primitives discussed in this section.

(1) Direct temporal transformation.
In this area of the video interaction space, a user directly interacts with the temporal properties of a video. The horizontal bar in the bottom of TbVP001 allows a user to change the speed of playing the video in the range of 0.1 (i.e., 10 times slower) to 10 (i.e., 10 times faster). The bar of TbVP002 allows a user to reverse the speed in addition to TbVP001, in the range of -5 (5 times faster playing backward) to 5 (5 times faster playing forward).

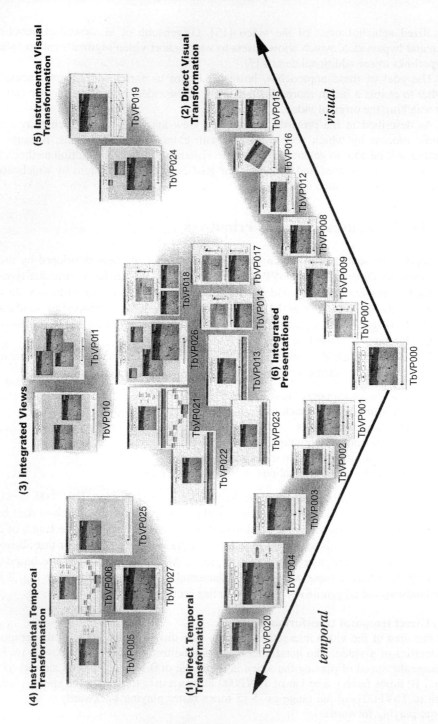

Fig. 2. The TbVP Landscape

The oval indicator of the second tracker bar in TbVP003 allows a user to specify the frame around which the viewer slows down when playing the video. When a user pushes the "focus now" button of TbVP004, the viewer quickly "rewinds" the video for 5 percent of the length of the entire movie, and then replays the rewound part at the slower speed, allowing a user to carefully examine frames that have just passed. TbVP020 allows a user to specify a certain period of time on the tracker bar for which the viewer slows down during the play.

(2) Direct visual transformation.
In this area of video interaction space, a user directly interacts with visual properties of a video. The vertical slider bar of the view allows a user to change the opacity (TbVP007) or the frame size (TbVP009) of the video in the viewer. With TbVP008, a user may directly grasp the corner of the movie viewer and resize it proportionally. TbVP012 is the same as TbVP008 except that the viewer does not keep the aspect ratio (proportions) of the original size. With TbVP016, a user can rotate the video image while playing it by dragging a corner of the frame window.

TbVP015 allows a user to specify and enlarge an area within the frame displayed in the lower frame pane and show it in the upper frame pane. The zooming factor can be changed by using its vertical slider.

(3) Integrated views.
Tools in the other four areas provide multiple frame views of a single video. In contrast, tools in this area can show multiple frame views of different videos. TbVP010 allows a user to freely position a frame in a 2D space. TbVP011 allows a user to freely position multiple frames in a 2D space. A set of trackers for each frame can be controlled in terms of the single tracker bar. Such free positioning of objects in a 2D space serves as a spatial hypertext representation allowing a user to gradually formalize emerging relationships among objects [11][13][22].

(4) Instrumental temporal transformation.
In (1) and (2), users manipulate the temporal and visual properties of a video by directly changing the objects. With tools in this area, a user would use an instrument to change temporal property values. The single-stroked line graph view of TbVP005 is a graphical interface to represent the transition of the playing-speed and the playing-direction (i.e., forward or backward) of the video while keeping the temporal continuity of video. The horizontal axis represents the original frames of the video, and the vertical axis represents the play forward/backward speed. Users drag line segments through the graph to indicate which parts of the video should be played at what speed and in which direction. TbVP006 is an extension of TbVP005. TbVP006 shows the thumbnail images on the graph that are derived from the corresponding frames in the video.

With TbVP025, the vertical position of the viewer in the space determines the speed of play. As a user drags the viewer toward the right edge of the space, the playing speed gets faster; placing the viewer around the middle stops the play, and moving the viewer toward the left edge reverses the direction, playing faster and faster. The horizontal bar of TbVP027 allows a user to change the size of the frame, which also changes the speed of play—the larger, the slower; and the smaller, the faster.

(5) Instrumental visual transformation.
With TbVP019, a user does not directly change the size of the frame window, but instead, the size dynamically changes as the playing speed changes, which can be specified through the line-graph interface described above. With TbVP024, the horizontal position of the viewer in the space determines the frame size. As a user drags the viewer toward the top edge, the size gets smaller; toward the bottom, the viewer becomes larger.

(6) Integrated Presentations.
The TbVP primitives in (1),(2),(4) and (5) presume that there is only one frame view for each moment. In contrast, the primitives in this area show two or more frame views simultaneously in their viewers.

TbVP013 shows a list of ten thumbnails extracted from the original video and placed along with the tracker bar as a sparse overview. A user can thus browse the rough overview of the entire video and decide which frame to look at.

TbVP022 and TbVP023 both show a list of two hundred frames (translucent frames in the case of TbVP023) extracted from the original video and overlaid and lined up along the tracker bar as a dense overview. Although a user is not able to distinguish each frame in the dense overview, slight color changes in the dense overview might indicate possible anomalies in the video.

Different from the above three primitive tools, TbVP014 provides two frame views. A user specifies the area from the bottom frame, which is overlaid on top of the frame view in the top. The two views can have different temporal manipulators; therefore, one can overlay a partial image of a forthcoming part of the video on top of the frame currently played. With TbVP018, a user can have two overlaying images. TbVP017 is similar to TbVP014 except that a user can resize the overlaid portion in the frame view in the top.

TbVP021 combines TbVP006 and TbVP025, where the speed is specified through the graph interface, and the change of the speed results in the change of the size of the frame. TbVP026 combines TbVP024 and TbVP025; moving a viewer toward the top right corner of the space makes the viewer get smaller and play faster.

4   Scenarios

This section presents five scenarios to illustrate how the TbVP primitives are combined and used for specific tasks. The five scenarios are: (1) a security person analyzes a video recorded by a surveillance camera, (2) a coach of a local soccer team analyzes the video of the team's last game, (3) an overseas tourist learns by video how to cook a Japanese pancake using a table-top BBQ, (4) a student learns how to juggle by watching the video of his expert buddy, and (5) a scientist designing a bio module system analyzes the behavior of paramecia in a charged petri dish. Those scenarios are chosen to emphasize different aspects toward richer video experiences.

(1) A Surveillance Video. When a security person analyzes a video recorded by a surveillance camera, the primary task is to quickly zap the entire video, and search for possible anomalies in long-term events recorded on the video. We use TbVP003, TbVP015, and TbVP022 to design a tool for such a scenario (Fig. 3).

The dense overview of TbVP022 gives the security person a rough idea of where to focus in the video. The security person can set the oval pointer of TbVP003 to view the part of the video around the frames of interest in slow speed. TbVP015 allows zooming-in a particular part of a frame in the video that seems suspicious.

Once the security person becomes aware of a suspicious part of the video, the rest of the video may not be of much interest and thereby viewers such as TbVP004 may not be necessary.

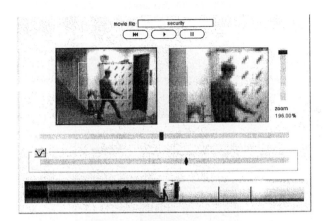

Fig. 3. A TbVP View for the Surveillance Video Scenario

(2) A Video of a Soccer Game. When the coach of a local soccer team analyzes the video of the team's last game, the primary task is to understand how the team's formation changed over time in terms of each player's position on the soccer field. We use TbVP001, TbVP003, TbVP004 and TbVP017 to provide such a macroscopic view for the coach (Fig. 4).

By using TbVP001, the coach may want to quickly browse the entire game on the video with a very fast playing speed. While browsing the game, whenever the coach notices an interesting phenomenon in a game, he/she can press the "focus now" button of TbVP004 to rewind and replay at a slower speed to further examine what was going on. If the coach notes a particular part of the video (such as a shooting scene), he/she can set the indicator with TbVP003 so that the viewer plays the video in fast speed, except it plays the shooting scene at the much slower speed, which allows the coach to concentrate on the scene. TbVP017 allows the coach to zoom-in on a particular player's play within a frame.

(3) A Video on a Cooking Procedure. When an overseas tourist learns by video how to cook a Japanese pancake using a table-top BBQ, the tourist is interested in knowing every detail of the procedure of how to mix ingredients, turn over a pancake, and top it with garnishes. At the same time, because the tourist is not familiar with the cuisine, he/she also wants to know the relationship between each step in the procedure and how the resulting cooked dish looks. We use TbVP011, TbVP013 and TbVP014 to design a viewer for such a situation (Fig. 5).

With TbVP011, the tourist can compare multiple phases of the cooking procedures, for instance, scenes after 1 minute, 3 minutes, and 10 minutes from the beginning of the cooking time. The sparse overview of TbVP013 gives the tourist a rough idea of what would happen in each phase of the procedure. TbVP014 allows the tourist to compare how the pancake would look when finished by overlaying a part of the pancake from different time on top of the currently displayed frame view.

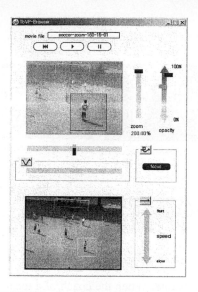

Fig. 4. A TbVP View for the Soccer Game Analysis Scenario

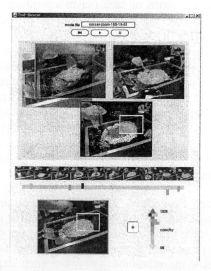

Fig. 5. A TbVP View for the Cooking Video Scenario

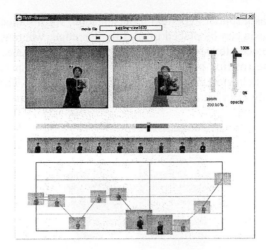

Fig. 6. A TbVP View for the Juggling Performance Video Scenario

(4) A Video on Juggling Performance. When a student wants to learn how to juggle by watching the video of his expert buddy, he/she wants to view particular parts of the video again and again to learn specific skills the expert plays in a video. We use TbVP006, TbVP013, TbVP017 and TbVP020 to design a video viewer for the student (Fig. 6).

With TbVP006, the student can program how to view the video by specifying the playing speed for the entire movie by using the line-graph interface. Thumbnails on the line-graph of TbVP006 together with the sparse overview of TbVP013 would help the student to have a rough idea of which times his expert buddy uses which techniques. TbVP017 allows the student to zoom-in on a particular part of the frame that shows the expert's hand movement. The student can repeat a certain part of the video many times by using TbVP020.

(5) A Video on Paramecia. Because the size of the body of a paramecium is very small (about 0.1 mm) and the movement of paramecia in a charged petri dish is very fast with constantly changing directions, a scientist analyzing the behavior of paramecia in such an environment to design a biomodule system needs to view the video from multiple perspectives, compare a number of frames, and zoom-in on particular parts of the frame. This type of video viewing task is in some sense the most challenging kind to support.

We use TbVP002, TbVP003, TbVP005, TbVP011, TbVP016, and TbVP017 to design a viewer for the scientist (Fig. 7). TbVP002 allows the scientist to play forward and backward at various speeds. When the scientist gets interested in a particular scene, he/she can indicate the frame with the TbVP003 indicator to play the scene at a slower speed. TbVP005 allows the scientist to save a particular mode of viewing the video so that he/she can share this viewing experience with peers in a research group. Most of the frames look alike, so thumbnail displays on a line-graph interface are unnecessary, eliminating the need for TbVP006. TbVP011 allows the scientist to freely position multiple video frames in a space, and he/she can use the space to organize hypotheses as a spatial hypertext representation; for instance, video frames for a particular hypothesis can be placed toward the top edge, whereas those for another hypothesis can be placed toward the bottom edge. Because paramecia keep moving in many directions, the rotation provided by TbVP016 would be necessary to compare some aspects of the behavior. Zooming into a part of a frame in TbVP017 would help the scientist to deeply examine the behavior of a particular paramecium.

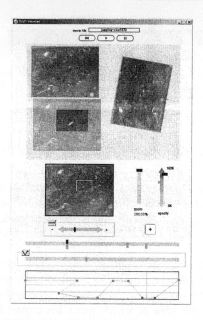

Fig. 7. A TbVP View for the Paramecia Analysis Scenario

5   Concluding Remarks

This paper has focused on interaction methods for users to actively be engaged in video viewing tasks to experience a variety of presentation styles of video data, rather than to edit and produce new video contents. Our approach is to develop the landscape of various types of interaction design primitives with which users could "talk about" their needs for a wide variety of rich video experiences through active watching. We have identified possible patterns of combining TbVP primitives for specific types of video viewing tasks, ranging from a monitoring task to a scientific investigation.

Our immediate future work includes developing a language and an environment to combine some of the primitives to design such a video viewing environment for a specific task. In doing so, we have to cope with design, technical, and psychological challenges, including how to handle complex user operations on multiple video views, how to solve conflicting operations (e.g., when visual properties are dynamically determined by more than one determinant), and how not to overwhelm a user's cognitive process and yet enable a rich video experience. We will continue this work through user observations and exploration of user interface devices that might be better suited for this kind of task.

Acknowledgements

The authors would like to thank Elisa Giaccardi for her valuable comments for organizing this paper. This research is supported by the Ministry of Education, Science, Sports and Culture, Grant-in-Aid for Scientific Research (A), 16200008, 2004-2007.

References

1. Adler, M. J. and Doren, C. V.: How to Read a Book, Simon and Schuster, New York, 1972.
2. Chiu, P., Girgensohn, A., Liu, Q.: Stained-Glass Visualization for Highly Condensed Video Summaries, Proceedings of 2004 IEEE International Conference on Multimedia and Expo (ICME 2004), June (2004)
3. Cockburn, A., Savage, J., Wallace, A.: Tuning and Testing Scrolling Interfaces that Automatically Zoom, Portland, OR., ACM Press, April (2005) 71-80
4. Correia, N. and Chambel, T.: Active video watching using annotation, in Multimedia'99 Proceedings (Part 2), ACM Press (1999) 151-154
5. Fels, S., Lee, E., Mase, K.: Techniques for Interactive Video Cubism. Proceedings of the Multimedia'00. Marina del Rey, CA. (2000) 368-370
6. Fukuchi, K., Mertens, S., Tannenbaum, E.: EffecTV: A Real-time Software Video Effect Processor for Entertainment. Lecture Notes in Computer Science, Vol. 3166. Springer-Verlag, Berlin Heidelberg New York (2004) 602-605
7. Girgensohn, A., Wilcox, L., Shipman, F., Bly, S.: Designing Affordances for the Navigation of Detail-on-Demand Hypervideo, Proceedings of the Working Conference on Advanced Visual Interfaces, AVI 2004, May (2004) 290-297
8. Hornbaek, K. and Fraekjaer, E.: Reading Patterns and Usability in Visualizations of Electronic Documents, ACM Transactions on Computer-Human Interaction (TOCHI), Vol. 10, No. 2 (2003) 119-149
9. Igarashi, T. and Hinckley, K.: Speed-dependent Automatic Zooming for Browsing Large Documents, in Proceedings of the 13th Annual ACM Symposium on User Interface Software and Technology, ACM Press (2000) 139-148
10. Li, F.C., Gupta, A., Sanocki, E., He, L.-W., Rui, Y.: Browsing Digital Video. Proceedings of the CHI'00. Hague, Netherlands. ACM Press (2000) 169-176
11. Marshall, C. C. and Shipman, F. M.: Spatial Hypertext: Designing for Change, in Communications of the ACM, Volume 38, Issue 8 (1995) 88-97
12. Nakakoji, K., Takashima, A., and Yamamoto, Y.: Cognitive Effects of Animated Visualization in Exploratory Visual Data Analysis, in IEEE Proceedings of Information Visualisation, (2001) 77-84
13. Nakakoji, K., Yamamoto, Y., Reeves, B.N., Takada, S.: Two-Dimensional Positioning as a Means for Reflection in Design of Interactive Systems (DIS 2000), ACM Press, New York (2000) 145-154
14. Nakakoji, K. Yamamoto, Y., Aoki, A.: Third Annual Special Issue on Interface Design, Interactions, ACM Press, Vol.IX.2, March+April (2002) 99-102
15. Nam, J. and Tewfik, A. H.: Dynamic Video Summarization and Visualization, in Proceedings of the Seventh ACM International Conference on Multimedia (Part 2) (1999) 53-56
16. Schilit, B. N., Golovchinsky, G., Price, M. N.: Beyond Paper: Supporting Active Reading with Free Form Digital Ink Annotations, in Proceedings of the SIGCHI Conference on Human Factors in Computing Systems, ACM Press / Addison-Wesley Publishing Co. (1998) 249-256

17. Spence, R.: Rapid, Serial and Visual: A Presentation Technique with Potential. Information Visualization, Vol.1, No.1 (2002) 13-19

18. Takashima, A., Yamamoto, Y., Nakakoji, K.: A Model and a Tool for Active Watching: Knowledge Construction through Interacting with Video, Proceedings of INTERACTION: Systems, Practice and Theory, Sydney, Australia, November (2004) 331-358

19. Uchihashi, S., Foote, J., Girgensohn, A., Boreczky, J.: Video Manga: Generating Semantically Meaningful Video Summaries, in Proceedings of the ACM Multimedia 99 (1999) 383-392

20. Wittenburg, K.B., Forlines, C., Lanning, T., Esenther, A.W., Harada, S., Miyachi, T.: Rapid Serial Visual Presentation Techniques for Consumer Digital Video Devices, ACM Symposium on User Interface Software and Technology (UIST), November (2003) 115-124

21. Yamamoto, Y., Nakakoji, K.: Interaction Design of Tools for Fostering Creativity in the Early Stages of Information Design, International Journal of Human Computer Studies (IJHCS), Special issue on Creativity, E.A. Edmonds, L. Candy (Eds.) (2005) (in print)

22. Yamamoto, Y., Nakakoji, K., Aoki, A.: Spatial Hypertext for Linear-Information Authoring: Interaction Design and System Development Based on the ART Design Principle, Proceedings of Hypertext2002, ACM Press, June (2002) 35-44

Temporal Magic Lens: Combined Spatial and Temporal Query and Presentation

Kathy Ryall[1], Qing Li[1,2], and Alan Esenther[1]

[1] MERL
201 Broadway, Cambridge, MA 02139   USA
{ryall, esenther}@merl.com
[2] Virginia Tech
Dept. of Computer Science, Blacksburg, VA 24061 USA
qili2@vt.edu

Abstract. We introduce the concept of a *Temporal Magic Lens*, a novel interaction technique that supports querying and browsing for video data. Video data is available from an increasing number of sources, and yet analyzing and processing it is still often a manual, tedious task. A Temporal Magic Lens is an interactive tool that combines spatial and temporal components of video, creating a unified mechanism for analyzing video data; it can be used for viewing real-time video data, as well as for browsing and searching archival data. In this paper, we define the Temporal Magic Lens concept and identify its four key components. We present a sample implementation for each component, and then describe two usage scenarios for a prototype surveillance application.

1 Introduction

Video data is available from an increasing number of sources, such as entertainment, web cams, home video, and surveillance systems. With more and more video data available, the task of understanding, analyzing, summarizing, or even finding an event of interest becomes a daunting task. Although there are a number of automatic techniques for event detection and object tracking, these do not solve the problem; while they may reduce the amount of data by converting a raw video stream into a set of abstract objects (e.g., events, people, and trajectories), there is still inherently a large amount of data for a person to deal with. Thus there is a need for interface and interaction support to deal with the abstract or meta-data extracted by the automatic techniques, as well as with the raw video data.

Analyzing and processing video data is still often a manual, tedious task. In particular, looking for a specific event in a large data stream can be very difficult. When dealing with "personal" video (i.e., content that you filmed, or a movie that you have seen before) it may be possible to exploit one's own knowledge to help manage the search. In contrast, when dealing with arbitrary video, such as surveillance video or a movie that you have not seen before, finding an individual event may be like looking for a needle in a haystack. While methods exist to support querying by time (e.g., show me all the people that entered a building between 1:00 and 1:15) or by location (e.g., show me all the people that entered a particular room) few techniques attempt to

M.F. Costabile and F. Paternò (Eds.): INTERACT 2005, LNCS 3585, pp. 809–822, 2005.

combine the spatial and temporal components inherent in video data into a unified query and presentation.

We introduce the concept of a *Temporal Magic Lens* to support a combined spatial and temporal query, enabling a novel presentation of the query results to aid people with their video data by serving as a "window in time" into their data. Users choose a *region* of interest and *a time period* of interest, and the computer provides a summary of that location in that particular time period. While a Temporal Magic Lens provides important dynamic information, and is intended to be used dynamically to query and browse streams of video data, it can also be used to provide static snapshots of different subsets of the data. The Temporal Magic Lens concept will be a powerful tool in video information exploration across many domains. For example, for any physical activity (e.g., sports, dance, T'ai Chi) users can quickly detect the minute difference between the body movements of coach's from time to time and thus learn it more quickly. In video editing, we can easily pick out frames in which big differences appear or detect small changes among a number of frames in which all objects seem to remain unchanged.

In Section 2 we present related work that has motivated our research. In Section 3 we define the Temporal Magic Lens concept along with a sample implementation of each of its four key components. We present two sample usage scenarios for our system in Section 4, and conclude in Section 5 with a summary of our work and a discussion of open issues and future directions.

2 Related Work

We first review general video summarization techniques, followed by visualization techniques focusing on the issues of video query, browsing and presentation. Finally, we discuss previous work on magic lenses.

2.1 Video Summarization Techniques

Rendering animated pictures is both time and space consuming. In some cases, there is a risk of exhausting the whole system if appropriate resources are not available (i.e., not enough memory) or if resources are not appropriately managed (i.e., memory leaks). To solve this problem it is often highly desirable to present appropriate summarization or abstraction of the raw video data to users.

Video summarization, sometimes referred to as video parsing, is the first step in video information processing. In this step an index is created and important features of the video are extracted for later analysis. In general it includes two parts: temporal segmentation and key-frame abstraction. Temporal segmentation detects boundaries between consecutive camera shots or event sequences. Key-frame abstraction maps an entire segment to some small number of representative images, usually called key-frames – still images which best represent the video content in an abstracted manner. An index may be constructed from key-frames, and retrieval queries may be directed at key-frames, which can subsequently be displayed for browsing purposes.

A common approach is to integrate the key-frame extraction process with the processes of segmentation. When a new shot is identified, the key-frame extraction process is invoked, using parameters calculated during segmentation [15]. The challenge, which is also the focus of much previous research, is how to generate video summarization automatically based on context. Summarization algorithms can either rely on low-level image features such as color (brightness and dominant color etc.) and motion activity, geometry (i.e., size and location) or more advanced semantic analysis such as pattern detection [4,11]. While this technique is useful and powerful, the time it takes to process the raw images may make it undesirable for a system requiring real-time analysis. As described in Section 3, a Temporal Magic Lens can be used for real-time analysis, when no additional information (or meta-data) is available; it can also exploit the extra information when it is available.

2.2 Video Visualization

We started our work by seeking appropriate visualization techniques to present video data, combining both the raw images and any extracted information (i.e., meta-data). Meta-data is usually associated with individual frames, and may include object counts, object bounding boxes, motion vectors or other derived information. The algorithms used to create the meta-data often require multiple frames, and may not run in real-time. We quickly found it is possible to use our techniques to summarize the raw data directly and present summary views without the help of meta-data.

There is a long history of work in creating efficient methods to present and browse video data. In the DIVA system, for example, the spatial view is arranged in the center and temporal views appear on the sides, which simulates 3D visualization to give a sense of past and future [9]. The side view displays data streams (or summaries). While this approach is suitable for displaying many kinds of data streams in parallel, it requires large display space and meta-data to be available. It can also only be used to visualize data from a particular point in one direction (e.g., the past or the future).

In the Rapid Serial Visual Presentation Techniques (RSVP) project, Wittenburg *et. al.* investigated various space layouts of video frames to help TV channel surfing and video summarization by frame selection [13]. Users can select a number of key frames by clicking the displayed frames. The system presents the video stream in temporal context in "time tunnels" and helps users to navigate to points of interest quickly and precisely. While RSVP provides convenient presentation and navigation methods for video streams, it does not support a direct query method in the same way that our Temporal Magic Lens does – RSVP is more concerned with navigation and browsing rather than posing or answering specific user-queries. We experimented with several RSVP techniques prior to developing our temporal magic lens concept.

Daniel and Chen presented a method for "summarizing" video sequences using opacity and color transfer functions in volume visualization [3]. In particular, they utilized color transfer functions to indicate different magnitudes of changes, or to remove parts of spatial object. This is one of the few examples that we have found that summarizes video data directly by solely utilizing visualization techniques. As with the DIVA system, this technique requires meta-data to be available.

Freeman and Zhang [5] introduced "shape-time photography," a novel method to describe shape relationships over time in a single photograph. Using data gathered from a stationary stereo camera, they compute a composite image that can be used to summarize events or for instructional materials (i.e., in lieu of illustrations). Their work shares many of the same goals as our current work, namely capturing changes in time in a single image, and determining which pixels to contribute to the final image. In our work, however, we focus on the interface and interaction technique that allow users to select the spatial and temporal regions of interest, and the larger context in which a compositing technique may be used. Freeman and Zhang focus on the compositing itself. While their compositing technique could be used as part of our temporal magic lens, it is not suitable for much of today's video as it requires stereo images.

For practical video analysis, it is important to present information at different temporal scales in video editing and analysis. For example, users may only have two minutes to view a half-hour video clip. The Hierarchical Video Magnifier provides users with a detail+context view by using successive timelines [10]. Initially it uses a timeline to represent the total duration of the video clip. Users can select a portion of the timeline and expand it to a second timeline. The timelines create an explicit spatial hierarchical structure of the video source. The disadvantage is that it is hard to scale up. As with the RSVP approach, this work is more concerned with browsing and navigation support rather than explicit querying. Alternatively, Silver2 [8] system applies a spatial magic lens to the timeline to support semantic zooming in the timeline, and hence provides a "fisheye" view.

2.3   Magic Lens

We propose a novel magic lens technique that can be integrated into video analysis systems to support video navigation and exploration with or without meta-data. The magic lenses with which we are familiar to date are spatial in nature – our Temporal Magic Lens adds a new dimension (time) to determine which content should be displayed in the lens. It combines temporal and spatial aspects of a video-based query, and provides a unified presentation of the query results.

The "magic lens" concept was introduced by Bier et. al. as a see-through interface in 1993. A magic lens is a screen region that semantically transforms the content underneath it; users can move the lens to control what region is affected. In practice, a magic lens is a composable visual filter that may be used as an interactive visualization technique [2]. A lens may act as a magnifying glass, zooming in on the content on which it is placed. It may also function as an x-ray tool to reveal otherwise hidden information. Multiple lenses may be stacked on top of one another to provide a composition of the individual functionality. In some cases, different lens ordering will generate different result. A Magic Lens interface offers many advantages over traditional controls. It reduces dedicated screen space while providing the ability to view context and detail simultaneously. It enhances data of interest and suppresses distracting information, and thus reduces execution errors. The Magic Lens concept has been used in many applications, such as Pad++ [1], Debugging Lenses [7] and Document Lens [12]. Our work builds upon this earlier work by providing access to temporal information, and is appropriate to help video querying, browsing and presentation.

3   Temporal Magic Lenses

A Temporal Magic Lens combines spatial and temporal query components into a single query. A user picks a region of interest and a time period of interest, and then the computer present a composite of some subset of the frames to give a summary of that location in that particular time period. The choice of parameter settings may be done manually (by the user) or more automatically (by the system). We believe a Temporal Magic Lens should also provide users with techniques and interactions to quickly understand and further analyze the data displayed within it. In this section, we first describe the concept of a Temporal Magic Lens by defining its four key components. We then describe a sample implementation of a Temporal Magic Lens for an example video surveillance application prototype.

3.1 Key Components

A Temporal Magic Lens has four key components: the spatial query, the temporal query, methods for rendering/compositing multiple video frames, and mechanisms to support drill-down in the data.

Spatial Query: The spatial query indicates the spatial region of interest. It is a contiguous set of pixels, and may be of any shape (e.g., rectangle, oval, blob, etc.); it defines the physical boundaries of the magic lens, and is also the area in which the query results are displayed. The user may select the region manually (i.e., by drawing directly over an image) or the system may automatically select the region (i.e., using an event or motion detection algorithm). To date we have only worked with fixed camera video data, and so the spatial query is specified relative to a fixed (geographical) window. The question of defining the spatial query for panning or mobile cameras is left for future work. We have found that while the initial region could be created using the same manual techniques described above, it is our experience that the region should track the camera's motion (or the motion of objects in the camera's view), and not remain fixed relative to the window frame. World-coordinate frames, if available, might also be useful.

Temporal Query: The temporal query indicates the temporal region of interest. Specifying the start time and duration of the time window may also be done using manual or automated methods. For real-time data the temporal window can only extend into the past. For archival data, it may extend into the past, future, or some combination of the two. In addition to the depth of the temporal window, there is also a question of the granularity of the data within that window – how much data to display or summarize. Within the temporal window we must also specify or determine how many frames (or layers) should be included in the summary.

Rendering/Compositing: Once we have the frames that result from the temporal and spatial query, we must consider the method for compositing the frames for presentation to the user. In essence, we will blend multiple frames to create a single frame, encapsulating or summarizing the query results. When compositing multiple images, the stacking order and the weighting of each frame controls the final appearance of the Temporal Magic Lens. Rather than composite the entire region of interest, it may also be advantageous to identify clipping regions within the larger spatial query. The compositing issue is addressed in more detail by Freeman and Zhang [5].

Drill-Down: The contents (i.e., composited image) of a Temporal Magic Lens contain data across a range of times. Users may want to distinguish which part of the frame comes from which point in time, and may want to further explore that time period in more detail. Thus the Temporal Magic Lens should provide easy interactions for a user to better understand and explore the summary data provided in the composited view, including methods to determine which frames objects/content came from, and easy visual indications of temporal distance. For example, in addition to the composited frame (in the Temporal Magic Lens area), the interface could provide a secondary region with thumbnails (one for each frame that contributed to the summary) or alternatively could provide some interactive feedback using mouse-overs.

3.2 Sample Temporal Magic Lens

We have implemented a sample Temporal Magic Lens for a video surveillance prototype. Here we describe implementations for each of the core components.

Spatial Query: We support manual specification of the spatial query, and use a rectangular lens shape. Users select the region of interest by drawing rectangular areas in the video player window. Its size and position may be adjusted at any time. A single Temporal Magic Lens is shown in the video player in Figure 1a.

Temporal Query: We have implemented a timeline slider widget (Figure 1b) to support specifying the temporal window along with the number of layers of interest within that window. We created our own specialized widget instead of using general sliders to enable pixel-based moving and selection. The vertical line represents the time pointer and will automatically move forward/backward in auto-play mode. It can also be moved freely along the timeline by the user, moving either forward or backward in time. This control is similar to existing widgets appearing in many popular video player applications with an additional function to set the temporal depth of the magic lens. In this implementation the current frame (longer vertical bar) serves as one end of the time interval while the black bar indicates the temporal depth – how far temporally the magic lens can go (the depth of layers). In an alternate version the time period can bracket the current frame, extending in both the past and the future directions. The slider also provides information such as the number of frames composited in the magic lens and their relative temporal distance and weightings.

In the example shown in Figures 1a-c, the temporal magic lens composites eight frames. Each frame is represented by a small rectangle between the temporal pointer and the temporal depth bar. The inter-bar spacing indicates relative temporal positioning, and the bars' gray-levels indicate their relative weighting for compositing. In this example the frames are evenly-spaced. The more "recent" frames are more heavily weighted, making them clearer in the final (composited) image displayed in the lens. The weighting, spacing and "recent" details are discussed in more detail below.

Rendering/Compositing: Choosing appropriate rendering opacity level is rather tricky when many images are overlaid together. Traditional methods primarily address compositing fixed, unrelated images [6, 14]. Their goal is to make either foreground or background more clear while maintaining the visual cues in the whole context. For video data, pictures taken over a time period are normally played sequentially, one by one. Compositing a series of pictures from video data which include moving objects requires us to not only be able to make a particular frame of interest

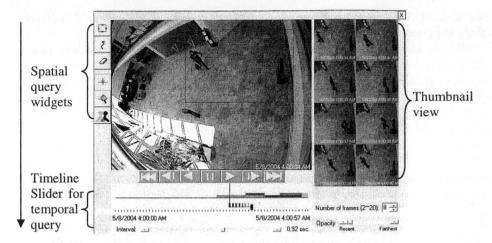

Spatial query widgets

Thumbnail view

Timeline Slider for temporal query

Fig. 1a. The Temporal Magic Lens includes four basic widgets: video player with spatial query widgets (upper left quadrant), timeline sliders to control the temporal query (bottom left corner), thumbnail views for drill down (right-hand side), and compositing/rendering techniques (inset of video player, and below in Figure 1c).

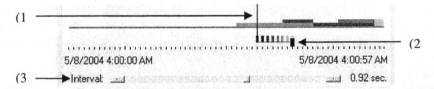

Fig. 1b. A closer look at the Timeline Slider from Fig. 2a: Our composite widget includes (1) Time Pointer, (2) Temporal Depth Bar, and 3) Interval Scrollbar.

Fig. 1c. Temporal Magic Lens detail from Fig 1a. Left: Defining the temporal magic lens. Right: Seeing through the temporal magic lens; the ghosting gives a preview of "future" events. The effect is more evident from the actual motion of the video in the prototype system when viewed interactively, than in the static images shown here.

the clearest (i.e., the most recent or the farthest away temporally), but also clearly show the continuous moving sequence as well.

We use an interpolation approach to composite the view of the magic lens. Given the starting and ending pictures (a time period) and the number of pictures to composite, we calculate the time interval between consecutive composite frames and select them from the disk. The selected images are further filtered by the number of objects detected in the frame. Currently frames containing no object (as determined by metadata, if available) are discarded as they are essentially background images and do not contribute any new information from the user's perspective. Their exclusion brings us a clearer view by minimizing any blurring or fading of the context. We also tried to only composite regions with objects (local compositing) in hope of further reducing the blurs. However, the result is not as good as expected due to the roughness of the meta-data. The detected object rectangles are so large that they overlap each other. As a result, local compositing does not make any big difference from global compositing and it brings even more confusion with sharp edges around each object rectangle.

We evaluated three techniques for creating an appropriate transparency effect when compositing multiple frames; ideally the temporal lens should enable users to see all composited frames as clearly as possible or with emphasis on a subset. Based on our experiment, we determined that simply applying a fixed opacity value is unacceptable. For a fixed opacity value, we observed that images will be perceived differently – images above will always be clearer than those below. This method can either show the most recent images or the farthest ones more distinctively than others, but showing all images with the same perceived opacity level, as might be desirable when users are interested in observing the overall motion sequence, is impossible.

The second method we tried composites images according to different orders to emphasize a subset of images (order switch method). We let the *Opacity* scrollbar control to the number of composited frames and assign a fixed alpha value to each image (0.5). When users want to see the farthest phantom (i.e., the least recent temporally), the system will draw image with the most recent timestamp first (i.e., closest to the time pointer), and less recent one next. As a result, the farthest image (which was drawn last) will be the clearest one since it is rendered on top of the others. For example, given a total of six overlaid frames, if the last frame is the most interesting frame, the overlaying order will be 1, 2, 3, 4, 5, 6 (from bottom to top); if the fifth one is the most interesting frame, the order should be 1, 2, 3, 6, 4, 5 and so on. This method makes the interesting frame and its peripherals distinct from others. The disadvantage is that it still cannot provide a balanced transparency view; even the neighborhood can be blurred and images far away will completely vanished. Users perceive fewer phantoms than the real number being composited.

In the third method, we used a heuristic equation to control the opacity level for each composited frame according to their overlaying order, so that all images can be perceived as with the same opacity value (Equation 1, 2).

$$\sum_{i=1}^{n} \alpha_i \times \frac{i}{n} = 1 \tag{1}$$

$$\alpha_i \times \frac{i}{n} = \alpha_j \times \frac{j}{n} \quad (i \neq j) \tag{2}$$

α_i represents the alpha value of a given pixel on the ith layer, n represents the number of total composited images. i/n stands for the weight of α_i and the multiplication stands for the heuristic value (user perceived value) on a certain layer. The condition when users perceived all composite images as with the same opacity level is defined as a balanced view. Thus we solve $\alpha_i = 1/i$. The equation maintains a continuous transparency spectrum, from the least recent (i.e., oldest) phantom being the clearest to a balanced view, and to the most recent image (i.e., newest) becoming most distinctive as shown in Figure 2.

Fig. 2a. The four single video frames to be composited into a single image

Farthest/oldest   Balanced view   Most recent/newest

Fig. 2b. The transparency spectrum illustrating the effect of different weightings. The frame on the left emphasizes the (temporally) most distant frame; the frame on the right emphasizes the most recent. The balanced view falls in the center. The five sample frames from different points along the spectrum *do not* represent a video sequence; each frame is a composite image showing the different weighting schemes. Only one frame would be displayed within the Temporal Magic Lens.

For example, when compositing two layers, both images are seen as clear as possible when the alpha value for the bottom image is equal to 100%, and the alpha value for the top image is equal to 50%, both images are perceived as having $\alpha = 50\%$. In an informal study, given three images, people perceived all three images to be equally weighted when in fact they are weighted with $\alpha_1 = 100\%$ (bottom), $\alpha_2 = 50\%$ (middle) and $\alpha_3 = 33\%$ (top). Starting from the balanced view, users can decide which side (most recently or farthest) should be more distinguished from others by dragging the Opacity scrollbar, located below the thumbnail view in Figure 1a.

Drill-Down: We provide thumbnails next to the video player to display frames contributing to the composited image in the Temporal Lens (Figure 1a) to enable users to interactively explore the data. Dynamically mousing over a thumbnail allows users to better understand the temporal nature of the data; the system's behavior depends upon the availability of meta-data. When no meta-data is available, it can reorder the layers of the composited image, moving that (active) thumbnail to the top so that it becomes more distinct. When meta-data is available, the system will only show the objects within that (active) thumbnail's frame in the video player. Users can observe the change sequence by moving the cursor over a series of thumbnails and hence get better understanding of the compositing process. We also draw object indicators on each thumbnail to show detailed information about the detected objects.

4 Example System

We applied the temporal magic lens concept in a surveillance system and the result is very promising. There are a number of tasks that any surveillance system should provide for its users: helping users to quickly search video frames (i.e. go to the pictures taken in a certain time period), detecting outliers quickly and precisely (i.e. decide whether an outlier exists, and if so when and where it happens), and identifying suspect objects easily.

To support these tasks, we extended the temporal magic lens by exploring alternative implementations of three of its components. Our investigation into compositing techniques was described in the previous section.

Spatial Query: We augmented the spatial query with a *trajectory query*, which defines a spatial region of interest, and a filter to further constrain the query. This tool allows users to define a pattern of movement (the path and the direction) so that only trajectories with similar patterns will be displayed in the magic lens. A trajectory query is specified by drawing a sample trajectory, a straight line (rather than a rectangle) in the video player. Future work will explore alternate methods for specifying arbitrary trajectories, including non-linear paths and changes in speed. Trajectory queries also require meta-data to be available.

Temporal Query: Two functions were added to support temporal queries. First, a *time compression control* enables users to see the video clip in different detail levels. This tool allows users to decide the time interval by scrolling the *Interval* scrollbar at the bottom of the timeline slider (Figure 1b). For example, a user is able to view a one-hour video clip in just three minutes by changing the time interval, in essence using "fast-forwarding." Instead of playing the frames one by one (taken every 0.05 second), the system plays every twentieth frame with a one second interval. Second we added *temporal zooming* support -- users can zoom into a given time period to see more detailed information. In 3a, the "zoom in" area is shown as a pink-shaded rectangle above the timeline slider. The time interval in the "zoom in" area is controlled by a separate interval scrollbar at the bottom of the object histogram.

Drill-Down: Due to the special characteristics of the surveillance system, we also incorporated an *object query* function, by modifying and extending three components. First, we added an object histogram as a background in the timeline, with the height representing the number of objects and colors distinguishing them. From it users can easily tell how many objects are in a given time period, when the object appears, and how long it lasts. Second, we added an interactive object histogram component (the lower right portion of Figure 3a). Once users select a particular time period in the timeline slider, the corresponding histograms are shown as an interactive histogram. Each object is assigned a distinct color. Users can select different bars in the histogram and a path will appear in the video player indicating its trajectory. Third, we added colorful dots in the lower left corner of each thumbnail to indicate how many objects are detected in the frame. Every object is assigned a unique color consistent with the object histogram. Mousing over a thumbnail will display a rectangle representing the locations and sizes of those objects in the video player. The object query itself merits a thorough study, and is beyond the scope of this paper.

4.1 Usage Scenario One

For the example shown in Figure 1, the video sequence records the event that a man left his bag in the courtyard. It is a one-minute video with pictures taken 25fps. A quick look at the histogram in the timeline slider tells us the activity happens in the later half of the video clip so it is reasonable for us to slide the time pointer directly to the interesting time period. Our task is to detect the actual movement of the man. We first defined the magic lens to let it only cover the center region of the picture. The default number of frames to composite with the magic lens is six with equal perceived opacity. Figure 1c displays the result; we can easily identify the path along which the man walked, and the location in which the man dropped his bag.

4.2 Usage Scenario Two

Another scenario is visualizing the pictures obtained from a highway surveillance system. This video clip covers footage taken for five minutes along a highway. Suppose we only want to take 6 seconds to look at the whole movie. We need to specify a longer time interval (play every 50th frame) using the time interval scrollbar. Figure 3a-b shows the initial interval scrollbar. In Figure 3c we have dragged the interval scrollbar to the right. The summarized result is much clearer than the initial data.

From the long pink bar in Figure 3c we detect that there is an outlier in the last quarter of the video; some object stayed for a long time in the highway. Highlighting that time period by selecting it with the mouse provides an object histogram. Mousing over the bar of interest shows the trajectory of that object (Figure 3a). We can see from the thumbnail in the upper left corner that it is a red car and it stopped on the right curb for quite a long time. In Figure 3a, the diameter of the circle indicates how long the object stays in a place.

Compositing many frames may compromise the clarity of the view. In Figure 4 we defined a rectangular magic lens and the task is to compare the current frame with one of the future frames to see the difference. We can put cursor over the given frame on the right side and objects detected in that frame will be displayed as a rectangle with unique colors in the video player (on the left side). The current frame contains two vehicles, but there will be four vehicles twenty-one seconds later. The red car will still be visible and has driven back a few yards.

Fig. 3a. Object query - putting the cursor onto the object histogram shows the trajectory of the corresponding object in the video player. The object histogram spans the bottom of the application window. The long cyan bar at the bottom of the object histogram indicates an object present for a long period of time. Mousing over that bar brings up a thumbnail of that object (a red car), shown in the upper left-hand corner.

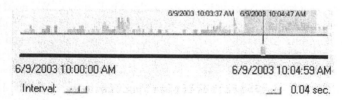

Fig. 3b. Larger view of the timeline slider with object histogram from Fig. 3(a)

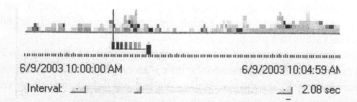

Fig. 3c. Timeline slider with object histogram after summarization (see Section 4.2). The interval scrollbar has been dragged to the right, indicating a longer time interval between frames (0.04 seconds in (a), 2.08 seconds in (b)). We can now see (from the long pink bar in the histogram) that some object lingered on the highway for a prolonged period of time.

Fig. 4. Object query. Moving cursor over a thumbnail will show the detected objects in the particular frame in the video player.

5 Conclusion

In this paper we have introduced the concept of a Temporal Magic Lens, a novel interaction technique that supports querying and browsing for video. It can be used to search and browse video surveillance data, home video, or any other recorded digital content. By combining spatial and temporal aspects of the data, it creates a unified display that supports people's browsing and querying, and provides both dynamic and static views into their video data. We have described its four key components, along with our first investigation into implementations for each. The two scenarios presented in this paper illustrate how to apply the Temporal Magic Lens concept in a surveillance system. Although our initial results are limited due to the roughness of the available meta-data, they suggest better results will follow with more accurate meta-data (e.g., enabling local instead of global compositing). More importantly, they illustrate that the Temporal Magic Lens may be used even in cases where no meta-data is available.

Our current prototype is an initial exploration of the Temporal Magic Lens concept; at present it is a vehicle for our own research rather than an end-user's tool (e.g., our compositing techniques still have many degrees of freedom). Additional study is needed to determine and evaluate the best implementations for each component. In the cases where multiple techniques should be supported (e.g., image compositing), easier-to-understand (and perhaps more intuitive) controls need to be developed. Moreover, by defining the Temporal Magic Lens concept and clearly delineating its four components, we provide a foundation for other researchers to apply their technology (e.g., meta-data extraction, object recognition, compositing techniques, and interactive timelines) to the domain of video.

There are a number of future directions to explore. We would like to support defining and viewing multiple temporal magic lenses simultaneously. In addition, integrating dynamic interaction to the Temporal Magic Lens concept will increase its query power; its filtering function should not only consider the existence of objects, but also the dwell time and other users-specific interests. Finally, to date we have only applied the tool to analyze data from a single, fixed camera. Compositing frames from multiple cameras may generate more interesting results. As previously noted, supporting non-fixed cameras (i.e., pan-tilt-zoom cameras) will require more sophisticated compositing techniques as well as additional meta-data. The Temporal Magic Lens provides a framework for video query and presentation for us and others to build upon, and for designing next-generation video information exploration systems.

Acknowledgements

We thank Tom Lanning and Kent Wittenburg for their suggestions and discussion on this project, Fatih Porikli and Ajay Divakaran for their data and input, Bill Buxton for his comments on this work, and Joe Marks for feedback on this paper.

References

1. Bederson, B. B. and Hollan, J. "Pad++: a zooming graphical interface for exploring alternate interface physics," *Proceedings of UIST '94*, pp. 17-26, 1994.
2. Bier, E. A., Fishkin, K., Pier, K. and Stone, M. C. "Toolglass and magic lenses: the see-through interface," *Proceedings of SIGGRAPH'93*, pp. 73-80, 1993.
3. Daniel, G. and Chen, M. "Video visualization," *Proceedings IEEE Visualization 2003*, pp. 409-416.
4. Divakaran, A., Peker, K. A., Radharkishnan, R., Xiong, Z. and Cabasson, R. "Video Summarization Using MPEG-7 Motion Activity and Audio Descriptors," *Video Mining*, Rosenfeld, A.; Doermann, D.; DeMenthon, D., October 2003.
5. Freeman, W., and Zhang, H. "Shape-Time Photography," *Proceedings of CVPR 2003*.
6. Harrison, B.L., Ishii, H., Vicente, K. and Buxton, W. "Transparent Layered User Interfaces: An Evaluation of a Display Design Space to Enhance Focused and Divided Attention," *Proceedgins of CHI'95*, pp. 317-324. .
7. Hudson, S., Rodenstein, R. and Smith, I. "Debugging Lenses: A New Class of Transparent Tools for User Interface Debugging," *Proceedings of UIST'97*, pp.179-187.
8. Long, A. C., Myers, B. A., Casares, J, Stevens, S. M. and Corbett, A. "Video Editing Using Lenses and Semantic Zooming," http://www-2.cs.cmu.edu/~silver/silver2.pdf, 2004.
9. Mackay, W.E., and Beaudouin-Lafon, M. "DIVA: Exploratory Data Analysis with Multimedia Streams," *Proceedings CHI'98*, pp. 416-423, 1998.
10. Mills, M., Cohen, J. and Wong, Y. "A Magnifier Tool for Video Data," *SIGCHI '92: Proceedings of Human Factors in Computing Systems,* Monterey, CA, pp. 93–98, 1992.
11. Radhakrishnan, R., Xiong, Z., Divakaran, A. and Memon, N. "Time Series Analysis and Segmentation Using Eigenvectors for Mining Semantic Audio Label Sequences", *IEEE International Conference on Multimedia and Expo (ICME)*, June 2004.
12. Robertson, G.G. and Mackinlay, J.D. "The document lens," *UIST'93*, pp. 101–108, 1993.
13. Wittenburg, K., Forlines, C., Lanning, T., Esenther, A., Harada, S., Miyachi, T. "Rapid Serial Visual Presentation Techniques for Consumer Digital Video Devices", *Proceedings of UIST 2003*, pp. 115-124.
14. Zhai, S., Buxton, W. and Milgram, P. "The partial-occlusion effect: Utilizing semitransparency in 3D human-computer interaction," *ACM Transactions on Computer-Human Interaction*, 3(3), 254-284, 1996.
15. Zhang, H., Low, C.Y., Smoliar S.W. and Wu, J. H. "Video Parsing, Retrieval and Browsing: An Integrated and Content-Based Solution," *ACM Multimedia 95*, pp. 15–24, 1995.

Logging Events Crossing Architectural Boundaries

Gregory S. Hartman[1] and Len Bass[2]

[1] Carnegie Mellon University, Institute for Software Research International, USA
gghartma@cs.cmu.edu
[2] Carnegie Mellon University, Software Engineering Institute, USA
ljb@sei.cmu.edu

Abstract. We describe an approach to study the long-term use of GUI applications that supplements a log of low-level events with additional data gathered at the applications' architectural boundaries. We implement a preliminary system based on this approach and apply it to two applications. For the second application, we compare the data collected with our technique to data collected with manual instrumentation. We demonstrate that our technique is easy to apply to new applications and captures information missed by manual instrumentation. This additional information is helpful in answering questions about the use of the application. However, our technique generates large logs and does not yet capture all of the information needed to study the use of applications. We conclude with proposals for rectifying these deficiencies in future systems.

1 Introduction and Problem

It is difficult to build usable applications. This problem can be addressed by involving users in the design of applications, which has been shown to increase their level of satisfaction with the final product [2]. When applications serve a large population of users, it may not be possible to involve a representative sample of users. Detailed records of the interactions between users and prior versions of the application could serve as a substitute for direct user involvement. Logging is a compelling way to gather these data, since it scales to a large number of users, does not require specialized hardware, and can support automatic analysis.

Existing approaches to logging require considerable investment in the process of designing and implementing the logs and/or the process of interpreting the logs to answer specific questions about the use of the application (called queries in this paper). We propose a method that exploits knowledge of the structure of GUI applications to reduce the cost of implementing and interpreting logs. While the initial effort needed to design this logging system is comparable to the effort to write application-specific instrumentation, the resulting logging system can be reapplied to other applications using the same GUI toolkit with relatively little effort. We demonstrate this by writing instrumentation for jEdit [10] (an open source text editor), and reapplying the same instrumentation to a drawing tool implemented for a computerized whiteboard. We compare the information gathered by our logging system to the information gathered by manual instrumentation in the drawing tool.

M.F. Costabile and F. Paternò (Eds.): INTERACT 2005, LNCS 3585, pp. 823–834, 2005.
© IFIP International Federation for Information Processing 2005

2 Existing Logging Techniques

Existing logging techniques, as outlined in [7] and [9], either gather data with application-specific changes (manual instrumentation) or gather GUI events and analyze these events to reconstruct interactions between the user and the application. The relative strengths and weaknesses of manual instrumentation and GUI event loggers become apparent when they are assessed against the selection, context, abstraction, reduction, and evolution problems described in [8]:

- What should be logged? This question has two parts: the approach must decide when to add an entry to the log (the *selection* problem) and what part of the application's state should be included in the entry (the *context* problem).
- How can the data be translated into terms that are appropriate to answer queries? This corresponds to Hilbert's *abstraction* problem.
- How can the data be processed to reduce its volume and highlight events that answer queries? This corresponds to Hilbert's *reduction* problem.
- How should the logging capability be maintained? Changes in the application may require new data to be logged, and changes in the logging may require new releases of the application. This corresponds to Hilbert's *evolution* problem.

In manual instrumentation, programmers solve the selection problem by first translating the queries into specific interactions between the user and the application. They then use these interactions to identify specific locations in the application's code that will execute when these interactions occur. They resolve the context problem by finding the parts of the application's state that are needed to answer the queries. The programmers then insert statements into the application to log execution of these sections of code. This work must be done carefully, since mistakes in the analysis of the selection or the context problems will produce logs that lack information needed to answer the queries. This approach also suffers from the evolution problem, since changes in the application after the logging is implemented may invalidate the analysis of the selection and context problems. In addition, modifications to the logging force a re-release of the application. Some projects attempt to avoid the evolution problem by postponing the implementation of logging, increasing the risk that defects in the logs may not be noticed before the application is released.

While these risks are substantial, manual instrumentation can return valuable data. For example, Cook and Kay employed application-specific changes to study the use of a text editor over a three year period [4]. This paper also illustrates the advantage of manual instrumentation; since the log messages are carefully designed based on the queries, the messages need little processing to provide answers to the queries. Therefore, manual instrumentation rarely suffers from the abstraction problem.

Approaches that log GUI events attempt to avoid the evolution problem by capturing information at the operating system level [5] or through modified GUI toolkits [1, 6, 13]. These approaches can also avoid the selection problem; it is typically possible to log every event and then filter out the unwanted events during analysis. There are two disadvantages to these approaches. First, no GUI event loggers provide a fully automated solution to the abstraction problem. In part, this is caused because the techniques work without detailed knowledge of the application. To solve the abstraction problem, programmers must develop a model of the users' expected behavior [6] or create a mapping between the low-level events and higher level concepts during the analysis [1].

A second weakness becomes apparent when we consider the context problem. Several of the tools provide a logging mechanism to capture the data needed to solve the context problem, but no GUI event loggers can capture this data without modifications to the application. In addition, the loggers do not specify what context would be useful in interpreting the logs. To work around these limitations, programmers must still analyze the queries to identify the context and make changes to the application to capture this context. As with manual instrumentation, these changes reintroduce the evolution problem.

To conclude, we are aware of several viable solutions to the selection problem, but we cannot find a solution to the context problem that does not involve application-specific modifications. In addition, there are few general guidelines that developers can use to identify the relevant context in their applications. The lack of automated support for capturing context also prevents a complete solution to the evolution problem; any change to the application may invalidate the analysis done by developers to collect context, creating new deficiencies in the logs. Finally, there are no fully automatic solutions to the abstraction problem: existing solutions rely on input from either programmers or analysts to create a mapping between low-level and high-level events.

3 Approach

We propose an approach that solves the selection problem by logging at four architectural boundaries present in applications implemented with modern GUI toolkits, such as MFC, Swing, and Motif. These boundaries are illustrated in figure 1. We solve the abstraction problem by associating the data captured at each boundary with the event being processed. Including data captured at the boundary crossed by marker 4 in the diagram partially addresses the context problem. Finally, we address our current approach to reduction. We discuss the evolution problem and readdress the context problem in the next section, which gives more details about our initial implementation of this approach in a system called LECAB.

In most GUI applications, events representing low-level user actions (such as key presses and mouse movements) travel through several well defined layers in the GUI toolkit and the application. In figure 1, events move from the lower layers toward the top layers, eventually reaching application-specific code. At each layer, the events are represented at a higher level of abstraction. Like many other GUI event loggers, we capture events at the lowest level of the architecture. Unlike other loggers, we also track these events as they travel to higher levels of the architecture, logging additional information about the code processing the events.

Given the importance of solving the abstraction and reduction problems, it seems that we should only capture data at the higher levels of the architecture, as is often done in manual instrumentation. In our experience, the data gathered at each level of the architecture are essential, since some of the events at the lower levels will not be dispatched to higher levels. For example, users may click on parts of the application

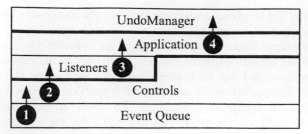

Fig. 1. The architecture of a typical Swing application. The numbered circles portray the path of a typical event through the application. Boxes below the bold line are part of the GUI toolkit; boxes above the line are part of the application.

windows where there are no controls to accept the event [12]. In this case, the GUI toolkit may silently drop the event. By capturing events in level 1, we record these events. Later, these events can be detected by searching logs for mouse clicks that did not translate to higher levels in the architecture. While users may occasionally click the mouse button without expecting a response from the application, a large cluster of these events in a particular location of the window may indicate a problem in the design of the user interface.

If the events are successfully dispatched to a control (reaching 2 in the diagram), we log the identity of the control that received the event. We identify the control by logging both the type of the control (scrollbar, button, etc), strings that are displayed on the screen, and the name of any icons on the screen. By associating this information with the low-level event, we solve part of the abstraction problem: the event is now described in the terms displayed in the user interface of the system.

This information also points to usability problems that are not visible at higher levels of the architecture. We encountered one of these problems when we observed actual use of a drawing application that provided a toolbar of buttons for selecting controls. Users occasionally attempted to insert shapes into their drawings by dragging these buttons into the drawing canvas. The buttons interpreted the drag as a canceled button press. Figure 2 indicates that all of these events were dispatched to a control; logging at level 1 would not have identified the problem. However, there are no activations at level 3 for the MouseToolBar, even though the user clicked in it at step A1. Once again, this pattern does not automatically point to a usability problem; users may make this gesture to cancel an unwanted button press. However, this sequence of events was often present when users were confused by the user interface of the drawing application.

At level 3, the event processing moves into application specific code. The GUI toolkit sends the event to the application by invoking one or more callbacks registered by the application (called listeners). When this happens, we log the name of the listener being invoked. The name of this listener is often closely associated with the name of one of the commands of the application. By logging the name of the command invoked by the low-level event, we complete our solution to the abstraction problem.

In general, we do not attempt to capture information in the application-specific code represented by layer 4 in the diagram. Capturing more information would require either modifications to the application or the use of application-specific

EventQueue	Control	Listener
A1.	User clicks on the textbox button in the toolbar	
MousePressed	MouseToolBar$1	
A2.	User drags into the canvas	
MouseDragged	MouseToolBar$1	
MouseDragged	JScrollPane	
MouseDragged	DocumentCanvas	SelectTool
A3.	User releases the mouse button	
MouseReleased	DocumentCanvas	

Fig. 2. Events showing a failed attempt to insert a new object in a drawing by dragging a button from the MouseToolBar into the drawing canvas. The EventQueue, Control, and Listener columns show what information we collect at these levels. The table is interrupted by lines explaining the user's action.

knowledge. Both of these approaches would necessitate additional work from developers, which we avoid.

However, we do identify information that will help to solve the context problem. The GUI applications that we have studied to date implement undo by representing changes to documents in a stack. This code is represented by the UndoManager layer on the architectural diagram. We provide an interface to allow changes to this state to be recorded. We discuss an application independent technique that allows this data to be captured for some Swing applications in the next section.

Unlike other approaches that solve the reduction problem by analyzing events as they are captured [6], we log every event and boundary crossing and rely on an application-specific post-processing script to reduce the volume of the data. Our approach minimizes the risk that useful information will be lost, and also allows a solution to the reduction problem to be tailored to specific queries. Unfortunately, this approach creates extremely large logs. However, application developers may choose to stop logging at levels 1 and 2 if they do not want to identify usability problems like the ones described in this section. Once we gain more understanding of the data that are needed to analyze typical queries, we hope to reduce the size of the logs by excluding common sequences of events that are not useful in analysis.

4 Implementing Our Approach in LECAB

Our initial implementation of this approach (LECAB) uses AspectJ [11] to automatically instrument Java applications implemented with the Swing GUI toolkit. AspectJ automates the instrumentation of the application, greatly reducing the evolution problem. The choice of Java and Swing simplifies the implementation of LECAB and reduces the programmer effort needed to gather information about changes in the undo state that LECAB uses to address the context problem.

LECAB avoids the evolution problem by relying on AspectJ to automate the instrumentation of the application. The AspectJ project provides a compiler that accepts standard Java source code and one or more aspects that describe changes to be woven into the code. These aspects are made up of two parts: fragments of Java code to be inserted, called advice, and patterns that trigger the insertion of the code, called pointcuts. These pointcuts match one or more well-defined points in the execution of the program code. The architectural boundaries that LECAB uses to instrument Swing applications are easy to represent in terms of pointcuts. For example, the pointcut that captures calls to the listeners in the application is shown in figure 3. We have developed similar aspects to capture interactions with the undo system provided by Swing and to initialize the event capture system when the application starts.

```
public aspect AWTListeners {
    pointcut action(EventObject e, EventListener l):
      execution(void *.*(*)) &&
      args(e) && target(l);

    before(EventObject e, EventListener l): action(e,l){
      AOPLoggerExt.LogListener(CrossType.ENTER, e, l);
    }

    after(EventObject e, EventListener l): action(e,l) {
      AOPLoggerExt.LogListener(CrossType.EXIT, e, l);
    }
}
```

Fig. 3. An aspect that inserts logging code that will be triggered when Swing calls one of the EventListeners defined by the application

Automatic instrumentation has several advantages. First, it reduces the effort needed to apply LECAB to new systems. Second, it reduces the chances for omissions and other errors in the instrumentation. Finally, it eliminates most of the evolution problem, since the automated placement is repeated whenever programmers recompile their application.

LECAB also benefits from patterns defined in the Java language. For instance, LECAB calls the toString method on each new listener and control that it encounters to extract information that describes the control. This method typically returns both the name of the class and much of the internal state of the object, such as the text string being displayed on the control. The class names are often sufficient to describe the purpose of the control. Programmers typically follow one of two patterns when they implement EventListeners. Often, programmers do not name the classes. In this case, the EventListener is assigned a name derived from the enclosing class at compile time. In other cases, programmers name the class after the command being implemented. For example, a listener attached to an undo button may be called UndoHandler. In either of these cases, associating the class name with the low-level GUI event solves the abstraction problem: it translates the low-level event into the terms that the programmers use to reason about the application.

Swing also dictates that all GUI processing must happen on a single thread. Therefore, LECAB can assume that any crossings of the architectural boundaries that occur while the event thread is processing a GUI event are caused by the event.

LECAB logs both calls and the returns that cross architectural boundaries, and assigns any messages that happen between these crossings to the event being processed.

Finally, LECAB benefits from Swing's approach to implementing undo. Unlike many other GUI toolkits, Swing provides a centralized UndoManager that is well integrated with some of the more complex controls in the toolkit. While the use of this manager is optional, many developers choose to use it to reduce the effort of implementing undo in their applications. In LECAB, we use the knowledge of this service to track changes made to the document, eliminating the need for programmers to provide information about their implementation of undo.

An example of a LECAB log is shown in figure 4. The top section of the log shows the descriptions of various events, controls, and listeners that LECAB gathers with the toString method. Each of these descriptions is given a short name that is used in other log entries. In a real log, the descriptions are interleaved with the messages; in this sample they were moved to the beginning of the fragment to improve the readability of the log. The second section shows the architectural boundary crossings for a single event. The first line corresponds to level 1 of the architecture, and indicates that the application is processing event E626. The definition of E626 indicates that it is a press of button 1 of the mouse. The second line shows that the event was sent to control C2, a TextAreaPainter. The TextAreaPainter informs the application of the event by calling listener L15, a MouseHandler defined in the JTextArea class of the application. While this listener is processing the event, some part of the application adds the record U2 to the UndoManager. This record indicates that the caret moved to location 25 in the document. This chain of reasoning from the low-level event to the high-level change in the state of the document represents a solution to the abstraction problem.

```
DEFINE E626 MouseEvent[MOUSE_PRESSED,(43,109),button=1…
DEFINE C2 TextAreaPainter[,4,0,638x420,alignmentX=…
DEFINE L15 JEditTextArea$MouseHandler@23bdd1
DEFINE E627 MouseEvent[MOUSE_PRESSED,(33,10),button=1…
DEFINE U25 caret move[start=25,end=25]

ENTER EVENT E626
   ENTER   CONTROL C2 EVENT E626
      ENTER   LISTENER L15 EVENT E627
         CREATED   UNDO U25
      EXIT   LISTENER L15 EVENT E627
   EXIT   CONTROL C2 EVENT E626
EXIT EVENT E626
```

Fig. 4. LECAB events for a click inside a jEdit document. This sample log has been reformatted: the timestamps and thread id on each entry have been removed, some of the statements have been abbreviated, and indentation has been added to illustrate the nesting that LECAB uses to solve the abstraction problem.

5 Applying LECAB to a Second Application

During the development of LECAB, we ran simple tests on jEdit to verify LECAB's solutions to the selection, abstraction, and context problems. To verify LECAB's application independence, we used the version of LECAB developed against jEdit to instrument a drawing application designed for an interactive whiteboard. This application was developed as part of a research effort by an outside group of developers. As part of their research, these developers added manual instrumentation to the application. Our prior experience studying these logs to answer queries highlighted several deficiencies in the data collected. Since the drawing application already contained a version of manual instrumentation and we already had a large list of queries, it was a good candidate for an initial test case.

When we examined the first set of logs created by LECAB, we realized that the logs lacked context information about the changes to the document being edited. After inspecting the code, we discovered that the developers did not make use of the undo functions provided by Swing. This new version of the undo system had a similar structure to the one provided by the Swing libraries, but used different class names. Therefore, we wrote an application-specific aspect to collect information from the application's undo system.

6 Comparing LECAB to Manual Instrumentation

We decided to compare LECAB to manual instrumentation by assessing their ability to count the number of times that users grouped multiple objects in the drawing application. We defined a simple user session that would simulate use of the drawing application. In this session, the user creates three simple objects, groups two of the objects, and then moves both the group and the ungrouped object. These actions and the resulting log messages are given in more detail in figure 5.

The events in these log messages correspond to five general categories. The messages marked with E1 and E5 represent simple clicks in the application's toolbar to select a tool. In both of these cases, the LECAB log is roughly identical to the manual log: both identify that a tool was selected (LECAB's log of the "MouseRelease heard by" is roughly equivalent to the manual log's "Selected Tool"), and both identify which tool was selected.

E2, E3, and E4 are logged as the user draws the shapes on the board. Both LECAB and the manual instrumentation identify the operation, but LECAB's instrumentation also captures unique identifiers for the objects being created (FH0, FH1, and FH2). While this is not valuable for this query, we have encountered other queries that could use the information. For instance, we wanted to count the number of times that a user immediately deleted a new object, since this is similar to an undo. This pattern can be detected by searching the log for create statements that are immediately followed by delete statements that reference the same features.

E6 marks a scenario where neither LECAB nor the manual log returns as much information as we would like. Here, the user has just completed a select operation. Ideally, we would like to know which objects were selected. Since this does not

User Action	LECAB Log	Manual Log
E1. User clicks on freehand drawing tool in the toolbar	MouseReleased heard by FreeHandTool	Whiteboard: Selected Tool: FreeHandTool
E2. User draws a line with the tool	MouseDragged heard by FreeHandTool that creates FH0	Whiteboard: Did Freehand draw
E3. User draws a second line	MouseDragged heard by FreeHandTool that creates FH1	Whiteboard: Did Freehand draw
E4. User draws a third line	MouseDragged heard by FreeHandTool that creates FH2	Whiteboard: Did Freehand draw
E5. User clicks on the select tool in the toolbar	MouseReleased heard by SelectTool	Whiteboard: Selected Tool: SelectTool
E6. User selects the first two lines	MouseReleased heard by SelectTool	Whiteboard: Used select tool
E7. User presses the "make group" button on the toolbar	MouseReleased heard by GroupHandler that deletes FH1, deletes FH0, creates PF0	Whiteboard: WB Action Button: Grouping figures
E8. User clicks on the grouped lines and begins to move them	MouseDragged heard by SelectTool that does nothing?	
E9. User releases the mouse button after moving the group	MouseReleased heard by SelectTool heard by SelectTool that changes PF0, …	Whiteboard: Used select tool
E10. User clicks on the third, ungrouped line and begins to move it	MouseDragged heard by SelectTool that does nothing?	
E11. User releases the mouse button after moving the line	MouseReleased heard by SelectTool heard by SelectTool that changes FH2…	Whiteboard: Used select tool

Fig. 5. This figure compares the data collected by LECAB to the manual instrumentation of the drawing application for a simple drawing session

change the state of the document, LECAB's instrumentation of the undo system does not see this change in the application state.

E7 demonstrates that LECAB's instrumentation of undo captures information missed in the manual instrumentation. The LECAB log shows that the group button removed the first two features in the document (FH0 and FH1) and inserted PF0. The manual instrumentation only indicates that the grouping figures button was pressed, it does not describe the effect that this operation had on the document.

E8 and E10 mark places where LECAB detected a bug in the undo system implemented in the drawing application. We were aware of this bug from prior studies that observed actual use of the application with video recording, but were unable to reproduce it. With the detailed information provided by LECAB we were able to see that the bug was triggered by moving objects on the drawing canvas.

E9 and E11 also illustrate a case where LECAB's log is superior to the manual instrumentation. Here, the user clicks on the new group of objects (E9) or the remaining ungrouped object (E11) and drags it to a new location. This operation is handled by the same callback that handles selecting objects. Therefore, both the LECAB log and the manual log record the use of the select tool. However, the instrumentation that LECAB adds to the undo handling in the application detects a change to the document and identifies the changed object.

This example illustrates that LECAB can return more of the data needed to answer queries than manual instrumentation. However, it also points to two limitations of LECAB. First, even after aggressive reduction, the log messages returned by LECAB are considerably more verbose than messages generated by manual instrumentation. Second, LECAB misses changes to the state of the application, such as the state tracking the current selection, that do not affect the document being edited. While this missing state did not adversely affect our ability to analyze this query, it could prevent the analysis of other queries.

7 Future Work

There are several limitations in our evaluation of LECAB. Before designing LECAB, we attempted to analyze queries by examining the logs generated by the manual instrumentation in the drawing application. The design of LECAB was informed by our knowledge of what information was not included in these logs. In addition, the developers of the manual instrumentation did not know about our queries when they designed the instrumentation. Given knowledge of our queries, they would have been more likely to design instrumentation that would capture the relevant data.

This study would be enhanced by looking at a wider assortment of applications and more queries. We intend to do this as part of our future work. This collection of applications should also help us to understand how often developers using Swing do not use the undo manager provided by the toolkit. If this is a common pattern, our approach to automatically collecting context will not be workable.

Based on our initial experiences with LECAB, we now realize that we need to find a way to reduce the volume of the data collected by the system (the reduction problem). This is a difficult problem to solve, since overly aggressive reduction could discard data needed to answer queries. We plan to examine approaches used in prior work that identify and eliminate the events that can be reconstructed from other data [3].

Logging systems must protect the privacy of users [12]. We have not addressed this in LECAB. We may be able to address privacy by discarding data about the content of documents, such as the information in a text box on a drawing, while retaining information about the documents' structure, such as the position of the text box in the drawing and the amount of information that it contains.

If we assume that developers can invest a small amount of effort to improve logging, we may be able to direct them to write aspects that would log context that is missed by LECAB. For example, developers may be able to identify the state in their applications that tracks the current selection and write aspects to log changes to this state.

Our current approach to logging changes to the document relies on a correct implementation of undo. If developers forget to implement undo for a specific command, LECAB will not log the corresponding changes in the document. In future work we intend to provide a toolkit to support developers as they implement features that cannot be isolated to one part of the application, such as cancel. This toolkit would isolate much of the state of the application, providing another interface that could be targeted by LECAB. Discrepancies between the crossings of the cancel interface and crossings of the undo interface would reveal defects in the implementation of undo.

8 Conclusion

We described a new approach to capturing interactions between users and GUI applications. Our approach augments a log of GUI events with class names and descriptions of document changes captured at architectural boundaries of the application. These additional data facilitate the interpretation of the logs; class names often correspond to features in the application and changes in the document often describe the application's response to the user's action. We implemented this approach in LECAB, a logger designed to capture information about Java applications using the Swing GUI toolkit, and use LECAB with two different applications. Simple tests demonstrate that the resulting logs address the selection and abstraction problems described by Hilbert [7]. In some cases, the LECAB logs provide more information about interactions between users and applications than manual instrumentation. However, the same tests indicate that additional logging is needed to capture the context. In addition, the reduction problem must be addressed during data capture to control the size of the logs. We plan to address these issues in future work.

Acknowledgements

This work was supported by the NASA High Dependability Computing Program under cooperative agreement NCC-2-1298. This material is based upon work supported by the Defense Advanced Research Projects Agency (DARPA) under Contract No. NBCHD030010. We thank Bonnie John for her help in forming the queries we used to evaluate the logging systems. We also thank the developers and other researchers working with the drawing application for their help in gathering data and reconstructing the development process.

References

1. Al-Qaimari, G., McRostie, D.: KALDI: a computer-aided usability engineering tool for supporting testing and analysis of human-computer interaction. In: Proceedings of the third international conference on Computer-aided design of user interfaces, Kluwer Academic Publishers. (1999) 337-355
2. Baroudi, J.J., Olson, M.H.,Ives, B.: An empirical study of the impact of user involvement on system usage and information satisfaction. Commun. ACM 29 (1986) 232-238
3. Chung, G., Dewan, P.: A mechanism for supporting client migration in a shared window system. In: UIST '96: Proceedings of the 9th annual ACM symposium on User interface software and technology. (1996) 11-20
4. Cook, R., Kay, J., Ryan, G.,Thomas, R.C.: A toolkit for appraising the long-term usability of a text editor. Software Quality Journal 4 (1995) 131-154
5. Gellner, M., Forbrig, F.: ObSys: a tool for visualizing usability evaluation patterns with mousemaps. In: HCI International. (2003)
6. Hilbert, D.M., Redmiles, D.F.: An approach to large-scale collection of application usage data over the internet. In: Proceedings of the 20th international conference on Software engineering, IEEE Computer Society. (1998) 136-145
7. Hilbert, D.M., Redmiles, D.F.: Extracting usability information from user interface events. ACM Comput. Surv. 32 (2000) 384-421
8. Hilbert, D.M., Redmiles, D.F.: Large-scale collection of usage data to inform design. In: Proceedings of the Eighth IFIP TC.13 Conference On Human-Computer Interaction (INTERACT 2001). (2001)
9. Ivory, M.Y., Hearst, M.A.: The state of the art in automating usability evaluation of user interfaces. ACM Comput. Surv. 33 (2001) 470-516
10. jEdit: Open source programmer's text editor.
11. Kiczales, G., Hilsdale, E., Hugunin, J., Kersten, M., Palm, J.,Griswold, W.G.: An overview of AspectJ. In: Proceedings of the 15th European Conference on Object-Oriented Programming, Springer-Verlag. (2001) 327-353
12. Nielsen, J.: Usability Engineering. Morgan Kaufmann Publishers Inc. (1993)
13. Uehling, D.L., Wolf, K.: User action graphing effort (UsAGE). In: Conference companion on human factors in computing systems, ACM Press. (1995) 290-291

Representing Unevenly-Spaced Time Series Data for Visualization and Interactive Exploration

Aleks Aris[1], Ben Shneiderman[1], Catherine Plaisant[1], Galit Shmueli[2]
and Wolfgang Jank[2]

[1] Human-Computer Interaction Laboratory
University of Maryland Institute for Advanced Computer Studies
{aris, ben, plaisant}@cs.umd.edu
[2] Department of Decision and Information Technologies,
Robert H. Smith School of Business
University of Maryland, College Park, MD 20742 USA
{gshmueli, wjank}@rhsmith.umd.edu

Abstract. Visualizing time series is useful to support discovery of relations and patterns in financial, genomic, medical and other applications. Often, measurements are equally spaced over time. We discuss the challenges of unevenly-spaced time series and present four representation methods: sampled events, aggregated sampled events, event index and interleaved event index. We developed these methods while studying eBay auction data with TimeSearcher. We describe the advantages, disadvantages, choices for algorithms and parameters, and compare the different methods for different tasks. Interaction issues such as screen resolution, response time for dynamic queries, and learnability are governed by these decisions.

1 Introduction

Time series data consist of measurements of a variable over time. In many cases, measurements are evenly-spaced over time. Muller & Schumann provide an extensive survey on visualizing real-valued multivariate time-dependent data, with the emphasis on evenly-spaced data [15]. Silva & Catarci's review extends to categorical data and shows examples of unevenly-spaced data [18]. Like many researchers ([1], [3], [19]) the designers of TimeSearcher 1 assumed equally spaced time series data [10]. Common examples are daily stock prices and electric potential measurements taken from electrocardiograms at regular short intervals. Van Wijk & Van Selow show how to visualize evenly-spaced data on multiple scales [20]. They visualize the number of employees working in a company at various time points on daily, weekly, monthly or yearly scale by using time series plots and a calendar. Several researchers show how to visualize evenly-spaced periodic data using spirals to discover patterns and relations ([7], [21]).

While evenly-spaced data occurs frequently, there are also examples where data are not spaced equally over time. Our current research looks at online auction data, which consist of series of bids with timestamps, dollar amounts, bidder ID etc. Other examples are traffic incident data on highways, blood test results in patient records,

M.F. Costabile and F. Paternò (Eds.): INTERACT 2005, LNCS 3585, pp. 835–846, 2005.
© IFIP International Federation for Information Processing 2005

and postings on Internet discussion boards. In these examples, the measurements are not scheduled beforehand and can occur at any time. We call such measurements "events". Their occurrence over time is unpredictable and in general, no simple formula can map natural numbers to the timing of these events which can be separated by seconds, days or years. We call such time series "unevenly-spaced", as opposed to the more common "evenly-spaced" time series.

While it is straightforward to plot an evenly-spaced time series, at least the ones with small cardinality, it is challenging to plot unevenly-spaced ones. The arbitrary spacing in such time series poses trade-offs and problems such as precision of data, encoding of timing, and representation of data, which may or may not result in data loss. For instance, consider visualizing eBay auction data that displays all the bids that were placed during an auction. Consecutive bids can be separated by as much as entire days or by as little as a single second as is often the case toward the end of the auction. Some auctions only have a few bids; other auctions have hundreds of bids. In order to see the real data with full precision, the time points on the x-axis would need to be 1 second apart from each other. Even though the longest eBay auction is only 10 days long, this would result in 864,000 time points for one auction which can lead to performance problems. The average screen has only between 1,024 and 1,600 horizontal pixels, so it also becomes a challenge to fit the data in this resolution. This paper investigates several methods to overcome this problem and discuss the issues surrounding them. Each of the methods presented transforms unevenly-spaced time series into evenly-spaced points on the x-axis of the visualization. Each representation is effective for addressing a subset of the problems and users' tasks, but we focus on representations that provide rich overviews of the data while minimizing data loss and required memory resources.

2 Characteristics of Time Series Under Consideration

Time series data is a general term that includes many variations, such as nominal, ordinal, and continuous values at evenly- or unevenly-spaced time points [15]. The data may consist of a single time series or multiple ones; it may consist of a single variable or multiple variables. For example, meteorological data may have multiple variables, such as temperature, barometric pressure, and rainfall for each day at multiple locations. Although TimeSearcher 2 now supports multiple variables (see [8] and www.cs.umd.edu/hcil/timesearcher), for simplicity, this paper focuses on multiple time series for a single variable.

To keep the illustrations readable we used a small sample of 3 auctions from www.eBay.com, which is the largest consumer-to-consumer electronic auction house. Each auction is a time series of bids placed throughout that auction. eBay uses a "second price" auction format with a "proxy bidding" mechanism. This means that the winner pays the second highest bid, and that at every point in the auction only the second highest bid is disclosed. Bidders, therefore, sometimes submit bids that are lower than the highest bid, and therefore the resulting time series is not necessarily monotonic. Table 1 describes the main characteristics of the 3 sample auctions:

Table 1. Auction characteristics

Auction Name	Length	Number of bids	Opening bid	Closing bid
A	3 days	13	99.00	224.72
B	5 days	29	9.99	232.50
C	10 days	18	5.00	172.50

The auctions start and end at different times, however, they occur close to each other such that all auctions fall within a 13-day period. This sample dataset is used in all the figures of the paper. Note that in all figures, the events (=placed bids) are connected via line segments. Although this has the disadvantage of making the detection of change in the y-value more difficult, the perception of which events belong to the same time series is much easier. There are alternatives (e.g. [16]) providing the reverse effect.

The data characteristics of time series varies enormously across applications, and the tasks that users need to perform vary greatly as well. Filtering and searching are likely to be insensitive to the type of representation chosen (except for general issues of performance and data loss) but browsing and more importantly close inspection of a small number of auctions – such as a result set – are the tasks where representation type will have a greater impact. Tasks might involve looking at the details of bid timing and value to study bidder strategies, comparing two or more concurrent auctions, looking for clues linking bids with world events or personal routines, and many other typical visual inspections tasks such as looking for abnormalities or patterns.

3   Description of Four Representation Methods

Our discussions led to several proposals for representation methods, and we selected four for implementation and detailed investigation: sampled events, aggregated sampled events, event index, and interleaved event index. The first two methods are more conventional, and their advantages and disadvantages become clearer after examination of the last two methods.

3.1 Sampled Events

In this representation, we sample the value at regular intervals. Fig. 1 illustrates the visualization of our sampled auction dataset with a sampling interval of 5 minutes. The y-axis reflects the bid amount ($) and the x-axis is an ordinary time scale.

We define the *cardinality of a time series* to be the number of time points a single time series contains, and define the *cardinality of the x-axis* to be the number of time points on the x-axis of the visualization of the multiple time series. Those numbers will be used to compare the four methods. Along with the number of time series, the cardinality of the x-axis is useful for estimating the memory and processing requirements of the representation. For our sample dataset (Fig. 1) the sampled events method at five minute intervals makes the cardinality of A = 866, B = 1444, C = 2880. The cardinality of the x-axis is 3851.

Sampling requires an algorithm to determine what y-value to use when no event occurred at the time of the sampling. In Fig. 1, the most recent event value is used. (Fig. 1 shows the data as it is visualized in TimeSearcher 2.1.) In auction data this makes sense as the most recent bid corresponds to the current auction price. As the sampling interval increases, the chance that events will not appear on the display increases, resulting in greater data loss.

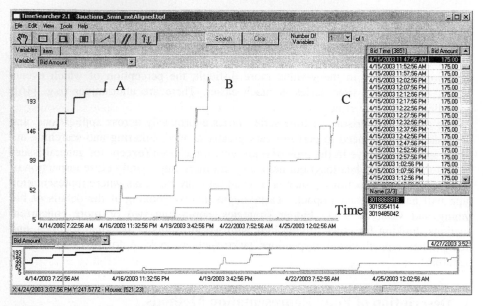

Fig. 1. Time series sampled at 5-minute intervals (not aligned), visualized in TimeSearcher 2.1. Bid amounts sometimes decline because eBay uses second-price auctions and does not disclose the highest bid.

Cardinality of time series: A = 866, B = 1444, C = 2880.
Cardinality of the x-axis: 3851 time points.

Advantages:
- Horizontal distance between time points accurately encodes time. When and how long a bid is placed before/after another can be perceived by the horizontal distance (up to the accuracy of the interval).
- Both the time-order relation and the length of time are conveyed, even though zooming might be required to see the order of close events.
- The visual length of a line indicates the actual duration of the corresponding time series.

Disadvantages:
- Many time points are generated.
- There may be data loss. Data loss will increase with the sampling interval. For example, if more than one bid occurred within the sampling interval, the presence and value of all the bids except for the last one will be lost.

- The y-values are exact but the time points (on the x-axis) are approximate. The error is bounded by the length of the sampling interval.

3.2 Aggregated Sampled Events

The sampled events representation generates many time points. When viewing time series over long periods with small sampling intervals, the number of pixels on the screen will not be sufficient for an overview to show all the data points. In such instances, aggregation can be used to allow the overview to fit into the screen, mitigate the amount of processing required and maintain interactivity. The main difference between aggregation and sampling is that a sampled value represents only one event, while an aggregated value represents a collection of events.

In order to implement aggregation for time series, the following parameters should be specified: 1) the *level of aggregation* is the number of consecutive values that an aggregated value represents. 2) an *algorithm (a summary statistic) to determine the aggregated y-value*: A common approach is to take the average. However, there are other choices such as the median, min or max. 3) an a*lgorithm to determine the aggregated x-value*: Many possibilities exist. Besides taking the first, last, or middle value of the time points, a totally new value could be generated as well. One motivation to use aggregation is to reduce the overhead for operations available in interactive visualization of time series. This is especially useful when the difference between the aggregated view and the sampled view is indiscernible. For example, when the data of Fig. 1 is aggregated with 12x aggregation level, the overview of the aggregated data has the same appearance as in Fig. 1. While the sampling interval is 5 minutes in Fig. 1, the granularity of every time point is 1 hour in the aggregated version with 12x level. We used the average function to determine the aggregated y-value. To determine the x-value, we used the last time point from the set of points that are aggregated. The cardinalities are greatly reduced: While the cardinality of x-axis reduced from 3851 to 321 time points, the cardinality of time series reduced from 866, 1444, and 2880 time points to 73, 121, and 240 time points, respectively, in the aggregated version.

The effect of aggregation becomes apparent when users zoom in. Fig. 2 shows three zoomed versions of a portion of the data in Fig. 1 with different aggregation levels, showing the impact of different aggregation levels: 6-hour, 2-hour and 5-minute intervals. As the aggregation level decrease, the precision improves. One possibility is to aggregate dynamically considering the amount of information to be displayed and available space on the screen to keep the differences unnoticeable. The algorithm for such a dynamic aggregation can become complex but several researchers implemented examples of dynamic aggregation [5], [7]. In Brodbeck & Girardin's TrendDisplay, the raw data is never shown, rather they are represented with one of the four different levels of detail, which are density distributions, thin box plots, box plots plus outliers, and bar histograms. Hence, they can be considered as some form of aggregation, and the aggregation level dynamically changes within these four levels according to the density of the data to be displayed [7]. This strategy is an implementation of semantic zooming [4]. In Berry & Munzner's BinX, the aggregation technique of binning is used, and users can choose the aggregation level interactively. There are visual cues to indicate the aggregation level, and evenly-spaced time series are used [5].

Sampling and aggregation both require a method to determine what value to use when no event occurred at all in the time interval. For applications with highly variable values, interpolated or moving average estimates are risky, making it necessary to have a special indicator for missing values [19].

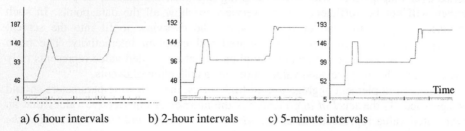

a) 6 hour intervals   b) 2-hour intervals   c) 5-minute intervals

Fig. 2. Three zoomed versions of a portion of Fig. 1 with various aggregation levels: a) uses 6-hour intervals (72x), b) 2-hour intervals (24x) and c) 5-min. intervals (1x)

Advantages:
- The cardinality of the time series and the x-axis are reduced, which increases performance.
- Both the time-order relation of events and the length of time are conveyed, although approximately.
- The visual length of a line indicates the actual duration of the corresponding time series.

Disadvantages:
- Besides the data loss due to sampling, the data is only approximate. Neither the y-values, nor the time points precisely reflect the reality. As the aggregation level increases, greater degradation occurs.
- Parameters of aggregation need to be changed according to the density of the data to minimize error. The algorithm for finding optimal parameters tends to be complex.

3.3 Event Index

Unlike the previous two methods, which represent time linearly on the horizontal x-axis, the event index method does not. This method distorts the x-axis and stretches it when there are more events by separating each event by an equal amount of space, regardless of the elapsed time between events. In our example of auctions, the event index method provides a simple and powerful representation when users are analyzing and comparing the number of bids and their amounts, independently from the time they took place.

In this method, the cardinality of an auction is equal to the number of bids in that auction (e.g. 13 for Auction A). The cardinality of the x-axis equals the largest time-series cardinality among all time series (here 29 because of auction B) (Fig. 3).

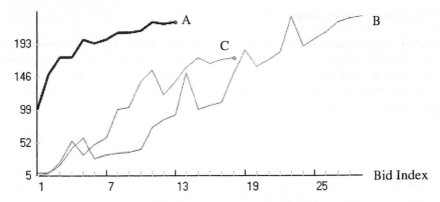

Fig. 3. Event index visualization of the same dataset

Cardinality of each time series: A = 13, B = 29, C = 18
Cardinality of the x-axis: 29

In Fig. 3, the horizontal length in each auction corresponds to the number of bids in that auction. Note that clock time is not encoded anywhere although the order of events is. Even though the nth bids of all auction are lined up vertically, this alignment does not imply that the bids were placed at the same time.

Advantages:
- The cardinality of the time series and the x-axis are kept as small as possible without loss of data in terms of bid amounts. To contrast with the sampled events method, which may have data loss, notice that while A looks monotone in Fig. 1, in reality, it is not monotone as we understand from the dip at the 6th index in Fig. 3. (Bid data from eBay are non-monotone as eBay uses second-price auctions, where the highest bid is hidden. This results in bids that might be lower than the previously placed bid.)
- Having the smallest number of data points maximizes performance in an interactive visualization setting.
- Comparing the nth bids across two or more auctions is easy.
- In the context of auctions, long lines with many bids represent more competitive auctions.

Disadvantages:
- Time is not conveyed, neither absolute nor relative. The inherent alignment of auctions results in no information on which auction started earlier.
- The order of bids, although preserved within an auction, is not preserved across auctions.
- In the context of auctions: the visual length of a time series doesn't indicate the duration of an auction. For example, C appears shorter than B because it has fewer bids, while in fact its duration is twice as long as B (10 days vs. 5 days).

3.4 Interleaved Event Index

Similar to the previous method, the Interleaved event index does not represent time linearly. On the contrary, it represents the sequence of events across multiple time series. In this method, all the time points of all the time series are collected, sorted by time, and indexed. This new index is used for the x-axis. It treats the time points as ordinal, but ignores the time interval information.

All events are shown in the order they occurred, therefore whenever an event appears to the right of another one - even on a different auction, it happened later in time. However, since the time duration information is not encoded, users cannot determine the duration between events. The resulting effect is the stretching of time series during the periods where they have many events, but also during the periods where they have no events while other series do (Fig. 4).

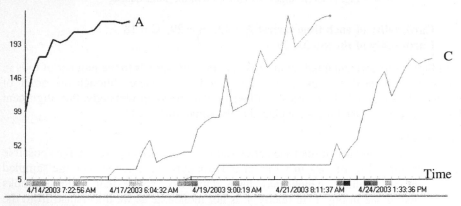

Fig. 4. Interleaved event index visualization of the same sample auction dataset. Dates are used to label the time axis but note that their spacing is not uniform.

Cardinality of each time series:
A = 16, B = 37, C = 44 (excluding the missing values at the beginning and end)
Cardinality of the x-axis: 60

In our example, there are 60 time points on the x-axis (13+29+18 = 60). The cardinality of the x-axis is bounded by the sum of the cardinality of the time series, but it is smaller when there are simultaneous events across auctions. Our count excludes the data points needed to mark the missing values, i.e. the normal lack of data before and after the auction period.

Advantages:
- Uses a small number of time points without any loss of data
- Preserves the temporal order of events across time series.
- The visual length of a time series is an indicator of its length in relation to other time series in terms of time. It conveys whether it is longer or not, but not how long.

Disadvantages:
- The time between two consecutive events is not conveyed.

- The granularity in time is arbitrary and changes from one time point to another. In Fig. 4, it is conveyed by labeling with date-time information; however, this is difficult for users to interpret. Nevertheless, it is possible to convey with cues such as the color intensity or thickness of the time point segments on the x-axis. Fig. 4 illustrates how shading the segments on the x-axis can be used to indicate density of intervals in terms of time. The darker the shade, the longer the time span the interval represents.
- It is difficult to tell which points are actual events, versus additional points introduced by the representation. In the auction example changes in angle in the line obviously correspond to bids, but bids of equal amount will not be visible. One solution is to mark events with a dot or a small shape.

4 Discussion

Each of the methods in Section 3 is specialized to deal with a subset of users' goals. There are trade-offs in choosing one method over another. The following table compares several features of the four visualizations:

Table 2. Comparison of the features of the four visualizations

	Sampled	Aggregated	Event index	Interleaved
# of points for our example	3851 time points	320 time points	29 indexed time points	60 indexed time points
Bid order preserved across auctions?	Yes	Yes	No	Yes
Time encoded?	Yes	Yes	No	No
Visual length of a line shows:	Time series length in time	Time series length in time	# of events in that time series	# of distinct time events in all time series
Event loss?	Yes	Yes (but used in aggregating)	No	No
Left alignment of time series	Optional	Optional	Inherent	Optional
Parameters required for the technique	Interval	level method,...	None	None

The event index representation is ideal when users want to compare the measurements across time series. For example, users might want to compare the 2nd or 3rd bid values across auctions, and they don't need to know the specific times that the bids are placed. In this case, event index visualization provides just the right amount of data and enables very fast processing.

If users do need to know the order of event arrivals over time, the interleaved event index representation is more appropriate. For a small total number of events dispersed over a long period of time, this representation will be ideal and will facilitate optimal processing times for visual exploration. However, as the number of events increases, or when the screen space for the x-axis is too small, it may be wiser to switch to the sampled events representation. The interleaved event index representation is also good when users do not care to know how far apart in time the events took place. One instance where this representation is ideal is when one is interested in only the consecutive values of bids in an auction, and needs to compare them and investigate how the bid amounts in one or more than one auctions parallel in time affect bidders' behavior.

If users do care about the length of time between events, it is best to use the sampled events visualization. They will need to carefully choose the sampling interval because as the sampling interval gets longer, the processing becomes faster due to decreased number of time points, however, loss of data and approximation errors increase. If sampling leads to slow performance, users should consider aggregation.

5 Other Representations

Viewing multiple unevenly-spaced time series has the inherent characteristic that an individual time series can have a varying start time, end time, and length. For example the auction start time is chosen by the seller and could be anytime of the day or night. eBay auctions vary in length from 1 to 10 days. An important design choice is to decide if absolute time (actual clock time) or relative time (time relative to the beginning of the auction) should be used in the visual representation. Absolute and relative time representations allow different hypotheses to be made about phenomena taking place between or across auctions. For instance, "last minute bidding" is a known phenomenon in eBay auctions. To study this we would use absolute time for auctions of all durations. In comparison, if we are interested in the percentage of bids achieved by mid-auction, then relative time should be used. Using relative time is likely to reduce the cardinality of the x-axis. For example, aligning the start times in the sampled events method results in a cardinality of 2880 (opposed to 3851 when not aligned). It is important to make clear to the user if alignment has been used or not.

Another alignment method is to stretch the time series so that both the start and end times of the time series are aligned [3]. Bapna, Jank and Shmueli [1] use a similar approach for auction data. They represent each time series (i.e., auction) by a smooth curve, which is derived by penalized smoothing splines. Then, they use a linear transformation to stretch and align the curves to start and end at the same time.

Hybrid techniques could be employed where different sections of the x-axis use different techniques. This is not appropriate for the two index techniques, but designers may consider using the sampled events method for sections that require detailed information and the aggregated sampled events method for other sections. Designers can also choose to use different parameters for different sections. For example, auctions typically have more events toward the end; therefore a smaller sampling interval will help convey the excitement of the final moments. Clearly indicating to users the location of those sections and their characteristics is crucial. Another completely different hybrid method would be aggregating indexed data (i.e. aggregating over a fixed number of events, not over a fixed time period).

There are certainly other methods for representing time series data, such as the Symmetric Aggregate Approximation (SAX), which could be adapted for unevenly-spaced time series [14]. Even more compact representations using iconic or glyph strategies could be helpful in getting a quick glance to see similar or different time series [10]. Other tasks such as motif finding or anomaly detection could inspire further novel methods [14] as could coping with uncertainty and frequent missing values.

6 Conclusions

This paper identifies the issues and problems with representing and visualizing time series with unevenly-spaced measurements. We considered four methods and illustrated each on a sample dataset to understand their implications. Finally, we compared them and discussed which situations are best to use in different cases. Each method has its strengths and weaknesses for certain tasks, so users must understand the tradeoffs. Our contribution is to present the features of various representations in order to help users decide which one(s) to use. We have implemented all of these four methods to be visualized in TimeSearcher. There is a preprocessing step for the data for each method to put it into TimeSearcher format. In other words, computations such as sampling, aggregation, and interleaving event indices are performed outside of TimeSearcher to produce an evenly-spaced time series data, which can then be loaded into TimeSearcher 2 [17]. We continue to investigate those methods and refine our understanding of their benefits and disadvantages by exploring new datasets.

Acknowledgements

We would like to thank the Center for Electronic Markets and Enterprises and the R.H. Smith School of Business at the University of Maryland for providing support for this project, as well the National Science Foundation thru grant NSF EIA 0129978 and Microsoft Research. We also thank Eamonn Keogh, Bill Kules, Harry Hochheiser and Paolo Buono for providing useful feedback on early drafts of the paper.

References

1. Bapna, R., Jank, W., Shmueli, G., Price Formation and its Dynamics in Online Auctions, *Working paper, Smith School of Business, Univ. of Maryland*, 2004.
2. Bar-Joseph, Z., Analyzing time series gene expression data, *Bioinformatics*, 20(16), 2004.
3. Bar-Joseph, Z., Gerber, G., Gifford, D.K., Continuous representations of time series gene expression data, *Journal of Comp. Biology*, 10(3-4): 241-256, 2003.
4. Bederson, B.B., Hollan, J.D., Pad++: a zooming graphical interface for exploring alternate interface physics, *Proceedings of the 7th annual ACM symposium on User interface software and technology*, 17-26, 1994.
5. Berry, L., Munzner, T., BinX: Dynamic exploration of time series datasets across aggregation levels, *IEEE Info. Visualization 2004, Posters Compendium*, 5-6.
6. Bettini, C., A glossary of time granularity concepts, *Temporal Databases: Research and Practice*, Etzion et al. (Eds), Springer, 406-413, 1998.
7. Brodbeck, D., Girardin, L., Trend analysis in large timeseries of high-throughput screening data using a distortion-oriented lens with semantic zooming, *IEEE Symposium on Information Visualization*, Seattle, October 19-21, 2003.

8. Buono, P., Aris, A., Plaisant, C., Khella, A. and Shneiderman, B., Interactive Pattern Search in Time Series, *Proceedings of Conference on Visualization and Data Analysis*, SPIE, Washington, DC (2005):175-186.
9. Carlis, J.V., Konstan, J.A., Interactive visualization of serial periodic data, *Proc. of ACM UIST'98, San Francisco, CA,* 29-38, 1998.
10. Hinneburg, A., Keim, D.A., Wawryniuk, M., HD-Eye: Visual mining of high-dimensional data, *IEEE Computer Graphics and Applications,* v.19 n.5, 22-31, September 1999.
11. Hochheiser, H., Shneiderman, B., Dynamic query tools for time series data sets: timebox widgets for interactive exploration, *Information Visualization*, Vol.3, Issue 1, Spring 2004, 1-18.
12. Keim, D.A, Information visualization and visual data mining, *IEEE Transactions on Visualization and Computer Graphics,*8(1), 1-8, 2002.
13. Keogh, E., Chakrabarti, K., Pazzani, M., Locally adaptive dimensionality reduction for indexing large time series databases, *ACM SIGMOD Record,* 30(2), 151-162.
14. Lin, J., Lankford, J., Keogh, E., Lonardi, S., Visually mining and monitoring massive time series, *Proc. ACM Conference on Knowledge Discovery and Data Mining*, ACM Press, New York, 460-469, 2004.
15. Muller, W., Schumann, H., Visualization methods for time-dependent data, *Proceedings of the 2003 Winter Simulation Conference*, 737-746, 2003.
16. Shmueli, G., Jank, Wolfgang, Visualizing online auctions, *Journal of Computational and Graphical Statistics*, 14 (2) 1-21, 2005.
17. Shmueli, G., Jank, W., Aris, A., Plaisant, C., and Shneiderman, B., Exploring Auction Databases through Interactive Visualization, *UMd HCIL Technical Report*, www.cs.umd.edu/hcil, 2005.
18. Silva, S.F., Catarci, T., Visualization of linear time-oriented data: a survey, *Proceedings of the First International Conference on Web Information Systems Engineering*, Vol.1, 310-319, 2000.
19. Troyanskaya O, Cantor M, Sherlock G, Brown P, Hastie T, Tibshirani R, Botstein D, Altman RB, Missing value estimation methods for DNA microarrays, *Bioinformatics*, 17(6):520-5, 2001.
20. Van Wijk, J. J., Van Selow, E. R., Cluster and calendar based visualization of time series data, *Proc. 1999 IEEE Symposium on Information Visualization*, IEEE Press, Piscataway, NJ, 4-9, 1999.
21. Weber, M., Alexa, M., Muller, W., Visualizing time series on spirals, *Proc. IEEE Symposium on Information Visualization,* IEEE Press, Piscataway, NJ, 7-14, 2001.

Multilevel Compound Tree - Construction Visualization and Interaction

François Boutin[1], Jérôme Thièvre[2], and Mountaz Hascoët[3]

[1] LIRMM, CNRS, Montpellier
francois.boutin@univ-montp1.fr
[2] INA, Paris
jthievre@ina.fr
[3] LIRMM – CNRS, Montpellier
mountaz@lirmm.fr

Abstract. Several hierarchical clustering techniques have been proposed to visualize large graphs, but fewer solutions suggest a focus based approach. We propose a multilevel clustering technique that produces in linear time a contextual clustered view depending on a user-focus. We get a tree of clusters where each cluster – called *meta-silhouette* – is itself hierarchically clustered into an inclusion tree of *silhouettes*. Resulting *Multilevel Silhouette Tree (MuSi-Tree)* has a specific structure called *multilevel compound tree*. This work builds upon previous work on a *compound tree* structure called *MO-Tree*. The work presented in this paper is a major improvement over previous work by (1) defining *multilevel compound tree* as a more generic structure, (2) proposing original space-filling visualization techniques to display it, (3) defining relevant interaction model based on both focus changes and graph filtering techniques and (4) reporting from case studies in various fields: co-citation graphs, related-document graphs and social graphs.

1 Introduction

Graph clustering objective is to minimize inter-connectivity (edges between clusters) and maximize intra-connectivity (edges inside clusters). A multilevel clustering technique is used to organize large graphs [5][7]. It provides a *hierarchical clustered graph* that consists of a graph of clusters where each cluster is itself hierarchically clustered. If we induce edges between clusters, we get a structure called *compound graph* (section 2.2) [16].

We are interested in multilevel clustering techniques that produce contextual graph views from any focus. The idea is to be able to organize information "around" a focus using graph connectivity.

Previous work on *MO-Tree* [3] introduced a focus based multilevel clustering technique that provides a *compound tree* structure (section 2.2). It is a tree of clusters, where each cluster is itself hierarchically clustered. For instance, considering a connected graph in Fig.1, a *MO-Tree* view from focus 1 is displayed in Fig.2.

In this paper we define *multilevel compound tree* which improves the concept of *compound tree*. We also provide an algorithm for the construction of such structure.

M.F. Costabile and F. Paternò (Eds.): INTERACT 2005, LNCS 3585, pp. 847–860, 2005.
© IFIP International Federation for Information Processing 2005

We further propose a space-filling visualization technique and an interaction model for displaying and interacting with this structure. Moreover, we report results of three case studies using co-citation graphs, related-document graphs and social graphs.

In the next section, we present a synthesis of related work on graph clustering, and multilevel visualization/interaction techniques. Section 3 further describes the new *multilevel compound tree structure* called *MuSi-Tree* and its construction algorithm. In section 4, we propose space-filling visualisation techniques to display this structure and an associated interaction model. Finally, in section 5, we report the results of three case-studies that aim at:

– Producing real graphs visualization and interaction from various perspectives.
– Applying filtering techniques to produce understandable *MuSi-Tree* structures.
– Providing qualitative results from a set of 56 users (section 5.4).

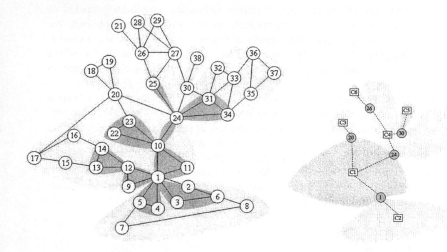

Fig. 1. (a) Graph clustering into silhouettes, (b) silhouette tree

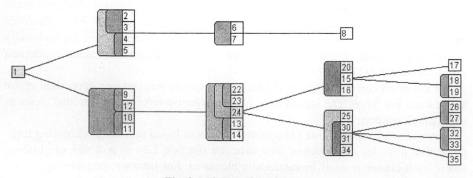

Fig. 2. MO-Tree from focus 1

2 Related Work

2.1 Graph Partitioning Techniques – A Review

There are different ways to classify partitioning techniques [1][6][8]. We propose main criteria and illustrate them with some methods (see table 1).

Firstly, geometrical techniques take into account nodes coordinates: for instance, *K-Means* [1][11] is a local clustering method that produces iteratively a k-partition using centroïds. Global geometric methods [6][8][13] are based on energy models, inertial algorithms or graph bisection (with hyperplans or spheres).

Secondly, structural algorithms are based on graph connectivity. The principle of a local clustering technique is to minimize inter cluster connectivity using nodes exchange, agglomeration or separation. Global structural [1][4][6][8] techniques use matrix operations: Markov clustering is a stochastic method based on flow computing while spectral techniques consist in mapping nodes into an eigenspace. Spectral techniques may be used to provide coordinates for geometric clustering methods.

Many algorithms [11][13] use both global and local methods to refine clustering. Choice of clustering technique may depend on graph propriety (size, connectivity…), but also clustering constraints (balanced clustering, edge crossing minimization…).

Table 1. clustering criteria and methods

Partitioning criteria	Centroïd based – K-Means [1][11]	Geometric segmentation [6][8]	Force directed based clustering [13]	Inertial algorithm [6][8]	Nodes exchanging – genetic [1][6]	Agglomerative - greedy [1][6][11]	Min Cut [1][4][8]	Spectral method [1][4][6][8]	Flow - Markov method [1][4][8]
geometric (x) vs. structural	x	x	x	x				→	
local (x) vs. global approach	x				x	x	x		
Iterative optimization (x) vs. exact	x	both	x		x	both	x		
hierarchical (x) vs. flat	→	both	both			x		both	both
matrix computing.(x) vs. graph				x			x	x	x
stochastic (x) vs. determinist	x	x	x		x	both			x

Multilevel clustering techniques were developed to organize large graphs into hierarchical clustered graph (section 2.2). For that purpose, some "flat" techniques are adapted. For instance *K-Means* can be applied recursively [11] (see → in Table 1). Cutting techniques depending on a threshold may be computed with many thresholds.

Otherwise, hierarchical clustering techniques proceeds iteratively with merging or splitting the most appropriate clusters according some metric. Resulting dendrogram can be cut at different levels to provide a *hierarchical clustered graph* [1][11].

According to our criteria, our method is a structural-local-exact-hierarchical-graph-based-determinist clustering technique.

2.2 Multiscale Structure – Definitions and Visualization

Now, we review and define new multilevel graph structures:

- A *hierarchical clustered graph* was defined [5] by a graph $G = (V, E)$ and a rooted tree T. Leaves of T are vertices of G. Other nodes in T are sets of nodes of G called *clusters*. T describes an inclusion relation between *clusters* so T is called inclusion tree. *2D* and *3D* views (see Fig.3) are proposed in [7]: inclusion tree T is described either by inclusion areas (Fig.3.a) or dotted arrows (Fig.3.b).
- A *compound graph* consists of a *hierarchical clustered graph* with edges between clusters [16]. *2D* and *3D* views are proposed in [5][7] (Fig.3.a,b). Edges between clusters are drawn in thin lines for small clusters and thick lines for large clusters: their removal induces a *hierarchical clustered graph*.
- We defined in [3] a *compound tree* as a *compound graph* with an adjacency tree of meta-clusters (largest clusters). For instance, (Fig.3.c) presents a *compound tree* since largest clusters belong to an adjacency tree. We proposed in [3] flat *compound tree* visualization (Fig.2) of G (Fig.1): to avoid a cluttered view, edges between meta-clusters are displayed unlike edges between clusters into meta-clusters.
- In this paper, we define a *multilevel compound tree* as a *compound tree* where each layer consists of an adjacency tree of clusters. For instance (Fig.3.d) meta-clusters but also small clusters belong to adjacency trees. We propose an algorithm that computes a specific *multilevel compound tree* structure called *MuSi-Tree*. This structure is general enough to be provided by other clustering techniques.

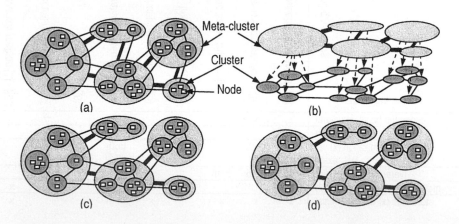

Fig. 3. (a) & (b) compound graph, (c) compound tree, (d) multilevel compound tree

2.3 Visualization and Interaction Concepts – Multilevel Approach

2D and *3D* views of hierarchical clustered graphs based on tree layouts are described in [5] and [7] respectively. These visualizations support multilevel views by allowing user to choose level of visibility of cluster hierarchy, or manually collapse/expand clusters. Fisheye and full zoom methods are compared in [14].

On the other hand, the use of upgraded force-directed models to layout clustered graphs has been studied in [10][17]. The main idea here is to use different forces for intra and inter clusters links and add an invisible attractor vertex to force vertices of the same cluster to keep close to each other.

Yee and al. propose a focus-based radial tree layout of non-clustered graphs [18]. The system builds a breadth-first spanning tree of the graph from a focus node selected by the user. The focus node is laid out at the centre of the display and the others nodes are located on concentric rings corresponding to their shortest distance to the focus. Angular position of a node depends on its parent position in the spanning tree. Angular width of each node is computed from the angle needed by its subtree. This system presents a particularly interesting work on animation of focus changes. When the user selects another focus, all nodes move to their new position, following an intuitive path with a smooth slow-in, slow-out timing. The *prefuse* toolkit [9] offers a smart implementation of this technique. Nevertheless, as mentioned earlier, neither particular visualization nor specific interactions have been implemented for multilevel data structures.

In this work we propose an add-on to *prefuse* [9] that supports the visualization of *multilevel compound trees* (Section 4). This technique is used with *MuSi-trees* that are produced from our clustering technique. A *MuSi-Tree* consists of a particular case of *multilevel compound tree*. Nevertheless our visualization technique is not limited to *MuSi-tree*. It can be used for any type of *multilevel compound tree*. Since *multilevel compound tree* structure is general enough, we believe that this technique can be used to visualize other clustering techniques results.

3   Multilevel Graph Clustering Technique

3.1   Main Principles and Definitions

Let us consider a connected graph $G = (V, E)$. A node is called *articulation node* if its removal disconnects G. Splitting (but not removing) articulation nodes disconnects G into maximal biconnected components or trivial components (two connected nodes). Indeed, any non trivial component is biconnected else it would be split up into components. Maximal biconnected or trivial components are called *silhouettes*.

Graph G is a *bipartite tree* that connects *articulation nodes* and *silhouettes*, see (Fig.1.b). Indeed, if there was a cycle between *silhouettes*, then *silhouettes* should belong to a same component, what is impossible since they are maximal.

The *silhouette tree* decomposition can be applied to graph G but also to any connected sub graph G' of G. Considering a *silhouette* of G', it naturally belongs to one *silhouette* of G. Consequently, we say that *silhouette tree* of G' belongs to *silhouette tree* of G. In Fig.1.a, we present two *silhouette trees*: one for graph G, another one for a connected sub graph G' (see darkest included areas).

Now, the purpose is to be able to choose interesting sub graphs of G, in order to apply our algorithm recursively. We present our approach in section 3.2.

3.2 Focus Based Clustering Approach

We propose a clustering technique that takes into account a focus-node. So, we get different graph perspectives depending on the focus we select. Resulting computing is very efficient as explained in section 3.3.

Nodes are displayed into K_{max} levels according to their distance to the focus. G_k is defined as the connected sub-graph of G that contains nodes at distance at most k from the focus. Sil_k is defined as the *silhouette tree* of G_k. The set of silhouettes trees $\{Sil_k\}$ is ordered with inclusion relation. It means that Sil_k includes Sil_i *if k is above i*.

$\{G_k\}$ is computed in linear time *using a breadth-first search*. Sil_{k+1} is also naturally computed from Sil_k (section 3.3) and resulting computing of $\{Sil_k\}$ is linear. The set of silhouettes $\{Sil_k, 0 \le k \le K_{max}\}$ is called *Multilevel Silhouette Tree (MuSi-Tree)*.

Sil_{Kmax} is called *meta-silhouette tree*. It is a tree of *meta-silhouettes*. Each *meta-silhouette* is itself an inclusion tree of *silhouettes*.

3.3 Optimized Algorithm

Let consider graph G organized into K_{max} levels from a focus node. We describe our *MuSi-Tree* optimized algorithm (Fig.4). $Sil_0 = \{focus\}$. Sil_{k+1} is computed using Sil_k:

− Level $k+1$ is first organized into connected components. See Fig.4, resulting connected components: $\{ab\}$, $\{cd\}$, $\{e\}$, $\{f\}$, $\{g\}$, $\{hij\}$, $\{k\}$, $\{lm\}$, $\{no\}$.
− If a connected component is related to only one node v on level k, v is an articulation node for Sil_{k+1} that connects a new *silhouette*. For instance, see Fig.4, $\{ab\}$, $\{cd\}$, $\{e\}$, $\{f\}$, $\{g\}$, $\{lm\}$ belong to new silhouettes.
− Else a large silhouette is created that includes silhouettes of Sil_k connected by this connected component. See Fig.4: components $\{hij\}$, $\{k\}$, $\{no\}$

So, the resulting *MuSi-Tree* structure is computed in linear time.

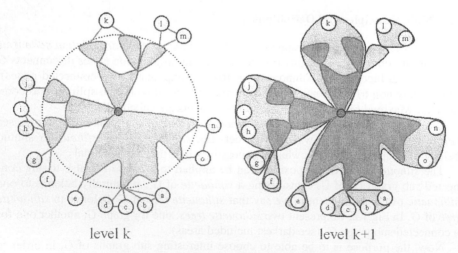

level k   level k+1

Fig. 4. Graph clustering algorithm – step k+1

3.4 Invariant Sets

We can get various MuSi-Trees depending on the focus we take. However, meta-silhouette tree structure remains the same. Indeed, global articulation nodes and meta-*silhouettes* are graph invariants. Focus changes will be used in the interaction model and will benefit this property as explained in the next section.

4 MuSi-Tree Visualization and Interaction

4.1 MuSi-Tree Layout

The nature of our clustering, based on a focus node and distances between nodes and this focus, leads us to choose a hierarchical layout. Among existing hierarchical layout, radial layout is really well-suited. Nodes are located on concentric rings around focus, which makes distance between each node and the focus explicit [18]. Moreover, radial layout makes a better use of screen space than classical top-down tree layout.

Our layout is quite similar to radial layout [18]. Our main contribution is in the drawing of silhouettes. To perform this, we started by transforming *MuSi-Tree* into a well-suited spanning tree. This mainly implies particular ordering of spanning tree nodes to ensure (1) silhouettes graphical cohesiveness and (2) non-overlapping. Once nodes locations have been computed with respect to ordering constraint, we perform a depth-first traversal and draw each silhouette as the bounding shape of its nodes.

Initial graph (Fig.5.a) is iteratively clustered by level into meta-nodes (light areas Fig.5.b) using a former technique introduced in [3]. Each silhouette is computed as a tree of meta-nodes (Fig.5.c). Geometric outline of this tree generates the drawing of silhouette (dark areas).

We attribute different colors to silhouettes trees to easily recognize non trivial bi-connected components in the graph. Each hierarchy of silhouettes is attached to an articulation node that is painted with the same color. Articulation nodes are not included in their corresponding silhouette to avoid multiple overlaps that would make the visualization too complex. The use of transparent colors to fill silhouettes helps to perceive their inclusion level: the deeper they are, the darker they look.

Visualization is built over the *prefuse* framework [9] that provides support for animated transformations on graph layout. It is used to animate our focus changes.

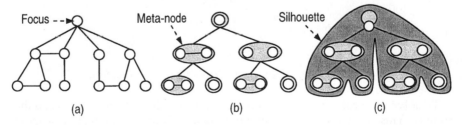

Fig. 5. (a) Initial graph: hierarchical view (b) clustering by level (c) silhouette drawing

4.2 Changing Focus

Transitions between focus changes are animated, to help the user in tracking objects of interest and keeping a coherent perception of graph structure [18]. At this moment, only nodes and links are animated. The silhouettes are not displayed during transition because it is quite hard to get smooth animation of their transformation since their shape can change completely between two states, but we keep working on this interesting problem.

4.3 Dynamic Filtering

Graph visualizations provide great information on data structures and relations, and some properties can be displayed by using visual attributes like colours, size and shape. However, it is very hard to show the complete information attached to a node inside the graph view, and it is especially true for textual information.

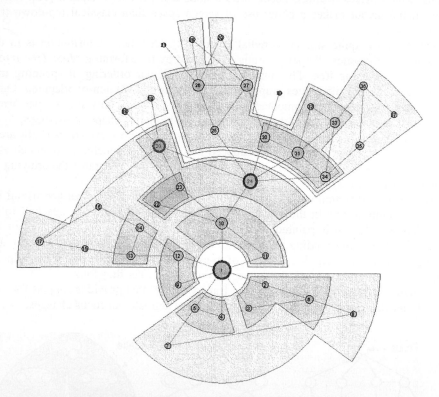

Fig. 6. Multilevel Silhouette Tree (MuSi-Tree) from focus 1

To solve this problem, we use a traditional data table to display nodes and their attributes. This widget supports multiple sorts and filters. Combination of these two features allows users to perform quick searches and selections over the whole dataset. We propose different filtering features depending of nodes and edges attributes types:

- Regular expressions for textual attributes,
- Minimum and maximum threshold for numeric attributes,
- Temporal intervals for dates.

Filtering is easily reversible and its effects (dynamic insertions, nodes and links removals) are animated to offers users a good perception of changes.

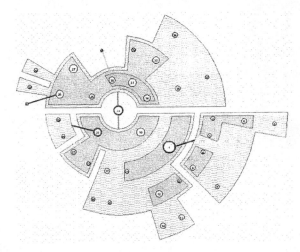

Fig. 7. Multilevel Silhouette Tree (MuSi-Tree) – compact view from focus 24

5   Case Studies

5.1   Citation Graph

We have clustered a connected citation graph including 122 papers and 206 links. It was collected on Research Index (CiteSeer) [12] from focus: "Navigation and interaction within graphical bookmarks" (Fig.8). Three large silhouettes are related to: information visualization, database visualization and document classification (Fig.9). All silhouettes and articulation nodes belong to a silhouette tree (Fig.9).

5.2   Related-Document Graph

The aim is to propose a map of conferences "around" Interact 2005. For that purpose, we use *TouchGraph GoogleBrowser* [15] that iteratively produces a *spring* view of 101 conferences related to www.interact2005.org (Fig.10.b). To manage a well connected graph, we consider nodes with 2 or more incoming edges. We get 200 edges.

We present *MuSi-Trees* from two foci: www.interact2005.org (Fig.10.a) and NYC 2004: www2004.org (Fig.11). Resulting views share five non trivial silhouettes that represent five specific domains: visualization/interaction, ergonomics, computational linguistic, digital library and image processing. We get different articulation nodes between domains: NYC 2004 and SIGIR 2004 introduce digital library and computational linguistic. VIS 2005 connects visualization/interaction with image processing. HCII 2005 is a bridge between visualization/interaction and ergonomic.

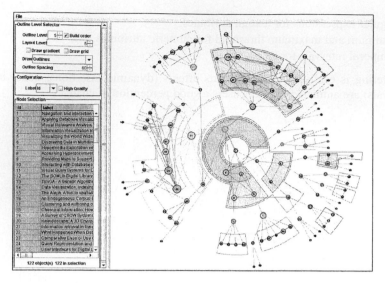

Fig. 8. MuSi-Tree Viewer – citation graph clustering

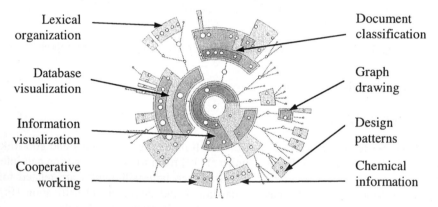

Lexical organization

Document classification

Database visualization

Graph drawing

Information visualization

Design patterns

Cooperative working

Chemical information

Fig. 9. MuSi-Tree – compact view

5.3 Social Graph

In this study, 56 medical students divided into four work groups were asked about their friendship relations (strong or weak). To begin with, whole social graph including all relations (unilateral and bilateral, strong and weak) is displayed in Fig.12. We get a single well connected component.

Then, a filtering algorithm is applied to include bilateral strong relations. Social graph is displayed from the same focus (Fig.13). We denote one large component in relation with four smaller components. In fact, each small group belongs more or less to a work group. Five students create relations between these groups.

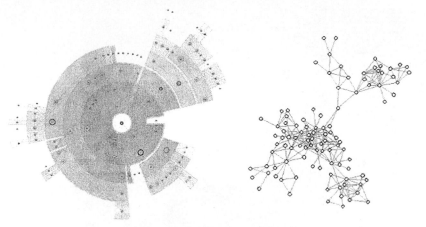

Fig. 10. (a) MuSi-tree from focus "Interact 2005", (b) TouchGraph view [15]

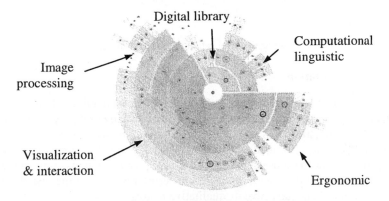

Digital library

Computational
linguistic

Image
processing

Visualization
& interaction

Ergonomic

Fig. 11. Organization from focus: "NYC 2004"

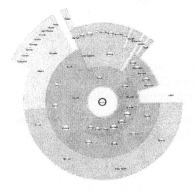

Fig. 12. Whole relations between students

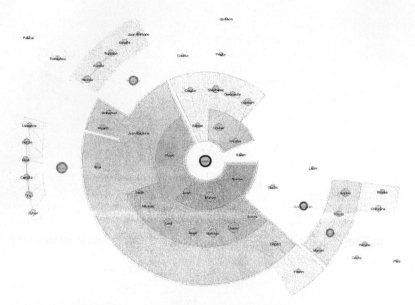

Fig. 13. Strong bilateral relations between students

5.4 Qualitative Evaluation

After collecting data, resulting social *MuSi-Trees* were presented to the four groups of medical students (without experience in information visualization). A five minutes show included visualization and interactive techniques: focus changing and group zooming. *MuSi-Tree* was presented as a "strong friendship map" around a student. No more explanation about the clustering algorithm was given. Students were invited to express themselves about their feeling on the clustering results, and the visualization/ interaction technique. The study reveals qualitative results:

- Majority of students considered the map as meaningful, even though they knew nothing about clustering technique.
- They recognized many natural groups of friends.
- They naturally understood dark areas as cohesive groups.
- Students were interested in changing focus to draw their own friendship map. They sometimes felt lost especially when focus moved from a silhouette to another.
- Students had sometimes difficulties to follow nodes when the graph was moving. Nevertheless, they often recognized silhouettes from their shape or their color.

This preliminary study invites us to practice a quantitative study to compare both our clustering technique, and our visualization/interaction technique with other ones.

6   Conclusion

In this paper we proposed a focus-based multilevel agglomerative technique. Resulting structure called *Multilevel Silhouette Tree* (*MuSi-Tree*) is easy to explore and easy to manage because of its features (*multilevel compound tree*).

We applied our algorithm to a citation graph, a related-document graph and a social graph. Citation graph was displayed in a compact view that reveals *silhouette tree* structure. We present a graph of related sites displayed from two foci. Resulting views share meta-silhouettes and articulation nodes. Applying filtering techniques help the user understanding clustering structure.

MuSi-Tree appeared to be particularly well suited to organize a *locally well articulated graph*. It consists of a graph with "some" articulation nodes in its various k-neighbourhood. It will be interesting to study *locally well articulated graph* indices. In order to improve visualisation of large graphs with high connectivity we propose to use filtering techniques in a pre-processing stage of our clustering technique. The objective will be to extract a "nice" *multilevel silhouette tree* structure.

More intensive evaluation is needed to better clarify conditions in which our clustering and visualization techniques can best benefit users interacting with large graphs. The question of what criteria should be used for the evaluation of clustering and visualization results is an open issue. A good evaluation of this work can only be a long and challenging task. We have already conducted many informal evaluations and studies on this work, but we are now deeply engaged into a more controlled evaluation approach. In this area, we plan to perform larger evaluation both in terms of analytical criteria [2] as in terms of controlled experiments involving real users.

References

1. Alpert C.J. and Kahng A.B. Recent Developments in Netlist Partitioning: A Survey, Integration: the VLSI Journal, vol. 19, pp. 1-81, 1995.
2. Boutin F. and Hascoët M., Cluster Validity Indices for Graph Partitioning, Proceedings of the Conference on Information Visualization IV'2004.
3. Boutin F. and Hascoët M., Focus Dependent Multi-level Graph Clustering. Proceedings of the Conference on Advanced Visual Interfaces, AVI 2004, ACM.
4. Brandes U., Gaertler M., and Wagner D.: Experiments on Graph Clustering Algorithms. Proc. ESA '03, LNCS 2832, pp. 568-579. © Springer-Verlag, 2003.
5. Brockenauer R. and Cornelsen S., Drawing Clusters and Hierarchies. In Michael Vaufmann and Dorothea Wagner (Eds.): Drawing Graphs: Methods and Models, LNCS 2025, pp. 194 - 228. © Springer-Verlag, 2001.
6. Chamberlain B.L. Graph Partitioning Algorithms for Distributing Workloads of Parallel Computations. Technical Report UW-CSE-98-10-03, Univ. of Washington, 1998.
7. Eades P., Multilevel Visualization of Clustered Graphs, Proceedings of Graph Drawing'96, Berkeley, California, September, 1996.
8. Elsner U. 1997. Graph partitioning - A survey. Technical Report 393, Technische Universitat Chemnitz.
9. Heer J., Card S.K., and Landay J.A., prefuse: a toolkit for interactive information visualization. In CHI 2005, Human Factors in Computing Systems, 2005.
10. Huang M. L., Eades P. A Fully Animated Interactive System for Clustering and Navigating Huge Graphs, Proceedings of the 6th International Symposium on Graph Drawing (GD'98), Springer LNCS 1547, pages 374-383, 1998.
11. Karypis G., Han E-H and Kumar V. CHAMELEON: A hierarchical clustering algorithm using dynamic modeling. IEEE Computer, 32(8): 68-75, 1999.
12. Lee Giles C., Bollacker K.D., Lawrence S.: CiteSeer: An Automatic Citation Indexing System. ACM DL 1998: 89-98.

13. Noack A. An energy model for visual graph clustering. In G. Liotta, editor, Proceedings of GD 2003, LNCS 2912, pages 425--436, Berlin, 2004. Springer-Verlag.
14. Schaffer D., Zhenping Z., Grreenberg, S. et al. Navigating Hierarchically Clustered Networks through Fisheye and Full-Zoom Methods, ACM Transactions on Computer-Human Interaction volume 3-2, pages 162-188, 1998.
15. Shapiro A., TouchGraph, Dynamic Graph Layout Tool, www.touchgraph.com
16. Sugiyama K., Tagawa S. and Toda M. Methods for Visual Understanding of Hierarchical System Structures. IEEE Transactions on Systems Man and Cybernetics, 1981.
17. Wang X., Miyamoto I. Generating Customized Layouts, Proceeding of the 3rd International Symposium on Graph Drawing (GD'95), Springer LNCS 1027, 504-515, 1995.
18. Yee K.P., Fisher D., Dhamija R. & Hearst M.A. Animated Exploration of Dynamic Graphs with Radial Layout. Proceeding of IEEE Symposium on Information Visualization, 2001.

Visualizing Missing Data:
Graph Interpretation User Study

Cyntrica Eaton, Catherine Plaisant, and Terence Drizd*

Human-Computer Interaction Laboratory,
University of Maryland, College Park, 20742
{ceaton, plaisant}@cs.umd.edu

Abstract. Most visualization tools fail to provide support for missing data. In this paper, we identify sources of missing data and describe three levels of impact missing data can have on the visualization: perceivable, invisible or propagating. We then report on a user study with 30 participants that compared three design variants. A between-subject graph interpretation study provides strong evidence for the need of indicating the presence of missing information, and some direction for addressing the problem.

1 Introduction

Information visualization provides an effective way for users to rapidly find trends in data and values of attributes of interest. The use of color, position, and shape contributes to helping users seeing patterns and outliers. Preserving the integrity of data exploration requires the use of visualization techniques that present data accurately without introducing misleading patterns or masking data properties. In particular, we believe that poor handling of missing and uncertain information can have a strong influence on users' interpretation of the data [1] (Fig. 1).

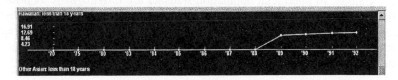

Fig. 1. In this figure the data seems to be stable, with a sharp increase starting in 88. Practically no data was collected until 89, so this interpretation is wrong.

When data is missing (e.g. there an empty cell in a data table), many tools will simply crash. Others will nicely inform users to "fix" the problem, which most users do by entering a value such as zero. As a result, it is often impossible for others to discriminate a value of zero from missing data. This paper categorizes possible

---

* At the time this research was conducted, Terry Drizd was working at the National Center for Health Statistics, Hyattsville, Maryland.

M.F. Costabile and F. Paternò (Eds.): INTERACT 2005, LNCS 3585, pp. 861–872, 2005.

reasons for data to be missing, differentiates three levels of impact missing data can have on visualization, and reports on a graph interpretation user study comparing three implementations.

2 Sources of Missing Data

As part of our research on making government statistics more accessible to the public (see Govstat project http://ils.unc.edu/govstat/) we found five main reasons for data to be missing:

Uncollected Data
The most common reason for missing data is that data was simply not collected. Equipment or sensors can malfunction, a survey can be misprinted, and files can be lost.

Data Source Confidentiality
Privacy protection can affect how findings are presented when publishing results of human-centric surveys or experiments. When the publication of a value might provide clues to the identity of individuals, that data must be omitted or presented aggregated at a higher level. For instance, when an organization publishes the average salaries of employees based on position and gender, the actual salary of the only female Vice President will be revealed.   Publishing an empty cell is a solution, but if the number of male Vice Presidents is known, the aggregated data by position will also indirectly reveal her salary and should be omitted as well.

Redefined Data Categories
In statistical and demographic computation, data is often aggregated into classes or ranges. Although aggregation is often necessary for efficient data presentation, problems arise when a class or range is redefined after data has been compiled.   For example, U.S. population surveys did not allow people to select multiple races until the 2000 Census, so interracial population statistics are missing in years prior to 2000 even though citizens are counted in other categories. New definitions or discoveries of illnesses can also create complex missing data cases where studies of trends need to look at data across definition boundaries periods and understand the implications of the redefinitions.

Mutually Exclusive Multivariate Combinations
There are instances when combinations of data variables are impossible or highly improbable. Consider the example where the two variables of a dataset are age and cause of death by a firearm. Since it is not realistic to determine that a child of less than five years of age committed suicide, such category of data could be described as non-existing instead of having a value of zero.

Uncertainty Deemed Excessive
In some cases problems with small sample size, flawed methodology, and lack of data to use for estimation can contribute to high uncertainty for certain data values.   The

authors of a study or report might decide to publish a simplified version of the dataset that does not include data with uncertainty over a certain threshold.

3   Three Levels of Missing Data Impact

We found that there are three levels of impact missing data could have on a visualization display, mostly depending on how the position of the graphic elements of the visualization is computed [2].   This attribute of the visualizations nicely complement the existing categorization of visualizations (e.g. [3, 4]).

Missing data can have a 1) perceivable impact, 2) an invisible impact, or 3) a propagating impact. The perceivable impact can be seen when the position of each graphic element is dedicated to the data item, independently of the attribute values. This is the case for simple line graph in which the graphic element representing a data value is a dot at a dedicated X location.   The values of other data items have no influence on the position of the graphic object. At most, the minimum and maximum values impact axis calibration.   Choropleth maps and techniques relying on ordering usually fall also in this category. For this type of visualization, if the data is missing then no object is displayed at the corresponding location, and the absence of data should be easily detected since users will be expecting to see a value there (Figure 2).

Fig. 2. Missing data is *perceivable* when there is a dedicated location for each data object

The second level - invisible impact - occurs when the position of the graphical element is entirely a function of the attribute value(s). An example is a scatter plot. In a scatter plot the position, color, and size of a graphical object is entirely based on the data item attribute values. If a data item is missing, there is nothing in the standard scatter plot that indicates the existence of missing data (Fig. 3).

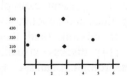

Fig. 3. In a scatter plot missing data is *invisible*

Fig. 4. In a pie chart, not only is missing data invisible but it also biases the other data items (by making the other wedges larger than they should really be), therefore *propagating* the impact of missing data

The third level of impact – propagating impact – occurs when a graphic element is function not only of the attributes values of the data item but also of the attribute values of neighboring items. Examples occur with pie charts and treemaps. Here, the size and placement of a wedge or box representing the data item is a function of the data item attribute values but also of values for all the other items. If a data item is missing, simply omitting it from the display not only goes completely unnoticed but it also biases the other items (Fig. 4). This is a characteristic of all the space-filling techniques.

Many hybrid cases exist as well. For example, with parallel coordinates, an omitted data item will go unnoticed because the position of the line is entirely a function of attribute values; but a missing attribute value is perceivable because the location for that attribute is dedicated and the line can be rendered broken or connected to a separate location for missing values.

We believe that three complementary enhancements that could be used to provide effective indication of missing data. They include:

- Dedicated visual attributes
- Annotation
- Animation

Dedicating visual attributes essentially involves associating a special color, texture, shape, or any combination of these in order to indicate missing values. Annotation allows users to gain further insight into missing and unreliable data through text or graphic information presented outside of the scope of graphic element appearance. Lastly, animation can provide a series of data display transitions that allow users to view several different perspectives in a short period of time. Animation can be helpful in temporary highlighting missing data, then adding estimated values, based on the preference and/or exploration goals of the user.

4 Related Work

Researchers in scientific or geographic visualization have given more attention than those in information visualization to missing data as well as uncertain data [4 to 9]. In addition to specifically identifying sources of uncertainty, Pang et al. [10] discuss a classification of methods, present an overview of visual attributes that can be modified to indicate uncertainty. Pham and Brown [11] propose a list of relevant visual features that can be used to indicate data value imprecision (including hue, luminance, size, transparency, depth, texture, and blur) and present examples of "fuzzy" data. Cedlink and Rheingans [12], also providing clues and annotations such as grid lines. Restorer [13] uses grayscale to indicate missing (and therefore estimated) data on color map. Djurcilov and Pang [14] discuss visualization techniques they used to analyze a sparsely populated meteorological dataset. Here a missing value is not an error but an indication that no phenomena were observable at a given point. They argue that missing data points should not be estimated (as is usually the case), but presented in a way that alerts the user of "non-observation". In contrast, Dybowski and Weller [15] address the problem of displaying missing information to users by computing estimates and ranges.

MANET[16] and XGobi[17] attempt to make users aware of missing data and uncertainty. They use complementary display that indicates the proportion of a missing data. For example in XGobi, a scatterplot is shown is two windows. One contains the data, the other displays a shadow plot that indicates the data values that are complete, or missing the x, the y, or both attributes. Our exploration of the existing techniques highlights diversity of techniques and the challenge of providing visualization techniques that alert, yet do not distract. A common problem with the existing technique is that missing or uncertain data often ends up catching users' eye more than the "good" data.

Empirical studies reporting on how users deal with missing or uncertain data are rare. Other studies involving graph interpretation (e.g. [18-20]) assume a complete data set that did not include missing data. The following section discusses the pilot study we conducted to better understand how users interpret and mis-interpret simple graphs that include missing data.

5 Empirical Study

Our goal was to study users' ability to compare data values and draw accurate conclusions about trends when data is missing, using three different displays. We wanted to be able to observe users dealing with missing data without making it obvious that missing data was the focus of our study, so each group of participants used only one of the three interfaces (i.e. we used a between subject design) and we asked them to answer some questions that involved missing data as well as some questions for which all the data was available.

Thirty people from the University of Maryland community participated in the study, 13 females and 17 males. Each participant was paid $5.00 for taking part in the 20 minute study; and to improve motivation we also gave an extra $5.00 to the participant with the highest accuracy and speed, in each of the three groups.

Microsoft Excel was used to create four separate time-sequence graphs. The graphs were then modified in a graphic presentation tool to transform them as necessary into one of the model variants. A tool was developed in C# to automate the presentation of the questions and displays, and collect time and preferences.

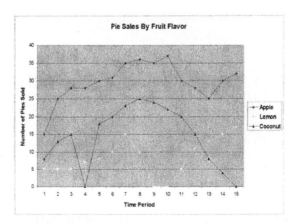

Fig. 5. *Misleading* Display - Missing data points are replaced by a default value (0)

Figures 5-7 show three displays of the same data. In the *Misleading* display (Fig. 5), data values are encoded as 0. In the *Absent* display (Fig. 6) missing data is completely omitted from the display, and the line graph appear as broken when no data exist. The *Coded* display (Fig. 7), also omits missing data points but it adds an icon on the next present data point in the series that indicates why the prior data points are missing from the data set.

We hypothesized that participants using *Coded* or *Absent* displays would be more accurate than participants using the *Misleading* display. We predicted that participants with *Absent* displays would have a shorter response time because they would have less information to digest, and that confidence and accuracy would be similar for users of both *Absent* and *Coded* displays and higher than *Misleading*. We thought that users would prefer the *Coded* version because it provides explanations.

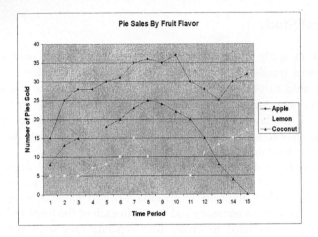

Fig. 6. *Absent* Display - Missing data points are omitted resulting in breaks in the lines

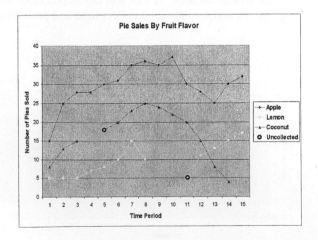

Fig. 7. *Coded* Display - Missing data points are omitted, and the next valid point in the series has a mark which provides the reason why prior points are missing

Procedure

Participants signed the Informed Consent form and watched a brief slide show which explained a sample graph of the type they would be using during study. Instructions for answering comparison-based questions were provided. More specifically, to ensure uniformity in responses, participants were advised to answer questions of the form "Compare the value of X to Y at time t" in the form "X is greater/lower than Y". Next, each participant was given a brief overview of how the study would be executed.

They answered 13 questions. For each question the procedure was the same. The written question appeared on the screen. Once they had read the question and felt that they were ready to continue, they would click a button and a graph was displayed for five seconds, then hidden. The question reappeared along with a set of multiple-choice responses. For every question users could reply that they didn't have enough information to answer. After they had selected an answer (based on recall) and provided a confidence rating from 1 to 10, the graph reappeared and they were given a second opportunity to answer the same question while viewing the graph. The 1st answer measured the accuracy attained after a rapid glance at the graph , while for the final answer users had time to study the graph more carefully. After completing the study (using only one type of display: *Misleading, Absent* or *Coded*), users were shown examples of the other 2 displays and asked to choose the display they would prefer to use to answer the type of questions they had been given.

During the entire 20-minute session, the experimenter was seated beside the participants. She answered questions before the start of the experiment, observed participants and then asked clarifying questions after the experiment. There were four types of questions: (the parenthesis contain the notation used in the result charts)

- Value **Comparisons** where both points were **Present** (CP)
- **Trend**-related questions concerning only **Present** data (TP)
- Value **Comparisons** where one of the two points was **Missing** (CM)
- **Trend**-related questions involving **Missing** data (TM.)

The data was made-up but realistic, carefully chosen so that it did not allow users to make conclusions based on their knowledge of the world, but based solely on the graph data they saw. For example data was about preferences of people from other planets, or imaginary illnesses. A complete list of sample graphs and questions used can be found at: www.cs.umd.edu/hcil/govstat/cyntricadata.html).

Results and Discussion

Fig. 8 shows the average number of correct answers based on recall after a 5 second glance at the data. For each display there were 10 participants so a value of 10 means that all participants answered the question correctly every time, and a value of 0 means that none of the participants were able to answer the question correctly. For questions where all the data was present (CP and TP) users made a few mistakes, but the striking result is that none of the users were able to answer correctly to any of the questions involving missing data (CM and TM) using the *Misleading* display (remember that this is a commonly used way to present missing data). In each instance, participants indicated a definite trend or made a comparison between values as opposed to indicating that there was not enough information to answer the question. Even after being given more time to look at the display, they rarely changed their answers (Fig. 9). Users performed better with the *Absent* and *Coded* displays, but trends were still a problem, with great variability among users.

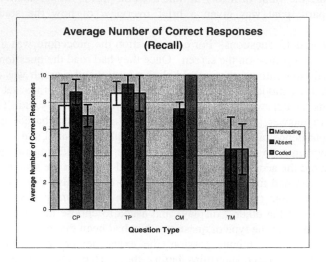

Fig. 8. The average number of correct responses based on recall after a 5 sec. glance at the data. The right 2 sets of bars show that users using the misleading display could not answer any of the questions correctly when missing data was involved (CM and TM).

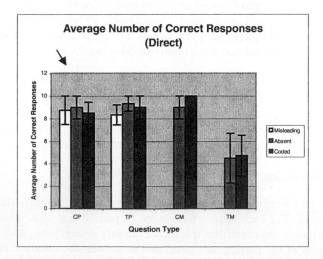

Fig. 9. The average number of correct final responses given while viewing the graph directly on the screen. Overall, users didn't change their answers when given more time. (Please notice the change of Y axis maximum value).

Our hypothesis that participants with *Coded* and *Absent* displays would be more accurate than their counterparts using the *Misleading* displays was verified. The differences were significant when users compared between a missing value and a present data point ($p < 0.05$ for CM questions) and but less so when users have to describe a trend that incorporates missing values ($p < 0.10$ for TM questions). A closer look at the results showed that none of the participants using the *Absent* display answered two questions correctly. Both of these questions involved trend lines in which data was missing from the display. In both cases, the majority of users seemed to have constructed a confident opinion about the trend in the data based only on a few points of data shown in the display, as opposed to concluding that they did not have enough information to decide.

This supports our initial claim that poor indication of missing values can have a negative impact on data interpretation, but also suggests that even when missing data is indicated clearly users may not resist the temptation to find trends in partial data.

No significant differences between displays were found for confidence (Fig. 10 and 11). Users were confident in their answers. The average confidence value was nearly 8 for each of the models and for all of the questions, after 5 seconds and also when given more time.

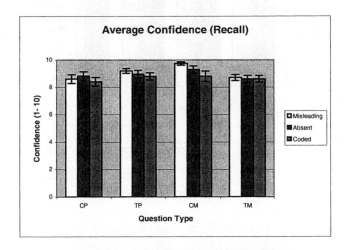

Fig. 10. Users were very confident after viewing the graphs for only 5 seconds, even in treatments where they made lots of errors (in CM and TM)

Concerning the time to answer, no significant differences where found either, contradicting our hypothesis (Fig 12). For six of the thirteen questions answered, users with *Coded* displays had longer average response times. For four questions *Absent* displays had the longest response times while only two questions required more time to answer with the *Misleading* displays. Users of the *Misleading* displays seemed to behave as if the display was relatively straightforward and did not feel that they needed an extended period of time to ponder a response while some users of the other displays seem to hesitate more, but not all of them did so.

Eight users never changed their mind between the first answer and the final answers, while seventeen users made one or two changes, and five users made three or more changes. On a category-by-category breakdown, of the eight participants who changed answers with the *Misleading* display, an average of two answers were modified with an average of one answer actually being changed to the correct answer. Users with *Absent* displays, changed an average of three questions, with an average of two modified to the correct response. Finally, users with *Coded* displays modified an average of two responses with an average of two actually being modified to the correct reply. Of the ten participants using the *Misleading* display, only one (a math major) commented at the end of the test that he was starting to suspect that missing data might have been an issue.

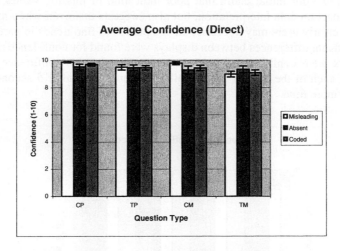

Fig. 11. The final confidence level remains very high

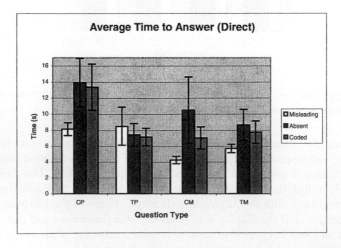

Fig. 12. The average time to give the final answer (while directly viewing the graphs). There were no significant differences.

When asked about their preference at the end of the test 27 users out of 30 selected the *Coded* display. They commented that they liked the idea of having more information available. Surprisingly two participants favored the *Absent* display over all three because they felt the *Coded* display was confusing. In the *Coded* display, the first present data point to appear after a series of missing points is encoded to convey the reason why previous data values were not available and this was found confusing. Finally, one user preferred the *Misleading* display because he liked the continuity of the graphs.

6 Conclusions

Accurately displaying missing and uncertain data presents an interesting challenge for information visualization. We hope that our general classification of visualization techniques will provide a useful basis for building and comparing techniques that represent missing data. Our study looked at how users interpret graphs with missing data. It suggests that users may not realize that data is missing when it is replaced by a default value. In real situations, the rate of error might be reduced because users can take advantage of their world knowledge to spot unlikely values. Furthermore, the study revealed that even if the missing data is noticeable, users are compelled to make general conclusions with partial data.

Participants preferred the *coded* display that provided additional information on the reason for the data to be missing. Some subjects voiced concern about the actual design of the *coded* display, suggesting that improvements could be made. Further studies of the impact of missing data on the more difficult cases of attribute dependant visualizations and neighbor dependant visualizations are needed as well.

Acknowledgments

This research was supported in part by the National Center for Health Statistics and the National Science Foundation thru grant NSF EIA 0129978 (Govstat http://ils.unc.edu/govstat/). We also thank Ben Shneiderman for his advice on the design of the experiment and early versions of this report.

References

1. Babad, Y.M., Hoffer, J.A., Even no data has a value. Communications of the ACM 27, 8 (1984) 748-756
2. Eaton, C., Plaisant, C., Drizd, T., The Challenge of Missing and Uncertain Data Poster Summary in the Visualization 2003 Conference compendium, IEEE (2003) 40-41
3. Shneiderman, B., The Eyes Have It: A Task by Data Type Taxonomy of Information Visualizations. IEEE Visual Languages, (1996) 336-343
4. Chi, E. H., A Taxonomy of Visualization Techniques Using the Data State Reference Model. Proceedings of IEEE Symposium on Information Visualization (2000) 69-76
5. Olston, C., and Mackinlay, J., Visualizing Data with Bounded Uncertainty. In Proceedings of the IEEE Symposium on Information Visualization (2002) 37-40

6. Gershon, N., Knowing What We Don't Know; How to Visualize an Imperfect World. ACM SIGGRAPH Computer Graphics 33, 3 (1999)39-41
7. Howard, D., MacEachren, A. Interface Design for Geographic Visualization: Tools for Representing Reliability. Cartography and Geographic Information Systems., 23, 2 (1996) 9-77
8. MacEachren, A. M., Brewer, C. A., and Pickle, L., Visualizing Georeferenced data: Representing reliability of health statistics. Environment and Planning: A 30 (1998) 1547-1561
9. Ehlschlaeger, C. Exploring Temporal Effects in Animations Depicting Spatial Data Uncertainty. Available at: http://www.geography.hunter.cuny.edu/~chuck/aag98/ (1998)
10. Pang, A. T., Wittenbrink, C. M., Lodha, S.K, Approaches to Uncertainty Visualization. Technical Report UCSC-CRL-96-21, University of California, Santa Cruz. (1996)
11. Pham, B., Brown, R., Visualization: An Analysis of Visualization Requirements for Fuzzy Systems. First International Conference on Computer Graphics and Interactive Techniques, (2003) 181-187
12. Cedlink, A., Rheingans, P., Procedural Annotation of Uncertain Information. IEEE Visualization (2000) 77-83
13. Twiddy, R., Cavallo, J., and Shiri, S., Restorer: A visualization technique for handling missing data. In IEEE Visualization (1994) 212-216
14. Djurcilov, S., Pang, A., Visualizing Gridded Datasets with large Numbers of Missing Values. IEEE Visualization (1999)405-408
15. Dybowski, R., Weller, P., Prediction Regions for the Visualization of Incomplete Datasets. Computational Statistics16, 1 (2001) 25-41
16. Unwin, A. Hawkins, G., Hofmann, Siegl, B. Interactive Graphics for Data Sets with Missing Values – MANET. Journal of Computational and Graphical Statistics 5(2), (1996) 113-122
17. Swayne, D. F., Buja, A., Missing Data in Interactive High-Dimensional Data Visualization. Computational Statistics 13, 1 (1998) 15-26
18. Beichner, R., Testing Student Interpretation of Kinematics Graphs. American Journal of Physics, 62(1994) 75-762
19. Roth, W., Gervase, M.B., When Are Graphs Worth Ten Thousand Words? An Expert-Expert Study. Cognition and Instruction 21,4 (2003) 429-473
20. Brassuer, L., The Role of Experience and Culture in Computer Graphing and Graph Interpretive Processes. Proceedings of the 17th annual international conference on Computer documentation. (1999) 9-15

High-Level Visualization of Users' Navigation in Virtual Environments

Lucio Ieronutti, Roberto Ranon, and Luca Chittaro

HCI Lab, Dept. of Math and Computer Science, University of Udine,
Via delle Scienze 206, 33100, Udine, Italy
{ieronutt, ranon, chittaro}@dimi.uniud.it
http://hcilab.uniud.it

Abstract. This paper presents the current status of VU-Flow (Visualization of Users' Flow), a software tool that is able to automatically record usage data in Virtual Environments and provide a set of 2D and 3D visualizations that make it easy for an evaluator to visually detect peculiar users' behaviors and navigability problems. The paper focuses on novel functionalities we recently added to the tool. More specifically, the new version of VU-Flow includes: (i) the possibility of visualizing predominant flow directions for multiple users or multiple visiting sessions, (ii) a visualization aimed at highlighting traffic congestion problems in multi-user VEs, (iii) the possibility of visualizing a replay of users' visits together with audio and video recordings of actual users (e.g. gathered during lab experiments), and (iv) the ability to derive, for each user, a list of quantitative data characterizing her behavior in the VE.

1 Introduction

A commonly used technique to study how people navigate in electronic information spaces is based on recording users' actions and then derive users' navigational patterns. Analyzing users' navigational behavior (e.g., identifying more/less accessed parts of the information space or recurrent navigation patterns) may help one in understanding the effects of design choices. Unfortunately, while several techniques and tools for such activity have been proposed in the contexts of Web sites or, more generally, hypermedia systems (e.g., see [1,2,3]), in the context of Virtual Environments (VEs) there are no established techniques and tools.

In this paper, we present a software tool, called *VU-Flow* (*Visualization of Users' Flow*), which is able to record users' movements in a VE and visualize them using various techniques that help one in deriving information about how users navigate in the VE, highlighting navigability problems, and making hypotheses about interests or preferences of users.

A first prototype of VU-Flow has been presented in [4]. This paper focuses on novel functionalities we recently added to the tool. In particular, the actual version of VU-Flow adds: (i) the possibility of visualizing predominant flow directions for multiple users or multiple visiting sessions, (ii) a novel visualization aimed at highlighting traffic congestion problems in multi-user VEs, (iii) the possibility of visualizing a replay of users' visits together with audio and video recordings of actual

M.F. Costabile and F. Paternò (Eds.): INTERACT 2005, LNCS 3585, pp. 873–885, 2005.
© IFIP International Federation for Information Processing 2005

users (typically gathered during lab experiments), and (iv) the ability to derive, for each user, a list of quantitative data (a *feature vector*) characterizing her behavior in the VE, and that can be later studied with other data analysis applications (e.g. spreadsheets or statistical tools) or machine-learning techniques.

The paper is structured as follows. In Section 2, we survey related work; Section 3 explains the main motivations of our research. Section 4 describes the architecture of VU-Flow, while in Section 5 we describe in detail its novel functionalities. Finally, Section 6 concludes the paper by discussing ongoing or future developments of VU-Flow.

2   Related Work

In this Section, we focus on the context of Web/Hypermedia systems, and summarize the main approaches that allow an evaluator to automatically record users' interactions with the system and then analyze them to evaluate usability or characterize users' behavior. In general, usage data can be collected during: (i) a remote evaluation, where users and evaluators are separated in space (and can be also separated in time), or (ii) by carrying out lab experiments, where the evaluator directly observe the user interacting with the system, and may also audio/visual record her.

Two main techniques are available for automatically recording information on users' actions. The straightforward one is based on using Web server logs. This approach, that has the advantage of being inexpensive and applicable to any Web site, has however some disadvantages: only some navigation data can be captured (e.g., in general, if one wants to record the browsing history, it cannot include other Web sites) and the impossibility to capture low-level user interactions with user interface elements (e.g., menus and buttons). A second technique requires to modify Web pages to include code (e.g., javascript and/or Java applets) able to record interface events (e.g., reset of forms, resize and scroll of browser windows); in this case, the acquired data can be sent through the Internet and stored into a remote database.

Starting from recorded usage data, there are mainly three kinds of techniques for deriving usability-related information in the context of Web/Hypermedia applications [5]: *metric-based*, *task-based*, and *inferential analysis*.

Metric-based approaches generate quantitative performance measurements that allow evaluators to identify performance bottlenecks (e.g., slow server response time) that may have a negative impact on the usability of a Web site. However, these approaches focus on server and network performance, and thus provide little insight into the usability of the Web site itself.

Task-based approaches analyze anomalies between the expected users' behavior and what users really do while using the system. For example, the WebRemUSINE tool [1] identifies a usability problem by the lack of correspondence between how users perform a certain task and the model of that task describing how it should be efficiently performed.

Inferential analysis of data includes statistical and visualization techniques to extract usability-related information. Statistical approaches are mainly based on traffic-based analysis (e.g., computing accessed pages per visitor or number of visitors per page) and time-based analysis (e.g., click-streams and page-view durations). By analyzing the number of accesses to Web pages and deriving recurrent patterns of visit, one can derive information on the usability of a Web site. For example, derived patterns may highlight non-optimal (e.g., too long) navigation paths frequently followed by users, and thus suggest design modifications. Some tools (e.g., [2,3,6]) facilitate analysis by also presenting results in graphical formats. For example, the VISVIP tool [2] represents paths followed by users during a site visit by visualizing the Web site as a directed graph (pages are represented with nodes and links with edges), and the paths followed by users through curved lines connecting nodes (different colors are used to represent paths followed by different users). Moreover, VISVIP visualizes the average time spent at each page as the length of a dotted vertical line positioned on the corresponding node. The WebQuilt tool [6] uses a similar graph-based visualization, but employs screenshots of Web pages for the nodes of the graph, and edges are drawn only for traversed links; the thickness of an edge indicates how many times the corresponding link has been followed, while its color indicates the average amount of time spent before clicking the link.

However, graph-based approaches can become visually confusing with large and complex Web sites, or when one wants to follow the usage evolution over time. An interesting visualization technique using 3D graphics to face this problem, called Time Tube [3], uses one or more *Disk Trees* representing the evolution of a Web site structure and usage in time. Time Tube provides the evaluator a sense of direction for users' flow, represents usage evolution in time and identifies significant users' paths.

3 Motivations

The same motivations for studying users' navigational behavior in Web/Hypermedia applications still hold in the context of VEs, since navigation is in both cases one of the fundamental user activities. Additionally, navigation in VEs is generally perceived as a difficult activity by users, and typical navigation problems, such as disorientation and difficulties in wayfinding, are exacerbated by well-known troubles in moving inside a 3D space.

Navigational problems in VE are therefore critical for usability, and typically result in users becoming rapidly frustrated and leaving the VE, missing interesting parts of it, or completing the visit with the feeling of not having adequately explored it.

Although some solutions to improve navigability of VEs (e.g., design guidelines [7] or electronic navigation aids [8,9]) have been proposed, in most cases, finding and correcting navigability problems requires one to observe and analyze how users really interact with the VE. Moreover, unlike in the context of Web/Hypermedia systems (or, more generally, 2D interfaces), there are no extensive and comprehensive sets of verified guidelines for designing navigable VEs.

The techniques and tools for studying the navigational behavior of users in Web/Hypermedia applications cannot be used in the context of VEs, because:

- the structure of the information space is different: while Web sites are mainly a collection of connected information items organized in a graph structure, VE content (e.g., 3D models, images, text and audio) is organized in a 3D space, following a possibly complex spatial arrangement (e.g., the 3D model of a building or an entire city): therefore, the graph-based visualizations mentioned in the previous Section are not effective in the context of VEs.

- while in Web sites users navigate from one item to another by simply selecting the desired one from a set of links, in VEs users typically navigate by continuously controlling the position of their viewpoint through mouse, arrow-keys or 3D pointing devices: therefore, usage data are different and, consequently, the techniques for acquiring them mentioned in the previous Section do not work in the context of VEs.

In the remaining part of the paper, we will propose usage data acquisition and visualization techniques that are effective in the context of VEs, and show how the VU-Flow tool implements them.

4 VU-Flow Architecture

VU-Flow is composed by two modules, called *Data Analysis* and *Visualization* (see Fig. 1). An external module, called *Data Acquisition*, is responsible for collecting navigation data from user's visits to a VE.

More specifically, the Data Acquisition module considers that users move into the VE in a "walking" mode (i.e. the typically adopted navigation modality), and samples a user's position and orientation at brief time intervals. Then, it stores the collected data into a database, together with proper identifiers for the considered VE, user and visiting session (this last data is needed to be able to separately analyze different visits to the same VE).

Since the Data Acquisition module has to capture application-specific events, its actual implementation depends on the technology used to build the VE. The Data Acquisition module we implemented works with VEs built with VRML [10] or X3D [11] technologies, and is also able to send the monitored data through the network, allowing to collect navigation data in the context of remote evaluations.

The Data Analysis module processes the navigation data stored in the database, allowing the evaluator to choose the subset of data to analyze by selecting the VE, set of users and set of visiting sessions of interest. For each VE, the Data Analysis module also needs:

- a *map* of the VE, in the form of a two dimensional matrix where each cell represents a (possibly small) square area of the VE, and where the cell value specifies if the corresponding area can be traveled by users or contains obstacles to navigation (e.g., objects and walls). This map can be automatically constructed from the VE itself, using the method described in [12].
- (optionally) locations in the VE of relevant *Points of Interest* (hereinafter, POIs), e.g. exhibits in a virtual museum or products in a virtual store.

The main task of the Data Analysis module is to compute additional values for the cells of the map that are then taken as input by the Visualization Module, which graphically represents them using two main types of visualizations: (i) by overlaying computed data onto a visual representation of the map (i.e., a 2D visualization), or (ii) by integrating computed data into the VE itself (i.e., a 3D visualization).

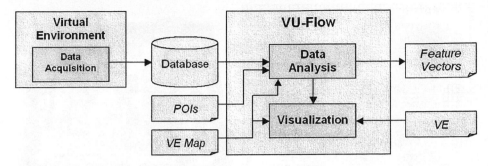

Fig. 1. VU-Flow Architecture

5 Main Functionalities of VU-Flow

VU-Flow provides the evaluator with six main functionalities:

- visualizing (over the map or in the VE), by using different shades of color, more/less traveled areas in the VE or areas where users stayed for more/less time (e.g., see Fig. 2 and 3);
- visualizing over the map the objects in the VE (possibly chosen among the given POIs) that were more/less seen by users during their visit(s) (e.g., see Fig. 4);
- replaying visits of single or groups of users, either employing points and colored lines over the map to draw the user's positions and paths (e.g., see Fig. 5), or visualizing them directly in the VE (e.g., see Fig. 6);
- visualizing over the map, for each part of the VE, the users' predominant flow direction (e.g., see Fig. 7);
- for multi-user VEs, highlighting and visualizing (over the map or in the VE) areas where traffic congestions occurred (see Fig. 8);

The first two functionalities are presented in [4]. The following Sections describe in detail the last three, novel, functionalities.

The new version of VU-Flow includes also the possibility of integration with other analysis and/or classification tools. More specifically, the Data Analysis module is able to derive (and export to a file) a *feature vector* characterizing the behavior of each user by values such as average and standard deviation of the user's speed, average and the standard deviation of the user's angular speed, number of intersections in the navigation path, how much time the user looked toward each POIs.

5.1 Replaying Users' Visits

VU-Flow allows one to replay visits of single or groups of users to a VE and visualize them using either a 2D or a 3D visualization. This functionality can be useful, for example, to review and analyze data collected during an evaluation with users. Since recorded navigational data are just position and orientation samples, VU-Flow employs interpolation techniques to derive navigation trajectories and smoothly replay user's movements.

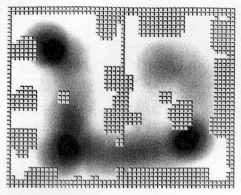

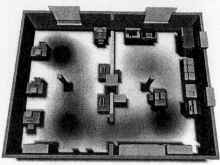

Fig. 2. Visualizing over the 2D map areas where users stayed for more/less time (darker grey highlights areas where users spent more time)

Fig. 3. Visualizing into the VE areas where users stayed for more/less time (darker grey highlights areas where users spent more time)

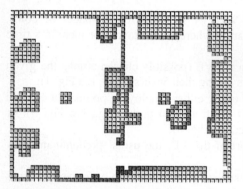

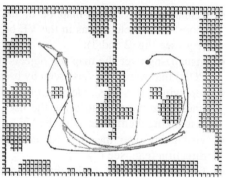

Fig. 4. Visualizing over the map objects in the VE that were more/less seen by users (darker grey highlights more seen objects)

Fig. 5. Drawing on the 2D map paths followed by three users during their visit

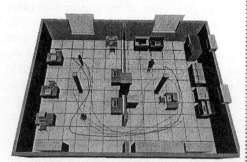

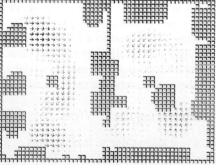

Fig. 6. Drawing into the VE paths followed by three users during their visit

Fig. 7. Visualizing the users' predominant flow directions (arrows indicate flow directions, darker grey arrows indicate more predominant flow directions)

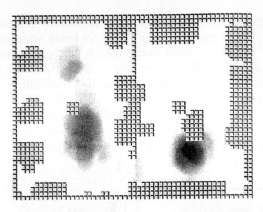

Fig. 8. Visualizing areas where traffic congestion occurred (darker grey indicates more critical traffic congestions)

In the 2D visualization (see Fig. 9a), the current position of the user is drawn on the map as a point, while orientation is represented by two lines that delimit the user's field of view. In this way, the evaluator is both able to observe users' positions in time and estimate where users looked at during the visit. One can choose also to visualize the entire path followed by users up to the current instant (as shown in Fig. 9b).

The 3D visualization replays users' visit into the original VE, by using a different avatar model for each user. The evaluator can observe the replayed visits either through a freely controlled viewpoint (see Fig. 10a), or directly "through the eyes" of one of the users by selecting a specific user's viewpoint (see Fig. 10b). The first solution allows the evaluator to choose the most suitable view of the 3D scene, while the second (that reproduces exactly what a user saw during a visit) may be useful, for example, to precisely identify which objects in the VE have been seen by each user.

To control replay, VU-Flow provides VCR-like controls, i.e. play, fast forward, rewind, pause, and fine tuning of replaying speed (see Fig. 11).

When experiments with users are video-recorded (or only user's voice is recorded, e.g. in a think-aloud experiment), it is possible to replay visits together with video and/or audio recordings. For example, in this way the evaluator can:

- relate users' verbal comments (and/or facial expressions) with interactions in the VE, e.g. to contextualize and disambiguate deictic comments such as "What is this?", "How can I open it?";
- better understand motivations for a particular user's behavior, e.g., when video data are available, in a situation where a user does not interact for many seconds with the application, to point out the real motivation (has the user encountered difficulties in using input devices or was she simply observing something?);
- identify specific areas of the VE where users had navigation difficulties.

Although the Data Acquisition module is not currently able to acquire video and audio data (and thus they have to be separately acquired and then manually synchronized with the navigational data), VU Flow allows the evaluator to display audio and video data during the replay of visits in both the 2D and 3D visualizations (e.g., see Fig. 12). When multiple users' visits are being replayed at the same time, reproducing audio recordings from every user is likely to result in unintelligible sounds. For this reason, VU-Flow allows the evaluator to select which user's audio comments to replay. However, when using the 3D visualization, another interesting option is to use positional audio sources in the VE, where each audio source reproduces comments for a specific user, and is located in the head of the user's avatar. In this case, by moving in the VE, the evaluator may focus on audio comment related with specific users or places, and at the same time perceive comments in the surroundings.

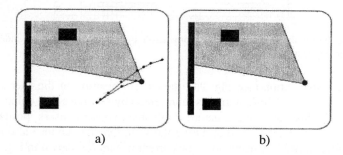

a)   b)

Fig. 9. Replay of user's movements using 2D visualizations

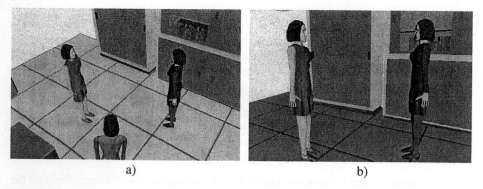

a)   b)

Fig. 10. The same visiting instant seen by employing a freely controlled viewpoint (a) and a user-viewpoint (b)

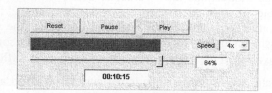

Fig. 11. VCR-like controls provided by VU-Flow to control replay

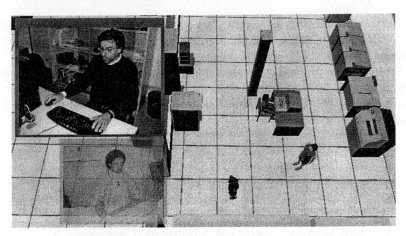

Fig. 12. Replaying visits video recordings of two users

5.2 Deriving and Visualizing Users' Predominant Flows

Visualizing detailed users' paths on the map might help one in identifying user's behavior, but the result is likely to be too visually confusing when one wants to consider a user's very complex and long path, or a population of users (e.g., see Fig. 13) and/or more visiting sessions.

For this reason, in [4], we introduced a set of techniques that, by coloring cells of the 2D map, are able to derive more effective visualizations, e.g. using different colors to visualize areas of the VE where users stayed for more/less time. However, these techniques are not able to visualize users' directions in the visits.

The current version of VU-Flow introduces a new visualization that displays information of predominant flow directions starting from a *vector field* computed by the Data Analysis module. More specifically:

- for each user and visiting session that are under consideration, we first compute a unit vector for each pair of successive navigation samples, where the vector direction is equal to the user movement direction; the computed vector is associated to the map cell where the first of the two navigation samples where taken;
- then, we sum together all vectors associated to the same cell.

As a result, for each cell of the map, the associated vector direction represents the predominant flow direction followed by users in the corresponding part of the VE, and the associated vector length shows the predominance of the computed direction.

VU-Flow visualizes the vector field by employing *hedgehog arrows* [13], a typical technique employed for this purpose. More precisely, an arrow is drawn for each cell of the map, where the arrow color is used to represent the associated vector length (darker means longer), while the arrow orientation corresponds to the associated vector direction. As a result, if an area of a VE was visited by users following a strongly predominant direction, the corresponding arrow will be darker, while the arrow will be lighter if users visited the same area without following a predominant direction.

To better understand the benefits offered by this visualization, in the following we provide a simple example showing parts of different visualizations of the same data recorded on a VE composed by two rooms (denoted by A and B) connected by two passages.

Figure 13 visualizes the recorded data by employing colored lines over the map to show detailed users' paths, Fig. 14 employs different shades of grey to highlight more/less traveled areas, while Fig. 15 visualizes the predominant flow directions. While the first visualization could be used to determine both more traveled areas and movement directions (by observing the recorded data as they are replayed), it is visually quite confusing; the second visualization is more effective in understanding the users' global behavior, since most traveled parts are clearly highlighted, but information on users' movement directions are completely lost. For example, one can determine that the left passage was more traveled than the top one, but cannot determine a predominant flow direction for any of the two passages, nor if the number of times users entered room B is greater than the number of times users exited the same room. By using the novel visualization (Fig. 15), one can easily discover that users predominantly entered room B through the top passage and visited room B following a clockwise direction, while a predominant direction through the left passage cannot be identified. Moreover, the number of times users entered room B is greater than the number of times of users exited the same room.

It is also interesting to note that additional information can be derived by synergically employing both the visualizations in Fig. 14 and 15; in particular, by observing that Fig. 15 does not highlight a predominant flow direction near the left passage, one could hypothesize that only a few users traveled through it; however, by considering also Fig. 14, and noting that the left passage was a highly traveled area, one can rule out the above hypothesis.

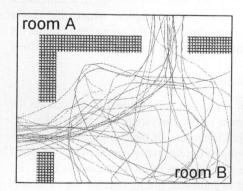 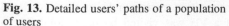 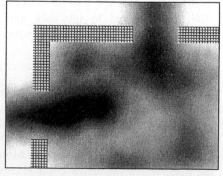

Fig. 13. Detailed users' paths of a population of users

Fig. 14. Areas more/less traveled by users

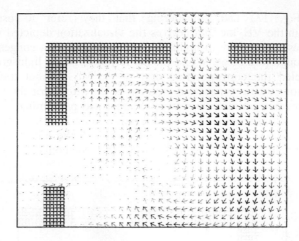

Fig. 15. Users' predominant flow directions (arrows indicate flow directions, darker grey arrows indicate more predominant flow directions)

5.3 Detecting and Visualizing Traffic Congestions

In the context of multi-user VEs, the simultaneous presence of several users navigating can introduce additional navigability issues. For example, navigation difficulties due to traffic congestions may occur when a user's movements are obstructed by the presence and movements of other users. This situation may be problematic when the environment includes narrow passages (e.g., doors or corridors) or when POIs are not effectively spatially distributed in the VE.

The current version of VU-Flow is able to detect and visualize areas where traffic congestions occurred during a multi-user session. Information on traffic congestions is internally represented by associating a real number in [0, 1] to each cell of the map, indicating how much critical a traffic congestion was in the corresponding area of the VE (0 means no congestion).

Intuitively, a traffic congestion occurs whenever an area of the VE is traveled by more than one user in the same time interval (whose length can be changed by the evaluator). Moreover, the criticality of the congestion depends on the number of these users.

More precisely, congestions are identified as follows:

- in a first step, the Data Analysis module groups navigational data such that samples that are mutually sufficiently close in time (i.e., sampling times are within the given temporal interval) and space (i.e., the distance between sampled positions is less than a given value) belong to the same group (note that a sample may belong to different groups). Only groups that contain more than one sample are passed to the second step.
- in a second step, each group is mapped to one or more adjacent map cells and the number of samples in the group is associated to the cell (0 is assigned to cells to which no groups are mapped).

The Visualization module then converts cell values into appropriate shades of a given color. For example, by processing the navigational data used in the previous

Section (see Fig. 13) and considering that they refer to users navigating simultaneously in the VE, the tool derives the visualization depicted in Fig. 16. The visualization uses darker gray to highlight more critical traffic congestion and white to identify no congestion areas. While for the left passage the light-grey areas shows that users traveled the corresponding part of the VE without traffic congestion problems, a serious traffic congestion problem is identified near the top passage. By using also information on more/less traveled areas and predominant flow directions, one can derive that: (i) several users tried to enter room B at the same time through the top passage, and (ii) several users walked through the left passage in opposite directions in different instants (then, without facing traffic congestion problems).

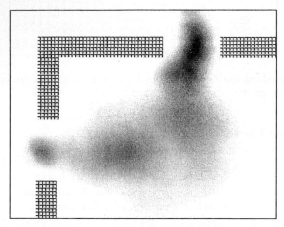

Fig. 16. Visualizing areas of traffic congestion (darker grey indicates more critical traffic congestions)

6 Conclusions

This paper proposed a tool, called VU-Flow, that is able to automatically record usage data in VEs and then visualize them in formats that help an evaluator to understand the effects of VE design on users' navigation.

With respect to future goals of this project, we plan to extend VU-Flow for studying users' behavior in real environments. In this context, the Data Acquisition module should be modified to record information on users' position and orientation through localization technologies, e.g., GPS. It must be noted, however, that while in VEs positions and orientations of users can be precisely determined, in real environments localization technologies usually provide partial and/or inaccurate positioning information.

We are also investigating which kind of feature vectors could be effectively used to identify users' visiting style [14]. To achieve this goal, we are developing a machine-learning system (similar to the one used in [15]) based on the combination of an unsupervised approach (similar vectors are automatically clustered in the same class) and a supervised approach (an expert has to label each vector with a certain class).

Acknowledgments

Our research has been partially supported by the Italian Ministry of Instruction, University and Research (MIUR) under the project "Web-based management and representation of spatial and geographical data", subproject "User Interfaces for the Visualization of Geographical Data on Mobile Devices".

References

1. Paganelli, L., Paternò, F.: Intelligent Analysis of User Interactions with Web Applications. In: Proc. Intelligent User Interfaces (IUI 02), ACM Press, New York (2002) 111-118
2. Cugini, J., Scholtz, J.: VISVIP: 3D visualization of paths through web sites. In: Proc. Database and Expert Systems Applications (DEXA 02), IEEE Computer Society Press (2002) 259-263
3. Chi, E., Pitkow, J., Mackinlay, J., Pirolli, P., Gossweiler, R., Card, S.: Visualizing the Evolution of Web Ecologies. In: Proc. Conference on Human Factors in Computing Systems (CHI 98), ACM Press, New York (1998) 400-407
4. Chittaro, L., Ieronutti, L.: A Visual Tool for Tracing Behaviors of Users in Virtual Environments. In Proc. Advanced Visual Interfaces (AVI 04), ACM Press, New York (2004) 40-47
5. Ivory, M., Hearst, M.: The state of the art in automating usability evaluation of user interfaces. ACM Computing Surveys (CSUR), ACM Press, New York (2001) 470-516
6. Hong, J., Landay, J.: Webquilt: A Framework for Capturing and Visualizing the Web Experience. In: Proc. World Wide Web. ACM Press, New York (2001) 717-724
7. Vinson, N. G.: Design Guidelines for Landmarks to Support Navigation in Virtual Environments. In: Proc. Conference on Human Factors in Computing Systems (CHI 99), ACM Press, New York (1999) 278-284
8. Chittaro, L., Burigat, S.: 3D Location-pointing as a Navigation Aid for Virtual Environments. In: Proc. Advanced Visual Interfaces (AVI 04), ACM Press, New York (2004) 267-274
9. Darken, R. P., Cevik, H.: Map Usage in Virtual Environments: Orientation Issues. In: Proc. IEEE Virtual Reality 99, IEEE Computer Society Press (1999) 133-140.
10. VRML. ISO/IEC 14772-2:2004, http://www.web3d.org/x3d/specifications/vrml/ISO-IEC-14772-IS-VRML97WithAmendment1/#ISO_IEC_14772Part2 (last access on April 2005).
11. X3D. ISO/IEC FDIS 19775, http://www.web3d.org/x3d/specifications/index.html (last access on April 2005).
12. Ieronutti, L., Ranon, R., Chittaro, L.: Automatic Derivation of Electronic Maps from X3D/VRML Worlds. In: Proc. International Conference on 3D Web Technology, ACM Press, New York (2004) 61-70
13. Post, F., van Wijk, J.: Visual Representation of Vector Fields: Recent Developments and Research Directions. In: Scientific Visualization: Advances and Challenges, Academic Press, London (1994) 367-390
14. Veron, E., Levasseur, M.: Ethnographie de l'Exposition. Bibliothque publique d'Information, Centre Georges Pompidou, Paris (1983)
15. Sas, C., O'Hare, G. M. P, Reilly, R.: Virtual Environment Trajectory Analysis: A Basis for Navigational Assistance and Scene Adaptivity. Future Generation Computer Systems, Special Issue on Interaction and Visualisation Techniques for Problem Solving Environments, Elsevier (2004)

How Do People's Concepts of Place Relate to Physical Locations?

Changqing Zhou, Pamela Ludford, Dan Frankowski, and Loren Terveen

Department of Computer Science and Engineering,
University of Minnesota,
200 Union ST SE, 4-192,
Minneapolis MN 55414
{czhou, ludford, dfrankow, terveen}@cs.umn.edu

Abstract. Advances in GPS and wireless networking technologies have enabled a new class of *location-aware* applications, including location tracking [10,2], location-enhanced messaging [3,9], location-based gaming(www.botfighters.com), and navigation aids for the visually impaired [12]. However, these applications typically represent places quite simply, as a geographical point or a point plus radius. We conducted an experiment that showed that this simple representation is not expressive enough to represent the full range of people's everyday places. We also present a set of more complicated physical *shapes* that our subjects found sufficient to cover their places. These results identify representational requirements for location-aware systems, have implications for systems that aim to acquire place representations, suggest enhanced applications, and open up interesting avenues for future research.

1 Introduction

Most existing location-aware systems, both research prototypes and commercial applications, represent locations as a point (e.g., a latitude/longitude) or point plus radius (e.g., 50 meters). A typical use of such information is for an application to take some action when a user crosses the "threshold" of a place. For example, GeoNotes [5] will present relevant notes, and uLocate(www.uLocate.com) can notify a "watching" user that a "watched" user has crossed a "geofence".

comMotion [14] took a step beyond the direct, simple relationship of places to physical locations. A comMotion device inferred the existence of a new place when it lost a GPS signal three different times at the same location (the intuition is that this often signaled entering a building, and many places correspond to buildings). When this happened, it presented its guess to the user (on a visual map interface) for labeling. Further, while each place by default was treated as a distinct place (for comMotion, this meant that it received its own "to-do" list), a user could choose to associate the same list with multiple locations; for example, someone might create a single grocery list for all grocery stores. Thus, users could create an entity consisting of distinct physical locations that the application treated somewhat like a single place.

M.F. Costabile and F. Paternò (Eds.): INTERACT 2005, LNCS 3585, pp. 886–898, 2005.
© IFIP International Federation for Information Processing 2005

We believe that the point + radius representation of a place is not always sufficient, and more complicated representations need to be introduced to accomendate places like "all grocery stores". Our first basis for this assertion is simply reflecting on our everyday places. A favorite bike route, any coffee shop in a small city, or even a five-block-long stretch of a street filled with interesting shops and nightclubs might be very meaningful places to a person and his friends. We also note that Geographical Information Systems offer a rich set of geometric representations, such as points, multiple points, and regions [19]. These data structures were developed to represent geographic features such as roads, rivers, and political boundaries. However, we suspect they will be useful for representing people's personal places, too. Finally, we observe that the GIS geometric representations and people's conceptual representations of places may not always agree. In virtual reality research, places are represented both symbolically and literally to give designers the freedom to present important details without worrying about the correct scale, ratio, etc [16]. A person may perceive a large city as a point simply because it is far away and his only memory about the city is the conference center he went to; by contrast, this person may perceive his grandparent's small town in many detailed shapes, such as the local roads, shops and restaurants, the river and streams that flow by, etc.

Research in environmental psychology has shown that people naturally structure their experience around socially meaningful places - home, office, school, church, coffee shop, pub, etc [6]. A number of research projects have taken steps toward discovering such places from location data. As we already have discussed, comMotion [14] was one such effort. Ashbrook and Starner [1] applied a clustering algorithm to group GPS readings into what they called "significant locations". Zhou et al. explicitly sought to discover meaningful places, presented an algorithm for discovering places from location data [21], and conducted an empirical evaluation of their algorithm data [22]. Other researchers have explored the use of methods such as Markov models and Bayesian networks to learn significant locations and probable transitions between them [15,13]. Based on the results of an empirical investigation of the actual descriptions people produce in mobile phone conversations, Wilenmann and Leuchovius proposed that location-based services should describe location in ways relevant to users, such as "I'm home", "Where we met last time", "So you'll be here in five minutes" [20].

If one believes that the concept of *place* is useful in location-aware systems, then a fundamental research question is:

How do people's concepts of place relate to the representations of physical locations used by computational systems?

We carried out an empirical study to answer this question; this paper reports the results.

The remainder of the paper is organized as follows. We first present some background concepts, then describe our experimental design. Next, we present our results and follow that with a discussion of design implications for location-aware applications. Finally, we close with a brief summary.

2   Background Concepts

In this section, we describe the data collection process and a set of place *shapes* that we used in our experiment.

2.1   Sources of Data

To attempt to answer our question, we needed two types of data: (1) information about people's everyday places, and (2) some computational representation of physical locations that correspond to these places. Details are given in the description of the experimental design below. However, at a high level, we obtained place information by having subjects keep a diary, and we obtained physical location information by giving subjects a GPS device that took frequent location readings. We then applied an algorithm [21] to generate a set of discovered places.

2.2   Proposed Place Shapes

We went into the study hypothesizing the existence of four place *shapes* representing possible physical representations a place could assume. We based these shapes on our intuitions and analysis of data from a pilot study. The four shapes are:

- *Dot*: the simplest category. A single physical location (or 'dot on a map') such as "my house" or "Mariucci Hockey Arena".
- *Multiple Dots(Multi-Dots)*. One conceptual place consisting of separate physical locations or dots on a map. Prototypical examples are chain stores like Starbucks or Barnes & Noble or generic places like a gas station or grocery store.
- *Region*: a geographic region. Prototypical examples include urban neighborhoods ("Soho", "Downtown"), recreational parks and University campuses.
- *Path*: a sequence of locations, e.g., a commuting route or biking/walking path.

3   Experiment

Subjects. Our intuition was that people's daily activities, and thus the types of places they visited, would depend on their life stage. For example, we expected 20-year-old college students, 40-year-old working parents, or 60-year-old retirees to frequent different types of places. Therefore, we recruited subjects from across this spectrum.

We recruited 28 subjects, all from a major U.S. metropolitan area. Some live in a core city, some in the suburbs. They used a variety of travel modes, including walking, biking, public transportation, and personal car. Their ages ranged from the early 20s to late 60s, with an average in the early 30s. Twenty were male, 8 female. Three subjects had preschool children, 4 had school aged children, and

2 had adult children not living with them. The subjects were highly educated, with two thirds having college or advanced degrees. They included 6 college students, 4 engineers, 4 information technology professionals, 4 teachers, a range of other professional and service jobs, as well as several retired people. Clearly our sample is limited and unrepresentative in certain ways. However, we believe it is appropriate since we were conducting formative research intended to better characterize a phenomenom and define more precise, quantitative questions for future study.

Data collection. We equipped subjects with a GPS-enabled cell phone (the Motorola i88s, with service from Nextel) that ran Accutracking software (www. accutracking.com). We set the software to take a GPS reading every minute and send it to a server for storage. Subjects carried the phone for about three weeks, and were instructed to keep the phone with them and turned on at all times. However, they could turn off the phone for privacy reasons whenever they wanted. Subjects also kept a diary [8,18] of the places they visited each day. They received a daily reminder (email, instant message or phone call); they could return their list of places via email or record it in a notebook. We met with all subjects at the beginning of the study to give them the phone, demonstrate its use, and instruct them in the data collection procedure. After data collection was complete, we conducted a semi-structured interview with each subject.

Interview preparation. We ran our discovery algorithm on each subject's personal location dataset (i.e., the GPS readings). For the purposes of this study, the key result of this was that it established a potential correspondence between users' places (as recorded in their diaries) and physical locations. For each subject, we printed out an overview map showing all the discovered places and a set of more detailed maps showing nearby groups of discovered places at a higher level of resolution (see Fig 4 and Fig 5). We also printed a table of each subject's places, shown in Table 1. Note that 1 is filled out to represent the data collected during the interview; initially, the "Shape" and "Comments" columns are blank).

Table 1. Excerpt from the interview table, showing data from one subject

Description	Shape	Comments
Home	Dot	
Cub Foods	Dot	Where I work
TCF Bank	Dot	
ME Building	Dot	Where I study
Neighbor's house	Dot	
Bus stop	Multi-Dots	I ride bus to work and school
Parking lot	Multi-Dots	Many places where I catch a ride from friends
Walk to bus stop	Path	I walk 3-4 blocks
Rosedale mall	Region	This is where I shop

Interviews. We conducted a semi-structured interview with each subject organized around the maps and table. We first led subjects through the process of matching their places (in the table) to the discovered places (on the map). Any discovered places that were not in the diary were added to the table. We then stepped through each place with each subject, asking them to tell us the physical shape of the place. While we presented our shape categories – *Dot, Multi-Dots, Region, Path, Other* – we also gave subjects the chance to describe places as having a different shape (which we categorized as *Other*). However, subjects scarcely exercised this option. We also kept notes of the subjects' comments.

4   Results

4.1   The Dataset

All 28 subjects logged their data for three weeks. Time constraints kept us from scheduling interviews for 3 subjects, so we discarded their data. Also, the interview with one subject was unsuccessful, so we discarded this data as well. Thus, we ended up with data for 24 subjects.

Table 2 summarizes the location readings collected from the subjects. This is a large amount of real data. We know of no other studies with samples of this size. Subjects followed the data collection procedure quite faithfully. The average number of readings per subject is 6,364, which represents over 100 hours of data. Fig. 1 illustrates a subject's GPS data in a metropolitan area collected in a period of 3 weeks.

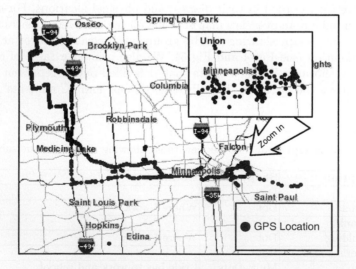

Fig. 1. One subject's GPS data in a metropolitan area collected in a period of 3 weeks. Each dot represents a GPS reading and most of the dots are distributed along major highways. The zoom-in section represents readings on a university campus, which contains 4 places where density of the dots is high.

Table 2. Personal location dataset: on average, 4.8 hours wirth of GPS data was tracked for each subject

Statistics	Readings	Data collect days	Mean readings per day
Total	152,741	516	7,008
Mean per subject	6,364	22	292
Std Dev	3,997	3	167

4.2 Occurrences of Different Place Shapes

Figure 2(a) summarizes the number of places that fell into each place shape. A large majority (79%) of the places were simple locations, or "dots". This may reflect the fact that people typically spend most of their time at relatively fixed and small locations, such as home, office, restaurant, etc. However, 21% were of more complicated shapes. Figure 2(b) gives the average numbers of places with different shapes: on average each subject has 25 *Dot* type places, 4 *Multi-Dots*, 2 *Region* and 1 *Path*.

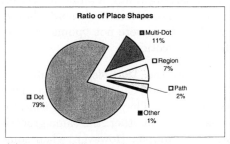
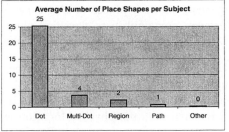

(a)Ratio of different shapes   (b)Average number of shapes per subject

Fig. 2. Occurrences of different place shapes: Figure(a) shows that 79% of the places are *Dot* type, while 21% of the places are not; Figure(b) shows that on average, each subject has 7 places that are either *Multi-Dots*, *Region* or *Path*

4.3 Occurrences of Subjects with Different Place Shapes

Fig 3(a) shows the number of subjects that had places of each of the different shapes. Again, not surprisingly, every subject has place shape *Dot*. Although the complicated shapes account for only 21% of the total shapes, 20 out of 24 subjects have *Multi-Dot*, 18 have *Region* and 13 have *Path*. Fig 3(b) illustrates the percentage of subjects with different number of shapes: 38% of the subjects have 3 shapes, 33% have 4 shapes, 21% have 2 shapes and only 4% have 1 shape.

These results suggest that people's everyday places do take on physical shapes that are more complex than simply a point or point + radius.

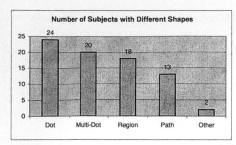
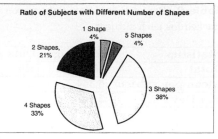

(a) Number of subjects with different place shapes

(b) Ratio of subjects with different number of shapes

Fig. 3. Number of subjects with different place shapes: Figure(a) shows more than two thirds of the subjects have *Multiple Dot* and *Region* type, and half of them have *Path* shape; Figure(b) shows that 71% of the subjects have 3 or 4 different types of place shapes

4.4   Examining the Place Shapes

Dot. This type typically represents an atomic geometry, such as home, work, a restaurant, a post office, a friend's house, a parking ramp, a store, a theater. Fig. 4(a) shows 2 places of *Dot* typs: a subject's home and her friend's house. However, some subjects classified places as *Dots* that were not "point" geometries. We discuss these situations in the following sections.

Multiple Dots. Subjects found it easy to apply the *Multiple Dots* category; they commonly placed chain stores (McDonalds, Target, Cub Foods) and generic places (restaurant, gas station, bank) in this category. They would note that, for many purposes, one physical location was as good as another: the same groceris could be bought at any Cub Foods store, for example. However, when some subjects always went to just one particular McDonalds, they classified this as

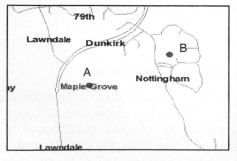
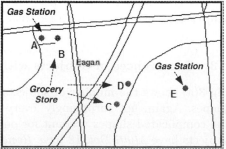

(a) Example of Dot type places

(b) Example of Multiple Dots type places

Fig. 4. Examples of Dot and Multiple Dots type of places: Figure(a) shows a subject's home(A) and friend's house(B); Figure(b) shows a subject's grocery stores(D, C, and B) and gas stations(A and E)

Dot. Another example is that one subject categorized Dairy Queen (a chain ice-cream store) as *Multiple Dots* because she and her daughter stop by more than one or a number of DQs, while she categorized PetMart(a chain pet store) as Dot because she goes only to the one in her neighborhood. Fig. 4(b) shows a section of one subject's map that contains two *Multiple Dots* places, "grocery store" and "gas station".

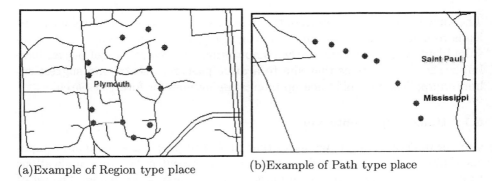

(a)Example of Region type place   (b)Example of Path type place

Fig. 5. Examples of Region and Path type places: Figure(a) shows a subject's neighborhood region; Figure(b) shows a subject's path for walking her dog in a no-leash dog park by a river

Region. Subjects also made use of the Region concept. Fig. 5(a) shows one subject's region, which consists of his neighborhood. Each of the dots is a specific place contained within the region, e.g., his house, friends' houses, etc.

Some subjects articulated a very interesting point, that is that the very definition of a place depends on the activities one does there. They saw a place as a region if multiple activities took place there, regardless of the size of the place.

> *"Cooke Hall [campus building] is a Region because that is where I work, teach, talk to my colleagues, and have meetings; MSU [another university] is a Dot because we just drove by and had a quick tour."*

> *"Duluth is a point [Dot] because I just stayed at my son's place; Wal-Mart is a Region because it's got several departments I shop every time."*

Note that *Regions* typically are seen not just as places in their own right but as containers of other places (usually *Dots*). For example, one subject mentioned that his bank is contained within the (very large) grocery store where he works. Another subject noted that a restaurant he goes to frequently is contained in a hotel some of his friends stayed at.

Path. Over half of the subjects had places of type Path. Typical examples were commuting routes, favorite walks, and bike paths. However, a subject categorized South Dakota(a state in the US) as Path because it represents the highway he drives to go camping each summer. One subject categorized Lake Calhoun as a *Path* because he saw it in terms of the trails around the lake that he rollerbladed on, while other subjects categorized it as *Region* because they included the parks, theaters and volleyball courts around the lake. Fig. 5(b) shows the path that one subject takes frequently to walk her dog.

5   Discussion

The knowledge we have gained of the relationship of places to physical locations leads to design implications and challenges for location-aware systems. Our results identify requirements for the computational representation of places, have implications for systems that aim to acquire place representations, suggest enhanced applications, and open up interesting avenues for future research.

5.1   Place Representation

Our results suggest that the places that matter to people take on more complicated physical shapes than prior systems have represented. For some applications to meet their full potential, they must represent these other shapes. The set of shapes we have discussed here can be represented easily by using OpenGIS data structures (www.opengis.org), e.g., as implemented in the PostgreSQL database system. OpenGIS also provides a powerful set of methods, e.g., to find the distance from a point to a region or to find out whether two paths intersect. As we discuss below, we expect these methods to be useful for emerging location-aware applications.

Our interviews also showed that different people may have different conceptions of "the same" place. Some subjects saw Lake Calhoun as a *Region*, while one saw it as a *Path*; some subjects think that the grocery chain Cub Foods is *Multiple Dots*, while others think it is a *Dot* because they shop at only one Cub Foods location. Our interviews also showed that their conceptions may differ from a "standard" map-based or Geographical Information Systems definition – recall that some subjects saw a state (a large geopolitical region in the USA) as a *Path*, others saw a city as a *Dot*, and some saw an office building as a *Region*. These findings highlight the requirement for *personal* representations of place. The physical geometry of well-known places is a useful resource, but interfaces and acquisition techniques (see below) must allow individual users to create the representations that make sense for them.

5.2   Place Acquisition

The more complicated place representations we propose raise challenges for place acquisition techniques. We consider these challenges from three perspectives, suggesting possible courses of action from each perspective.

Algorithms. Existing algorithms [1,15,13,11,14,21] are all point-oriented discovering techniques. We need to enhance existing algorithms or develop new ones to discover more complicated shapes. Because these shapes contain multiple *Dots*, knowledge of the associations of individual dots in the group must be extracted. Spatial and temporal data mining techniques, such as motion pattern detection algorithms [7], may be employed to address these problems. Specifically, for *Paths*, extending existing spatial clustering algorithm to incorporate temporal data processing may be a viable solution. *Multiple Dots* and *Regions* could perhaps be discovered by incorporating background knowledge, either of standard places or of places previously acquired for other users (however, recall the caveats about the need for place personalization above). However, we believe that acquisition of the latter two shapes is best done interactively.

Interactive acquisition. It is crucial to give users a role in the acquisition process. This is necessary not just to overcome limits of (even the most advanced) algorithms but also to allow people to express their place concepts as they find easiest. Thus, a discovery algorithm must be embedded in a larger interactive system. A well-designed interface can make it easy for people to indicate that a set of dots really all belong to a *Region*, or that a sequence of dots really represents a *Path*. In our work, we are adding interactive capabilities to map-based visualizations like those shown in Fig. 4 and Fig. 5.

Social acquisition. Many places are meaningful not just to a single person but to social groups of varying sizes. In our experiment, we found some students share the same class rooms, study area, lunch places, bus stops and night clubs; some parents share the same community center, city parks, bike trails and grocery stores. Although (as we have noted) one person may not view a particular place the same way as another person, shared places are at least a valuable resource for getting started. For example, suppose Jeff is a student visiting a university campus, and he wants to acquire a set of relevant places to help him in getting around. He might obtain them from his friends who live in the area, for example, a set of restaurants from Joan, some challenging bike routes around campus from Tom, and interesting shopping malls from Jack. Note that *collaborative filtering* or *social matching* techniques are useful here, too. That is, even if Jeff doesn't yet know anyone in the area, he could be matched with the people above if (say) he and Joan were both vegetarians, he and Tom were both cyclists, and he and Jack live in the same neighborhoods.

When socially acquiring places, we must note that descriptions of a single place may vary widely, ranging from generic ("a grocery store") to specific ("Cub Foods") to idiosyncratic ("the place we met last time"). Espinoza et al. [5] have provided some anecdotal descriptions of labels people give places when using GeoNotes. Wilenmann and Leuchovius argue that location-based services should describe location in ways relevant to users, such as "I'm home" [20]. In 'Smart Mobs', Rheingold [17] describes a number of applications that will require individuals to share names of their places with others. Consolvo et al. [4] studied factors that impact people's decision to disclose their locations. In our recent study [23], we investigated the types of descriptions people naturally produce for places, the extent to which they tailor these descriptions for different audiences, and the factors they consider in deciding how to tailor their descriptions.

5.3 Opportunities for New Applications

Existing applications certainly can benefit from this more expressive representation. Consider a virtual notes system, like comMotion or GeoNotes. It is plausible that a user will want to associate her grocery list with any grocery store (*Multiple Dots*), that her tips for finding a good parking place in the Downtown area should be associated with a broad geographic area (*Region*), and that people at the beginning of a *Path* such as a bike route might want to know information about later parts of the path, such as where to get a drink.

New applications may also benefit by incorporating different place shapes. For example, we are interested in the design of navigation aids for visually impaired people. Such users often want to learn routes in a new environment before navigating through it. A user may have certain questions that require complex places to answer, such as: how long is this route? Which routes does this route intersect? How do I get to the emergency exits? What is my relative position in the building?

Different place shapes also empower location-ware social matching applcations to exploit new sharable space and experiences; for example, carpooling applications require representation, identification and matching of drivers' commuting routes (*paths*).

6 Summary

We performed an experiment to investigate how people's concepts of place relate to physical loactions. First, we found that places come in more complex shapes than "points"; in particular the shapes *Multiple Dots*, *Region* and *Path* were common across subjects. Twenty-one percent of all places observed in the study were of these more complex shapes; more than two thirds of the subjects had *Multiple Dots* and *Regions* type, and half had *Paths*. Second, we identified a need for *personal* representations of palce: different people view places in different ways, and these personal conceptions may not match standard map-based representations.

These findings lead to various implications for the design of location-aware applications. First, place representations must include more complicated shapes. Since people's concepts of place shapes do not always match exactly with the physical shape and people have different concepts for the same place, personal representations and interactive acquisition techniques are required. Second, for a system to acquire more complicated place shapes, algorithms must be improved, interactive techniques must be provided, and social acquisition methods should be explored. Finally, new place shapes and acquisition techniques will empower designers to design new applications in new doamins, such as navigation aids for the visually impaired.

Acknowledgements

This work was partially supported by grants from the NSF (IIS 03-07459 and IIS 03-08018). We would like to thank the reviewers for their valuable insights.

References

1. D. Ashbrook and T. Starner. Learning significant locations and predicting user movement with GPS. In *Proc. IEEE Sixth International Symposium on Wearable Computing*, 2002.
2. L. Barkhuus and A. Dey. Location-based services for mobile telephony: a study of users privacy concerns. In *Proc. Interact*, 2003.
3. J. Blom, A. Kankainen, T. Kankainen, and S. Tiitta. Location-aware multiuser messaging: Exploring the evolution of mobile text-based communication services. Technical report, Helsinki Institute for Information Technology (HIIT), 2003.
4. S. Consolvo, I. E. Smith, T. Matthews, A. LaMarca, J. Tabert, and P. Powledge. Location disclosure to social relations: Why, when, & what people want to share. In *Proc. CHI*, 2005.
5. F. Espinoza, P. Persson, A. Sandin, H. Nystrm, E. Cacciatore, and M. Bylund. Geonotes: Social and navigational aspects of location-based information systems. In *Proc. UbiComp*, 2001.
6. K. A. Franck and L. H. Schneekloth, editors. *Ordering space: types in architecture and design*. Van Nostrand Reinhold, 1994.
7. J. Gudmundsson, M. van Kreveld, and B. Speckmann. Efficient detection of motion patterns in spatio-temporal data sets. In *Proc. ACMGIS*, 2004.
8. J. Hightower. From position to place. In *Proc. Workshop on Location-Aware Computing*, 2003.
9. Y. Jung, P. Persson, and J. Blom. Dede: Design and evaluation of a context-enhanced mobile messaging system. In *Proc. CHI*, pages 351–360, New York, NY, USA, 2005. ACM Press.
10. E. Kaasinen. User needs for location-aware mobile services. *Personal and Ubiquitous Computing*, 7:70–79, 2003.
11. J. H. Kang, W. Welbourne, B. Stewart, and G. Borriello. Extracting places from traces of locations. In *Proc. WMASH*, pages 110–118, New York, NY, USA, 2004. ACM Press.
12. P. Klante, J. Krsche, S. Boll, and AccesSights. A multimodal location-aware mobile tourist information system. In *Proc. International Conference on Computers Helping People with Special Needs(ICCHP)*, 2004.
13. L. Liao, D. Fox, and H. Kautz. Learning and inferring transportation routines. In *Proc. AAAI*, 2004.
14. N. Marmasse and C. Schmandt. Location-aware information delivery with commotion. In *Proc. HUC*, pages 157–171, 2000.
15. D. Patterson, L. Liao, D. Fox, and H. Kautz. Inferring high-level behavior from low-level sensors. In *Proc. UbiComp*, 2003.
16. J. S. Pierce and R. Pausch. Navigation with place representations and visible landmarks. In *Proc. IEEE VR*, 2004.
17. H. Rheingold. *Smart Mobs - The Next Social Revolution*. Basic Books, 2003.
18. J. Rieman. The diary study: a workplace-oriented research tool to guide laboratory efforts. In *Proc. CHI*, 1993.

19. S. Shekhar and S. Chawla. *Spatial Databases: A Tour.* Prentice Hall (ISBN 0-7484-0064-6), 2003.
20. A. H. Weilenmann and P. Leuchovius. I'm waiting where we met last time: exploring everyday positioning practices to inform design. In *Proc. NordiCHI*, 2004.
21. C. Zhou, D. Frankowski, P. Ludford, S. Shekhar, and L. Terveen. Discovering personal gazetteers: An interactive clustering approach. In *Proc. ACMGIS*, 2004.
22. C. Zhou, P. Ludford, D. Frankowski, and L. Terveen. An experiment in discovering personally meaningful places from location data. In *Proc. CHI, Extended Abstract*, 2005.
23. C. Zhou, P. Ludford, D. Frankowski, and L. Terveen. Talking about place: An experiment in how people describe places. In *Proc. Pervasive, Short Paper*, 2005.

The Territory Is the Map: Exploring the Use of Landmarks in Situ to Inform Mobile Guide Design

Nicola J. Bidwell[1] and Jeff Axup[2]

[1] School of IT, James Cook University, Cairns, Queensland, Australia 4878
nic@it.jcu.edu.au
[2] School of IT and Electrical Engineering, University of Queensland, Australia 4172

Abstract. People have difficulties interacting with external representations designed to guide navigating physical environments. We derive theory to inform design by probing users' experience and use of their "internal" representations in a temporally evolving wayfinding activity in situ. Interactions with environmental landmarks are explored by analyzing spatial concepts in SMSs used by a group collaborating to wayfind to an unfamiliar rendezvous. Results show differences between landmarks provoking actions and contributing to abstract concepts; and, effects of direct or induced perspective in situ. Design recommendations account for orientation dependence and use of ambiguity in user-world-representation mappings. These include tactics to enable users' to induce perspectives appropriately: with accuracy for recognising landmarks along routes and agility to situate landmark use in naturally evolving wayfinding goals.

1 Introduction

People encounter difficulties interacting with *external* representations designed to guide wayfinding physical environments [e.g. 1, 2]. Here, we derive theory to inform design by probing users' experience and use of their *internal* representations in situ. First, we note close couplings between wayfinding and more global goals and the importance of landmarks in mappings between people and terrain. Then we describe an approach exploring mappings in "naturally" evolving interactions in situ. This analyses spatial concepts in Short Message Service (SMS) communicated and used by a group collaborating to wayfind to an unfamiliar rendezvous. We summarise the method and a narrative of the activity. Next, we describe generalities of landmarks use and themes abstracted by grouping observations related to perspective and different wayfinding goals. This illustrates the effect of orientation and situated goals on mappings and their relations with users' directly experienced or induced perspective. We conclude with design recommendations to assist users in reconciling their internal representations and experience in situ and relate these to situated and collaborative wayfinding. We propose specific tactics to guide perspective enabling landmark recognition en route and to confer agility in using landmarks for naturally evolving wayfinding goals.

1.1 Landmarks in Mappings Between People and the World While Wayfinding

Wayfinding encompasses going to both familiar and unfamiliar destinations and exploring unfamiliar terrain. While wayfinding may be implicit to all mobile activity it

M.F. Costabile and F. Paternò (Eds.): INTERACT 2005, LNCS 3585, pp. 899–913, 2005.
© IFIP International Federation for Information Processing 2005

is rarely the goal. Instead, it is an activity which is closely coupled with the person and their environment and more global goals (e.g. go to work, meet friends, sight-see). A person's interactions while fluidly traversing familiar terrain are "thrown" [e.g. 3]. This implies wayfinding perceptions and actions in such, "ready-to-hand", terrain are unreflective and peripheral to other goals, perceptions and actions. Reliable "thrown" interactions depend on effective mappings [4] between the environment represented internally and experienced in situ. In unfamiliar terrain people interact more reflectively and focus on wayfinding perceptions and actions. Mappings with the environment in situ also reflect dynamic and subjective contextualisation [e.g. 5] of internal representations by perceptions, conceptions and actions associated with people's global goals. Consider a pair of tourists agreeing to meet for ice-cream and explore Australia's famous Bondi Beach for the first time. For example, either's internal representation may be contextualised by semantics conferred to gelateries; physical relations between gelateries, clusters of people and promenades; and, temporality and intersubjectivity such as anticipating their, and the other person's, time and direction of arrival etc.

Landmarks are locational cues that link internal representations to perceptions and actions in the physical environment. The conception of space as sets of familiar landmarks has been shown cognitively, behaviourally and phenomenologically [6, 7, 8]. Landmarks are salient to acquiring, communicating and applying spatial knowledge in wayfinding. People use landmarks to learn [9], use and describe [10] routes between places and for higher-level cognitive concepts allied with wayfinding (e.g. selecting an area in which to dine or shop [11]). Landmarks in route guidance are most effective when they are proximal to a route [12, 13] and relate to prescribed actions [14]. However, meta- and structural information in people's route descriptions [2] seems to express an appreciation of the recipient's global navigation goal [15]. This may contribute to internal representations of landmarks which differ from route sequences.

External representations designed to support wayfinding in mobile devices explicitly or implicitly integrate landmarks [e.g. 16]. Landmarks act as decision points and/or spatial references in route *descriptions* of different modalities, graphical *depictions*, (e.g. annotated maps) and, photographic or simulated, transcendent or immanent views. Interaction difficulties suggest external representations of landmarks may not map closely to users' internal representations and experience in situ. This may relate to the salience of landmarks for effective wayfinding. Landmark salience includes its visual characteristics, semantics (e.g. purpose) and its relative location in the structure of the environment [17]. Differences arise between the types of landmarks described from memory and during route creation in situ [18]. Since external representations tend to be designed outside of an environment they favour a landmark's salience for *recall* and particular semantic concepts associated with places and routes. This may not map well to a user's internal representation and immanent experience of landmarks along unfamiliar routes. Evidence identifying the effect of perspective on internally representing objects [19] suggests mappings are prone to conflicts between the perspectives of users in situ and those of external representations. In unfamiliar terrain, users have difficulties or make errors when matching their perspective with immanent 2-D views [13, 20], and dynamically transposing [1] or self-reporting their position [21] with extrinsic depictions (e.g. aerial-view maps). Further, salience may be subjective [17], which may account for differences noted between users [20] and is likely to temporally evolve with global or situated goals. People refer to external representations of landmarks during situated, as well planned, wayfinding; for example, tourists use landmarks in situ as loci to pivot exploring interesting areas [11].

2   Interactions During an Evolving Wayfinding Activity

2.1   Probing Users' Experience and Use of *Internal* Representations in Situ

To develop insight into people's mappings during wayfinding we drew upon two inter-action design approaches: phenomenological games and technology probes. We sought to provoke foregrounded perceptions and actions in the environment by framing way-finding as a spatially-authentic, mobile, collaborative problem solving experience. This contrasts with studies which foreground activity around an external representation by accounting for users' interactions with a system (e.g. a mobile guide) and the world [e.g. 11, 20]. A group of "wayfinders", starting from separate undisclosed locations, searched for and rendezvoused at an unfamiliar target, a small park (Fig. 4a). They were guided only by a brief description of the target (Fig. 1b) and their interactions with the physical environment and each other. We used mobile SMS to capture data on spatial concepts associated with wayfinding during the activity. Wayfinders communicated with each other using SMS only, even if they were in sight of each other. Every SMS was broad-cast to the other wayfinders and could be referred to repeatedly. Ethnographic evidence suggests people often collaborate to wayfind [11], use SMS to rendezvous [22] and evolve plans amongst groups from numerous short messages [23]. In logging each SMS the device acted as a technology probe, by possessing "embedded, invisible, non-intrusive functionality enabling ongoing use of the technology" [24]. In addition to for-mative, holistic understandings, as commonly yielded by probes, we also systematically analysed the situated use of spatial concepts to inform interpreting mappings. We pos-ited that SMS content would verbally describe conceptual categories and linguistic structures [in: 17] associated with wayfinders' perceptions and actions in the environ-ment and temporally evolving activity. Thus, SMSs may embody some "thrown" inter-actions and situated and global goals. Length constraints on SMS restrict verbosity. To inform interpreting indexicality [25] we captured detailed in situ observations and spa-tio-temporal and post-activity reflective data.

2.2   Method

Mobile activity covered an 8km^2 extent in Palmerston, Northern Territory, Australia. This included parts of the Central Business District (CBD) and two proximal suburbs, comprising single-story family homes with gardens. The city, purpose-built in 1981, has a small population, is set in bushland and was planned to account for motor traffic [26]. Wayfinders, referred to as A, B and C, were males in their 20s who volunteered, as a group, via a WiFi gaming community website. All had been to Palmerston but only C knew parts of the suburbs. B and C had walked around the CBD but A had only driven "across some of these main junctions".

The SMS interface to a Nokia 3650 mobile phone was customized as a discussion list between the 3 wayfinders (Fig. 1a). Each wayfinder's SMS was sent to an address book item labelled 'Mobile group'. This was the number of a phone connected, via Bluetooth, to an SMS server running on a laptop in a car parked in the CBD. The

SMS server [27] recorded the message text, sender and time of arrival of incoming SMSs. It then prefixed "Member [*A*, *B*, or *C*] says:" to the SMS and sent it, via the attached phone, to the other two wayfinders without returning a copy to the sender.

Wayfinders and the research team drove to the main shopping centre in the CBD via main roads at least 1.5Km from the target. Wayfinders were driven individually to separate locations where they waited until an SMS indicated the start of the activity. *A*, *B*, *C* started from the University bus-stop, central bus terminus and in the suburb of Grey respectively (Fig. 2a). Wayfinders were observed passively and occasionally expressed their thoughts and intentions using the Think Aloud protocol. Observers took time-stamped notes and photographs. Each of the 184 photos showed the wayfinder's orientation and what they might be viewing when they received or composed SMSs, or appeared to examine the terrain; or, other notable objects. The next day a pair of observers retraced each wayfinder's route using the notes and photos rendered on a Hewlett Packard Tablet computer (Fig. 1c). They plotted, on a map, each photo's exact position and orientation. Later this data, indexed with times and SMS sent and received, was transposed to an aerial photo from 1,000m (Fig. 2a).

Pre- and post- activity briefings and interviews took place 20km east of Palmerston and were recorded on paper and audio. Before the activity, wayfinders were briefed and practiced using the SMS interface. Experiences relevant to the activity were collected by interview and questionnaire. In a post-activity workshop wayfinders scrolled through the SMSs on their phones and photographs of their surroundings at the time were projected onto a wall. Wayfinder's read out each SMS and commented on their actions and experiences related to this. After individual journey reflections, the group discussed confluences and conflicts in their narratives, decisions and SMSs. The reflections prompted specific questions on individual situated perspectives, shared location awareness and usage issues for mobile, group communication.

Fig. 1. (a) Mobile phone interface to the group SMS; (b) Description of the target destination; (c) Observer retracing a wayfinder's route using photos rendered on a Tablet PC

2.3   Results and Interpretations

Results, first emerging phenomenally, were analysed by integrating the diverse data set. A comprehensive account, incorporating the multiple, distributed data sources, enabled hermeneutically interpreting subtleties of situations. Detailed analysis of the SMS text related to wayfinder's goals, situations and experiences emerging, spatiotemporally, during the activity. The first author's analysis was verified by the second author. Here, we emphasise analysis of the use of landmarks and Frame of Reference (FOR) in SMS. A FOR is any co-ordinate system which spatially relates objects and components of objects. It is specified by its origin, orientation and the relationship between its axes. FORs varied with the sender's situation and experience in the environment. Several themes, arising from grouping analyses of landmarks' FORs and indexicality, afford insight into mappings between wayfinders' internal representations and the world. These are discussed (2.4), with example situations according to the use and efficacy of different perspectives of landmarks for various aspects of wayfinding.

Goals of the Wayfinding Activity

All wayfinders reached the target within 1.5 hours after the first SMS. Their situated wayfinding activity evolved around a set of goals which emerged "naturally" in 5 chronological phases: localize others; primed rendezvous; naïve search for the target; localize target; and, route to target (Figs. 2b,c,d).

Localise Others and Primed Rendezvous: In the first few minutes the majority of SMSs referred to what wayfinders could see, or knew about, their respective starting locations (Fig. 2b). The remainder related to a strategy to deduce the target's location by triangulation. Wayfinders spent time scanning the vicinity of locations. Then each undertook wayfinding which we refer to as "primed" since the all headed to the unanimously familiar water tower (Fig. 2b).

Naïve Search for the Target: From the water tower wayfinders dispersed until *A* discovered the target (Fig. 2c). *A* walked north, *B* walked west and *C* south-east. Each headed towards different areas that they already knew existed. They intended to check promising areas or to explore unknown areas. Wayfinders "naïvely" searched for the target as they had no direct experience of either its location or appearance. *A* and *B* also explored areas naively, commenting "Where the hell [sic] am I?" When *A* found the target, *C*, who was some distance away, asked if it was in the suburb of Driver. Both *A* and *B* had been in Driver for the past 30 minutes, but neither knew its name. Locating the target was difficult for wayfinders. *A* said "The hard part is working out the end point" and *B* felt as if he was "aimless[ly] wandering". As, a group, wayfinders maintained distance between each by drawing on having seen each other (e.g. near the water tower *A* saw *B* head towards a park so did not check it) or tracking each other using SMS information combined with existing area knowledge. Individual strategies differed according to wayfinder's familiarity with Palmerston. *A* paused little and operated "on the principle of moving as quickly as possible". This corresponds with people in unfamiliar terrain who modify hastily constructed routes, opportunistically [11, 28]. Possibly, *C* moved most slowly as he had better familiarity and sought to limit his time en route by *a priori* route creation [28].

Localise Target and Route to Target: *A* found the target 50 minutes after the first SMS was sent (Figs. 4a, f, g). In the final 37 minutes *A* attempted to guide *B* and *C* to the target (Fig. 2d). He started by describing the target's location but by the end included specific route guidance.

Landmarks Referred to in SMSs

The majority (83%) of the 56 SMSs exchanged were reports, questions or instructions relating to location and/or direction. Of these 72% referred to one or more landmarks and the remainder contained non-specific locational and/or directional information (e.g. "where to now?"). Current or intended self movement was specified in 12 reports relating a landmark to verbs (e.g. search, turn, pass). There were 9 instructions for a direction of heading by another wayfinder which related a landmark to the verbs: head, check, go and look. Throughout wayfinding SMSs referred to landmarks that the sender both was or was not currently able to see. Of all instances of landmarks described in SMSs the sender was able to see or had very recently seen, 43%; or had previously seen 37% which were not currently visible. The remaining 19% had not yet been seen by the sender during the activity. Only 14% of landmarks mentioned were never seen by the sender during the activity. The frequency of referring to a landmark did not correlate with time spent in its vicinity (e.g. wayfinders walked on University Avenue across the longest duration but referred to it only at the start and end).

Landmarks were used to refer to a location in 60% of all SMSs. The landmarks can be classified according to Lynch's schema [7]. The most frequent class was a "node", where people undertake activities. Eight nodes were visible, and one was signposted, from main arterial roads. The 3 nodes that were not visible or sign posted from main arterial roads required fuller description by relating to other landmarks. SMSs mentioned 8 "districts", or larger entities with particular semantic identities [7]: 6 visible from main arterial roads and, 2 signposted from main arterial roads. All of the 6 "edges" indicated in SMSs had fuller descriptions by relating to other landmarks; 4 were road features and 2 were distinctly labelled entrances. All 4 "paths" were road names. There was one Lynchian "landmark", the water tower.

Approximately half (56%) of SMSs which used landmarks to describe a location expressed directional information. A total of 29 different landmarks were each specified between 1 and 10 times (mean = 3 per landmark). Landmarks were described by name or function in equal proportion. Those described by name included districts such as suburbs (e.g. "Driver"); paths, such as roads (e.g. "University Avenue"); or nodes such as shops (e.g. "Woolworths"). Name usage closely related to functional uniqueness (e.g. 3 supermarkets were individually named). Landmarks described by function included areas (e.g. "golf course"), buildings (e.g. "shopping centre"), distinct features (e.g. "water tower") or road features (e.g. roundabout) (Figs. 2b,c,d). Parts of landmarks described specifically were considered distinct (e.g. 13th hole [of golf course]; Corner of [Chung Wah Terrace]). SMSs frequently described locational and/or directional information by combining several landmarks which are considered distinct. For example, "Oasis-Target roundabout" contains: Oasis, Target and roundabout. Composite descriptions were used to provide specific locational descriptions and/or directional information. Some SMSs described two locations to provide directional information. For example, "Circling Coles to water tower" refers to a direction of movement towards another location. Such a SMS is considered to contain one directional and two locational information items. Some SMSs contained several locational and/or directional information items. For example," Check the skate park then head towards fairway waters, ℬ check near golfpark I'll go down main middle road" contains 4 locational items (skate park, golf park, fairway waters and main middle road) and one explicit directional information item: "then head towards".

Perspectives of Frames of Reference (FORs)
SMSs tended to refer to landmarks with an explicit FOR (total = 54 information items). The majority of SMSs explicitly referred to landmarks with intrinsic FORs, with co-ordinates within the world (e.g. Table 1). Many information items (48%) with explicit FORs related landmarks to the sender's own, egocentric, perspective (e.g. "The first left before the golf course"). Other information items (33%) with explicit FORs described the landmark, allocentrically from the landmark's perspective (e.g. "Inside Fairway Waters"). Many intrinsic FORs were induced [29] indirectly as the sender was not insight of the landmark at the time. Wayfinders must have induced at least 44% of egocentric and 32% of allocentric FORs in SMS as they referred to landmarks that the sender had not yet seen in the activity. One SMS used extrinsic FOR with co-ordinates lying outside of the world and induced from experience (Table 1). However, wayfinders were uncertain in relating locations to absolute directions.

Table 1. Examples of SMS (referred to in text), landmarks and FORS

SMS Text	Landmarks	FOR	
omw [on my way]	-		
Circling coles 2 tower	Coles; Watertower	Egocentric	
Bhind the shopin centre target	Shopping centre; Target	Allocentric	Direct
I am in the housing estate opposite	House estate; Watertower	Allocentric	
the water tower moving back to Oasis-Target roundabout	Oasis; Target, Roundabout	Allocentric	In-duced
I am approx 200 m SSE fm coles h2o tower	Coles; Watertower	Extrinsic	
4 b. Goto 13th hole	13th hole [of golfcourse]	Egocentric	

2.4 Mappings Between Internal Representations and the World

Allocentric FORS Convey Abstract Wayfinding Concepts
References to landmarks using allocentric (object-centred) FORs appear to reflect awareness of holistic and abstract wayfinding contexts. Wayfinders developed awareness of other's respective locations using imprecise allocentric FORs. These appeared to assist sharing a spatial conceptualization of wayfinding. Wayfinders used landmarks to describe location, rather than direction, in SMSs on their starting locations, for rendezvousing at a known location and during naïve search for the target. In brief initial SMSs (2-6 terms) wayfinders referred to landmarks that they expected others would know (Figs. 2b) (e.g. *A* chose the "shopping centre", some distance from his starting location, because it was "a large centralized location with no houses"). SMSs carried relatively low locational specificity (Fig. 3a) but efforts were made to avoid ambiguity (e.g. 4 SMSs were exchanged to clarify that *B* was at the bus terminus not a

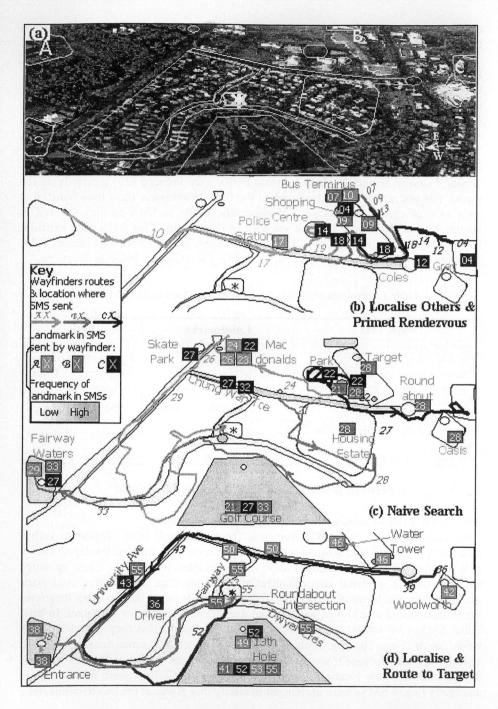

Fig. 2. (a) Aerial view of terrain showing starting locations and example landmarks. Wayfinders' routes and locations where example SMS, referred to in text, were sent during the naturally evolving phases (b, c, d,) of the activity (see key).

bus stop, Fig. 2b). Imprecise location information was used to co-ordinate rendez-vousing at a known place (Figs. 3b, 2b). While no wayfinder was in sight of the water tower, all headed immediately to it without explicating its location or route directions. They said "everyone knows the water satellite tower". Wayfinders used coarse existing knowledge to identify others' locations. When searching for the target (Fig. 2c) they avoided areas others may be, or have been (e.g. "I knew $\mathcal{A}$ was in proximity so moved away from him"). Often wayfinders referred to previous SMSs "to see where [others] said they had been". These expressed imprecise locational information (Fig 3b) but, as $\mathcal{A}$ commented, "visualizing where other people are is easy...".

During the naïve search for the target, wayfinders described and used landmarks with allocentric FORS to spatially relate several districts with course granularity (Figs. 3, 2b). These landmarks often related to semantics about a district. Wayfinders associated the target with public or residential spaces where children might be (e.g. while exploring a housing estate, $\mathcal{B}$ said "single mothers need parks"). Shared allocentric FORs were prone to ambiguity and failed to guide wayfinders' individual searches precisely. When referred to allocentrically, the water tower was misinterpreted twice by different people as a rendezvous rather than a spatial reference. They sought richer descriptions and directional information about headings. Landmarks associated with "nodes" and "districts" seem to contribute to a spatial context for wayfinding that differs from route

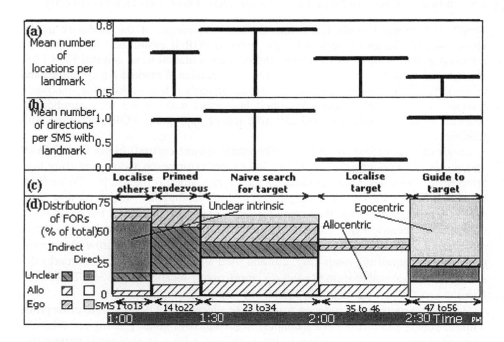

Fig. 3. Characteristics of the use of landmarks in SMS in each (c) phase of wayfinding: (a) Mean number of locations associated with a landmark; (b) Mean number of directions associated with a landmark; (d) Frequency of direct (solid) and indirect (stippled) egocentric, allocentric and non-explicit intrinsic FORs associated with landmarks

following. Wayfinders primed their search for the target with knowledge limited to places visible from main arterial roads (e.g. McDonalds) or from a hill-top which A and C used to "see other features" and gain inspiration.

Egocentric FORs Are Associated with Action

Egocentric (viewer-centred) FORs appeared to relate to movement and direction more directly than allocentric FORs. Wayfinders most accurately and effectively described directional information by describing landmarks with egocentric FORs (Figs. 3b, c). Egocentric structures are thought to more strongly associate with actions than abstract reasoning [28] and correspond more closely with the physical environment than allocentric structures [29]. Conveying a landmark's affordance in verbal route descriptions connects perception to actions [12]. Wayfinders most accurately described and understood route directions when they had direct experience of the landmark relative to that route. This may imply that a landmark's efficacy as a cue en route is relative to subjective perception of it in a route (e.g. B was able to visualize his heading parallel to a route along the golf course as he had previously walked along the course, Fig. 2d). Generally wayfinders favoured more visual landmarks over road names (e.g. in the CBD's commercial setting, Fig. 2b). However, to describe routes they referred to road names to increase locational specificity (Fig. 2d).

2.5   Induced FORs Are More Error Prone Than Those Experienced Directly

Wayfinders induced FORs from limited visual experience of the landmark and/or knowledge of classes of landmarks. An induced FOR is established by performing rotations and relocations of the origin and/or the orientation of an original FOR [30]. Wayfinders tended to induce mentally. On one occasion A marked a map in the sand to visually assist inducing extrinsic FORs. He described landmarks using, incorrect, compass bearings. Wayfinders described landmarks with similar total numbers of intrinsic FORs but induction and effective use of appropriate FORs increased with familiarity.

Landmarks described by inducing allocentric (object-centred) FORs from limited egocentric (viewer-centred) experience were more error prone and/or confusing than allocentric FORs describing landmarks that were visible to the sender. To increase locational specificity wayfinders combined multiple landmarks, which tended to be on distant arterial roads rather than close to their locales (Figs. 2c, 3a). For example, B generated allocentric FORs from his limited experience of distal landmarks to report on location and heading. A arrived at the target by traversing the suburb without scrutinizing interconnecting roads (Fig. 2c) and used allocentric FORs for landmarks denoting routes accessible from B's and C's approximate locations (Fig. 3d). These confused B and C who were unable to induce the target's location.

Egocentric routes were induced from course allocentric FORs but were error prone without robust knowledge. For example, A attempted to guide C along an unknown route between two known landmarks by describing it from an egocentric perspective which he incorrectly inferred from allocentric information. Allocentric knowledge may derive from experience or knowledge of spatial relations holding on a class of landmarks. The golf course offered a set of edges and nodes proximal to the target (Fig. 2d). When asked that the golf course entrance be a reference, A correctly induced egocentric perspectives for the route relative to the golf course from allocentric FOR using the landmarks: entrance to, end of and 13th hole. These were not in his sight and he had not seen all of them before. The golf course was the most frequently referenced landmark, used as an initial trajectory and to limit the search extent (Figs. 2b,c,d). This suggests some of its characteristics were functionally significant to the wayfinders. Egocentric perspectives induced from allocentric knowledge of classes of landmarks affected recognition. Wayfinders had difficulty identifying the target as they approached it from an orientation where, as $\mathcal{A}$ said, its "Swings and slides are hidden ... so its park features are obscured" (Fig. 4). $\mathcal{A}$'s attention was drawn to the target from 50m when he saw a plaque matching the description. $\mathcal{B}$ had previously walked in view without noticing the park; a roundabout obscured his view of the plaque. C was guided to the target from the same direction as $\mathcal{B}$ when $\mathcal{B}$ had missed it.

Landmark Saliency for Memorability: Recalled Landmarks Relate to Decisions
Differences were observed between landmarks wayfinders used in situ and those they recalled from a route. In the final phase, instructions to guide others to the target, related to edges and paths more than in other phases. $\mathcal{A}$ and $\mathcal{B}$ constructed routes to guide C by describing landmarks from memory and by checking road names in the vicinity. Yet, when wayfinders retraced their own steps they recognized places but were unaware of road names. $\mathcal{B}$ said "I don't remember road names well [but].. I easily remembered where I had come from". It is proposed that the wayfinders tended to emphasize edges and paths because they were remembered as decision points within the relatively homogeneous suburb. While, this corresponds with saliency when people recall routes; salience for using such directions in situ correlates more strongly with landmarks' appearance than those generated from memory [31].

Fig. 4. (a) Park features are visible from limited orientations; (b) Target depicted on a city map; (c) Orientation of wayfinders close to the target; (d, e) $\mathcal{A}$ noticed the plaque from 50m; (f) $\mathcal{B}$ did not see the target when first in its vicinity; (g) $\mathcal{B}$ and (h, i) C were guided to the target

3 Mappings Between External Representations and the World

Mappings between a user's internal representations and the world during wayfinding exhibit a dynamic, situated dependency with their environment and subjective way-finding goals. Such dependencies can be resolved only by gathering data in the specific environments in which people think, reason and act [32]. However, careful analysis of meticulously detailed data which captures user's internal representations created and used in situ can yield generalized patterns to theoretically inform aspects of design.

3.1 Supporting 'Thrown" Interactions

Designs enabling accurate direct mapping support "thrown" interactions en route in unfamiliar terrain. We propose that errors in inducing FORs may impede recognizing landmarks in situ from external representations. People will induce some FORs from external representations when they construct internal representations before traversing unfamiliar terrain [e.g. 33]. For example, a person anticipates a landmark's appearance from their intended direction of approach. However, recognising landmarks in situ depends on experience and orientation. People first form egocentric (viewer-centred) FORs for an object and these depend on their orientation relative to it during exposure [19]. Tourists are better at recognizing a destination when they view its landmarks from the direction of their first encounter [34] and anecdotes imply that they may not realize they have reached a destination if they are familiar with a single iconic image of it from another angle. Mapping egocentric perspectives delayed identifying features when observers reconstructed wayfinders' routes from images (Fig. 1c) if precise orientation was absent. Users are able to more accurately follow guidance by Global Positioning Systems when it is accompanied by images of proximal landmarks en route [35]. Egocentric representations of objects that can be recognised from any orientation can support users' direct mappings. Users of image-only sequences to follow routes realigned to correspond with an image's orientation and found and recognized features more easily when images contained familiar or predictably shaped objects [36]. Such objects are less easily recalled than unusual objects [7, 37].

3.2 Perspectives and Paradoxes

We propose that linking route descriptions to coarser graphical depictions of more distal landmarks assists inducing perspectives appropriately. *Appropriate induction* enables effective "thrown" interactions or more discretionary interactions contextualised by the user's situated and/or global goals. In situ users maintain confidence in route descriptions and their orientation from information between decision points [12] and from distal landmarks and matched landmarks to images which contained multiple features more easily [36]. Coarser depictions of distal landmarks can support accurately inducing FORs to recognise proximal landmarks en route. These should use allocentric FORs to relate proximal to distal landmarks visually and/or semantically. For example depicting prominent, distant landmarks (e.g. mountains, shopping areas) from the perspective of a landmark en route. They should also emphasise "ambiguity of information" [38] if a user's orientation relative to a represented landmark is unpredictable. Users following routes using image-only sequences tended to assume that image perspective implied heading and rarely noted triangulating several landmarks [36]. Thus, exposing inconsistency may thwart inducing ineffective FORs.

Emphasising "ambiguity of information" also confers agility in using landmarks for temporally evolving wayfinding goals. Uncertain approximations of landmark position enable sharing abstract wayfinding concepts. For example: by wayfinders to limit the extent of their search and visualise other's trajectories; and, in location-based games, to conceptualise remote player position [21]. Thus, facilitating appropriate induction can support contingent and situated wayfinding [e.g. 11] and enhance communication and decision making during co-located or distributed, collaborative wayfinding [e.g. 21]. A mixed reality game which exposed inconsistencies in locational information engaged player' interpretation of ambiguity [38]. The depictional form of prominent distal landmarks which are allocentrically related and expose inconsistency remains to be explored. We conjecture that caricatures and impressionistic sketches present fertile opportunities for exploring appropriation in situated wayfinding [11]. We propose that exploring such depictions created by users in situ for "naturally" evolving wayfinding goals promises an interesting contribution to research in embodied interactions [5].

4 Conclusion

Representations created and used in situ to wayfind can theoretically inform mobile guide design. They identify a need to enable direct mapping to user's perspectives in situ and guide *appropriate* induction of perspective. Verbal or visual route descriptions from egocentric perspectives should emphasise the salience of proximal landmarks for recognition and action not recall. Co-ordinating these with, macro depictions of distal landmarks will guide perspective and expose ambiguity for situated use.

Acknowledgements. We thank: Darwin Wireless wayfinders for their time and energy; SMSNow for the server; Computer Sciences Corp and Charles Darwin University for support; NC, MP, BP, SV and CL for research assistance and suggestions; CK, CG$_1$ and CG$_2$, for insightful critique and review; and, CG$_1$ for patience and inspiration.

References

1. Brown, B., Chalmers, M. Tourism and Mobile Technology. Proc. of the VIIIth European Conference of Computer Supported Cooperative Work Kluwer (2003) 335-354
2. Geldof, S., Dale, R. Improving Route Directions on Mobile Devices. Proc. ISCA workshop on Multi-Modal Dialogue in Mobile Environments Kloster Irsee, Germany (2002)
3. Winograd, T., Flores, F. Understanding Computers and Cognition. Reading, MA, USA: Addison-Wesley Publishing Company (1986)
4. Graham, C., Cheverst, K. Guides, Locals, Chaperones, Buddies and Captains: Managing Trust Through Interaction Paradigms. Workshop on Mobile Guides, Vth Int. Symposium on Human-Computer Interaction with Mobile Devices and Services (2004)

5. Dourish, P. Seeking a Foundation for Context-Aware Computing. Human-Computer Interaction, (2001).16: 23
6. Siegal, A.W., White, S.H. The development of spatial representations of large-scale environments. Advances in Child Development & Behavior 10. Academic Press (1975) 10-55.
7. Lynch, K. The Image of the City. MIT-Press, Cambridge, (1960)
8. Thorndyke, P.W. Performance models for spatial and locational cognition. Rand, Washington (1980)
9. Golledge R., Wayfinding Behaviour. John Hopkins UP Baltimore & London (1999)
10. Taylor, H.A., Tversky, B. Perspectives in Spatial descriptions. J. Memory & Language (1996)20(5):483-496
11. Brown B., Laurier, E., Designing electronic maps: an ethnographic approach. Map-based mobile services: Theories, Methods and Implementations. Springer-Verlag (2005)
12. May A.E., Ross T., Bayer S.H., Tarkiainen M.J. Pedestrian navigation aids: information requirements and design implications. Pers Ubiquit Comput (2003) 7:331
13. Bidwell, N.J.,Lueg, C Creating a Framework for Situated Way-Finding Research. APCHI New Zealand (2004)
14. Denis, M., Pazzaglia, F., Cornoldi, C., Bertolo, L. Spatial Discourse and Navigation: An Analysis of Route Directions in the City of Venice. App. Cog. Psych. (1999) 13: 145-1
15. Weissensteiner, E., Winter, S. Landmarks in the Communication of Route Directions. GIScience: Lecture Notes in Computer Science, Springer Berlin (2004)
16. Kray, C., Baus J., A Survey of Mobile Guides. Workshop on Mobile Guides, Vth Int. Symposium on Human-Computer Interaction with Mobile Devices and Services (2003)
17. Raubal, M.,Winter, S. Enriching wayfinding instructions with local landmarks. GISscience Lecture Notes in Computer Science Springer, Berlin(2002)
18. Freksa, C., C. Habel C.,Wender K. F. Spatial cognition: An Interdisciplinary Approach to Representing & Processing Spatial Knowledge, Springer-Verlag, Berlin (1998) 157-175.
19. Iachini, T, Logie R. H. The Role of Perspective in Locating Position in a Real-World, Unfamiliar Environment. Applied Cognitive Psychology (2003) 17:904
20. Goodman, J., Brewster, S. Gray, P. How can we best use landmarks to support older people in navigation Behaviour and Information Technology (2005)
21. Benford, S., Seager, W., Flintham, M., Anastasi R., Rowland D., Humble, J., Stanton D., Bowers, J., Tandavanitj, N., Adams M., Farr, J.R., Oldroyd, A., Sutton J., The Error of Our Ways: The Experience of Self-Reported Position in a Location-Based Game. Proc. Ubiquitous Computing: 6th International Conference, Lecture Notes in Computer Science Springer-Verlag Heidelberg (2004) 3205:70 – 87
22. Grinter, R. E., Eldridge, M. Wan2tlk?: Everyday Text Messaging. Proc. CHI. ACM Press (2003)
23. Ling, R., Birgitte, Y. Hyper-coordination via mobile phones in Norway. In: Perpetual Contact: Mobile Communication, Private Talk, Public Performance Cambridge University Press, Cambridge: (2002) 139-169.
24. Cheverst, K. Fitton, D., Rouncefield, M., Graham, C., 'Smart Mobs' and Technology Probes: Evaluating Texting at Work. Proc. of 11th European Conference on Information Technology Evaluation Royal Netherlands Academy of Arts & Sciences (2004) 11-12
25. Garfinkel, H., Studies in Ethnomethodology, Englewood Cliffs: Prentice-Hall (1967)
26. www.pcc.nt.gov.au/devdem/Statistical%20Comparisons%201986%20to%202001.pdf
27. SMSNow http://www.nowsms.com
28. Freksa, C. Spatial and temporal structures in cognitive processes. Foundations of Computer Science. Potential Theory Cognition, Springer-Verlag, Berlin (1997) 379-387

29. Chalmé, S., Visser, W., Denis, M. Cognitive aspects of urban route planning. International Conference on Traffic and Transport Psychology (2000) 145
30. Kray, C Inducing Frames of Reference Workshop on Spatio-Temporal Reasoning at ECAI04, Valencia, Spain (2004)
31. Lovelace, K, Hegarty, M., Montello, D., Elements of Good Route Directions in Familiar & Unfamiliar Environments. Proc. Int. Conference COSIT, Springer-Verlag (1999) 65-82
32. Suchman, L. Plans and situated actions: the problem of human-machine communication. Cambridge U.P (1987)
33. Michon PE., Denis, M. When and Why are Visual Landmarks Used in Giving Directions? Proc. Int. Conference COSIT, Springer Verlag (2001) 292
34. Allen, G.L., Kirasic, K.C. Effects of the Cognitive Organization of Route Knowledge on Judgments of Macrospatial Distances. Memory & Cognition (1985) 3: 218-227
35. Schilit, B., LaMarca, A., Borriello, G., Griswold, McDonald, D., Lazowska, E., Balachandran, A., Hong J., Iverson V. Challenge: Ubiquitous Location-Aware Computing and the Place Lab Initiative. First ACM Int. Workshop on Wireless Mobile Applications & Services on WLAN San Diego, US (2003)
36. Bidwell, N.J., Pictures Made for Walking: Pilots & Orienteers 1. Proc. Australasian Conference on Computer Human Interaction, Woolongong, Australia (2004)
37. Evans, G. W., Smith, C., Pezdek, K. Cognitive maps and urban form. J. American Planning Associations (1982) 48:232-244
38. Gaver, W.W., Benford, S., Beaver, J., Ambiguity as a resource for design Proc. Conference on Human Factors in Computing Systems ACM Press NY, US (2003) 233 – 240

Technology in Place:
Dialogics of Technology, Place and Self

John McCarthy[1] and Peter Wright[2]

[1] Department of Applied Psychology, University College Cork, Ireland
john.mccarthy@ucc.ie
[2] Department of Computer Science, University of York, York Y010 5DD, UK
peter.wright@cs.york.ac.uk

Abstract. Ubiquitous and ambient computing – computationally enhanced built environments and portable products that aim to make computing available anytime-anywhere – has somewhat paradoxically put place at the heart of Interaction Design. In this paper, foundations are laid for a dialogical approach to place as an expression of the experienced relationship between people and space. Building on McCarthy and Wright's dialogical conceptualisation of technology as experience, place is described in terms of the plurality of histories, interactions and meanings that characterise people's different engagements with particular spaces. Implications of a dialogical approach to place are considered with respect to the further development within Interaction Design of concepts such as context, engagement, and interactivity.

1 Introduction

The focus of attention for Interaction Design is no longer just a box on a desk. Visions for the future of interaction such as 'Ubiquitous Computing' [1] and 'The Invisible Computer' [2], accompanied by the integration of information and communication technologies, have ensured that. Nowadays many people's primary encounters with technology are in their incidental interactions with computationally and digitally enhanced portable products, buildings, and public spaces. In order to make a meaningful contribution to understanding people's experiences and relationships with technology in these fluid contexts, Interaction Design needs to expand its conceptual repertoire. As well as attending to the relative certainties of planned interaction, it needs to develop an understanding of the immanent potentiality and possibility of incidental interaction in ambient environments. Interaction Design is only beginning to understand ambient computing. This paper, by drawing on philosophical, cultural, and psychological treatments of people's experience and sense of place as they in turn settle and wander, suggests some foundations for a relational account of technology, place, and self that is a requirement for understanding ambient computing.

This is not only a conceptual task. It bears strongly on how we see Interaction Design practice developing in a world of context aware and ambient computing. As these technologies develop, practice is increasingly concerned with designing interaction spaces, not just devices. In this interaction paradigm, the user is embedded in a computational environment, and interaction may no longer involve deliberate and

M.F. Costabile and F. Paternò (Eds.): INTERACT 2005, LNCS 3585, pp. 914–926, 2005.
© IFIP International Federation for Information Processing 2005

conscious input from the user but instead may be triggered by incidental interactions or movements detected by sensors. With the obvious potential that ambient and location sensitive technologies offer for the personalisation and user-customisation of spaces, a theoretical understanding of relations between space and place, and a design practice geared towards enriching people's sense of place through digitisation seem to be central to ensuring a user-centred approach to ambient technology, situated displays, and location sensitive information systems.

Take students' experiences with technology as an example of the kind of dynamic, reciprocal relationship between people and portable, ubiquitous, ambient technology that motivates many of the concerns of this paper. Many students walk to college listening to their MP3 player. Some, who find the walk uninteresting, use music to take them out of their immediate surroundings. They may shuffle through their collection, play their favourites, or select a musician who suits their current mood or whom they know will get them energised for the day. Arriving on campus, still listening to the music, they go to one of the computer rooms, to check email and announcements on Blackboard (the teaching-learning support system) that might affect their lecture schedule today. Some log onto their chat rooms for a few minutes to see who's there and to say hello. Then they go toward the lecture room lingering in the hall until a track finishes before going into their first lecture. After the lecture, they walk to the library or the cafe, listening to music again, and texting friends to get in touch and to arrange to meet them later. In a laboratory in computer science some research students are having a video-conference with project collaborators in another country, demonstrating tools they have developed and discussing the technical problems encountered. Others down the hallway are looking at a display that is showing information on their lectures and meetings for the day, this information having been triggered by sensors that recognised them as they passed [3].

People interact with a variety of technologies, some experimental and some prosaic. In their interactions with them, they participate in defining what those technologies are and what they do. For example, at different times, they may use their MP3 players to evoke particular moods, make boring spaces more acceptable, create a personal or intimate space in a crowded street, and conjure up memories [4]. They may use their mobile phones to say hello, stay in touch, make arrangements to meet, store personal text messages, take and send photos, and play at taking photos of friends [5]. These interactions with technology can sometimes be planned, sometimes routine and almost ritualistic, and sometimes entirely incidental. In the light of this variety of interactions and relationships between people and technology, with technology deeply embedded in the ways in which people live their lives, the primary concern for HCI – and related activities such as Interaction Design and Computer Supported Cooperative Work – has become User Experience. When the technologies of interest are portable, distributed and embedded in our physical and social environment, people's experience of place and its mediation by technology becomes central.

For about two decades now, HCI and Interaction Design have documented the analysis and development of distributed technologies that mediate people's experience of space, for example: EuroPARC's work on media spaces [6]; Ciolfi and Bannon's [7] use of humanistic geography to provide a technologically augmented experience of a museum; Turner et al's [8] phenomenological approach to enhancing the sense of place in virtual environments. Interaction Design has also, more recently, shown some interest in people's use of portable technologies [9]. This work has been influenced by contributions from areas such as architecture [10,11] and human geography. It has also resulted in interesting discussions on the relative importance of space and place in interaction design. For example, a seminal contribution by Harrison and Dourish [12] argues that place is central to understanding human behaviour and should inform the design and evaluation of interactive systems. From their geographical perspective on place, which proposes that a sense of place can only emerge through physical immersion in a space, Ciolfi and Bannon distance themselves from Harrison and Dourish's notion of place, which can indeed be 'spaceless'.

Whereas different conceptualisations of space, place, and technology have obvious implications for thinking about virtual environments as places, they have less obvious but equally important implications for thinking about the experience of space and place more generally in Interaction Design. However, some characteristics of current conceptualisations limit their more general application and certainly limit their value in analysing the kinds of (student) experiences described above where movement between interactions with portable technologies and in digitally enhanced spaces is unremarkable. These characteristics include the following:

1. In some conceptualisations, 'place' seems to be restricted to stable structures such as buildings and public squares. This may be too restrictive, as Interaction Design needs to think about space and place in a way that addresses locative aspects of interaction with portable and fixed technologies, in bricks-and-mortar, and in virtual environments.
2. Understanding of 'experience' is uneven in conceptualisations of place in Interaction Design. In some cases it is underdeveloped and in others its development is unnecessarily tied to a particular methodology. A pragmatic approach prepared to address multiple dimensions and aspects of experience may be more useful.
3. The concept of 'agency' in people's experience of technologically mediated place is also underdeveloped. Given that one of the impetuses for developing the concept of place in Interaction Design was to elaborate the increasingly influential model of interaction as 'person-acting-in-context', this lacuna is curious and needs to be addressed.

The aim of this paper is to begin to address some of the limitations mentioned above and, in the process, to begin to develop a more inclusive language of space and place in Interaction Design. Specific objectives are:

− To suggest a way of conceptualising experience that clarifies some of the uncertainties about space and place in Interaction Design. In this regard, McCarthy and Wright's [13] conceptualisation of technology as experience will be used as the basis for a dialogical interpretation of place.
− To introduce the idea of the possibility of experiencing space and place while in transit to discussion of place as a way of integrating experiences of portability and experiences of augmented built space.
− To draw conclusions about how Interaction Design might progress understanding of the dialogue between technology, place and self and how this understanding might illuminate important questions about context, engagement, and interactivity.

2 Conceptualising Experience

In order to think about experience in a way that gives due weight to its social, individual and personal aspects, McCarthy and Wright [13] conceptualise it as an irreducible, dynamic interrelationship between person and environment, in which meaning has sensory, affective, and emotional dimensions as well as cognitive and sociocultural aspects. They distinguish between the immediate experience that a person has and the meaning of that experience as it becomes known and thereby appropriated personally and communally. This draws attention to the ways in which immediate experience is associated with personal, social, and cultural sense making processes, specifically relational aspects of interpretation and reflection, and communal processes such as telling others of our experiences. Implicit in much of the foregoing is a sense of experience unfolding across time and space. This can be seen in both the transitoriness of the immediate experience and the spatio-temporal relations between the immediate and the lifelong.

McCarthy and Wright describe their approach to experience as dialogical. The dialogical approach starts with the idea that experience is a bit like a conversation that always involves at least two consciousnesses. Conversation is a useful metaphor for the dynamic aspects of experience as it is now well understand that, in a conversation, meaning is always changing as a consequence of what comes next. Even as both parties to a conversation seem to settle on an understanding of a point that has arisen in the conversation, the utterance being made by one of them may unsettle that understanding and suggest an alternative sense or meaning. One of the reasons for this of course is that each utterance has many meanings, a history of use, and a number of voices associated with it. So the dialogical approach to experience draws attention to the ways in which people engage in activity with half an eye to what might be about to happen and half an ear to the nuances of what already has happened. In this sense, experience is responsive to the other and to the future, it is in relation to or in dialogue with the other and anticipating or oriented to possible futures.

The dialogical metaphor can usefully be taken further in conceptualizing experience. Dialogically all unity is accomplished and not given, and moreover it is always accomplished relationally. In terms of the focus of this paper, this suggests that any unified or settled sense of place, or indeed of self–in-place, is accomplished through the relationship between self and place, and increasingly in Interaction Design through the relationship between space and place. Dialogically, buildings and their walls are understood in terms of the relations that sustain them – as are selves and their boundaries with others and places and their boundaries with other places. Dialogicality insists that any unity – such as the unity of place, technology, or self - is composed of many voices in conversation, for example the voices of past experience in that place or with that technology or the voices of one's own past that evoke a past self who is resistant to or embracing of change. It also insists that that unity is unfinalised, always open to being changed by the next event.

In terms of understanding user experiences with technology, dialogicality stretches the analyst's imagination in a number of directions. It draws attention to anticipation of experience, reflection on experience, and the dynamic relations between them including the possibility of reflection influencing anticipation and vice versa. For example, reflection on similar past experiences colours anticipation of a new experience but anticipation of how one might reflect on experience not yet had can also colour the experience and its anticipation. It also takes corporeality – which is very influential in phenomenal accounts of place – into meaning making and back such that a sense of the distinction between self and other is as much due to the sensation of boundary and the inability to see self in the world as it is to interaction with others. A dialogical perspective takes evaluation into areas concerned with the quality of experience and, in the case of the issues so far raised in this paper, with the relationship between technology, place, and self in experience – for example toward consideration of whether particular technologies extend or diminish spaces of possibilities for people, and enrich or impoverish their sense of self [14]. In adopting such a perspective, interaction design and evaluation would exercise creativity by giving shape to a world that is always open and unfinished. Among other things, people do this by constructing spaces, places and theories.

3 Dialogics of Place and Technology

Making a contrast between space and place begins to clarify the role place (and space) can play in Interaction Design. Space is an abstract, disembodied description of the world. According to Descartes, it can be expressed in terms of the dimensions of height, breadth and depth or even further reduced to the X, Y and Z axes of analytical geometry. From an Interaction Design perspective therefore space describes structure and abstract possibilities for interaction. The basic idea that human activity is influenced by the physical environment has been appropriated by Interaction Design in a number of ways, one of the most influential of which has been the use of Alexander's architectural theory of patterns [15].

With space in focus, attention is on the physical environment as a container-like context of interaction. The underlying assumption is that the spatial properties of an environment can be designed to influence the way people act in and use that environment. A simple example might be the way in which a space, such as a football ground, is designed for efficient entry and egress of large numbers of people and to provide as good a view of the football as possible for as many people as possible. These aims may be met by having a large number of entrances-exits with clear, unambiguous routes to the seating areas and steeply banked all-seater stands to provide a clear view for as many people as possible. While this approach to design might be well and good in theory, it is not so straightforward in practice. When football grounds in Britain were being re-designed in this way in the 1980s – for crowd safety and control reasons – there was strong resistance from die-hard football fans. Many of them had a very strong attachment to their grounds just as they were. They had a particular attachment to the standing-only terraces where, in some cases for many years, they had stood week after week in teeming crowds and rain. Abstract, structural, spatial descriptions of interaction miss this kind of experience of place.

Whereas space describes abstract possibility, place describes histories of experiences, interactions, and meanings. It can be construed in terms of the expectations, intentions, needs, desires, history, and feelings that people bring to a particular space or environment. For example, some football fans go to matches to be part of the club and often go to a particular part of the ground – the part of the ground frequented by the same group of fans for years. For these fans, the ground is not abstract possibility but a living place full of history, memories, and friends. It is the place where they express deeply-felt loyalties and commitments and where they have made and sustain longstanding friendships. They think about it during the week and feel at home there on Saturdays to the extent that they would feel displaced anywhere else if there was a match on at that time in their ground. Other equally loyal football fans are less committed to the history of the ground and more concerned with its suitability for the current team and its safety for those attending.

In contrast with some earlier Interaction Design approaches to place, the dialogical approach attempts to deal with the complexity and plurality of experience of place, engaging with material and ideal, corporeal and cultural, sensory and reflective, as well as the constitutive relations between these perspectives. According to the dialogical approach, analysis of the experience of a place requires attention to both the immediate sensory transaction and the ways in which the immediate experience transforms in the telling. For example, in a football ground, the excitement of the noise and the fear of the pressing crowd become highlights in the story of the event and moments of achievement in the construction of an identity. In this sense, place interpenetrates the play of identity and the playful construction of self, always embodied and also always languaged.

Take the sense of place associated with the coffee house or café culture, for example. From the 17th century, coffee houses were places where people engaged in critical discourse on the times, politics, social conventions, and art of the day. They were community places where people would expect to become engaged in conversations with friends, acquaintances and strangers. Contrast this sense of the place with the sense contrived by contemporary coffee house chains. Starbucks might create a comfortable space, but not a socially, culturally, and politically engaging place. It may be that virtual cafes and chat rooms provide something closer to the public place created in the 17th century coffee houses (see [16] for a detailed discussion of coffee house culture). In this case, it is the sense and quality of engagement that makes the place, regardless of the physical environment and physical immersion.

Emphasising place has implications for Interaction Design. In general, it directs designers and analysts toward the experiential concerns of users as they relate to the spaces in which they live. The following specific implications of a focus on place are particularly noteworthy.

- It draws attention away from physical structures and structural constraints toward community, identity, familiarity, feelings, relationships, and discourse. It also draws attention to people dwelling, however temporarily, feeling the security of rules and boundaries respected. This suggests an experiential starting point for designing and critically evaluating technological interventions in places such as homes and public squares, and for analysing people's use of mobile technologies.
- It suggests that the physical environment should no longer be seen as a container-like context shaping the way people act in and use space, rather as a participant in a dialogue between person and environment (including technology).
- From this perspective, the context of activity and interaction refers to a transaction between person and environment/technology, which, in Interaction Design,

has been primarily characterised as *engagement*. Laurel [17] defined engagement as "a desirable – even essential – human response to computer mediated activities" and it is clearly the characteristic response of many people to computer games, MP3 players, and mobile phones.

– It suggests that any attempt to design for engagement has to address the interaction space, not just the technology.
– It also suggests a critical edge for analyses of interactivity. For example, some engagement in football grounds is positively toned with community and intimacy and other engagement negatively toned with violence between those committed to different communities or with the passivity of a distraction from another reality. This kind of analysis may also provide a useful means of identifying positive and negative absorption with mobile phones and MP3 players.
– It accommodates chat rooms and other virtual places. The dialogic of place depends on located sensory and cultural transaction, not just physical placement. It follows the cultural understanding that people experience a sense of place in films and novels and that the author's success or failure at creating a sense of place (and time) can often be a critical point. In Interaction Design, this might also be the pragmatically more useful conclusion as it enables analysts to also make place-space distinctions in analyses of Internet or VR interactions.

Whereas a commitment to the importance of place in Interaction Design raises the above issues and suggests tentative directions for addressing them, a closer analysis of the dialogical experience of place – the sense of being in place – will help further to explore these issues for Interaction Design.

4 Being in Place

As an experiential construct, the category 'place' is generated by the ways in which people live in the world and the sense they make of their living. Experience involves acting and being acted upon, sensing and feeling both, and transforming them into an emotional and intellectual sense. The particular embodied aspect of human experience requires place [18]. More than that, the sense people make of their experience, individual and collective, makes use of place. These aspects of experience of place are dialogically engaged. The sense of being at home in a particular place or not at home in another is a sensory and affective sense, given cultural expression and meaning in reflection and recounting, and transformed in future by those emotional and intellectual threads of experience. In this way, as sensory and affective experience becomes transformed in thought and story, a building, the top of a mountain, and a chat room can become significant places for people – not just physical structures, natural landscapes, or digital discourses, but also meaningful and heartfelt places. When they become places, they become encultured, such that the natural landscape – as a place - is no longer just natural but also cultural. Dialogically, place and culture depend on each other, one not being possible without the other.

What can Interaction Design learn from spaces in which people don't easily feel at home or in place? People can enjoy a couple of hours in an airport reading a book or on a motorway mindlessly getting from one place to another. But when this happens, it is the enjoyment of not being engaged, the temporary sense of release from the weight of community and identity. Marc Augé [19] called these spaces 'supermodern spaces', arguing that, although they can offer pleasant temporary freedom, as they lack the quality of place, they contribute little to the quality of experience and the growth of self. In fact, one of the characteristics that contributes both to their potential for the momentary pleasure of disengagement and to their lack of any sense of being in place is the way in which people are abstracted in them. They don't have the quality of place in part because they receive people as anonymous units without identity into a contractual relationship that may indeed require the user to identify themselves by producing 'papers' – passport, ticket, or driving licence. In these supermodern spaces, people may be reminded of the terms of the contractual relationship if they step out of line. It is clearly not their place, they are not even fully acknowledged as a person there. In this sense, a sense of place and a sense of personhood dialogically constitute each other.

5 Dwelling, Being in Place, and Wandering

There is a danger with the way it has been discussed so far that the sense of being in place will be associated with being in a fixed location. Casey [18], in his analysis of the two ways to dwell – dwelling as residing and dwelling as wandering – suggests that being in place is not a static thing. Building a place to call home, a stable habitable location, that becomes a particular dwelling place, trades freedom of movement and the possibility of displacement for constrained movement and a clear definition of what is here and near. In building residences, people not only change the look and meaning of the landscape, they also change themselves as subjects from body subjects into making subjects or agents. As makers or fabricators of places – from homes to cities – people also become social and societal subjects by creating places that people inhabit together. These places also bring the density of lasting value to life experience, as dwelling opens up new possibilities for future experiences of education, contemplation, being together for a time, and organising futures together.

But people can also have a sense of place as they wander. People can in some meaningful way dwell in public spaces like arcades and parks as they move about them, shopping or just hanging out. People can clearly have a strong sense of place about a city as they wander around its winding streets. Increasingly, people dwell on street corners and in the buses, trains or cars in which they spend hours travelling to and from work. But the experience of wandering can be considered dwelling only if the people involved feel settled. In contrast, if people's wandering is exploratory, if they are trying to find a place, get oriented, or simply moving between places, there is no dwelling or being in place. Casey identifies two characteristic features that give people the sense of being settled or in place: repeated return or re-accessibility and familiarity. For him, being in place involves the kind of familiarity that comes from continually returning to the place and on each return knowing that it is the same place.

Augé's suggests that in supermodernity, people spend much of their time wandering in supermarkets, airports, hotels and on motorways. According to Augé, spatial overabundance in supermodernity makes the construction of bounded spaces of signification, places that people experience as meaningful without having to think about their meaning – familiar and accessible places perhaps - difficult. This is so at a number of levels. Seeing somebody walk on the moon can make walking in our own patch seem trivial and the construal of the personal significance of that patch problematic. When the location of products in a supermarket is regularly changed, people can feel disoriented even if it is their regular supermarket. It can be difficult at times to even know the direction in which one is travelling on motorways that are undifferentiated except for the occasional appearance of a road sign. Airports offer few places for quiet time alone or for meaningful social encounters – hard to have in serried rows of seats in a warehouse-like lounge. A question for Interaction Design then is whether ubiquitous and portable computing and communications technologies can be used to enrich these experiences by promoting a sense of place.

Interaction designers, working with ubiquitous computing, have a choice. Like the architects who have gone before them into these spaces, they can impoverish people's experience or enrich it. They inevitably intervene in people's experience of space and place but can do so in a manner that is sensitive to people's creation of places of signification and their experience of collective, community and individual identity or they can ignore these processes and put people heavily in parentheses, to borrow another evocative phrase from Augé. Think about the airports you have been through. How many of them have facilitated the creation of places of signification and how many of them have been more like warehouses, with the people passing through them treated as objects in transit? Interactive technologies can be used to support either construction of airport space. If interactive technologies are to be used to support the creation of places of signification, they can also be designed to support experiences of place and being in place.

6 Technology and Place

If interaction designers want to help people feel in place, they need to engage them at the level of their personhood, not just treat them as anonymous and equivalent units. Mobile phones and MP3 players seem to facilitate this kind of engagement by enabling users to personalise the products and their use of them. For example, MP3 users create tailored music collections and listening preferences, and use their players to manage space – by creating bubbles of familiarity in unfamiliar spaces and by creating zones of comfort in crowded spaces [4]. Mobile phone users treat some texts as very personal gifts [9]. Mobile phones also allow people to capture the intimacy of interpersonal relations while moving from one place to another in a public sphere blurring traditional boundaries between public and private, intimate and extraneous [20]. Designs have also attempted to make use of some of these qualities of mobile phones and their technical capabilities to create places populated with 'familiar strangers' in generally anonymous urban spaces [21].

The 'familiar strangers' project creates place anew each day by lightly connecting people who simultaneously use a particular public space. Similarly the RIOT!1831 project [22], re-made place in Queen Square, a large Georgian square in the heart of Bristol, England. It used hand held computing technology and GPS to stage an interactive play about a riot that took place in 1831 in that square, connecting people in that square in 2004 to the events in that same square in 1831. People enjoyed the experience on the old Bristolean dialect and the sense of privacy that they had in a public space. In interviews, people talked about being immersed in the riots: *"I didn't even see people. I kind of switched off and I was there at the riots"*. Others referred to the importance of being in the right place for the action in the play: *"one of the clips we got in the centre was of them climbing up on the statue on the horses back when you were standing next to the statue."*

'Familiar strangers', RIOT!1831, and people's experiences with mobile phones and MP3 players show how technologies can be used to take advantage of the unfinalisability of place and its constitutive cultural relationship with personhood. According to Casey, it is the cultural and experiential being in a place that give a place a sense of reality or as he puts it a felt density, the sense that there is something of lasting value in it. A mountain-top may becomes a place of lasting significance because of the quality of experience associated with it. Initially there is the sensory and affective thrill of climbing it. This is the dialogue of acting on and being acted upon that gives sensory evidence of lived experience. The social context, the people with whom the climb was made, for example, gives the achievement another equally important dialogical grounding. Finally there is the reflection and recounting, the dialogue extended over time that makes it a communal and cultural experience. Through the lived experience, the experiment of climbing and recounting, a concept becomes a place. Now instead of being an image to behold it is a place to experience. For Augé, place "is in one sense… an invention: it has been discovered by those who claim it as their own" (p.43). People create physical and social boundaries to mark what would otherwise remain unmarked and perhaps unrecognised. In this very strong sense, people and the contexts that they act in and experience make each other. This is the dialogical context, born of engagement, that was referred to earlier – and 'familiar strangers' and RIOT!1831 are example of how Interaction Design can intervene in the dialogical process of person-place making.

One of the interesting features of these interventions, in terms of the design of place, is their stretching of the temporal boundaries of engagement. Laurel's [17] characterisation of engagement as bounded by the start and end of a discrete experience is challenged by experiences of place that include anticipation based on previous experience of the place or the story of the event (e.g. Queens Square and/or the 1831 riots in the RIOT!1831 case) and the potential for reflection and recounting that is likely to change future experiences of the same place. Interaction Design informed by the dialogics of place, technology and self should think of engagement in this extended manner.

In turn, a perspective on extended engagement throws further light on how relatively stable, ontologically pre-existent notions of place emerge. Having created their boundaries or contexts, the fantasy of those who inhabit a place is that it is a closed world about which everything that can be known is already known – a kind of provisional finalisation. For those who inherit them, places constitute "a means of recognition, rather than knowledge" (p.33). A place then is a space of signification in which inhabitants recognise themselves, the codes, sounds, sights, rules, and boundaries. They don't have to be told them or learn to know them. If they belong to this place they recognise them, if not they don't. Invention and fantasy notwithstanding, people experience and treat place as real. People experience places as welcoming, homely or comforting, and they try to re-create place. As Augé notes, people manage space to symbolise different aspects of identity. People create public spaces in which shared identity can be symbolised and experienced (e.g. public parks, museums, and cinemas) particular spaces in which community identity can be experienced (e.g. parish halls, seating areas, and local shops), and singular spaces in which individual identity can be symbolised and experienced (e.g. homes, work spaces, gardens). However a notion of engagement bounded by cycles of activity or even the materiality of action can result in a reified conceptualisation of place that misses its dialogical invention or construction. Appropriating such conceptualisations for Interaction Design runs the risk of missing the potential for creativity and invention in the relationship between technology, place and self.

Missing the potential for creativity and invention takes attention away from a final critical point – mentioned earlier – which refers to the attention Interaction Design pays (or does not) to the extent to which particular technologies extend or diminish spaces of possibilities for people, and thereby enrich or impoverish their sense of self. This goes to the heart of what kind of interactivity – or interaction spaces – are being designed. A hypothetical distinction might be helpful here, between places such as Queen's Square or an airport being technologically augmented and people's experience of public space being mediated by their use of their MP3 players. McCarthy and Wright [23] have argued that this use of MP3 players can be seen as interpassive rather than interactive. To the extent that activity with and through technology replaces engaged, felt, responsible relating with a substitute that extracts some aspect of relating from fully felt form, it reveals passivity, not agency or activity. In this context, it might not be too far-fetched to think of the process of engaging people with the history and feel of a place, as RIOT!1831 did with Queens Square, as mutually interactive, and the process of blocking out the feel of a place with an MP3 player as one-sided interpassivity – engagement without feelings of mutually relating. There is an agency in it but it is the agency of resistance or avoidance rather than engagement. However, it is important to note that these concepts are also dialogical, as apparently one-sided relationships can in fact involve a subtle, expressive response, where for instance disengagement with lifeless space is replaced with engagement with living music.

7 Conclusions

This paper has outlined some of the key features of a dialogics of technology, place and self. The dialogical approach described and used in the paper is concerned with the work involved in creating space and place, the relationships that sustain them, and the potential entailed in their unfinalisability. In this novel contribution to Interaction Design, place is both material and ideal, corporeal and cultural, stable and mobile.

Making place central in the Interaction Design of ubiquitous, ambient, portable, and virtual computing draws attention to the sensations and feeling, thoughts and emotions, and the plurality of voices in situated interaction. The implications of this re-centring of place for a number of concepts that have been influential in Interaction Design for the last decade or so - context, engagement, and interactivity for example - have been considered.

As place and personhood constitute each other in the dialogical approach to place, the approach creates the potential for Interaction Design to contribute to discourse on whether technological interventions extend or restrict spaces of possibility for people and for their sense of self. This can be seen as a response to the need, identified earlier in the paper, for a strong conceptualization of people's experience of space and place as the basis for a user-centred design of pervasive and ambient computing. However, as was clear from this paper, if Interaction Design is to fulfil this potential, it has to attend to both personal experience and cultural and historical understandings of self and place.

References

1. Weiser, M.: The Computer of the 21st Century. Scientific American, 265 (1991) 19-25.
2. Norman, D.: The Invisible Computer. Basic Books, New York (1998)
3. Sawhney, N., S. Wheeler and Schmandt, C.: Aware Community Portals: Shared Information Appliances for Transitional Spaces. Proc. CHI'2000, Workshop on Situated Interaction in Ubiquitous Computing. ACM, New York (2000)
4. Bull, M.: Sounding out the City. Berg (2000)
5. Katz, J.E. and Aakhus, M. (eds.): Perpetual Contact: Mobile Communication, Private Talk, Public Performance. Cambridge University Press, Cambridge (2002)
6. Dourish, P. and Bellotti, V: Awareness and Coordination in Shared Workspaces. Proc. CSCW'1992. ACM, New York (1992)
7. Ciolfi, L. and Bannon, L.: Designing Interactive Museum Exhibits: Enhancing Visitor Curiosity Through Augmented Artefacts. Proc. ECCE11, European Conference on Cognitive Ergonomics, Consiglio Nazionale delle Ricerche, Roma (2002)
8. Turner, P., McGregor, I., Turner, S. and Carroll, F.: Using Soundscapes to Create a Sense of Place. Proc. Int. Conference on Auditory Display (2003)
9. Taylor, A.S. and Harper, R.: Age-old Practices in the New World: A Study of Gift-giving Between Teenage Mobile Phone Users. Proc. CHI'2002. ACM Press, New York (2002)
10. Coyne, R.: Technoromanticism: Digital Narrative, Holism, and the Romance of the Real. MIT Press, Cambridge, Mass. (1999)
11. McCullough, M.: Digital Ground: Architecture, Pervasive Computing, and Environmental Knowing. MIT Press, Cambridge, Mass. (2004)
12. Harrison, S. and Dourish, P.: Re-Place-ing Space: the Roles of Place and Space in Collaborative Systems. Proc. CSCW'1996. ACM, New York (1996)
13. McCarthy, J. & Wright, P.: Technology as Experience. MIT Press, Cambridge, Mass. (2004a)
14. Benson, C.: The Cultural Psychology of Self: Place, Morality, and Art in Social Worlds. Routledge (2001)
15. Alexander, C.: The Timeless Way of Building. Oxford University Press, Oxford (1971)
16. Ellis, M.: The Coffee-House: A Cultural History. Weidenfield and Nicolson, London (2004)
17. Laurel, B.: Computers as Theatre. Addison-Wesley (1991)
18. Casey, E.: Getting Back into Place: Toward a Renewed Understanding of the Place-World. Indiana University Press (1993)
19. Augé, M.: Non-Places. Introduction to an Anthropology of Supermodernity. Verso, London-New York (1995)
20. Fortunati, L.: Italy: Stereotypes, true and false. In Katz, J.E. and Aakhus, M. (eds), Perpetual Contact: Mobile Communication, Private Talk, Public Performance. Cambridge University Press, Cambridge (2002)

21. Paulos, E. and Goodman, E.: Familiar strangers: Anxiety, comfort and play in public places. Proc. Chi'2004. ACM Press, New York (2004) 223-230.
22. Blythe, M., Reid, J., Geelhood, E., and Wright, P.: Intedisciplinary criticism: Analysing the experience of RIOT!1831, a location sensitive digital narrative. Submitted to Behavious and Information Technology, Special Issue, Empirical Studies of the User Experience. (submitted)
23. McCarthy, J. and Wright, P.: Putting felt-life at the centre of HCI. In ECCE'12: Proc. ECCE12, 12th European Conference on Cognitive Ergonomics (2004b).

Interaction and End-User Programming with a Context-Aware Mobile Application

Jonna Häkkilä[1], Panu Korpipää[2], Sami Ronkainen[1], and Urpo Tuomela[1]

[1] Nokia Multimedia,
Yrttipellontie 6, 90230 Oulu, Finland
firstname.lastname@nokia.com
[2] VTT Electronics,
Kaitoväylä 1, P.O. Box 1100, FI-90571 Oulu, Finland
panu.korpipaa@vtt.fi

Abstract. In this paper we present the user interface design and evaluation of a tool for customizing mobile phone applications with context-aware features. The tool enables the user to program a set of context-action rules, defining the behavior of the device when a selected context is recognized and/or some other user-defined conditions are met. The tool user interface design is described starting from an early paper prototype and its evaluation, leading to a functional software implementation in a mobile phone. Finally, the usability evaluation of the functional prototype, and other relevant findings from the user test, are presented.

1 Introduction

Context-awareness has recently been intensively studied in mobile computing. Context-awareness concerns proactive actions, such as user interface adaptation or evoking appropriate application functions in certain external conditions. The literature gives several studies on location-aware applications, which have been demonstrated in, for instance, the Lancaster tourist guide *GUIDE*, the Aware Campus at Cornell University [3], or in offering location and presence information in Active Campus [2]. Sensor–based context recognition systems have been presented in [5] and [11].

Despite the extensive research in the field, several problems remain in developing usable context-aware applications. Uncertainties in context recognition or ambiguity may lead to erroneous conclusions of current context [4], and objective and explicit definition of context attributes and their values is often problematic. Moreover, using contextual information for automated actions has led to concern about whether context-awareness will take the control away from the end user [1]. Enabling end-user programming of context-aware features in mobile phone applications solves the problem of user control, but brings other challenges; end-user programming is an unknown concept for most mobile phone users. Moreover, mobile phones are commonly used because of their easy accessibility and ability to perform multi-tasking – but it is as yet unclear how large a percentage of users would like to configure their phones, even if significant personalization and usability efficiency advantages were offered. Hence end-user programming is a challenging field, and so far has been very little

M.F. Costabile and F. Paternò (Eds.): INTERACT 2005, LNCS 3585, pp. 927–937, 2005.

studied among mobile handheld devices. Automated capture has been investigated in [6], and its usage linked to end-user programming in [16].

In this paper we present the user interface and usability evaluation of a mobile phone application, Context Studio, the concept of which was originally introduced by Mäntyjärvi et al. [12] and further developed by Korpipää et al. [8, 9]. Context Studio is a tool that enables the user to define context-action rules in order to activate mobile phone functions when the rule conditions are fulfilled. The user-centric design practices were emphasized in the user interface design process. The main contribution of this paper is the description of the user interface design and results of the user test, which was arranged to evaluate the final design with a functional prototype in a mobile phone. The tool was developed on a Symbian Series 60 platform following its style guides.

The paper is organized as follows. First, the background and experience from the Context Studio development are shared. Then the tool functionality and user interface are introduced. This is followed by the evaluation of the functional tool against the criteria based on standard usability guidelines. Finally, a discussion and conclusions, with plans for future work, are presented.

2   Context Studio

Mobile phones are used in many different kinds of situations, i.e. in numerous different contexts, where the priorities of the device functions and most applications vary according to the situation. Furthermore, mobile phones are personal devices usually constantly carried by the user, and thus adapting the device behavior to the specific user is a relevant goal. The ways of using a mobile phone differ significantly among individuals. The aim is to provide more flexibility of use for various user groups.

2.1   Development Background

As mentioned earlier, selecting incorrect contextual information sources may lead to inappropriate actions being performed by the device. It is thus important to select relevant information sources in the design phase, or enable customization of the sources. In sensor-based interaction the recognition of correct patterns from the measured signals is crucial for success.

User control and visibility of system status are two important issues in Nielsen's usability heuristics [13], which is a commonly used guideline in usability evaluation. In the design of the tool, one of the main goals was to provide the sense of user control, which has been one of the usability concerns with context-aware applications [1]. In addition to this, the visibility of system status is a design challenge, as the current state of the device (and user) context may be hard to define explicitly as a union of all available context types [12].

The approach to these problems was to let the user decide which context types they wanted to apply to each situation [8], instead of having to define all context types that describe the situation. The tool provided a selection of contextual triggers and application actions, which were presented in a hierarchical folder structure for a scalable representation and to aid the user navigation.

The experiences from the previous studies [12, 8] were utilized in developing the tool user interface. According to the previous experiences, we decided to leave out complex rule structures, including a set of Boolean operators, as they were found to complicate the rule definition for most users. On the other hand, the idea of defining trigger-action rules had been perceived as understandable and intuitive. It was found that users generally prefer making simple rules. However, by not using Boolean operators, setting expressive rules would become problematic. As a compromise, the Boolean operator AND was included as the default operator between multiple triggers in the same rule, while OR was made available by allowing the user to define parallel rules for the same set of triggers.

Context Studio was designed and implemented for the Nokia Series 60 platform phones, which sets certain restrictions, such as screen size and style. The Nokia Series 60 user interface style guide was utilized for defining the look-and-feel and general interaction style for the tool.

An iterative HCI design was employed during the development process. The first evaluation of the Context Studio user interface was done with paper prototypes early in the development process, and feedback was used to iterate the user interface design before the software implementation was started. In the next section, the Context Studio user interface is described as it was in the final evaluation.

2.2 User Interface

Context Studio is a mobile phone tool that enables the user to define context-action rules. The condition (context) part of the rule is called a trigger for clarity. The rules take a simple predicative format:

> *When the trigger condition is fulfilled,*
> *the action is executed.*

For instance:

> *When the environment sound intensity is loud,*
> *set phone ringing tone volume up.*

The user can also combine multiple triggers with the AND operator, for instance:

> *When the location is home and the phone battery is charging,*
> *save new images into an image album.*

The triggers can include implicit (context) inputs - such as location, environment sound and device activity - or explicit input actions - such as gestures, if gesture recognition is supported - or RFID-based commands. Figure 1 shows an example screenshot from the Context Studio rule view.

In Figure 1 the screenshot of the Series 60 mobile phone display shows the basic elements of a user-defined rule. The first row presents the name of the rule, which is automatically generated from the *action* and *trigger*. Although the automatically generated name appears when the user selects the elements for the rule, (s)he can also edit the name. If the user defines the name before setting the action and trigger(s), the name is not automatically generated.

User-defined rule for a gesture-triggered phone action

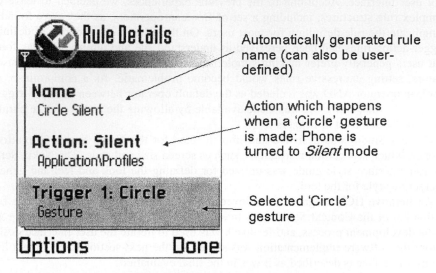

Rule Details

Name
Circle Silent

Action: Silent
Application\Profiles

Trigger 1: Circle
Gesture

Options   Done

Automatically generated rule name (can also be user-defined)

Action which happens when a 'Circle' gesture is made: Phone is turned to *Silent* mode

Selected 'Circle' gesture

Fig. 1. Rule view in Context Studio

Below the rule name are the *action* and *trigger* fields. The user selects the triggers and actions from a hierarchical folder structure, where the items are named and grouped according to their meaning and resemblance. Below the attribute values, which are marked with bold text in Figure 1, the path to the value, describing the attribute type, is shown. This provides the user with additional information on the attribute value, and helps the user to remember the overall folder structure. An example of the folder structure appearance is presented in Figure 2. Folders describe the attribute type, and can contain subfolders, which the user can navigate to find the desired attribute value. For example, the Environment folder in Figure 2 contains the subfolders Temperature, Light, and Humidity. The Light folder contains the subfolders Intensity, Type, and SourceFrequency. The last folder in the path contains the attribute values to select from. Hence the folder hierarchy enables a scalable representation of a large number of triggers and actions to choose from, instead of, e.g., displaying a very long list of values.

To enable the setting of more complex and sophisticated rules, the user can include more than one trigger in the rule. This is done by selecting 'Add Trigger' from the 'Options' menu, which results in a 'Trigger 2' field appearing below the 'Trigger 1' field. The defined triggers are connected with the Boolean operator AND.

In order to keep the rules understandable and relatively simple, it was decided that a single rule could contain only one *action*. However, to provide a quick way of enhancing the automated action with the same contextual triggers, we wanted to provide a shortcut for creating the rules, and included a rule copy function. The user can also activate, deactivate, delete, send, and edit rules. Active rules are marked with an icon in the main rule list, and active attributes are marked with an icon in the attribute value list. The color of the icon indicates the state of the corresponding attribute. Furthermore, a set of phone joystick and keypad controls were implemented for each user interface view to allow flexible use of the tool.

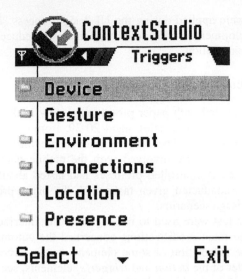

Fig. 2. The folder structure in the *triggers* view. The folders describe the attribute type and can contain subfolders, which the user can navigate to find the desired attribute value.

2.3 Enabling the Functional System

A functional prototype system was implemented to enable the user to create rules with the tool and after that use the features defined in the rule. After the user has created the desired context-action rule, the context framework handles the background monitoring of contexts and the triggering of actions according to the rules [9]. Context management is based on the blackboard-based context framework for mobile devices. For example, after the user has created the rule shown in Figure 1, (s)he can change the profile of the phone to silent at any time by making a circle-shaped gesture with the phone.

The folder hierarchies for *actions* and *triggers* are automatically generated based on a context ontology model, described in detail in [8]. The ontology vocabulary hierarchy is transformed into a folder-file model representation in the UI. The ontology, with an enhanced vocabulary model, offers a scalable information representation, and easy navigation of context and action information in the UI, and enables straightforward updating of the UI elements according to changes in the vocabularies - i.e., without programming any changes to the tool itself. Furthermore, the ontology supports the utilization of a formal rule model. Rules are represented as Context Exchange Protocol (CEP) XML scripts, which can be executed by an inference engine [10].

3 Evaluation

Before evaluating the functional prototype, the user interface of the tool was tested with two iterations of paper prototypes (the latter is briefly described in section 3.1) during the development process, and improved accordingly [12, 8]. Nielsen's usability heuristics [13] were applied during the UI design process. The iterative user testing during the development is considered valuable as it reduces the need for corrections after the implementation.

3.1 Early Evaluation with Paper Prototypes

A user test was conducted with paper prototyping early in the development process. Eight subjects (4 male and 4 female), aged 20-39, from different fields of study or work participated in the test. The subjects had no previous experience of context-aware systems, and none were involved with the mobile phone industry. Each test session was conducted at controlled premises and lasted about 1.5–2 hours. During the test the subjects conducted given tasks with the paper prototype user interface according to given usage scenarios.

The results of the test were used to redesign the user interface before the software implementation. The main modifications concerned the automated name generation for the rules and the disposition of some elements in the screen layouts. The results also affected the order of the *action* and *trigger(s)* elements, see Figure 1, since it was discovered that it was preferable to have both elements of the rule in the same view. Thus the *Action* field was placed above the *Trigger 1* as the user might select several triggers, even though placing the triggers first would have been more logical.

3.2 Final Evaluation – The Evaluation Criteria

According to the standard on Human-Centred Design Processes for Interactive Systems, usability is defined as the 'extent to which a product can be used by specified users to achieve specified goals with effectiveness, efficiency and satisfaction in a specified context of use' [14]. The criteria for the evaluation were adopted from an ergonomic requirements standard's usability guidelines [15], and were complemented with case-specific measures. The goal of the user study was to verify the selected fundamental customisation approach and the tool UI, and to gain possible feedback for further development. Moreover, initial user feedback was collected from the novel customisable smartphone interaction modalities. The evaluation criteria were the following.

Easy to learn: Formally, learnability is the resources expended before a specified level of proficiency in terms of effectiveness and efficiency is attained, or the speed at which proficiency increases over time. Learnability was assessed with two measurements: the ability to operate the tool without instructions on the first try, and the number of tasks that were required before reaching the ability to use the tool without errors. Folder searching was not considered an error. The measurements were based on usage monitoring, and oral and written feedback.

Effectiveness: According to the ISO 9241 standard on usability, effectiveness is the accuracy or completeness with which users achieve specified goals. The main measurement here was the ability of the user to complete a given task successfully.

Efficiency: Efficiency is the expenditure of physical and mental resources with which users achieve specified goals. It concerns time and the physical and cognitive effort that needs to be spent to successfully complete the given task. In this case, physical and cognitive effort can be measured as, e.g., the number of errors, re-doing basic actions, or consulting the manual or asking advice.

Satisfaction: Satisfaction refers to the level of comfort when using the tool, and is measured as the user's attitudes (positive or negative) towards the tool. The measurement was based on the subjective written feedback given by the test participants after the tests.

3.3   Test Set-Up

The evaluation of the application was done with user tests by ten participants (4 male, 6 female), none of whom worked in the mobile phone industry. The test was carried out with a Series 60 Nokia mobile phone, see Figure 3. The tests were video recorded with a screen camera. The users were encouraged to think aloud during the test, and their comments were recorded. After completing the tasks, the users completed a questionnaire that charted their opinions on the tool and the modalities, and their ideas for development.

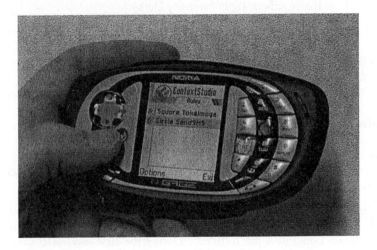

Fig. 3. The tool user interface in the mobile phone used in the user tests

The test consisted of five scenarios, based on which the users were asked to use the briefly introduced customisation tool without further advice. The scenarios only implicitly referred to making rules, such as scenario 1:

You often call your best friend, Anna, and you want to be able to make the call quickly and without watching the phone, as you often call her while riding a bike. The phone recognizes a 'circle' movement. Now you want to determine that when you make a circle with the phone, it starts calling Anna.

Table 1 presents the contexts and actions that were used in the rules. In each table cell the attribute type (folder) is the first element and the attribute value is the second element. Optional rule elements are in brackets. The scenarios in Table 1 can be read as, for instance, scenario 1: When the user makes a Gesture with value Circle, perform an Application function Call with value Anna.

The context and action vocabularies, transformed into a UI directory hierarchy, consisted of over a hundred name-value pairs, which the users navigated in order to select the elements of the rule.

Table 1. The user customised five features. In scenarios 1,3, and 5 the user could perform the actual interaction with the smartphone after the customization.

Scenario	Context trigger(s)	Action
1	Gesture Circle	Application\Call Anna
2	Gesture Square (& Location Home)	ExternalDevice\TV On
3	Device\Movement\Swing SwingRight	Application\Profiles Silent
4	Location OuluCenter & Environment\Sound\Intensity Loud (& Environment\Light\Intensity Dark)	Application\Profiles Loud
5	Connections\RFTag Jonna	Call Jonna

In addition to the scenarios the users were asked to perform separate tasks, such as training personal gestures. The aim was to collect feedback on how the users responded to the possibility of customising personal triggers, in addition to the rules.

3.4 Results

Results According to the Criteria
In the following, the results of the test are discussed separately for each criterion presented in each section.

Easy to learn. The idea of constructing context-action rules was understood by 9/10 users at the beginning of the first task on a general level: 'one must design what happens when certain conditions are fulfilled'. During the first task, 4/10 users needed clarification of the terms *action* and *trigger*. All ten participants could complete the tasks without help after performing the first task. Use of the tool is easy to learn.

Effectiveness. All participants were able to complete all given tasks. All participants were able to complete the task given in scenario 1, although one participant required help with the fundamental idea of rule building. For scenarios 2-5, all ten participants could perform the given tasks. In scenario 4, the task was given so that it involved the users setting several trigger options in more detail. Here the results showed some variations in the selected triggers. This result is consistent with earlier research on user perceptions and context-awareness - i.e., the users tend to have a subjective definition for what is meant by context [12]. Moreover, another finding was that the participants were not eager to define long settings, even if they understood that this would result in more precise rules. Thus, to summarize, the usage of the tool is effective.

Efficiency. The number of errors was small after the first task, and the users did not have to ask advice or redo basic actions. However, since the content of the context trigger and action directories was unknown to the users beforehand, they initially had to perform some searches to find the required rule elements. This behaviour was obvious as the participants used the application for the first time. The choice of ontology concepts is crucial for the UI navigation efficiency. The usage of the tool is quite efficient.

Satisfaction. In the written feedback, 8/10 participants said that they would benefit from the application. When they were asked to rate the general usability of the application on a scale from 1 (worst) to 5 (best), the average was 3.7 with a standard deviation of 0.8. Median of the rating was 4, minimum 2 and maximum 5. The usage of the tool is quite satisfactory.

User Feedback

The users were asked which of the features in the test they liked the most. All ten subjects answered the question, and four of them gave more than one answer. Gesture control was preferred in six answers, implicit interaction based on sensed contexts in five, and three most liked controlling external devices with the phone. RF tag-based physical selection was not mentioned as a most-liked feature, which may be due to the currently required extra hardware and the difficulty in quickly perceiving the possibilities of an interaction concept completely unknown to users. In this sense, gestures have the advantage that they are innately natural to human communication. Concerning implicit control, the users had different opinions about the subjective contexts, such as Environment\Sound\Intensity Loud. This suggests that subjective contexts should either be defined by the users themselves, or omitted, or at least the description of the meaning of the subjective context value should be accessible. The result confirms our earlier experience [12].

For gesture control, the users were asked which method of gesture recognition they preferred; the user marks the gesture by pressing a button, or continuous recognition without marking the gesture with a button. The participants unanimously perceived user-initiated activation of gesture recognition as better than continuous. The main reason for this was a concern about unintended gesture commands. Two female participants were worried about false commands when the phone was carried in a handbag. Moreover, training personal gestures was appreciated because it was assumed to improve the recognition accuracy and enable the use of intuitive and natural gestures. This is in line with our earlier results [7]. When asked to comment freely, one user proposed training of location context, e.g. *'I would [like to] go to the bar and press a button, and the device would remember the place'* (user #10). Customised locations could then be used as triggers for rules.

As a summary of the evaluation results, the user study verified the feasibility of the customisation approach. The implemented tool was found to be usable, and targets for further development were acquired. Moreover, initial user feedback was collected about the new modalities for phone control. The users most liked the idea of freely trainable gestures, controlling external devices with the phone, and implicit context-based interaction.

4 Discussion

A few general observations based on the user tests are in order. The subjects were more willing to construct short and simple rules than more complex ones, even though they were advised that they could define several triggers. Configuring the phone settings was generally perceived as an additional hassle, and people tended to set rules with just one trigger. Perceptions of the usefulness of Context Studio differed depending on the given scenarios. The perceived usefulness of the tool depended on whether the scenario appealed to the personal needs and usage experiences of each test subject. The ability to personalize the phone and provide shortcuts to the actions corresponding to their usage style and behavior was generally appreciated.

Thus the users had preferences on which triggers and actions they liked. The underlying software design enables tailoring the available triggers and actions - i.e., it is possible that the user may delete unnecessary triggers and actions from the folder structure. This has not yet been implemented, but is considered future work.

An alternative to explicit rule setting would be to model contexts based on examples, which is feasible when an example contains a single, chosen type of context. When one example contains multiple types of contexts, the programming-by-demonstration approach may lead to functionality that the user did not intend to have, if the user cannot control exactly which contexts are relevant for the intended action. Hence the explicit rule definition approach gives the user better control over creating the intended device functionality.

Although the user tests give a good indication of a successful interaction design, the true value of the tool and the ways in which the users would use it can only be revealed by observing long-term usage, which is relevant further work. However, the evaluation shows that the resulting user interface is both understandable and usable. Furthermore, the tool was evaluated with a functional prototype developed on a widely used mobile platform by applying a novel software framework and information representation methods, thereby demonstrating the feasibility and potential for utilization by large user groups.

5 Conclusions

This paper presented the user interface design and user evaluation of a tool for end-user programming of context-aware applications developed for a Series 60 mobile phone platform. The tool enables the user to define context-action rules that cause the mobile phone to perform actions when the rule conditions are fulfilled. The design process and rationale for the interaction design were discussed, and the resulting mobile device user interface was presented. The tool user interface and the fundamental customization approach were evaluated with user tests. The results were analyzed against criteria based on standard usability guidelines. The results indicate that the tool is easy to learn and efficient to use.

The study provides a good basis for further studies. Future work related to interaction design includes user-initiated capture of context attributes, more flexible personalization of the contextual information to better support the user's individual needs, and a large-scale user deployment to study the utility of the tool in daily life.

References

1. Barkhuus, L., and Dey, A.: Is Context-Awareness Taking Control Away from the User? Three Levels of Interactivity Examined. Proceedings of Ubicomp (2003) 159-166
2. Barkhuus, L, and Dourish, P.: Everyday Encounters with Context-Aware Computing in a Campus Environment. Proceedings of Ubicomp (2004) 232-249
3. Burrell, J., Gay, G. K., Kubo, K., Farina, N.: Context-Aware Computing: A Test Case. Proceedings of Ubicomp (2002) 1-15
4. Erickson, T.: Some Problems with the Notion of Context-Aware Computing. Communications of the ACM, Vol. 5, No. 2 (2002) 102-104
5. Gellersen, H.W., Schmidt, A., Beigl, M.: Multi-Sensor Context-Awareness in Mobile Devices and Smart Artefacts. Mobile Networks and Applications Vol. 7 (2002) 341-351
6. Hayes, G. R., Kientz, J. A., Truong, K., N., White, D. R, Abowd, G. D., Pering, T.: Designing Capture Applications to Support the Education of Children with Autism. Proceedings of Ubicomp (2004) 161-178
7. Kela, J., Korpipää, P., Mäntyjärvi, J., Kallio, S., Savino, G., Jozzo, L., Di Marca, S.: Accelerometer-based gesture control for a design environment. Personal and Ubiquitous Computing special issue on Multimodal Interaction with Mobile and Wearable Devices, Springer-Verlag, In Press
8. Korpipää, P., Häkkilä, J., Kela, J., Ronkainen, S. & Känsälä, I.: Utilising context ontology in mobile device application personalisation. Proceedings of International Conference on Mobile and Ubiquitous Multimedia, ACM (2004) 133-140
9. Korpipää, P., Malm, E., Salminen, I., Rantakokko, T., Kyllönen, V. & Känsälä, I.: Context management for end-user development of context-aware applications. Proceedings of International Conference on Mobile Data Management MDM'05 (2005), In Press
10. Lakkala, H.: Context Exchange Protocol Specification, Context Script Specification. (2003), Available: http://www.mupe.net
11. Michahelles, F., and Samulowitz, M.: Smart CAPs for Smart Its – Context Detection for Mobile Users. Personal and Ubiquitous Computing Journal, Vol. 6, Springer-Verlag London Ltd. (2002) 269-275
12. Mäntyjärvi, J., Tuomela, U., Häkkilä, J., Känsälä, I.: Context-Studio - Tool for Personalizing Context-Aware Applications in Mobile Terminals. In Proceedings of Australasian Computer Human Interaction Conference OZCHI'03 (2003) 64-73
13. Nielsen, J. & Mack, R.L.: Usability Inspection Methods. Canada: John Wiley & Sons, Inc (1994)
14. Standard: ISO 13407 (3.3)
15. Standard: ISO 9241-11:1998. Ergonomic requirements for office work with visual display terminals (VTDs). Part 11: Guidance on usability. (1998)
16. Truong, K. N., Huang, E. M., Abowd, G. D.: CAMP: A Magnetic Poetry Interface for End-User Programming of Capture Applications for the Home. Proceedings of Ubicomp (2004) 143-160

Large Visualizations for System Monitoring of Complex, Heterogeneous Systems

Daniel M. Russell, Andreas Dieberger, Varun Bhagwan, and Daniel Gruhl

IBM Almaden Research Center,
650 Harry Road, San Jose, CA 95120 USA
{daniel2, andreasd, vbhagwan, dgruhl}@us.IBM.com
http://www.Almaden.IBM.com

Abstract. As systems grow larger in size and complexity, it becomes increasingly difficult for administrators to maintain some shared sense of awareness of what's going on in the system. We implemented a large public display with appropriately designed visualizations that allow for rapid assessment and peripheral awareness of system health. By placing the visualizations on a large display in a shared, commonly used team location, system administrators can monitor behavior as they walk past. Such a display helps administrators identify emerging problems early on and be a focal point for discussions of the system. It allows them not only to share information with colleagues on an "as-noticed" basis, but also highlights interconnected problems that would not be otherwise evident. We found that this approach significantly reduces the workload of individual system administrators, changing the nature of their work by radically simplifying a complex task through social sharing of peripherally noticed state.

1 Introduction

Complex systems exhibit complex failure modes. Traditional system monitoring tools work well for small and isolated problems, but they quickly become swamped when cascading faults occur. System admin experience teaches us that the sheer number of things going wrong in a very short period of time requires novel approaches to monitoring and information sharing. Such approaches are not meant as a replacement but as a complement to traditional methods of administering these systems.

As an example of a large, heterogeneous system with complex behaviors, the Web-Fountain [3] system developed at the IBM Almaden Research Center is ideal: it is a large, loosely coupled system of over 500 multi-processor computers working on very large-scale text analytic problems WebFountain has shown a wide variety of complex problem modes which have proven very difficult to diagnose using traditional tools.

To address these issues we built Shepherd, a visualization tool running on a large display, to help us gain a high-level overview and awareness of the health of the entire cluster. The tool does not show all details about every aspect of the system, but instead provides a global overview of the cluster. It runs on a large, public display located in a space shared by all sysadmins. Shepherd's goal is to give admins a one-glance view of the overall system health such that they can notice if something is peculiar or out-of-balance, and a touch-screen to allow immediate drill-down to details.

M.F. Costabile and F. Paternò (Eds.): INTERACT 2005, LNCS 3585, pp. 938–941, 2005.
© IFIP International Federation for Information Processing 2005

2 Shepherd: A Tool to Monitor Large System Behavior

Over the past several years the cost basis of running large systems has significantly shifted from large hardware and software costs to the point where people costs now dominate the cost of large systems infrastructure. The more time people spend waiting for a problem to develop, the less time they can spend actually running and tuning the system, performing upgrades, isolating problematic subsystems, etc.

Therefore, a monitoring solution based on a low-level awareness of system state, that allows operators to notice problems as they develop without time-consuming conscious monitoring would allow for tremendous time and cost savings. [2] Once a problem is noted, an analysis needs to be made as to the extent of it, and a solution strategy quickly developed and implemented – as soon as the issue is resolved the operations staff needs to get back to their "day job." [1]

Shepherd is built around a simple visualization designed to be rapidly perceivable. People can easily spot asymmetry in a field of small multiples. Shepherd represents each machine in the cluster using a star visualization, where each point indicates a relevant status value for that machine, such as free memory, or CPU load. The values are normalized such that a "healthy" machine results in a mostly symmetric star.

Each row of small stars in Figure 1 corresponds to a numbered rack. Shepherd runs on a display with touch screen so administrators can just tap a star and it will move into the detail area on the right. There the visualization is shown larger and additional details on the machine are displayed below. With another double screentap, admins can open a secure shell connection to a machine shown in detail.

The physical layout of machines in the rack corresponds to the visualization layout, allowing problems stemming from local common resource problems (e.g., in-rack network bandwidth, in-rack cooling issues, a whole rack being down due to PDU issues, etc.) as well as point problems, or randomly distributed issues (unbalanced load on the cluster, for example) to be quickly understood as physical, not network, problems.

Shepherd is implemented in Macromedia Flash talking to a Java-based backend using XML Socket connections. It is deployed on an BlueBoard [4], a large display with basic touch screen capability provided by a touch overlay. The display was placed at the entrance to the sysadmin cubicle farm where it could be easily seen whenever entering or exiting the common workspace, but also from any point in the farm when standing up.

After Shepherd had been in place for six months, we conducted a set of semi-structured, in situ interviews with half of the end user population (6 admins) to discover their use patterns and war stories when the Shepherd display had been especially useful or problematic. These interviews revealed several strikingly consistent results:

Simplified task: The admins we interviewed uniformly told us that Shepherd simplified the task of correlating application problems and process tracing. For instance, if one node in the cluster is down, a quick visual scan will find other nodes may be down as well. The history line might indicate that network load recently was/is high and might suggest a diagnosis. The admin's interaction with Shepherd allows one to trace the entire path without going through tedious logs and notifications. Users have found it is far simpler to see the patterns of failure using Shepherd than to mentally correlate co-failures of nodes with arbitrary names.

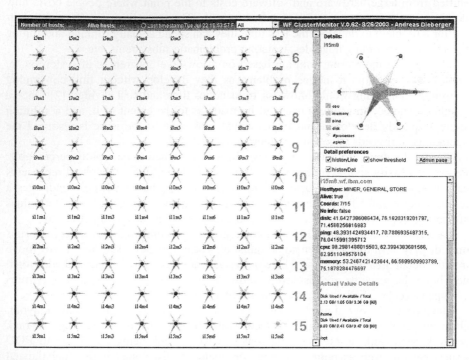

Fig. 1. The Shepherd cluster status visualization takes advantage of symmetric displays to permit rapid determination of variance from standard server behavior. The star's points show current values and the gray lines show a 30 minute average of the same value, providing trend information. Blue dots make the end of the gray lines more visible from a distance. Alert thresholds are shown as red curves on the spikes. The center circle indicates special situations (crashes, alerts) by changing color.

Shows large-scale state effectively: In several cases, an administrator was able to spot a rapid rise in disk utilization (caused by an incorrectly configured link) early on because an obvious spike appeared on one of the stars. The spike became immediately visible to passing admins, and the problem was caught before it became serious.

Social sharing of task information: A somewhat unanticipated effect of Shepherd was social sharing of team information. As admins walked by they would glance at the display, informally noting the current status of the system. Since their job involves continuously moving about, the net effect was that they noticed not just problems that affected their own task assignments, but also those of their colleagues. Telling someone to "look at the big display" became a common way to let someone else know that a significant change in their part of the system was underway. In the end, this meant that more eyes were watching for common problems in the cluster, but each person spent less time doing so. [5]

Focal point for team discussions: Teams also found that they would gather at the big display to talk over what was going on with the system in the large. Since the display wasn't owned by any one person and constantly showed overall system state, teams would gather at the display, discussing the visualization and using the access tools to get more information to investigate ideas about what was going on and why.

Daily time savings: The consensus of opinion among the admins is that Shepherd saved them typically one hour a day per admin. This estimate is based on time saved by debugging complex problems faster, in turn made possible by having a dedicated public display resource with constantly updating performance monitoring data. This freed up time from repeatedly looking up information that was instantly available.

3 Summary

The utility of placing an "ambient" monitoring system in the ops room cannot be overstated in terms of its effects on the performance of the sysadmin team. We found that an overview visualization of a complex system allows administrators to gain a general awareness of system health and allows them to discover emerging problems in a cluster early on.   Large groupwork displays are becoming common in practice and research settings. Typically, these systems are either public displays of personal information, group work space or generic displays for common awareness purposes. By contrast with other system state display visualizations [6], we have shown that Shepherd dramatically changes admin behavior by providing peripheral awareness of critical system status and a place to interact with the information.

References

1. Barrett, R., Kandogan, E., Maglio, P., Haber, E., Takayama, L. A., Prabaker M. "Cases from the field: Field studies of computer system administrators" Proc. 2004 ACM Conf. on Computer supported cooperative Work (2004)
2. Card, S. K., Mackinlay, J. D., Shneiderman, B. *Information visualization, Readings in information visualization: using vision to think* Morgan Kaufmann Publishers Inc., San Francisco, CA, (1999)
3. Gruhl, D., Chavet, L., Gibson D., Meyer, J., Pattanayak, P., Tomkins, A., Zien, J. " How to build a WebFountain: An architecture for very large-scale text analytics" IBM Systems Journal, v 43, n 1 (2004) , p. 64-77
4. 4. Russell, D., Sue, A., "Large interactive public displays: Use patterns, support patterns, community patterns" in O'Hara, K., Perry, M., Churchill, E., Russell, D. M. (eds.) *Public and Situated Displays: Social and Interactional Aspects of Shared Display Technologies.* Kluwer Academic Publishers. (2003)
5. Russell, D. M., Drews, C., Sue, A. "Social aspects of using large public interactive displays for collaboration" Proceedings of Ubiquitous Computing (UBICOMP) Conference, Goteborg, Sweden (2002), 229-236
6. Skog, T. & Holmquist, L.E. WebAware: Continuous Visualization of Web Site Activity in a Public Space. In Extended Abstracts of Computer-Human Interaction Conf. (CHI) (2000)

The Challenge of Visualizing Patient Histories on a Mobile Device

Carmelo Ardito, Paolo Buono, and Maria Francesca Costabile

Dipartimento di Informatica, Università degli Studi di Bari, Italy
{ardito, buono, costabile}@di.uniba.it

Abstract. This paper presents a tool to display patient histories and to visually query patient data, stored in the hospital database, using a mobile device. Employing Information Visualization techniques, the developed tool is able to accommodate on the screen a good amount of information that physicians require in their analysis of the clinical cases. This work has been motivated by specific requests of physicians of a pediatric hospital treating children with neurological diseases.

1 Introduction and Motivation

Patient records are an important source of information for the physicians; they can be multifaceted and collected in time periods ranging from days to decades. For several diseases, physicians need to interpret rapidly a large number of clinical data collected during the patient disease history in order to formulate an accurate diagnosis and plan a treatment. Often a doctor needs to check such data out of the hospital, for instance when he is called on the phone for an emergency.

This paper presents a tool designed for a mobile device that displays he patient histories and permits to visually query patient data stored in the hospital database. The work is motivated by specific requests of physicians of a pediatric hospital treating children with neurological diseases. The challenge is to capture as much as possible information about the patient history on a limited display space, providing overview data as well as details. The employed visualization technique is inspired to Shneiderman's "information-visualization-seeking mantra": *Overview first, zoom and filter, then details-on-demand*[5]. Providing data overview gives users indication of content and interconnections within an information domain. Zooming and filtering mechanisms allow users to concentrate on some portion of data, while mechanisms for showing details, when users request them, must also be included.

The work has been inspired from LifeLines, a general technique for visualizing summaries of personal histories [4]. Displaying on a single screen the overview of multiple facets of records, this technique provides users with a better sense of type and volume of the available data. Other systems have been proposed to support medical personnel in their work. In particular, the systems presented in [1] and [3] use handhelds PC connected, via Wireless Networks, to centralized databases to allow doctors and nurses to check patient clinical records. However, these works do not provide details about user interface features.

M.F. Costabile and F. Paternò (Eds.): INTERACT 2005, LNCS 3585, pp. 942–945, 2005.
© IFIP International Federation for Information Processing 2005

The development of the mobile application we describe in this paper is carried out in collaboration with physicians of "Giovanni XXIII" pediatric hospital in Bari, Italy. A field study with contextual interviews has been performed during the requirements analysis to better understand the medical domain, how the physicians operate and the main features of the application to be implemented. User observation methods and principles of participatory design have proven to be effective in user interface design. To our knowledge, our application is the first one adapting LifeLines on a PDA, thus visualizing on a small screen as much as possible patient data useful to the physicians in their analysis of the clinical cases. More details on the field study and on the requirement analysis can be found in [2]. In the remainder of this paper, we will briefly describe the visualization technique to display patient histories on a PDA.

2   PHiP: Patient History in Pocket

PHiP is a tool designed to support the neurologists in the treatment of patients with epilepsy; it is intended to make available on mobile devices some sections of patient records and to implement features and functionality that neurologists consider needful to treat such neurological diseases. Several important indications emerged from the field study performed during the requirements analysis. First of all, it is very important for neurologists to analyze the patient history and have information such as periods during which the patient was hospitalized, frequency of seizures, different combinations of drugs the patient took during his/her disease history. Another indication is that the drugs that really work for children affected by epilepsy are a small number, less than twelve; some combinations of them are prescribed to the patients during periods of time and neurologists must know what was prescribed. We therefore realized that neurologists could greatly benefit from having an overview of multi-dimensional, time-oriented data related to all patient hospitalizations, medical controls, therapies. After designing and evaluating with users several prototypes, the main screen of the current PHiP interface is shown in Figure 1. This screen is displayed once the user (we suppose a male neurologist) has specified the name of the patient and the history period he wants to see: the default is the last five years (or the whole history if it covers less than five years). The name of the patient is shown at the very top of the screen. The display is divided in two main areas: the bottom one, below the green bar with 6/1996 and 1/2001 at the sides, is the *overview area* of the patient history; the top larger area is the *focus area* and shows a zoom in a five months time period.

Let us first concentrate on the bottom area that, in Figure 1, indicates that the overview spans from August 1996 to December 2000. The user can change the range of the displayed time period by clicking on the green bar and selecting a value from a combo box that will appear. In this overview area, various information is summarized through colored line segments that we call bars. The bars along a line immediately below the ticker green bar represent hospitalizations or medical controls, in red and green respectively. The bars on the lines below represent the drugs prescribed in the shown time period. The white strip in the overview area represents a lens that permits to zoom on the information covered by the lens, which spans over five months, and shows it in the focus area. The user can quickly move the lens by clicking on another point in the overview area, or gradually move it by clicking on the single-arrow buttons at the extremes of the overview area. The slide bar at the left of the overview area permits to modify the thickness of the colored bars choosing among three different sizes: this because interacting with previous prototypes, some doctors said that it was difficult to distinguish the bars. This overview area can be eliminated by simply clicking on the button above this slide bar. In this way the focus area will be enlarged. Another click will show the overview again.

Detailed information is displayed in the focus area. As for the overview area, the user can change the range of the displayed interval by clicking on the green bar and selecting a value from a combo box. In this way, the user can visualize even a short interval if he wants more details in that time interval. The lens in the overview area is updated accordingly. Hospitalizations and medical controls are shown along the top line below the month bar using red and green colors: they never overlap because a patient might either be hospitalized or go to the outpatient clinic for a medical control. To help the user recall that red indicates hospitalizations, the icon representing a bed at the left of the line is in red, while med-

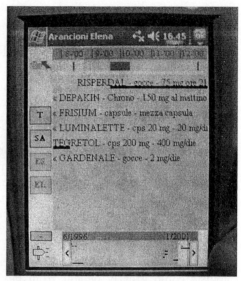

Fig. 1. An example of PHiP interface

ical controls are in green, which is the same color of the folder icon at the left of the bed icon. In Figure 1, in the period August-December 2000 the patient had two medical controls, one in August and one in December, and was hospitalized from end of September to beginning of October.

In the remaining part of the focus area, details about prescribed drugs are shown. Each drug is indicated by a label that explains the name and the posology. If a drug was prescribed in the displayed period, a black bar starts from the day in which the patient took it and ends when he/she stopped the treatment. For example, Figure 1 shows that from the second half of September, the drug RISPERDAL is taken daily in a quantity of 75 milligrams at 9 pm. If a drug was prescribed in a period that is not displayed, the label is shown without the bar and an arrow indicates if it was taken in a previous or in a following period. In Figure 1, DEPAKIN is a drug that was taken before August 2000. Two arrows, one at left and one at right, are shown if the drug was taken in a previous period as well as in a following one. This because for the neurologist it is important to know if a patient already got a drug during a certain time of his/her life.

In Figure 1, two buttons on the left of the focus area are active: one has the T label, since the focus area shows the patient therapy in the selected time interval. The button with SA label allows the user to display patient personal data. The other two buttons become active if the user requires detailed information. More specifically, a click on a period in which the patient was hospitalized, or on a medical control, allows the physician to see details related to that event. This click has several effects. First of all, the drugs prescribed in the clicked period change color and become blue. The ES an EL buttons on the left of the focus area are activated. By clicking on EL, the list of laboratory tests referring to the selected hospitalization or medical control appears in the focus area, replacing the previously visualized data. The user can also query such data to see more details on the tests. Similarly, by clicking on ES, the physician obtains the list of instrumental tests. Such detailed views can be seen in [2].

3   Conclusion

The aim of PHiP, Patient History in Pocket, is to increase the quality of neurological diseases treatment, by supporting physicians with a tailored tool.

The field study carried out in a hospital revealed that the primary need for neurologists is the availability, in different contexts, of patient histories. Thus, a mobile device is suitable to query patient data stored in the hospital database. The main challenge was to accommodate the patient data, on the small screen of the PDA, providing an overview of the most significant data and their temporal sequence. Prototype testing and interviews with neurologists are confirming that the developed application satisfies their needs. They appreciate very much that the tool is useful, easy to understand and use much more than they expected.

References

1. M. Ancona, G. Dodero, V. Gianuzzi, F. Minuto, and M. Guida. Mobile computing in a hospital: the WARD-IN-HAND project. In *Proceedings of the 2000 ACM Symposium on Applied Computing, SAC 2000*, pages 554–556, 2000.
2. C. Ardito, P. Buono, and M. F. Costabile. Visualizing patient histories on mobile devices. Technical Report TR 05-03-01, LACAM - IVU group, Department of Computer Science, University of Bari, Italy, March 2005.
3. J. Bardram, T. A. Kjaer, and C. Nielsen. Supporting local mobility in healthcare by application roaming among heterogeneous devices. volume 2795 of *Lecture Notes in Computer Science*, pages 161–176. Springer-Verlag, 2003.
4. C. Plaisant, B. Milash, A. Rose, S. Widoff, and B. Shneiderman. Lifelines: Visualizing personal histories. In *Proceedings of the ACM Conference on Human Factors in Computing Systems, CHI-1996*, pages 221–227. ACM Press, 1996.
5. B. Shneiderman and C. Plaisant. *Designing user interfaces*. Addison Wesley, Washington, D.C., 2004.

Static Visualization of Temporal Eye-Tracking Data

Kari-Jouko Räihä, Anne Aula, Päivi Majaranta, Harri Rantala, and Kimmo Koivunen

Tampere Unit for Computer-Human Interaction, Department of Computer Sciences,
FIN-33014 University of Tampere, Finland
Tel. +358-3-35518871
{kjr, aula, curly, hjr, kimmo}@cs.uta.fi

Abstract. Existing static visualization techniques for eye-tracking data do not make it possible to easily compare temporal information, that is, gaze paths. We review existing techniques and then propose a new technique that treats time as the prime attribute to be visualized. We successfully used the new technique for analysing the visual scanning of web search results listings. Based on our experiences, the new visualization is a valuable tool when the temporal order of visiting Areas of Interest (AOI) is the main focus in the analysis, the AOIs have a natural linear order, there are many AOIs to produce interesting patterns, and the AOIs fill most of the coordinate space being studied.

1 Introduction

Eye-tracking is increasingly being used to provide insight on a variety of tasks involving visual perception. Eye-trackers provide massive amounts of data that needs to be summarized to make it useful. A variety of numerical metrics, such as fixation duration, number of fixations, and saccade length, are used for this purpose [6].

Before the data can be analyzed statistically with appropriate metrics, it is essential to understand the characteristics of gaze behaviour in the current context. A number of gaze data visualization techniques have been developed for this purpose. They are currently being supported by commercial analysis tools [4, 8].

The problem of visualizing temporal gaze data (that is, gaze paths) statically in a compact and usable way still remains a challenge. We first present the existing solutions and then propose a new technique, *time plots*, that focus on static visualization of the temporal data without cluttering the visualization.

2 Existing Visualization Techniques

Most current eye-trackers are based on video technology. They produce coordinates that indicate where the user is looking at using typically a sampling rate from 50 Hz to 250 Hz. Thus, new coordinates are produced every 20 ms to every 4 ms, respectively.

A straightforward way of visualizing eye-tracking data is to plot the coordinate stream on top of the observed target. However, this is often problematic for visual analysis of the data: the individual data points carry little information, and in these

M.F. Costabile and F. Paternò (Eds.): INTERACT 2005, LNCS 3585, pp. 946–949, 2005.
© IFIP International Federation for Information Processing 2005

visualizations there are 50 to 250 of them per second. It is a challenging task for the human analyzer to make sense of this stream because of the sheer volume of data. Therefore, the most common way of representing eye-tracking data is to draw a *scan path* on top of the target image. It consists of fixations, typically shown as circles, and saccades, shown as lines connecting the circles. Figure 1 (a) shows a scan path of a user viewing a web search result listing.

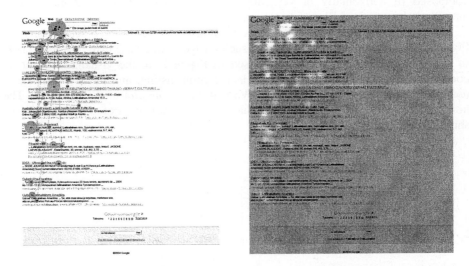

Fig. 1. (a) On the left, a scan path. (b) On the right, the same data visualized as a fixation map.

Scan path visualizations are typically more useful than visualizations of the individual data points, since they group the information into meaningful chunks. However, Figure 1 (a) illustrates the typical problem of gaze path visualizations: the fixations and saccades overlap, making it difficult to figure out the order in which the fixations occurred. The fundamental reason for this problem is that a two-dimensional image is used to represent three-dimensional data: *x*-coordinates, *y*-coordinates, and *time*. To solve this problem, the third dimension (time) is usually handled in some special way, such as by using colour coding to indicate the order of the saccades. However, as there is no natural ordering of colours for the human observer, the interpretation of the coding is cognitively demanding. Moreover, colour can only give a rough illustration of the order, as these visualizations typically contains tens of saccades.

Another possibility is to collapse the time dimension, so that only the fixations are visualized, not their order. This is a useful way of summarizing numerous gaze paths, even from different users, and it can be effectively used to highlight the points of interest. When such cumulative data is displayed smoothly using *fixation maps* by David Wooding [9] or its variations, the result is expressive and informative. A sample fixation map is shown in Figure 1 (b). The visualization is less cluttered than the gaze path on the left, but the time dimension has completely disappeared.

3 Static Visualization of Temporal Gaze Data

In some situations the timing information is the crucial aspect in the analysis. Our visualization technique is especially suitable for situations where (1) the exact locations of the fixations are less important than how they land on predefined *areas of interest* (AOI) in the stimulus; and when (2) the AOIs have a natural linear ordering. This is the case, for instance, when studying gaze behaviour on web pages that are composed of horizontally or vertically arranged blocks of information. Another natural application is studies of menu usage [2, 3].

Prime examples of such web pages are the result listings of web search engines. Figure 2 shows a miniaturized image of such a page, with a gaze path positioned next to it. The data is the same that was used in Figure 1. In the visualization, the y-coordinate corresponds to the position in the result listing, and the x-coordinate is used to visualize the ordering in time. We call this a *time plot* of the gaze data. The horizontal location of where the gaze has landed within the area of interest is not shown.

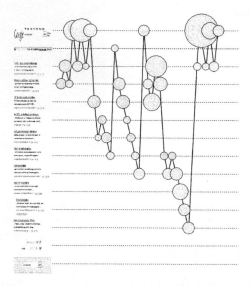

Fig. 2. A time plot of the scan path shown in Figure 1 (a)

Time plot visualizations make it possible to visually observe differences in the gaze behaviour of different users. We have used the technique for analyzing how users perceive search result listings (see [2] for more examples).

The basic time plot approach can be used with variations. For instance, the y-coordinate could denote the exact position of the AOI in the coordinate space, and similarly, the x-coordinate could denote a relative point in time. In Figure 3 we are visualizing only the order of AOIs, both for the vertical locations (y) and for their visiting order (x). For this analysis task, this solution was found to work well.

4 Discussion

We have proposed a simple new way of visualizing gaze data that facilitates the analysis of gaze paths. We have used it successfully for analyzing the scanning of web search result listings, and believe it to be useful for other visual search tasks as well. Figure 3 illustrates another study where we tried to use this technique. Here the objective was to study the differences of gaze behaviour of designers and consumers while viewing design products. Figure 3 shows that in this case the time plot was less illustrative.

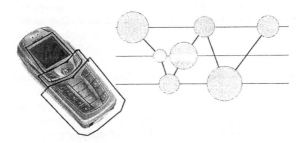

Fig. 3. Time plot (on the right) of a user inspecting the image of a mobile phone. AOIs are highlighted with polygons.

Based on our experiences, we believe the time plot to be a valuable tool when (1) the temporal order of visiting AOIs is the main target of the analysis, (2) the AOIs have a natural linear order, (3) there are sufficiently many AOIs to produce interesting patterns in the time plot, and (4) the AOIs fill most of the coordinate space being studied.

References

1. Aaltonen, A., Hyrskykari, A., and Räihä, K.-J.: 101 spots, or how do users read menus? In Proc. CHI 1998, ACM Press (1998) 132-139
2. Aula, A., Majaranta, P., and Räihä, K-J.: Eye-tracking reveals the personal styles for search result evaluation. In Proc. INTERACT 2005, Rome, September 2005
3. Byrne, M.D., Anderson, J.R., Douglass, S., and Matessa, M.: Eye tracking the visual search of click-down menus. In Proc. CHI 1999, ACM Press (1999) 402-409
4. Eye Response Technologies: GazeTracker. Available at http://www.eyeresponse.com/
5. Feusner, M.: Eye-tracking visualizations. Available at http://www.hci.cornell.edu/eyetracking/visualizations.php
6. Jacob, R.J.K., and Karn, K.S.: Eye tracking in human-computer interaction and usability research: Ready to deliver the promises (section commentary). In The Mind's Eye: Cognitive and Applied Aspects of Eye Movement Research, ed. by J. Hyönä, R. Radach, and H. Deubel, pp. 573-605, Amsterdam, Elsevier Science, 2003
7. Outing, S., and Ruel, L.: The Best of Eyetrack III: What We Saw When We Looked Through Their Eyes. Available at http://www.poynterextra.org/eyetrack2004
8. Tobii Technology: ClearView. Available at http://www.tobii.com/
9. Wooding, D.: Fixation maps: quantifying eye-movement traces. In Proc. ETRA'02, ACM Press (2002), 31-36

Analytic Worksheets: A Framework to Support Human Analysis of Large Streaming Data Volumes

Grace Crowder[2], Sterling Foster[2], Daniel M. Russell[1],
Malcolm Slaney[1], and Lisa Yanguas[1]

[1] IBM Almaden Research Center, 650 Harry Rd., San Jose, CA, 95120
[2] U.S. Department of Defense, 9800 Savage Rd., Fort Meade, MD 20755
{gacrowder, ssfoster}@afterlife.ncsc.mil, daniel2@us.ibm.com,
malcolm@ieee.org, lryangu@us.ibm.com

Abstract. Worksheets are a new user-interface framework to support analysis of streaming data by combining streaming data queries with visualization objects in a composable document framework. A worksheet lets users work at human speeds with large quantities of streaming data by creating a persistent, literate, dynamic document that flows data into analysis patterns of filters and visual presentations. The worksheet provides basic support for analysis created, as well as buffering and managing streaming data as it continually arrives.

1 Motivation and Approach

A significant problem most analysts face is the volume, velocity and variety of data they must manage and manipulate in a timely manner. Such pressure constantly works against careful and through analysis, creating a tension between completeness and publication timeliness for a comprehensive story based on the synthesis of this data and information.

Traditional intelligence analysis schemes have relied on stored data or information in databases, which analysts and other users subsequently access to make queries. Yet current analysts find themselves being buried under a constant onslaught of information pushes. Thus we focus on a way to work with the streaming aspect of data, a situation more closely resembling actual information flows in practice, where data constantly comes into the system, and where decisions are made on data while it is in motion rather than at rest. This adds to the complexity of the analytic task, but provides real benefits for more up-to-date and valid interpretations of the information stream.

In addition, collaboration within and among multiple users is an age-old problem. While there are many impediments to collaboration, an obvious one is the dearth of tools that truly support a collaboration environment as it would best serve users and their tasks. Analysts typically create a "sandbox" area while they are assessing data and information and creating a strategy to understand that data. Such models are often tentative and exploratory. They are typically not shared early on, but results are developed to a more finished form before being shared with others. However, once

M.F. Costabile and F. Paternò (Eds.): INTERACT 2005, LNCS 3585, pp. 950–953, 2005.
© IFIP International Federation for Information Processing 2005

users have formed an assessment, it would be helpful to be able to show what specific pieces or aspects of data, analyses, thought processes, queries, etc. went into the user's making that particular assessment.

Our goals in designing analytic worksheets are to (a) provide tools to manage streaming data tasks, (b) to create and capture analysis patterns as a way to express the intent and context of a particular kind of analysis in progress, (c) form the basis for collaboration between analysts working on shared or similar problems.

A worksheet is a view of relevant data streams, packaging together data with contextualizing information that helps organize and communicate the work being done. It not only supports analysts in sharing information among themselves but also allows information to be shared with others involved in the analytic process. An analyst working on a particular problem can see in the worksheet what others working on similar or related issues have done, what queries they have levied on the system, what actions have been taken and how they manage incoming information (i.e., data streams).

2 Worksheets: A Way to Handle Large Volumes of Data for Analysis

Figure 1 shows an example of a worksheet. A worksheet is an easily authored, persistent, live document that is built up out of *inquiries* (persistent queries over streams of live data, continually filtering the stream for records that match their query specifications), *annotations* (user-editable text and graphics to document or comment on the analysis process or context), *visualizations* (linked to the data streams coming out of inquiries to filter and visually present the output of the inquiries), and *notifications* (that cause an email or IM to be sent out when a specified, exceptional condition in the data stream is reached). A user creates a hierarchy of these components by creating inquiries on specific data source streams, then attaching visualizations and notifications to that inquiry. Like any hierarchy, subsections of the worksheet can be minimized to hide details of the document that the reader does not want to see at the moment. In this way a worksheet seems very much like an outline tool, where inquiries form section headings with visualizations and notifications below as parts of the section.

One inquiry can produce a wealth of data for which a number of visualizations might be appropriate. A user creates an inquiry, embedding it in the worksheet, then specifies as many visualizations as necessary to understand the data, providing multiple views of the data that might filter or reorganize the collected data. In our prototype these visualizations include tabular views of records, geospatial maps, image viewers and simple graphical representations (e.g., line graphs and histograms); data sources include news wire stories, stock prices and realtime sensor data.

Intrinsic to the worksheet model is its ability to handle streaming data. The worksheet manages streaming data to provide a match between the incessant push of data and the need for users to slow down, pause and even back up in the collected data. That is, in order to operate with multiple, parallel inquiry streams, the worksheet buffers content streaming in from active inquiries to provide flow management and received data storage. When working with live streaming data, the capability to pause the inquiry stream, extract a portion of the data, and back up to do a historical review of earlier data is critical.

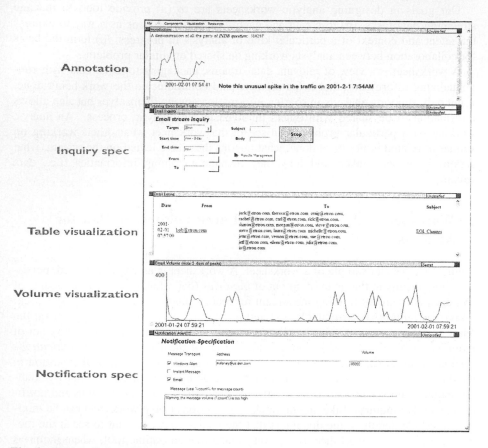

Fig. 1. This worksheet fragment shows an inquiry and two visualizations within the scope of the inquiry. Each visualization is linked to the inquiry, which in turn is updated by a stream of results coming from the Worksheet server. Worksheets provide basic capabilities to handle multiple live data streams with pause, flow management and the ability to back up for historical review of streamed data.

The worksheet promotes collaboration by allowing individual and groups of widgets to be selected, copied and pasted into a new worksheet. A portion of the worksheet, containing any number of text, inquiry, or visualization components can be copied as a group and sent to another user. A portion of the worksheet might address a particularly difficult question, and can be shared by simply copying and pasting into a new worksheet. Since the worksheet model is persistent, the entire structure of annotations, visualizations, inquiries and notifications can be copied and shared as a document.

3 Summary

Our worksheet model combines a few existing interface techniques: the persistent notebook, data flow graphs and component-style visualizations embedded in an organizing framework a la OpenDoc [6]. The Virtual Notebook [3] is a composite document holding interactive components in a persistent document-like object that can be edited, read, manipulated and monitored by the user.

The notebook was popularized in Mathematica [2], which provided a notebook interface as its primary interface model. Users combine text and graphics with mathematical expressions to display interactive results. If you change the definition of an equation, the display updates immediately showing its new values.

The worksheet-style interface has several advantages. It is *literate*, capturing the steps of the analysis, exposing intermediate work and assumptions. In this way the worksheet is a document that is meant to be read, like a book, instead of executed like a computer program [4, 5]. A worksheet is *dynamic*, continuously reflecting changes in the streaming environment as new information arrives.

The worksheet becomes a tool for sensemaking [1] when it captures the knowledge patterns of analysts. That is, a user can easily construct a tree of inquiry objects that import data from streams and then provide visualization tools to look at, examine and work with the data stream. The constructed worksheet is then a representation of the analytic framework, illustrating what works for this kind of problem.

Finally, worksheets are a way to do real analysis work over data streams; not simply collecting and organizing evidence, but also providing support for comparing evidence – pro and con. As data streams through the worksheets, we want to be able to create the best possible interpretation based on *currently* available information. The inherently live streaming nature of the worksheet approach allows users to keep these analyses up-to-date and accurate.

References

1. Russell, Daniel M., Stefik, Mark J., Pirolli, Peter, Card, Stuart. K. The cost structure of sensemaking. In Proc. of ACM INTERCHI'93 Conference on Human Factors in Computing Systems, 269—276 (1993)
2. Wolfram, Stephen *Mathematica: A System for Doing Math by Computer,* Addison Wesley (1990)
3. Burger, Andrew M., Meyer, Barry D., Jung, Cindy P., Long, Kevin B. The Virtual Notebook System, Proceedings of ACM Hypertext Conference, 395—402 (1991)
4. Slaney, Malcolm Interactive Signal Processing Documents, in *Symbolic and Knowledge-Based Signal Processing*. A. Oppenheim, H. Nawab (eds.), Prentice Hall, NJ (1992)
5. Knuth, Donald E. *Literate Programming*, Center for the Study of Language and Information Press, Stanford, CA (1992)
6. Feiler, Jesse; Meadow, Anthony *EssentialOpenDoc*. Addison Wesley, Reading, MA. (1996)

Hundreds of Folders or One Ugly Pile – Strategies for Information Search and Re-access

Anne Aula and Harri Siirtola

Tampere Unit for Computer-Human Interaction (TAUCHI),
Department of Computer Sciences, FIN-33014 University of Tampere, Finland
{anne.aula, harri.siirtola}@cs.uta.fi

Abstract. Previous research has identified information search and re-access strategies used by experienced web users, but not the popularity of these strategies. To fill this gap, we collected data from 236 experienced web users via a questionnaire. A cluster analysis of the data revealed three distinct user groups, each having different search and re-access strategies. The group of "professional searchers" was the only one to use Boolean operators in searching and most of the advanced strategies for information re-access. In contrast, the strategies of the other two groups were much simpler. These results show that the previous findings on advanced search and re-access strategies may describe the strategies of information professionals, but not those of other web users, regardless of their extensive experience.

1 Introduction

Previous studies have shown that information professionals or "expert users" commonly utilize advanced strategies for information search and re-access. Most of these studies have used observational methods [6,7,9] and have suggested the following strategies: e-mailing URLs, saving URLs in files or adding them to a website, saving documents as files or printing them out, using a search engine or directly the URL, adding bookmarks, using the History tool, and writing down queries or URLs. The problem with using observational methods is the expense of data acquisition, which typically results in small sample sizes.

The questionnaire approach (previously used by [1,2,3,4]), makes it possible to reach hundreds of users, and to acquire data about the use of all different applications. Although the absolute frequencies of different strategies should not be measured with questionnaires (because this approach depends on the users' memory), we believe that people can reliably evaluate their relative frequencies.

We compiled a comprehensive list of the search and re-access strategies and conducted a questionnaire study about the usage frequencies of them among experienced web users. The results concerning the strategies of the respondents as a whole are presented in a separate paper [3]; the current paper presents the strategies of three subgroups of experienced users.

M.F. Costabile and F. Paternò (Eds.): INTERACT 2005, LNCS 3585, pp. 954–957, 2005.

2   The Questionnaire and Methods for Data Analysis

To receive responses from experienced web users with different backgrounds (not only information professionals), we sent the URL of the questionnaire to CHI-WEB and SIGCHI-Finland mailing lists in August 2004. In addition, the URL was sent to seven personal contacts from a large IT company who distributed it in their organization.

The questionnaire had 7 background questions and 9 questions about computer, web, and search engine use. The respondents were asked to think of a typical work-related information search task when answering the questions. In relation to this task, the frequency of using 14 different search and re-access strategies was asked on a 5 point scale (*almost always, often, sometimes, rarely,* or *never*). In addition, 10 questions addressed bookmark use and the frequency of using operators or modifiers in queries. Three open-ended questions elicited the participants' understanding of their primary search engine, strategies not listed in the questionnaire, and other comments. The questionnaire can be accessed from http://www.cs.uta.fi/~aula/questionnaire.php.

The 31 (questions) × 236 (respondents) table with 6 ratio, 22 ordinal, and 3 nominal scale variables was analyzed. The dissimilarities between observations were computed with algorithm daisy. Then, the hclust package of statistical system R was used for a hierarchical clustering [8]. For the pairwise comparisons between the clusters, Tukey's multiple comparisons with exact *t*-distribution were used.

3   Results

The cluster analysis resulted in three top-level groups of respondents. In the remainder of this paper these groups will be called *professionals, frequent searchers,* and *regular searchers*. In Figures 1 and 2, the boxes denote the region between the first and the third quartile (50% of the responses) and the black dots are the median values. Fig. 1 summarizes the search frequency of these groups. Professionals (37 respondents) were mainly librarians (35.1%) and managers (21.6%) with an average of 11.7 years of experience in their profession. Frequent searchers (111 respondents) were mainly designers (21.1%), researchers (18.0%), and librarians (17.1%), with an average of 6.0 years of professional experience. Regular searchers (88 respondents) were mainly researchers (23.9%), designers (20.5%), and usability specialists (15.9%) with an average of 7.8 years of professional experience.

Fig. 2 shows the frequency of using operators and modifiers, as well as the use of information re-access strategies. Quotes were the most common modifier, and they were used *often* in all groups. The use of the other modifiers and operators was *rare*, only professionals used all of them *sometimes*. In their use of operators, regular searchers were the least active of the three groups as most of them *never* used the operators OR and NOT, and also the use of AND, +, and − was *rare*. Frequent searchers seemed to use the operators and modifiers slightly

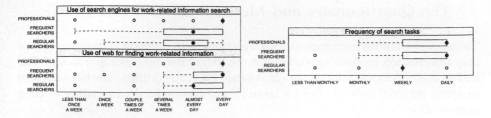

Fig. 1. Search frequency in the three groups

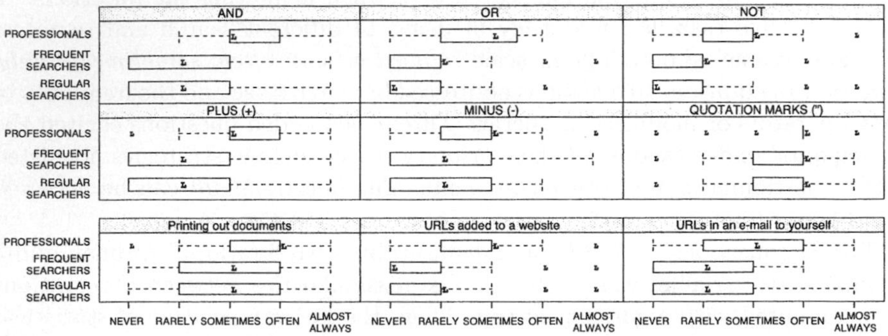

Fig. 2. Frequency of using query operators and strategies for information re-access

more often, the median usage frequency being *rarely* for all of them. Statistically, the only significant difference between the frequent and regular searchers was in the use of the NOT operator.

In information re-access strategies, statistically significant differences were found between the two less experienced groups (frequent and regular searcher) and professionals. The professionals email URLs to themselves, add URLs to websites, and print out documents more often.

Bookmark collection sizes seem to increase with experience. Professionals had collections of 400 files, on average; the collections of frequent and regular searchers had an average of 213 and 167 files, respectively. The number of folders pointed to the same direction with professionals having an average of 33 folders, and frequent and regular searchers having 25 and 31 folders (difference *n.s.*).

4   Discussion

The three groups differed in their use of the strategies. Professionals used the advanced strategies most frequently, whereas the use of them was relatively rare in the other groups. The differences in the strategies of the two less experienced groups were subtle, but their search frequencies differed significantly.

The use of some strategies was rare in all of the groups (e.g., writing down web addresses or queries). As most of the strategies were used frequently by professionals only, it seems that these strategies are truly advanced strategies – only used by information professionals or others with similar needs. However, the other user groups might also benefit from the advanced strategies, but are currently unable to use them efficiently. *"IE makes it so hard to organize 'favorites' that I leave them all in an ugly pile and don't rely on them as much as I'd like."* Professionals, on the other hand, may be in a position where they must go through some trouble for making information useful for them. *"I have organized bookmarks in subject alphabetical based folders [sic] with subfolders and links below... Yes it has been highly successful for my needs ... I literally have hundreds of folders."*

All of the groups use quotes *often*. Otherwise, the queries are simple. The regular searchers, in particular, employ a "just-type-in-words" strategy. In contrast, professionals use all of the listed operators *sometimes*. Frequent searchers were in the middle, using them *rarely*. Thus, it seems that professionals are the only notable exceptions to the just-type-in-words strategy.

The strategies of professionals are not unquestionably better than those of less experienced users. However, as there is evidence that the effectiveness in information search tasks increases with experience [5], we feel safe to make this assumption. Thus, the focus in developing interfaces for information search and re-access should be in making these strategies *accessible* for all users and for the time being, set aside the question of whether they will be used by them. If we do not try and make the strategies accessible, the "lazy sort of guy", as one respondent described himself, will never get to see their possible benefits.

References

1. Abrams, D., Baecker, R., and Chignell, M. Information archiving with bookmarks: personal web page construction and organization. In P. Isaías and N. Karmaker (eds.), Proc. CHI 1998, ACM Press (1998), 41–48.
2. Aula, A. Query Formulation in Web Information Search. In Proc. WWW/Internet 2003, IADIS Press (2003), 403–410.
3. Aula, A., Jhaveri, N., and Käki, M. Information search and re-access strategies of experienced web users. Proceedings of WWW 2005, May 10-14, 2005, pp. 583–592.
4. Bruce, H., Jones, W., and Dumais, S. Keeping and re-finding information on the web: What do people do and what do they need? In Proc. ASIST 2004, (2004).
5. Hölscher, C., and Strube, G. Web search behavior of internet experts and newbies. In H. Maurer & R.G. Olson (eds.), Proc. 9th Int. WWW conference, (2000), 337–346.
6. Jones, W., Bruce, H., and Dumais, S. Keeping found things found on the Web. In H. Paques et al. (eds.), Proc. Information and Knowledge Management, (2001), 119–126.
7. Jones, W., Bruce, H., and Dumais, S. How do people get back to information on the web? How can they do it better? In M. Rauterberg et al. (eds.), Proc. INTER-ACT'03, IOS Press (2003), 793–796.
8. R Development Core Team and R Foundation for Statistical Computing. R: A language and environment for statistical computing, (2004).
9. Wen, J. Post-valued recall web pages: User disorientation hits the big time. IT & Society, 1, 2 (2003), 184–194.

Exploring Results Organisation for Image Searching

Jana Urban and Joemon M. Jose

Department of Computing Science, University of Glasgow, Glasgow G12 8RZ, UK
{jana, jj}@dcs.gla.ac.uk

Abstract. An explorative study of an image retrieval interface with respect to the support it offers the user to organise their search results is presented. The evaluation, involving design professionals performing practical and relevant tasks, shows that the proposed approach succeeds in encouraging the user to conceptualise their tasks better.

1   Introduction and Motivation

Content-based image retrieval (CBIR) systems have still not managed to find favour with the public even after more than a decade of research effort. There are two main reasons for their lack of acceptability: first, the images' low-level feature representation does not reflect the high-level concepts the user has in mind (*semantic gap*) [1]; and – partially due to this – the user tends to have major difficulties in formulating and communicating their information need effectively (*query formulation problem*) [2]. Moreover, current interfaces are limited to providing query facilities and result presentation. Our approach, in contrast, encourages the user to group and organise their search results and thus provide more fine-grained feedback for the system. It combines the search and management process, which – according to our hypothesis – helps the user to conceptualise their search tasks and to overcome the query formulation problem. The system assists the user by recommending relevant images for selected groups. This way, the user can concentrate on solving specific tasks rather than having to think about how to create a good query in accordance with the retrieval mechanism. In this paper we explore how useful the organisation of search results is for the user to solve their work tasks.

2   The EGO Interface

The EGO system is an image management and retrieval tool that learns from and adapts to a user by the way they interact with the image collection. A workspace is provided in the interface allowing the user to organise their search results. Images can be dragged onto the workspace and organised into groups. The grouping can be achieved in an interactive fashion with the help of a recommendation system. For a selected group, the system can recommend new images based on their similarity with the images already in the group. The user then has

M.F. Costabile and F. Paternò (Eds.): INTERACT 2005, LNCS 3585, pp. 958–961, 2005.
© IFIP International Federation for Information Processing 2005

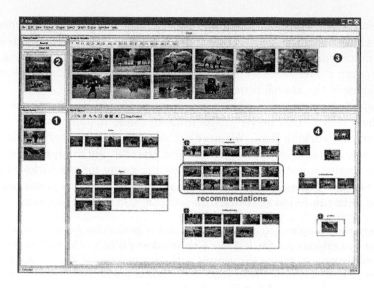

Fig. 1. Annotated EGO interface

the option of accepting any of the recommended images by dragging them into the group. An image can belong to multiple groups simultaneously. The query facilities available in the EGO interface are: (1) manually constructed queries by providing one or more image examples (QBE), and (2) user-requested recommendations. The underlying retrieval system is described in [3] and [4]. The learning strategy involves calculating an ideal query and the parameters of the matching function based on the provided images. The interface depicted in Figure 1 comprises the following components:

1. *Given Items Panel* contains a selection of images (three per task) provided for illustration purposes and that can be used to bootstrap the search;
2. *QBE Panel* provides a basic query facility by allowing the user to compose a search request by adding example images to this panel.
3. *Results Panel* displays the search results from a query constructed in the QBE panel. Any result image can be dragged onto the workspace to start organising the collection or into the QBE panel to change the current query.
4. *Workspace Panel* serves as the organisation ground for the user. Also, the recommendations will be displayed close to the selected group on the workspace.

3   Experimental Methodology

This study's objective is to analyse how people make use of the workspace, depending on the task nature, in order to judge the workspace's usefulness for helping the user to conceptualise their task. We conducted a task-oriented, user-centred evaluation [5], employing a collection of 12800 photographs (CD 1, CDs 4-6 of the Corel 1.6M dataset).

Our sample user population consisted of post-graduate design students and young design professionals (20-30 years; 9 male, 3 female). Responses to an entry questionnaire indicated that our participants could be assumed to have a good understanding of the tasks we were to set them, but a more limited knowledge or experience of the search process.

We adopted a simulated work task situation [6], which allows the users to evolve their information needs in the same dynamic manner as they might do so in their real working lives. We have created two different task scenarios: the category search scenario and the design task scenario. By analysing the number of groups created and the number of images per group for the various tasks, we can identify how these numbers relate to task complexity. The participants were presented with the following work task scenario and task description:

Task Scenario *Imagine you are a designer with responsibility for the design of leaflets on various subjects for the Wildlife Conservation (WLC). The leaflets are intended to raise awareness among the general public for endangered species and the preservation of their habitats. These leaflets [...] consisting of a body of text interspersed with up to 4–5 images selected on the basis of their appropriateness to the use to which the leaflets are put.*

Category Search Task: *You will be given a leaflet topic [...] Your task involves searching for as many images as you are able to find on the given topic, suitable for presentation in the leaflet. [...] You have 10 minutes to attempt this task.*

Design Task: *[...] you're asked to select images for a leaflet for WLC presenting the organisation and a selection of their activities [...] Your task is to search for suitable images and then make a pre-selection of 3-5 images for the leaflet. (20 minutes)*

4 Results Analysis

Concerning the number of groups created in the design task, we could identify two different types of behaviour. About half the people saved all candidates on the workspace organised in 4-9 groups reflecting different aspects of the task before making the final selection. The other half only added a small number of images, mostly all in the same group. The average number of images saved on the workspace for the first selection strategy was 53 images in 6.5 groups. On the other hand, the other group of users saved only 14 images in 1.5 groups.

It is also interesting to highlight differences in behaviour in the design task and the category search task. The average number of groups per task is shown in Table 1. We can clearly see a dependency between the number of groups and the nature of the task. Tasks 1-3 are very focused (e.g. "Mountainous landscapes"), while Tasks 4-6 are composite/multi-faceted (e.g. "African Wildlife").

Table 1. Average Number of groups created per task

	Task 1	Task 2	Task 3	Task 4	Task 5	Task 6	Task AVG	Design
Avg Nr Groups	1.5	1.0	1.0	7.0	2.0	4.0	3.4	4.0

In addition, the questionnaire data points to differences in user perception depending on the task nature. The responses suggest they had a clearer idea of the images relevant for the task in the category search scenario (average 4.4, on a scale from 1-5), compared to the design scenario (3.7). However, the organisation of images into groups seems to be more helpful in the design scenario than in the category search scenario. The average of the responses to the statement, whether the system organisation of images into groups helps them express different aspects of the task, is 4.42 and 3.92 for the design task and category search task, respectively. The difference is even more pronounced comparing the different task groups for the category search tasks. The average response is 3.0 for the focused tasks and 4.83 for the more complex tasks. So, while the organisation is helpful in general, it is dependent on, and reflects the nature of, the task.

5   Conclusion

In this study, we found a correlation between the number of groups created and the complexity of the task set. Further, user responses showed that the management of search results was more helpful in the design scenario, which is more flexible and open to interpretation than the category search scenario. In the latter, the usefulness of the organisation also depended on the task's complexity: the more facets the task comprised, the more useful the workspace was considered. The dependency between both the number of groups created and the users' perception of the workspace's usefulness, led us to the conclusion that our approach indeed helps in conceptualising the task better.

In the future, the user should be assisted in determining task aspects and create groups (semi-) automatically. For a multi-aspect task, we could then group results into the various aspects and present recommendations for each group. The category task aims at maximising recall, while the design task aims at finding a selection of good quality images that work well together. The interface should have a way to be tailored to these contrasting requirements to adapt to its users.

References

1. Smeulders, A.W., Worring, M., Santini, S., Gupta, A., Jain, R.: Content-based image retrieval at the end of the early years. IEEE Trans. Pattern Analysis and Machine Intelligence **22** (2000) 1349–1380
2. ter Hofstede, A.H.M., Proper, H.A., van der Weide, T.P.: Query formulation as an information retrieval problem. The Computer Journal **39** (1996) 255–274
3. Urban, J., Jose, J.M.: EGO: A personalised multimedia management tool. In: Proc. of the 2nd Int. Workshop on Adaptive Multimedia Retrieval. (2004) 3–17
4. Urban, J., Jose, J.M.: Evidence combination for multi-point query learning in content-based image retrieval. In: Proc. of the IEEE 6th Int. Symposium on Multimedia Software Engineering (MSE 2004). (2004) 583–586
5. Ingwersen, P.: Information Retrieval Interaction. Taylor Graham, London (1992)
6. Jose, J.M., Furner, J., Harper, D.J.: Spatial querying for image retrieval: A user-oriented evaluation. In: Proc. of the ACM SIGIR Conf. (1998) 232–240

The SenseMS: Enriching the SMS Experience for Teens by Non-verbal Means

Alia K. Amin, Bram Kersten, Olga A. Kulyk, Elly Pelgrim,
Jimmy Wang, and Panos Markopoulos

Design School of User System Interaction, Eindhoven University of Technology,
Den Dolech 2, 5600 MB Eindhoven, The Netherlands
{a.k.amin, b.t.a.kersten, o.a.kulyk, p.h.pelgrim,
c.m.wang}@tm.tue.nl
p.markopoulos@tue.nl

Abstract. The paper presents a design exploration into emotional communication through mobile phones for teenagers. A participatory design approach was followed, that lead to the development of two potential enhancements to text messaging services that are feasible with today's mobile phones. These enhancements refer to using MMS technology for: identifying callers through personalized avatars which are also coupled with context related information for the caller and using semi-automated text enhancements. Preliminary evaluation results are encouraging regarding the value of the emotional and contextual cues that can be conveyed in this way.

1 Introduction

Teeners use Short Messaging Service (SMS) to stay in touch with their peers and it is very popular among this group. The main reasons for this popularity are that it is fast, cheap, easy, and convenient. Teens consider the use of SMS as more convenient, because they can do it in private, silently in public places or late in bed. SMS also helps teens to avoid long and unwanted conversations and save costs.

However, short messaging has several drawbacks. The most obvious restriction is the absence of non-verbal communication support. In addition, text messaging lacks expressiveness [1] and human embodiment (e.g. usage of avatars in Instant Messaging [2]). In face-to-face situations, non-verbal aspects account for a great proportion of the total communication (e.g. facial expressions, body posture, gestures, etc.). Due to the fact that a receiver tends to interpret the intentions of the sender based on the non-verbal cues she/he perceives from the message, the absence of those makes the correct interpretation difficult for receivers, without sufficient indications.

In this paper we report the user study results and design concepts of a new messaging application for teens. Section 2 describes the user study of teens' behavior regarding informal communication. Section 3 presents our enhanced SMS design concept, the SenseMS. Section 4 describes the preliminary user evaluation, which focuses on comparing teens' understanding of emotion in using SMS and SenseMS. Section 5 concludes the paper and discusses perspectives in a view of recent developments.

M.F. Costabile and F. Paternò (Eds.): INTERACT 2005, LNCS 3585, pp. 962–965, 2005.

2 User Study

A user study was conducted to get insight into teens' communication and life style. Our aim was to gain insight into teens' communication needs, as well as to establish the necessary empathy with our target users. Two participatory design workshops were conducted, part of which was inspired by the Cultural Probes technique [3]. The probes were designed as creative tasks in a colorful booklet, which were adapted to teens' interests and preferences (see figure 1). Two groups of teens (one group of 4 girls and one group of 5 boys) participated in the workshops, which took place in their home environment.

The results showed that it is common for teens to add emoticons to their messages to express their emotions and intentions. Illustrative was that during the assignments a lot of pictures and cartoons of facial expressions were used to express how they were feeling. Still, it is essential to mention that, when they had a choice, the teens preferred to also include text. In addition, the workshops demonstrated that context information is an important aspect in communication for teens, because it was also noticed that often during phone calls (e.g. in the train or in shops) the teens first ask each other where they are.

Fig. 1. The teen's craftwork from left to right: a result from "this is me" of girl (age 17) and of boy (age 15), a result from "the holiday" assignment, and a result of the "them and me" assignment

3 The Design Concept

From the findings of the user study and literature about teenagers' behavior, we propose an enhanced SMS design based on the following four elements, which are very essential in teen's communication:

1. *Identity:* The use of avatars is one way for people to visually represent themselves in the virtual world. Especially among teens, avatars are popular and widely used. What makes avatars favorable is that they give teens a possibility to be represented in a real or surreal (e.g. caricatures, cartoons, idols) way.
2. *Personalization:* When teens use Internet text applications (chat and instant messaging) they are very creative in expressing themselves with various text colors and sizes. Oksman et al. [4] found that teens have become large-scale consumers of personalized mobile services (logos and ringing tones).

3. *Facial expression:* A crucial part of non-verbal communication is body language. Facial expressions especially help in the interpretation of the intention of the communication content.

4. *Location awareness:* The workshop showed that teens expressed the location information in the environment to elaborate their messages.

The complete design composes of two parts, the stamp and the enhanced text message. The stamp (see figure 2) is the first part the user sees when he/she receives a message. It provides the situational and environmental context (the stamp background) and the psychological context (the emotion displayed by the avatar). In addition, the sender's name, and the time and date the message was send are displayed as usual. This way the receiver of the message has a lot of information at a glance, before the actual text message is even read. Teens can personalize the avatar and the background picture. The avatar's facial expressions can be adjusted according to the user's preference.

The second part of the SenseMS is enhanced text. The sender of a SenseMS can customize the text appearance, by changing the background color, the font type, and the font color.

In addition to the above, the application filters the content of a text message as it is typed, prompting the user with suggestions for the presentation of special words. In a manner comparable to automatic word completion or detection of emoticons in instant messaging, words that are typically associated with a specific emotion will be provided with a pop-up providing different text styles and adorned with graphics. For example, like with the word "jarig" in figure 2.

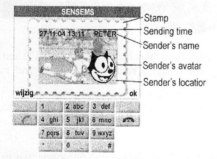

Fig. 2. The design of stamp (on the left) and enhanced text (on the right) of SenseMS application

4 Prototype Evaluation

Based on the design concept, we developed a SenseMS prototype on a Pocket PC platform to simulate the mobile phone usage. A preliminary evaluation was conducted with 8 teens to test if they could understand the emotion and context of the sender more easily using SenseMS compared to SMS. We asked participants to compose emotionally charged messages to each other and then interpret the emotion and context conveyed in the messages.

The test results show that teens interpreted the emotion conveyed in SenseMS better than SMS, especially negative emotions. Teens reported that they enjoyed receiving a SenseMS, because of the possibility to communicate emotions and context, which makes them feel closer. Teens also indicated different usage scenarios for SMS and SenseMS, namely sending ordinary messages with SMS and messages for special occasions with SenseMS, because the composing time for SMS is shorter than SenseMS.

5 Conclusion and Future Work

This study has identified shortcomings of current messaging services with regards to communicating emotions and contextual information regarding the caller. We have proposed two design concepts that can enrich non-verbal communication allowing the expression of emotion, the efficient communication of contextual cues and the personalisation of messages. Clearly, our evaluation was of a small scale and a more extensive field trial involving a fully functional service is needed to consolidate our findings. Further, an improved input method should be implemented in the application.

The concepts proposed were designed to be feasible with current technology. A direct improvement of today's services in line with our findings would be for network operators to provide real time context information that can be used to construct the Stamp as shown in this work. Future developments in context awareness through the use of sensor and GPS technology as, for example, explored by Marmasse [5], also promise to enrich the contextual information adding no extra tasks to the sender of the message.

References

1. Berg, S., Taylor, A.S., Harper, R.: Mobile Phones for the Next Generation: Device Designs for Teenagers. Proceedings of Human factors in computing systems, Ft. Lauderdale, Florida, USA (2002) 433 – 440
2. Takahashi, T., Bartneck, C., Katagiri, Y.: Show Me What You Mean – Expressive Media for Online Communities. Proceedings of the CHI Workshop on Subtle Expressivity of Characters and Robots, Fort Lauderdale (2003)
3. Gaver, B., Dunne, T., Pacenti, E.: Cultural probes. Interactions 1 (1999) 22-29
4. Oksman, V., Malinen, S., Utriainen, A., Rautiainen, P., Liikala, H.: Mobile Communication Culture of Children and Teenagers in Finland. A research project based on qualitative fieldwork 1997-2001, University of Tampere (2001)
5. Marmasse N., Schmandt S., Spectre D.: WatchMe: Communication and Awareness Between Members of a Closely-Knit Group. Proceedings of UbiComp, Nottingham, England (2004)

TextTone: Expressing Emotion Through Text

Ankur Kalra and Karrie Karahalios

University of Illinois at Urbana-Champaign
{kalra2, kkarahal}@cs.uiuc.edu

Abstract. An increasingly large part of online communication is inherently social in nature. This social interaction is limited by the modalities of online communication, which do not convey tone or emotion well. Although some solutions have evolved or have been proposed, they are inherently ambiguous. We present a system, TextTone, for the explicit expression of emotion in online textual communication. TextTone incorporates reader-specific preferences for the visualization of tone and emotion. We describe social interaction and visualization scenarios that TextTone can be meaningfully used for and discuss an initial implementation. Finally, we present the results of a preliminary evaluation of this implementation of TextTone.

1 Introduction

An increasingly large part of online communication is inherently social [11]. Blogs, instant messaging, IRC chat rooms and the like are new forms of social communication, and even predominantly non-social interactions online have a significant social component [6, 8].

However, the modalities of online social interaction are much more limited than those of face-to-face social interaction, and provide no good way to convey non-verbal cues [3], which make up 93% of face-to-face interaction [7]. Online communities have appropriated the use of emoticons and other textual representations to help address this issue, but the lack of a standard set of expressive and versatile representations introduces ambiguity, which limits their usefulness [10].

TextTone aims to provide a means for unambiguously expressing emotion through text. It does this by dynamically switching representations based off of the preferences of the reader. Instead of forcing all the users to 'speak a common language', TextTone picks the most meaningful representation based on the audience, the environment, and the platform, so that two users reading the same text would each see the representations that made the most sense to them in their own environment.

2 Current Representations

The inability to convey emotion through text greatly limits the effectiveness of textual communication from a social perspective. Not surprisingly, therefore, numerous attempts have been made to address the issue, both by interaction researchers and the online community [1, 4, 5, 9, 13]. However, expressive representations, such as

M.F. Costabile and F. Paternò (Eds.): INTERACT 2005, LNCS 3585, pp. 966–969, 2005.
© IFIP International Federation for Information Processing 2005

kinetic or *animated text*, have met with limited success in practice, largely due to difficulties in interaction and archival [1, 4, 5]. Our system overcomes these kinds of issues through an easy-to-use authoring environment (Figure 1) and representations that can be naturally archived.

Currently, the most successful representation by far is the use of *emoticons* [9, 13]. However, studies have shown that only four emoticons account for almost all of the common emoticon usage online, with the prototypical smiley face – :) or :-), accounting for more than half [9]. This suggests that the set of emoticons that can be widely used is very limited. Additionally, different cultures sometimes adopt different representations for the same emotion – the textual representation of 'angry' in Japan is >.< , and is very different from the :@ commonly used in the United States[1]. Consequently, there is an inherent ambiguity in the usage of all but a very few emoticons, and expressing any kind of non-trivial emotion textually is unfeasible with these representations.

3   TextTone

TextTone attempts to address these issues by dynamically picking a representation that the reader has chosen to be meaningful and appropriate for that emotion, in that environment and on that platform. The author of a body of text semantically indicates tones in the text – much as emoticons are used today, and TextTone represents this text in an intermediate plain-text format that can be distributed to readers. When viewed, TextTone transforms the text in this format into the appropriate representation chosen locally by each reader. For example, a blogger could indicate that a certain line was written in anger, and everyone who read that line would see it represented to them in a way that indicated anger to them personally – be it with bold text, or red text, or large text, or whatever representation meant 'anger' to them.

This allows the author to select the tones that need to be conveyed, but delays the encoding of those tones until the text is viewed by the reader, thereby allowing the system to use each reader's preferred representation.

As an initial exploration into the space, TextTone was implemented as an IM client based on the open-source DAIM library [12] for the AOL Instant Messaging (AIM) architecture. We felt that an IM client would allow us to study a wide enough variety of textual social interactions to be able to meaningfully evaluate the system.

Our implementation allows the user to connect to the AIM network and to communicate with people on their buddy list. In their instant messages, users can indicate tone by demarcating blocks of text with the corresponding emoticon. Alternatively, users can select text and choose the tone from a drop-down menu. The preset tones are: *happy, very happy, upset, disappointed, angry, very angry, shocked, confused, winky, tongue-in-cheek, embarrassed* and *'none'* (the default no-tone option). The corresponding emoticons are also displayed. These tones were chosen as they represent the emoticons most commonly included with commercial IM clients. In

---

[1] In reality, :@ is not always used to represent angry. We found other emoticons for angry (and other meanings for :@) on different systems. This only serves to further illustrate our point.

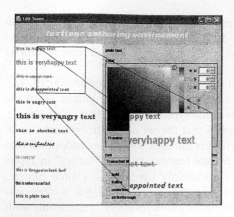

Fig. 1. The interface used to assign representations to tones in TextTone, showing the 'very happy' tone

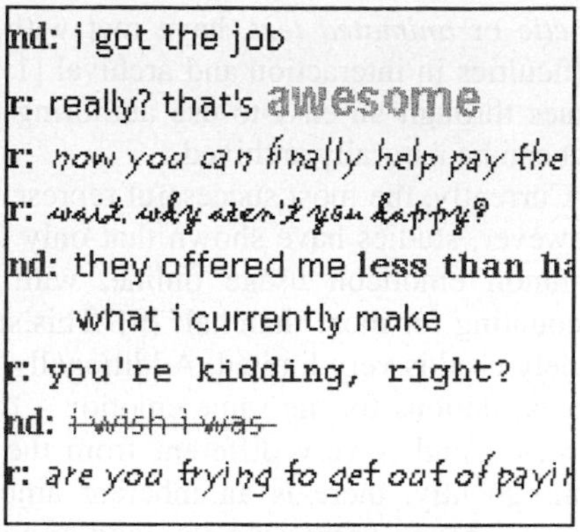

Fig. 2. An archive of one side of a conversation on TextTone. The word 'awesome' uses the 'very happy' tone

choosing a representation for emotion, users can control the text's *font-size, font-color*, and *font-face*, and whether the text is *bold, italicised, underlined* or has a *strike-through* (Figure 1).

4   Usage Scenarios

We identified several key usage scenarios where we expect TextTone to be particularly useful. These scenarios can be broadly divided into two categories – *social interaction scenarios* and *visualization scenarios*.

From a social interaction standpoint, we expect TextTone to be used in situations similar to the ones that emoticons are currently used in – *emphasis* and the *resolution of ambiguity*. For emphasis, the analogous use of emoticons would be 'Lunch is finally here! :)' or 'I had an exam today :('. Resolution of ambiguity, on the other hand, frequently occurs in situations of sarcasm or humor, such as 'I hate you ;)' or 'You're crazy :)'. Although not strictly ambiguity resolution, we will consider this to include the case when an explicit tone is used to indicate tone where none is implied, such as 'I hope I get into INTERACT 2005! :)'.

By using mappings that the users have specified to be meaningful to them, TextTone facilitates the development of a visual vocabulary of tones, which can be leveraged from a visualization perspective. Through TextTone, users can rapidly infer the tone of parts of a conversation by the style of the text used to archive it, without having to actually read the content (Figure 2). We also feel that TextTone makes it easier for users to retrieve earlier conversations based on the tones of the conversation, and not on the exact words used. For example, it is easier to find out what it was that your best friend said to make you feel better when you were upset last week, or the conversation from last month that quickly went from happy to sour.

5 Evaluation and Future Work

We conducted a preliminary qualitative evaluation of TextTone with 20 participants (8 female), with ages ranging from 18 to 32. Users were brought in pairs, were introduced to the existing AIM system and to TextTone, and were asked to interact with each other for 10-15 minutes on each system.

Results from the evaluation were decidedly positive about the use of TextTone for the expression of emotion. An analysis of the qualitative feedback revealed that most of our users (17/20) found it advantageous to use TextTone over the existing system to express emotion; and questionnaires revealed that a significant number (16/20) found it more satisfying to use. The most common disadvantage that users identified, apart from minor technical issues, was the need for extended use of the system to be able to build mappings between tones and the corresponding visual representation. We intend to conduct an extended diary study to account for this and to study more of the complex usage scenarios we have identified, such as archival and visualization.

Users commented on the similarity of the representations to actual speech, where the tone affects the delivery of the content. Users also commented that the representations were "more expressive and less annoying than emoticons", and that they "didn't have to worry about how the message may sound".

We are currently exploring automatic means of inferring tone in bodies of text. Despite the need to explicitly indicate tone in this iteration, all our users expressed a significant interest (mean=5.3/7.0, min=4.0) in using TextTone again.

References

1. Gromala, D. BioMorphic Typography. Available: http://lcc.gatech.edu/~gromala/excretia/
2. Donath, J. Karahalios, K. and Viegas, F. Visualizing Conversations. In Proceedings of the 32nd Hawaii International Conference on Systems, 1998.
3. Kiesler, S., Siegel, J., & McGuire, T.W. (1984). Social psychological aspects of computer-mediated communication. American Psychologist, 39, 1123-1134.
4. Lee, G. (2002). Typorganism: Communication Experiments focused on Interactive Kinetic Typography and Communal Interactivity in the Web Environment. MFA thesis.
5. Lee, J., Forlizzi, J., Hudson, S. E. The kinetic typography engine: An extensible system for animating expressive text. UIST02 Conference Proceedings (Paris, France), 81 - 90.
6. McCormick, N. B., & McCormick, J. W. (1992). Computer friends and foes: Contents of undergraduates' electronic mail. Computers in Human Behavior, 7, 137-147.
7. Mehrabian, A. Nonverbal Communication. Chicago: Aldine-Atherton, 1972
8. Reid, Elizabeth. (1991). Electropolis: Communication and Community on Internet Relay Chat. Thesis, Dept. of History, University of Melbourne.
9. Rezabek, L. L., & Cochenour, J. J. (1998) Visual cues in computer-mediated communication: Supplementing text with emoticons. Journal of Visual Literacy, 201-215.
10. Sarbaugh-Thompson, J.S. and Feldman, M.S. (1998) Electronic mail and organizational communication: Does saying "hi" really matter? Organization Science, 9(6), 685-698.
11. Sproull, L. & Kiesler, S. (1991). Connections. Cambridge, MA: MIT Press.
12. Walluck, D. DAIM Available: https://daim.dev.java.net/
13. Walther, J. B., & D'Addario, K. P. (2001). The Impacts of Emoticons on Message Interpretation in Computer-Mediated Communication. SSCR, 19(3), 323-345.

Lock-on-Chat: Boosting Anchored Conversation and Its Operation at a Technical Conference

Takeshi Nishida[1] and Takeo Igarashi[1,2]

[1] Department of Computer Science, The University of Tokyo
[2] PREST JST
tnishida@ui.is.s.u-tokyo.ac.jp, takeo@acm.org

Abstract. This paper introduces a text-based chat system designed to support conversations anchored to specific locations of shared images and reports our experience in operating it at a technical conference. Our system is unique in that it focuses on supporting communications scattered around among multiple images, while other systems for anchored conversations are designed for deeper discussions within a single document. Our system was used in a technical conference as a space for anchored conversations over presentation slides and we observed that audiences actively participated in discussions during the presentation. The detailed chat log was also useful for both audiences and presenters.

1 Introduction

Most synchronous and asynchronous online communications are still primarily based on texts as seen in instant messaging, BBS, and online chat. This is because text-based communication has several advantages over other communication methods such as videos or voices. One reason is that texts can show long conversation history in a single view, which is difficult with streaming media. Another reason is that texts make it possible to have simultaneous multiple conversation sessions and also to interleave them with other activities such as web browsing. Finally, they require less equipments and mental preparation.

Some text based communication systems support communications anchored into documents. Shared annotation systems (e.g. Microsoft Office Web Discussions) provide a web-based front-end for digital annotations created by readers and writers. These systems not only offer opportunities for asynchronous conversations around documents, but also encourage collaborative writing. Anchored conversations [3] is a synchronous version of such communication, providing a text-chat window anchored to a specific point in a document.

These systems are appropriate for deep discussions within a document. However, they are not suitable for communications over multiple documents because it is difficult to monitor the whole communication when messages are scattered around various locations. In a study of a shared web annotation system, Cadiz et al. reported the users' slow response time using the system [2]. Improving the notification system is one way to facilitate the conversation [1], yet it is not appropriate for synchronous systems.

M.F. Costabile and F. Paternò (Eds.): INTERACT 2005, LNCS 3585, pp. 970–973, 2005.

We have built a system called Lock-on-Chat, to support fluid transition among conversational threads anchored to multiple images. The key idea is to gather all activities and provide an interactive summary of these activities. This paper describes its user interface and reports our experience with the system at a 3-day technical conference.

2 Design Details

Lock-on-Chat allows image sharing and anchored conversation over shared images. Figure 1 shows its screenshot. The user can upload still images to the server by drag-and-drop to the client window and the uploaded images are shared by all clients. Once images are shared, the user can easily switch to different images by clicking the corresponding thumbnail in the list. Initiating a new anchored conversation is also easy; all the user has to do is to click the point of interest in an image and type the first message. We call such an anchored thread, *lock-on*.

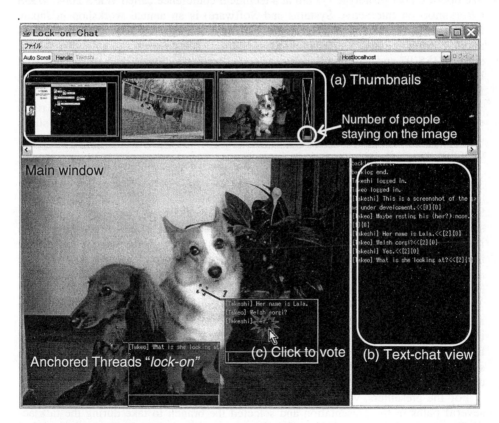

Fig. 1. Screenshot of Lock-on-Chat

Lock-on-Chat provides three features to boost anchored conversations. First, a thumbnail indicates the location of anchored threads and the number of people looking at the image (Figure 1(a)). It helps the user to detect where hot conversations are taking place at a glance.

Second, all messages are gathered and shown in chronological order just like an ordinary text-chat client in the right pane (Figure 1(b)). The user can jump to a lock-on by simply clicking the corresponding message. Messages not locked on to an image are also shown in this part; conversations are not required to be anchored.

Third, each lock-on has a simple vote function (Figure 1(c)). To vote for a lock-on, the user clicks repeatedly on it. The vote count is shown beside the lock-on and on the thumbnail. This can be used for many purposes; for example, choosing from several candidates, attracting people to the lock-on, or just expressing the excitement.

3 Experience at a Technical Conference

We operated our prototype system at a technical conference called WISS 2004. WISS (Workshop on Interactive Systems and Software) is an annual workshop in Japan, focusing on user interface technologies [6]. It is a single-track conference and has about 150 participants. Presentation sessions have been augmented by a chat system since WISS'97 and various chat systems have been tested since then. In the first trial by Rekimoto et al [5], Comic Chat [4] was operated, resulting in the strong support from participants for further trials.

During the presentations, most attendances were in the main conference room equipped with their own note PC. The contents of the main screen (presentation slides and demonstrations) were manually captured and uploaded to the server by an operator.

3.1 Results and Observations

98 people (about two-thirds of the entire participants) have connected to the chat server and sent messages at least once. Messages were sent 6.24 times/minute and images were uploaded 1.33 times/minute on average during the sessions. 48.4% of the messages were anchored to images, although the conversation was not restricted to be anchored. This heavy traffic indicates that people were able to follow and participate in the fast conversation scattered to a number of presentation slides.

For the audience, sharing the presentation slides was truly helpful. Many commented that easy access to previous slides was very helpful to follow the talk. In addition, simply having a slide at hand was helpful for people sitting a seat toward the back because the main screen was rather small compared to the room size. Moreover, some felt that they were concentrated on the presentation than usual. One reason could be that people were more attentive in order not to miss a chance to lock-on.

For the presenters, vote function seemed to be appealing. One presenter prepared several paths in the presentation and selected the branch to take during the talk according to the vote result. This attempt was successful, demonstrating the potential of dynamic, interactive presentation. The current system does not provide any assistance for the presenters, so the operator had to report the vote result each time. It is our future work to provide such functionality. Supporting the presenters to monitor the conversation would also enable them to answer questions during the presentation.

Chat log was also very beneficial to both the audience and the presenters. All captured slides (except the ones that were told as confidential by a presenter) were included in the published chat log. The chat log anchored to slides helped them to report the activities at the conference to their group and to review their presentations for improvement.

4   Conclusion and Future Work

We introduced the Lock-on-Chat system, which boosts anchored conversations with three additional features; rich thumbnails, text-chat view, and vote function. We have also reported its application to a technical conference as a chat system running in parallel with the presentation session. The results suggest that the proposed features are effective for communications over multiple documents. In addition, we have observed the importance of sharing the presentation slides and the need of supporting presenters in monitoring the conversation.

We are planning to enhance the visual effects to boost the conversation furthermore. For example, some visual effect for the vote count would attract people to the thread. We are also planning to provide assistance for presenters to monitor the conversation without controlling the GUI.

References

1. Brush, A. J. B. Bargeron, D. Jonathan, G. and Gupta, A. Notification for Shared Annotation of Digital Documents, In Proc of CHI2002.
2. Cadiz, J. Gupita, A. and Grudin, J. Using Web Annotations for Asynchronous Collaboration Around Documents, In Proc. of CSCW2000.
3. Churchill, E. F., Trevor, J., Bly, S., Nelson, L., and Cubranic, D. Anchored Conversations: Chatting in the Context of a Document, In Proc. of CHI2000.
4. Kurlander, D. Skelly, T. and Salesin, D. Comic Chat, In Proc. of SIGGRAPH96.
5. Rekimoto, J. Ayatsuka, Y. Uoi, and H. Arai, T. Adding Another Communication Channel to Reality: An Experience with a Chat-Augmented Conference, In the Conference Summary of CHI98.
6. WISS website available at http://www.wiss.org/

BROAFERENCE - A Next Generation Multimedia Terminal Providing Direct Feedback on Audience's Satisfaction Level

Uwe Kowalik, Terumasa Aoki, and Hiroshi Yasuda

Research Center of Advanced Science and Technology,
The University of Tokyo,
4-6-1 Komaba, Meguro-ku, Tokyo, 153-8904, Japan
{uwe, aoki, yasuda}@mpeg.rcast.u-tokyo.ac.jp

Abstract. In this paper we present BROAFERENCE, a test bed for studying future oriented multimedia services and applications in distributed environments. The BROAFERENCE system provides a method of direct feedback of audience satisfaction level by means of real-time smile-detection. We describe the real-time system components and we will show the result of our approach to record and transmit the data of smile intensity as a hint for 'how much the audience enjoys" the TV program.

1 Introduction

Definitely interesting for content and service providers is the feedback of the audience' satisfaction level and watching behavior. Tracking this information will be means for providing higher quality and customized contents to the audience in the future. Against this background we present a study of a new type of multimedia terminal called BROAFERENCE. The system is equipped with a module, which tracks the user's face in order to detect facial expressions of 'joy'. We are using the 'smile'-intensity as an indicator for the 'joy' emotion. Current tracking systems for TV audience' watching behavior provide only manual feedback of appreciation. The observed subjects have to give the feedback by themselves and the awareness about giving the feedback is required. This will influence the preciseness of the result and moreover in will effect the user's experience negatively. The advantage of our approach within the BROAFERENCE system is deriving the information of appreciation from the user's face. The system provides a direct feedback of a spontaneous emotion compared to current methods. Based on a vision based tracking SDK' provided by NVision we developed a real-time smile detection module, which continuously outputs a value proportional to the smile intensity while the user is watching TV. The smile intensity value is synchronized with the program time, recorded or transmitted and can be used as a hint how much the audience enjoyed the program. In the following first an overview of related work will be given. Than our implementation approach of BROAFERENCE will be introduced to the reader and described in detail.

M.F. Costabile and F. Paternò (Eds.): INTERACT 2005, LNCS 3585, pp. 974–977, 2005.

2 Related Work

Many different approaches and combinations of algorithms have been proposed for the purpose of face detection and face feature detection. Color based approaches try to detect the face by skin color 1. The approach of 2 directly locates eyes, mouth, and face boundary based on measurements derived from the color-space components of an image. 3 uses an invariant feature based approach exploiting the geometrical structure of a face to detect facial feature points in gray level images by graph matching. A combination of feature-based and image-vector-based approach is presented in 4 combining Higher-order Local Auto-Correlation features and fisher weight maps to detect facial expressions of smile. The BROAFERENCE system uses a commercial face detection module that provides face features. In this paper we focus on deriving a facial expression of smile describing intensity value in real-time under near-reality conditions (i.e. lighting conditions may change).

3 System Overview and User Feedback

The block diagram of the BROAFERENCE terminal and the feedback module can be seen in Fig. 1. Media streams can be received over a network connection. The composition of media streams and other data is described by contents description, rendered by a compositor and displayed at the screen. A camera takes the video of the person in front of the terminal and hands the images to the feedback analyzer that analyzes the expressions shown at the user's face in real-time. The face tracker module finds the user's face and provide the geometric information of specific points (e.g. mouth corners, eye center, etc.). Fig. 2 visualizes the output of the tracker module. The output builds a vector of 44 elements consisting of the x- and y-components of the features. In addition to the facial features, we obtain the global position of the face' projection in the image plane determined by $P(x, y)$ with $0<=x, y<=1.0$ independent of the image size. A scale factor z with $z \sim d$, where d is the distance of the face to the camera plane. The Euler-angles for the rotation of the face around the x-, y- and z-axis are provided too. The smile detection module provides an intensity value of smile calculated from the tracked mouth points. The smile intensity value is in the range between 0.0 and 1.0, whereas a value of 0.0 means 'no smile' and a value of 1.0 is related to 'big smile' expression. A compensation of head translation, rotation and scale is performed before applying a neural network classifier to the mouth feature set. The resulting feature vector is 16-dimensional. For classification of the mouth shape represented by the 16-dimensional input vector a feed-forward network with three layers has been designed. The input layer consists of sixteen neurons to fit the feature vector's dimension. A hidden layer with two neurons and an output layer with one neuron complete the network. A training set of 268 samples has been used for training. 50% of the input pattern have been labeled as 'smile' and 50 % have been labeled as 'no smile.

The training patterns have been extracted semi-automatically from video sequences taken from three persons posing 'smile' and 'no smile' expressions. The whole video database consists of sequences of six people. Each sequence contains about one minute of video. A set of three sequences has been used to extract the data for 'untrained' patterns to verify the performance. During the pattern generation step the video of facial expressions is presented to the test person. In the case the person recognizes a smile in the video sequence, he/she clicks a button for smile. The same procedure has been applied to 'no smile' expressions. Doing so ensures a natural judgment by a human observer.

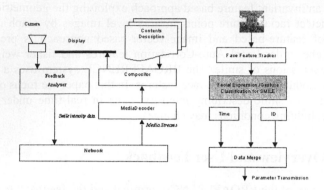

Fig. 1. Block diagram of BROAFERENCE terminal and feedback system

Fig. 2. The system tracks 22 features, 8 mouth features are used

In Fig. 3 sample images taken from our video database are shown. The upper row images were used to train the network. The lower row images have been used for verification. For training the network we used the 'Resilient Propagation' method (Rprop). A detailed description of the algorithm can be found in 5 .

Fig. 3. Sample images of our video database

4 Experiments and Results

After training the network classifier the video sequences of previously unknown persons have been presented to the system. The processing time for classifying the extracted mouth features has been measured and takes 3 ms in average per video frame. The performance of the used tracker is satisfying also under darker lighting conditions, but it heavily depends on the used camera model.

Fig. 4. Smile intensity values

In Fig. 4 a sample pictures taken during the verification process can be seen. The intensity of the smile recognized by the system is represented by the colored bar in the right images. The polygon is the shape of the mouth formed by the tracked features.

5 Summary

In this paper we introduced the new feature for providing direct feedback of audience' satisfaction level by automatically recognizing the facial expression of smile in order to provide a hint of how much the audience enjoyed the program. The future work will focus on facial expressions taking other emotions like boredom or sadness into account. We believe that our approach of direct feedback will help to improve the quality of future TV programs and multimedia presentations which will finally improve the user experience and contribute to a richer life by exploiting latest technology advances.

References

1. S.Singh, D.S. Chauhan, A Robust Skin Color Based Face Detection Algorithm, Tamkang Journal of Science and Engineering, Vol.6, No.4, pp227-234, 2003
2. R.-L. Hsu, M. Abdel-Mottaleb, A. K. Jain, Face detection in color images, IEEE Trans. Pattern Analysis and Machine Intelligence, vol. 24, no. 5, May 2002
3. J.Buhmann, J.Lange, C.von der Mahlsburg, Distortion invariant Object Recognition Matching Hierarchically Labeled Graphs, Proc. Int. Joint Conf. Neural Networks, 1989
4. Y.Shinohara, N.Otsu, Facial Expression Recognition Using Fisher Weight Maps, Sixth IEEE International Conference on Automatic Face and Gesture Recognition, Soul, 2004
5. M Riedmiller. Untersuchungen zu Konvergenz und Generalisierungsverhalten überwachter Lernverfahren mit dem SNNS. Proc. of the SNNS workshop, 1993

ChatAmp: Talking with Music and Text

M. Ian Graham and Karrie Karahalios

Department of Computer Science,
University of Illinois,
Urbana, IL 61801 U.S.A.
{mgraham2, kkarahal}@cs.uiuc.edu

Abstract. Current systems for synchronous, text-based communication offer more varied interactions than e-mail, but cannot easily convey non-verbal or emotional information in an unobtrusive and intuitive manner. In this report we introduce ChatAmp, a new chat system which incorporates music as a central part of social interaction. Music is used in order to create an unobtrusive ambient soundscape that gives information about conversational activity and emotion using changes to instrument behavior. This soundscape acts as a peripheral channel to let a multitasking user monitor the conversation while focused elsewhere without being interrupted by jarring alert sounds. By combining this with non-sequential visualization which groups all of a user's activity in his area of the screen, ChatAmp provides "at-a-glance" information through both auditory and visual channels. Informal user tests support the effectiveness of integrating music and conversation in achieving the goals above and suggest directions for further research.

1 Introduction

Instant messaging (IM) and chat systems have potential for much richer social interaction than asynchronous mediums such as e-mail. However, this potential has been largely unfulfilled by modern text-based interfaces which use bare sequential text. Conveying social cues or emotional information is difficult, and alerts that indicate events while users are focused elsewhere are distracting and uninformative. With this as a problem to be solved, we created a new system called ChatAmp which integrates text, visuals, and music to produce a new style of chat. Unlike existing systems, sound does not act as a mere decoration or distracting alert bell, but provides an unobtrusive ambient channel (reinforced by corresponding visuals) for relaying emotional cues and activity information.

Many past systems have used visualization or sonification to change the experience of chat. The Palace [6] visualizes users with portrait-based avatars that converse through speech bubbles. Closer in spirit to our project are pieces like Chat Circles and Talking in Circles [7] which provide an abstract visual avatar in the form of a circle whose location influences social dynamics. ChatAmp aims to use dynamic positioning of bare text in space to provide at-a-glance information and reinforce musical cues. Sonification projects like Listening Post [2] produce music from chat rooms, but are made to depict thousands of conversations, not to be used during a single chat.

M.F. Costabile and F. Paternò (Eds.): INTERACT 2005, LNCS 3585, pp. 978–981, 2005.
© IFIP International Federation for Information Processing 2005

Recent ubiquitous computing research involves the use of an ambient soundscape to convey peripheral information to the user, as in A Whisper in the Woods [3]. ChatAmp provides a similar ambient channel specifically for chat, using music as a more natural sound environment than abstract sounds.

Fig. 1. Shot of an example conversation in ChatAmp. Usernames and corresponding messages are grouped in clusters and arranged in a roughly circular configuration.

2   ChatAmp

ChatAmp's visualization (see Fig. 1) arranges text in 2D to give activity information and support musical cues. Users are identified by "clusters" of text that consist of any recent messages plus the username indicated in a different color. Presence of these clusters on-screen gives an immediate indication of the number of people participating (and thus the size of one's audience). Messages fade and disappear over time, and when all are gone a user is considered inactive—this causes his instrument to stop playing. When an instrument is playing, the username on-screen comes to life, shifting back and forth with each note. Thus, both visual and auditory cues let the user see and hear who is talking, and give a brief history of activity.

Our design centers around the integration of music into a conversation, and uses changes to existing music data to enhance communication rather than generating new music algorithmically. The main issue we addressed is how to convey information through and give meaning to this music in the context of a text-based conversation.

To truly enrich users' communication, a mutual relationship between music and conversation is needed. We designed for such a relationship as follows:

- Given an arbitrary song, instruments are split among users of the chat space, and each participant is associated with the sound of a specific instrument.
- Music is audible to all users and is affected in real time by user activity. Instruments of active users produce sound while instruments of inactive users are silent.
- Visualization of the conversation is directly affected by the music. The visuals associated with one user will move in time with the sound of her instruments.

The effect of music on the visual display serves to strengthen the mapping between user and instrument. It is easier for a user to detect the effects of his activity if feedback is received through both visual and auditory information, and if these two are in concert then the outcome should be further improved [4].

Using music in this manner also allows for the communication of information to the user unobtrusively in the periphery, while her attention is on another application. Rather than using sudden discrete alert sounds as in current IM and chat systems, ChatAmp makes changes to music that is always present in the background. Because each user is associated with an instrument, an "auditory glance" will yield immediate information about who is active and who is inactive.

The association of a user with specific sounds also introduces the possibility of communicating emotion through the peripheral audio channel. An early approach to this which we take as a preliminary experiment is to detect a basic set of emoticons in a user's messages and respond with a simple operation on their instrument output. In our first attempt we use a simple pitch bend: an instrument bends up for happy emoticons and down for sad. Pitch bends were chosen because pitch-based representations of data like Earcons [1] have been proven effective as information displays.

ChatAmp was implemented as a Java Swing application. MIDI was selected as our music format to make real-time manipulation of songs straightforward.

3 Evaluation

Preliminary, informal evaluation of ChatAmp was conducted by letting ten students use the program and collecting feedback through verbal interviews. After brief testing of different genres, electronic music was selected for use with the program, as the removal of arbitrary instruments is much more likely to leave a coherent song.

With no instruction, users immediately intuited the function of text clusters in identifying individuals. Due to the motion of usernames, several users described their roles as "dancers" against the backdrop of their own words. Based on this feedback, the "avatar" in ChatAmp appears to arise not from spatial representation but rather from kinetic properties of text: users described each other as having different personalities based on a song's instruments. This seems to indicate that personality can be embodied in forms other than avatars based on static 2D images or 3D models [5], and prompts reconsideration of the nature of online avatars.

Testers found it very easy to judge approximately how many users are active at a given time by listening to the program's music output or glancing at the visualization. Determining the identity of specific individuals from the sound of their instruments was a much harder task, with limited success. Whether this would improve with extended use is a question for future investigation.

Emotional cues through music were the one element of ChatAmp that users did not learn on their own. After being informed about pitch changes in response to emoticons, however, testers easily identified emotional events from prominent instruments in the song.

An unexpected finding is that the silence of inactivity is perceived as awkward and results in pressure on users to keep typing. This causes tension if messages fade too quickly. The fade time in our first implementation was 10 seconds, and this proved to be much too fast for relaxed conversation.

4 Future Work

Immediate work to follow in ChatAmp's development will involve detailed studies to determine its effect on users in comparison to current chat applications. Two important items to test are satisfaction levels and impact on productivity for tasks performed with different types of peripheral audio channels. Also, by comparing the number of messages sent with and without audio, we hope to quantitatively measure the effect of ChatAmp's music on user activity. Finally, a survey-based study will yield information about how an individual perceives others differently when their spatial or musical configuration changes.

The next important step is to consider how to redesign the UI of ChatAmp to provide users further ability to express themselves in new ways. Giving users more explicit musical control may allow for richer and more intuitive interaction.

References

1. Brewster, S., Wright, P., Edwards, A. An Evaluation of Earcons for Use in Auditory Human-Computer Interfaces. Proceedings of INTERCHI 1993
2. Hansen, H., Rubin, M. and B. Listening Post: Giving Voice to Online Communication. Proceedings of ICAD 2002
3. Kilander, F., Lonnqvist, P. A Whisper in the Woods – An Ambient Soundscape for Peripheral Awareness of Remote Processes. Proceedings of ICAD 2002
4. McGrath, M., Summerfield, Q. Intermodal Timing Relations and Audio-Visual Speech Recognition by Normal-Hearing Adults. Journal of the Acoustic Society of America. Vol. 77, Iss. 2. February 1985
5. Suler, J. The Psychology of Avatars and Graphical Space in Multimedia Chat Communities. http://www.rider.edu/~suler/psycyber/psyav.html
6. The Palace. http://www.thepalace.com
7. Viegas, F., Donath, J. The Chat Circles Series: Explorations in designing abstract graphical communication interfaces. Proceedings of Designing Interactive Systems (DIS) 2002

The Optimal Focus Position When Scrolling Using a Small Display

James Whalley and Andrew Monk

CUHTec, Department of Psychology, University of York,
York, YO10 5DD, UK
A.Monk@psych.york.ac.uk
http://www.cuhtec.org.uk/

Abstract. When scrolling through a list on a small display, such as that on a cell phone, the "focus" is the currently highlighted item that would be selected were the user to stop scrolling and choose select. When scrolling through a list that is longer than the number of items that may be displayed simultaneously, the focus position becomes stationary and the items scroll under it. An experiment is reported which varies this stationary focus position in a five item display. It was either: the last item in window (end stop scheme), the next to last (view forward one item) or the centre (view forward two items). The centre position allowed significantly faster scrolling than the other two positions.

1 Introduction

Scrolling is the term used to describe various interaction techniques for varying the window of displayed material onto a sequential object such as a document or list that is too large to be displayed all at once. For example, there are well established conventions for using a scroll bar in graphical user interfaces utilising a mouse or stylus. This paper is concerned with small devices such as cell phones where conventions for scrolling are still developing.

With these very small digital displays there is often no pointing device to parallel the mouse and hence no way to select an item with a single action. The alternative is to display a "focus". This is the item that is visually highlighted as being the one that would be selected were the user to choose "select". In the first panel of Fig. 1, item 3 is under the focus in the centre of the display. Subsequent panels in Fig. 1 show how, initially, the focus moves down the display as the user scrolls. When the focus reaches the bottom of the window it remains stationary and the list moves under it (see last two panels in Fig. 1). This "end stop" scheme is commonly used on cell phones. Fig. 2 depicts a small variation on this interaction technique to provide "view forward" which is found on some phones. Here the focus becomes stationary and the list starts to move when the focus reaches the penultimate item in the display. This provides the user with a fleeting opportunity to see an item before it becomes the focus. Still other phones keep the focus stationary at the centre of the display. This paper reports an experiment which varies the focus position in a five item display: last item visible, next to last and centre. The aim was to identify the optimal focus position for rapid scrolling through a large list such as an address list.

M.F. Costabile and F. Paternò (Eds.): INTERACT 2005, LNCS 3585, pp. 982–985, 2005.

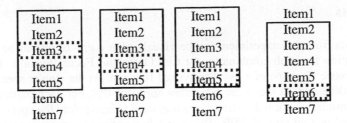

Fig. 1. Standard scrolling scheme (end stop), the solid box is the window displayed, the dotted box is the focus

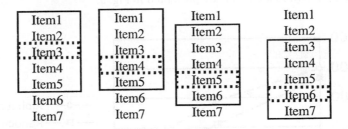

Fig. 2. View forward scheme, see Fig. 1 for explanation

2 Method

A 50 item list was constructed consisting of randomly paired first and second names. These were presented at 1.5, 2.5, 3.5, and 4.5 items per second on a small display simulated on a PC. Pressing the mouse button commenced scrolling, letting it go stopped it. On each trial the user was given a target name and asked to stop scrolling with this target in focus. Any trial when they did this on the first press was counted as a hit.

As suggested above, analysis of the user's task suggested that focus positions 3 and 4 might have advantages over position 5 because the target could be seen before it came under the focus. This advantage would be expected to be most evident when the user has no knowledge of what is coming next in the list. This was the case in the randomly presented lists, where the list order was randomised separately for each trial. However, this is not very natural. An address list, for example, will generally be alphabetised and hence always appear in the same order. For this reason half the trials used a list presented in the same alphabetical order each time.

Six experimental conditions were formed by factorially combining the three focus positions with the two list orders. With 20 replications this means each of the 6 users completed 480 trials. Testing was split into 120 trial blocks. Within each block there were 10 replications of each Focus Position by Speed of Scrolling condition random-ised separately for each participant. Two blocks (one alphabetic and one random) would be completed on one day with a half-hour gap between, with the remaining two blocks a week later, The order participants received the blocks was counterbalanced between days and participants. The 6 participants in this experiment were all under-graduate students.

3 Results

The raw data from this experiment can be visualised as a plot of hit rate against speed of presentation for each combination of List Order and Focus Position. These plots have the classic 'S' shape of a psychophysical function. At the slower speeds hit rates approach 100% and at the faster rates they approach 0%. For each participant curve fitting (a cumulative normal distribution) was used to interpolate the speed that would have resulted in a hit rate of 75%. This was taken as the maximum acceptable scrolling speed for that experimental condition. These rates in items per second were then submitted to analysis of variance. Means items per second for the three Scrolling Positions and the two List Orders are presented in Fig. 3.

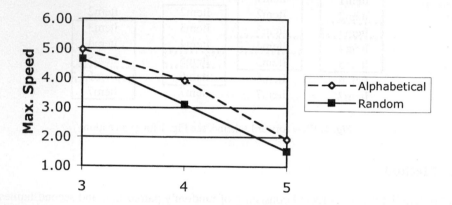

Fig. 3. Mean interpolated maximum speed in items per second for random and alphabetical lists. Position 3 is the centre of the display, and position 5 is the last.

These results can be straightforwardly interpreted as a main effect of Focus Position ($F(2, 10) = 44.513$, $p < .05$) and a smaller main effect of List Order ($F(1, 10) = 18.313$, $p < .05$). There was no significant interaction, i.e., the effect of focus position is the same for both list orders ($F(2, 10) = 1.501$, n.s.). The effect of focus position is considerable, moving it up from position 5 to position 4 doubles the speed at which users can scroll. There was a similar increase in the estimated maximum speed moving from position 4 to position 3. Tukey's HSD test showed that all pairwise comparisons of these three means were statistically significant.

4 Implications for Design

Users can scroll faster when they have preview of the items before they fall under the cursor and having preview of two items permits faster scrolling speeds than having one. On this basis it is recommended that the focus position should be at least two items up, and not the last item in the window as is commonly the case with cell phones.

It is not clear how this result arises. It could be because users are then able to fixate the bottom line of the display, allowing for reaction time when the target comes in view. If this were the case, then one might expect it to be reflected in the rates expressed as seconds per item rather than items per second. In fact, the difference between two items preview (centre position) and one item (penultimate) is only .077 s/item as compared with .296 s/item for the difference between no preview (last) and one item. Alternatively the users may be fixating the focus and extracting information about the up coming items in peripheral vision. The results of Eriksen and Eriksen (1974) indicate that this is possible with the display used here. The likely answer is that there is some complex combination of peripheral vision and fixation strategy going on here that can only be properly explored with eye movement monitoring.

Five items per second is faster than the average phone currently scrolls. Of course there will be large differences in acceptable scrolling rates across individual users and so to take advantage of the faster rates that are possible the user needs to be given control of the scrolling rate. How this may is done depends very much on the hardware controls available. An isometric joystick where pressure maps onto speed of scrolling would be very advantageous and could potentially make the phone a Fitts' Law device (MacKenzie, 2003). Thus, when scrolling an alphabetised list the user could use knowledge of the approximate position of the target item to vary the speed of scrolling efficiently.

Of course, there are other factors than scrolling speed governing the position of the cursor such as ease of learning and ease of use. The next step is to test such a scheme with new and experienced users and using real phones to check there are no unforeseen side effects of making such a change.

References

1. Eriksen, B.A. and Eriksen, C.W. (1974) Effects of noise letters upon the identification of a target letter in a nonsearch task. Perception and Psychophysics, 16, 143-149.
2. MacKenzie, I.S. (2003) Motor behaviour models for human-computer interaction, in Carroll, J.M. (Ed.) *HCI Models, theories and frameworks,* San Francisco: Elsevier Science, pp27-54.

Collaboration with DiamondTouch

Stephen G. Kobourov, Kyriacos Pavlou, Justin Cappos, Michael Stepp,
Mark Miles, and Amanda Wixted

Department of Computer Science,
University of Arizona

Abstract. We study the performance of collaborative spatial/visual
tasks under different input configurations. The configurations used are a
traditional mouse-monitor, a shared-monitor with multiple-mice, and a
multi-user input device (DiamondTouch). Our experiments indicate that
there is a significant variation in performance for the different configurations with pairs of users, while there is no such variation with individual
users. The traditional configuration is not well-suited for collaborative
tasks, and even after augmenting it to a shared monitor with multiple-
mice it is still significantly inferior to the multi-user input device.

1 Introduction

The traditional mouse-monitor-keyboard configuration was designed for a single user and it does not lend itself easily to collaborative spatial/visual tasks.
When more than one users interact with one computer, typically there is one
user interacting and the others are "back-seat drivers." Moreover, augmenting
a mouse-monitor setup to a shared monitor with multiple mice and keyboards
is also unlikely to significantly improve performance in collaborative tasks, compared to input devices designed for collaborative use.

The DiamondTouch table [2] is a touch-sensitive input device which supports
concurrent operation by up to four users. The table detects multiple and simultaneous tactile events and can distinguish between each user's touch. The users
interact with the table by placing their finger(s) on the touch-sensitive surface
while sitting or standing upon a receiver pad, which closes a low signal circuit.
The DiamondTouch table offers advantages for applications that benefit from
collaboration, as well as applications that allow interaction through more than
one contact point at a time. These properties make it especially attractive for
design, architecture and 3D modeling applications.

One of the earliest uses of the DiamondTouch table was for a collaborative
game, TetraTetris [1]. In the early days of touchscreen research and development,
Schneiderman listed some of the desirable qualities of being able to use one's
fingers directly on the display screen [4]. The relationship between group size
and table size in collaborative work has also been studied [3].

We compared the user-pairs performance of spatial/visual problems using
three different input configurations: one-mouse and one-monitor, two-mice and

M.F. Costabile and F. Paternò (Eds.): INTERACT 2005, LNCS 3585, pp. 986–989, 2005.
© IFIP International Federation for Information Processing 2005

one-monitor, and the DiamondTouch table. Despite the familiarity of the traditional mouse interactions, the DiamondTouch setup yielded the best performance thus confirming that it offers a significant advantage for collaborative work on spatial/visual problems. To ensure that the results are not due to other differences between the DiamondTouch and the mouse-monitor configurations, we also tested individual users. There was no significant difference in individual performance on the mouse-monitor versus the DiamondTouch configurations.

2   Experimental Setup

In order to compare the different hardware configurations for collaborative work on spacial/visual problems, we presented user-pairs with a series of three graph problems (crossings removal) with increasing difficulty. We measured the time required to solve each problem, and recorded the mean time to completion over the three problems. We performed the experiments on three input configurations:

One-mouse and one-monitor: The first configuration was the standard one-mouse and one-monitor setup. In all the experiments we used the same computer (Dell Pentium 4 desktop running Windows XP) with a 52cm diagonal LCD display. Typically, the users ended up with one dominant user manipulating the input with the other one in a "back-seat driver" role.

Two-mice and one-monitor: The second configuration was a two-mice and one-monitor set-up, allowing both users to simultaneously interact with the system. Note that just attaching a second mouse the the computer is not a good solution as it defeats the purpose of collaboration. When two mice are attached to the same computer, one "steals" the cursor from the other, whenever movement is detected. Therefore, we modified our system to allow two mouse-cursors, each independently controlled by its own mouse, using the CPNMouse project drivers (`http://cpnmouse.sourceforge.net`).

DiamondTouch table: The DiamondTouch hardware used in this study has a surface with a 79cm diagonal and a 4:3 aspect ratio. The table is connected through a USB cable to a Dell Pentium 4 desktop PC running Windows XP. All images, which normally appear on the display monitor,

Fig. 1. Physical setup

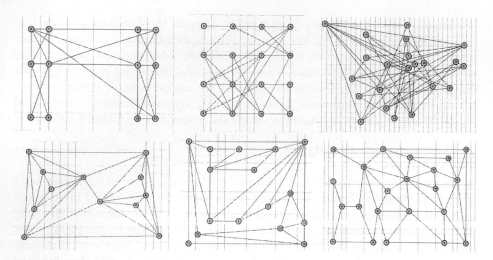

Fig. 2. Each column contains an input graph and one of the possible plane drawings

are routed to a video projector that projects them onto the table surface with the aid of a mirror; see Fig. 1.

The task: Each of the three problems featured a 2-dimensional straight-line representation of a planar graph with crossings; the task was to "untangle" this graph by moving the vertices until a representation without crossings was found. Since there is no unique planar representation for the test graphs, any planar representation arrived to by the users was considered a valid solution. All graphs were constructed and solved using custom-built software which allows for easy click-and-drag manipulation of graphs. The GUI was identical in all configurations, except that in the two-mice case there were two mouse-cursors on the screen. Clicking on a node (or placing a finger on it) selects the node and dragging the mouse (finger) moves the node. The graphs are shown in Fig. 2.

The test subjects: Our users were college students who were proficient computer users. The test subjects did not necessarily have knowledge of graphs or graph theory. All test subjects were initially given a short training session (less than 5 minutes) using an easy graph problem, to allow them to familiarize themselves with the experimental setup, the software and the task at hand. The assignment of the user-pair to one of the three hardware configurations was done at random and in all three configurations user-pairs sat side by side. The users were presented with the same series of graph problems and were asked to collaborate in solving the problems. Times for each of the three graph problems were recorded and their mean was taken.

3   Experimental Results

The seven user-pairs who worked on the DiamondTouch table averaged 302 seconds per problem. The eight user-pairs who worked on the two-mouse and

Result Summary			
Test type	Sample size	Mean	Standard Deviation
one-mouse (pairs)	8	480	223
two-mice (pairs)	8	464	119
DiamondTouch (pairs)	7	302	119
one-mouse (individuals)	9	536	313
DiamondTouch (individuals)	9	558	197

Fig. 3. Summary of experimental results

one-monitor configuration averaged 464 seconds per problem. Finally, the eight user-pairs who worked on the one-mouse and one-monitor configuration averaged 480 seconds per problem. We used the robust two-sample t-test to verify that there is a statistically significant difference in the population means; see Fig. 3. The test yielded a p-value of 0.011, so at a 95% confidence level the hypothesis that the DiamondTouch setup outperformed the two-mouse and one-monitor setup for the collaborative untangling of graphs, was accepted.

There is a possibility that the better performance of the user-pairs on the DiamondTouch table is the result of the display size, or display orientation, or speed of touch-interactions compared to mouse-interactions. In an effort to eliminate these possibilities, we also compared the performance of single users on the DiamondTouch table versus the traditional one-mouse and one-monitor setup. We conjectured that the improvement in the case of collaborative use on the DiamondTouch table will not be seen in single-user interactions. With this in mind, we performed the same experiments as in the case of user-pairs and found that in the case of individual users, there was no significant difference in the mean completion time. The nine single-users who worked on the DiamondTouch table averaged 558 seconds per problem, while the nine single-users who worked on the one-mouse and one-monitor configuration averaged 536 seconds per problem. Again, using the two-sample t-test (p-value = 0.567) we verified that at a 95% confidence level there is no statistically significant difference in the performance of the DiamondTouch table versus the traditional mouse-monitor setup for the individual untangling of graphs.

References

1. C. Collberg, S. G. Kobourov, S. Kobes, B. Smith, S. Trush, and G. Yee. Tetratetris: An application of multi-user touch-based human-computer interaction. In *9th Intl. Conf. on Human-Computer Interaction (INTERACT)*, pages 81–88, 2003.
2. P. Dietz and D. Leigh. Diamondtouch: A multi-user touch technology. In *14th ACM Symp. on User Interface Software and Technology (UIST)*, pages 219–226, 2001.
3. K. Ryall, C. Forlines, C. Shen, and M. Ringel-Morris. Exploring the effects of group size and table size on interactions with tabletop shared-display groupware. In *ACM Conference on Computer Supported Cooperative Work*, pages 284–293, 2004.
4. B. Shneiderman. Touchscreens now offer compelling uses. *IEEE Software*, 8(2):93–94, 107, 1991.

Preference-Based Group Scheduling

Jiang Hu and Mike Brzozowski

Stanford University
{huj, zozo}@Stanford.edu

Abstract. Traditional group scheduling applications often treat users' availability as binary: free or busy. This is an unrealistic representation because not all times are equally free or busy. The inflexibility makes it difficult to find times with which everyone is truly satisfied. We present an online group scheduling approach by which users indicate four-tier preferences for meeting times on a calendar, which dynamically adjusts to provide instant feedback and suggests optimal meeting times for all participants. Our prototype is geared toward college students and the scheduling is done through a democratic and open negotiation process where everyone's preference is heard. Students who evaluated the prototype thought that the scheduling process was more efficient than the widely-used e-mail scheduling among college students, which is largely based on binary availability.

1 Introduction

Even though many group scheduling applications are commercially available [1], they are still considered "the least useful groupware application" [2]. Group scheduling has come to be viewed, as Palen [3] describes it, as "less an 'optimizing' task and more often a 'satisficing' task." A primary limitation of traditional group scheduling systems is that they treat users' time as binary: *free* or *busy*. The inflexibility of such treatments tends to make group scheduling a lengthy and frustrating process. In reality, not all free times are created equal, nor are all busy times absolutely immutable. This is especially true for college students.

Unlike business users, college students have very erratic schedules and often find themselves "at work" 24x7. During academic quarters/semesters, students have to meet in groups for class projects, assignments, social activities, and so on. However, when the meeting involves multiple students who are not often in the same place to discuss availability, scheduling becomes difficult.

Current groupware scheduling systems are expensive and typically designed for corporate users. Our own experience and interviews with fellow students, however, suggest that college students also desire a way to easily schedule meetings with a minimum of effort, and without constant maintenance of an additional calendar. In fact, many universities nowadays provide students with online registration services that generate weekly schedules on a quarter or semester basis. Group scheduling systems for students can readily tap into existing online registration systems and directly address many of Grudin's concerns over groupware [2].

M.F. Costabile and F. Paternò (Eds.): INTERACT 2005, LNCS 3585, pp. 990–993, 2005.

2   Preference-Based Group Scheduling

Beard *et al.*'s Visual Scheduler [4] introduced a "priority-based" scheduling system, allowing users to mark any given *busy* time slots with five levels of gray shading to indicate "low" to "highest" priority. However, no attempt was made to distinguish between better or worse *free* times. In general, Visual Scheduler and similar systems operate within the relatively controlled domain of an office environment.

Here we introduce a scheduling system based not on users' absolute *availability* as a traditional "free/busy" binary but rather on users' *preferences*, extending the Visual Scheduler model by allowing users to indicate their better and worse free times as well as busy times. The system is designed so that it is to each user's advantage to respond quickly to a meeting request.

2.1   Contextual Inquiry

In order to have a clear picture of students' group scheduling behaviors, we observed and interviewed some students from an introductory HCI class at Stanford University. We found that students in general use e-mail to schedule meetings when it is impractical do so face-to-face. To simulate the common scenario where a professor groups students in project teams, we e-mailed five groups of four randomly selected student volunteers, asking each group to find a good time for an ostensibly "focus group" meeting on interface design.

To our surprise, only three groups finished the scheduling task and they all used e-mail as the primary means of communication. Inferring from our correspondence with the failing groups, the frustration associated with the e-mail scheduling process appeared to be a significant barrier to completing the task.

Most importantly, we observed that asynchronous group scheduling typically takes one of two routes: 1) *Negotiation:* One student initiates an e-mail thread by enumerating several potential meeting times he/she is free to seek other students' opinions on those times. As others respond, a consensus is reached by process of elimination; 2) *Aggregation:* One student from the group sends an e-mail asking for everyone's availabilities. After getting every member's schedule, the student manually combines them and selects a meeting time for the group. In either case, the inherent problem with binary availability was frequently pronounced in the form of multiple rounds of negotiation and involuntary acceptance of sub-optimal times.

2.2   The Prototype

Our prototype blends the two strategies by *aggregating* user calendars to automatically select optimal meeting times and then letting users *negotiate* through providing additional information about their time constraints and preferences. The prototype takes the form of an Excel workbook. Each worksheet of the workbook contains a grid of a user's schedule for the following week. Every cell in this grid represents a 30-minute block and can be marked/colored with one of the following labels (borrowed from Evite [5]):

- *Works Great:* "This is one of the best times for me."
- *Is OK:* "I could come, but there are other times that work better."

- *Rather Not:* "I'd rather not do it then but I could come if I had to."
- *Can't Make It:* "There is no way I can meet then."

Depending on the color assigned, each cell is assigned a numeric value from 0 (Can't Make It) to 3 (Works Great). Cells without a color are treated as "Is OK," receiving the value of 2, because people are generally apathetic about times that are acceptable to them. Also, this provides extra incentive to people to correct the model if it is actually a bad time.

On the worksheet that aggregates all group members' schedules, each cell's score is computed as the average of the value each user labeled it, and the optimal time periods for meeting are those that span the maximal set of scores, as those are the times that maximize overall satisfaction within the group. To avoid confusion, we restrict the best times selected so that they do not overlap.

During the set-up stage, users are encouraged to label their firm time commitments with one of the latter two categories so the coloring closely corresponds to their quarterly schedules. When a user receives a workbook during the negotiation process, the application has suggested five times that it thinks are optimal. The user can respond by coloring cells in and near the proposed time. Upon making any change, the system automatically re-computes the best options, so the user can ensure that the proposed times are acceptable before forwarding the workbook on to the next user.

3 Evaluation and Results

Twenty students from an introductory communication class participated in the user study for course credit. Upon signing up, the 12 male students and 8 female students were randomly assigned to five groups of four students.

There are three major steps. First, each group was given instructions similar to those used in our initial contextual inquiry except that these five new groups had to identify *two* possible times for a focus group meeting. Second, during the meeting at a scheduled time, participants used our prototype to schedule another hour-long meeting for the coming week. Their first subtask was to label firm time commitments based on their quarterly schedules as if this was done at the start of the quarter/semester. The second subtask was to check the top five meeting times recommended by the prototype, and to modify their schedules for the coming week so as the prototype could adjust its recommendations based on accurate schedules and time preferences. The order in which they took turns to modify their calendars was identical to the order in which they first started/responded to their scheduling e-mail threads. Lastly, the participants filled out an online questionnaire to compare the second subtask with e-mail scheduling.

In the first step, four of the five groups were able to identify only one possible meeting time via e-mail; one of the four groups did not evaluate the prototype due to the absence of one group member. E-mail records indicate that all four groups went through *negotiation* instead of *aggregation*. On average, each student had to read about seven e-mails before a mutually acceptable meeting time was selected.

With the help of the prototype's aggregation, however, three of the four groups finished their scheduling task with five possible meeting times after only one round of negotiation. This is far more efficient than e-mail scheduling. As a result, participants compared the prototype favorably with conventional scheduling using e-mail: they thought the prototype was "easy to use" [M_{easy} = 8.31, SD = 1.71, on a 10-point Likert scale], and "user-friendly" [$M_{friendly}$ = 8.13, SD = 1.25]. They also indicated high likelihood to try out an application based on our prototype and to recommend it to friends and classmates.

4 Conclusion

Our preference-based scheduling system shortens the negotiation process during group scheduling and recommends multiple, ranked, meeting times. We have identified a new segment of users underserved by current scheduling solutions, and applied the insights gained through contextual inquiry to construct the prototype. As our evaluation indicates, greater satisfaction with the meeting times should be expected, potentially contributing to harmonious and productive collaborations among meeting attendees.

We evaluated our prototype against scheduling through e-mail, but the advantages the prototype holds may well extend to other scheduling systems based on binary availability. The preference-based principle can be applied to other contexts than college campus. If synchronized with actively used personal or group calendars such as Microsoft Outlook or a PDA, such a system could become even more powerful.

The model we present also provides a framework for automated optimal scheduling, potentially based on incomplete information. We demonstrated that users are comfortable negotiating with this model, providing a platform on which to test probabilistic and empirical techniques for hypothesizing about preferences.

References

1. Palen, L, Grudin, J.: Discretionary Adoption of Group Support Software: Lessons from Calendar Applications. Implementing Collaboration Technologies in Industry. Springer-Verlag, Berlin Heidelberg New York (2003) 159-179
2. Grudin, J.: Groupware and Social Dynamics: Eight Challenges for Developers. Comm. of the ACM January (1994) 93-105
3. Horvitz, E., Koch, P., Kadi, C. M. Jacobs, A.: Coordinate: Probabilistic Forecasting of Presence and Availability. Proc. Of the 18th Conference on Uncertainty and Artificial Intelligence. Morgan Kaufman (2002) 224-233
4. Beard, D., Palaniappan, M., Humm, A, Banks, D., Nair, A., Shan, Y.: A Visual Calendar for Scheduling Group Meetings. *Proc. of the 1990 ACM Conference on CSCW.* ACM Press (1990) 279-290
5. Evite. http://www.evite.com
6. Tullio, J., Goecks, J., Mynatt, E.D., Nguyen, D. H.: Augmenting Shared Personal Calendars. *Proc. of the 15th Annual ACM Symposium on UIST.* ACM Press (2002) 11-20

Under My Finger: Human Factors in Pushing and Rotating Documents Across the Table

Clifton Forlines[1], Chia Shen[1], Frédéric Vernier[1,2], and Mike Wu[1,3]

[1] MERL, 201 Broadway, Cambridge, MA, USA
[2] University of Paris 11, LIMSI-CNRS, BP 133, 91403 Orsay, France
[3] University of Toronto, 10 King's College Road Toronto Ontario
`{forlines, shen}@merl.com,`
`frederic.vernier@limsi.fr, mchi@dgp.toronto.edu`

Abstract. When passing a document to someone across a table, the person passing the document often rotates it to face the receiver. In this paper, we present the results of a user evaluation of three *Push-and-Rotate* schemes that offer different underlying control semantics for how an electronic document can automatically rotate as it is pushed across an interactive tabletop surface. The effects of document size are also discussed.

1 Introduction

Moving digital documents on vertical displays, such as desktop monitors or electronic white boards, involves dragging operations with only two degrees of freedom in the XY plane. Vertical displays rely on everyone sharing a common "up" vector with the display; digital documents that are translated are still readable. However, no such assumption can be made for horizontal displays because a horizontal display may be viewed simultaneously by many people sitting around it. Thus, a multi-user digital tabletop that aims to support around-the-table collaboration with digital documents must support not only the positioning, but also the orientation of documents [4].

Simultaneously moving and rotating a digital document is the subject of this paper. Specifically, we focus on techniques that map the 3 DOF into one single control point (thus requiring only one finger). Although multi-finger and multi-hand techniques can also be developed [5], by combining movement and rotation into a single finger operation, designers can use the more sophisticated gestures for issuing other commands.

There are two approaches for single-finger tabletop document repositioning and reorientation. One is to decompose the interaction into two steps by providing separate widgets for each of the tasks (such as a title bar for movement and rotation handle). An alternative approach that more naturally matches a user's basic perceptual structure of the task [1] would be to integrate the two together in a single step. With one action, the user can push and rotate a document to the desired location and orientation [2][3]. In our system, the orientation of a document is a function of the point where a user touches the document and the position of the document with respect to the table's center. The directness of under-the-finger manipulation leads to a high sensitivity to subtle variations in the constraint function. In building [4], we developed a number of functions, three of which, shown in Figure 1, are described below.

M.F. Costabile and F. Paternò (Eds.): INTERACT 2005, LNCS 3585, pp. 994–997, 2005.
© IFIP International Federation for Information Processing 2005

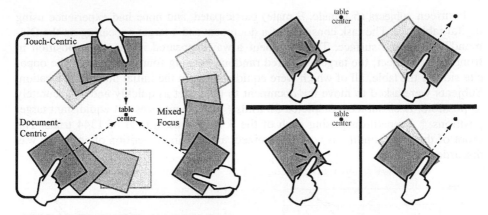

Fig. 1. (*on the left*) The three constraint functions differ in how documents follow the finger and how they auto-orient. (*on the top-right*) When touched, Document-Centric documents "slide" to center themselves with the touch point. (*on the bottom-right*) Touch-Centric documents "slide" when touched to constrain their orientation with a line between the touch point and the table center.

Document-Centric. When the user touches a document, it instantly slides to center itself on the touch point, as shown in Figure 1 (*top-right*). As the finger drags the document on the table, the document continues to center itself to the touch point and the document's orientation is constrained by lining up the center of the document, the center of its top edge, and the center of the table, as shown in Figure 1 (*left*).

Touch-Centric. When the user touches a document it instantly constrains its orientation using a line between the touch point and the center of the table that is perpendicular to the document's top edge, shown in Figure 1 (*bottom-right*). As the finger moves around the table, the document orients itself using this line and moves itself so that the initial touch point is always under the finger, as shown in Figure 1 (*left*).

Mixed-Focus. This function is a hybrid of the other two techniques. It is touch-centric for movement, and document-centric for rotation. When the user touches a document, it follows the movement of the user's finger relative to where it was first touched; however, the document orients itself using a line between the center of the table and the center of the top edge of the document, as shown in Figure 1 (*left*).

2 User Evaluation

Our hypotheses were:

H1. Subjects will be able to position documents at a desired location on the tabletop *faster* using some techniques as compared to others.

H2. The size of a document will influence the *speed* with which subjects reposition it on the tabletop.

H3. Subjects will be able to *more accurately* position documents at a desired location on the tabletop using some techniques as compared to others.

H4. The size of a document will influence the *accuracy* with which subjects reposition it on the tabletop.

Fourteen subjects (5 female, 9 male) participated, and none had experience using digital tabletops. The task consisted of a document and a target appearing on the DiamondTouch input surface. The document always appeared in the same position in front of the subject; the target appeared randomly among four positions on the opposite side of the table, all of which were equidistant from the initial document location. Subjects were asked to move the document to the target as quickly and as accurately as possible. Each subject completed 32 trials (4 document sizes * 4 equidistant target positions * 2 repetitions) using each of the 3 conditions; a total of 1344 trials. The order of the three conditions was randomized, and the first repetition of each task was discarded.

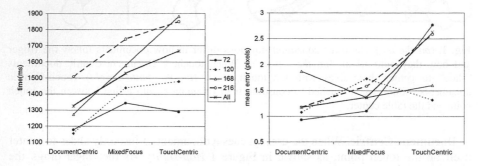

Fig. 2. (*on the left*) Task time by technique and document size. Smaller documents tend to lead to shorter times. (*on the right*) Task error by technique and doc size.

2.1 Results

Our experimental data confirmed all four hypotheses.

H1: For each trial, the testing application recorded the speed with which subjects moved a document to the target position. A repeated measures ANOVA of the recorded data suggests that the technique used significantly affected the task time ($F(2,13)=13.75$, $p=0.003$, $d=0.92$). The average task times for the three techniques were 1.32, 1.67, and 1.53 seconds for Document-Centric, Touch-Centric, and Mixed-Focus respectively. The relative task times for all document sizes are shown in Figure 2.

H2: The size of the documents significantly affected the speed with which subjects repositioned them ($F(2,13)=42.99$, $p<0.001$, $d=1.0$). In general, the smaller the document, the faster the subjects were able to reposition it. Furthermore, there was a significant interaction between document size and condition ($F(6,12)=5.20$, $p=0.042$, $d=0.55$).

H3: At the end of each trial, the testing application recorded the distance in pixels between the document center and the target center. The constraint function used significantly affected this task error ($F(2,13)=13.6$, $p=0.004$, $d=0.92$). The average errors for the three techniques were 1.95, 3.54, and 2.13 pixels for Document-Centric, Touch-Centric, and Mixed-Focus respectively. Figure 2 shows the mean task errors broken down by the four document sizes.

H4: The size of the documents significantly affected the accuracy with which subjects repositioned them ($F_{(2,13)}=3.9$, $p=0.045$, d=0.53). Again, in general subjects performed better with smaller documents. There was a significant interaction between document size and condition ($F_{(6,12)}=7.19$, $p=0.02$, d=0.69).

After each session, we asked subjects which of the three techniques they preferred the most and the least. As a whole, subjects disliked the Touch-Centric condition, expressing that it was hard to predict the orientation of the document as it moved across the table. While they (correctly) felt that they performed well with the Document-Centric technique, many subjects disliked the initial "sliding" of the document in this condition. Most subjects named Mixed-Focus as their favorite of the three.

3   Discussion and Design Recommendations

While Document-Centric was the fastest and least error prone, it received the lowest user preference score. We are left with the question, "What is the appropriate measure for comparing these types of tabletop interaction techniques?" Future study is needed to help decide if the modest performance gains outweigh user satisfaction.

With all 3 techniques, smaller documents lead to quicker and more accurate results. We speculate that this may be because larger documents are more sensitive to small changes in angle and that this made adjustment more difficult (i.e. a small change in angle resulted in greater displacement of pixels). This led us to look at the relationship between performance and the position where the subject touched the document. In the Mixed-Focus and Touch-Centric conditions, the distance between the center of the document and the touch point was correlated with the task time and error. Therefore, a title bar that runs along the full length of the document may not be the optimal design. Rather, a design that encourages the user to touch near the center of the document when repositioning it could be a better alternative. This specific example provides weight to the argument that the design of many desktop GUI components should be scrutinized before they are brought to tabletop interfaces.

References

1. Jacob, R. J. K., Sibert, L. E., McFarlane, D. C., and Mullen Jr., M. P. Integrality and separability of input devices, *ACM Trans. Computer-Human Interaction 1* (1994), 3-26.
2. Kruger, R., Carpendale, S., Scott, S.D. and Tang, A., Fluid integration of rotation and translation. in *Proceeding of the SIGCHI conference on Human factors in computing systems*, (Portland, Oregon, USA, 2005), ACM Press, 601-610.
3. Rekimoto, J., SmartSkin: an infrastructure for freehand manipulation on interactive surfaces. in *Proceedings of the SIGCHI conference on Human factors in computing system*, (Minneapolis, Minnesota, USA, 2002), ACM Press, 113-120.
4. Shen, C., Vernier, F., Forlines, C. and Ringel, M., DiamondSpin: an extensible toolkit for around-the-table interaction. in *Proceedings of the SIGCHI conference on Human factors in computing systems*, (Vienna, Austria, 2004), ACM Press, 167-174.
5. Wu, M. and Balakrishnan, R., Multi-finger and whole hand gestural interaction techniques for multi-user tabletop displays. in *Proceedings of the 16th annual ACM symposium on User interface software and technology*, (Vancouver, Canada, 2003), ACM Press, 193-202.

DocuBits and Containers: Providing e-Document Micro-mobility in a Walk-Up Interactive Tabletop Environment

Katherine Everitt, Chia Shen, Kathy Ryall, and Clifton Forlines

Mitsubishi Electric Research Laboratories, 201 Broadway, Cambridge, MA, USA
everitt@cs.washington.edu, {shen, ryall, forlines}@merl.com

Abstract. A key challenge in supporting face-to-face collaborative work is e-document micro-mobility: supporting movement of digital content amongst shared display surfaces and personal devices at arbitrary levels of document granularity. Micro-mobility is a dexterity that physical paper artifacts afford – the ability to be handled with any position and placement, to be dismantled, cut and torn apart, marked up, reassembled and sorted. To support micro-mobility for electronic content and group work, we propose *DocuBits* and *Containers*. *DocuBits* offer the metaphor of a paper-cutter and a scanner for electronic documents. A portion of screen 'bits' from any application or any parts of visible display can be cut, grabbed, sent and launched onto a different display surface or device with minimal interaction – merely three mouse/stylus click-select. Once arrived on the target display surface, DocuBits can be arbitrarily positioned, re-oriented, marked up, and pulled into other documents, or again sent to other display surfaces. A *Container* is a composite draft of DocuBits and other documents, usually composed as the outcome of a collaborative meeting.

1 Introduction

When collaborating in a face-to-face setting, people often use large surfaces such as tables as the physical location for paper-based information, making information easily viewable and accessible by all. In contrast, electronic documents (e-documents) are usually located on devices designed for individual use, accessed by single user input mechanisms such as mice and keyboards. Today's e-documents do not support dynamic mobility-related techniques such as decomposition, on-the-spot sorting or piling – actions typical in many group settings such as brainstorming sessions or content design and creation meetings where the electronic artifacts to be used are often brought in by each participant; groups then work together with e-documents in-situ to create composite draft documents. In such multi-device environments, e-documents lack some of the basic capabilities of their paper (physical) counterparts.

Paper documents afford the ecological dexterity [2] of re-orientation, markup, ease of passing amongst participants, and even the option of tearing off part of a page of a document so it can be re-arranged and reassembled with respect to other pages. E-documents lack support for this type of interaction and composition. Current interactive tabletop and roomware such as [5, 6, 7] do not provide the

M.F. Costabile and F. Paternò (Eds.): INTERACT 2005, LNCS 3585, pp. 998–1001, 2005.

necessary micro-mobility of artifacts (as paper documents do) – it is often *not* possible to move *arbitrary* portions and granularities (e.g., a line, a word or a section of a screen) of digital data in a simple yet holistic interaction style across device boundaries. Most current systems support only whole document movement amongst display devices.

Some recent work touches on micro-mobility of documents in a desktop setting. WinCuts [8] offers a mechanism to carve out any portion of an active window for spatial organization of information. WinCuts are synchronized with the original content, and so support alternate visual presentation but not version comparison. Synchronizing Clipboards [3] allow two computers to share a system clipboard. This supports mobility of files and ASCII text in an "invisible" fashion, and is best suited to a single user with multiple machines. ScreenCrayons [4] collects annotations of screen captures and provides capability to annotate, classify, and highlight notes. It is designed for use by a single user on a desktop machine.

In this paper, we present our initial design and prototype of Docubits in an interactive walk-up multi-user tabletop environment [1, 6], as shown in Fig. 1 (*left*).

2 DocuBits and Containers: Design and Prototype

DocuBits mechanisms allow users to easily carve out any portions of documents or any portion of visible screen display and operate with them as full documents. We support the amalgamation of documents and DocuBits into composite documents, called "Containers," which are saved as HTML for easy after-meeting portability.

DocuBits: Figures 1, 2 and 3 illustrate the sequence of interaction of Docubits creation and movement. A DocuBit is a portion of the visible screen, including both the content and its layout in the workspace. A portion of screen from any application or arbitrary portion of the visible display can be cut, grabbed, sent and launched onto a different display surface or device. We currently support two forms for the captured DocuBits: images and editable text, making DocuBits portable to any platform. DocuBits provide a quick and fluid way for multiple people to bring their own draft documents or bits and pieces of ideas onto the meeting table, and can be used to clarify spatial relationships between content, highlight a point, and remove private information. They can represent many levels of granularity: from a word or a section of a window, to an entire window or even the spatial relationships between windows.

DocuBits are designed to be lightweight, and easy to create and send. The interaction in creating DocuBits approximates WYSIWYG; users select any region from what can be seen and immediately make it into a new DocuBit. When the user starts a new visual DocuBit by clicking the "New Screen Section" button (Fig 1 *right*), a screenshot is taken and the user selects the relevant screen subsection with a rectangular selection gesture (Fig 2 *left*). Text-based DocuBits use the system clipboard in the same way as conventional text copy. DocuBits appear in Java frames, and are sent between devices using sockets. A preview window is provided with three buttons: "Send", "Discard" and "Save" (Fig 2 *right*), to allow the user to easily cancel, save a copy, and/or send the DocuBit to a different display surface. DocuBits are not tethered to the original documents or screen content. As they are not synchronized with other versions of the same content, but are effectively a snapshot in time, they can be compared to each other like different paper drafts. Each DocuBit stores meta-data about its creation location and time. This allows users to later determine *when* and *where* the DocuBit was created. They can easily be reorganized using the Container described below. Both DocuBits and Containers are implemented in Java.

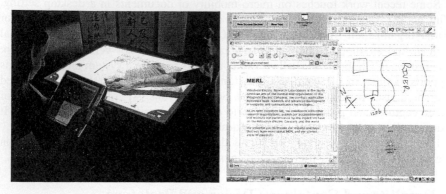

Fig. 1. Sample Setup: *Left*: Meeting around an interactive UbiTable [6] tabletop. *Right*: TabletPC desktop screen with "New Screen Section" button on top left of desktop display.

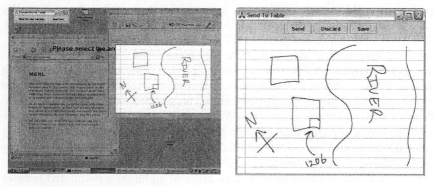

Fig. 2. "New Screen Section" button grays out the screen: Left: User selects a portion of screen area which becomes un-grayed. Right: Selected screen bits automatically become a DocuBits preview window with three buttons (Send, Discard, Save).

Containers: A container object supports micro-mobility by providing a mechanism to *recombine* objects. We have prototyped the Container in two forms: as a list of objects and a more flexible collage of items. A user can "drop" an object into the Container list by sliding an object over it and releasing. Containers can be copied, deleted, and moved between the display surfaces; in essence they are a new e-document. When saved on a personal device, a Container, in the form of an HTML document with meta-data, contains a record of where the pieces came from, the document type of each piece, and could also contain information about who edited which parts. This can be easily viewed later on other devices.

Linking Devices: Portable devices (e.g., laptops or TablePCs) can be linked to the table on-the-fly using portals similar to those used in [6]. This creates a virtual link between the corner on the table closest to the device's user and the device (see Fig 3). Objects dragged onto a portal will be copied and a representation will appear on the linked device. DocuBits can be moved between devices in this way.

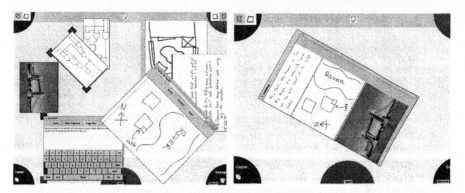

Fig. 3. On the TableTop: *Left*: Screenshot of a tabletop with DocuBits. Corners of the tabletop are wormhole portals to personal devices. *Right*: DocuBits are combined into a Container on the tabletop comprised of a diagram, some text and an image.

3   Conclusions and Future Work

DocuBits raise a number of interesting directions for future work. We would like to explore different usage patterns, expand selection beyond rectangular boxes, and explore the idea of synchronization of items. Synchronization could potentially improve speed of collaboration but might also cause confusion with so many objects and increase difficulty of document comparison. The question is still open as to whether making the system functionally more sophisticated in this way would benefit the user or would merely make the system overwhelmingly complex.

References

1. Everitt, K., Forlines, C., Ryall, K., Shen, C., "Observations of a Shared Tabletop User Study," Interactive Poster, ACM CSCW 2004.
2. Luff, P., Heath, C., "Mobility in Collaboration,". Proc. ACM Computer Supported Cooperative Work (CSCW), 1998. pp. 305-314.
3. Miller, R., Myers, B., "Synchronizing Clipboards of Multiple Computers," Proc. ACM UIST 1999.
4. Olsen, D., Taufer, T., Fails, J.A., "ScreenCrayons: annotating anything," Proc. ACM UIST 2004.
5. Rekimoto, J., Saitoh, M., "Augmented Surfaces: A Spatially Continuous Work Space for Hybrid Computing Environments," Proc. ACM CHI 1999.
6. Shen, C., Everitt, K.M.; Ryall, K., "UbiTable: Impromptu Face-to-Face Collaboration on Horizontal Interactive Surfaces," Proc. UbiComp 2003. LNCS 2864. 281-288.
7. Streitz, N.A., Tandler, P., Muller-Tomfelde, C., Konomi, S. "i-LAND: An Interactive Landscape for Creativity and Innovation," Proc. ACM CHI 1999.
8. Tan, D.S., Meyers, B., Czerwinski, M. "WinCuts: Manipulating Arbitrary Window Regions for More Effective Use of Screen Space," Extended Abstract, ACM CHI 2004.

Transcription Table: Text Support During Meetings

Joris van Gelder, Irene van Peer, and Dzmitry Aliakseyeu

Faculty of Industrial Design,
Eindhoven University of Technology,
Den Dolech 2, Eindhoven, The Netherlands
J.M.v.Gelder@student.tue.nl, {i.p.v.peer, d.aliakseyeu}@tue.nl

Abstract. In this paper we present the design of a tool that allows a hearing-impaired person to participate in a meeting. The tool combines speech recognition with a table top augmented reality system. One of the foremost requirements was that the tool should not stigmatize the hearing-impaired user. Therefore the tool supports features that are attractive to all participants in the meeting. The final prototype has the following features: it can convey (some of) the meeting content to the hearing-impaired person, it supports eye contact between participants, it allows an interaction with words and sentences, it provides a meeting history and instant minutes.

1 Introduction

Sudden deafness is a condition where someone who already knows how to talk becomes deaf at a later age [1]. Since the life of these people is not organized to function with deafness they usually are not able to continue their social and professional life and consequently suffer from isolation.

There are several communication products available for hearing-impaired people. Unfortunately none of them is a substitute for direct communication. One instance of professional activity where direct communication is very important is in meetings. When an employee can not participate in a meeting he/she has no share in many important decisions. An interview with several hearing-impaired people confirmed that this is indeed one of the biggest problems that they encounter.

We believe that by employing a combination of speech and tabletop augmented reality technologies we can at least partially resolve this problem. We particularly focus on small (work) meetings, since they are the most common meetings in a professional environment. Small meetings are the base for personal contact between co-workers and deal with the day-to-day organization of the work.

When developing a tool for such a group of users, an important requirement is that the tool should not stigmatize the hearing-impaired user. Therefore this project focuses not only on the perspective of the hearing-impaired user, but also on that of the other participants in the meeting. The tool should enable the hearing-impaired person to take part in a meeting and also provide an added value for the hearing participants of the meeting.

When all participants use the tool, the hearing-impaired person is not in a different position from the rest of the team.

M.F. Costabile and F. Paternò (Eds.): INTERACT 2005, LNCS 3585, pp. 1002–1005, 2005.

In summary, makes the design goals for the project are twofold: the tool has to be a translation device, i.e. convey (some of) the meeting content to the hearing-impaired, person and the tool needs to support the position of the hearing-impaired person in the group with features that are also attractive to the other participants in the meeting.

The remainder of the paper is organized as follows. First we describe a first exploratory user study that served to motivate some of the design choices. Next we discus the final design, expected problems and potential benefits.

2 Exploratory User Study

In order to study how people react on real-time transcriptions during a meeting, a wizard of Oz user study was performed. More precisely, we wanted to obtain answers to the following questions. First can a hearing-impaired person participate in a meeting using a speech-to-text translating device? Second, which influence does the added visual information have on the meeting?

The test consisted of two 15-minute sessions, with and without the transcription tool. Both sessions were video-taped and all participants were interviewed after the experiment. During the second session (without the transcriptions) the hearing participants used pen and paper to communicate their conversation to the hearing-impaired participant.

A simple tabletop projection setup was used. The transcriptions were displayed on the middle of the table in two orientations (toward and away from the speaker) so that participants on both sides of the table could read the transcriptions. The transcription subsequently moved towards the speaker.

Speech recognition was not implemented in this setup. Instead a human operator inserted transcriptions that were synchronized with the meeting.

The result of the exploratory study showed that: a hearing-impaired person was able to participate in the discussion; participants had little eye contact during the meeting; participants made little use of the transcriptions during their own story, they only read it when it appeared on the table. These results indicates that a possible tool, in addition to supporting transcription, should also stimulate and enable interaction with the words, and stimulate eye contact between the participants of the meeting.

3 Prototype Design

The results of the user study were used as a starting point for the prototype design.

From the user study, we conclude that interaction with the transcriptions is vital. To improve this interaction, we decided that text feedback should be displayed within hand reach of the speaker. Such text position can also stimulate eye contact (see Figure 1).

In addition to the eyes, the hands are an important communication tool. With their hands, users can emphasize words and sentences.

The transcription table has four functions: (I) Display the transcriptions for the users. (II) Display who is speaking. (III) Enable the participants to have interaction with the transcriptions. (IV) Hold items like cups of coffee or papers.

The layout of the tabletop consists of a communication field (Figure 1.1), the soumaine, where the speaker can put his personal items (Figure 1.2), the touch screen (Figure 1.3) is the area where a speaker can see his own words and emphasize them by touch. This setup is equal for every participant of the meeting (Figure 1.4). Note that the current translation is only shown in the communication area of the speaker (Figure 1.5). Otherwise the other participants would not be able to see who is speaking. The transcription is displayed in multiple orientations to give all participants a comfortable view (Figure 1.6). The transcription is also displayed in the touch area of the speaker (Figure 1.7). When a transcription is replaced with a new transcription the old one is copied to the history which is also within the touch area (Figure 1.8). All participants have a copy of this history which consists of the four most recent sentences.

Two main points for interaction came out of the user study – the ability to emphasize words (sentences) and the ability to correct errors that can occur in the speech recognition. The users can emphasize sentences during the meeting. There are two types of emphasis, intonation and main clause emphasis. Intonation emphasis is the emphasis of single words to stress their importance or clarify their meaning. Intonation emphasis can only be executed by the speaker by touching the relevant word within the touch area. Main-clause emphasis is emphasizing a complete sentence to stress its importance. Main-clause emphasis can be executed by all participants of the meeting by touching a sentence in the history. The intonation emphasis still needs to be implemented in the prototype.

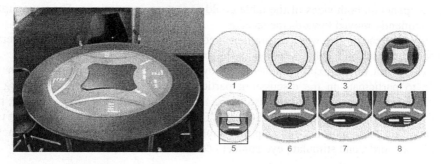

Fig. 1. Final prototype and step by step layout of the tabletop

Currently the speech recognition is controlled by a java program. The speech input is regulated by a microphone switch. The switch converts four microphone inputs into a single audio output. The input with the highest loudness is connected to the output.

The tool also provides instant minutes after the meeting. Since the computer has to translate all the spoken words into written sentences to be displayed on the table, they can also be saved. This transcription file can be printed right after the meeting is finished and be used as a basis for the minutes.

4   Related Work

There exists a lot of literature on supporting collaborative work with tabletop displays [7]. However most of this work does not consider speech as one of the input modalities. In terms of the technology, the most commonly used input devices are a touch sensitive surface (for example DiamondTouch [4]), or vision-based recognition [5].

Another area of related research is speech recognition, including the research on using speech recognition for disabled people [3]. Nevertheless there are not a lot of systems that combines both speech and tabletop display or touch input. One example is the Quickset [2], a speech/gesture multimodal system, which consists of parallel recognizers for the speech and gesture input modalities.

5   Conclusions and Future Work

The first prototype of the transcription table can convey (some of) the meeting content to the hearing-impaired person without stigmatizing him or her, it supports the eye-contact between participants, it allows an interaction with words and sentences, provides a meeting history and instant minutes.

A next step in this project is user testing with hearing-impaired users. Experiments with different turn taking setups would be interesting as well; an example is that the speaker remains connected to the computer as long as he is speaking.

References

1. Association of Late-Deafness Adults. http://www.alda.org/.
2. Cohen, P.R., Johnston, M., McGee, D.R., Oviatt, S.L., Pittman, J.A., Smith, I., et al. Quick-Set: Multimodal interaction for distributed applications. In *Proc. of the IEEE International Multimedia Conference*, Seattle, WA, Nov. 1997), pp. 31–40.
3. Cox, s., Lincoln, M., Tryggvason, J., Nakisa, M., Wells, M., Tutt, M., Abbott, S. Tessa, a system to aid communication with deaf people. In *Proc. of Assets'02*, Edinburgh, Scotland, ACM Press (2002), pp. 205–212.
4. Deitz P., Leigh D. DiamondTouch: A Multi-User Touch Technology. In *Proc. of UIST'01*, Orlando, Florida, 2001, pp. 219-226.
5. Fitzmaurice, G. W., Ishii, H., Buxton, W. Bricks: Laying the Foundations for Graspable User Interfaces. In *Proc. of CHI'95*, May 1995, Denver, ACM Press (1995), pp. 442 – 449.
6. ScanSoft - Dragon NaturallySpeaking. http://www.scansoft.com/naturallyspeaking/
7. Scott, S.D., Grant, K.D., & Mandryk, R.L. System Guidelines for Co-located, Collaborative Work on a Tabletop Display. In *Proc. of ECSCW'03*, European Conference Computer-Supported Cooperative Work 2003, Helsinki, Finland, 2003.

Common Ground to Analyse Privacy Coordination in Awareness Systems

Natalia A. Romero and Panos Markopoulos

Eindhoven University of Technology,
User Centred Design Group, Industrial Design Department,
Eindhoven, 5600MB, The Netherlands
{n.a.romero, p.markopoulos}@tue.nl

Abstract. This paper discusses how Clark's theory of Common Ground can be applied to analyse how individuals connected by Awareness Systems conjointly meet and coordinate their privacy needs. Relevant aspects of Common Ground theory for the analysis of human communication behaviours are used in this study to understand privacy as a *collaborative coordination process*. The exposition illustrates how Awareness Systems are a mechanism for helping individuals to meet their privacy needs rather than as a privacy threat, as a first impression might suggest.

1 Introduction

A core function of awareness systems is to push information about one' colleagues or social network to the periphery of one' attention and a vice versa. The decision of which information to share concerns the design and subsequently the daily use of awareness systems. At a first reading, awareness appears to be the flip side of privacy: a gain in awareness of another individual comes at a cost of that person' privacy.

This view though is rather simplistic. There are clear occasions when people desire to share information about themselves, desire to engage in social interactions while at other moments they may prefer solitude, isolation or to keep some information about themselves private in order to manage how they present themselves to others. The variables attitude and the behaviour of people pertain to their privacy needs and the mechanisms they adopt to manage their privacy. The term privacy is not used here in its colloquial sense of secrecy or confidentiality of one's own personal data from third parties (often assumed to be government organizations). Rather, we are concerned with privacy as understood in social psychology as "an interpersonal boundary process by which a person or group regulates interaction with others..."([1], p.6) or as a "selective control of access to the self or to one's group..."([1], p.18).

Social psychologists have examined needs, attitudes and mechanisms people use to manage their privacy in the domain of face-to-face interactions. There is little work yet that will provide a theoretical understanding of how individuals manage their privacy needs in the context of computer-mediated communication. This work aims to address this problem. More specifically, we try to understand the role in privacy management of an awareness system, broadly seen as an always on, lightweight

M.F. Costabile and F. Paternò (Eds.): INTERACT 2005, LNCS 3585, pp. 1006–1009, 2005.
© IFIP International Federation for Information Processing 2005

communication channel that aims to place information about one individual at the periphery of the attention of another, so that this information will be easily recruited but also easily ignored.

In the context of CMC, extant communication behaviours and privacy mechanisms (see Altman [1]) that are part of our interpersonal social skills are severely constrained. A successful solution for privacy management would require that both sender and receiver's needs have to be addressed in tandem when disclosing private information [5] in what becomes a collaborative activity. For an effective collaboration, participants have to mutually develop a shared understanding that helps them jointly negotiate their meanings and understandings, i.e., senders' intentions and receivers' recognition of those intentions. Note that we do not concern ourselves with the related problem, of information security, where the confidentiality of one's information is considered to be under threat by external parties.

In this paper, we apply Common Ground theory [2] to describe how awareness systems can support privacy negotiation as a joint activity. In the following sections we summarise some key elements of Common Ground theory and we discuss how they can help explain some known empirical results regarding the negotiation of privacy needs in the context of CMC.

2   Common Ground Theory

Clark's theory states that all communication behaviours are *joint activities* where participants share a common goal and the responsibility to achieve that goal. Every joint activity used *coordination mechanisms* that give participants shared basis for believing that they are all converging to the same joint goal. Those *shared basis* are what Clark calls *common ground*: "...a great mass of knowledge, beliefs, and suppositions they [participants] believe they share" ([2], p.12). The process of developing common ground, *grounding process*, involves a series of *contributions* each consisting in a pair of *presentation and acceptance*. In a contribution speaker presents an utterance to express a *meaning* and addressee gives evidence of *understanding* of that presentation.

The stronger the common ground that participants shared, the higher the possibilities to *cooperate* in the design of their presentations and acceptances, the lower *the collaborative effort* needed to succeed in their communication goal. People engage in two parallel tracks of actions when communicating. Track I attempts to carry out the official business while track II attempts to create a successful communication. It is in track II that speakers ask for confirmation and addressees provide evidences of understanding. Track II is a central component of Clark's theory to facilitate the grounding process.

Four characterizations of track II guarantee lightweight presentations and acceptances of collateral signals and tacit actions: backgrounding (signals in track I should be prominent), simultaneity (actions in both tracks at the same time should be performing signals in both tracks in parallel), brevity (signals in track II should carry little information and should be limited in variety), and differentiation (signals of track I should be distinguishable from signals of track II). The concept of the two tracks has, to the best of our knowledge, not so far been used in analyses of CMC using common ground. Nevertheless, the definitions above relate closely to what is described by Nardi [4] as "interaction" and "outeraction".

The different aspects of track II support different representations of common ground, which are used as coordination devices. The *initial state* represents the shared assumptions, cultural practices, etc., used as conventions. The *current state* corresponds to the shared external representations of the current situation used as explicit agreements. The *track of public events* represents the shared perceptual salient events used as precedents.

Considering privacy negotiation as a communication activity we borrow three concepts from Clark's theory as our basic vocabulary to identify the level of support of privacy negotiation in awareness systems: track II, common ground representations and least collaborative effort. The latter concept refers to the willingness of people to use "evidences enough for current purposes" to achieve an agreement. We consider that, representations of common ground in track II can provide "evidences enough for current purposes" so people can cooperatively ground their privacy/awareness needs.

The vocabulary helps us to describe the level of support of awareness systems to represent the different states of common ground (initial, current, track public events) in terms of the four requirements of track II: background, brief, simultaneously, distinguishable. To demonstrate how Common Ground theory helps describe and analyse privacy mechanisms manifested in the usage of CMC, we relate two published empirical studies to the elements of Common Ground identified above.

2.1 Analysis: Push-to-Talk (PTT)

Push-to-talk is a half duplex, lightweight cellular radio communication. A study done by Woodruff [6] found that the half-duplex, and lightweight aspects of the medium create a sense of reduced interactional commitment where users appreciated the immediate access to another person and the relatively low interactional demands of the various conversation styles afforded. The benefits observed relate to reduced openings and closings, delayed or omitted responses, reduced feedback, and interleaved interaction. Controversially, participants were reluctant to use PTT with others than very close friends.

In terms of track II support on one side the system provides lightweight presentation and acceptance mechanisms signalling briefly and in the background privacy/awareness needs. On the other side, in situation where the initial state of common ground represents a more competitive relation between the participants there is a need to ground more information about the current and recorded states that is not supported by PTT. The lack of support of track II to represent common ground *simultaneously* and *distinguishable* from track I obliged users to use mechanisms in track I to signal their privacy/awareness needs clearly increasing the interactional commitment.

2.2 Analysis: Media Space

Media spaces are CMC tools of audio and video equipment to support synchronous collaboration. Dourish, et al [3] analyses personal experiences over a long period of use of a v/a link connecting two physical offices (share office). The study reports that users jointly created and developed new social norms to deal with the emergent communicative practices afforded by media spaces. Nevertheless, lack of context cues did not facilitate collaboration between users in the adoption of new norms.

Analysing how media spaces support track II to provide context cues, we identify a lack of *background* features (use of image size, blurriness, etc.) damaging the exchange information in the periphery and a lack of support of *brief* non-verbal signals to control lightweight communication devices such as preambles, plausible deniability, etc. The lack of support of track II to represent background and brief context cues, as shared basis, did not facilitate a joint decision process on how to behave under unfamiliar situations.

3 Conclusions

Awareness systems can be seen as a source of Common Ground that can help to develop a sufficient shared basis to help users to mutually agree on their privacy/awareness expectations. In track II communicators can use collateral signals and tacit actions to present their privacy/awareness needs. The discussion above illustrates that different CMC designs can be analysed with respect to how they support negotiation of privacy and awareness needs through track II. It suggests that common ground can provide a much needed theoretical framework for analysing Privacy negotiation processes in CMC. Our current research seeks to collect empirical evidence to demonstrate this possibility and to suggest a method for evaluating computer mediated communication systems with respect to how well they support individuals satisfy their privacy needs, whether these concern the will to share information and to interact socially or conversely, to avoid interaction and to keep information private.

References

1. Altman, I. *The Environment and Social Behaviour*. Brooks/Cole, Monterey, CA, 1975.
2. Clark, H.H. *Using Language*. Cambridge University Press, Cambridge, UK, 1996.
3. Dourish, P., Adler, A., Bellotti, V. and Henderson, A. Your Place or Mine? Learning from Long-Term Use of Audio-Video Communication. *Journal CSCW*, 5 (1), 1996, 33-62.
4. Nardi, B.A., Whittaker, S. and Bradner, E., Interaction and Outeraction: Instant Messaging in Action. in *Proceedings of the 2000 ACM conference on Computer supported cooperative work*, 2000, ACM Press, 79-88.
5. Petronio, S. *Boundaries of Privacy: Dialectics of Disclosure*. State University of New York Press, Albany, 2002.
6. Woodruff, A. and Aoki, P.M., How push-to-talk makes talk less pushy. in *Proceedings of the 2003 international ACM SIGGROUP conference on Supporting group work*, 2003, ACM Press, 170 - 179.

3D Syllabus: Interactive Visualization of Indexes to Multimedia Training Content

Kyuman Song[1], Surapong Lertsithichai[2], and Patrick Chiu[3]

[1] General Dynamics C4 Systems, 2100 Wharton st. Pittsburgh, PA 15203 USA
ksong@post.harvard.edu
[2] Faculty of Architecture, Silpakorn University, Bangkok, Thailand
surapong@post.harvard.edu
[3] FX Palo Aloaratory, 3400 Hillview Ave., Bldg. 4, Palo Alto, CA 94304 USA
chiu@fxpal.com

Abstract. Indexes such as bookmarks and recommendations are helpful for accessing multimedia documents. This paper describes the 3D Syllabus system, which is designed to visualize indexes to multimedia training content along with the information structures. A double-sided landscape with balloons and cubes represents the personal and group indexes, respectively. The 2D ground plane organizes the indexes as a table and the third dimension of height indicates their importance scores. Additional visual properties of the balloons and cubes provide other information about the indexes and their content. Paths are represented by pipes connecting the balloons. A preliminary evaluation of the 3D Syllabus prototype suggests that it is more efficient than a typical training CD-ROM and is more enjoyable to use.

1 Introduction

Digital multimedia documents are becoming more widely available with rapid advances in technologies for content creation and distribution. For accessing and browsing documents in a collection, indexes are helpful and often indispensable. Examples of indexes are bookmarks, annotations, recommendations by other users, and sequences prescribed by an instructor.

This paper describes techniques for 3D visualization and interaction with indexes to multimedia training documents. These techniques were developed in response to a multimedia system used to train technicians in the maintenance and repair of printers and copiers from the Fuji-Xerox Company. This multimedia content is distributed on a CD-ROM and produced with Macromedia Authorware. The user interface has hyperlinks and buttons for page turning. The content is organized hierarchically. At the top level are modules, and within each module is a tree diagram (Fig. 1-A and B). The leaves of a tree diagram are pages that can be accessed and viewed. The pages contain text, images, and video clips (Fig. 1-C).

There are several problems with this visualization and user interface, which also occur with typical hyperlinked training CD-ROMs. For the training application in Fig. 1, the complicated hierarchical structure is time-consuming to navigate. Limited

M.F. Costabile and F. Paternò (Eds.): INTERACT 2005, LNCS 3585, pp. 1010–1013, 2005.

information is displayed; the tree view for each module shows the structure, but the screen does not have room to show all the trees. Learning paths are inflexible because they are determined by the tree structures, and instructors and users cannot create customized paths. The interactions restrict the user to clicking on hyperlinks for navigation and page turning. Knowledge sharing between students is not supported.

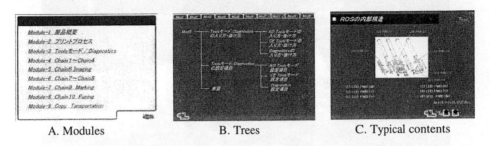

A. Modules   B. Trees   C. Typical contents

Fig. 1. Screen shots of the Fuji-Xerox Training CD-ROM

The 3D techniques presented in this paper address these problems. An overview of the entire content structure and relationships can be displayed. A property of 3D space is that it is scalable and essentially infinite. Consequently, through 3D navigation, the user can vary the viewpoint to obtain better views of the entire content or certain parts of the content. Paths are better supported in 3D than in 2D, since paths that crisscross or pass over nodes cause difficulties in a 2D visualization. For the specific problem of showing personal and group indexes, we have designed a double-sided 3D landscape.

Other visualizations for multimedia or hyperlinked contents are surveyed in [1]. None of these utilizes a double-sided landscape. Alternatively, a simple listing of multimedia data (e.g. [2]) is easy to use but does not provide a view of the information structures. Context maps like the Learning Landscape [3] provide different views (by topic, faculty, people, places); however, distortion and instability are drawbacks with this type of mapping.

2 3D Syllabus

A screen shot of the 3D Syllabus is shown in Fig. 2. The content visualized is taken from the Fuji-Xerox training CD-ROM. The content set is organized as a table that is represented by a grid of square tiles (see Fig. 3). These tiles are set on the flat ground plane in the 3D landscape. Spaces between the tiles allow the user to see the objects above and below ground. Part names are listed along one axis and task types are listed along the other axis.

A balloon (or sphere) represents an index to the multimedia content; a balloon has a string connecting it to the square tile beneath it. Clicking on a balloon accesses or plays the content corresponding to the square (i.e. one of the content pages in Fig. 1C). A balloon's size indicates the amount of content for that lesson; the size can be computed from the number of pages or the file size. The color patches on a balloon indicate the number and type of media. After content has been accessed, the user can give it a rating by directly manipulating the balloon's height (or through a dialog box). The height of a balloon indicates the rating: very low, low, medium, high, very high.

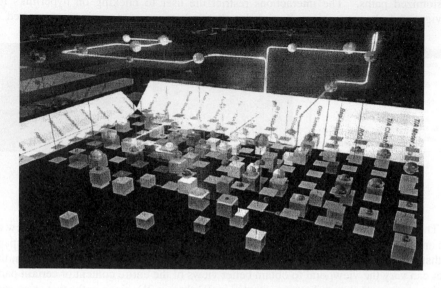

Fig. 2. 3D Syllabus

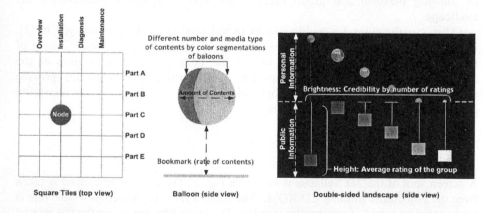

Fig. 3. Concept diagram of 3D Syllabus

It is sometimes useful to know whether a balloon has been visited and its content viewed. A visited balloon has a red circle painted on its square tile (shown in Fig. 2). Color is used to visually group tiles of related content. For example, tiles of the same color belong to the same training module. When the cursor hovers over a balloon or tile, tooltips can be used to provide text information about the title, content size, height, tile group, etc. The pipes connecting the balloons represent paths through the content. For example, an instructor can prescribe a course by using a path.

Alternatively, a path can show the history of the lessons taken by a user studying independently. Arrows on the pipes can indicate direction (not shown in figure).

The visualization is a double-sided landscape with one side for personal indexes and the other side for group indexes. See Fig. 2 and 3. Examples are bookmarks (personal index) and recommendations by other students (group index). The side with the balloons is the personal side, and the side with the cubes is the group side. For the training application, the group can comprise the students in the class. The height of a cube is given by the average rating of the group. The brightness indicates how many people rated the content; this is important to know since an average rating from a small number of people may be less reliable. Clicking on a cube accesses group content such as the annotations created by other people.

3   Prototype Evaluation

A prototype of this system built in Macromedia Director has been tested in comparison with the existing system by five people. After a five-minute introduction, users were asked to find five particular topics in both systems. For the first given task, users spent 5-20 seconds finding the topic in the 3D syllabus compared to 60–500 seconds using the current system. After the test, users were asked to draw a mental map of the location of specific information. Significantly, users recalled the location of contents more precisely from their mental map of the 3D grid system. On the other hand, users couldn't remember the location of information on more than two topics from the existing system. Another benefit of 3D has to do with the user experience. From our informal user testing of an early prototype, users commented that 3D interfaces are more enjoyable to use. While the response to the 3D Syllabus has been encouraging, further testing with real users at Fuji-Xerox will be needed to ascertain the usefulness of the system.

Acknowledgements. We thank Laurent Denoue, Tohru Fuse, and Lynn Wilcox for their help and comments.

References

1. Benford, S., Taylor, I., Brailsford, D., Koleva, B., Craven, M., Fraser, M., Reynard G. Greenhalgh, C. Three dimensional visualization of the World Wide Web. *ACM Computing Surveys* 31(4), Dec. 1999.
2. Girgensohn, A., Boreczky, J., Wilcox, L., Foote, J.   Facilitating   video   access   by visualizing automatic analysis. *Proceedings of Interact '99*, pp. 205-212.
3. Learning Landscape, ETH (Federal Institute of Technology Zurich), http://www.dgj.ch/ ethworld

A Navigation and Examination Aid for 3D Virtual Buildings

Luca Chittaro, Vijay Kumar Gatla, and Subramanian Venkataraman

HCI Lab, Dept. of Math and Computer Science, University of Udine,
Via delle Scienze 206, 33100, Udine, Italy
{chittaro, gatla, venkatar}@dimi.uniud.it

Abstract. In this paper, we present the Interactive 3D BreakAway Map (I3BAM), an extension of Worlds In Miniature (WIM) that works not only as a navigation aid for virtual buildings but also provides a means of examining any floor of a virtual building without having to navigate it.

1 Introduction

In several virtual environment (VE) applications, users navigate 3D buildings. Typical examples can be virtual shopping malls, virtual museums, 3D games, simulations where users learn routes and building structure to be applied in real life scenarios [1], virtual models of complex real buildings where structural changes to rectify design defects are not feasible, thus creating the need for alternative solutions [2]. This paper presents the I3BAM, an extension of WIM that works not only as a navigation aid for virtual buildings but also provides a means of examining any floor without having to navigate it.

2 Related Work and Motivations

Several aids have been proposed in the literature to provide navigation support in VEs (e.g., [3,5,6,7]). Buildings are one of the most common types of VEs. Navigation within a virtual building (to learn a route to a particular location or gain structural knowledge) is often not the only task and the user's cognitive resources can be needed for additional tasks (e.g., object manipulation, collecting information etc.). The WIM is a well-known metaphor that uses 3D miniature maps to provide the user with object manipulation and locomotion capabilities [5]. A WIM is a 3D miniature version of the VE, floating in front of the user, as if it were in her virtual hand. User's position and orientation are indicated in the WIM. Although intuitive, the WIM has shortcomings especially related to navigation [5,6], e.g., merely presenting a WIM of an entire building would not provide a means of studying both the external and internal structure of the building (floor wise), the importance of which has been stressed in building structure visualization [4]. No previous attempts have been made to apply the WIM to virtual buildings (except for a prop based technique [7]). The I3BAM extends the WIM and applies it to virtual buildings aiming at providing both: i) a navigation

M.F. Costabile and F. Paternò (Eds.): INTERACT 2005, LNCS 3585, pp. 1014–1017, 2005.

aid – for users who travel in the VE by walking; ii) a means of studying any floor without having to navigate it.

3 The Interactive 3D BreakAway Map

For designing the I3BAM we aimed at providing: i) easy to understand information to help the user gain route and survey knowledge of a building; ii) easy interaction; iii) the capability of studying the structure of any floor without having to navigate it; iv) multiple views of the building, including a view of user's immediate surroundings with respect to the global context; v) enhancements to the user's exploration and discovery process.

The I3BAM provides the user with knowledge about the external and overall structure (e.g., the number of floors, exits,...) and also the internal structure of the building (e.g., how the floors are connected by staircases, where staircases are located, structural details of each floor,...). The I3BAM is a miniature 3D model of the building that constantly floats in front of the user. It can be moved and resized to avoid unwanted occlusions and it can be flipped to gain the best (ranging from a front to a top down) view of the building, by means of slider controls (Fig 1). Three different views (described in the following) are provided by the I3BAM, each one presenting the building at varying amounts of visual complexity. Operating on the views does not affect the virtual building in any manner.

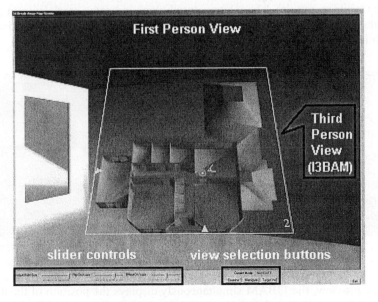

Fig. 1. The I3BAM (center of the screen) with the related controls (bottom of the screen)

Examine: In this view, the user can interact with the I3BAM via mouse clicks. All floors are visualized. Each floor slides out (horizontally) when clicked. This allows the user to move floors obstructing the view to a particular floor and study its structure. It also helps to understand how the floors are organized to form the complete building. The floor sliding action is toggle-controlled: one click slides a floor outward from its initial position, another click slides it back to the initial position, e.g. being on floor 1 (below the white rectangle in Fig 2 and 3), the user can examine the structure of other floors: she clicks on floor 4 which slides out in the direction of the arrow (Fig 2) revealing the structure of floor 3, then she clicks on floor 3 to reveal floor 2 (Fig 3).

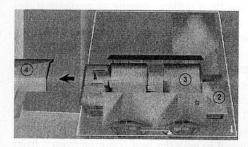
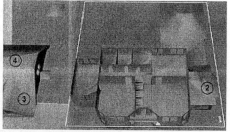

Fig. 2. Examine View (before click on floor 3)   **Fig. 3.** Examine View (after click on floor 3)

Floor: In this view, the I3BAM displays mainly the floor on which the user is walking. The rest of the building becomes semi-transparent, making it possible to use the view as a 3D map to navigate the current floor. In Fig 4, the I3BAM shows floor 1 (below the white rectangle). The white colored glyph indicates user's current position and orientation. The two white arrowheads along the sides are user's position along the length and breadth of the floor.

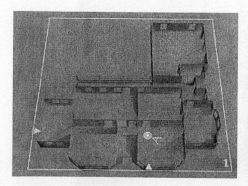
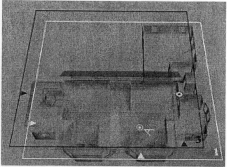

Fig. 4. Floor View   **Fig. 5.** Target View

Target: In this view, the I3BAM simultaneously displays the position of the user and a selected target within the global context of the entire building, enabling the user to assess her own position with respect to the target and decide how to reach it, by navigating. In Fig 5, the I3BAM shows the user's glyph is on floor 1. The target floor is outlined by the black rectangle and the target position by the black and white spot. The arrowheads (white for user's position and black for target position) further help the user to reach the target: once on the target floor, the user moves towards the target position until both the white and black arrow pairs coincide. The transparencies of floors are varied to provide the best possible view to the user. Let us call 'Higher' as the higher among the user and target floors and the other one as 'Lower'. All floors below the Lower floor are completely opaque, those between the Lower and Upper floor are rendered 90% transparent. The Higher floor is rendered 50% transparent. All floors above the Higher floor are rendered completely transparent.

The three views are easily differentiated visually and the name of the active view is also shown in text. Transitions among views are animated. Route knowledge can be gained by using the I3BAM because the user is made aware of the possible directions she can take and her own bearings with respect to the target as she travels towards it. Furthermore, survey knowledge can be gained both by studying (e.g., using the examine view) and actively exploring the building.

4   Conclusions and Future Work

The I3BAM extends the WIM (and attempts to overcome some of its shortcomings), applying it to virtual buildings both as a navigation aid and as a tool to study the building. We are now evaluating it on users and preliminary results are promising. We are also currently working on the development of tools to apply the I3BAM to previously created building models and on the integration of a path planning algorithm to provide detailed route indication capabilities. Finally, we plan to carry out a training transfer study based on routes to offices in our university building.

References

1. Bliss, J.P., Tidwell, P.D, Guest, M. The effectiveness of virtual reality for administering spatial navigation training to firefighters. Presence: Teleoperators and Virtual Environments 6, 1, pp.73-86, 1997.
2. Kalkusch, M., Lidy, T., Knapp, M., Reitmayr, G.,Kaufmann, H.,Schmalstieg, D. Structured visual markers for indoor pathfinding. Proc. of 1st IEEE International Augmented Reality Toolkit Workshop, IEEE Press, 2002.
3. Ruddle, R.A., Payne, S.J., Jones, D.M. The effects of maps on navigation and search strategies in very-large-scale virtual environments. Journal Of Experimental Psychology: Applied 5, pp.54-75, 1999.
4. Niederauer, C., Houston, M., Agrawala, M., Humphreys, G. Non-invasive interactive visualization of dynamic architectural environments. Proc. of the 2003 Symposium on Interactive 3D Graphics, ACM Press, New York, pp.55-58, 2003.
5. Stoakley, R., Conway, M., Pausch, R. Virtual reality on a WIM: Interactive worlds in miniature. Proc. of CHI95, ACM Press, New York, pp.265-272, 1995.
6. Pausch, R., Burnette, T., Brockway, D., Weiblen, M.E. Navigation and Locomotion in virtual worlds via flight into hand held miniatures, Proc. of SIGGRAPH '95, ACM Press, New York, pp.399-400, 1995.
7. Brooks, A. Aids for training real-world spatial knowledge using virtual environments. In Thompson B.J. (ed.) Research Papers of the Link Foundation Fellows (3), University of Rochester Press, 2003.
8. Murphy, M. "Home 07", (Public Domain) Building Model, www.pacranch.com

Virtual Reflections and Virtual Shadows in Mixed Reality Environments

Frank Steinicke, Klaus Hinrichs, and Timo Ropinski

WWU Münster, Institut für Informatik, Einsteinstrasse 62,
48419 Münster, Germany
{fsteini, khh, ropinski}@math.uni-muenster.de
http://viscg.uni-muenster.de

Abstract. In this paper we propose the concepts of virtual reflections, lights and shadows to enhance immersion in mixed reality (MR) environments, which focus on merging the real and the virtual world seamlessly. To improve immersion, we augment the virtual objects with real world information regarding the virtual reality (VR) system environment, e.g., CAVE, workbench etc. Real-world objects such as input devices or light sources as well as the position and posture of the user are used to simulate global illumination phenomena, e.g., users can see their own reflections and shadows on virtual objects. Besides the concepts and the implementation of this approach, we describe the system setup and an example application for this kind of advanced MR system environment.

1 Introduction

Seamlessly merging the real and the virtual world created within a computer is a challenging topic in current *virtual reality* (VR) research. Technology that superimposes the real world by computer-generated images is called *augmented reality* (AR) whereas the enhancement of virtual worlds using real-world data is called *augmented virtuality* (AV). In both cases, the goal is seamlessly merging of the real and virtual world. The term *mixed reality* (MR) ([3]) encompasses both augmented reality as well as augmented virtuality. As mentioned in [4], the main issues of MR environments are consistency of geometry, time, and illumination. Of course, one of the most important tasks is that superimposed objects have to be placed at the exact position where they would exist in the real world. Likewise, reflections, light sources and shadows must match in both worlds to obtain consistent global illumination; hence movements in the two worlds must be synchronized.

Recent approaches blend both synthetic as well as real objects to excellent quality images. However, the addressed global illumination is applicable only under specific limitations, e.g., non real-time performance, or if certain requirements are satisfied, e.g., a geometric computer model of the real scene is required or light sources need to be static [2]. The strategies proposed in [4] which improve the usage of virtual lights and shadows in MR use special hardware that is usually not accessible in most MR system environments. The effect of virtual reflections with respect to immersion in AR environments has been examined in [5]. This approach approximates reflections of real-world objects on virtual objects by extracting environment information from the background.

M.F. Costabile and F. Paternò (Eds.): INTERACT 2005, LNCS 3585, pp. 1018–1021, 2005.

Fig. 1. Captured video frame of the working area (left). Reflection from the user's point of view (right).

Our approach and system setup presented in this paper combines global illumination phenomena in MR system environments in order to blur the borders between the real and the virtual world. Hence we add visual information of the real environment surrounding the user to the virtual objects, e.g., objects dynamically mirror the environment, and thus users can see their own reflections and cast shadows in the virtual world. The proposed concepts and application scenario support the realization of an MR environment that provides a novel way of visual interaction.

In Section 2 we describe implementation and setup of our MR system environment. Section 3 presents an example application and discusses the benefits of our approach. Section 4 concludes the paper and gives an overview about future work.

2 Mixed Reality Environment Setup

2.1 Virtual Reflections

Reflective surfaces such as glass, metal or water reflect their environments. Usually an environment map is constructed in order to apply reflections in real-time computer graphics. For this purpose two types of maps have been proposed in [1]: *spherical environment maps* and *cubic environment maps*. In a spherical map a sphere with a single spherically distorted texture surrounds the virtual scene. Using cube maps the virtual environment is approximated by the six faces of a cube having an appropriate texture map; the cube is centered at the camera position. To simulate reflections rays are cast through the environment map. Green ([1]) preferred the usage of cubic environment maps because of the easier integration into 3D graphics hardware. Cubic environment maps are created by rendering a virtual scene or capturing real-world information with a 90-degree field of view (FoV) camera resulting in left, right, front, back, top and bottom textures. Since the textures are static images that are unaffected when the environment changes, interaction results in an inconvenient behavior in a highly interactive MR system environment. Thus, to further improve immersion in interactive MR applications changes of the real-world environment have to be considered. Hence a dynamic environment map representing the complete surrounding of the MR system environment is desirable. In our approach we simplify this idea and use a single USB camera that records the main working area of the user, i.e., the area in front of the screen in our projection-based MR system environment. The remaining areas, which are not subject to change, are given by static images of the surrounding generated by rendering a geometric model of the MR system environment.

In our setup the camera is attached to the top of a responsive workbench (RWB) (see Figure 2 (left)). Figure 1 (left) shows an image of a user in the working area captured from a live stream. This image is part of the cubic environment map containing the remaining areas. A resulting reflection based on this environment map is shown in Figure 1 (right). By using this approach, virtual objects with a reflective surface mirror other virtual objects and the static environment as well as the varying working area in front of the screen. Although the lighting conditions in MR system environments are often insufficient, users experience an adequate reflection (see Figure 1 (right)) because additional light is dispersed from the projection screen.

2.2 Virtual Shadows

Besides reflections the usage of virtual light sources and virtual shadows enhances the realism of virtual objects. In order to apply and modify direct lighting in MR environments in an intuitive way, we propose the following light interaction of real and virtual objects. Passive markers are attached to a real floor lamp for real-time tracking via our optical tracking system. Position and orientation of the tracked lamp are exploited to place the virtual light source accordingly. Thus a user simply moves the floor lamp, and the virtual light is positioned in the virtual scene in the same way as the real-world light source and illuminates the scene.

In the real world a user, moving in-between light source and an illuminated object, casts a shadow on the object. Because the user is usually not defined as geometry in the visualization system, it is difficult to calculate a corresponding shadow. In general, however, the user's head and at least one hand are tracked to allow an immersive direct interaction. In our approach we augment the virtual scene with a geometric model approximating the user's posture used for shadow generation. Therefore the depth information of this geometry is rendered into a depth texture, which is applied later on during shadow mapping. Using this approach no special hardware devices are necessary for shadow generation. The tracked floor lamp is illustrated in Figure 2 (left), while the resulting shadow of the user's hand in combination with the described reflection can be seen on the engine hood of the car in Figure 2 (right).

3 Application Scenario

To evaluate the described concepts we have implemented an example application that supports the advanced exploration of different car models (see Figure 2). The virtual cars can be illuminated intuitively by naturally positioning the previously described tracked floor lamp. The surrounding of the VR laboratory can be seen in the reflection and thus the surface structure of the car looks more realistic. The virtual car seen from the user's point of view is illustrated in Figure 2 (right), which shows clearly visible reflections and shadows on the engine hood.

 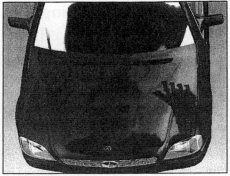

Fig. 2. Responsive workbench environment with tracked head, hand, and floor lamp (left). Reflections and shadows on the engine hood from the user's point of view (right).

4 Conclusion and Future Work

We have proposed the concepts of an advanced MR system environment that considerably increases realism of virtual objects as well as an example application which underlines the benefits. We are confident that the described approach enhances the VR-based design of cars in automotive industry since surface properties are displayed more realistic, and an intuitive positioning of light sources is possible.

An evaluation of the described system setup will show in how far the usage of virtual reflections and virtual shadows increases the users' immersion and improves object interaction. To further enhance this approach more high-resolution cameras could be attached to the setup, and additional information about the user's posture could be used to generate more precise shadow models.

References

1. Greene, N.: Environment Mapping and Other Applications of World Projections. IEEE Computer Graphics and Applications 6(11) (1986) pp. 21-29.
2. Jacobs, K., Loscos, C.: Classification of Illumination Methods for Mixed Reality. Eurographics 2004, State of the Art Report (2004) pp. 95-118.
3. Milgram, P., Kishino, F.: A Taxonomy of Mixed Reality Visual Displays. IEICE Trans. on Information Systems E77-D (12) (1994) pp. 1321-1329.
4. Naemura, T., Nitta, T., Mimura, A., Harashima, H.: Virtual Shadows in Mixed Reality Environment Using Flashlight-like Devices. Trans. of Virtual Reality Society of Japan 7(2) (2002) pp. 227-237.
5. Ropinski, T., Wachenfeld, S., Hinrichs, K.: Virtual Reflections for Augmented Reality Environments. Int. Conference on Artificial Reality and Telexistence (2004) pp. 311-318.

Cooking with the Elements:
Intuitive Immersive Interfaces
for Augmented Reality Environments

Leonardo Bonanni, Chia-Hsun Lee, and Ted Selker

MIT Media Laboratory,
20 Ames Street, Cambridge MA 02139 (USA)
{amerigo, jackylee, selker}@media.mit.edu
http://www.media.mit.edu/~amerigo

Abstract. The glut of information produced by ubiquitous computing in augmented reality environments requires that the resulting information displays be tailored to the attention of users and mapped directly to the objects and surfaces of the space. This paper proposes a method for designing and implementing ambient information displays combining ambient displays and augmented reality to produce useful intuitive interfaces that are concretely mapped to architectural spaces for the purposes of expanding and enriching the quality and sensuality of user experience.

1 Introduction

Ubiquitous computing in architectural space is making it possible to gather information about people and their tasks that can be applied to augmenting and enriching the experience of users. As the interface possibilities made possible by the widespread use of computer sensors and effectors grow, it becomes possible to map information on all the surfaces and tools of a space to orient and assist users and make possible entirely new experiences within conventional environments. In order to be effective these spatial interfaces must be designed and implemented in accordance with the attention of users and their performance so as to assist and enrich user experience without distracting or confusing basic tasks. Ambient interfaces offer a minimally

Fig. 1. Cooking with the Elements: Multimedia projections enrich a conventional kitchen by projecting intuitive displays to reveal the status of tools and surfaces

M.F. Costabile and F. Paternò (Eds.): INTERACT 2005, LNCS 3585, pp. 1022–1025, 2005.
© IFIP International Federation for Information Processing 2005

taxing means of distributed information display, while augmented reality interfaces seek to provide useful task-based information. This paper proposes a new type of interface that concentrates on creating intuitive immersive interfaces that inform activity without interfering with tasks.

2 Related Work

Ambient displays have been prototyped and produced for the purpose of displaying information throughout the built environment in a manner that does not tax the attention of users. Ishii's Windmills and Ambient Devices' Stock Orb are two systems that display a limited amount of information in the form of decorative objects [1,2]. These devices purportedly communicate simple information in a language only understood by their trained owners; for example, the Orb requires users to know that its color refers to stock market values and that red indicates decreasing market performance while yellow indicates no change. Similarly, Kaye's InStink utilizes computer-dispensed perfumes as an ambient interface that maps information to the more salient but still unintuitive olfactory sense [4]. Nevertheless, ambient interfaces have the benefits of using the minimum possible attentional "bandwidth" to communicate information and organizing the information by distributing it throughout a physical space.

At the other extreme, spatial information displays have been implemented to orient and assist users in tasks by presenting, for example, projected desktop instruments in an office [6] or recipes in a kitchen [3]. In our evaluations of such text- and graphic-heavy displays, it was determine that they had no benefit and in some cases performed worse than standard screen- or paper-based displays. Reasons include the cognitive weight of text and graphics, especially when distributed over large areas, and the inability to reference multiple sources of information simultaneously. However these displays have the distinct advantage of mapping digital information directly to the physical space where tasks are being performed; for example, in Microsoft's Kitchen of the Future users measure out flour by pouring it onto a projected circle until it is completely covered [4].

3 Implementation

Our interfaces seek to combine the attention-based design of ambient interfaces with the utility of one-to-one projected augmentation by overlaying an environment with intuitive, immersive information interfaces. Our test bed is a kitchen because it stands as the epitome of a feedback-less modern space. Centuries of innovation in hygiene and automation have eliminated most sensory experience from modern kitchens while filling them with ubiquitous computers, sensors and effectors. In our kitchen, we have installed a system of sensors and projectors specifically for the purpose of overlaying the existing space with sensory feedback to assist and enrich the user's experience. The research on which this paper is based originates with a case study that considers the faucet alone, and expands to consider the appliances and countertops of the space.

3.1 HeatSink

In the kitchen, users have come to depend on remote controls and indicators to know the temperature of food and water or the status of the stove. For example, how often do we scald ourselves at the faucet or wait arbitrarily for tap water to reach a desired temperature? HeatSink is a simple solid-state circuit that projects colored light into the stream of tap water to indicate its temperature intuitively: red for hot fading to blue for cold. During design one iteration was considered that maps temperature to a full red-green-blue spectrum like the Stock Orb. The final choice of simple red and blue was based on the fact that people do not intuitively understand the temperature of 'green' water; their main concern is to determine whether the water is colder or hotter than their hands before touching it. By using various intensities of only two colors, HeatSink displays only the minimum essential information and does not inconvenience the task at hand or require prior knowledge. Taking a cue from projected augmented reality interfaces, the projection of colored light directly into the stream proves more successful than remote indicators like the control knob because the information is overlaid directly on the user's focus of attention (see Fig. 2).

Fig. 2. HeatSink: LEDs mounted to the faucet aerator and driven by a PIC-based microcircuit project modulated colored light into the stream of tap water

3.2 Cooking with the Elements

The modern kitchen is a technological marvel that combines the elements of fire, water, ice and earth in a compact hygienic space. Following from HeatSink, Cooking with the Elements maps intuitive multimedia textures to the countertops of a conventional kitchen to enrich and inform tasks in the space. Common problems such as knowing if the oven is hot or keeping the refrigerator door open too long can be intuitively annotated with dynamic audiovisual textures projected onto the surfaces of the appliances themselves. Likewise, the countertop can serve as a control panel that communicates the status of tools and surfaces intuitively in an ambient way that responds to the attention of users according to their performance and position in space.

Cooking with the elements consists of tiled multimedia projections that seamlessly cover all the countertops of the kitchen. Proximity sensors situated along the countertop edge locate users while temperature and water sensors and micro-switches detect the status of the cabinets, countertops, sink, and appliances. A Director movie is generated across three seamlessly tiled projections that maps dynamic multimedia textures to the space depending on the status of tools and the performance of users. When someone opens the refrigerator, the sound of a cold wind plays and projected snow begins to accumulate as an indication of how long the door is open and the energy wasted. When the electric range is on or the stove reaches desired temperature, a dynamic fire is projected while the crackling of a wood fire is heard. If the sink is left running, a projected pool of water grows to cover the countertop while the sound of a creek fills the room. Depending on where users are located, these displays grow or shrink to remain in the periphery of their attention and never to detract from their current task. In case a user forgets the water running or the stove on, the displays grow so that anyone entering the space is immediately aware that something is wrong. Although the displayed textures only convey limited information (hot, cold, wet) they seek to do so in a completely intuitive manner that is always accessible and never annoying. Cooking with the Elements enriches the sensory nature of cooking and returns some of the feedback that was lost when kitchens became modern and hermetic (see Fig. 1).

4 Conclusion

As computers become ubiquitous in the built environment, interfaces that interact at the scale of architectural space will be commonplace. Rather than fill the space with text and graphics, these immersive multimedia displays have the power to transform and augment human experience so that mundane experiences become exciting and users understand information with minimal cognitive effort or prior knowledge. While screen- and paper-based devices will continue to provide us with highly informative interfaces, the space around us can become simpler and more beautiful with immersive interfaces. Imagine waking up to a projected sunrise rather than a beeping alarm or smelling fresh food from the market when you open the refrigerator – computer interfaces can actively enrich and augment our daily experiences by calmly and intuitively enhancing the bland textures of our built environment with dynamic sensory experiences as we once had and as we never before dreamed.

References

1. Ambient Devices: www.ambientdevices.com
2. Ishii, H., Ren, S. and Frei, P., Pinwheels: Visualizing Information Flow in an Architectural Space (short paper), in *Proc. CHI '01*, 111-12.
3. Ju, W. et. al. (2001). "Counteractive: An Interactive Cookbook for the Kitchen Counter," *in Extended Abstracts CHI 2001*, 269-70.
4. Kaye, J. N. (2001) *Symbolic Olfactory Display*. Master's Thesis, MIT Media Lab, 2001.
5. Microsoft Kitchen of the Future as seen in the Food Network's documentary 'Kitchens of the Future,' 2003.
6. Wellner, P. "The DigitalDesk calculator: Tangible Manipulation on a Desk Top Display," in *Proc. UIST '91*, 27-34.

Learners' Perceived Level of Difficulty of a Computer-Adaptive Test: A Case Study

Mariana Lilley, Trevor Barker, and Carol Britton

University of Hertfordshire, School of Computer Science,
College Lane, Hatfield, Hertfordshire AL10 9AB, United Kingdom
{M.Lilley, T.1.Barker, C.Britton}@herts.ac.uk

Abstract. A computer-adaptive test (CAT) is a software application that makes use of Item Response Theory (IRT) to create a test that is tailored to individual learners. The CAT prototype introduced here comprised a graphical user interface, a question database and an adaptive algorithm based on the Three-Parameter Logistic Model from IRT. A sample of 113 Computer Science undergraduate students participated in a session of assessment within the Human-Computer Interaction subject domain using our CAT prototype. At the end of the assessment session, participants were asked to rate the level of difficulty of the overall test from 1 (very easy) to 5 (very difficult). The perceived level of difficulty of the test and the CAT scores obtained by this group of learners were subjected to a Spearman's rank order correlation. Findings from this statistical analysis suggest that the CAT prototype was effective in tailoring the assessment to each individual learner's proficiency level.

1 Introduction

Computer-adaptive tests (CATs) are computer-assisted assessment applications in which the level of difficulty of the questions is dynamically tailored to the proficiency level of individual learners. Wainer [8] suggests that CATs mimic aspects of an oral interview in which the tutor would adapt the interview by choosing questions appropriate to the proficiency level of individual learners. Jettmar & Nass [5] describe CATs as a special case of intelligent user interfaces, in which user performance is unobtrusively monitored and the level of difficulty of the questions adapted accordingly. Brusilovsky [2] cites CATs as one of the elements of a paradigm shift within educational software development, from "one size fits all" to one capable of offering higher levels of interaction and personalisation. Conejo et al. [3], Fernandez [4], Lilley et al. [6] amongst others have reported on the benefits of the CAT approach in a range of educational contexts.

The main aim of a CAT software application is to provide learners with questions that are sufficiently challenging, and yet not so difficult that could lead to frustration or bewilderment on the part of the learners.

CATs are based on Item Response Theory (IRT). IRT is a family of mathematical functions that attempts to predict the probability of a user successfully completing a task or, more specifically, answering a question correctly. An overview of our CAT prototype is provided in the next section of this paper.

M.F. Costabile and F. Paternò (Eds.): INTERACT 2005, LNCS 3585, pp. 1026–1029, 2005.

2 Prototype Overview

The CAT prototype described here comprised a graphical user interface, a question bank and an adaptive algorithm based on the Three-Parameter Logistic (3-PL) Model from IRT [7, 8].

Equation 1 [7] shows the 3-PL Model function used to predict the probability of a test-taker with an unknown proficiency level θ correctly answering a question of difficulty b, discrimination a and pseudo-chance c. In Equation 1, questions with greater values for the difficulty b parameter require greater proficiency on the part of the test-taker to answer the question correctly than those questions with lower values. The discrimination a parameter describes the question's usefulness when distinguishing amongst test-takers near a proficiency level θ [7]. The pseudo-chance c parameter indicates the probability of a test-taker answering a question correctly by chance.

$$P(\theta) = c + \frac{1-c}{1 + e^{-1.7a(\theta-b)}} \tag{1}$$

A typical CAT starts with a question of medium difficulty. In general terms, a correct response will cause a more difficult question to be administered next. Conversely, an incorrect response will cause a less difficult question to follow. As the test proceeds, the mathematical function shown in Equation 1 is employed to estimate the test-taker's proficiency level. The proficiency level estimate is then used to select the question to be administered next. A detailed description of IRT is beyond the scope of this paper and the interested reader is referred to Lord [7] and Wainer [8].

3 The Study

A sample of 113 Computer Science undergraduate students participated in a summative assessment session using the CAT application. The assessment session took place in computer laboratories, under supervised conditions. Participants had 35 minutes to answer 24 objective questions organised into 4 topics within the Human-Computer Interaction (HCI) subject domain. Participants' performance on this assessment is summarised in Table 1.

In Table 1, the value for the proficiency level ranged from -3 (lowest) to +3 (highest). In a CAT, we are not concerned with the number of correct responses. Indeed most participants are expected to answer approximately 50% of the questions correctly, as it is anticipated that the questions administered to each individual test-taker would be tailored to that individual's proficiency level within the subject domain. The focus is therefore on the level of difficulty of the questions answered correctly by each individual test-taker.

Table 1. Summary of test-takers' performance (N=113)

	Mean	Standard Deviation
Proficiency Level	0.08	1.07
% Correct responses	47.64	10.37

At the end of the assessment session, all participants were asked to rate the difficulty of the test that they had just taken from 1 (very easy) to 5 (very difficult). The mean test difficulty, as perceived by the participants, was 3.37 (SD=0.60, N=113). Their ratings are illustrated in Table 2.

Table 2. Level of difficulty of the test as perceived by the participants (N=113)

1 (Very easy)	2	3 (Just right)	4	5 (Very difficult)	Total
0	2	72	34	5	113

It was important to investigate whether or not the correlation between participants' performance and their perceptions on the level of difficulty of the overall test was statistically significant. Such statistical analysis is the focus of the next section of this paper.

4 Perceived Test Difficulty According to Learner's Performance

Participants' results and their perception of the test's difficulty were subjected to a Spearman's rank order correlation.

No statistically significant correlation was found between participants' proficiency levels and the test's difficulty rating, such as rs = -0.092, Sig. (2-tailed) = 0.333, N=113. The data gathered in this study was also subjected to a Kruskal-Wallis Test, where Chi-Square = 0.736, df = 2, Asymp. Sig. = 0.692. The results from this statistical analysis are summarised in Table 3.

Table 3. Level of difficulty of the test as perceived by the participants, according to test performance (N=113)

	Group	N	Mean Rank
Rating	Low-performing participants	38	58.96
	Intermediate-performing participants	36	58.24
	High-performing participants	39	53.95

The results shown in Table 3 were taken to indicate that the participants' performance on the test had no effect on the perceived difficulty of test. This is of particular importance, since one of the goals of our CAT prototype was that test-takers would be presented with tasks that are challenging and motivating, rather than tasks that are either too difficult and therefore frustrating, or too easy and thus uninteresting.

5 Summary and Concluding Remarks

Interactive software applications that adapt to their users have been rapidly gaining in importance within the HCI field. CATs are an example of such interactive applications, as the level of difficulty of the tasks is adapted to the proficiency level of individual users. Despite the substantial amount of work that has been conducted in this area, it can be argued that users' perceptions of the CAT approach have been under represented in the literature.

In previous studies we have shown that our CAT prototype supports accurate measurement of learners' proficiency levels [1, 6]. This paper is concerned with users' perceptions of the level of difficulty of an assessment session that was interactively created using our CAT prototype. Findings from this empirical study were taken to indicate that the CAT approach was effective in providing individual users with a sufficient challenge whilst using the application. An important assumption of our work was that an appropriate degree of challenge would enhance test-takers' motivation. This could, in turn, contribute towards an enhancement of their learning experience. The use of computers alone is not sufficient to motivate users of educational software applications. Interaction is a valuable tool to maintain learners' motivation and therefore whenever possible, educational software should adapt to the learner's proficiency levels and skills.

References

1. Barker, T. & Lilley, M. Are Individual Learners Disadvantaged by the Use of Computer-Adaptive Testing? In *Proceedings of the 8th Learning Styles Conference*. University of Hull, European Learning Styles Information Network (ELSIN), pp. 30-39, 2003.
2. Brusilovsky, P. Knowledge Tree: A Distributed Architecture for Adaptive E-Learning In *Proceedings of the 13th World Wide Web Conference*, May 17-22, New York, New York, USA, pp. 104-113, 2004.
3. Conejo, R., Millán, E., Pérez-de-la-Cruz, J. L. & Trella, M. An Empirical Approach to On-Line Learning in SIETTE In Proceedings of the 2000 Intelligent Tutoring Systems Conference, LNCS **1839**, pp. 605-614, 2000.
4. Fernandez, G. Cognitive Scaffolding for a Web-Based Adaptive Learning Environment In *Proceedings of 2003 International Conference on Web-based Learning*, LNCS **2783**, pp. 12–20, 2003.
5. Jettmar, E. & Nass, C. Adaptive testing: effects on user performance In *Proceedings of the SIGCHI conference on Human factors in computing systems: Changing our world, changing ourselves*. Minneapolis, Minnesota, USA, pp. 129-134, 2002.
6. Lilley, M., Barker, T. & Britton, C. The development and evaluation of a software prototype for computer adaptive testing. *Computers & Education Journal* **43**(1-2), pp. 109-122, 2004.
7. Lord, F. M. *Applications of Item Response Theory to practical testing problems*. New Jersey: Lawrence Erlbaum Associates, 1980.
8. Wainer, H. *Computerized Adaptive Testing (A Primer)*. 2nd Edition. New Jersey: Lawrence Erlbaum Associates, 2000.

How to Communicate Recommendations?
Evaluation of an Adaptive Annotation Technique

Federica Cena[1,2], Cristina Gena[2], and Sonia Modeo[1,2]

[1] CSP Innovazione nelle ICT s.c. a r.l., Torino, Italy
{modeo, cena}@csp.it
[2] Dip. di Informatica, Università di Torino, Torino, Italy
cgena@di.unito.it

Abstract. In this paper we present an evaluation of an adaptive annotation technique (the use of icons to help the user in the selection of the most relevant suggested item), using the Grounded Theory methodology. The goal of the evaluation was to find out the best icon in order to communicate the system recommendations in the most effective way.

1 Introduction

Information overload is one of the most serious problems that user suffers in every day life, especially during Internet navigation. Recommender systems help the user to choose within this large amount of information. This could be especially helpful in a mobile context where the interaction can be very challenging for the user due to: device limitations (display, battery, connection, I/O devices, etc.), and difficulties of interaction (movement, noisy or badly illuminated environment, etc.). These difficulties requires not only the personalization of the user interaction with the system [10][2], but also the communication of the personalization in the most effective way, as the user must be always aware of the personalization features of the system.

We faced these problems during the development of UbiquiTO, a multi-device mobile tourist guide that provides recommendations adapted to the individual user, her location, her device and the current context conditions (for more details see [1]). Usually, in adaptive systems, recommended items are emphasized with adaptive annotation, a navigation support that consists in attaching various visual cues (e.g., enlarging font, changing color, adding icons, etc.) to the suggested items in order to help the user to select the most relevant one [3]. Empirical studies of adaptive annotation in educational context demonstrate that it could reduce navigation overhead and improve learning activity [4]. Adaptive annotation is also largely exploited in recommender systems (see, for example, [5]), even if there is a lack of empirical studies on the correct way to annotate items (one of them is [6]).

2 Testing and Results

We decided to communicate the UbiquiTO recommendations by means of the adaptive annotation technique. In particular, we decided to add meaningful icons to every

M.F. Costabile and F. Paternò (Eds.): INTERACT 2005, LNCS 3585, pp. 1030–1033, 2005.

suggested item. In order to choose the best kind of icon, we presented the icons commonly used in adaptive systems to real users: (Fig. 1): *traffic light circles*, which are mainly used in adaptive learning systems [4]; *stars*, which are mainly used in recommender systems to express a quantitative assessment and two other less exploited icons (*circles* and *asterisks*) sharing a similar meaning; *emoticons,* which have been used both in recommender and in adaptive learning systems; *full-half full-empty colour,* which are often added to enforce the meaning of adaptive icons [6]. We also presented to the subjects a seventh choice: a percentage associated to each item since our previous prototype used this option. Notice that we used well-known and common icons to facilitate user's recognition rather than recall [7]. Thus, we did not consider creative icons from commercial systems in order to increase the usability of our interface: icons have to be easily recognizable and understandable. The user does not have to think too much working out from memory what an icon is about.

In particular, the goal of the evaluation were to find out: *i*) if the users understand the way the system communicates the strength of recommendations; *ii*) which is the most appropriate symbol for representing the system recommendations; *iii*) which meaning the users attribute to each group of symbols.

In order to evaluate point *i*) we provided the subjects with a set of PDA screenshots with the symbols associated to a non-significant text ("foo"), equal in every screenshot. Each screenshot contained the 3 symbols belonging to the same group (Fig. 2), ordered in a randomized way. We asked the subjects to choose "the item you think the system is recommending as the best one for you". For instance, in the emoticon group, the smiling face suggests the best choice, while in case of stars the three stars are the right choice, and so on. To evaluate point *ii*), we asked the subjects which group of symbols best represents the system personalization and why. Finally, to test point *iii*) we asked the subjects to associate a meaning to every symbol.

We involved in the evaluation 34 subjects, 20 males and 14 females, 25-34 aged, with different types of background and occupation, and being familiar with computer, Internet and new devices (PDA, smartphone, Digital Terrestrial Television). Regarding point *i*), subjects correctly understood the way the system communicates the strength of recommendations: in fact, most of the times they chose the symbols we associated to the best recommendations (69%). They rarely chose symbols referring to the recommendations with medium strength (15%) and worst strength (16%) and the differences were significant ($\chi^2(66)=129.83$, $p<0.001$). The type of symbol (*stars, balls, emoticons,* etc.) does not influence in a significant way the choices of the best items ($\chi^2(10)=13.92$). Concerning the evaluation of point *ii*), the group of symbols best representing recommendations were the *stars* (chosen by 18 subjects), followed by *emoticons* (6 choices), *traffic light circles* (5 choices), *full-half full-empty circles* (2 choices), *asterisks* (1 choice), *percentage* (1 choice), and *circles* (1) and the differences were significant ($\chi^2(6)=54.5$, $p<0.001$). Finally, to evaluate the meaning the subjects associate to the symbols (point *iii*), we related these results to the subjects' explanations about the symbols best representing the system personalization, to find possible correlations. Since we gained both quantitative and qualitative results, we decided to apply the Grounded Theory methodology [11], where collected data may be qualitative or quantitative or a combination of both types, since an interplay between qualitative and quantitative methods is advocated. Moreover, as a recent study pointed out [8], statistical analyses are often false, misleading and too narrow, while insights and qualitative studies do not suffer from these problems as they strictly rely to the users' observed behavior and reactions. Even if our quantitative analysis reported significant results, the actual preferences of the users could be different.

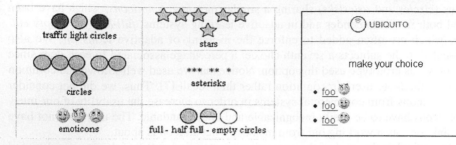

Fig. 1. The evaluated icons groups   Fig. 2. A PDA screenshot

Three phases of data analysis are involved in the Grounded Theory. In the **open coding** phase we identified the concepts the subjects associate to the symbols and their properties (*traffic light circles* = user actions, *stars* = qualitative assessment, *circles* = quantitative assessment, *asterisks* = context-dependent meaning, *emoticons* = system emotion and opinion, *full-half full-empty circles* = quantity, *percentage* = numeric estimate). In the **axial coding** phase we related categories to their subcategories, linking categories at the level of properties and dimensions. For instance, we noticed that *circles* and *stars* share the same category (assessment) by considering different points of views (respectively quantitative and qualitative). In the **selective coding** phase we phrased the theory: the core category that best represents the communication of personalized suggestions is the "non-verbal communication", since the non-verbal hints express those emotional states necessary to make the system-user communication as personalized as possible. In our context we have to disambiguate that the system suggestions are not absolutely the best ones, but they are the best ones for a specific user, and emoticons are able to express feelings that make the interaction more human-like.

3 Discussions

The analysis carried on showed that the symbols that best represent emotional states are the emoticons: they represent opinions and emotions the system aims at communicating to the users. As it can be noticed, the last finding is in contrast to the quantitative evaluation results, which showed that stars are the best symbols for recommendations. Stars usually express a qualitative evaluation associated to an expert opinion or to a general assessment (e.g., 3 stars associated to a restaurant mean that the restaurant received good rates by a somewhat guide, not that it is good for me). When users explained their choices, they associated stars to a general qualitative judgment, while they related emoticons to feelings expressed by the system itself. In addition, the usual context where stars are used (e.g., newspapers, books, etc.) is different from a personal interaction, whereas emoticons are able to express positive, neutral or negative feelings. Even if some web sites, such as Amazon, use stars to communicate personalization, our subjects seem to have some difficulties in associating them to a personalization concept. We think that the reported quantitative results oversimplified the discussion about users choices, thus we gave more weight to qualitative results emerged from subjects explanations.

Therefore, we have used emoticons in UbiquiTO, as they seem to be able to communicate personalized messages. Moreover, in a small device with limited screen capabilities, the exploitation of emoticons allows us to use a single icon instead of a group of icons, thus reducing the amount of required space. Last but not least, our results are similar to the "The Media Equation" theory [9], which claims that as humans treat computer socially, the main goal of interface design has to be the replication of human-human communication.

References

1. I. Amendola, F. Cena, L. Console, A. Crevola, C. Gena, A. Goy, S. Modeo, M. Perrero, I. Torre, and A. Toso. UbiquiTO: a Multi-Device Adaptive Guide. In *the Proceedings of conference MobileHCI'04*, Sept. 13–16, Glasgow, Scotland (2004) 409-114.
2. D. Billsus, C. Brunk, C. Evans, B. Gladish, and M. Pazzani. Adaptive Interfaces for Ubiquitous Web Access. *Comm. of the ACM 45*(5), 2003, pp. 34-38.
3. P. Brusilowsky. Adaptive Hypermedia. *UMUAI 11* (1-2): 2001, pp 87-110
4. P. Brusilovsky, S. Sosnovsky, and O. Shcherbinina. QuizGuide: Increasing the Educational Value of Individualized Self-Assessment Quizzes with Adaptive Navigation Support. In the *Proceedings of World Conference on E-Learning*, E-Learn 2004, Washington, DC, USA, November 1-5, 2004, pp. 1806-1813
5. GroupLens Research Projects, http://www.grouplens.org, 2005.
6. S. M. McNee, K.S. Lam, C. Guetzlaff, J. A. Konstan, and J. Riedl. Confidence Displays and Training in Recommender Systems. In the *Proceedings of INTERACT '03 IFIP TC13 International Conference on Human-Computer Interaction*, 2003, pp. 176-183.
7. J. Nielsen. Usability Engineering. Boston, MA.Academic Press, 1993.
8. J. Nielsen. Risks of Qualitative Studies. http://www.useit.com/alertbox/20040301.html, 2004.
9. B. Reeves and C. Nass. The Media Equation: How People Treat Computers, Televisions, and New Media as Real People and Places. Cambridge University Press, New York, 1996.
10. B. Smyth and P.Cotter. The Plight of the Navigator: Solving the Navigation Problem for Wireless Portals. In the *Proceedings of the 2nd International Conference on Adaptive Hypermedia and Adaptive Web Systems*. Malaga, Spain, 2002, pp. 328-337.
11. A. L. Strauss and J. M. Corbin. Basics of qualitative research: techniques and procedures for developing grounded theory. SAGE, Thousand Oaks, 1998.

Adaptive User Interfaces Development Platform

Jing-Hua Ye and John Herbert

Department of Computer Science,
Kane Building,
University College Cork,
College Road,
Cork, Republic of Ireland
{jhy1, j.herbert}@cs.ucc.ie

Abstract. Most documents dynamically generated by a web server are in HTML format. However the use of dynamic HTML documents severely limits the amount of user interface (UI) validation that can be done. In order to generalize the abstract UI platform and strengthen the UI validation process, we developed a novel platform to support both UI adaptation and dynamic UI construction. It provides a generic architecture for runtime adaptive UI development based on various XML technologies. As well as making use of different built-in modules, one can extend the platform by adding new functionalities into it. The ease of use of the platform is illustrated using a case study of an on-line accommodation booking form based on the official web site of the English town of Windsor.

1   Introduction

With the increasing availability of wireless technologies people can now use a variety of hand-held computing devices, such as PDAs, smart phones and pagers to access the same information from any place at any time. Due to varying input/output techniques, modalities, interaction mechanisms, as well as physical constraints, the UIs used to access this information across devices are often drastically different. It is very difficult to build UIs that work across multiple devices without duplicating development effort. The difficulty in designing UIs for multiple devices prompts the need for the development of a multi-device adaptive UI. The goal of this work is to facilitate UI development for devices with restrictive capabilities. An innovative generic software architecture has been developed as a framework. It provides various adaptation mechanisms and provides an XML-based dynamic UI generation mechanism that is a significant feature of the framework.

2   Software Architecture for Adaptation

Figure 1 shows the main building blocks of this framework, which has been designed and implemented with an Xalan-XSLT-processor [1], the Apache web server and the JAXP package [2].

M.F. Costabile and F. Paternò (Eds.): INTERACT 2005, LNCS 3585, pp. 1034–1037, 2005.

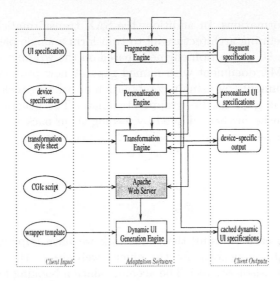

Fig. 1. Generic architecture for a runtime adaptive UI Development System

The UI and device specifications, the associated transformation style sheet, the CGIc script [3], and the wrapper template are required as the inputs to the adaptation software. Each specification is created by UI developers at design time. Developers can use XUL to specify the logical structure of the UI in a UI specification. It is prudent for developers to explicitly specify whether each XUL element can be split or not by giving a yes/no value to the "breakable" attribute of each one. All physical constraints on the target device (i.e. memory capacity, screen size, resolution etc) are specified in a standard XML format. All elements in the UI specification can be transformed to some corresponding device-specific ones by applying the rules specified in an XSL based transformation style sheet. A CGIc script is a standard C program imported from the CGI library. It wraps up user requests submitted via the Apache web server into a standard XML file. A wrapper template is a standard XML file containing a set of named gaps and source code for a target page that will be constructed dynamically.

The fragmentation engine runs a new fragmentation technique [4] to paginate a complex UI by using SAX APIs to index each abstract XUL element in order to minimize the mismatch between the presentation of a UI and a device's capabilities to present it. This fragmentation engine provides developers with the convenience of UI development for multiple devices.

The personalization engine deals with personalizing the adaptive UIs according to the user requests received from the external personalization request handlers. In particular, this engine has adopted a controller-filter architecture [5] so that various types of personalization can be supported by a single module. Link personalization, user-based personalization, and context personalization are supported by this engine.

The transformation engine transforms a UI specification into a device-specific one. The most important feature of this engine is that it supports both the DOM and SAX transformations. In addition, the SAX transformation engine uses a special filter pipelining architecture [6] to transform a single page.

The dynamic UI generation engine is based on the wrapper template, which is a standard XML document with named gaps. A new process constructs dynamic XML documents by using a combination of pruning techniques and plug operations for the gaps in the wrapper template. The generated dynamic UI specifications can be further adapted by feeding them back into any one of the engines (e.g. the personalization engine). This pruning-plugging process effectively provides a flexible means of constructing abstract dynamic UIs prior to a validation process.

3   Evaluation

To illustrate the ease of using the framework we have implemented a simple accommodation booking form for the official web site of the English town of Windsor (www.windsor.gov.uk). The accommodation booking form available on this site is in a hard-coded HTML format. Consequently, it can only be displayed on regular desktop PCs. However, it would be more desirable for holiday-makers to reserve their accommodations anytime, anywhere with their small screen devices. This problem can be easily overcome with our framework.

We re-coded the Windsor accommodation booking form in the XUL language. This booking form can be adapted to the various needs of UI developers. There are three important possible scenarios for this adaptation. The first scenario is to directly transform the form into HTML format. The second scenario is to paginate the XUL-encoded accommodation booking form into a seven-page PDA presentation. The third scenario is to personalize the XUL-encoded accommodation booking form according to the developer's requests, for example, a developer might wish to remove all the images from the booking form. Besides these three scenarios, a web page can also be dynamically generated by submitting the completed booking form to the web server that is supported in our framework. Due to lack of space, we show the result of the third scenario only in figure 2.

4   Conclusions

This paper presents a general framework that provides an innovative generic software architecture for a runtime adaptive UI development system. An abstract UI can be fragmented into a set of UI fragments that satisfies the constraints of the target device. An abstract UI can also be personalized according to the developer's needs and be transformed into a device-displayable UI. This framework also provides a dynamic UI generation engine that allows one to automatically generate a dynamic XML-based UI. Various functionalities can be easily integrated into this architecture in a modular fashion. This framework allows one to easily update or create a new UI for a new application. One can combine the modules provided in this framework according to one's needs. This framework makes available sophisticated technologies for UI adaptation in a re-usable extensible architecture that make it easy for UI developers to design, experiment with, and change an adaptable UI.

References

1. Apache XML Project: Xalan home page. http://xml.apache.org/xalan-j/index.html.
2. Sun Microsystems, Inc.: The JavaTM Web Service Tutorial v1.2.4. (2003), http://java.sun.com/.
3. Boutell.com: CGIc: An ANSI C library for CGI programming. (August 5th 2004) http://www.boutell.com/cgic/.
4. Jing-Hua Ye and John Herbert: User Interface Tailoring for Mobile Computing Devices. 8th ERCIM Workshop "User Interfaces for All". (28th June 2004), Vienna Austria.
5. Jing-Hua Ye and John Herbert: A Generic Architecture for User Interface Personalization. Proceedings of the Workshop on Environments for Personalized Information Access, Working Conference on Advanced Visual Interfaces (AVI 2004) (May 25th, 2004)
6. Jing-Hua Ye and John Herbert: Framework for User Interface Adaptation. 8th ERCIM Workshop "User Interfaces for All". (28th June 2004), Vienna Austria.

A   Windsor's Accommodation Booking Form

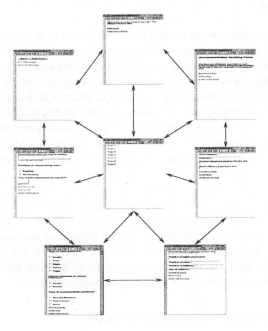

Fig. 2. Fragmented personalized accommodation booking form rendered on a PDA

Adapting the ADS for High Volume Manufacturing

Connor Upton and Gavin Doherty

Distributed Systems Group, Trinity College Dublin, Ireland
{connor.upton, gavin.doherty}@cs.tcd.ie

Abstract. Cognitive Work Analysis (CWA) is a methodology for analysing complex socio-technical systems. It aims to structure system information in a manner that is meaningful for human control and interaction. The Abstraction Decomposition Space (ADS) in an important tool used during the first phase of CWA to describe the work domain. In this paper we create an ADS for a Semiconductor Fabrication Plant. This is a High Volume Manufacturing environment and its complexity necessitates a number of adjustments to the original ADS technique. The physical decomposition of the system is de-emphasised and a number of alternative decomposition hierarchies are used instead. The analysis aims to produce artifacts that aid in the design of decision support systems. These artifacts not only help to assess the information needs of workers, but also structure the work domain in a manner that will inform display design.

1 Introduction

The correct visual representation of data has been shown to improve user performance and reduce human error in a range of domains [1] and many guidelines exist for the correct visual encoding of quantitative data [2]. Advances in sensor and communications technology means that more data is now being generated than ever before. Automated control systems are frequently used to process this data but human operators are often relied on to step in and assume system control if required. In these cases operators must examine data to evaluate the system state and make decisions. The complexity of these domains means that the challenge is not only how to encode the data visually, but also how to decide what data is required for the tasks at hand and how to navigate through the information space. These complex socio-technical systems, generally involve: large problem spaces, multiple users, conflicting constraints, dynamic data, coupled components and unanticipated events. These attributes make it difficult to apply a purely task-oriented analysis approach when designing user interfaces. Cognitive Work Analysis (CWA) [3] is an alternative approach that attempts to structure system information in a manner that is meaningful for human control and interaction. It produces a number of design artifacts that can inform a UI designer about both the system and the user's information requirements.

2 The Abstraction-Decomposition Space

CWA structures system information using means-ends relationships across multiple levels of abstraction. The aim is to support reasoning about a system rather than providing a set path of interaction towards a predefined goal. The Abstraction

M.F. Costabile and F. Paternò (Eds.): INTERACT 2005, LNCS 3585, pp. 1038–1041, 2005.
© IFIP International Federation for Information Processing 2005

Decomposition Space (ADS) is a tool used in CWA to analyse the work domain. The ADS combines two views of a system, a functional means-end hierarchy, ranging from high-level functional purpose to low-level physical form, and a physical decomposition hierarchy, ranging from overall system to individual components. These hierarchies are placed orthogonally in a matrix, essentially mapping function to form at different levels of granularity. Each cell in the resulting matrix describes the entire system at a different level of abstraction. This tool allows us to chart the information requirements of a user at various levels of abstraction during a problem solving task. The ADS has been frequently applied to the design of process control systems in microworld examples. Here we attempt to use it to generate an information navigation and monitoring system for a large and complex domain.

3   Applying the ADS to High Volume Manufacturing

Modern High Volume Manufacturing (HVM) environments are examples of extremely complex socio-technical systems. They combine sophisticated factory automation with the changing demands of dynamic markets. A common constraint across HVM is the conflicting goals of achieving high volumes of production while ensuring that machinery continues to operate within acceptable control limits. High production volumes place machinery under stress, requiring them to receive more maintenance and repair. Repair causes more downtime leading to lower levels of production. This conflict is resolved by humans who must reconcile manufacturing-focused and engineering-focused priorities. A visualisation that could present system state information from both perspectives would benefit users trying to deal with such conflicts. We attempt to construct an ADS for a HVM environment to structure system information in a way that can inform our visualisation design.

Our study focuses on a Semiconductor Fabrication Plant (Fab), involving hundreds of machines (described as tools) and a highly complex process-flow. The overall *process* is divided into a number of *segments*. Segments consist of a number of functional *operations* that build components of the semiconductor. These operations may be repeated with slight variations in different segments, introducing circulation and re-entries into the process-flow. Operations are carried out on specific *tools* which are categorised according to specific functional activities. Multiple tools carrying out the same operation are gathered together into a *toolset*. Groups of toolsets that carry out the same general function form a *functional area*. This complex relationship between process-flow and functional areas is shown in fig.1a.

Two basic structures are evident. A Process hierarchy organises the system into different levels of granularity based on position in the process-flow. This equates to the manufacturing view mentioned earlier giving a horizontal view across the process-flow. A Functional hierarchy structures the system in terms of functional areas. It equates to an engineering view giving a vertical view into areas, toolsets and tools.

4   Adaptation of the ADS

The ADS combines a functional abstraction hierarchy with a physical decomposition, but in this case the physical decomposition has limited use. While physical tools match functional operations at the lowest levels, recirculation in the process-flow

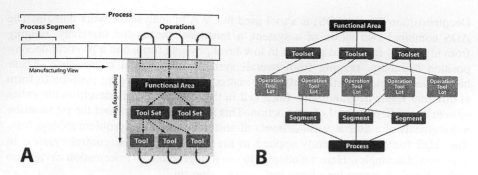

Fig. 1. A) Process-Flow & Functional Area Structures, B) Abstraction Lattice

Decomposition ⟶

Abstraction ↑

	Process	Segment	Operation
Functional Purpose	Efficient Product Manufacturing		
Abstract Function	Move Product through Process	Advance wafer production	
Generalised Function		Carry out Operations	Carry out an operation
Physical Function			Lot/Tool States (Production)
Physical Form			Wafer in Tool

Abstraction ↑

	Func Areas	Toolsets	Tool
Functional Purpose	Maximise Tool Availablility		
Abstract Function		Max. Uptime Min. Downtime	
Generalised Function		Toolset Health Toolset Availability	Carry out PM's Find Faults Fast
Physical Function			Tool States (Health)
Physical Form			Wafer in Tool

	Process	Segment	Operation
Functional Purpose	Produce a Technology		
Abstract Function	Move Product through Process	Advance wafer production	
Generalised Function		Carry out Operations	Carry out an operation
Physical Function			Lot/Tool States (Production)
Physical Form			Tool, Lot Operation
Physical Function			Tool States (Health)
Generalised Function		Toolset Health Toolset Availability	Carry out PM's Find Faults Fast
Abstract Function		Maximise Uptime Minimise Downtime	
Functional Purpose	Maximise Tool Availablility		
	Func Areas	**Toolsets**	**Tool**

Fig. 2. Two ADS's for alternate views & Final ADS

means that physical and functional relationships no longer equate at higher levels of abstraction, i.e. segment variables do not equate to toolset variables. Lind [4] points out the limitation of an ADS based on a single physical decomposition noting that a physical component within a functional subsystem may belong to multiple functions at the same time. Multilevel Flow Modelling (MFM) provides a technique for dealing with this by replicating the physical components in multiple subsystems. Our problem is somewhat different. Here the process flow is just too large and too complex. This makes a physical model unfeasible to work with. We propose replacing the physical decomposition within the ADS with one based on functional constraints. However, this system features two conflicting functional constraints at the highest level. These are the manufacturing and engineering views discussed earlier. Both of these are valid system decompositions but their relationship is non-analogous. The question is how can we generate a single model of the system that encompasses both structures?

As a first step, two ADS's (fig.2) were constructed and examined, one for each view. While they are very different at the abstraction level of functional purpose, they share the same properties at the level of physical form. This commonality can act as a bridging point between the two views. While a single physical decomposition causes us to think of the ADS as an Abstraction hierarchy, using two conceptual decompositions allows us to think of the ADS in terms of an Abstraction Lattice (fig.1b). An Abstraction Lattice allows us to reason our way down through levels of abstraction in one view and then up through levels of abstraction in an alternative view of the same system. This approach allows us to reflect the Abstraction Hierarchy across the level of physical form joining up the two ADS representations. Our new ADS (fig.2) captures all of the system variables from both view at multiple levels of abstraction.

5 Evaluation and Observations

In order to evaluate our adjustments we mapped a use-case scenario for shutting down an Out-of-Control Tool to our ADS. The mapping revealed a number of interesting observations. Firstly, although the user was operating in the engineering area, information from both sides of the ADS was referred to during the use-case. Secondly, information at different levels of abstraction was combined from different sides of the ADS in order to gain a better understanding of the system state. Thirdly, while causal reasoning enables movement between states of knowledge in either view, this cannot explain movement between abstraction-levels that occurs independently in both views. These observations are particularly interesting for display design as they force us to think about visual representations that can encompass different levels of information abstraction within a display and movement between different displays.

6 Conclusion

While the ADS is a useful tool for structuring system information it has difficulty dealing with the Fab environment. Conflict at the level of functional purpose and circulation in the process-flow makes physical/functional relationships problematic at higher levels of abstraction. MFM attempts to deal with this problem and has been successfully applied to plant process control. However the scale and complexity of our domain encourages us to move away from physical decompositions altogether. Our approach prioritises functional constraints over physical ones. By combining functional decompositions of the system it becomes possible to structure information in a manner that is meaningful to users. This modified ADS allows us to chart users information needs when interacting with the system. While a preliminary use-case mapping has been completed, more are being carried out to further test the ADS. This is being used as part of an approach to the analysis and design of displays for a HVM environment.

References

1. Woods DD, Johannesen L, Cook RI, Sarter N. Behind Human Error: Cognitive Systems, Computers and Hindsight. CSERIAC, WPAFB, Dayton OH. (1994).
2. Tufte, E. R. The Visual Display of Quantitative Information. Graphics Press, Conn. (1983)
3. Vicente, K. J., Cognitive Work Analysis: Towards Safe, Productive, and Healthy Computer-based Work, Mahwah, NJ: Erlbaum (1999).
4. Lind, M. Plant Modeling for Human Supervisory Control. Transactions of the Institute of Measurement and Control, Vol 21. No 4/5, pp. 171-180. (1999).

Immersive Live Sports Experience
with Vibrotactile Sensation

Beom-Chan Lee, Junhun Lee, Jongeun Cha, Changhoon Seo, and Jeha Ryu

Human-Machine-Computer Interface Lab.,
Dept. Mechatronics, Gwangju Institute of Science and Technology, Gwangju, Korea
{bclee, junhun, gaecha, search, ryu}@gist.ac.kr

Abstract. This paper presents a vibrotactile display system designed with an aim of providing immersive live sports experience. Preliminary user studies showed that with this display subjects were 35% more accurate in interpreting an ambiguous visual stimulus showing a ball either entering or narrowly missing a football net. About 80% of subjects could judge the correct ball paths in the presences of ambiguous visual stimuli. Without the tactile display, only 60% correct paths are judged from the visual display.

1 Introduction

The rapid development of broadcasting technology has made it possible to provide TV viewers with high quality visual and auditory services yielding a more realistic and impressive experience of digital content. However, we believe, there exists futher potential. Specifically we are concerned with the possibilities afforded by the additional of haptic information to a broadcast stream [1], [2].

In TV broadcasting of live sports, sometimes confusing situations occur. For example, when a soccer ball passes close to the edge of a goalpost, viewers may be unable to determine whether or not a goal was scored because the visual scene gives only 2D information. For radio broadcasting, this problem is increased as listeners cannot see the position and direction of the ball and just rely on the dictations of a commentator. For this situation, more accurate directional information about the ball could help viewers and listeners judge its path.

This paper presents a vibrotactile display for an immersive live sports experience and an overall system concept including tactile data in broadcasting. A vibrotactile display can be easily used to detect the motion of specific object [3], [4], [5]. The prior work allows us to test the feasibility of using a tactile display for sensory compensation in a soccer game scenario in a prototype system. In addition, we propose a methodology for path display that assists a user in recognizing directional movements.

This paper is organized as follows: Section 2 describes the system configuration, and the mapping between the vibrotactile device and the goal area. Section 3 presents a preliminary user study and results. Finally, Section 4 draws some conclusions, and highlights opportunities for future work.

M.F. Costabile and F. Paternò (Eds.): INTERACT 2005, LNCS 3585, pp. 1042–1045, 2005.

2   System Configuration and Mapping Rule

The system configuration is shown in Fig 1(a). As this is a feasibility study (and for simplicity) we used a virtual, rather than a real, soccer game for our experiment. The system is divided into two parts: a desktop computer and a tactile device. The desktop computer calculates the movement of the virtual ball and transmits the tactile data to the vibrotactile device through Bluetooth to control the vibrating motors sequentially. The vibrotactile device has its own micro controller [6] which controls the vibrators.

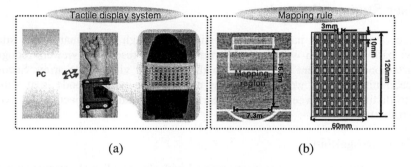

(a)   (b)

Fig. 1. System configuration

As is shown in Fig 1(b), the tactile array is composed of a (7×10) array and attached on the forearm in order to display directional movement of the ball. As they are relatively ergonomic and comfortable for the viewer, the coin type pager motors widely in use cell phones were used in our hardware. They have the additional qualities of being small, light, cheap and low power.

Due to the limited resolution of the tactile display, it was important to carefully select the region of the soccer pitch that would correspond to the device. Since the most interesting event of a soccer game is a goal, the front of the goal (shown in Fig 1(b)) was chosen for the actuator mapping area. We chose a region with a width of 7.3 meters and a length of 16.5 meters. The vibrotactile array is 60 millimeters by 120 millimeters. Therefore, each vibrator represents 1.05 meters width and 1.65 meter length.

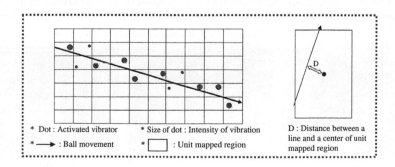

Fig. 2. Control rule of vibrotactile actuator

The vibrating motors are controlled sequentially to display the movement of a soccer ball on the ground. After some user studies, we found that a "path display" to give correct directional information on the forearm can be effectively achieved by "tracing mode", in which two vibrators along the ball motion trajectory are excited simultaneously with different intensities that are proportional to the distance from the center of the mapped region to the virtual ball position (See Fig. 2). The tracing mode, therefore displays a flow of vibration. Note that each motor is controlled by a PWM (Pulse Width Modulation) signal with duty ratio from 10% to 90% for generating different intensities.

3   User Study and Results

Two recognition rates have been investigated through preliminary user studies. Firstly, path recognition where we determine at what resolution viewers recognizes the directional movement of a ball with the proposed vibrotactile array. Secondly, goal recognition where we examine how effective the tracing mode is at allowing users to distinguish between goals and near misses. A total 10 subjects were involved in the user studies.

3.1   Path Recognition

For path recognition, each subject was trained with six established patterns (Fig 3(a)), experiencing each pattern 3 times. They were then exposed to the patterns again and asked to identify which they were experiencing. The patterns were randomly displayed at eighteen times. Since the vibrotactile device has spatially limited resolution, patterns were established at intervals of five degrees from each other in order to display distinguishable paths. Both tracing and non-tracing mode were tested. The user studies show that although it is difficult for some participants to discriminate adjacent path, most participants could discriminate the directions of a ball in Fig 3(a). While path recognition rate without the tracing mode reached around 81% mean, the tracing mode shows about 4% higher recognition rate than the non-tracing mode. In addition, most participants said that they could feel the flow of vibration as if someone scanned their forearm with a fingertip.

3.2   Goal Recognition

For goal recognition, cases of the confusing ball motion are established by the trajectories shown in Fig 3(c). When a subject sees a ball motion from the perspective

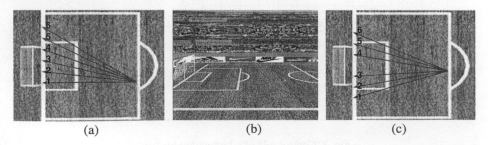

(a)   (b)   (c)

Fig. 3. User study environments

shown in Fig 3(b), the simulated 3D soccer playing ground, if can be challenging to judge whether the ball is heading towards the goal or not. Each subject was asked to make this decision in trials with and without the vibrotactile device. Without tactile compensation, accuracy was around 60% mean. In particular, most subjects had difficulty with cases 2 and 3. However recognition rate with tactile compensation increased by 33% (to 80% accuracy), indicating the tactile cues substantially disambiguated this situation.

4 Conclusions and Future Works

We designed a prototype vibrotactile display system to compensate for visually confusing movements of a ball in a soccer match. We also proposed a tactile display method termed tracing mode that accurately displays the directional information of a moving ball. By displaying a seemingly true ball path on the 2D vibrotactile display plane that maps to the front area of the goal in a soccer pitch, subjects could feel the correct ball paths with an accuracy rate of about 80%. This shows the feasibility of the proposed system. The next phase of this work is to display the 3D movement of a ball in two vibrotactile display planes and to conduct a more comprehensive human factors study to inform the design of future generations of device (perhaps including vertical as well as horizontal 3D compensation). Furthermore, a statistical analysis of the user's responses will be performed. In the long run, the proposed system will be extended to a realistic broadcasting system with image processing, editing, and networking.

Acknowledgment

This work was supported by the Ministry of Information and Communication through the Realistic Broadcasting IT Research Center at GIST and by the next generation PC project.

References

1. S. O'Modhrain and I. Oakley, "TouchTV: Adding Feeling to Broadcast media", Proc. the 1st European Conf. Interactive Television: from Viewer to Actors, pp.41-47, 2003.
2. J. Cha, J. Ryu, S. Kim, S. Eom, and B. Ahn, "Haptic Interaction in Realistic Multimedia Broadcasting", Proc. 5th Pacific Rim Conf. Multimedia on Advances in Multimedia Information Processing, Part III, pp.482-490, 2004.
3. H.Z. Tan and A. Pentland, "Tactual Display for Wearable Computing", Int, Sympo, Wearable Computers, pp.84-89, 1997.
4. Y. Yanagida, M. Kakia, R.W. Lindeman, Y. Kume, and N. Tetsutani, "Vibrotactile Letter Reading using a Low-Resolution Tactor Array", Proc. of the 12th Symp. on Haptic Interfaces for Virtual Environment and Teleoperator Systems, pp.400-406, 2004.
5. U. Yang, Y, Jang, and G.J. Kim, "Designing a Vibro-Tactile Wear for "Colse Range" Interaction for VR-based Motion Training", Proc. 12th International Conference on Artificial Reality and Telexistence(ICAT2002), pp.4-9, 2002.
6. http://www.atmel.com/dyn/resources/prod_documents/doc2467.pdf

Smooth Haptic Interaction
in Broadcasted Augmented Reality

Jongeun Cha[1], Beom-Chan Lee[1], Jong-phil Kim[1], Seungjun Kim[2], and Jeha Ryu[1]

[1] Human-Machine-Computer Interface Lab.,
{gaecha, bclee, ryu}@gist.ac.kr
Dept. Mechatronics, Gwangju institute of Science and Technology, Gwangju, Korea
[2] System Integration Lab.,
zizone@gist.ac.kr

Abstract. This paper presents smooth haptic interaction methods for an immersive and interactive broadcasting system combining haptics in augmented reality. When touching the broadcasted augmented virtual objects in the captured real scene, problems of force trembling and discontinuity occur due to static registration errors and slow marker pose update rate, respectively. In order to solve these problems, threshold and interpolation methods are proposed respectively. The resultant haptic interaction provides smoother continuous tremble-free force sensation.

1 Introduction

Rapid growth of computing and telecommunication technology allows recent digital multimedia systems to incorporate users' immersion and interactions. Physical touch to the digital multimedia may play an important role for immersion and interactions. O'Modhrain and Oakley [1] explored how haptic interaction might enhance and enrich the experience of broadcast contents. Moreover, much attention is newly given to the augmented reality (AR) technology [2] in broadcasting media production because of its simple but excellent interactive display and tracking potential. BBC [3] also introduced AR technology in broadcasting production. The haptic interaction in AR-based broadcasting system, however, may cause force trembling and discontinuity problems as observed in [4]. Virtual objects that are augmented in the captured scene showed trembling due to static registration errors. Moreover, touch to the moving objects generated abrupt change of force sensation because of the slow marker pose update rate compared to the high haptic rendering rate. In order to solve these problems, this paper presents smooth haptic interaction methods by threshold and interpolation techniques for haptically enhanced broadcast contents, which can be produced and broadcasted.

2 Broadcasting System Chain with Haptics in Augmented Reality

This section presents brief summary of the haptically enhanced broadcasting system that we proposed earlier [4] for explaining overview of the data flow. In Fig. 1, a captured video is analyzed in the **AR process** to detect fiducial markers in it in order

M.F. Costabile and F. Paternò (Eds.): INTERACT 2005, LNCS 3585, pp. 1046–1049, 2005.
© IFIP International Federation for Information Processing 2005

to derive their 3D spatial relationship with respect to the camera coordinate system. ARToolKit [5] can facilitate this process. The **3D media database** contains 3D object model information: geometry, texture, and even material properties for haptic sensation. In the proposed system, the 3D model data is downloaded to clients prior to video streaming because the 3D object model is not needed for every scene. Then the viewer can explore and manipulate the object at designated haptic interaction session that can be indicated on the screen by a producer. In the client site, the object is augmented to the scene and is displayed. Then haptic probe is overlaid on it. The control unit processes the video media and the 3D model data to control haptic device by using haptic rendering algorithm that is the main functions of **haptic process**. In our system, we have used the 6-dof haptic devices, Phantom [6].

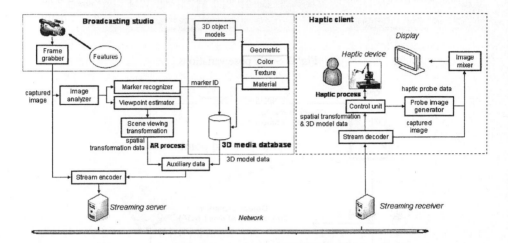

Fig. 1. The broadcast system chain

3 Smooth Haptic Interaction in Augmented Haptics

Implementation of the proposed haptically enhanced broadcasting system showed some abrupt and trembling force sensation to users. The first problem is that static registration errors occur from optical distortion, tracking errors, mechanical misalignments, and incorrect viewing parameters even when nothing is moving in the scene [2]. These errors lead to force trembling when viewers touch an augmented virtual object with a haptic interface. The estimated accuracy of ARToolKit for a single marker showed that the farther the marker distance from the camera and the smaller the tilt angle, the less the accuracy [7]. In order to estimate the maximum pose error to cut off, we measured the marker (8×8 cm) pose fixed on the wall that is 70cm distant from and perpendicular to the camera. Then we obtained the maximum static errors in the 70 cm camera workspace. Fig. 2 shows the results, where the left column indicates the x-y-z position variations and the right column indicates roll-pitch-yaw angle variations. Then we have applied the threshold to almost completely eliminate the trembling based on the maximum pose variations given by equation in Fig. 2.

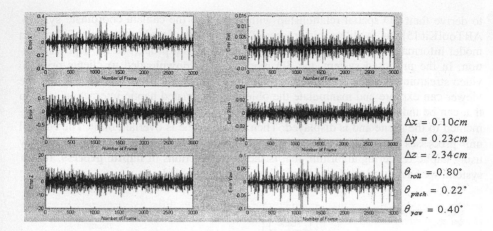

$$\Delta x = 0.10cm$$
$$\Delta y = 0.23cm$$
$$\Delta z = 2.34cm$$
$$\theta_{roll} = 0.80°$$
$$\theta_{pitch} = 0.22°$$
$$\theta_{yaw} = 0.40°$$

Fig. 2. Static pose variations

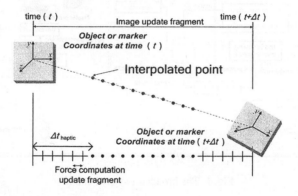

Fig. 3. Pose interpolation in haptic interaction

Humans can sense force vibrations well in excess of 300Hz. For smoother and more stable force feeling, generally, high haptic update rate (>1000Hz) is required. But the estimated marker pose, that is the virtual object pose, is updated at around 20Hz, much slower than haptic update rate. This performance gap may cause the contact force discontinuous, that is to say, humans can perceive the discrete change of the virtual object. The haptic rendering loop calculates the interaction force in about 1kHz rate while the virtual object pose is updated in about 20Hz. In other words, between the two consecutive graphic rendering time (t) and time ($t+\Delta t$) in Fig. 3, the haptic rendering loop computes the interaction force about 50 times with the virtual object that is statically posed at time (t). When the virtual object pose jumps to the next pose at time ($t+\Delta t$), therefore, the viewer grabbing the haptic interface and contacting the virtual object feels uneven jumping force. Therefore, the virtual object pose must be interpolated between the poses at (t) and ($t+\Delta t$) in the haptic rendering loop. This interpolation is possible because when we display the augmented scene at (t), we already have the virtual object poses at (t) and ($t+\Delta t$) because the streamed data is buffered in advance. Each interpolation pose in the haptic rendering loop between (t) and $(t+\Delta t)$ was calculated by adding the pose at (t) and the pose variation during (Δt_{haptic}). The results indicate that the interpolation process is sufficient to give the apparent continuous force when the virtual object is moving.

4   Conclusions and Future Works

This paper presented smooth haptic interaction methods for an immersive and interactive broadcasting system combining haptics in augmented reality. Threshold and interpolation methods showed more stable and smoother force in haptic interaction. The estimated threshold values are a little sensitive to light condition and background scene. We will design and implement robust low-pass filter to eliminate the static registration errors in changing environments.

Acknowledgement

This work was supported by the Ministry of Information and Communication (MIC) through the Realistic Broadcasting IT Research Center (RBRC) at Gwangju Institute of Science and Technology (GIST).

References

1. S. O'Modhrain and I. Oakley,: TouchTV: Adding Feeling to Broadcast media, Proc. the 1st European Conf. Interactive Television: from Viewer to Actors, Dec. (2003) 41-47
2. R. Azuma,: A survey of augmented reality, Presence : Teleoperators and Virtual Environments, Vol. 6, No. 4 (1997) 355-385
3. A. Woolard, V. Lalioti, N. Hedley, N. Carrigan, M. Hammond and J. Julien,: Case Studies in Application of Augmented Reality in Future Media Production, Proc. the Second IEEE and ACM Int. Symp. Mixed and Augmented Reality, Oct. (2003)
4. J. Cha, J. Ryu, S. Kim, S. Eom and B. Ahn,: Haptic Interaction in Realistic Multimedia Broadcasting, Proc. 5th Pacific Rim Conf. Multimedia on Advances in Multimedia Information Processing, Part III, Nov./Dec. (2004) 482-490
5. ARToolKit, http://www.hitl.washington.edu/artoolkit
6. Phantom, SensAble Technologies, http://www.sensable.com
7. D. F. Abawi and J. Bienwald,: Accuracy in Optical Tracking with Fiducial Markers: An Accuracy Function for ARToolKit, Proc. the Third IEEE and ACM Int. Symp. Mixed and Augmented Reality, Nov. (2004)

A Laser Pointer/Laser Trails Tracking System for Visual Performance

Kentaro Fukuchi

Graduate School of Information Systems,
The University of Electro-Communications Choufu-shi, Tokyo, Japan 182-8585
fukuchi@megaUI.net

Abstract. Visual performance with a large video projection screen is popular for various entertainment events such as DJ events. Some performers use computers to generate visuals, but using a keyboard or a mouse to control the visuals in front of a large screen is neither exciting nor intuitive for performers and audiences. We developed an interactive display system using camera-tracked laser pointers that enables performers to interact with the screen directly. The system can also detect shapes of the laser trails that enables the performer to move the laser pointers quickly. Most of existing systems employ color and pattern matching techniques that are not suitable for visual performance.

1 Background

Interactive techniques to improvise live visual images are an important challenge for a stage performance. For that purpose, computers are commonly used on-stage to generate real-time rendered computer graphics, and most of the systems are controlled via mice or keyboards. The problem is that using such interactive devices in front of a large screen on the stage lacks the feeling of direct manipulation for a performer. Besides, it is difficult for an audience to recognize the relationship between a body action of the performer and the result on the screen. In addition, it is not very entertaining to see a performer manipulating a mouse or tapping a keyboard. The goal of our research is to make the relationship between performer and screen clear for both the performer and the audience. We believe this goal is attained with our laser pointer tracking system.

2 Laser Trails Tracking System

2.1 System Requirements

An effective laser pointer tracking system for visual performance must satisfy some requirements that differ from requirements for desktop applications or interactive presentation systems. First, its scan rate should be high and its latency should be low because the visual on the screen must be synchronized to the motion of the performer's action. Second, the system must track lasers accurately

M.F. Costabile and F. Paternò (Eds.): INTERACT 2005, LNCS 3585, pp. 1050–1053, 2005.

during a performance. Third, the system should be able to apply to any kind of visual presentation without restriction of color or image.

Because of these requirements, we did not adopt the previous approaches[1][2]: background subtraction or color matching techniques are not versatile because they restrict the presentation of the visual, while pattern matching techniques are not robust if the laser spots move quickly.

2.2   Implementation

We developed a laser pointer tracking system and applied it to a live visual performance. This system was designed to meet the requirements described above.

Fig.1 shows an overview of the system. Its basic approach is the same as that of previous systems: the computer is connected to a projector and a camera that observes the screen. We used an IEEE1394 digital camera (Fire-i, Unibrain S.A.) that can deliver uncompressed 640×480 pixels at 30 frames per second. The projector was a standard 2000–2500 ANSI lumen XGA projector.

In order to bypass expensive image processing techniques for laser detection, we used very bright green laser pointers (532nm wave length, class 3a, 5mW), and attached an ND-4 or ND-8 filter that decreases the power of an incoming ray to 1/4 or 1/8. By using this filter, we could eliminate environmental light and image on the screen from the camera's view completely because the luminosity contrast is very high. All of the automatic parameter controls (brightness, white balance, exposure) of the camera were turned off to avoid unexpected parameter shifts during a performance. We set the exposure to almost 1/30 second, the same as the scan rate of the camera. This causes the image of a laser spot moved quickly to become a blurred and slightly dimmed trail (fig.2). This has been considered less suitable for laser spot tracking[3], but we feel justified in using the laser trails because the laser motion by performers is captured as trails. We discuss this approach in section 2.4.

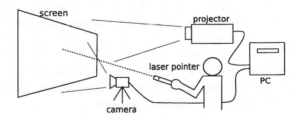

Fig. 1. An illustration of the laser tracking system

2.3   Calibration

A calibration process is needed before a performance to map the detected positions and shapes of laser trails in the camera image to the corresponding positions and shapes on the screen. We employ a simple solution that uses a perspective transformation.

At the beginning of the calibration process, the user points to four corners of the screen with a laser pointer for a second (30 frames) for every corner. The system measures centroids of the laser spots in the camera image and chooses a *mode* position among 30 recognized positions.

After the four corner positions are given, a three-dimensional transformation matrix is obtained by using standard linear algebra techniques.

2.4   Using Laser Trails

Most of the previous systems use a centroid of a laser spot to estimate its position and track its motion. In many cases this strategy works well enough to track the motion of the laser for a presentation or a desktop application. But sometimes, as seen in fig.2, a laser trail can be large and skewed. This means that a set of centroids of the trails makes a rough estimation of the motion of the laser pointer, and sometimes this is not desirable for visual performances.

Our approach to solve this problem uses bitmap image of a laser trail. If tracking positions are not needed by the application, using a bitmap has advantages over position tracking. First, it is able to use the entire information of a laser trail, some of which is omitted by the position tracking process. Second, we could avoid delay caused by position tracking process.

As we described in section 2.2, our approach allows us to get a bitmap image of a laser trail. This is sufficient for a painting application. To get a whole stroke of the laser pointer, we compose all the bitmap images of the trails by adding RGB values of pixels with saturation.

To extend this approach to Graphical User Interface, we implemented an experimental GUI button for bitmap image-based interaction. Traditional GUI widgets and interaction techniques (e.g., buttons or sliders, click or drag & drop mechanisms) are not usable with this approach because the GUI depends on a position-based input system.

In fig.3, a rectangle and a circle frame represent buttons, and a filled rectangle and a circle represent *pressed* buttons. When a trail image is captured, every button on the screen scans its region inside its shape (rectangle or circle) and counts the number of pixels of laser trails. If it is non-zero, the button is pressed, or it is *released*. It does not lose touch with the laser trails even if the laser moves quickly (fig.3). At this time, if a button is touched with two or more laser pointers simultaneously, it is not able to detect them, but there would be chance to detect them by counting the increasing number of pixels.

Fig. 2. Sequential shots of a fast moving laser trail

Fig. 3. Button widgets for bitmap image-based interaction

3   Case Study

We have not evaluated this interaction technique precisely, but we have used the laser tracking system for visual performances and observed the impact of this approach for a performance.

We observed that this approach satisfied our design goal in presenting a clear relationship between a performer's action and a visual result. Especially in a club space, the room was filled with smoky air, but the beams of the laser pointers were clearly visible, and the audience understood that the visuals on the screen were controlled directly by the lasers. Some members of the audience were given laser pointers to use, and these enabled them to interact directly with the screen.

We used both position tracking-based and image-based applications. We consider that the two approaches have different advantages. Position-based interaction is good for making some geometrical graphics or for manipulating graphical objects on a screen by laser interaction. On the other hand, the image-based approach produced an 'action painting-like' performance. For that purpose, we observed that a delay of visuals is fatal for a performance. Our system always causes 1/30 second delay because of the camera interface. If there is an additional one frame delay, it causes around 0.1 second delay in total, and it is not acceptable for a performance with music.

References

1. Kirstein, C., Müller, H.: Interaction with a Projection Screen Using a Camera-tracked Laser Pointer. Proceedings of The International Conference on Multimedia Modeling (1998) 191–192
2. Sukthankar, R., Stockton, R.G., Mullin, M.D.: Self-Calibrating Camera-Assisted Presentation Interface. Proceedings of International Conference on Automation, Control, Robotics and Computer Vision (2000) 33–40
3. Oh, J.Y., Stuerzlinger, W.: Laser Pointers as Collaborative Pointing Devices. Proceedings of Graphics Interface (2002) 141–149

Effects of Display Layout on Gaze Activity During Visual Search

Jérôme Simonin, Suzanne Kieffer, and Noëlle Carbonell

LORIA, Campus Scientifique, BP 239, F54506, Vandœuvre-lès-Nancy Cedex France
{Jerome.Simonin, Suzanne.Kieffer, Noelle.Carbonell}@loria.fr

Abstract. We report an experimental study that aims at investigating the influence of spatial layout on visual search efficiency and comfort. 4 layouts were used for displaying 120 scenes comprising 30 realistic colour photos each: random, elliptic, radial and matrix-like. Scenes (30 per structure) were presented to 5 participants who had to select a pre-viewed photo in each scene using the mouse. Eye-tracking data indicate that elliptic layouts provided better visual comfort than any of the other layouts (shortest scan paths), and proved to be more efficient than matrix layouts (shorter search times). These results are statistically significant (paired t-tests).

1 Introduction

Entertainment and commercial Web-sites, information kiosks and public terminals tend to display a growing number of pictures simultaneously: video and movie stills, CD sleeves, book covers, etc. Personal electronic archives and directories are increasingly cluttered with collections of photos, scanned documents, videos. It is a standard practice for designers of image browsers, to display information items in the form of 2D arrays that users browse through, using horizontal and vertical scrollbars. Current products (e.g., ACDSee, PhotoSuite or ThumbsPlus) make general use of scrollable 2D arrays of file icons or miniatures for displaying folder contents. Research prototypes of multimedia news summaries [5] or "zoomable" image browsers [1] also use 2D array presentations exclusively. Designers and researchers seem to take it for granted that 2D arrays are more efficient and comfortable than any other structure for presenting picture sets.

However, the prevalent use of 2D array layouts for displaying collections of images has yet to be grounded on established ergonomic criteria. Empirical and experimental studies are needed to determine the actual efficiency and visual comfort of possible display layouts. To our knowledge, this ergonomic issue has not yet been addressed. Published research on the usability of picture browsers amounts to a few studies meant to assess the overall ergonomic quality of specific products [3] or research prototypes, for instance Shoebox [6] and PhotoMesa [4]. The aim of the experimental study presented here is to obtain a meaningful insight into the actual influence of display layout on visual search performance and comfort, for picture sets.

Experimental design and set-up, which take advantage of the conclusions of an earlier pilot study [2], are first described. Then, quantitative and qualitative results are presented and discussed. The paper ends with a summary of conclusions stemming from these results together with a brief sketch of future research directions.

M.F. Costabile and F. Paternò (Eds.): INTERACT 2005, LNCS 3585, pp. 1054–1057, 2005.
© IFIP International Federation for Information Processing 2005

2 Experimental Design and Set-Up

Five experienced computer users with ages between 24 and 29 and normal sight (Bioptor test kit) carried out 120 visual search tasks in scenes displayed on a 21'' screen (1280 x 1024 pixel resolution). Each scene included 30 realistic colour photos arranged along four different symmetrical structures (see figure 1): *Matrix*-like (2D array), *Elliptic* (two concentric ellipses), *Radial* (eight radii along medians and diagonals of the screen), and *Random* (i.e., random placing). *Elliptic* and *Radial* structures were meant to schematise information presentation layouts often used in everyday life (e.g., dials).

For each scene, participants had to locate a pre-viewed photo in the scene, and to select it as fast as they could using the mouse. The isolated target was first displayed in the centre of the screen during three seconds; then participants clicked on a button in the centre of the screen for launching the scene display; thus, mouse initial position was identical for all search tasks. Participants' gaze activity was recorded using a head-mounted eye-tracker (ASL). After a short presentation followed by a calibration stage (5 min.), participants carried out 6 trial tasks, then the 120 experimental tasks (30 per structure).

3600 photos pulled from popular Web sites were sorted out into 40 themes or so (e.g., sports, animals, monuments) and sub-themes. Each scene was made up of photos belonging to the same theme or sub-theme in order to reduce intra-scene variability in visual saliency and subjective appeal; thus, "pop out" effects that might interfere with the possible influence of display layout on gaze activity were avoided. For this reason also, each target was chosen among photos with medium visual saliency in the scene. Photos were placed randomly in the scenes save for targets which were placed manually in all possible locations in the 120 scenes; thus, possible effects of target

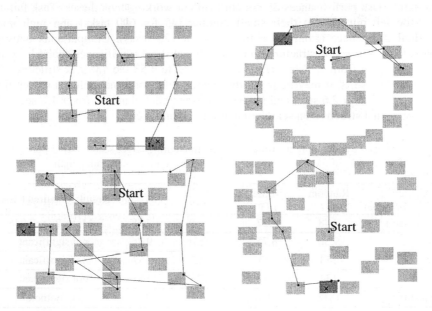

Fig. 1. Standard scan paths for each spatial structure. The target is represented by a dark gray box, the selection click by a cross, fixations by black dots.

position on visual search efficiency were prevented. Scenes were ordered randomly, regardless of their structure, and a different order was assigned to each participant so as to neutralize possible sequence and task learning effects.

Display layout was the main independent variable. Overall task efficiency and effectiveness were assessed using target selection time and task failure rate as dependent variables. To evaluate visual search efficiency and comfort, five measures were computed over the time interval (st) ranging from scene display onset to first fixation on the target offset: duration of st (D_st), number and duration of fixations (Nf and Df), saccade duration (Ds), scan path length (Lsp). All these measures are useful for assessing visual search efficiency; some of them also contribute to evaluating visual comfort, since longer search times, higher fixation numbers and longer scan paths imply higher gaze activity, hence greater visual fatigue.

Results are presented in the next section. We discuss their contribution to validating the two following working hypotheses which are based on the general assumption that display structure influences eye movements during visual search. Given our visual material, we expect worse performances for unstructured displays (c.f. the *Random* structure) than for any structured display since, if spatial structure influences scan paths it will favour thorough systematic search and limit useless backtracking (hypothesis 1). In addition, best performance results will be obtained for *Elliptic* layouts which have a greater influence on gaze trajectories than *Matrix* layouts and do not favour backtracking like the *Radial* structure; worst results are expected for *Matrix* layouts which influence scan paths least (hypothesis 2).

3   Results: Presentation and Discussion

Participants' task performances do not confirm our working hypotheses. Task failures had to be left out, due to their small number (45 for 600 tasks) and high inter-individual differences (from 2.5% to 11.7% of 120 tasks). Comparisons between target selection times by structure do not reach statistical significance (paired t-tests), averages ranging from 4.17 sec. (*Elliptic* structure) to 4.53 sec. (*Matrix* structure). To explain these results, it may be put forth that, as selection time includes search time for the target (about 2.6 sec.) and mouse move-and-click duration (over 1.6 sec.), the effects of spatial structure on search time might go unnoticed.

Table 1. Averaged eye-tracking measures per structure during target search (st), 5 participants: duration of st, number of fixations, fixation and saccade duration, scan path length

Variables *Number of values*	Random *141*	Ellipse *143*	Matrix *142*	Radial *141*	Results of paired t-tests
D_st (sec.)	2.48	2.27	2.89	2.68	E-M: t=-2; p=0.0462
Nf	9.38	8.75	10.78	9.76	not significant
Df (ms.)	153	153	157	157	not significant
Ds (ms.)	134	130	129	143	not significant
Lsp (pixels)	1818	1440	1951	1973	see footnote[1]

[1] Rand.-E : t=2.08; p=0.0380 / M-E : t=2.53; p=0.0119 / Rad.-E : t=2.44; p=0.0462

Eye-tracking data (see table 1) support this interpretation. Target localization time is significantly shorter for *Elliptic* layouts than for *Matrix* layouts. In addition, scan path length is significantly smaller for *Elliptic* layouts compared to the three other structures. These results validate hypothesis 2 partly, while they contradict hypothesis 1. Qualitative analyses of participants' gaze activity during target search help to interpret them (see figure 1). Scan paths seem to have been more influenced by *Radial* and *Elliptic* layouts than by *Matrix* layouts: only 17% of saccades or so are jumps from one ellipse to the other or from one radius to a non neighbouring one, whereas saccade directions are more varied for *Matrix* layouts (34% of saccades follow lines, 28% diagonals, and 23% columns) with higher inter-individual differences (e.g., from 21% to 35% for moves along diagonals). Besides, two strategies were used for exploring *Radial* structures, one with few backtrackings (2 participants), the other with many (see figure 1). These observations explain why hypothesis 2 was only partly confirmed by quantitative results. As for hypothesis 1, scan path analysis shows that participants moved from one "cluster" of photos to another in a *Random* structured scene, suggesting that *Random* layouts cannot be viewed as unstructured layouts.

4   Conclusion

We performed an experimental study that aimed at investigating the influence of spatial layout on visual search efficiency and comfort. 4 layouts were used for displaying sets of 30 realistic colour photos: random, elliptic, radial and matrix-like. 120 scenes (30 per structure) were presented to 5 participants who had to select a previewed photo in each scene using the mouse. Eye-tracking data analyses indicate that *Elliptic* layouts provided better visual comfort than any of the other layouts (shortest scan paths), and proved to be more efficient than *Matrix* layouts (shorter search times). These results are significant (paired t-tests). They may be useful for improving the design of photo visualization and browsing. Future work will focus first on modelling user gaze strategies in order to refine the comparison between *Radial* and *Elliptic* layouts, then on testing whether similar results are obtained for displays of sensibly larger collections of visual items.

References

1. Bederson, B.B. (2001). PhotoMesa: a Zoomable Image Browser Using Quantum Treemaps and Bubblemaps. Proc. 14th ACM Annual Symposium on User Interfaces Software and Technology (UIST'01), CHI Letters, 3(2), 71-80.
2. Carbonell, N., Kieffer, S. (2005). Do oral messages help visual exploration?", in J. van Kuppevelt, L. Dybkjaer, N. Bernsen (Eds.), Advances in Natural, Multimodal Dialogue Systems, Springer (Boston: Kluwer Inc.), 27 pp. (to appear).
3. Combs, T.T., Bederson, B.B. (1999). Does Zooming Improve Image Browsing. Proc. ACM Conference on Digital Liraries (DL'99), ACM Press, New York, pp. 130-137.
4. Khella, A., Bederson, B. (2004). Pocket PhotoMesa: a Zooming Image Browser for the Pocket PC. Technical Report, University of Maryland HCI Lab, 9 pp.
5. Maybury, M. (2000). News on demand. Communications of the ACM, 43(2), 32-34.
6. Shneiderman, B., Kang, H., Kules, B., Plaisant, C., Rose, A., Rucheir, R. (2002). A Photo History of SIGCHI: Evolution of design from personal to public. Interactions, 9(3), 17-23.

Eye-Tracking Reveals the Personal Styles for Search Result Evaluation

Anne Aula, Päivi Majaranta, and Kari-Jouko Räihä

Tampere Unit for Computer-Human Interaction (TAUCHI),
Department of Computer Sciences, FIN-33014 University of Tampere, Finland
{aula, curly, kjr}@cs.uta.fi

Abstract. We used eye-tracking to study 28 users when they evaluated result lists produced by web search engines. Based on their different evaluation styles, the users were divided into *economic* and *exhaustive* evaluators. Economic evaluators made their decision about the next action (*e.g.*, query re-formulation, following a link) faster and based on less information than exhaustive evaluators. The economic evaluation style was especially beneficial when most of the results in the result page were relevant. In these tasks, the task times were significantly shorter for economic than for exhaustive evaluators. The results suggested that economic evaluators were more experienced with computers than exhaustive evaluators. Thus, the result evaluation style seems to evolve towards a more economic style as the users gain more experience.

1 Introduction and Related Work

To date, the process of evaluating result lists of web search engines has received little attention. Eye-tracking is a promising method for this purpose as it provides information on visual information processing. In HCI, eye-tracking has been used to study the usability of web pages [3], menu searching [1, 2], and information searching from web pages [4] and hierarchical displays [6], among others. Three previous eye-tracking studies have specifically focused on search result evaluation.

Salojärvi et al. [9] aimed at inferring the relevance of newspaper headings from the features of eye-tracking data. The features they found useful for the relevancy prediction were, for example, fixation count, total fixation duration, and pupil size.

Granka et al. [5] studied how users browse result listings and how they select links. In their study, the participants entered their own queries for 10 tasks. Their results suggested that users spend most of the time fixating on the first and the second result before their initial click. The third and following results get significantly less fixation time. Their results also indicated that users tend to follow a sequential strategy in scanning the results by going from top to bottom until they follow a link.

In Klöckner et al. [7], all participants saw the same result page with 25 results. Their task was to collect information from this list for one open-ended search task. A majority of the users (65%) used a *depth-first strategy* where only the results above the selected link are evaluated before the selection. 15% of the users used a *breadth-first strategy* where they looked through all the results before opening any documents. The remaining 20% of the participants used a mixture of these strategies.

M.F. Costabile and F. Paternò (Eds.): INTERACT 2005, LNCS 3585, pp. 1058–1061, 2005.

Our aim was to deepen the understanding of the results evaluation process with a semi-controlled study. Our participants first saw a pre-defined search result page for each task making it possible to compare their gaze data when viewing exactly the same stimulus. However, we aimed for as realistic gaze behaviour as possible. Thus, immediately after seeing the pre-defined page, the participants could modify the query, enter a URL, or select a result from the pre-defined page. This semi-controlled method enabled us to find the differences in the participants' evaluation styles in a realistic search situation while also preserving the control over the first stimulus.

2   Methods

All of the pre-defined queries were submitted to Google and the corresponding result pages were saved as local files. The 10 queries were chosen so that three of them were poor (no relevant results in the list), three were good (more than five relevant results), and the remaining four were mixed. We used Tobii 1750 remote eye-tracker with its default 17 inch TFT monitor with a resolution of 1280 × 1024. 42 students from different majors participated. Due to technical problems, data from 4 participants was excluded. This paper reports the preliminary results from the first 28 participants (11 females 17 males; average age 23.7 years), who were all experienced in using Google.

The participants were told that the purpose was to study their normal information searching with search engines, as well as to test the eye-tracker for pupil size measurements during web use. The cover story ensured that the participants did not concentrate on their eye-movements. The eye-tracker's calibration was tested before each task and it was re-calibrated if needed. The tasks were presented on slips of paper in random order. The participant proceeded to the task-specific result listing by selecting it from a list and then continued the searching normally. In the end, the participants filled in a background questionnaire. Finally, they were debriefed.

3   Data Analysis and Results

The results are based on the gaze data in the pre-defined result page until the user selected a result, formulated a new query, or exited the page otherwise. For the analysis, we defined Areas of Interest (AOI) in ClearView eye-gaze analysis software provided by Tobii. The area above the result listing formed one AOI, as did each individual result. We then collected all successive fixations to each AOI and calculated their cumulative fixation duration.

For analysing the evaluation styles, we developed a static visualization that presents the order in which each AOI is visited [8]. To enable comparison of the evaluation styles of different individuals and the effects of good and poor result lists, all the visualizations (280 visualizations in total) were printed out on paper and visually inspected by each author, first separately and then in face-to-face meetings. The goal of the inspection was to find patterns in the evaluation styles and to group the visualizations accordingly. As a result of this analysis, two groups of users with different result evaluation styles were identified. We call these groups *economic* (46% of the participants) and *exhaustive evaluators* (54% of the participants).

In the pre-defined result lists, there were six or seven results visible in the result list without scrolling. In over 50% of the tasks, economic evaluators scanned at most half (three) of those results before their first action. Exhaustive evaluators, on the other hand, evaluated in most of the tasks more than half of the visible results or even scrolled the results page to view all of the results before performing the first action. Examples of economic and exhaustive evaluation strategies are presented in Fig 1.

User 1: Exhaustive evaluation style		User 2: Economic evaluation style	
Task A	Task B	Task A	Task B

Fig. 1. Examples of evaluation styles. The *y* axis shows the vertical position in the search result page with a compact representation of the result page shown on the left side. The *x* axis shows the order in which different AOIs were visited. The size of the circle corresponds to the time spent on each AOI, the largest circles are approximately 3 seconds. In task A, the results were irrelevant to the task (both users chose to reformulate the query) and in task B, most of them were relevant (both users followed the second link).

An independent samples t-test showed that the time before the first action was significantly shorter for economic than for exhaustive evaluators, $t(26) = -3.1$, $p < .01$. In computer experience (measured by multiplying the frequency of computer use and the years of usage), a marginal difference between the two groups was found with economic being more experienced than exhaustive evaluators, $t(26) = -1.9$, $p = .07$. There was also a correlation between the average fixation duration and the evaluation style: the more economic the searcher was, the shorter were the fixations (Pearson's two-tailed $r = -.44$, $p < .05$).

In the result pages differing in quality, we found that when the query was good and most of the results were relevant, the economic evaluation style was especially beneficial. In this case, the task times of economic evaluators were shorter than those of exhaustive evaluators (average times 74.9 and 109.0 seconds), $t(26) = -2.0$, $p = .05$. In tasks with poor results, the task times did not differ.

4 Discussion

Our results suggested that economic evaluation style was more efficient in search tasks, especially when the quality of the results was good. Thus, it seems that it is beneficial to quickly click on the relevant-looking result instead of carefully trying to choose the best one. The results also identified a large group of exhaustive evaluators.

They, possibly due to their lack of expertise, carefully evaluate the results before following a link or re-formulating a query. Thus, they are more dependent on the result summaries given by the search engine.

Economic and exhaustive evaluation styles resemble the depth-first and breadth-first strategies by Klöckner et al. [7]. However, their participants scanned a list of 25 results with a task of selecting relevant results from the list. In contrast, our participants could go through the pre-defined result list, select results, or modify the query according to their will. This setup presumably enabled them to employ their normal scanning styles. Therefore our results cannot be directly compared with those by Klöckner et al. However, our results indicated a large group of less-experienced users who evaluate results below the one that gets selected and even thoroughly scan irrelevant results. Granka et al. [5] suggested that users tend to scan only the results above the selected link. As they did not report the computer experience of the participants, it is possible that their participants were experienced and thus, employed economic strategies as suggested by our results.

The data analysis is still ongoing. We are analyzing the data from the rest of the participants and in other pages than the pre-defined ones. We are also developing metrics for analyzing the differences in the gaze paths of the users with different evaluation styles. In the quest for *proactive search interfaces* [9], we will analyze the data in order to infer the relevance of the individual results from the gaze data.

References

1. Aaltonen, A., Hyrskykari, A., and Räihä, K.-J.: 101 spots, or how do users read menus? In Proc. CHI 1998, ACM Press (1998) 132-139
2. Byrne, M.D., Anderson, J.R., Douglass, S., and Matessa, M.: Eye tracking the visual search of click-down menus. In Proc. CHI 1999, ACM Press (1999) 402-409
3. Ellis, S., Cadera, R., Misner, J., Craig, C.S., and Lankford, C.P.: Windows to the soul? What eye movements tell us about software usability. In Proc. 7th Annual Conf. Usability Professionals Association, Washington D.C. (1998)
4. Goldberg, J.H., Stimson, M.J., Lewenstein, M., Scott, N., and Wichansky, A.M.: Eye tracking in web search tasks: Design implications. In Proc. ETRA'02, ACM Press (2002) 51-58
5. Granka, L., Joachims, T., and Gay, vcG.: Eye-tracking analysis of user behavior in WWW search. In Proc. SIGIR'04, ACM Press (2004) 478-479
6. Hornof, A.J., and Halverson, T.: Cognitive strategies and eye movements for searching hierarchical computer displays. In Proc. CHI 2003, ACM Press (2003) 249-256
7. Klöckner, K., Wirschum, N., and Jameson, A.: Depth- and breadth-first processing of search result lists. In Proc. CHI 2004, ACM Press (2004) 1539
8. Räihä, K.-J., Aula, A., Majaranta, P., Rantala, H., and Koivunen, K.: Static visualization of temporal eye-tracking data. In Proc. INTERACT 2005, Rome, September 2005
9. Salojärvi, J., Kojo, I., Jaana, S., and Kaski, S. Can relevance be inferred from eye movements in information retrieval? In Proc. WSOM'03 (2003) 261-266

Hotspot Components for Gesture-Based Interaction

Alejandro Jaimes and Jianyi Liu

FXPAL Japan, Fuji Xerox Co., Ltd.
alex.ajimes@fujixerox.co.jp

Abstract. We present a novel camera-based adaptable user interface system that uses hotspot components for 2D gesture-based interaction. A camera points to the desktop and the image captured by the camera appears on the user's screen. A hotspot area is activated when a user's hand passes *through* the rectangle that defines it. For example, a *right_left* hotspot activates when the user moves his hand from right to left, entering and exiting the rectangle. Our system is highly flexible because it allows the user to customize the interface as follows: (1) hotspot areas can be created anywhere within the camera-captured image; (2) new commands can be assigned to particular hotspots or composite hotspot sequences (e.g., *right_left* for previous webpage; *up+right+down* for webpage reload); (3) a physical workspace on the desktop can be defined by pointing the camera to any location; (4) different hotspot layouts for different applications can be created and saved. The system works with an inexpensive webcam in real time and uses machine learning to automatically detect skin areas for robust gesture recognition.

1 Introduction

Lower hardware costs and higher computational power (webcams are standard in many new PCs and laptops) make camera-based interaction techniques promising. Gesture-based interaction is of particular interest because humans use gestures to communicate naturally, but defining a set of meaningful and computationally recognizable 3D gestures can be difficult. Two-dimensional gestures, on the other hand, can be easily defined, assigned application or user-dependent meanings, and recognized using simple computer vision techniques.

In this paper, we present a novel camera-based, adaptable user interface system that uses hotspot components for 2D gesture-based interaction. In our approach, a camera points to the user's desktop. The user defines an interaction area within the desktop by pointing the camera to a desired location, defines new commands by configuring hotspot areas, and executes them by moving his hand across them. For example, to move to the previous page in a document, the user moves his hand from left to right across a hotspot area (Fig. 1). The framework has many applications, as the desk can become a large interactive space in which a rich set of hotspot configurations can be created with different meanings. For instance, imagine an instrument in which each hotspot or hotspot configuration represents a different sound; a desk with multiple displays so that different parts of the desk can be used to simultaneously interact with multiple documents; hand gestures similar to "mouse gestures" for browsing; or special gestures for people with disabilities.

M.F. Costabile and F. Paternò (Eds.): INTERACT 2005, LNCS 3585, pp. 1062–1066, 2005.

Work related to our system includes frameworks where physical devices are used as interface components [3], tangible interfaces [5], and systems that learn objects for interaction [2]. We do not use physical devices as in [35] and the system does not learn new interface objects for programmers as in [2]. The framework of [9] uses modular "Visual Interface Cues" and Hidden Markov Models to learn gesture dynamics. Our approach does not require training (except for the skin filter), and focuses on allowing the user to combine simple hotspot components for desktop gesture recognition. Most gesture recognition approaches [67] image the entire hand to model different postures. Instead, we use small hotspot areas that respond only to simple 2D actions (e.g., entered from right to left, etc.). The framework in [1] is also based on the idea of camera-based interaction, but three types of widgets are used: button, linear, and circular. We use only one camera, and interaction is based on 2D *configurations* of simple, directional hotspot components. A similar framework was presented in [4], but using skin and face detection for video indexing.

The advantages of our system can be summarized as follows: (1) individual components can be very robust and easily combined for different purposes; (2) users do not need to learn complex gestures (simple 2D motion gestures suffice); and (3) users do not need to remember gestures (hotspots are visible on the screen).

2 The User Interface

In our system, a camera is placed above the desktop (for example, on top of the computer monitor) and the corresponding video captured by the camera appears in a resizable window on the computer screen (Fig. 1). The user defines the interface area by

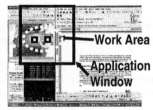

Fig. 1. System setup. The camera (left) points at a physical work area on the desktop. The interface image as viewed by the user (middle) can be resized as desired and shows the captured video images and hotspots (right image).

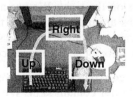

Fig. 2. Screen shot of captured image. On the right image a composition of hotspots represents a single command (e.g., re-load a webpage), whereas on the left each hotspot represents a different command (back, forward).

moving the camera to point at a desired physical location: in Fig. 1 (left) the main capture area is behind the keyboard—a user might prefer to point the camera elsewhere (e.g., in front of the keyboard as in Fig. 1, right).

A hotspot area is a 2D area in the video image that is activated when the user moves his hands or fingers *across* the area in a particular direction. In the application window (Fig. 1, middle) the user can draw new hotspot rectangles and assign commands either to individual hotspots or combinations. Fig. 2 (right) shows a composite sequence of hotspots combined to represent a single action (e.g., reload a webpage). Such configurations can be saved, so the user could have a library of configurations for different applications if desired.

3 Gesture Recognition

Our recognition approach is based on the idea of simple and easily re-configurable 2D hotspot components: a gesture is recognized as a sequence of hotspot area activations. This approach yields effective and robust results because the gestures that each individual hotspot recognizes are very specific. This contrasts with approaches that image the entire hand or hands and use algorithms to disambiguate between different hand postures and movements.

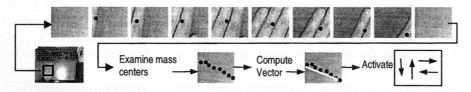

Fig. 3. Hotspot activation starts when a skin area is detected (frame 2) and ends when no skin is present (frame 10). In each sample, skin is detected and the center of mass is computed.

Hotspots are rectangular areas on a video image, defined by four coordinate points *(x1, y1, x2, y2)*, and an activation constraint. A hotspot is *activated* only when its activation constraint is met. Our system includes a basic library of 2D directional activation constraints: a hotspot is activated when a skin area enters the hotspot and exits it in one of four directions: *left_to_right, right_to_left, top_to_bottom,* and *bottom_to_top.* In order to increase robustness, a hotspot is assigned only one constraint. For example, the hotspot of 0 Fig. 1 (right) activates *only* if a skin area enters it from the left and exits on the right. We use a skin filter so that hotspots are activated only when hands/limbs are used to perform the gestures. The skin filter can be trained for each user (to increase robustness), or a standard one trained by the system developers can be used. The hotspot activation process, described next, is depicted in Fig. 3.

- **Skin filter construction:** first, we obtain a set of skin images and a set of images that do not contain skin. We convert each image to HSV color space (because it is perceptually uniform: points that are close in HSV space are also perceptually similar). This yields a training set of skin and non-skin pixels. We use a machine learning algorithm from Weka [8] to build a skin classifier.

- **Skin detection:** the area corresponding to each hotspot is processed every t milliseconds. In order to make processing more efficient, we examine only a subset of the pixels *inside* each hotspot rectangle: a pixel every d pixels is classified into skin or not-skin using the skin filter. Then we compute the center of mass of the detected skin pixels within the hotspot area (black spots in Fig. 3).
- **Hotspot activation:** activation of a hotspot starts with the first frame in which skin pixels are found (hand enters hotspot) and ends when no skin pixels are found (hand leaves hotspot). This yields a sequence of center of mass points. We use the first n points in the sequence to compute a motion start point, and the last m points to compute a motion end point. Using the two points we estimate the motion vector. The hotspot is activated only if the vector's direction corresponds to the hotspot's constraint.
- **Gesture recognition:** a gesture is detected when all of its corresponding hotspots are activated in a particular sequence (e.g., Fig. 2, right).

We have performed quantitative skin detection experiments. Using 12 training images we obtain approx. 32,000 pixels. This yields the following results (using separate training (66%) and testing sets (34%)): Naïve Bayes [8] yields 90.23% accuracy, and 1-Nearest Neighbor [8] yields 98.6% accuracy (with $d=n=m=2$). Quantitative evaluation of the activations or gestures is difficult since the results depend on the speed of the hand motions and on whether the user's hand properly enters the hotspot areas. However, we have found that individual hotspots are accurate close to 100% of the time (as long as the speed of the hand motion is reasonable).

4   Conclusions and Future Work

We presented a novel camera-based adaptable user interface system that uses hotspot components for 2D gesture-based interaction. The proposed component-based framework to interaction has two advantages: (1) combinations of simple components can yield higher accuracy than what may be achieved with gesture recognition frameworks that require segmentation and tracking, and (2) it allows high user customization so the user can create several hotspot configurations and save them for a wide range of different applications. Since the user views the image being captured by the camera, remembering specific gestures for particular applications is not necessary.

Future work includes integrating the prototype we have built with other applications, investigating ways to determine hotspot area sizes, integration with audio commands (e.g., to select different hotspot templates), experiments with users, and implementation on mobile devices (e.g., camera phones).

References

1. J. Alan, D.R. Olsen, "Light Widgets: Interacting in Every-day Spaces," in *proc. ACM 7th Intl. Conference on Intelligent User Interfaces 2002*, San Francisco, CA, Jan. 2002.
2. J.A. Fails, D.R. Olsen, "A Design Tool for Camera-based Interaction," *CHI: ACM Conf. on Human Factors in Computing Systems, CHI Letters 5(1)*, pp. 449 – 56, 2003.

3. S. Greenberg and C. Fitchett, "Phidgets: easy development of physical interfaces through physical widgets," in proc. *UIST 2001*, pp. 209-218, Orlando, Florida, Nov. 11-14, 2001.
4. Jaimes, Q. Wang, N. Kato, H. Ikeda, and J. Miyazaki, "Visual Trigger Templates for Knowledge-Based Indexing," in *ACM/IEEE PCM 2004*, Toyko, Japan, Dec. 2004.
5. S.R. Klemmer J.Li, J. Lin, and J.A. Landay, "Papier-Mâché: Toolkit Support for Tangible Input," in *proc. ACM CHI 2004, Vienna, Austria, April 24-29*, 2004.
6. S. Marcel, "Gestures for multi-modal interfaces: A Review," *T.R. IDIAP-RR* 02-34, 2002.
7. V.I. Pavlovic, R. Sharma and T.S. Huang, "Visual interpretation of hand gestures for human-computer interaction: a review", *IEEE Trans. on PAMI*, 19(7):677-695, 1997.
8. I.H. Witten and E. Frank, *Data Mining: Practical Machine Learning Tools and Techniques with Java Implementations*, Morgan Kaufmann, 1999.
9. G. Ye, J.J. Corso, D. Burschka, and G.D. Hager, "Vics: A modular hci framework using spatio-temporal dynamics," *Machine Vision and Applications*, 16(1):13-20, 2004.

Development of Multi-modal Interfaces in Multi-device Environments

Silvia Berti and Fabio Paternò

ISTI-CNR,
Via G.Moruzzi 1, 56124 Pisa, Italy
{silvia.berti, fabio.paterno}@isti.cnr.it

Abstract. Recent technological evolution has enabled environments accessible through a wide variety of interactive devices. Such devices can differ also in terms of interaction modality. In this paper we show how it is possible to generate multi-modal interfaces for different platforms starting with logical user interface descriptions. This approach simplifies the development of applications that can be accessed through a variety of interactive devices and modalities.

1 Introduction

In recent years, there has been an increasing availability of interactive devices, including mobile phones, personal digital assistants (PDAs), pagers, and so on. This poses a number of challenges for designers and developers of multi-device interfaces. To further complicate this issue, such devices can use different modalities (graphical, vocal, gestural, and so on). Indeed, although several real multimodal systems have been built, their development still remains a difficult task [1].

To address such complexity, a promising solution is to use logical device-independent, XML-based [2][4], languages able to represent relevant concepts, such as user tasks and communication goals, along with intelligent transformers able to generate user interfaces in different implementation languages for different platforms depending on their interaction resources, including modalities. Such intelligent rendering can be incorporated in authoring environments to decrease the cost of development of multiple interface versions for the various target platforms, allowing designers to concentrate on the logical decisions without learning a variety of low-level detailed implementation languages. However, the design of such transformations has to take into account the features of the target platforms and identify how to exploit the available modalities. Some authors have proposed a component-based approach to ease development of user interfaces [1], exploiting the CARE logical properties for multimodal interfaces. We use logical descriptions that can generate implementations in component-based environments or using other approaches.

In the paper, we discuss how multimodal interfaces (using graphical and vocal modalities) for desktop and PDA can be designed following this approach and show an example application. Lastly, we draw some conclusions and indications for future work.

M.F. Costabile and F. Paternò (Eds.): INTERACT 2005, LNCS 3585,, pp. 1067 – 1070, 2005.
© IFIP International Federation for Information Processing 2005

2 The Method

Our approach exploits a number of transformations that allow designers to move through various views of interactive systems. It allows designers to focus on the logical tasks to accomplish and then transform their descriptions into a user interface description, which incorporates the design decisions but is still in a modality format independent. This is then used to derive a modality-dependent interface description that is used to generate the final code of the user interface. For each logical level considered a XML-based language has been defined. The advantage of this approach is that designers can focus on logical aspects and make design decisions without having to deal with many low-level implementation details. The environment provides support to make concrete design decisions that take into account the target platforms and automatically generate the code where all the low-level details are specified (currently it is able to generate implementations in XHTML, XHTML Mobile Profile, VoiceXML, SVG, X+V). This type of support is particularly useful when a variety of devices should support access to the interactive application. On the other hand, it is worth noting that in order to make effective decisions designers should be aware of the target platforms and modalities even since the early stages of the design process. They do not need to know the implementation details of all the targeted devices but they still should know their main features (through the platform concept).

Indeed, there are tasks that may be meaningful only when using some specific platform or modality. For example, watching a long movie makes sense only in a multimedia desktop system whereas accessing information from a car in order to know directions to avoid a traffic jam can be done only through a mobile device and if this task should be performed while driving it can be supported only through a vocal interface. The available modality may also have an impact on how to accomplish a task, for example a vocal interface or a graphical mobile phone interface can require to perform sequentially tasks that can be performed concurrently in a desktop graphical interface.

In our approach a user interface is structured into a number of presentations. The presentation is structured into interactors (logical descriptions of interaction techniques) and composition operators that indicate how to put together such interactors. While at the abstract level such interactors and their compositions are identified in terms of their semantics in a modality independent manner, at the concrete level their description and the values of the attributes depend on the available modality. When both vocal and graphical support are available, the multimodality can be exploited in different manners. The modalities can be used alternatively to perform the same interaction. They can be used synergistically within one basic interaction (for example, providing input vocally and showing the result of the interaction graphically) or within a complex interaction (for example, filling in a form partially vocally and partially graphically). Some level of redundancy can be supported as well, for example when feedback of a vocal interaction is provided both graphically and vocally.

The composition operators are associated with a communication goal. A communication goal is a type of effect that designers aim to achieve when they want to structure presentations. Grouping is an example of composition operator that aims to highlight the logical relation amongst a group of interface elements. It can be implemented in the graphical channel through one or multiple attributes (fieldset, colour, position...), whereas in the vocal channel it is possible to group elements by inserting a sound or a pause at the beginning and the end of the grouped elements. In case of multimodal interfaces we have to consider the actual resources available for the modalities. Designing a multimodal interface for a desktop is different from designing one for a PDA because the graphical resources available are different. The composition operators such as grouping are implemented graphically in desktop interfaces because the graphical modality is dominant, whereas in mobile devices they are supported both graphically and vocally.

If we consider the interactors the reasoning is similar. In the case of multimodal interfaces for a desktop platform we have decided to employ the graphical representation for only-output interactors, because the interface has a lot of space available, while for PDAs we have decided to use either modality or both in a complementary manner depending on the specific case (for example, the vocal modality is used for long texts). In interactive elements, in the case of desktop the prompt, input, and feedback are graphical (and the input can be also vocal), whereas in the case of PDA in addition the prompt can be vocal and the feedback is also always vocal unless the designer specifies otherwise.

3   A Sample Application and Concluding Remarks

In this section we show an example multimodal application for a multi-hall cinema designed with our environment. This example aims to highlight different and similar aspects between a PDA and a desktop multimodal interface. In both versions users can check the movies currently being shown or coming soon and book a ticket.

The main difference is that in the PDA version the vocal modality is more used than in the desktop version because handheld devices have limited graphics capabilities, and a small screen. As you can see in Figure 1, the movie description page of the desktop version provides more information, for example "user rating" or the film trailer. In addition, all tasks that do not require user interaction (only output interactors) are implemented using graphical modality. Differently, in the PDA version some tasks are not supported because the PDA screen is small and it is very tedious to scroll down so much, and some more important tasks are supported in the vocal modality, for example the plot summary. When users access the film description page with the PDA, they start to listen a little summary while some general information is shown. It is also interesting to highlight that users can provide input through either graphical or vocal modalities. In both versions it is possible to access the booking page using vocal commands or graphical selection. In case there are two or more input interactors in the same presentation, users can provide all information with only one vocal command or can select graphically each object. For example, in the booking page the user can say the time and the hall number together ("I would like to book a ticket for a screening in the Hall 3 at 9 p.m.") or can select graphically the two options. This features is very useful when users interact with PDAs, where there is no keyboard, because the interaction becomes much faster. In this example you can notice the different techniques adopted for grouping elements: in the multimodal desktop interface it is obtained through a graphical field set, whereas in the PDA version is obtained using both a sound (for the vocal comment) and a background colour at the same time to delimit the grouped elements.

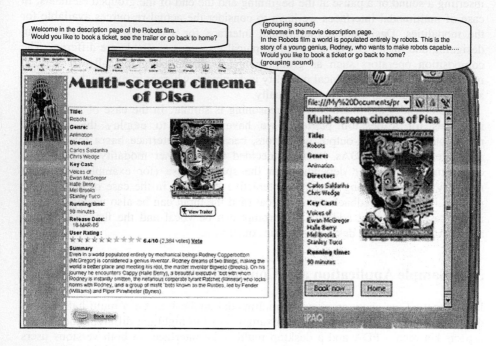

Fig. 1. Two multi-modal versions (desktop and PDA) for the cinema application

We have presented an environment supporting design of multimodal interfaces in multi-device environments. In particular, we have considered development of graphical and vocal interfaces in desktop and PDA devices. The approach is based on the use of logical, device-independent descriptions and transformations that incorporate multi-modal design criteria. An example application has been shown. Future work will be dedicated to extending the approach to consider other modalities, such as gestural interaction.

References

1. Bouchet J., Nigay L., ICARE: A Component-Based Approach for the Design and Development of Multimodal Interfaces, Adjunct Proceedings CHI 2004, pp.1325-1328.
2. Mori, G., Paternò, F., Santoro, C., Design and Development of Multi-Device User Interfaces through Multiple Logical Descriptions, IEEE Transactions on Software Engineering, August 2004, Vol.30, N.8, pp.507-520, IEEE Press.
3. Coutaz, J. Nigay, L. Salber, D. Blandford, A. May, J. Young, R.,. Four Easy Pieces for Assessing the Usability of Multmodal Interaction: the CARE properties. Proceedings INTERACT 1995, pp.115-120
4. Puerta, A., Eisenstein, XIML: A Common Representation for Interaction Data, Proceedings ACM IUI'01, pp.214-215.

Analysing Trans-Modal Interface Migration

Renata Bandelloni, Silvia Berti, and Fabio Paternò

ISTI-CNR,
Via G.Moruzzi 1, 56124 Pisa, Italy
{renata.bandelloni, silvia.berti, fabio.paterno}@isti.cnr.it

Abstract. While new solutions for supporting migratory interfaces are emerging, there is still a lack of analysis of their impact on users. In this paper we discuss the design of a solution for trans-modal migratory interfaces in multi-device and results obtained testing it with users. We conducted a study aimed at evaluating the user impact of a migration service applied to platforms supporting different interaction modalities (graphic vs. vocal) in Web environments.

1 Introduction

Migratory interfaces are interfaces able to support device changes and still allow the user to continue the task at hand. Device adaptation, interface usability and task continuity are the main goal. In particular, we are interested in migratory services in multi-device environments, characterised by a variety of devices, both mobile and stationary. Due to the novelty of transmodal interface migration, studies on the resulting usability are lacking. Indeed, no public service currently supports such migration and even at research level there is a lack of sufficiently engineered prototypes for end-user testing. We have designed and implemented an infrastructure for trans-modal migration [2] and performed a first test to better understand the impact on users in terms of disorientation due to interaction modality change and different support for task performance. The goal is to support users in multi-device environments, allowing migration even among different interaction-modality devices (currently graphical and vocal). While other contributions focus on migration through activation of different applications for the same service depending on the current device features [4]; or on distributed user interfaces, where users change interaction resources (such as the screen) but not the device [3], we manage to consider different interaction modalities. A conceptual framework for such issues is presented in [1].

2 The Trans-Modal Migration Service

Our trans-modal migration service is based on a server able to receive requests for migration, identify the target device and activate a specifically adapted user interface, maintaining the state resulting from the user interactions on the source device. This is obtained through logical descriptions of the tasks to support and of the user interfaces, used to perform interface adaption to the target platform, map the state from the source interface to the target one and identify the point where the target interface

M.F. Costabile and F. Paternò (Eds.): INTERACT 2005, LNCS 3585, pp. 1071–1074, 2005.
© IFIP International Federation for Information Processing 2005

should be activated. In order to facilitate users in continuing the interaction through the vocal platform when migrating from a graphic one, the migration service inserts an initial audio feedback summarising the information already entered. The message is built by collecting all the feedback messages concerning the tasks already performed by users and moving them at the beginning of the vocal interface. The migration service was tested on the "Restaurant" application, which allows users to select a restaurant, accessing its general information and make a reservation. The interfaces of the test application for desktop, PDA and vocal platforms differ both in the number of tasks and their implementation. For example, the date insertion is a text field in the desktop version and a selection object in the PDA version, while the insertion of free comments was removed from the vocal interface.

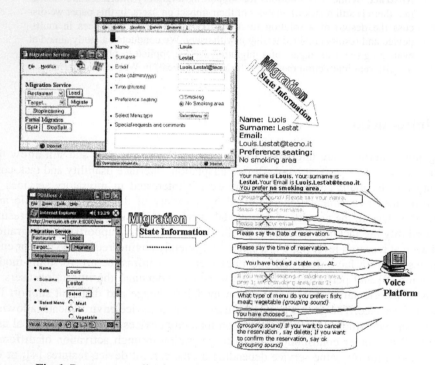

Fig. 1. Restaurant application and migration client interfaces used in the test

Figure 1 shows both the migration client and the "Restaurant" application interface. The migration client allows users to load applications and send migration requests. With the desktop, users could work on two different windows: one for the migration client interface and the other for the "Restaurant" application, while on the PDA they were presented in two frames of the same browser window.

3 The User Test

Since we are interested in considering multi-device environments, both a desktop PC and a PDA were used as graphic source platforms. This is useful for understanding if the features of the platform can influence the user because of the different interaction resources and, consequently, the different set of tasks supported. The 20 users involved were divided into two groups. The first one started with migration from PDA to vocal platform and repeated the experiment starting with the desktop. The second started with the desktop and repeated the test using the PDA. Users were asked to load the "Restaurant" application on the graphic device and start booking a table at a restaurant. At some point, they had to ask for migration towards the available vocal device and there complete the Restaurant Reservation task. After the session the users filled in the evaluation questionnaire. The average user age was 33.5 years (min 23 - max 68). Thirty percent of them were females, 65% had undergraduate degrees or higher and 55% had previously used a PDA. Users had good experience with graphic interfaces but far less with vocal ones: on a scale of 1 to 5, the average self-rating of graphic interface skill was 4.30 and 2.05 for vocal interfaces. For each migration experiment, users were asked to rate from 1 to 5 the parameters shown in Table 1.

Table 1. User rating for transmodal migration attributes

Parameters	Desktop to vocal	PDA to vocal
Interaction continuity easiness	4.35	4.65
Initial vocal feedback usefulness	4.1	4.2
Vocal feedback usefulness	4.25	4.25

Vocal feedback was provided via both the initial message, recalling the information inserted before migration, and a final message at the end of the session about the information inserted after migration. We chose this solution as the most likely to reduce user memory load. After the test, we asked the users if they would have preferred only total final feedback instead. Finally, we asked whether they noticed any difference between the graphic and vocal interface with the aim of finding out whether they could perceive the different number of supported tasks. The numeric test results were interpreted taking into account the answer justifications and free comments left in the questionnaire and considering user comments while performing the test.

Table 2. User preferences and salience of task differences

Parameters	Desktop to vocal	PDA to vocal
Only final vocal feedback preferred	Yes 20% - No 80%	Yes 20% - No 80%
Noticed different task set	Yes 25% - No 75%	Yes 20% - No 80%

4 Result Discussion and Conclusions

The service in itself was appreciated by users. Many judged it interesting and stimulating. The users had never tried any migration service before and interacted with it more easily in the second experiment, thus, showing it was easy to learn through practise, once the concepts underlying migration were understood. Interaction continuity received a slightly higher score in the PDA-to-vocal case. Indeed, the PDA and the vocal versions were more similar in terms of number of tasks than the desktop and the vocal ones. The difference in ease of continuity between the two platforms is small, thus the interaction continuity ease is influenced, but not compromised. Both the initial and the overall feedback through the vocal application were judged positively (Table 1). The vocal feedback design was appreciated and 80% of the users would not want to change its style. One concern was the potential user disorientation in continuing interaction, not only by the change in modality, but also in the different range of possible actions to perform. Only 20-25% noticed the difference and it was perceived more in the desktop-to-vocal case (Table 2).

While further empirical work will certainly be needed to investigate usability of migratory interfaces, this first study provides some useful suggestions to keep in mind while designing user interface transmodal migration. The modality change does not cause disorientation but must be well supported by proper user feedback balancing completeness while avoiding boredom. The differences in interaction objects used to support the same task were not noticed at all, while the difference in the number of task supported was. Changing the number of actions that the user can perform can not be avoided due to the different capabilities of the platforms involved. However, this must be well designed in order to reduce as much as possible any sudden disruption in user's expectation. It is worth considering not supporting migration among devices in which the user interfaces implement a high number of different tasks, unless there is a particular need for it. A further interesting study could concern a new version of the migration environment supporting a richer set of modalities and their combinations.

References

1. Balme, L., Coutaz, J., Demeure, A., Calvary, G. CAmeleon-RT: a Software Architecture Reference Model for Distributed, Migratable, and Plastic User Interfaces, European Symposium on Ambient Intelligence, EUSAI 04, LNCS 3295, Springer Verlag, pp. 291-302.
2. Bandelloni, R., Berti, S., Paternò F., Mixed-Initiative, Trans-Modal Interface Migration, Proceedings Mobile HCI 2004, Glasgow, September 2004, Lecture Notes Computer Science 3160, pp.216-227, Sprinter Verlag.
3. Coninx, K., Vandervelpen, C. Towards Model-based Design Support for Distributed User Interfaces. In Proceedings of the Third Nordic Conference on Human Computer Interaction (NordiCHI'04)(October23-27, 2004, Tampere, Finland), ISBN:1-58113-857-1, 61-70.
4. Garlan, D., Siewiorek, D., Smailagic, A., Steenkiste, P. Project Aura: Toward Distraction-Free Pervasive Computing. IEEE Pervasive Computing, Vol 21, No 2 (April-June 2002), 22-31.

Inferring Relations Between Color and Emotional Dimensions of a Web Site Using Bayesian Networks

Eleftherios Papachristos, Nikolaos Tselios, and Nikolaos Avouris

Human-Computer Interaction Group, Electrical and Computer Eng. Dept.,
University of Patras, GR-265 00 Rio Patras, Greece
{epap, nitse}@ee.upatras.gr, avouris@upatras.gr

Abstract. In this paper, a novel methodology for selecting appropriate color scheme for a web site is presented. The methodology uses a machine learning algorithm for generating a network that relates the color model of a web site with the emotional values that are attributed to it by its users. The approach involves an empirical study to collect data, used to train the algorithm. A preliminary case study has been conducted to validate the applicability of the methodology. Description of the framework and of a set of tools that were built to support the methodology is also included.

1 Introduction

Various factors contribute to the effectiveness of a web site, such as structure, content hierarchy, styles, text format and navigational elements position. Additionally to these, one of the most important design factors that influence the usability of a site is effective color usage. Recent work has shown that the design space is affected by both engineering and aesthetic usability issues. Also, visual aesthetics of computer interfaces seem to be a strong determinant of users' satisfaction and pleasure [1]. The design has to communicate broader values such as sense of professionalism, skillfulness and credibility. Color plays various roles ranging from the aesthetic to the utilitarian. However, most prior studies and recent survey studies for design guidelines focus on cognitive efficiency evaluation of websites [2]. In addition, existing color guidelines are often of limited use. Experiential advice tends to be non-representative, contradictory or even obsolete [3]. Even assuming that relevant guidelines exist, they are of little value to web designers with limited background on color theory and art. Furthermore, many issues remain unresolved, such the relationship between colors, the optimal number of colors for each case, etc.

The research goal described in this paper is to identify methodologically the color combinations which communicate effectively desired emotional values. For example, a news web site should effectively communicate values such as 'consistent', 'reliable', 'subjective', etc. Due to the fact that a direct evaluation of each color is heavily subjective, the methodology tackles this problem by indirectly evaluating the emotional influence of selected color combinations, and then breaking down the underlying influence of each factor via Bayesian Belief Networks. Tools have been developed to support the data collection and preprocessing stage, and to suggest appropriate chromatic combinations according to the desired communicating values.

M.F. Costabile and F. Paternò (Eds.): INTERACT 2005, LNCS 3585, pp. 1075 – 1078, 2005.
© IFIP International Federation for Information Processing 2005

In the rest of the paper, the proposed methodology and the explicit research goals are presented first. Then, a case study, carried out to validate the effectiveness of the proposed framework, is described, together with the developed tools that support it.

2 Color Scheme Selection Framework

Our goal is to determine relations between color characteristics and affective, emotional descriptors. The result of this approach is a formal methodological process to select the appropriate color combination. In addition, for a web site of a given scope we can elicit the appropriate color characteristics. The proposed methodology is partially inspired from a similar research by Guerin et al. [4], who examined color usage in the frame of designing internal spaces. The subjects of the experiment had to evaluate computer generated interior environments with a list of 21 words, selected for this purpose, using a Likert scale from 1 to 5.

In our study, a model of color has been developed, combining physical, aesthetic and artistic dimensions for various color combinations. A number of users (representing the expected users' characteristics) have been requested to characterize these color combinations according to a set of emotional descriptors. The 12 most distinctive terms were chosen: *Pleasant, Formal, Fresh, Modern, Friendly, Aggressive, Professional, Attractive, Calming, Dynamic, Reliable and Sophisticated*. These emotional dimensions are compatible with the thirteen emotional dimensions that have been used by Kim et al. [5]. This process led to a formal selection of chromatic combinations, in aspects such as *dominant* and *secondary color selection*, recommendation on *number of colors* to use, appropriate *color scheme* and *secondary color* scheme attributes such as *degree of saturation* and *brightness*. By simply asking the participants for their preferences in colors, their answers would present highly subjective character, thus leading to non meaningful or contradictory conclusions. Therefore, we constructed an indirect approach to gather their evaluations concerning the attributes of the color model of a specific layout. The data collected have been used for training a Bayesian belief network (BBN). A BBN is an annotated directed acyclic graph that encodes a joint probability distribution and is considered as a significant knowledge representation and reasoning tool, under conditions of uncertainty [6], [7]. The proposed framework is supported by two tools. The first to facilitate user data collection. The second tool allows the user to choose which emotional descriptor has to be present on her web site and at what degree. According to user's emotional preferences, the system proposes a list of color characteristics coupled with detailed explanations on the results.

3 Validation of the Proposed Framework

An experiment took place with the objective to validate the feasibility of the proposed framework. Forty six (46) participants (35 male and 11 female), aged 21 to 31, most of them experienced Internet users, evaluated eight color schemes each. Most participants were students of our Department. All of the characteristics referring to color selections were encoded to uniquely identify each layout. These comprise a color model that contains attributes related to the physical properties of the primary and secondary color (e.g. color hue, saturation and brightness), as well as aesthetic properties (e.g. perceived warmth of the primary color, color scheme). The data collected was 4416 evaluations (=46 participants x12 descriptors x8 layouts).

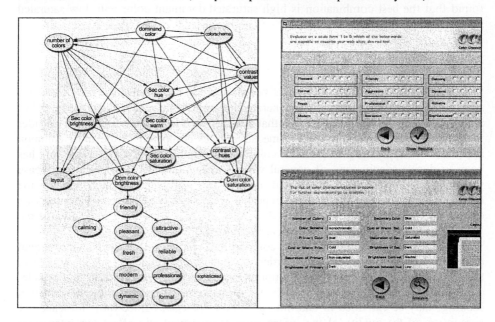

Fig. 1. The Bayesian Belief Network derived (left). Color Selector Tool (right). (a) the user has to select the desired emotional values. (b), the system infers the appropriate color characteristics using the trained Bayesian Belief Network

The result of the experiment is expressed through the Bayesian Belief Network constructed (Figure 1). With the help of the BBN construction and testing tool, *Hugin Expert*, the Bayesian Network built was analyzed. The diagrammatic nature of the BBN, allows recognition of the relations between the variables of the experiment (color scheme attributes and emotional descriptors). Furthermore, the method allows us to gain an insight on how a change in the value of one variable affects the attributes of other variables of the Network. In general, conclusions from the BBN are both structural and statistical. For example, according to the tree structure, the *brightness* of the dominant color has a stronger emotional effect than its *hue*.

Further analyzing the BBN structure, lead to a categorization of influence of color factors, into 4 levels of importance. The design attribute with the strongest effect is the *brightness* of the dominant color. Secondly, the *brightness* level of the secondary color and its type (warm or cold), the *number of colors*, *contrast* between hues. Thirdly, the *two primary colors,* the *color scheme* and the *contrast level*. Finally the *dominant color's saturation* and its type (warm or cold).

Besides observations on the structure of the network, or performing sensitivity studies on various nodes, other significant relationships have been derived. For example, it seems to be preferable to use more than four colors or monochromatic and analogical chromatic combinations. Additionally to this, it seems to be preferable to use low contrast levels between colors. Cold colors are perceived as more suitable than warm ones. And, if we would like to adopt a monochromatic color scheme, it is preferable to have high contrast in brightness. Finally, regarding saturation, it was found that the best combination is high saturated dominant color with low saturated secondary color.

4 Conclusions

In this paper, a novel framework has been presented that relates the web site color scheme to its emotional impact. It generates a network that relates the color model of a web site with the emotional values that are attributed to it by its users. We consider the proposed framework to have some advantages compared to the most common approach, i.e. applying guidelines for color usage. The objective of the framework has been to derive conclusions, of general value and applicability. The preliminary case study reported here was conducted mainly to certify the applicability of the methodology. Many of the findings reported here confirm earlier empirical rules on color and current tendencies in web design, which is a significant indication of the validity of the proposed methodological framework.

An additional research goal is to compare our results with expert's views about best color usage in web design in order to establish the reliability of our approach. Finally, one may put the issue of appropriate chromatic combination to a broader context. We argue that various models of typical web user behavior, like information seeking, may be extended to take into account color issues since they influence our perception of the quality of the information environment and affect our interaction with it[1].

References

1. Lavie, T. and Tractinsky, N., Assessing Dimensions of Perceived Visual Aesthetics of Web Sites, Int. J. of Human-Computer Studies, 60 (3):269-298, 2004
2. Wang, P., A survey of design guidelines for usability of web sites. Proceedings of the 2001 Human-Computer Interaction International Conference 1, 183-187, 2001.
3. Schwier, R.A. and Misanchuk, E.R., The art and science of color in multimedia screen design Proc. of Conf. of the Assoc. for Educ. Comm. and Technology, Anaheim, CA., 1995
4. Guerin, D. A., Park, Y., & Yang, S., Development of an instrument to study the meaning of color in interior environments. Journal of Interior Design, 20 (2), 31-41, 1995.
5. Kim J., Lee J., Choi D., Designing emotionally evocative homepages: an empirical study of the quantitative relations between design factors and emotional dimensions, Int. J. Human-Computer Studies, 59, pp. 899–940, 2003.
6. Jensen F. V.. "Bayesian Networks and Decision Graphs". Springer. 2001.
7. Glymour C., Cooper G. (eds.). Computation, Causation & Discovery. AAAI Press/The MIT Press, Menlo Park, 1999.

[1] The reported research here is funded by the Hellenic Ministry of Education under the Pyhtagoras II-EPEAEK program, project:"Study and Development of models of information search in the web".

Abbrevicons: Efficient Feedback for Audio Interfaces

Matthew Hockenberry, Sharon Cohen, Zachary Ozer, Tiffany Chen,
and Ted Selker

The Media Laboratory, 20 Ames St. E15-322, Cambridge MA 02139
{hock, selker}@media.mit.edu
{sbcohen, zozer, chent}@mit.edu

Abstract. Abbrevicons are a technique for encoding audio information efficiently while still providing the user with useful and appropriate feedback. Ideally, abbrevicons are targeted towards audio interfaces that are infrequently used and where the user doesn't have the opportunity to develop a strong model of the system or make sense of rich encoding schemes. Abbrevicons allow us to present natural language feedback that is identifiable and comprehensible, while taking significantly less time than traditional verbal feedback. Abbrevicons can decrease the speed of short descriptive feedback by up to 200% while still ensuring user comprehension. These techniques seek to provide richer user feedback in audio interfaces while still keeping in mind the need for efficient user interactions.

1 Introduction

In audio interfaces such as telephone trees, tones are often used to provide confirmation of user actions. These systems are inefficient because these tones provide little feedback or information to the user's specified action – they only indicate that an action has occurred. [1]

Abbrevicons are intended to replace these generic tones in audio interfaces. Abbrevicons are created by compressing a base word or phrase so that it plays significantly faster than normal speed. Abbrevicons can provide significantly more information to the user than a generic tone and has the potential to significantly improve the efficiency and quality of feedback in audio interfaces. A generic tone provides only awareness that the user has made a selection from the menu; it does not confirm their choice. Our goal in creating abbrevicons is to provide the user with as much information as possible within a very compressed space.

1.1 Existing Approaches

There is a large body of work in the literature on providing feedback mechanisms for audio interfaces. Audio icons and earcons both represent established methods for providing feedback based on user interactions, but neither offers feedback that is *both* innately meaningful and can be mechanically synthesized for occasional-use audio interfaces.

Audio icons are rich naturalistic sounds that encode underlying system mechanics in sound. The classic example of this is the ARKOLA simulation where Gaver used the sounds of a bottling factory to offer feedback on the state of the system. [2]

M.F. Costabile and F. Paternò (Eds.): INTERACT 2005, LNCS 3585, pp. 1079–1082, 2005.

Generally, audio icons are well received by users and can communicate a lot of information. The difficulty comes in their construction; there has been little success in creating effective audio icons that can be generated through purely mechanical methods. [3]

Earcons are generated synthetic tones that can vary in rhythm, pitch, timbre, register, and dynamics. Earcons can use these five factors to encode different kinds of information such as the type of application, family, or number of a file on a desktop. Although they can be very flexible and computer generated, they require that the user learn how each of the factors encodes or alters the encoding of information. [4] This is quite unlike audio icons that have an obvious meaning that relates directly to the encoded information. Still once the system has been learned they offer a lot of opportunity for improved efficiency in presentation speed. [5]

1.2   Creating Abbrevicons

Abbrevicons are created by starting with a 'base phrase' recorded either directly from a human speaker or (ideally) through a speech generation tool. This base phrase is then processed to drop frames of audio content. The result is an abbrevicon which shares the same tonal properties of the base phrase, but which sounds as though it was spoken very quickly. We chose to drop frames so that we could keep the natural sound of the base phrase without distortion (such as changes to pitch, etc...). This process is relatively simple and can be performed with a large number of audio editing programs (such as soundforge, audacity, and so on).

2   Evaluation

We have run a series of studies in our exploration of the effectiveness of abbrevicons. We have had over 100 subjects complete 100 trials for each of three conditions studying both recognition and recall of abbrevicons. Our recognition conditions presented the subject with an abbrevicon and a set of either five visual or five auditory cues. We also did a flat recall that required the subjects record what they believed they heard. The abbrevicons were constructed from a fixed, known lexicon with which the subjects were familiar. We found that the comprehensibility of abbrevicons depends on four main factors: the amount of compression of the base phrase, the number of syllables in the base words, the presence of distinct spaces between words, and the consonant sounds within the base words. For our purposes a "comprehendible" abbrevicon is one for which the subjects were able to identify its meaning in more than 95% of trials.

One of the largest influences on the level of comprehension of abbrevicons is the amount that the base phrase is compressed. The difficulty of comprehension increased as the base phrases were increasingly compressed. Speeding the base phrase up by 75-150% tended to create reasonably understandable abbrevicons (the mean error rate is .866% for a 75% increase and 1.088% for a 150% increase with 99.5% confidence), while increases of speed by 200-250% rendered abbrevicons that were significantly less comprehensible (though still acceptable, the error rate for 225% was 3.053% with 99.5% confidence). Tripling the speed of the abbrevicons was the maximum limit of any comprehension and we see the error rate rise exponentially at this point. Subjects also reported feeling uncomfortable listening to audio at this rate.

Increasing the number of syllables within a word increases the difficulty of comprehension. Abbrevicons that consisted of single-syllable base words were generally easier to comprehend, even at higher speeds, than abbrevicons of multiple syllable base words. Abbrevicons that contained two or three-syllable base words were not only harder to understand, but also had less potential to be compressed further and retain comprehensibility. For example, of the abbrevicons "confirm selection" and "confirm choice," the latter abbrevicon demonstrated higher clarity at the same compression rate of 100%. We attributed this easier understanding to "choice" having fewer syllables than "selection."

To make Abbrevicons more comprehensible at higher speeds, we found that intentionally adding spaces between words allowed for greater clarity, even at higher speeds. This was especially effective when using computer-synthesized voices, rather than human recordings of abbrevicons. For example, the abbrevicon "please hold" could be heard with much more clarity if a deliberate pause was added in between the two words. With the added pause, the Abbrevicon could be easily comprehensible even at 150% or 200% compression (with an error rate of 1.088% as reported earlier), whereas without the space, the Abbrevicon was only readily understandable at 75-100% increase in speed (with an error rate of 2.097%).

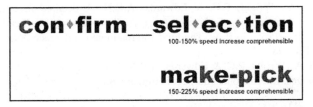

Fig. 1. 'Confirm selection', because of its lack of harsh consonants and multiple syllables can only be increased by 100-150%, while a base phrase like 'make pick' can achieve an increase of 150-225% and remain comprehensible

Another interesting conclusion about abbrevicons is that words with hard consonant sounds were easier to comprehend. In the previously discussed abbrevicon "confirm choice," the beginning "k-" and middle "-ch-" sounds are both weak consonant sounds. Abbrevicons with these weak consonant sounds tend to be readily understandable at 100-150% increase in speed. However, words with hard consonant sounds tended to be greater in clarity. "Make pick" consists of the "m" and "k" harsh consonants for the first word as well as the "p" and "-ick" harsh consonant sounds for the second word. The two words combined with a deliberate space in between, this abbrevicon had high clarity even after being speed up by 150-200%. Once again, computer-synthesized voices, which emphasized the harsh consonant sounds, were easier to comprehend at higher speeds than human recordings.

3 Conclusions and Future Work

From our studies, we concluded that the most easily comprehensible abbrevicons consisted of words with harsh consonant sounds and few syllables. In addition, a clear space between words increases clarity even at high compression rates. Using these methods, we can compress information to up to 360 words per minute, twice the speed of normal conversational, without significantly hindering comprehension. Unlike other methods for providing feedback in audio interfaces, abbrevicons have both intrinsic meaning (assuming the listener can understand the language) and the capacity for computer generation (by scripting sound applications with text-to-speech engines). This could allow us to use abbrevicons as a method for providing feedback in general purpose audio interfaces with little effort on the part of the interface or system developer. The goal is that we can use these techniques to generate feedback that is useful to the user while still presenting information as efficiently as possible.

References

1. Resnick, P., and Virzi, RA. Relief from the Audio Interface Blues: Expanding the Spectrum of Menu, List, and Form Styles. ACM Transactions on Computer-Human Interaction, 2, 2 (1995), 145-176.
2. Gaver, W. W., & Smith, R. B., O'Shea, T. Effective sounds in complex systems: the ARKOLA simulation. In Proc. SIGCHI conference on Human factors in computing systems: Reaching through technology. (1991), p. 85-90.
3. Gaver, W. W. Synthesizing Auditory Icons. In Proc. INTERCHI. (1993).
4. Brewster, S. A., Wright, P.C. & Edwards, A.D.N. A detailed investigation into the effectiveness of earcons. In G. Karmer (ed.), Auditory display, sonification, audification and auditory interfaces. In Proc. The First International Conference on Auditory Display. (1992) pp. 471-498.
5. Brewster, S. A., Wright, P.C. & Edwards, A.D.N. Parallel Earcons: Reducing the length of Audio Messages. International Journal of Human-Computer Studies, (1995).

Icon Use by Different Language Groups: Changes in Icon Perception in Accordance with Cue Utility

Siné McDougall[1], Alexandra Forsythe[2], and Lucy Stares[1]

[1] University of Wales Swansea, Swansea SA2 8PP
{s.mcdougall, l.a.stares}@swansea.ac.uk
[2] Queen's University Belfast, Belfast BH10 1TT
a.forsythe@qub.ac.uk

Abstract. This study shows that both icon and function label characteristics combine subtly to affect the way that individuals perceive icons. Icon users unconsciously use the cues available to them: the perce to which these cues are utilised depends on the language background of the user. In order to optimise design we therefore need know more, not only about the effects of function label characteristics, but also about how they merge with icon and user characteristics to affect usability.

1 Introduction

It has been assumed that icons offer a universal and international mode of communication [2] [5] and they are used in airports, stations, and other public spaces for this reason. However, although some icons appear to be universally recognised (see Figure 1(a)), others are more culturally specific (see Figure 1(b) [3]). Furthermore, when Smith & Siringo [6] asked participants to match an icon with its function they found considerable differences between nationalities (India, Turkey, Singapore and the United States). Given that icons are typically presented along with their function written underneath to optimise comprehension [7], this study examines the extent to which different language groups are able to use function labels.

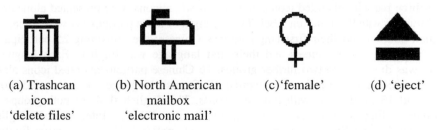

| (a) Trashcan icon 'delete files' | (b) North American mailbox 'electronic mail' | (c) 'female' | (d) 'eject' |

Fig. 1. Examples of icons

Bates and her colleagues [1] suggest that language perception and comprehension depends on the information value of the cues available and the amount and type of

M.F. Costabile and F. Paternò (Eds.): INTERACT 2005, LNCS 3585, pp. 1083–1086, 2005.
© IFIP International Federation for Information Processing 2005

processing associated with using each cue. We assumed that the same principles would hold true for icons and that icon *perception* would change depending on the utility of the cues available. The perceptions of two language groups were compared: one whose first language was English and another group from China who were acquiring English as their second language. Participants were asked to provide ratings of their subjective perceptions of the concreteness, or pictorialness, of icons when they were presented alone or when they were presented with the function label in English underneath. Our first hypothesis was that native English speakers' ratings would be more affected by the presentation of both icon and function since they would make more use of the function cue. Non-native English speakers were more likely to rate concreteness solely on the basis of pictorial cues in the icon than on concreteness of the function label since this cue would provide less information for them.

Other, more detailed, predictions were also made. Our second hypothesis was that the magnitude of the change in concreteness ratings for native English speakers would depend on the difference between the concreteness of the icon itself and the concreteness of the function label (i.e. on the combined use of both cues). Figure 1(c) and (d) illustrate how the icon and function label may, or may not, differ: 'female', a function rated as highly concrete, is depicted using an abstract icon while 'eject', an abstract function, is also depicted abstractly. For 'female', we might expect a large difference between 'icon only' and 'icon and function' concreteness ratings if English speakers are utilising both icons and function labels as cues, while differences between rating conditions would be minimal for 'eject'. A third hypothesis was that non-native English speakers would be more likely to use the function as a cue in their concreteness ratings if the words used in the function label occurred more frequently in English (i.e. were highly familiar). The assumption in both these hypotheses is that cue use is not all-or-none but is probabilistic, based on the combined information value of the cues available.

2 Method

2.1 Participants

A total of 99 participants took part in this study and all were student volunteers. Fifty-three participants rated icon concreteness when icons were presented alone or in combination with the function label. Twenty eight of these participants were attending English courses and their first language was Chinese; the remaining 25 participants were attending other courses and their first language was English. Each language group was divided into two further groups: 16 Chinese participants rated icons alone and 12 rated icons with function words; 12 English language speakers rated icons alone and 13 rated icons with function words. The English skills of both groups of non-native English speakers were equated using IELTS (International English Language Testing System) scores (t(26) = 0.31, p>0.05). Forty-six native English speakers provided additional ratings: 25 rated the concreteness of the function label alone and 21 participants rated their familiarity with the function label alone.

2.2 Materials and Procedure

Participants were asked to rate 239 icons from a corpus used by McDougall et al [4] for which concreteness ratings had already been obtained. In contrast to the original ratings procedure for the corpus, where only icons without their functions were rated, two groups of participants were also presented with icons with the function label underneath. Ratings were on a 1-5 scale (5=definitely concrete, 1=definitely abstract)[1]. Icons were rated as concrete if they depicted real objects, materials or people; those that did not were rated as abstract. Additional ratings of the concreteness of the function label alone were also obtained using identical instructions. Ratings of familiarity with the function label were also obtained using a 1-5 scale (1=very unfamiliar, 5=very familiar). The icons and ratings obtained can be seen at http://psy.swan.ac.uk/staff/mcdougall/additionalratings.htm.

3 Results and Discussion

In line with our first hypothesis, ratings for native English speakers differed between conditions (M(icon only)=3.20, M(icon+function)=3.02) while non-native speakers were remarkably similar irrespective of whether the function was shown underneath the icon or not (M(icon only)=3.30, M(icon+function)=3.31). By-items analysis of variance with language (Chinese/English) and rating condition (icon only/ icon+function) as factors revealed a significant effect of language on ratings, $F(1,238)=41.69$, MSE=9.12, $p<0.01$, since concreteness ratings were generally lower for English speakers. The effect of rating condition was also significant, $F(1,238)=5.39$, MSE=2.12, $p<0.05$, as was the interaction between language and rating condition, $F(1,238)=12.17$, MSE=1.76, $p<0.01$. This interaction shows that, as predicted, native speakers are more likely to change their perceptions of the icons given function cues than non-native speakers.

The second hypothesis stated that as the difference between icon and function concreteness increased (e.g. Figure 1(c)), so the difference in ratings obtained between the icon only and icon+function conditions would increase. This was examined by first computing the difference between the original norms (icons alone; see [4]) and ratings of the concreteness of the function name alone. This provided a measure of the difference between icon and function concreteness. The difference between ratings in the icon only and icon+function conditions was then calculated. Both of these difference scores were then correlated on the assumption that a significant correlation would occur if participants modified their ratings more given a greater difference between the concreteness of the icon and the concreteness of the function label. Correlations for both native and non-native speakers were significant (r=.71and r=.43 respectively). When Fisher's z_r transformation was used to examine the difference between these two correlations, it revealed that the correlation for native speakers was significantly higher than for non-native speakers. This shows that subjective perceptions of icon concreteness are based on the difference in concreteness between icon and function for both groups but that native speakers use the function label cues more to adjust their perceptions of concreteness.

---

[1] Our thanks to Dr Chris Shei for translating ratings instructions for Chinese participants.

Our final hypothesis was that Chinese speakers may be better able to use the cues provided by function labels if they were highly familiar. Icons whose function label familiarity ratings were in the top quartile were regarded as familiar (n=59) and those in the bottom quartile were regarded as unfamiliar (n=62). The same correlations were carried out as for Hypothesis 2 for non-native speakers for familiar and unfamiliar functions. Correlations for icons with familiar and unfamiliar functions were r=.58 and .48 respectively. Fisher's z_r transformations were used to compare these correlations with that for the whole icon set (r =.43). While no differences were found between the whole sample and unfamiliar icons, the correlation was significantly higher when icons were familiar. This shows that second language English speakers are able to make better use of function names as cues when they occur more frequently.

4   Conclusions

The data obtained suggests that cross-linguistic differences in icon interpretation can be very subtle and affect the way icons are perceived. Even when not explicitly asked to do so, individuals use cues from icon and function in accordance with their ability to utilise those cues. At a practical level, designers need to know more about how icon and function characteristics act together to affect icon perception and interpretation and how the balance in the use of these cues changes with language and cultural background. Although our study showed that concreteness and familiarity are important cues, future research needs to examine the role of other cues such as the phonological and orthographic complexity of the function label and the closeness of the semantic relationship between icon and function.

References

1. Bates, E., Devescovi, A. & Wulfeck, B.: Psycholinguistics: A cross-language perspective. Annual Review of Psychology, Vol. 52, (2001) 369-396
2. Bocker, M.: A multiple index approach for the evaluation of pictograms. Proceedings of the 14th International Symposium of Human Factors in Telecommunication (1993) 73-843.
3. Marcus, A.: Icon and symbol design issues for graphical user interfaces. In del Galdo, E.M., & Nielsen, J. (eds.) International user interfaces, John Wiley & Sons, New York (1996) 257-270
4. McDougall, S.J.P., Curry, M.B. & de Bruijn, O.: Measuring symbol and icon characteristics: Norms for concreteness, complexity, meaningfulness, familiarity, and semantic distance for 239 symbols.   Behavior Research Methods, Instruments & Computers, Vol. 31. (1999) 487-519
5. Rogers, Y.: Icon design for the user interface. International Review of Ergonomics, Vol. 2. (1989) 129-154
6. Smith, J.A. & Siringo, M.P. (1997). The acceptability of icons across countries. In G. Salvendy, M.J. Smith & R.J. Koubek (eds.), Design of computing systems: Cognitive considerations: Advances in Human Factors/ Ergonomics Vol. 21A. Elsevier, New York (1997) 177-180
7. Weidenbeck, S.: The use of icons and labels in an end user application program: An empirical study of learning and retention. Behaviour & Information Technology, Vol.18. (1999) 68-82

User Aspects of
Explanation Aware CBR Systems

Jörg Cassens

Department of Computer and Information Science (IDI),
Norwegian University of Science and Technology (NTNU),
7491 Trondheim, Norway
jorg.cassens@idi.ntnu.no

Abstract. This paper addresses the problem of embedding explanation-aware intelligent systems into a workplace environment. We outline an approach with three different perspectives, focusing on the work process as a whole as well as user interaction from an interface and a system view. The theoretical background consists of Actor Network Theory, Semiotics, and Activity Theory. We further propose to integrate this workplace analysis into a design process for knowledge-intensive and explanation-aware Case-Based Reasoning systems.

1   Introduction

Explanations are an important vehicle to convey information in everyday human-human interaction. They help us to understand one another and enhance the knowledge of the communication partners in such a way that they accept certain statements. The partners understand more, allowing them to make informed decisions. The need for explanations provided by knowledge-based systems is well documented [1,2,3]. The adequacy of explanations is dependent on pragmatically given background knowledge. What counts as a good explanation in a certain situation is determined by context-dependent criteria [4].

Research on explanation is of interest today because it can be argued that the whole scenario on research on Knowledge-Based Systems (KBS) has changed: KBS are no longer considered as black boxes that provide a full solution to a problem. Instead, problem solving is seen as an interactive process (a socio-technical process). Problem descriptions as well as other input can be incomplete and changing. As a consequence, there has to be communication between human and software agents. Communication requires mutual understanding that can be essentially supported by explanations. Such explanations can improve the problem solving process to a large degree.

Case-Based Reasoning (CBR, [5]) is a research area in the field of AI. Its aim is to understand and build systems which are able to use previous experience in order to solve new problems. A CBR system is able to learn by storing experience in the form of so called cases, which describe problems and their solutions. When a new problem arises, a sufficiently similar previous problem has to be identified

M.F. Costabile and F. Paternò (Eds.): INTERACT 2005, LNCS 3585, pp. 1087–1090, 2005.

and the former solution has to be adapted to the new problem. The new solution might also be based on more than one previous case.

We are suggesting a framework for the design of explanation-aware CBR systems which takes the usage of the system into account. We are therefore in need of methodologies which can describe the workplace environment in which the system is going to be used on the human-computer interaction level. This analysis is then integrated into the design process as a whole, as described in [6].

In order to understand how the system fits into a workplace situation, we propose a theoretical framework which is focusing on three different perspectives:

- Work process view: Actor Network Theory,
- HCI interface view: Semiotics, and
- HCI system view: Activity Theory.

2   Work Process View: Actor Network Theory

We model the context in which the system is implemented with the help of the Actor Network Theory, ANT [7,8]. The basic idea here is fairly simple: whenever you do something, many influences on *how* you do it exist. For instance, if you visit a conference, it is likely that you stay at a hotel. How you behave at the hotel is influenced by your own previous experience with hotels, regulations for check-in and check-out, the capabilities the hotel offers you (breakfast room, lifts), amongst others.

In effect, you are not performing from scratch, but are influenced by a wide range of factors. The aim of ANT is to provide an unified view on these factors and your own acting. According to Monteiro, an actor network in this notion is 'the act linked together with all of its influencing factors (which again are linked), producing a network' (see [8, p. 4]).

In this network, you find both technical and non-technical elements. By this, the ANT avoids the trap of either overstating the role of technological artifacts in a socio-technological system or underestimating their normative power by applying the same framework to both human actors and technological artifacts.

This makes it possible for us to understand how technological artifacts influence the doing of human actors in much the same way as other human actors.

3   HCI Interface View: Semiotics

When focusing on the interaction of a particular user with the system, we use the semiotics approach [9,10] to understand the peculiarities of interaction with intelligent systems. In the terminology of semiotics, human communication is a sign process. In contrast, conventional computer systems are only processing signals, lacking the necessary interpreting capabilities humans have.

We argue that in order to make intelligent systems work not merely as tools or media, but as actors to whose decision making abilities a human user can subscribe, the system must appear to the user as if it was capable of a meaningful interaction. Since both processes, sign and signal, have to be coupled, the goal is to make an intelligent system behave in such a way that the user ascribes to the system the ability to participate in a sign process. The upper-level analysis of the work process helps in defining the aspects of user interaction where this ascription has to succeed in order to make the user believe in the system's capabilities.

One important challenge here is the ability of the system to show its capabilities. This can be described as a communication problem: the system has to interpret the actions of the user in a meaningful way and itself present results that make sense for the user. This process of sense-making is highly interactive: an intelligent partner in a communication process asks (meaningful) questions if an unclear situation occurs and is able to explain its own actions. The semiotic approach is useful to analyse this sense-making process with the help of transferring knowledge about similar processes from other semiotic domains.

4 HCI System View: Activity Theory

In our framework, we use Activity Theory (AT, [11]) to analyse the use of artifacts as instruments for achieving a predefined goal in the work process and especially to understand the transformation of the artifact itself and the individual and collective work practice during this process.

Since an AI system is more a partner in a work process than a tool, its role in the user interaction changes. Whereas a classical informatics system is a passive translator and memory of praxis, the intelligent system is constantly re-shaping praxis through its use. Looking at a decision support system, the decision making process itself is transformed by the ability of the system to react differently, e.g. through accumulated experience and usage context.

But since AT itself models artifacts as being preformed as socio-cultural entities, we can describe the artifacts in a way which takes this modification into account. Again, our upper-level model helps us to identify the mediation process and the role of both human and non-human actors in the usage process.

The ability of an intelligent system to adapt to the user is very important. In the process of re-shaping praxis, a user expects from an (as-if) intelligent system that it adapts to the changed situation. In the beginning of the usage of a Case-Based diagnostic system, it will be important to explain to the user in detail why a particular case was matched to a new problem, but the user expects from an intelligent partner that the same match will be explained in less detail when occurring very frequently (since the artifact should be changed by the changed praxis, that is here the accumulated knowledge on both parts). On the other hand, in the event of a breakdown situation, the level of detail in explanations given by the system should be increased again.

In addition, the notion of action cycles [12] is helpful for mapping the CBR system model to existing work processes. For example, identifying those situations where feedback to the system is both required and fits into the existing work process helps in avoiding obtrusive system behaviour.

5   Conclusions

The three perspectives presented allow system designers to analyse different socio-technical aspects of the targeted workplace environment. They can be used together to get a more complete model, but this is not always possible or even necessary. For example, in recent work we have investigated how Activity Theory alone can be used to model the knowledge needed in context-aware systems [13].

On the other hand, combining these three approaches allows modelling different aspects of human-computer interaction ranging from the socio-technical network to the design of the user interface itself on the knowledge level. Our goal is therefore to integrate these perspectives further and combine them with other steps of the CBR system lifecycle [6].

References

1. Swartout, W.: What Kind of Expert Should a System be? XPLAIN: A System for Creating and Explaining Expert Consulting Programs. Artificial Intelligence **21** (1983) 285–325
2. Buchanan, B.G., Shortliffe, E.H.: Rule-Based Expert Systems: The MYCIN Experiments of the Stanford Heuristic Programming Project. Addison Wesley, Reading (1984)
3. Swartout, W., Smoliar, S.: On Making Expert Systems More Like Experts. Expert Systems **4** (1987) 196–207
4. Leake, D.B.: Goal-Based Explanation Evaluation. In Ram, A., Leake, D.B., eds.: Goal-Driven Learning. MIT Press/Bradford Books, Cambridge (1995) 251–285
5. Aamodt, A., Plaza, E.: Case-Based Reasoning: Foundational Issues, Methodological Variations, and System Approaches. AI Communications **7** (1994) 39–59
6. Roth-Berghofer, T.R., Cassens, J.: Mapping Goals and Kinds of Explanations to the Knowledge Containers of Case-Based Reasoning Systems. In Muñoz-Avila, H., Ricci, F., eds.: Proceedings ICCBR 2005 (to appear). (2005)
7. Latour, B.: Technology is Society made Durable. In Law, J., ed.: A Sociology of Monsters. Routledge (1991) 103–131
8. Monteiro, E.: Actor-Network Theory. In Ciborra, C., ed.: From Control to Drift. Oxford University Press (2000) 71–83
9. Nake, F.: Human-Computer Interaction – Signs and Signals Interfacing. Languages of Design **2** (1994) 193–205
10. Andersen, P.B.: What Semiotics Can and Cannot do for HCI. Knowledge-Based Systems **14** (2001) 419–424
11. Bødker, S.: Activity Theory as a Challenge to Systems Design. In Nissen, H.E., Klein, H., Hirschheim, R., eds.: Information Systems Research: Contemporary Approaches and Emergent Traditions. North Holland (1991) 551–564
12. Fjeld, M., Lauche, K., Bichsel, M., Voorhoorst, F., Krueger, H., Rauterberg, M.: Physcial and Virtual Tools: Activity Theory Applied to the Design of Groupware. CSCW **11** (2002) 153–180
13. Kofod-Petersen, A., Cassens, J.: Activity Theory and Context-Awareness. In Schulz, S., Leake, D.B., Roth-Berghofer, T.R., eds.: IJCAI Workshop Proceedings: MRC 2005 (to appear). (2005)

Mobile Reacher Interface for Intuitive Information Navigation

Yuichi Yoshida, Kento Miyaoku, Takashi Satou, and Suguru Higashino

Nippon Telegraph and Telephone Corporation, NTT Cyber Communications
Laboratory Hikari-no-oka 1-1 Yokosuka, Kanagawa, Japan
{yoshida.yuichi, miyaoku.kento, satou.takashi,
higashino.suguru}@lab.ntt.co.jp

Abstract. We propose Mobile Reacher Interface (MoRIn) that is a new interface with a visual tag for a mobile device. MoRIn allows users to navigate sophisticated information structures by making natural hand gestures while holding a camera-equipped mobile terminal. The structure of an item of interest is acquired via a visual tag. The user can then navigate the structure as if he/she is handling physical objects. MoRIn greatly eases the user's cognitive loads. For instance, the user can alter the volume of an announcement by twisting terminal as if he/she were turning a dial. We describe MoRIn, some applications, and the results of a preliminary experiment.

1   Introduction

Many new services are being created that utilize the user's mobile device as a display system. The user sees public media and acquires a visual tag which loads a URL into the terminal which then accesses the corresponding information source[1,2].

Early services provided just a simple link to go to an advertisement but more sophisticated variants are emerging. The current information structure of tag-based services is a simple pointer which brings the typical menu list. That is, the real world is not linked directly to the cyber world and the user is forced to turn away from the real world and remember the control operations needed to access the information in the menu list, see Fig.1-(a). This poses a problem since most terminals provide non-intuitive interaction devices such as buttons. A more effective interface is needed.

We believe that this unduly restricts the services available and prevents wide-spread adoption. Our approach is to replace the pointer with three structures that mirror the real world: the line, surface, and space, see Fig.1-(b). User can intuitively navigate the information structure which is indicated by the visual tag as if directly manipulating a real world object with a "Mobile Reacher".

To implement MoRIn, we utilize the terminal's camera to acquire the visual tag and use the physical movements of the terminal as user input to navigate the information structure indicated by the tag. The extraction of physical movement from visual field processing with the tags has already been reported; six Degrees

M.F. Costabile and F. Paternò (Eds.): INTERACT 2005, LNCS 3585, pp. 1091–1095, 2005.

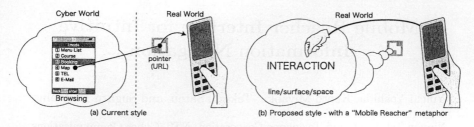

Fig. 1. Current and proposed style

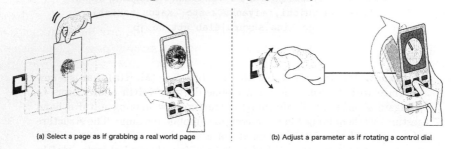

(a) Select a page as if grabbing a real world page   (b) Adjust a parameter as if rotating a control dial

Fig. 2. Example of MoRIn

Of Freedom (DOF) are available. For instance, the research has examined the impact of overlaying the camera image with the information acquired through the tag[3,4].

MoRIn permits a wide range of intuitive operations. For instance, the user can select one of several "pages" as if grabbing a real world page, see Fig.2-(a). Fig.2-(b) shows another example, the user can adjust a parameter, such as audio volume, by rotating the terminal as if rotating a control dial. MoRIn allows users to control virtual attributes with real world actions.

We constructed a prototype MoRIn system and evaluated its performance. In this paper, we describe MoRIn, several applications, and the results of a preliminary evaluation.

2   MoRIn - Mobile Reacher Interface

2.1   Basic Operations

A MoRIn system consists of mobile devices with digital cameras, content servers, and public media, like a poster, magazine, large screen, holding the visual tags. Each visual tag is structured to provide content ID and operation ID. The operations reflect the six DOF as shown in Fig.3. Besides, the more complex operations can be composed of these basic operations.

2.2   Applications

MoRIn services consist of three layers: (1)content layer, (2)logical operation layer, and (3) operation layer. Two typical MoRIn services are shown in Fig.4.

position	operation		description	operation		description
	slide		move vertically or horizontally.	sink		move perpendicularly to a target
pose	spin	roll	rotate about roll degree	tilt	yaw · pitch	tilt about yaw, pitch degree

Fig. 3. Basic operations

Restaurant Map. The restaurant map shows the physical locations of the restaurants and their visual tags. Each tag calls up and displays the dishes, ordered by price, offered by that restaurant. The logical operation provided, sink, allows the user to flip through the dishes by changing the desired price. The user can lower (raise) the desired price by moving the terminal towards (away from) the tag, see Fig.4-(a).

Automatic Dis-paper(dispenser). MoRIn allows a poster to become an automatic dis-paper through the metaphor of the automatic dispenser. The poster shows several CD jacket pictures and their corresponding visual tag. The contents layer holds songs. The logical operation layer allows the user to select a song, adjust volume, and purchase a song. The user can select an album by horizontal slide, select a song by sink, adjust volume by spin, and buy a song by vertical slide as shown in Fig.4-(b).

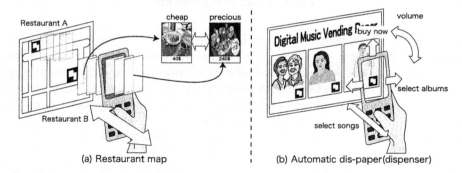

(a) Restaurant map   (b) Automatic dis-paper(dispenser)

Fig. 4. Example of applications

3   Prototype System

We constructed a prototype terminal that is as small as the current cellular phones and used it to evaluate the performance of MoRIn (Fig.5-(a)). The prototype terminal was connected to a PC by a cable in order to process MoRIn software operation. Fig.5-(b) shows the flowchart of MoRIn software operation; QR Code was used as the visual tag[2].

4   Experiments and Results

We asked 3 adult subjects with no previous experience of MoRIn to use the prototype terminal to find virtual pages via visual tags as described below. The

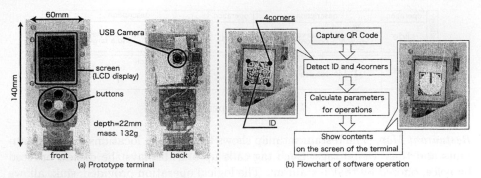

Fig. 5. Prototype system

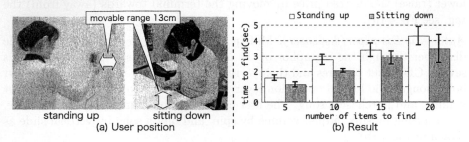

Fig. 6. Result of experiments

tags yielded information structures that consisted of 5, 10, 15, and 20 pages arranged as a vertical stack; the only operation provided was sink. The visual tags were placed on a wall and on a desk so user's position was either standing up or sitting down. For each tag in each position, the subjects were shown a number on the screen of the prototype and then told to "find the page that shows the same number." In each trial the pages were randomly ordered. Each subject repeated this action 10 times and we measured the time it took for the subjects to find the correct page. Figure 6-(a) shows the appearance of the trials and Fig.6-(b) shows the mean time taken, the bars in the figure show the standard deviation.

The results show that the subjects could page through the information structures with 10 and 15 pages in approximately 3 seconds in both positions. Two subjects commented that MoRIn could be used in the real world. We note that system performance may be degraded if the camera (currently at the center of the terminal) is placed off-center.

5   Conclusion and Future Work

We proposed MoRIn that was a new interface with a visual tag for mobile devices. MoRIn allows users to employ intuitive hand movements to navigate complex information structures and retrieve digital content. We described examples of MoRIn applications, and a preliminary evaluation of the performance of sink using a prototype system. The results confirm that visual tags, printed on posters and magazines, can realize the MoRIn service. We intend to evaluate the performance of other basic operations, and the performance of practical applications of MoRIn.

References

1. Arai, T., Aust, D. and Hudson, S. E.: PaperLink:a technique for hyperlinking from real paper to electronic content. Proceedings of the SIGCHI. (1997)327–334
2. http://www.qrcode.com
3. Kato, H. and Billinghurst, M.:Marker tracking and HMD calibration for a video-based augmented reality conferencing system:In Proc. IEEE International Workshop on Augmented Reality. (1999)125–133
4. Rekimoto, J. and Ayatsuka, Y.: CyberCode:Designing Augmented Reality Environments with Visual Tags. Designing Augmented Reality Environments. (2000)

Recognition Errors and Recognizing Errors – Children Writing on the Tablet PC

Janet Read, Emanuela Mazzone, and Matthew Horton

Child Computer Interaction Group, University of Central Lancashire,
Preston, PR1 2HE, UK
{jcread, emazzone, mplhorton}@uclan.ac.uk
http://www.chici.org

Abstract. The paper describes a research study to determine the usability of handwriting recognition technology on a tablet PC for free writing by children. Results demonstrate that recognition error rates vary according to the metrics used, and the authors discuss how some of the errors are created concluding that the error rates say very little about what was happening at the interface and that with research of this type (novel interfaces and young users) researchers need to be immersed in the context in order to produce useful results.

1 Introduction

Over recent years there has been a significant increase in the published work relating to children and interaction design. However as the discipline of Child Computer Interaction (CCI) is still quite new [1] the methods used by researchers are generally derived from HCI and many of these have not been well tested with children. Using handwriting recognition for text entry on a tablet device is a relatively new form of interaction that has relied on evaluation methods from discrete text input and from speech recognition; the suitability of these methods for handwritten input have also not been well researched [2].

The tablet PC is a variation of the notebook PC incorporating a touch screen that can be written on by the user with a special stylus, in a similar way to writing on paper. This technology has recently been evaluated for use in learning environments and with children writing [3], [4]. Using a tablet PC, writing can be done in the user's regular script (handwriting) and software provided with the tablet PC is then able to change the writing into ASCII text (handwriting recognition) so that it can be manipulated in any text or word processing package.

It is common to evaluate the effectiveness of any text input method by measuring the accuracy of the process. The de-facto measure for the accuracy of any text input method is generated from two text strings; usually called the presented text (PT) and the transcribed text (TT). These two strings are compared, and each 'error' in the transcribed text is classified as either an insertion (I), a deletion (D) or a substitution (S). This measure can exist in two forms, as a word error rate (WER) (typically used in speech recognition) or as a character error rate (CER) (typically used in handwriting recognition as well as in discrete text input as is done at a keyboard) [5].

M.F. Costabile and F. Paternò (Eds.): INTERACT 2005, LNCS 3585, pp. 1096–1099, 2005.

2 The Empirical Study

The small study that is described here was intended to determine the usability of the tablet PC for children writing. In particular, the intention was to look at the accuracy of the handwriting recognition that was supplied with the Windows Journal® application (as shipped with the tablet PC). Ten children aged 7 and 8 were recruited to the study that took part in school time. They came to the room individually and used the tablet PC to write their own stories using ideas that had already been developed in the classroom. Each child stayed for around fifteen minutes and the researchers, who were on hand to assist with any hardware problems, supervised the writing tasks. Children had the technology demonstrated to them before they began and had a chance to do a short piece of practise writing before they started writing their story.

2.1 Analysis and Results

There were three outputs from each instance of use. The first was a journal file that showed the writing of the child. This was used to generate an image of the child's writing; an example is seen in Fig. 1. The second output (PT, presented text) was created by the lead researcher and was a text file of what the child wrote (as seen in Fig. 3). A related text file (TT, transcribed text) was created from the journal file by the recognition software (shown in Fig. 4).

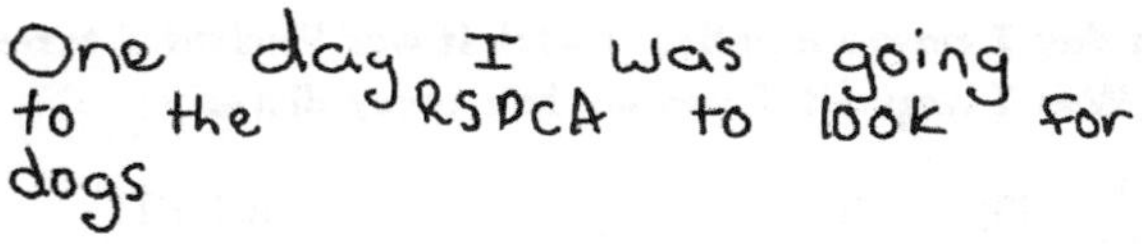

Fig. 1. Writing as collected in the Windows Journal Application

Outputs PT and TT were aligned in two ways using minimum string distance (MSD) algorithms [6] and from these, two error rates, word error rate (WER) and character error rate (CER) were derived. Each was calculated in a similar way where: *Error Rate* $= (S + I + D) / N$ where N is the number of words or characters The error rates from the work of the children are shown in Table 1.

On average, around one in every six letters was inaccurately recognized. The average WER was 30%; this was considerably less favorable than the CER at 17%, and for around half of the children, the difference between the CER and WER was quite pronounced. Reasons for these discrepancies are briefly explored in the next section.

Table 1. Recognition rates from the text pairs (N = number of characters written)

Child	1	2	3	4	5	6	7	8	9	10	Avg
N	38	172	31	132	83	121	79	122	45	86	
WER (%)	0	19	37	28	60	24	42	21	36	35	30
CER (%)	0	10	41	13	25	12	11	7	42	12	17

3   Discussion

The discussion that follows uses (as an example) the writing from child number 5 (seen in Fig. 2.) to demonstrate some of the problems with the derivation of error rates.

Fig. 2. The writing as it was done

The first process that was carried out was the interpretation of this writing into text (to create a text string for the error rate calculations), and the resulting text (PT) can be seen in Fig. 3.   There is a problem at this point as this is the '*researchers guess*' about the child's writing.   For example, the character that follows '**wen**' was assumed to be a capital **I**, but without using the contextual clues (provided by the sense of the sentence), it could be easily considered as a '**t**' and this would have had an impact on the recognition results.

> **one day I mayed a potion. wotsh it was Finnisht I tested
> it Wen I wrenckit I saw my holl bodey distepiy**

Fig. 3. The writing once it was interpreted (PT)

The recognizer that was used in this experiment uses a dictionary to assist in the recognition process.   This has an effect on the recognition results (shown in Fig. 4) as, for instance, when the word '**distepiy**' is recognized, the characters would individually make a word sufficiently close to the word '**distensile**' to convince the recognition software that this is what was written.

> **one hay I may tell a potion wets, it was Finnis ht tested
> it Went wryneck-I saw m holy they distensile.**

Fig. 4. The writing once it was recognized (TT)

The teacher of the child (and the researcher) assumed that the child wrote '**distepiy**' to mean '**disappear**'; a phonetically designed matching algorithm (spell checker) would have had a much better chance of getting this word right.   It is in a similar way that '**bodey**' ('**body**') turns into '**they**'.

4 Conclusion

From this very simple study it is evident that the reported error rate numbers fail to say it all. Firstly, the CER and the WER metrics were not consistent, it is easy to see how one or other of these figures could be reported and could present conflicting results. Secondly, the small investigation of a single child's writing demonstrates the impact of several factors, the included dictionary, the text creation task, the knowledge of the researcher and the diversity of the child population. It appears that for this study there was a real need for the researcher to be immersed in the context related to the single task as well the overall context of learning, school setting, and user experience, calligraphy, and child motivation [7].

Some of these findings translate into other studies; any study which relies on written (or to a lesser extent) spoken language with child users will be influenced by their developmental stage and the researchers knowledge and studies using other novel applications that 'borrow' metrics from related domains need to be investigated to determine the appropriateness of the metrics and to determine which metrics are most valid.

Further work that is planned in relation to this study includes an investigation of the impact of phrase choices when children use copied phrases for handwritten text input and a study with older children to determine whether the disparity between the CER and WER measures is reduced as children gain common knowledge in language.

References

1. Read, J.C., *The ABC of CCI*. Interfaces, 2005. **62**: p. 8 - 9.
2. Plamondon, R. and S.N. Srihari, *On-line and Off-Line Handwriting Recognition: A Comprehensive Survey*. IEEE Transactions on Pattern Analysis and Machine Intelligence, 2000. **22**(1): p. 63 - 84.
3. McFall, R., E. Dahm, D. Hansens, C. Johnson, and J. Morse. *A Demonstration of a Collaborative Electronic Textbook Application on the Tablet PC*. in *World Conference on Educational Multimedia, Hypermedia and Telecommunications*. 2004: AACE.
4. Read, J.C. and M. Horton. *The Usability of Digital Tools in the Primary Classroom*. in *Ed-Media2004*. 2004. Lugano: AACE.
5. MacKenzie, I.S. and R.W. Soukoreff, *Text Entry for Mobile Computing: Models and Methods, Theory and Practice*. Human-Computer Interaction, 2002. **17**(2): p. 147 - 198.
6. MacKenzie, I.S. and R.W. Soukoreff. *A Character-Level Error Analysis for Evaluating Text Entry Methods*. in *NordiChi2002*. 2002. Aarhus, Denmark: ACM Press.
7. Nardi, B., *Context and Consciousness : Activity Theory and Human-Computer Interaction*. 1996, Cambridge, MA: MIT Press.

The Design of an Authoring Interface to Make eLearning Content Accessible

Silvia Gabrielli, Valeria Mirabella, Massimiliano Teso, and Tiziana Catarci

Università di Roma "*La Sapienza*",
Dipartimento di Informatica e Sistemistica,
via Salaria 113, 00198 Roma, Italy
{gabrielli, mirabell, teso, catarci}@dis.uniroma1.it

Abstract. This paper presents the rationale and design process of an authoring interface that enables didactic experts to create or modify eLearning content to make it accessible by learners with special needs. The tool has been designed according to a methodological framework and a set of guidelines for eLearning accessibility previously developed by our group. A key aspect of our framework consists in helping authors to preserve the didactic quality of the eLearning experiences provided to disabled learners (in particular, visually impaired ones) beyond assuring their mere physical access to online materials. A user-centred design process has been adopted to develop a usable prototype of the authoring interface, named *aLearning,* that we describe below.

1 Introduction

Developing accessible web products and services is becoming a main commitment for many organizations, as it is strongly recommended by the law [1][2]. In the field of eLearning, in particular, accessibility assumes special importance, since large repositories of Learning Objects and resources need to be created, shared, reused to deliver courses that should fit the requirements of different learners, including also students with some kinds of impairment or disability. Relevant to this objective is an effective support of didactic authors during the preparation of eLearning material. Unfortunately, most of the authoring tools currently available provide technical advice on how to design web pages that are 'physically' accessible by users with special needs, but do not specify to authors how to transform critical contents into didactically effective alternatives for disabled learners. As part of the VICE project [I], we are experimenting with a methodology and a design process that should better support the development of high quality eLearning experiences for these types of learners. Section 2 introduces the methodological framework for eLearning accessibility that we have proposed; in Section 3 we report a brief description of *aLearning,* a prototype interface we have designed to make it easier for authors the deployment of our methodological framework when developing accessible eLearning contents. We conclude by envisioning some next directions of our research, to further improve the prototype developed.

M.F. Costabile and F. Paternò (Eds.): INTERACT 2005, LNCS 3585, pp. 1100–1103, 2005.

2   Methodological Approach

Many recommendations for the design of accessible eLearning contents have been delivered by international standard organizations, as well as private educational initiatives worldwide [6][7][8][12]. However, their level of abstraction as well as their quantity, can make it very hard for educators, who might not have prior expertise on accessibility, to effectively incorporate them into their everyday authoring practices [9]. Also, compliance of a specific web content to guidelines, as it might be assessed by the most commonly used accessibility checkers, like Bobbly [3], Lift [4], A-Prompt [5] etc., is not sufficient for eLearning material, since these tools mainly perform a syntactic assessment of web pages, but say nothing about the adequacy of any equivalent-alternative contents created, to enable effective access to this materials by disabled users during learning.

To remove this type of difficulties our work has focused, initially, on developing a methodological approach and a set of eLearning-centred guidelines for accessibility, to steer and simplify the authoring process. The method developed, that we named a 'no-frills' approach [13], is based on prompting authors to remove any content that might be considered as not essential for reaching the objectives of a learning module by learners with some level of impairment or disability. When this step has been performed and all relevant or mandatory content has been identified, the next move consists in checking if this is accessible not only from a physical point of view (like, an image described to become accessible by visually impaired learners), but also from a didactic point of view (i.e., if the content description provided does not deteriorate, in some way, the overall quality of the learning experience for a disabled learner). To develop specific guidelines or indications enabling authors to create more effective equivalent-alternative representations of critical contents, we started by analysing and selecting contents from the IEEE Learning Object Metadata (LOM) classification scheme [12], that were compliant with the criteria of format independence, such as: diagram, figure, graph and table. From the classification of learning content types provided by the CPB/WGBH National Centre for Accessible Media (NCAM) [11] we also identified and selected multimedia and math-scientific expressions. For each of these types of learning resources we analysed its impact with respect to the main typologies of impairment-disabilities that may be found in the learners' population, like visual, hearing, physical, cognitive-language ones. Each relevant match identified was then elaborated in the form of detailed guidelines for accessible eLearning content development. Due to the types of contents selected, most of the matches we have identified by now are particularly relevant to visual disabilities, however, our approach already addresses the other types of disabilities mentioned above and will be extended in the near future to include further typologies of learning resources.

The methodology and guidelines provided were initially evaluated during a formative study we conducted [10], whose main findings were fed into the design of *aLearning* prototype.

3   The User-Centred Design of *aLearning* Prototype

For developing *aLearning* prototype, beyond taking into account the guidelines for accessible authoring tools development delivered by W3C [14], we adopted a user-centred design approach, focused on involving several didactical experts, including also our colleagues at the university department, in providing comments and suggestions about the interface layout and functionalities.

A main motivation of our work was to develop a domain specific accessibility tool for the field of eLearning, that was intuitive to use even for authors without specific expertise on accessibility and/or that might not have a technical kind of background. The tool is meant to facilitate their creation of more accessible and usable eLearning contents, by making automatic or semiautomatic any technical step of the methodology that would not benefit from human intervention or expertise (such as the identification of critical contents within the eLearning material), but prompting, informing and capitalizing on authors' knowledge and decision making when addressing the non technical steps of the method (e.g., creating an alternative-equivalent version of the content). A representation of our methodological approach and guidelines by means of task analysis was carried out, leading to subsequent phases of low-mid tech prototyping of the interface features required. We also applied walkthrough evaluation techniques to assure consistency of the prototype and to make its exploration as familiar and intuitive as possible from a user perspective.

3.1 Overview of *aLearning* Prototype

Currently, *aLearning* interface mainly supports authors in:

- automatically identifying and marking any critical and inaccessible content within the eLearning material. Differently from other existing accessibility tools, it considers didactically relevant categories of contents (such as diagrams, figures, graphs, etc.), instead of web domain ones (like framesets, scripts, links, etc).
- Enabling the user to select and start repairing that content (e.g., a graph) by choosing among three alternative modalities: i) directly clicking on the critical content as marked within the course pages, ii) selecting that content from the list of learning resource categories reported on a frame window, iii) starting a step-by-step repairing procedure for the whole sequence of inaccessible contents identified. These different modalities are expected to provide authors more flexibility on how to complete the repairing process (also in terms of its timescale), differently from the file-by-file repairing process enabled by other tools.
- Explaining to the user why a specific content is inaccessible, prompting the user to classify it as optional or mandatory for the objectives of the course, supporting different ways of creating alternative versions of the content if it is mandatory, providing links to more detailed information (guidelines and examples) on how to create an appropriate alternative representation of it.

Our efforts are also addressed towards refining and improving the quality of user-system communication implemented so far, to speed up not only any repairing process performed by the user, but also authors' acquisition of expertise on accessibility by means of use and navigation through the prototype functionalities.

The tool is being developed in Java, we expect to integrate it with a content management system which receives XML pages as input and transforms them into XHTML.

4 Conclusions and Future Work

We are planning a series of empirical user studies, involving different authors working on different topics and types of Learning Objects, to evaluate the effectiveness, quality of performance, and user satisfaction during the authoring of accessible eLearning materials supported by our prototype. In addition, we are investigating if other accessibility functionalities should be added, like for instance, authors' specification of accessibility metadata for the materials they have created or modified.

We expect that all these future steps will enable us to improve our design outcomes in terms of their usability and level of contribution to the accessibility research field.

Acknowledgments. This work is supported by the VICE project [Comunità Virtuali per la Formazione, CNR-MIUR, Italy].

References

1. Section 508 of the Rehabilitation Act; see http://www.section508.gov
2. Law 9 January 2004, n. 4; http://www.pubbliaccesso.it/normative/legge_20040109_n4.htm
3. Bobby, Watchfire Corporation; see http://bobby.watchfire.com/
4. LiFT, http://www.usablenet.com/
5. A-Prompt, University of Toronto, http://aprompt.snow.utoronto.ca/
6. Web Content Accessibility Guidelines 2.0, W3C Recommendations, Working Draft 19 November 2004, http://www.w3.org/TR/WCAG20
7. Advanced Distributed Learning , http://www.adlnet.org/
8. IMS Guidelines for Developing Accessible Learning Applications, Version 1.0, White Paper 2002, http://www.imsproject.org/accessibility
9. Bennett, S., Hewitt, J., Kraithman, D., Britton, C.: Making Chalk and Talk Accessible. Proc. of the ACM Conf. on Universal Usability (2003) 119-125
10. Gabrielli, S., Mirabella, V., Kimani, S., Catarci, T.: Steering the Development of Accessible e-Learning Content. In Proc. of the 3rd ECEL Conf. (2004) Paris (F) 517-526
11. Freed, G., Rothberg M., Wlodkowski T. (Eds.): Making Educational Software and Web Sites Accessible. Design Guidelines Including Math and Science Solutions (2003), http://ncam.wgbh.org/cdrom/guideline
12. Hodgins, W. & Duval, E. (Eds.): IEEE LTSC Learning Object   Meta-data LOM_1484_12_1_v1_Final_Draft, (2002), http://ltsc.ieee.org/wg12/files/
13. Mirabella, V., Kimani, S., Gabrielli, S., Catarci, T.: Accessible e-Learning Material: A No-Frills Avenue for Didactical Experts, The New Review of Hypermedia and Multimedia, Vol.10 N.2 (Dec. 2004) 1-16
14. Treviranus, J., McCathieNevile, C., Jacobs, I., Richards, J. (Eds.): Authoring Tool Accessibility Guidelines 1.0. W3C Recommendation (2000), http://www.w3.org/TR/ATAG10/

Reducing the Risk of Abandonment of Assistive Technologies for People with Autism

Peter Francis[1], Lucy Firth[1], and David Mellor[2]

[1] Department of Information Systems, The University of Melbourne, Australia
psfran@pgrad.unimelb.edu.au
[2] Department of Psychology, Deakin University, Australia

Abstract. This paper reports on an investigation that found that conventional techniques for including users in technology design are likely to fail if the user has autism. The heterogeneity of autistic symptomatology across cognitive, social, behavioural and communication domains suggests a 'single user' environment, while rendering typical design interaction techniques meaningless, making the need for assistive technologies great, and the risk of abandonment high. This complex problem of urgency and constraint was addressed through a Delphi study with a panel of psychologists critiquing design activities for people with autism. The major finding is that while each of the activities may work if modified, all require that the designer is well acquainted with autism in general and has a close working relationship based on trust with the individual user. If these requirements are met, there is no reason that the abandonment rate cannot be reduced.

1 Introduction

There is a demonstrated need by people with cognitive disorders for visual tools [1]. These tools provide assistance with organisation, memory and other activities and, as such, contribute greatly to the independence of the user. Such tools, however, are often paper-based and bulky so, while functional, they are likely to present social problems for the self-aware user.

With the increasing availability of suitable handheld platforms, such as personal digital assistants (PDAs) and mobile phones, there is great potential to offer more discrete and socially acceptable versions of existing visual supports, in addition to supporting the user in ways previously not possible.

User acceptance, however, is not assured. It has been reported [2] that one-third of all assistive devices are abandoned (citing a range of 8% for life-saving devices to 75% for hearing aids). That research also noted that user involvement in selection and design is a key factor in adoption. Importantly, co-design activities should go beyond functionality into preferences as devices "must be aesthetically pleasing, age appropriate, fashionable, and culturally and socially acceptable. Devices that look 'handicapped' are not adopted" ([2] p.6). The additional associated tendency of people with autism toward rigidity and resistance to change strongly suggests that

M.F. Costabile and F. Paternò (Eds.): INTERACT 2005, LNCS 3585, pp. 1104–1107, 2005.

user-centered and participatory approaches be adopted in the design of assistive digital technologies for this group if high rates of abandonment are to be avoided.

1.1 The Problem with Direct Involvement

Autism presents traits that should be considered before working directly with this group. Here those traits are discussed in terms of their potential to cause failure to achieve a technology that will be adopted and not abandoned by the user, and (more importantly) cause harm to those participating in the design process.

Harm to the participant:

- Management of expectations can be a consideration with any design process that directly involves users [3]. Given that people with autism have a greater potential for misunderstandings, coupled with the difficulties of dispelling misconceptions [4], additional care must be taken in allowing expectations to be developed. Additionally, many design processes involve a degree of learning by the user-subject (e.g. prototyping), this can be disconcerting, even distressing for this group if at the end of the design 'experiment' the prototype is then withdrawn and the newly acquired skills no longer have an outlet.
- As the onset of depression among the target group has been attributed in part to 'negative life events' [5] care should be taken that the experience of participation in research and design activities be a positive one, importantly from the viewpoint and perception of the target user, not from the researcher's perception. Reports of suicidal tendencies [6] would indicate that care should be taken not to exacerbate such negative emotions by using techniques and procedures that have not been first the subject of careful examination.

Design failure:

- Poor imaginative, communication and cognitive skills [7] may render the design interaction too difficult for the user-subject.
- Fear of failure [4] and motivational difficulties may make it difficult to engage people with autism in the design process.
- Interpretation of the level of understanding or emotional state of the user can be difficult. For example, laughter or giggling may reveal that the person is anxious or stressed [4]. This may be misinterpreted by the untrained designer.
- Variability of traits in the group means that the designer is unable to make assumptions about the abilities of the subject-user's abilities.

Therefore, an empirical study was designed to find ways to overcome these problems in engaging people with autism in the design of assistive digital technologies specifically for their needs.

2   Method

Given the above traits it was deemed appropriate to design a method for this exploratory study that did not directly involve people with autism. Moreover, due to the stress on families coping with autism and the fact that they, and carers, typically have experience of only one person with autism it was decided to design a method around a third expert group – psychologists. The Delphi Method was considered appropriate for data collection as it enabled the time for panelists to consider and reflect upon the application of unfamiliar processes to a domain that they were considered expert in. The experts in this study were each given outlines of design techniques placed in the context scenario of a youth with autism transitioning from school to work, and asked to comment on the suitability of those design techniques given the traits of autism. The panelists did not know who the other Delphi panelists were, and only communicated to the researcher, not to one another. The material thus gained, were analysed, a summary produced including dissenting comments, and used as the basis for questions for the next Delphi round. The Delphi study ran for three rounds. The involvement of 7 panelists is consistent with recommendations [8].

Data collection was mainly in the form of written responses to mostly open questions, therefore qualitative techniques such as identification of themes and clustering of issues were used in the analysis. In order to facilitate the involvement of expert panelists who were dispersed geographically, and were busy, an online Delphi Method was developed using a commercial online survey tool (QEDML).

Four scenarios were developed to describe the use of four techniques by a technology designer at the requirements stage of a user-centered design project. The choice of techniques was based upon offering a variety of different levels of user-designer interaction. They also required a variety of different skills of the user, and were situated in a range of locations from laboratory to field. In addition to being techniques used in technology design, the essential elements of all four activities had some precedence for use with people with autism (see for example, [4] and [9]). The four techniques were:

- a designer and video-recordist follows the subject-user throughout the day for latter discussion with the subject-user (field location; low level of user participation and control)
- the subject-user thinks aloud while the designer listens for later discussion with the designer (field location; moderate level of user participation and control)
- the subject-user self photographs throughout the day for later discussion with a designer (field location; high level of user participation and control)
- the subject-user role-plays (using models in a doll's house setting) while the designer watches (laboratory location; high level of user participation and control)

The Delphi panelists were asked to comment on the likely impact of the techniques on the subject-user, and on the potential for the process to produce usable, credible and meaningful data for the designer.

Although most of the questions put to the panelists were scenario-specific (e.g. how well would the subject-user cope with the need to role play in the doll's house) the majority of the responses were general. Therefore, the draft guidelines developed are general in flavour, and require the designer to become well acquainted with the subject-user's unique individual condition and abilities. This is consistent with findings in a study investigated appropriate educational practices for students with autism that, as the target group is heterogeneous in nature, no single practice would be likely to suit all students [10].

3 Discussion and Conclusion

It is possible to include users with autism directly in the design process, but:

- Care must be taken to conduct a thorough assessment of the user and their abilities, motivators and behaviours **prior** to commencement of the design process, no matter which technique is adopted.
- Development of a solid and trusting working relationship is paramount when working with this user group.
- The designer should be experienced in the disorder. This is especially relevant as interpretation of the user's emotions and level of understanding may be difficult.
- Each of the four techniques that were investigated would appear to work with some of the target group if the techniques are modified in accordance with the individual's condition. This conclusion is dependent, of course, on the three preceding conclusions: thorough assessment and planning by a designer experienced with the target group and with the user.

The literature and our study suggest no reason why the likely high rate of abandonment of assistive technologies by users with autism cannot be significantly reduced by appropriate inclusion of users in the design process.

References

1. Hodgdon, L.: Visual Strategies for Improving Communication: Practical Supports for School & Home. Quirkroberts Pub.; Michigan (1996)
2. Kintsch, A., and dePaula, R.: A Framework for the Adoption of Assistive Technology. SWAAAC 2002: Supporting Learning Through Assistive Technology, Winter Park, CO, USA. [http://www.cs.colorado.edu/~l3d/clever/assets/pdf/ak-SWAAAC02.pdf] (2002)
3. Preece, J., Rogers, Y. and Sharp, H.: Interaction design: beyond human-computer interaction. John Wiley & Sons.: New York (2002)
4. Attwood, T.: Asperger's Syndrome: A guide for parents and professionals. Jessica Kingsley Publishers.; London (1998)
5. Ghaziuddin,M. Ghaziuddin, N. and Greden, J.: Depression in persons with autism: implications for research and clinical care. Journal of Autism and Developmental Disorders, Aug; 32(4):299-306 (2002)
6. Barnhill, G.: Social attributions and depression in adolescents with Asperger syndrome. Focus on Autism and Other Developmental Disabilities; Spring; 16, 1; 46-53 (2001)
7. Griswold, D. E., Barnhill, G. P., Myles, B. S., Hagiwara, T. and Simpson, R. L.: Asperger syndrome and academic achievement. Focus on Autism and Other Developmental Disabilities, Summer, 17, 2, 94-102 (2002)
8. Delbecq, A. L., Van den Ven, A. H. and Gustafson, D. H.: Group techniques for program planning: a guide to nominal group and Delphi processes. Scott, Foresman.; Glenview, Ill. (1975)
9. Danielsson, H. and Svensk, A.: Digital Pictures as Cognitive Assistance. AAATE 2001, September 3-6, Ljubljana, Slovenia. [http://www.english.certec.lth.se/isaac/] (2001)
10. Iovannone, R., Dunlap, G., Huber, H. and Kincaid, D.: Effective educational practices for students with autism spectrum disorders. Focus on Autism and Other Developmental Disabilities, Fall, Vol.18, No.3, 150-165 (2003)

From Extraneous Noise to Categorizable Signatures: Using Multi-scale Analyses to Assess Implicit Interaction Needs of Older Adults with Visual Impairments

Kevin P. Moloney, V. Kathlene Leonard, Bin Shi,
Julie A. Jacko, Brani Vidakovic, and François Sainfort

School of Industrial & Systems Engineering, Georgia Institute of Technology,
765 Ferst Drive NW, Atlanta, GA, 30332-0205, USA
{kmoloney, vkemery, bshi, jacko, brani,
sainfort}@isye.gatech.edu

Abstract. The holistic understanding of human-computer interaction (HCI) is increasingly important, especially given the impending influx of older users who present dynamic needs that evolve with age. This study explores pupillary response behavior (PRB) during computer interaction to identify underlying differences between older adults of varying ocular profiles. PRB was measured from two groups of individuals diagnosed with Age-related Macular Degeneration (AMD) and a visually healthy control group. Unconventional analytical techniques – wavelet-based multifractal analyses – were used to identify PRB anomalies resulting from the effects of aging and/or ocular pathology. A distribution of regularity indices was extracted from the data signals to reveal signatures of PRB change patterns. One characteristic of the multifractal spectrum, Left Slope (LS), fully distinguished the user groups, revealing trends of increasing PRB irregularity with increasing levels of ocular dysfunction.

1 Introduction

The holistic characterization of users, including both implicit and explicit interactions, has potential to inform system design in order to better anticipate and account for user needs across HCI scenarios. This is critical considering the impending influx of older adult users who present a highly dynamic array of needs and capabilities that evolves with age. A recent study [1] revealed consistent performance differences between users with and without Age-related Macular Degeneration (AMD), despite the absence of significant user differences on traditional demographic and clinically-assessed measures of visual function (e.g., visual acuity). This suggests that aspects of users' visual health and capabilities can manifest themselves as impediments to HCI, while remaining undisclosed through traditional user profiling efforts.

One popular objective method to convey covert aspects of HCI is the interpretation of psychophysiological responses to stimuli, including examination of constriction and dilation of the iris (i.e., pupillometry) during task performance. Research has long supported that changes in pupil diameter correspond to information acquisition, processing and cognitive workload (e.g., larger pupil = higher levels of processing) [2].

M.F. Costabile and F. Paternò (Eds.): INTERACT 2005, LNCS 3585, pp. 1108–1111, 2005.

More recently, research in HCI has used pupillary activity during computer-based interactions to predict the cognitive demands experienced by users during performance of varying tasks to help inform interface and interaction design [3].

However, the proper measurement and interpretation of pupillary response behavior (PRB) is not straightforward. PRB is affected by a variety of factors, including ambient light, fatigue, and medication use [2]. Moreover, aging naturally leads to ocular changes, such as shrinking pupil size and slower, smaller responses to visual stimuli [2]. Ophthalmologic research has also revealed that ocular disease (e.g., AMD) can decrease controlled, sustained movement of the iris [2]. Thus, powerful analytical tools are needed to detect these muted or irregular PRB change patterns.

The most commonly used statistical methods for analyzing PRB include: mean task-evoked pupillary response (TEPR); averaging measures of pupil diameter for a given post-stimulus time period; and frequency, power and spectral analyses. These approaches, however, do not adequately account for the seemingly erratic nature of PRB intrinsic to the pupil's physiological control mechanisms. Furthermore, they cannot resolve the amplified PRB complexity and irregularity exhibited by older adults with visual impairment. The richness of PRB in these individuals requires more sophisticated statistical techniques to improve the ability to examine this facet of HCI.

This study uses an advanced statistical concept – wavelet-based analysis of multifractality – to leverage the richness of this population's pupillary response data. The multifractal spectrum refers to the probability distribution of Hölder regularity indices (α's) from the raw data signal [4]. These regularity indices represent estimations of signal smoothness, based on fluctuations and correlations within local neighborhoods of time-series data points. Geometric attributes of multifractal spectra can be used to describe the richness of signal irregularity across scales of resolution. One such measure is Left Slope (LS), with a steeper slope indicative of decreasing multifractality and a smoother data signal with smaller, slower, or more persistent changes.

2 Methods

Pupillary response behavior was measured from older adults (mean age = 76 yrs) diagnosed with AMD, the leading cause of visual impairment in the US and UK. As summarized in Table 1, participants were grouped according to ocular disease and visual acuity, including two user groups of individuals diagnosed with AMD and one visually healthy control group. Comprehensive ophthalmologic exams were provided to ensure the clinical diagnosis of AMD and knowledge of current visual capabilities. Tasks were performed under conditions of best-corrected vision. PRB was measured with the Applied Science Laboratories® Model 501® head-mounted optics system.

Table 1. User group characterization

Group	n	Visual Acuity (Range)	AMD Diagnosis?
Control	14	[20/20 – 20/32]	No
Group 1	8	[20/32 – 20/70]	Yes
Group 2	6	[20/80 – 20/200]	Yes

Participants performed 105 trials of a computer-based task; a single trial entailed the drag and drop of a Microsoft® Word file icon to a Window folder icon, integrated with different types of multimodal feedback to assist the participants' drop of file into the folder. Task-based PBR of each participant was recorded at a rate of 60 Hz. This study employed a repeated-measures, within-subjects design, with each participant receiving all experimental conditions (e.g., feedback forms). User group was the independent, between-subjects variable. A more detailed methodological description and performance summaries can be found in related work [1].

The wavelet-based multifractal analysis approach is best summarized by a five-step procedure, including: 1) The preparation and segmentation of individual pupillary response behavior data signals; 2) The application of a discrete wavelet transform; 3) The generation and characterization of a multifractal spectrum for each data set; 4) The regression-based estimate of the LS measure; and 5) ANOVA and post-hoc analysis of group-based differences. As a comprehensive account is not permissible within this brief manuscript, interested readers are directed to related work [4, 5].

3 Results and Conclusions

Analysis revealed that decreases in LS correspond to decreases in the ocular condition (in terms of both disease and acuity) of users. Figure 1 illustrates this clear monotonic trend between the LS multifractal summary and ocular condition. One-way analyses of variance (ANOVA) confirmed significant group-based differences with respect to LS (F = 32.258, p < 0.01). Post-hoc comparisons (Games-Howell) further revealed significant differences in LS between all user groups (p < 0.05), in accordance with the monotonic trend. Group 2's PBR can be classified as the most multifractal, with a relatively rough PBR signal containing larger, faster, and anti-persistent changes in pupil diameter, followed by Group 1 and then the Control Group.

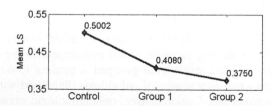

Fig. 1. Monotonic relationship between multifractality and ocular profile

To further reveal the contribution of this novel analytical approach, Figure 2 presents a comparison of individuals without and with AMD. Traditional statistical methods (e.g., the TEPR) would produce an interpretation that these individuals exhibit equivalent PRB and experience similar cognitive load during task performance (see Figures 2a and 2b). However, using multifractal analysis to examine the underlying signatures of irregularity, a clearer distinction can be made between these individuals (see Figures 2c and 2d). The individual with AMD (Figure 5d) exhibits PRB that is much more multifractal, based on LS and the resultant multifractal spectrum.

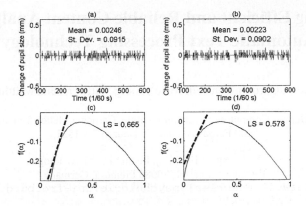

Fig. 2. Illustration of the utility of multifractal analysis. Figures (a) and (b) plot the PRB of individuals without and with AMD, respectively, during computer-based task performance. Figures (c) and (d) illustrate the corresponding multifractal spectra from these same datasets.

This research has potentially far-reaching implications for the examination of cognitive workload via PRB and furthering the understanding of the interaction needs and behaviors of users who are aging and/or have visual impairment. Multifractal analyses provide a new window through which the implicit subtleties of PRB can be utilized by HCI researchers. Additional efforts are underway to classify these individuals on the basis of other attributes of fractality. These novel analytical methods extend HCI user characterization beyond the use subject demographics or performance measures. The application of these analytical techniques holds great promise for utilizing the richly informative PRB of older adults with visual impairment in the context of HCI.

Acknowledgments

This research was made possible through funding from the National Science Foundation (BES-9896304), and the National Security Agency (NSA E24-60R).

References

1. Jacko, J.A., Moloney, K.P., Kongnakorn, T., Barnard, L., et al.: Multimodal feedback as a solution to ocular disease-based user performance decrements in the absence of functional visual loss. Int. J. of HCI **18**(2) (2005) 183-218
2. Loewenfeld, I.E.: The Pupil: Anatomy, Physiology, and Clinical Applications. 2nd edn. Butterworth-Heinemann, Oxford, UK (1999)
3. Iqbal, S.T., Zheng, X.S., Bailey, B.P.: Task-evoked pupillary response to mental workload in human-computer interaction. In: Proceedings of CHI'04. ACM Press (2004) 1477-1480
4. Gonçalvès, P., Riedi, R., Baraniuk, R.: A simple statistical analysis of wavelet-based multifractal spectrum estimation. In: Proceedings of the 32nd Asilomar Conference on Signals, Systems and Computers. IEEE (1998)
5. Vidakovic, B.: Statistical Modeling by Wavelets. John Wiley & Sons, New York, NY (1999)

Supporting Efficient and Reliable Content Analysis Using Automatic Text Processing Technology*

Gahgene Gweon[1], Carolyn Penstein Rosé[1], Joerg Wittwer[2], and Matthias Nueckles[2]

[1] Human-Computer Interaction Institute, Carnegie Mellon University,
5000 Forbes Avenue, Pittsburgh PA 15213
{ggweon, cprose}@cs.cmu.edu
[2] Universitaet Freiburg, Institut Fuer Psychologie,
Engelbergerstr. 41, 79085 Freiburg, Germany
{wittwer, nueckles}@psychologie.uni-freiburg.de

Abstract. Text categorization technology can be used to streamline the process of content analysis of corpus data. However, while recent results for automatic corpus analysis show great promise, tools that are currently being used for HCI research and practice do not make use of it. Here, we empirically evaluate trade-offs between semi automatic and hand labeling of data in terms of speed, validity, and reliability of coding in order to assess the usefulness of incorporating this technology into HCI tools.

1 Introduction and Background

A wide range of behavioral researchers in the field of Human Computer Interaction, such as social psychologists studying communication in Computer Supported Cooperative Work settings, painstakingly code by hand and analyze large quantities of natural language corpus data as an important part of their research. Similarly, research in Computer Supported Collaborative Learning often depends upon quantitative process analyses through multi-dimensional coding schemes such as those described in [3]. Another instance, more relevant for HCI practitioners than researchers, is labeling of Contextual Inquiry data in order to mark instances relevant for different types of models or instances of standard types of critical incidents.

In this paper we explore issues related to the use of technology for supporting such coding by making automatic predictions about those codes. Despite the availability of such technology, none of the tools that are commonly used in the HCI community make use of it. For example, specialized software for supporting text, audio, and video data analysis such as HyperResearch, MacShapa, and Nvivo offer well designed interfaces for hand annotation and cataloguing of codes. Yet, none of them go as far as to support automatic assignment of codes. In this paper, we investigate the possibility of incorporating automatic classification of text into data analysis applications widely used in HCI research and practice. Since automatic coding technology is not perfect, and the data analyzed in HCI research requires subjective judgments, before such technology

---

* This work was supported by NSF SGER REC-0411483.

M.F. Costabile and F. Paternò (Eds.): INTERACT 2005, LNCS 3585, pp. 1112–1115, 2005.

can safely be accepted into common practice, it is essential to measure precisely how the accuracy of the classification affects user performance.

2 Technical Approach

Automatic text classification technology for supporting automatic analysis of corpus data shows great potential benefit to HCI researchers and practitioners [1]. Here we offer a brief introduction to this technology. Applying a categorical coding scheme can be thought of as a text classification problem where a computer decides which code to assign to a text based on a model built from examining "training examples" that were coded by hand. Some machine learning techniques that have successfully been applied to this problem are regression models, nearest neighbor classifiers [7], decision trees [4], and Bayesian classifiers [2]. Success at automatic coding can be evaluated by comparing predicted codes to those in a Gold Standard corpus, which is a corpus that has been annotated with a coding scheme, and the coding has been verified to be reliable. For example, in comparison with a hand-coded Gold Standard of a 1200 sentence test corpus coded with the 7 dimensional coding scheme used for the analysis in [5], it is possible with state-of-the-art technology to achieve an acceptable level of agreement (Cohen's K > .7) along 6/7 of the dimensions between automatically generated codes and hand coded codes when we commit only to the portion of the corpus where the predictor has the highest certainty [1]. Along 5 of those dimensions, the percentage of the corpus where the predictor was confident enough to commit a code was at least 88% of the corpus. Thus, fully automatic coding is a viable option for the greater portion of the corpus, but not the whole thing.

3 Formal Study

When fully automatic coding is not a viable choice, there are two primary options: (a) Limit automatic predictions to the subset of the data where the predictor can confidently assign a code with high reliability; or (b) Have the system make predictions about everything, and the analyst checks and corrects the codes for dimensions where the reliability is not at an acceptable level. The purpose of our study is to measure the impact of automatic predictions in terms of speed, validity, and reliability of human judgment when the predictions are not accurate enough for fully-autmatic coding. The coding scheme used in the study presented in this paper was established in a study by Wittwer, Nückles and Renkl who examine computer-mediated communication between experts and laypersons in the context of asynchronous help-desk support [6]. 20 participants, students and staff at nearby universities, were randomly assigned to 2 conditions. In the control condition, participants worked with the coding interface with no predicted code (Hand-Code). In the experimental condition, participants worked with the minimally adaptive coding interface that displays predicted codes in such a way that 50% of the sentences were randomly selected to agree with the Gold Standard, and the rest were randomly assigned (Auto-Code-And-Correct). This proportion of correct versus incorrect predictions was selected based on timing results from a small pilot study conducted before the study reported here. In a small pilot study with 3 expert analysts coding 141 sentences each, we measured the average time required to code a sentence depending upon the selected strategy (Hand-Code vs. AutoCode-And-Correct) and (in the AutoCode-And-Correct case) whether the predicted code is correct. On average the analysts spent 11 seconds/ sentence when they agreed with the prediction. They spent on average 21.5 seconds/ sentences where they did not agree with it. And they spent 17 seconds on average per sentence when no prediction was offered. Thus, the advantage of the automatic predictions in terms of coding time may depend upon the % of time that the coder agrees with the automatic codes.

Procedure. Participants first spent 20 minutes reading the 6 page coding manual. They then spent 20 minutes working through 28 training exercise sentences using the coding manual. They were instructed to think aloud about their decision making process. They then received coaching from an experimenter to help them understand the intent behind the codes and compared their answers with a Gold Standard set of codes. After a 5 minute break, they spent up to 90 minutes coding 76 sentences.

Interface. Participants coded sentences using a menu-based interface. For the standard coding interface, the sentences were arranged in a vertical list. Next to each sentence was a menu containing the complete list of codes. No code was selected as a default. In contrast, a minimally adaptive version was used in the experimental condition. The only difference between this and the standard version was that a predicted code was selected by default for each sentence, which appeared as the initial element of the menu list and was always visible to the analyst.

4 Results and Recommendations

First we evaluated the reliability of coding of each of the two conditions. Average pairwise Kappa measures of agreement were significantly higher in the experimental condition (p < .05). Mean pairwise Kappa(K) in the control condition was .39, whereas it was .48 in the experimental condition. As a measure of the best we could do with novice analysts and 50% correct predicted codes, we also analyzed the pairwise K measures of the 3 participants in each condition whose judgments were the most similar to each other. With this carefully chosen subset of each population, we achieved an average pairwise K of .54 in the control condition and .71 in the experimental condition. This difference was significant (p < .01). The average agreement between these analysts' codes from the experimental condition and the Gold Standard was also high, an average K of .70. Thus, the analysts who agreed most with each other also produced valid codes in the sense that they agreed well with the Gold Standard. Next, evaluating the validity of coding more stringently, we found analysts in the experimental condition were significantly more likely to agree with the prediction when it was correct (74% of the time) than when it was incorrect (16% of the time). This difference was significant using a binary logistic regression with 760 data points, one for each sentence coded in the experimental condition (p<.001). Average K agreement with the gold standard across the entire population was marginally higher in the experimental condition than in the control condition (p=.1). Average agreement in the unsupported condition was a K measure of .48. In the experimental condition, average agreement with the gold standard was a K measure of .56. The raw percent agreement with the gold standard was significantly higher in the experimental condition than in the control condition ($p < .001$). Thus, we conclude that analysts were not harmfully biased by incorrect codes. Coding time did not differ significantly between control (67min 36sec) and experimental (66min 10sec) conditions, thus providing some confirmation of the estimate that 50% correct predictions is a reasonable break even point for coding speed.

In this paper we have described some investigations towards developing a tool for providing automatic coding support for human corpus analysts. Our evaluation demonstrates that a savings of time with AutoCode-And-Correct over Hand-Code only occurs when percent agreement between predicted codes and the analyst's selected codes is greater than 50%. At that percent agreement level, we demonstrate that the AutoCode-And-Correct option leads to an increase in reliability while maintaining validity of human judgments by novice coders. Making use of predictions to boost reliability with less skilled, and thus cheaper, analysts may be an advantage in terms of research costs as long as the coding scheme itself is properly evaluated for reliability first. Since 50% prediction is feasible with technology available in the computational linguistics community, the next step would then be to integrate technology with tools used in HCI community for easy, reliable and faster coding.

References

1. Donmez, P., Rosé, C. P., Stegmann, K., Weinberger, A., and Fischer, F. Supporting CSCL with Automatic Corpus Analysis Technology, to appear in the Proceedings of Computer Supported Collaborative Learning'05, forthcoming.
2. Dumais, S., Platt, J., Heckerman, D. and Sahami, M. *Inductive Learning Algorithms and Representations for Text Categorization*, Technical Report, Microsoft Research, 1998.
3. Fischer, F., Bruhn, J., Gräsel, C., & Mandl, H. Fostering collaborative knowledge construction with visualization tools. *Learning and Instruction*, 12, 213-232, 2002.
4. Lewis, D., Ringuette, R. A Comparison of teo learning algorithms for text classification, In *3rd Annual Symposium on Document Analysis and Information Retrieval*, pp. 81-93, 1994.
5. Weinberger, A. Scripts for Computer-Supported Collaborative Learning Effects... 2003, From http://edoc.ub.uni-muenchen.de/archive/00001120/01/Weinberger_Armin.pdf
6. Wittwer, J., Nückles, M., Renkl, A. Can experts benefit from information about a layperson's knowledge for giving adaptive explanations?. In K. Forbus, D. Gentner, T. Regier (Eds.), *Proc. 26th Annual Conf of the Cognitive Science Society*, 2004. 1464-1469.
7. Yang, Y. and Pedersen, J. Feature selection in statistical learning of text categorization, In *the 14th Int. Conf. on Machine Learning*, pp 412-420, 1997.

Multi-platform Online Game Design and Architecture

JungHyun Han[1,*], Ingu Kang[1], Chungmin Hyun[1],
Jong-Sik Woo[2], and Young-Ik Eom[3]

[1] Department of Computer Science and Engineering,
Korea University, Seoul, Korea
[2] Korea Game Development and Promotion Institute,
Ministry of Culture and Tourism, Seoul, Korea
[3] School of Information and Communications Engineering,
Sungkyunkwan University, Suwon, Korea

Abstract. Contemporary Multi-player online games (MOGs) support only a single game platform. Our research goal is to provide an MOG service to 'users from different platforms.' This paper presents the architecture of the world-wide first multi-platform online game, which consists of 3D game engines and a multi-platform game server. The experimental results through the prototype implementation show the feasibility of simultaneously supporting multiple game platforms.

1 Introduction

Recently, 3D *multi-player online games* (MOGs) have experienced an amazing success, especially in East Asia. In Korea, for example, a large number of MOGs are currently in service that can accommodate tens or hundreds of thousands simultaneous players, and there is also a long line of MOGs which are scheduled for commercial release. Initially, MOGs were running on only PCs, but now are running on game consoles (e.g., PlayStation2 and Xbox), arcade game machines, or mobile devices (including mobile phones, PlayStation Portable and Nintendo DS). However, such an MOG can currently be serviced for a single platform. Our research goal is to provide an MOG service to 'users from different platforms,' e.g. to allow a PC user and a mobile phone user to interact in an MOG.

This paper presents the architecture of the 'world-wide first' *multi-platform* online game, supported by the Korean government. The game service environment is illustrated in Fig. 1, which encompasses six types of platforms. The core components of a multi-platform MOG service consists of 3D game engines[1][2] and multi-platform game server. The game platforms are classified into *high-end* and *low-end* machines, depending on their computing capabilities, and we have developed both of the high- and low-end 3D game engines. The game server has also been developed, and an FPS (first-person shooting) MOG has been developed as a prototype implementation of the multi-platform game.

---

* Corresponding Author.

M.F. Costabile and F. Paternò (Eds.): INTERACT 2005, LNCS 3585, pp. 1116–1119, 2005.

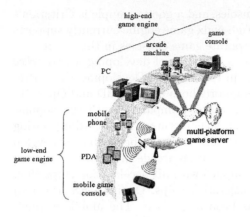

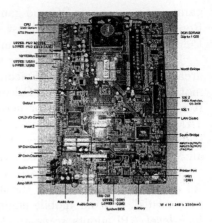

Fig. 1. Multi-platform online game   **Fig. 2.** Falcon3D game board

2   Game Design

Three challenges in a multi-platform game design can be described as follows:
(1) the hardware performance gap between low-end and high-end platforms, (2)
the network latency gap between wired and wireless networks, and (3) the user
expectation gap between different platforms.

First, the hardware performances of the low-end and high-end platforms are
significantly different. However, we have to also note that the *hardware accelerators* for mobile 3D graphics are coming to market.

Second, the latencies of the wireless and wired networks are also different.
For example, a game player through the wireless network may not be able to
perform *realtime* actions, which are nicely supported in the wired environment.

Third, game players from different platforms usually have different expectations. For example, a game player on the arcade machine would expect *immersion* or *virtual reality* while mobile users would not. However, it is important
to provide the same or similar *look-and-feel* of the game to all game players,
regardless of the platforms through which they are connected.

In designing multi-platform game contents, the above-mentioned features
should be carefully considered. To tackle the first feature, we designed lightweight mobile 3D game engine that can yet incorporate upcoming mobile 3D
acceleration hardware. We have handled the second and third features by assigning different *roles* to wired users and wireless users.

3   Game Engines for Multi-platform Support

Computing capabilities of PCs, arcade machines and game consoles are comparable, especially in hardware 3D acceleration. It is a trend that a high-end

game engine supports PC and game consoles, and a good example is Criterion's Renderware engine[3]. In contrast, our high-endx game engine currently supports PC and arcade hardware, and can incorporate game consoles in the future.

The 4th author of this paper has been in charge of developing a *networked* arcade game board, named Falcon3D[4], in Korea Game Development and Promotion Institute. See Fig. 2. Falcon3D supports both of Direct3D and OpenGL. It also supports TCP/IP for networking, and is compatible with the popular JAMMA (Japanese Amusement Machine Manufacturers' Association) wiring standard for arcade machines. With Falcon3D, we have been able to develop an MOG, which can be played either on PCs or on arcade machines.

Recently, mobile phones are being equipped with 3D acceleration chips[5][6]. As a standard interface for the 3D acceleration chips, OpenGL ES has been proposed[7], and our mobile engine has been built on it. The mobile engine's *high-level* API adopts *scene-graph*[8], which hierarchically organizes geometric models, transformations, textures, light sources, rendering state information, levels of detail (LOD), etc.

4   Multi-platform Game Server

The multi-platform game server's architecture is illustrated in Fig. 3. The front-end system, called the *ubiquitous game framework*, is composed of the *game container* which provides the game service API and the actual game logic is mounted on, and the *gateway server* working as a request-response broker. The back-end system consists of game database, billing server, CRM server, etc.

Together with the game engines discussed in Section 3, the game server enables developing a multi-platform game, which is always accessible if any of PCs, arcade game machines, desktop or mobile game consoles, PDAs and mobile phones is available.

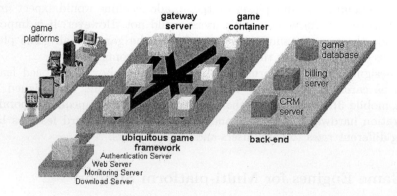

Fig. 3. Multi-platform game server

5   Prototype Implementation and Conclusion

We have designed and implemented an FPS (first-person shooting) game, which currently can be connected through PCs, arcade machines, PDAs, and mobile phones. The user from a PC or an arcade machine plays on the ground in the FPS game world. In contrast, the mobile users can play the game only in a stealth fighter. The mobile users are not supposed to do realtime actions, but do non-realtime actions such as bomb-dropping. However, the PC/arcade-machine users can do all kinds of realtime shooting actions. Fig. 4 and Fig. 5 show the snap-shots of the FPS game.

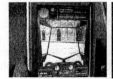

Fig. 4. Game snap-shots from PC   **Fig. 5.** Game snap-shots from PDA

Unlike a few existing *turn-based* (not *realtime*) MOGs mostly in the casual board game genre, the authors aim at an MOG, where PC/arcade-machine users are connected through wired Internet and play a realtime FPS game whereas mobile users are connected through wireless network and play special roles which do not require realtime actions. The experimental results show the feasibility of supporting multiple platforms simultaneously. The authors believe that this work is the first of its kind in the field of multi-platform MOGs.

Acknowledgements

This work was sponsored and funded by Korea Game Development & Promotion Institute as Korean government project. (Ministry of Culture and Tourism)

References

1. Bishop, L., Eberly, D., Finch, M., Shantz, M., Whitted, T., "Designing a PC Game Engine," *IEEE CG&A*, Vol. 18, No. 1, Feb. 1998, pp. 46-53.
2. Eberly, D., *3D Game Engine Architecture*, Morgan Kaufmann Publishers, 2005.
3. Renderware, http://www.renderware.com/
4. Falcon3D, http://www.uniondigital.com/
5. ATI IMAGEON 2300, http://www.ati.com/kr/products/imageon2300
6. NVIDIA GoForce 3D 4500, http://www.nvidia.com/page/goforce_3d_4500.html
7. OpenGL ES, http://www.khronos.org/opengles/
8. Sowizral, H., Rushforth, K., Deering, M., The Java 3D API Specification, Addison Wesley, 1998.

Segment and Browse: A Strategy for Supporting Human Monitoring of Facial Expression Behaviour

Michael J. Lyons, Mathias Funk, and Kazuhiro Kuwabara

ATR Intelligent Robotics & Communication Laboratories,
2-2-2 Hikaridai, Seika-cho, Soraku-gun, Kyoto, Japan 619-0288
mlyons@atr.jp

Abstract. We describe a system to ease long-term human monitoring of mood via facial expressions. Video images are processed in real-time to isolate the area of the face and record facial expressions. Optic flow is used to annotate motion of the face. A simple-to-use browser is used to navigate the facial expression record. A preliminary evaluation of both components is reported.

1 Introduction

An increasingly large fraction of the population of many nations is aged and no longer capable of a self-sufficient lifestyle. In Japan such seniors often live with family members and can require many hours of attention each day. Our team is investigating technologies to assist the caregivers of dependent seniors as well as improve the quality of life for all concerned. A sub-goal is to develop methods to aid the assessment of the emotional status of the dependent person. This could reduce the need for continuous monitoring of a dependent, as well as improve efficiency in responding to their needs. Fully automatic systems are under investigation, however it is also very important to also consider partially-automatic systems which augment human propensities to assess another's emotional status and needs. Facial expressions provide salient information on mood [2, 4]. There has been substantial progress on the research problem of classifying facial expressions [3], however automatic systems are not very effective at combining contextual information with facial expression data in judging affect [4]. A major design goal in this project is to create a system which augments human capabilities at judging affect from facial expressions. We automate the long-term observation of facial expressions and format the image data so it can be evaluated quickly by a caregiver. Here we describe a complete working prototype for monitoring and browsing facial expressions over extended periods.

2 System Design and Implementation

The system consists of vision and browser modules. The **vision module**: (a) ambiently acquires images of a person (b) segments the face from the image (c) calculates motion sensitive features (d) stores facial images with motion attribute data. The **browser module** aids a caregiver to navigate the large dataset quickly and assess mood.

M.F. Costabile and F. Paternò (Eds.): INTERACT 2005, LNCS 3585, pp. 1120–1123, 2005.
© IFIP International Federation for Information Processing 2005

2.1   Vision Module

Video input from a camera is reduced from 640x480 pixels to 320x240. A face detection algorithm determines whether or not there is a face in view of the camera and, if so, where it is. The optical flow field of the image is calculated on multiple time scales to detect motion in the video frame. The segmented faces are saved with averages of the optic flow over the entire internal region of the face.

We use a powerful and widely popular algorithm for face detection [5] known as cascade-correlation. The algorithm automatically registers a rectangle of fixed aspect ratio with the head with the face centered in the interior. It detects faces accurately for out of plane rotations of up to roughly 30 degrees and roughly the same amount of in plane rotation of the head. The facial image is scaled to a standard size and stored with timestamp at up to 30 fps. Normalizing the size and position of the face and isolating it from a complex background makes the face data easier to browse.

Optic flow measures displacements of image areas due to motion in the visual scene. For a fixed camera and approximately constant illumination, the optic flow field gauges the local velocities. The method we use for calculating optic flow is known as *block matching* or *block correlation* [1]. With the block correlation technique, a region from one image frame is matched to a region of the same size in the subsequent frame. The velocity vector is calculated from the displacement of the block between frames. To gauge motion at a range of velocities we calculate the optic flow field between frames separated by 1,3,5,7, and 10 video frames. Flow values are

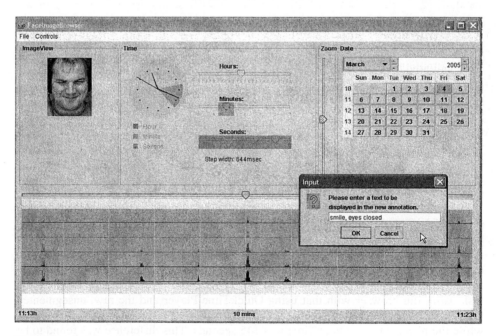

Fig. 1. The facial expression data browser. A detailed description of the components is given in section 2.2.

average over regions corresponding to the internal part of the face as detected by the face detection module. The optic flow values are saved to index file which also contains facial image filenames.

2.2 Browser Module

Figure 1 shows a screen shot of the browser module. The components of this module are (clockwise from upper left corner) (a) normalized display of the facial image at the selected time (b) time range display in clock and linear form (c) a time resolution zoom control to select range of the timeline (d) a calendar for selecting images of a certain date and (from middle to bottom) (e) a timeline for scrolling the time (f) a display of average optic flow value at different velocity scales for each point in time (g) bar indicating the presence of user annotations. A sample annotation window is shown overlapping the optic flow display.

The user selects the date and then zoom the time range control to choose the timeline range. Images are browsed with the timeline scroller. Presence or absence of facial images is indicated by red or grey colour in the optic flow indicator giving an immediate estimate of whether the subject was present. The optic flow annotations provide indication of whether motion of the face occurred. The distribution of activity over the five velocity levels indicate whether the motion corresponds to large rigid body motion of the entire face or more subtle movements corresponding to expressions and speech. Short text annotations may be added and edited or removed by clicking on the lowest active zone below the timeline.

3 Evaluation

We evaluated the capability of the vision module to properly segment facial images in realistic situations. Video of three senior citizens suffering from various stages of dementia was collected in actual domestic situations by our research team. The subject watched television while a roughly frontal view (±45 degrees) of the upper body and face was recorded. The backgrounds were typically complex. To protect the privacy of these patients, images from this dataset cannot be shown here. The performance of the automatic face detection and segmentation algorithm was found to be more than adequate for our needs, with very few facial views being lost over the course of approximately 30 total minutes recording.

A preliminary user study of the browser module was conducted to test the hypothesis that segmentation of the facial image and annotation with motion data would allow users to navigate facial expression more efficiently. We videotaped 4 subjects while they watched a 20 minute cartoon. Five experimental users had to search these video tapes for target facial expression images selected from the video data. There were 4 target images for each of the 4 videos. We compared average time to complete the task using our browser with that using QuickTime Player and the raw, unsegmented video. Average time to complete a search task using the browser was 58 seconds while the average using QuickTime was 145 seconds. This difference was found to be significant to better than 5% using the Wilcoxin signed ranks test. In addition, accuracy was higher with our browser than with the QuickTime player.

4 Conclusion

We have developed a system to support the monitoring of mood from ambiently captured video data of facial expression behaviour. By segmenting the face from a complex scene, normalizing it, and annotating it with motion data we were able to greatly increase the efficiency of navigation of a large facial expression dataset. In our continuing work on this project we plan to conduct more extensive field and user studies.

Acknowledgement

This work was supported in part by the National Institute of Information and Communications Technology.

References

1. Barron, J. L., Fleet, D. J., Beauchemin, S. S.: Performance of optical flow techniques. The International Journal of Computer Vision, 12 (1994) 43-77
2. Ekman, P. , Friesen, W.V.: Unmasking the Face. Prentice Hall, Englewood Cliffs (1975)
3. Lyons, M.J., Budynek, J., Akamatsu, S.: Automatic Classification of Single Facial Images. IEEE Transactions on Pattern Analysis and Machine Intelligence 21 (1999) 1357-1362
4. Russell, J.A.: Core Affect and the Psychological Construction of Emotion. Psychological Review 110 (2003) 145-172
5. Viola, P., Jones, M.: Rapid object detection using a boosted cascade of simple features. In Proc. IEEE Conference on Computer Vision and Pattern Recognition (2001) 511-518

iDwidgets: Parameterizing Widgets by User Identity

Kathy Ryall[1], Alan Esenther[1], Katherine Everitt[2], Clifton Forlines[1],
Meredith Ringel Morris[3], Chia Shen[1], Sam Shipman[1], and Frederic Vernier[4]

[1] MERL, 201 Broadway, Cambridge, MA, USA
[2] University of Washington, 185 Stevens Way, Seattle, WA, USA
[3] Stanford University, 353 Serra Mall, Stanford, CA, USA
[4] University of Paris 11, LIMSI-CNRS, BP 133, 91403 Orsay, France
{ryall, esenther, forlines, shen, shipman}@merl.com
everitt@cs.washington.edu, merrie@cs.stanford.edu,
frederic.vernier@limsi.fr

Abstract. We introduce the concept of *identity-differentiating widgets* (iDwidgets), widgets parameterized by the identity of their user. Although multi-user applications have become more common, most support only traditional "single-user" widgets. By adding user-identity information we allow interactions with today's widgets to be dynamically customized on a per-user basis in a group usage setting. The concept has inspired the design of new widgets as well. In this paper we describe example iDwidgets and define a conceptual framework based on what is being customized in the widget. iDwidgets can support novel interaction techniques in collaborative settings.

1 Introduction

WIMP interfaces provide a consistent look and feel across different computer platforms and applications. Widgets, standard reusable GUI elements, are a staple in that environment. To date most widgets have been designed to be used by one person at a time; within a single session, a widget will behave the same regardless of who is using it. Pebbles [5] and MMM [1] were two of the first systems to extend widgets, adding user identity information. Much of their focus is on the visual representation needed to distinguish people (and their actions/interactions) in shared-display settings. We further exploit user identity information, extending and generalizing the concept to encompass a larger set of functionality, and providing a conceptual framework in which the use of identity to customize interaction can be designed and analyzed.

iDwidgets (*identity-differentiating widgets*) are basic GUI building blocks for user-aware environments; the iDwidget's novelty is that its function, contents and/or appearance are parameterized by the identity of its current user amongst a group of co-present (local or remote) users. Thus an iDwidget may look or behave differently for different user identities. By identity we mean a person with particular preferences and privileges, or a tool associated with such a person (e.g., the stylus the person is using). A person may have multiple identities (e.g., Dad and Senior Engineer).

Although we focus our discussion on shared-display groupware (SDG) settings [7], iDwidgets are applicable in any multi-user environment. A number of toolkits have been developed for these spaces. Multi-rodent systems (e.g., MID [3]) give multiple people simultaneous access to traditional widgets. DiamondSpin [6] provides multiple

M.F. Costabile and F. Paternò (Eds.): INTERACT 2005, LNCS 3585, pp. 1124–1128, 2005.
© IFIP International Federation for Information Processing 2005

toolbars (one for each user) and simultaneous interactions with traditional single-user widgets, and has recently added support for some iDwidgets concepts [4]. Likewise, the SDG Toolkit [8] supports group interaction, but does not introduce any new widgets. Tool-based systems may provide support for multiple people to work in parallel, but each tool is not inherently user-aware; it behaves the same regardless of who is using it. The goal of iDwidgets is to increase a widget's utility and to support widget reuse. A single widget instance serves multiple people, helping reduce clutter in shared-display groupware applications. In cases where widget replication may have advantages, iDwidgets do not preclude widget replication.

While our concept originates with the use of multi-user touch surfaces that can identify who is touching (e.g., DiamondTouch [2]), iDwidgets are applicable in any system that can provide identity information. Many ubiquitous computing environments exploit identity-differentiating technology (e.g., face recognition, biometrics, RFID) to build applications for multi-user environments; we propose embedding the identity information at a lower level, encapsulating it into reusable iDwidgets, rather than at the application or system level.

2 Customizing Idwidgets

The ability to identify the user of a widget is the key feature that enables iDwidgets to be defined; user-id becomes a parameter (or a tag on input) to the widget. iDwidget versions can be made of many traditional widgets by extending and customizing them in up to four dimensions: function, content, appearance, and group input.

Customizing Function: The widget can pass along the identity information to its event handler; the widget looks the same to all users, but behaves differently.

Multi-User Buttons: a single traditional pushbutton would perform a different function based on who is touching the button. For example, a multi-user 'Undo' button, when pushed by a particular person, causes the last action of that person to be undone. While the system is responsible for keeping track of the multiple undo stacks [5], the user identity parameter indicates which stack to access.

Semantic Interpretation: a single string (or graphic) may denote different objects for different people. For example, 'Dad' is a different alias for most people – only identifying the same person for siblings. In a photo-browsing application with a search feature, if John entered 'Dad' in the search box, the system would return pictures of his father; if Mary entered 'Dad' it would return all pictures of her father.

Differentiated Behavior: a single instance of a widget performs the same action, but behaves differently based on the user's identity. For example, a scroll bar may provide continuous scrolling for one user and discrete scrolling for another, based on their pre-specified preferences, or a paintbrush may vary in its numerical values of brush thickness range (e.g., thin, medium, broad) on a per-user basis.

Privileged Access: a particular widget may only work for some special subset of users. It may only respond when a specific individual interacts with it. A security widget, for example, might respond only to a senior member of the group touching it.

Customizing Content: When activated, the contents of the widget will look different to different people, potentially providing different options.

Custom Lists: a traditional list widget whose contents vary depending on who is accessing the list. A list of Bookmarks (web browsing), for example, varies across users. The contents of the displayed list may be generated on the fly depending on who is interacting with the widget.

Custom Menus: a traditional pull-down menu whose contents are the same across users, but access to certain menu items (or sub-menus) is determined based on who is interacting with the menu. Menu items may be reordered (e.g., most recently used items appear closer to the top as in Windows), inactive (e.g., grayed out) depending on who is using the menu, or even be removed, making it more of a custom list.

Customizing Appearance: A widget's appearance (e.g., fonts, colors) may be customized using identity information without changing its behavior or function.

Properties and Aesthetics: the colors, fonts, languages and other traditional graphical features of a widget may also be customized based on the user, while the widget functionality remains unaffected. While some might argue that label language on a widget may impact its functionality, we prefer to think of it as a user preference or a usability issue. Adapting some of the widget properties (e.g., large type) is especially important for elderly and disabled individuals.

Orientation: a widget's orientation may also be customized based on identifying information, which is especially relevant for horizontal displays. Combining user identity with location information would allow widgets to dynamically orient themselves to a particular user. Automatic handle positions may also be determined by user identity and location.

Customizing Group Input: iDwidgets may support or require group input, enabling interaction from multiple people. We distinguish these iDwidgets from previous multi-input widgets (e.g., two-handed input), which are typically used by one person. Multi-input widgets could, of course, be extended to exploit the identity information provided to an iDwidget.

Cumulative Effect: an iDwidget could require interaction from a number of people before taking some action. A voting widget, for example, may require all users to respond before tallying the result; as an alternative, it might only require a quorum to agree, without requiring everyone to respond. The number of distinct users interacting with the widget (as indicated by the identity information) would be the distinguishing factor.

Simultaneous Input: iDwidgets may also require simultaneous interaction in order to activate a widget. Two people, for example, may be needed to turn virtual silo keys in order to launch a missile. Other examples include large surface interactions, where one person cannot directly reach all the needed objects or regions.

Modal Input Sequences: iDwidgets can support parallel moded-interactions. By tracking identity information they can support the interleaving of different people's actions. One person can be in 'Delete' mode while another person is simultaneously in 'Annotate' mode. With traditional widgets once the 'Delete' mode is activated, the next object touched would be deleted. With iDwidgets only the next touch of the person in 'Delete' mode would delete an object.

Audit and Logging: iDwidgets also support easy logging and audit trail creation. Because the widget knows who is touching, the identification information can be added to the log file. Many other systems provide such multi-user audit support (such as MS Word's 'Track Changes' feature); iDwidgets incorporate it at the widget level.

In general, any attributes or behaviors that are customizable in traditional (single-user) computing environments (typically via user-profiles or resource files) can be exploited by iDwidgets. Rather than creating multiple tool bars or other controls (one per person) a single instance of an iDwidget may be used, providing flexible and customizable interaction for different people, and in some cases screen space savings.

3   Conclusions and Future Work

The power of a widget lies in encapsulating a set of behaviors and packaging them up along with graphical attributes so that it can easily be used and reused. The iDwidget concept, adding user identity as a parameter in order to customize a widget in a multi-user setting, enables interactions with widgets to be dynamically adapted on a per-user basis in a group usage setting. In addition to the benefits of personalized interactions, iDwidgets support widget reuse (or sharing).   When and how it is appropriate to allow shared widgets, and which dimension(s) of customization should be used are two application-dependent questions, and should be left as a policy question for the application developer. While some fragments of the iDwidget concept are present in a number of other systems, iDwidgets promotes identity to a first-class widget parameter, providing a unifying framework for specifying the customization of shared widgets.

iDwidgets also raise new feasibility and usability issues. Which widgets lend themselves to identity differentiation, and which do not? What happens when two people simultaneously access a menu – do one user's preferences take priority, or do we temporarily replicate the menu? What effects will dynamically adapting widgets have on interactions with an application? When will customizing a widget enhance performance or hinder learnability?

iDwidgets represent a generalization of ideas already in practice today. The enabling technology is already available and in use, most notably in ubiquitous computing environments; many applications already incorporate fragments of the iDwidgets idea. By extending and generalizing the use of identity in widgets introduced in earlier work and moving the identity information out of the application or system level and into the widgets, iDwidgets provides a conceptual framework in which to think about the use of identity information to customize interaction, and opens the door for new application development and new lines of research.

References

1. Bier, E., and Freeman, S., "MMM: a user interface architecture for shared editors on a single screen," In Proc. of UIST 1991, pp. 79-86.
2. Dietz, P., and Leigh, D., "DiamondTouch: A multi-user touch technology," In Proc. of UIST 2001, pp. 219-226.

3. Hourcade, H.P., and Bederson, B.B., "Architecture and Implementation of a Java Package for Multiple Input Devices (MID)," HCIL Tech Report No. 99-08, 1999.
4. Morris, M.R., Ryall, K., Shen, C., Forlines, C., and Vernier, F., "Beyond 'Social Protocols': Multi-User Coordination Policies for Co-located Groupware," In Proc. of CSCW 2004.
5. Myers, B., Stiel, H., and Gargiulo, R. "Collaboration Using Multiple PDAs Connected to a PC," In Proc. of CSCW 1998, pp. 285-294.
6. Shen, C., Vernier, F.D., Forlines, C., and Ringel, M. "DiamondSpin: An Extensible Toolkit for Around-the-Table Interaction," In Proceedings of CHI 2004, pp. 167-174.
7. Stewart, J. Bederson, B., and Druin, A., "Single Display Groupware: A Model for Co-present Collaboration," In Proc. of CHI 1999, pp. 286-293.
8. Tse, E., and Greenberg, S. "SDGToolkit: A Toolkit for Rapidly Prototyping Single Display Groupware." Poster session. CSCW 2002.

Rater Bias: The Influence of Hedonic Quality on Usability Questionnaires

Stefanie Harbich and Sonja Auer

Siemens AG, CT IC 7, User Interface Design, Otto-Hahn-Ring 6, 81730 Munich, Germany
stefanie.harbich@dokusoft.de
sonja.auer@siemens.com

Abstract. In this study of various evaluation-instruments, subjects fulfilled several tasks on two different operating systems and answered several questionnaires, among them AttrakDiff[TM] and ISONORM 9241/10, and objective measures were taken. A correlation between the "hedonic quality - identity"-scale of the AttrakDiff[TM] and the ISONORM 9241/10 was found. As the ISONORM 9241/10 measures usability as described in ISO 9241-10 and not hedonic quality, the hedonic quality seems to have an influence on the tester ratings of usability. This is supported by the finding, that the hedonic quality does not correlate with the objective measures and therefore does not have any effective influence on the efficiency component of usability.

1 Introduction

Usability testing often relies on questionnaires, as they are known to be easy to handle, reliable, statistically objective, economical and easy to evaluate. They allow products to be compared and usability questions can be answered in an effective way. Though questionnaires have the advantage of being highly efficient and low in cost, they have disadvantages, too, like adulterations by biases in answering the checkmark items.

A well proven effect is the halo effect. After subjects judged one main aspect of the tested software, which had a quite big effect, they tend to judge all other aspects dependent on that main aspect. They seem to be unable to differentiate between different categories and therefore rate them all in an equal way [1]. This may negatively affect usability ratings, as one aspect of a software may easily cause a deep impression on the testers, which disables them to rate other aspects objectively.

Besides usability, an additional aspect in testing products is their appeal. Hassenzahl developed a questionnaire called AttrakDiff[TM] using a semantic differential with the four scales pragmatic quality, appeal, hedonic quality - stimulation and hedonic quality - identity [2]. Hedonic quality comprises the fulfillment of the need for novelty and change and the need to communicate and express oneself through objects [3]. "Hedonic quality - stimulation" means the human need for individual development, i.e. improvement of knowledge and skills. Another human need - identity - is the expression of the self through objects by identifying with them [2].

The concept of hedonic quality is different from the concept of usability, so these two should not correlate. But as this quality is an attribute of the tested software that

M.F. Costabile and F. Paternò (Eds.): INTERACT 2005, LNCS 3585, pp. 1129 – 1133, 2005.

needs to be rated on a very subjective basis, it may very easily bias the users perception of other attributes like the usability of a software. In this case, testers would not rate usability itself but would be influenced by the hedonic quality of the software.

Are participants influenced by the hedonic quality of a product when rating its usability? To test this, a usability test was conducted. Two questionnaires were employed, one measuring usability, one measuring hedonic quality. These subjective measures were complemented by a set of objective measurements, namely performance time, clicks and success in task performance. These objective methods operationalize effectiveness and efficiency as defined in ISO 9241-11 [4].

The questionnaire for measuring usability was the ISONORM 9241/10 question-naire [5], which represents an operationalisation of the ISO 9241-10 [6]. As hedonic quality is not part of ISO 9241-10, this questionnaire is not supposed to measure any-thing similar to hedonic quality. Thus a high correlation between objective task per-formance measures and the ISONORM 9241/10 results should be expected, if the questionnaire measures were not influenced by hedonic quality.

Considering the possibility of an influence of hedonic quality on the ratings of a usability questionnaire because of the halo effect, it may be presumed that a higher correlation between the hedonic scales of the AttrakDiff^{TM} and the ISONORM 9241/10 will occur than between the hedonic scales and the objective measures.

2 Method

32 clerks participated in this study, 30 female, 2 male. Their average age was 42 years, with a minimum of 24 and a maximum of 58 years, $s = 9.3$.

Participants were told they should test the two operating systems Windows XP Professional and SuSE Linux 9.2 with KDE 3.3. Every participant was currently working with Windows and had not previously worked with Linux. This ensured a predictable result to the effect that Windows would receive better ratings. Participants were given the same nine tasks for each system. Two observers sat behind a one-way mirror and watched the testers and their monitors by cameras and a scan converter. They rated the task achievement, stopped the needed time and counted the clicks.

Participants were instructed to work through the tasks and questionnaires listed in their testers' manual. Tasks were for example: "Save the attachment of this mail to [path] without renaming." or "Open the data browser and copy the file [filename] to [path]". After having completed the tasks participants answered the AttrakDiff^{TM} and the ISONORM 9241/10.

Success was rated "1" (without errors), if the task was completed faultlessly, i.e. straightly without any mistake. "2" (noncritical errors) was assigned, if the participant completed the task successfully within seven minutes and without aid of the instructors. The observers rated success "3" (critical error), if the participants gave up or did not complete the task successfully within seven minutes.

In order to normalize the time and clicks, as they may depend on the specific hard- and software used, the times and clicks of four 'experts' were taken. These 'experts' knew the two systems and how to solve the tasks. Every expert's task was rated the best achieveable value. The participants' data was divided by the experts' value to calculate a ratio of time and clicks.

Some participants gave up before they completed the task or quitted because they thought erroneously they did complete the task. As these time and clicks measures do not represent the real time and clicks, that would have been measured, if the tasks were completed, every value corresponding with a critical error ("3") was substituted by a missing.

3 Results

All measures used were able to distinguish between the two systems. This holds for the usability questionnaire and averaged objective usability measures as well as for averaged hedonic quality.

Table 1. Means and standard deviations for usability ratings of the two operating systems Windows and Linux

Method	Windows (n = 32)		Linux (n = 32)		total (n = 64)	
	M	SD	M	SD	M	SD
Usability questionnaire	4.90 *	0.92	4.56	0.83	4.73	0.89
Hedonic quality - stimulation	4.07 **	0.87	4.59	0.95	4.33	0.94
Hedonic quality - identity	4.78	0.63	4.60	0.70	4.69	0.66
Success	1.74 **	0.29	2.06	0.21	1.90	0.30
Time	4.10	1.65	4.44	1.50	4.27	1.57
Clicks	1.70	0.45	1.63	0.53	1.66	0.49

Note. Usability questionnaire and hedonic quality scales based on Likert-type scale with "1" indicating strong disagreement and "7" indicating strong agreement. Windows' means with asterisks differ significantly from Linux' means.

   $* p < .1$
   $** p < .01$

Table 2. Comparison of correlations between usability questionnaire and hedonic qualities and correlations between hedonic qualities and objective measures

Method	Hedonic quality				Hedonic quality - identity				Hedonic quality - stimulation			
	Obj.	Success	Time	Clicks	Obj.	Success	Time	Clicks	Obj.	Success	Time	Clicks
r	-.14	.10	-.02	-.27	-.14	-.02	-.06	-.22	-.15	.21	.03	-.31
HQ .39	*	**	*	-								
HQ-I .54					**	**	**	*				
HQ-S .21									-	-	-	-

(left margin label: Usability questionnaire)

Note.   Obj.: Objective measures (mean of success, time and clicks) $**: p < .01$
       HQ: Hedonic quality (mean of identity and stimulation) $*: p < .05$
       HQ-I: Hedonic quality - identity $-: p > .05$
       HQ-S: Hedonic quality - stimulation

Table 3. Correlations between usability questionnaire and objective measures

Method	Usability questionnaire
Objective measures	-.02
Success	-.18
Time	.08
Clicks	.04

Correlations between the different methods support the rater bias hypothesis: Table 2 shows high correlations between usability and hedonic quality (mean of "hedonic quality - identity" and "hedonic quality - stimulation" after a Fishers-Z-transformation), $r = .39$, but low correlations between hedonic quality and object0ive measures, $r = -.14$. Surprisingly, as can be seen in Table 3, there is almost no correlation between the usability questionnaire and the (after a Fishers Z - transformation) averaged objective measures, $r = -.02$, and between the usability questionnaire and the single objective measures, i.e. success, $r = -.18$, time, $r = .08$, and clicks, $r = .04$.

Comparing the single correlations in Table 2, the correlation between usability and hedonic quality, $r = .39$ is significantly bigger than the correlation between hedonic quality and objective measures, $r = -.14$, $p < .05$ (one-tailed). This holds especially for the correlation between the objective measure success and hedonic quality, $r = .10$, versus the correlation between the usability questionnaire and hedonic quality, $p < .01$ (one-tailed), and also for the objective measure time, $r = -.02$, $p < .05$ (one-tailed), but not for the objective measure clicks, $r = -.27$, $p > .05$ (one-tailed).

As for the averaged hedonic quality, the correlation between "hedonic quality - identity" and the usability questionnaire, $r = .54$, also is significantly bigger than between "hedonic quality - identity" and averaged objective measures, $r = -.14$, $p < .01$ (one-tailed). This again is true for success, $r = -.02$, $p < .01$ (one-tailed), and time, $r = -.06$, $p < .01$ (one-tailed), and clicks, too, $r = -.22$, $p < .05$, (one-tailed).

These findings suggest an influence of hedonic quality (specifically the "hedonic quality - identity") on the usability questionnaire, but not on the objective measures. There is no evidence for such a difference in influence of "hedonic quality - stimulation" on the usability questionnaire compared to the objective measures. The correlation of "hedonic quality - stimulation" and the usability questionnaire, $r = .21$, does not significantly differ from the correlation of "hedonic quality - stimulation" and the averaged objective measures, $r = -.15$, or success, $r = .21$, or time, $r = .03$, or clicks, $r = -.31$, $p > .05$.

The results were analyzed separately for the two operating systems, too. Similar effects were found.

4 Discussion

The hedonic quality and usability questionnaires correlate to a big extent, whereas there seems to be no correlation between the usability questionnaire and objective measures, even though the ISONORM 9241/10 questionnaire and the objective measures indicate to measure usability and not hedonic quality. A possible explanation is the halo effect of hedonic quality on usability. Testers are influenced by the hedonic quality of a software and rate usability depending on their ratings of hedonic quality.

Hedonic quality means "hedonic quality - identity" here. The "hedonic quality - stimulation" does not have such a big effect. Participants rated usability higher, when they identified highly with the tested software. When they were stimulated by the soft-ware, they rated usability higher, too, but to a lesser extent.

Another explanation may be that the objective instruments measure something different from usability, as the usability questionnaire and the objective measures do not correlate. This seems unplausible, as the objective measures operationalize the ISO 9241-11 - definition of efficiency and effectivity. Solely satisfaction was not covered by the objective measurements time, clicks and success. Maybe satisfaction influences both usability and hedonic quality in an extensive way. Of course, this would be a halo effect, too, as satisfaction then outshines other aspects of the software.

For the future, the influence of satisfaction on usability questionnaires *and* the hedonic quality should be analyzed.

Depending on the goals of testing, usability questionnaires should be used and analyzed carefully. Though they seem to rate usability in an objective way, other aspects may influence these ratings and give a false impression of the usability of the product.

References

1. Bortz, J. & Döring, N. (2002). Forschungsmethoden und Evaluation, Berlin: Springer.
2. Hassenzahl, M., Burmester, M.& Koller, F. (2003). AttrakDiff: Ein Fragebogen zur Messung wahrgenommener hedonischer und pragmatischer Qualität. In J. Ziegler & G. Szwillus (Eds.), Mensch & Computer 2003. Interaktion in Bewegung (pp. 187-196). Stuttgart, Leipzig: B.G. Teubner.
3. Hassenzahl, M., Beu, A. & Burmester, M. (2001). Engineering Joy. In: IEEE Software, 2-8, (pp 70-76).
4. ISO 9241-11 (1998). Ergonomic requirements for office work with visual display terminals (VDTs) - Part 11: Guidance on usability. Brüssel: CEN.
5. Prümper, J. (1993). Software-Evaluation based upon ISO 9241 Part 10. In: T. Grechenig & M. Tscheligi (Eds.), Human Computer Interaction (pp 255-265), Berlin: Springer.
6. ISO 9241-10 (1996). Ergonomic requirements for office work with visual display terminals Part 10: Dialogue Principles. Brüssel: CEN.

Towards the Maturation of IT Usability Evaluation (MAUSE)

Effie L.-C. Law[1], Ebba T. Hvannberg[2], Gilbert Cockton[3], Philippe Palanque[4], Dominque Scapin[5], Mark Springett[6], Christian Stary[7], and Jean Vanderdonckt[8]

[1] ETH Zürich, Switzerland [2] University of Iceland, UK [3] University of Sunderland, UK [4] Universite Paul Sabatier, France [5] INRIA Rocquencourt, France [6] University of Middlesex, UK [7] University of Linz, Austria [8] Catholic University of Louvain, Belgium

Abstract. This article describes a new initiative MAUSE of which the ultimate goal is to bring more science to bear on usability evaluation methods. This overarching goal will be realized through scientific activities of four Working Groups (WGs) with each of them having specific objectives, rationales, tasks and expected outcomes. Outlook for MAUSE's development is described.

1   Introduction

MAUSE (Towards the **MA**turation of Information Technology **US**ability **E**valuation), COST294, is a recent initiative with the mission of bringing more science to bear on the development, evaluation and comparison of Usability Evaluation Methods (UEMs), aiming to drive this young and significant Research & Development area towards maturity and to yield results that can be transferred to industry and educators.

A UEM is defined as any systematic method or technique employed to perform usability evaluation of any interactive design at any stage of its development. The objective of usability evaluation is to determine whether a system fulfils a set of usability requirements. The output is a set of deviations from the requirements, which may be a list of usability problems (UPs), expressed as undesirable design features, scenarios or improvement suggestions, but these deviations may also be described with other measures that indicate problematic usages. Usability evaluation research has been poorly focused and the findings are inconclusive. Consequently, many serious UPs still occur in all kinds of software products. This fact also suggests that the integration of software design and usability evaluation in industrial software development has largely been unsuccessful. Indeed, there are a number of definitional, theoretical and methodological issues in usability research. Furthermore, the emerging landscape of Information Technologies (IT) such as Ambient Intelligence and Pervasive Computing calls for the adaptation as well as extension of existing UEMs. Basic and intricate problems in usability research need to be resolved by extensive co-operation among a community of usability professionals and researchers with diversified backgrounds. MAUSE-COST294 is a structured four-year action being operated under the auspices of the European Science Foundation to orchestrate collaborative efforts of usability experts from a number of European countries (http://www.cost294.org). The action was launched in January 2005.

M.F. Costabile and F. Paternò (Eds.): INTERACT 2005, LNCS 3585, pp. 1134–1137, 2005.

2   Objectives and Four Working Groups

The main objective of MAUSE is threefold:

- To deepen understanding about the inherent strengths and weaknesses of individual Usability Evaluation Methods (UEMs);
- To identify reliable and valid methods for comparing different UEMs in terms of their effectiveness, efficiency and scope of applicability;
- To develop effective strategies for extracting useful information from the results of UEMs in order to improve the systems tested

MAUSE comprises four WGs with each of them having specific objectives, rationales, tasks and expected outcomes. They are interdependent to a certain extent; results from one can facilitate the progress of the others and vice-versa.

WG1: Critical Review and Analysis of Individual UEMs

Objective: To build a refined, substantiated and consolidated knowledge-pool about usability evaluation based on the expertise, experiences and research work of the participating partners.

Rationale: The fundamental problem is that most UEMs are not strongly rooted in a clearly defined and sound theoretical framework [8], but are rather pragmatic. Further, no effective strategies are yet available to manage (never mind eradicate) systematically the user/evaluator effect [5], which are known to substantially undermine the reliability and validity of results of UEMs. How variants of think-aloud methods (concurrent vs. retrospective) [9] and sets of usability guidelines (Nielsen vs. Gerhardt-Powals) [6] influence UEM results entail more empirical data.

Tasks: UEMs of interest are critically reviewed and analyzed on various attributes:

- underlying theoretical background – explaining the effect of a UEM
- scope of application – range of conditions and contexts where a UEM is deployed
- cost-effectiveness – person-hours versus effectiveness as specifically defined
- user/evaluator effect – means to measure and mitigate this undesirable effect
- limitations of the techniques – identifying remedial strategies
- level of acceptance – extent of usage in the industry and academic community
- possible extension – increasing scope of application and effectiveness

Outcome: A database is created to record the findings of individual project teams involved in MAUSE with regard to the aforementioned attributes of different UEMs. These data serve as important reference points from which insights into the future development of UEMs can be gained. Best practices of different UEMs, covering operational, organizational as well as cultural dimensions, can be derived from records of this database and rendered accessible to researchers and practitioners.

WG2: Comparing UEMs: Strategies and Implementation

Objective: To identify effective strategies to compare different UEMs.

Rationale: There is currently poor understanding of the scope of different UEMs in terms of who, when, how and where they are used. UEMs tend to yield different insights into usability issues and these differences are not well understood or articulated [cf. 7]. There is a need for well-defined and tested methods for establishing that scope. Further, in the literature [2, 3] different comparison criteria have been proposed, but they are loosely defined and thus measured differently.

Tasks: Empirical, analytic and model-based UEMs will be compared. Major tasks are:

- To conduct meta-data analysis of the empirical studies implemented in the context of MAUSE and those available in the literature
- To develop comprehensive, consistent and robust means to compute different comparison criteria, especially thoroughness, validity and reliability
- To implement comparisons among different UEMs or among different usage conditions of a single UEM as it is applied to different software systems. Multi-sited experiments involving different project teams will be coordinated to carry out both types of comparisons
- To develop quality models for the Web to enable a benchmarking comparing different UEMs

Outcome: Recommendation on the deployment of a particular UEM, under certain conditions and contexts with the expected effectiveness, can be proposed to usability practitioners.

WG3: Refining and Validating Classification Schemes for Usability Problems

Objective: To improve and substantiate the tools for classifying and analyzing usability problems with the goal of enhancing feedback to design and process improvement

Rationale: There is a lack of a thoroughly validated defect classification scheme (DCS) specifically designed for analyzing usability problems based on the integration of basic concepts of HCI and software engineering. Such a scheme is crucial for identifying origins of usability problems, for extracting useful information to improve the systems evaluated and for facilitating the communication between usability specialists and software developers.

Tasks: (i) To review and compare existing DCSs (e.g. CUP [4], UAF [1]) for their suitability and adaptability for isolating causes of usability problems and for proposing re-design solutions; (ii) To validate CUP with various types of software applications, ranging from mobile PDA to large screen display devices, by evaluators with different expertise and experience; (iii) To explore the possibility of developing a robust DCS by integrating the findings to be obtained in (i) and (ii).

Outcome: Refined and validated DCSs will be disseminated to other usability professionals. Deeper understanding of the origins of UPs can shed some light on the significant issue of integrating usability into the systems development lifecycle.

WG4: Review on Computational and Definitional Approaches in Usability Evaluation

Objective: To review systematically the existing models and procedures for estimating certain key usability test parameters and the traditionally defined usability quality metrics. Of primary interest are the capabilities of formal representations.

Rationale: Several fundamental definitions and standard approaches entail further systematic investigations and refinements.

Tasks: The work will be guided by six strategic principles: (i) Computational UEM Relevance – a meta-model for computing indicators and prospective indices for human behaviour and system performance; (ii) Definitional Primacy – a real and broadly accepted UP specification; (iii) Fine-grain UEM Specification – identifying a comprehensive list of UEM attributes; (iv) Baseline Specificity Exploitation – addressing user, system and organizational baseline measures; (v) Explication of Semantic Encodings – mapping a usability-parameter definition to a computational scheme; rendering the semantic relationships between the three traditional usability metrics transparent; (vi) UEM Accuracy Determination – the adequacy of the means for capturing interactive software quality

Outcome: With the improved models and algorithms, more accurate estimations of key usability test parameters can be obtained. Practitioners might re-arrange usability evaluation accordingly, based on revised usability metrics, operational criteria for UPs and in line with other quality attributes upheld by other professionals.

3 Outlook

MAUSE-COST294 brings together leading HCI researchers from different European countries with each of them being highly knowledgeable in usability evaluation. The concerted efforts being contributed by these experts will lead to fruitful outcomes. Apart from the Working Groups, other instruments for fostering the attainment of MAUSE's overarching goal are Short-Term Scientific Missions and Training Schools for young researchers. Further, given the wide networks that the partners are continuously extending to the academic community, standardization bodies and industry for exchanging knowledge and practice, results from MAUSE-COST294 can be disseminated effectively, thereby enabling their uptake. Since the action is still in its infancy, concrete outcomes with respect to the problems addressed above are not yet available and will become more visible during its course of development.

References

1. Andre, T.S., Hartson, H.R., Belz, S.M., & McCreary, F.A. (2001). The user action framework. *International Journal Human-Computer Studies*, 54: 107-136.
2. Cockton, G., D. Lavery, & A. Woolrych (2003). Inspection-based evaluation. In J. A. Jacko & A. Sears (Eds.), *Human-Computer Interaction Handbook* (pp. 1118-1138). Erlbaum.
3. Hartson, H.R., Andre, T.S., Williges, R.C. (2003). Criteria for evaluating usability evaluation methods. *Int. J. Human and Computer Interaction 15*(1): 145-181.
4. Hvannberg, E.T., & Law, E.L.-C. (2003).Classification of Usability Problems (CUP) Scheme. In *Proceedings of INTERACT 2003*.
5. Law, E. L.-C., & Hvannberg, E.T. (2004a). Analysis of combinatorial user effect in international usability tests. *In Proceedings* of *CHI 2004*.
6. Law, E. L.-C., & Hvannberg, E.T. (2004b). Analysis of strategies for improving and estimating the effectiveness of heuristic evaluation. In: *Proceedings of NordiCHI 2004*.
7. Molich R., Ede M., Kaasgaard K., & Karyukin B.(2004). Comparative usability evaluation. *Behaviour and Information Technology,* 23(1): 65-74.
8. Rogers, Y. (2004). New theoretical approaches for HCI. *Annual Review of Information Science and Technology* (ARIST), Volume 38.
9. Van den Haak, M.J., de Jong, M.D.T., Schellens, P. (2003). Retrospective vs. concurrent think-aloud protocols. *Behaviour and Information Technology, 22* (5), 339-351.

An X-Ray of the Brazilian e-Gov Web Sites

Cristiano Maciel, José Luiz T. Nogueira, and Ana Cristina Bicharra Garcia

Universidade Federal Fluminense,
Rua Passos da Pátria, 156 sl 326, Niterói, RJ, Brazil
{cmaciel, nogueira, bicharra}@ic.uff.br

Abstract. The digital inclusion promotes the reduction of social inequalities. Based on this principle, the Brazilian Government has been setting up an increasing number of Web access locations to render virtual support to its citizens. However, there are no guidelines for the construction and assessment of these electronic Government (e-Gov) sites. In this article we measure the web site quality in the e-Gov domain with the following proprieties: usability, accessibility, interoperability, security, privacy, information reliability, and service agility. We implemented our method, by using a checklist tool, in the evaluation of 127 Brazilian government sites (federal, state and municipal). Our method proved itself efficient in the diagnosis and identification of specific problems in the e-Gov site domain.

1 Introduction

Electronic government (e-gov) means the use of information and communication technology: 1) to meet the citizens' needs regarding government information acquisition; 2) to render services (it allows on-line transactions of government products and services); 3) and to participate in government decisions (it permits citizen's participation through interaction with the government).

Brazil ranks eighteenth [1] in the group of countries that have top qualification in "e-government", presenting a higher rating than Italy, Japan and Austria. Nevertheless, several Brazilian studies indicate that these e-Gov sites do not meet Brazilian citizen needs [2]. Although these studies indicate that the sites are not good, they do not determine which are the specific problems, when applied to the information, services and citizen's participation categories..

This research is based on the indirect usability evaluation method, known as Heuristic Evaluation, and in Brazilian documents on eletronic government [5][6]. The heuristics, as defined by Nielsen [3][4], that were used to measure the usability property were: visibility of system status, match between system and the real world, user control and freedom, consistency and standards, error prevention, recognition rather than recall, flexibility and efficiency of use, aesthetics and minimalist design, help users recognize, diagnose, and recover from errors, and help and documentation. For the electronic government domain, the Nielsen's heuristics evaluation were not sufficient for site evaluations and, thus, require extensions to measure the quality of the e-Gov Web sites[07][08][09][10]. See in the Table 1 all properties investigated.

M.F. Costabile and F. Paternò (Eds.): INTERACT 2005, LNCS 3585, pp. 1138–1141, 2005.

Table 1. Proprieties to e-Gov Web site assessment

Proprieties	Description	Justification
Usability (Us)	Traditionally associated with these attributes: Learnability, Efficiency, Memorability, Errors e Satisfaction [4].	This principle is ideal to interface evalution.
Accessibility (Ac)	The site must be devised so as to ensure its content is accessible to those with special needs and from different environments.	Digital inclusion of citizens with special needs makes electronic government accessible to all.
Interoperability (In)	Ability to interchange information between different systems, allowing data exchange based on the government standard [6].	Allows a broader scope and minimizing physical strain of citizens who used other systems.
Security and Privacy (SP)	Personal information requiring privacy should travel on the net security, without risk for the users.	Visibility of site security allows users to interact with confidence.
Information Reliability (IR)	Inform last update on each page of the site.	Up-to-date pages convey content credibility and promote required trust for interaction.
Service Agility (SA)	The site's response time should be brief or even instantaneous and denotes transparency in governmental processes.	Citizens expect prompt response and any delay diminishes trust on the site and increases intolerance.

To implement the method, the proprieties were charted on an evaluation table, with several items, in a manual *checklist*, used by specialists evaluators. This also quantified the migration scope, to the Web environment, in the three categories - information, services, and participation.

The evaluation method was applied to 127 government domain sites [11]. The results demonstrated the method's efficiency, not only to diagnose but, also, to identify specific problems in e-Gov sites.

2   Case Study

In this section, to test the efficiency of the e-gov Web sites quality assessment a case study was presented. The proposed method was implemented to analyze the quality of Brazilian e-Gov sites, with the following breakdown: 9 federal sites, 91 municipal sites (all of them in Rio de Janeiro state) and 27 municipal sites (from Brazilian state capitals). All Web sites were evaluated in the totality of their pages. The quantitative data was presented in tables and graphs, so as to facilitate their qualitative analyses.

Figure 1 showed the behavior of the proprieties used in the evaluation. The checklist was composed of several sub-items for each property. Some of these were argued in this session.

Considering only "Usability" (Us) property, through the evaluation of the ten Nielsen's heuristics, there was 44,93% average, with the exception of the "usage flexibility and efficiency"(1.95%) and "help and documentation" (13,91%) heuristics. The best was the "consistency and standards" heuristic, with 68,55% of the sites.

The "Accessibility" (As) property was fundamental for this domain. No need of concern was found not even within federal sites. The checklist sub-item with "allows visual perception through text markers" was not taken into account by 83.70 % of the sites. Meanwhile, the sub-item "Uses easy access resources through various means, cellular and palmtop" is not considered by 98.91 %, while 94.81 % of the sites do not even "comply with W3C recommendations".

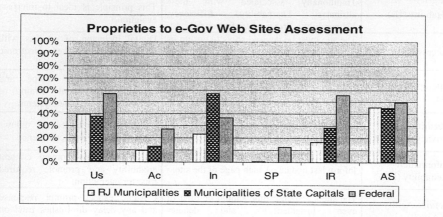

Fig. 1. Assessment of e-Gov Web Sites Proprieties

The "Interoperability" (In) property, in the analyzed federal sites, it was observed intense usage of proprietary formats. For the checklist sub-item "makes document available under patterns xml, swx, rtf, pdf , txt, htm or html", less than de 56 % of the federal sites comply with this norm, while, in the overall evaluation, 69.74 % of the evaluated sites were in compliance.

In the "Security and Privacy" (SP) property, evaluation results were much closer to 0 (zero), this being a noteworthy problem for this kind of domain. Upon analyzing the checklist sub-items, was found that 96.10 % of the sites did not use "digital certification", while 100 % did not "use virtual keyboard".

Looking into the "Information Reliability" (IR) property, 9 municipal sites were highly rated. In spite of this, as it could be observed, several municipalities show no concern with this issue, and this may generate a credibility failure towards the site, on the citizen's part. Upon analyzing the checklist sub-items, if was seen that 76.82 % of the sites do not meet the sub-item "when necessary, informs last update of each page".

When it comes to the "Service Agility" (SA) property, less than 50% of the sites meet this requirement satisfactorily. Upon analyzing the sub-items individually, it was verified that 21.74 % of the sites do not "make available e-mail contact". Another hurdle is that 81.25 % of the analyzed sites did not reply e-mails within the following 48 hours and, a month later, the situation was practically the same. The checklist sub-items "renders public accout to citizens" and "it demonstrates the budgetary execution" had indicated low transparency in governmental processes.

3 Discussions

This study presents a Web sites quality assessment of government sites. The exclusive use of Nielsen Heuristics does not guarantee usability of electronic government sites, hence the incorporation of specific proprieties for the evaluation of this domain.

Regarding the evaluated sites, it can be perceived that, in general, those of the federal sphere present better percentages in proprieties to e-gov Web sites assessment. It was observed the existence of sites that purport to be official but are, in fact, business-oriented, portraying a totally distorted image of electronic government. Such proprieties - acessibility, information reliability and service agility - are absolutely necessary for the implementation of a viable electronic government system which users trust and feel at ease with. Another issue that should be highlighted is the lack of security of government sites. Provision of government services depends on strict security. Therefore, this proprieties is extremely important since citizens interacting with these systems need to feel totally secure.

During visits to sites evaluated in this research, it could be verified the existence of many important governamental information, but the citizen participation is limited, in most instances, to expressing opinion via e-mail (though it was verified that this option is not always available), and voting in restricted polls.

When issues are raised, which are relevant to both the citizen, and the government, a set of measures must be stablished t evaluate e-Gov sites, so as to provide better quality. It is hoped that this research contributes to the process by raising new indicators to improve electronic government systems.

References

1. Benchmarking E-government: A Global Perspective. Assessed in July 2004. Available on http://www.unpan.org/.
2. Chalin, A. et all. E-gov.br: a próxima revolução brasileira: eficiência, qualidade e democracia. São Paulo: Prentice Hall. (2004). 380p. /in portuguese/
3. Nielsen, J. Usability Engineering. Boston: Academic Press, Cambridge, MA. (1993).
4. Nielsen, J. Usability Metrics. Assessed in May 2004. Available on http://www.useit.com/ alertbox/ 20010121.html.
5. e-Ping - Versão 1.0 do documento e-Ping. Assessed in October 2004. Available on http://www.governoeletronico.e.gov.br/governoeletronico/index.html. /in portuguese/
6. Governo Federal. Assessed in July 2004.Cartilha de Usabilidade para Sítios e Portais do Governo Federal - Versão 01 – 30/06/2004. /in portuguese/
7. Holliday, I; Kwok, R.C. Governance in the information age: building e-government in Hong Kong. New Media&Society, 6(4), (2004) 549-570.
8. Mahammed, S.N. Self-presentation of small developing countries on the World Wide Web: A study of official Web sites. New Media & Society, 6(4), (2004), 469-486.
9. Zazenlenchuk, T,. In Search of the Holy Grail: Alternatives to Nielsen's Heuristics. Assessed in Setember 2004. Available on http://www.indiana.edu/~usable/utips/ february_03.htm.
10. Zeithaml, V. A., Parasuraman, A. and Malhotra, A.. Service Quality Delivery through Web Sites: A Critical View of Extant Knowledge. Journal of the Academy of Marketing Science, Vol. 30, No. 4 (2002) 362-375.
11. Garcia, A.C.B.; Maciel, C.; Pinto, F. B. A Quality Inspection Method to evaluate e-Government Sites. Lecture Notes in Computer Science, 2005.

An Experiment to Measure the Usefulness of Patterns in the Interaction Design Process

N.L.O. Cowley and J.L. Wesson

P.O. Box 77000, Nelson Mandela Metropolitan University,
Port Elizabeth, South Africa, 6031
{Janet.Wesson, Lester.Cowley}@nmmu.ac.za

Abstract. Interaction design patterns have yet to prove themselves in interaction design in the way that design guidelines have. This paper describes an empirical study comparing the use of patterns and guidelines. The study involved a heuristic evaluation of a web site, the redesign of the web site, and the design of a new web site. Preliminary results suggesting that developers find patterns useful in the interaction design process are presented. Further analysis using heuristics to compare the quality of the designs produced using patterns and guidelines will provide an objective assessment of the usefulness of patterns.

1 Introduction

Interaction design (ID) is concerned with designing interactive products to support people in their everyday lives. ID consists of four activities: identifying user needs and establishing requirements, developing alternative designs, building interactive versions, and evaluating the usability of these versions. Successful ID requires a user-centered focus, iterative design and evaluation. The design activity involves the design of the conceptual model and the physical design.

Design guidelines are a commonly used and generally accepted aid for physical design and can be used as heuristics for expert evaluation of existing systems. Guidelines summarize good practice, are easy to understand and apply, but are sometimes contradictory. Interaction design patterns have been proposed as alternatives to guidelines. Various researchers have described the advantages of patterns, including Griffiths and Pemberton [1], Tidwell [2], Dearden *et al.* [3], and Van Welie and van der Veer [4].

Empirical evidence about pattern use is limited. As an evaluation aid, there is evidence that guidelines may be easier to use and more effective than patterns [5]. There is little evidence that interfaces designed using patterns are better than the equivalent interfaces designed using guidelines [2, 6]. Existing pattern collections are works in progress and the patterns may be deficient in form or content. The pattern languages (PLs) in the collections may be lacking, fragmentary or inconsistent.

An investigation into the use of interaction design patterns was conducted in 2004. The aim of the investigation was to evaluate the use of patterns in interaction design, the quality of the patterns used and the interfaces produced. An experimental group

M.F. Costabile and F. Paternò (Eds.): INTERACT 2005, LNCS 3585, pp. 1142–1145, 2005.
© IFIP International Federation for Information Processing 2005

used selected patterns to evaluate and redesign an existing website and to design a new website. A control group used similar guidelines to carry out the same tasks.

2   Research Design

Several research questions were formulated (Table 1). The primary research question was to determine to what extent patterns are a useful interaction design aid.

Table 1. Interaction Design Patterns Research Questions

Question	To what extent are patterns:
1-3	An efficient, effective and satisfying evaluation aid?
4-6	An efficient, effective and satisfying redesign aid?
7-9	An efficient, effective and satisfying design aid?
10-11	Useful in terms of their format and content?
12	Useful when linked together into a pattern language?
13	Easy to become familiar with when first encountered?
14-15	A personal and shared design language?

Thirty-three Computer Science masters and honours students registered for a postgraduate E-commerce course were recruited for the study. Stratified sampling was employed to split the group into equivalent experimental and control groups. A pre-test questionnaire was used to record the participants' biographical data. The Porcupine Ceramics website (http://www.porcupine.co.za/) was chosen as a suitable E-commerce web site for evaluation and redesign.

The pattern collections selected for use by the experimental group were van Welie's Amsterdam Pattern Collection [7] and van Duyne *et al.*'s Design of Sites Pattern Browser [8]. The design guidelines selected for use by the control group were Barnard's E-commerce guidelines [9], which are based on those proposed by Nielsen *et al.* [10]. Permission to use these resources was obtained from their owners.

The experimental group carried out three tasks using patterns while the control group carried out the same tasks using guidelines. The first task was to perform a heuristic evaluation of the Porcupine Ceramics website. The second task was to redesign the Porcupine Ceramics website and to evaluate the content of the design aids used. The third task was to design a new E-commerce website from specifications, and to evaluate the form of the design aids. The groups documented their designs using sitemaps and detailed wireframes (as high-fidelity prototypes).

Each group was provided with a list of suggested patterns or guidelines to use. Suggested patterns included Shopping Experience, Shopping Cart, Product Page, Login and Register (from the Amsterdam Pattern Collection). Suggested guidelines included Customer Support, Shopping Cart & Placing Order and Product Pages (from Barnard's E-commerce guidelines). The participants used project diaries to record their mental processes and experiences while they carried out the tasks.

A post-test questionnaire was used to record quantitative and qualitative data about the participants' attitudes towards the design aids used. The items were grouped into five categories: Evaluation, Redesign, New Design, Format and Content, and General

Experience. Several statements were presented in each category, relating to the research questions in Table 1. The participants rated the statements in the five categories, using a five-point Likert scale, with 1 indicating Strongly Disagree and 5 indicating Strongly Agree. Open-ended items were used to collect qualitative data.

3 Preliminary Research Results

Preliminary results obtained for the post-test questionnaire items are summarised in Table 2. Interval-data descriptive statistics were calculated for each of the statements, including means and standard deviations. The N values indicate the number of data items used in the calculations. Initial estimates of whether the pattern hypotheses can be accepted (A) or not accepted (N) appear in the Result column.

Table 2. Results of Analysis of Post-Test Questionnaire Quantitative Data

Category	Property	R Question	Guideline Users			Pattern Users			Result
			N	Mean	Std Dev	N	Mean	Std Dev	
Evaluation	Efficiency	1	20	3.8	0.6	30	3.6	1.0	A
	Effectiveness	2	20	4.0	0.8	30	3.5	0.9	A
	Satisfaction	3	19	3.5	0.8	30	3.1	1.3	N
Re-design	Efficiency	4	20	3.6	0.8	31	3.6	0.9	A
	Effectiveness	5	20	3.7	0.7	31	3.6	0.9	A
	Satisfaction	6	20	3.3	0.8	31	3.3	1.2	N
New Design	Efficiency	7	40	3.3	0.8	60	3.5	1.1	A
	Effectiveness	8	20	3.7	0.8	29	3.8	0.8	A
	Satisfaction	9	20	3.3	0.9	30	3.6	1.1	A
Format/ Content	Form	10	21	3.4	1.2	34	3.4	1.1	A
	Content	11	20	3.3	1.3	34	3.5	1.0	A
	Organisation	12	10	4.3	0.7	33	3.5	1.0	A
General Experience	Learnability	13	33	3.4	1.0	48	3.4	1.0	N
	Personal Lang.	14	11	3.5	0.7	16	3.7	0.9	A
	Shared Lang.	15	8	3.1	1.0	15	3.1	1.1	N

Based on the above results, we can conclude that designers consider patterns to be an efficient and effective aid for evaluation, redesign and new design; that the form and content of the pattern collections is generally seen as useful; and that designers consider patterns to be a personal design language. It is noteworthy that both groups were equally strongly positive about using the different design aids in future projects.

4 Conclusions and Future Work

This paper has presented some empirical evidence that designers consider patterns to be useful for interaction design. Analysis of the post-test qualitative data and the project diaries will provide additional information about the attitudes and design rationales of the two groups, in order to better understand the interaction design process. Future work using heuristics to compare the quality of the designs produced using patterns and guidelines will provide an objective assessment of the usefulness of patterns in the interaction design process.

References

1. Griffiths, R.N. and Pemberton, L: Don't Write Guidelines Write Patterns! (2000) [cited 30 March 2005]; Available from: http://www.it.bton.ac.uk/staff/lp22/guidelinesdraft.html
2. Tidwell, J.: Common Ground: A Pattern Language for Human-Computer Interface Design. (1998) [cited 30 March 2005]; Available from: http://www.mit.edu/~jtidwell/common_ground.html
3. Dearden, A., Finlay, J., Allgar, E. and McManus, B.: Using Pattern Languages in Participatory Design. In Binder, T., Gregory, J. & Wagner, I (eds.): PDC 2002, Proceedings of the Participatory Design Conference. CPSR, Palo Alto, CA., (2002). 104 - 113
4. Van Welie, M. and van de Veer, G.C.: Pattern Languages in Interaction Design: Structure and Organisation. In IFIP INTERACT '03. 2003. Zurich, Switzerland: IOS Press.
5. Wesson, J.L. and Cowley, N.L.O.: Designing with Patterns: Possibilities and Pitfalls. in IFIP INTERACT'03 Workshop on Software & Usability Cross-Pollination: The Role of Usability Patterns. (2003). Zurich, Switzerland.
6. Kok, D. and Wesson, J.L.: Designing Transaction Processing Systems: A Patterns Approach. In South African Institute of Computer Scientists & Information Technologists Conference (SAICSIT) 2002. (2002). Port Elizabeth, South Africa.
7. Van Welie, M. and Trætteberg, H.: The Amsterdam Collection of Patterns in User Interface Design. (2001) [cited 30 March 2005]; Available from: http://www.cs.vu.nl/~martijn/patterns/PLoP2k-Welie.pdf
8. Van Duyne, D.K., Landay, J.A. and Hong, J.I.: The Design of Sites: Patterns, Principles, and Processes for Crafting a Customer-Centered Web Experience. Addison-Wesley, Pearson Education, Boston (2003)
9. Barnard, L.: An Investigation into Usability Issues for E-Commerce in South Africa. PhD thesis, University of Port Elizabeth (2004)
10. Nielsen, J., Molich, R., Snyder, C. and Farrell, S.: E-Commerce User Experience: High-level Strategy. Nielsen Norman Group (2001).

Testing New Alarms for Medical Electrical Equipment

Alexandra Wee and Penelope Sanderson

School of Information Technology and Electrical Engineering,
The University of Queensland,
St Lucia, Queensland, Australia 4072
{alexwee, psanderson}@itee.uq.edu.au

Abstract. This paper reports the first of several tests of new auditory alarms originally proposed by Block et al. [1] and formalized in IEC 60601-1-8 for use in medical electrical equipment. We test whether participants who are supplied with the IEC-recommended mnemonics while learning label-alarm associations can more accurately identify the alarms after short periods of learning. Results for 18 participants strongly indicate that there is a mutual confusability between certain alarm pairs in both learning conditions, but that mnemonics may strengthen rather than diminish certain key confusions.

1 Introduction

It has been a concern for many years that alarms in the Intensive Care Unit—and in other critical care areas in the hospital, such as the operating room—are too numerous and are often inappropriate and confusing [2]. It is reported that even in low stress conditions humans do not readily learn and retain more than eight sounds [3].

Block et al. [1] have proposed new alarm sounds that comply with existing standards from the International Organization for Standardization (ISO), European Committee for Standardization (CEN) and the American Society for Testing and Materials (ASTM). To help distinguish the alarm sounds, each alarm sound has been given a melody and assigned a mnemonic, which is a small phrase that can be "sung" to the alarm melody and that might suggest the nature of the device. Each alarm conforms to the same rhythmic pattern, as defined by stringent existing equipment standards, and varies only in its melodic pattern. The alarm sounds also have to be identifiable within the first few notes, and high and medium priority alarms must be distinguishable.

To date, there appears to be no indication that the alarms as proposed in these standards have been formally tested for discernability and memorability. This would seem to be a considerable oversight given that the proposed alarms are part of an international standard for a safety critical domain. In our study we aim to provide this information. In our study two key issues were investigated: (1) whether the varying melody is sufficient for users to readily discern the differences between one alarm and another and (2) whether the mnemonics suggested in the IEC 60601-1-8 standard help learning.

M.F. Costabile and F. Paternò (Eds.): INTERACT 2005, LNCS 3585, pp. 1146–1149, 2005.

2 Method

Participants. Participants were 18 first year undergraduate students from The University of Queensland, recruited through the School of Psychology research sign-up system. Although no formal hearing tests were administered, participants were asked prior to the experiment whether they had any known hearing problems.

Apparatus and Stimuli. Based on criteria outlined in the recently published IEC standard for medical equipment (IEC 60601-1-8) 16 auditory warnings were created using Csound. Sounds were processed on a Pentium® 4 1.9 GHz PC compatible with Soundblaster live 5.1 digital soundcard. The sounds were presented via Harmon/Kardon HK695 speakers at a mean amplitude of 60dB SPL(A), located about one meter from the participant. Alarm labels and mnemonics were displayed on a 19 inch touch screen monitor, which also recorded the participants' responses.

Procedure. The experiment required the participant to learn the 16 different alarm sounds (8 medium priority and 8 high priority) proposed by Block et al (2000) for auditory alarms in anesthesia machines. Learning proceeded in a series of learning phase-test phase cycles until the participant satisfied the learning criterion of achieving two consecutive sets of correct tests or until 35 minutes had passed— whichever came first.

In the learning phase the experimenter introduced the sound and meaning of each alarm. A screen was then presented that displayed the alarm labels categorized by priority. Participants learned the alarms by touching the label of the alarm they wished to hear. They were allowed to listen to each alarm only once and could choose the order in which they listened to the alarms. (Participants who had already mastered certain alarm sounds could elect not to hear them again during a subsequent learning session.) Half the participants were randomly assigned to a group who learned with the help of mnemonics given in [1] [4] whereas the other half did not use mnemonics.

The test phase required the participant to identify alarms played in a random order. For each alarm, the participant indicated which label, out of a list of 16 provided, was the correct one. If the learning criterion was not reaching during the test phase, the participant returned to the learning phase screen to review any alarms they were unsure about before attempting another testing phase.

3 Results

Learnability. Mean accuracy across the different alarms was poor. The exception was the very simple general alarm, which had a mean accuracy across all conditions of 91%. Participants' accuracy at identifying alarms was tested in a mixed-design ANOVA with factors of learning condition (mnemonic vs. no mnemonic) and alarm type (excluding the general alarm due to its near-perfect recognisability). There was a significant effect of alarm type, $F(6, 96) = 3.025$, $p = .009$. Some alarms were learned more easily; accuracy and RT were better for them compared with other alarms. A significant interaction of alarm type and learning condition was also found, $F(6, 96) = 2.843$, $p = .014$. The basis of this interaction still needs to be explored. Reaction time results are consistent with accuracy and do not show any speed-accuracy tradeoffs.

In the 35-minute learning period, only 9 out of 18 participants were able to complete at least one test with 100% accuracy, and only 7 of those 9 could fulfill the requirement of achieving 100% in two successive trials. Some participants found the alarm sounds very easy to learn whereas others were having difficulty in learning them, even showing very little signs of improvement over trials (see Figure 1).

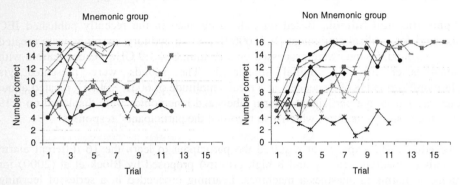

Fig. 1. Successive test results for participants showing test trial and number correct in each test trial. Each line represents a different participant.

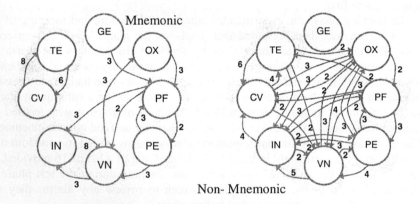

Fig. 2. Pattern of confusions between alarms. See text for description.

Confusions and mnemonics. We examined each participant's confusions between different alarms. We noted the strongest confusion and second strongest (in cases where confusions between first and second were close) for each participant. Figure 2 shows the eight alarms. Links indicate that the alarm at the origin of the arrow is confused for the alarm at the end of the arrow. Numbers on the links indicate the number of participants for whom the confusion was the strongest or near-strongest confusion. Links were included only when two or more participants were confused. Participants in the mnemonic condition appear to be confused about a relatively small number of parameters (principally CV/TE and IN/VN) but these confusions are shared by many participants. In contrast, participants in the non-mnemonic condition have a broader and more idiosyncratic pattern of confusions.

4 Discussion

To date, our results suggest that if no mnemonic is provided when participants are learning the IEC 60601-1-8 alarms, then they develop their own strategies. This leads to a wider variety of confusions between alarms across the group. For the mnemonic group, the confusion between some pairs of alarms seems more consistent. The mnemonics seem to have an effect of restricting confusions to a smaller number, but these confusions are then strong. This could result in more people stumbling over those few pairs and never learning the full set. Finally, some pairs of alarms were more easily confused with each other whether or not mnemonics were used. Overall, these results are unexpected. In ongoing work, 22 additional participants are being tested to increase statistical power. Long-term retention and alarm discrimination while performing dual tasks are being assessed in follow-up test sessions.

The results also raise the issue of how much training is required for the majority of participants to attain 100% learning. In the present results three distinct groups appear to be forming: (1) participants who quickly learn all alarms, (2) participants who take a while to learn and (3) participants who do not seem to learn at all. It is important to focus on the latter two groups to discover the most effective ways in which we can help them learn the alarms faster and more accurately.

If they are robust, these results indicate there may be problems when healthcare providers use equipment with the new alarm sounds. In a followup study we plan to test the IEC 60601-1-8 alarm sounds with healthcare professionals over more prolonged periods of exposure to see whether confusions endure or lessen with time.

Acknowledgements

We thank Philippe Lacherez for preparing the alarm stimuli and for his input on the project. Thanks also to members of the Cognitive Engineering Research Group at The University of Queensland for their input on the manuscript.

References

1. Block, F. E., Rouse, J. D., Hakala, M., & Thompson, C. L. (2000). A proposed new set of alarm sounds which satisfy standards and rationale to encode source information. *Journal of Clinical Monitoring, 16*, 541-546.
2. Meredith C. & Edworthy J. (1995) Are there too many alarms in the intensive care unit? An overview of the problems. *Journal of Advanced Nursing* 21, 15-20.
3. Patterson R.D. & Milroy R. (1980) *Auditory Warnings on Civil Aircraft: The learning and Retention of Warnings.* CAA paper 7D/S/0142. Civil Aviation Authority, London.
4. IEC 60601-1-8 (2003-08-14). *Medical electrical equipment - Part 1-8.* Geneva, Switzerland: International Electrotechnical Commission.

Relevance of Prior Experience in MHP Based Interactive TV Services

Regina Bernhaupt, Bernd Ploderer, and Manfred Tscheligi

ICT&S Center, University of Salzburg
{regina.bernhaupt, bernd.ploderer, manfred.tschelgi}@sbg.ac.at

Abstract. Despite its rising success, interactive TV (iTV) has found very little attention in the field of HCI. Therefore, the aim of this paper is to investigate the usability of iTV services. It presents the results of a usability test and discusses the implications for further developments. The results show, that prior knowledge of Internet and mobile phones supports the usability of iTV services regarding navigation and text input, while the lack of it leads to great difficulties. Difficult tasks, such as writing a text message, had a success rate of only 20%, while guided tours proofed to be more usable with a success rate of 70%.

1 Introduction

Interactive television (iTV) has taken off with extensive field tests in the US in the late 1970ies and is now slowly paving its way to TV households all over the world with the UK as precursor [4]. The HCI community started to pay attention to the design of user interfaces for iTV in the mid-1990ies [5, 7, 10] but since then the topic has received relatively sparse attention. Evaluations took place largely in industrial environments and led to the development of guidelines for iTV services [1, 9], but few publications originate from research in scientific environments. Therefore, we are aiming at filling parts of this gap by reporting usability issues on iTV discovered in a usability test within the scope of a 4 months field test.

2 Field Test

The iTV Salzburg field test ran from December 2004 to March 2005 aiming at the investigation of the technical feasibility of interactive TV with DVB-C and the acceptance of interactive services based on the MHP standard. 80 households were equipped with a galaxis set-top box and a cable modem (back channel). They were provided with a bundle of services containing news, real video on demand, e-mail and SMS communication, games and online shopping (ticket reservation and food ordering). The design process was partly based on a user-centered approach [3] doing heuristic evaluation based on guidelines [1, 9] and paper prototyping. Online questionnaires, interviews and event logging of all households accompanied the field test phase. The results from usage statistics of 80 households are expected in May 2005. While the latter mentioned activities partially dealt with the issue of acceptance,

M.F. Costabile and F. Paternò (Eds.): INTERACT 2005, LNCS 3585, pp. 1150–1153, 2005.
© IFIP International Federation for Information Processing 2005

we conducted a usability test to further explore the usability of the MHP-services. This article focuses on the results of the usability test carried out in February 2005 using the same iTV set up as in the households.

3   Usability Test

The usability test focused on the investigation of several factors influencing user-acceptance. We explored the following relationships:

- [ ] task completion rate in text input tasks and prior experience with similar text input on other media
- [ ] task completion rate of services with strict (guided) navigation and prior media experience
- [ ] relation of long waiting times and real system failures

Participants

11 persons agreed to participate on a voluntary basis. Due to technical problems one participant had to be excluded from the analysis as only a small part of the test could be conducted. Thus six male and four female users took part (age M= 30,6 SD=4,6), which is an appropriate sample size for the purpose of usability testing for our target group of young, technophile users [8]. The participants all owned a cell phone and a TV. To be able to determine the influence of prior knowledge we surveyed the users' media use. Users watch TV M=1,6 hours per day (SD=1,2), send M= 5,5 SMS per week (SD=7,8) and have a high usage rate of computers with M=37 hours per week (SD = 40) including 11 hours per week mean usage of the Internet (SD = 8,3).

Table 1. Tasks of the usability test

#	Task	Service
1	Select the latest news item on the iTV Portal	iTV Portal
2	Read through the news article about the new BMW Formula One car and find out its horsepower	News Service
3	Play the weather forecast video clip of yesterday's news program	Video on Demand
4	Login to the TV-mail service and read the latest mail message	TV-Mail Service
5	Send a text message to your own mobile phone	SMS
6	Order two tickets for the André Rieu concert	Ticket Service

Procedure and Material
All participants were tested individually. We tried to overcome the reported shortcomings of artificial iTV test settings [8] by equipping the usability lab with comfortable furniture to give the impression of a domestic lounge. Sweets, drinks and magazines were placed on a coffee table. A loose conversation by participant and instructor should lead to a relaxing atmosphere.

The test began with a questionnaire, followed by a short introduction to iTV and the request to the participants to give us feedback whenever they thought they would decide to stop the task. We guided the participants to the so called iTV Portal (first and main page bundling all iTV services) and carried out the actual usability test. The usability test consisted of 6 tasks, ordered by difficulty (see table 1). After filling out a post-test questionnaire, the participants were asked to wait approximately 10 minutes for a first data capture (this was the official reason for the break). During this time they had the free choice either using iTV or reading the newspaper in front of them. After this free exploration phase the participants could tell us their impressions on iTV.

The setting used two cameras for monitoring the participants: first in full perspective, second with a focus on the remote control. All key strokes and events of the interactive service were additionally monitored by the iTV System (database-logging).

4 Results

The estimated difficulty of tasks was reflected by the task completion rates. Overall only 55% of the tasks were completed successfully without the help of the instructor. 90% of the participants could successfully read the news entries (task 2), but only 50% handled watching a video clip.

Even more problematic were the e-mail and SMS services: only two from ten participants succeeded in reading an e-mail. Most of them struggled when being asked to input their user ID and user code. The text input was designed according to a multi-tap used on cell-phones. The two successful users had the highest SMS usage rates on cell phones (about 20 per week). Here higher usage of SMS services on cell phones helped the user to successful accomplish the task. The same two users were successful in writing a text message. The task completion rate in text input tasks is thus closely related to prior experience with similar text input on other media (like cell phones).

Computer usage seems to support a strict (guided) navigation. Buying tickets in a guided sequence of screens was successfully accomplished by seven participants. The successful users did have a mean computer usage time of 39,3 hours per week, not successful users had 33,0 hours mean computer usage per week.

The mean perceived system failure per participant was 1.34 times, which is identical with the mean real system failures gained in the log file analysis. Thus long waiting times (more than 30 seconds) do not lead to misinterpretations of system state. From a technical point of view fast loading times and quick feedback in MHP-services is very difficult to achieve. Technical induced waiting times for MHP-services are thus not related to the system stability perceived by the user.

During the waiting time at the end of the test half of the participants decided to use and further explore iTV, while the other half preferred reading a newspaper or a magazine.

5 Discussion and Conclusions

The usability test indicates that the successful accomplishment of tasks seems to be partly influenced by prior experience. In the case of sending short messages participants with high SMS usage (about 20 SMS/week) were successful; all others failed to accomplish the SMS task. When designing text input, the prior experience of users from other media use must be taken into account. Therefore the design of services building on text input should clearly focus on a specific target group. Generally, particular services for specific target groups and contexts seem to be a seminal direction for iTV [11]. For services addressing a broader audience we encourage the use and development of alternative and more easy to use text input methods than multi-tap, e.g. TNT [6],when no keyboard is available.

Most of the participants stated, that they would not pay for any of the services except Internet access and personalized services and news. Furthermore 50 % of the users prefer an ordinary newspaper instead of reading news with interactive services. Thus a further goal for the future must be to develop new kinds of services. Such services should not aim at the remediation [2] of the Internet on TV. Instead they should make use of and contribute to the specific strengths of the medium TV.

The analysis of the usage statistics will be used to further validate the findings of the usability test and we will take all three discussed issues as an agenda for further research in a follow-up project. Firstly we will investigate the design of alternative interaction techniques, secondly we will investigate specific user groups in ethnographic studies and finally we aim at the development and evaluation of new interactive services.

Acknowledgements

The iTV Salzburg Field trial was supported by the EFRE project of the country of Salzburg and the European Union. We would like to thank all our partners within this project for their support and cooperation.

References

1. BBCi: Interactive Television Style Guide. (2002) available on http://www.bbc.co.uk/commissioning/newmedia/itv.shtml
2. Bolter, J. D. and Grusin, R.: Remediation: Understanding New Media. MIT Press, Cambridge, MA (2001)
3. Eronen, L.: User Centered Research for Interactive Television. Proceedings of the 1st European Conference on Interactive Television. Brighton (2003) 5–12
4. Gawlinski, M.: Interactive Television Production. Focal Press, Oxford (2003)
5. Herigstad, D. and Wichansky, A.: Designing user interfaces for television. ACM CHI 98 conference summary on Human factors in computing systems, Los Angeles (1998) 165-166
6. Ingmarsson, M., Dinka, D. and Zhai, S.: TNT: a numeric keypad based text input method. Proceedings of ACM CHI: Conference on Human Factors, Vienna (2004) 639–646
7. McDonald, S.: Learning from diversity: interactive TV, computers, and the frontier of the cognitive sciences. ACM CHI: Conf. companion on Human factors in comp. systems, Denver (1995) 197
8. Pemberton L. and Griffiths, R. N.: Usability Evaluation Techniques for Interactive Television. HCI International conference, Crete (2003)
9. Serco Usability Services: Interactive TV And Electronic Programme Guides: Usability Guidelines. Report (2001) available on http://usability.serco.com/research/research.htm
10. Teasley, B., Lund, A. and Bennett, R.: Interactive television: a new challenge for HCI. ACM CHI: Conf. companion on Human factors in comp. systems, Vancouver (1996) 356
11. Van Dijk, J., De Vos,: L. Searching for the Holy Grail: Images of interactive television. New Media & Society (2001) Vol 3(4), 443-465

Author Index

Adcock, John   781
Agrawala, Maneesh   69
Ahtinen, Aino   227
Aliakseyeu, Dzmitry   1002
Alpert, Sherman R.   117
Als, Benedikte S.   443
Amin, Alia K.   962
Andersen, Tue Haste   144
Aoki, Terumasa   974
Ardito, Carmelo   942
Aris, Aleks   835
Auer, Sonja   1129
Aula, Anne   946, 954, 1058
Avouris, Nikolaos   1075
Axup, Jeff   899

Baauw, Ester   457
Badi, Rajiv   130
Bae, Soonil   130
Bailey, Brian P.   337, 699
Ball, Robert   350
Bandelloni, Renata   1071
Banerjee, Satanjeev   643
Barendregt, Wolmet   457
Barker, Trevor   1026
Bass, Len   823
Bastide, Rémi   170
Beirekdar, Abdo   281
Bekker, Mathilde M.   457
Bernhaupt, Regina   1150
Berti, Silvia   1067, 1071
Betiol, Adriana Holtz   470
Beymer, David   741, 767
Bhagwan, Varun   938
Bicharra Garcia, Ana Cristina   1138
Bidwell, Nicola J.   899
Biehl, Jacob T.   699
Bonanni, Leonardo   1022
Boutin, François   847
Brewster, Stephen   6, 253
Britton, Carol   1026
Brna, Paul   295
Brodie, Carolyn   671
Brzozowski, Mike   990
Buono, Paolo   942

Burigat, Stefano   213
Buxton, William   1

Campos, Pedro   158
Cappos, Justin   986
Carbonell, Noëlle   1054
Carpendale, Sheelagh   615
Cassens, Jörg   1087
Castellani, Stefania   377
Catarci, Tiziana   1100
Cena, Federica   1030
Cesta, Amedeo   657
Cha, Jongeun   1042, 1046
Chen, Tiffany   1079
Chittaro, Luca   213, 482, 873, 1014
Chiu, Patrick   1010
Ciravegna, Fabio   309
Cockton, Gilbert   1134
Cohen, Sharon   1079
Connelly, Kay H.   267, 588
Conti, Giuseppe   94
Cooper, Matthew   781
Cortellessa, Gabriella   657
Costabile, Maria Francesca   942
Cowley, N.L.O.   1142
Coyette, Adrien   550
Crowder, Grace   950
Cutrell, Edward   565

Danis, Catalina   522
Darroch, Iain   253
de Abreu Cybis, Walter   470
De Amicis, Raffaele   94
De Angeli, Antonella   405
De Marco, Luca   213, 482
de Ruyter, Boris   510
Dieberger, Andreas   938
Doherty, Gavin   1038
Dressler, Armin   364
Drizd, Terence   861

Eaton, Cyntrica   861
Eom, Young-Ik   1116
Esenther, Alan   809, 1124
Everitt, Katherine   998, 1124

Feng, Jinjuan   671
Firth, Lucy   1104
Ford, Gabrielle   713
Forlines, Clifton   536, 994, 998, 1124
Forsythe, Alexandra   1083
Foster, Sterling   950
Francis, Peter   1104
Frankowski, Dan   886
Freitas, Carla M.D.S.   170
Fröhlich, Bernd   601
Fukuchi, Kentaro   1050
Funk, Mathias   1120

Gabrielli, Silvia   1100
Gatla, Vijay Kumar   1014
Gena, Cristina   1030
Girgensohn, Andreas   781
Giuliani, Vittoria   657
Goodman, Joy   253
Graham, M. Ian   978
Grasso, Antonietta   377
Gray, Phil   253
Grayson, Andrew   753
Grolaux, Donatien   198
Gruhl, Daniel   938
Gweon, Gahgene   431, 1112

Hagita, Norihiro   685
Hakala, Tero   227
Häkkilä, Jonna   927
Han, JungHyun   1116
Han, Li   94
Harada, Susumu   240
Harbich, Stefanie   1129
Harrison, Michael D.   184
Hartman, Gregory S.   823
Hascoët, Mountaz   847
Herbert, John   1034
Higashino, Suguru   1091
Hinrichs, Klaus   1018
Hochstrate, Jan   601
Hockenberry, Matthew   1079
Hornecker, Eva   30
Horton, Matthew   1096
Hsieh, Haowei   130
Hsieh, Tony   240
Huckauf, Anke   601
Hu, Jiang   106, 990
Hvannberg, Ebba T.   1134
Hyun, Chungmin   1116

Ieronutti, Lucio   873
Igarashi, Takeo   970
Iivari, Netta   418
Imamiya, Atsumi   18
Inkpen, Kori M.   80
Inoue, Hiroshi   57
Ishiguro, Hiroshi   685
Ishihara, Masami   18

Jacko, Julie A.   1108
Jacucci, Giulio   43
Jaimes, Alejandro   1062
Jank, Wolfgang   835
Jensen, Janne J.   443
Jose, Joemon M.   958

Kalra, Ankur   966
Kanda, Takayuki   685
Kang, Ingu   1116
Karahalios, Karrie   966, 978
Karat, Clare-Marie   671
Karat, John   117, 671
Keita, Marc   281
Kersten, Bram   962
Khalil, Ashraf   588
Kieffer, Suzanne   1054
Kim, Jong-phil   1046
Kim, Seungjun   1046
King, Alison   6
Kjeldskov, Jesper   496
Klein, David   579
Kobourov, Stephen G.   986
Koivunen, Kimmo   946
Korhonen, Hannu   227
Korpipää, Panu   927
Kotzé, Paula   713
Kowalik, Uwe   974
Krüger, Hans-Peter   364
Kulyk, Olga A.   962
Kunert, André   601
Kuwabara, Kazuhiro   1120
Kwok, Misa Grace   18

Lanfranchi, Vitaveska   309
Laqua, Sven   295
Law, Effie L.-C.   1134
Lee, Alison   522
Lee, Beom-Chan   1042, 1046
Lee, Chia-Hsun   1022
Lee, Junhun   1042
Lehikoinen, Juha   227

Leonard, V. Kathlene   1108
Lertsithichai, Surapong   1010
Leshed, Gilly   579
Li, Qing   809
Lilley, Mariana   1026
Liu Jianyi   1062
Loer, Karsten   184
Ludford, Pamela   886
Lyons, Michael J.   1120

Maciel, Cristiano   1138
Majaranta, Päivi   946, 1058
Mandryk, Regan L.   80
Mannonen, Petri   727
Mariage, Céline   281
Markopoulos, Panos   510, 962, 1006
Marshall, Catherine C.   130
Mazzone, Emanuela   1096
McCarthy, John   914
McDougall, Siné   1083
Meintanis, Konstantinos   130
Mellor, David   1104
Miles, Mark   986
Minocha, Shailey   753
Mirabella, Valeria   1100
Miyahara, Kosuke   57
Miyaoku, Kento   1091
Modeo, Sonia   1030
Moloney, Kevin P.   1108
Monk, Andrew   982
Moore, J. Michael   130

Nakakoji, Kumiyo   795
Nass, Clifford   106
Navarre, David   170
Nedel, Luciana P.   170
Ngai, Jane   431
Nielsen, Christian M.   391
Nishida, Takeshi   970
Nogueira, José Luiz T.   1138
Noirhomme, Monique   281
Nomura, Tatsuya   685
North, Chris   350
Nueckles, Matthias   1112
Nunes, Michael N.   80
Nunes, Nuno J.   158

Omata, Masaki   18
O'Neill, Eamonn   629
O'Neill, Jacki   377

Orton, Peter Z.   741
Oulasvirta, Antti   43
Overgaard, Michael   391
Ozer, Zachary   1079

Paay, Jeni   496
Paepcke, Andreas   240
Palanque, Philippe   170, 1134
Papachristos, Eleftherios   1075
Parker, J. Karen   80
Paternò, Fabio   1067, 1071
Patil, Sameer   117
Pavlou, Kyriacos   986
Pedersen, Michael B.   391
Pelgrim, Elly   962
Pemberton, Steven   4
Petre, Marian   753
Petrelli, Daniela   309
Plaisant, Catherine   835, 861
Ploderer, Bernd   1150
Psik, Thomas   30, 43

Qvarfordt, Pernilla   767

Räihä, Kari-Jouko   946, 1058
Raj, Bhiksha   536
Randolet, Frédéric   281
Rangos, Jenica   431
Ranon, Roberto   873
Rantala, Harri   946
Read, Janet   1096
Ringel Morris, Meredith   1124
Rogers, Yvonne   267
Romero, Natalia A.   1006
Ronkainen, Sami   927
Ropinski, Timo   1018
Rosé, Carolyn Penstein   323, 643, 1112
Rudnicky, Alexander I.   643
Russell, Daniel M.   741, 938, 950
Ryall, Kathy   809, 998, 1124
Ryu, Jeha   1042, 1046

Sainfort, François   1108
Saini, Privender   510
Salovaara, Antti   43, 727
Sanderson, Penelope   1146
Satou, Takashi   1091
Scapin, Dominque   1134
Schmidt-Nielsen, Bent   536

Scholz, Sascha   364
Schyn, Amélie   170
Scopelliti, Massimiliano   657
Selker, Ted   1022, 1079
Seo, Changhoon   1042
Shami, N. Sadat   579
Shen, Chia   994, 998, 1124
Shi, Bin   1108
Shilman, Michael   69
Shiomi, Masahiro   685
Shipman, Frank M.   130
Shipman, Sam   1124
Shmueli, Galit   835
Shneiderman, Ben   835
Siek, Katie A.   267
Siirtola, Harri   954
Simon, Andreas   364
Simonin, Jérôme   1054
Skov, Mikael B.   443
Slaney, Malcolm   950
Song, Kyuman   1010
Sonnet, Henry   615
Sparacino, Flavia   2
Speed, Alexander   601
Springett, Mark   1134
Stage, Jan   391
Stares, Lucy   1083
Stary, Christian   1134
Steinicke, Frank   1018
Stepp, Michael   986
Strothotte, Thomas   615
Su, Ramona E.   337
Sugimoto, Masanori   57
Sutcliffe, Alistair   405

Takashima, Akio   795
Tasaki, Takugo   685
Terveen, Loren   886
Teso, Massimiliano   1100
Thièvre, Jérôme   847
Tolmie, Peter   377
Torrey, Cristen   323
Tscheligi, Manfred   1150
Tselios, Nikolaos   1075
Tsunesada, Yuji   57

Tuomela, Urpo   927
Tzanidou, Ekaterini   753

Upton, Connor   1038
Urban, Jana   958

van Breemen, Albert   510
van Gelder, Joris   1002
van Peer, Irene   1002
Van Roy, Peter   198
Vanderdonckt, Jean   198, 281, 550, 1134
Venkataraman, Subramanian   1014
Vernier, Frédéric   994, 1124
Vidakovic, Brani   1108

Wagner, Ina   43
Wang, Jimmy   962
Wang, QianYing   106, 240
Warr, Andrew   629
Wee, Alexandra   1146
Wesson, J.L.   1142
Whalley, James   982
Wilcox, Lynn   781
Wilson, Andrew D.   565
Winckler, Marco   170
Wind, Jürgen   364
Wittenburg, Kent   536
Wittwer, Joerg   1112
Wixted, Amanda   986
Wolf, Catherine   117
Wolf, Peter   536
Woo, Jong-Sik   1116
Wright, Peter   914
Wu, Mike   994

Yamamoto, Yasuhiro   795
Yanguas, Lisa   950
Yasuda, Hiroshi   974
Ye, Jing-Hua   1034
Yoshida, Yuichi   1091

Zacchi, Anna   130
Zhai, Shumin   767
Zhou, Changqing   886

Lecture Notes in Computer Science

For information about Vols. 1–3603

please contact your bookseller or Springer

Vol. 3728: V. Paliouras, J. Vounckx, D. Verkest (Eds.), Integrated Circuit and System Design. XV, 753 pages. 2005.

Vol. 3718: V.G. Ganzha, E.W. Mayr, E.V. Vorozhtsov (Eds.), Computer Algebra in Scientific Computing. XII, 502 pages. 2005.

Vol. 3714: H. Obbink, K. Pohl (Eds.), Software Product Lines. XIII, 235 pages. 2005.

Vol. 3712: R. Reussner, J. Mayer, J.A. Stafford, S. Overhage, S. Becker, P.J. Schroeder (Eds.), Quality of Software Architectures and Software Quality. XIII, 289 pages. 2005.

Vol. 3710: M. Barni, I. Cox, T. Kalker, II.J. Kim (Eds.), Digital Watermarking. XII, 485 pages. 2005.

Vol. 3703: F. Fages, S. Soliman (Eds.), Principles and Practice of Semantic Web Reasoning. VIII, 163 pages. 2005.

Vol. 3702: B. Beckert (Ed.), Automated Reasoning with Analytic Tableaux and Related Methods. XIII, 343 pages. 2005. (Subseries LNAI).

Vol. 3698: U. Furbach (Ed.), KI 2005: Advances in Artificial Intelligence. XIII, 409 pages. 2005. (Subseries LNAI).

Vol. 3697: W. Duch, J. Kacprzyk, E. Oja, S. Zadrożny (Eds.), Artificial Neural Networks: Formal Models and Their Applications - ICANN 2005, Part II. XXXII, 1045 pages. 2005.

Vol. 3696: W. Duch, J. Kacprzyk, E. Oja, S. Zadrożny (Eds.), Artificial Neural Networks: Biological Inspirations - ICANN 2005, Part I. XXXI, 703 pages. 2005.

Vol. 3693: A.G. Cohn, D.M. Mark (Eds.), Spatial Information Theory. XII, 493 pages. 2005.

Vol. 3691: A. Gagalowicz, W. Philips (Eds.), Computer Analysis of Images and Patterns. XIX, 865 pages. 2005.

Vol. 3690: M. Pĕchouček, P. Petta, L.Z. Varga (Eds.), Multi-Agent Systems and Applications IV. XVII, 667 pages. 2005. (Subseries LNAI).

Vol. 3687: S. Singh, M. Singh, C. Apte, P. Perner (Eds.), Pattern Recognition and Image Analysis, Part II. XXV, 809 pages. 2005.

Vol. 3686: S. Singh, M. Singh, C. Apte, P. Perner (Eds.), Pattern Recognition and Data Mining, Part I. XXVI, 689 pages. 2005.

Vol. 3684: R. Khosla, R.J. Howlett, L.C. Jain (Eds.), Knowledge-Based Intelligent Information and Engineering Systems, Part IV. LXXIX, 933 pages. 2005. (Subseries LNAI).

Vol. 3683: R. Khosla, R.J. Howlett, L.C. Jain (Eds.), Knowledge-Based Intelligent Information and Engineering Systems, Part III. LXXX, 1397 pages. 2005. (Subseries LNAI).

Vol. 3682: R. Khosla, R.J. Howlett, L.C. Jain (Eds.), Knowledge-Based Intelligent Information and Engineering Systems, Part II. LXXIX, 1371 pages. 2005. (Subseries LNAI).

Vol. 3681: R. Khosla, R.J. Howlett, L.C. Jain (Eds.), Knowledge-Based Intelligent Information and Engineering Systems, Part I. LXXX, 1319 pages. 2005. (Subseries LNAI).

Vol. 3679: S.d.C. di Vimercati, P. Syverson, D. Gollmann (Eds.), Computer Security – ESORICS 2005. XI, 509 pages. 2005.

Vol. 3678: A. McLysaght, D.H. Huson (Eds.), Comparative Genomics. VIII, 167 pages. 2005. (Subseries LNBI).

Vol. 3677: J. Dittmann, S. Katzenbeisser, A. Uhl (Eds.), Communications and Multimedia Security. XIII, 360 pages. 2005.

Vol. 3675: Y. Luo (Ed.), Cooperative Design, Visualization, and Engineering. XI, 264 pages. 2005.

Vol. 3674: W. Jonker, M. Petković (Eds.), Secure Data Management. X, 241 pages. 2005.

Vol. 3672: C. Hankin, I. Siveroni (Eds.), Static Analysis. X, 369 pages. 2005.

Vol. 3671: S. Bressan, S. Ceri, E. Hunt, Z.G. Ives, Z. Bellahsène, M. Rys, R. Unland (Eds.), Database and XML Technologies. X, 239 pages. 2005.

Vol. 3670: M. Bravetti, L. Kloul, G. Zavattaro (Eds.), Formal Techniques for Computer Systems and Business Processes. XIII, 349 pages. 2005.

Vol. 3666: B.D. Martino, D. Kranzlmüller, J. Dongarra (Eds.), Recent Advances in Parallel Virtual Machine and Message Passing Interface. XVII, 546 pages. 2005.

Vol. 3665: K. S. Candan, A. Celentano (Eds.), Advances in Multimedia Information Systems. X, 221 pages. 2005.

Vol. 3664: C. Türker, M. Agosti, H.-J. Schek (Eds.), Peer-to-Peer, Grid, and Service-Orientation in Digital Library Architectures. X, 261 pages. 2005.

Vol. 3663: W.G. Kropatsch, R. Sablatnig, A. Hanbury (Eds.), Pattern Recognition. XIV, 512 pages. 2005.

Vol. 3662: C. Baral, G. Greco, N. Leone, G. Terracina (Eds.), Logic Programming and Nonmonotonic Reasoning. XIII, 454 pages. 2005. (Subseries LNAI).

Vol. 3661: T. Panayiotopoulos, J. Gratch, R. Aylett, D. Ballin, P. Olivier, T. Rist (Eds.), Intelligent Virtual Agents. XIII, 506 pages. 2005. (Subseries LNAI).

Vol. 3660: M. Beigl, S. Intille, J. Rekimoto, H. Tokuda (Eds.), UbiComp 2005: Ubiquitous Computing. XVII, 394 pages. 2005.

Vol. 3659: J.R. Rao, B. Sunar (Eds.), Cryptographic Hardware and Embedded Systems – CHES 2005. XIV, 458 pages. 2005.

Vol. 3658: V. Matoušek, P. Mautner, T. Pavelka (Eds.), Text, Speech and Dialogue. XV, 460 pages. 2005. (Subseries LNAI).

Vol. 3655: A. Aldini, R. Gorrieri, F. Martinelli (Eds.), Foundations of Security Analysis and Design III. VII, 273 pages. 2005.

Vol. 3654: S. Jajodia, D. Wijesekera (Eds.), Data and Applications Security XIX. X, 353 pages. 2005.

Vol. 3653: M. Abadi, L. de Alfaro (Eds.), CONCUR 2005 – Concurrency Theory. XIV, 578 pages. 2005.

Vol. 3652: A. Rauber, S. Christodoulakis, A M. Tjoa (Eds.), Research and Advanced Technology for Digital Libraries. XVIII, 545 pages. 2005.

Vol. 3649: W.M.P. van der Aalst, B. Benatallah, F. Casati, F. Curbera (Eds.), Business Process Management. XII, 472 pages. 2005.

Vol. 3648: J.C. Cunha, P.D. Medeiros (Eds.), Euro-Par 2005 Parallel Processing. XXXVI, 1299 pages. 2005.

Vol. 3646: A. F. Famili, J.N. Kok, J.M. Peña, A. Siebes, A. Feelders (Eds.), Advances in Intelligent Data Analysis VI. XIV, 522 pages. 2005.

Vol. 3645: D.-S. Huang, X.-P. Zhang, G.-B. Huang (Eds.), Advances in Intelligent Computing, Part II. XIII, 1010 pages. 2005.

Vol. 3644: D.-S. Huang, X.-P. Zhang, G.-B. Huang (Eds.), Advances in Intelligent Computing, Part I. XXVII, 1101 pages. 2005.

Vol. 3642: D. Ślezak, J. Yao, J.F. Peters, W. Ziarko, X. Hu (Eds.), Rough Sets, Fuzzy Sets, Data Mining, and Granular Computing, Part II. XXIII, 738 pages. 2005. (Subseries LNAI).

Vol. 3641: D. Ślezak, G. Wang, M. Szczuka, I. Düntsch, Y. Yao (Eds.), Rough Sets, Fuzzy Sets, Data Mining, and Granular Computing, Part I. XXIV, 742 pages. 2005. (Subseries LNAI).

Vol. 3639: P. Godefroid (Ed.), Model Checking Software. XI, 289 pages. 2005.

Vol. 3638: A. Butz, B. Fisher, A. Krüger, P. Olivier (Eds.), Smart Graphics. XI, 269 pages. 2005.

Vol. 3637: J. M. Moreno, J. Madrenas, J. Cosp (Eds.), Evolvable Systems: From Biology to Hardware. XI, 227 pages. 2005.

Vol. 3636: M.J. Blesa, C. Blum, A. Roli, M. Sampels (Eds.), Hybrid Metaheuristics. XII, 155 pages. 2005.

Vol. 3634: L. Ong (Ed.), Computer Science Logic. XI, 567 pages. 2005.

Vol. 3633: C. Bauzer Medeiros, M. Egenhofer, E. Bertino (Eds.), Advances in Spatial and Temporal Databases. XIII, 433 pages. 2005.

Vol. 3632: R. Nieuwenhuis (Ed.), Automated Deduction – CADE-20. XIII, 459 pages. 2005. (Subseries LNAI).

Vol. 3631: J. Eder, H.-M. Haav, A. Kalja, J. Penjam (Eds.), Advances in Databases and Information Systems. XIII, 393 pages. 2005.

Vol. 3630: M.S. Capcarrere, A.A. Freitas, P.J. Bentley, C.G. Johnson, J. Timmis (Eds.), Advances in Artificial Life. XIX, 949 pages. 2005. (Subseries LNAI).

Vol. 3629: J.L. Fiadeiro, N. Harman, M. Roggenbach, J. Rutten (Eds.), Algebra and Coalgebra in Computer Science. XI, 457 pages. 2005.

Vol. 3628: T. Gschwind, U. Aßmann, O. Nierstrasz (Eds.), Software Composition. X, 199 pages. 2005.

Vol. 3627: C. Jacob, M.L. Pilat, P.J. Bentley, J. Timmis (Eds.), Artificial Immune Systems. XII, 500 pages. 2005.

Vol. 3626: B. Ganter, G. Stumme, R. Wille (Eds.), Formal Concept Analysis. X, 349 pages. 2005. (Subseries LNAI).

Vol. 3625: S. Kramer, B. Pfahringer (Eds.), Inductive Logic Programming. XIII, 427 pages. 2005. (Subseries LNAI).

Vol. 3624: C. Chekuri, K. Jansen, J.D.P. Rolim, L. Trevisan (Eds.), Approximation, Randomization and Combinatorial Optimization. XI, 495 pages. 2005.

Vol. 3623: M. Liśkiewicz, R. Reischuk (Eds.), Fundamentals of Computation Theory. XV, 576 pages. 2005.

Vol. 3622: V. Vene, T. Uustalu (Eds.), Advanced Functional Programming. IX, 359 pages. 2005.

Vol. 3621: V. Shoup (Ed.), Advances in Cryptology – CRYPTO 2005. XI, 568 pages. 2005.

Vol. 3620: H. Muñoz-Avila, F. Ricci (Eds.), Case-Based Reasoning Research and Development. XV, 654 pages. 2005. (Subseries LNAI).

Vol. 3619: X. Lu, W. Zhao (Eds.), Networking and Mobile Computing. XXIV, 1299 pages. 2005.

Vol. 3618: J. Jedrzejowicz, A. Szepietowski (Eds.), Mathematical Foundations of Computer Science 2005. XVI, 814 pages. 2005.

Vol. 3617: F. Roli, S. Vitulano (Eds.), Image Analysis and Processing – ICIAP 2005. XXIV, 1219 pages. 2005.

Vol. 3615: B. Ludäscher, L. Raschid (Eds.), Data Integration in the Life Sciences. XII, 344 pages. 2005. (Subseries LNBI).

Vol. 3614: L. Wang, Y. Jin (Eds.), Fuzzy Systems and Knowledge Discovery, Part II. XLI, 1314 pages. 2005. (Subseries LNAI).

Vol. 3613: L. Wang, Y. Jin (Eds.), Fuzzy Systems and Knowledge Discovery, Part I. XLI, 1334 pages. 2005. (Subseries LNAI).

Vol. 3612: L. Wang, K. Chen, Y. S. Ong (Eds.), Advances in Natural Computation, Part III. LXI, 1326 pages. 2005.

Vol. 3611: L. Wang, K. Chen, Y. S. Ong (Eds.), Advances in Natural Computation, Part II. LXI, 1292 pages. 2005.

Vol. 3610: L. Wang, K. Chen, Y. S. Ong (Eds.), Advances in Natural Computation, Part I. LXI, 1302 pages. 2005.

Vol. 3608: F. Dehne, A. López-Ortiz, J.-R. Sack (Eds.), Algorithms and Data Structures. XIV, 446 pages. 2005.

Vol. 3607: J.-D. Zucker, L. Saitta (Eds.), Abstraction, Reformulation and Approximation. XII, 376 pages. 2005. (Subseries LNAI).

Vol. 3606: V. Malyshkin (Ed.), Parallel Computing Technologies. XII, 470 pages. 2005.

Vol. 3605: Z. Wu, M. Guo, C. Chen, J. Bu (Eds.), Embedded Software and Systems. XIX, 610 pages. 2005.

Vol. 3604: R. Martin, H. Bez, M. Sabin (Eds.), Mathematics of Surfaces XI. IX, 473 pages. 2005.